ECONOMICS

# ECONOMICS

## LIPSEY &
## CHRYSTAL

ELEVENTH EDITION

**OXFORD**
UNIVERSITY PRESS

# OXFORD
### UNIVERSITY PRESS

Great Clarendon Street, Oxford OX2 6DP

Oxford University Press is a department of the University of Oxford.
It furthers the University's objective of excellence in research, scholarship,
and education by publishing worldwide in

Oxford  New York

Auckland  Cape Town  Dar es Salaam  Hong Kong  Karachi
Kuala Lumpur  Madrid  Melbourne  Mexico City  Nairobi
New Delhi  Shanghai  Taipei  Toronto

With offices in

Argentina  Austria  Brazil  Chile  Czech Republic  France  Greece
Guatemala  Hungary  Italy  Japan  Poland  Portugal  Singapore
South Korea  Switzerland  Thailand  Turkey  Ukraine  Vietnam

Oxford is a registered trade mark of Oxford University Press
in the UK and in certain other countries

Published in the United States
by Oxford University Press Inc., New York

© Richard G. Lipsey and K. Alec Chrystal 2007

The moral rights of the authors have been asserted
Database right Oxford University Press (maker)

First published 2007

British Library Cataloguing in Publication Data
Data available

Library of Congress Cataloging in Publication Data
Data available

Typeset by Graphicraft Limited, Hong Kong
Printed in Italy
on acid-free paper by Rotolito Lombarda

ISBN 978-0-19-928641-6

1 3 5 7 9 10 8 6 4 2

# CONTENTS

## MICROECONOMICS

# MACROECONOMICS

# DETAILED CONTENTS

## MICROECONOMICS

# WHY STUDY ECONOMICS?

Some of you may already be excited by the prospect of studying economics, but others among you will answer the question posed in the heading with 'It was part of my course of study, so I had no choice.' To both the reluctant conscripts and the willing volunteers we offer hope and encouragement.

Economics studies topics that are highly relevant both to decision-making in most jobs that you are likely to do in life and to understanding many of the most pressing issues facing today's world—free markets versus government intervention, resource exhaustion, pollution and environmental degradation, global warming, the revolution in digital communications media, government taxes and spending, employment and unemployment, inflation, the EU, the euro, changing living standards in advanced nations, growth and stagnation among many of the world's poorest nations. Thus, economics is both a preparation for taking day-to-day decisions in a firm or other organization, and training in the analysis of many of the 'big issues' of our time.

One of the most important events in the first three quarters of the twentieth century was the rise of communism. One of the most important events in the last quarter of that century was communism's fall. By the first decade of the twenty-first century, the century-long battle between free markets and government planning as alternatives for organizing economic activity had been settled in almost all countries with a degree of decisiveness that is rare for great social issues. Understanding why market-oriented, capitalist economies perform so much better than fully planned or highly government-controlled economies is a core issue in economics. Economic theories are expressly designed to help us understand the successes (and, where they occur, the failures) of free-market economies.

The triumph of market-oriented economies suggests that income- and wealth-creating activities are usually best accomplished through the efforts of private citizens operating in largely unregulated markets. But this is not the end of the story, for at least three fundamental reasons.

First, although market economies certainly work better than fully planned economies, they do not work perfectly. One of today's great social issues is how best to allocate the responsibilities of government, leaving it to do what it can do best and leaving free markets to do what they can do best. We ask: 'What are the important roles that governments can play in improving the functioning of a basically market-oriented economy?'

Second, market economies produce severe short-term cycles as well as long-term growth. Long-term growth has raised the living standards of the ordinary working person from the horrors and degradations in the early and mid-nineteenth century and described by Charles Dickens to those of the property-owning workers of today, whose living standards are higher than those of 99.9 per cent of all the people of all classes who ever lived on Earth. Yet capitalist growth is uneven growth because economic activity cycles around its rising trend. In recessions, unemployment is high and living standards typically stand still or even fall. Although each cycle tends to leave living standards higher than all previous cycles, the ups and downs of uneven market-driven growth can be upsetting to those affected by it.

Third, capitalist growth is unequal growth. Although it is desirable to create national income and wealth, we also care about how these are distributed among all citizens. Poverty for a minority in the midst of plenty for the majority has always been a problem in wealthy countries—just as poverty for the majority has always been a problem for poor countries. We ask: 'What can governments do to alleviate the poverty and suffering of those who do not share in the income and employment that well-functioning market economies create for the majority?'

Economists have been in the forefront of analysing, explaining, and, where appropriate, offering solutions to all of the issues mentioned above—and many more. They have often succeeded in these tasks, mainly because economics has a core of useful theory that explains how markets work and evaluates their performance. Although some economic analysis is extremely abstract, and sometimes even economists wonder about its value, the basic core of economic theory that is the secret of the subject's success can be understood by anyone who is willing to make the effort. This basic theory has an excellent record in illuminating issues in ways that lead both to deeper understanding and to useful policy recommendations.

When you start to read this book, you are setting out on the study of a subject that, as the above discussion suggests, is highly relevant to understanding and improving the world in which we live. Approached in the right way, your study will be an adventure. The basic theory must be mastered. Whether or not you find this effort fun in itself, you will find surprisingly early in your studies that theories can be used to understand many practical issues. The world is complex, and fully understanding its economic aspects requires much more economic theory than can be packed into one elementary textbook. But mastery of the subject to the level of this one book will contribute greatly to your understanding of many important issues and many of the policies directed at dealing with them. It will also provide you with a toolbox that will prove useful in the world of work, whatever occupation you eventually enter.

Good luck and good studying!

RICHARD LIPSEY and ALEC CHRYSTAL
*Vancouver, BC, and London, England*
November 2006

# HOW TO USE THIS BOOK

Lipsey and Chrystal's *Economics* is enriched with a range of features designed to help support and reinforce your learning. This guided tour shows you how to fully utilise your textbook and get the most out of your study.

## Learning objectives

In particular, you will learn that:

- Real-world firms can adopt one of several different legal structures, but for most this book firms are assumed to have a very simple structure.
- There is a difference between economists' measure of profit and accountants' m
- For economists, profit is the difference between total cost and total revenue, wh includes the opportunity cost of owners' capital.
- The production function relates physical quantities of inputs to the quantity of
- Cost curves show the money cost of producing various levels of output.
- In the version of the theory of the firm we develop here, the short-run cost curve because some inputs are being held constant and the law of diminishing return that are allowed to vary.

Each chapter begins with a bulleted list of learning objectives outlining the main concepts and ideas you will encounter in the chapter. These serve as a helpful signpost for learning and revision.

## Boxes

 **Box 11.2  Why are women paid less than men?**

Wage discrimination can affect women (or any other group that is discriminated against) in at least two ways. They may earn less than men when doing the same job, or they may be forced into jobs that typically pay lower wages than the jobs from which they are excluded. Non-discriminatory wage differentials arise when men and women differ on average in relevant labour market characteristics. For example, men and women differ significantly in their average educational qualification and in their labour market experience, with women typically spending somewhere between five and ten years out of the labour market raising children.

due to part-time
less work experi
being concentra
• *Travel patter*
*muting than me*
*to balancing wo*
*on women's pay*
*and/or lots of wo*
*to where they liv*
• *Occupational*
*concentrated in*

Boxes have been included throughout the book to provide illustrations of the theory described in the main body of the text. These take the form of examples of real life applications of economic theory, empirical illustrations to ensure deeper understanding or more detailed elaboration of points made in the text.

## Key terms

money that
carton. The
bles might be
, 1,800 *dozen*
60 *dozen* at a

e define the
of eggs that
time-period.

is explained
e influences
ed by forces

ships that helps us analyse the supply side of markets. It shows how the amount of output is related to the quantities of inputs used to produce it. This relationship is specified in what is called a production function, which sets out an equation for the relationship between inputs and output.

Conditions of application

Assumptions are often used to specify the conditions under which a theory is meant to hold. For example, a theory that assumes there is 'no government' does not mean literally the absence of government, but only that the theory is meant to hold when governments are not significantly affecting the situation being studied. Another

The first time a key term is used in the text it is printed in bold to draw your attention to it. These terms are then defined in the Glossary at the end of the book.

CASE STUDIES

1. The earnings of superstars

Small groups of people in many professions are often paid extraordinarily large salaries. In July 2006 Chelsea signed Andre Shevchenko from AC Milan for a transfer fee reported to be in excess of £30 million. He was given a four-year contract which was said to include a wage in excess of £110,000 per week. In 2004 David Beckham was transferred to Real Madrid from Manchester United for £25 million and Beckham himself was

surgeon, you
but not the be
the Premier L
coming seco
those who ar
the bunch be
wage premiu
being the bes

## Case studies

All chapters except for 1 and 2 conclude with a minimum of 2 short case studies. These are designed to reinforce your understanding of core chapter themes and to encourage you to apply your learning to real life situations.

SUMMARY

**Wage differentials**

- Equilibrium wage differentials can arise between jobs because (a) each requires different degrees of physical or mental abilities, (b) each requires different amounts of human capital acquired through costly formal education or on-the-job training, (c) some jobs are closed to people who could fill them as a result of discrimination, and (d) the markets for the types of worker needed in different jobs have different competitive structures.

■ Minim
wages
minim
raised
expen
the af

**Hetero**
■ Today

## End of chapter summaries

The central points and concepts covered in each chapter are distilled into summaries at the ends of chapters. These provide a mechanism for you to reinforce your understanding and can be used as a revision tool.

TOPICS FOR REVIEW

- Causes of equilibrium wage differentials
- Human capital
- Formal education and on-the-job training
- Wage differentials arising from the departure from perfect competition on the demand and the supply sides of labour markets

■ Relati
■ Princip
■ Efficie
■ Signall
■ Intern

## Topics for review

Each chapter ends with a list of topics for review which are designed as a prompt for you to check your understanding of these subjects. They also serve as a helpful revision tool.

QUESTIONS

1 If inflation cannot occur without money, does this mean that changes in the money stock always cause changes in inflation and that controlling the money stock is the only way to control inflation?

2 What is the relationship between the short-run Phillips curve and the *SRAS* curve?

3 What is the relationship between the long-run Phillips curve and the *LRAS* curve?

4 Starting from equilibrium, explain what happens to

5 Repeat
author
output
6 Using t
and un
at the
aggreg
the mo
7 Repeat

## End of chapter questions

Problem questions and essay type questions at the end of each chapter will help you to develop analysis and problem solving skills. These can be tackled to check your understanding of the topics before moving on to the next chapter, or for group discussion or revision.

# ABOUT THE ONLINE RESOURCE CENTRE

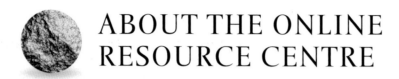

The Online Resource Centre that accompanies this book provides students and lecturers with ready-to-use teaching and learning resources. They are free of charge and are designed to maximise the learning experience. **www.oxfordtextbooks.co.uk/orc/lipsey11e/**

## For Students

### Self-test questions

A suite of questions has been provided for each chapter in the book to allow you to test your knowledge of the key themes in each chapter. These consist of a mix of short answer, multiple choice and problem based questions.

### Economics in the News

Current news stories have been selected by the authors in order to help illustrate how the theory in the book can be seen in action in the real world. This feature will be regularly updated.

### Interactive chapters

Additional course material is provided in an interactive format to assist learning.

## Web links

A selection of annotated web links chosen by the authors to allow you to easily research those topics that are of particular interest to you. These links are checked regularly to ensure they remain up to date.

## Flashcard glossary

The key glossary terms from the text are presented in a flashcard format.

# For Lecturers

## PowerPoint slides

A suite of customisable PowerPoint slides has been included for use in lecture presentations. Arranged by chapter theme, the slides may also be used as handouts in class.

## Instructor's manual

Discussion of the main themes in each chapter is included in a comprehensive guide for instructors. It also incorporates the answers to all of the questions set in the textbook.

## Test bank

A ready-made electronic testing resource which you can customise to meet your teaching needs is included for every chapter in the book.

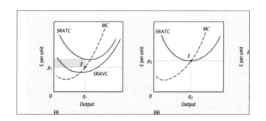

## Figures from the text

All of the figures in the textbook are available to download electronically for use in lectures to aid student understanding.

## Approaches to studying economics

You need to study a book on economics in a different way from how you would study a book on, say, history or English literature. Economic theory has a logical structure that builds on itself from stage to stage. Thus, if you understand some concept or theory only imperfectly, you will run into increasing difficulty when, in subsequent chapters, this concept or theory is taken for granted and built upon. Because of its logical structure, quite long chains of reasoning are encountered; if A then B; if B then C; if C then D; and if D then E. Each step in the argument may seem simple enough, but the cumulative effect of several steps, one on top of the other, may be bewildering on first encounter. Thus when, having followed the argument step by step, you encounter the statement 'It is now obvious that if A then E', it may not seem at all obvious to you. This is a problem that everyone encounters with chains of reasoning. The only way to deal with it is to follow the argument through several times. Eventually, as the reasoning becomes familiar, it will become obvious that *if A then E.*

Economics has its own technical language or jargon. At first you may feel that you are merely being asked to put complicated names to commonsense ideas. To some extent this is true. It is a necessary step, however, because loose thinking about vaguely formed ideas is a quick route to error in economics. Furthermore, when you begin to put several ideas together to see what follows from them, jargon—a clearly defined term to refer to each idea—becomes a necessary part of your equipment.

A book on economics is to be worked at, and understood step by step. It is usually a good procedure to read a chapter quickly in order to see the general run of the argument, and at this stage you might omit the captions to the figures. You then need to re-read the chapter carefully, making sure that the argument is understood step by step. On this reading, you *must* study the captions to all the figures carefully. If you do not understand the captions, you have not understood the economics. You should not be discouraged if, occasionally at this stage, you find yourself spending quite a bit of time on only a few pages.

A pencil and paper are valuable adjuncts to your reading. Difficult arguments should be followed by building up your own diagram while the argument unfolds, rather than relying on the printed diagram, which is, perforce, complete from the beginning. Numerical examples can be invented to illustrate general propositions.

In short, the technical vocabulary aside, you must seek to *understand* economics, not to memorize it. Theories, principles, and concepts are always turning up in slightly unfamiliar guises. If you have understood your economics, this poses no problem; if you have merely memorized it, it spells disaster.

## Write to us

Economics is a subject about which one never stops learning. We are grateful to many users—students and teachers—who have taken the trouble to write to us pointing out possible errors, making comments, and offering suggestions. We hope that readers will continue to teach us with as many further comments and criticisms as they have in the past. We try to acknowledge every such letter.

# OUTLINES FOR SHORT OR MODULAR COURSES

This book provides a comprehensive coverage of basic economics suitable for a full one-year course. We have, however, designed the text to be flexible enough to cover shorter courses, and we have considerably simplified the chapter structure for this edition and moved much supplementary material to our website. To illustrate, we give our suggestions for the chapter content of several shorter courses.

### A short Introduction to Economics course (20 weeks)

Chapters 1–14 for basic micro, and 15–22 for basic macro

### An Introduction to Microeconomics course (one semester)

Chapters 1–14

### An Introduction to Macroeconomics course (one semester)

Chapters 1 and 2, and 15–22, with more advanced material appearing in Chapter 23 and more detail on inflation and unemployment in Chapters 24 and 25. (Alternatively, for a course with a growth emphasis include Chapter 26; for a course with an international emphasis, the key chapters are 22 and 27, with addition of our web-based material on developing countries.)

# ACKNOWLEDGEMENTS

Finally we wish to say a word of thanks to some people who have helped make this book possible. Sue Hughes has been insightful and creative in editing the manuscript. At OUP we are indebted to Kirsty Reade, Nicola Bateman, and Sarah Brett for their organization and guidance of the project. Kjell Horn has provided essential administrative support in London. This edition has also benefited from many students, especially Cass undergraduates, who have pointed out mistakes or unclear passages in the previous edition. We are particularly grateful to Iqbal Ibrahim Bhamani who pointed out some errors that had survived through several editions of this book. The usual disclaimer of course holds here: for all remaining shortcomings and mistakes, the authors may blame each other, but readers should blame us both.

R.G.L.
K.A.C.

# Chapter 1

# ECONOMIC ISSUES AND CONCEPTS

Economics studies how basic resources are transformed by producers into all the many goods and services that modern consumers want. In this chapter you will learn:

- That a modern market economy uses price signals to solve the complex problems involved in using resources to produce the goods and services that people want
- How economics studies the choice between competing demands for scarce resources
- How production, employment, and consumption decisions interact
- That the market economy generally delivers outcomes desired by consumers
- That governments step in when markets fail to produce results that are regarded as successful

A modern economy makes available millions of goods and services for people to choose from. It provides jobs for most people who want to work. It allows us to travel and communicate easily with anybody anywhere in the world. Yet no one has sat down and planned how all this will work. It has evolved as a response to economic forces interacting with individuals and institutions. One of our main tasks in this book is to understand how such an economy works, how well it works, and what can be done when it does not work well.

If you want a pint of milk, you go to the shop and buy it. The shop owner is just one part of a complex supply chain that makes this milk available when you want it. When the shop owner needs more milk, she orders it from the distributor, who in turn gets it from the bottling plant, which in its turn gets it from the dairy farmer. The dairy farmer buys cattle feed and electric milking machines, and gets power to run all his equipment by putting a plug into a wall socket where the electricity is supplied as he needs it. The milking machines are made from parts manufactured in several different countries throughout the world, while these parts in their turn are made from materials mined and refined in a dozen or more different countries.

As it is with the milk you drink, so it is with everything else that you buy. When you go to the appropriate shop, what you want is normally in stock. Those who make these products find that all the required components and materials are available when needed—even though these things typically come from many different parts of the world and are made by people who have no direct dealings with each other. The economy is so good at delivering what we want when we want it that we only tend to notice when it goes wrong.

## The complexity of the modern economy

The sales and purchases in which you are involved are only a small part of the fantastically complex set of transactions that take place every day in a modern society. Shipments arrive daily at our seaports and airports. These include raw materials such as iron ore and logs, parts such as computer chips and circuit boards, tools such as screwdrivers and digging equipment, perishables such as fresh flowers and fruits, and all kinds of manufactured goods such as washing machines and TV sets. Rail and road shippers receive and dispatch these goods to thousands of destinations. Some go directly to consumers; others are used by domestic firms as inputs into the manufacture of their own products—of which some will be sold in the home market and some exported.

Most people who want to work have a job. By working they earn incomes, which they then spend on the goods and services that they, and other workers, produce. Some people own businesses that employ workers to assist in the making and selling of their products. Business owners earn part of their income as profit from their enterprises, though they may also pay themselves some salary as managers if they work in their own firms.

Some activity takes place in the public sector, where the services produced are provided free to consumers and where wages and salaries are paid for by the government out of general taxation. Public-sector workers then spend their incomes on a wide range of goods, just as other types of worker do.

## Self-organization

Economics as a subject began when thoughtful observers asked themselves how such a complex set of transactions making up a modern economy is organized. Who co-ordinates the vast array of production, employment, and consumption decisions? Who makes sure that all the activities fit together, providing jobs to produce the goods and services that people want and delivering them to where they are wanted?

The answer is: no one!

**The great insight of the early economists was that an economy based on free-market transactions is self-organizing.**

By following their own self-interest, doing what seems best and most profitable for themselves, and responding to the incentives of prices set on open markets, people produce a spontaneous social order. In that order, literally thousands of millions of transactions and activities fit together to produce the things that people want within the constraints set by the resources that are available to the nation.

The great Scottish economist and political philosopher Adam Smith, who was the first to develop this insight fully, put it this way:

*It is not from the benevolence of the butcher, the brewer, or the baker, that we expect our dinner, but from their regard to their own interest. We address ourselves, not to their humanity but to their self-love, and never talk to them of our own necessities*

*but of their advantages. Nobody but a beggar chuses to depend chiefly upon the benevolence of his fellow-citizens. (Smith 1776, pages 26–7 of 1976 edn)*

Smith is not saying that benevolence is unimportant—indeed, he praises it in many passages. He is saying, however, that the massive number of economic interactions that characterize a modern economy cannot all be motivated by benevolence. Although benevolence does motivate some of our actions, such as when we donate to earthquake, famine, and tsunami relief funds, the majority of our everyday actions are motivated by self-interest. The individual pursuit of self-interest is, therefore, the main behavioural incentive that drives a market economy to behave as it does.

## Efficient organization

Another great insight, which was hinted at by Smith and fully developed over the next century and a half, was that this spontaneously generated social order is relatively efficient. Loosely speaking (we will be more precise later), efficiency means that the resources available to a nation are organized to produce the maximum possible total output of the types of goods and services that people wish to consume.

An economy organized by free markets behaves almost as if some superior power had guided it. This does not literally mean that a supernatural presence runs economic affairs. Instead, it refers to the relatively efficient order that emerges spontaneously out of many independent decisions made by those who make, sell, and buy goods and services. The key to explaining this market behaviour is that these people all respond to the same set of prices, which are determined in markets that reflect the overall conditions of scarcity or plenty. Much of economics is devoted to understanding how this market outcome is generated, and to assessing the efficiency of that outcome.

## A planned alternative

A century after Adam Smith, another great economist and political philosopher, Karl Marx, argued that, although this market system would produce high total output, it would distribute that output in such a way that, over time, the rich would get richer and the poor poorer. He also argued that when societies became rich enough they should dispense with the spontaneous social order. They should then replace it with a consciously created system, called a command economy, or communism, in which the government would plan all of the economic

**Box 1.1  The failure of central planning**

The abandonment of communism by many countries at the end of the 1980s signalled to the world what many economists had long argued: the superiority of a market-oriented price system over central planning as a method of organizing economic activity. The failure of central planning had many causes, but four were particularly significant.

### The failure of co-ordination

In centrally planned economies, a body of planners tries to co-ordinate all the economic decisions about production, investment, trade, and consumption made by the producers and consumers throughout the country. This proved impossible to do with any reasonable degree of efficiency. Bottlenecks in production, shortages of some goods, and gluts of others plagued the Soviet economy for decades. For example, in 1989 much of a bumper harvest rotted on the farm because of shortages of storage and transportation facilities, and for years there was an ample supply of black-and-white television sets and severe shortages of toilet paper and soap.

### Failure of quality control

Central planners can monitor the number of units produced by any factory and reward those who overfulfil their production targets and punish those who fall short. It is much harder, however, for them to monitor quality. A constant Soviet problem was the production of poor-quality products. Factory managers were concerned with meeting their quotas by whatever means were available, and once the goods passed out of their factory, what happened to them was someone else's headache. The quality problem was so serious that in the 1990s very few Eastern European-manufactured products were able to stand up to the newly permitted competition with superior goods produced in the advanced market societies.

In market economies poor quality is punished by low sales, and retailers soon give a signal to factory managers by shifting their purchases to other suppliers. The incentives that obviously flow from such private-sector purchasing discretion are generally absent from command economies, where purchases and sales are planned centrally.

### Misplaced incentives

In market economies relative wages and salaries provide incentives for labour to move from place to place, and the possibility of losing one's job provides an incentive to work diligently. This is a harsh mechanism that punishes shirkers with loss of income (although social programmes provide floors to the amount of economic punishment that can be suffered). In planned economies workers usually have complete job security. Industrial unemployment is rare, and even when it does occur new jobs are usually found for those who lose theirs. Although the high level of security is attractive to many, it proved impossible to provide sufficient incentives to work reasonably hard and efficiently under such conditions. In the words of Oxford historian Timothy Garton Ash, who wrote eyewitness chronicles of the developments in Eastern Europe from 1980 to 1990, the social contract between the workers and the government in the Eastern countries was 'We pretend to work, and you pretend to pay us.'

### Environmental degradation

Fulfilling production plans became the all-embracing incentive in planned economies, to the exclusion of most other considerations, including the environment. As a result, environmental degradation occurred in all the countries of Eastern Europe on a scale unknown in advanced Western nations. A particularly disturbing example occurred in central Asia, where high quotas for cotton output led to indiscriminate use of pesticides and irrigation; birth defects were found there in nearly one child in three. This is but one example of a general phenomenon that included toxic chemical dumps and atomic waste scattered throughout the land.

The failure to protect the environment stemmed from a combination of pressure to fulfil plans and lack of a political marketplace. The democratic process allows citizens to express views on the use of scarce resources for environmental protection. Imperfect though the system may be in democratic economies, their record of environmental protection has been vastly better than that of the command economies.

transactions and, in so doing, create a more equal and just distribution of the total output.

Beginning with the USSR in the 1920s, many nations listened to Marx and established systems in which conscious government central planning largely replaced the spontaneous order of the free market. For much of the twentieth century two systems—the centrally planned and the market—competed with each other for the favour of undecided governments. Then, within the last two decades of the century, governments of one communist country after another abandoned their central planning apparatus. More and more economic transactions and activities were left to the market. Seldom has a great social issue been settled with such conclusiveness.

**Adam Smith was right and Karl Marx was wrong.**

Box 1.1 explains some of the reasons for the failure of centrally planned economies. Marx was right about many things, including the importance of technological change in raising living standards over the centuries. Where he was wrong, however, was in believing that the market could be replaced by central planning as a way of organizing all of a nation's economic activities.

In contrast to the failures of command economies, the performance of the free-market price system is impressive. One theme of this book is the success of the market—how the price system works to co-ordinate with relative efficiency the decentralized decisions made by millions of private consumers and producers. However, this does not mean that doing things better implies doing things perfectly. Another theme of this book is market failure—how and why the unaided market economy can fail to produce socially desirable outcomes.

In short, economists seek to understand how well the market economy works, and to identify where governments may need to intervene to correct specific aspects of market failure.

## Main characteristics of market economies

What then are the main characteristics of market economies that produce this spontaneous self-organization?

- Individuals pursue their own self-interest, buying and selling what seems best for themselves and their families.

- People respond to incentives. Other things being equal, sellers seek high prices while buyers seek low prices.

- Prices are set in open markets in which suppliers compete to sell to potential buyers.

- People earn their incomes by selling their services to those who wish to use them—their labour services—or by selling things they have produced, or by selling the services of the property that they own.

- All of these activities are governed by a legal framework largely created and administered by the state.

## Resources and scarcity

All of the issues discussed so far would not matter much if we lived in an economy of plenty where there was enough of everything for everybody. But instead we live in a world of scarcity. Most of us want better food, clothing, housing, schooling, holidays, hospital care, and entertainment. But there is not enough to go around. Even the richest economy can produce only a small fraction of the goods and services that people would like to have if all were free. Hence economics is concerned with the problem of choice under conditions of scarcity. We cannot have everything we want, so we must choose what we will and will not have.

At this stage, it is helpful to clarify a few terms and concepts that you will use in studying economics.

### Kinds of resources

An economy's resources can be divided into four main categories:

- All those gifts of nature, such as land, forests, minerals, etc., commonly called natural resources and called by economists **land**, for short.

- All human resources, mental and physical, both inherited and acquired, which economists call **labour**.

- All those man-made aids to further production, such as tools, machinery, and factories, that are used in the process of making other goods and services rather than being consumed for their own sake. Economists call these **capital**.

- Those who take risks by introducing new products and new ways of making old products, developing new businesses and forms of employment. They are called **entrepreneurs** or **innovators**, and the resource they provide is **entrepreneurship**.

Traditionally these resources have been called **factors of production**, but we shall more frequently refer to them just as different types of **input** into the production process. Part 3 of this book focuses explicitly on **resource allocation**; that is, why are resources drawn into one activity rather than another—why do some people work in agriculture, others in manufacturing, and yet others in services, for example?

### Ownership of resources

Private property is a key institution of a market economy. Individuals own the majority of the nation's resources. They also own the goods that they produce and the things that they buy. Some assets are owned by the state—roads, schools, public buildings, etc.—but most are, and must be, in private hands. People cannot make contracts to buy and sell what is not theirs. So without private ownership the market economy cannot function.

### Kinds of production

The resources of the economy are used in a production process to make goods, which are tangible, in that they have a physical existence, such as cars and shoes. They also produce services, which are intangible, for example haircuts, TV programmes, education and telephone calls. Throughout this book we use the term 'goods' to cover both goods and services, unless we explicitly make a distinction between the two.

The nation's total output of all goods and services over one year is called its gross domestic product or GDP for short. The act of making goods and services is called production, and the act of using up these goods and services to satisfy wants is called consumption. Anyone who makes goods or provides services is called a producer, and anyone who consumes them to satisfy his or her wants is called a consumer.

## Choice and opportunity cost

You might want a mobile phone so that you can call your friends or an MP3 player so that you can listen to your favourite music. Your parents might have a car to get them to work or to visit your grandparents at the weekend. In general, people value specific goods and services because these help them to satisfy their needs. Goods and services are thus regarded as a means to an end, which is the satisfaction of wants. Because no economy can produce enough goods and services to satisfy all of its citizens' wants, choices must be made.

Most of us have only a specific amount of income that we can spend. If we want to have more of one thing, then we must have less of something else. For example, suppose someone you know is considering whether to go out and have a few drinks with friends. The cost of these extra drinks could be measured as the money cost of so much per pint of beer or glass of juice. A more revealing way of looking at the cost, however, is in terms of what other consumption this person must forgo in order to pay for the drinks. Suppose that she decides to give up going to the cinema and use the money saved to buy the drinks. If the price of one drink is, say one third the price of a cinema seat, then the cost of three drinks is one cinema visit; put the other way around, the cost of one cinema visit is three drinks.

Now think of the same problem at the level of a whole society. If the government decides to build more roads, and finds the required money by deciding to build fewer schools, then the cost of the new roads can be expressed as so many schools per hundred miles of road.

Opportunity cost is a measure of costs expressed as alternatives given up, rather than in terms of money. If

some course of action is adopted, there are typically many alternatives that might have to be sacrificed. For example, once the government has decided on its total spending for any given year, this provides it with an aggregate resource constraint, and it must then decide how to allocate that spending between various competing parts of the public sector such as health, education, and the police. So it could be, for example, that if the government decides that it wants to hire 1000 extra police it will have to reduce spending on education so that 900 fewer teachers can be afforded. The opportunity cost of 1000 police, therefore, would be 900 teachers.

Of course, it would not necessarily have to be the education budget that was cut: it could be the health budget or the defence budget or some other part of the public sector. Indeed, it might be that a little bit is cut off all the other spending components. The point is that, for any given aggregate resource constraint, if you want more of one thing you have to give up something else. The something else given up is the opportunity cost of the new good or service that is obtained.

The concept of opportunity cost highlights the choices that must be made by measuring the cost of anything that is chosen in terms of the alternative that could have been chosen instead.

## The production-possibility boundary

We can illustrate on a diagram some of the issues surrounding economic choices. As you will soon see, diagrams or figures pervade elementary economics books. If you find them difficult to follow, you should study the section on graphs in Chapter 2 (pages 24–30).

All the things that governments provide, such as schools, national defence, and roads, are produced in the public sector. Everything else, including all the goods and services that consumers buy, is produced in the private sector. How should the nation's productive resources be divided between these two sectors? To illustrate this choice we put all the goods and services that governments provide into one group called 'public sector goods'. The rest are provided by non-government organizations and we call these 'private sector goods'. The balance between public and private provision is determined through the political process by government tax and spending policies. Higher public provision requires higher taxes, and higher taxes reduce private consumption.

The choices that each country must make are illustrated in Figure 1.1. The horizontal axis measures the quantity of public sector goods while the vertical axis measures

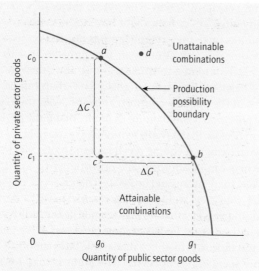

**Figure 1.1  A production possibility boundary**
The negatively sloped boundary shows the combinations that are just attainable when all of the society's resources are efficiently employed. The quantity of public sector goods produced is measured along the horizontal axis, the quantity of private sector goods along the vertical axis. Any point on the diagram indicates some amount of each kind of good produced. The production possibility boundary separates the blue-shaded attainable combinations, such as $a$, $b$, and $c$, from unattainable combinations, such as $d$. It is negatively sloped because in a fully employed economy more of one good can be produced only if resources are freed by producing less of other goods. Moving from point $a$ (whose coordinates are $c_0$ and $g_0$) to point $b$ (whose coordinates are $c_1$ and $g_1$) implies producing an additional amount of public sector goods, indicated by $\Delta G$ in the figure, at an opportunity cost of a reduction in private sector goods by the amount indicated by $\Delta C$. Points $a$ and $b$ represent efficient uses of society's resources. Point $c$ represents either an inefficient use of resources or a failure to use all the resources that are available.

the quantity of private sector goods. The blue curve shows all those combinations of public and private goods that can be produced if all the nation's resources are fully employed. It is called a **production-possibility boundary**. Points outside the boundary show combinations that cannot be obtained because there are not enough resources to produce them. Points on the boundary are just obtainable: they are the combinations that can just be produced using all the available supplies of resources.

## Choice, scarcity, and opportunity cost illustrated

A single production-possibility boundary illustrates three concepts that we have already discussed: scarcity, choice,

and opportunity cost. Scarcity is shown by the unattainable combinations beyond the boundary. There are some things we just cannot have. Choice arises because of the need to select one of the attainable points on or inside the boundary. No economy can be at more than one point at one time. Any combination of public sector and private sector goods that is within the blues shaded area is achievable and anything outside is not. *Opportunity cost* is shown by the negative slope of the boundary. As the economy moves along that boundary, more of one type of good is being obtained at the cost of fewer of the other type.

### Increasing opportunity cost

The production-possibility boundary of Figure 1.1 is drawn with a slope that gets steeper as one moves along it from left to right. The increasing slope indicates increasing opportunity cost as more and more private goods have to be given up for each additional unit of public goods. Starting, for example, at the vertical axis, where all production is of private sector goods, a small increase in the production of public goods moves the economy along a fairly flat part of the curve, indicating a small reduction in the production of private sector goods. But the loss of private goods gets greater (for each additional unit of public good) as we move further along the boundary.

The figure can also be used to illustrate another three important economic issues.

### Three key issues

#### What should be produced

How should the nation's scarce resources be allocated between the various possible kinds of production? Where to locate on the production-possibility boundary is the graphical representation of this key question. Each point on the boundary indicates a specific combination of the possible outputs. Alternative points indicate different allocations of the nation's resources, producing different combinations of outputs.

#### Efficient production

If an economy is located inside its boundary, then more of everything could be produced. There are two main reasons why an economy may produce inside its production boundary. First, some of its resources may be unemployed. Putting them back to work would raise the production of some goods without having to lower the production of anything else. Second, although its resources are fully employed, some of them may be employed inefficiently. If they could be used more efficiently, the production of some goods could be increased without having to produce less of anything else. We will have

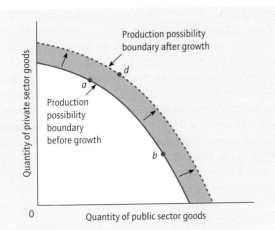

**Figure 1.2** The effect of economic growth on the production possibility boundary

Economic growth shifts the production possibility boundary outward, allowing more of all commodities to be produced. Before growth in productive capacity, points *a* and *b* were on the production possibility boundary and point *d* was an unattainable combination. After growth, point *d* becomes attainable, as do all points within the dark blue band.

much more to say about inefficient uses of resources in later chapters.

These two possibilities help to reveal the source of opportunity cost.

If all of the nation's resources are fully employed, and none is employed inefficiently, then more of one good can be produced only by taking resources away from the production of another good.

The lost production of the other good is the opportunity cost of the first.

### Economic growth

There is one other way an economy can get more of everything without having less of anything. If the economy's capacity to produce goods is increasing through time, the production-possibility boundary will be moving outwards over time, as illustrated in Figure 1.2. More of all goods can then be produced. This is what economic growth has accomplished from one decade to the next over the last

 **Box 1.2** The terminology of production possibilities

We have used the term 'production possibility boundary'. 'Boundary' emphasizes that the points on the line are maximum points. It is always possible to produce at points inside the line by not employing some factors of production, or by using them inefficiently. Two other terms, 'frontier' and 'curve', are often used instead of 'boundary'.

The words 'production possibility' emphasize the alternative possibilities available to a society. However, the term 'transformation' is often used instead. The idea behind the term 'transformation' is that society can, in effect, 'transform' one product into another by moving resources from the production of one product into the production of the other. Speaking of transforming one product into another involves the idea of opportunity cost. Of course, one good is not literally transformed into another, but, by moving resources from producing one type of good to producing another, quantities of the first type of good are sacrificed to gain quantities of the second type.

You can make up six terms by combining the following words:

Production-possibility *or* Transformation } *with* { Curve *or* Boundary *or* Frontier

All six terms mean the same thing. All six are commonly used.

several hundred years—and sporadically before then, back to the beginning of history. We will study this growth later in the book. In the meantime, we merely note that in the long term growth is driven by technological change. Over the years we learn to make existing products better and more cheaply, and also to make many new products that satisfy old needs in new ways and create altogether new needs.

Box 1.2 deals with some of the sometimes confusing terminology that surrounds the concept of the production-possibility boundary.

# Who makes the choices and how

Economic choices have to be made—but who makes them, and how are they made?

## The flow of income and expenditure

Figure 1.3 shows the main players in the economy and the flows of income and spending that they generate. Individuals own most of the resources that are used in production, including their own labour. They sell the services of these resources to producers and receive payments in return: these are their incomes. Producers use the inputs that they buy to make goods and services for consumption. They sell these to individuals, receiving payments in return: these are the incomes of producers. These basic flows of income and spending pass through markets. Individuals sell the resources that they own in the labour and capital markets. Producers sell their outputs of goods and services in consumption goods markets. The prices that are set in these markets determine the incomes that are earned and the purchasing power of those incomes. People who get high prices for their services earn high incomes; those who get low prices earn low incomes.

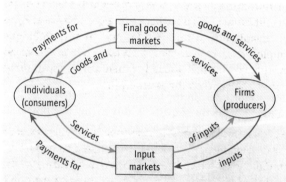

**Figure 1.3 The circular flow of income and expenditure**

**The green line shows the flows of goods and services while the blue line shows the payments made to purchase these.** Inputs flow from individuals who own the resources (including their own labour), which they sell to firms, which use them to make goods and services. These then flow through goods markets to those who consume them. Money payments flow from firms to individuals in the form of wages to workers or profits to shareholders. This becomes the individuals' income. When they spend this income buying goods and services, money flows through the goods markets back to the producers.

The **distribution of income** indicates how the nation's total income is distributed among its citizens. This is largely determined by the price that each type of resource input can command and by how evenly the endowments of these resources are distributed. It could be thought that labour is equally endowed to individuals, because each person has only one body. However, talents are not equally endowed and people acquire varying skill levels. Ownership of land and other property may also vary considerably among people.

### Maximizing decisions

In this story of what drives economic outcomes, the basic decision-makers are individuals and firms. Later we shall also discuss the role of the government. The most important characteristic that economists assume about how individuals and firms take their decisions is that everyone tries to do as well as possible for themselves. In the jargon of economics, they are assumed to be *maximizers*. When individuals decide how much of their labour services to sell to producers and how many products to buy from them, they are assumed to make choices designed to maximize their well-being. When managers of firms decide how many inputs to buy from individuals and other firms, and how many of their own products to make and sell to them, they are assumed to be seeking to maximize their profits.

### Marginal decisions

Individuals and firms make most of their choices *at the margin*. When you enter a shop to buy a newspaper and a pint of milk, you are deciding to buy one more newspaper and one more pint of milk. You do not have to decide which product to spend your entire income on, and neither do you have to decide what to spend your income on next week or next year. You can, and do, decide to spread your spending around and to make these decisions incrementally (more or less) one at a time. Today you could buy two newspapers and a half-pint of milk; tomorrow you might buy one newspaper, six eggs and two pints of milk. These are marginal decisions—decisions to buy a bit more or a bit less. The decisions are made sequentially, not all at once.

Individuals and firms are constantly taking marginal decisions about whether to buy or produce a bit more or a bit less of the things that they consume or make. These decisions are assumed to be taken in order to achieve the most desirable outcome, that is, to maximize some objective.

## Production choices

Managers of businesses decide what to produce and how to produce it. Some products, like haircuts, are quite simple to produce. But other production processes can be very complex. A typical car manufacturer assembles a product out of thousands of individual components. It makes some of these components itself, but most are sub-contracted to other parts manufacturers, and many of the major parts manufacturers subcontract some of their work out to smaller suppliers. This kind of production displays two characteristics noted two centuries ago by Adam Smith and one that is more recent: these are specializa-tion, the division of labour, and globalization.

### Specialization

In ancient hunter–gatherer societies, and in modern sub-sistence economies, most people make most of the things they need for themselves. However, from the time (about 10,000 years ago) that people first engaged in settled agriculture and some of them began to live in towns, people have specialized in doing particular jobs. Farmers, carpenters, soldiers, and priests had some of the earliest specialized occupations. The allocation of different jobs to different people is known as **specialization of labour**, or the **division of labour**. There are two fundamental reasons why specialization is extraordinarily efficient compared with self-sufficiency.

First, individual abilities differ, and specialization allows each person to do what he or she can do relatively well while leaving everything else to be done by others. Even when people's abilities are unaffected by the act of specializing, production is greater with specialization than with self-sufficiency. This is one of the most funda-mental principles in economics. It is called the principle of **comparative advantage**. An example is given in Box 1.3 and a much fuller discussion is found in Chapter 27.

The second reason is that people's abilities change when they specialize. A person who concentrates on one activ-ity becomes better at it than could a jack-of-all-trades. This is called **learning by doing**. Learning by doing is very important in many jobs today where complex tasks are required.

### The division of labour

Throughout most of history, each worker who specialized in making some product made the whole of that product. Over the last several hundred years, many technical advances in methods of production have made it efficient to organize agriculture and manufacturing into large-scale firms organized around a division of labour. There is job specialization within the production process of a particular product. Today few people work alone to make a whole product. Instead, most individuals specialize in making one bit of the final product, which is the outcome of the contributions of the labours of many specialist workers and machines. This is obviously true of most manu-factured products including cars, TV sets and washing machines, which have many components, and many individuals play different roles in the assembly process. It is also true of most service industries, where individuals work in teams to deliver a complex product.

#### Mass production

In a mass-production factory, work is divided into specialized tasks using specialized machinery. Each indi-vidual repeatedly does one small task that is a small part of the total number of tasks necessary to produce the product. This is an extreme case of the division of labour.

#### Craft workers and flexible manufacturing

Two recent developments have significantly altered the degree of specialization found in many modern produc-tion processes. First, individual craft workers have recently reappeared in some lines of production. Craft workers are highly skilled manufacturing workers who are well trained and do much more that purely routine or repetitive opera-tions. They are responding to a revival in the demand for individually crafted, rather than mass-produced, products. Second, many manufacturing operations have been reorgan-ized along new lines called 'lean production' or 'flexible manufacturing', which was pioneered by Japanese car manufacturers. It has led back to a more craft-based form of organization within the factory. In this technique employees work as a team; each employee is able to do every team member's job rather than one very specialized task at one point on the assembly line.

### Globalization

Market economies constantly change, largely as a result of the development of new products and new technologies. One important recent development is referred to as **global-ization**. Globalized trade is not new—it has been around for hundreds, and in some areas thousands, of years. Since the industrial revolution, the usual pattern was of manufactured goods being sent from Europe and North America to the rest of the world, with raw mater-ials and primary products being brought back in return. What is new in the last few decades is the globalization of manufacturing, and in particular the rapid growth of manufacturing, mainly in China, but also in India and some of the countries of SE Asia.

Two major causes of globalization are the rapid reduction in transportation costs and the revolution in information

**Box 1.3 Absolute and comparative advantage**

A simple case will illustrate the important principles involved in the gains from specialization.

## Absolute advantage

Suppose that, working full-time on his own, Peter can produce either 100 sweaters *or* 40 suits per year, whereas Jane can produce 400 sweaters *or* 10 suits. These productive abilities are shown in the first two columns of Table i. Jane has an absolute advantage in making sweaters because she can make more per year than Peter can. However, Peter has an absolute advantage over Jane in producing suits for the same reason. If they both spend *half* their time producing each commodity, the results will be as given in the columns (3) and (4) of Table i.

Now let Peter specialize in suits, producing 40 of them, and Jane specialize in sweaters, producing 400. Columns in (5) and (6) of the table i, labelled 'Full specialization', show that production of both commodities has risen because each person is better than the other at his or her speciality: sweater production rises from 250 to 400, while suit production goes from 25 to 40.

### Table (i)

| | Time spent fully on one or other | | Time divided equally between the two | | Full specialization | |
|---|---|---|---|---|---|---|
| | Sweaters (1) | Suits (2) | Sweaters (3) | Suits (4) | Sweaters (5) | Suits (6) |
| Peter | 100 | 40 | 50 | 20 | | 40 |
| Jane | 400 | 10 | 200 | 5 | 400 | |
| Total | | | 250 | 25 | 400 | 40 |

## Comparative advantage

Now make things a little less obvious by giving Jane an absolute advantage over Peter in both commodities. We do this by making Jane more productive in suits, so that she can produce 48 of them per year, with all other productivities remaining the same. This gives us the new data for productive abilities shown in the first two columns of Table ii. Now, compared with Peter, Jane is four times more efficient at producing sweaters and 20 per cent more efficient at producing suits. Columns (4) and (5) in Table ii gives the outputs when Peter and Jane both divide their time equally between the two products.

It is possible to increase their combined production of both commodities by having Jane increase her production of sweaters and Peter increase his production of suits. The final pair of columns in Table ii gives an example in which Peter specializes fully in suit production and Jane spends 25 per cent of her time on suits and 75 per cent on sweaters. (Her outputs of suits and

### Table (ii)

| | Time spent fully on one or other | | Time divided equally between the two | | Peter fully specialized; Jane 75%/25% on sweaters v. suits | |
|---|---|---|---|---|---|---|
| | Sweaters (1) | Suits (2) | Sweaters (3) | Suits (4) | Sweaters (5) | Suits (6) |
| Peter | 100 | 40 | 50 | 20 | | 40 |
| Jane | 400 | 48 | 200 | 24 | 300 | 12 |
| Total | | | 250 | 44 | 300 | 52 |

sweaters are thus 25 and 75 per cent of what she could produce of these goods if she worked full time on one or the other.) Total production of sweaters rises from 250 to 300, while total production of suits goes from 44 to 52.

In this latter example Jane is absolutely more efficient than is Peter in both lines of production, but her margin of advantage is greater in sweaters than in suits.

Jane has a **comparative advantage** over Peter in the line of production in which her margin of advantage is greatest (sweaters, in this case). Peter has a comparative advantage over Jane in the line of production in which his margin of disadvantage is least (suits, in this case).

This example is only an illustration. The principles can be generalized in the following way:

- When two trading partners each have a comparative advantage over the other in one of two traded products, there is an obvious gain from each specializing in their most productive activity and trading for the other product.

- However, absolute advantages are not necessary for there to be gains from specialization.

- Gains from specialization occur whenever there are *differences* in the margin of advantage that one producer enjoys over another in various lines of production.

- Total production can always be increased when each producer becomes more specialized in the production of the commodity in which it has a comparative advantage.

A more detailed study of the important concept of comparative advantage and its many applications to international trade and specialization must await our discussion of international trade (Chapter 27). In the meantime, it is worth noting that the comparative advantage of individuals and of whole nations may change. Jane may learn new skills and develop a comparative advantage in suits that she does not currently have. Similarly, whole nations may develop new abilities and know-how that will change their pattern of comparative advantage.

technology. First, the cost of moving products around the world fell greatly in the last half of the twentieth century, owing to air travel and also to containerization and the increasing size of ships. Second, our ability to transmit and to analyse data has been increasing even more dramatically over the past fifty years, while the costs of doing so have been decreasing, equally dramatically. For example, today £1,000 or so buys a computer that fits into a briefcase and has the same computing power as one that in 1970 cost £5 million and filled a large room.

This revolution in information and communication technology (ICT) has made it possible to co-ordinate economic transactions around the world in ways that were difficult and costly fifty years ago and quite impossible a hundred years ago. This, combined with falling costs of transport, has allowed manufacturing activities to be decentralized. Fifty years ago, if a car was to be assembled in Birmingham all the parts had to be made nearby. Today it is possible to make parts anywhere in the world and get them to Birmingham exactly when they are required. As a result, manufacturing, which was formerly concentrated in the advanced industrial countries of Europe and North America, now takes place all over the world. A typical CD player, TV set, or car contains components made in literally dozens of different countries. Cars, for example, are made up of tyres, wheel hubs, windows, seats, computers, clocks, CD players, speedometers, petrol gauges, locks, doors, handles, pistons, gears, distributors, wiper blades, brakes, brake liners, switches, steering wheels, etc., and we have not even started listing the components of the engine. All of these can be made by different suppliers which may be in different parts of the world. We still know where a product is *assembled*, but it is becoming increasingly difficult to say where it is *made*.

Also, many *markets* are globalizing. For example, as some fashions have become universal, we can see the same designer jeans, brand labels, and fast food outlets in virtually all big cities. Many *corporations* are globalized, as more and more of them become what the UN calls **transnationals**, but which are also known as **multinationals**. These are massive firms with a physical presence in many countries. MacDonald's restaurants are as visible in Moscow or Beijing as in London or New York. Many other brands are also virtually universal, such as Coca Cola, Kelloggs, Heinz, Nestlé, Guinness, Toyota, Mercedes Benz, Rolls-Royce, Sony, and Hoover.

The pros and cons of globalization have recently been a subject of great controversy. Notice, however, that globalization is not the only game in town. While globalization has affected financial markets and manufacturing, an ever-increasing proportion of employment is in service industries, many of which, by the nature of the product, remain very local. How far, for example, would you be prepared to travel for an evening meal, a haircut, a concert, or a trip to the theatre? Most people shop in their local town and visit their local doctor and local hospital, though in cases of highly specialized needs some purchase products on the internet from anywhere in the world and others will travel great distances to consult a Harley Street specialist or a US medical expert at the Mayo Clinic.

### Markets and money

People who are specialized in doing only one thing, whether they are factory workers or computer programmers, must satisfy most of their needs by consuming goods and services produced by other people. In early societies exchange of products took place by simple mutual agreement between neighbours. In the course of time, however, trading became centred on particular gathering places called *markets*. For example, the French markets, or trade fairs, of Champagne were well known throughout Europe as early as the eleventh century. Even now, many towns have regular market days. For economists, however, the term 'market' has a much broader meaning. We use the term **market economy** to refer to a society in which people specialize in productive activities and meet most of their material wants through voluntarily agreed exchanges. Most employed people, for example, work for a single employer (at any one time) and buy goods and services in a wide range in outlets (such as shops and restaurants, or by phone, internet, etc.).

**Specialization must be accompanied by trade. People who produce only one thing must trade most of it to obtain all of the other things they require.**

Early trading was by means of **barter**, the trading of goods directly for other goods. But barter is costly in terms of time spent searching out satisfactory exchanges. If a farmer has wheat but wants a hammer, he must find someone who has a hammer and wants wheat. A successful barter transaction thus requires what is called a *double coincidence of wants*.

Money eliminates the restrictive system of barter by separating the transactions involved in the exchange of products. If a farmer has wheat and wants a hammer, she does not have to find someone who has a hammer and wants wheat: she merely has to find someone who wants wheat, and takes money in exchange. Then she finds a person who wishes to trade a hammer and gives up the money for the hammer.

**The existence of 'money' greatly expands the possibilities of specialization and trade.**

# Is there a practical alternative to the market economy?

The answer is: yes and no. 'No' because the modern economy has no practical alternative to reliance on market determination for most of its functions; but 'yes' because a market economy cannot deliver all the outcomes we generally desire without some role for interventions by government.

There are four main types of economic system.

## Traditional systems

A **traditional economic system** is one in which behaviour is based primarily on tradition, custom, and habit. Young men follow their fathers' occupations—typically, farming, hunting, fishing, and tool-making. Women do what their mothers did—typically, cooking, mending, and fieldwork. There are few changes in the pattern of production from year to year, other than those imposed by the vagaries of nature. The techniques of production also follow traditional patterns, except when the effects of an occasional new invention are felt. The concept of private property is often not well defined, and property is frequently held in common, such as common grazing land. Finally, production is allocated between the members of society according to long-established traditions. In short, the answers to the economic questions of what to produce, how to produce, and how to distribute are determined by what has happened in the past. Such a system works best in an unchanging environment. Under static conditions, a system that does not continually require people to make choices can prove effective in meeting economic and social needs.

Traditional systems were common in earlier times. The feudal system under which most people lived in medieval Europe was a largely traditional society. Today only a few small, isolated, self-sufficient communities still retain mainly traditional systems; examples can be found in some of the most isolated parts of the Canadian Arctic, the Himalayas, the Amazon jungle, and isolated parts of Papua New Guinea.

## Command systems

We have already seen that in command systems some central authority determines economic behaviour. It makes most of the necessary decisions concerning what to produce, how to produce it, and who gets to consume it. Because centralized decision-makers usually lay down elaborate and complex plans for the behaviour they wish to impose, the terms **command economy** and **centrally planned economy** are usually used synonymously.

The sheer quantity of data required for the central planning of an entire economy is enormous, and the task of analysing it to produce a fully integrated plan can hardly be exaggerated, even in the age of computers. Moreover, the plan must be a rolling process, continually changing to take account not only of current data but also of future trends in labour supplies, technological developments, and people's tastes for various goods and services. This involves the planners in the notoriously difficult business of forecasting the future.

Three decades or so ago, over one-third of the world's population lived in countries that relied heavily on central planning to deal with the basic economic questions. Today the number of such countries is small. Even in countries where central planning is the official system, as in China, rapidly increasing amounts of market determination are being accepted and encouraged.

## Pure market systems

Earlier in this chapter we discussed the basics of a free-market economy. Millions of consumers decide what products to buy and in what quantities. A large number of firms produce those products and buy the inputs that are needed to make them. Individual decisions collectively determine the economy's allocation of resources between competing uses and the distribution of its output among individual citizens.

In a **pure market economy** all of these decisions, without exception, are made by buyers and sellers acting through unhindered markets. The state provides the legal structure and external defence, but beyond that markets determine all resource allocation and income distribution.

## Mixed systems

Fully traditional, fully centrally controlled, and fully free-market economies are useful concepts for studying the basic principles of resource allocation. When we look in detail at any real economy, however, we discover that its economic behaviour is the result of some mixture of central control and market determination, with a certain amount of traditional behaviour as well. The term **mixed** economy refers to an economy in which both free markets and governments have significant effects on the allocation of resources and the distribution of income.

In practice, every economy is a mixed economy in the sense that it combines significant elements of all three systems—traditional, command, and market—in determining economic behaviour.

The proportions of the mixture of free-market determination and government control vary from economy to economy and over time. There is more free-market determination in the UK and the USA than in France and South Korea. There is more free-market determination in the UK today than there was forty years ago. The mix also varies from sector to sector within any one economy. For example, European agricultural markets have a substantial amount of government control. Under market determination, the average size of a farm would be much larger and agricultural prices much lower than they now are. In contrast, the markets for information and computer technologies are largely free from government intervention. Even the economies closest to free markets have a significant role for government; so it appears that there is no real alternative to a mixed system with major reliance on markets but with a substantial government presence in many aspects of the economy.

## Government in the modern mixed economy

Modern market economies in advanced industrial countries are based primarily on market transactions between people who voluntarily decide whether or not to transact. Private individuals have the right to buy and sell what they wish, to accept or refuse work that is offered to them, and to move where they want when they want. But governments create the legal framework that governs transactions.

Key institutions are private property and freedom of contract, both of which must be maintained by active government policies. The government creates laws of ownership and contract, and then provides the courts to enforce these laws. Governments are also responsible for provision of a stable-valued money which is the measuring rod for all prices.

In modern mixed economies governments go well beyond these important basic functions. They intervene in market transactions to correct what are called 'market failures'. These are identifiable situations in which free markets do not work well. For example, natural resources such as fishing grounds and common pastureland tend to be overexploited to the point of destruction under free-market conditions. Some products, called **public goods**, are not provided at all by markets because, once produced, no one can be prevented from using them. So their use cannot be restricted to those who are willing to pay for them. Defence and law and order are public goods. In other cases private agents impose costs called **externalities** on others by their economic activities, such as when factories pollute the air and rivers—the public is harmed but has no part in the producers' decisions about what to make and how to make it. These are some of the reasons why free markets sometimes fail to function in desirable ways. They explain why citizens want governments to intervene and alter the outcome that would result if everything were left to the market.

There are also some products, like health and education, that could be provided through the market, but which governments have decided should be provided by the state and (in some cases) free of charge. These are not pure public goods, but many countries' governments have decided that some level of minimum provision must be available to all, so this cannot be left to the market. These are sometimes referred to as **merit goods**.

Also, there are important equity (or fairness) issues that arise from letting free markets determine people's incomes. Some people lose their jobs because firms are reorganizing in the face of new technologies. Others may keep their jobs, but the market values their services so poorly that they face economic hardship. The old and the chronically ill may suffer if their past circumstances did not enable them to save enough to support themselves. For many reasons of this sort, we accept government intervention to redistribute income by taking something from the 'haves' and giving it to the 'have-nots'. Almost everyone accepts that there should be some redistribution of incomes. Care must be taken, however, not to kill the goose that lays the golden egg. Taking too much from the 'haves' risks eliminating their incentive to work hard and produce income, some of which would be redistributed to the 'have-nots'.

Governments also play a part in influencing the overall level of prices and in attempting to stabilize the economy against extreme fluctuations in income and employment. A stable price level and full employment are the two major goals of what is called the government's macroeconomic policy. These are dealt with in the second half of this book.

These are some of the reasons why all modern economies are mixed economies. Throughout most of the twentieth century, in advanced industrial societies the mix was altering towards more and more government participation in decisions about the allocation of resources and the distribution of income. In the last two decades of the century, however, there was a worldwide movement to lower the degree of government participation. The details of this shift in the market/government mix, and the reasons for it, are among the major issues that you will study in this book.

# SUMMARY

### The complexity of the modern economy

- A market economy is self-organizing in the sense that, when individuals act independently to pursue their own self-interest, responding to prices set on open markets, they produce co-ordinated and relatively efficient economic outcomes.

### Resources and scarcity

- Scarcity is a fundamental problem faced by all economies because not enough resources—land, labour, capital, and entrepreneurship—are available to produce all the goods and services that people would like to consume. Scarcity makes it necessary to choose among alternative possibilities: what products should be produced and in what quantities?

- The concept of opportunity cost highlights scarcity and choice by measuring the cost of obtaining a unit of one product in terms of the number of units of other products that could have been obtained instead.

- A production-possibility boundary shows all of the combinations of goods that can be produced by an economy when its resources are fully employed. Movement from one point to another on the boundary shows a shift in the amounts of goods being produced, which requires a reallocation of resources.

### Who makes the choices and how

- Modern economies are based on the specialization and division of labour, which necessitate the exchange of goods and services. Exchange takes place in markets and is facilitated by the use of money. Markets work to co-ordinate millions of individual, decentralized decisions.

- Three pure types of economy can be distinguished: traditional, command, and free-market. In practice, all economies are mixed economies in that their economic behaviour responds to mixes of tradition, government command, and price incentives.

- Governments play an important part in modern mixed economies. They create and enforce important background institutions such as private property. They intervene in an attempt to increase economic efficiency by correcting situations where markets do not effectively perform their co-ordinating functions. They also redistribute income and wealth in the interests of equity.

# TOPICS FOR REVIEW

- Kinds of resources
- Self-organization
- Goods and services
- Scarcity, choice, and opportunity cost
- Production-possibility boundary

- Resource allocation
- Growth in productive capacity
- Specialization and the division of labour
- Command, traditional, market, and mixed economic systems

## QUESTIONS

1 Make a list of all the economic activities that contribute to each of the following: (*a*) delivering the evening news bulletin to your television or radio, (*b*) providing cotton shirts on sale in your local high street stores, (*c*) providing a hamburger in a local fast-food restaurant.

2 What is the opportunity cost to you of each of the following: (*a*) studying at weekends, (*b*) doing charity work two evenings a week, (*c*) working in paid employment during every vacation?

3 List some of the choices you make on a daily basis in terms of how you spend your time and how you spend your money.

4 Make a list of all the different goods and services you typically buy in a normal week. In how many different markets does this suggest that a typical individual trades on a regular basis?

5 Explain the concept of opportunity cost and discuss how it relates to the problem of choice between scarce alternatives.

6 Outline the differences between traditional, command, and market economies and explain why the former two have been superseded.

7 In what ways does money facilitate specialization and the division of labour?

8 Why do governments have a role in a market economy? (Revisit this question once you have studied Chapters 13 and 14.)

9 Economics used to be known as the 'dismal science' because it pointed out that choices had to be made between scarce alternatives. Assess the prospects of scarcity being eliminated in the foreseeable future.

# Chapter 2

# HOW ECONOMISTS WORK

In this chapter you will learn some of the language and methods of economics.[1] In particular you will discover:

- The difference between positive and normative statements
- How economists set out their theories
- How economic data are handled and graphed
- How economic relationships are represented in diagrams

Economics seeks to understand many important issues in the world around us. What makes some countries grow richer while others seem to get poorer? Why do we sometimes have recessions? When should the government try to influence markets? What are the costs and benefits of globalization? Will some new technology eliminate many jobs? In order to get a handle on such big issues, economists have developed ways of setting out and testing their theories. They also seek to use what they have learned in order to provide advice on how things could be improved.

We start this chapter by discussing an important distinction relating to types of statement that are used in giving advice. We then outline how theories are built in economics and discuss some of the tools that will be used to analyse and illustrate economic relationships, not only in this book, but throughout your study of economics.

## Economic advice: positive and normative statements

Economists give advice on a wide variety of topics. If you read a newspaper, watch television news, or listen to commentaries on the radio you will often notice some economist's opinions being reported, perhaps on the prospects for unemployment, inflation, or interest rates, on some new tax, or on the case for privatization or regulation of an industry.

Advice comes in two broad types: normative and positive. **Normative** statements depend on value judgements.

They involve issues of personal opinion, which cannot be settled by recourse to facts. In contrast, **positive** statements do not involve value judgements. They are statements about what is, was, or will be: that is, statements that are about matters of fact.

It is difficult to have a rational discussion of issues if positive and normative issues are confused. Much of the success of modern science depends on the ability of scientists to separate their views on *what does*, or *might*, *happen* in the world, from their views on *what they would like to happen*. For example, until the eighteenth century almost everyone believed that the Earth was only a few thousand years old. Evidence then began to accumulate that the

---

[1] We provide some more advanced material relating to economists' methods on our web page: www.oxfordtextbooks.co.uk/orc/lipsey11e/

**Table 2.1 Positive and normative statements**

| Positive | Normative |
|---|---|
| A Higher interest rates cause people to save more. | G People should save more. |
| B High income tax rates discourage effort. | H Governments should tax the rich to help the poor. |
| C High taxes on cigarettes discourage smoking. | I Smoking should be discouraged. |
| D Road-use charges would increase traffic. | J The tax system should be used to reduce traffic. |
| E People are more worried about inflation than unemployment. | K Technical change is a bad thing because it puts some people out of work. |
| F The burning of fossil fuels is causing global warming. | L Governments should do more to reduce carbon emissions in order to save the planet from global warming. |

Earth was thousands of millions of years old. This evidence was hard for most people to accept since it ran counter to a literal reading of many religious texts. Many did not want to believe the evidence. Nevertheless, scientists, many of whom were religious, continued their research because they refused to allow their feelings about what they wanted to believe to affect their search, as scientists, for the truth. Eventually all scientists came to accept that the Earth is about 4,000 million years old.

Distinguishing what is true from what we would like to be, or what we feel ought to be, depends to a great extent on being able to distinguish between positive and normative statements.

Examples of normative and positive statements are given in Table 2.1. All six statements listed in the table as 'positive' assert things about the nature of the world in which we live. In contrast, the six statements listed as 'normative' require value judgements.

Notice two things about the positive–normative distinction. First, positive statements need not be true. Statement D is almost certainly false; yet it is positive, not normative. Second, the inclusion of a value judgement in a statement does not necessarily make the statement normative. Statement E is about the preferences that people hold, that is, about their value judgements. We could, however, check to see if people really do worry more about inflation than unemployment. We can observe their answers to survey questions, and we can observe how they vote for parties that give different priority to these objectives. There is no need to introduce a value judgement in order to check the validity of the statement itself.

You can decide for yourself why each of the other statements is either positive or normative. Remember to apply two tests: (1) Is the statement only about actual or alleged facts? If so, it is a positive one. (2) Are value judgements necessary to assess the truth of the statement? If so, it is a normative statement.

# Economic theorizing

Why has the computer and internet revolution of the last few decades not led to an increase in the trend growth rate of most major economies? Does globalization help to raise living standards in the developing countries? These are important questions. In order to address them (and many more such questions) economists have developed an approach that involves developing theories and building models. What do we mean when we use words like 'theory' and 'model'?

## Theories

Theories are constructed to explain things. For example, what determines the number of eggs sold in Liverpool in a particular week? As part of the answer to this question, and others like it, economists have developed a theory of *demand*—a theory that we study in detail in Chapter 3. Like any other theory, the theory of demand is built around definitions, assumptions, and predictions.

## Definitions

The basic elements of any theory are its variables. A **variable** is something or factor of influence that can take on a range of different possible values.

In our theory of egg purchases, the variable *eggs* might be defined as a one-dozen box of large free-range eggs. The variable *price of eggs* could be the amount of money that must be given up to purchase the one-dozen carton. The particular values taken on by those two variables might be *2,000 dozen* at a price of £1.80 on 1 July 2006, *1,800 dozen* at a price of £2.00 on 8 July 2007, and *1,950 dozen* at a price of £1.90 on 15 July 2008.

For a theory of the demand for eggs, we define the variable *demand* as the number of cartons of eggs that consumers wish to purchase during a particular time-period.

### Endogenous and exogenous variables

An **endogenous variable** is a variable that is explained within a theory. An **exogenous variable** influences endogenous variables but is itself determined by forces outside the theory. For example, the quantity of eggs purchased is an endogenous variable in our theory of the demand for eggs. The forces at work within the theory determine it. Indeed, the whole point of the theory is to explain what makes the quantity of eggs purchased change. The state of the weather is an exogenous variable. It may affect the number of eggs people demand, but we can safely assume that the state of the weather is not determined by anything going on in the egg market.[2]

## Assumptions

A theory's assumptions concern motives, physical relationships, lines of causation, and the conditions under which the theory is meant to apply.

### Motives

In what is called *neoclassical economics*, it is generally assumed that individuals pursue their own self-interest when making economic decisions. People are assumed to know what they want, and to know how to go about getting it within the constraints set by the resources at their command. Similarly, firms are assumed to maximize profit.[3]

### Physical relationships

Suppose that an egg producer buys 20 more hens, rents another 50 square meters of land, and buys an extra £20 worth of chicken feed per week, and that this has enabled her to produce an extra 200 eggs per week. This is an example of one of the most important physical relationships that helps us analyse the supply side of markets. It shows how the amount of output is related to the quantities of inputs used to produce it. This relationship is specified in what is called a **production function**, which sets out an equation for the relationship between inputs and output.

### Conditions of application

Assumptions are often used to specify the conditions under which a theory is meant to hold. For example, a theory that assumes there is 'no government' does not mean literally the absence of government, but only that the theory is meant to hold when governments are not significantly affecting the situation being studied. Another example is that we often study the market for one product assuming that prices of all other products, and the range of all other products available, are held constant.

The purpose of specifying that some other factors are held constant is not to say that these other things do not matter, but merely to focus on one effect at a time. If many influences can change at the same time, then many alternative outcomes are possible

### Direction of causation

When economists assume that one variable is related to another, they are assuming some causal link between the two. For example, when the amount that consumers spend on holiday travel is assumed (and observed) to increase as their incomes increase, the causation is assumed to run from income to holiday travel. Consumers spend more on holiday travel *because* they have more income; they do not get more income *because* they spend more on holiday travel—it would be great if they did! Two terms are used to indicate this direction of causation. The variable that *does the causing* is called the **independent variable** and the variable that *is caused* is called the **dependent variable**. In the above example, income is the independent variable and spending on holiday travel is the dependent variable.

## Predictions

A theory's predictions are the propositions that can be deduced from it. For example, a proposition in the theory of demand states, 'If the price of eggs rises, consumers will purchase fewer eggs.' This negative relationship between

---

[2] Other words are sometimes used to make the same distinction. One frequently used pair is 'induced' for endogenous and 'autonomous' for exogenous. ('Autonomous' means self-governing or independent.)

[3] In Chapter 1 we discussed the pursuit of self-interest on page 2, and we return to the motivation of individuals in Chapter 5 and to that of firms in Chapter 7.

**Box 2.1** Prediction, prophecy, and forecasting

A scientific prediction is a conditional statement that takes the form '*If* something is done, *then* such and such will follow.' For example, if the government cuts taxes on firms, then investment will increase.

**Prediction versus prophecy**

A prediction of this sort is different from the statement 'I prophesy that in two years' time there will be a large increase in investment because I believe the government will decide to cut tax rates.' The government's decision to cut tax rates in two years' time will be the outcome of many influences, both economic and political. If the prophecy about investment turns out to be wrong because in two years' time the government does not cut tax rates, then all that has been learned is that the person was not good at guessing the behaviour of the government. However, if the government does cut tax rates (in two years' time or at any other time) and investment does not then increase, a conditional scientific prediction in economic theory will have been contradicted.

**Prediction versus forecasting**

Conditional prediction should not be confused with forecasting. Forecasting attempts to predict the future by discovering relationships between economic variables such as that the value of *Y* at some future date depends primarily on the value of *X* today. If so, future *Y* can be predicted by observing present *X*. Many conditional predictions are not of this form. Some theories relate the *current value* of *Y* to the current value of *X*. These theories provide significant and useful relationships that allow us to predict 'if you now do this to *X*, *Y* will change now in some specified way', without allowing us to forecast the future. Second, other theories show that the value of *X* is one important determinant of the future value of *Y* without being the only determinant. These theories allow us to influence *Y* in the future without being able to forecast its precise value—because we cannot predict the changes in all the other forces that influence *Y*. The analogy often drawn between economics and weather forecasting relates to economic forecasting rather than to the wider and more interesting class of conditional *if* . . . *then* economic predictions.

a product's price and the amount that people wish to buy applies to all commodities. These propositions are then taken as predictions about real-world events. For example, if the price of CDs is reduced, consumers will buy more of them. Box 2.1 discusses the distinction between predictions, forecasts, and prophecies.

## Models

Economists often proceed by constructing what they call **economic models**. This term has several different but related meanings.

Sometimes the term 'model' is used as a synonym for a theory, as when economists speak of the model of the determination of national income. Sometimes it may refer to a particular subset of theories, such as the Keynesian model or the neoclassical model of income determination.

More often, a model means a specific quantitative formulation of a theory. In this case, specific numbers are attached to the mathematical relationships defined by the theory, the numbers often being derived from observations of the economy. The specific form of the model can then be used to make precise predictions about, say, the behaviour of prices in the potato market, or the course of national income and total employment. Forecasting models used by the Bank of England and the International Monetary Fund (IMF) are of this type.

The term 'model' is often used to refer to an application of a general theory in a specific context. So if we take our theory of consumer demand and apply it to the egg market in southern England, we might speak of a model of the southern English egg market.

Finally, a model may be an illustrative abstraction, not meant to be elaborate enough to be tested. The circular flow in Figure 1.3 on page 8 is a model of this sort. Illustrating how income flows between consumers and producers helps us to understand how the decisions of these two groups influence each other through labour markets and goods markets. However, the actual flows in any real economy are vastly more complex than the simple flows shown in the figure. The model helps us to understand what is going on without being detailed enough to yield specific testable predictions about real-world behaviour. In some ways, a model of this sort is like a political caricature. Its value is in the insights it provides that help us to understand key features of a complex world.

Box 2.2 gives another example of how an illustrative model may be used to understand some tendencies by studying them in isolation.

## Evidence

Economists make much use of evidence, or, as they usually call it, empirical observation. Such observations can

**Box 2.2  An illustrative model**

It has been observed that the amount of research that goes into improving a new product often depends on the product's current sales—since the profits that finance much of a firm's research and development (R&D) are generated by its sales. To gain insight into some possible consequences of this relationship, we can build a very simple model in which the amount of current research to improve some product is positively related to the amount of that product's current sales. This creates what is called *positive feedback*, because the larger current sales are, the more research is done; the more research is done, the more rapidly the product improves; the more rapidly the product improves, the more current sales rise.

We may then elaborate the model by adding a second product, which competes with the first one. The model then shows that the product that gets the larger sales initially (for whatever reason) will attract more R&D, and hence will be improved more rapidly than the product with the smaller initial sales. This model will reveal one key tendency of positive feedback systems: initial advantages tend to be reinforced, making it more and more difficult for competitors to keep up. No one believes that this simple model catches everything about the complex interactions when various new products compete with each other in the early stages of their development. But it does alert us to certain forces to watch for when we build more complex models or create more general theories of competition among new products and new technologies.

Interestingly, these self-reinforcing characteristics have been observed in many actual cases. These include the competition to be the power source of the first motor cars early in the twentieth century, the competition among alternative technologies to produce nuclear power in the middle of the century, and the recent competition to produce the operating system of personal computers (which was won by Microsoft). All of these are cases in which early success helped a particular technology to build up an unbeatable lead over competing technologies.

be used to test a specific prediction of some theory and to provide observations to be explained by theories.

### Tests

A theory is tested by confronting its predictions with evidence. Are events of the type contained in the theory followed by the consequences predicted by the theory? For example, is an increase in the price of eggs met by a fall in the quantity of eggs that consumers wish to buy? Generally, theories tend to be abandoned when they are no longer useful. A theory ceases to be useful when it

cannot predict better than an alternative theory. When a theory consistently fails to predict better than an available alternative, it is either modified or replaced.

### Theory and evidence: which came first?

The old question of the chicken and the egg is often raised when discussing economic theories. In the first instance, it was observation that preceded economic theories. People were not born with economic theories embedded in their minds: instead, economic theories first arose when people observed the co-ordination of market behaviour and asked themselves how such co-ordination occurred. But now that a body of economic ideas exists, theories and evidence interact with each other. It has become impossible to say that one now precedes the other. In some cases empirical evidence may suggest inadequacies that require the development of better theories. In other cases an inspired guess may lead to a theory that has little current empirical support but is subsequently found to explain many observations.

Box 2.3 discusses some more detailed aspects of testability.

## Theories about human behaviour

So far we have talked about theories in general. But what about theories that purport to explain and predict human behaviour? A scientific study of human behaviour is possible only if humans respond in predictable ways to things that affect them. Is it reasonable to expect such stability? After all, we humans have free will and can behave in capricious ways if the spirit moves us.

Think, however, of what the world would be like if human behaviour were really unpredictable. Neither law, nor justice, nor airline timetables would be more reliable than the outcome of a single spin of a roulette wheel. A kind remark could as easily provoke fury as sympathy. Your landlady might evict you tomorrow or let you off the rent. One cannot really imagine a society of human beings that could work like this. In fact, we live in a world that is a mixture of the predictable, or average, or 'most of the people most of the time', and of the haphazard, or contrary, or random.

How is it that human behaviour can show stable responses even though we can never be quite sure what one individual will do? Successful predictions about the behaviour of large groups are made possible by the statistical 'law' of large numbers. Very roughly, this 'law' asserts that (under a carefully specified set of conditions) random movements of a large number of items tend to offset one another.

**Box 2.3 Testability**

The way in which a positive statement can be tested against facts varies with the kind of positive statement that is under consideration.

A statement that something exists can be proved by finding a confirming example. But it cannot be conclusively disproved, because it is always possible that we have not looked hard enough and that someone will find a confirming example in the future. For example, the statement that extraterrestrials exist and frequently visit Earth in flying saucers could be proved if well documented sightings were repeated in situations in which they could be confirmed by scientific measuring techniques—instead of occurring on isolated country roads to single individuals or small groups, as the alleged close-up sightings now do. But it can never be disproved. For, no matter how long we look and wait, there always exists the possibility that in the future sightings will occur in a convincing form. In the meantime believers say the statement is true while sceptics say 'not proven'.

In contrast, a statement that some relationship always holds true can be refuted by one well documented case in which it is does not hold. But it can never be proved, because there always exists the possibility that in the future we will observe a case in which it does not hold. For example, the theory of consumer demand predicts that the relationship between a commodity's price and the amount consumers wish to purchase is negative—the lower the price, the higher are desired purchases. Occasional exceptions have been alleged (and we will study some of them in later chapters), but they have not been well documented or repeated enough to satisfy contemporary observers. So we can say that the evidence is consistent with the theory, but we cannot say that the theory is proved, because we cannot rule out the possibility that at some future date a case will be documented in which a price reduction reduces desired purchases.

The general point is:

A statement that something exists can be proved but not refuted. A statement that something always exists can be refuted but not proved.

The statement may refer to the existence of some phenomenon or a relationship between two or more variables of the sort that we find in the theories of economics and other fact-based disciplines. In other words, we can show our theories to be consistent with observed facts, but we cannot establish that they are true with certainty.

For example, we might wonder if there is a relationship between motorway speed limits and road accidents. When the speed limit is actually lowered, it will be almost impossible to predict in advance what changes will occur in any single individual's driving record. One individual whose record had been good may have a series of accidents after the speed limit is lowered because of a deterioration in his physical or emotional health. Another person may have an improved accident record for reasons not associated with the alteration in the speed limit, for example because she has purchased a more reliable car. Yet others may have altered driving records for no reasons that we can discern.

If we study only a few individuals, we will learn nothing about the effects of the altered speed limit, since we will not know the importance of all the other causes that are at work. But if we observe 1,000 individuals, the effects of the change in the speed limit—if such effects do exist—will tend to show up in the average. If a lowered speed limit does discourage accidents, the group as a whole will have fewer accidents even though some individuals may have more. Individuals may do peculiar things that, as far as we can see, are inexplicable, but the group's behaviour will none the less be predictable, precisely because the odd things that one individual does will tend to cancel out the odd things that some other individual does.

## Why do economists often disagree?

When all their theories have been constructed and all their evidence has been collected, economists still disagree with each other on many issues. If you hear a discussion among economists on *Newsnight* or the *Today Programme*, or if you read about their debates in the daily press or weekly magazines, you will find that economists frequently disagree with each other. What should we make of this disagreement? Here are five of the many possible sources of disagreement.

First, different economists may be using *different benchmarks*. For example, inflation may be up compared with last year but down compared with the 1980s. When this sort of thing happens the disagreement is more apparent than real, although it can be confusing to observers.

Second, economists often fail to make it clear to their audience whether they are talking about *short-term or long-term consequences*. For example, one economist may be noting that a tax cut will stimulate consumption at the cost of lowering savings in the short run, while another is pointing out that it will stimulate investment and saving in the long run. Here again the disagreement is more apparent than real, since both these short- and long-run effects command much agreement among economists.

Third, economists often fail to acknowledge the full *extent of their ignorance*. There are many things about which we know little, and even more on which our evidence is far from conclusive. Informed judgements are then required before an economist takes a position on even a purely positive question. If two economists' judgements differ, the disagreement is real. Evidence is not sufficient, and different people can come to different conclusions on the basis of such evidence as is available. What a responsible economist will do in such cases is to make clear the extent to which informed judgement is involved in any position she is taking.

Fourth, different economists have *different values*, and these normative views play a large part in most public discussions of policy. Many economists stress the importance of individual responsibility, while others stress the need for collective action to deal with certain issues. Different policy advice may stem from such differences in value judgements about what is socially important.

A fifth reason lies in the desire of *the media* to cover both sides of any contentious issue. As a result the public will usually hear one or two economists on each side of a debate, regardless of whether the profession is divided right down the middle or is nearly unanimous in its support of one side. Thus, the public will not know that in one case a reporter could have chosen from dozens of economists to present each side, whereas in another case the reporter had to spend three days finding someone willing to take a particular side because nearly all the economists supported the other side. In their desire to show both sides of all cases, however, the media present the public with the appearance of a profession equally split over all matters.

Anyone seeking to discredit some particular economist's advice by showing that there is disagreement among economists will have no trouble finding evidence of some disagreement. But those who wish to know if there is a majority view, or even a strong consensus, will find one on a surprisingly large number of issues.

Because the world is complex, and because no issue can be settled beyond any doubt, economists are never in *unanimous* agreement on any issue. None the less, the methods we have been discussing in this chapter have produced an impressive amount of agreement on many aspects of how the economy works and what happens when governments intervene to alter its workings. For example, a survey published in the *American Economic Review* showed strong agreement among economists on many propositions, including 'Rent control leads to a housing shortage' (85 per cent yes). Other examples of these areas of agreement will be found in countless places throughout this book.

## Economic data

Economists seek to explain observations made of the real world. Why, for example, did the price of wheat rise in some years even though the wheat crop increased? We would be aware of this issue only if we had numbers for the wheat crop and the price of wheat, and we would need a lot of additional data (such as on incomes and other prices) to come up with a comprehensive answer.

Real-world observations are also needed to test the predictions of economic theories. For example, did the amount that people saved in a particular year rise—as the theory predicts it should have—when a large tax cut increased after-tax incomes? To test this prediction, we need reliable data for people's incomes and their savings.

Political scientists, sociologists, anthropologists, and psychologists all tend to collect much of the data they use to formulate and test their theories. Economists are unusual among social scientists in mainly using data collected by others, often government statisticians. In economics there is a division of labour between collecting data and using it to generate and test theories. The advantage is that economists do not need to spend much of their scarce research time collecting the data they use. The disadvantage is that they are often not as well informed about the limitations of the data collected by others as they would be if they collected the data themselves.

Once data are collected they can be displayed in various ways, all of which we will examine later in this chapter. For example they can be laid out in tables; they can be displayed in the various types of graph that we study later in this chapter; and where we are interested in relative movements rather than absolute ones, they can be expressed in index numbers.

**Table 2.2** Price of cocoa and coffee (average price in each quarter; US cents per kg)

| Period | Cocoa | Coffee |
|--------|-------|--------|
| 2001 Q1 | 100.4 | 146.7 |
| 2001 Q2 | 104.5 | 146.4 |
| 2001 Q3 | 100.8 | 129.7 |
| 2001 Q4 | 121.8 | 126.4 |
| 2002 Q1 | 149.0 | 136.6 |

*Source*: World Bank; www.worldbank.org

## Index numbers

Table 2.2 shows how the prices of cocoa and coffee beans varied during five quarters of 2001 and 2002. How do these two sets of prices compare in volatility? It may be difficult to tell from the table because the two prices start at different levels. It is easier to compare the series if we concentrate on relative rather than absolute price changes. (The *absolute change* is the actual change in the price; the *relative change* is the change in the price expressed in relationship to some base price.)

### Index numbers as relatives

Comparisons of relative changes can be made by expressing each price series as a set of **index numbers**. To do this we take the price at some point of time as the base with which prices in other periods will be compared. We call this the *base period*. In the present example we choose the first quarter of 2001 as the base period for both series. The price in that quarter is given a value of 100. We then take the price of coffee in each subsequent quarter and express it as a ratio of its price in the base year and multiply the result by 100. This gives us an index number of coffee prices. We then do the same for cocoa. The details of the calculations for coffee are shown in Table 2.3.

The results, which are shown in Table 2.4, allow us to compare the relative fluctuations in the two series. It is apparent from the figures that cocoa prices rose by nearly 50 per cent over the period while coffee prices fell by nearly 14 per cent before recovering slightly.

The formula of any index number is:

$$\text{Value of index in period } t = \frac{\text{value in period } t}{\text{value in base period}} \times 100$$

An index number merely expresses the value of some series in any given period as a percentage of its value in the base period. Thus, the 2002 Q1 index of cocoa prices,

**Table 2.3** Calculation of an index of coffee prices

| Quarter | Index |
|---------|-------|
| 2001 Q1 | $(146.7/146.7) \times 100 = 100$ |
| 2001 Q2 | $(146.4/146.7) \times 100 = 99.8$ |
| 2001 Q3 | $(129.7/146.7) \times 100 = 88.4$ |
| 2001 Q4 | $(126.4/146.7) \times 100 = 86.2$ |
| 2002 Q1 | $(136.6/146.7) \times 100 = 93.1$ |

Index numbers are calculated by dividing the current price by the base-year price and multiplying the result by 100. For example, the coffee price in 2001 Q4 was 126.4 cents per kg. Dividing by the base year price of 146.7 cents (in 2001 Q1) and multiplying by 100 gives an index of 86.2 for this quarter.

**Table 2.4** Index of cocoa and coffee prices

| Period | Cocoa | Coffee |
|--------|-------|--------|
| 2001 Q1 | 100 | 100 |
| 2001 Q2 | 104.1 | 99.8 |
| 2001 Q3 | 100.4 | 88.4 |
| 2001 Q4 | 121.3 | 86.2 |
| 2002 Q1 | 148.4 | 93.1 |

*Source*: Tables 2.2 and 2.3.

which is 148.4, tells us that the 2002 Q1 price of cocoa was 48.4 per cent higher than the 2001 Q1 price. By subtracting 100 from any index we get the change from the base to the given year, expressed as a percentage of the base year. To take a second example, the coffee index of 93.1 in 2002 Q1 tells us that the price of coffee at this time was only 93.1 per cent of the 2001 Q1 price—or, what is the same thing, that the price had fallen by 6.9 per cent over the year.

### Index numbers as averages

Index numbers are particularly useful if we wish to combine several different series into some average. Say, for example, that we want an index of hot-drinks beans, and that cocoa and coffee are the only two commodities we are interested in.

#### Unweighted indexes

For any one year, we could add the price indexes for cocoa and coffee and average them. This would give us a hot-drinks beans index. But the index would give the two prices equal weight in determining the value of the overall index. Such an index is often called an unweighted index, but that is misleading. Actually, it is

**Table 2.5  Two indexes of hot drinks beans prices**

|  | Equal weights | Coffee = 0.9; Cocoa = 0.1 |
|---|---|---|
| 2001 Q1 | 100 | 100 |
| 2001 Q2 | 101.9 | 100.2 |
| 2001 Q3 | 94.2 | 89.6 |
| 2001 Q4 | 103.7 | 89.7 |
| 2002 Q1 | 120.7 | 98.6 |

**Weights really matter.** The equal-weight index is calculated for each period by adding the cocoa and coffee indexes from Table 2.4 and dividing by 2. The second index is calculated for each period by multiplying the coffee index by 0.9 and the cocoa index by 0.1 and then adding the results. The two series behave quite differently as a result of using different weights, as shown in Figure 2.3.

an equal-weight index. It would be sheer luck if this were the appropriate thing to do.

In practice, we need to weight each price by some measure of its relative importance, letting the more important prices have more weight than the less important prices in determining what happens to the overall index.

### Output-weighted indexes

Coffee is a much more important commodity than cocoa in the sense that a much greater volume of coffee is produced. For purposes of illustration, we assume that 9 kg of coffee is produced for every 1 kg of cocoa. To get our weighted index of bean prices, we multiply the coffee index value in Table 2.4 by 0.9 and the cocoa index by 0.1 and sum the two to obtain the final index. The results are shown in Table 2.5. The quite different behaviour of the two indexes shows the importance of the choice of weights.

An index that averages changes in several series is the weighted average of the indexes for the separate series, the weights reflecting the relative importance of each series.

### Price indexes

Economists make frequent use of indexes of the price level which cover a broad group of prices across the whole economy. One of the most important of these is the retail price index, RPI, which covers goods and services that individuals buy. This is described in detail in Chapter 15 on page 251.

All price indexes are calculated using the same procedure. First, the relevant prices are collected. Then a base year is chosen. Then each price series is converted into index numbers. Finally, the index numbers are combined to create a weighted average index series where the weights indicate the relative importance of each price

series. For example, in any retail price series the price of sardines would be given a much smaller weight than the price of living accommodation, because what happens to the price of accommodation is much more important to consumers, all of whom spend much more on accommodation than on sardines.

## Graphing economic data

A single economic variable such as unemployment or GDP can be graphed in two basic forms.

### Cross-sectional graphs

**Cross-sectional data** are a number of different observations on one variable all taken in different places at the same point in time. Figure 2.1 shows an example. The variable in the figure is unemployment as a percentage of the workforce. It is shown for ten selected countries for September 2005.

### Time-series graphs

**Time-series data** are observations taken on one variable at successive points in time. The data in Figure 2.2 show the unemployment rate for the UK from 1950 to 2005. The large variations, with two peaks in the mid-1980s and mid-1990s, are readily apparent. Figure 2.3 shows another time-series, this time for the two indexes of hot-drinks beans that we calculated in the section on index numbers.

### Scatter diagrams

Another way in which data can be presented is in a **scatter diagram**. This type of chart is more analytical than those above. It is designed to show the relationship between two different variables, such as the price of eggs and the quantity of eggs sold. To plot a scatter diagram,

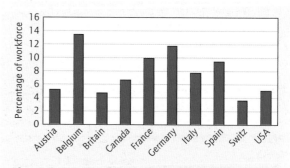

**Figure 2.1  Unemployment for ten countries, September 2005**

*Source: The Economist*, 29 October 2005. © The Economist Newspaper Ltd, London.

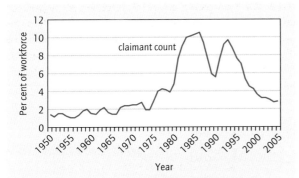

**Figure 2.2** **UK unemployment claimant count as a percentage of the workforce, 1950–2005**

*Source*: ONS, *Economic Trends annual supplement*, 2005, and ONS website.

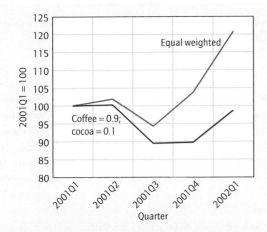

**Figure 2.3** **Two indexes of hot-drinks bean prices**

**Weights matter.** The two series are constructed from the same prices for cocoa and coffee. The difference is only in the weights. The equal-weighted series is a simple average of the indexes for each type of bean. The output-weighted series is constructed by multiplying the coffee price index by 0.9 and the cocoa price index by 0.1. These weights conform roughly to the relative proportion that each contributes to the total value of production.

*Source*: Table 2.5.

**Table 2.6** **Income and savings for ten selected households**

| Household | Annual income | Annual savings |
|-----------|---------------|----------------|
| 1 | £70,000 | £10,000 |
| 2 | 30,000 | 2,500 |
| 3 | 100,000 | 12,000 |
| 4 | 60,000 | 3,000 |
| 5 | 80,000 | 8,000 |
| 6 | 10,000 | 500 |
| 7 | 20,000 | 2,000 |
| 8 | 50,000 | 2,000 |
| 9 | 40,000 | 4,200 |
| 10 | 90,000 | 8,000 |

**Savings tend to rise as income rises.** The table shows the amount of income earned by ten selected households together with the amount they saved during the same year.

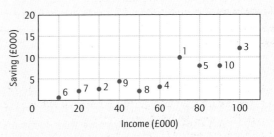

**Figure 2.4** **Savings and income**

**Saving tends to rise as income rises.** The figure plots the incomes and savings for the ten households listed in Table 2.6. The number on each dot refers to the household in the corresponding row of the table. (Note that the scales are not the same on the two axes.)

values of one variable are measured on the horizontal axis and values of the second variable are measured on the vertical axis. Any point on the diagram relates a specific value of one variable to a corresponding specific value of the other.

The two series plotted on a scatter diagram may be either cross-sectional or time-series. An example of a cross-sectional scatter diagram would be a scatter of the price of eggs and the quantity sold in July 2007 at two dozen different places in England. Each dot would show a price–quantity combination observed in a different place at the same time. An example of a scatter diagram using time-series data would be the price and quantity of eggs sold in Liverpool for each month over the last ten years. Each of the 120 dots would show a price–quantity combination observed at the same place in one particular month.

Table 2.6 shows data for the income and the savings of ten households in one particular year.[4] They are plotted on a scatter diagram in Figure 2.4. Each point in the figure stands for one household, showing its income and its saving. The positive relationship between the two stands out. The higher income is, the higher saving tends to be.

---

[4] Although our theory refers to individuals, data are often gathered for households, which are defined as a group of individuals who live under the same roof and make joint financial decisions.

# Graphing economic relationships

Theories are built on assumptions about relationships between variables. For example, the quantity of eggs purchased is assumed to fall as the price of eggs rises, and the total amount that an individual saves is assumed to rise as her income rises. How can such relationships be expressed? When one variable is related to another in such a way that to every value of one variable there is only one possible value of the second variable, we say that the second variable is *a function* of the first. When we write this relationship down, we are expressing a functional relationship between the two variables.

A functional relationship can be expressed in words, in a numerical schedule, in an equation, or in a graph.

To illustrate, we take a specific example of a relationship between a family's annual income, which we denote by the symbol $Y$, and the total amount the family spends on goods and services during that year, which we denote by the symbol $C$.

### Verbal statement

When income is zero, the family will spend £800 a year (either by borrowing the money or by consuming past savings), and for every £1 of income that it obtains it will increase its spending by £0.80.

### Schedule

This shows selected values of the family's income and the amount it spends on consumption:

| Annual income | Consumption | Reference letter |
|---|---|---|
| 0 | 800 | $p$ |
| 2,500 | 2,800 | $q$ |
| 5,000 | 4,800 | $r$ |
| 7,500 | 6,800 | $s$ |
| 10,000 | 8,800 | $t$ |

### Mathematical (algebraic) statement

$C$ = £800 + 0.8$Y$ is the equation of the relationship described above in words. As a check, you can first see that when $Y$ is zero $C$ is £800. Then you can substitute any two values of $Y$ that differ by £1, multiply each by 0.80, and add 800, and see that the corresponding two values of consumption differ by £0.80.

**Figure 2.5 Income and consumption**

**Consumption spending rises as income rises.** The figure graphs the schedule and the equation for the consumption function discussed in the text.

### Geometrical (graphical) statement

Figure 2.5 shows both the points from the schedule above and the line representing the equation given in the above paragraph.

Comparing the values on the graph with the values in the schedule, and with the values derived from the above equation, you can see that they are alternative expressions of the same relationship between $C$ and $Y$. All four of these modes of expression refer to the same relationship between total consumption spending and total income.

## Functions

Let us look in a little more detail at the algebraic expression of this relationship between income and consumption spending. To state the expression in general form, detached from the specific numerical example above, we use a symbol to express the dependence of one variable on another. Using 'f' for this purpose, we write

$$C = \mathrm{f}(Y). \tag{1}$$

This is read '$C$ is a function of $Y$'. More fully, it reads 'The amount of consumption spending depends upon the household's income.'

The variable on the left-hand side is the dependent variable, since its value depends on the value of the variable on the right-hand side. The variable on the right-hand side is the independent variable, since it can take on any value. The letter 'f' tells us that a **functional relationship** is involved. This means that a knowledge of the value of the variable (or variables) within the parentheses on the right-hand side allows us to determine the value of the variable on the left-hand side. Although in this case we have used 'f' (as a memory-aid for 'function'), any convenient symbol can be used to denote the existence of a functional relationship.

Functional notation can seem intimidating to those who are unfamiliar with it, but it is helpful. Since the functional concept is basic to all science, the notation is worth understanding.

## Functional forms

The expression $C = f(Y)$ states that $C$ is related to $Y$. It says nothing about the form that this relationship takes. The term 'functional form' refers to the specific nature of the relationship between the variables in the function. The example above gave one specific functional form for this relationship:

$$C = £800 + 0.8Y. \qquad (2)$$

Equation (1) expresses the general assumption that consumption spending depends on the consumer's income. Equation (2) expresses the more specific assumption that $C$ rises by 80p for every £1 that $Y$ rises. A second form for the function in (1) would be $C = £600 + 0.9Y$. You should be able to say in words the behaviour implied in this relationship.

There is no reason why either of these assumptions must be true; indeed, neither may be consistent with the facts. But that is a matter for testing. What we do have in each equation is a concise statement of a possible relationship.

## Graphing relationships

Different functional forms have different graphs, and we will meet many of these in subsequent chapters. Figure 2.5 is an example of a relationship in which the two variables move together. When income goes up, consumption goes up. In such a relationship the two variables are *positively related* to each other. (Figure 16.2 on page 365 shows the actual relationship for the UK over the period 1955–2005.)

Figure 2.6 gives an example of variables that move in opposite directions. As the amount spent on abating smoke pollution goes up, the amount of pollution goes down. In such a relationship the two variables are *negatively related* to each other.[5]

Both of these graphs are straight lines. In such cases we say that the variables are *linearly related* to each other.

## The slope of a straight line

Slopes are important in economics. They show you how fast one variable is changing as the other changes. The *slope* is defined as the amount of change in the variable measured on the vertical or $y$-axis per unit change in the variable measured on the horizontal or $x$-axis. In the case of Figure 2.6 it tells us how many tonnes of smoke pollution, symbolized by $P$, are removed per pound spent on pollution control, symbolized by $E$. As the figure shows, if we spend £2,000 more we get 1,000 tonnes less pollution. This is 0.5 tonne per pound spent. On the graph the extra £2,000 is indicated by $\Delta E$, the arrow indicating that $E$ rises by £2,000. The 1,000 tonnes of pollution reduction is indicated by $\Delta P$, the arrow showing that pollution falls by 1,000. (The Greek uppercase letter delta $\Delta$ stands for a change in something.) To get the amount of abatement per pound of spending we merely divide one by the other. In symbols this is $\Delta P/\Delta E$.

**More generally, if we let $X$ stand for whatever variable is measured on the horizontal axis and $Y$ for whatever variable is measured on the vertical axis, the slope of a straight line is $\Delta Y/\Delta X$.**

In Figure 2.5 the two variables change in the same direction, so both changes will always be either positive or

**Figure 2.6  Linear pollution abatement**

**Pollution falls linearly as spending on abatement rises.** The slope of the line indicates the marginal reduction in pollution for every increase of £1 of abatement spending. It is constant at −0.5, indicating that every extra £1 spent on abatement reduces pollution by half a tonne.

---

[5] We refer to the slopes of curves as *positive* if both variables change in the same direction along the curve (i.e. if they both increase or both decrease) and as *negative* if the variables change in opposite directions along the curve (i.e. if one increases while the other decreases). Economists often read curves from left to right, calling negatively sloped curves 'downward-sloping' and positively sloped curves 'upward-sloping'. We stick mainly to the unambiguous terminology of positive and negative slopes.

negative. As a result their ratio, which is the slope of this line, is positive.

In Figure 2.6 the two variables change in opposite directions: when one increases the other decreases. So the two Δs will always be of opposite sign. As a result their ratio, which is the slope of the line, is always negative.

Notice also that straight lines have the same slope no matter where on the line you measure that slope. This tells us what inspection of the chart reveals: that the change in one variable in response to a unit change in the other is the same anywhere on the line. We get 0.5 tonne of additional pollution abatement for every additional £1 that we spend on abatement, no matter how much we are already spending.

## Nonlinear relationships

The world is seldom as simple as linear relationships would make it seem. Although it is sometimes convenient to simplify a real relationship between two variables by assuming them to be linearly related, this is seldom the case over their whole range. Nonlinear relationships are much more common than linear ones. In the case of pollution abatement, it is usually quite cheap to eliminate the first units of pollution. Then, as the smoke gets cleaner and cleaner, the cost of further abatement tends to increase because more and more sophisticated and expensive methods need to be used. As a result, the graph relating spending on abatement and amount of pollution usually looks more like Figure 2.7 than Figure 2.6.

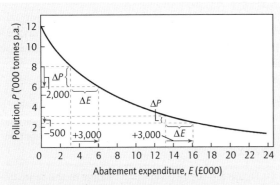

**Figure 2.7  Nonlinear pollution abatement**

**Pollution falls nonlinearly as abatement spending rises.** When pollution is 8,000 tonnes per year, an additional spending of £3,000 reduces pollution by 2,000 tonnes. The marginal return for £1 additional spending is ΔP/ΔE or 2,000/3,000, which is two-thirds of a tonne per £1 spent on abatement. However, when pollution has already been reduced to 3,000 tonnes, an extra £3,000 spent on abatement reduces pollution by only 500 tonnes. The marginal return for £1 of additional spending, ΔP/ΔE, is now only 500/3,000 or one-sixth of a tonne per £1 spent.

Inspection of this figure shows that, as more and more is spent, the benefit in terms of extra abatement for an additional £1 of abatement spending gets smaller and smaller. This is shown by the diminishing slope of the curve as we move rightward along it. As the figure shows, an extra £1 of spending yields two-thirds of a tonne of abatement (2,000/3,000) when pollution is 8,000 tonnes but only one-sixth of a tonne of abatement (500/3,000) when pollution is 3,000 tonnes.

Economists call the change in abatement when a bit more or a bit less is spent on it the *marginal* change. The figure shows that the slope of the curve at each point measures this marginal change. It also shows that, in the type of curve illustrated, the marginal return per pound spent is diminishing as abatement proceeds. There is always a payoff to more spending over the range shown in the figure, but the return diminishes as more is spent. This relationship can be described as *diminishing marginal response*. We will meet such relationships many times in what follows, so we emphasize now that diminishing marginal response does not mean that the total response is diminishing. In the figure the total amount of pollution continues to fall as more and more is spent on abatement. But diminishing marginal response does mean that the amount of abatement obtained for *each additional unit of expense* is diminishing as more and more pollution is abated.

In Figure 2.8 the graph shows marginal return increasing. It relates spending on navigational aids to the number of safe passages. At low levels of spending the curve is nearly flat. An additional unit of spending does not yield much additional protection, but as more and more is spent it becomes possible to employ more efficient navigation aids that work together as a whole system. Each extra unit of spending yields more additional protection than each previous unit. In this case we have what economists call *increasing marginal response*. The reason is that navigation aids encounter what are called network externalities. They are most effective not as single stand-alone bits, such as one lighthouse, but as an integrated whole. Each aid becomes more effective the more complex and interrelated is the whole system of which it is a part.

## Maxima and minima

So far all the graphs we have shown have had either a positive or negative slope over their entire range. But many relationships change direction as the independent variable increases. Figures 2.9 and 2.10 extend our navigation and pollution examples over a larger range of the independent variables. You can see that, as more and more is

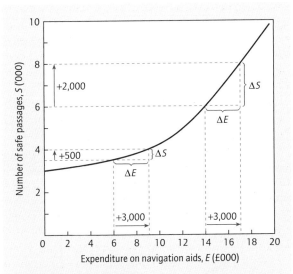

**Figure 2.8** Navigation aids

**Safe passages increase at an increasing rate as navigation aids are increased.** The figure shows the number of safe passages varying positively with the amount spent on navigation aids. Because of network externalities, the number of safe passages increases at an increasing rate as more is spent on navigation aids. An increase in spending on navigation aids by £3,000 when spending is £6,000 raises safe passages by 500, from 3,500 to 4,000. The marginal return to £1 extra spent on navigation aids is then 500/3,000 or 0.167; in other words, it takes £6 to get one more safe passage (3,000/500). When £14,000 is already being spent, a further increase of £3,000 increases safe passages by 2,000 from 6,000 to 8,000. The marginal return from £1 spent on aids is now 2,000/3,000 or 0.667; in other words, it only takes £1.50 extra spending to get one more safe passage (3,000/2,000).

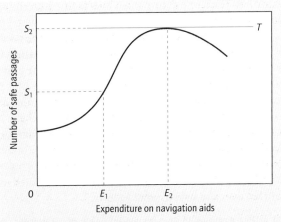

**Figure 2.9** Aid saturation

**Eventually increases in spending on navigation aids serve to reduce the number of safe passages.** Up to $E_1$ spending on navigation aids encounters increasing marginal returns; each additional £1 of spending allows a larger increase in safe passages than each previous £1 of spending. Between $E_1$ and $E_2$ spending encounters decreasing marginal returns; each additional £1 spent increases the number of safe passages by less than the previous £1 of spending. At $E_2$ safe passages reach a maximum of $S_2$. Further spending encounters negative marginal returns; each additional £1 spent lowers the number of safe passages. At the maximum point the slope of the tangent $T$ (the straight line that just touches the curve at that point) is zero. At that point the number of safe passages shows no response to small changes in spending on navigation aids.

spent on navigation aids, not only does the marginal contribution of each additional £1 spent begin to decline, but eventually the total safety begins to decline. The reason is that the signals begin to interfere with each other and confuse rather than aid navigators. So as spending on navigation aids increases, eventually the safety achieved reaches a maximum after which it begins to decline.

At the maximum point the curve is flat—it has a zero slope. Up to that point each £1 spent does increase safety —it has a positive marginal contribution. But beyond that point each additional unit lowers safety—it has a negative marginal contribution. At the maximum point the marginal contribution is zero.

Now look at Figure 2.10, which extends the pollution abatement example. Here we see that each £1 spent on pollution control adds to abatement up to the amount $E_1$, but after that abatement begins to decline. The reason in this case may be that the regulations become so costly that

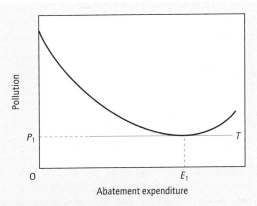

**Figure 2.10** Abatement saturation

**Beyond a certain point additional abatement spending increases pollution.** Up to $E_1$ each additional £1 of spending reduces pollution, but at a diminishing amount for each £1. At spending $E_1$ pollution reaches a minimum of $P_1$. If further amounts are spent, pollution actually rises. At the minimum point the slope of the tangent line $T$ is zero; at that point pollution shows no response to small changes in abatement spending.

firms find ways of evading them and total enforcement gets less effective. Pollution reaches a minimum when $E_1$ is spent but rises thereafter. Notice that up to $E_1$ the curve has a negative slope, indicating that more spending is associated with less pollution, but that after $E_1$ the curve has a positive slope, indicating that more spending is associated with more pollution. At the point of minimum pollution the tangent to the curve shown by the line $T$ has a slope of zero. (A *tangent* is a straight line that just touches a curve at some point and lies everywhere above or below the curve near that point.)

These two cases illustrate an important point, which we will see over and over in what follows:

**At either a minimum or a maximum value of a function, its slope, or marginal value, is zero.**

Figure 2.11 summarizes what we have seen so far. The three lines in part (i) are all positively sloped, making $Y$ positively related to $X$. The first is a straight line, which means it has a constant slope: the change in $Y$ for a given change in $X$, the marginal value of $Y$, is the same no matter where on the line we measure it. The slope of the second line gets steeper as we move along it to the right: the response of $Y$ to a change in $X$, the marginal value of $Y$, is increasing. The third line gets flatter as we move along it: the response of $Y$ to a change in $X$, the marginal value of $Y$, is decreasing as we move along the line.

In part (ii) the three lines are all negatively sloped, so that $Y$ is negatively related to $X$. Along the line labelled (4) the response of $Y$ to a change in $X$ is constant. On the line labelled (5) the response is increasing as the slope gets steeper and steeper. On the line labelled (6) the response of $Y$ to a change in $X$, its marginal value, is decreasing as we move along it, as shown by the flattening of the curve.

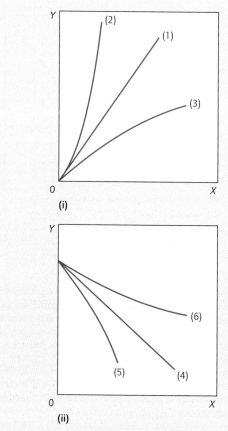

**Figure 2.11** Positive and negative relationships

*Y* is positively related to *X* in all three curves in part (i) and negatively related in all three curves in part (ii). The lines on the two graphs show the response of *Y* to a change in *X*. In curves (1) and (4) this response is constant. In curves (2) and (5) the response is increasing as we move along the curve to the right. In curves (3) and (6) the response is diminishing.

## Conclusion

This chapter has outlined some background issues and introduced some methods that will be helpful in studying economics. We take this further on our website: www.oxfordtextbooks.co.uk/orc/lipsey11e/

You may find it helpful to refer back to this chapter at later stages in your study of the remaining parts of this book.

# SUMMARY

### Economic advice: positive and normative statements

- A key to the success of scientific inquiry lies in separating positive questions about the way the world works from normative questions about how one would like the world to work.

### Economic theorizing

- Theories are designed to explain and predict what we see. A theory consists of a set of definitions of the variables to be employed, a set of assumptions about how things behave, and the conditions under which the theory is meant to apply.

- A theory provides conditional predictions of the type 'if one event occurs, then another event will also occur'. An important method of testing theories is to confront their predictions with evidence.

- The term 'model' has a number of meanings, including (a) a synonym for theory, (b) a precise realization of a general theory, with a specific numerical relationship in place of each general relationship posited by the theory, (c) an application of a general theory to a specific case, and (d) a simplified set of relationships designed to study one specific force in isolation.

### Economic data

- Index numbers express economic series in relative form. Values in each period are expressed in relation to the value in the base period, which is given a value of 100.

- Economic data may be graphed in three different ways. Cross-section graphs show observations of a specific variable for different agents taken at the same time. Time-series graphs show observations on one variable taken over time. Scatter diagrams show points each one of which refers to specific observations on two different variables at the same point in time.

### Graphing economic theories

- A functional relationship can be expressed in words, in a schedule giving specific values, in an equation, or in a graph.

- A graph of two variables has a positive slope when they both increase or decrease together and a negative slope when they move in opposite directions.

- The marginal value of a variable gives the amount it changes in response to a small change in a second variable.

- The maximum or minimum point of a function will be where its marginal value is zero. On a graph this will occur where the curve is flat either because it is passing from a positive to negative slope (maximum) or from a negative to positive slope (minimum).

# TOPICS FOR REVIEW

- Positive and normative statements
- Endogenous and exogenous variables
- Theories and models
- Variables, assumptions, and predictions
- Time-series and cross-sectional graphs and scatter diagrams
- Functional relationships

- Ways of expressing a relationship between two variables
- Positive and negative relationships between variables
- Positively and negatively sloped curves
- Marginal values
- Maximum and minimum values

## QUESTIONS

1 Which of the following statements are positive and which are normative?
  (a) The health of poor people is worse than the health of rich people.
  (b) Economic growth in sub-Saharan Africa is affected by the AIDS epidemic.
  (c) Rich countries should provide medicine more cheaply to Africa.
  (d) Protectionist policies in rich countries are hurting poor countries and should be abolished.

2 Draw graphs of the following relationships, where $Y$ is on the vertical axis and $X$ is on the horizontal axis:
  $Y = X$
  $Y = 10X$
  $Y = 0.5X$
  $Y = 100 + 3X$
  $Y = 100 + 3X^2$
  $Y = 100 - 4X$
  $Y = -100 + 4X$

3 The UK retail price index for the four years 1998–2001 was 160.6, 164.3, 170.3, and 171.3, where the base year was 1987 (that is, the RPI in 1987 = 100). Express the RPI for 1998–2001, using 1998 as the base year. If the RPI for 2002, using 1998 as the base year, is 109, what will the 2002 RPI be using 1987 as the base year?

4 A batsman in cricket has had five successive innings where he scored 100. He now scores 50, 20, and 0 in his next three innings. Explain what happens to his total run score for the season, his average score, and his marginal score after the fifth and each subsequent inning. Repeat the exercise using instead the next three scores of 120, 140 and 160. What relationship is revealed between the marginal score and the average?

5 Why does the distinction between positive and normative statements matter for economics?

6 Why do economists use models in order to help explain how the economy works?

7 Discuss the view that economic analysis cannot generate predictions as human behaviour is unpredictable.

8 Economists are often criticized for making simplifying assumptions or holding 'other things equal'. Discuss whether you think these criticisms are justified. (You may wish to return to this issue once you have finished the course.)

# MICRO
# ECONOMICS

# PART ONE

# MARKETS AND CONSUMERS

# Chapter 3

# DEMAND, SUPPLY, AND PRICE

Why does the price of computers keep falling while house prices keep rising? This is a question about how markets work and what factors influence the outcomes. To answer it we need to understand how markets function. This is one of the most important topics in economics. You will see that we can go a long way in understanding how markets work with some very simple tools.

In particular, you will learn:

● Who are the participants in markets and what motivates them

● What are the main factors that influence how much of a product consumers wish to buy

● What are the main factors that influence how much producers wish to sell

● How consumers and producers interact to determine the market price

● While demand and supply forces are present in all markets, many different institutional structures also affect market outcomes.

Growers of crops come to a town to sell their produce in farmers' markets. High street stores stock a wide range of goods for individuals to buy. Commodity markets determine world-wide prices for products such as oil, copper, and wheat. Potential buyers or renters of housing units deal with sellers of houses or landlords in housing markets. Workers sell their services to employers in labour markets. Indeed, a market exists whenever buyers and sellers exchange goods or services—usually for money.

Markets do not necessarily occur in just one place. The housing markets and the labour market operate throughout the country. The stock market and the foreign exchange market operate globally using computers and telephones. The book market works partly through bookshops and partly by internet or mail order.

We need to understand all of these different types of market. But we start by focusing on a market in which the buyers, also called *demanders*, are households and the suppliers, often called *producers*, are firms. The product whose market we analyse is a good that has a physical existence so it has to be grown or made by the producing firm. Any person who makes decisions relevant to our theory is called an **agent**. To make the study of their behaviour more manageable, we deal with just three types of agent: individuals, firms, and government. In this chapter you will encounter individuals as demanders and firms as suppliers. In a later chapter when we study the labour market you will find individuals supplying and firms demanding. Governments also play a role in some markets, either as producers or demanders. They too can intervene in markets by taxing transactions (with a sales tax, a value-added tax, or an excise tax) or by imposing regulations that impose maximum or minimum prices. In this chapter and the next we ignore the potential role of governments, but we shall return to it later.

# Demand

## Individuals and motives

In formulating our demand theory, the agents are all assumed to be adult individuals who earn income, and who spend this income purchasing various goods and services.[1]

Most economic theories assume that each individual consumer seeks maximum *satisfaction*, or *well-being*, or *utility*, as the concept is variously called. The consumer is assumed to 'maximize utility' within the limits set by his or her available resources. Utility cannot be observed directly, but we only need to assume that typical consumers know what they like, and make spending choices that give them as much personal satisfaction as possible.

## The nature of demand

The amount of a product that consumers wish to purchase is called the **quantity demanded**. Notice two important things about this concept. First, quantity demanded is a *desired* quantity. It is how much consumers *wish* to purchase, not necessarily how much they actually succeed in purchasing. We use phrases such as **quantity actually purchased** or **quantity actually bought and sold** to distinguish actual purchases from the quantity demanded. Second, note that quantity demanded is a *flow*. We are concerned not with a single isolated purchase, but with a continuous flow of purchases. We must, therefore, express demand as so much per period of time—for example 1 million oranges *per day*, or 7 million oranges *per week*, or 365 million oranges *per year*. The important distinction between stocks and flows is discussed in Box 3.1.

The concept of demand as a flow appears to raise difficulties when we deal with the purchases of durable consumer goods (often called 'consumer durables'). It makes obvious sense to talk about a person consuming oranges at the rate of 30 per month, but what can we say of a consumer who buys a new television set every five years? This apparent difficulty disappears if we measure the demand for the *services* provided by the consumer durable. Thus, at the rate of a new set every five years, the television purchaser is using the service (viewing TV programmes) at the rate of 1/60 of a set per month.

## The determinants of quantity demanded: the demand function

Five main variables are assumed to influence the quantity of each product that is demanded by each individual consumer:

1. The price of the product
2. The prices of other products
3. The consumer's income and wealth
4. The consumer's tastes
5. Various individual-specific or environmental factors

Making use of the functional notation that was introduced in Chapter 2, the above list is conveniently summarized in what is called a **demand function**:

---

  **Box 3.1  Stocks and flows**

Economics makes extensive use of both stock variables and flow variables, and it is important not to confuse the two. A *flow variable* has a time dimension: it is so much per unit of time. The quantity of free-range eggs purchased in Glasgow is a flow variable. Being told that the number purchased was 2,000 dozen eggs conveys no useful information unless we are also told the period of time over which these purchases occurred. For example, 2,000 dozen per hour would indicate an active market in eggs, while 2,000 dozen per month would indicate a sluggish market.

A *stock variable* has no time dimension; it is just so much. Thus, the number of eggs in an egg producer's warehouse at a certain time—for example 20,000 dozen eggs—is a stock variable. All those eggs are there at one time, and they remain there until something happens to change the stock held by the producer. The stock variable is just a number, not a rate of flow of so much per day or per month.

Economic theories use both flow variables and stock variables, and it takes a little practice to keep them straight. The amount of income earned is a flow—so much per year or per month or per hour. The amount of a consumer's expenditure is also a flow—so much spent per week or per month. In contrast, the amount of money in your bank account is a stock—just so many pounds sterling. The key test for a variable being a flow is that a time dimension is required to give it meaning. Other variables are neither stocks nor flows: they are just numbers, for example the price of eggs.

---

[1] When real-world data are studied, the spending unit analysed is often not the individual but the household. A *household* is defined as all the people who live under one roof and who make joint financial decisions or are subject to others who make such decisions for them. For purposes of developing our analysis of markets, however, we view consumers as individuals.

$$q_n^d = D(p_n, p_1, \ldots, p_{n-1}, Y, S).$$

The term $q_n^d$ stands for the quantity that the consumer demands of some product, which we call 'product $n$'. The term $p_n$ stands for the price of this product, while $p_1, \ldots, p_{n-1}$ is a shorthand notation for the prices of all other products. The term $Y$ is the consumer's income. The term $S$ stands for a host of factors that will vary from individual to individual, such as age, number of children, place of residence (e.g. big city, small town, country), and other assets. (Car owners, for example will demand petrol while non-car owners will demand train tickets.) There are also some environmental factors that will affect demand patterns, such as the state of the weather and the time of year. Although these factors matter in real markets, they are not central to our current analysis. Finally, the precise way in which the variables listed above affect demand is determined by the tastes of the consumer.

The demand function is just a shorthand way of saying that quantity demanded, which is on the left-hand side, is assumed to depend on the variables that are listed on the right-hand side. The form of the function determines the nature of that dependence. (Recall that the 'form of the function' refers to the precise quantitative relation between the variables on the right-hand side of the equation and the variable on the left.)

We will not be able to understand the separate influences of each of the above variables if we ask what happens when all of them change at once. To avoid this difficulty, we consider the influence of the variables one at a time. To do this, we use a device that is frequently employed in economic theory. We assume that all except one of the variables on the right-hand side of the above expression are held constant. Then we allow this one variable, say $p_n$, to change and see how the quantity demanded ($q_n^d$) changes. We are then studying the effect of changes in one influence on quantity demanded, *assuming that all other influences remain unchanged*—or, as economists are fond of putting it, *ceteris paribus* (which means 'other things being equal' or 'holding others things constant').

We can do the same for each of the other variables in turn, and in this way we can come to understand the effect of each variable. Once this is done, we can add up the separate influences of each variable to discover what will happen when several variables change at the same time—as they often do in practice.

## Demand and price

We are interested in developing a theory of how products get priced. To do this, we hold all other influences constant and ask, 'How will the quantity of a product demanded vary as its own price varies?'

A basic economic hypothesis is that the lower the price of a product, the larger the quantity that will be demanded, other things being equal.

This negative relationship between the price of a product and quantity demanded is sometimes referred to as the **law of demand**. Why might this law be true? A major reason is that there is usually more than one product that will satisfy any given desire or need. Hunger may be satisfied by meat or vegetables; a desire for green vegetables may be satisfied by broccoli or spinach. The need to keep warm at night may be satisfied by several woollen blankets, or one electric blanket, or a bedsheet and an efficient central heating system. The desire for a holiday may be satisfied by a trip to the Scottish Highlands or to the Swiss Alps; the need to get there by an aeroplane, a bus, a car, or a train; and so on. Name any general desire or need, and there will usually be several products that will contribute to its satisfaction.

Now consider what happens if we hold income, tastes, population, and the prices of all other products constant and vary the price of only one product.

First, suppose the price of the product rises. The product then becomes a more expensive way of satisfying a want. Some consumers will stop buying it altogether; others will buy smaller amounts; still others may continue to buy the same amount; but no rational consumer will buy more of it. Because many consumers will switch, wholly or partially, to other products to satisfy the same want, less will be bought of the product whose price has risen. For example, as meat becomes more expensive, consumers may switch some of their expenditure to meat substitutes; they may also forgo meat at some meals and eat less meat at others.

Second, let the price of a product fall. This makes the product a cheaper method of satisfying any given want. Consumers will buy more of it and less of other similar products whose prices have not fallen. These other products have become expensive *relative to* the product in question. For example, when a bumper tomato harvest drives prices down, shoppers buy more tomatoes and fewer other salad ingredients, which have now become relatively more expensive than tomatoes.

### The demand schedule and the demand curve

#### An individual's demand

A **demand schedule** is one way of showing the relationship between quantity demanded and price. It is a numerical

Table 3.1 Alice's demand schedule for eggs

| Reference letter | Price (£ per dozen) | Quantity demanded (dozen per month) |
|---|---|---|
| a | 0.50 | 7.0 |
| b | 1.00 | 5.0 |
| c | 1.50 | 3.5 |
| d | 2.00 | 2.5 |
| e | 2.50 | 1.5 |
| f | 3.00 | 1.0 |

The table shows the quantity of eggs that Alice demands at each selected price, other things being equal. For example, at a price of £1.00 per dozen she demands 5 dozen per month, while at a price of £2.50 per dozen she demands only 1.5 dozen.

Figure 3.1 Alice's demand curve

This curve relates the price of a commodity to the amount that Alice wishes to purchase. Each point on the figure relates to a row in Table 3.1. For example, when the price is £3.00, 1 dozen eggs are bought per month (point f), while when the price is £0.50, 7 dozen are bought (point a).

tabulation that shows the quantity that will be demanded at some selected prices.

Table 3.1 shows one consumer's demand schedule for eggs. Alice often eats boiled eggs for breakfast, and, living on her own, she often finds omelettes a convenient evening meal. But she does not have a lot of money, so she keeps an eye on the price of eggs when she does her weekly supermarket shopping. The table shows the quantity of eggs that she wishes to buy each month at six selected prices. For example, at a price of £1.50 per dozen, Alice demands 3.5 dozen per month. For easy reference, each of the price–quantity combinations in the table is given a letter.

Next we plot the data from Table 3.1 in Figure 3.1, with price on the vertical and quantity on the horizontal axis.[2] The smooth curve drawn through these points is called the **demand curve**, even though it may often be drawn as a straight line. It shows the quantity that Alice would

like to buy at every possible price, and its *negative slope* indicates that the quantity demanded increases as the price falls.

A single point on the demand curve indicates a single price–quantity relationship. *The whole demand curve shows the complete relationship between quantity demanded and price.* Economists often speak of the conditions of demand in a particular market as 'given' or as 'known'. When they do so they are referring not just to the particular quantity that is being demanded at the moment (i.e. not just to a particular point on the demand curve) but to the whole demand curve. The whole demand curve remains in one place so long as all variables other than the price of the product itself remain unchanged.

### The market demand curve

So far we have discussed how the quantity of a product demanded by one consumer depends on the product's price, other things being equal. To explain market behaviour, we need to know the total demand of all consumers. To obtain a market demand schedule, we sum the quantities demanded by each consumer at a particular price to obtain the total quantity demanded at that price. We repeat the process for each price to obtain a schedule of total, or market, demand at all possible prices. A graph of this schedule is called the *market demand curve*.

To avoid unnecessary complication, Figure 3.2 illustrates the summation graphically for only two consumers, Sarah and William. The figure illustrates the proposition

---

2 Readers trained in other disciplines often wonder why economists plot demand curves with price on the vertical axis. The normal convention, which puts the independent variable (the variable that does the explaining) on the horizontal axis and the dependent variable (the variable that is explained) on the vertical axis, calls for price to be plotted on the horizontal axis and quantity on the vertical axis. The axis reversal, now enshrined by a century of usage, arose as follows. The analysis of the competitive market that we use today stems from the French economist Leon Walras (1834–1910), in whose theory *quantity* was the dependent variable. Graphical analysis in economics, however, was popularized by the English economist Alfred Marshall (1842–1924), in whose theory *price* was the dependent variable. Economists continue to use Walras's theory and Marshall's graphical representation, and thus draw the diagram with the independent and dependent variables reversed—to the everlasting confusion of readers trained in other disciplines. In virtually every other graph in economics the axes are labelled conventionally, with the dependent variable on the vertical axis.

### Table 3.2 A market demand schedule for eggs

| Reference letter | Price (£ per dozen) | Quantity demanded ('000 dozen per month) |
|---|---|---|
| U | 0.50 | 110.0 |
| V | 1.00 | 90.0 |
| W | 1.50 | 77.5 |
| X | 2.00 | 67.5 |
| Y | 2.50 | 62.5 |
| Z | 3.00 | 60.0 |

The table shows the quantity of eggs that would be demanded by all consumers at selected prices, *ceteris paribus*. For example, row *W* indicates that, if the price of eggs were £1.50 per dozen, consumers would want to purchase 77,500 dozen per month.

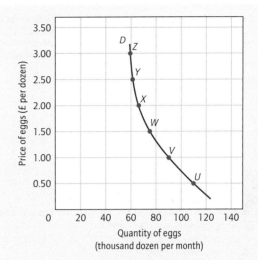

### Figure 3.3 A market demand curve for eggs

**The negative slope of the curve indicates that quantity demanded increases as price falls.** The six points correspond to the six price–quantity combinations shown in Table 3.2. The curve drawn through all of the points and labelled *D* is the demand curve.

that the market demand curve is the horizontal sum of the demand curves of *all* the individuals who buy in the market.

In practice, our knowledge of market demand is usually derived by observing total quantities of sales directly. The derivation of market demand curves by summing individual curves is a theoretical operation. We do it to understand the relation between curves for individual consumers and market curves.

In Table 3.2 we assume that we have data for the market demand for eggs. The schedule tells us the total quantity that will be demanded by all buyers of that product at selected market prices. The data are plotted in Figure 3.3, and the curve drawn through these points is the market demand curve.

### Market demand: a recap

We now summarize what we have learned about demand.

The total quantity demanded depends on the price of the product being sold, on the prices of all other products, on the incomes of the individuals buying in that market, and on their tastes. The market demand curve relates the total quantity demanded to the product's own price, on the assumption that all other prices, total income, tastes, and all other environmental factors are held constant.

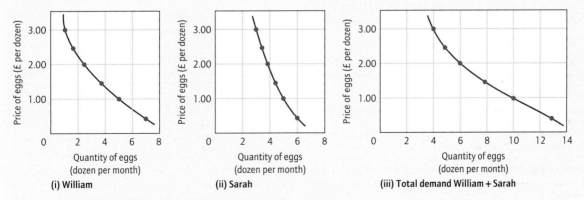

### Figure 3.2 The relation between individual and market demand curves

**The market demand curve is the horizontal sum of the demand curves of all consumers in the market.** The figure illustrates aggregation over two individuals, William and Sarah. For example, at a price of £2.00 per dozen, William purchases 2.4 dozen eggs, Sarah purchases 3.6 dozen, and together they purchase 6 dozen.

**Table 3.3** Two alternative market demand schedules for eggs

| (1) | Price of eggs (£ per dozen) (2) | Quantity of eggs demanded at original level of personal income ('000 dozen per month) (3) | Quantity of eggs demanded when personal income rises to new level ('000 dozen per month) (4) | (5) |
|---|---|---|---|---|
| U | 0.50 | 110.0 | 140.0 | U' |
| V | 1.00 | 90.0 | 116.0 | V' |
| W | 1.50 | 77.5 | 100.0 | W' |
| X | 2.00 | 67.5 | 90.0 | X' |
| Y | 2.50 | 62.5 | 81.3 | Y' |
| Z | 3.00 | 60.0 | 78.0 | Z' |

**An increase in total consumers' income increases the quantity demanded at each price.** When income rises, quantity demanded at a price of £1.50 per dozen rises from 77,500 dozen per month to 100,800 dozen per month. A similar rise occurs at every other price. Thus, the demand schedule relating columns (2) and (3) is replaced by the one relating columns (2) and (4). The graphical representations of these two schedules are labelled $D_0$ and $D_1$ in Figure 3.4.

## Shifts in the demand curve

The demand schedule and the demand curve are con-structed on the assumption of *ceteris paribus* (other things held constant). But what if other things change, as surely they must? What, for example, if consumers find themselves with more income? If they spend their extra income, they will buy additional quantities of many prod-ucts *even though market prices are unchanged*, as shown in Table 3.3. But if consumers increase their purchases of any product whose price has not changed, the new purchases cannot be represented by the original demand curve. The rise in consumer income *shifts* the demand curve to the right, as shown in Figure 3.4. This shift illustrates the operation of an important general rule.

A demand curve shifts to a new position in response to a change in any of the variables that were held constant when the original curve was drawn.

Any change that increases the quantity of a product consumers wish to buy at each price will shift the demand curve to the right, and any change that decreases the quantity consumers wish to buy at each price will shift the demand curve to the left.

### Changes in other prices

We saw that demand curves have negative slopes because the lower a product's price, the cheaper it becomes relat-ive to other products that can satisfy the same needs. Those other products are called **substitutes**. A product becomes cheaper relative to its substitutes if its own price falls. This also happens if the substitute's price rises. For example, eggs can become cheaper relative to pizzas either

**Figure 3.4** Two demand curves for eggs

The rightward shift in the demand curve from $D_0$ to $D_1$ indicates an increase in the quantity demanded at each price. The lettered points correspond to those in Table 3.3. When the curve shifts from $D_0$ to $D_1$, more is demanded at each price and a higher price is paid for each quantity. For example, at price £1.50, quantity demanded rises from 77,500 dozen (point $W$) to 100,000 dozen (point $W'$); while the quantity of 90,000 dozen, which was formerly bought at a price of £1.00 (point $V$), will be bought at a price of £2.00 after the shift (point $X'$).

because the price of eggs falls or because the price of pizzas rises—either change will increase the amount of eggs that consumers are prepared to buy. For example, Alice may eat more omelettes and fewer pizzas whenever she wants a quick meal.

A rise in the price of a product's substitute shifts the demand curve for the product to the right. More will be purchased at each price.

Thus, a rise in the price of pizzas may shift the demand curve for eggs from $D_0$ to $D_1$ in Figure 3.4, just as did a rise in income.

Products that tend to be used jointly with each other are called **complements**. Cars and petrol are complements; so are golf clubs and golf balls, bacon and eggs, electric cookers and electricity, or an aeroplane trip to Austria and tickets on the ski lifts at St Anton. Since complements tend to be consumed together, a fall in the price of either will increase the demand for both. For example, a fall in the price of cars that causes more people to become car owners will, *ceteris paribus*, increase the demand for petrol.

A fall in the price of one product that is complementary to a second product will shift the second product's demand curve to the right. More will be purchased at each price.

## Changes in total income

If consumers receive more income, they can be expected to purchase more of most products even though product prices remain the same. Such a shift is illustrated in Table 3.3 and Figure 3.4. A product whose demand increases when income increases is called a **normal good**.

A rise in consumers' incomes shifts the demand curve for normal products to the right, indicating that more will be demanded at each possible price.

For a few products, called **inferior goods**, a rise in consumers' income leads them to reduce their purchases (because they can now afford to switch to a more expensive, but superior, substitute).

A rise in income will shift the demand for inferior goods to the left, indicating that less will be demanded at each price.

## The distribution of income

If total income and all other determinants of demand are held constant while the distribution of income changes (i.e. some become richer and others become poorer), the demands for normal goods will rise for consumers gaining income and fall for consumers losing income. If both gainers and losers buy a good in similar proportions, these changes will tend to cancel out. This will not, however, always be the case.

When the distribution of income changes, demand will rise for those goods favoured by those gaining income and fall for those goods favoured by those losing income.

## Individual characteristics

Changes in the characteristics of the individuals who make up the market will cause demand curves to shift. For example, a reduction in the typical number of children per family, as happened in the twentieth century, will reduce the demands for the things used by children or in childcare. If the number of retired people increases, there will be a rise in the demands for goods consumed during leisure times.

## Environmental factors

Demand for some products is different at different times of year. Some of this is due to weather; for example, demand for electricity is higher in the winter when days are short and the weather is cold,[3] and demand for cold lager and ice cream is higher in the summer during hot weather. Other variations may be due to traditions associated with annual festivals, such as buying presents at Christmas, or the timing of school holidays. From the point of view of our theory of demand these are exogenous forces—things that lie outside the theory, affecting demand, sometimes greatly, but not themselves being explained by the theory. Box 3.2 illustrates the major influence that weather can exert on demand.

## Changes in tastes

If there is a change in tastes in favour of a product, more will be demanded at each price, causing the demand curve to shift to the right. In contrast, if there is a change in tastes away from a product, less will be demanded at each price, causing the entire demand curve to shift to the left.

Figure 3.5 summarizes our discussion of the causes of shifts in the demand curve. Notice that, since we are generalizing beyond our example of eggs, we have relabelled our axes 'price' and 'quantity', dropping the qualification 'of eggs'. The term *quantity* should be understood to mean quantity per period in whatever units the goods are measured. The term *price* should be understood to mean the price measured in pounds per unit of quantity for the same product.

### Movements along demand curves versus shifts

Suppose you read in today's newspaper that carrot prices have soared because more carrots are being demanded, perhaps following a report that carrot consumption gives protection against some disease. Then tomorrow you read that the rising price of carrots is greatly reducing the typical consumer's demand for carrots as shoppers switch to

---

[3] In some hot countries, demand for electricity may be even greater in summer than in winter owing to the use of air-conditioners.

**Box 3.2  Weather matters**

Other things than price and incomes influence demand, and sellers have to keep abreast of these non-economic causes—which have distinct economic effects.

A recent article in the *Guardian* newspaper quotes a person responsible for getting groceries to the stores at the right time and in the right quantities on the effects of a sudden turn in the weather from cold to hot: 'The trigger point is 80 degrees, especially if it is sustained for more than three days. For products such as ice cream, soft drinks, and salads sales can rise by between 70 per cent and 225 per cent on a big change in temperature.' As a result of a sudden upturn in the weather he had recently had to organize another million cases of soft drinks and additional lorry loads of salad and other fast-selling products 'if the shelves [were] not to be bare by lunchtime'.

Here are some of the ways in which the article said the weather affects UK demand:

- Drink sales respond immediately to temperature change.

- After two days of good weather we might think about buying a bike, but it has to be nice for more than a week before we start buying suntan lotion.

- Curiously, hot weather increases the sales of plain coleslaw much more than coleslaw with pineapple.

- Soft drink sales depend not only on heat but also on humidity.

- Rain and mild temperatures suit insurers best—we drive less and so have fewer and less serious prangs.

- Builders like storms—they interrupt work but generate huge business volumes repairing and replacing roofs.

- Every one degree colder adds 4 per cent to gas demand and increases electricity demand by about 5,000 megawatts —enough to supply the whole of Sheffield.

**Figure 3.5  Shifts in the demand curve**

A shift in the demand curve from $D_0$ to $D_1$ indicates an increase in demand; a shift from $D_0$ to $D_2$ indicates a decrease in demand. An increase in demand can be caused by a rise in the price of a substitute, a fall in the price of a complement, a rise in income, a redistribution of income towards groups that favour the commodity, or a change in tastes that favours the commodity.

A decrease in demand can be caused by a fall in the price of a substitute, a rise in the price of a complement, a fall in income, a redistribution of income away from groups that favour the commodity, or a change in tastes that disfavours the commodity.

potatoes, courgettes, and peas. The two statements appear to contradict each other. The first associates a rising price with a rising demand; the second associates a rising price with a declining demand. Can both statements be true? The answer is that they can be, because they refer to different things. The first refers to a *shift* in the demand curve; the second refers to a movement *along a* demand curve in response to a change in price.

Consider first the statement that the increase in the price of carrots has been caused by an increased demand for carrots. This statement refers to a shift in the demand curve for carrots. In this case, the demand curve must have shifted to the right, indicating more carrots demanded at each price. This shift will, as we will see later in this chapter, increase the price of carrots.

Now consider the statement that fewer carrots are being bought because carrots have become more expensive. This refers to a movement along a given demand curve and reflects a change between two specific quantities being bought, one before the price rose and one afterwards.

So what lies behind the two stories might be something like the following.

1. A rise in the perceived health-giving properties shifts the demand curve for carrots to the right as more and more are demanded at each price. This in turn raises the price of carrots (for reasons we will soon study in detail). This was the first newspaper story.

2. The rising price of carrots causes each individual consumer to cut back on his or her purchase of carrots. This causes a movement upward to the left along any particular demand curve for carrots. This was the second newspaper story.

To prevent the type of confusion caused by our two newspaper stories, economists have developed a specific vocabulary to distinguish shifts of curves from movements along curves. **Demand** refers to the *whole* demand curve. **Change in demand** refers to a *shift* in the whole curve, that is, a change in the amount that will be bought at *every* price.

An increase in demand means that the whole demand curve has shifted to the right; a decrease in demand means that the whole demand curve has shifted to the left.

Any one point on a demand curve represents a specific amount being bought at a specified price. It represents, therefore, a particular quantity demanded. A movement along a demand curve is referred to as a **change in the quantity demanded**.

A movement down a demand curve is called an increase (or a rise) in the quantity demanded; a movement up the demand curve is called a decrease (or a fall) in the quantity demanded.

To illustrate this terminology, look again at Table 3.3. First, at the original level of income, a decrease in price from £2.00 to £1.50 increases *the quantity demanded* from 67,500 to 77,500 dozen a month. Second, the increase in average consumer income *increases demand* from what is shown in column (3) to what is shown in column (4). The same contrast is shown in Figure 3.4, where a fall in price from £2.00 to £1.50 increases the quantity demanded from the quantity shown by point $X$ to the quantity shown by point $W$. An increase in total consumers' income increases demand from curve $D_0$ to curve $D_1$.

# Supply

We now look at the supply side of markets. The suppliers are firms, which are in business to make the goods and services that consumers want to buy.

## Firms' motives

Economic theory gives firms several attributes.

First, each firm is assumed to make consistent decisions, as though it were run by a single individual decision-maker. This allows the firm to be treated as the agent on the production or supply side of product markets, just as the consumer is treated as the individual unit of behaviour on the consumption or demand side.

Second, firms hire workers and invest capital and entrepreneurial talent in order to produce goods and services that consumers wish to buy. (There are some markets in which firms sell to other firms, or the government, and in the labour market individuals sell their services to firms. But here we focus on consumer goods markets for simplicity.)

Third, firms are assumed to make their decisions with a single goal in mind: to make as much profit as possible. This goal of *profit maximization* is analogous to the consumer's goal of utility maximization.

## The nature of supply

The amount of a product that firms are able and willing to offer for sale is called the **quantity supplied**. Supply is a desired flow: it indicates how much firms are *willing to sell* per period of time, not how much they actually sell.

Here we make a start on the analysis of supply, establishing only what is necessary for a theory of price. In later chapters we study the behaviour of individual firms, and

then aggregate individual behaviour to obtain the behaviour of market supply. For present purposes, however, it is sufficient to go directly to market supply, the aggregate behaviour of all the firms in a particular market.

## The determinants of quantity supplied: the supply function

Three major determinants of the quantity supplied in a particular market are:

1. The price of the product
2. The prices of inputs to production
3. The state of technology

This list can be summarized in a **supply function**:

$$q_n^s = S(p_n, F_1, \ldots, F_m),$$

where $q_n^s$ is the quantity supplied of product $n$; $p_n$ is the price of that product; $F_1, \ldots, F_m$ is shorthand for the prices of all inputs into production; and the state of technology determines the form of the function S. (Recall, once again, that the form of the function refers to the precise quantitative relation between the variables on the right-hand side of the equation and the one on the left.)

## Supply and price

For a simple theory of price, we need to know how quantity supplied varies with a product's own price, all other things being held constant. We are only concerned, therefore, with the *ceteris paribus* relationship, $q_n^s = S(p_n)$, that is, between the quantity that firms wish to supply and the price of the product itself. We will have much to say in later chapters about this relationship. For the moment, it is sufficient to state the hypothesis that, holding other things constant, *the quantity of any product that firms will produce and offer for sale is positively related to the product's own price, rising when the price rises and falling when the price falls.*

In Chapter 6 we link this hypothesis to the profit-maximizing behaviour of firms. In the meantime, all we need to note is that the basic reason behind this relationship is the way in which costs behave as output changes. Typically, the cost of increasing output by another unit tends to be higher the higher is the existing rate of output. So, for example, if the firm is already producing 100 units per week, the cost of increasing output to 101 units per week might be £1, while if 200 units were already being produced, the cost of increasing output to 201 units might be £2. Clearly, the firm will not find it profitable to increase output if it cannot at least cover the additional costs that are incurred. As the price of the product rises, the firm can cover the rising costs of more and more additional units of output. As a result, higher and higher prices are needed to induce firms to make successive increases in output. The result is a positive association between market price and the firm's output. Do not worry if this does not seem obvious; we set out a stronger justification in Chapter 6.

The **supply schedule** given in Table 3.4 is analogous to the demand schedule in Table 3.2. It records the quantity that all producers wish to produce and sell at a number of alternative prices, rather than the quantity consumers wish to buy.

The six points corresponding to the six price–quantity combinations shown in the table are plotted in Figure 3.6.

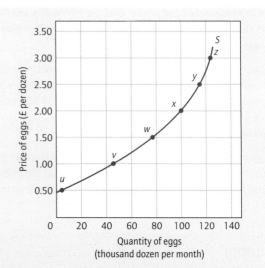

**Figure 3.6** A supply curve for eggs

This supply curve relates quantity of eggs supplied to the price of eggs; its positive slope indicates that quantity supplied increases as price increases. The six points correspond to the price–quantity combinations shown in Table 3.4. The curve drawn through these points, labelled *S*, is the supply curve.

The curve drawn through the six points is a **supply curve** for eggs. It shows the quantity produced and offered for sale at each price.[4]

The supply curve in Figure 3.6 has a positive slope. This is a graphical expression of the following assumption:

**The market price and the quantity supplied are positively related to each other.**

### Shifts in the supply curve

A shift in the supply curve means that, at each price, a different quantity is supplied. An increase in the quantity supplied at each price is illustrated in Table 3.5 and plotted in Figure 3.7. This change appears as a rightward shift in the supply curve. A decrease in the quantity supplied at each price causes a leftward shift.

For supply-curve shifts there is an important general rule similar to the one stated earlier for demand curves:

**When there is a change in any of the variables (other than the product's own price) that affect the amount of a product that firms are willing to produce and sell, the whole supply curve for that product will shift.**

**Table 3.4** A market supply schedule for eggs

| Reference letter | Price (£ per dozen) | Quantity supplied ('000 dozen per month) |
| --- | --- | --- |
| *u* | 0.50 | 5.0 |
| *v* | 1.00 | 46.0 |
| *w* | 1.50 | 77.5 |
| *x* | 2.00 | 100.0 |
| *y* | 2.50 | 115.0 |
| *z* | 3.00 | 122.5 |

The table shows the quantities that producers wish to sell at various prices, *ceteris paribus*. For example, row *y* indicates that if the price were £2.50 per dozen, producers would wish to sell 115,000 dozen eggs per month.

---

[4] Since we are not considering individual firms in this chapter, all supply curves are market curves showing the aggregate behaviour of the firms in the market. Where that is obvious from the context, the adjective 'market' is usually omitted.

**Table 3.5** Two alternative market supply schedules for eggs

| (1) | Price of eggs (£ per dozen) (2) | Original quantity supplied ('000 dozen per month) (3) | New quantity supplied ('000 dozen per month) (4) | (5) |
|---|---|---|---|---|
| u | 0.50 | 5.0 | 28.0 | u' |
| v | 1.00 | 46.0 | 76.0 | v' |
| w | 1.50 | 77.5 | 102.0 | w' |
| x | 2.00 | 100.0 | 120.0 | x' |
| y | 2.50 | 115.0 | 132.0 | y' |
| z | 3.00 | 122.5 | 140.0 | z' |

An increase in supply means a larger quantity is supplied at each price. For example, the quantity that is supplied at £2.50 per dozen rises from 115,000 dozen to 132,000 dozen per month. A similar rise occurs at every price. Thus, the supply schedule relating columns (2) and (3) is replaced by the one relating columns (2) and (4).

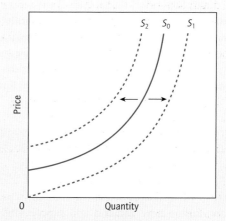

**Figure 3.8** Shifts in the supply curve

A shift in the supply curve from $S_0$ to $S_1$ indicates an increase in supply; a shift from $S_0$ to $S_2$ indicates a decrease in supply. An increase in supply can be caused by improvements in technology or decreases in the costs of inputs that are important in producing the commodity. A decrease in supply can be caused by increases in the costs of inputs that are important in producing the commodity, or by changes in technology that increase the costs of production (although such changes are rare).

**Figure 3.7** Two supply curves for eggs

The rightward shift in the supply curve from $S_0$ to $S_1$ indicates an increase in the quantity supplied at each price. For example, at the price of £1.00, the quantity supplied rises from 46,000 dozen to 76,000 dozen per month.

The major possible causes of such shifts are summarized in the caption of Figure 3.8 and are considered briefly below.

### Prices of inputs

All things that a firm uses to produce its outputs—such as, in the case of an egg producer, chicken feed, labour, and egg-sorting machines—are called the firm's *inputs*. Other things being equal, the higher the price of any input used to make a product, the less will be the profit from making that product. Thus, the higher the price of any input used by a firm, the lower will be the amount that the firm will produce and offer for sale at any given price of the product.

A rise in the price of any input shifts the supply curve to the left, indicating that less will be supplied at any given price; a fall in the price of inputs shifts the supply curve to the right.

### Technology

At any time, what is produced and how it is produced depend on the technologies in use. Over time, knowledge and production technologies change; so do the quantities of individual products that can be supplied.

A technological change that decreases costs will increase the profits earned at any given price of the product. Since increased profitability leads to increased production, this change shifts the supply curve to the right, indicating an increased willingness to produce the product and offer it for sale at each possible price.

### Movements along supply curves versus shifts

As with demand, it is essential to distinguish between a movement along the supply curve (caused by a change in the product's own price) and a shift of the whole curve (caused by a change in something other than the product's own price). We adopt the same terminology as with demand: **quantity supplied** refers to a particular quantity actually supplied at a particular price of the product, and **supply** refers to the whole relationship between price and quantity supplied. Thus, when we speak of an *increase* or a *decrease in supply*, we are referring to shifts in the supply curve such as the ones illustrated in Figures 3.7 and 3.8. When we speak of a *change in the quantity supplied*, we mean a movement from one point on the supply curve to another point on the same curve.

# The determination of price

So far we have considered demand and supply separately. We now outline how demand and supply interact to determine price.

## The concept of a market

For present purposes, a **market** may be defined as an area over which buyers and sellers negotiate the exchange of some product or related group of products. It must be possible, therefore, for buyers and sellers to communicate with each other and to make meaningful transactions over the whole market. Some markets are local, such as the farmers' market in a county town, while others cover the entire world, such as the market for petroleum or wheat. In recent times the technology of computers has greatly increased the number of world markets. For example, many commodities are advertised for sale to a world-wide audience on E-bay.

Individual markets differ in the degree of competition among the various buyers and sellers. In the next few chapters we will confine ourselves to markets in which the number of buyers and sellers is sufficiently large that no one of them has any appreciable influence on price. This is a very rough definition of what economists call *perfectly competitive markets*. Starting in Chapter 8, we will consider the behaviour of markets that do not meet this competitive requirement.

## The graphical analysis of a market

Table 3.6 brings together the demand and supply schedules from Tables 3.2 and 3.4. Figure 3.9 shows both the demand and the supply curves on a single graph; the six points on the demand curve are labelled with upper-case letters, while the six points on the supply curve are labelled with lower-case letters, each letter referring to a common price on both curves.

### Quantity supplied and quantity demanded at various prices

Consider first the point at which the two curves in Figure 3.9 intersect. Both the figure and Table 3.6 show that

**Table 3.6** Demand and supply schedules for eggs and equilibrium price

| Price per dozen (£) | Quantity demanded ('000 dozen per month) | Quantity supplied ('000 dozen per month) | Excess demand (quantity demanded minus quantity supplied) ('000 dozen per month) |
|---|---|---|---|
| 0.50 | 110.0 | 5.0 | 105.0 |
| 1.00 | 90.0 | 46.0 | 44.0 |
| **1.50** | **77.5** | **77.5** | **0.0** |
| 2.00 | 67.5 | 100.0 | −32.5 |
| 2.50 | 62.5 | 115.0 | −52.5 |
| 3.00 | 60.0 | 122.5 | −62.5 |

**Equilibrium occurs where quantity demanded equals quantity supplied so that there is neither excess demand nor excess supply.** These schedules are repeated from Tables 3.2 and 3.4. The equilibrium price is £1.50. For lower prices there is excess demand; for higher prices there is excess supply, which is shown as negative excess demand.

**Figure 3.9** **Determination of the equilibrium price of eggs**

**The equilibrium price corresponds to the intersection of the demand and supply curves.** Point *E* indicates the equilibrium. At a price of £1.50 per dozen, quantity demanded (point *W*) equals quantity supplied (point *w*). At prices above equilibrium there is excess supply and downward pressure on price. At prices below equilibrium there is excess demand and upward pressure on price. The pressures on price are represented by the vertical arrows.

the market price is £1.50, the quantity demanded is 77,500 dozen, and the quantity supplied is the same. At that price consumers wish to buy exactly the same amount as producers wish to sell. Provided that the demand curve is negatively sloped and the supply curve positively sloped throughout their entire ranges, there will be no other price at which the quantity demanded equals the quantity supplied.

Now consider prices below £1.50. At these prices consumers' desired purchases exceed producers' desired sales. It is easily seen that at all prices below £1.50 the quantity demanded exceeds the quantity supplied. Furthermore, the lower the price, the larger is the excess of the one over the other. The amount by which the quantity demanded exceeds the quantity supplied is called the **excess demand**, which is defined as quantity demanded *minus* quantity supplied ($q^d - q^s$). This is shown in the last column of Table 3.6.

Finally, consider prices higher than £1.50. At these prices consumers wish to buy less than producers wish to sell. Thus, quantity supplied exceeds quantity demanded. It is easily seen—and again you should check a few examples—that for any price above £1.50 quantity supplied exceeds quantity demanded. Furthermore, the

higher the price, the larger is the excess of the one over the other. In this case there is negative excess demand ($q^d - q^s$ < 0). This is also shown in the last column of Table 3.6.

Negative excess demand is usually referred to as **excess supply**, which measures the amount by which supply exceeds demand ($q^s - q^d$).

### Changes in price when quantity demanded does not equal quantity supplied

Whenever there is excess demand, consumers are unable to buy all they wish to buy; whenever there is excess supply, firms are unable to sell all they wish to sell. In both cases some agents will not be able to do what they would like to do. How will they react?

There is a key driving force in markets, which is called the **law of price adjustment** (not to be confused with the *law of demand* that we introduced earlier, which says that demand curves have a negative slope). This law predicts what will happen to the market price when there is either excess demand or excess supply.

When supply exceeds demand, the market price will fall. When demand exceeds supply, the market price will rise.

Excess supply means that producers cannot sell all that they wish to sell at the current price. They may then begin to offer to sell at lower prices, such as through clearance sales or discounts. If purchasers observe the glut of unsold output they may begin to offer to pay lower prices. For either or both of these reasons, the price in the market will fall.

If, at the current price, consumers are unable to buy as much as they would like to buy, they may offer higher prices in an effort to get more of the available supply for themselves. Suppliers are unable to produce a greater quantity of the product in the short run, but they can ask higher prices for the quantities that they are producing, and will make more profit if they do so. For either or both of these reasons, prices will rise.

This law of price adjustment makes considerable sense and conforms to common experiences of how markets work—shortages of any product tend to lead to price rises while gluts tend to lead to price falls. Most importantly, it implies that prices will move towards the level at which demand and supply will be equal.

This is a necessary condition for the market to exhibit *stability*. Whenever the current price is not the one that equates demand and supply, the law of price adjustment ensures that the price will move towards the market-clearing price rather than away from it. Thus, it is not enough that there exists a price for which demand is equal to supply. Stability of the market also requires some

**Box 3.3  Prices in periods of inflation**

Up to now we have developed the theory of the prices of individual products under the assumption that all other prices remain constant. Does this mean that the theory is inapplicable during an inflationary period when almost all prices are rising? Fortunately, the answer is no.

We have mentioned several times that what matters for demand and supply is the price of the product in question relative to the prices of other products. The price of the product expressed in money terms is called its **money price**; the price of a product expressed in relation to other prices is called its **relative price**.

In an inflationary world changes in a product's relative price can be measured by changes in the product's own price relative to changes in the average of all other prices, which is called the **general price level**. If, during a period when the general price level rose by 40 per cent, the price of oranges rose by 60 per cent, then the price of oranges rose relative to the price level as a whole: oranges became *relatively* expensive. However, if the price of oranges had risen by only 30 per cent when the general price level had risen by 40 per cent, then their relative price would have fallen: although the money price of oranges rose, oranges became *relatively* cheap.

In Lewis Carroll's famous story *Through the Looking-Glass*, Alice finds a country where everyone has to run in order to stay still. So it is with inflation. A product's price must rise as fast as the general level of prices just to keep its relative price constant.

It has been convenient in this chapter to analyse a change in a particular price in the context of a constant price level. The analysis is easily extended, however, to an inflationary period. Any force that raises the price of one product when other prices remain constant will, given general inflation, raise the price of that product relative to the average of all other prices. Consider the example of a change in tastes in favour of eggs that would raise their price by 20 per cent when other prices were constant. If, however, the general price level goes up by 10 per cent, then the price of eggs will rise by 32 per cent.* In each case, the price of eggs rises 20 per cent *relative to the average of all prices*.

In price theory, whenever we talk of a change in the price of one product, we mean a change *relative to* the general price level.

* Let the price level be 100 in the first case and 110 in the second. Let the price of eggs be 120 in the first case and $x$ in the second. To preserve the same relative price, we need $x$ such that $120/100 = x/110$, which makes $x = 132$.

---

mechanism to return the price to the market-clearing level whenever it is away from that point. The combination of a negatively sloped demand curve and positively sloped supply curve with the law of price adjustment will guarantee a stable market, so long as any market in this product exists (that is, so long as the demand and supply curves intersect at some positive price and quantity).

### The equilibrium price

In our hypothetical example, for any price of eggs above £1.50 the price will fall, while for any price below £1.50 the price will rise. At a price of £1.50 there is neither excess demand associated with a shortage, nor excess supply associated with a glut: the quantity supplied is equal to the quantity demanded. Once supply and demand are equal, there is no tendency for the price to change because suppliers are just able to sell all that they want and demanders are just able to buy all that they want. Nobody has any incentive to change the price.

The price of £1.50, where the supply and demand curves intersect, is the price towards which the actual market price will tend. It is called the **equilibrium price**: the price at which quantity demanded equals quantity supplied. The amount that is bought and sold at the equilibrium

price is called the **equilibrium quantity**. The term 'equilibrium' means a state of balance; it occurs when desired purchases equal desired sales and there are no forces tending to make anything change. Box 3.3 discusses the implications of inflation for our interpretation of market price.

When quantity demanded equals quantity supplied, we say that the market is in **equilibrium**. When quantity demanded does not equal quantity supplied, we say that the market is in **disequilibrium**.

### Summary

We have now developed one of the most famous and powerful theories in all of economics, and it is worth summarizing what we have done.

#### Assumptions concerning a competitive market

- **The law of demand:** demand curves have negative slopes throughout their entire range.

- **The theory of supply:** supply curves have positive slopes throughout their entire range.

- **The law of price adjustment:** prices rise when demand exceeds supply, and fall if supply exceeds demand. They remain unchanged when demand and supply are equal.

## Implications

- There is only one price at which quantity demanded equals quantity supplied: equilibrium is unique.
- Only at the equilibrium price will the market price remain constant.
- When the demand or the supply curve shifts, the equilibrium price and quantity will change.
- The market is stable in the sense that forces exist to move the price towards its market-clearing level.

Collectively, these forces are sometimes known as the *laws of demand and supply*.

## The predictions of demand and supply analysis

Earlier in this chapter, we studied shifts in demand and supply curves. Recall that a rightward shift in the relevant curve means that more is demanded or supplied *at each market price*, while a leftward shift means that less is demanded or supplied *at each market price*. How does a shift in either curve affect price and quantity?

The answers to this question are the predictions of our supply and demand theory. We wish to see what happens when an initial position of equilibrium is upset by some shift in either the demand or the supply curve, and a new equilibrium position is then established. This will enable us to derive predictions about what will happen in any market when something changes, and this is why we study economics: so that we can anticipate what will happen in specific markets when some change occurs.

To discover the effects of the demand and supply shifts that we wish to study, we use the method known as **comparative statics**. We start from a position of equilibrium and then introduce the change to be studied. The new equilibrium position is determined and compared with the original one. The differences between the two positions of equilibrium must result from the change that was introduced, for everything else has been held constant.

The four main predictions of demand and supply are derived in Figure 3.10. The analysis of that figure generalizes our specific discussion about eggs. Because it is intended to apply to any product, the horizontal axis is simply labelled 'quantity' and the vertical axis, 'price'.

(i) The effect of shifts in the demand curve

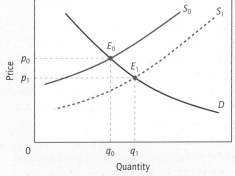

(ii) The effect of shifts in the supply curve

**Figure 3.10 The predictions of demand and supply analysis**

**The predicted effects on equilibrium price and quantity of shifts in either demand or supply are as follows.**

*Increase in demand.* In part (i) above, assume that the original demand and supply curves are $D_0$ and $S$, which intersect to produce equilibrium at $E_0$, with a price of $p_0$ and a quantity of $q_0$. An increase in demand shifts the demand curve to $D_1$, taking the new equilibrium to $E_1$. Price rises to $p_1$ and quantity rises to $q_1$.

*Decrease in demand.* In part (i), assume that the original demand and supply curves are $D_1$ and $S$, which intersect to produce equilibrium at $E_1$, with a price of $p_1$ and a quantity of $q_1$. A decrease in demand shifts the demand curve to $D_0$, taking the new equilibrium to $E_0$. Price falls to $p_0$ and quantity falls to $q_0$.

*Increase in supply.* In part (ii), assume that the original demand and supply curves are $D$ and $S_0$, which intersect to produce an equilibrium at $E_0$, with a price of $p_0$ and a quantity of $q_0$. An increase in supply shifts the supply curve to $S_1$, taking the new equilibrium to $E_1$. Price falls to $p_1$ and quantity rises to $q_1$.

*Decrease in supply.* In part (ii), assume that the original demand and supply curves are $D$ and $S_1$, which intersect to produce an equilibrium at $E_1$, with a price of $p_1$ and a quantity of $q_1$. A decrease in supply shifts the supply curve to $S_0$, taking the new equilibrium to $E_0$. Price rises to $p_0$ and quantity falls to $q_0$.

## Box 3.4 Demand and supply: what really happens

Just in case you might think at this stage that we are being abstract and theoretical and you feel that the world is 'not like that', here are some examples of recent newspaper headlines or extracts that illustrate how markets actually work. In the last section of this chapter we address some other doubts about how generally applicable our analysis might be.

• OPEC countries once again fail to agree on output quotas. Output soars and prices plummet.

• Oil prices rise as demand from China and India continues to grow.

• Oil and gas prices surge as hurricane Katrina cuts production on the US Gulf Coast.

• The price of cashew kernels has fallen nearly 6 per cent in 10 months as Vietnam has begun to challenge India and Brazil, the world's two largest exporters.

• How deep is the art market's recession? In today's unforgiving economic climate, the sales of contemporary, impressionist, and modern works of art took hits at this week's auctions. Sales totalled just under £60 million compared with £500 million just one year ago. Many paintings on offer went unsold, and those that did sell went for well under their predicted price.

• Coffee prices at the London Commodity Exchange staged another spectacular rise, putting them above their level at the start of the year. The president of the Association of Coffee Producing Countries said that the supply shortages that are underpinning prices would last quite some time.

• Increased demand for macadamia nuts causes price to rise above competing nuts. A major producer now plans to double the size of its orchards during the next five years.

• The world copper price reaches a ten-year high as high demand from China leads to demand outrunning the limited supply capacity.

The predictions of supply and demand theory are:

1. A rise in the demand for a product (a rightward shift of the demand curve) causes an increase in both the equilibrium price and the equilibrium quantity bought and sold.

2. A fall in the demand for a product (a leftward shift of the demand curve) causes a decrease in both the equilibrium price and the equilibrium quantity bought and sold.

3. A rise in the supply of a product (a rightward shift of the supply curve) causes a decrease in the equilibrium price and an increase in the equilibrium quantity bought and sold.

4. A fall in the supply of a product (a leftward shift of the supply curve) causes an increase in the equilibrium price and a decrease in the equilibrium quantity bought and sold.

In Figures 3.5 and 3.8 we summarized the many events that cause demand and supply curves to shift. Using the four predictions derived in Figure 3.10, we can understand the link between these events and changes in market prices and quantities. To take one example, a rise in the price of butter will lead to an increase in both the price of margarine and the quantity bought. This is because a rise in the price of one product causes a rightward shift in the demand curves for its substitutes, and prediction 1 tells us that such a shift causes price and quantity to increase.

The theory of the determination of price by demand and supply is beautiful in its simplicity and yet powerful in its range of applications. Box 3.4 gives some simple applications of demand and supply to real market events.

## But markets are not really like that!

As we built up our analysis of markets in this chapter, you might have been saying to yourself: 'This is all very well in theory, but the markets I know about are not like that.' There is one important respect in which you would be absolutely correct. But we now want to persuade you that the doubts you might have about this analysis are not a real problem. Demand and supply analysis helps us understand *all* markets, even though the details of how they actually work vary considerably from market to market.

### Administered prices and auction prices

The worry that we hope you had when reading the analysis of markets is that most of the markets in which consumers operate, including you and us, do not work in the way we describe. For example, if you wish to attend your local cinema for a peak-time showing of a much-hyped film, you may find queues outside the cinema to buy tickets. There may be more people who want to see the film at that time than the number of seats available for sale. According to our theory, this means that there is an excess demand and so the price of cinema seats should rise until enough people are discouraged and all those left in the queue are just able to obtain a seat.

Of course, this does not happen. What actually happens is that the cinema continues to sell tickets at its existing prices until it has sold all the seats, and it then puts up a notice saying: 'Sold Out' or 'House Full'.

Similarly, if you go into your local supermarket or department store, you will find the prices of all the goods clearly labelled. You can buy as much of each product as you like at the price set by the store, but the price does not change according to how many people are buying the product on a particular day. If some product is very popular the store will run out and the shelf will be empty, but the store does not adjust the price to ensure that there is just enough supply to meet the demand.

So have we been lying to you when we have said that prices adjust to clear markets? The answer is an overwhelming No. However, we do have to understand that market institutions vary with product and participants. Prices do adjust to clear markets, but they do not do it in the same way in all types of market. Let us think about different ways in which prices are set, and then we shall try to give some reasons for these differences.

The prices that most obviously fit our theory are referred to as **flexible prices** or **auction prices**, as they adjust on a continuous basis to equate demand and supply. Prices in the foreign exchange market and in the markets for petroleum, minerals, and grains are flexible, as they can change minute by minute while the market is open. Prices that are set by the supplier, who then just waits to see how much of the product sells at that price, are known as **administered prices** or **fixed prices**. Most consumer goods and services are sold at administered prices.

### Administered prices do adjust

Although prices in most retail outlets are set by the retailer, this does not mean that these prices do not adjust over time to market forces. On any particular day we find that all products have a specific price ticket on them. However, this price may be different from day to day or week to week. If, for example, bad weather leads to a poor potato crop, then the price that supermarkets have to pay for potatoes will go up and this will be reflected in the prices they mark on potatoes in their stores. Thus, these prices do reflect the interaction of demand and supply in the wider marketplace for potatoes. Similarly, fresh strawberries sell at very different prices in mid-winter and mid-summer. In

the summer they are locally grown, but in winter they will have been flown in from the other side of the world.

Even within a supermarket that sets prices on all its produce, there will be times when they mark prices down in order to get rid of stock. This may be as the stock approaches its sell-by date, or if the supermarket has new lines arriving the next day. Department stores have sales at regular intervals in order to get rid of stock that has not sold at higher prices and to make room for new products. When the costs of producing such durable consumer goods as TV sets and refrigerators rise or fall, their prices follow, even if there is a substantial interval between the two sets of changes. Cinemas will have lower prices at off-peak times. However, in all these cases, the supplier is still setting a price and then (in effect) saying: 'Take it or leave it at this price.'

### Why are some prices administered?

If administered prices do eventually adjust to reflect demand and supply conditions, why are they set at a fixed price in the first place? The answer is that this is a more efficient way to organize a retail marketplace. Auction markets work well where all the potential buyers can be assembled in one place (the auction room) or are connected by communication equipment (telephones or computers), so that they can simultaneously bid for the product. The price is set so that the highest bidder gets the goods, and all the goods available are sold.

Imagine the chaos, however, if all the people who ever shop in your local supermarket have to turn up at the same time and make bids for their weekly shopping basket. This is clearly not feasible. Imagine also what the checkout queues would be like if every shopper had to negotiate the price of each item in their shopping trolley when they reach the checkout. Again, this would be a very time-consuming way of shopping. There have been some recent attempts to organize certain retail markets by collecting bids through the internet, such as via E-bay. However, it seems very unlikely that this form of shopping will replace the supermarket and the department store any time soon.

### Mixed pricing

Some markets do have a mixture of administered prices and a degree of price negotiation. This is efficient because these are usually markets for items that are large and which you do not buy very often. Motor cars, for example, have 'list prices', but there is usually some leeway for negotiation, either about the price of the car itself, the extras it includes, or the trade-in price of your old car. When new models are introduced, stocks of the old models may be sold off at lower than the original list price. Houses too are typically listed at an 'asking price', but there is some negotiation around this price, and if several people are chasing the same house there may be what amounts to an auction where the house goes to the highest bidder. Indeed, in Scotland a sealed-bid auction system is the norm: bidders have to enter a written bid on the same day without knowing what others have bid, and the highest bidder gets the property.

Many manufactured goods are put on sale in shops at a fixed price. But these prices already reflect supply factors such as costs of production, and the rent and wages paid by the retailer. Demand influences will certainly affect the price. A very popular item that the retailer is finding hard to get may have its ticket price raised, while unsold items will be marked down for clearance at some stage. Clothing and other fashion items also typically stay for a period at a fixed price but are then sold off in clearance sales to make way for new fashions or new styles. Indeed, while most clothes retailers have 'sales' around twice a year, many have permanent racks of discounted items within their store. A similar example is wine shops, which regularly have 'bin end' sales of unwanted stock to make space for their new stock.

## Relationships between different markets

Although each of the individual markets referred to above is distinct, all are interrelated, and we need to see why.

### The separation of individual markets

Markets are separated from each other in three main ways: by the product sold, by natural economic barriers, and by barriers created by governments. Here is one example of each type of separation:

1. The market for men's shirts is different from the market for refrigerators because different products are sold in each.

2. The market for cement in the United Kingdom is distinct from the market for cement in the western United States. The costs of transporting cement are so high that UK purchasers would not buy American cement even if its market price in the western United States were very much lower than its market price in Britain.

3. The market for textiles used to be separated between many countries because government-imposed trade restrictions severely limited either the amount that firms in one country could sell to consumers in another or the prices at which they could sell.

Because markets are distinct, we can use demand and supply analysis to study the behaviour of markets one at a time.

### The interlinking of individual markets

Although all markets are to some extent separated, most are also interrelated. Consider again the three causes of market separation: different products, spatial separation, and government intervention. First, the markets for different kinds of product are interrelated because all products compete for consumers' income. Thus, if consumers spend more in one market, they will have less to spend in other markets. Second, the geographical separation of markets for similar products depends on transport costs. Products whose transport costs are high relative to their production costs tend to be produced and sold in geographically distinct markets. Products whose transport costs are low relative to their production costs tend to be sold in what amounts to one world market. But whatever the transport costs, there will be some price differential at which it will pay someone to buy in the low-priced market and ship to the high-priced one. Thus, there is always some potential link between geographically distinct markets, even when shipping costs are high. Third, markets are often separated by policy-induced barriers, such as tariffs (which are taxes paid when goods come into a country from abroad). Although high tariffs tend to separate markets, they do not do so completely. If price differences become large enough, it will pay buyers in the high-price market to import from the low-price market and producers in the low-price market to export to the high-price one, even though they have to pay the tariff as a result.

Because markets are interrelated, we must treat them as a single interrelated system for many purposes. *General equilibrium analysis* studies markets as a single interrelated system in which individual demands and supplies depend on all prices, and what happens in any one market will affect many other markets—and in principle could affect all other markets.

# Government intervention in markets

We now introduce a third set of players on the economic stage. We have called decision-takers *agents*, and earlier in this chapter we introduced two sets of agents: consumers and firms. The third set is most accurately called the *central authorities*, but is more commonly, if loosely, referred to as the **government** or the state.[5]

Governments play an important role in modern mixed economies. Among other things, they sometimes seek to alter market outcomes. They can influence the prices at which goods are sold by taxing or subsidizing either their production or their consumption. They can influence the terms on which goods and services are offered for sale by imposing quality standards or regulating product prices. These, and many other methods that we will encounter throughout this book, are collectively referred to as *government intervention*.

## Price controls

If the government wishes to influence the price at which some product is bought and sold, it has two main alternatives. First, it can change the equilibrium price by altering the product's demand or supply. Second, it can enact legislation that regulates the price. **Price controls** refer to the latter alternative: influencing price by laws, rather than by market forces.

### Disequilibrium trading

If controls are used to hold price at a disequilibrium level, what determines the quantity actually traded on the market?

Any voluntary market transaction requires both a willing buyer and a willing seller. Thus, if quantity demanded is less than quantity supplied, demand will determine the amount actually traded, and the excess supply will remain in the hands of the unsuccessful sellers. If quantity supplied is less than quantity demanded, however, supply will determine the amount actually traded and the excess demand will take the form of desired purchases by unsuccessful buyers. This is shown graphically in Figure 3.11.

At any disequilibrium price, the quantity exchanged is determined by the lesser of quantity demanded and quantity supplied.

This result is often expressed by the maxim that in disequilibrium the short side of the market dominates (i.e. determines what is bought and sold).

### Maximum-price legislation

In this section we concentrate on laws setting *maximum* permissible prices, which are often called 'price ceilings'. Over the years, such laws have had many purposes. Governments of medieval cities sometimes sought to protect their citizens from the consequences of crop failures by fixing a maximum price at which bread could be sold. In modern times, many governments have employed rent controls in an attempt to make housing available at a price that could be afforded by lower-income groups. Governments in many poor countries set the prices of some basic foodstuffs well below their market equilibrium values.

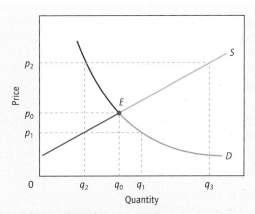

**Figure 3.11  Disequilibrium quantity**

In disequilibrium, quantity exchanged is determined by the lesser of quantity demanded and quantity supplied. Market equilibrium is at point $E$. For prices below $p_0$ the quantity exchanged will be determined by the supply curve. For example, $q_2$ will be exchanged at price $p_1$ in spite of the excess demand of $q_1 - q_2$. For prices above $p_0$ the quantity exchanged will be determined by the demand curve. For example, $q_2$ will be exchanged at price $p_2$ in spite of the excess supply of $q_3 - q_2$. Thus, the dark blue and dark pink portions of the $S$ and $D$ curves show the actual quantities exchanged at each price.

---

[5] It is *not* a basic assumption of economics that the central authorities always act in a consistent fashion as if they were a single individual. Indeed, conflict among different central authority agencies is often an important component in theories that analyse government intervention in the economy.

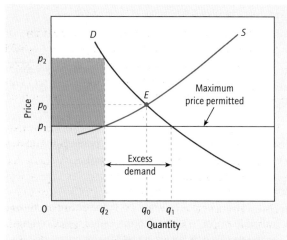

**Figure 3.12 Price ceilings and black market pricing**

A price ceiling set below the equilibrium price causes excess demand and invites a black market. Equilibrium price is at $p_0$. If a price ceiling is set at $p_1$, the quantity demanded will rise to $q_1$ and the quantity supplied will fall to $q_2$. Quantity actually exchanged will be $q_2$. Excess demand is $q_1 - q_2$. Black marketeers would buy $q_2$ at the controlled price of $p_1$, paying the amount shown by the light blue area $p_1 q_2$. They would sell at the price $p_2$, earning profits shown by the dark blue area between $p_1$ and $p_2$.

## The effects on price and quantity

Most price ceilings actually specify the highest permissible price that producers may legally charge. If the ceiling is set above the equilibrium price it has no effect, since the equilibrium remains attainable. If, however, the ceiling is set below the equilibrium price, it determines the price—in which case the ceiling is said to be *binding*. The key consequences of price ceilings are shown in Figure 3.12.

The setting of a maximum price has no effect if the price is set at or above the equilibrium price. If the maximum price is set below the equilibrium price, a shortage will develop and quantity actually bought and sold will fall below its equilibrium value.

## Allocation of available supply

In the case of a binding price ceiling, production is insufficient to satisfy everyone who wishes to buy the product. Since price is not allowed to rise so as to allocate the available supply among the would-be purchasers, some other method of allocation must be found. Theory does not predict what this other method will be, but experience has shown several possibilities.

If shops sell to the first customers who arrive, people are likely to rush to those stores that are rumoured to have any stocks of the scarce product. Long queues will develop, and allocation will be on the basis of luck, or to

those knowing enough to gain from the principle of 'first come, first served'. This system was commonly found in the command economies of Eastern Europe during the Communist era, where queuing was a way of life.

Sometimes shopkeepers themselves decide who will get the scarce products and who will not. They may keep products under the counter and sell only to regular customers or only to people of a certain colour or religion. Such a system is called allocation by **sellers' preferences**.

If the government dislikes the allocation that results from price ceilings, it can ration the goods, giving out coupons sufficient to purchase the available supply. The coupons might be distributed equally, or on criteria such as age, sex, marital status, or number of dependants. Rationing by coupons was used in Britain and most of the other belligerent countries during the Second World War (1939–45). Rationing persisted in Britain for another nine years after the war, until 1954.

Any official rationing scheme substitutes the government's preferences for the sellers' preferences in allocating a product that is in excess demand because of a binding price ceiling.

## Black markets

A binding price ceiling, with or without rationing, is likely to give rise to a **black market**. This is a market in which goods are sold illegally at prices that violate the legal restrictions. Many products have only a few manufacturers but many retailers. Although it is easy to police the producers, it is difficult even to locate, much less to control, all those who are, or could be, retailing the product.

Figure 3.12 shows the result of a price ceiling that determines the price that producers get but does not control the price at which retailers sell to the public. Output is restricted by the low price received by producers, while consumers must pay the high price that equates demand to the available supply. The difference between what consumers pay and what producers get goes as profits to the black marketeers.

It is unlikely that all of the output will be sold on the black market—both because there are many honest people in every society and because the government usually has some power to enforce its price ceilings on retailers. Thus, the normal case is not the extreme result shown in the figure. Instead, some of the limited supplies will be sold at the controlled price and some at the black-market price.

If the purpose of an intervention policy is to keep prices down, the policy is a failure to the extent that black marketeers succeed in raising prices; it is a success to the extent that sales actually occur at the controlled prices. If, however, the government wishes to restrict production in order to release resources for other, more urgent needs, such as war production, the policy works effectively, if somewhat unfairly.

### Evidence

There is plenty of evidence confirming these predictions. During the First and Second World Wars governments set binding ceilings on many prices. The legislation of maximum prices was always followed by shortages, then by either the introduction of rationing or the growth of some private method of allocation (such as sellers' preferences), and then by the rise of some sort of black market. The ceilings were more effective in limiting consumption than in controlling prices, although they did restrain price increases to some extent. Until the early 1990s, many of the former socialist countries of Eastern Europe followed a policy of controlling food prices at levels that were below the equilibrium prices. Chronic shortages, queues, allocation by sellers' preferences, and black markets were the result.

Another example of the effects of price controls arises in the market for rented accommodation. Rent controls have now been largely eliminated in the United Kingdom, but rent controls introduced during the First World War distorted the UK housing market for much of the twentieth century. They have also been (and are being) used in other countries.[6]

### Price floors and price support policies

Another common form of price intervention occurs when a government decides that it wants a price to be held above the market-clearing price. Agriculture is a common example, and it has been used both to guarantee incomes for farmers and to secure domestic supplies of agricultural supplies.

Figure 3.11 can be used to illustrate the problems that arise. An intervention price such as $p_2$ in the figure is above what the market-clearing price would be. At this price supply will exceed demand, and this excess supply will have to be managed somehow. In the EU this excess production was associated with what were called 'butter mountains' and 'wine lakes', which represented the production surpluses that were bought up by the authorities in order to sustain the higher-than-market price.

In addition to dealing with domestic production surpluses, a policy that aims to hold prices artificially high in a specific local market also has to make sure that cheaper imports do not enter from abroad; otherwise, the price support policy will fail to hold prices at their target level. We discuss this problem further in the third case study below and we offer more detail on agricultural price support policies on our website.

# CASE STUDIES

## 1. The market for steel

Figure 3.13 shows the price of steel from 1970 to 2004 as it appeared in an article in the *Financial Times* (*FT*) in September 2004. It shows both the actual price in US dollars and the price adjusted by inflation in the general price index. The latter is known as the *real price*, and it indicates changes in the relative price of steel and all other goods and services in the price index.

There are three features of this evolution of steel prices that need to be explained. First, there is a cycle in the price. Second, between the early 1970s and the early 2000s there was a downward trend in the relative price of steel. Third, there was a sharp upturn in steel prices in 2004.

The cycle in steel prices coincides roughly with the cycle in activity in the major economies of the world. Supply conditions in the steel industry are fairly stable, so that movements in price

tend to be driven by swings in demand. Demand for steel is high when consumer demand for durable goods such as cars and refrigerators is high, and when there is a lot of construction work going on. Hence the cycle in steel prices reflects the business cycle in the world economy. We say that demand for steel is *procyclical*, and steel prices are also procyclical: when the world economy is booming, demand for steel is high and steel prices are high.

The *FT* article explains the downward trend in steel prices by the fact that steel producers for much of this period continued to have excess capacity. As the article reported, 'Companies have shown an unfailing ability in recent years to misjudge demand growth and add too much capacity at times, creating oversupply that has caused prices to remain low.' The article reported that between 1970 and 2000 steel demand worldwide rose by only 1–2 per cent a year on average.

So what caused the sharp upturn in steel prices in 2004? One element of the answer is that growth in demand for steel rose to 6 per cent a year between 2001 and 2004. This occurred despite

---

[6] We discuss rent controls further on our website: www.oxfordtext books.co.uk/orc/lipsey11e/

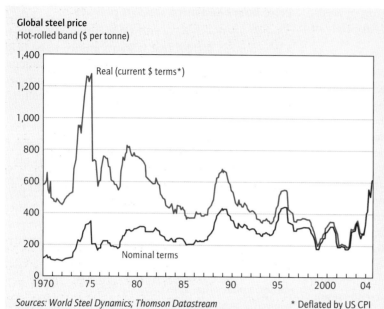

**Global steel price**
Hot-rolled band ($ per tonne)

**Figure 3.13**  **The world price of steel**

*Sources: World Steel Dynamics; Thomson Datastream*          * Deflated by US CPI          *Source: Financial Times*, 29 September 2004.

only modest growth in the major industrial countries during this period. The missing ingredient to the explanation is dramatic growth in demand for steel from China, whose national output was growing at a rate of nearly 10 per cent a year at this time: in 1998 China consumed 17 per cent of world steel production, but in 2004 it was projected to consume 29 per cent.

What is not shown in the chart is that in 2005 steel prices came down somewhat from the highs of 2004, and this was despite continued growth in China. The reason for this seems to be that by 2005 China had increased it own production capacity and so no longer needed to import so much steel from the rest of the world.

## 2.  The Channel Tunnel

In 2001 around 7 million passengers took journeys by Eurostar trains through the Channel Tunnel, and 2.5 million tonnes of freight were shipped on trains. In addition, the Shuttle service carried 2.5 million cars and 75,000 coaches. The equivalent figures for each year before 1994 were zero. The opening of the Channel Tunnel to full passenger and freight services had a big impact on the cross-Channel travel market as it involved a massive increase in capacity, that is, an increase in supply.

We now know a lot about the impact of the Tunnel. However, when we first analysed this issue in the 8th edition of this book the Tunnel was not open. In the 10th edition we were able to retain our earlier analysis virtually intact, adding to it some evidence from our 9th edition, which proves that jokes about the failure of economists to make accurate predictions are very far from the truth (at least some of the time).

### The impact of the Tunnel

We deal with the market in cross-Channel journeys. Although things other than price, such as speed and convenience, will affect the division of demand among the various types of travel, we hold these factors constant and focus on the average price of cross-Channel journeys. The supply comes from the Tunnel, several shipping firms, hovercraft, and airlines. [*This is what we wrote in 1994. The hovercraft service ceased in October 2000, and the number of ferry companies has fallen largely in response to competition from the tunnel.*] Although firms operating each of these types of travel have power over price, it is safe to assume that the total amount they will all wish to supply will vary positively with the price, that is to say that the supply curve of cross-Channel transport is positively sloped.

Figure 3.14 analyses the market. Part (i) shows the total demand and supply for cross-Channel journeys. Part (ii) shows the demand for journeys on air and sea services, which were the only suppliers before the tunnel opened. Initially the demand curve facing sea and air operators was the same as the total market demand curve. The opening of the Tunnel shifted the market supply curve to the right in part (i) while shifting the demand curve for air and sea journeys to the left in part (ii). (One way to think of the effect on demand for air and sea journeys is that the price of a substitute, Tunnel journeys, has fallen from infinity to some positive number.) Notice that it does not matter for the general analysis whether Tunnel journeys are cheaper or more expensive than other methods of travel, although the quantitative effects will depend on this. All that matters is that Tunnel travel is cheap enough that some passengers who would have gone by air or sea now go by rail.

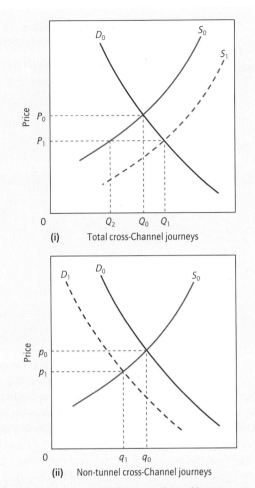

**(i)** Total cross-Channel journeys

**(ii)** Non-tunnel cross-Channel journeys

**Figure 3.14 The market for cross-Channel journeys**

**The opening of the Tunnel added to total supply but reduced demand for non-Tunnel travel.** Before the Tunnel opened, the demand and supply curves were $D_0$ and $S_0$ in both parts of the figure. Price and quantity are thus the same in both parts, shown as $P_0, Q_0$ in part (i) and $p_0, q_0$ in part (ii). The opening of the Tunnel shifted the supply curve to the right from $S_0$ to $S_1$ in part (i). With a given demand curve $D_0$ this lowered price and increased quantity from $P_0$ and $Q_0$ to $P_1$ and $Q_1$. Part (ii) shows the demand and supply curves for non-Tunnel journeys (air and sea). The availability of a new substitute, Tunnel travel, shifted the demand curve for other forms of travel to the left from $D_0$ to $D_1$. The price and quantity accordingly fell to $p_1$ and $q_1$. In part (i) the total of cross-Channel journeys $Q_1$ is split between $Q_2$ going by air and sea and $Q_1 - Q_2$ going via rail.

The first prediction derived from Figure 3.14 is that the opening of the Tunnel would cause a fall in the average price of cross-Channel journeys and an increase in the quantity purchased. The size of the increase would depend on the size of the price reduction and the sensitivity of demand to price (which we will later call the *elasticity of demand*).

The second prediction is that the air and sea operators would experience a fall in demand because there will be a new substitute: Tunnel journeys. Initially, this would be seen entirely in empty seats and car decks, because prices are set in advance (though some lower prices may have been set in anticipation of a demand fall). Very soon, however, there would be special cut-price deals, and, eventually, sustained price-cutting even for regular fares.

It was estimated (prior to the Tunnel being built) that the Tunnel might take a market share of about 40 per cent. Up to about half of these journeys were expected to be diverted from air and sea services, and the rest were expected to be new journeys stimulated by the new lower prices.

## What happened?

The above predictions, based on the application of simple demand and supply analysis, turned out to be remarkably accurate. In 1998 and 1999 the Channel Tunnel carried almost exactly 40 per cent of passengers and accompanied cars crossing the Channel by surface transport. Passengers travelling to Europe from Thames and Kent ports fell from 23.7 million in 1994 to 16.6 million in 2000, while over the same period passengers travelling on the shuttle rose from 315,000 to 17 million (with around a further 7 million travelling on the Eurostar train service).

Newspaper reports at the time illustrate other aspects of our predictions. In September 1995, shortly after the Tunnel came into full operation, the *Financial Times* wrote:

*Eurotunnel has grabbed a big slice of the ferry operators' business on the cross-Channel market over the crucial summer months. Stena Sealink, the second largest ferry company on the Dover–Calais route, admitted its passenger volume fell 10 per cent and freight volumes 13 per cent in July compared with the same month last year. These trends have continued during August.... Eurotunnel's own July traffic figures showed an 11.5 per cent increase over the previous month in the number of cars carried.... The price war in the cross-Channel market is growing in intensity, with the ferry companies maintaining discounts of up to 25 per cent on published prices throughout the summer. Eurotunnel has also offered a number of incentives to customers. (Financial Times, August 1995)*

Two months later *The Economist* had this to say:

*In June ... the number of passengers flying from London's Heathrow to Paris's Charles de Gaulle—traditionally the world's busiest airline route—was down 35 per cent from the same time last year.... On the London–Brussels route, the numbers fell by 6 per cent from Heathrow and 22 per cent from Gatwick. Worse still ... Eurostar has forced down average airline economy fares by 25–30 per cent. (The Economist, London, October 1995)*

In May 1996 the *Financial Times* wrote:

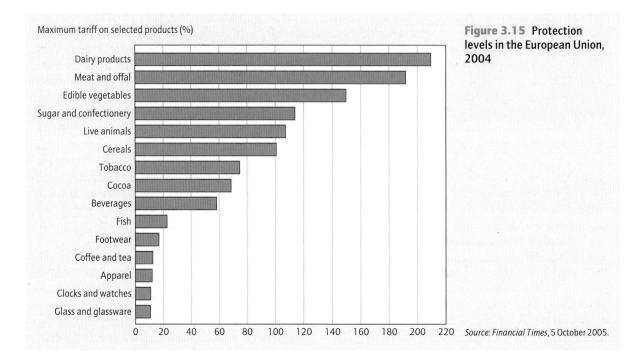

Maximum tariff on selected products (%)

**Figure 3.15** Protection levels in the European Union, 2004

*Source: Financial Times, 5 October 2005.*

*The cut-throat cross-Channel price war intensified yesterday when Eurotunnel, the Anglo-French operator of the Channel Tunnel, announced that it is to halve the standard return fare over the summer to £129. The main ferry companies responded immediately, saying they would match any bargain fares offered by Eurotunnel for comparable trips. . . . Eurotunnel has a market share of Dover–Calais traffic of about 45 per cent . . . (Financial Times, May 1996)*

The price war took place in the context of an overall growth in the cross-Channel journey market (as predicted by the negative slope of the overall market demand curve). The *Investors' Chronicle* (12 April 1996, page 10) estimated that this market had grown by 25 per cent in 1995 and by a further 20 per cent in 1996. Also, the *Economist* article referred to above quotes the total seat capacity on the London–Paris/Brussels routes as being 690,000 per week in July 1994 but having risen to 1,297,000 in July 1995. The latter information tells us by how much the supply curve shifted.

### Assessment

The subsequent data and the events referred to in the newspaper reports show that the predictions of our demand and supply analysis were amply borne out in practice. First, the prices of cross-Channel journeys fell and the quantity demanded increased. Second, the airlines, ferry, and hovercraft companies suffered a fall in demand. They all responded with aggressive price-cutting. The airlines also shifted some of their capacity on to other routes, and air travel to France did not recover to 1994 volumes until 1999.[7] In 1998 the two major ferry companies, P&O and Stena, merged their cross-Channel operations, so that

they could co-ordinate their competition with the other forms of transport and manage the needed capacity reduction. In 2000, the hovercraft service closed down owing to lack of demand.

The impact of the Channel Tunnel continued to be felt by its competitors for some time. In September 2004 the BBC News website reported: 'P&O to slash workforce by 1,200'. At this time the P&O group had announced the closure of four of its 13 ferry routes. The reason given was rising competition from no-frills airlines and from Eurotunnel. The chief executive of P&O was reported as saying: 'Clearly, the Channel Tunnel has had a major impact on our business and has taken substantial market share.'

### 3. Agricultural intervention: the EU Common Agricultural Policy[8]

The Common Agricultural Policy of the European Union, nick-named the CAP, illustrates many of the problems generated by sustained attempts by governments to intervene in markets. The policy has held agricultural prices well above their market equilibrium values within the EU. To prevent the flood of imports that would have been attracted by these high prices, the imports of all agricultural goods that receive EU price support have been subject to a high tariff. Figure 3.15 shows tariff protection levels for a range of goods in 2004.

---

[7] This was against a background of rapidly growing demand for air travel. Passenger numbers to all destinations from UK airports doubled between 1990 and 2000.

[8] We provide more analysis of agricultural support policies and their implication on our website: www.oxfordtextbooks.co.uk/orc/lipsey11e/

The high European prices cause EU production to exceed EU consumption. Surpluses pile up, only to be sold abroad at a fraction of their production costs, or even given away. EU farmers gain, while taxpayers, consumers, and efficient foreign producers lose out. The payments to farmers rose so much over the years that they put serious strain on the EU budget. Expenditure on agriculture reached a peak of nearly 65 per cent of the entire EU budget in 1986, but fell back over the next two decades, reaching around 50 per cent in the early 2000s. In contrast, in 2000 agriculture accounted for a little less than 2 per cent of total EU production of all goods and services (down from 4.8 per cent in 1973), and just over 4 per cent of EU civilian employment.

Many of the world's poorer countries have efficient agricultural sectors, and in a world of free trade they would export large quantities to the EU and the USA, earning good and rising incomes for their farmers. Instead, farmers in these developing countries have found their livelihoods threatened by subsidized exports of surplus EU products. The attempt to restrain these exports has caused great strains on the relations between the EU and other agricultural producing countries. These were a matter of contention in the long-running Uruguay Round of trade negotiations which concluded in 1994, as a result of which the EU agreed to relatively minor alterations to the CAP. They were an even more important issue in the Doha Round of trade talks which started in 2001 and were still running in 2006. However, as Figure 3.16 shows for the case of sugar, even proposed cuts in EU intervention prices were unlikely to do much to increase market access for non-EU producers.

A phased reduction in intervention prices started in the mid-1990s, and this helped to reduce the proportion of total EU budget devoted to agricultural support, with further reductions planned (as indicated for the case of sugar in the figure). Price

**Figure 3.16  The price of raw sugar**

*Source: Financial Times*, 15 August 2005, from *Thomson Datastream*; EC; ISO.

supports are partly being replaced by direct subsidies. In some cases these subsidies are payments for non-production. For example, the 'set-aside' policy pays farmers to keep some of their land idle. Thus, while the nature of intervention in the EU is changing, it is not disappearing. Consumers may gain from the price reductions planned (over time), but taxpayers will continue to carry the burden of the costs of intervention, and foreign producers continue to be penalized by lack of access to EU markets.

# Conclusion

Whatever the market in which we are interested, the analysis of how demand and supply interact to determine the market-clearing price is an essential tool. It is applicable to all situations in which some maker or owner of a product wishes to exchange the product with a potential user.

All the more detailed analysis that we are going to do between now and Chapter 14 is designed to build a fuller and fuller understanding of the forces affecting different types of market and market structure, and the motives and behaviour of market participants. But we have already gone a long way towards understanding how markets work, and the problems caused by government intervention.

# SUMMARY

- The decision-taking units in economic theory are called agents. They are (a) individuals, for demand in goods markets and for supply in labour markets; (b) firms, for supply in goods markets and demand in labour and capital markets; and (c) governments, for supply of some goods and for regulation and control of the private sector. Given the resources at their command, each individual is assumed to maximize his or her satisfaction, and each firm is assumed to maximize its profit.

## Demand

- An individual consumer's demand curve shows the relation between the price of a product and the quantity of that product the consumer wishes to purchase per period of time. It is drawn on the assumption that all other prices, income, and tastes remain constant. Its negative slope indicates that the lower the price of the product, the more the consumer wishes to purchase.

- The market demand curve is the horizontal sum of the demand curves of all the individual consumers. The demand curve for a normal good shifts to the right when the price of a substitute rises, when the price of a complement falls, when total income rises, when the distribution of income changes in favour of those with large demands for the product, and when tastes change in favour of the product. It shifts to the left with the opposite changes.

- A movement along a demand curve indicates a change in quantity demanded in response to a change in the product's own price; a shift in a demand curve indicates a change in the quantity demanded at each price in response to a change in one of the conditions held constant along a demand curve.

## Supply

- The supply curve for a product shows the relationship between its price and the quantity that producers wish to produce and offer for sale per period of time. It is drawn on the assumption that all other forces that influence quantity supplied remain constant, and its positive slope indicates that the higher the price, the more producers wish to sell.

- A supply curve shifts in response to changes in the prices of the inputs used by producers, and to changes in technology. The shift represents a change in the amount supplied at each price. A movement along a supply curve indicates that a different quantity is being supplied in response to a change in the product's own price.

## The determination of price

- At the equilibrium price the quantity demanded equals the quantity supplied. Graphically, equilibrium occurs where the demand and supply curves intersect. At any price below equilibrium there will be excess demand and price will tend to rise; at any price above equilibrium there will be excess supply and price will tend to fall.

- A rise in demand raises both equilibrium price and quantity; a fall in demand lowers both. A rise in supply raises equilibrium quantity but lowers equilibrium price; a fall in supply lowers equilibrium quantity but raises equilibrium price.

- Price theory is most simply developed in the context of a constant price level. Price changes discussed in the theory are changes relative to the average level of all prices. In an inflationary period, a rise in the relative price of one product means that its price rises by more than the rise in the general price level; a fall in its relative price means that its price rises by less than the rise in the general price level.

## But markets are not really like that!

- Most retail markets do not appear to have prices adjusting to differences between demand and supply. Prices are set at a specific level and shoppers can buy as much as they want at this price. Prices are administered by the seller.

- Even administered prices adjust to demand and supply forces, but it would not be efficient for these prices to be set either by auction or by negotiation, or to change every minute. Price changes do happen in response to persistent changes in the conditions affecting both demand and supply, but they do not do so instantaneously.

## Government intervention in markets

- Effective price ceilings lead to excess demand, black markets, and non-price methods of allocating the scarce supplies among would-be purchasers.

- Effective price floors lead to excess production and often require tariff protection to exclude cheaper foreign imports.

## TOPICS FOR REVIEW

- Quantity demanded and the demand function
- The demand schedule and the demand curve for an individual and for the market
- The law of demand
- Shifts in the demand curve and movements along the curve
- Substitutes and complements
- Quantity supplied and the supply function
- The supply schedule and the supply curve

- Shifts in the supply curve and movements along the curve
- Excess demand and excess supply
- Equilibrium and disequilibrium prices
- The law of price adjustment
- Auction prices and administered prices
- Government intervention to impose maximum or minimum prices

## QUESTIONS

1 What is the equilibrium market price and quantity for each of the following pairs of demand and supply curves:
   Demand: $p = £100 - 2q$; supply: $p = £0 + 3q$
   Demand: $p = £100 - 2q$; supply: $q = 30$
   Demand: $p = £100$;        supply: $p = £20 + 5q$

2 Use demand and supply curves to analyse what is happening in each of the following situations:
   - The price of coffee has risen because of a frost in Brazil reducing the coffee crop.
   - A fall in air fares from the UK has raised demand for hotel rooms on the Spanish costas.
   - Further falls in chip prices have led to a reduction in the price of laptop computers.
   - An exceptionally cold winter in North America leads to a higher price of oil.
   - A disease in British beef necessitates the slaughtering of large numbers of cattle.

3 List all the 'markets' in which you regularly buy goods or services. How are the price and quantity determined during your transaction? Do these prices change on a day-to-day basis or only infrequently? If prices do not adjust, what happens when there is an excess demand or supply?

4 Outline the main determinants of quantity demanded and quantity supplied, and explain how these interact to determine the market price.

5 Explain the main differences between administered prices and auction prices, and discuss which markets are most suitable for these two different mechanisms.

6 Outline the conditions that are required to achieve equality between demand and supply at a market-clearing price.

7 Explain the effect on market price and quantity in the market for mobile phone handsets of each of the following:
   (a) Consumer incomes rise.
   (b) Technical improvements reduce production costs.
   (c) The price of fixed-line calls falls sharply.

# Chapter 4

# ELASTICITY OF DEMAND AND SUPPLY

In this chapter we develop some very important concepts that will help you to understand how markets work.

In particular, you will learn:

- How the sensitivity of quantity demanded to a change in price is measured by the elasticity of demand and what factors influence it
- How elasticity is measured at a point or over a range
- How income elasticity is measured and how it varies with different types of good
- How elasticity of supply is measured and what it tells us about conditions of production
- Some of the difficulties that arise in trying to estimate various elasticities from sales data

The demand and supply analysis of the previous chapter helps us to understand the direction in which price and quantity will change in response to shifts in demand or supply. In most real-world situations economists and business analysts are not going to get away with saying things like 'If we raise our price sales will fall' or 'If incomes rise this year our demand will increase.' The question they need to answer is: 'By how much?' Fortunately, tools exist to help them—and you—answer this question in the many different circumstances in which it may be asked. These tools measure the responses of the quantity demanded and the quantity supplied to changes in the variables that determine them, particularly prices and incomes.

To illustrate why we want to have these measures, consider the effects of a new government tax on each litre of petrol refined (perhaps aimed at reducing emissions of greenhouse gases). This will shift the supply curve of petrol to the left because less will be offered at each price; equivalently, any specific quantity will be offered only at a higher price. If the demand for petrol is as shown in part (i) of Figure 4.1, the effect of the government's policy will be to increase petrol prices slightly, while greatly reducing the quantity refined and consumed. If, however, the demand is as shown in part (ii) of the figure, the effect of the policy will be to increase petrol prices greatly but to reduce petrol production and consumption by only a small amount. If the purpose of the tax is to reduce the amount that is produced and consumed, then the policy will be a great success when the demand curve is similar to the one shown in part (i), but a failure when the demand curve is similar to that shown in part (ii). If, however, the main purpose of the tax is to achieve a large increase in the price of petrol, the policy will be a failure when demand is as shown in part (i) but a great success when demand is as shown in part (ii).

This example shows that it is often not enough to know whether quantity rises or falls in response to some change. It is important to know by how much. To measure this we use the concept of *elasticity*.

**Figure 4.1  The effect of the shape of the demand curve**

The flatter the demand curve, *ceteris paribus*, the less the change in price and the greater the change in quantity. Both parts of the figure are drawn on the same scale. Both show the same initial equilibrium price $p_0$ and quantity $q_0$, the same shift of the supply curve from $S_0$ to $S_1$, and a new equilibrium at $p_1$ and $q_1$. In part (i) the effect of the shift in supply is a slight rise in the price and a large fall in quantity. In part (ii) the effect of the identical shift in the supply curve is a large rise in the price and a relatively small fall in quantity.

# Demand elasticity

In the first part of this chapter we deal with quantity demanded, and we start by considering its response to changes in a product's own price.

## Price elasticity of demand

In Figure 4.1 we were able to compare the responsiveness of quantity demanded along the two demand curves because they were drawn on the same scale. You should not try to compare two curves without making sure that the scales are the same. Also, you must not leap to conclusions about the responsiveness of quantity demanded on the basis of the apparent steepness of a single curve. The hazards of so doing are illustrated in Figure 4.2. Both parts of the figure plot the same demand curve, but the choice of scale on the 'quantity' and 'price' axes serves to make one curve look steep and the other flat.

### Measuring the responsiveness of demand to price

In order to get a measure of responsiveness that is independent of the scale we use, so that it can be compared across products, we need to deal in percentage changes. A given percentage change in the amount of petrol purchased will be the same whether we measure it in gallons or litres. Similarly, although we cannot easily compare the absolute changes in kilos of carrots and barrels of oil, we can compare their two percentage changes.

These considerations lead us to the concept of the **price elasticity of demand**, which is defined as the percentage change in quantity demanded *divided by* the percentage change in price that brought it about.[1] This elasticity is usually symbolized by the lower-case Greek letter eta, $\eta$:

$$\eta = \frac{\text{percentage change in quantity demanded}}{\text{percentage change in price}} \quad (1)$$

Many different elasticities are used in economics. To distinguish $\eta$ from the others, the full term 'price elasticity of demand' can be used. Since $\eta$ is by far the most commonly used elasticity, economists often drop the adjective 'price' and refer to it merely as *elasticity of demand*, or sometimes just *elasticity*. When more than one kind of elasticity could be involved, however, $\eta$ should be given its full title.

---

[1] Elasticity is an example of what mathematicians call a *pure number*, which is a number whose value is independent of the units in which it is calculated. Slope, $\Delta p / \Delta q$, is not a pure number. For example, if price is measured in pence, $\Delta p / \Delta q$ will be 100 times as large as $\Delta p / \Delta q$ along the same demand curve where price is measured in pounds sterling.

**Figure 4.2 One demand curve drawn on two different scales**

**Suitable choice of scale can make any demand curve appear steep or flat.** Parts (i) and (ii) plot the same demand curve. Because the same distance on the quantity axes stands for twice as much in part (ii) as in part (i), and the same distance on the price axes stands for half as much, the curve is steeper when plotted in graph (ii) than when plotted in graph (i).

**Table 4.1  Calculation of two demand elasticities**

|  | Original | New | % change | Elasticity |
|---|---|---|---|---|
| *Good A* |  |  |  |  |
| Quantity | 100 | 95 | −5% | $\left.\begin{array}{c}\\\\\end{array}\right\}\dfrac{-5}{10}=-0.5$ |
| Price | £1 | £1.10 | 10% |  |
| *Good B* |  |  |  |  |
| Quantity | 200 | 140 | −30% | $\left.\begin{array}{c}\\\\\end{array}\right\}\dfrac{-30}{20}=-1.5$ |
| Price | £5 | £6 | 20% |  |

**Elasticity is calculated by dividing the percentage change in quantity by the percentage change in price.** With good A, a rise in price of 10p on £1, or 10 per cent, causes a fall in quantity of 5 units from 100, or 5 per cent. Dividing the 5 per cent reduction in quantity by the 10 per cent increase in price gives an elasticity of −0.5. With good B, a 30 per cent fall in quantity is caused by a 20 per cent rise in price, making elasticity −1.5.

## The sign of the measure

Because of the negative slope of the demand curve, price and quantity will always change in opposite directions. One change will be positive and the other negative, making the measured elasticity of demand negative. This would pose no problem except for two unfortunate habits of economists. First, either by carelessness or by design, the minus sign is often dropped and elasticity is reported as a positive number. Second, it is almost universal practice when comparing two elasticities to compare their absolute, not their algebraic, values.[2] For example, if

product $X$ has an elasticity of −2 while product $Y$ has an elasticity of −10, economists will say that $Y$ has a greater elasticity than $X$ (in spite of the fact that −10 is *less than* −2). As long as it is understood that absolute and not algebraic values are being compared, this usage is acceptable. After all, the demand curve with the larger absolute elasticity *is* the one where quantity demanded is more responsive to price changes. For example, an elasticity of −10 indicates greater response of quantity to price than does an elasticity of −2.

This need not cause confusion so long as you remember the following:

Demand elasticity is measured by a ratio: the percentage change in quantity demanded divided by the percentage change in price that brought it about. For normal, negatively sloped, demand curves elasticity is negative, but the relative size of two elasticities is usually assessed by comparing their absolute values.

Table 4.1 shows the calculation of two demand elasticities, one that is quite large and one that is smaller. The larger elasticity indicates that quantity demanded is highly responsive to a change in price. The smaller elasticity indicates that the quantity demanded is relatively unresponsive to a change in price.

## Interpreting price elasticity

The value of price elasticity of demand ranges from zero to minus infinity. In this section, however, we concentrate on absolute values, and so ask by how much the absolute value *exceeds zero*.

---

[2] The absolute value is the magnitude without the sign. Thus, for example, −3 is smaller in algebraic value than 2 but larger in absolute value.

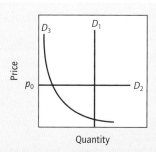

**Figure 4.3 Three constant-elasticity demand curves**

**Each curve has a constant elasticity.** $D_1$ has *zero elasticity*: the quantity demanded does not change at all when price changes. $D_2$ has *infinite elasticity at the price $p_0$*: a small price increase from $p_0$ decreases quantity demanded from an indefinitely large amount to zero. $D_3$ has *unit elasticity*: a given percentage increase in price brings an equal percentage decrease in quantity demanded at all points on the curve; it is a rectangular hyperbola for which price *times* quantity is a constant.

Elasticity is zero if quantity demanded is unchanged when price changes, namely when quantity demanded does not respond to a price change. A demand curve of zero elasticity is shown as curve $D_1$ in Figure 4.3. It is said to be *perfectly* or *completely* inelastic.

As long as there is some positive response of quantity demanded to a change in price, the absolute value of elasticity will exceed zero. The greater the response, the larger the elasticity. Whenever this value is less than one, however, the percentage change in quantity is less than the percentage change in price and demand is said to be **inelastic**.

When elasticity is equal to one, the two percentage changes are then equal to each other. This case, which is called **unit elasticity**, is the boundary between elastic and inelastic demands. A demand curve having unit elasticity over its whole range is shown as $D_3$ in Figure 4.3.

When the percentage change in quantity demanded exceeds the percentage change in price, the elasticity of demand is greater than one and demand is said to be **elastic**. When elasticity is infinitely large, there exists some small price reduction that will raise quantity demanded from zero to infinity. Above the critical price, consumers will buy nothing. At the critical price, they will buy all that they can obtain (an infinite amount, if it were available). The graph of a demand curve with infinite price elasticity is shown as $D_2$ in Figure 4.3. Such a demand curve is said to be *perfectly* or *completely* elastic. (This unlikely looking case will turn out to be important later when we study the demand for the output of a single firm with many competitors all producing an identical product.)

Box 4.1 summarizes the discussion of this and subsequent sections. The terminology in the table is important, and it is worth becoming familiar with it at some stage, but you may want to come back to it once you have read the rest of the chapter.

### Elasticity and total spending

How does consumers' total spending on a specific product react when the price of the product is changed? The total spending of the product's buyers is equal to the money received by the product's sellers plus any taxes that the government levies on the product. For simplicity, we ignore any taxes, so that sellers' receipts are equal to buyers' spending.

A simple example can be used to show that buyers' total spending and sellers' receipts may rise or fall in response to a decrease in price. Suppose 100 units of a product are being sold for £1 each. The price is then cut to £0.90. If the quantity sold rises to 110, the total spent falls from £100 to £99. But if quantity sold rises to 120, total spending rises from £100 to £108.

The change in total spending brought about by a change in price is directly related to the elasticity of demand. If elasticity is less than unity (so demand is inelastic), the percentage change in price will exceed the percentage change in quantity. The price change will then be the more influential of the two changes, so that total spending will change in the same direction as the price changes. If, however, elasticity exceeds unity (demand is elastic), the percentage change in quantity will exceed the percentage change in price. The quantity change will then be the more influential change, so that the total amount spent will change in the same direction as quantity changes (that is, in the opposite direction to the change in price).

1. When elasticity of demand exceeds unity (demand is elastic), a fall in price increases total spending on the good and a rise in price reduces it.

2. When elasticity is less than unity (demand is inelastic), a fall in price reduces total spending on the good and a rise in price increases it.

3. When elasticity of demand is unity, a rise or a fall in price leaves total spending on the good unaffected.[3]

---

[3] Algebraically, total spending is price *times* quantity. If, for example, the equilibrium price and quantity are $p_1$ and $q_1$, then total spending is $p_1 q_1$. On a demand-curve diagram, price per unit is given by a vertical distance and quantity by a horizontal distance. It follows that on such a diagram total spending is given by the *area* of a rectangle the length of whose sides represent price and quantity. Total revenue (receipts) to the supplier and total spending by consumers are identical in these examples.

## ⬤ ⬤ ⬤ Box 4.1 The terminology of elasticity

| TERM | SYMBOL | NUMERICAL MEASURE OF ELASTICITY | VERBAL DESCRIPTION |
|---|---|---|---|
| **Price elasticity of demand (supply)** | $\eta(\varepsilon_s)$ | | |
| Perfectly or completely inelastic | | Zero | Quantity demanded (supplied) does not change as price changes |
| Inelastic | | Greater than zero, less than one | Quantity demanded (supplied) changes by a smaller percentage than does price |
| Unit elasticity | | One | Quantity demanded (supplied) changes by exactly the same percentage as does price |
| Elastic | | Greater than one, but less than infinity | Quantity demanded (supplied) changes by a larger percentage than does price |
| Perfectly, completely, or infinitely elastic | | Infinity | Purchasers (sellers) are prepared to buy (sell) all they can at some price and none at all at a higher (lower) price |
| **Income elasticity of demand** | $\eta_y$ | | |
| Inferior good | | Negative | Quantity demanded decreases as income increases |
| Normal good | | Positive | Quantity demanded increases as income increases: |
| Income-inelastic | | Less than one | less than in proportion to income increase |
| Income-elastic | | Greater than one | more than in proportion to income increase |
| **Cross-elasticity of demand** | $\eta_{xy}$ | | |
| Substitute | | Positive | The quantity demanded of some good and the price of a substitute are positively related |
| Complement | | Negative | The quantity demanded of some good and the price of a complement are negatively related |

You can check points 1 and 2 for yourself using the example in Table 4.1. Calculate what happens to total spending on the product when price changes in each case. In the case of good A, whose demand is inelastic, you will see that a rise in price raises total spending (and thus also the revenue of sellers). In contrast, the rise in the price of good B, whose demand is elastic, lowers total spending (and sellers' revenue).

### Some complications

We now need to look a little more closely at the elasticity measure. Let us first write out in symbols the definition that we have been using, which is percentage change in quantity divided by percentage change in price:

$$\eta = \frac{\dfrac{\Delta q}{q} \cdot 100}{\dfrac{\Delta p}{p} \cdot 100}.$$

We can cancel out the 100s and multiply the numerator and denominator by $p/\Delta p$ to get

$$\eta = \frac{\Delta q}{q} \cdot \frac{p}{\Delta p}$$

Since it does not matter in which order we do our multiplication (i.e. $q \cdot \Delta p = \Delta p \cdot q$), we may reverse the order of the two terms in the denominator and write

$$\eta = \frac{\Delta q}{\Delta p} \cdot \frac{p}{q}. \tag{2}$$

We have now split elasticity into two parts: $\Delta q/\Delta p$, the ratio of the *change* in quantity to the change in price, which is related to the slope of the demand curve; and $p/q$, which is the ratio of the *level* of the price and quantity at which we make our measurement.

Figure 4.4 shows a straight-line demand curve. If we wish to measure the elasticity at a point, we take our $p$ and $q$ at that point and consider a price change, taking us to another point, and measure our $\Delta p$ and $\Delta q$ between those two points. The slope of the straight line joining the two points is $\Delta p/\Delta q$. (If you are not sure about this, see the explanation on page 27.) The term in equation (2), however, is $\Delta q/\Delta p$, which is the reciprocal of $\Delta p/\Delta q$. (This

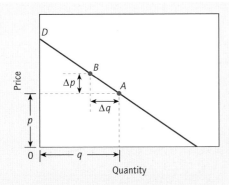

**Figure 4.4** Elasticity on a linear demand curve

**Elasticity depends on the slope of the demand curve and the point at which the measurement is made.** Starting at point $A$ and moving to point $B$, the ratio $\Delta p/\Delta q$ is the slope of the line, while its reciprocal $\Delta q/\Delta p$ is the first term in the percentage definition of elasticity. The second term is $p/q$, which is the ratio of the coordinates of point $A$. Since the slope $\Delta p/\Delta q$ is constant, it is clear that the elasticity along the curve varies with the ratio $p/q$, which is zero where the curve intersects the quantity axis and 'infinity' where it intersects the price axis.

**Figure 4.5** Two intersecting demand curves

**At the point of intersection of two demand curves, the steeper curve has the lower elasticity.** At the point of intersection $p$ and $q$ are common to both curves, and hence the ratio $p/q$ is the same. Therefore, elasticity varies only with $\Delta q/\Delta p$. The absolute value of the slope of the steeper curve, $\Delta p_2/\Delta q$, is larger than the absolute value of the slope, $\Delta p_1/\Delta q$, of the flatter curve. Thus, the absolute value of the ratio $\Delta q/\Delta p_2$ on the steeper curve is smaller than the ratio $\Delta q/\Delta p_1$ on the flatter curve, so that elasticity is lower.

involves just turning the ratio upside down. So the reciprocal of 2/3 is 3/2, and the reciprocal of a whole number is its inverse: the reciprocal of 4 is 1/4.) Thus, the first term in the elasticity formula (2) is the reciprocal of the slope of the straight line joining the two price–quantity positions under consideration. The second term is the ratio of price to quantity at the point where elasticity is measured.

Now we can use the expression in (2) to discover a number of things about our elasticity measure.

First, the elasticity of a negatively sloped straight-line demand curve varies from infinity at the price axis to zero at the quantity axis. A straight line has a constant slope, so that the ratio $\Delta p/\Delta q$ is the same anywhere on the line. Therefore, its reciprocal, $\Delta q/\Delta p$, must also be constant. We can now infer the changes in $\eta$ by inspecting changes in the ratio $p/q$ as we move along the demand curve. At the price axis $q = 0$ and $p/q$ is undefined. However, if we let $q$ approach zero, without ever quite reaching it, we see that the ratio $p/q$ becomes very large. Thus elasticity increases without limit as $q$ approaches zero. Loosely, we say that elasticity is infinity when $q$ is zero. Now move the point at which elasticity is being measured down the demand curve. As this happens, $p$ falls and $q$ rises steadily; thus the ratio $p/q$ is falling steadily, so that $\eta$ is also falling. At the $q$-axis the price is zero, so the ratio $p/q$ is zero. Thus elasticity is zero.

Second, with a straight-line demand curve the elasticity measured from any point $(p, q)$, according to equation (2) above, is independent of the direction and magnitude of the change in price and quantity. This follows immediately from the fact that the slope of a straight line is a constant. If we start from some point $(p, q)$ and then change price, the ratio $\Delta q/\Delta p$ will be the same whatever the direction or the size of the change in $p$.

Our third point takes us back to the beginning of this chapter, where we warned against judging elasticity from the apparent shape of a demand curve. We often want to compare elasticities of two different demand curves, but we have just seen that the elasticity of a straight-line demand curve varies as we move along it. So how can we compare two numbers both of which are ranging from zero to infinity for every straight line demand curve? Fortunately, if two demand curves intersect, their elasticity can be compared *at the point of intersection* merely by comparing the slopes of the two curves. The steeper curve is the less elastic. Figure 4.5 shows two intersecting curves and proves that the steeper curve is less elastic than the flatter curve when elasticity is measured at the point where the two curves intersect. The intuitive reason is that at the point of intersection $p$ and $q$ are common to both curves, so all that differs in the elasticity formula is their relative slopes. This is a valuable result, which we will use many times in later chapters.

Measured at the point of intersection of two demand curves, the steeper curve has the lower elasticity.

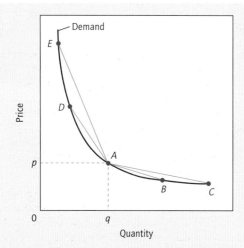

**Figure 4.6** Elasticity on a nonlinear demand curve

Elasticity measured from one point on a nonlinear demand curve and using the percentage formula varies with the direction and magnitude of the change being considered. Elasticity is to be measured from point $A$, so the ratio $p/q$ is given. The ratio $\Delta p/\Delta q$ is the slope of the line joining point $A$ to the point reached on the curve after the price has changed. The smallest ratio occurs when the change is to point $C$ and the highest ratio when it is to point $E$. Since the term in the elasticity formula, $\Delta q/\Delta p$, is the reciprocal of this slope, measured elasticity is largest when the change is to point $C$ and smallest when it is to point $E$.

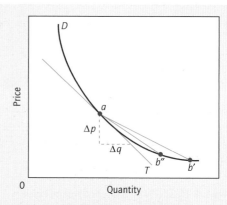

**Figure 4.7** Elasticity by the exact method

When elasticity is related to the slope of the tangent to the demand curve at some point, there is a unique measured value of elasticity at that point. In this method the ratio $\Delta q/\Delta p$ is taken as the reciprocal of the slope of the line that is tangent to point $a$. Thus, there is only one measured elasticity at point $a$: it is $p/q$ multiplied by $\Delta q/\Delta p$ measured along the tangent $T$. There is no averaging of changes in $p$ and $q$ in this measure because only one point on the curve is used.

The fourth point is that, when equation (2) is applied to a nonlinear demand curve, the elasticity measured at any one point varies with the direction and magnitude of the change in price and quantity. Figure 4.6 shows a nonlinear demand curve with elasticity being measured at one point. The figure makes it apparent that the ratio $\Delta q/\Delta p$, and hence the elasticity, will vary according to the size and the direction of the price change. This result is very inconvenient. It happens because the ratio $\Delta q/\Delta p$ gives the average reaction of $q$ to a change in $p$ over a section of the demand curve, and, depending on the range that we take, the average reaction will be different.

### A more precise measure

The measure defined in (2) gives the elasticity over some range, or *arc*, of the demand curve. This measure is sometimes used in empirical work where elasticity is measured between two observed price–quantity situations. In theoretical work, however, it is normal to use a concept that gives a unique measure of the elasticity at each specific point on the demand curve. Instead of using the changes in price ($\Delta p$) and quantity ($\Delta q$) over some range of the curve, this elasticity measure uses the concept of how

quantity is *tending* to change as price changes at each specific point on the curve.

If we wish to measure the elasticity in this way, we need to know the reaction of quantity to a change in price at each point on the curve, not over some range on the curve. We use the symbol d$q$/d$p$ to refer to this concept and define it as *the reciprocal of the slope of the straight line (i.e. $\Delta q/\Delta p$) that is tangent to the demand curve at the point in question*. Figure 4.7 illustrates the use of this measure to calculate the elasticity of demand at the point $a$. It is the ratio $p/q$ (as it has been in all previous measures), now multiplied by the ratio $\Delta q/\Delta p$ measured along the straight line, that is tangent to the curve at $a$.[4] This definition may now be written as

$$\eta = \frac{\mathrm{d}q}{\mathrm{d}p} \cdot \frac{p}{q}. \qquad (3)$$

This elasticity measure is the one normally used in economic theory. Elasticity measured by the percentage formula $(\Delta q/\Delta p)(p/q)$ may be regarded as an approximation to this expression. It is obvious from inspecting Figure 4.7 that the elasticity measured from $(\Delta q/\Delta p)(p/q)$ will come

---

[4] Although the expression d$q$/d$p$, as we have defined it, is the differential-calculus concept of the derivative of quantity with respect to price at the point $(p, q)$, you can understand the concept without knowing calculus.

**Box 4.2** Measuring elasticity over a range

We have seen that the percentage formula gives different answers for the elasticity at any point on a nonlinear demand curve depending on the size and the direction of the change being considered. Many textbooks just give the percentage elasticity formula, without warning the reader of this property. Inquisitive students usually discover this property with a shock the first time they try to calculate some elasticities from numerical data.

One common way in which students discover the problem is when they try to calculate the elasticity on a unit-elasticity curve. Using the percentage formula, the answer never comes out to be 1. For example, the demand curve

$$p = £100/q \qquad \text{(i)}$$

is a unit-elastic curve because expenditure, $pq$, remains constant at £100 whatever the price. But if you substitute any two prices into the above equation and calculate the elasticity according to the percentage formula, you will *never* get an answer of 1, whatever two prices you take. For example, the equation tells us that if price rises from £2 to £3, quantity falls from 50 to 33.3. If we take the original price as £2, we have a price change of 50 per cent and a quantity change of $-33.3$ per cent, making an elasticity of $-0.667$. If we take the original price as £3, the elasticity comes out to be $-1.5$.

This is unsatisfactory. The problem can be avoided when measuring elasticity between two separate points on the curve by taking $p$ and $q$ as the average values between the two points on the curve. This measure has two convenient properties. First, it is independent of the direction of the change; second, it gives a value of unity for any point on a demand curve whose true value is unity.

In the above example the average $p$ is £2.50 and the average $q$ is 41.667. This makes the percentage change in price 40 per cent ($(1/2.5) \times 100$) and the percentage change in quantity also 40 per cent ($(16.667/41.667) \times 100$). So elasticity is correctly measured as 1. Whatever two prices you put into equation (i), you will always get a value of unity for the elasticity, provided you use the average of the two prices and of the two quantities when calculating the elasticity. Readers who enjoy playing with algebra can have fun proving this proposition.*

**The best approximation to the correct measure when elasticity is measured between two separate points on a demand curve is obtained by defining $p$ and $q$ as the average of the prices and quantities at the two points on the curve.**

The above is the best way to measure elasticities given readings from any two points on a curve when that is all that is known. As we have seen in the text, for theoretical purposes the way out of the problem is to measure the ratio $\Delta q/\Delta p$ as the slope of the tangent to one point on the curve rather than between two points on the curve. To do this, we need to know a portion of the demand curve around the point in question.

In practice, economists do not usually estimate elasticity on the basis of only one observation. It is more common to report an elasticity measure that is valued at the mean of two $p$ and $q$ data points. This is analogous to the averaging we suggest here.

---

\* What you need to prove is that

$$\frac{q_2 - q_1}{p_2 - p_1} \cdot \frac{(p_1 + p_2)/2}{(q_1 + q_2)/2} = 1$$

---

closer and closer to that measured by $(dq/dp)(p/q)$, the smaller the price change used to calculate the value of $\Delta q/\Delta p$. Thus, if we consider the percentage definition of elasticity as an approximation to the precise definition, the approximation improves as the size of $\Delta p$ diminishes. Box 4.2 further investigates some of the properties of the percentage definition and shows a practical way of avoiding some of its undesirable aspects.

### What determines elasticity of demand?

The main determinant of elasticity is the availability of substitutes. Some products, such as margarine, cabbage, Coca Cola, and the Peugeot 406, have quite close substitutes—butter, other green vegetables, Pepsi, and the VW Passat. When the price of any one of these products changes, *the prices of the substitutes remaining constant*, consumers will substitute one product for another. When the price falls,

consumers buy more of the product and less of its substitutes. When the price rises, consumers buy less of the product and more of its substitutes. More broadly defined products, such as all foods, all clothing, tobacco, and petrol, have few if any satisfactory substitutes. A rise in their price can be expected to cause a smaller fall in quantity demanded than would be the case if close substitutes were available.

A product with close substitutes tends to have an elastic demand; one with no close substitutes tends to have an inelastic demand.

Closeness of substitutes—and therefore measured elasticity—depends both on how the product is defined and on the time-period under consideration. This is explored in the following sections. One common misconception about demand elasticity is discussed in Box 4.3.

**Box 4.3  Elasticity and income**

It is often argued that the demand for a product will be more inelastic the smaller the proportion of income spent on it. The argument runs as follows. When only a small proportion of income is spent on some product, consumers will hardly notice a price rise. Hence they will not react strongly to price changes one way or the other.

The most commonly quoted example of this alleged phenomenon is salt. Salt is, however, a poor example for the argument being advanced. Although it does take up a very small part of consumers' total expenditure, it also has few close substitutes. Consider another product, say one type of mint. These mints no doubt account for only a small portion of the total expenditure of mint-suckers, but there are many close substitutes—other types of mint and other sucking sweets. The makers of Polo mints, for example, know that if they raise Polo prices greatly mint-suckers will switch to other brands of mint and to other types of sucking sweets. They thus face an elastic demand for their product.

Similar considerations apply to any one brand of matches. If the makers of Swan Vesta matches raise their prices significantly, people will switch to other brands of matches rather than pay the higher price.

What this discussion shows is that *goods with close substitutes will tend to have elastic demands whether they account for a large or a small part of consumers' incomes.*

There is, however, another aspect of the influence of income. To see this, consider any good that has an inelastic demand. A rise in its price causes more to be spent on it. If consumers spend more on that product, they must spend less on all others taken as a group. But the higher is the proportion of income spent on the product, the less likely are they to spend more on it when its price rises. After all, if a consumer spends all of his or her income on potatoes, demand must have unit elasticity. As price rises, purchases must then fall in proportion, since the consumer has only a given income to spend. Thus, *for a good to have a highly inelastic demand it must have few good substitutes—and it must not take up too large a proportion of consumers' total expenditure.*

---

### Definition of the product

There is no substitute for food: it is a necessity of life. Thus, for food taken as a whole demand is inelastic over a large price range. It does not follow, however, that any one food—say Weetabix or Heinz tomato soup—is a necessity in the same sense. Each of these has close substitutes, such as Kellogg's Cornflakes and Campbell's tomato soup. Individual food products can have quite elastic demands, and they frequently do.

Durable goods provide a similar example. Durables as a whole have less elastic demands than do individual durable goods. For example, after a rise in the price of TV sets, some consumers may replace their personal computer or their hi-fi system instead of buying a new TV. Thus, although their purchases of television sets fall, their total purchases of durables fall by much less.

Because many specific manufactured goods have close substitutes, they tend to have price-elastic demands. A particular Marks and Spencer own-brand raincoat could be expected to be price elastic, but all clothing taken together will be inelastic. This is because, while it is easy to substitute a Marks and Spencer raincoat with a John Lewis, or Selfridge raincoat, you have to wear something in the winter and you cannot avoid wearing clothing altogether when its price in general rises relative to, say, the price of food.

**Any one of a group of related products will tend to have an elastic demand, even though the demand for the group as a whole may be inelastic.**

### Long-run and short-run elasticity of demand

Because it takes time to adjust fully to some price change, a demand that is inelastic in the short run may prove elastic when enough time has passed. For example, before the first OPEC oil price shocks of the mid-1970s, the demand for petrol was thought to be highly inelastic because of the absence of satisfactory substitutes. But the large price increases over the 1970s led to the development of smaller, more fuel-efficient cars and to less driving. The elasticity of demand for petrol was measured as –0.6 soon after the price rose. However, when the first five years of quantity adjustment had been allowed for, the elasticity had become –1.2.

**For many products the response of quantity demanded to a given price change, and thus the measured price elasticity of demand, will tend to be greater the longer the time-span considered.**

The different quantity responses can be shown by different demand curves. Every demand curve shows the response of consumer demand to a change in price. For such products as cornflakes and ties, the full response occurs quickly and there is little reason to worry about longer-term effects. For these products a single demand curve will suffice. Other products are typically used in connection with highly durable appliances or machines. A change in price of, say, electricity or petrol may not have its major effect until the stock of appliances and machines

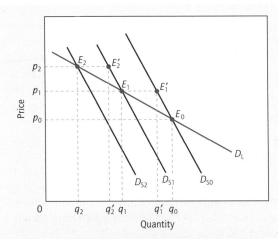

**Figure 4.8 Short-run and long-run demand curves**

The long-run demand curve is more elastic than the short-run curves. $D_L$ is the long-run demand curve showing the quantity that will be bought after consumers become fully adjusted to each given price. Through each point on $D_L$ there is a short-run demand curve. It shows the quantities that will be bought at each price when consumers are fully adjusted to the price at which that particular short-run curve intersects the long-run curve. So at every other point on the short run curve consumers are not fully adjusted to the price they face, possibly because they have an inappropriate stock of durable goods.

When consumers are fully adjusted to price $p_0$, they are at point $E_0$ consuming $q_0$. Short-run variations in price then move them along the short-run demand curve $D_{S0}$. Similarly, when they are fully adjusted to price $p_1$, they are at $E_1$ and short-run price variations move them along $D_{S1}$. The line $D_{S2}$ shows short-run variations in demand when consumers are fully adjusted to price $p_2$.

using these products has been adjusted. This adjustment may take a long time, making it useful to identify two kinds of demand curve for such products. A *short-run demand curve* shows the response of quantity demanded to a change in price, *given* the existing quantities of the durable goods that use the product, and *given* existing supplies of substitute products. A different short-run demand curve will exist for each such structure of durable goods and substitute products. The *long-run demand curve* shows the response of quantity demanded to a change in price after enough time has passed to allow all adjustments to be made.

The relation between long-run and short-run demand curves is shown in Figure 4.8. Assume, for example, that there is a large rise in the price of electricity. The initial response will be along the short-run demand curve. There will be some fall in quantity demanded, but the percentage drop is likely to be less than the percentage rise in

price, making short-run demand inelastic. Over time, however, many people will replace their existing electric cookers with gas cookers as they wear out. New homes will be equipped with gas rather than electric appliances more often than they would have been before the price rise. After further time, factories will switch to relatively cheaper sources of power. When all these types of long-run adaptation have been made, the demand for electricity will have fallen a great deal. Indeed, over this longer period of time the percentage reduction in quantity demanded may exceed the percentage increase in price. If so, the long-run demand for electricity will be elastic.

The long-run demand curve for a product that is used in conjunction with durable goods will tend to be substantially more elastic than any of the short-run demand curves.

This insight will prove valuable in several of the chapters that follow.

## Other demand elasticities

So far we have discussed *price elasticity of demand*, the response of the quantity demanded to a change in the product's own price. The concept of demand elasticity can, however, be broadened to measure the response to changes in *any* of the factors that influence demand. How much, for example, do changes in income and the prices of other products affect quantity demanded?

### Income elasticity

Economic growth has raised the real income of the average citizen of Europe and North America quite dramatically over the past two centuries. At low levels of income most money is spent on such basics as food, clothing, and shelter. As income rises an increasing proportion of expenditure tends to fall on manufactured goods, particularly such durables as cars, TV sets, and refrigerators. At yet higher levels of income more and more of any additional income goes to services such as foreign travel, entertainment, and education.

The responsiveness of demand for a product to changes in income is termed **income elasticity of demand**, and is defined as

$$\eta_y = \frac{\text{percentage change in quantity demanded}}{\text{percentage change in income}}.$$

For most products, increases in income lead to increases in quantity demanded, and income elasticity is therefore positive. If the resulting percentage change in quantity demanded is larger than the percentage increase in income, $\eta_y$ will exceed unity. The product's demand is then said to be **income-elastic**. If the percentage change in quantity demanded is smaller than the percentage change in income, $\eta_y$ will be less than unity. The product's demand is then said to be **income-inelastic**. In the boundary case, the percentage changes in income and quantity demanded are equal, making $\eta_y$ unity: the product is said to have a *unit income elasticity of demand*.

We have already encountered the link between income changes and demand on page 43, where we argued that a change in income would shift the demand curve for a product. If the product is a normal good, a rise in income causes more of it to be demanded, other things being equal, which means a rightward shift in the product's demand curve. If the product is an inferior good, a rise in income causes less of it to be demanded, which means a leftward shift in the product's demand curve. So normal goods have positive income elasticities while inferior goods have negative income elasticities. Finally, the boundary case between normal and inferior goods occurs when a rise in income leaves quantity demanded unchanged, so that income elasticity is zero.

While virtually all observed price elasticities are negative, income elasticities are observed to be both positive and negative.

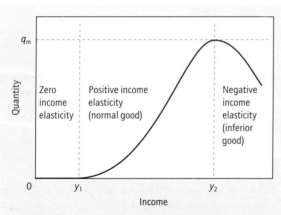

**Figure 4.9 The relation between quantity demanded and income**

Normal goods have positive income elasticities; inferior goods have negative elasticities. Nothing is demanded at income less than $y_1$, so for incomes below $y_1$ income elasticity is zero. Between incomes of $y_1$ and $y_2$, quantity demanded rises as income rises, making income elasticity positive. As income rises above $y_2$, quantity demanded falls from its peak at $q_m$, making income elasticity negative.

The important terminology of income elasticity is summarized in Figure 4.9 and in Box 4.1 on page 68. It is worth spending a bit of time familiarizing yourself with this terminology. Figure 4.9 illustrates all possible reactions by showing a product whose income elasticity goes from zero to positive to negative. No specific good is likely to show a pattern exactly like this. Most goods will have a positive income elasticity at all levels of income—people demand more as they get richer. (It should be obvious that no good can have a negative income elasticity at *all* levels of income.) A graph that directly relates quantity demanded to income, such as Figure 4.9, is called an *Engel curve* after Ernst Engel (1821–96), the German economist who used this device to display the relationship between household income and spending on necessities.

### Cross-elasticity

The responsiveness of quantity demanded of one product to changes in the prices of other products is often of considerable interest. Producers of, say, beans and other meat substitutes find the demands for their products rising when cattle shortages force the price of beef up. Producers of large cars find their sales falling when the price of petrol rises dramatically after a large oil price rise.

The responsiveness of demand for one product to changes in the price of another product is called **cross-elasticity of demand**. It is defined as

$$\eta_{xy} = \frac{\text{percentage change in quantity demanded of product } x}{\text{percentage change in price of product } y}.$$

Cross-elasticity can vary from minus infinity to plus infinity. Complementary goods have negative cross-elasticities, and substitute goods have positive cross-elasticities.

Mobile phones and the calls that can be made on them, for example, are complements. A fall in the price of calls causes an increase in the demand for both handsets and calls. Thus, changes in the price of calls and in the quantity of handsets demanded will have opposite signs—price of calls goes down and demand for handsets goes up. In contrast, mobile calls and fixed-line calls are substitutes: a fall in the price of mobile calls increases the quantity of mobile calls made but reduces the quantity demanded of fixed-line calls. Changes in the price of mobile calls and in the quantity of fixed-line calls demanded will, therefore, have the same sign. The terminology of cross-elasticity is also summarized in Box 4.1.

Box 4.4 provides some examples of the importance of taking elasticity into account when making many practical decisions.

**Box 4.4 Elasticity matters**

Elasticities may seem like rather boring concepts to learn about and to calculate. But they are powerful tools. Practical people who scorn theory ignore elasticity considerations at their peril. Here are a few cautionary tales.

• Many years ago the government of the former USSR was trying to earn enough US dollars to buy some strategic materials that it lacked at home. It had few exports at the time but it did have large stocks of gold, which it sold on the world market to earn US dollars. Since it was desperate for the money it adopted desperate measures, selling a large amount quickly. This drove the price down substantially. Indeed, the price fell more than in proportion to the increased quantity brought to the market. If you had been advising the Communist government just after reading this chapter, you would have known enough to point out the error of its ways. Since the world demand was inelastic, it was important not to try to sell too much. The government could have earned more by selling less!

• Not long ago the treasurer of a professional association introduced a motion at the annual meeting 'to increase membership fees by 10 per cent so as to increase our revenues by 10 per cent'. You could have told her that she was optimistically assuming that the elasticity of demand for membership was zero. If the elasticity differed at all from zero, revenues would rise by less than 10 per cent. If the elasticity proved to be greater than unity, the association would actually suffer a loss of revenue as a result of the rise in fees.

• A local bus company raised its prices by 10 per cent in an attempt to cover increased costs. It was pleased to see its revenues rise by 5 per cent. The next year it confidently raised its prices again and was surprised and dismayed to find that its revenues fell by 2 per cent. The manager was reported in the local press as saying, 'It is hard to do business when our customers are so erratic.' You could have told him that there was nothing erratic about the customers' behaviour. The manager was unreasonably assuming that the elasticity of demand for bus rides was constant over the whole relevant range. All that happened is that the second increase took fares into the range where the market demand curve was elastic.

# Supply elasticity

We have seen that elasticity of demand measures the response of quantity demanded to changes in any of the variables that affect it. Similarly, elasticity of supply measures the response of quantity supplied to changes in any of the variables that influence it. Because we wish to focus on the product's own price as a variable influencing its supply, we will be concerned mainly with *price elasticity of supply*. The usual practice is to drop the adjective 'price', referring to 'elasticity of supply' or 'supply elasticity' whenever there is no ambiguity in this usage.

Supply elasticities are important in economics. Our treatment is brief for two reasons: first, much of what has been said about demand elasticity carries over to the case of supply elasticity and does not need repeating; second, we will have more to say about the determinants of supply elasticity later in this book when we have looked more closely at the production decisions of firms.

## A definition

The **price elasticity of supply** is defined as the percentage change in quantity supplied divided by the percentage change in price that brought it about. Letting the lower-case Greek letter epsilon, $\varepsilon$, stand for this measure, its formula is

$$\varepsilon_S = \frac{\text{percentage change in quantity supplied}}{\text{percentage change in price}}$$

Supply elasticity is a measure of the degree of responsiveness of quantity supplied to changes in the product's own price.

Since supply curves normally have positive slopes, supply elasticity is normally positive.

## Interpreting supply elasticity

Figure 4.10 illustrates three cases of supply elasticity. The case of zero elasticity is one in which the quantity supplied does not change as price changes. This would be the case, for example, if suppliers persisted in producing a given quantity and dumping it on the market for whatever it would bring. Infinite elasticity occurs at some price if nothing is supplied at lower prices but an indefinitely large amount will be supplied at that price. Any straight-line supply curve drawn through the origin, such as the one shown in part (iii) of the figure, has an elasticity of unity. The reason is that, for any positively sloped straight

**Figure 4.10  Three constant-elasticity supply curves**

**All three curves have constant elasticity.** Curve $S_1$ has a *zero elasticity*, since the same quantity, $q_1$, is supplied whatever the price. Curve $S_2$ has an *infinite elasticity at price* $p_1$; nothing at all will be supplied at any price below $p_1$, while an indefinitely large quantity will be supplied at the price of $p_1$. Curve $S_3$, as well as all other straight lines through the origin, has a *unit elasticity*, indicating that the percentage change in quantity equals the percentage change in price between any two points on the curve.

line, the ratio of $p/q$ at any point on the line is equal to the ratio $\Delta p/\Delta q$ that defines the slope of the line. Thus, in the formula $(\Delta q/\Delta p)(p/q)$ the two ratios cancel each other out.

The case of unit supply elasticity illustrates that the warning given earlier for demand applies equally to supply. Do not confuse the geometric steepness of supply curves with elasticity. Since *any* straight-line supply curve that passes through the origin has an elasticity of unity, it follows that there is no simple correspondence between geometrical steepness and supply elasticity. The reason is that varying steepness (when the scales on both axes are unchanged) reflects varying *absolute* changes, while elasticity depends on *percentage* changes. The terminology of supply elasticity is summarized in Box 4.1 on page 68.

## What determines elasticity of supply?

What determines the response of producers to a change in the price of the product that they supply? First, the size of the response depends in part on how easily producers can shift from producing other products to producing the one whose price has risen. If agricultural land and labour can be readily shifted from one crop to another, the supply of any one crop will be more elastic than if labour cannot easily be shifted. Here also, as with demand, length of time for response is critical. It may be difficult to change quantities supplied in response to a price increase in a matter of weeks or months, but easy to do so over a period of years. An obvious example concerns the planting cycle of crops. Also, new oilfields can be discovered, wells drilled, and pipelines built over a period of years, but not in a few months. Thus, the elasticity of supply of oil is much greater over five years than over one year, and greater over one year than over one month. Second, elasticity is strongly influenced by how costs respond to output changes. This issue will be looked at in more detail in later chapters.

## Measurement of demand and supply

Much of what economists do to earn a living uses measurements of demand and supply elasticities. Will a fare increase help to ease the deficit of London Underground or the Panama Canal? The answer requires knowledge of price elasticity of demand. The United Nations Food and Agriculture Organization (FAO), and producers' co-ops, use income elasticities of demand to predict future changes in demand for food. Over the past decade, many industries have estimated their products' cross-elasticities of demand with petroleum in order to predict the effects of sharply changing petroleum prices. Members of the Organization of Petroleum Exporting Countries (OPEC) may wish to know supply elasticities in non-member countries in order to predict the reaction to price increases manipulated by OPEC. The methods for obtaining this information are dealt with in econometrics courses.[5] Solutions to two of the most troubling problems concerning demand measurement are discussed below.

## Problems of demand measurement

The explosion of knowledge of elasticities in recent decades came about when econometricians overcame major problems in measuring demand (and supply) relationships.

### Everything is changing at once

When quantity demanded changes over time, it is usually because a number of the influences that affect demand have been changing at the same time. How, then, can the separate influence of each variable be determined?

What, for example, is to be made of the observation that the quantity of butter consumed per capita rose by 10 per cent over a period in which average consumer income rose by 5 per cent, the price of butter fell by 3 per cent, and the price of margarine rose by 4 per cent? How much of the change is due to income elasticity of demand, how much to price elasticity, and how much to the cross-elasticity between butter and margarine? If this is all we know, the question cannot be answered. If, however, there are many observations showing, say, quantity demanded, income, price of butter, and price of margarine every month for four or five years, it is possible to discover the separate influences of each of the variables. The standard technique for doing so is called *multiple regression analysis*.

### Separating the influences of demand and supply

A second set of problems concerns the separate estimation of demand and supply curves. We do not observe directly what people wish to buy and what producers wish to sell at each possible price. Rather, we see what they do buy and what they do sell. So in any specific market we observe a price and quantity that is a point on both the supply and demand curve. For example, Marks and Spencer might sell 1,000 white shirts at £30 each in a particular week. These shirts were both demanded and supplied, so the price–quantity combination is a point on both the demand curve and on the supply curve. If in the subsequent week 1,100 shirts are sold at £32 each, what can we conclude about elasticity of demand or supply? The answer is 'nothing'—unless we know whether it is the demand curve or the supply curve that has shifted. If both

have shifted, then the observation tells us nothing about demand or supply elasticity.

The problem of how to estimate demand and supply curves from observed market data on prices and quantities actually traded is called the **identification problem**.

To illustrate the problem, we assume in Figure 4.11 that all situations observed in the real world are equilibrium ones, in the sense that they are produced by the intersection of demand and supply curves. The first two parts of the figure show cases where only one curve shifts. Observations made on prices and quantities then trace out the curve that has not shifted. The third part of the figure, however, shows that when both curves are shifting observations of prices and quantities are not sufficient to identify the slope of either curve.

The identification problem is surmountable. The key to identifying the demand and supply curves separately is to bring in variables other than price, and then to relate demand to one set and supply to *some other* set. For example, supply of the product might be related not only to price of the product but also to its cost of production, and demand might be related not only to price of the product but also to consumers' incomes. Provided that these other variables change sufficiently, it is possible to determine the relation between quantity supplied and price as well as the relation between quantity demanded and price. The details of how this is done will be found in a course on econometrics.

Econometricians allow for the identification problem when estimating demand curves. In more popular discussions, however, the problem is sometimes ignored. Whenever you see an argument such as 'We know that the foreign elasticity of demand must be very low because the price of whisky rose by 10 per cent last year while whisky exports hardly changed at all', you should ask if the author has really identified the demand curve. If the rise in price was due to a rise in foreign demand for whisky, we may actually have discovered that the short-run *supply curve* of whisky is very inelastic (since whisky takes several years to manufacture). The general proposition to keep in mind is:

Unless we know that one curve has shifted while the other has not, price and quantity data alone are insufficient to reveal anything about the shape of either the demand or the supply curve.

## Measurements of specific elasticities

The solution of the statistical problems associated with demand measurement has led to a large accumulation of

---

[5] *Econometrics* is the application of statistical methods to measurement and testing in economics.

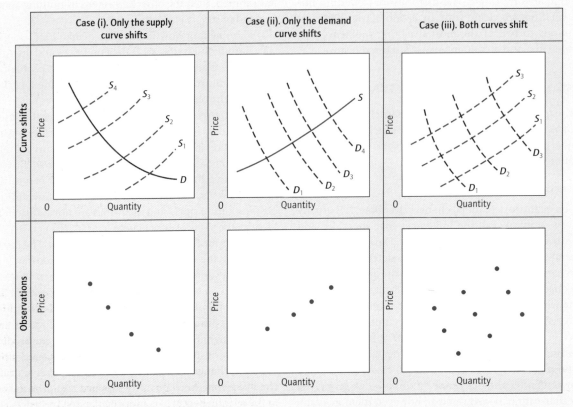

**Figure 4.11 The identification problem**

Observations on prices and quantities are sufficient to identify the slope of one of the curves only when it is stationary while the other shifts. In each case the curves in the top row shift randomly from one numbered position to another, generating the observations shown by the points in the corresponding bottom row. In case (i) the observations trace out the shape of the demand curve. In case (ii) they trace out the supply curve. In case (iii) neither curve can be identified from the observed prices and quantities.

data on demand elasticities. The value of these data to the applied economist shows the usefulness of demand theory.

### Price elasticities

Much of the early work on demand measurement concentrated on the agricultural sector. Large fluctuations in agricultural prices provided both the incentives to study this sector and the data on which to base estimates of price elasticities of demand. Nobel Laureate Professor Richard Stone in the United Kingdom (1913–91) and Professor Henry Schultz (1893–1938) in the United States did much of the pioneering work. Many agricultural research centres extended their work and even today are making new estimates of the price elasticities of foodstuffs. The resulting data mostly confirm the existence of low price

elasticities for food products as a whole, as well as for many individual products. The policy payoff of this knowledge in terms of understanding agricultural problems has been enormous; it represents an early triumph of empirical work in economics.

Although the importance of the agricultural problem led early investigators to concentrate on the demand for foodstuffs, modern studies have expanded to include virtually the whole range of products on which consumers spend their incomes. The demands for consumer durables such as cars, radios, refrigerators, television sets, and houses are of particular interest because they constitute a large fraction of total demand, and because they can vary markedly from one year to the next. A durable product can usually be made to last for another year; thus, purchases can be postponed with greater ease than can

**Table 4.2** Price and income elasticities of UK food items

|  | Price elasticity | Income elasticity |
| --- | --- | --- |
| Milk and cream | −0.36 | 0.05 |
| Cheese | −0.35 | 0.23 |
| Carcase meats | −0.69 | 0.2 |
| Fresh fish | −0.69 | 0.27 |
| Eggs | −0.28 | −0.01 |
| Fresh green vegetables | −0.66 | 0.27 |
| Fresh potatoes | −0.12 | 0.09 |
| Fresh fruit | −0.29 | 0.3 |
| Fruit juices | −0.55 | 0.45 |
| Bread | −0.4 | 0.12 |
| Beverages | −0.37 | 0.1 |

*Source: Expenditure and Food Survey*, DEFRA 2002. Available on www.defra.gov.uk. Data for price elasticities are for 1988–2000 and for income elasticities 1998–2000. Estimates are derived from panel data, that is, cross-section data for several periods of time.

purchases of non-durables such as food and services. If enough consumers decide simultaneously to postpone purchases of durables for even six months, the effect on the economy can be substantial.

Durables as a whole have an inelastic demand, while many individual brands of durable have elastic demands. This is another example of the general proposition that the broader the category, the fewer the close substitutes and hence the lower the elasticity. Indeed, whether durable or non-durable, many specific manufactured goods have close substitutes, and studies show that they tend to have price-elastic demands. This is why many firms try to build strong brands so that consumers of their product remain loyal. It helps them to raise price without losing substantial market share.

Table 4.2 shows some recent measures of price elasticity for food products.

Notice that all the price elasticities shown in Table 4.2 are negative, and staples like potatoes and eggs have relatively low price elasticities. What is not clear from the table is that, within categories shown in the table, the elasticity for a subset of that category can be much higher than for the product class as a whole. Carcase meats, for example, have a price elasticity of −0.69, but the price elasticity for lamb is −1.29, for pork it is −0.82, and for bacon it is −0.78. This indicates that carcase meats are closer substitutes for each other than are other foods for carcase meats as a whole.

## Income elasticities

Table 4.2 also shows some measured income elasticities for the United Kingdom. Note the low income elasticities for all of the food products. The income elasticity for food as a whole (not shown in table) is estimated at 0.2; this says that, for every one per cent increase in incomes, there is only a 0.2 of one per cent increase in spending on food. Notice, however, that all the estimates in the table except one show a positive income elasticity. Eggs have a negative income elasticity but this number is not significantly different from zero, so we should not conclude from this that eggs are an inferior good. The only clear estimate of an inferior good among food products (not shown in the table but from the same source) is margarine, which has an estimated income elasticity of −0.37.

## Cross-elasticities

Cross-elasticities are much harder to estimate as there are many more of them. Each product has only one own-price elasticity and one income elasticity, but it has a (potential) cross-elasticity with every other product. The source for Table 4.2 does report estimates of cross-elasticities for the same food products but most of them are insignificant. One that is not, however, is the positive cross-elasticity of bread and cheese (of 0.34), which indicates that bread and cheese are substitutes.

Though hard to measure, the concept of cross-elasticity is important. In many countries monopoly is illegal. Measurement of cross-elasticities has helped courts to decide on the allegation that a monopoly exists. To illustrate, assume that the competition authority of a particular country brings a suit against a company for buying up all the firms making aluminium cable, claiming the company has created a monopoly of the product. The company replies that it needs to own all the firms in order to compete efficiently against the several firms producing copper cable. It argues that these two products are such close substitutes that the firms producing each are in intense competition, so that the sole producer of aluminium cable cannot be said to have an effective monopoly over the market for cable. Measurement of cross-elasticity can be decisive in such a case. A cross-elasticity of 10, for example, would support the company by showing that the two products were such close substitutes that a monopoly of either would not be an effective monopoly of the cable market. A cross-elasticity of 0.5, on the other hand, would support the contention that the monopoly of aluminium cable *was* a monopoly over a complete market.

### Elasticities and economic growth

One of the most interesting constants in the behaviour of elasticities is the tendency for both income and price elasticities of demand for food to fall as nations get richer. Over the decades, economic growth has been increasing the real incomes of many countries throughout the world. As this happens the demand for foodstuffs increases, but at a slower and slower rate. At the same time, the demand becomes less and less sensitive to price fluctuations. For example, the price elasticity of demand for food is only about 0.1 in the USA, the country with the highest per capita income. As we go down the income scale, price elasticities rise, being about 0.3 in the UK, 0.45 in Israel, 0.55 in Peru, and around 0.7 in India. Over the same income range, income elasticities also rise; they go from about 0.15 in the USA, 0.2 in the UK, 0.5 in Israel, and 0.65 in Peru to almost 0.8 in India.

### Other variables

Research shows that demand is often influenced by a wide variety of socioeconomic factors—family size, age, religion, geographical location, type of employment, wealth, and income expectations—not included in the traditional theory of demand. Although significant, the total contribution of all these factors to changes in demand tends to be small. Typically, less than 30 per cent of the variations in demand are accounted for by these 'other' factors and a much higher proportion is explained by the traditional variables of current prices and incomes.

## Why the measurement of demand is important

The empirical measurements of demand elasticity help to provide the theory of price with empirical content. If we knew *nothing* about demand elasticities, then all of the exercises we have gone through in previous chapters would have very little application to the real world. As time goes by, further evidence accumulates, and economists are far beyond merely wondering if demand curves have negative slopes. Not only do we now know the approximate shape of many demand curves; we also have information about how demand curves shift. Our knowledge of demand relations increases significantly every year.

This knowledge has two general uses. First, in our study of economics it helps us to understand much more about how individual markets and the market economy work. This is helpful for understanding the world around us, and for informing debates about whether, for example, the market outcome can be trusted or whether government should intervene. Second, those of you who work in business after you have finished in college will find that your employer is competing with other firms in some markets and you will be expected to suggest ways in which the firm can be more successful. This will require you to build a detailed knowledge of the markets in which your firm operates, so that you can analyse issues like pricing of existing products and potential impact of new products.

 # CASE STUDIES

### 1. The coffee market

Judging from the growing number of Starbucks and Costa Coffee outlets, you might think that the market for coffee is booming. So it is for the final product, whether your preference be for a tall skinny latte or a machiatto grande. However, nothing could be further from the truth in the market for coffee beans. There are two main varieties of coffee bean—arabica and robusta—and their price movements are broadly similar, so we focus on arabica, which provides over 70 per cent of consumption.

Figure 4.12 shows the price of Brazilian arabica coffee beans in US dollars per pound in weight from January 1976 to December 2005. The price history shows a nearly flat long-term trend, with, if anything a slight downward drift. This means that the real price (relative to other consumer goods, whose prices in money terms have generally risen over time) of coffee is clearly trending downwards. Also there are several episodes of a sharp upward jump in the price. The price of coffee beans fell to a historic low level in late 2001 and early 2002. It recovered somewhat in 2003–5 but fell again in 2006 (not shown). The price all-time low (in 2002) was the lowest price of coffee in real terms (i.e. adjusted for inflation) in the last hundred years, and the lowest nominal price in at least the past four decades. So what was the reason for this fall?

Not surprisingly, the answer is that, although demand has been increasing over time, supply has been increasing even faster, thereby tending to create excess supply at whatever the current market price is, and this has tended to drive the price down even further.[6]

---

[6] Note that we are analysing demand for coffee beans here and not demand for prepared coffee-based drinks in retail outlets, which has a very different market.

**Figure 4.12** The price of Brazilian arabica coffee, 1976–2005

*Source*: International Coffee Organization: http://www.ico.org/

Demand for coffee has grown over time, but only slowly. The World Bank has estimated that the worldwide income elasticity of demand for coffee was about 0.6 up to the mid-1990s, and that this figure falls as per capita income rises; for example, in the United States, which has the highest per capita income in the world, the income elasticity is estimated to be close to zero. This means that demand rises at a slower rate than do incomes in the coffee-importing countries. An income elasticity of demand of 0.6, for example, means that a 10 per cent increase in incomes would lead to a 6 per cent increase in demand for coffee (other things being equal). An annual trend growth rate of about 2 per cent (such as is the case for the UK) would imply a growth in demand for coffee of about 1.2 per cent per annum.[7]

On the supply side, there has been a steady increase in output capacity as traditional coffee-producing countries such as Brazil have expanded their capacity and newer suppliers such as Vietnam have also become big producers. The excess of supply over demand at current market prices between 1998 and 2002 led to growing stocks of coffee beans in consuming countries. When stocks are already high, consumer countries become increasingly unwilling to accumulate more, so only a fall in price can discourage further excess supply. However, the World Bank also estimates that supply elasticities are very low in the short term, which means that, despite sharp falls in prices, the quantity supplied falls only slightly. Hence, unless there is a crop failure (typically because of bad weather) in a major producing country such as Brazil (as happened in 1977, 1986, 1994 and 1997), the prospects are for coffee prices to stay low unless these low prices at some stage lead to land being diverted into other uses, thereby reducing supply. The price rises in 2004–5 also seem to be the result of bad weather conditions in Brazil affecting supply, but the supply disruption was not as bad as in some of the earlier episodes. Low prices do little to encourage an increase in quantity demanded in consumer countries, as the own-price elasticity of demand is also low.

In summary, the demand curve is shifting slowly to the right as income increases, but only slowly (owing to a low income elasticity) and it is fairly steep (owing to a low price elasticity). The supply curve, however, has been shifting more quickly to the right over time (owing to new production methods and greater planting). This means that prices will be tending to fall in normal times, but to rise sharply in abnormal times, such as when there is a crop failure in a major producer country, perhaps because of bad weather. Coffee prices cannot fall for ever, since producers at some point will divert their land to other uses and divert their labour to other activities. When growth in supply is not greater than growth in demand, the price will tend to stabilize.

This is a good illustration of the interaction of demand and supply forces. There are other elements to the story which should not be totally ignored, but we do not have the space to discuss them fully here. First, the low coffee price causes severe problems for many of the world's poorest countries—coffee provides 76 per cent of export revenue for Burundi, 68 per cent for Ethiopia, 62 per cent for Rwanda, and 60 per cent for Uganda. Second, much of the recent growth in capacity has been in 'sun grown' plantations, which have no tree cover (as the forests have been cut down to provide the space) and use chemicals to enhance yields. These plantations can produce high yields quickly, but environmental groups argue that they are bad for the environment as they do not use the tree cover of traditional 'shade grown' coffee plantations and this is harmful to bird life (as well as involving destruction of forests). Third, the low coffee price has been particularly harmful to the traditional 'shade-grown' producers of Central America, who have not been covering costs and so have cut output (but not enough to affect the price significantly) and suffered lower prices, thereby dramatically reducing incomes.

---

[7] This is assuming an income elasticity of demand of 0.6, though it could be lower (or higher).

**Table 4.3** Changes in the demand for newspapers

| | Price | | Average daily sales | | Percentage change | |
|---|---|---|---|---|---|---|
| | Pre-Sept. '93 | Post-Sept. '93 | Pre-Sept. '93 | Post-Sept. '93 | Price | Sales |
| *The Times* | 45p | 30p | 376,836 | 448,962 | −40.0 | +17.5 |
| *Guardian* | 45p | 45p | 420,154 | 401,705 | 0.0 | −4.5 |
| *Daily Telegraph* | 45p | 45p | 1,037,375 | 1,017,326 | 0.0 | −1.95 |
| *Independent* | 50p | 50p | 362,099 | 311,046 | 0.0 | −15.2 |
| | | | 2,196,464 | 2,179,039 | | |

*The Times* **led but no one followed.** The table shows the fall in the price of *The Times* and the less-than-proportionate increase in sales. It also shows the constant prices of the other papers, with declining sales as they lost readers to *The Times*. Percentage changes in the last two columns are calculated from the initial position, but calculations of elasticity in the text are made at the mid point between the initial and ultimate position.

*Source*: Audit Bureau of Circulation. The sales figures are daily average circulation for September 1992 to February 1993 and for September 1993 to February 1994.

## 2. Free museums

In November 2001 the UK government abolished admission charges on many museums. Entrance charges that had ranged up to £9 for adults with lower prices for children and pensioners were all set to zero overnight. What would you expect to happen when charges were abolished? Yes, admissions should rise.

Fortunately for economics textbook writers, admissions really did rise, and quite substantially in many cases. Comparison of December 2001 monthly attendances with those in December 2000 (and thereby controlling for seasonal influences) shows a huge increase in museum visits at the lower price. The Victoria and Albert Museum (V&A) experienced the biggest increase, with visitor numbers rising from 42,600 in December 2000 to 174,000 in December 2001, an increase of 309 per cent. Similarly, though not so dramatically, the Museum of London saw an 88 per cent increase, the Natural History Museum an 82 per cent increase and the Museums of Science and Industry in Manchester a 75 per cent increase.

You might think that we cannot calculate demand elasticity when a price of zero is involved, as $\Delta P/P$ would be undefined. However, in this case we are measuring the price change over a range, so we would use the price, $P$, at the mid-point of the price change and $Q$ at the mid-point of the change. (To review the reasons for this see Box 4.2 on page 71.)

Let us take the case of the V&A. The entry price fell from £5 to £0 and we know that admissions increased from 42.6 thousand to 174 thousand. We take $P$ to be the mean of the price before and after the change, which is £2.50. The percentage change in price is $(-5/2.5) \times 100 = -200$ per cent.[8] We take $Q$ to be the mean of admissions before and after the price change

((174 + 42.6)/2), which is 108.3 thousand. The change in admissions is 131.4 thousand, so the percentage change in admissions is $(131.4/108.3) \times 100 = 121.3$. The elasticity is the percentage change in quantity divided by the percentage change in price, or $121.3/-200 = -0.61$.

So the elasticity of demand for visits to the V&A on this basis is calculated as −0.61. This might seem very low given the huge increase in attendance; however, note that the price change was large too.

Notice also that we have not, strictly speaking, calculated the demand elasticity for any one museum, as many museums changed their prices at the same time. The response might have been different if one museum had cut its entry charge at a time when no others did. In this case its demand elasticity could have been larger, as the elasticity of demand for a single museum is likely to be larger than that for museums as a whole. (See the discussion of elasticity of demand for meat on page 79.) On the other hand, numbers may have been boosted by the free publicity that the nationwide cutting of entry charges generated, so these two effects could be offsetting.

We now turn to an example in which one supplier cut its price but no other competitors followed for some time.

## 3. Keeping up with *The Times*

In September 1993 the owners of *The Times* newspaper unilaterally lowered the price of *The Times* by one-third. Initially all the major competing newspapers kept their prices constant and carried on as if nothing had happened. Only later did a price war break out.

Table 4.3 provides price and sales figures for the four major national broadsheet[9] newspapers—*The Times*, the *Guardian*,

---

[8] Among other admission charges abolished, the Natural History Museum had charged £9 and the Science Museum £7.75. So the big increase in numbers attending the V&A was not because it had a higher charge than others before abolition.

[9] We continue to refer to then as 'broadsheets' even though three of the four had changed their format by 2006.

**Figure 4.13** Demand for *The Times* and the *Independent*

A cut in the price of *The Times* shifted the *Independent's* demand curve to the left. Part (i) shows the price cut for *The Times*. When its price was lowered from 45p to 30p, sales rose from 377,000 to 449,000 copies per day. Part (ii) shows the shift in demand for the *Independent* as a result of the fall in the price of *The Times*. At a constant price of 50p, sales fell from 362,000 to 311,000.

the *Daily Telegraph*, and the *Independent*. Since consumers' average incomes changed only slightly over the period and newspapers have a low income elasticity, we would expect total sales to have remained constant, unless there had been a major change in tastes over the period in question. The data suggest that tastes did not change significantly, since the combined sales of all the newspapers held constant at around 2.5 million copies daily. Hence the existing suppliers were fighting for a share of a stable market. If one gained more customers, it had to be at the expense of rival suppliers.

## Observed price elasticities

Table 4.3 shows us that a 40 per cent price reduction of the price of *The Times* led to a 17.5 per cent increase in its sales.[10] This indicates a price elasticity of demand for *The Times* of −0.44 (calculated as percentage change in quantity divided by percentage change in price, or 17.5/−40). As a result, *The Times*'s daily sales revenue fell from £169,576 (376,836 × £0.45) to £134,689 (448,962 × £0.30). Only if the price elasticity had been greater than 1 would total revenue have increased.

The competing papers suffered, and the *Independent* suffered most, with a 15.2 per cent loss of sales. This would suggest that the *Independent* was the closest substitute for *The Times*. The cross-elasticity of demand implied by these figures was −15.2/−40 = 0.38. (This is positive, as both sales and price changes were negative.) The cross-elasticity for the *Guardian* was −4.5/−40 = 0.11, and the cross-elasticity for the *Daily Telegraph* was −1.95/−40 = 0.05.

---

[10] Note that we are measuring the price and quantity (*P* and *Q*) used in our elasticity calculations as the mid-point between the initial price and quantity and the ultimate price and quantity. The reasons for doing it this way are explained in Box 4.2 on page 71. Use of the mid-point as the base applies to all calculations in this section.

## Applying demand and supply

The theory of demand and supply developed in Chapter 3 assumes that there are many buyers and many sellers, each one of whom must accept the price that is determined by overall demand and supply. Newspapers fit this theory on the demand side, since there are tens of thousands of buyers each of whom can do nothing to affect the price. On the supply side, however, there are only a few newspapers and each sets the price of its own product. In the terminology of Chapter 3, it is an *administered price*. We can, however, handle the supply side if we note that each newspaper sells all the copies that are demanded at the price that it sets. Graphically, this is shown by a horizontal supply curve at each newspaper's fixed price. The elasticity of supply is effectively infinite at the set price.

Figure 4.13 illustrates the effect of the price cut both on *The Times* and on the *Independent*. Notice that, since each newspaper is a distinct product, there is no industry supply curve for newspapers. Each supplier simply sets a price and lets demand determine its sales.

Rival newspapers may not have followed *The Times* in cutting prices because they believed that their demands would prove as inelastic as those for *The Times*. If so, they would have lost more revenue by cutting their prices than they did by leaving prices unchanged. As it was, the *Independent* suffered a daily loss of revenue of a little over £25,000 (just over 50,000 sales at 50p each).

The puzzle is why *The Times* persisted with its price drop even though it lost sales revenue. One possibility is that the increased circulation led to an increase in advertising revenue. Newspapers' advertising rates are related to their circulation. If *The Times* increased its advertising revenue by more than about £35,000, the price reduction would have increased its profit.

The *Independent* was known to be in financial difficulty, and it is possible that the managers of *The Times* thought that their price cut might force the *Independent* out of business—a strategy sometimes referred to as *predatory pricing*. Had it succeeded, a high proportion of *Independent* readers would have moved over to *The Times*, since the cross-elasticities show that the *Independent* was the closest substitute for *The Times*. Soon after, however, the *Independent* was taken over by the Mirror Group, which had more financial resources. Hence if *The Times* had been following a predatory strategy it failed. Later the Mirror Group sold the *Independent* to an Irish newspaper group.

A third possibility is that its managers expected that *The Times*'s demand elasticity would increase over time. If so, sales could eventually have risen sufficiently to compensate for the price cut. Indeed, *The Times* did continue to increase its market share beyond the period studied in Table 4.3. In June 1994 the *Telegraph* reacted to *The Times*'s growing market share by cutting its price, and the *Independent* followed. *The Times* responded to this by cutting its own price still further, although prices settled down at slightly higher levels soon after. To some extent this third explanation has proved correct. By July 1998 *The Times*'s price was 35p while the *Guardian*, *Telegraph*, and *Independent* were at 45p. *The Times*'s sales were around 800,000, almost double what they had been just after the first gains following the outbreak of the price war. In contrast, the *Independent*'s sales were 210,000, less than 60 per cent of what they were just before the price war began.

These relative positions stayed more or less unchanged for the next five years. By the spring of 2002 there had been a small decline in the overall market for UK broadsheets. Sales of *The Times* were running just over 700,000 daily, the *Guardian* at just under 400,000, the *Independent* at about 220,000 and the *Telegraph* remained remarkably stable at just over 1 million.

Between 2002 and 2006 there was a significant decline in the market for this group of newspapers, probably as a result of the growth of the internet and of 24 hours news TV channels. The nature of competition seems to have changed as a result. Price competition took a back seat: *The Times* raised its price to 60p in 2005, the same as the *Guardian*, the *Independent* and the *Telegraph*. But in 2004 the *Independent* introduced a new tabloid format and this gained it some share, so *The Times* and *Guardian* introduced new formats of their own in 2005. The big loser in this new style of war was the *Telegraph*: its average daily sales fell from over 1 million to under 850,000 (by October 2005). Sales of *The Times* at this time were about 660,000, the *Guardian* 380,000 and the *Independent* 230,000 per day.

The aggressive pricing strategy adopted by *The Times* in the early 1990s does appear to have had a very long-lasting effect on the sales pattern of UK newspapers. The changes in sale patterns established in the mid-1990s were still evident a decade later, even though the price war that increased sales of *The Times* was clearly over. In January 2007 *The Times* was priced at 65p while the *Telegraph*, *Guardian* and *Independent* were all 70p. We discuss some further episodes of newspaper competition in Chapter 9.

# SUMMARY

### Demand elasticity

- Elasticity of demand (also called price elasticity of demand) is defined as the percentage change in quantity divided by the percentage change in price that brought it about.

- When the percentage change in quantity is less than the percentage change in price, demand is inelastic and a fall in price lowers the total amount spent on the product. When the percentage change in quantity is greater than the percentage change in price, demand is elastic and a fall in price raises total spending on the product.

- A more precise measure, which gives a unique value for elasticity at any point on any demand curve, replaces $\Delta q/\Delta p$ measured between two points on the curve with $\Delta q/\Delta p$ measured along the tangent to the curve at the point in question (symbolized by $dq/dp$).

- The main determinant of the price elasticity of demand is the availability of substitutes for the product. Any one of a group of close substitutes will have a more elastic demand than the group as a whole.

- Elasticity of demand tends to be greater the longer the time over which adjustment occurs. Items that have a few substitutes in the short run may develop ample substitutes when consumers and producers have time to adapt.

- Income elasticity is the percentage change in quantity demanded divided by the percentage change in income that brought it about. The income elasticity of demand for a product will usually change as income varies.

- Cross-elasticity is the percentage change in quantity demanded divided by the percentage change in the price of some other product that brought it about. Products that are substitutes for one another have positive cross-elasticities; products that complement one another have negative cross-elasticities.

### Supply elasticity

- Elasticity of supply measures the ratio of the percentage change in the quantity supplied of a product to the percentage change in its price.

■ A commodity's elasticity of supply depends on how easy it is to shift resources into the production of that commodity and how the costs of producing the commodity vary as its production varies.

## Measurement of demand and supply

■ Over the years, economists have measured many price, income, and cross-elasticities of demand. Being able to do so requires the use of statistical techniques to measure the separate influences of each of several variables when all are changing at once. It also requires a solution of the identification problem, which refers to measuring the separate shapes of the demand and supply curves. This cannot be done from price and quantity data alone.

## TOPICS FOR REVIEW

■ Price, income, and cross-elasticity of demand

■ Zero, inelastic, unitary, elastic, and infinitely elastic demand

■ The relation between price elasticity and changes in total expenditure

■ Determinants of demand elasticity

■ Income elasticities for normal and inferior goods

■ Cross-elasticities between substitutes and complements

■ Long- and short-run elasticity of demand

■ Elasticity of supply and its determinants

## QUESTIONS

1 Calculate the elasticity of demand for the demand curve $P = 100 - 5Q$ at each of the following price and quantity levels:
$P = 90$ and $Q = 2$;
$P = 50$ and $Q = 10$;
$P = 5$ and $Q = 19$.

2 Calculate the elasticity of supply for the supply curve $P = 10 + 3Q$ at each of the following price and quantity levels:
$P = 25$ and $Q = 5$;
$P = 40$ and $Q = 10$;
$P = 70$ and $Q = 20$.

3 In one particular month 1.2 million kilos of potatoes are sold at £1.20 per kilo. In the next month 1.5 million kilos are sold at £1.40 per kilo. Which of the following explanations is consistent with this observation (there may be more than one or none at all)?
(a) The price of carrots has risen, and carrots are a close substitute for potatoes.
(b) The price of fish has risen, and fish is a complement to potatoes.
(c) Bad weather has reduced the potato crop.
(d) Consumer incomes have risen, and potatoes are an inferior good.
(e) Newspapers have reported that potatoes have health-giving properties, and this has generated a shift of tastes towards potatoes.

4 Suggest products that you think might have the following patterns of elasticity of demand:
(a) high income elasticity, high price elasticity;
(b) high income elasticity, low price elasticity;
(c) low income elasticity; low price elasticity;
(d) low income elasticity, high price elasticity.

5 Define the elasticity of demand and explain why this concept should be of interest to anyone in business who has a choice to make about the price at which to sell their products.

6 Why is demand likely to be more elastic in the long run than in the short run?

7 Outline the main determinants of demand and supply elasticity.

8 What is the identification problem? How does it affect the interpretation of observed price and quantity changes, and what does it imply that we need to know before we can say whether any specific price and quantity change contains information about either demand or supply elasticity?

9 Explain the concept of income elasticity. Why does the income elasticity of demand for food tend to be low in rich countries? Give examples of types of goods and services the demand for which you would expect to have a high income elasticity in rich countries. How would the last answer differ in poorer countries?

# Chapter 5

# CONSUMER CHOICE: INDIFFERENCE THEORY

In this chapter we look more closely at the determinants of consumer demand. In particular, we discuss the concept of utility and how we can use this to gain insights into how consumers choose to allocate their spending. We first explain some key insights that were achieved by thinking about utility as if it can be measured. We then outline the approach that does not require utility to be measurable but that yields many similar insights into the determinants of demand. In particular, you will learn that:

- Consumers will maximize their overall satisfaction when the marginal utility per pound spent is equal for all products purchased.
- A theory of demand can be built by focusing on bundles of goods between which the consumer is indifferent.
- Indifference curves show combinations of goods that give the same level of satisfaction.
- A budget constraint shows what the consumer could buy with a given income.
- A consumer optimizes by moving to the highest indifference curve that is available with a given budget constraint.
- The response to a price change can be decomposed into an income and a substitution effect.
- For a good to have a negatively sloped demand curve, it is necessary (but not sufficient) that it be an inferior good.

In this chapter we will first explain some important insights that come from early analyses of utility in the nineteenth century. We then explain how modern economics uses indifference curves to develop a theory of consumer choice. We show how indifference curves can be used to describe consumers' tastes, and then introduce a budget line to describe the consumption possibilities open to a consumer who has a given income. After that, we show how consumers reach equilibrium by consuming the bundle that allows them to reach the highest possible levels of satisfaction. We can then see how any consumer alters behaviour when either income or prices change, and we go on to derive the negative slope of the demand curve.

This approach to consumer behaviour has two great advantages. First, it allows us to distinguish between two effects of a change in price, called the income effect and the substitution effect; this distinction has important practical applications. Second, it allows us to understand the rare but interesting exception to the prediction that all demand curves are negatively sloped, which arises with a so-called Giffen good.

All of the theories in this chapter use the basic assumption that consumers are motivated to make themselves as well off as they can—or, as economists like to put it, to maximize their satisfaction.

# Early insights

All units of the same product are identical; for example, one tin of Heinz baked beans is the same as another tin of Heinz baked beans. But the satisfaction that a consumer gets from each unit of a product is not the same. If you are hungry you will get great satisfaction from a good meal, but you will not get the same satisfaction from having a second identical meal immediately. This suggests that the satisfaction that people get from consuming a unit of any product varies according to how many of this product they have already.

Economists and philosophers thinking about consumer choice and satisfaction in the nineteenth century developed the concept of utility and so were sometimes called *utilitarians*.[1] But the big breakthrough for economics came in the 1870s with what is known as the *marginal revolution*, which gave birth to *neoclassical economics*.[2] For a long time it was thought that utility could not be measured and therefore that utility theory was based on unverifiable concepts. Recently, however, economists and psychologists have succeeded in measuring utility. They have used these measurements to verify, among other things, two of the basic assumptions of utility theory: (1) that the marginal utility of any one good declines when more of it is consumed, with the consumption of all other goods held constant, and (2) that the marginal utility of income declines as people earn more of it.[3]

## Marginal and total utility

What we want to think about first is how an individual consumer's satisfaction changes as he or she alters the amount consumed of a single product. The satisfaction a consumer receives from consuming that product is called *utility*. **Total utility** refers to the *total satisfaction* derived from all the units of that product consumed. **Marginal utility** refers to the *change in satisfaction* resulting from consuming one unit more or one unit less of that product. For example, the total utility of consuming 14 cups of coffee a week is the sum total satisfaction provided by all

14 cups of coffee. The marginal utility of the fourteenth cup of coffee consumed is the addition to total satisfaction provided by consuming that extra cup. Put another way, the marginal utility of the fourteenth cup is the addition to total utility gained from consuming 14 cups of coffee per week rather than 13.

### Diminishing marginal utility

A basic assumption of utility theory, which is sometimes called the *law of diminishing marginal utility*, is as follows:

**The marginal utility generated by additional units of any product diminishes as an individual consumes more of it, holding constant the consumption of all other products.**

The way in which most of us use water provides a good example of diminishing marginal utility. We consume it in many forms: tap water, soft drinks, bottled water, or water flavoured with such things as tea leaves and coffee grounds. Whatever the form in which we consume it, we consume it: water is necessary to our very existence, and anyone denied water will not survive very long. So we value the minimum of water needed to sustain life as much as we value life itself. We would be willing, therefore, to pay quite a lot if this were the only way to obtain the amount of water needed to stay alive. The total utility of that much water is therefore extremely high, as is the marginal utility of the first few units drunk. More than this bare minimum will be drunk, but the marginal utility of successive amounts of water drunk over any period of time will decline steadily.

Furthermore, water has many uses other than for drinking. A fairly high marginal utility will be attached to some minimum quantity for bathing, but much more than this minimum will be used for more frequent baths or showers. The last weekly gallon used for bathing is likely to have a low marginal utility. Again, some small quantity of water is necessary for tooth brushing, but many people leave the water running while they brush. The water going down the drain between wetting and rinsing the brush surely has a low utility. When all the many uses of water by the modern consumer are considered (washing machines, dishwashers, lawn sprinklers, car washing, etc.), it is certain that the marginal utility of the last, say, 10 per cent of all units consumed is very low and falling, even though the total utility of all the units consumed is extremely high.

---

[1] Leading members of the utilitarian school were Jeremy Bentham (1748–1832), James Mill (1773–1836), and John Stuart Mill (1806–73).

[2] Key contributors to the marginal revolution were: the English economist William Stanley Jevons (1835–82), the Austrian Carl Menger (1841–1910), and the Swiss Leon Walras (1834–1910).

[3] See e.g. Layard (2005).

## Maximizing utility

We can now ask: what does diminishing marginal utility imply for the way a consumer who has a given income will allocate spending in order to maximize total utility? How should a consumer allocate his or her income in order to get the greatest possible satisfaction, or total utility, from that spending?

If all products had the same price, the answer would be easy. A consumer should simply allocate spending so that the marginal utility of all products was the same. If the marginal utility of all products were not equal, then total utility could be increased by choosing a different spending pattern. For example, if one product had a higher marginal utility than the others, expenditure should be reallocated so as to buy more of this product, and less of all others that have lower marginal utilities. By buying more, the product's marginal utility would fall. Only when the last unit of all products bought gives the same satisfaction is the consumer getting the greatest possible total utility from his or her spending pattern.

How does this work if products have different prices? Again the same principles apply, but now the best a consumer can do is to rearrange spending until the last unit of satisfaction per pound spent on each product is the same. For example, suppose that a consumer is deciding to allocate income between going to football matches and going to the cinema, and that tickets to football cost £30 while a cinema ticket costs £10. If a consumer gets more than three times as much extra satisfaction from another football match as another movie, then off to more football matches he or she should go. This consumer will be maximizing total utility from her income only when the last match attended generates extra utility that is just three times that generated by the last film.

To maximize utility, consumers allocate spending between products so that equal utility is derived from the last unit of money spent on each.[4]

The conditions for maximizing utility can be stated more generally. Denote the marginal utility of the last unit of product X by $MU_X$ and its price by $p_X$. Let $MU_Y$ and $p_Y$ refer respectively to the marginal utility of a second product, Y, and its price. The marginal utility per pound spent on X will be $MU_X/p_X$. For example, if the last unit adds 30 units to utility and costs £2, its marginal utility per pound is $30/2 = 15$.

The condition required for any consumer to maximize utility is that the following relationship should hold, for all pairs of products:

$$MU_X/p_X = MU_Y/p_Y \qquad (1)$$

This merely says in symbols what we earlier said in words. Consumers who are maximizing their utility will allocate spending so that the utilities gained from the last £1 spent on both products are equal.

This is the fundamental equation of utility theory. Each consumer demands each good up to the point at which the marginal utility per pound spent on it is the same as the marginal utility of a pound spent on each other good. When this condition is met, the consumer cannot shift a pound of spending from one product to another and increase total utility.

### Consumers choose quantities not prices

If we rearrange the terms in equation (1), we can gain additional insight into consumer behaviour:[5]

$$MU_X/MU_Y = p_X/p_Y \qquad (2)$$

The right-hand side of this equation states the relative price of the two goods. This is determined by the market and is beyond the control of individual consumers, who react to the market prices but are powerless to change them. The left-hand side of the equation states the relative contribution of the two goods to add to satisfaction if a little more or a little less of either of them were consumed, a choice that is available.

If the two sides of equation (2) are not equal, the consumer can increase total satisfaction by changing their spending pattern. Assume, for example, that the price of a unit of X is twice the price of a unit of Y $(p_X/p_Y = 2)$, while the marginal utility of a unit of X is three times that of a unit of Y $(MU_X/MU_Y = 3)$. Under these conditions, it pays to buy more of X and less of Y. For example, reducing purchases of Y by two units frees enough purchasing power to buy a unit of X. Since one extra unit of X bought yields 1.5 times the satisfaction of two units of Y forgone, the switch is worth making. What about a further switch of X for Y? As the consumer buys more X and less Y, the marginal utility of X falls and the marginal utility of Y rises. In this example the consumer will go on rearranging purchases—reducing Y consumption and increasing X consumption—until the marginal utility of X is only twice that of Y. At this point, total satisfaction cannot be further increased by rearranging purchases between the two products.

Think about what the utility-maximizing consumer is doing. She is faced with a set of prices that cannot be

---

[4] By the 'last unit' we do not mean money spent over successive time-periods: instead, we are talking about buying more or fewer units at one point in time, that is, alternative allocations of spending at a moment in time.

[5] This is done by multiplying both sides of the equation by $p_X/MU_Y$.

changed. She responds to these prices and maximizes satisfaction by adjusting the things that can be changed—the quantities of the various goods purchased—until equation (2) is satisfied for all pairs of products.

We see this sort of equation frequently in economics—one side representing the choices the outside world presents to decision-takers and the other side representing the effect of those choices. It shows the equilibrium position reached when decision-takers have made the best adjustment they can to the external forces that constrain their choices.

When they enter the market, all consumers face the same set of market prices. When they are fully adjusted to these prices, each one of them will have identical ratios of their marginal utilities for each pair of goods. Of course, a rich consumer may consume more of each product than a poor consumer and get more *total utility* from it. However, the rich and the poor consumer (and every other consumer who is maximizing utility) will adjust their relative purchases of each product so that the relative *marginal utilities* are the same for all. Thus, if the price of X is twice the price of Y, each consumer will purchase X and Y to the point at which their marginal utility of X is twice the marginal utility of Y. Consumers with different tastes, however, will derive different marginal utilities from their consumption of the various commodities, so they will consume differing relative quantities of products. But all will have declining marginal utilities for each commodity and hence, when they have maximized their utility, the ratios of their marginal utilities will be the same for all of them.

A very important insight can be derived from this analysis. It is that marginal, not average, values are what matter for maximization. We will return to this idea in subsequent chapters when we see that marginal values are also important for the profit-maximizing behaviour of firms. Box 5.1 reinforces just how important marginal utility is as a concept, in that it helps explain what used to be known as the 'paradox of value'. The key point to notice from this is that market prices reflect marginal utilities of various products and not total or average utilities. Hence market prices are not a measure of the total value to society of one good or service as compared with that of some other good or service.

---

 **Box 5.1  The paradox of value**

Early thinkers about the economy struggled with the problem of what determines the relative prices of products. They encountered the *paradox of value*: many essential products without which we could not live, such as water, have relatively low prices. On the other hand, some luxury products, such as diamonds, have relatively high prices, even though we could easily survive without them. Does it not seem odd that water, which is so important to us, has such a low market value while diamonds, which are much less important, have a much higher market value? It took a long time to resolve this apparent paradox, so it is not surprising that even today similar confusions about the determinants of market values persist and cloud many policy discussions.

The key to resolving the 'paradox' lies in the distinction between total and marginal utility. We have already seen in this chapter that a utility-maximizing consumer will adjust his or her spending pattern so that the marginal utility per pound spent is equal for all products. It follows that the value consumers place on the last unit consumed of any product, i.e. its marginal utility, is equal in equilibrium to the product's price.

We will explain in Box 5.2 (on page 91) that the area under the demand curve above market price represents the total benefit consumers get from consuming a product. We will call this benefit *consumers' surplus*, and we can think of consumer surplus as an indicator of the value of the total utility that consumers get from a product.

Now look at the total amount spent to purchase the product—the price paid for it multiplied by the quantity bought and sold—which we can call its total market value or sale value. The figure shows the markets for two goods, one for which total market value is a very small fraction of its total utility and another for which total market value is a much higher fraction of total utility.

The resolution of the paradox of value is that a good that is very plentiful, such as water, will have a low price. It will be consumed, therefore, to the point where all purchasers place a low value on the last unit consumed, whether or not they place a high value on their total consumption of the product; in other words, marginal utility will be low whatever the value of total utility. On the other hand, a product that is relatively scarce will have a high market price. Consumption will, therefore, stop at a point at which consumers place a high value on the last unit consumed whatever value they place on their total consumption of the good; that is, marginal utility will be high whatever the value of total utility.

This analysis leads to an important conclusion:

The market price of a product depends on demand and supply. Hence no paradox is involved when a product on which consumers place a high total utility sells for a low price, and hence has only a low total market value (i.e. a low amount spent on it).

→

**Box 5.1** *continued*

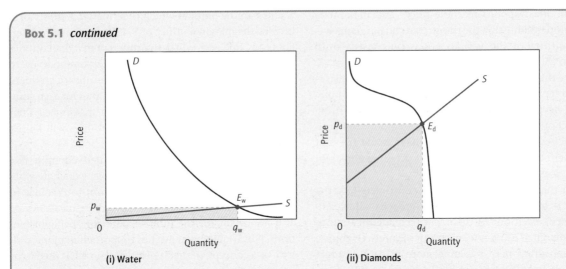

**(i) Water**  **(ii) Diamonds**

**Total utility versus market value**

**The market value of the amount of some commodity bears no necessary relation to the total utility that consumers derive from that amount.** The total utility that consumers derive from water, as shown by the area under the demand curve in part (i), is great—indeed, we cannot possibly show the curve for very small quantities, because people would pay all they had rather than be deprived completely of water. The total utility that consumers derive from diamonds is shown by the area under the demand curve in part (ii). This is less than the total utility derived from water. The supply curve of diamonds makes diamonds scarce and keeps their price high. Thus, when equilibrium is at $E_d$, the total market value of diamonds sold, indicated by the blue area of $p_d q_d$, is high. The supply curve of water makes water plentiful and makes water low in price. Thus, when equilibrium is at $E_w$, the total market value of water consumed, indicated by the blue area of $p_w q_w$, is low.

## Implication of marginal utility theory for demand curves

The assumption that all products exhibit diminishing marginal utility has a simple implication for demand curves: they are all negatively sloped. This is because, if consumers were already maximizing utility and the price of one product fell, then in order to restore equation (2) above, consumers would have to buy more of the product whose price had fallen and less of all other products.

In the twentieth century economists moved away from relying upon the assumption of diminishing marginal utility as a key building block in their theory of demand. The reason is that it was harder to take the theory much further without being able to measure of utility, which seemed impossible at the time. However, considerable progress was made without having to measure utility. All

that was needed was to assume that consumers could rank alternative bundles of products in order of preference without necessarily being able to say by *how much* they preferred one to another.

We now outline this modern approach to consumer choice. In it the two key insights that we have just discussed remain valid:

1. Marginal comparisons are what matter for consumer choice, and equations (1) and (2) above remain valid as optimization conditions for consumers whether or not utility is assumed to be measurable.

2. Market prices are determined by marginal utilities and not by total or average utilities.

Box 5.2 outlines a concept known as 'consumers' surplus', which is related to diminishing marginal utility.

**Box 5.2 Consumers' surplus**

The negative slope of the demand curve has an interesting consequence:

All consumers pay less than they would be willing to pay for the total amount of any product that they consume.

The difference between what they would be willing to pay—which is the value of the total utility that they derive from consuming the product—and what they do pay—which is their total spending on that product—is called **consumers' surplus**.

This concept is important and deserves further elaboration. The table gives hypothetical data for the weekly consumption of milk by one consumer, Ms Green. The second column, labelled 'Total utility', gives the total value she places on consumption of so many glasses per week (when the alternative is zero). Column (3), labelled 'Marginal utility', gives the amount she would pay to add the last glass indicated to weekly consumption. Thus, for example, the marginal utility of £0.80 listed against four glasses gives the value that Ms Green places on increasing consumption from three to four glasses. It is the difference between the total utilities she attaches to consumption levels of three and four glasses per week.

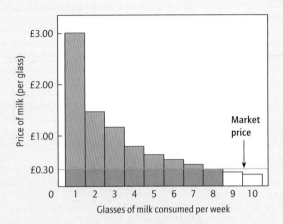

**(i) Consumer's surplus for an individual**

Consumer's surplus is the sum of the extra valuations placed on each unit above the market price paid for each. This figure is based on the data in Table (i). Ms Green pays the pink area for the 8 glasses of milk she consumes per week when the market price is £0.30 a glass. The total value she places on these 8 glasses of milk is the entire shaded area (pink and blue). Hence her consumer's surplus is the blue area.

**(i) Consumer's surplus**

| Glasses of milk consumed per week (1) | Total utility (2) | Marginal utility (3) | Consumer's surplus on each glass if milk costs £0.30 per glass (4) |
|---|---|---|---|
| 1 | £3.00 | £3.00 | £2.70 |
| 2 | 4.50 | 1.50 | 1.20 |
| 3 | 5.50 | 1.00 | 0.70 |
| 4 | 6.30 | 0.80 | 0.50 |
| 5 | 6.90 | 0.60 | 0.30 |
| 6 | 7.40 | 0.50 | 0.20 |
| 7 | 7.80 | 0.40 | 0.10 |
| 8 | 8.10 | 0.30 | 0.00 |
| 9 | 8.35 | 0.25 | — |
| 10 | 8.55 | 0.20 | — |

Consumer's surplus on each unit consumed is the difference between the market price and the maximum price the consumer would pay to obtain that unit. The table shows the value that Ms Green puts on successive glasses of milk consumed each week. As long as she is willing to pay more than the market price for any glass, she obtains a consumer's surplus when she buys it. The marginal glass of milk is the eighth. This is the one she values at just the market price and on which she earns no consumer's surplus.

If Ms Green is faced with a market price of £0.30, she will maximize total utility by consuming eight glasses per week, because she values the eighth glass just at the market price, while valuing all earlier glasses at higher amounts. Because she values the first glass at £3.00 but gets it for £0.30, she makes a 'profit' of £2.70 on that glass; that is, she gets £3.00 worth of satisfaction for £0.30. Between her £1.50 valuation of the second glass and what she has to pay for it, she clears a 'profit' of £1.20. She clears £0.70 on the third glass. And so on. These 'profits', which are called her consumer's surpluses on each unit, are shown in the final column of the table. The total surplus is £5.70 per week. In the table, we calculate Ms Green's surplus by summing the surpluses on each glass. We arrive at the same total, however, by first summing the maximum that Ms Green would pay for all the glasses bought (which is £8.10 in this case) and then subtracting the £2.40 that she does pay.

The value placed by each consumer on his or her total consumption of some product can be estimated in at least two ways. The valuation that the consumer places on each successive unit may be summed, or the consumer may be asked the maximum that he or she would pay to consume the amount in question if the alternative were to have none. While other consumers would put different numerical values into the table, diminishing marginal utility implies that the figures in the final column would

**Box 5.2** *continued*

**(ii)  Consumer's surplus for the market**

**Total consumers' surplus is the area under the demand curve and above the price line.** The area under the demand curve shows the total valuation that consumers place on all units consumed. For example, the total value that consumers place on $q_0$ units is the entire area shaded pink and blue under the demand curve up to $q_0$. At a market price of $p_0$ the amount paid for $q_0$ units is the pink area. Hence consumers' surplus is the blue area.

be declining for each person. Since a consumer will go on buying further units until the value placed on the last unit equals the market price, it follows that there will be a consumers' surplus on every unit consumed except the last one.

The data in columns (1) and (3) of the table give Ms Green's demand curve for milk. This is her demand curve, because she will go on buying glasses of milk as long as she values each glass at least as much as the market price she must pay for it. When the market price is £3.00 per glass she will buy only one glass; when it is £1.50 she will buy two glasses; and so on. The total consumption value is the area below her demand curve, and consumers' surplus is that part of the area that lies above the price line. This is shown in Figure (i).

Figure (ii) shows that the same relationship holds for the smooth market demand curve that indicates the total amount all consumers would buy at each price.*

---

\* Figure (i) is a bar chart because we allowed the consumer to vary her consumption only in discrete units, one at a time. Had we allowed her to vary her consumption continuously, we could have traced out a continuous curve for Ms Green similar to the one shown in Figure (ii).

## Consumer optimization without measurable utility

The basic assumption here about consumer *motivation* is not changed from the last section. Consumers are assumed to maximize their satisfaction by allocating a given budget between the various goods and services that they wish to buy. Each consumer may be aware of exactly how much satisfaction is delivered by each of the goods consumed (though we do not need to assume this).

The key difference in this section is that, in explaining the consumer's behaviour, we do not need to know *how much* satisfaction he or she derives from consuming each product—nor indeed does the consumer need to know this. All that is needed is that each consumer can order any two bundles of goods by saying which gives more satisfaction and hence is the preferred bundle. Faced with a choice between many bundles, the maximizing consumer will then choose the one in the highest rank order of preference—and hence the one that is the most preferred of all available bundles.[6]

First, we ask how we can find the consumer's equilibrium allocation of spending in this new framework. Once that is done, we will be able to study consumers' responses to changes in such things as prices and incomes.

### The consumer's preferences

In the analysis that we are about to develop, the consumer's tastes or preferences, as they are variously called, are shown by indifference curves.

#### A single indifference curve

We start by deriving a single indifference curve. To do this we give an imaginary consumer, Kevin, some quantity of each of two products, say 18 units of clothing (*C*) and 10 units of food (*F*). This bundle is plotted as point *b* in Figure 5.1. Now think about the alternative combinations of these two products in the two shaded areas created by drawing vertical and horizontal lines through *b*. Would Kevin prefer the bundles of goods in these two shaded areas? To help answer this, we introduce our first assumption about tastes.

---

[6] This approach was originally due to the Italian economist Vilfredo Pareto (1848–1923). It was introduced to the English-speaking world (and greatly elaborated) by two British economists, John Hicks (1904–89) and R. G. D. Allen (1906–83).

**Figure 5.1  Some consumption bundles compared**

According to assumption 1, bundle *b* is superior to bundles that have less of both goods and inferior to all bundles that have more of both. All points in the dark blue area are regarded as inferior to bundle *b* because they contain less of both commodities (except on the boundaries, where they have less of one and the same amount of the other).

*Assumption 1.* Other things being equal, the consumer always prefers more of any one product to less of that same product.

This allows us to rank the bundles of goods represented by the two shaded areas in Figure 5.1. Combinations on the edges of this space to the north-east of point *b* all have more of one good and no less of the other, while points inside this area represent bundles containing more of both goods. All points in this space, apart from *b* itself, will thus be preferred to *b*. By similar logic, all points to the south-west of *b* represent either fewer of both goods or fewer of at least one and no more of the other. These points will all be inferior for the consumer as they deliver a lower level of satisfaction.

But what about bundles that have more of some products and less of others? At point *b*, Kevin consumes 18 units of clothing and 10 of food. Let us ask how much extra clothing we would have to give him to make him equally satisfied if we took away one unit of food. The answer might be that 20 units of clothing and 9 units of food would leave Kevin just as satisfied as with the initial combination. If we do this again, taking away another unit of food, there will be some further increase in clothing that could just compensate. Table 5.1 shows that if we have taken away 5 units of food, Kevin will require 30 units of clothing to leave him feeling just as satisfied as at point *b*. This is also illustrated by point *a* in Figure 5.2. These combinations of fewer units of food and increased

**Table 5.1  Bundles conferring equal satisfaction**

| Bundle | Clothing | Food |
| --- | --- | --- |
| *a* | 30 | 5 |
| *b* | 18 | 10 |
| *c* | 13 | 15 |
| *d* | 10 | 20 |
| *e* | 8 | 25 |
| *f* | 7 | 30 |

Since each of these bundles gives Kevin equal satisfaction, he is indifferent between them. None of the bundles contains more food and more clothing than any of the other bundles. Kevin's assumed indifference among these bundles is not, therefore, in conflict with the assumption that more is preferred to less of each product.

**Figure 5.2  An indifference curve**

The indifference curve shows combinations of food and clothing that yield equal satisfaction and among which the consumer is indifferent. Points *a* to *f* are plotted from Table 5.1 and an indifference curve is drawn through them. Compared with any point on the curve, point *g* is superior while point *h* is inferior. The slope of the tangent *T* gives the marginal rate of substitution at point *b*. Moving down the curve from *b* to *f*, the slope of the tangent flattens, showing that the more food and the less clothing Kevin has, the less willing he will be to sacrifice further clothing to get more food.

quantities of clothing that leave Kevin just as satisfied trace out the line segment from *b* to *a* in the figure.

Starting again at point *b*, we can now move in the opposite direction and ask how much extra food would Kevin need to leave him equally satisfied as we take successive units of clothing away from him. The answer to this question traces out the line through points *c*, *d*, *e*, and *f*.

By construction, the curved line drawn out in Figure 5.2 shows combinations of clothing and food all of which give Kevin the same level of satisfaction. He is indifferent between all of the different bundles of goods represented by that line (some specific combinations of which are listed in Table 5.1). For this reason this pink line is called an **indifference curve**. The line joining points *a–f* in Figure 5.2 is one indifference curve.

An indifference curve shows combinations of products that yield the same satisfaction to the consumer. Thus, a consumer is indifferent between the combinations indicated by any two points on one indifference curve.

Points above and to the right of the indifference curve in Figure 5.2 show combinations of food and clothing that Kevin would prefer to combinations indicated by points on the curve. Consider, for example, the combination of 20*F* and 20*C*, which is represented by point *g* in the figure. Although it might not be obvious that this bundle is preferred to bundle *a* (which has more clothing but less food), Assumption 1 tells us that *g* is preferred to bundle *c*, because *g* has more clothing *and* more food than *c*. Inspection of the graph shows that *any* point above the curve will be obviously superior to *some* points on the curve in the sense that it will contain both more food and more clothing than those points on the curve. But since all points on the curve are equally valuable in Kevin's eyes, any point above the curve must, therefore, be superior to *all* points on the curve. By a similar argument, points such as *h*, which are below and to the left of the curve, represent bundles of goods that Kevin regards as inferior to all bundles on the curve. These comparisons are summarized in Figure 5.3.

### Diminishing marginal rate of substitution

What is the shape of a typical indifference curve? To answer this we need a second assumption.

*Assumption 2.* The less of one product that is presently being used by a consumer, the smaller the amount of it that the consumer will be willing to forgo in order to increase consumption of a second product.

This is called the assumption of a **diminishing marginal rate of substitution**. The *rate of substitution* tells how much more of one product we need to compensate for successive lost units of the other. The *diminishing* of this rate of substitution may seem intuitively akin to diminishing marginal utility; however, for the latter we hold consumption of all but one good constant, while here we have more of one good compensating for fewer of the other.

Diminishing marginal rate of substitution is illustrated in Table 5.2, which is based on the example of food and clothing shown in Table 5.1. As we move down the table

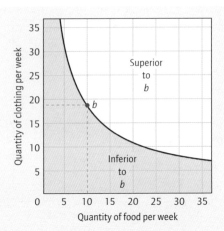

**Figure 5.3  Consumption bundles compared**

The indifference curve allows any bundle such as *b* to be compared with all others. Kevin regards all bundles in the blue area as inferior and all bundles in the white area as superior to *b*. The indifference curve is the boundary between these two areas. All points on the curve yield equal satisfaction and Kevin is, therefore, indifferent among them.

**Table 5.2  Diminishing marginal rate of substitution**

| Movement | Change in clothing (1) | Change in food (2) | Marginal rate of substitution (3) |
|---|---|---|---|
| From *a* to *b* | −12 | 5 | 2.4 |
| From *b* to *c* | −5 | 5 | 1.0 |
| From *c* to *d* | −3 | 5 | 0.6 |
| From *d* to *e* | −2 | 5 | 0.4 |
| From *e* to *f* | −1 | 5 | 0.2 |

The marginal rate of substitution measures the amount of one product a consumer must be given to compensate for giving up one unit of the other. This table is based on the data in Table 5.1. When Kevin moves from *a* to *b*, he gives up 12 units of clothing and gains 5 units of food, a rate of substitution of 12/5 or 2.4 units of clothing sacrificed per unit of food gained. When he moves from *b* to *c*, he sacrifices 5 units of clothing and gains 5 of food (a rate of substitution of 1 unit of clothing for each unit of food). Note that the marginal rate of substitution (MRS) is the absolute value of the ratio of Δ*C* to Δ*F*. Since these two changes always have opposite signs, the MRS is obtained by multiplying this ratio by −1.

through points *a* to *f*, Kevin has bundles with fewer and fewer units of clothing and more and more food. In accordance with the hypothesis of diminishing marginal rate of substitution, he is willing to give up smaller and smaller amounts of clothing further to increase his consumption of food by one unit. When Kevin moves from *c* to *d*, for example, the table tells us that he is prepared to give up 0.6 unit of clothing to get a further unit of food. When he moves from *e* to *f*, he will give up only 0.2 unit.

The geometrical expression of this hypothesis is found in the shape of the indifference curve. Look closely, for example, at the slope of the curve in Figure 5.2. Its negative slope indicates that, if Kevin is to have fewer units of one product, he must have more of the other to compensate. Diminishing marginal rate of substitution is shown by the curve being convex viewed from the origin: moving down the curve to the right, its slope gets flatter and flatter. The absolute value of the slope of the curve is the marginal rate of substitution, the rate at which the consumer is willing to reduce his consumption of the product plotted on the vertical axis in order to increase his consumption of the product plotted on the horizontal axis.

The slope of the indifference curve at any point is measured by the slope of the tangent to the curve at that point. The slope of tangent *T* drawn to the curve at point *b* shows the marginal rate of substitution at that point. It can be seen that, moving down the curve to the right, the slope of the tangent gets flatter and flatter, and hence the marginal rate of substitution is diminishing.[7]

### The indifference map

So far we have constructed only a single indifference curve. There must, however, be a similar curve passing through any of the other points in Figure 5.2, in addition to those points on the single curve drawn. Starting at another point, such as *g*, and going through the same exercise, there will be other combinations that will yield Kevin equal satisfaction. If the line joining all of *these* combinations is drawn, another indifference curve will be constructed. This exercise can be repeated many times, generating a new indifference curve each time.

It follows from the comparisons given in Figure 5.3 that the further away any indifference curve is from the origin, the higher is the level of satisfaction given by the consumption bundles that it indicates. We refer to a curve that confers a higher level of satisfaction as a *higher curve*.

A set of indifference curves is called an **indifference map**. An example is shown in Figure 5.4. It specifies Kevin's tastes by showing his complete ordering of preferences between different bundles of these two products, and it

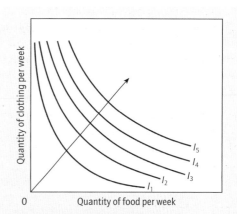

**Figure 5.4 An indifference map**

A set of indifference curves is called an indifference map. The further the curve from the origin, the higher the level of satisfaction it represents. If Kevin moves along the arrow, he is climbing a 'utility mountain', moving to ever-higher utility levels and crossing ever-higher equal-utility contours, which we call *indifference curves*.

shows his rate of substitution between them at each specific point. When economists say that a consumer's tastes are *given*, they do not mean merely that the consumer's current consumption pattern is given: rather, they mean that the consumer's entire indifference map is given.

Of course, there must be an indifference curve through *every* point in Figure 5.4. To graph them, we only show a few, but all are there. Thus, as Kevin moves upwards to the right starting from the origin, his utility is rising continuously. As he follows a route such as the one shown by the arrow, consuming ever more of both products, he can be thought of as climbing a continuous utility mountain. We show this 'mountain' by selecting a few equal-utility contours, labelled $I_1$ to $I_5$. But every point between each of the contours shown must also have a curve of equal utility passing through it. Thus, an indifference map is really like the continuous surface of one half of a cone, rather than a set of discrete lines.

In indifference theory we do not need to make any assumptions about how big the difference is between the level of satisfaction on one indifference curve and the next; i.e., we do not need to assume that utility can be quantified. Instead, all we assume is that the utility attached to $I_5$ exceeds that attached to $I_4$, which in turn exceeds the utility attached to $I_3$, and so on. We can say that the consumer is climbing a utility mountain as he moves along the arrow starting from the origin, but we do not need to know if the mountain is gentle or steep.

Box 5.3 shows some specific shapes of indifference curves that correspond to some specific taste patterns.

---

[7] Table 5.2 calculates the rate of substitution between distinct points on the indifference curve. Strictly speaking, these are the incremental rates of substitution between the two points. Geometrically, the slope of the chord joining the two points gives this incremental rate. The marginal rate refers to the slope of the curve at a single point and is given by the slope of the tangent to the curve at the point.

## Box 5.3 Shapes of indifference curves

Any taste pattern can be illustrated with indifference curves. This box gives a few examples that will help you understand how indifference curves work. In each case the curve labelled $I_2$ indicates a higher utility than the curve labelled $I_1$.

**Perfect substitutes: part (i)** Drawing pins that came in red packages of 100 would be perfect substitutes for identical pins that came in green packages of 100 for a colour-blind consumer: he would be willing to substitute one type of package for the other at a rate of one for one. The indifference curves would thus be a set of parallel lines with a slope of $-1$, as shown in part (i) of the figure. *Indifference curves for perfect substitutes are straight lines whose slopes indicate the rate at which one good can be substituted for the other.*

**Perfect complements: part (ii)** Left- and right-hand gloves are perfect complements, since one of them is of no use without the other. This gives rise to the indifference curves shown in part (ii) of the figure. There is no rate at which any consumer will substitute one kind of glove for the other when she starts with equal numbers of each. *Indifference curves for perfect complements are L-shaped.*

**A good that gives zero utility: part (iii)** When a good gives no satisfaction at all, a person will be unwilling to sacrifice even the smallest amount of other goods to obtain any quantity of the good in question. Such would be the case regarding meat for a vegetarian consumer, whose indifference curves are horizontal straight lines. *Indifference curves for a product yielding zero satisfaction are parallel to that product's axis.*

**An absolute necessity: part (iv)** There is some minimum quantity of water, $w_0$, that is necessary to sustain life. As consumption of water falls towards $w_0$, increasingly large amounts of other goods are necessary to persuade the consumer to cut down on his water consumption. Thus, each indifference curve becomes steeper and steeper as it approaches $w_0$, and the marginal rate of substitution increases. *The marginal rate of substitution for an absolute necessity approaches infinity as consumption falls towards the amount that is absolutely necessary.*

**A good that confers a negative utility after some level of consumption: part (v)** Beyond some point, further consumption of many foods and beverages, films, plays, or cricket matches would reduce satisfaction. Figure (v) shows a consumer who is *forced* to eat more and more food. At the amount $f_0$ she has all the food she could possibly want. Beyond $f_0$ her indifference curves have positive slopes, indicating that she gets *negative* value from consuming the extra food, and so will be willing to sacrifice some amount of other products to avoid consuming it. *When, beyond some level of consumption, the consumer's utility is reduced by further consumption, the indifference curves have positive slopes.*

This case does not arise if the consumer can dispose of the extra unwanted units at no cost. The indifference curves then become horizontal.

**A good that is not consumed: part (vi)** Typically, a consumer will consume only one or two of all the available types of cars, TV sets, dishwashers, or tennis rackets. If a consumer is in equilibrium when consuming a zero amount of say, green peas, she is in what is called a *corner solution* (as shown in part (vi) of the figure by the budget line *ab* and the curve $I_1$). *When a good is not consumed, the indifference curve cuts the axis of the non-consumed good with a slope flatter than the budget line.*

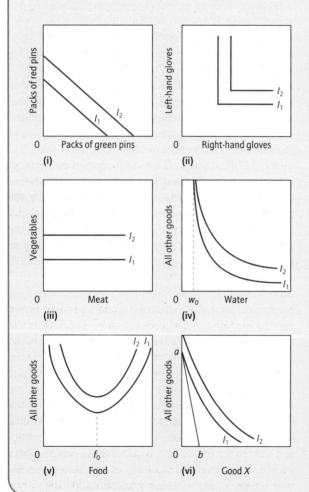

Table 5.3 Data for Jane's budget line

| Quantity of food | Value of food | Quantity of clothing | Value of clothing | Total expenditure |
|---|---|---|---|---|
| 60 | £120 | 0 | £0 | £120 |
| 50 | 100 | 5 | 20 | 120 |
| 40 | 80 | 10 | 40 | 120 |
| 30 | 60 | 15 | 60 | 120 |
| 20 | 40 | 20 | 80 | 120 |
| 10 | 20 | 25 | 100 | 120 |
| 0 | 0 | 30 | 120 | 120 |

The table shows combinations of food and clothing available to Jane when her income is £120 and she faces prices of £4 for clothing and £2 for food. Any row indicates a bundle of food and clothing that exactly exhausts Jane's income.

## The choices available to the consumer

An indifference map tells us what any consumer *would like* to do: reach the highest possible indifference curve, that is, be as high up the utility mountain as possible. To see what that consumer *can* do, we need another construction, called the budget line.

We start by considering a single consumer, Jane, who is allocating the whole of her money income between two goods, food and clothing.[8]

### The budget line

The **budget line** shows all those combinations of the goods that are just obtainable, given Jane's income and the prices of the products that she buys.[9]

Assume initially that Jane's income is £120 per week, the price of food is £2 per unit, and the price of clothing is £4 per unit. As in the earlier discussion, we denote food by $F$ and clothing by $C$. Thus, for example, a bundle containing 20 units of food and 10 units of clothing is written as $20F$ and $10C$. Table 5.3 lists a few of the bundles of food and clothing available to Jane, while the blue line

Figure 5.5 Jane's budget line

The budget line shows the quantities of goods available to Jane, given her money income and the price of the goods she buys. With an income of £120 a week and prices of £2 per unit for food and £4 per unit of clothing, the blue line is Jane's budget line, showing all combinations of $F$ and $C$ that are obtainable. Bundle $u$ ($10C$ and $20F$) does not use all of her income. Bundle $v$ ($35C$ and $40F$) requires more than her present income.

If Jane moves from point $y$ ($20F$ and $20C$) to point $x$ ($40F$ and $10C$), she consumes 20 more $F$ and 10 fewer $C$. These amounts are indicated by $\Delta F$ and $\Delta C$ in the figure. Thus, the opportunity cost of each unit of $F$ added to consumption is $10/20 = 0.5$ unit of clothing forgone. This is the absolute value of $\Delta C/\Delta F$, which is the slope of the budget line $zw$ in the figure.

running from $z$ to $w$ in Figure 5.5 shows all the possible bundles that she could buy with her income. At point $w$, for example, Jane is spending all her income to buy $60F$ and no clothing, while at point $z$ she is spending all her income to buy $30C$ and no food. Points on the line between $z$ and $w$ indicate how much Jane could buy of both products.

### The slope of the budget line

Marked on Figure 5.5 as points $x$ and $y$ are two of the specific spending combinations from Table 5.3. It is clear from the figure that the absolute value of the slope of the budget line measures the ratio of the change in $C$ to the change in $F$ as we move along the line. This ratio, $\Delta C/\Delta F$, is 0.5 in our present example ($10/20$).

How does the slope of the budget line relate to the prices of the two goods? This question is easily answered if we remember that all points on the budget line represent bundles of goods that just exhaust Jane's whole income. It follows that, when she moves from one point on the budget line to another, the change in expenditure on $C$ must be of equal value, but opposite in sign, to the change in expenditure on $F$. Letting $\Delta C$ and $\Delta F$ stand for the changes in the quantities of clothing and food respectively, and $p_c$ and $p_f$ stand for the money prices of

---

[8] These assumptions are not as restrictive as they at first seem. Although just two goods are used so that the analysis can be handled graphically, the argument can easily be generalized to any number of goods with the use of mathematics. Savings are ignored because we are interested in the allocation of expenditure among commodities for current consumption. Saving and borrowing can be allowed for, but doing so affects none of the results in which we are interested here.

[9] A budget line is analogous to the production possibility boundary shown in Figure 1.1 on page 6. The budget line shows the combinations of commodities available to one consumer given her income and prices, while the production possibility curve shows the combination of commodities available to the whole society given its supplies of resources and techniques of production.

clothing and food respectively, we can write this relation as follows:

$$\Delta C p_c = -\Delta F p_f.$$

There is nothing difficult in this. All it says is that, if any amount more is spent on one product, the same amount less must be spent on the other. A given income imposes this discipline on any consumer.

If we divide the above equation through, first by $\Delta F$, and then by $p_c$, we get the following:

$$\frac{\Delta C}{\Delta F} = \frac{p_f}{p_c}.$$

So the slope of the budget line is the negative of the ratio of the two prices (with the price of the good that is plotted on the horizontal axis appearing in the numerator).

Notice that the slope of the budget line depends only on the ratio of the two prices, not on their absolute values. To check this, consider an example. If clothing costs £4 and food costs £2, then Jane must forgo 0.5 unit of clothing in order to be able to purchase one more unit of food. If clothing costs £8 and food costs £4, Jane must still forgo 0.5 unit of clothing to be able to purchase one more unit of food. As long as the price of clothing is twice the price of food, Jane must forgo half a unit of clothing in order to be able to purchase one more unit of food.

More generally, the amount of clothing that must be given up to obtain another unit of food depends only on the *ratio* of their two prices. If we take the money price of food and divide it by the money price of clothing, we have the opportunity cost of food in terms of clothing (the quantity of clothing that must be forgone in order to be able to purchase one more unit of food). This may be written:

$$\frac{p_f}{p_c} = \text{opportunity cost of food in terms of clothing.}$$

It is apparent that changing income and/or changing both prices in the same proportion leaves the ratio $p_f/p_c$ unchanged.

This discussion helps to clarify the distinction between money prices and relative prices. Both $p_f$ and $p_c$ are money prices, while the ratio $p_f/p_c$ is a relative price.

## The consumer's equilibrium

The budget line tells us what consumers *can* do: they can select any consumption bundle on, or below, the line— but not above it. This means that they can spend only within the limits of a given income. To see what consumers *want* to do, we introduce our third assumption:

*Assumption 3.* Consumers seek to maximize total satisfaction, which means reaching the highest possible indifference curve.

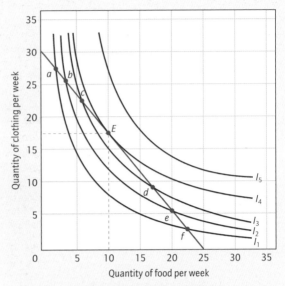

**Figure 5.6 The equilibrium of a consumer**

Equilibrium occurs at *E*, where an indifference curve is tangent to the budget line. Paul has an income of £150 a week and faces prices of £5 a unit for clothing and £6 a unit for food. A bundle of clothing and food indicated by point *a* is attainable, but by moving along the budget line to points such as *b* and *c*, higher indifference curves can be reached. At *E*, where the indifference curve $I_4$ is tangent to the budget line, Paul cannot reach a higher curve by moving along the budget line. If he did alter his consumption bundle by moving from *E* to *d*, for example, he would move to the lower indifference curve $I_3$ and thus to a lower level of satisfaction.

We have now developed representations of a consumer's tastes and available choices. Figure 5.6 brings together the budget line and the indifference curves for another consumer, Paul. Any point on the budget line can be attained. Which one will Paul actually choose?

Will Paul choose to consume 25 units of food and no clothing, as he could do with his income? Will he instead choose to consume 30 units of clothing and no food? The answer is no in both cases. By moving away from either of these combinations, he can move to a higher indifference curve. Indeed, he can get to higher and higher indifference curves by moving from each of the corners into the middle until he reaches point *E*, which is just touching— i.e. is tangent to—the highest possible indifference curve. When Paul is at this point of tangency between the indifference curve and the budget line, he cannot reach a higher indifference curve by varying the bundle consumed. Any move from this point that remains within the budget constraint will lead him to a lower indifference curve and thus to lower satisfaction.

Satisfaction is maximized at the point where an indifference curve is tangent to a budget line. At that point, the slope of the indifference curve—which measures the consumer's marginal rate of substitution—is equal to the slope of the budget line—which measures the opportunity cost of one good in terms of the other as determined by market prices.

Notice that Paul is presented with market prices that he cannot change. He adjusts to these prices by choosing a bundle of goods such that, at the margin, his own relative valuation of the two goods conforms to the relative valuations given by the market. Paul's relative valuation is given by the slope of his indifference curve, while the market's relative valuation is given by the slope of his budget line.

When Paul has chosen the consumption bundle that maximizes his satisfaction, he will go on consuming that bundle unless something changes. The consumer is thus in equilibrium.

It is also worth noting that the equilibrium position we have just derived has the same characteristics as the one the utilitarians discovered and is expressed in equations (1) and (2) on page 88. The price ratio $p_x/p_y$ is the slope of the budget line in Figure 5.6. The slope of each indifference curve, which we have called the *marginal rate of substitution*, is the ratio of the marginal utilities of the two products, $MU_x/MU_y$; and so where the budget line is tangent to the highest possible indifference curve (i.e. where the consumer is maximizing utility) it will also be true that $MU_x/MU_y = p_x/p_y$.

# The consumer's response to price and income changes

How do consumers change their spending patterns when there is a change in goods prices or in available income? To answer this, we take another hypothetical consumer called Karen. Karen's tastes are given, and are represented by an indifference map that does not change. We first show that changes in her income and the prices she faces can be represented as a shift in the budget line. We then investigate the change in spending induced by price and income changes.

## Parallel shifts in the budget line

### A change in money income

A change in Karen's money income will, other things being equal, shift her budget line. For example, if income rises Karen will be able to buy more of both goods. Her budget line will, therefore, shift out parallel to itself to indicate this expansion in her consumption possibilities. (The fact that it will be a parallel shift is established by our demonstration on page 97 that the slope of the budget line depends only on the relative price of the two products.)

A change in the consumer's income shifts the budget line parallel to itself—outwards when income rises and inwards when income falls.

The effect of income changes is shown in Figure 5.7. For each level of income, there is an equilibrium position at which an indifference curve is tangent to the relevant budget line. Each such equilibrium position means that Karen is doing as well as she possibly can for that level of

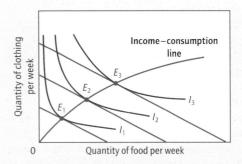

**Figure 5.7  An income–consumption line**

This line shows how Karen's purchases react to changes in income with relative prices held constant. Increases in income shift the budget line out parallel to itself, moving the equilibrium from $E_1$ to $E_2$ to $E_3$. The blue income–consumption line joins all these points of equilibrium.

income. If we join up all the points of equilibrium, we trace out what is called her **income–consumption line**. This line shows how the consumption bundle changes as income changes, with prices held constant.[10]

---

[10] This income–consumption line can be used to derive the curve relating quantity demanded to income that was introduced on page 74. This is done by plotting the quantity of one of the goods consumed at the equilibrium position against the level of money income that determined the position of the budget line. Repeating this for each level of income produces the required curve.

## A proportionate change in all prices

If all prices are cut in half, Karen can buy twice as much of both products. This causes the same shift in the budget line as when Karen's income doubles with prices held constant. On the other hand, a doubling of all prices will cause her budget line to shift inwards in exactly the same way as if her money income had halved with prices held constant.

This illustrates a general result:

An equal proportionate change in all money prices, with money income held constant, shifts the budget line parallel to itself—towards the origin when prices rise and away from the origin when prices fall.

From this point on the analysis is the same as in the previous section, since changing money prices proportionately has the identical effect to changing money income.

## Offsetting changes in money prices and money incomes

The results in the last two sections suggest that we can have offsetting changes in money prices and money incomes. Consider a doubling of Karen's money income, shifting her budget line outwards. Let this be accompanied by a doubling of all money prices, which shifts her budget line inwards. The net effect is to leave her budget line where it was before the changes in her income and in the market prices. This illustrates a general result:

Multiplying money income by some constant $\lambda$, and simultaneously multiplying all money prices by $\lambda$, leaves the budget line unaffected and hence leaves consumer purchases unaffected.

The symbol $\lambda$ is the lower-case Greek letter lambda, which is often used for some constant multiple. This result is sometimes referred to as the *homogeneity condition*.

## Changes in the slope of the budget line

### A change in relative prices

We already know that a change in the relative prices of the two goods changes the slope of the budget line. At a given price of clothing, Karen has an equilibrium consumption position for each possible price of food. Connecting these

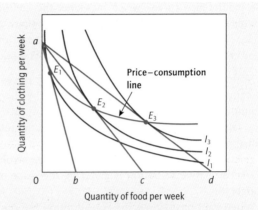

**Figure 5.8  The price–consumption line**

This line shows how a consumer's purchases react to a change in one price with money income and other prices held constant. Decreases in the price of food (with her money income and the price of clothing constant) pivot Karen's budget line from *ab* to *ac* to *ad*. Her equilibrium position moves from $E_1$ to $E_2$ to $E_3$. The blue price–consumption line joins all such equilibrium points.

positions traces out a price–consumption line, as is shown in Figure 5.8. Notice that, as the relative prices of food and clothing change, the relative quantities of food and clothing purchased also change. In particular, as the price of food falls, Karen buys more food.

## Real and money income

The preceding analysis allows us to look deeper into the important distinction between two concepts of income. Money income measures a consumer's income in terms of some monetary unit, for example so many pounds sterling or so many dollars. Real income measures the *purchasing power* of the consumer's money income. A rise in money income of *x* per cent combined with an *x* per cent rise in all money prices leaves a consumer's purchasing power, and hence their real income, unchanged. When we speak of the *real value* of a certain amount of money, we are referring to the goods and services that can be bought with the money, that is, the purchasing power of the money.

Box 5.4 discusses the importance of relative prices and the problems created by inflation.

**Box 5.4** Relative prices and inflation

**Allocation of resources: the importance of relative prices**

Price theory shows why the allocation of resources depends on the structure of relative prices. If the money value of all prices, incomes, debts, and credits were doubled, there would, according to our theory, be no noticeable effects. We have already seen that doubling money income and all money prices leaves each consumer's budget line unchanged. So, according to the theory of consumer behaviour, the combination of these changes gives the consumer no incentive to vary any purchases. As far as producers are concerned, if the prices of all outputs and inputs double, the relative profitabilities of alternative lines of production will be unchanged. Thus, producers will have no incentive to alter production rates so as to produce more of some things and fewer of others. The same set of relative prices and real incomes would exist, and there would be no incentive for any reallocation of resources. The economy would function as before.

In contrast, a change in *relative* prices will cause resources to be reallocated. Consumers will buy more of the relatively cheaper products and less of the relatively more expensive ones, and producers will increase production of those products whose prices have risen relatively, and reduce production of those whose prices have fallen relatively (since the latter will be relatively less profitable lines of production).

The theory of price and resource allocation is a theory of relative, not absolute, prices.

**Inflation and deflation: the importance of absolute prices**

The average level of all money prices is called the general price level, or more usually just the **price level**. If all money prices double, we say that the price level has doubled. An increase in the price level is called an **inflation**; a decrease is called a **deflation**. If a rise in all money prices and incomes has little or no effect on the allocation of resources, it may seem surprising that so much concern is expressed over inflation. Clearly, people who spend all their incomes, and whose money incomes go up at the same rate as money prices, lose nothing from inflation. Their real income is unaffected.

Inflation, while having no effect on consumers whose incomes rise at the same rate as prices, none the less does have many serious consequences. These arise mainly because all prices do not rise at the same rate and some assets are denominated in money terms, so that their value falls as the price level rises. These consequences are studied in detail later in this book. In the meantime, *we assume that the price level is constant*.

Under these circumstances, a change in one money price necessarily changes that price *relative to* the average of all other prices. The theory extends to situations in which the price level is changing. Under inflationary conditions, whenever shifts in demand or supply require a change in a product's relative price, its price rises *faster* (its relative price rising) or *slower* (its relative price falling) than the general price level is rising. Explaining this each time can be cumbersome. It is, therefore, simpler to deal with relative prices in a theoretical setting in which the price level is constant. It is important however to realize that, even though we develop the theory in this way, it is not limited to such situations. The propositions we develop can be applied to changing price levels merely by making explicit what is always implicit: in the theory of relative prices, 'rise' or 'fall' *always* means rise or fall *relative to the average of all other prices*.

# The consumer's demand curve

We now establish the link between the above analysis of indifference curves and budget constraints, and the consumer's demand curve. To derive the consumer's demand curve for any product, we need to depart from the world of two products. We are now interested in what happens to the consumer's demand for some product, say petrol, as the price of that product changes, *all other prices being held constant*. We can do this with the tools developed above simply by making the bundle of 'all other goods' take the place of the second product.

## Derivation of the demand curve

In part (i) of Figure 5.9 a new type of indifference map is plotted in which the horizontal axis measures litres of petrol and the vertical axis measures the value of all other goods consumed. We have in effect used *everything but petrol* as the second product. The indifference curves now give the rate at which another hypothetical consumer, Philip, is prepared to substitute petrol for money (which allows him to buy all other goods).

(i)

(ii)

**Figure 5.9** Derivation of an individual's demand curve

The points on a price–consumption line provide the information needed to draw a demand curve. In part (i) Philip has an income of £200 per month and alternatively faces prices of £0.75, £0.50, and £0.25 per litre of petrol, choosing positions $E_0$, $E_1$, and $E_2$. The information concerning the number of litres he demands at each price is then plotted in part (ii) to yield his demand curve. The three points $x$, $y$, and $z$ in (ii) correspond to the three equilibrium positions $E_0$, $E_1$, and $E_2$ in (i).

**Figure 5.10** The income and substitution effects

The substitution effect is defined by sliding the budget line around a fixed indifference curve; the income effect is defined by a parallel shift of the budget line. The original budget line is $ab$ and a fall in the price of petrol takes it to $aj$. The original equilibrium is at $E_0$ with $q_0$ of petrol consumed, and the final equilibrium is at $E_2$ with $q_2$ of petrol consumed. To remove the income effect, imagine reducing Philip's income until he is just able to attain his original indifference curve at the new price. We do this by shifting the line $aj$ to a parallel line nearer the origin until it just touches the indifference curve that passes through $E_0$. The intermediate point $E_1$ divides the quantity change into a substitution effect, $q_1 - q_0$, and an income effect, $q_2 - q_1$. The point $E_1$ can also be obtained by sliding the original budget line $ab$ around the indifference curve until its slope reflects the new relative prices.

The derivation of a demand curve is illustrated in part (ii) of Figure 5.9. For a given income, each price of petrol gives rise to a particular budget line and a particular spending choice. Plotting the quantity of petrol that Philip consumes for the specific budget line at any given price yields one point on his demand curve. Every other possible price yields a different point. The resulting price–quantity combinations trace out Philip's whole demand curve.

## The slope of the demand curve

The price–consumption line in part (i) of Figure 5.9 indicates that, as price decreases, the quantity of petrol demanded increases. But it is possible to draw Philip's indifference curves in such a way that his response to a decrease in price is for less to be consumed rather than more. A positively sloped demand curve for a good is referred to as a **Giffen good** after the Victorian economist

Sir Robert Giffen (1837–1910), who is reputed to have documented such a case. We now show how this case can be analysed using indifference curves.

### Income and substitution effects

The key is to distinguish between *the income effect* and *the substitution effect* of a change in price. The separation of the two effects according to indifference theory is shown in Figure 5.10. We can think of it as occurring in the following way. After the price of the good has fallen, we reduce money income *until the original indifference curve can just be obtained*. Philip is now on his original indifference curve but facing the new set of relative prices. His response is defined as the **substitution effect**: the response of quantity demanded to a change in relative price, real income being held constant (i.e. staying on the original indifference curve). Then, to measure the income effect, we restore money income. Philip's response to this is defined as the **income effect**: the response of quantity

**Box 5.5** **The Slutsky decomposition of income and substitution effects**

The discussion of income and substitution effects in the text is based upon the analysis of English Nobel Laureate Sir John Hicks (1904–89). An alternative approach was developed by the Russian mathematician Evgeny Slutsky (1880–1948).

Hicks's decomposition was derived in the context of developing the concept of indifference curves, so it was natural for him to ask the question: following a price change, how much income must be taken away in order that the consumer can return to the original indifference curve and thus have the same level of utility or satisfaction as prior to the price change?

Slutsky, when thinking about the same issue, did not have at his disposal the tool of indifference curves. Instead he asked the question: following a price change, how much income must be taken away so that the consumer is just able to buy the initial bundle of goods (and therefore could not be any worse off than in the initial position)?

The figure illustrates the difference between these two approaches. There is a fall in the price of good 1 holding the price of good 2 constant. The initial consumption points is at A and after the price fall the consumption point is at B.

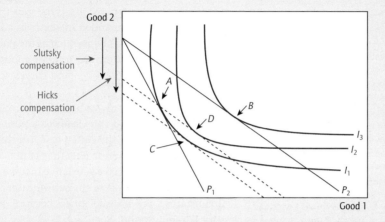

As we saw in the discussion of Figure 5.10, Hicks's decomposition generates an income compensation that returns the consumer to the original indifference curve $I_1$ following the fall in price of good 1 and the associated shift of the budget constraint from $P_1$ to $P_2$. This is achieved by shifting the new budget line $P_2$ towards the origin until it is just tangent to the original indifference curve. Thus, the Hicks substitution effect takes the consumer from point A to point C, and the income effect takes her from C to B.

To find the Slutsky decomposition, we shift the new budget constraint inwards parallel to its new position until it just passes through the original consumption bundle at point A. If the

consumer had faced this budget constraint with the original level of disposable income but at the new relative prices, she would have chosen to be at point D, which is on indifference curve $I_2$ and is thus at a higher utility level than the initial position.

There is no general reason why one of these methods is to be preferred to the others. They are answering slightly different questions. The Slutsky compensation is easier to calculate as it relies on observable income and prices, but the Hicks compensation is useful for welfare comparisons because it tells us the income change that leaves the consumer *feeling* just as well off as before. The choice of methods should therefore depend on the purpose to which it is put.

demanded to a change in real income, with relative prices held constant.

Box 5.5 explains an alternative method of isolating the income and substitution effects.

In Figure 5.10 the income and substitution effects work in the same direction, both tending to increase quantity demanded when price falls. Is this necessarily the case? The answer is no. It follows from the convex shape of indifference curves that the substitution effect is always in the same direction: more is consumed of a product whose

relative price has fallen. The income effect, however, can be in either direction: it can lead to more or less being consumed of a product whose price has fallen. The direction of the income effect depends on the distinction between normal and inferior goods.

### The slope of the demand curve for a normal good

For a *normal good*, an increase in any consumer's real income, arising from a decrease in the price of the product, leads to increased consumption, reinforcing the

**(i) Non-Giffen good**

**(ii) Giffen good**

**Figure 5.11 Income and substitution effects for inferior goods**

A large enough negative income effect can outweigh the substitution effect and lead to a decrease in consumption in response to a fall in price. In each part of the diagram Philip is in equilibrium at $E_0$, consuming a quantity $q_0$ of the good in question. The price then decreases and the budget line shifts to $aj$, with a new equilibrium at $E_2$ and quantity consumed $q_2$. In each case the substitution effect increases consumption from $q_0$ to $q_1$. In (i) there is a negative income effect of $q_1 - q_2$. Because this is less than the substitution effect, the latter dominates, so good X has a normal, negatively sloped demand curve. In (ii) the negative income effect $q_1 - q_2$ is larger than the substitution effect, and quantity consumed actually decreases. Good Y is a Giffen good.

substitution effect. Because quantity demanded increases, the demand curve has a negative slope.[11] This is the case illustrated in Figure 5.9.

### The slope of the demand curve for an inferior good

Figure 5.11 shows indifference curves for inferior goods. The income effect is negative in each part of the diagram. This follows from the nature of an *inferior good*: as income rises, less of the good is consumed. In each case the substitution effect serves to increase the quantity demanded as price decreases and is offset to some degree by the negative income effect. The final result depends on the relative strengths of the two effects. In part (i) the negative income effect only partially offsets the substitution effect, and thus quantity demanded increases as a result of the price decrease, though not as much as for a normal good. This is the typical pattern for inferior goods, and it too leads to negatively sloped demand curves, usually relatively inelastic ones.

In part (ii) the negative income effect outweighs the substitution effect and thus leads to a positively sloped demand curve. This is the Giffen case. For this to happen the good must be inferior. But that is not enough: the change in price must have a negative income effect *strong enough* to more than offset the substitution effect. These circumstances are unusual ones, because strong inferiority is rarely found. Such goods, if they ever existed, would tend to disappear from use as consumers get richer. Most goods are normal goods. A positively sloped market demand curve is thus a rare exception to the general rule that demand curves have negative slopes.

### Equivalent and compensating variations

There are further concepts associated with the income effect of a price change that are commonly used in economics. These are known as **equivalent variation** and **compensating variation**.

---

[11] A possible exception to this arises from the *endowment income effect*. This arises in some models where the consumer is assumed to have an initial endowment of goods and may choose to be a net seller of some goods. If the price of these goods rises, the consumer has a higher income and therefore can buy more of all normal goods, including the goods for which he or she is a net seller. A practical example would be as follows. Suppose the price of haircuts rises (all other price remaining constant). For most consumers we would predict that the quantity demanded of haircuts would fall. However, hairdressers are now richer, so for them the price rise has generated a positive rather negative income effect. So for the hairdressers the income effect goes the other way, inasmuch as incomes rise as the price of haircuts rises.

**Figure 5.12 Equivalent variation of income**

**The equivalent variation is the change in income that leaves the consumer just as well off as some specific change in the price of a good.** The consumer is initially at point $A$ on budget line $P_1$. The price of good 1 falls, the budget line shifts to $P_2$ and the consumer shifts her spending pattern to $B$, which is on a higher indifference curve. The equivalent variation in income is given by the size in the parallel shift in the original budget line that would have taken the consumer to the level of utility indicated by the higher indifference curve (which is achieved after the fall in the price of good 1.) The equivalent income variation would have generated consumption point $C$ as the optimal choice, but the consumer is indifferent between points $B$ and $C$.

### Equivalent variation

The equivalent variation is the answer to the question: if we had given the consumer a sum of money instead of a lower price of one product, how much extra income would have made her feel just as well off? This is illustrated in Figure 5.12. It is calculated by shifting outwards the original budget line parallel to itself until it just touches the new indifference curve achieved after a price fall of one good.

### Compensating variation

This works backwards rather than forwards. It is the same as the income effect shown in Figure 5.10, and is measured by the distance $a$–$a_1$ in that figure. It is the amount of income that has to be taken away from the consumer following a price fall of one good in order to return the consumer to the initial indifference curve, and thus leave her feeling just as well off as before.

The difference between these two effects is whether the income adjustment is made relative to the consumption bundle chosen at the original prices or that chosen at the new prices.

# CASE STUDIES

## 1. Income and substitution effects in practice

Although they sound highly abstract and 'theoretical' when first encountered, the income and substitution effects turn out to be useful tools. They help us to deal with many problems such as: Do high rates of income tax act as disincentives to work? Would cutting the rate of income tax increase the amount of work people will do? Would raising the wage rate of workers in some industry lead to a reduction in absenteeism?

Such questions frequently face decision-takers and they are often surprised at the results that the market produces. For example, many years ago the National Coal Board, which used to run the UK coal industry, raised miners' wages in an attempt to boost coal production and was surprised to find miners working fewer rather than more hours. In several countries increases in rates of income tax (within a moderate, not a confiscatory, range) have been found to be associated with people working more hours rather than fewer even though they earn less after-

tax income for each hour worked; at other times reductions in tax rates seem to have caused people to work less even though they earn more after-tax income for each hour worked. The surprise in all these cases was the same. Intuition suggests that if you pay people more they will work more; experience shows that the result is sometimes the opposite: more pay, less work; less pay, more work.

The explanation of this surprising behaviour lies in distinguishing the income effect from the substitution effect of a change in the reward for work.

Think of Luke, starting with an endowment of 24 hours per day and deciding to consume some of it as 'leisure' (including sleeping time) and to trade the rest for income by working. If Luke works 9 hours a day at an after-tax rate of £10 per hour, he is consuming 15 hours a day of leisure and trading the other 9 for £90 worth of income which can be used to buy goods and services.

Now let the after-tax wage rate rise to £12 an hour, either because the wage rate rises or because the rate of personal income tax falls to produce that increase in after-tax earnings. Luke's response to this change will have an income and a substitution component.

The substitution effect works the way intuition suggested: more wages, more work. Gaining income is now cheaper in terms of the leisure Luke must sacrifice per £1 worth of income gained. At the new wage rate, 1/12 of an hour (i.e. 5 minutes) of work earns Luke £1 worth of income, whereas before it took 1/10 of an hour (6 minutes). Looked at the other way around, consuming leisure is now more expensive per amount of income that Luke must give up. An extra hour of leisure consumed requires sacrificing £12 of income instead of £10. The substitution effect leads to an increased consumption of the thing whose relative price has fallen—everything that income can buy, in this case—and to a reduced consumption of the thing whose relative price has risen—leisure.

So far so good. The surprise lies in the income effect. The rise in the after-tax wage rate has an income effect in the sense that Luke can have more goods *and* more leisure. He could, for example, consume an extra hour of leisure by cutting his hours worked from 9 to 8 while at the same time raising his income from £90 a day (9 hours @ £10) to £96 a day (8 hours @ £12). The income effect leads him to consume more goods and more leisure, that is to work fewer hours.

Only if the substitution effect is strong enough to overcome the income effect will the rise in the wage rate induce Luke to work more. If the substitution effect is strong enough, Luke might for example work 9.5 hours instead of 9 and increase his income from £90 to £114 a day. However, this means choosing this combination of income and leisure in preference to all combinations that give more income and more leisure, such as 8.5 hours of work (down from 9) and £105 of income (up from £90).

So we should not be surprised if increases in the after-tax hourly wage lead to less work; this merely means that the income effect is stronger than the substitution effect.

The above analysis helps to explain why employers separate higher overtime rates from normal rates of pay. If the normal rate of pay is increased the income effect is quite large, whereas if only the overtime rate is raised the income effect is much smaller but the substitution effect is unchanged. In the above example, raising the normal wage rate from £10 to £12 increases Luke's income by £18 if he continues to work an unchanged 9 hours a day. But introducing an overtime rate has an income effect only in so far as overtime hours are already being worked. If, in the previous example, the employer introduced a £15 hourly rate for work of over 9 hours a day, the income effect would be zero; Luke must work more in order to gain any benefit from the higher overtime rate.

## 2. Experimental economics and the concern for fairness

In the past decade or so economists and other scientists have co-operated in designing experiments to determine how people actually respond to various choices. This line of inquiry has provided evidence that individuals do not invariably maximize their own utility with no regard for what others around them are doing. The following extract summarizes the results of one such experiment.

*Imagine that somebody offers you $100. All you have to do is agree with some other anonymous person on how to share the sum. The rules are strict. The two of you are in separate rooms and cannot exchange information. A coin toss decides which of you will propose how to share the money. Suppose that you are the proposer. You can make a single offer of how to split the sum, and the other person—the responder—can say yes or no. The responder also knows the rules and the total amount of money at stake. If her answer is yes, the deal goes ahead. If her answer is no, neither of you gets anything. In both cases, the game is over and will not be repeated. What will you do?*

*Instinctively, many people feel they should offer 50 per cent, because such a division is 'fair' and therefore likely to be accepted. More daring people, however, think they might get away with offering somewhat less that half of the sum.*

*Before making a decision, you should ask yourself what you would do if you were the responder. The only thing you can do as the responder is say yes or no to a given amount of money. If the offer were 10 per cent, would you take $10 and let someone walk away with $90, or would you rather have nothing at all? What if the offer were only 1 per cent? Isn't $1 better than no dollars? And remember, haggling is strictly forbidden. Just one offer by the proposer: the responder can take it or leave it.*

*So what will you offer?*

*According to utility maximizing theory you should keep the majority of the money for yourself and offer a very small amount to the responder. After all, her alternative is to get nothing. So if she is a maximizer, she will accept any offer greater than zero. But this is not what happens in such experiments!*

*Instead, between two thirds of the offers are between 40 and 50 per cent of the total sum. Only four in 100 people offer less than 20 per cent. Also more than half of all responders reject offers that are less than 20 per cent.*

*The motive of the person making the offer may be mixed. On the one hand, he may be concerned with what he thinks is fair. On the other hand, he may know that very small offers are likely to be refused because the responder will react strongly to what she perceives as an unfair offer.*

*But the motivation of the responder is not so complicated. She either accepts or rejects whatever offer she receives. According to maximization theory, there is a puzzle here: why should anyone reject* *an offer as 'too small'? The responder has just two choices: take what is offered or receive nothing at all. The only rational option for a maximizing individual is to accept any offer. Even $1 is better than nothing. A maximizing proposer who is also sure that the responder is also a maximizer will therefore make the smallest possible offer. In response, the responder will accept any offer greater than zero. The predictions of maximizing theory are clear on this one: offer as little as possible and accept anything positive, no matter how meagre.*

*The resolution of the puzzle in the case of both players is that they care about fairness almost as much as they care about doing as well as they can for themselves.*

*The scenario just described, called the Ultimatum Game, belongs to a small but rapidly expanding field called experimental economics. . . . For a long time, theoretical economists postulated a being called* Homo economicus—*a rational individual relentlessly bent on maximizing a purely selfish reward. But the lesson from the Ultimatum Game and similar experiments is that real people are a cross-breed of* Homo economicus *and* Homo emoticus, *a complicated hybrid species that can be ruled as much by emotion as by cold logic and selfishness. . . .*

*Centuries ago philosophers such as David Hume and Jean-Jacques Rousseau emphasized the crucial role of 'human nature' in social interactions. Theoretical economists, in contrast, long preferred to study the selfish* Homo economicus. *They theorized about how an isolated individual—a Robinson Crusoe on some desert island—would choose among different bundles of commodities. We are, however, not Robinson Crusoes. Our ancestors' line has been social for hundreds of millions of years. And in social interactions, our preferences turn out to be far from selfish. (Sigmund, Fehr, and Nowak 2002).*

The above extract does not imply that the assumption that individuals maximize their own utility or self-interest is useless. In everyday decisions, such as how many potatoes or holidays in Switzerland to buy, self-interest explains behaviour quite well. But the self-interest assumption is not applicable to many forms of group behaviour. We care about others as well as ourselves, and we also care about what others think of us. This often affects our behaviour, altering it from what a purely selfish individual would do.[12]

# Conclusion

The demand curves for most products have negative slopes. Knowledge of the precise nature of the demand curve for a product is obviously important for firms that want to be able to predict the likely quantity demanded at various prices. An understanding of demand is also important for policy-makers, who might wish to impose taxes, intervene in markets in other ways, or predict the effects of sudden shortages of such things as food or energy. For economists, an understanding of demand is one important step along the road to understanding the detailed workings of a market economy.

---

[12] For a fascinating discussion of the wider implications of altruistic behaviour, see Barber (2004).

# SUMMARY

### Early insights

- Consumers will maximize utility where the ratio of marginal utility to price is equal for all products.

- The paradox of value can be resolved when it is realized that marginal utilities and not total utilities determine market price.

### Consumer optimization without measurable utility

- Indifference theory assumes only that individuals can order alternative consumption bundles, saying which bundles are preferred to which but not by how much.

- A single indifference curve shows combinations of products that give the consumer equal satisfaction, and among which he is therefore indifferent. An indifference map is a set of indifference curves.

- The basic assumption about tastes in indifference curve theory is that of a diminishing marginal rate of substitution: the less of one good and the more of another good the consumer has, the less willing she will be to give up some of the first good to get more of the second. This implies that indifference curves are negatively sloped and convex to the origin.

- While indifference curves describe the consumer's tastes, and therefore refer to what he or she *would like* to purchase, the budget line describes what the consumer *can* purchase.

- Each consumer achieves an equilibrium that maximizes his satisfaction at the point at which an indifference curve is tangent to his budget line.

### The consumer's response to price and income changes

- The income–consumption line shows how quantity consumed changes as income changes with relative prices constant.

- The price–consumption line shows how quantity consumed changes as relative prices change. The consumer will normally consume more of the product whose relative price falls.

- The price–consumption line, relating the purchases of one particular product to all other products, contains the same information as an ordinary demand curve. The horizontal axis measures quantity, and the slope of the budget line measures price. Transferring this information to a diagram whose axes represent price and quantity leads to a conventional demand curve.

### The consumer's demand curve

- A change in price of one product, all other prices and money income constant, changes both relative price and the real incomes of those who consume it. The effect of changes on consumption is measured by the substitution effect and the income effect.

- Demand curves for normal goods have negative slopes because both income and substitution effects work in the same direction, a decrease in price leading to increased consumption.

- A decrease in price of an inferior good leads to more consumption via the substitution effect and less consumption via the income effect. In the exceptional case of a Giffen good, the income effect more than offsets the substitution effect, causing the product's demand curve to have a positive slope.

# TOPICS FOR REVIEW

- Marginal and total utility
- The paradox of value
- An indifference curve and an indifference map
- Slope of an indifference curve and diminishing marginal rate of substitution
- Budget line
- Absolute and relative prices, and the slope of the budget line

- Response of a consumer to changes in income and prices
- Derivation of the demand curve from indifference curves
- Income and substitution effects
- Hicks and Slutsky decomposition
- Normal goods, inferior goods, and Giffen goods
- Equivalent and compensating variations of income

# QUESTIONS

1 Suppose a consumer's disposable income is £200 per week and she has a choice between spending this on meals and concerts. Concerts are £10 each and meals are £20 each. List the possible combinations of meals and concerts that could be bought with the income.

2 Using the same information as in question 1, the price of meals now falls to £10. What combinations of meals and concerts can now be purchased with the same income?

3 Assuming that (facing the prices in question 1) the consumer chose to consume 10 concerts and 5 meals per week, what change in income would leave the consumer still just able to consume this same combination of meals and concerts while facing the prices set in question 2? Would you expect this consumer to purchase the same combination of meals and concerts as before if faced by the new prices but with income lower by this amount?

4 Which of the following statements is true (there may be more than one or none)?

 If the price of good X rises holding all other prices and income constant:

 (a) the substitution effect alone will make a consumer buy more of X if X is inferior.

 (b) the income effect alone will make a consumer buy more of X if it is a normal good.

 (c) the income effect alone will make a consumer buy less of X if it an inferior good.

 (d) the substitution effect will make a consumer buy less of X and it is irrelevant whether X is a normal or inferior good.

 (e) the consumer will buy less of good X unless it is an inferior good, in which case she will always buy more.

5 Explain the difference between the income effect and substitution effect of a price change.

6 What is a Giffen good? Explain, using indifference curves, how it could arise.

7 Indifference curve analysis is not much use because it only tells us that demand curves slope down except when they don't. Discuss.

8 A company that normally pays its workers £400 per week in money decides to pay them instead with £400 worth of a specific good. Assume that there is no second-hand market in these goods, so that they cannot be sold for cash, but also assume that the workers would choose to consume some of these goods anyway. Using budget constraints and indifference curves, analyse whether the workers are likely to be just as happy with this arrangement as they were when they received their wages in money.

# PART TWO

# MARKETS AND FIRMS

# Chapter 6

# THE COST STRUCTURE OF FIRMS

In Chapter 1 we discussed how the price system coordinates the actions of large numbers of independent agents: consumers and producers. How does this system induce firms to produce the things consumers want? Can firms exploit consumers by changing more or less any price they wish? How do firms respond to changes in costs and in demand? These are questions about the supply decisions of firms that we will analyse in this and the next three chapters. Here we focus mainly on the cost structures of firms.

In particular, you will learn that:

- Real-world firms can adopt one of several different legal structures, but for most of our analysis in this book firms are assumed to have a very simple structure.

- There is a difference between economists' measure of profit and accountants' measure of profit.

- For economists, profit is the difference between total cost and total revenue, where total cost includes the opportunity cost of owners' capital.

- The production function relates physical quantities of inputs to the quantity of output.

- Cost curves show the money cost of producing various levels of output.

- In the version of the theory of the firm we develop here, the short-run cost curve is U-shaped because some inputs are being held constant and the law of diminishing returns applies to those that are allowed to vary.

- The long-run cost curve can take on various shapes depending on the scale effects when all inputs are allowed to vary at once.

- Costs in the very long run are altered by technical change.

We begin by comparing the firms that we see in the real world with those that we shall assume for the purposes of our analysis throughout this book. We then introduce the concepts of costs, revenues, and profits, and outline the key role that profits play in determining which goods and services get produced. In order to identify the most profitable level of production for a firm, we need to see how its costs vary with its output. This we do in the last three sections of the chapter. The first of these deals with the short run, when a firm can vary only some of its inputs and output is governed by the famous '*law of diminishing returns*'. The third section deals with the long run, when the firm can alter all of its inputs. Here we pay special attention to scale economies, where increases in total output lead to reductions in the cost of producing each unit of output. In the final section, we discuss how firms alter their production capabilities by research and development, in response to such economic signals as rising costs of particular inputs.

## Firms in practice and theory

The firm is the agent in the economy that makes decisions about the production of specific goods or services in which it specializes.

## Firms in reality

Real-world firms come in many sizes and shapes. The most important distinction is between firms, sole traders, and ordinary partnerships, where the owners bear full liability for everything that the firm does, and those, mainly joint-stock, companies where the owners' liability is restricted to the amount of money they have invested in the firm. The details of the various ways of organizing firms are covered in more detail in Box 6.1

The finance that firms need to carry on their business is provided in two basic ways: through **equity**, i.e. funds

---

   **Box 6.1  Organization of producers**

The majority of production in a market economy is in the hands of firms. These can be organized in any one of five different ways. A **single proprietorship**, or **sole trader**, has one owner–manager who is personally responsible for everything that is done. A **partnership** has two or more joint owners, each of whom is personally responsible for all of the partnership's debts. A **limited partnership**, which is less common than ordinary partnerships, provides for two types of partner. *General partners* take part in the running of the business and are liable for all the firm's debts. *Limited partners* take no part in the running of the business, and their liability is limited to the amount they actually invest in the enterprise.* A **joint-stock company** (called a *corporation* in the United States) is a firm regarded in law as having an identity of its own; its owners are not personally responsible for anything that is done in the name of the firm, though its directors may be.

In the United Kingdom joint-stock companies are indicated either by the initials plc after the firm's name, standing for *public limited company*, or by Ltd (limited), which indicates a *private* limited-liability company. 'Private' in this context means that its shares are not traded on any stock exchange, while 'public' means that shares are traded on some public exchange. In the UK many limited companies are wholly owned subsidiaries of plcs, while most plcs own many subsidiary companies. A **public corporation** is set up to run a nationalized industry. It is owned by the state but is usually under the direction of a more or less independent, state-appointed board. Although its ownership differs, the organization and legal status of such a public corporation are similar to those of a joint-stock company.

A sixth type of organization, one that does not involve firms, comprises those governmental or charitable institutions that provide free goods and services, such as hospitals and schools. These are an important part of the economy, but we do not include them in our study of 'firms' as they typically provide their product free, while their costs are met out of general taxation. Their output therefore is not part of the market sector of the economy (though many of their input purchases will be).

Joint-stock companies that have operations in more than one country are often called **multinational enterprises (MNEs)**, or **transnational corporations (TNCs)**. Their number has been increasing steadily over the years. Although large firms still dominate the TNC scene, the role of medium-sized and small TNCs is significant and growing.

In 2001 there were about 60,000 TNCs in the world and they controlled about 820,000 foreign affiliates.[†] Ninety per cent of these TNCs are headquartered in developed countries; the three major home bases being the EU, Japan, and the United States. Together they owned a stock of about $6 trillion worth of direct foreign investments, about 20 per cent of which are in developing countries.

There are many reasons for a company to transfer some of its production beyond its home base (thereby becoming a TNC) rather than producing everything at home and then exporting the output. First, products become more sophisticated and differentiated; locating production in large local markets allows more flexible responses to local needs than can be achieved through centralized production 'back home'. Second, trade barriers make location in large foreign markets, such as the United States and the European Union, less risky than sending exports from the home base. Third, many TNCs are in the rapidly developing service industries such as advertising, marketing, public management, accounting, law, and financial services, where a physical presence is needed to produce a service in any country. Fourth, the computer and communications revolutions have allowed components of any one product to be manufactured in many countries, each component being made where its production is cheapest.

The globalization of production has brought benefits to many less developed countries. They have gained increasing employment at wages that are low by world standards but high by their own. As the United Nations put it, 'the growth of TNCs is one of the major channels by which economic change is spread throughout the world'.

---

\* Limited partnerships are used mainly for high-tech start-ups, where inventors have full liability and backers risk only what they have invested. However, it is in the interest of the general partner (inventor) to convert to 'Ltd' status fairly quickly.

† The data source is *World Investment Report* (UNCTAD 2001).

provided by the owners, and **debt**, i.e. funds borrowed from outside the firm. For a sole trader and a partnership, the owners provide the equity. A joint-stock company acquires its equity from its owners in return for stocks, shares, or equities (as they are variously called). These are basically ownership certificates. The money goes to the company and the shareholders become owners of the firm, risking the loss of their money, and gaining the right to share in the firm's profits. Profits that are paid out to shareholders are called **dividends**.

One easy way for an established firm to raise equity funds is to retain current profits rather than pay them out to shareholders. Financing investment from *undistributed profits* has become an important source of funding in modern times. Reinvested profits add to the value of the firm, and hence raise the market value of existing shares.

The second main way in which funds can be acquired is through borrowing funds from an external lender, which creates debt. Two characteristics are common to all forms of debt. First, there is an obligation to repay the amount borrowed, called the **principal** of the loan. Second, there is an obligation to pay **interest** to the lender. The day when the principal is to be repaid is called the **redemption date** or *maturity date* of the debt. The amount of time between the issue of the debt and its redemption date is called its **term**. There are many different forms of loan agreement. Some involve a financial intermediary such as a bank, which lends money to firms. Others involve the issuance of **debt instruments**, such as **bonds**. Box 6.2 discusses a variety of different forms of

these debt instruments. For simplicity, later in this book we refer to all forms of interest-bearing debt instrument (including bank loans) as *bonds*.

Firms are in business to make profits. They earn income by making and selling goods and services, but they must pay all their costs of production. The cost of labour includes wages, pension contributions, and other payments that must be made whenever labour is employed. In addition to the wage bill, firms have also to pay the cost of interest on debts, the cost of goods and services bought from other firms, and the cost of any rented inputs such as land and buildings. Firms must also impute costs for using their own capital equipment such as buildings, machinery, and office equipment. This cost, which is called *depreciation*, is correctly measured by the reduction in the value of the assets that will occur if the firm uses them over the period in question. After deducting all these costs, the remainder is what firms call their profits. This is the return to their owners' capital. Some of this may be distributed to the shareholders in the form of dividends while the rest is retained for reinvestment. If the investments are sound, the value of the firm increases and this adds to the owners' capital.

## Firms in theory

In Chapter 3 we defined the firm as the unit that takes decisions regarding the production and sale of goods and services. This theoretical concept of the firm includes all types of business organization, from sole trader to joint-

---

 **Box 6.2  Kinds of debt instrument**

Most debt instruments can be grouped into three broad classes. First, some debt is in the form of *loans* from financial institutions. These are private agreements between the firm and the institution, usually calling for the periodic payment of interest and repayment of the principal, either at a stipulated future date or 'on demand', meaning whenever the lending institution requests repayment.

Second, *bills* and *notes* are commonly used for short-term loans of up to a year. They carry no fixed interest payments, only a principal value and a redemption date. Interest arises because the borrowing firm sells the new bills that it issues at a price below their redemption value. If, for example, a bill promising to pay £1,000 in one year's time is sold to a lender for £950, this gives the lender an interest payment of £50 in one year's time when the bill that he bought for £950 is redeemed for £1,000. This makes an interest rate of 5.26 per cent per year ((50/950) × 100). Bills are *negotiable or marketable*, which means they can be

bought and sold. So if I buy a 90-day bill from some firm and want my money back 30 days later, I can sell the bill on the open market. The purchaser must be prepared to assume the loan to the firm for the 60 days that it still has to run, or else can sell it on to another party before maturity.

The third type of instrument carries a fixed redemption date, like a bill, and the obligation to make periodic interest payments, like most loans. These instruments have many different details and correspondingly many different names, such as *bonds*, *stocks*, or *debentures*. They are commonly used for long-term loans—up to 20 or 30 years. A firm that issues a 7 per cent 30-year instrument of this sort with redemption value of £1,000 is borrowing money now and promising to pay £70 a year for 30 years and then to pay £1,000. All such instruments are negotiable. This is important, because few people would be willing to lend money for such long periods of time if there were no way to get it back before the redemption date.

**Box 6.3** **The boundaries of the firm**

If firms require some specific input such as a specialized part, or a service such as cleaning their shop floor, they have two options. Either they can do it themselves—making the part or providing their own service—or they can buy what they need from some other firm. The boundary between what firms do for themselves and what they buy from outside differs among firms and changes over time. Why is this so?

The answer was provided by British-born economist Ronald Coase, who received the 1991 Nobel Prize in economics for this, and other, path-breaking work. His analysis is based on the concept of **transaction costs**, which are the costs associated with all market transactions. For example, when a firm purchases some good or service, it must identify the market and then find what different quantities and qualities are available at what prices. This takes time and money, and it usually involves some uncertainty. When the firm decides to do the job itself 'in house', it uses the *command principle*: it orders the product to be made, or the service to be performed, to its desired specifications. The market transaction costs are avoided, but the advantages of buying in a competitive market are lost. Furthermore, as the firm gets larger, the inefficiencies of the command system tend to rise relative to efficiencies involved in decentralizing decision-taking through the market system.

All firms must choose when to transact internally and when to transact through the market. For example, a car manufacturer must decide whether to purchase a certain component from an independent parts manufacturer or to produce the component itself. Most firms do both, buying many of their components from other firms and producing others for themselves.

Coase's insight was to see the firm as an institution that economizes on transaction costs. The market works best when transaction costs are low. When transaction costs are high, there is an incentive for the firm to reduce these by using the internal mechanisms of the command system in place of market transactions.

Firms exist as an alternative to a pure market structure of transactions. Inside a firm there is a command economy. Managers of firms have always to be asking what activities should be done inside the firm and what should be obtained in the market from other suppliers.

Changes in technology alter the relative advantages of these two types of activity. For example, the modern information and communications revolution, centred on the computer and the internet, has greatly reduced the transaction costs associated with many market activities. So the costs of obtaining things through the market have fallen relative to the costs of doing them in-house. As a result, firms do many fewer things in-house than they used to do. Instead, they 'contract out' both the production of many parts and the performance of many services. Large firms are then able to concentrate on what they call their 'core competencies', the main things they do. Smaller firms that specialize in producing single services, such as lift maintenance, office cleaning, accounting, and product design, are often able to perform these services more efficiently than a large multipurpose business unit can.

---

stock company. It also covers the whole variety of business sizes and methods of financing, from the single inventor operating in his garage and financed by whatever he can extract from a reluctant bank manager, to vast undertakings with many thousands of shareholders and customers.

To theorize about the firm we make two key assumptions.[1] First, all firms are profit-maximizers, seeking to make as much profit for their owners as is possible. Second, each firm can be regarded as a single, consistent decision-taking unit.

The desire to maximize profits is assumed to motivate all decisions taken within a firm, and such decisions are assumed to be unaffected by the peculiarities of the people taking the decisions and by the organizational structure in which they work.

These assumptions allow us to ignore the firm's internal organization and its financial structure. They also allow us to derive predictions about the behaviour of firms. To do this, we first study the choices open to the firm, establishing the effect that each choice would have on the firm's profits. We then predict that the firm will select the alternative that produces the largest profit. Box 6.3 discusses the determinants of what firms produce internally and what they buy from others.

---

[1] The approach is known as the *neoclassical theory* of the firm.

# Production, costs, and profits

We must now define a little more precisely the concepts of production, costs, and profits that we need for our analysis of the firm.

## Production

In order to produce the goods or services that it sells, each firm needs inputs. Hundreds of inputs enter into the production of any specific output. Among the many inputs entering into car production, for example, are sheet steel, rubber, spark plugs, electricity, the work space of the factory, machinists, cost accountants, spray-painting machines, forklift trucks, painters, and managers. These can be grouped into four broad classes: (1) inputs to the car firm that are outputs from some other firm, such as spark plugs, electricity, and sheet steel; (2) inputs provided directly by nature, such as land and air; (3) efforts of people, such as the services of workers and managers; and (4) the use of plant and machines.

The items that make up the first class of inputs, goods and services produced by other firms, are called **intermediate products**. These appear as inputs only because different firms are involved at different stages of production. For example, one firm mines iron ore and sells it to a steel manufacturer. Iron ore is an intermediate product: an output of the mining firm and an input for the steel plant. The output of the steel maker is then an input for the car manufacturer.

If all production were in the hands of a single firm, there would be no intermediate inputs. In this case, or if we merely view the entire chain of production as a whole, all production can be accounted for by the services listed as (2)–(4) above. These were first discussed in Chapter 1 as the gifts of nature, such as soil and raw materials, called *land* (item 2 above); physical and mental efforts provided by people, called *labour* (item 3 above); and the services of factories, machines, and other man-made aids to production, called *capital* (item 4 above). These are traditionally called *factors of production*, though we also refer to them more simply as *inputs*.

The **production function** relates inputs to outputs. It describes the technological relation between the inputs that a firm uses and the output that it produces. A production function is written as

$$q = \psi(f_1, \ldots, f_m), \tag{1}$$

where $q$ is the quantity of output of some good or service and $f_1, \ldots, f_m$ are the quantities of $m$ different inputs used in its production, everything being expressed as rates per period of time. The Greek letter $\psi$ (psi) tells us that $q$ is a function of the $f$s; that is, the $f$s determine $q$.

When using the production function, remember that it relates flows of inputs to flows of outputs: so many units *per period of time*. For example, if it is said that production rises from 100 to 101 units, this does not mean that 100 units are produced this month and 1 unit next month: rather, it means that the rate of production has risen from 100 units *each month* to 101 units *each month*.

## Costs and profits

Real firms arrive at what they call profits by taking the revenues they obtain from selling their output and deducting all the costs associated with their inputs, including depreciation of their own capital. When all costs have been correctly deducted, the resulting 'profits' are the return to owners' capital.

In economics the concepts of costs and profits differ from that used by firms because economists count the opportunity cost of the owner's capital as part of the firm's costs. This opportunity cost is not just the depreciation of the capital, but also includes an estimate of what the capital, and any other special advantages owned by the firm, could have earned in their best alternative uses. When this larger set of costs is deducted from revenues, the remainder is called **pure** or **economic profits**—or, where there is no room for ambiguity, simply **profit**.

The owners' opportunity cost of the financial capital that they have tied up in their firm can be divided into two parts. The first part can be determined by asking what could be earned by lending that capital to someone else in a riskless loan. For example, the firm could have purchased a government bond, which has no significant risk of default. Suppose the return on this is 6 per cent per annum. This rate is called the **pure return**, or risk-free rate of return on capital. It is clearly an opportunity cost, since the firm could close down operations, lend out its money, and earn a 6 per cent return. To determine the second part of the opportunity cost, ask what the firm could earn in addition to this amount by lending its money to another firm where risk of default was equal to the firm's own risk of loss. Say this is an additional 5 per cent. This is called the **risk premium**, and it is clearly also a cost. If the firm does not expect to earn this much in its own operations, it could close down and lend its money out to some other

**Table 6.1** Profit and loss account for XYZ Company for the year ending 31 December 2008

| Expenditure | | Income | |
|---|---|---|---|
| *Variable costs* | | | |
| Wages | £200,000 | Revenue from sales | £1,000,000 |
| Materials | 300,000 | | |
| Other | 100,000 | | |
| Total VC | 600,000 | | |
| *Fixed costs* | | | |
| Rent | 50,000 | | |
| Managerial salaries | 60,000 | | |
| Interest on loans | 90,000 | | |
| Depreciation allowance | 50,000 | | |
| Total FC | 250,000 | | |
| Total costs | 850,000 | | |
| Profit | | | 150,000 |

**The profit and loss account shows profits as defined by the firm.** The table gives a simplified version of a real profit and loss statement. The total revenue earned by the firm, minus what it regards as costs, yields profits. (Note that costs are divided into those that vary with output, called variable costs, and those that do not, called fixed costs. This distinction is discussed later in this chapter.)

**Table 6.2** Calculation of pure profits

| | |
|---|---|
| Profit as reported by the firm | £150,000 |
| *Opportunity cost of capital* | |
| Pure return on the firm's capital | –100,000 |
| Risk premium | –40,000 |
| Pure or economic profit | 10,000 |

**The economist's definition of profit excludes the opportunity cost of capital.** To arrive at the economist's definition of profit, the opportunity cost of capital—the return on a riskless investment plus any risk premium—must be deducted from the firm's definition of profit. What is left is pure profit.

Since there are two different concepts, it would be better if two different terms were used to denote them. But we are stuck with the fact that in economics we are using a slightly different definition of 'profit' than that used by firms and accountants. When there is any possibility of confusion, we speak of 'economic' or 'pure profit'. It is a standard convention in academic economics to use the word 'profit' to mean the return to the firm over and above all costs including the opportunity cost of capital (the pure risk-free return *and* the risk premium).[3]

Neither of the two alternative definitions of profit is better or worse than the other: instead, each is appropriate for different purposes. Firms are interested in the return to their owners and seek to maximize this, which is what they call profit. They must also conform to tax laws and accounting standards, which define profit this way. In contrast, in economics we are interested in how profits affect resource allocation, and the definition we use is best for that purpose.[4]

### Profits and resource allocation

When resources are valued by the opportunity-cost principle, their costs show how much these resources would earn if they were used elsewhere in the economy. If the revenues of all the firms in some industry exceed opportunity cost, the firms in that industry will be earning pure

equal-risk use earning 11 per cent (6 per cent pure return plus 5 per cent risk premium).[2]

Tables 6.1 and 6.2 compare the concepts of cost and profit as used by firms in practice and in economic analysis. (Notice that Table 6.1 divides the firm's costs between those that vary with output, called *variable costs*, and those that do not, called *fixed costs*, a distinction that is considered in detail later in this chapter.)

What firms call profit is the return to the owners' capital. In economics we deduct from this profit figure the imputed opportunity cost of the owners' capital (and any marketable special advantages owned by the firm) to obtain pure or economic profits.

---

[2] A firm may also own a valuable patent or a highly desirable location, or a popular brand name such as Gucci, Rolex, Polo, or Porsche. Each of these involves an opportunity cost to the firm in production (even if it was acquired free), because if the firm did not choose to use the special advantage itself, it could sell or lease it to others. The firm must, therefore, impute a charge to itself for using the special advantage.

---

[3] An alternative terminology avoids the potential confusion arising from using the same term to refer to two different things. You may encounter it elsewhere, since it is still used in some elementary textbooks—but seldom in more advanced theory. This terminology calls the opportunity cost of capital *normal profit*. Any excess of revenue over normal profits is then called *supernormal profit*.

[4] Note that any activity that maximizes one concept of profit also maximizes the other. The only difference is that, by subtracting the opportunity cost of capital from the firm's concept of profit, economists make positive or negative pure profit the signal for resources to enter or leave an industry.

profits; that is, the returns will be higher than in other industries with comparable risks. Thus, the owners of resources will want to move into this industry, because the earnings potentially available to them are greater there than in alternative activities. If, in some other industry, firms are incurring economic losses, some or all of this industry's inputs will earn higher rewards by moving to new activities.

**Profits and losses play a crucial signalling role in the workings of a free-market system.**

Positive profits in an industry are the signal that resources can profitably be moved into the industry. Losses are the signal that the resources can profitably be moved elsewhere. Only if there are zero economic profits is there no incentive for resources to move into or out of an industry.

## Profit-maximizing output

To develop a theory of supply, we need to determine the level of output that will maximize a firm's profit, to which we give the symbol $\pi$ (the lower-case Greek letter pi). This is the difference between the revenue each firm derives from the sale of its output, $R$, and the cost of producing that output, $C$:

$$\pi = R - C.$$

Thus, what happens to profit as output varies depends on what happens to revenue and costs. In the rest of this chapter we analyse how input costs vary with output. This analysis is common to all firms, irrespective of the market structure in which they operate. In the chapters that follow we consider how revenue varies with output. Costs and revenues are then combined to determine the profit-maximizing equilibrium for firms in various market situations. The resulting theory can then be used to predict the outcome of changes in such things as demand, costs, taxes, and subsidies. This may seem like quite a long route to get to a theory of supply, *and it is*—but the payoff when you get there is that you will be able to understand a big part of the working of a market economy.

We start with inputs. Suppose that a firm wishes to increase its rate of output. To do so, it must increase the use of at least some of its inputs. For the rest of this chap-

ter, we consider a very simple example relating to the production of some manufactured product. However, the approach is the same for any product. Even in service industries, for example, there will be various inputs that are combined to produce the output. A haircut requires the labour of a hairdresser (or barber) plus the services of a chair, shop space, scissors, dryers, basins, mirrors, electricity, hair spray, etc. Practically any business you can think of involves the combination of human effort (labour), some equipment or tools (capital), and some materials (intermediate inputs).

To keep things as simple as possible, we analyse a hypothetical firm that has only two inputs. The first is labour, to which we give the symbol $L$. The second is capital, to which we give the symbol $K$. This means that we are ignoring land and all intermediate inputs[5] and are dealing with the simplified version of the production function introduced earlier in this chapter:

$$q = \psi(L, K), \tag{2}$$

where $q$ is quantity of output per period of time, $L$ is labour employed in production (measured as worker hours per period—10 men working an 8-hour day is 80 worker-hours per day), and $K$ is units of capital services used (measured as machine-hours per period). The Greek letter $\psi$ again stands for the relationship that links the inputs to the outputs; here it links $K$ and $L$ to $q$.

A firm cannot vary all of its inputs with equal speed. It can usually vary labour at short notice, but time is needed to install more machinery or buildings. To capture the fact that different inputs cannot be varied with the same ease, we abstract from the more complicated nature of real decisions and think of each firm as making three distinct types of decision: (1) how best to employ its existing plant and equipment; (2) what new plant, equipment, and production processes to select, using currently available technology; and (3) what to do about encouraging the development of new technology. The first set of decisions is said to be made over the *short run*; the second over the *long run*; and the third over the *very long run*.

---

[5] Nothing is lost by this simplification, as it is easy to generalize our results to the case of multiple inputs at a later stage.

# Costs in the short run

The **short run** is defined as the period of time over which some inputs, called **fixed factors** or *fixed inputs*, cannot be varied.[6] The input that is fixed in the short run is usually capital (such as plant and equipment), but it might be land, or the services of management, or even the supply of skilled, salaried labour. What matters for the analysis is that at least one significant input is fixed; it cannot be increased, and all of it must be used. The inputs that can be varied in the short run are called *variable inputs*, or **variable factors**.

The short run is not of the same real-time duration in all industries. In the electric power industry, for example, it takes three or more years to build new power stations, so an unforeseen increase in demand must be served as well as possible with the existing capital equipment for several years. At the other end of the scale, a machine shop can acquire new equipment in a few weeks, and so the short run is correspondingly short. The length of the short run is influenced by technological considerations such as how quickly equipment can be manufactured and installed. These things may also be influenced to some extent by the price the firm is willing to pay to increase its capacity quickly.

## Short-run variations in input

In the short run we are concerned with what happens to output and costs as more, or less, of the variable input is set to work with a given quantity of the fixed input. In the simplified production function given above, we assume that capital is fixed and labour is variable. Our firm starts with a fixed amount of capital equipment. It then contemplates using various amounts of labour to work with it. Table 6.3 shows three different ways of looking at how output varies with the quantity of the variable input. We now need to define some terms.

**Total product (*TP*)** means just what it says: the total amount produced during some period of time by all the inputs that the firm uses. If all but one of the inputs is held constant, the total product will change as the variable input is changed. This variation is illustrated in

Table 6.3 Total, average, and marginal products in the short run

| Quantity of labour (*L*) (1) | Total product (*TP*) (2) | Average product (*AP*) (3) | Marginal product (*MP*) (4) |
|---|---|---|---|
| 1 | 43 | 43 | 43 |
| 2 | 160 | 80 | 117 |
| 3 | 351 | 117 | 191 |
| 4 | 600 | 150 | 249 |
| 5 | 875 | 175 | 275 |
| 6 | 1,152 | 192 | 277 |
| 7 | 1,372 | 196 | 220 |
| 8 | 1,536 | 192 | 164 |
| 9 | 1,656 | 184 | 120 |
| 10 | 1,750 | 175 | 94 |
| 11 | 1,815 | 165 | 65 |
| 12 | 1,860 | 155 | 45 |

**The relation of output to changes in the quantity of the variable input can be looked at in three different ways.** Capital is assumed to be fixed at 10 units. As the quantity of labour increases, the rate of total output increases, as shown in column (2). The average product in column (3) is found by dividing the total product in column (2) by the labour requirement shown in the corresponding row of column (1). The marginal product is positioned between the rows because it refers to the change in output from one level of labour input to another.

column (2) of Table 6.3, which gives a total product schedule. Figure 6.1(i) shows such a schedule graphically. (The shape of the curve will be discussed shortly.)

**Average product (*AP*)** is the total product *per unit* of the variable input, which is labour in the present illustration:

$$AP = \frac{TP}{L}.$$

Average product is shown in column (3) of Table 6.3. Notice that as more of the variable input is used, average product first rises and then falls. We argue below that this is one likely pattern, but other patterns are possible. The point where average product reaches a maximum is called the *point of diminishing average returns*. In the table, average product reaches a maximum when 7 units of labour are employed.

---

[6] 'Factors' in this context refers to factors of production as defined above, not the common usage of the term to mean items of influence. We shall more commonly refer to factors of production as 'inputs', as this is a more familiar terminology for most readers.

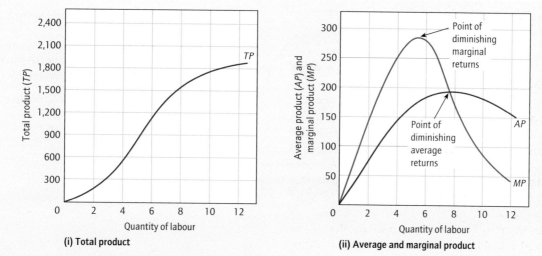

**Figure 6.1 Total, average, and marginal product curves**

Total product (*TP*), average product (*AP*), and marginal product (*MP*) curves often have these shapes. The curves are plotted from the data in Table 6.3. In part (i) the *TP* curve shows the total product steadily rising, first at an increasing rate, then at a decreasing rate. This causes both the average and the marginal product curves in part (ii) to rise at first and then decline. Where *AP* reaches its maximum, *MP* = *AP*.

Marginal product (*MP*) is the change in total product resulting from the use of one more (or one less) unit of the variable input:[7]

$$MP = \frac{\Delta TP}{\Delta L}$$

where Δ*TP* stands for the change in the total product and Δ*L* stands for the change in labour input that caused *TP* to change.

Computed values of the marginal product appear in column (4) of Table 6.3. Marginal product in the example reaches a maximum between *L* = 5 and *L* = 6 and thereafter declines. The level of output for which marginal product reaches a maximum is called the *point of diminishing marginal returns*.

Figure 6.1(ii) shows the average and marginal product curves plotted from the data in Table 6.3. Notice first that *MP* reaches its maximum at a lower level of *L* than does

*AP*, and second that *MP* = *AP* when *AP* is a maximum. These relations are discussed in more detail below.

Finally, bear in mind that the schedules of Table 6.3, and the curves of Figure 6.1, all assume a specified quantity of the fixed input that is fully used at all times. If the quantity of capital had been, say, 14 instead of the 10 units that were assumed, there would be a different set of total, average, and marginal product curves. The reason is that, if any specified amount of labour has more capital to work with, it can produce more output: its total, average, and marginal products will be greater.

### The law of diminishing returns

We now consider the variations in output that result from applying different amounts of a variable input to a given quantity of a fixed input. These variations are the subject of a famous hypothesis called the **law of diminishing returns**.

The law of diminishing returns states that, if increasing quantities of a variable input are applied to a given quantity of a fixed input, the marginal product, and the average product, of the variable input will eventually decrease.

The law of diminishing returns is consistent with marginal and average product curves that decline over the whole range of output (as illustrated in part (i) of Figure 6.2), or that increase for a while and diminish only later

---

[7] Strictly speaking, the text defines what is called 'incremental product', that is, the rate of change of output associated with a discrete change in an input. Marginal product refers to the rate at which output is tending to vary as input varies at a particular output. Students familiar with calculus will recognize the marginal product as the partial derivative of the total product with respect to the variable input. In symbols, $MP = \partial q/\partial L$. In the text we refer only to finite changes, Δ*L* and Δ*TP*, but the phrase 'a change of one unit' should read 'a very small change'.

**Figure 6.2** Alternative average and marginal product curves

**According to the law of diminishing returns, average and marginal product must eventually decline as output increases.** The law of diminishing returns permits the average and marginal product curves to decline at all positive levels of output, as shown in part (i). The law also allows the average and marginal products to rise over an initial range of output and only then decline, as shown in part (ii).

(part (ii) of the same figure). The latter case arises when it is impossible to use the fixed input efficiently with only a small quantity of the variable input (if, say, one man was trying to farm 1,000 acres). In this case increasing the quantity of the variable input would make possible a more efficient division of labour, so that the addition of another unit of the variable input would make all units more productive than they were previously. According to the hypothesis of diminishing returns, the scope for such economies must eventually disappear, and sooner or later the marginal and average product of additional workers must decline.

Notice that, when various amounts of labour are applied to a fixed quantity of capital, the proportion in which the two types of input are used is being varied.

The law of diminishing returns is also called the 'law of variable proportions', because it predicts the consequences of varying the proportions in which input types are used.

The common sense of diminishing marginal product is that the fixed input limits the amount of additional output that can be obtained by adding more of the variable input. Were it not for the law of diminishing returns, there would be no need to fear that rapid population growth would cause food shortages in poorer countries. If the marginal product of additional workers employed on a fixed quantity of land were constant, then a country's food production could be expanded in proportion to the increase in population merely by keeping the same proportion of the population on farms. As it is, diminishing returns means an inexorable decline in the marginal product of each additional labourer as an expanding population is applied, with static techniques, to a fixed supply of agricultural land. Thus, unless there is a continual improvement in the techniques of production, a

population increase among subsistence farmers in a poor country must bring with it declining living standards.[8]

### The relation between marginal and average product curves

Notice that in Figure 6.2(ii) the *MP* curve cuts the *AP* curve at the latter's maximum point. It is important to understand why. The key is that the average product curve slopes upward as long as the marginal product curve is above it; it makes no difference whether the marginal curve is itself sloping upwards or downwards. The common sense of this relation is that, if an additional worker is to raise the average product of all workers, the worker's addition to total output must be greater than the average output of all existing workers. It is immaterial whether his contribution to output is greater or less than the contribution of the worker hired immediately before him: all that matters is that his contribution to output exceeds the average output of *all* the workers hired before him. Since *AP* slopes upwards or downwards depending on whether *MP* is above or below *AP*, it follows that *MP* must equal *AP* at the highest point on the *AP* curve.

This relationship between marginal and average values is a mathematical one that is thus not restricted to economics. A cricketer, for example, will raise his batting average if his next score is above his current average, and he will lower his average if his next score is below the current average.

---

[8] This has not happened everywhere in the world, because rapid technological advances have increased productivity in agriculture faster than population has increased. However, in many poorer countries farmers subsist mainly on what they themselves grow, and they use relatively static techniques. For them, rising population in combination with the law of diminishing returns means declining output per person and hence declining living standards.

# Short-run variations in cost

We have now seen how output varies with changes in just one of the inputs in the short run with a fixed amount of the other being used. By costing these inputs, we can discover how the cost of production changes as output varies. For the time being we consider firms that are not in a position to influence the prices of their inputs, so they take the prices of these inputs as given.

We now define cost concepts that are closely related to the product concepts introduced earlier.

**Total cost (*TC*)** means just what it says. It is the total cost of producing any given rate of output. Total cost is divided into two parts: total fixed costs (*TFC*) and total variable costs (*TVC*). **Fixed costs** are those costs that do not vary with output; they will be the same if output is 1 unit or 1 million units. These costs are also often referred to as *overhead costs* or *unavoidable costs*. All of those costs that vary positively with output, rising as more is produced and falling as less is produced, are called **variable costs**. In our present example, since labour is the variable input, the cost of labour is a variable cost. Variable costs are often referred to as *direct costs* or *avoidable costs*. The latter term is used because the costs can be avoided by not hiring the variable input.

**Average total cost (*ATC*)** is the total cost of producing any given output divided by the number of units produced, that is, the cost per unit. *ATC* may be divided into **average fixed costs (*AFC*)** and **average variable costs (*AVC*)** in just the same way as total costs were divided.

**Marginal cost (*MC*)** is the increase in total cost resulting from raising the rate of production by one unit. The marginal cost of the tenth unit, for example, is the change in total cost when the rate of production is increased from 9 to 10 units per period.

These three measures of cost are merely different ways of looking at a single phenomenon, and they are mathematically interrelated.[9] Which measure we use depends on the task in hand.

## Short-run cost curves

The relations just outlined are most easily understood if we show them as cost curves. To illustrate how this is done, we take the production relationships in Table 6.3 and assume that the price of labour is £20 per unit (worker hours) and the price of capital is £10 per unit (machine

hours). In Table 6.4 we present the cost schedules computed for these values. Figure 6.3(i) shows the total cost curves; Figure 6.3(ii) plots the marginal and average cost curves that are derived in Table 6.4.[10]

### How cost varies with output

Since total fixed cost (*TFC*) does not vary with output, average fixed cost (*TFC/q*) is negatively related to output, while marginal fixed cost is zero. In contrast, variable cost is positively related to output, since to produce more requires more of the variable input. Average variable cost may, however, be negatively or positively related to output. Marginal variable cost is always positive, indicating that it always costs something to increase output; but, as we will soon see, marginal cost may rise or fall as output rises.

Notice that the marginal cost curve cuts the *ATC* and *AVC* curves at their lowest points. This is another example of the relation (discussed above) between a marginal and an average value. The *ATC* curve, for example, slopes downwards as long as the marginal cost curve is below it; it makes no difference whether the marginal cost curve is itself sloping upwards or downwards.

In Figure 6.3 the average variable cost curve reaches a minimum and then rises. With fixed input prices, when average product per worker is at a maximum, average variable cost is at a minimum. The common sense is that each new worker adds the same amount to cost but a different amount to output, and when output per worker is rising the cost per unit of output must be falling, and vice versa.

Short-run *AVC* curves are often drawn U-shaped. This reflects the assumptions (1) that average productivity is increasing when output is low, but (2) that average productivity eventually begins to fall fast enough to cause average total cost to increase.

**The law of diminishing returns implies eventually increasing marginal and average variable cost.**

### The definition of capacity

The output that corresponds to the minimum short-run average total cost is very often called **capacity**. Capacity in this sense is not an upper limit on what can be produced, as you can see by looking again at Table 6.4. In the example, capacity output is between 1,536 and 1,656 units, but higher outputs can be achieved. A firm

---

[9] Mathematically, average total cost is total cost divided by output, while marginal cost is the first derivative of total cost with respect to output.

[10] The calculation here involves discrete changes, while calculating marginal values requires very small changes. We are therefore producing an approximation to the true marginal value calculated over a specific range.

**Table 6.4** Variation of costs with capital fixed and labour variable

| Inputs | | Output (q) | Total cost | | | Average cost | | | Marginal cost (MC)[d] |
|---|---|---|---|---|---|---|---|---|---|
| Capital (1) | Labour (L) (2) | (3) | Fixed (TFC) (4) | Variable (TVC) (5) | Total (TC) (6) | Fixed (AFC)[a] (7) | Variable (AVC)[b] (8) | Total (ATC)[c] (9) | (10) |
| 10 | 1 | 43 | £100 | £20 | £120 | £2.326 | £0.465 | £2.791 | £0.465 |
| | | | | | | | | | 0.171 |
| 10 | 2 | 160 | 100 | 40 | 140 | 0.625 | 0.250 | 0.875 | |
| | | | | | | | | | 0.105 |
| 10 | 3 | 351 | 100 | 60 | 160 | 0.285 | 0.171 | 0.456 | |
| | | | | | | | | | 0.080 |
| 10 | 4 | 600 | 100 | 80 | 180 | 0.167 | 0.133 | 0.300 | |
| | | | | | | | | | 0.073 |
| 10 | 5 | 875 | 100 | 100 | 200 | 0.114 | 0.114 | 0.228 | |
| | | | | | | | | | 0.072 |
| 10 | 6 | 1,152 | 100 | 120 | 220 | 0.087 | 0.104 | 0.191 | |
| | | | | | | | | | 0.091 |
| 10 | 7 | 1,372 | 100 | 140 | 240 | 0.073 | 0.102 | 0.175 | |
| | | | | | | | | | 0.122 |
| 10 | 8 | 1,536 | 100 | 160 | 260 | 0.065 | 0.104 | 0.169 | |
| | | | | | | | | | 0.167 |
| 10 | 9 | 1,656 | 100 | 180 | 280 | 0.060 | 0.109 | 0.169 | |
| | | | | | | | | | 0.213 |
| 10 | 10 | 1,750 | 100 | 200 | 300 | 0.057 | 0.114 | 0.171 | |
| | | | | | | | | | 0.308 |
| 10 | 11 | 1,815 | 100 | 220 | 320 | 0.055 | 0.121 | 0.176 | |
| | | | | | | | | | 0.444 |
| 10 | 12 | 1,860 | 100 | 240 | 340 | 0.054 | 0.129 | 0.183 | |

**The relation of cost to the rate of output can be looked at in several different ways.** These cost schedules are computed from the product curves of Table 6.3, given the price of capital of £10 per unit and the price of labour of £20 per unit. Marginal cost (in column (10)) is positioned between the other rows because it refers to the *change* in cost divided by the *change* in output that brought it about. Marginal cost is calculated by dividing the increase in costs by the increase in output when one additional unit of labour is used. This gives the increase in cost per unit of output over that range of output. For example, the MC of £0.08 is the increase in total cost of £20 (from £160 to £180) divided by the 249 unit increase in output (from 351 to 600). This tells us that when output goes from 351 to 600 (because labour inputs go from 3 to 4), the increase in costs is £0.08 per unit of output. In constructing a graph, marginal costs should be plotted midway in the interval over which they are computed. The MC of £0.08 would thus be plotted at output 475.5.

ᵃ Col. (4) ÷ col. (3).     ᶜ Col. (6) ÷ col. (3) = col. (7) + col. (8).
ᵇ Col. (5) ÷ col. (3).     ᵈ Change in col. (5) from one row to the next ÷ corresponding change in col. (3).

(i) Total cost curves

(ii) Marginal and average cost curves

**Figure 6.3** Total cost, average cost, and marginal cost curves

Total cost (TC), average cost (AC), and marginal cost (MC) curves often have the shapes shown here. These curves are plotted from Table 6.4. Total fixed cost does not vary with output. Total variable cost and the total of all costs (TC = TVC + TFC) rise with output, first at a decreasing rate, then at an increasing rate. The total cost curves in (i) give rise to the average and marginal curves in (ii). Average fixed cost (AFC) declines as output increases. Average variable cost (AVC) and average total cost (ATC) fall and then rise as output increases. Marginal cost (MC) does the same, intersecting the ATC and AVC curves at their minimum points. Capacity output is at the minimum point of the ATC curve, which is an output of 1,500 in this example.

**Box 6.4** Short-run cost curves when firms have excess capacity

Ever since economists began measuring the cost curves of manufacturing firms more than half a century ago, they have reported flat, short-run variable cost curves. The evidence is now clear that in most manufacturing industries, and in many services, cost curves are shaped like the *AVC* curve shown in the figure, with a long, flat portion and a rising section only after capacity output had been achieved. For such a cost curve, there is a large range of output over which average variable costs are constant and marginal and average costs are equal.

Why are many cost curves shaped like this rather than U-shaped? The answer is that firms design plants to have this property so that they can accommodate the inevitable seasonal and cyclical swings in demand for their products.

To see how a firm can choose the shape of its short-run average cost curve, consider again the law of diminishing returns. The U-shaped, short-run cost curve arises when a variable amount of one input, say labour, is applied to a fixed amount of a second input, say capital. Imagine starting from zero output and zero use of the variable input and then increasing output. As more of the variable input is used, a more nearly optimal combination with the fixed input is achieved. Once the optimal combination is obtained, the use of further units of the variable input will lead to too much of that input being used in combination with the fixed input. This will cause average variable costs to begin to rise. Only one quantity of labour leads to the least-cost input proportions.

These changing combinations of fixed and variable inputs must occur in the short run whenever all of the fixed input must be used all of the time—in other words, when the fixed input is *indivisible*. This, however, is not usually the case. Even though

the firm's plant and equipment may be fixed in the short run, so that *no more* than what exists is available, it is often possible to use *less than* this amount.

Consider, as a simple example, a factory that consists of 10 sewing machines in a shed, each of which has a productive capacity of 20 units per day when operated by one operator for one shift. If 200 units per day are required, then all 10 machines would be operated by 10 workers on a normal shift. If demand falls to 180, then one operator could be laid off. There is no need, however, to have the 9 remaining operators dashing about trying to work 10 machines. Clearly, one machine could be 'laid off' as well, leaving constant the ratio of *employed* labour to *employed* machines.

Production could go from 20 all the way to 200 units per day without any change in the proportions in which the employed inputs are used. In this case, we would expect the factory to have constant marginal and average variable costs from 20 to 200 units per day. Only beyond 200 units per day would it begin to encounter rising costs, because production would have to be extended by overtime and other means of combining more labour with the maximum available supply of 10 machines.

In such a case, the fixed input is *divisible*. Because some of it can be left unemployed, there is no need to depart from the most efficient ratio of *labour used* to *capital used* as production is decreased. The *divisibility* of the fixed input means that diminishing returns does not apply, because variations in output below full capacity are accomplished by reducing the input of both labour and capital. Thus, average variable costs can be constant over a large range, up to the point at which all of the fixed input is used.

A similar situation occurs when a firm has many plants. For example, a manufacturer with 10 plants may choose to reduce its output by temporarily closing one or more plants (or operating them on a limited-time basis) while operating the rest at normal-capacity output. Another firm can choose to put its factory on short time, working 6 hours a day or 4 days a week, thereby reducing its use of both capital and labour. In such cases the *firm's* short-run variable costs tend to be constant over a large range of output because there is no need to depart from the optimal combination of labour and capital in the plants that are kept in operation.

The figure shows the type of cost curve that is observed when the fixed input is divisible. At outputs below capacity, the *AVC* curve is flat because output is varied by using more or less labour and capital in constant proportions. When output reaches capacity, the fixed stock of capital is fully employed, and further increases in output can be achieved only at rising cost as more labour is applied to a fixed quantity of capital.

producing *below capacity* is producing at a rate of output less than the one for which average total cost is a minimum. A firm producing *above capacity* is producing more than this amount; it is thus incurring costs per unit of output

that are higher than the minimum achievable. Box 6.4 discusses the shape of short-run cost curves when firms can operate at below capacity output, a situation that many firms find themselves in much of the time.

### A family of short-run cost curves

A short-run cost curve shows how costs vary with output for a given quantity of the fixed input—say, a given size of fully used plant. A small plant for manufacturing nuts and bolts will have its own short-run cost curve. A medium-sized and a very large plant will each have their own short-run cost curves. If a firm expands by replacing its small plant with a medium-sized plant, it will move from one short-run cost curve to another.

There is a different short-run cost curve for each quantity of the fixed input.

This change from one size of plant to another is a long-run change. We now study how the short-run cost curves of different-sized plants are related to each other.

## Costs in the long run

In the short run, with only one input variable, there is only one way to produce a given output: by adjusting the use of the variable input until the optimal rate of output is achieved. Thus, once the firm has decided on a rate of output, there is only one technically possible way of achieving it.

By contrast, in the long run all inputs can be varied. The firm must decide both on a level of output *and* on the best input mix to produce that output. Specifically, this means that firms in the long run must choose the nature and amount of plant and equipment, as well as the size of their labour force.

Long-run decisions are risky because the firm must anticipate what methods of production will be efficient—not only today, but also for many years in the future, when the costs of labour and raw materials will no doubt have changed. The decisions are also risky because the firm must estimate how much output it will want to produce. Is the industry to which it belongs growing or declining? Will new products emerge to render its existing products less useful than an extrapolation of past sales suggests?

### Profit maximization and cost minimization

In making the choice of inputs, the profit-maximizing firm will wish to avoid being technically inefficient, which means using more of *all* inputs than is necessary. Being technically efficient is not enough, however. To be economically efficient the firm must choose, from among the many technically efficient options, the one that produces a given level of output at the lowest possible cost. This implication of the hypothesis of profit maximization is called **cost minimization**: from the alternatives open to it, the profit-maximizing firm will choose the least costly way of producing whatever specific output it chooses.

### Choice of input mix

If it is possible to substitute one input for another in such a way that output remains constant while total cost falls, the firm is not using the least-cost combination of inputs. The firm should then substitute one input for another input. Such cost-reducing substitutions are always possible whenever the marginal product of one input per £1 spent on it is greater than the marginal product of the other input per £1 spent on it. The firm has not minimized its costs as long as these two magnitudes are unequal. For example, if an extra £1 spent on labour adds more to output than an extra £1 spent on capital, the firm can reduce costs by spending less on capital and more on labour.

If we use $K$ to represent capital, $L$ to represent labour, and $P_K$ and $P_L$ to represent the prices of a unit of each, the necessary condition for cost minimization is as follows:

$$\frac{MP_K}{P_K} = \frac{MP_L}{P_L} \qquad (3)$$

Whenever the two sides of equation (3) are not equal, there are possibilities for input substitutions that will reduce costs.

To see why this equation must be satisfied if costs of production are to be minimized, consider a situation where the equation is not satisfied. Suppose, for example, that the marginal product of capital is 20 and its price is £2, making the left side of equation (3) equal to 10. Suppose that the marginal product of labour is 32 and its price is £8, making the right side of equation (3) equal to 4. Thus, the last £1 spent on capital adds 10 units to output, whereas the last £1 spent on labour adds only 4 units to output. In such a case the firm could maintain its output level and reduce costs by using £2.50 less of labour and spending £1.00 more on capital. Making such a substitution of capital for labour would leave output unchanged and would reduce costs by £1.50. Therefore, the original position was not cost-minimizing.[11]

We can take a different look at cost minimization by multiplying equation (3) by $P_K/MP_L$ to obtain

$$\frac{MP_K}{MP_L} = \frac{P_K}{P_L} \qquad (4)$$

The ratio of the marginal products on the left-hand side of the equation compares the contribution to output of the last unit of capital and the last unit of labour. If the ratio is 4, this means that 1 unit more of capital will add 4 times as much to output as 1 unit more of labour. The right-hand side of the equation shows how the cost of 1 unit more of capital compares with the cost of 1 unit more of labour. If the ratio is also 4, the firm cannot reduce costs by substituting capital for labour or vice versa. Now suppose that the ratio on the right-hand side of the equation is 2. Capital, which is four times as productive as labour, is now only twice as expensive. It will pay the firm to switch to a method of production that uses more capital and less labour. If, however, the ratio on the right-hand side is 6 (or *any* number greater than 4), it will pay to switch to a method of production that uses more labour and less capital.

We have seen that when the ratio $MP_K/MP_L$ exceeds the ratio $P_K/P_L$ the firm will substitute capital for labour. This substitution is measured by changes in the **capital–labour ratio**, which is the amount of capital per worker. So if the firm uses £1 million worth of capital and employs 100 workers, its capital–labour ratio is 10,000 (1,000,000/100), indicating that there is £10,000 worth of capital for each worker.

How far does the firm go in making this substitution? There is a limit, because the law of diminishing returns tells us that, as the firm uses more capital, the marginal product of capital falls, and as it uses less labour the marginal product of labour rises. Thus, the ratio $MP_K/MP_L$ falls. When it reaches 2, the firm does not need to substitute further. The ratio of the marginal products is equal to the ratio of the prices.

Equation (4) shows how the firm can adjust the elements over which it has control (the quantities of inputs used, and hence the marginal products of those inputs) according to the market prices of the inputs.

### Long-run equilibrium of the firm

The firm will have achieved its equilibrium capital–labour ratio when there is no further opportunity for cost-reducing substitutions. This occurs when the marginal product per pound spent on each input is the same (equation (3)) or, equivalently, when the ratio of the marginal products of inputs is equal to the ratio of their prices (equation (4)).

## The principle of substitution

Suppose that a firm is meeting the cost-minimizing conditions shown in equations (3) and (4) and that the cost of labour increases, while the cost of capital remains unchanged. The least-cost method of producing any output will now use less labour and more capital than was required to produce the same output before the input prices changed.

Methods of production will change if the relative prices of inputs change. Relatively more of the cheaper input and relatively less of the more expensive input will be used.

This is called the **principle of substitution**, and it follows from the assumption that firms minimize their costs.

The principle of substitution plays a central role in resource allocation, because it relates to the way in which individual firms respond to changes in relative input prices that are caused by the changing relative scarcities of factors of production in the economy as a whole. When some resource becomes scarcer to the economy as a whole, its price will tend to rise. This motivates individual firms to use less of that input. When some other input becomes more plentiful to the economy as a whole, its price will tend to fall. This motivates individual firms to use more of it. Firms need never know the relative national scarcities of the various factors of production. As long as relative prices reflect relative scarcities, firms will tend to substitute plentiful inputs for scarce inputs. They do this through their own cost-minimizing responses to the changes in the prices of their inputs. Box 6.5 discusses the broader significance of the principle of substitution.

## The long-run cost curve

When all inputs can be varied, there is a least-cost method of producing each possible level of output. Thus, with given input prices, there is a minimum achievable cost for each level of output; if this cost is expressed as a quantity per unit of output, we obtain the long-run average cost of producing each level of output. When this least-cost method of producing each output is plotted on a graph, the result is called a **long-run average cost curve** (*LRAC*). Figure 6.4 shows one such curve.

---

[11] The argument in this paragraph assumes that the marginal products do not change when expenditure changes by a small amount.

## Box 6.5 The economy-wide significance of the principle of substitution

In free markets, relative input prices reflect the relative scarcities (in relation to demand) of different factors of production. Abundant factors have prices that are low relative to the prices of factors that are scarce. Firms seeking their own private profit and responding to relative input prices will be led to make lavish use of the inputs with which the whole country is plentifully endowed, and to be frugal in their use of the inputs that are in scarce supply.

For example, a country with a great deal of land and a small population will experience a low price of its plentiful land and a high price of its scarce labour. Firms producing agricultural goods will tend to make lavish use of the cheap land and to economize on the expensive labour. In contrast, a small country with a large population will have expensive land and cheap labour. Firms producing agricultural goods will tend to economize on land by using a great deal of labour per unit of land.

In recent decades construction workers' wages have risen sharply relative to the wages of factory labour and the cost of machinery. In response, builders have shifted from on-site construction to *panelization*, a method of building that uses standardized modules. The wiring, plumbing, insulation, and painting of these standardized modules are all done at the factory. The bulk of the factory work is performed by machinery and by assembly-line workers whose wages are only half those of on-site construction workers.

These are examples of the price system operating as an automatic control mechanism. No single firm need be aware of national resource surpluses and scarcities. Since these are reflected in relative market prices, individual firms that never look beyond their own private profits are led to economize on inputs that are scarce in the nation as a whole. We should not be surprised, therefore, to discover that methods of producing the same product differ in different countries. In Europe, where labour is highly skilled and very expensive, a manufacturer may use very elaborate equipment to economize on labour. In China, where labour is abundant and capital scarce, a much less mechanized method of production may be appropriate. The Western engineer who feels that the Chinese are behind because they are using methods abandoned in the West as inefficient long ago may be missing the significance of economic efficiency.

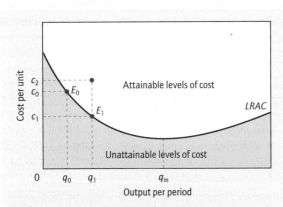

## Figure 6.4 A long-run average cost curve

The long-run average cost (*LRAC*) curve is the boundary between attainable and unattainable levels of cost. Since the lowest attainable cost of producing $q_0$ is $c_0$ per unit, the point $E_0$ is on the *LRAC* curve. Suppose a firm producing at $E_0$ desires to increase output to $q_1$. In the short run it will not be able to vary all inputs, and so unit costs above $c_1$, say $c_2$, must be accepted. In the long run, a plant that is the optimal size for producing output $q_1$ can be built and costs of $c_1$ can be attained. At output $q_m$ the firm attains its lowest possible per-unit cost of production for the given technology and input prices.

This cost curve is determined by the industry's current technology and by the prices of the inputs. It is a 'boundary' in the sense that points below it are unattainable; points on the curve, however, are attainable if sufficient time elapses for all inputs to be adjusted. To move from one point on the *LRAC* curve to another requires an adjustment in all inputs, which may, for example, require building a larger, more elaborate factory.

**The *LRAC* curve is the boundary between cost levels that are attainable, with known technology and given input prices, and those that are unattainable.**

Just as the short-run cost curves discussed earlier in this chapter are derived from the *production function* describing the physical relationship between inputs and output, so is the *LRAC* curve. The difference is that in deriving the *LRAC* curve there are no fixed inputs, so all inputs are treated as variable. Because all input costs are variable in the long run, we do not need to distinguish between average variable cost (*AVC*), average fixed cost (*AFC*), and average total cost (*ATC*), as we did in the short run. In the long run, there is only one long-run average cost (*LRAC*) for any given set of input prices.

### The shape of the long-run average cost curve

As the firm varies its output, average cost may vary for two distinct reasons. First, the prices of its inputs may change. Second, the physical relationship between its inputs and outputs may change. To separate these two effects, we assume for the moment that all input prices remain constant.

Now look at the *LRAC* curve shown in Figure 6.4. This curve is often described as U-shaped, although empirical studies suggest it is often 'saucer-shaped'.

### Decreasing costs

Over the range of output from zero to $q_m$, the firm has falling long-run average costs: an expansion of output permits a reduction of costs per unit of output. Technologies with this property are said to exhibit **economies of scale**. (Of course, when output is increased, such economies of scale will be realized only after enough time has elapsed to allow changes to be made in all inputs.) Recall that the prices of inputs are assumed to be constant for the moment. Therefore the decline in long-run average cost must occur because output is increasing *more than* in proportion to inputs as the scale of the firm's production expands. Over this range of output, the decreasing-cost firm is often said to enjoy long-run **increasing returns**. This is an extremely important phenomenon, and its sources are discussed in the next section. Ouput $q_m$ is called the **minimum efficient scale**, defined as the lowest level of output at which all scale economies are exploited.

### Increasing costs

Over the range of outputs greater than $q_m$, the firm encounters rising long-run unit costs. An expansion in production, even after sufficient time has elapsed for all adjustments to be made, will then be accompanied by a rise in average costs per unit of output. Since input prices are still assumed to be constant, the firm's output must be increasing *less than* in proportion to the increase in inputs. When this happens, the increasing-cost firm is said to encounter long-run **decreasing returns**. Decreasing returns imply that the firm is suffering some diseconomy of scale; as its scale of operations increases, diseconomies are encountered that increase its per-unit cost of production.

These diseconomies may be associated with the difficulties of managing and controlling an enterprise as its size increases. For example, planning problems do not necessarily vary in direct proportion to size. At first there may be scale economies as the firm grows, but sooner or later planning and co-ordination problems may multiply more than in proportion to the growth in size. If so, management costs per unit of output will rise. Another source of scale diseconomies concerns the possible alienation of the labour force as firm size increases. Also, providing appropriate supervision becomes difficult as more and more tiers of supervisors and middle managers come between the person at the top and the workers on the shop floor. Control of middle-range managers may also become more difficult. As the firm becomes larger, man-

agers may begin to pursue their own goals rather than devote all of their efforts to making profits for the firm. (This is the principal–agent problem, which is discussed in detail in Chapter 11.)

### Constant costs

In Figure 6.4 the firm's long-run average cost falls until output reaches $q_m$ and rises thereafter. Another possibility should be noted. The firm's *LRAC* curve might have a flat portion over a range of output around $q_m$. With such a flat portion, the firm would be encountering constant costs over the relevant range of output. This means that the firm's long-run average costs per unit of output do not change as its output changes. Because input prices are assumed to be fixed, the firm's output must be increasing *exactly in proportion to* the increase in inputs. A firm in this situation is said to be encountering **constant returns**.

## Sources of increasing returns

Whenever a firm finds that it can increase its output per unit of input, it is enjoying economies of large-scale production. These economies are important, and wherever they exist they encourage large plants and/or large firms. Three important sources of scale economies are geometrical relations, one-time costs, and the technology of large-scale production.

### Geometric relationships

One important source of scale economies lies in the geometry of our three-dimensional world. To illustrate how geometry matters, consider a firm that wishes to store liquid. The firm is interested in the *volume* of storage space. However, the amount of material required to build the container is related to the *area* of its surface. When the size of a container is increased, the storage capacity, which is determined by its volume, increases faster than its surface area.[12] This is a genuine case of increasing returns—the output, in terms of storage capacity, increases proportionately more than the increase in the costs of the required construction materials. Another of the many other similar effects concerns smelters. The heat loss is proportional to the smelter surface area, while the amount of ore smelted depends on its volume. Thus, there is a scale economy in heat needed per tonne of ore smelted as smelters get

---

[12] For example, consider a cubic container with metal sides, bottom, and lid, all of which measure 1 metre by 1 metre. To build this container, 6 m² of metal is required (six sides, each 1 m²), and it will hold 1 cubic metre of gas or liquid. Now increase all of the lengths of each of the container's sides to 2 m. Now 24 m² of metal is required (six sides, each 4 m²), and the container will hold 8 m³ of gas or liquid (2 m × 2 m × 2 m). So increasing the amount of metal in the container's walls fourfold has the effect of increasing its capacity eightfold.

larger. In practice, however, the size of the smelter is limited by the need to deliver a smooth flow of air to all of the molten ore. When improved forced-air pumps were invented in the nineteenth century, smelters could be built larger and unit costs fell.

### One-time costs

A second source of increasing returns consists of inputs that do not have to be increased as the output of a product is increased, even in the long run. For example, the research and development (R&D) costs to design a new generation of aeroplanes, or a more powerful computer, have to be incurred only once for each product. Hence they are independent of the scale at which the product is subsequently produced. Even if the product's *production costs* increase in proportion to output in the long run, average total costs, including *product development costs*, will fall as the scale of output rises. The influence of such once-and-for-all costs is that, other things being equal, they cause average total costs to be falling over the entire range of output.[13]

### The technology of large-scale production

A third and very important source lies in technology. Large-scale production can use more specialized and highly efficient machinery than smaller-scale production. It can also lead to more specialization of human tasks, with a resulting increase in human efficiency.

Even the most casual observation of the differences in production techniques used in large and small plants will show that larger plants use greater specialization. These differences arise because large, specialized equipment is useful only when the volume of output that the firm can sell justifies employment of that equipment. For example, assembly-line techniques, body-stamping machinery, and multiple-boring engine block machines in car production are economically efficient only when individual operations are repeated thousands of times. Use of elaborate harvesting equipment (which combines many individual tasks that would otherwise be done by hand and by tractor) provides the least-cost method of production on a big farm but not on a few acres. Typically, as the level of planned output increases, capital is substituted for labour and complex machines are substituted for simpler ones.

---

[13] This phenomenon is popularly referred to as 'spreading one's overhead'. It is similar to what happens in the short run when average fixed costs fall with output. The difference is that fixed short-run production costs are variable long-run production costs. If the firm increases its scale of output for some product, it will incur more capital costs in the long run as a larger plant is built. However, its costs of developing that product are not affected.

Robotics is a contemporary example. Electronic devices can handle huge numbers of operations quickly, but unless the level of production requires such a large volume of operations, robotics or other forms of automation will not provide the least-cost method of production.

Until very recently, large-scale production meant mass production, sometimes referred to as 'Fordism', a system that was introduced early in the twentieth century. This was based on a very detailed division of jobs, often on a production line, in which each person did one repetitive task in co-operation with very specialized machinery (called *dedicated machinery*). In this technology, size was very important. Very high rates of output were required in order to reap all the scale economies available to this type of production.

In the later decades of the twentieth century production technology was revolutionized by *flexible manufacturing*. This is a much less specialized type of production in which workers do many tasks in co-operation with machinery that is also less specialized. One of its most important characteristics is its ability to achieve maximum efficiency with low average costs at much smaller rates of output than are required for mass production techniques.

## The relationship between long-run and short-run costs

The short-run cost curves and the long-run cost curves are all derived from the same production function. Each curve assumes given prices for all inputs. In the long run all inputs can be varied; in the short run some must remain fixed. The long-run average cost (*LRAC*) curve shows the lowest cost of producing any output when all inputs are variable. Each short-run average total cost (*SRATC*) curve shows the lowest cost of producing any output when one or more factors are held constant at some specific level.

No short-run cost curve can fall below the long-run curve, because the *LRAC* curve represents the lowest attainable cost for each possible output. As the level of output is changed, a different-sized plant is normally required to achieve the lowest attainable cost. This is shown in Figure 6.5, where the *SRATC* curve lies above the *LRAC* curve at all outputs except $q_0$.

As we observed earlier in this chapter, a short-run cost curve such as *SRATC* in Figure 6.5 is one of many such curves. Each curve shows how costs vary as output is varied from a base output, holding the fixed input at the quantity most appropriate to that output. Figure 6.6 shows a family of short-run average total cost curves along a single long-run average cost curve. The long-run average

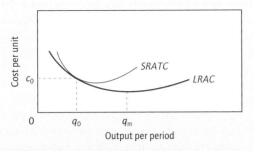

**Figure 6.5** Long-run average cost and short-run average total cost curves

The short-run average total cost (*SRATC*) curve is tangent to the long-run average cost (*LRAC*) curve at the output for which the quantity of the fixed input is optimal. The curves *SRATC* and *LRAC* coincide at output $q_0$, where the fixed plant is optimal for that level of output. For all other outputs there is too little or too much plant and equipment, and *SRATC* lies above *LRAC*. If some output other than $q_0$ is to be sustained, costs can be reduced to the level of the long-run curve when sufficient time has elapsed to adjust the size of the firm's fixed capital.

The output $q_m$ is the lowest point on the firm's long-run average cost curve. It is called the firm's *minimum efficient scale* (MES), and it is the output at which long-run costs are minimized.

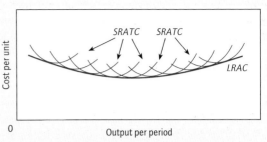

**Figure 6.6** The envelope long-run average cost curve

For every point on the long-run average cost (*LRAC*) curve there is an associated short-run average total cost (*SRATC*) curve tangent to that point. Each short-run curve shows how costs vary if output varies, with the fixed input held constant at the level that is optimal for the output at the point of tangency. As a result, each *SRATC* curve touches the *LRAC* curve at one point and lies above it at all other points. This makes the *LRAC* curve the envelope of the *SRATC* curves.

cost curve is sometimes called an **envelope** because it encloses a series of short-run average total cost curves by being tangent to them. Each *SRATC* curve is *tangent* to the long-run average cost curve at the level of output for which the quantity of the fixed input is optimal, and lies above it for all other levels of output.

## Shifts in cost curves

The cost curves derived so far show how cost varies with output, given constant input prices and fixed technology. Changes in input prices will cause the entire family of short-run and long-run average cost curves to shift. If a firm has to pay more for any input that it uses, the cost of producing each level of output will rise; if the firm has to pay less for any input that it uses, the cost of producing each level of output will fall.

A rise in input prices shifts the family of short-run and long-run average cost curves upward. A fall in input prices, or a technological advance, shifts the entire family of average cost curves downward.

Although input prices usually change gradually, sometimes they change suddenly and drastically. For example, between February 1999 and mid-2000 oil prices rose dramatically, from around $10 per barrel to around $35 per barrel. As a result there was a rise in the cost curves of all firms that used oil and oil-related products as inputs. By early 2002 this price had fallen back to around $20 so cost curves shifted back down again. In 2006 oil prices reached even higher levels, around $70 per barrel, before falling somewhat.

# The very long run: endogenous technical change

In the long run, profit-maximizing firms do the best they can to produce known products with the techniques and the resources currently available. This means being *on*, rather than above, their long-run cost curves. In the very long run, production techniques change. This means that the production function itself alters so that the same inputs produce more output. This in turn causes long-run cost curves to shift.

The decrease in costs that can be achieved by choosing from among the available inputs, known techniques, and alternative levels of output is necessarily limited. In contrast, improvements by invention and innovation are potentially limitless. Hence sustained growth in living standards is critically linked to *technological change*, which allows the same output to be produced with fewer inputs, and hence more output to be produced with society's limited amount of resources. Technological change was once thought to be mainly a random process, brought about by inventions made by ingenious individuals and eccentric scientists working in garages and scientific laboratories. However, research over the past few decades has shown that this is an incorrect view.

Changes in technology are usually *endogenous responses* to changing economic signals; that is, they result from responses by firms to the same things that induce the substitution of one input for another within the confines of a given technology.[14]

In our discussion of long-run demand curves in Chapter 3, we looked at just such technological changes in response to rising relative prices when we spoke of the development of smaller, more fuel-efficient, cars in the wake of rising petrol prices. Similarly, much of the move to substitute capital for labour in manufacturing, transportation, communications, mining, and agriculture in response to rising wage rates has taken the form of inventing new labour-saving methods of production.

Most microeconomic theory analyses only the short- and long-run responses of the firm to various changes. In the short run, firms can change price and output within the confines of fixed plant and equipment. In the long run they can change all inputs, but within the confines of fixed technology. Such an analysis is incomplete whenever technological change is an endogenous response to economic signals. Consider, for example, a rise in the price of an important input in one country. In the short run, firms that use the input will cut back production in response to the rise in costs. In the long run, they will substitute other inputs for the one whose price has risen. When all adjustments have been made, however, firms still find themselves at a cost disadvantage compared with competitors in other countries who have not suffered the rise in the price of their inputs. In the very long run, the

domestic firms may engage in research and development designed further to reduce the use of the newly expensive inputs. If the firms succeed, they may develop processes that allow them to lower costs below those of their competitors in other countries who did not suffer the increased input prices and so did not have the same incentive to innovate.

Modern research into induced technological development has documented many such instances. As a result, the response of firms to changes in such economic signals as output prices and input costs must be studied in three steps:

1. the short-run response that changes the variable input;

2. the long-run response that consists of adjusting *all* inputs; and

3. the R&D response, in which firms seek to innovate their way out of difficulties caused by reductions in their product prices and/or increases in their input prices.

Studies that ignore the third set of responses ignore what are often the most important effects, once several years have elapsed.

In this context, it is interesting to note that flexible manufacturing, which revolutionized production in most industrialized countries in the later part of the twentieth century, was first developed by the Japanese car producers in response to a scale disadvantage. They were unable to reach the efficient scale of production when they were selling only in their small, protected home market. In response, they innovated their way out of these difficulties by developing techniques that allowed them to produce a superior product at lower prices than their American and European competitors, and so turned a long-run disadvantage into a very-long-run advantage.

 # CASE STUDIES

## 1. Economies of scale in the electricity industry

In the 1940s, 1950s, and 1960s major economies of scale in electricity generation in the UK came from the use of larger and larger generators: from 30 MW (= 30,000 kilowatt) generating sets in 1948 to 100 MW sets in 1956, 200 MW sets in 1959, and 500 MW sets in 1966.

Since the 1970s there has been little increase in the size of generators, with the largest now being installed at 660 MW. Furthermore, total generating capacity has been declining since 1980. The cause is a decline in the demand for energy, because of the decline of British manufacturing and the superior energy efficiency of newer technologies such as chips and fibre optics.

In spite of the absence of further economies in the size of generators after 1970, and in spite of the decline in overall capacity after 1980, methods of gaining scale economies were still being found. The new method was to reduce the *number* of power stations, each station having several generators. As a result, the

---

[14] For a recent summary of the incorporation of endogenous technical change into economics, see Warsh (2006).

average capacity of each power station has continued to rise significantly, bringing a different type of economy of scale. The number of power stations fell from 233 in 1965 to 174 in 1978 to 78 in 1987; the average capacity of these stations rose from 147 MW in 1965 to 324 MW in 1974 to 671 MW in 1987.

Costs were also reduced by exploring economies of scale in bulk transmission of electricity. The 'Supergrid' of 400 kV (= 400,000 volt) transmission lines which was built in the 1960s replaced three lines operating at 275 kV and 18 lines operating at 132 kV, without a corresponding increase in costs.

Economies of scale have allowed the industry to cope with rising *real* prices of its main inputs—coal and labour—without raising the real price of electricity. During the 1960s the real price of oil, the major alternative fuel, was falling owing to the increasing exploitation of economies of scale in oil tankers delivering crude oil from the Middle East. In response, the UK electricity industry was able to reduce the real price of electricity, which is one of the reasons why electric heating was adopted more and more widely in preference to other fuels.

Privatization did not change the cost structure of the industry immediately, partly because producers were locked into three-year contracts to buy coal. After this period however shifts were made to cheaper, imported coal and, where new capacity was required, to the adoption of the cheaper technology of combined cycle gas turbines (CCGTs). There are mild economies of scale with current technology (in 2006) as size increases from 240 MW to 480 MW, but bigger generators do not deliver significant further scale economies.

Strictly speaking, 'scale economies' refer to the effects of increasing output *along* a negatively sloped *LRAS* curve as a result of rising output within the confines of known technology, while changes in technological knowledge *shift* the *LRAS* curve. As this example shows, the two forces usually become mixed in most real-world applications. The rise in demand for electricity in the three decades of the 1950s, 1960s, and 1970s required an increase in output. The rise in output made the use of higher-capacity equipment possible and thereby provided an incentive for the development of such equipment. No fundamental new knowledge was required, but the details of the technology of larger generators had to be developed through research rather than being taken from already existing blueprints.

Competitive forces continue to put pressure on producers to reduce costs. The main pressures now are on cutting costs through productivity gains rather than exploiting further economies of even-larger-scale production of individual plants and distribution systems.

## 2. Endogenous materials design: a new industrial revolution?

A new industrial revolution has been in progress in the past two decades or so: the 'Materials Revolution'. Throughout history, an important source of technological advancement has been the development of new materials. Indeed, we label stages of history by the materials that were used—the Stone Age, the Bronze Age, and the Iron Age. Many key twentieth-century advances in manufacturing would not have been possible without materials such as steel and hydrocarbons. Today, important technical progress is built upon polymers, composites, and ceramics.

Previous materials advances were usually the outcome of a process of trial and error—Edison allegedly tried thousands of different materials and designs before he 'invented' the light bulb. Today, however, scientists are able to use knowledge of the microstructure of matter, combined with advanced computing power, to design the materials to be used in production simultaneously with the engineering of production itself. This is having profound effects on the design of most new products and processes.

An example is found in a long-term co-operative venture between Audi and Alcoa to develop an aluminium-intensive car:

*The result has been a quantum leap in weight reduction technology and automotive structural manufacturing. This revolution is embodied in the development of the aluminium space frame (ASF) and in the ability to integrate the design of the material, the product, and the manufacturing process. The ASF concept breaks away from design and manufacturing mindsets and requirements associated with steel monocoque car body structures. Moreover, the aluminium-intensive vehicle introduced by Audi in 1994 represents a significant first step towards the development of a 'green' car which is cost effective, high-performance, low emission and recyclable. Lower weight facilitates greater fuel efficiency and the reduction of carbon dioxide emissions while at the same time increasing stiffness and passenger safety. . . . Despite a minimum 40 per cent reduction in weight in the space frame, it is an extremely strong structure and provides exceptional safety for the car occupants. Aluminium absorbs more energy, on a weight to weight basis, than steel. The aluminium body structure absorbs more energy in a collision than today's steel monocoque body structures. Audi claims that the standard of safety and crashworthiness offered by the ASF has not been seen before in conventional cars.*
(Kaounides 1995)

Another example of new materials technology can be found in sports equipment. When Björn Borg won the Wimbledon tennis tournament five times in the late 1970s, he played with a wooden racket. Jimmy Connors won it in 1982 playing with an aluminium alloy racket. Roger Federer, the three-time men's champion in 2004–6, played with a new type of racket, a product of the materials revolution. The frame material of modern rackets is made most commonly from graphite and fibreglass, and sometimes other materials as well, such as titanium and kevlar, mixed with a plastic resin. The stiffness and cost of composite frames varies depending on the exact mix of materials and can be adjusted to meet the needs of individual players.

# SUMMARY

### Firms in practice and theory

- Production is organized either by private sector firms, which take four main forms—sole traders, partnerships, limited partnerships, and joint-stock companies—by state-owned enterprises called public corporations, and by non-profit units, mostly government-owned bodies, that distribute goods and services free, or at least substantially below cost.

- Firms are in business to make profits, which they define as the difference between what they earn by selling their output and what it costs them to produce that output. This is the return to owners' capital.

### Production, costs, and profits

- The production function relates quantities of inputs to quantities of outputs.

- In addition to what firms count as their costs, economists include the imputed opportunity costs of owners' capital. This includes the pure return, or what could be earned on a riskless investment, and a risk premium, or what could be earned over the pure return on an equally risky investment. Pure or economic profits are the difference between revenues and all these costs.

- Pure profits play a key role in resource allocation. Positive pure profits attract resources into an industry; negative pure profits induce resources to move elsewhere.

### Costs in the short run

- Short-run variations in output are subject to the law of diminishing returns: equal increments of the variable input sooner or later produce smaller and smaller additions to total output and, eventually, a reduction in average output per unit of variable input.

- In the theory presented here, short-run average and marginal cost curves are U-shaped, the rising portion reflecting diminishing average and marginal returns. The marginal cost curve intersects the average cost curve at the latter's minimum point, which is called the firm's capacity output.

- There is a family of short-run average and marginal cost curves, one for each amount of the fixed input.

### Costs in the long run

- In the long run, the firm can adjust all inputs to minimize the cost of producing any given level of output.

- Cost minimization requires that the ratio of an input's marginal product to its price be the same for all inputs.

- The principle of substitution states that, when relative input prices change, firms will substitute relatively cheaper inputs for relatively more expensive ones.

- Long-run cost curves are often assumed to be U-shaped, indicating decreasing average costs (increasing returns to scale) followed by increasing average costs (decreasing returns to scale).

- The long-run cost curve may be thought of as the envelope of the family of short-run cost curves, all of which shift when factor prices shift.

### The very long run

- In the very long run, innovations introduce new methods of production that alter the production function.

- These innovations often occur as response to changes in economic incentives such as variations in the prices of inputs and outputs. They cause cost curves to shift downwards.

# TOPICS FOR REVIEW

- Forms of business organization
- Imputed costs
- Alternative definitions of profits
- The production function
- Short, long, and very long runs
- The law of diminishing returns

- Short-run average, marginal, fixed, and total costs
- Conditions for long-run cost minimization
- The principle of substitution
- The long-run envelope cost curve
- Constant, increasing, and decreasing long-run costs
- Invention and innovation in the very long run

# QUESTIONS

1 The following series of scores in successive innings is made by a batsman in cricket: 10, 20, 50, 60, 80, 100, 100, 100, 70, 50, 0, 10, 20, 0. Calculate the cumulative total of runs scored after each innings and the average score after each innings. Each successive score tells us the marginal score. Say what happens to the average when the marginal score is above the previous average, and what happens to the average when the marginal score is below that average. Notice that these relationships between marginal and average values are not applicable just to economics.

2 Suppose the production function is $Q = 20(K^{0.5} L^{0.5})$ and the value of capital is 100. Calculate the total product for the following values of labour input: 1, 5, 10, 20, 40, 50, 80, 100, 150, 200. Calculate the average product at each of these levels of output. How does marginal product vary over this range of output?

3 Here are data for total production costs of a manufacturing firm at various levels of output:

| Output (units) | Total cost (£) |
| --- | --- |
| 0 | 1,000 |
| 20 | 1,200 |
| 40 | 1,300 |
| 60 | 1,380 |
| 100 | 1,600 |
| 200 | 2,300 |
| 300 | 3,200 |
| 400 | 4,300 |
| 500 | 5,650 |
| 1,000 | 13,650 |

(a) Calculate average variable cost (AVC), average total cost (ATC), and average fixed cost (AFC). (Hint: fixed costs have to be incurred even when output is zero and do not vary with the production level in the short run.)

(b) Calculate marginal or incremental cost over each production range for which data are given.

(c) [You may attempt this and subsequent parts now, but alternatively you could return to them after reading Chapter 7.] If this firm can sell as much as it wants at a price of £11, what is its profit-maximizing output?

(d) How much profit is made?

(e) At output levels shown in the table immediately on either side of the profit-maximizing output, what is the level of profit?

4 Using the production function $Q = 20(K^{0.5} L^{0.5})$, where K is machine-hours per week, L is worker-hours week, and Q is output per week, calculate five different combinations of capital and labour that will generate each of the following levels of output: 20, 100, 1,000, 2,000.

5 Suppose that capital is £10 per machine-hour and labour £5 per worker-hour. What would be the cost-minimizing combination of capital and labour that could be used to produce each of the four levels of output listed in question 4?

6 Holding capital constant at 100 and varying labour input accordingly, calculate the short-run average cost of producing the levels of output listed in question 4 (and using the input prices set out in question 5). Repeat the exercise for the following levels of capital: 16, 25, 36, 49, 64, 81.

7 Explain the difference between economists' and accountants' definitions of profit.

8 What is the law of diminishing returns, and what does it imply about the likely shape of short-run cost curves?

9 Explain the differences between economies of scale, constant returns to scale, and diminishing returns to scale.

# Chapter 7

# PERFECT COMPETITION

In Chapter 6 we studied the determinants of firms' costs and how these vary with the output of the firm. In this and the next two chapters we build on what we have learned about costs and study how the markets in which firms operate (combined with cost conditions) also affect what they do. The influence of the market depends on the nature of the product involved and the number of firms competing for market share. In this chapter we study a market structure in which a large number of firms produce an identical product. In Chapter 8 we study a market in which there is only one large firm, and in Chapter 9 we study intermediate cases in which a small number of firms produce differentiated products.

In all market structures we ask: what determines the amount of output that firms will supply? What does maximization of profit imply for the behaviour of the whole market? Does this behaviour serve the interests of consumers as well as that of firms?

In particular, in this chapter you will learn that:

- The impact of the product market on firms' prices and output choices is determined by the nature of the product and the market structure in which they operate.

- In perfect competition firms produce a homogeneous product and are price-takers in their output markets.

- All profit-maximizing firms choose their output to equate marginal cost and marginal revenue.

- Under perfect competition marginal cost will equal the market price, so the supply curve of firms will be determined by the marginal cost curve.

- The long-run supply curve of a competitive industry may be positively sloped, horizontal, or negatively sloped depending on how input prices are affected by the industry's expansion.

- Perfect competition maximizes the benefit that consumers receive from the output of the product in question.

Our main task in this chapter is to derive the supply curve for a perfectly competitive industry. We then go on to study how such an industry reacts to various forces that affect it, including changes in demand and costs.

In perfectly competitive industries, all firms produce an identical product and there are so many firms that no one of them can affect the market price by varying its own output. Since each firm can sell as much as it wants at the going price, its sales revenue is proportional to its output. For example, doubling the amount produced and sold at any constant price doubles sales revenue. In contrast, when the sale price changes as more is produced the relationship between production and revenue is more complicated. Firms that can influence their own product price are studied in Chapters 8 and 9.

The degree to which firms can influence the price of their product through their own actions depends upon market structure, a concept that needs discussion at the outset.

# Market structure and firm behaviour

Does Shell compete with BP in the sale of petrol? Does HSBC Bank compete with Barclays? Does a wheat farmer from Essex compete with a wheat farmer from Somerset? If we use the ordinary meaning of the word 'compete', the answer to the first two questions is plainly yes, and the answer to the third is no.

Shell and BP both advertise extensively to persuade car drivers to buy *their* products. Gimmicks such as new mileage-stretching additives and free airmiles are used to tempt drivers to buy one brand of petrol rather than another. Most larger towns in England and Wales have not only Barclays and HSBC Banks but also others such as LloydsTSB, NatWest, HBOS and Abbey. In Scotland the choices look to be different, but many of the institutions are linked. The Royal Bank of Scotland, for example, owns NatWest, and HBOS was formed from a merger between the Bank of Scotland and the Halifax. Banks all provide similar services but work hard to attract business from each other. For example, they often offer incentives for students to open bank accounts in the hope that they will stay with that bank for life. If one bank is very successful in attracting business, it will do so at the expense of its rival banks.

In the wheat market, however, there is nothing that the Essex farmer can do to affect either the sales or the profits of the Somerset farmer, and the sales and profits of the Somerset farm have no effect on those of the Essex farm.

To understand who is competing with whom and in what sense, it is useful to distinguish between the behaviour of individual firms and the *type of market* in which they operate.

## Market structure and behaviour

The term **market structure** refers to the type of market in which firms operate. Markets can be distinguished by the number of firms in the market and the type of product that they sell.

### Competitive market structure

The competitiveness of the market depends on the power of individual firms to influence market prices. *The less power an individual firm has to influence the market in which it sells its product, the more competitive that market is.*

The extreme form of competitive structure occurs when each firm has zero market power. In such a case many firms sell an identical product and each must accept the price set by the forces of market demand and market supply. The

firms can sell as much as they choose at the prevailing market price and have no power to influence that price.

This extreme is called a *perfectly competitive market structure*. (Usually the term 'structure' is dropped and economists speak of a *perfectly competitive market*.) In it, there is no need for individual firms to compete actively with one another, since one firm's ability to sell its product does not depend on the behaviour of any other firm. For example, Essex and Somerset wheat farmers operate in a perfectly competitive market over which they have no power. The price of wheat is set in world markets, and there are thousands of suppliers to that market in many different countries.[1]

### Competitive behaviour

In everyday language, the term 'competitive behaviour' refers to the degree to which individual firms actively compete with one another. For example, Shell and BP certainly engage in competitive behaviour. Both companies also have some real power over their market. Either firm could raise its price of petrol at the pumps and still continue to attract customers. Each has the power to decide, within limits set by buyers' tastes and the prices of competing products, the price that people will pay for their petrol and oil. So, although they actively compete with each other, they do so in a market that does not have a perfectly competitive structure.

In contrast, Essex and Somerset wheat farmers do not engage in competitive behaviour, because the only way they can affect their revenues is by changing their outputs of (or their costs of producing) wheat.

### Behaviour versus structure

The distinction that we have just made explains why firms in perfectly competitive markets (e.g. Essex and the Somerset wheat farmers) do not compete actively with each other, whereas firms that do compete actively with each other (e.g. Shell and BP) do not operate in perfectly competitive markets.

## The significance of market structure

The firms that make a product, or a closely related set of products, constitute an **industry**. The market demand

---

[1] Of course government agencies may intervene to influence the price, such as in the EU Common Agricultural Policy, but this does not change the fact that individual farmers are price-takers.

curve for any particular product is the demand curve facing the *industry*.

When firms take their production and sales decisions, they need to know what quantity they can sell at various prices. Their concern, therefore, is not with the *market* demand curve for the whole industry, but rather with the demand curve for their own output. If a firm's managers know the demand curve that their firm faces, they know the sales that the firm can make and the revenue it will earn at each possible price. If they also know their costs of production, they can calculate the profits that will be associated with each rate of output. With this information, they can choose the output that maximizes their profits.

The structure of the market in which a firm operates determines the relationship between the market demand curve for the product and the demand curve facing each individual firm in that industry. To reduce the analysis of market structure to manageable proportions, we analyse four theoretical market structures: perfect competition, monopoly, monopolistic competition, and oligopoly. Monopoly and perfect competition lie at the two extremes of market structure. In monopoly the industry contains only one firm, which can, therefore, set its price without concern about how competing firms in the industry will react (since there are none). In perfect competition there are so many firms in the industry that no one of them has any power to influence the market price for its product. Most real markets are somewhere in between these extreme cases. Firms operate in market structures that are either monopolistically competitive or oligopolistic.

Perfect competition will be dealt with in the rest of this chapter; the other market structures will be dealt with in the chapters that follow.

## Perfectly competitive markets

The perfectly competitive market structure—usually referred to simply as *perfect competition*—applies directly to a number of real-world markets. It also provides an important benchmark for comparison with other market structures.

### Assumptions of perfect competition

Our analysis of **perfect competition** is built on a number of key assumptions relating to the firm and to the industry.

• **Assumption 1.** All the firms in the industry sell an identical or **homogeneous product**.

• **Assumption 2.** Buyers of the product are well informed about the characteristics of the product being sold and the prices charged by each firm.

• **Assumption 3.** The output of each firm, when it is producing at its minimum long-run average total cost, is a small fraction of the industry's total output.

• **Assumption 4.** Each firm is a **price-taker**. This means that each firm can alter its output without significantly affecting the market price of its product. Each firm must passively accept the existing market price, but it can sell as much as it wants at that price.[2]

• **Assumption 5.** There is *freedom of entry and exit*, which means that any new firm is free to enter the industry and start producing if it so wishes, and any existing firm is free to cease production and leave the industry.

The difference between the wheat farmers that we considered earlier and Shell is in their *degree of market power*. Each firm that is producing wheat is an insignificant part of the whole market and so has no power to influence the price of wheat. The oil company, on the other hand, does have power to influence the price of petrol, because its own sales represent a significant part of the total sales of petrol, even though all the firms in the industry are selling a product that is close to homogeneous.[3] Box 7.1 explores further the reasons why each wheat-producing firm finds the price of wheat to be beyond its influence.

A perfectly competitive market is one in which individual firms have zero market power.

---

[2] To emphasize its importance, we identify price-taking as a separate assumption, although strictly speaking it is implied by the first three assumptions.

[3] Even homogeneous commodities come in different types, for example different varieties of wheat or coffee bean. Any firm may produce more than one variety, but across firms each type and grade of a commodity is the same, e.g. super unleaded petrol or number 1 grade durum wheat.

**Box 7.1** Demand under perfect competition: firm and industry

Because all products have negatively sloped market demand curves, *any* increase in the industry's output will cause *some* fall in the market price. The calculations given below show, however, that any conceivable increase that one wheat farm could make in its output has such a negligible effect on the industry's price that the farmer correctly ignores it. (For our purposes, the farm is a firm producing wheat.*)

The calculations given below arrive at the elasticity of demand facing one wheat farmer in two steps. Step 1 shows that a 200 per cent variation in the farm's output leads to only a very small percentage variation in the world price. Thus, as step 2 shows, the elasticity of demand for the farm's product is very high: 71,429!

Although the arithmetic used in reaching these measures is unimportant, understanding why the wheat farmer is a price-taker in these circumstances is vital.

Here is the argument that the calculations summarize. The market elasticity of demand for wheat is approximately 0.25. This means that, if the quantity of wheat supplied in the world increased by 1 per cent, the price would have to fall by 4 per cent to induce the world's wheat buyers to purchase the extra wheat.

Even huge farms produce a very small fraction of the total world crop. In a recent year, one large farm produced 1,750 metric tonnes of wheat; this was only 0.00035 per cent of the world production of 500 million metric tonnes. Suppose that the farmer decides one year to produce nothing and the next year manages to produce twice his normal output of 1,750 metric tonnes; this is an extremely large variation in one farm's output. The increase in output from zero to 3,500 metric tonnes represents a 200 per cent variation measured around the farm's average output of 1,750 metric tonnes. Yet the percentage increase in world output is only $(3,500/500,000,000) \times 100 = 0.0007$ per cent. The calculations show that this increase would lead to a decrease in the world price of 0.0028 per cent (2.8p in £1,000) and would give the farm's own demand curve an elasticity of over 71,000. This is an enormous elasticity of demand. The farm would have to increase its output by over 71,000 per cent to bring about a

1 per cent decrease in the price of wheat. It is not surprising, therefore, that the farmer regards the price of wheat as unaffected by any change in output that his one farm could conceivably make. For all intents and purposes, the wheat-producing firm faces a perfectly elastic demand curve for its product: *it is a price-taker.*

We will now proceed with the calculation of the firm's elasticity of demand ($\eta_f$) from market elasticity of demand ($\eta_m$), given the following figures:

World elasticity of demand ($\eta_m$) = 0.25
World output = 500,000,000 metric tonnes

A large farm with an average output of 1,750 metric tonnes varies its output between 0 and 3,500 tonnes. The variation of 3,500 tonnes represents 200 per cent of the farm's average output of 1,750 metric tonnes. This causes world output to vary by only $(3,500/500,000,000) \times 100 = 0.0007$ per cent.

**Step 1: Find the percentage change in world price.** We know that the market elasticity is 0.25. This means that the percentage change in quantity must be one-quarter as great as the percentage change in price. Put the other way around, the percentage change in price must be four times as large as the percentage change in quantity. We have just seen that world quantity changes by 0.0007 per cent, so world price must change by $0.0007 \times 4 = 0.0028$ per cent.

**Step 2: Find the firm's elasticity of demand.** This is the percentage change in its *own output* divided by the resulting percentage change in the world price, i.e. 200 per cent divided by 0.0028 per cent. Clearly, the percentage change in quantity vastly exceeds the percentage change in price, making elasticity very high. Its precise value is 200/0.0028 or 2,000,000/28, which is 71,429.

* Strictly speaking, this box applies to wheat farmers outside of the EU. It will apply directly when the EU lowers its support price to the world price or removes it altogether. In the meantime, EU wheat farmers do face a perfectly elastic demand curve, because the Commission stands ready to buy all the wheat that is legally produced at its support price.

## Demand and revenue for a firm in perfect competition

A major distinction between firms operating in perfectly competitive markets and firms operating in any other type of market is in the shape of the firm's own demand curve.

In perfect competition each firm faces a demand curve that is horizontal, because variations in the firm's output have no noticeable effect on price.

The horizontal (perfectly elastic) demand curve does not mean that the firm could actually sell an infinite amount at the going price. What it does mean is that the variations in output *that it will normally be possible for the firm to make* will leave price virtually unchanged because they have only a negligible effect on the industry's total output. Figure 7.1 contrasts the demand curve for the product of a competitive industry with the demand curve facing a single firm in that industry.

To study the revenues that each firm receives from the sales of its products, we use total, average, and marginal revenue. These are the revenue counterparts of total, average, and marginal cost that we considered in Chapter 6.

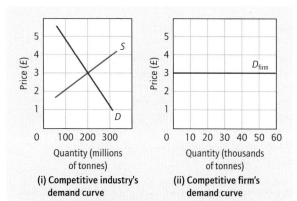

**Figure 7.1 The demand curve for a competitive industry and for one firm**

The industry's demand curve is negatively sloped; the firm's demand curve is virtually horizontal. Notice the difference in the quantities shown on the horizontal scale in each part of the figure. The competitive industry has output of 200 million tonnes when the price is £3. The individual firm takes that market price as given and considers producing up to, say, 60,000 tonnes. The firm's demand curve in part (ii) is horizontal because any change in output that this one firm could manage would leave price virtually unchanged at £3.

**Table 7.1 Revenue concepts for a price-taking firm**

| Quantity sold (units) (q) | Price (p) | TR = p·q | AR = TR/q | MR = ΔTR/Δq |
|---|---|---|---|---|
| 10 | £3.00 | £30.00 | £3.00 | |
| 11 | 3.00 | 33.00 | 3.00 | £3.00 |
| 12 | 3.00 | 36.00 | 3.00 | 3.00 |
| 13 | 3.00 | 39.00 | 3.00 | 3.00 |

**When price is fixed, average revenue, marginal revenue, and price are all equal to each other.** The table shows the calculation of total (*TR*), average (*AR*), and marginal revenue (*MR*) when market price is £3.00 and the firm varies its quantity over the range from 10 to 13 units. Marginal revenue is positioned between the rows because it represents the change in total revenue in response to a change in quantity. For example, when sales rise from 11 to 12 units, revenue rises from £33 to £36, making marginal revenue $(36 - 33)/(12 - 11) = £3$ per unit.

**Total revenue** (*TR*) is the total amount received by the seller from the sale of a product. If *q* units are sold at a price of *p* pounds each, $TR = p \times q$.[4]

**Average revenue** (*AR*) is the amount of revenue per unit sold. This is equal to the market price of the product.

**Marginal revenue** (*MR*), sometimes called *incremental revenue*, is the change in a firm's total revenue resulting from the sale of one extra unit. Whenever output changes by more than one unit, the change in revenue must be divided by the change in output to calculate marginal revenue. For example, if an increase in output of three units per month is accompanied by an increase in revenue of £1,500, the marginal revenue resulting from the sale of *one extra unit* per month is £1,500/3, or £500.[5]

To illustrate each of these revenue concepts, consider a firm that is selling an agricultural product in a perfectly competitive market at a price of £3 per tonne. Because every tonne brings in £3, the average revenue per tonne sold is clearly £3. Furthermore, because each *additional* tonne sold brings in £3, the marginal revenue of an extra tonne sold is also £3. Table 7.1 shows calculations of these revenue concepts for a range of outputs between 10 and 13 tonnes.

The important point illustrated in the table is that, as long as the market price is unaffected by the amount the firm sells, its marginal revenue is equal to its average revenue (which is *always* equal to the price at which the output is sold). Graphically, as shown in part (i) of Figure 7.2, average revenue and marginal revenue are the same horizontal line drawn at the level of market price. Because the firm can sell any quantity it chooses at this price, the horizontal line is also the *firm's demand curve*; it shows that any quantity the firm chooses to sell will be associated with this same market price.

If the market price is unaffected by variations in the firm's output, the firm's demand curve, its average revenue curve, and its marginal revenue curve all coincide in the same horizontal line.

This result can be stated in a slightly different way, which turns out to be important for our later work:

For a firm in perfect competition, price equals marginal revenue.

This means, of course, that total revenue rises in direct proportion to output, as shown in part (ii) of Figure 7.2.

---

[4] Four common ways of indicating that two variables such as *p* and *q* are to be multiplied together are $p \cdot q$, $p \times q$, $(p)(q)$ and $pq$.

[5] Because we use discrete changes in the text, we are, strictly speaking, using *incremental revenues*, $\Delta TR/\Delta q$. Marginal revenue is defined geometrically as the slope of the tangent to the total revenue curve at the point in question. For those readers who know some calculus, it is the first derivative of total revenue with respect to output, $dTR/dq$. For small changes, incremental revenue may be regarded as an approximation of marginal revenue, as we do in the text.

**Figure 7.2 Revenue curve for a firm**

**The demand curve for a perfectly competitive firm is a horizontal straight line.** The graph shows the data in Table 7.1. Because price does not change, neither marginal nor average revenue varies with output—both are equal to price. When price is constant, total revenue is a straight line through the origin whose positive slope is the price per unit.

# Short-run equilibrium

The next step is to combine information about the firm's costs and revenues to determine the level of output that will maximize its profits. We have just seen how the revenue of each price-taking firm varies with its output. In the short run, the firm has one or more fixed inputs such as its plant and machinery, and the only way in which it can change its output is by altering its variable inputs such as labour. In effect, the firm has to choose where it wants to be on its short-run cost curve (the curve we derived in Chapter 6).

## Rules for all profit-maximizing firms

We start by stating three rules that apply to *all* profit-maximizing firms, whether or not they operate in perfectly competitive markets.

### Should the firm produce at all?

The firm always has the option of producing nothing. If it exercises this option, it will have an operating loss that is equal to its fixed costs. If it decides to produce, it will add the variable cost of production to its costs and the income from the sale of its product to its revenue. Therefore, it will be worthwhile for the firm to produce as long as it can find some level of output for which revenue exceeds variable cost. However, if its revenue is less than its variable cost at *every* level of output, the firm will actually lose more by producing than by not producing.

*Rule 1.* A firm should not produce at all if, for *all* levels of output, the total variable cost of producing that output exceeds the total revenue derived from selling it or, equivalently, if the average variable cost of producing the output exceeds the price at which it can be sold.

### The shutdown price

The sale price at which the firm can just cover its average variable cost when producing at its most profitable level of output is called the **shutdown** or **break-even price**. At that price it is indifferent between producing and not producing. At any price below it, the firm will shut down. Such a price is shown in part (i) of Figure 7.6 on page 144. At the price of £2, the firm can just cover its average variable cost by producing $q_0$ units. Any other output would not produce enough revenue to cover variable costs. For any price below £2, there is no output at which variable costs can be covered. The price of £2 in part (i) is thus the shutdown price.

Box 7.2 deals with an interesting case of what to do with some parts of a firm's production facilities when their variable costs cannot be covered.

### How much should the firm produce?

If a firm decides that (according to rule 1) production is worth undertaking, it must decide how much to produce. Common sense dictates that, on a unit-by-unit basis, if any unit of production adds more to revenue than it does to cost, then producing and selling that unit will increase profits. However, if any unit adds more to cost than it does to revenue, producing and selling that unit will decrease profits. Using the terminology introduced earlier, a unit of production raises profits if the marginal revenue obtained

**Box 7.2 Scrap or store: what do airlines do in a downturn?**

The terrorist attack on New York's World Trade Center on 11 September 2001 led to a sharp downturn in demand for air travel. Many airlines quickly reduced their number of flights and the number of aircraft in service. Those planes that were not expected to be put back in service for some time, if at all, were parked in the desert in the Southwest of the United States. (The dry air of the desert means that the metal planes will not rust as they would in a damp climate.) The airlines could have considered selling their unwanted planes, but their second-hand value would have been very low when most other airlines had excess capacity at the same time. Moreover, the planes that were 'parked' tended to be older models which had already had many years of service.

Eventually, however, decisions have to be taken about whether these planes should be sold, put back into service, or broken up for the value of the spare parts that can be stripped out. This decision will clearly be based on whether average variable cost of running (and restoring) an old plane will be less than the average variable cost of running other planes in the fleet, which in turn remains less than the average total cost of buying new planes.

The following is an extract from a newspaper article on this subject:

*Airlines will be forced to scrap planes worth $1.3 billion (£910 million) that were grounded during the traffic downturn caused by the September 11 terrorist attack.*

*Research by Boeing, the aircraft maker, reveals that two-thirds of the 2,000 planes grounded after the attacks will not return to the skies. They are likely to be used for spares or scrapped altogether.*

*Airline analysts said the aircraft would be worth about $1 million each as scrap.... A new aircraft can cost up to $80 million.*

*The cut will be the largest cull of the world's commercial fleet. Usually, about 250 aircraft are scrapped each year.... Large American firms have used the downturn to bring forward the retirement of swathes of their fleet. American Airlines, for example, has decided to rationalise its fleet from 11 plane types to six.* (Dominic O'Connell, Sunday Times, 24 March 2002, page 3 of Business Section.)

from selling it exceeds the marginal cost of producing it; it lowers profits if the marginal revenue obtained from selling it is less than the marginal cost of producing it.

Now let a firm with some existing rate of output consider increasing or decreasing that output. If a further unit of production will increase the firm's profits, the firm should expand its output. However, if the last unit produced reduces profits, the firm should contract its output. From this it follows that the only time the firm should leave its output unaltered is when the last unit produced adds the same amount to costs as it does to revenue. These results yield the second rule:

*Rule 2.* Whenever it is profitable for the firm to produce some output, it should produce the output at which marginal revenue equals marginal cost.

### Maximization not minimization

Figure 7.3 shows that it is possible to fulfil rule 2 and yet have profits at a minimum. Rule 3 is needed to distinguish minimum-profit from maximum-profit positions:

*Rule 3.* An output where marginal cost equals marginal revenue may be either profit-maximizing or profit-minimizing. Profit maximization requires that marginal cost be less than marginal revenue at slightly lower outputs and that marginal cost exceed marginal revenue at slightly higher outputs.

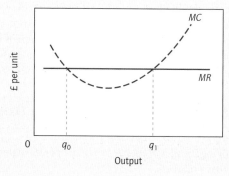

**Figure 7.3 Two outputs where marginal cost equals marginal revenue**

The equality of marginal cost and marginal revenue is necessary, but not sufficient, for profit maximization. $MC = MR$ at outputs $q_0$ and $q_1$. Output $q_0$ is a minimum-profit position because a change of output in either direction would increase profit: for outputs below $q_0$ marginal cost exceeds marginal revenue and profits can be increased by *reducing* output; while for outputs above $q_0$ marginal revenue exceeds marginal cost and profits can be increased by *increasing* output. Output $q_1$ is a maximum-profit position, since at outputs just below it marginal revenue exceeds marginal cost and profit can be increased by *increasing* output towards $q_1$; while at outputs just above it marginal cost exceeds marginal revenue and profit can be increased by *reducing* output towards $q_1$.

The geometric implication of this condition is that, at the profit-maximizing output, the marginal cost curve should intersect the marginal revenue curve from below. This ensures that *MC* is less than *MR* to the left of the profit-maximizing output and greater than *MR* to the right of the profit-maximizing output.

### The optimum output

The above three rules determine the output that will be chosen by any firm that maximizes its profits in the short run. This output is called the firm's **profit-maximizing output**, and sometimes its **optimum output**:

- The firm's optimum output is zero if total revenue is less than total variable cost at all levels of output; the optimum output is positive if there is any output for which total revenue equals or exceeds total variable cost.

- When the firm's optimum output is positive, it is where marginal cost equals marginal revenue.

- If output is reduced slightly from the optimum level, marginal cost must be less than marginal revenue; if output is increased slightly from the optimum level, marginal cost must exceed marginal revenue.

### Rule 2 applied to price-taking firms

Rule 2 tells us that any profit-maximizing firm that is in production will produce at the point where marginal cost equals marginal revenue. However, we have already seen that for price-taking firms marginal revenue is the market price. Combining these two results, we can arrive at an important conclusion:

A firm that is operating in a perfectly competitive market will produce the output that equates its marginal cost of production with the market price of its product (as long as price exceeds average variable cost).

In a perfectly competitive industry, the market determines the price at which the firm sells its product. The firm then produces the output that maximizes its profits. This is the output for which price equals marginal cost.

When the firm has reached a position where its profits are maximized, it has no incentive to change its output, because it is doing as well as it can do given the market situation. Therefore, unless prices or costs change, the firm will continue to produce that output. The firm is in *short-run equilibrium*, as illustrated in Figure 7.4. (The long run is considered later in this chapter.) In summary:

In a perfectly competitive market, each firm is a price-taker and a quantity-adjuster. A firm pursues its goal of profit maximization by producing the output that equates its short-run

**Figure 7.4** **The short-run equilibrium of a firm in perfect competition**

The firm chooses the output for which *p* = *MC* above the level of *AVC*. When price equals marginal cost, as at output $q_E$, the firm loses profits if it either increases or decreases its output. At any point left of $q_E$—say $q_2$—price is greater than the marginal cost, and it pays to increase output (as indicated by the left-hand arrow). At any point to the right of $q_E$—say $q_1$—price is less than the marginal cost, and it pays to reduce output (as indicated by the right-hand arrow).

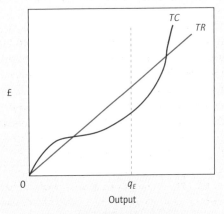

**Figure 7.5** **Total cost and revenue curves**

The firm chooses the output for which the gap between the total revenue and the total cost curves is the largest. At each output the vertical distance between the *TR* and *TC* curves shows by how much total revenue exceeds or falls short of total cost. In the figure the gap is largest at output $q_E$, which is therefore the profit-maximizing output.

marginal cost with the price of its product, which is determined by the market.

Figure 7.4 shows the equilibrium of the firm using average cost and revenue curves. We can, if we wish, show the same equilibrium using total cost and revenue curves. Figure 7.5 combines the total cost curve first drawn in

Figure 6.3 with the total revenue curve first shown in Figure 7.2. It shows the profit-maximizing output as the output with the largest positive difference between total revenue and total cost. This must of course be the same output as we located in Figure 7.4 by equating marginal cost and marginal revenue.

## Short-run supply curves

We have seen that in a perfectly competitive market the firm responds to a price that is set by the forces of demand and supply. By adjusting the quantity it produces in response to the current market price, the firm helps to determine the market supply. The link between the behaviour of the firm and the behaviour of the competitive market is provided by the *industry supply curve*, which is also called the *market supply curve*.

### The supply curve for one firm

The firm's supply curve is derived in part (i) of Figure 7.6, which shows a firm's marginal cost curve and four alternative prices. The horizontal line at each price is the firm's demand curve when the market price is at that level. The firm's marginal cost curve gives the marginal cost corresponding to each level of output. We require a supply curve that shows the quantity that the firm will supply at each price. For prices below average variable cost, the firm will supply zero units (rule 1). For prices above average variable cost, the firm will equate price and marginal cost (rule 2, modified by the proposition that $MR = p$ in perfect competition). This leads to the following conclusion:

In perfect competition, the firm's supply curve is its marginal cost curve for those levels of output for which marginal cost is above average variable cost.

### The supply curve of an industry

To illustrate what is involved, Figure 7.7 shows the derivation of an industry supply curve for an industry containing only two firms. The general result is as follows:

In perfect competition, the industry's supply curve is the horizontal sum of the marginal cost curves of all firms in the industry (above the level of average variable cost).

The reason for summing the marginal cost curves is that each firm's marginal cost curve shows how much it will supply at each given market price, and the industry supply curve is the sum of what each firm will supply. The reason for the qualification 'above the level of average variable cost' is that, as rule 1 shows, the firm will not produce at all if price is less than its average variable cost.

(i) Marginal cost and average variable cost curves

(ii) The supply curve

**Figure 7.6  The supply curve for a price-taking firm**

For a price-taking firm the supply curve has the same shape as its *MC* curve above the level of *AVC*. The point $E_0$, where price $p_0$ equals *AVC*, is the shutdown point. As price rises from £2 to £3 to £4 to £5, the firm increases its production from $q_0$ to $q_1$ to $q_2$ to $q_3$. If for example price were £3, the firm would produce output $q_1$ and would be earning the contribution to fixed costs shown by the shaded rectangle.

The firm's supply curve is shown in part (ii). It relates market price to the quantity the firm will produce and offer for sale. It has the same shape as the firm's *MC* curve for all prices above *AVC*.

This supply curve, based on the short-run marginal cost curves of all the firms in the industry, is the industry's supply curve that was first encountered in Chapter 3. We have now established the profit-maximizing behaviour of individual firms that lies behind that curve. It is sometimes called a **short-run supply curve** because it is based on the short-run, profit-maximizing behaviour of all the firms in

**Figure 7.7 The supply curve for a group of firms**

The industry supply curve is the horizontal sum of the supply curves of each of the firms in the industry. At a price of £3, firm A would supply 4 units and firm B would supply 3 units; together, as shown in part (iii), they would supply 7 units. In this example, because firm B does not enter the market at prices below £2, the supply curve $S_{A+B}$ is identical to $S_A$ up to price £2 and is the sum of $S_A$ and $S_B$ above £2.

the industry. This distinguishes it from a *long-run supply curve*, which relates quantity supplied to the price that rules in long-run equilibrium when firms are free to enter and exit and all inputs can be varied.

### Short-run equilibrium price

The price of a product sold in a perfectly competitive market is determined by the interaction of the industry's short-run supply curve and the market demand curve. Although no one firm can influence the market price significantly, the collective actions of all firms in the industry (as shown by the industry supply curve) and the collective actions of consumers (as shown by the market demand curve) together determine the equilibrium price. This occurs at the point where the market demand curve and the industry supply curve intersect.

At the equilibrium price, each firm is producing and selling a quantity for which its marginal cost equals price. Given their fixed inputs, all firms are maximizing their profits and so have no incentive to alter output in the short run. Because total quantity demanded equals total quantity supplied, there is no reason for market price to

change. Thus, the market and all the firms in the industry are in short-run equilibrium.

### Short-run profitability of the firm

We know that when an industry is in short-run equilibrium each firm is maximizing its profits. However, we do not know *how large* these profits are. It is one thing to know that a firm is doing as well as it can, given its particular circumstances; it is another thing to know how well it is doing.

Figure 7.8 shows three possible positions for a firm in short-run equilibrium. In all three cases the firm is maximizing its profits by producing where price equals marginal cost, but the size of the profits is different in each case: in part (i) the firm is suffering losses; in part (ii) it is just covering all of its costs—it is breaking even; in part (iii) it is making pure profits because average revenue exceeds average total cost. In part (i) we could say that the firm is minimizing its losses rather than maximizing its profits, but both statements mean the same thing. In all three cases the firm is doing as well as it can, given its costs and the market price.

## Long-run equilibrium

In perfect competition, the forces that produce long-run equilibrium of the industry are created by the entry and exit of firms and by the option of varying the capital stock. The incentive for entry or exit comes from the existence of profits or losses.

### The effect of entry and exit

Firms in *short-run equilibrium* may be making profits, suffering losses, or just breaking even. Because costs include the opportunity cost of capital, firms that are just breaking

**Figure 7.8** Alternative short-run equilibrium positions for a firm in perfect competition

**When it is in short-run equilibrium, a competitive firm may be suffering losses, breaking even, or making profits.** The diagram shows a firm with given costs faced with three alternative prices, $p_1$, $p_2$, and $p_3$. In each part $E$ is the point at which $MC = MR$ = price. Since in all three cases price exceeds $AVC$, the firm is in short-run equilibrium.

In part (i) price is $p_1$. Because price is below average total cost, the firm is suffering losses shown by the blue area. Because price exceeds average variable cost, the firm continues to produce in the short run. Because price is less than $ATC$, the firm will not replace its capital as it wears out. In part (ii) price is $p_2$ and the firm is just covering its total costs. It *will* replace its capital as it wears out since its revenue is covering the full opportunity cost of its capital. In part (iii) price is $p_3$ and the firm is earning pure profits in excess of all its costs, as shown by the blue area. As in part (ii), the firm will replace its capital as it wears out.

even are doing as well as they could do by investing their capital elsewhere. Thus, there will be no incentive for such firms to leave the industry. Similarly, if new entrants expect just to break even, there will be no incentive for firms to enter the industry, because they can earn the same return on their capital elsewhere in the economy. If, however, existing firms are earning revenues in excess of all costs, including the opportunity cost of capital, new capital will enter the industry attracted by these profits. If existing firms are suffering losses, capital will leave the industry because a better return can be obtained elsewhere in the economy. This process of entry and exit is an important driver of the dynamics of a market economy, so it is worth looking at in a little more detail.

### An entry-attracting price

First, suppose that all firms in a competitive industry are in the position of the firm shown in part (iii) of Figure 7.8. Attracted by the profitability of existing firms, new firms will enter the industry. If, for example, in response to the high profits that the 100 existing firms are making, 20 new firms enter, the market supply curve that formerly added up the outputs of 100 firms at each price must now add up the outputs of 120 firms. At any price, more will be supplied because there are more producers.

With an unchanged market demand curve, this shift in the short-run industry supply curve means that the previous equilibrium price will no longer prevail. The increase in supply will lower the equilibrium price, and both new and old firms will have to adjust their output to

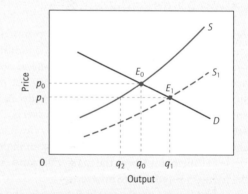

**Figure 7.9** New entrants shift the supply curve

**The supply curve shifts to the right and the equilibrium price falls.** The entry of new firms shifts the supply curve to $S_1$, the equilibrium price falls from $p_0$ to $p_1$, while output rises from $q_0$ to $q_1$. Before entry only $q_2$ would have been produced at this price. The extra output is supplied by the new firms.

this new price. This is illustrated in Figure 7.9. New firms will continue to enter, and the equilibrium price will continue to fall, until all firms in the industry are just covering their total costs. Firms will then be in the position of the firm shown in part (ii) of Figure 7.8, which is called a *zero-profit equilibrium*.

Profits in a competitive industry create an incentive for the entry of new firms; the industry will expand, pushing price down until the profits fall to zero.

## An exit-inducing price

Now suppose that the firms in the industry are in the position of the firm shown in part (i) of Figure 7.8. Although the firms are covering their *variable* costs, the return on their capital is less than the opportunity cost of capital. They are not covering their *total* costs. This is a signal for firms to exit. Old plants and equipment will not be replaced as they wear out. As a result, the industry's short-run supply curve shifts leftward, and the market price rises. Firms will continue to exit, and the market price will continue to rise, until the remaining firms can cover their total costs, that is until they are all in the zero-profit equilibrium illustrated in part (ii) of Figure 7.8. The exit of firms will then cease.

Losses in a competitive industry create an incentive for the exit of firms; the industry will contract, driving the market price up until the remaining firms are just covering their total costs.

## The break-even price

Firms exit an industry when they are making losses and enter when they are attracted by positive profits. There is no further entry or exit when firms are just covering all their costs. This means that:

The long-run equilibrium of a competitive industry occurs when firms are earning zero profits.

The firm in part (ii) of Figure 7.8 is in a zero-profit, long-run equilibrium. For that firm, the price $p_0$ is its shutdown or break-even price. It is the price at which all costs, including the opportunity cost of capital, are being covered. The firm is just willing to stay in the industry. It has no incentive to leave, nor do other firms have an incentive to enter.

Profit-seeking generates movement of resources between different industries. Freedom of entry combined with profit-seeking tends to push profit towards zero in any industry, whether or not it is perfectly competitive.

Box 7.3 uses the theory just developed to investigate the costs and benefits of changes in input prices.

## Marginal and intramarginal firms

If firms have an incentive to exit from an industry which ones will leave? Here it is useful to distinguish marginal from intramarginal firms. The marginal firm is just covering its full costs and would exit if price fell by even a small amount. The intramarginal firm is earning profits and would require a larger fall in price to persuade it to exit. In the pure abstract model of perfect competition, however, all firms are marginal firms in long-run equilibrium. All firms have access to the same technology, and all, therefore, will have identical cost curves when enough time has passed for full adjustment of all capital to be made. In long-run industry equilibrium, all firms are thus in position (ii) in Figure 7.8. If price falls below $p_2$ in that figure, all firms will wish to withdraw. Exit must then be by some contrived process, such as random lot, since there is nothing in the theory to explain who will exit first.

In real-world situations firms are not identical, since technology changes continually and different firms have different histories. A firm that has recently replaced its capital is likely to have more efficient, lower-cost plant, and hence lower cost curves, than a firm whose capital is ageing. The details of each practical case will then determine the identity of the marginal firm that will exit first when price falls. For example, assume that all firms have identical costs and differ only in the date at which they entered the industry. In this case, the firm whose capital comes up for replacement first will be the marginal firm. It will exit first because it will be the first to confront the long-run decision about replacing its capital in a situation where no firms are covering long-run opportunity costs.

Box 7.4 shows how the theory can be used to understand some of the effects of technological changes that lower production costs.

## The effect of making capital a variable input

Consider the position of the firms and the industry when both are in long-run equilibrium. There is no change that any firm could make over the short or the long run that would increase its profits. This requirement can be stated as three distinct conditions:

1. *No firm wants to vary the output of its existing plants.* Short-run marginal cost (*SRMC*) is equal to price.

2. *Profits earned by existing plants are zero.* This implies that short-run *ATC* is equal to price—that is, firms are in the position of the firm in Figure 7.8(ii).

3. *No firm can earn profits by building a plant of a different size.* This implies that each existing firm must be producing at the lowest point on its long-run average cost curve.

We have already seen why the first two conditions must hold. The reasoning behind the third condition is shown in Figure 7.10. Although the firm with the average cost curve $SRATC_0$ is in short-run equilibrium, it is not in long-run equilibrium because its *LRAC* curve lies below the market price at some higher levels of output.[6] The firm can, therefore, increase its profits by building a plant of

---

[6] Because all inputs are variable in the long run, no distinction is needed between variable and fixed costs. There is only one long-run average cost curve.

## Box 7.3 Who benefits and loses from changes in input costs?

A fall in the cost of production causes a downward shift in each firm's marginal cost curve. As a result the short-run supply curve, which is the sum of the individual firms' marginal cost curves, shifts downwards. This leads to a higher output and a lower price. The price will fall, however, by less than the fall in costs, while profits will now be earned because of the lower costs of production. These changes are shown in the figure.

A fall in costs in a competitive industry leads to a fall in price, an increase in output, and the emergence of profits. In part (i) the original demand and supply curves of $D$ and $S_0$ intersect at $E_0$ to yield a price and quantity of $p_0$ and $q_0$. When each firm's production costs fall, the supply curve—which is the sum of the marginal cost curves of all firms in the industry—shifts downward by the amount of the fall in costs, to $S_1$. If price fell by the full amount that costs had fallen, price would become $p_2$. Instead, price falls to $p_1$ while quantity rises to $q_1$, at the new equilibrium $E_1$.

In part (ii) the typical firm is shown in equilibrium at price $p_0$ with cost curves $SRATC_0$ and $MC_0$. The cost curves then shift to $SRATC_1$ and $MC_1$. The firm would be willing to produce output $q_0$ at price $p_2$. Instead, price falls only to $p_1$, and the firm increases its output to $q_1$. At this price–quantity combination it earns profits shown by the dark blue area.

In the short run under perfect competition, a fall in variable cost causes price to fall, but by less than the reduction in marginal cost. The benefit of the reduction in cost is thus shared between consumers, in terms of lower prices, and producers, in terms of profits.

In the long run, however, profits cannot persist in an industry with freedom of entry. New firms will enter the industry, increasing output and reducing price until all profits are eliminated. Entry shifts the short-run supply curve to the right. Now each firm, old and new, just covers its total costs by producing at the minimum point on its average total cost curve.

Under perfect competition, all of the benefits of lower costs are passed on to consumers in terms of higher output and lower prices in the long run.

The case of a rise in costs is just the reverse. In the short run the effects will be shared between consumers, in terms of higher prices, and producers, in terms of losses. In the long run, however, firms will leave the industry until those remaining can cover all their costs. Therefore, the long-run effects of higher costs are fully borne by consumers in terms of lower output and higher prices.

(i)

(ii)

---

larger size, thereby lowering its average total costs. Since the firm is a price-taker, this change will increase its profits.

A price-taking firm is in long-run equilibrium only when it is producing at the minimum point on its *LRAC* curve.

All three of the conditions listed above are fulfilled when each firm in the industry is in the position shown in Figure 7.10 by the short-run cost curve *SRATC\**.[7]

[7] The text discussion implies that all existing firms and all new entrants face identical *LRAC* curves. This means that all firms face the same set of input prices and use the same technology. We are in the long run, *where technological knowledge is given and constant*, and where all firms have had a chance to adjust their capital to the best that is available. This is a theoretical construction designed to analyse tendencies. In any industry in which technological change is ongoing, full long-run equilibrium will never be established and a variety of technologies will be used by different firms at each point in time.

**Box 7.4** The effects of changing technology

### A once-and-for-all change

To see the effects of a single advance in an industry's production technology, let the industry start in long-run equilibrium where each firm is earning zero profits. Some technological development in the industry's production process now lowers the production costs of newly built plants. In this case, as with many technological changes, old production facilities cannot use the technology because it must be embodied in new plant and equipment. Since initially the price was just equal to the average total cost for the existing plants, new plants will be able to earn profits and so will be built immediately. But this expansion in capacity shifts the industry's short-run supply curve to the right and drives price down.

The expansion in capacity and the fall in price will continue until price is equal to the average total cost of the new plants. At this price old plants will not be covering their long-run costs. As long as price exceeds their average variable cost, however, they will continue in production. As the outmoded plants wear out, they will gradually disappear. Eventually a new long-run equilibrium will be established in which all plants are using the new technology. Output will be larger, price will be lower, and the new plants will be just covering their total costs.

### Ongoing changes

Now ask what happens in a competitive industry in which this type of technological change occurs more or less continuously. Plants built in any one year will tend to have lower costs than plants built in any previous year. The figure illustrates such an industry. Plant 1 is the oldest plant in operation. It is just covering its average variable costs, and will close down when price falls below $p_0$. Plant 2 is of intermediate age. It is covering its variable costs, and earning some contribution towards its fixed costs, as shown by the shaded area in part (ii). Plant 3 is the newest plant with the lowest costs. It is fully covering its fixed costs, as shown

by the dark shaded area in (iii). It is also making additional profits (shown by the light shaded area) which will offset the losses it expects to suffer later, when firms with newer technology enter the industry.

Such an industry typically has a number of interesting characteristics. First, plants in operation will be of many different ages and will be operations at different levels of efficiency. This is dramatically illustrated by the variety of types and vintages of generator found in any long-established electricity industry. Critics who observe the continued use of older, less efficient plants and urge that the industry be modernized miss the point of economic efficiency. If the plant is already there, it can be operated profitably as long as it can cover its variable costs.

A second characteristic of such an industry is that price will be governed by the minimum average total cost of the most efficient plants. Entry will continue until plants of the latest vintage are just expected to cover the opportunity cost of their capital over their lifetime. This means that new plants must earn pure profits when they enter to balance the losses they expect later in life when newer firms with superior technologies enter the industry. The benefits of the new technology are passed on to consumers, because all units of the product, whether produced by new or old plants, are sold at a price that is related solely to the average total costs of the new plants. Owners of older plants find their returns over variable costs falling steadily as increasingly efficient plants drive the price down.

A third characteristic is that old plants will be discarded when the price falls below their average total costs. This may occur well before the plants are physically worn out. In industries with continuous technical progress, capital is usually discarded because it is economically obsolete, not because it has physically worn out. This illustrates the economic meaning of 'obsolete'.

Old capital is obsolete when its average variable cost exceeds the average total cost of new capital.

(i) Plant 1

(ii) Plant 2

(iii) Plant 3

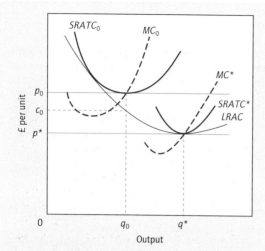

**Figure 7.10 Short-run and long-run equilibrium of a firm in perfect competition**

A perfectly competitive firm that is not at the minimum point on its *LRAC* curve cannot be in long-run equilibrium. The firm's existing plant has short-run cost curves $SRATC_0$ and $MC_0$ while market price is $p_0$. The firm produces $q_0$, where $MC_0$ equals price and total costs are just being covered. Although the firm is in short-run equilibrium, it can earn profits by building a larger plant and so moving downwards along its *LRAC* curve. Thus, the firm cannot be in long-run equilibrium at any output below $q^*$, because average total costs can be reduced by building a larger plant.

If all firms do this, industry output will increase and price will fall until long-run equilibrium is reached at price $p^*$. Each firm is then in short-run equilibrium with a plant whose average cost curve is $SRATC^*$ and whose short-run marginal cost curve, $MC^*$, intersects the price line $p^*$ at an output of $q^*$. Because the *LRAC* curve lies above $p^*$ everywhere except at $q^*$, the firm has no incentive to move to another point on its *LRAC* curve by altering the size of its plant. The output $q^*$ is the firm's minimum efficient scale.

## Long-run response to a change in demand

What will happen if demand for the product increases? Price will rise to equate demand with the industry's short-run supply. Each firm will expand output until its short-run marginal cost once again equals price. Each firm will earn profits as a result of the rise in price, and the profits will induce new firms to enter the industry. This will shift the short-run supply curve to the right and force down the price. Entry will continue until all firms are once again just covering average total costs.

What if demand falls? The industry starts with firms in long-run equilibrium as shown in Figure 7.10, and the market demand curve shifts left so that price falls. There are two possible consequences.

First, the decline in demand may force price below $ATC$ but leave it above $AVC$. Firms are then in the position

shown in Figure 7.8(i). They can cover their variable costs and earn some return on their capital, so they remain in production for as long as their existing plant and equipment last. Exit will occur, however, as old capital wears out and is not replaced. As firms exit, the short-run supply curve shifts left and market price rises. This continues until the remaining firms in the industry can cover their total costs. At this point it will pay to replace capital as it wears out, and the industry will stop declining. This adjustment may take a long time, for the industry will shrink in size only as existing plant and equipment wear out.

The second possibility is that the decline in demand is large enough to push price below the level of $AVC$. Now firms cannot even cover their variable costs, and some will shut down immediately. Reduction in capital devoted to production in the industry occurs rapidly because some existing capacity is scrapped or shifted to other uses. The decline in the number of firms reduces supply and raises the equilibrium price. Once the price rises enough to allow the remaining firms to cover their variable costs, the rapid withdrawal of capital ceases. Further exit occurs more slowly, as described in the previous paragraph.

Entry of new capital into a profitable industry can take place only as fast as new plants can be built and new equipment installed. Exit of existing capital from an unprofitable industry with losses will occur very quickly when price is less than average variable cost, but only at the rate at which old plant and equipment wear out when price exceeds average variable cost.

Box 7.5 applies what we have just learned to the case of declining industries.

## The long-run industry supply curve

Possible adjustments of the industry to the kind of changes in demand just discussed are shown by the **long-run industry supply (LRS) curve**. This curve shows the relationship between equilibrium market price and the output that firms would be willing to supply after all desired entry or exit has occurred.

The long-run supply curve shows the quantity supplied at each market price in long-run equilibrium, that is, after all demand-induced changes have occurred and the incentives for exit and entry have been eliminated.

For given input prices, the long-run supply curve of a competitive industry will be horizontal. But when induced changes in input prices are considered, it is possible for the *LRS* curve to be positively or negatively sloped. The various cases are illustrated in Figure 7.11.

**Box 7.5 Declining industries**

What happens when a competitive industry begins to suffer losses because the demand for its output starts to decline? The market price will begin to fall, and firms that were previously covering average total costs will no longer be able to do so. They find themselves in the position shown in part (i) of Figure 7.8 on page 146. Firms suffer losses instead of breaking even; the signal for the exit of capital is given, but exit takes time.

The economically efficient response to a steadily declining demand is to continue to operate with existing equipment as long as variable costs of production can be covered. As equipment becomes obsolete because average variable cost cannot be recovered, it will not be replaced unless the extra revenue generated from use of new equipment exceeds the firm's average total cost. As a result, the capacity of the industry will shrink. If demand keeps declining, capacity must keep shrinking.

Declining industries typically give a depressing impression. Revenues are below long-run total costs, and as a result new equipment is not brought in to replace old equipment as it wears out. The average age of equipment in use therefore rises steadily. An observer of the industry's plight is likely to blame it on the old equipment.

The antiquated equipment in a declining industry is often the effect rather than the cause of the industry's decline.

Governments are often tempted to support declining industries because they are worried about the resulting job losses. Experience suggests, however, that propping up genuinely declining industries only delays their demise—at significant national cost. When the government finally withdraws its support, the decline is usually more abrupt, and hence more difficult to adjust to, than if the industry had been allowed to decline gradually under the market force of steadily declining demand.

Once governments recognize the decay of certain industries and the collapse of certain firms as an inevitable aspect of economic growth, a more effective response is to provide temporary income support and retraining schemes that cushion the impacts of change. These can moderate the effects on the incomes of workers who lose their jobs and make it easier for them to transfer to expanding industries. Intervention that is intended to increase mobility while reducing the social and personal costs of mobility is a viable long-run policy. In contrast, trying to freeze the existing industrial structure by shoring up a declining industry is not viable in the long run.

(i)

(ii)

(iii)

**Figure 7.11 Long-run industry supply curves**

**The long-run industry supply curve may be horizontal, or positively or negatively sloped.** In all three parts the initial curves are at $D_0$ and $S_0$, yielding equilibrium at $E_0$ with price $p_0$ and quantity $q_0$. A rise in demand shifts the demand curve to $D_1$, taking the short-run equilibrium to $E_1$. New firms now enter the industry, shifting the short-run supply curve outwards and pushing price down until pure profits are no longer being earned. At this point the supply curve is $S_1$ and the new equilibrium is $E_2$ with price at $p_2$ and quantity $q_2$.

In part (i) price returns to its original level, making the long-run supply curve horizontal. In part (ii) profits are eliminated before price falls to its original level, giving the *LRS* curve a positive slope. In part (iii) the price falls below its original level before profits return to normal, giving the *LRS* curve a negative slope.

In Figure 7.11(i) the long-run supply curve is horizontal. This indicates that, given time, the industry will adjust its size to provide whatever quantity is demanded at a constant price. That price is set by the minimum point of the firms' long-run average cost curves. An industry with a horizontal long-run supply curve is said to be a *constant-cost industry*.

This situation occurs when a change in the size of the industry leaves the long-run cost curves of existing firms unchanged, which requires that the industry's input prices do not change as the whole industry's output expands or contracts. Since all firms are assumed to have access to the same technology and to face the same input prices, all firms have identical cost curves. Under these circumstances, the long-run equilibrium with price equal to minimum long-run average total cost of each and every firm can be re-established after a change in demand only when price returns to its original level.

### Changing input prices and rising long-run supply curves

When an industry expands its output it needs more inputs. The increase in demand for these inputs may bid up their prices.[8]

If costs rise with increasing levels of industry output, so too must the price at which the producers are able to cover their costs. As the industry expands, the short-run supply curve shifts outwards, but the firms' *SRATC* curves shift upward because of rising input prices. The expansion of the industry comes to a halt when price is equal to minimum *LRAC* for existing firms. This must occur at a higher price than was the case before the expansion began, as illustrated in Figure 7.11(ii). A competitive industry with rising long-run supply prices is often called a *rising-cost industry*.

### Can the long-run supply curve decline?

So far we have suggested that the long-run supply curve may be horizontal or positively sloped. Could it ever decline, thereby indicating that higher outputs are associated with lower prices in long-run equilibrium?

It is tempting to answer 'yes', because of the opportunities of more efficient scales of operation using greater mechanization and more effective specialization of labour.

---

[8] In a fully employed economy, the expansion of one industry implies the contraction of some other industry. What happens to input prices depends on the proportions in which the expanding and the contracting industries use the inputs. The relative price of the input that is used intensively by the expanding industry will rise, causing the costs of the expanding industry to rise relative to those of the contracting industry. In a two-sector, two-input model, a rising long-run industry supply curve is normal because of the effect that changes in industry outputs have on relative input prices.

But this answer would not be correct for perfectly competitive industries, because each firm in long-run equilibrium must already be at the lowest point on its *LRAC* curve. If a firm could lower its costs by building a larger, more mechanized plant, it would be profitable to do so without waiting for an increase in demand. Since any single firm can sell all it wishes at the going market price, it will be profitable to expand the scale of its operations as long as its *LRAC* is falling.

The scale economies that we have just considered are within the control of the firm; they are said to be **internal economies**. A perfectly competitive industry might, however, have falling long-run costs if industries that supply its inputs have increasing returns to scale. Such effects are outside the control of the perfectly competitive firm and are called **external economies**. Whenever expansion of an industry leads to a fall in the prices of some of its inputs, the firms will find their cost curves shifting downwards as they expand their outputs.

As an illustration of how the expansion of one industry can cause the prices of some of its inputs to fall, consider the early stages of the growth of the car industry. As the output of cars increased, the industry's demand for tyres grew considerably. This increased the demand for rubber and tended to raise its price, but it also provided the opportunity for tyre manufacturers to build larger plants, which exploited some of the economies available in tyre production. These economies were large enough to offset any input-price increases, and tyre prices charged to car manufacturers fell. Therefore car costs fell, because of the lower prices of an important input. This case is illustrated in part (iii) of Figure 7.11. An industry that has a negatively sloped long-run supply curve is often called a *falling-cost industry*.

Notice that, although the economies were external to the car industry, they were internal to the tyre industry. However, if the tyre industry had been perfectly competitive, all its scale economies would already have been exploited. So this is a case of a perfectly competitive industry that uses an input produced by a non-competitive industry, whose own scale economies have not yet been fully exploited because demand is insufficient. Another example is provided by perfectly competitive agricultural industries; they buy their farm machinery from the farm-implement industry, which is dominated by a few large firms.

## Can perfectly competitive industries have unexploited scale economies?

The key to answering this question lies in the size of the firm relative to the size of the market.

A competitive firm will never be in equilibrium on the falling part of its *LRAC*—if price is given and costs can be reduced by increasing the scale of output, profits can be increased by doing the same. Thus, firms will grow in size until all scale economies are exhausted. Provided that the output that yields the minimum *LRAC* for each firm is small relative to the industry's total output, the industry will contain a large number of firms and will remain competitive. If, however, reaching the minimum *LRAC* makes firms so large that each one has significant market power, they will cease to be price-takers and perfect competition

will cease to exist. Indeed, scale economies may exist over such a large range that one firm's *LRAC* is still falling when it serves the entire market. That firm will then grow until it monopolizes the entire market. This case, which economists call a *natural* monopoly, is considered further in later chapters.

A necessary condition for a long-run perfectly competitive equilibrium is that any scale economies that are within the firm's control should be exhausted at a level of output that is small relative to the whole industry's output.

## The allocative efficiency of perfect competition

We saw in Chapter 1 that resources are allocated by markets in which people make independent decisions motivated by self-interest. Under certain conditions, this market outcome is *optimal* or *efficient*. (The two words mean the same thing in this context.) Resources are efficiently allocated if there is no other allocation that would allow someone to be made better off while no one was made worse off. To put this statement the other way around, resources are *inefficiently* allocated if the allocation could be changed in such a way as to make at least one person better off while making no one worse off. For example, if resources could be reallocated so as to make fewer hats and more shoes and someone could be made better off by the change while no one would be made worse off, then the current allocation cannot be efficient.

It can be shown that a perfectly competitive economy would allocate its resources efficiently. However, a number of other conditions also need to be fulfilled, as we will see in Chapter 13. In the meantime we will show one way in which the tendency for perfect competition to produce an optimal allocation of resources can be established. We do this using the concepts of consumers' and producers' surplus.

We first introduced the idea of consumers' surplus in Box 5.2 on page 91. **Consumers' surplus** is the difference between the total value that consumers place on all the units consumed of some product and the payment that they actually make for the purchase of that product. This surplus arises because each consumer, who has a negatively sloped demand curve for each product, is prepared to pay more for the first unit of a product consumed than for the second, and a decreasing amount for each subsequent unit. Take, for example, my demand for visits to the cinema each month. If tickets cost £30, I would go once

per month (and £30 is the value I place on that first visit); at £20 I would go twice per month (and still value the first visit at £30 and the second visit at £20), and at £10 I might go three times per month (valuing the first visit at £30, the second at £20 and the third at £10). If the market price is £10, then I will go to the cinema three times a month and pay £30 for these visits (three tickets at £10 each). But I will value these visits at £60 (£30 for the first visit, £20 for the second visit and £10 for the third visit). This is because I would have been prepared to pay £30 for the first visit but only had to pay £10, and I would have been prepared to pay £20 for the second visit but only had to pay £10, and so on. Thus, the value of my consumer surplus from purchases of cinema tickets is £30 per month (the £60 of value that I place on these visits minus the £30 I actually paid at £10 per ticket).

Put another way, consumers pay the same amount for each unit that they purchase, but, given diminishing marginal utility, they value every unit that they purchase at more than that price—with the exception of the last marginal unit, which they value at just the price they pay for it. The difference is the *consumers' surplus*, which is positive for each unit purchased except for the last unit, where the value they get is just equal to the price that they pay.

For consumers in general, the total value that they place on the amount they consume of a specific product is the area under the demand curve, which represents the summation of all the marginal valuations they place on each successive unit consumed. What they pay is the area representing the price multiplied by the quantity consumed. The difference between these two is shown in Figure 7.12 as consumers' surplus.

Producers' surplus is analogous to consumers' surplus. It occurs because all units of each firm's output are sold at

**Figure 7.12  Consumers' and producers' surplus**

**Consumers' surplus is the area under the demand curve and above the market price line.** Producers' surplus is the area above the supply curve and below the market price line. The equilibrium price and quantity are $p_0$ and $q_0$. The total value that consumers place on $q_0$ units of the product is given by the sum of the dark pink, light pink, and blue areas. The amount that they pay is $p_0q_0$, the rectangle that consists of the light pink and blue areas. The difference, shown as the dark pink area, is *consumers' surplus*.

The receipts to producers from the sale of $q_0$ units are also $p_0q_0$. The area under the supply curve, the blue-shaded area, is total variable cost, the minimum amount that producers require to supply the output. The difference, shown as the light pink area, is *producers' surplus*.

**Figure 7.13  The allocative efficiency of perfect competition**

**Competitive equilibrium is allocatively efficient because it maximizes the sum of consumers' and producers' surplus.** At the competitive equilibrium $E$ consumers' surplus is the dark pink area above the price line, while producers' surplus is the light pink area below the price line.

Reducing the output to $q_1$ but keeping price at $p_0$ lowers consumers' surplus by area 1 and lowers producers' surplus by area 2. If producers are forced to produce output $q_2$ and to sell it to consumers, who are in turn forced to buy it at price $p_0$, producers' surplus is reduced by area 3 (the amount by which variable costs exceed revenue on those units), while consumers' surplus is reduced by area 4 (the amount by which expenditure exceeds consumers' satisfactions on those units). Only at the competitive output, $q_0$, is the sum of the two surpluses maximized.

the single market price, while, given a rising supply curve, the marginal cost of all but the last unit is less than the market price. **Producers' surplus** is defined as the amount that producers are paid for a product less the total variable cost of production. The total variable cost of producing any output is shown by the area under the supply curve up to that output, which represents the summation of the marginal costs of producing each unit of output.[9] Thus, producers' surplus, which is shown in Figure 7.12, is the area between the supply curve and the market price line. (All firms are either directly or indirectly owned by people, so producers' surplus is really owners' surplus.)

If the total of consumers' and producers' surplus is not maximized, the industry's output could be altered to increase that total. The additional surplus could then be

used to make some people better off without making any others worse off.

**Allocative efficiency occurs where the sum of consumers' and producers' surplus is maximized.**

The allocatively efficient output occurs under perfect competition where the demand curve intersects the supply curve, that is, at the point of equilibrium in a competitive market. This is shown graphically in Figure 7.13. For any output that is less than the competitive output, the demand curve lies above the supply curve, which means that the value consumers put on the last unit of production exceeds its marginal cost of production. Suppose, for example, that an additional pair of shoes costs £60 to make but is valued by consumers at £70. If the shoes are sold at any price between £60 and £70, both producers and consumers gain; there is £10 of potential surplus to be divided between the two. In contrast, the last unit produced and sold at competitive equilibrium adds nothing to either consumers' or producers' surplus. This is because

---

[9] The area under a marginal cost curve up to any output is the total variable cost of producing that output. Graphically, taking the area under a marginal cost curve is equivalent to summing all the marginal costs to get total variable cost. Similarly, summing the area under the demand curve yields the total amount that consumers would be willing to pay if offered each unit one at a time, i.e. the total valuation they place on all the units.

consumers value it at exactly its market price, and it adds the full amount of the market price to producers' cost.

If production were pushed beyond the competitive equilibrium, the sum of the two surpluses would fall. Assume, for example, that firms were forced to produce and sell further units of output at the competitive market price and that consumers were forced to buy these extra units at that price. (Neither group would do so voluntarily.) Firms would lose producers' surplus on those extra units because their marginal costs of producing them would be above the price that they received for them. Purchasers would lose consumers' surplus because the valuation that they placed on these extra units, as shown by the demand curve, would be less than the price that they would have to pay.

The sum of producers' and consumers' surplus is maximized when a perfectly competitive industry is in equilibrium with demand equal to supply. The resulting level of output is allocatively efficient.

 # CASE STUDIES

The markets that best fit the assumptions of perfect competition are those for primary commodities. These are homogeneous products; they typically sell on world markets; and each individual supplier is small in the sense that it cannot influence the world market price by acting alone. In Chapter 4 we discussed some features of the market for coffee beans, which at the level of individual coffee farmers fits into our classification of a perfectly competitive market. We now look at two others: the markets for cocoa beans and the market for copper.

## 1. Cocoa: 'the food of the gods'[10]

Cocoa beans are the main natural ingredient used to make chocolate. Cocoa beans grow on trees that require a tropical climate and substantial rainfall. They also require the shade of other trees, but once matured a cocoa tree will bear fruit for up to a hundred years or so. The plant is a native of South America but its cultivation has spread to Africa and Asia. In the early 1970s cocoa production was concentrated in Cote d'Ivoire, Ghana, Nigeria, and Brazil, but a high world market price encouraged entry for other producer countries such as Indonesia and Malaysia. In 2005, these six countries plus Ecuador and Cameroon accounted for 95 per cent of the world market supply.

While there are eight major producing countries, within these countries production is fragmented into a mixture of medium-sized estates and small farms. In some cases, such as Ghana, the national government has created a marketing board to buy the beans from domestic farmers (and guarantee a price each year to these farmers). In other cases, private agents buy from the farmers and then sell in the world market. But in all cases the farmers themselves are price-takers and are unable to influence the price that they receive.

Figure 7.14 shows the world price of cocoa beans since 1980. The world market price reached an all time high of around $3,700 per tonne in the late 1970s and this encouraged a significant increase in planting, as mentioned above. The result of this was that supply growth outstripped demand growth for much of the 1980s and 1990s. On several occasions the world price fell below $1,000 per tonne.

As with many food products (it is worth re-reading the discussion of the coffee market at this point on pages 80–1) the demand side of the cocoa market is dominated by two important economic characteristics: a low income elasticity, and a low price elasticity. Low income elasticity means that, even when real incomes are growing significantly in consumer countries, demand for cocoa beans grows only very slowly. Low price elasticity means that, when the price falls, this does not encourage a proportionate increase in quantity demanded. Indeed, cocoa beans contribute only a small component of the total cost of finished chocolate products; so, for example, a significant fall in the price of wholesale cocoa beans will have a very small effect on the price of a half-pound box of Cadbury's Milk Tray.

One characteristic of the coffee market that is noticeable in Figure 4.12 on page 81 is that there are occasional big supply shocks that lead to dramatic upward spikes in the market price. These are largely explained by adverse weather events in major producer countries such as Brazil. Cocoa is not subject to such adverse weather events. This is because it is grown in tropical regions, whereas coffee is grown in cooler locations which can be subject to unseasonal frosts. However, there was a clear price spike in the cocoa market in 2002 and this was caused by a reduction in supply due to a civil war in Cote d'Ivoire, the largest producer country.

It is easy to imagine the main decisions that cocoa farmers have to make. First, if they decide to go into the business of growing

---

[10] This is the name given to cocoa by the Spanish conquistadors when they first came across it in South America around 500 years ago. We are grateful to Juan Berg for this information.

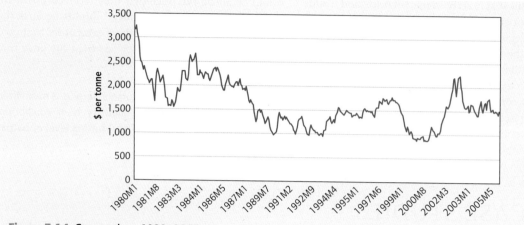

**Figure 7.14** Cocoa prices, 1980–2005

cocoa trees, how much land should be devoted to this crop? A high world price is likely to encourage new planting. Once the trees are planted, however, it is the fertility of the trees that will determine the size of the crop, and then world market conditions that will determine what the crop will be worth. When prices are low it is hard to shift the land into other uses. The farm could be sold, but would not fetch much if covered in low-value producing cocoa trees. Alternatively, the cocoa trees and the surrounding shade-giving trees could be chopped down and the land converted to another use. However, this is expensive, hard to reverse, and alternative crops may be few and just as low yielding. Hence in the short term a typical cocoa farmer has little choice but to live as best he can off whatever revenue the crop generates each year. This is not a perfect world, but it is one example of perfect competition at work. The world market price is determined by the global interaction of demand and supply, and each producer has to accept whatever price is so determined.

## 2. Copper

*Copper is a key metal used in global industrial development. Its unique chemical and physical properties, including a high electrical conductivity, resistance to corrosion, and excellent malleability and ductility, make it a superior material for use in the building construction, electrical energy, telecommunications, transportation and industrial machinery businesses. Wire and cable products, used principally as energy cable, building wire and magnet wire, account for as much as 75% of copper consumption. Copper is also an important metal in non-electrical applications such as plumbing, roofing and, when alloyed with zinc to form brass, in many industrial and consumer applications. The building and construction industry accounts for approximately 37% of worldwide copper usage. . . . The principal source of global copper supply is from mine production, with recycled*

*scrap comprising the balance of approximately 12%. Latin America is the largest contributor to mine production at 45%, followed by the former Eastern Bloc countries at 19%, Oceania at 18% and North America at 12%. (AUR Resources on http://www.aurresources.com/copper.htm)*

The copper market shares some characteristics with the steel market that we discussed on pages 57–8. Both metals are inputs into industries in the major countries of the world. In common with other markets that have a perfectly competitive structure, there is a homogeneous product and the world price is determined in the aggregate by the interaction of demand and supply. In the cases of both copper and steel (as compared with coffee and cocoa) it is less obvious that all the assumptions of perfect competition are satisfied, because there are some very large producers in these markets. However, in both cases the world market is so large compared with the output of even the largest firms that each firm is a price-taker. Also, both copper and steel can be produced in many different parts of the world.

Figure 7.15 shows world copper prices since 1980. As copper is an input into virtually all construction projects, demand tends to rise when there is a construction boom in the main consuming countries. Thus, demand was high in the late 1980s and mid-1990s. In a period of slack demand, such as the mid-1980s and 1998–2002, there is an excess of production over final demand which leads to a big build-up of stocks. Rundowns of stocks in periods of high demand help to moderate the resulting price rises. This feature of the copper market—that inventories are built up when demand is low and run down when it is high —serves to moderate price fluctuations, and it makes this market rather different from that of a perishable commodity. It does not however violate the assumptions of perfect competition, because all that is required is that individual producers know

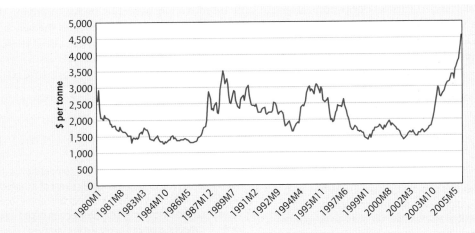

**Figure 7.15** World copper prices, 1980–2005

about the price fluctuations and prefer to maintain production and build up stocks when they perceive that demand is low and to sell these off when they perceive that demand is high.

In 2003 world copper demand started to grow ahead of new production, and accumulated inventories of copper ran down rapidly. This demand growth came largely from the rapid growth in demand for construction in China, India, and other Asian countries. By 2004 stocks reached historically low levels and prices started to rise sharply. This increase in price ultimately led to greater production, but the expansion of production capacity takes considerable time, so industry experts expect the price to remain high for several years to come.

For individual firms, the choices posed by the market in which they operate fit well with the perfect competition model. They take the world market price as beyond their control and then have to decide how much to produce. Firms in this industry own mines or mining rights, but extracting copper is expensive as it lies deep underground and requires much labour and machinery to excavate. Production bears increasing marginal costs even in existing mines. The opening up of new mines carries high marginal costs, and considerable time must pass before sales can increase. When prices are low, therefore, firms cut back on their production and cease operation in any mines that do not cover average variable costs. (This is similar to the decision by airline operators to park their planes when demand is low, discussed in Box 7.2 on page 142.) When prices are high, firms expand production up to the point where marginal cost is equal to price. They may also investigate the opening up of new mines. In general, they will go ahead with such investment decisions if the expected extra revenue exceeds the extra cost. (The precise calculation involved in such an investment decision is discussed in Chapter 12 below.)

As the world price is given, the main incentive for profit-maximizing firms is to seek ways of reducing their costs of production. This means looking for improved extraction technology, hiring more productive workers, or reducing costs of management and distribution. The perfect competition model is more than adequate to help us understand the context of these decisions.

## Conclusion

Perfect competition is a special case that exists in only a few sectors where the product is homogeneous and there are so many buyers and sellers that no one of them can influence the market price by altering the amount that she buys or sells. This applies to primary commodity industries but it does not apply to most of the goods and services purchased by consumers. The bread and washing powder in Sainsbury's and Tesco may be identical, but supermarkets are not operating under perfect competition as they have some power over their prices, and their own-brands do seek to differentiate what is the same generic product. Most other consumer products are affected even more by brands and actual product differentiation. Hence the perfect competition model is not directly applicable to most markets for goods and services.

None the less, the model of perfect competition gives us some key insights into the working of any market economy. It gives us a simple example within which to understand the principles of profit maximization. It highlights the incentive role played by profits in driving the entry and exit of firms. Finally, it provides the benchmark for the optimal allocation of resources. All of these insights have a payoff in later chapters.

## SUMMARY

### Market structure and firm behaviour

- Competitive *behaviour* refers to the extent to which individual firms compete with each other to sell their products. Competitive *market structure* refers to the power that individual firms have over the market, with perfect competition occurring where firms have no market power and hence no need to react to each other.

### Perfectly competitive markets

- The theory of perfect competition is based on the following assumptions: (i) firms sell a homogeneous product; (ii) customers are well informed; (iii) each of the industry's many firms is a price-taker; and (iv) firms are free to enter or leave the industry.

### Short-run equilibrium

- Any firm maximizes profits by producing the output where its marginal cost curve intersects the marginal revenue curve from below—or by producing nothing if average variable cost exceeds price at all possible outputs.

- A perfectly competitive firm is a quantity-adjuster, facing a perfectly elastic demand curve at the given market price and maximizing profits by choosing the output that equates its marginal cost to price.

- The supply curve of a firm in perfect competition is its marginal cost curve, and the supply curve of a perfectly competitive industry is the horizontal sum of the marginal cost curves of all its firms. The intersection of this curve with the market demand curve for the industry's product determines market price.

### Long-run equilibrium

- Long-run industry equilibrium requires that each individual firm produce at the minimum point of its *LRAC* curve and make zero profits.

- The long-run industry supply curve for a perfectly competitive industry may be (i) positively sloped, if input prices are driven up by the industry's expansion, (ii) horizontal, if plants can be replicated and input prices remain constant, or (iii) negatively sloped, if some other industry that is not perfectly competitive produces an input under conditions of falling long-run costs.

### The allocative efficiency of perfect competition

- Perfect competition produces an optimal allocation of resources because it maximizes the sum of consumers' and producers' surplus by producing equilibrium where marginal cost equals price.

## TOPICS FOR REVIEW

- Competitive behaviour and competitive market structure
- Behavioural rules for the profit-maximizing firm
- Price-taking and a horizontal demand curve
- Average revenue, marginal revenue, and price under perfect competition
- Relation of the industry's supply curve to its firms' marginal cost curves
- The role of entry and exit in achieving long-run equilibrium
- Exhaustion of scale economies in perfectly competitive long-run equilibrium

# QUESTIONS

1 A firm sells its product at £15 each. Calculate its total, average, and marginal revenue at sales levels of 100, 500, and 10,000.

2 Suppose that total fixed costs of the firm in question 1 are £300 and total variable costs for production levels between 100 units of output and 108 units of outputs are:

100 = £1,000
101 = £1,010
102 = £1,021
103 = £1,033
104 = £1,046
105 = £1,060
106 = £1,075
107 = £1,091
108 = £2,108.

What is the profit-maximizing level of output, given a sale price of £15 as in question 1?

3 Calculate the average variable cost and the average total cost associated with the output levels in question 2. How much profit is made at the profit-maximizing level of output? How much profit would be made at the two higher and two lower levels of output? What would be the profit-maximizing output and profit at a sales price of £12?

4 Which of the following observed facts about an industry are inconsistent with its being perfectly competitive?
(a) Different firms use different methods of production.
(b) The industry's product is extensively advertised by a trade association. (c) Individual firms devote a large fraction of their sales receipts to advertising their own product brands. (d) There are 24 firms in the industry. (e) All firms made economic profits in 2006. (f) All firms are charging the same price.

5 What are the three rules of profit maximization? Explain these rules in the context of a firm that is in a perfectly competitive market structure.

6 Suppose all of the potentially arable land in some country is currently being used for growing either wheat or barley. Both crop markets are in equilibrium. Discuss exactly how decentralized competitive markets would respond in order to shift resources following a report that barley helps reduce the risk of cancer.

7 Why would the existence of entry barriers make it unlikely that an industry would be perfectly competitive? What types of entry barriers do you think are important in practice? How can the existence of economies of scale affect the degree of competitiveness in a market?

8 How does technical progress affect the equilibrium of a firm and of the perfectly competitive industry in which it operates? Why do some industries decline while others grow? At what point should firms quit a declining industry?

9 What factors determine the shape of the long-run supply curve of an industry?

10 What is allocative efficiency? Why is the outcome under perfect competition allocatively efficient?

# Chapter 8

# MONOPOLY

How does a firm choose its profit maximizing output when it is the only producer and so faces the downward sloping market demand curve? What price would this firm set? Does a monopolist have unlimited power to exploit consumers by charging them whatever price it pleases? These are some of the questions that we address in this chapter.

In particular, you will learn that:

- A monopolist sets marginal cost equal to marginal revenue, but marginal cost is less than price.
- Output is lower under monopoly than under perfect competition.
- Profit can be increased for a monopolist if it is possible to charge different prices to different customers or in separate markets.
- Pure profits exist in the long run under monopoly, so long as there are entry barriers.
- Cartels can increase the profits of colluding firms, but individual members have an incentive to cheat.

Monopoly is at the opposite extreme from perfect competition. A **monopoly** occurs when one firm, called a monopolist or a monopoly firm, produces an industry's entire output. In contrast to perfectly competitive firms, which are price-takers, a monopolist sets the market price.

In the first part of this chapter we show that, when a monopoly firm must charge a single price for its output, it will produce less, charge a higher price, and earn greater profits than firms operating under perfect competition. Next, we explain why all monopoly firms have an incentive to charge different prices to different classes of users or on different units sold to the same user. We also see that monopoly profits provide a strong incentive for new firms to enter the industry and that this will happen unless there are effective barriers to entry, of either a natural or a man-made variety. In the final part of the chapter we analyse how groups of firms can band together to form a cartel, which raises profits by acting as if it were a monopoly.

In this chapter we mainly analyse the positive implications of monopoly. In Chapter 13 we discuss the normative public policy issues posed by monopoly.

## A single-price monopolist

We first analyse the price and output decision of a monopoly firm that charges a single price for its product. The firm's profits, like those of all firms, will depend on the relationship between its production costs and its sales revenues.

### Cost and revenue in the short run

In Chapter 6 we assumed that firms had U-shaped short-run cost curves. Since the conditions of cost are the same no matter what type of market the firms sells its product in, we can assume that monopoly firms also have U-shaped short-run cost curves.[1]

Because the monopoly firm is the only firm in its industry, there is no distinction between the market demand curve and the demand curve facing a single firm, as there is in perfect competition. Thus, the monopoly firm faces a negatively sloping market demand curve and can set its own price. However, this negatively sloped market demand curve presents the monopoly firm with a trade-off: sales can be increased only if price is reduced, and price can be increased only if sales are reduced.

### Average and marginal revenue

When the monopoly firm charges the same price for all units sold, average revenue per unit is identical to price. So the market demand curve is also the firm's *average revenue curve*. But unlike the firms in perfect competition, the monopoly firm's demand curve is not its marginal revenue curve, which would show the change in total revenue resulting from the sale of an additional (or marginal) unit of production. Because its demand curve is negatively sloped, the monopoly firm must lower the price that it charges on *all* units in order to sell an *extra* unit.

It follows that the addition to its revenue resulting from the sale of an extra unit is less than the price that it receives for that unit (less by the amount that it loses as a result of cutting the price on all the units that it was selling already).

**The monopoly firm's marginal revenue is less than the price at which it sells its output.**

This proposition is illustrated in Figure 8.1.

To clarify these relationships, we use a numerical example of a specific straight-line demand curve. Some points on this curve are shown in tabular form in Table 8.1 while the whole curve is shown in Figure 8.2. Notice in the table that the change in total revenue associated with a change of £0.10 in price is recorded *between* the rows corresponding to three different prices: this is because the data show what happens when the price is changed from the value shown in one row to the value shown in the adjacent row.

Notice also from Figure 8.2 that, when price is reduced starting from £10, total revenue rises at first and then falls. The maximum total revenue is reached in this example at a price of £5. Since marginal revenue is the change in

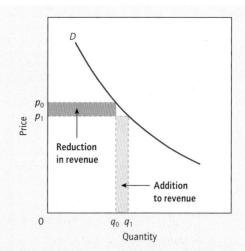

**Figure 8.1 The effect on revenue of an increase in quantity sold**

Because the demand curve has a negative slope, marginal revenue is less than price. A reduction of price from $p_0$ to $p_1$ increases sales by one unit from $q_0$ to $q_1$ units. The revenue from the extra unit sold is shown as the light blue area. But to sell this unit, it is necessary to reduce the price on each of the $q_0$ units previously sold. The loss in revenue is shown as the dark blue area. Marginal revenue of the extra unit is equal to the *difference* between the two areas.

**Table 8.1 Total, average, and marginal revenue**

| Price<br>$p = AR$ | Quantity<br>$q$ | Total revenue<br>$TR = p \cdot q$ | Marginal revenue<br>$MR = \Delta TR / \Delta q$ |
|---|---|---|---|
| £9.10 | 9 | £81.90 | |
| | | | £8.10 |
| 9.00 | 10 | 90.00 | |
| | | | 7.90 |
| 8.90 | 11 | 97.90 | |

**Marginal revenue is less than price because price must be lowered to sell an extra unit.** The marginal revenue of the eleventh unit is total revenue when 11 units are sold minus total revenue when 10 units are sold. This is £7.90, which is less than the price of £8.90 at which all 11 units are sold. Marginal revenue is the £8.90 gained from selling the extra unit at £8.90 minus £0.10 lost on each of the 10 units already being sold when their price falls from £9.00 to £8.90.

total revenue resulting from the sale of one more unit of output, marginal revenue is positive over the range in which total revenue is increasing, and it is negative where total revenue is falling.[2]

---

[1] Some monopolies may arise because the minimum efficient scale of production is large relative to the market demand. We discuss this case, which is known as *natural monopoly*, later in the chapter, and we return to a discussion of the public policy issues that arise in Chapter 13.

[2] Notice that the marginal revenue shown in the table is obtained by subtracting the total revenue associated with one price from the total revenue associated with another, lower, price and then apportioning the change in revenue among the extra units sold. In symbols, it is $\Delta TR / \Delta q$.

**Figure 8.2  Revenue curves and demand elasticity**

Rising *TR*, positive *MR*, and elastic demand all go together, as do falling *TR*, negative *MR*, and inelastic demand. In this example, for outputs from 0 to 50 marginal revenue is positive, elasticity is greater than unity, and total revenue is rising. For outputs from 50 to 100 marginal revenue is negative, elasticity is less than unity, and total revenue is falling. (All elasticities refer to absolute, not algebraic, values.)

The proposition that marginal revenue is always *less than* average revenue, which has been illustrated numerically in Table 8.1 and graphically in Figure 8.2, provides an important contrast with perfect competition. Recall that in perfect competition the firm's marginal revenue from selling an extra unit of output is *equal to* the price at which that unit is sold. The reason for the difference is not difficult to understand. The perfectly competitive firm is a price-taker; it can sell all it wants at the given market price. The monopoly firm faces a negatively sloped demand curve; in order to increase its sales it must reduce the market price.

### Marginal revenue and elasticity

In Chapter 4 we discussed the relationship between the elasticity of the market demand curve and the total

revenue derived from selling the product. Figure 8.2 summarizes this earlier discussion for a linear demand curve and extends it to cover marginal revenue.

Over the range in which the demand curve is elastic, total revenue rises as more units are sold; marginal revenue must, therefore, be positive. Over the range in which the demand curve is inelastic, total revenue falls as more units are sold; marginal revenue must, therefore, be negative.

## Short-run monopoly equilibrium

To show the profit-maximizing equilibrium of a monopoly firm, we bring together information about its revenues and its costs and then apply two rules developed in Chapter 7. First, the firm should not produce at all unless there is some level of output for which price is at least equal to average variable cost. Second, if the firm does produce, its output should be set at the point where marginal cost equals marginal revenue. At this point, marginal cost should be rising relative to marginal revenue, so that if any additional units were to be produced they would add more to cost than to revenue, and so would reduce profit.

When the monopoly firm equates marginal cost with marginal revenue, it produces an outcome such as that shown in Figure 8.3. The profit-maximizing output is the level at which marginal cost equals marginal revenue. The point on the demand curve vertically above that output is the price at which that output can be sold, as this is the price that demanders are willing to pay for that quantity. (We normally think of this the other way round: at price $p_0$ demanders would choose to buy quantity $q_0$.)

We have explained the monopolist's decision as if it were taken in two steps: first set the quantity that is determined by $MC = MR$; then see what price can be charged for that quantity. This is not how it works in practice, as the position of *MR* is itself determined by the demand curve. So what is really happening is that the monopolist is choosing price and quantity simultaneously from the interaction of cost and demand conditions. The monopolist is solving the following problem: given the constraints of costs and demand, what is the profit-maximizing combination of price and quantity that it is feasible to achieve? The answer to this question is the same whichever way we look at it: set marginal cost equal to marginal revenue and then determine the price to be charged, or determine the price–quantity combination that maximizes profit.

An important characteristic of the outcome under monopoly is that the market price of the product exceeds the marginal cost of producing it. In the next section we discuss why this may be regarded as an undesirable outcome.

## Figure 8.3 The equilibrium of a monopoly

**The monopoly maximizes its profits by producing where marginal cost equals marginal revenue.** The monopoly produces output $q_0$ for which marginal revenue equals marginal cost (rule 2). At this output the price of $p_0$—which is determined by the demand curve—exceeds the average variable cost (rule 1). Total profits are the profits per unit of $p_0 - c_0$ multiplied by the output of $q_0$, which is the blue area.

When the monopoly firm is in profit-maximizing equilibrium, equating marginal revenue with marginal cost, both are less than the price it charges for its output.

This is because the firm's marginal revenue curve is always below the demand curve.

### Elasticity of demand for a monopolist

The relationship between elasticity and revenue discussed above has an interesting implication for the monopoly firm. Because marginal cost is always greater than zero, a profit-maximizing monopoly (which must produce where $MR = MC$) will always produce where marginal revenue is positive, that is, where demand is elastic. If the firm were producing where demand was inelastic, it could reduce its output, thereby driving up the price sufficiently to increase its total revenue while reducing its total costs and hence increasing its profits. No such restriction applies in perfect competition. Each firm faces a perfectly elastic demand curve whatever the elasticity of the market demand curve at the market price. So the aggregate market equilibrium can occur where the market demand curve is either elastic or inelastic.

## Figure 8.4 Alternative profit possibilities for a monopolist

**Profit maximization means only that the monopoly is doing as well as it can do.** The figure shows one demand curve and three alternative cost curves. With the curve $ATC'''$ there is no positive output at which the monopolist can avoid making losses. With the curve $ATC''$ the monopolist covers all costs at output $q_1$, where the $ATC$ curve is tangent to the $D$ curve. With the curve $ATC'$ profits can be made by producing at any output between $q_2$ and $q_3$. (The profit-maximizing output will be some point between $q_2$ and $q_3$, where $MR = MC$, which is not shown on the diagram.)

### Monopoly profits

The fact that a monopoly firm produces the output that maximizes its profits tells us nothing about how large these profits will be, or even whether there will be any profits at all. Figure 8.4 illustrates this by showing three alternative average total cost curves: one where the monopoly firm can earn pure profits, one where it can just cover its costs, and one where it makes losses at any level of output.

### No supply curve for a monopoly

In perfect competition the industry short-run supply curve depends only on the marginal cost curves of the individual firms. This is true because, under perfect-competition, profit-maximizing firms equate marginal cost with price. Given marginal costs, it is possible to know how much will be produced at each price. In contrast, a monopoly firm's output is not solely determined by its marginal cost. Let us see why.

As with all profit-maximizing firms, the monopolist equates marginal cost to marginal revenue; but marginal revenue does not equal price. Hence the monopolist does *not* equate marginal cost to price. In order to know the amount produced at any given price, we need to know the market demand curve as well as the marginal cost curve. Under these circumstances, it is possible for different demand conditions to cause the same output to be sold at

**Figure 8.5  No supply curve under monopoly**

There is no unique relation between price and the quantity sold. The demand curves $D'$ and $D''$ both have marginal revenue curves that intersect the marginal cost curve at output $q_0$. But because the demand curves are different, $q_0$ is sold at $p_0$ when the demand curve is $D'$, and at $p_1$ when the demand curve is $D''$.

different prices. This is illustrated in Figure 8.5 by an example in which two monopolists facing the same marginal cost curves but different demand curves sell identical outputs at different prices. An important conclusion follows from this

For a monopoly firm, there is no unique relationship between market price and quantity supplied.

### Firm and industry

Because the monopolist is the only producer in an industry, there is no need for separate analysis of the firm and the industry, as there is with perfect competition. The monopoly firm *is* the industry. Therefore, the short-run, profit-maximizing position of the firm, as shown in Figure 8.3, is also the short-run equilibrium of the industry.

Box 8.1 deals with an interesting variation of monopoly theory: the pricing of limited editions.

---

### Box 8.1  Demand for once-off production

An interesting case of monopoly pricing occurs with 'limited editions'. These are sometimes works of art, such as lithographs, prints, etchings, or woodcuts by famous artists. But limited editions are also produced of other things, from cars to T-shirts and briar pipes. In 2001 the Singer Company offered a limited-edition gold-coloured sewing machine with a 22k gold badge, to commemorate the 150th anniversary of the invention of the original machine. Our favourite recent example, however, is a limited edition model of a prize-winning goat called Mostyn Minival: 'A beautifully crafted limited edition of 100, each individually numbered. £110 for members and £120 for non-members'.

Here is an extract from a recent advert for a limited edition mobile phone:

*Responding to the demands of urban sophisticates, Nokia has introduced an exclusive, limited edition Nokia 7200 phone. With tailored, pure white leather covers, the Nokia 7200 Limited Edition offers state-of-the-art technology—including an integrated camera, colour screen and FM radio—in an haute couture, folding design.*

*The Nokia 7200 Limited Edition blends contemporary fashion, modern design and mobile communications in a must-have collector's package. Only 7200 units of this latest offering from the award-winning Nokia Design studio will be produced. The Nokia 7200 Limited Edition is available only in select fashion boutiques and Nokia concept stores, beginning in May.*

*Adding a touch of luxury and a hint of the unexpected, the leather covers of the Nokia 7200 Limited Edition are available in pure white, or with added embellishments like embroidered designs or geometric patterns. Presented in distinctive all-white packaging, the Nokia 7200 Limited Edition is completed by a white leather wrist strap and matching pouch—the perfect accessories for*

*fashion-focused consumers.* (http://www.3g.co.uk/PR/April2004/6916.htm, 8 April 2004)

A recent ( 2006) internet search for 'limited edition offers' produced over 27 million hits. This suggests that limited edition offers are a way of adding value to products, especially collectibles, by creating an image of restricted supply, which may make the product seem unusual and therefore more valuable in future.

What is the economics of all this? The normal demand curve is for a repeated flow of purchases, period after period. In the case of limited editions, the demand is for a stock to be produced and purchased once only. The smaller the total number of items produced, the more people value each item and the higher the price that can be charged. This gives rise to a negatively sloped demand curve.

If producers know the curve exactly and know their marginal cost of production, choosing the profit-maximizing price–quantity combination is simple. They equate marginal cost with marginal revenue. But since limited-edition production and sales are not repeated period after period, producers have no chance to learn the shape of the demand curve. They must guess, on the basis of the sales of earlier, more or less similar, limited editions. If they set the price too low, they will sell all their output but not at its profit-maximizing price. If they set the price too high, they will be left with unsold output, which they must destroy or re-advertise at considerable expense. Most importantly, perhaps, the limited edition promotion is a way of creating a demand for something that would have very little intrinsic demand in the absence of scarcity value. Selling art work is a hard job for all but the most famous artists, but at least if the work is rare it has a chance of having some market value in future. We do not expect many readers to make their living out of making models of champion goats—why not try something even more unusual?

## A multi-plant monopoly

So far we have implicitly assumed that the monopoly firm produces all of its output in a single plant. The analysis can easily be extended to a multi-plant monopolist. Assume, for example, that the firm has two plants. How will it allocate production between them? The answer is that any given output will be allocated between the two plants so as to equate their marginal costs. Assume, for example, that plant A is producing 30 units per week at a marginal cost of £20, while plant B is producing 25 units at a marginal cost of £17. Plant A's production could be reduced by one unit, saving £20 in cost, while plant B's production is increased by one unit, adding £17 to cost. Overall output is held constant while costs are reduced by £3. The generalization is that, whenever two plants are producing at different marginal costs, the total cost of producing their combined output can be reduced by reallocating production from the plant with the higher marginal cost to the plant with the lower marginal cost.

A multi-plant, profit-maximizing monopoly firm will always operate its plants so that their marginal costs are equal.

It is worth noting that the message that a multi-plant firm should equate marginal cost in each plant does not apply only to monopolies: it applies to all firms. For any given output and any market structure, if the firm is not equating the marginal cost of production of an identical product between plants then it is not maximizing profit. It could reduce total cost for the same output by rearranging production between its plants.

How does the multi-plant monopoly firm determine its overall marginal cost? Assume, for example, that both plants are operating at a marginal cost of £10 per unit and that one is producing 14 units per week while the other is producing 16. The firm's overall output is 30 units at a marginal cost of £10. This illustrates the following general proposition:

The monopoly firm's marginal cost curve is the horizontal sum of the marginal cost curves of its individual plants.

It follows that the analysis in this chapter applies to any monopolist, no matter how many plants it operates. The marginal cost curve we use is merely the sum of the marginal cost curves of all the plants. In the special case in which there is only one plant, the *firm's MC* curve is that *plant's MC* curve.

## The allocative inefficiency of monopoly

We showed in Chapter 7 that the perfectly competitive equilibrium maximizes the sum of consumers' and producers' surpluses. Output under monopoly is lower and so must result in a smaller total of consumers' and producers' surpluses.

When the monopoly chooses an output below the competitive level, market price is higher than it would be under perfect competition. As a result, consumers' surplus is diminished, and producers' surplus is increased. In this way, the monopoly firm gains at the expense of consumers. This is not, however, the whole story.

When the output between the monopoly and the competitive levels is not produced, consumers give up more surplus than the monopolist gains. There is thus a net loss of surplus for society as a whole. This loss of surplus is called the *deadweight loss of monopoly*. It is illustrated in Figure 8.6.

**Figure 8.6 The deadweight loss of monopoly**

Monopoly is allocatively inefficient because it does not maximize the sum of consumers' and producers' surpluses. At the perfectly competitive equilibrium $E_c$ consumers' surplus is the sum of the pink shaded areas 1, 5, and 6. When the industry is monopolized, price rises to $p_m$ and consumers' surplus falls to area 5. Consumers lose area 1 because that output is not produced; they lose area 6 because the price rise has transferred it to the monopolist. Producers' surplus in a competitive equilibrium is the sum of the blue areas 7 and 2. When the market is monopolized and price rises to $p_m$, the surplus area 2 is lost because the output is not produced. However, the monopolist gains area 6 from consumers. Area 6 is known to be greater than 2 because $p_m$ maximizes profits. Thus, areas 1 and 2 are lost to society. They represent the deadweight loss resulting from monopoly and account for its allocative inefficiency.

It follows that there is a conflict between the private interest of the monopoly producer and the public interest of all the nation's consumers. This creates a rational case for government intervention to prevent the formation of monopolies if possible—and if that is not possible to control their behaviour.

# A multi-price monopolist: price discrimination

So far in this chapter we have assumed that the monopoly firm charges the same price for every unit of its product, no matter where or to whom it sells that product. We now show that a monopoly firm will also find it profitable to sell different units of the same product at different prices whenever it gets the opportunity.[3]

Raw milk is often sold at one price when it is to be used as fluid milk but at a lower price when it is to be used to make ice cream or cheese. Doctors in private practice often charge for their services according to the incomes of their patients. Cinemas often have lower admission prices for children and pensioners than for adults. Railroads charge different rates per tonne per kilometre for different products. Electricity producers sell electricity at one rate to homes and at a lower rate to firms. Airlines often charge less to people who stay at their outward-bound destination over a Saturday night than to those who come and go within the week.

Price discrimination occurs when a seller charges different prices for different units of the same product for reasons not associated with differences in cost. Not all price *differences* represent price *discrimination*. Quantity discounts, differences between wholesale and retail prices, and prices that vary with the time of day or the season of the year may not represent price discrimination, because the same product sold at a different time, in a different place, or in different quantities may have different costs. If an electric power company has unused capacity at certain times of the day, it may be cheaper for the company to provide service at those hours than at peak demand hours. If price differences reflect cost differences, they are not discriminatory. In contrast, when a price difference is based on different buyers' valuations of the same product, price discrimination does occur.

Some forms of price discrimination may be illegal or contrary to regulations in an industry. We make no moral judgements about whether price discrimination is a good or a bad thing. The analysis is merely designed to show that a firm that has some market power has an incentive to segment its market and charge a different price in each segment if it can.

## Why price discrimination is profitable

Why should it be profitable for a firm to sell some units of its output at a price that is well below the price that it receives for other units of its output? Persistent price discrimination is profitable either because different buyers are willing to pay different amounts for the same product or because one buyer is willing to pay different amounts for different units of the same product. The basic point about price discrimination is that, in either of these circumstances, sellers may be able to capture some of the consumers' surplus that would otherwise go to buyers.

### Discrimination between units of output

Let us revisit the example we used in Chapter 7 on page 153 where one of us expressed a demand for cinema visits per month such that there would be one visit if the entry price was £30, two visits if it were £20, and three visits if it were £10. At a market price of £10 per visit, I would go three times per month and would have value of consumer surplus of £30 (because the first visit would have been undertaken at an entry price of £30 but only £10 was charged, and the second visit would have been undertaken at an entry price of £20 but again only £10 was charged; so the surplus for this consumer on the first visit was £20 and on the second visit £10).

Perfect price discrimination occurs when the firm obtains the entire consumers' surplus. In this example, the managers of the cinema could increase their revenue if they charged £30 for the first visit, £20 for the second visit and £10 for the third visit, thereby increasing total revenue by £30 and converting what had previously been a surplus benefit to a movie buff into profit for the cinema.

Of course, achieving a pricing structure that is able to distinguish how many times each customer has visited each month is not easy, but the point we are making here is that, if each unit sold could be separately priced, the

---

[3] Because this practice is also prevalent in markets that contain a few large firms, called *oligopolistic* markets, the range of examples quoted covers both types of market structure.

seller could increase total revenue by extracting some or all of the consumers' surplus.

### Discrimination between buyers in one market

If different buyers have different demand curves for some commodity, a monopoly producer can profitably discriminate by charging more to those with a higher demand for the commodity and less to those with a lower demand. Here is a simple example.

Think of the demand curve in a market that is made up of individual buyers, each of whom has indicated the maximum price that she is prepared to pay for the single unit that each wishes to purchase. Suppose, for the sake of simplicity, that there are only four buyers, the first of whom is prepared to pay any price up to £4, the second of whom is prepared to pay £3, the third £2, and the fourth £1. Suppose that the product has a marginal cost of production of £1 per unit for all units. If the selling firm is limited to a single price, it will maximize its profits by charging £3, thereby selling two units and earning profits of £4. If the seller can discriminate among each of the buyers, it could charge the first buyer £4 and the second £3, increasing its profits from the first two units to £5. Moreover, it could also sell the third unit for £2, increasing its profits to £6. It would be indifferent about selling a fourth unit, because the price would just cover marginal cost.

### Discrimination between markets

Many monopoly firms sell in two different markets. A firm might be the only seller in a tariff-protected home market but a price-taker in foreign markets where there is much competition. The firm would then equate its marginal cost to the price in the foreign market, as would any perfect competitor. But in the domestic market it would equate marginal costs to marginal revenue, as would any monopolist. As a result, it would charge a higher price on sales in the home market than on sales abroad. This case is elaborated in the appendix to this chapter.

### Price discrimination more generally

One reason why demand curves have a negative slope is because different units are valued differently by consumers. For example, if tastes or incomes differ, the same unit will be valued differently by different individuals. These facts, combined with a single price for a product, are what give rise to consumers' surplus.

The ability to charge multiple prices gives a seller the opportunity to capture some (or, in the extreme case, all) of the consumers' surplus.

The larger the number of different prices that can be charged, the greater is the firm's ability to increase its revenue at the expense of consumers.

It follows that, if a selling firm is able to discriminate through price, it can increase revenues received (and hence also profits) from the sale of any given quantity. However, price discrimination is not always possible, even if there are no legal barriers to its use.

## When is price discrimination possible?

Discrimination between units of output sold to the same buyer requires that the seller be able to keep track of the units that a buyer consumes in each period. Thus, the tenth unit purchased by a given buyer in a given month can be sold at a price that is different from the fifth unit *only* if the seller can keep track of who buys what. This can be done by an electricity supplier through meter readings, or by a magazine publisher by distinguishing between renewals and new subscriptions. It can also be done by distributing certificates or coupons that allow, for example, a car wash at a reduced price on a return visit.

Discrimination between buyers is possible only if the buyers who face the low price cannot resell the goods to the buyers who face the high price. Even though the local butcher might like to charge the banker twice as much for steak as he charges the taxi driver, he cannot usually succeed in doing so—the banker can always shop for meat in a supermarket, where her occupation is not known. Even if the butcher and the supermarket agreed to charge her twice as much, she could hire someone to shop for her. The surgeon, however, may succeed in discriminating (especially if other reputable surgeons do the same) because it will not do the banker much good to hire the taxi driver to have her operation for her.

Price discrimination is possible if the seller can either distinguish individual units bought by a single buyer or separate buyers into classes such that resale between classes is impossible.

The ability to prevent resale tends to be associated with the character of the product or the ability to classify buyers into readily identifiable groups. Services are less easily resold than goods; goods that require installation by the manufacturer (e.g. heavy equipment) are less easily resold than movable goods such as household appliances.

Of course, it is not enough to be able to separate different buyers or different units into separate classes. The seller must also be able to control the supply going to each group. There is no point, for example, in asking more than the competitive price from some buyers if they can simply go to other firms who are selling the good at the competitive price.

Transportation costs, tariff barriers, and import quotas separate classes of buyers geographically and may make discrimination possible.

## Consequences of price discrimination

A monopoly firm that is able to discriminate between two markets will allocate its output between those two markets so as to equate the marginal revenues in the two. If this is not done, total revenue can always be increased by reducing sales by one unit in the market with the lower marginal revenue and raising sales by one unit in the market with the higher marginal revenue. This reallocation of sales raises total revenue by the difference between the two marginal revenues. If the demand curves are different in the two markets, having the same marginal revenues means charging different prices.

Two important consequences of price discrimination follow from this result.

**1. For any given level of output, the most profitable system of discriminatory prices will provide higher total revenue to the firm than will the profit-maximizing single price.**

Remember that a monopolist with the power to discriminate could produce exactly the same quantity as a single-price monopolist and charge everyone the same price. Therefore, it need never receive *less* revenue, and it can do better if it can raise the price on even one unit sold, so long as the price need not be lowered on any other.

**2. Output under price discrimination will generally be larger than under a single-price monopoly.**

Remember that a monopoly firm that must charge a single price for a product will produce less than would all the firms in a perfectly competitive industry, because it knows that selling more will depress its price. Price discrimination allows the firm to avoid this disincentive. To the extent that the firm can sell its output in separate blocks, it can sell another block without spoiling the market for the block that is already being sold. In the case of perfect price discrimination, in which every unit of output is sold at a different price, the profit-maximizing monopolist will produce every unit for which the price charged is greater than or equal to its marginal cost. It will therefore produce the same quantity of output as does the perfectly competitive industry.

Figure 8.7 illustrates the output-expanding effects of price discrimination. It shows a case in which a monopoly

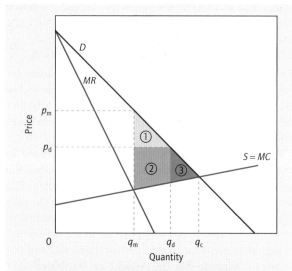

**Figure 8.7 A price-discriminating monopolist**

**Price discrimination reduces the deadweight loss of monopoly.** Initially the monopolist produces output $q_m$ where $MC = MR$, instead of the competitive output $q_c$ where $MC$ equals demand (which is consumers' marginal utility). The deadweight loss is the sum of the three blue shaded areas labelled 1, 2, and 3. A second group of consumers is then isolated from the first. This group, who would buy nothing at the original price of $p_m$, will buy an amount that would increase total output to $q_d$ at a price of $p_d$. The monopoly firm's profits now rise by the shaded area 2, which is the difference between its cost curve and the price $p_d$ that is charged to the new group, which buys the amount between $q_m$ and $q_d$. Consumers' surplus rises by the shaded area labelled 1 and total deadweight loss falls to the shaded area labelled 3.

firm has maximized profits selling at a single price. The firm then finds that it can isolate a group of potential buyers who were unwilling to purchase at the monopoly price, perhaps by forming a buying club from which existing customers are excluded. A lower price can then be used to attract the isolated group of potential new buyers without having to lower the price charged to its original customers. As long as the new price exceeds the marginal cost of producing the extra output, the monopoly firm adds to its profits. But consumers' surplus is also increased, since a new group of buyers is now in the market. So both the monopolist and consumers earn additional surplus.

## Normative aspects of price discrimination

There are two quite separate issues involved in evaluating any particular example of price discrimination. The first concerns the effect of discrimination on the level of output. Discrimination usually results in a higher output than would occur if a single price were charged. As we saw in Figure 8.7, price discrimination tends to reduce the deadweight loss of monopoly and therefore leads to a more efficient allocation of resources than does a single-price monopoly.

Often, however, it is the effect on income distribution that accounts for people's strong emotional reactions to price discrimination. Compared with perfect competition, price discrimination transfers income from buyers to sellers. When buyers are poor and sellers are rich, this may seem undesirable. However, some cases are more complex. For example, doctors in countries with market-based medical systems often vary their charges with their patients' incomes. This enables them to serve their poorer patients in ways that they could not if they had to charge everyone a single price for their services. Another example is the prevalent practice of giving discounts to old-age pensioners or airline passengers who stay on at their travel destination over a weekend. These practices often allow lower-income persons to buy a product that they would be unable to afford if it were sold at the single price that maximized the producers' profits.

Box 8.2 outlines some interesting cases of price discrimination.

---

  ## Box 8.2 Examples of price discrimination

The principle of charging different customers different prices has been around for a very long time. The earliest example we have come across is from the Egyptian kingdom of Rameses the Great in the period 1304–1237 BC.* In what is now southern Lebanon, the Egyptians maintained a toll road on an important route across a range of hills. There were other routes, but they were considerably more tortuous than this one. The servant of the Egyptian ruler sent to administer this toll road found that he had some discretion over pricing. He wrote to his employers asking for guidelines on charges. The reply came back: 'Charge what the traffic will bear.' So famous is this instruction that the phrase has become something of a cliché. It is based upon the insight, set out in the text, that setting different prices increases revenue. In practice, the discriminating monopolist charges each traveller the maximum that she would be prepared to pay to use the road.

Here are two more recent examples from transport. The first describes price discrimination in action. The second explains how problems can arise when price discrimination does not occur.

### Air fares

In February 2006 a standard economy fare on BA from London Heathrow to Rome was £618.40. This fare permitted return the same day or within the week. However, if you stayed in Rome over a Saturday night and were prepared to fly from Gatwick, you could go for £123.90! This difference for the same class of fare on the same planes discriminates between the business traveller and the tourist. Such discrimination is profitable because the elasticities of demand for these two types of travel are different, being lower for business than for leisure travel.

Similar price discrimination applies to transatlantic airfares. In early 2006 a standard economy return fare between London and Chicago on the major airlines (such as BA, United and American) cost around £1,040. However, the fare with the same carriers, if booked 14 days in advance and for a stay of at least seven days, was around £330. Again, these substantial differences reflect a segmentation of the market between business travellers, who presumably get their fares paid by their company, and tourists, who are paying out of their own pocket. Business people do not want to use up more time than is necessary on a business trip, as the opportunity cost of their time is high, so the seven-day minimum keeps them from taking advantage of the low fare.

### British Rail

This case illustrates the problems that arise when segmentation is not allowed even though both producers and consumers could be better off if it were. Some years ago British Rail (the nationalized industry that once operated all British railways) was not allowed to charge different prices to passengers travelling on different lines. In the interest of equity, a fixed fare per passenger mile was laid down by government and had to be charged on all lines, whatever the density of their passenger traffic and whatever the elasticity of demand for their services. In the interests of economy, branch lines were closed down when they could not cover their costs. This meant that some lines closed, even though the users preferred rail transport to any of the available alternatives and the strength of their preferences was such that they would voluntarily have paid a price sufficient for the line to cover its costs. None the less, the lines were closed because it was thought inequitable to charge the passengers on one line more than the passengers on other lines.

Since privatization of the railways in the 1990s, differential pricing has been permitted. For example, train companies such as the operators of the Gatwick Express are able to charge higher prices for trips from London Victoria to Gatwick Airport than were being charged by other companies running on the same route—the only difference being the non-stop journey of the former.

---

* We are grateful to Professor Arie Melnik of Haifa University for this example.

# Long-run monopoly equilibrium

In both monopolized and perfectly competitive industries, profits and losses provide incentives for entry and exit.

If a profit-maximizing monopoly firm is suffering losses in the short run, it will continue to operate as long as it can cover its variable costs. In the long run, however, it will leave the industry unless it can find a scale of operations at which its full opportunity costs can be covered.

If the monopoly firm is making profits, other firms will wish to enter the industry in order to earn more than the opportunity cost of their capital. If such entry occurs, the equilibrium position shown in Figure 8.3 will change, and the firm will cease to be a monopolist.

## Entry barriers

Impediments that prevent entry are called **entry barriers**; they may be either natural or created.

If a monopoly firm's profits are to persist in the long run, effective entry barriers must prevent the entry of new firms into the industry.

### Barriers determined by technology

Natural barriers most commonly arise as a result of economies of scale. When the long-run average cost curve is negatively sloped over a large range of output, big firms have significantly lower average total costs than small firms.

You will recall from Chapter 7 that perfectly competitive firms cannot be in long-run equilibrium on the negatively sloped segment of their long-run average cost curve (see Figure 7.10 on page 150).

Now suppose that an industry's technology is such that any firm's minimum achievable average cost is £10, which is reached at an output of 10,000 units per week. Further, assume that at a price of £10 the total quantity demanded is 11,000 units per week. Under these circumstances only one firm can operate at or near its minimum costs.

A **natural monopoly** occurs when, given the industry's current technology, the demand conditions allow no more than one firm to cover its costs while producing at the minimum point of its long-run cost curve. In a natural monopoly, there is no price at which two firms can both sell enough to cover their total costs.

Another type of technologically determined barrier is *setup cost*. If a firm could be catapulted fully grown into the market, it might be able to compete effectively with the existing monopolist. However, the cost to a new firm of entering the market, developing its products, and establishing such things as brand image and a dealer network may be so great that entry would be unprofitable.

### Policy-created barriers

Many entry barriers are created by conscious government action and are, therefore, officially condoned. Patent laws, for instance, may prevent entry by conferring on the patent-holder the sole legal right to produce a particular product for a specific period of time.

A firm may also be granted a charter or a franchise that prohibits competition by law. Regulation and licensing of firms, often in service industries, can restrict entry severely. For example, the 1979 Banking Act required all banks in the UK to be authorized by the Bank of England. The 1986 Financial Services Act required all sellers of investment products to be authorized by the Securities and Investment Board (SIB) or some other recognized regulatory body. Regulation and authorization of all financial firms, including banks, was formally transferred to the Financial Services Authority in December 2001.

Other barriers can be created by the firm or firms already in the market. In extreme cases the threat of force or sabotage can deter entry. The most obvious entry barriers of this type are encountered in the production and sale of illegal goods and services, where operation outside the law makes available an array of illegal but potent barriers to new entrants. The drug trade is a current example. In contrast, legitimate firms must use legal tactics such as those that are intended to increase a new entrant's setup costs. Examples are the threat of price-cutting, designed to impose unsustainable losses on a new entrant, and heavy brand-name advertising. (These and other created entry barriers will be discussed in much more detail in Chapter 9.)

### The significance of entry barriers

Because there are no entry barriers in perfect competition, profits cannot persist in the long run.

Profits attract entry, and entry erodes profits.

In monopoly, however, profits *can* persist in the long run whenever there are effective barriers to entry.

Entry barriers frustrate the adjustment mechanism that would otherwise push profits towards zero in the long run.

### 'Creative destruction'

In the very long run technology changes. New ways of producing old products are invented, and new products are created to satisfy both familiar and new wants. This has important implications for entry. A monopoly that succeeds in preventing the entry of new firms capable of producing its current product will sooner or later find its barriers circumvented by innovations. One firm may be able to use new processes that avoid some patent or other barrier that the monopolist relies on to bar entry of competing firms. Another firm may compete by producing a new product that, although somewhat different, still satisfies the same need as the monopoly firm's product. Yet another firm might get around a natural monopoly by inventing a technology that produces the good at a much lower cost than the existing monopoly firm's technology. (The cost curve may be lowered throughout its range, and/or the minimum level of costs may be reached at a lower output than previously.) The new technology may subsequently allow several firms to enter the market and still cover costs.

Joseph Schumpeter (1883–1950) argued that entry barriers were not a serious problem in the very long run. According to Schumpeter, the possibility of obtaining monopoly profits provides a major incentive for people to risk their money by financing inventions and innovations. The large short-run profits of a monopoly encourage others to try to capture some of these profits for themselves. If a frontal attack on the monopolist's barriers to entry is not possible, the barriers will be circumvented by such means as the development of similar products against which the monopolist will not have entry protection.

Schumpeter called the replacement of an existing monopoly by one or more new entrants through the invention of new products or new production techniques the *process of creative destruction*. He argued that this process precludes the very-long-run persistence of barriers to entry into industries that earn large profits.

It is worth noting that the same argument apples to an oligopolistic industry with a few firms of the sort we will consider in the next chapter. If they are making profits and succeed in barring entry, potential new firms may circumvent the entry barriers by inventing new technologies in the very long run.

The telephone market provides a good example of this process at work. British Telecom (BT) used to have a virtual monopoly of the provision of telephone services through its network of cables to every house and office building in the country. Originally, operators used to connect people by hand (through plugging wires into sockets) or through a mechanical switching device. More recently, however, the switching technology began using computers, and this enabled regulators to insist that other telephone providers should be able to compete via the BT telephone lines. On top of this, new wireless technology led to the production of mobile phones. The barriers to entry were suddenly dramatically reduced, allowing new providers, such as Vodafone and Orange, to become big players in the UK telephone market.

## Cartels as monopolies

Up to this point in our discussion, a *monopoly* has meant that there is only one firm in an industry. A second way in which a monopoly can arise is for firms in an industry to agree to co-operate with one another, i.e. to behave as if they were a single seller, in order to maximize joint profits by eliminating competition among themselves. Such a group of firms is called a **cartel**, or sometimes just a *producers' association*. A cartel that includes *all* firms in the industry can behave in the same way as a single-firm monopoly that owned all of these firms. The firms can agree among themselves to restrict their total output to the level that maximizes their joint profits.[4]

### The effects of cartelization

Perfectly competitive firms take the market price as given and increase their output until their marginal cost equals price. In contrast, a monopoly firm knows that increasing its output will depress the market price. Taking account of this, the monopolist increases its output only until marginal revenue is equal to marginal cost. All the firms in an industry can achieve the same result by grouping together into what is called a cartel to take collective action to reduce output and drive up price. They can agree to restrict industry output to the level that maximizes

---

[4] In this chapter we deal with the simple case in which *all* of the firms in a perfectly competitive industry form a cartel in order to act as if they were a monopoly. Cartels are sometimes formed by a group of firms (or countries) that account for a significant part, but not all, of the total supply of some commodity. The most famous example of this type is the Organization of Petroleum Exporting Countries (OPEC), and we discuss this further in the case study at the end of this chapter.

(i) Market equilibrium                    (ii) Firm equilibrium

**Figure 8.8  Conflicting forces affecting cartels**

**Co-operation leads to the monopoly price, but individual self-interest leads to production in excess of the monopoly output.** Market conditions are shown in part (i), and the situation of a typical firm is shown in part (ii). (Note the change of scale between the two graphs.) Initially the market is in competitive equilibrium, with price $p_0$ and quantity $Q_0$. The individual firm is producing output $q_0$ and is just covering its total costs.

   The cartel is formed, and then enforces quotas on individual firms that are sufficient to reduce the industry's output to $Q_1$, the output that maximizes the joint profits of the cartel members. Price rises to $p_1$. The typical firm's quota is $q_1$. The firm's profits rise from zero to the amount shown by the blue area in part (ii). Once price is raised to $p_1$, however, the individual firm would like to increase output to $q_2$, where marginal cost is equal to the price set by the cartel. This would allow the firm to earn profits shown by the blue hatched area. If all firms violate their quotas, industry output will exceed $Q_1$, and the profits earned by all firms will fall.

their joint profits (where the industry's marginal cost is equal to the industry's marginal revenue). One way to do this is to establish a quota for each firm's output. Suppose that a cartel is formed in what was a perfectly competitive industry and that the joint profit-maximizing output is two-thirds of the perfectly competitive output. When the cartel is formed, each firm could be given a quota equal to two-thirds of its competitive output.

   The effect of cartelizing a perfectly competitive industry and of reducing its output through production quotas is shown in part (i) of Figure 8.8.

## Problems facing cartels

Cartels encounter two characteristic problems. The first is ensuring that members follow the behaviour that will maximize the industry's *joint* profits, and the second is preventing these profits from being eroded by the entry of new firms.

### Enforcement of output restrictions

The managers of any cartel want the industry to produce its profit-maximizing output. Their job is made more

difficult if individual firms either stay out of the cartel, or enter and then cheat on their output quotas. Any one firm has an incentive to do just this: to be either the one that stays out of the organization or the one that enters and then cheats on its output quota. For the sake of simplicity, assume that all firms enter the cartel, so enforcement problems are concerned strictly with cheating by its members.

   If Firm X is the only firm to cheat, it is in the best of all possible situations. All other firms restrict output and hold the industry price near its monopoly level. They earn profits, but only by restricting output. Firm X can then reap the full benefit of the other firms' output restraint and sell some additional output at the high price that has been set by the cartel's actions. However, if all of the firms cheat, the price will be pushed back to the competitive level, and all of the firms will return to their zero-profit position.

   This conflict between the interests of the group and the interests of the individual firm creates the cartel's dilemma. Provided that enough firms co-operate in restricting output, all firms are better off than they would be if the industry remained perfectly competitive.

However, any one firm will be even better off if it remains outside the cartel, or joins it and then cheats by exceeding its output quota. If all firms act on this incentive, all will be worse off than if they had joined the cartel and restricted output.

**Cartels tend to be unstable because of the strong incentives for individual firms to violate the output quotas needed to enforce the monopoly price.**

The conflict between the motives for co-operation and for independent action is analysed in more detail in part (ii) of Figure 8.8.

Cartels and similar output-restricting arrangements have a long history. For example, schemes to raise farm incomes by limiting crops bear ample testimony to the accuracy of the predicted instability of cartels. In the past, industry agreements to restrict output often broke down as individual farmers exceeded their quotas. This is why most crop-restriction plans are now operated by governments rather than by private cartels. Production quotas backed by the full coercive power of the state can force monopoly behaviour on existing producers and can effectively bar the entry of new ones.

### Restricting entry

A cartel must not only police the behaviour of its members, but must also be able to prevent the entry of new producers. In an industry with no strong natural entry barriers, to maintain its profits in the long run the cartel must create its own barriers; otherwise new firms will enter and force down price until the profits disappear. Successful cartels are often able to license the firms in the industry and to control entry by restricting the number of licences. At other times the government has operated a quota system and has given it the force of law. If no one can produce without a quota and the quotas are allocated among existing producers, entry is precluded.

 # CASE STUDIES

### 1. OPEC: a case study of a cartel

Cocoa producers in West Africa, farmers in the European Union, coffee growers in Brazil, oil producers, taxi drivers in many cities, and labour unions throughout the world have all sought to obtain, through collective action, some of the benefits of departing from the price-taking aspects of perfect competition. In all of these cases, the sellers were so numerous that no single seller had any individual market power. Acting separately, each had to accept the market price that was determined by forces beyond its control. Acting collectively, they were able to influence prices by restricting supply. Cases of this sort are worth studying because they occur frequently and in various guises.

In the previous section we analysed the behaviour of perfectly competitive firms that organized themselves into a cartel. We reached two important conclusions:

1. **It always pays the producers in a perfectly competitive industry to enter into an output-restricting agreement (at least so long as it is legal).**

2. **Each individual cartel member can increase its profits by violating the output restrictions, provided the other members do not violate theirs.**

These two conclusions highlight the dilemma of any cartel that is composed of firms that, acting individually, would be price-takers—whether it be the Organization of Petroleum Exporting Countries (OPEC) or a local producers' association. Each firm is better off if the cartel is effective in restricting output and thereby raising price. But each is even better off if everyone else co-operates while it cheats. Yet, if all cheat, all will be worse off.

The behaviour of OPEC over the past several decades provides an example of the cartelization of an industry. As we shall see, OPEC did not control the whole supply side of the oil industry, but its experience helps us understand the forces affecting cartels in general.

### Early success

In contrast with today's market, throughout the twentieth century there was the capacity to produce more oil than was demanded. As a result, output rose until the market price was approximately equal to the marginal costs of production and distribution. In this context OPEC was formed in 1960. It did not, however, attract world attention until 1973, when its members voluntarily agreed to restrict their outputs by negotiating quotas. At the time OPEC countries accounted for over half of the world's supply of crude oil and an even bigger proportion of world oil exports. So, although it was not a complete monopoly, the cartel had substantial market power. As a result of the output restrictions, the world price of oil nearly quadrupled within a year, from about $3 to nearly $12 a barrel. (Oil prices are customarily stated in US dollars.) The demand and supply analysis of what happened (in simplified terms) is analysed in Figure 8.9.

### Figure 8.9 OPEC as a successful cartel

**Given a rising non-OPEC supply curve of oil, OPEC could determine equilibrium price by choosing its contribution to total supply.** The curve $S_N$ represents the non-OPEC supply curve of oil. When the OPEC countries were prepared to supply all that was demanded at the world price $p_W$, the world supply curve was $S_W$. At that price production was $q_1$ in non-OPEC countries and $q_0 - q_1$ in OPEC countries.

By lowering its production, OPEC shifted the world supply curve to $S'_W$, where the horizontal distance between $S_N$ and $S'_W$ is OPEC's production. The world price rose to $p'_W$. Production became $q_3$ in non-OPEC countries and $q_2 - q_3$ in the OPEC countries.

OPEC increased its oil revenues because, although sales fell, the price rose more than in proportion. Non-OPEC countries gained doubly because they were free to produce more and to sell it at the new, higher world price.

OPEC's policy succeeded for several reasons. First, the member countries provided a significant part of the total world supply of oil. Second, other producing countries could not quickly increase their outputs in response to price increases. Third, as Figure 8.9 shows, the world demand for oil proved to be highly inelastic in the short run. Data for oil prices over time are shown in Figure 8.10.

The higher prices were maintained for the remainder of the decade. As a result, OPEC countries found themselves suddenly enjoying vast wealth. The increase in their wealth was so great that the temptation to cheat, in order to gain even more, was small during the rest of the 1970s. By the end of the decade, however, the OPEC countries had become used to their vast wealth and were spending more and more on arms, as well as on economic development. Eager for yet more income, they engineered a second output restriction that pushed prices from the $10–$12 range to over $30 a barrel. New income poured in, and OPEC's power to hold the oil-consuming world to ransom seemed limitless.

Longer-term market forces, however, were working against OPEC.

### Pressure on the cartel

Monopolistic producers always face a long-run dilemma. The closer their prices are to the profit-maximizing level, the greater their short-term profits—but also the greater the incentive for market reactions that will reduce their profits in the longer term. In OPEC's case, the market reactions came from both the demand and the supply sides of the market.

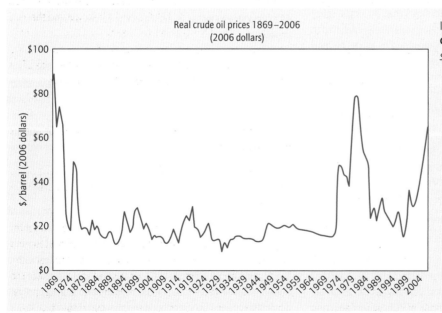

### Figure 8.10 Long-run price of oil 1869–2006

*Source*: WTRG Economics.

**Figure 8.11** OPEC share of world oil production, 1973–2004

*Source*: Energy Information Administration.

### Increasing world supply

The high prices and high profits achieved by the OPEC cartel spurred major additions to the world's oil supply by non-OPEC producers. This was, in effect, new entry and resulted in a rightward shift in the non-OPEC supply curve. In 1973 OPEC was producing more than half of the world's oil; by 1979 its share was well under half, and by 1985 it was only just over one quarter (see Figure 8.11). The increased supply of non-OPEC oil tended to drive the world price down. To maintain the price, OPEC had to reduce its own output more and more.

### Declining world demand

The market demand curve for oil in Figure 8.9 shows how variations in the price of oil affect purchases, holding other variables constant. Other things being equal, there was little that users could do in the short run to reduce their consumption of petroleum products in response to the price rise. Over a longer period of time, however, other things did not remain equal. A host of long-term adaptations—including smaller cars, more efficient insulation on oil-heated buildings, and more economical diesel engines—economized on petroleum products within known technology. The long-run demand curve proved to be much more elastic than the short-run demand curve. (See Figure 4.8 on page 73, for an elaboration of the distinction between short- and long-run demand curves.) UK inland deliveries of petroleum, for example, fell from 107 million tonnes in 1973 to 72 million tonnes in 1981, and even two decades later (in 2000) it had recovered only to 76 million tonnes.

Very-long-run forces were also unleashed. The high price of petroleum led to a burst of scientific research to develop more petroleum-efficient technologies and alternatives to petroleum. Solar-heating technology was advanced, as was technology con-

cerning many longer-term alternatives such as tidal power and heat from the interior of the Earth. Had the price of petroleum remained at its 1980 peak, this research would have continued at an intense pace and would have borne increasing fruits in the decades that followed.

The shrinking market for OPEC oil at the high world price necessitated ever-stiffer production limitations if the cartel was to maintain that price. By 1981 OPEC exports were only 18 million barrels per day, two-thirds of the 1973 level, and by 1985 to maintain this price production had to be cut to only 15 million barrels.

### The pressure to cheat

As world output of oil grew, OPEC output had to be reduced substantially to maintain the high prices. As a result, incomes in OPEC countries declined sharply and the instabilities inherent in any cartel began to be felt. In 1981 the cartel price was about five times as high as the 1972 price (measured in constant dollars), but production quotas were less than half of OPEC's capacity. Upset by declining incomes, OPEC producers began to violate their quotas. They met every few months to debate quotas, deplore cheating, and argue about strategy. But the agreements that were reached proved impossible to enforce, and at the end of 1985 OPEC eliminated production quotas. The price fluctuated considerably and then settled down near $18 a barrel, which is a little higher than the price before OPEC's restrictions began (allowing for inflation)—the slightly higher price being accounted for by the modest output restrictions that OPEC was still able to enforce.

Recently OPEC has got its act together again. This is not surprising, as world consumption particularly in the United States rose and discovery of new supplies fell, so that non-OPEC production levelled off and OPEC came to have a rising share of the market. Now it has real market power again and is using it. This time it is aided by rapidly rising demand from such growing economies as China and India, and by declining reserves of oil that can be brought online in response to higher prices.

### The relevance of the OPEC experience

OPEC's experience illustrates some basic problems of output restriction schemes.

**1. Where demand is inelastic, restriction of output to below the competitive level can lead to immense profits in the short term.**

However, supply is likely to increase when, as Schumpeter long ago predicted, new producers find ways of overcoming entry barriers in order to share in the large profits. Furthermore, demand is likely to decrease as substitutes are invented and produced. These long-term adjustments limit the market power of monopolies and cartels, but only with a significant time-lag.

2. Maintaining market power becomes increasingly difficult as time passes.

The closer the cartel pushes price to the monopoly level, the higher are the short-run profits, but the greater is the incentive for longer-term, profit-reducing reactions from both the supply side and the demand side of the market.

3. Producers with market power face a basic trade-off between profits in the short term and profits in the longer term.

When there are many producers it is difficult to force them all to maintain the output restrictions, because each one has an incentive to cheat. This is particularly so if declining demand and increasing competition from new sources, or new products, lead to a steadily shrinking share of the market and falling profits.

4. Output restriction by voluntary agreement among several producers is difficult to maintain over any long period of time.

For a while OPEC massively exploited the non-OPEC world; then the forces of the free market came to the rescue. But now, as demand increases while new discoveries are on the decline, oil prices will remain high without OPEC's intervention. Although they might be somewhat lower in the short run if OPEC did not exist, high and rising world prices are dictated by the free market—at least until alternative sources of fuel come on line in a big way.

## 2. Tamiflu: a monopoly that may not last[5]

Tamiflu is an antiviral drug that was created and patented by a US pharmaceutical company, Gilead Sciences. In 1996 Gilead signed an exclusive licensing agreement for marketing and manufacture with Roche, a Swiss pharmaceutical company. The patent and the licensing agreement run to 2016. A patent gives legal protection to the inventor of a product so that they have exclusive rights to benefit from the sale of that product for some period of time, normally 20 years. A patent, in effect, creates a legal monopoly.

In 2005 an outbreak of bird flu hit the world headlines when a virulent strain, known as the H5N1 virus, was caught by some humans who subsequently died. There was a serious concern that the virus could mutate into a form that would be transmitted from human to human, and thereby possibly initiate a world-wide influenza pandemic. This could be especially virulent as there was no human resistance to this strain and no available vaccine.

Tamiflu was one of only two known antiviral drugs with proven results at treating influenza-like conditions. In 2005

Roche's sales of Tamiflu increased by 370 per cent from 2004 and revenue rose from about $220 million to well over $1 billion as health authorities around the world bought in stocks of the drug in case of a major flu outbreak.

Clearly this monopoly position was hugely beneficial to Roche and to Gilead, which received a percentage on all sales. However, the position is nothing like as simple as portrayed in our analysis earlier in the chapter of a monopolist who sells directly to a large number of individual consumers. First, in many countries drug purchases are undertaken on behalf of government-controlled health authorities, and these authorities have some power in the negotiation of prices. So the seller of a drug has to negotiate a price that is acceptable to both parties, rather than one that maximizes its own profit. Second, health issues are of major political concern and governments can change the law if they wish to, including imposing taxes on companies, overturning patents, and compulsorily purchasing a company or any of its assets. In 2003 the World Trade Organization stated that, in cases of a national health crisis, patent protection of specific drugs could be violated. Third, while Roche and Gilead have a patent on Tamiflu until 2016, they cannot stop other companies developing a drug that is even more effective or a vaccine that would make Tamiflu redundant.

Hence the problem for Roche was not as simple as just maximizing profit during the period of patent protection, given current conditions of demand and supply. Rather, it had to walk a fine political line as well as an economic one. It did not want to be seen as overcharging for a drug at a time of a health crisis, as this would encourage governments to withdraw patent protection. Taiwan did just this in 2005, but at the time of writing no other country had followed. A further problem was that the surge in demand initially left Roche with inadequate production capacity, and this itself led to political criticism. Roche proceeded to negotiate sub-licence agreements with other producers in countries such as India and China, but this looked likely to be leading to a legal dispute with Gilead as to whether the original licence agreement had been violated. In order to head off political criticism (or perhaps for entirely altruistic reasons), Roche donated 5 million doses of Tamiflu to the World Health Organization in 2005.

The prospects for Tamiflu looked very good in 2006 as most governments were committed to further buildup of their stocks of this drug. But two major threats remained. First, it is possible that a future major influenza outbreak could lead governments to violate the patent and authorize generic copies of the drug. Second, it is possible (indeed, quite likely) that, if there is a major outbreak of influenza in humans, a new vaccine will be quickly developed. There already exists a vaccine for the H5N1 virus, but it is not clear whether this would be the virus at the heart of human outbreak.

---

[5] This case study has drawn on an excellent project written by Cass Business School students Gintare Sribykyte, Seonghee Yang, and Lina Landelius.

Fortunately for Roche, Tamiflu is not the only drug in its product portfolio. Its fastest sales growth in 2005 was of a treatment for lung cancer called Tarceva. Big pharmaceutical companies are used to living in a world in which they seek to develop a 'block buster' drug that generates large profits for a period and then becomes unprofitable once the patent expires or a superior substitute is developed. The anti-ulcer drug Zantac was just such a product and made huge profits for Glaxo, but since the expiry of its patent it has been cheaply available in generic form.

Government policy in this area needs to tread a fine line between creating incentives for the invention of new drugs and making sure that the best treatments currently known are available and affordable for those who need them. In the drug industry, monopolies come and go under patent protection, but they do not last for ever—20 years is the maximum length under current laws, but under political pressure the window of opportunity could become much shorter.

## Conclusion

A monopoly has power over the market in which it sells. Monopolies faced with a large number of consumers can force up the market price by restricting their output. As a result, monopolies are rarely left alone by government, and monopoly profits create incentives for others to invent new products. Few monopolies last for very long, and if they do their actions are generally heavily restricted by regulation or public ownership. We discuss the response of government to monopoly further in Chapter 14.

## SUMMARY

### A single-price monopolist

■ A monopoly is an industry containing a single firm. The monopoly firm maximizes its profits by equating marginal cost to marginal revenue, which is less than price. Production under monopoly is less than it would be under perfect competition, where marginal cost is equated to price.

### The allocative inefficiency of monopoly

■ Monopoly is allocatively inefficient. By producing less than the perfectly competitive output, it transfers some consumers' surplus to its own profits and also causes deadweight loss of the surplus that would have resulted from the output that is not produced.

### A multi-price monopolist

■ If a monopolist can discriminate between either different units or different customers, it will always sell more and earn higher profits than if it has to charge a single price.

■ For price discrimination to be possible, the seller must be able to distinguish individual units bought by a single buyer or to separate buyers into classes between whom resale is impossible.

### Long-run monopoly equilibrium

■ A monopoly can earn positive profits in the long run if there are barriers to entry. These may be man-made, such as patents or exclusive franchises, or natural, such as economies of large-scale production and large setup costs.

### Cartels as monopolies

■ The joint profits of all firms in a perfectly competitive industry can always be increased if they agree to restrict output. After agreement is in place, each firm can increase its profits by violating the agreement. If they all do this, profits are reduced to the perfectly competitive level.

## TOPICS FOR REVIEW

- Relationship between price and marginal revenue for a monopolist
- Relationships among marginal revenue, total revenue, and elasticity for a monopolist
- Short- and long-run monopoly equilibrium
- Natural and created entry barriers
- Price discrimination among different units and different buyers
- Individual versus group profits in a cartel

## QUESTIONS

1 Using the same cost information as for the firm described in question 3 of Chapter 6 (page 135), you are now given information about demand. The prices and corresponding quantities that can be sold are as follows:

| Sales (units) | Price (£) |
| --- | --- |
| 20 | 19.20 |
| 40 | 18.40 |
| 60 | 17.60 |
| 100 | 16.00 |
| 200 | 12.00 |
| 300 | 8.00 |
| 400 | 4.00 |
| 500 | 0.00 |
| 1,000 | — |

(You might like to know that this is a straight-line demand curve which can be expressed as $p = 20 - 0.04q$, where $p$ is price and $q$ is quantity sold.)

(a) What is the marginal revenue for each level of sales?

(b) What are the approximate profit-maximizing levels of sales and price?

(c) Draw a graph showing total costs, total revenue, and profit at each level of sales.

2 Suppose now that the firm in question 1 above has constant marginal costs of £4.00 per unit (i.e. ignore previous information about costs) and that it faces two segmented markets. One has the demand curve above in question 1, and the other has the following demand curve:

| Sales (units) | Price (£) |
| --- | --- |
| 20 | 9.60 |
| 40 | 9.20 |
| 60 | 8.80 |
| 100 | 8.00 |
| 200 | 6.00 |
| 300 | 4.00 |
| 400 | 2.00 |
| 500 | 0.00 |
| 1,000 | — |

(If it helps, this demand curve can be written $p = 10 - 0.02q$.)

(a) What quantity will the firm sell in each market?

(b) What price will be charged in each market?

3 For the two demand curves listed in questions 1 and 2 above, calculate the price elasticity of demand at each of the listed sales levels. What is the elasticity at the sales level that maximizes total revenue? Are there any sales levels for which demand is inelastic? What is total revenue at this level of sales?

4 Compare the price and output levels under monopoly and perfect competition.

5 Explain why monopoly is allocatively inefficient.

6 Explain how a cartel can raise the joint profit of its members. Why are cartels likely to be unstable?

7 If a firm produces an identical product in two separate plants, explain how it should decide the profit-maximizing production levels in each plant.

8 Why can a monopolist increase profit by segmenting its markets and charging different prices in each segment?

9 Explain why a profit-maximizing monopolist will never be selling on an inelastic portion of its demand curve.

# **Appendix**  Price discrimination between two markets

Consider a monopoly firm that sells a single product in two distinct markets, A and B, with demand, marginal revenue, and cost curves as shown in Figure 8A.1. Resale among customers is impossible, and a single price must be charged in each market.

What is the best price for the firm to charge in each market? The simplest way to discover this is to imagine the firm deciding how best to allocate any given total output $Q^*$ between two markets. Since output is fixed arbitrarily at $Q^*$, there is nothing the monopolist can do about costs. The best it can do, therefore, is to maximize the revenue that it gets by selling $Q^*$ in the two markets. *To do this it will allocate its sales between the markets until the marginal revenues are the same in each market.* Consider what would happen if the marginal revenue in market A exceeded the marginal revenue in market B. The firm could keep its overall output constant at $Q^*$ but reallocate a unit of sales from B to A, gaining a net addition in revenue equal to the difference between the marginal revenues in the two markets. Thus, it will always pay a monopoly firm to reallocate a given total quantity between its markets as long as marginal revenues are not equal in the two markets.

If we assume that marginal cost is constant, we can determine the profit-maximizing course of action from Figure 8A.1. The *MC* curve in both parts shows the constant marginal cost. The firm's total profits are maximized by equating *MR* in each market to its constant *MC*, thus selling $q_A$ at $p_A$ in market A and $q_B$ at $p_B$ in market B.

Marginal revenue is the same in each market ($c_A = c_B$), so that the firm has its total output correctly allocated between the two markets, and marginal cost equals marginal revenue, showing that the firm would lose profits if it produced more or less total output.

Next, assume that marginal cost varies with output, being given by *MC'* in Figure 8A.2(iii). Now we cannot just put the *MC* curve on to the diagram for each market, since the marginal cost of producing another unit for sale in market A will depend on how much is being produced for sale in market B and vice versa. To determine what overall production should be, we need to know overall marginal revenue. To find this, we merely sum the separate quantities in each market that correspond to each particular marginal revenue. If, for example, the tenth unit sold in market A and the fifteenth unit sold in market B each have a marginal revenue of £1 in their separate markets, then the marginal revenue of £1 corresponds to overall sales of 25 units (10 units in A and 15 in B). This example illustrates the general principle: the overall marginal revenue curve for a discriminating monopolist is the horizontal sum of the marginal revenue curves in each of its markets. This overall curve shows the marginal revenue associated with an increment to production on the assumption that sales are divided between the two markets so as to keep the two marginal revenues equal.

This overall *MR* curve is shown in Figure 8A.2(iii) and is labelled *MR'*. The firm's total profit-maximizing

(i) Market A

(ii) Market B

**Figure 8A.1**

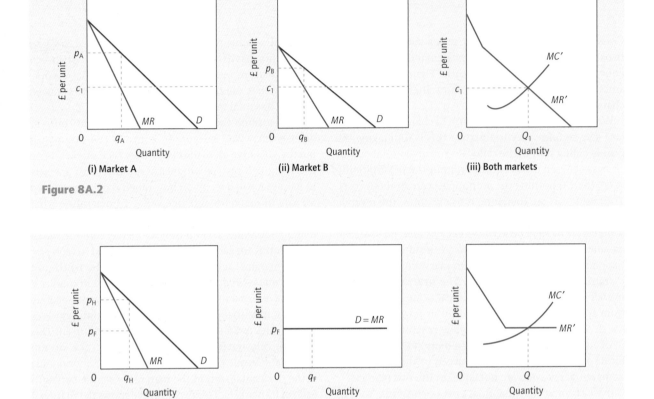

**Figure 8A.2**

**Figure 8A.3**

output is at $Q_1$, where $MR'$ and $MC'$ intersect (at a value of $c_1$). By construction, marginal revenue is $c_1$ in each market although price is different. To find the equilibrium price and quantity in each market, find the quantities, $q_A$ and $q_B$, that correspond to this marginal revenue; then find the prices in each market that correspond to $q_A$ and $q_B$. All of this is illustrated in parts (i) and (ii) of the figure.

## An application

In some industries firms sell competitively on international markets while enjoying a home market that is protected from foreign competition by tariffs or import quotas. To illustrate the issues involved, consider the following extreme case. A firm is the only producer of product X in country A. There are thousands of producers of X in other countries, so that X is sold abroad under conditions of perfect competition. The government of country A grants the firm a monopoly in the home market by prohibiting imports of X. The firm is now faced with a negat-

ively sloped demand curve at home and a perfectly elastic demand curve abroad at the prevailing world price of X.

What will it do? To maximize profits, the firm will divide its sales between the foreign and the home markets so as to equate marginal revenues in the two. On the world market its average and marginal revenues are equal to the world price. So the firm will equate marginal revenue in the home market with the world price, and, since price exceeds marginal revenue at home (because the demand curve slopes downwards), price at home must exceed price abroad.

The argument is illustrated in Figure 8A.3. The home market is shown in (i), the foreign market in (ii), and the sum of the marginal revenue curves in (iii). Provided that the marginal cost curve cuts the marginal revenue curve to the right of the kink (i.e. $MC$ does not exceed the world price when only the home market is served), the two markets will be served at prices of $p_H$ at home and $p_F$ abroad. The total quantity sold will be $Q$, of which $q_H$ is allocated to the home market and the rest ($q_F = Q - q_H$) is sold abroad.

# Chapter 9

# IMPERFECT COMPETITION

Perfect competition and monopoly are extreme cases that do not involve active competition at all. In the former, firms have no influence over the market price, while in the latter there is only one producer. In neither case do they need to worry about what other firms are doing. So what about the intermediate cases, where firms do have some market power but also have competitors? These cases are the subject of this chapter.

In particular, you will learn that:

- Concentration of production varies among industries, but firms in all intermediate industry types have some power to influence their price.

- In industries where there are many producers but of differentiated products, free entry will tend to eliminate profits in the long run.

- Where there is a small group of dominant producers (oligopoly), strategic interaction is important because the market for one is affected by what its rivals do.

- Insights into the choices available and the nature of outcomes in small-group situations can be achieved using game theory.

- Oligopoly can be associated with pure profits in the long run if there are barriers to entry.

Most real firms operate under intermediate market structures rather than the two extremes of perfect competition and monopoly. On the one hand, they are not monopolies because their industries contain several firms, which often compete actively against each other. Firms manufacturing cars, refrigerators, TV sets, breakfast cereals, and many other consumer goods are in industries containing several close rivals, usually both foreign and domestic. Even in small towns, residents find more than one chemist, garage, hairdresser, and supermarket competing for their patronage. On the other hand, these firms do not operate in perfectly competitive markets because the number of competing firms is often small and, even when the number is large, *the firms are not price-takers*.

In this chapter we study firm behaviour in two intermediate market structures. One, which is called monopolistic competition, is close to perfect competition with one important difference: firms do not sell a homogeneous product. The second, called oligopoly, deals with industries that typically contain a few large firms that compete actively with each other.

## Patterns of concentration in manufacturing

One measure of the extent to which firms in some industry have potential market power is a **concentration ratio**. This measures the fraction of total sales in the nation that is controlled by some specified number of the industry's largest sellers. Common types of concentration ratio cite the share of an industry's total market sales made by the largest three or five firms. For example, the UK five-firm concentration ratio for leather and leather products

| | Turnover of largest five enterprises as a % of the turnover of the sector |
|---|---|
| Food products and beverages | 15 |
| Tobacco products | 100 |
| Textiles | 12 |
| Wearing apparel; dressing and dyeing of fur | 16 |
| Leather and leather products | 43 |
| Wood and wood products | 12 |
| Pulp, paper and paper products, publishing and printing | 22 |
| Publishing, printing, and reproduction of recorded media | 14 |
| Coke, refined petroleum products, and nuclear fuel | 90 |
| Chemicals, chemical products, and man-made fibres | 19 |
| Rubber and plastic products | 9 |
| Non-metallic mineral products | 18 |
| Basic metals | 48 |
| Fabricated metal products (excl. machinery and equipment) | 6 |
| Machinery and equipment | 11 |
| Office machinery and computers | 63 |
| Electric machinery and apparatus (not covered elsewhere) | 18 |
| Radio, TV, and communication equipment | 46 |
| Medical, precision/optical instruments, and watches/clocks | 20 |
| Motor vehicles, trailers, and semi-trailers | 59 |
| Other transport equipment | 62 |

**Table 9.1** Concentration ratios for UK manufacturing sub sectors

*Source*: Office of National Statistics, ABI 2000.

is 43 per cent; this means that the largest five firms in that industry account for 43 per cent of the industry's total sales.

Table 9.1 gives the five-firm concentration ratios for 21 sub-sectors of UK manufacturing. The data show that in many of these industries the largest five firms are too large a part of the total market to be price-takers. Yet none of these industries is a single-firm monopoly. The most concentrated (by this measure) is tobacco products, where the five largest firms account for the entire turnover.

Although national concentration ratios provide useful information, care must be taken in interpreting them. For example, markets often extend across national borders. A single firm operating in the United Kingdom does not have a monopoly if it is competing in the UK market against products imported from several foreign producers. The globalization of competition, brought about by the falling costs of transportation and communication, has been one of the most significant developments in the world economy in recent decades. Global competition has greatly reduced the number of secure monopolies that exist in national markets. This important development is discussed further in Box 9.1.

**The extent of competition in any market depends not just on the number of domestic producers, but also on the ability of foreign producers to compete effectively in that market.**

# Imperfectly competitive market structures

The market structures that we are now going to study are termed *imperfectly competitive*. The word 'competitive' emphasizes that we are not dealing with monopoly, and the word 'imperfect' emphasizes that we are not dealing with perfect competition.

Some patterns of firm behaviour are typical of all imperfectly competitive market structures. We outline these first, before looking at specific models of imperfect competition.

**Box 9.1 Globalization of production and competition**

A mere 150 years ago people and news travelled by sailing ship, so that it took months to communicate across various parts of the world. Advances in the twentieth century sped up both communications and travel. In the past several decades the pace of change in communications technology has accelerated. The world has witnessed a communications revolution that has dramatically changed the way business decisions are made and implemented.

Fifty years ago telephone links were laboriously and unreliably connected by operators; satellites were in the dreams of rocket scientists; photocopying, fax and email were completely unknown, as was the internet. Hand-delivered mail was the only way to send hard copy, and getting it to overseas destinations often took weeks. Computers were in their infancy and accessible only to an elite few academics and military scientists. Jets were just beginning to replace the much slower and less reliable propeller aircraft. Today direct dialling is available to most parts of the world, at a fraction of what long-distance calls cost forty years ago. Internet, faxes, satellite TV links, fast jet travel, email, cheap courier services, and a host of other developments have made communication that is reliable, and often instantaneous, available throughout the world.

The communications revolution has been a major contributor to the development of what has become known as the 'global village', three important characteristics of which are a *disintegration* of production, an increase in competition, and a decline in the power of the nation-state.

**Production**

The communications revolution has allowed many large international companies, known as transnational corporations (TNCs), to decentralize their production process (see Box 6.1 on page 114). They are now able to locate their research and development (R&D) where the best scientists are available. They can produce various components in dozens of places, locating each activity in the country where costs are cheapest for that type of

production. They can then ship all the parts, as they are needed, to an assembly factory where the product is 'made'.

The globalization of production has brought employment, and rising real wages, to people in many less developed countries. At the same time, it has put less skilled labour in the developed countries under strong competitive pressures.

**Competition**

The communications revolution has also caused an internationalization of competition in many industries. National markets are no longer protected for local producers by high costs of transportation and communication or by consumers' ignorance of similar foreign products. Walk into a local supermarket or department store today, and you will have no trouble in finding products representing most of the UN member states.

Consumers gain by being able to choose from an enormous range of goods and services. Firms that are successful gain worldwide sales. Firms that fall behind even momentarily may, however, be wiped out by competition coming from many quarters. Global competition is fierce, and firms that want to survive must be fast on the uptake of their own and other people's new ideas.

**Economic policy**

The globalization of production, and consequently of competition, has greatly reduced the scope for individual countries to implement distinctive economic policies. Today, firms of all sorts, from large transnationals to individuals operating out of their homes through computer links, can relocate production easily. So tough national policies that reduce local profitability are often self-defeating, as firms move production elsewhere.

Globalization and international capitalism have recently been the object of political demonstrations whenever there is an international economic conference in a vulnerable location. We discuss the economic issues associated with this disquiet on pages 622–3.

## Firms create their own products

If a new farmer enters the wheat industry, the full range of products that can be produced is already in existence. If he decides to produce No. 1 durum wheat, it will be the same as the No. 1 durum wheat produced by all other farmers. In contrast, if a new firm enters the computer software industry, it must decide on the characteristics of the new computer programs that it is to produce. It will not produce programs that are identical to those already in production: rather, it will develop new programs, each of which will have its own distinctive characteristics. This

is true of firms in virtually all consumer and capital goods industries. As a result, firms in these industries sell a range of differentiated products. The term **differentiated product** refers to a group of products that are similar enough to be considered variations on one generic product but dissimilar enough that they can be sold at different prices; for example, Ford and Mercedes both make cars but their models are different.

**Most firms in imperfectly competitive market structures sell differentiated products. In such industries, the firm itself must decide on the characteristics of the products it will sell.**

## Firms choose their prices

In imperfectly competitive markets, firms typically have several product lines that differ more or less from each other and from the competing product lines of other firms. No market sets a single price for jeans, television sets, MP3 players, mobile phones, or computer games. Instead, *each* variety of the differentiated product has a price that must be set by its maker, and then some mark-up is set by the retailer (whenever the product is sold through a retailer, rather than direct to the consumer). These are the administered prices that we discussed in Chapter 3. Having set the price, firms wait to see how much is sold at that price.

In market structures other than perfect competition, firms set their prices and then let demand determine sales. Changes in market conditions are signalled to the firm by changes in the quantity that the firm is selling at its current administered price.

The changed conditions may then lead firms to change their prices—but they may instead decide to change their level of production.

## Short-run price stability

In perfect competition, prices change continually in response to changes in demand and supply. In markets for differentiated products, prices often change less frequently. Manufacturers' prices for cars, computers, television sets, and i-Pods do not change with anything like the frequency of price changes in markets for basic materials, company shares, and foreign exchange.

Modern firms that sell differentiated products typically have hundreds, or even thousands, of distinct products on their price lists. Changing such a long list of administered prices involves costs. These include the costs of printing new list prices and notifying all customers, the difficulty of keeping track of frequently changing prices for purposes of accounting and billing, and the loss of customer and retailer goodwill owing to the uncertainty caused by frequent price changes.

Because firms producing differentiated products must administer their own prices, they must decide on the *frequency* with which they will change these prices.

In making this decision, each firm will balance the cost of making price changes against the revenue lost by not making price changes. Clearly, the likelihood that the firm will make costly price changes rises with the size of the disturbance to which it is adjusting and the probability that the disturbance will not be reversed. Thus, transitory fluctuations in demand may be met by changing output with prices constant, while changes in costs that are thought to be permanent are passed on through price increases. With the rise of internet sales, of course, there is much more price flexibility than there used to be in some products. Compare for example the prices of airline seats, which now may change hourly, with those of the pre-computer days, which were posted in a printed brochure and changed only rarely.

## Non-price competition

Many firms spend large sums of money on advertising. They do so in an attempt both to shift the demand curve for the industry's product and to attract customers from competing firms. Firms often offer competing standards of quality and product guarantees. Any kind of sales promotion activity undertaken by a single firm would not happen under perfect competition, since each firm can sell any amount at the going market price. Any such scheme directed at competing firms in the same industry is, by definition, inconsistent with monopoly. Firms also use advertising to signal their commitment to quality and service, in order to generate customer loyalty to their brand. Again this is something a perfect competitor would never do, and something a pure monopolist is unlikely to need to do.

## Unexploited scale economies

Many firms in imperfectly competitive industries appear to be operating on the downward-sloping portions of their long-run average cost curves.[1] One reason for this is the high development costs and short product lives of many modern products. Some popular software products, for example, did not exist five years ago and will almost certainly have been superseded in five years' time. A computer program takes a lot of time and effort to write but further copies of it can be run off very cheaply. Similarly, a new drug typically requires years of R&D costs to discover and test, but will often be inexpensive to manufacture once the correct formula has been arrived at. In such cases, firms face steeply falling long-run average total cost curves. The more units they sell, the lower are their fixed development costs per unit. If they were in perfect

---

[1] Although this is also possible under monopoly, firms in perfect competition must, in the long run, be at the minimum point of their long-run average cost curves (see Figure 7.10 on page 150).

competition, these firms would go on increasing outputs and sales until rising marginal costs of production just balanced their falling average fixed costs, bringing their average total cost to a minimum. But under imperfect competition firms often face falling average total cost curves throughout each product's life. Such industries are sometimes referred to as **increasing returns industries**.

## Entry prevention

Firms in many industries engage in activities that are designed to hinder the entry of new firms, thereby preventing existing pure profits from being eroded by such entry. We discuss these activities in much more detail later in the chapter.

# Monopolistic competition

One easily tractable model of imperfect competition is monopolistic competition. Tractability of this model is achieved by limiting the form of interdependence between producers. We deal with this case first before discussing more general types of strategic interactions between firms in oligopolistic market structures.

**Monopolistic competition** refers to a market in which there are many firms but each sells a differentiated product and so faces a downward sloping demand curve for its own product.[2]

## The theory

### Assumptions

The theory is based on four key assumptions.

1. *Each firm produces one specific variety, or brand, of the industry's differentiated product.* Each firm thus faces a demand curve that, although negatively sloped, is highly elastic, because many close substitutes are sold by other firms.

2. *The industry contains so many firms that each one ignores the possible reactions of its many competitors when it makes its own price and output decisions.* Each firm makes decisions based on its own demand and cost conditions, and does not take any account of potential reactions by other firms.

3. *There is freedom of entry and exit in the industry.* If existing firms are earning profits, new firms have an incentive to enter. When they do, the demand for the industry's product must be shared among more brands.

4. *There is symmetry.* When a new firm enters the industry selling a new version of the differentiated product,

it draws customers equally from all existing firms. For example, a new entrant that captured 5 per cent of the existing market would do so by capturing 5 per cent of the sales of each existing firm.

### Equilibrium

#### Short-run equilibrium

Because each firm's product has some features that differ from those of competitors, each firm faces a negatively sloped demand curve. But the curve is rather elastic because similar products sold by other firms provide many close substitutes. The negative slope of the demand curve provides the potential for monopoly profits in the short run, as illustrated in part (i) of Figure 9.1.

#### Long-run equilibrium

Freedom of entry and exit forces profits to zero in the long run. If existing firms in the industry are earning profits, new firms will enter. Their entry will mean that the demand for the product must be shared among more and more brands. Thus, the demand curve for each existing firm's brand shifts to the left.[3] Entry continues until profits fall to zero as shown in part (ii) of Figure 9.1.

### Excess capacity

The absence of positive profits requires that each firm's demand curve be nowhere above its long-run average total cost curve. The absence of losses, which would cause exit, requires that each firm be able to cover its costs. Thus, average revenue must equal average total cost at some output. Together these requirements imply that, when a monopolistically competitive industry is in long-run equilibrium, each firm will be producing where its demand

---

[2] US economist Edward Chamberlin (1899–1967) was the originator of the theory of monopolistic competition.

[3] The amount of the shift in the demand curve is determined by the *symmetry assumption*: a new entrant takes sales in equal proportion from all existing firms.

**(i) Short-run equilibrium**  **(ii) Long-run equilibrium**

**Figure 9.1 Equilibrium of a typical firm in monopolistic competition**

**In the short run a typical firm may make pure profits, but in the long run it will only cover its costs.** In part (i) a typical monopolistically competitive firm is shown in short-run equilibrium at point $E_S$. Output is $q_S$, where $MC = MR$, price is $p_S$, and profits are the blue area.

In part (ii) the firm is in long-run equilibrium at point $E_L$. Entry of new firms has pushed the existing firm's demand curve to the left until the curve is tangent to the $ATC$ curve at output $q_L$. Price is $p_L$, and total costs are just being covered. Excess capacity is $q_C - q_L$. If the firm were to produce at capacity, its costs would fall from $p_L$ per unit of output to $p_C$.

Note that, to make the points $q_L$ and $q_C$ visually distinct, the demand curve in part (ii) has been drawn as more steeply sloped than in part (i). The flatter demand curve of part (i) is what is expected in monopolistic competition. If it were drawn on part (ii), $q_L$ would more realistically be closer to $q_C$, but the differences being illustrated by the figure would be harder to see.

curve is tangent to (i.e. touching at just one point) its average total cost curve.

Two curves that are tangent to each other have the same slope at that point. If a negatively sloped demand curve is to be tangent to the long-run average cost (*LRAC*) curve, the latter must also be negatively sloped at the point of tangency. This situation is shown in Figure 9.1(ii): the typical firm is producing an output less than the one at which its *LRAC* reaches its minimum point.

This is the **excess capacity theorem** of monopolistic competition. Each firm is producing its output at an average cost that is higher than it could achieve by producing its capacity output. In other words, each firm has *unused* or *excess* capacity. So:

The theory of monopolistic competition shows that an industry can be competitive, in the sense of having numerous competing firms and no pure profits, and yet contain unexploited scale economies, in the sense that each firm is producing on the negatively sloped portion of its average total cost curve.

This implies that firms typically invest in capacity that is not fully utilized.

### Is excess capacity wasteful?

The long-run equilibrium of a monopolistically competitive industry might seem inefficient. Production costs are not as low as they could be if firms produced at the lowest

point on their average cost curves, and firms typically invest in some capacity that goes unused.

But this is not necessarily inefficient, because people value diversity and are prepared to pay a price for it. For example, each brand of breakfast food, shampoo, car, and jeans has its sincere devotees. Increasing the number of differentiated products has two effects. First, it increases the amount of excess capacity in the production of each product, because the total demand must be divided between more products. Second, the increased diversity of available products will better satisfy diverse tastes.

How will consumers' satisfaction be maximized in these circumstances?

Consumers' satisfaction is maximized when the number of differentiated products is increased until the marginal gain in consumers' satisfaction from an increase in diversity equals the loss from having to produce each existing product at a higher cost.

For this reason, among others, the prediction that large-group monopolistic competition would lead to inefficiency in the use of resources is not proven: it might and it might not.

## Empirical relevance

Is there any empirical relevance of the monopolistic competition model? Although, product differentiation is an

**Box 9.2**  The price of haircuts and the profits of hairdressers

Suppose that there are many hairdressers and freedom of entry into the industry: anyone can set up as a hairdresser. Assume that the going price for women's haircuts is £10 and that at this price all hairdressers believe their incomes are too low.

The hairdressers hold a meeting and decide to form a trade association. The purpose of the association is to impose a price of £12 for women's haircuts. What is the result?

We need to distinguish between the short-run and long-run effects of an increase in the price of haircuts. In the short run the number of hairdressers is fixed. Thus, in the short run the answer depends only on the elasticity of the demand for their services. If demand elasticity is less than 1, total expenditure will rise and so will the incomes of hairdressers; if demand elasticity exceeds 1, the hairdressers' revenues will fall. Thus, to answer the question we need some knowledge about the elasticity of demand for haircuts. Assuming it to be inelastic, hairdressers will be successful in raising incomes in the short run.

What about the long run? If hairdressers were just covering costs before the price change, they will now be earning economic profits. Hairdressing will become an attractive trade relative to other trades requiring equal skill and training, and there will be a flow of new entrants into the industry. As the number of hairdressers rises, the same amount of business must be shared among more and more of them, so the typical hairdresser will find business —and hence earnings—decreasing.

Profits may also be squeezed from another direction. With fewer customers coming their way, hairdressers may compete against one another for the limited number of customers. Their agreement does not allow them to compete through price cuts, but they can compete in service. They may spruce up their shops, offer their customers expensive magazines to read, and so forth. This kind of non-price competition will raise operating costs.

These changes will continue until hairdressers are just covering their opportunity costs, at which time the attraction for new entrants will vanish. The industry will settle down in a new long-run equilibrium in which individual hairdressers make incomes only as large as they did before the price rise. There will be more hairdressers than there were in the original situation, but each one will be working for a smaller fraction of the day and will be idle for a larger fraction. (The industry will have excess capacity.) Customers will have shorter waits even at peak periods, and they will get to read a wide choice of magazines, but they will be paying £12 for haircuts.

If the association adopted the plan in order to raise the average income of hairdressers, it will have failed. It has created more jobs for hairdressers, but not a higher income for each.

**The general lesson is clear: one cannot raise income by raising price above the competitive level unless one can prevent new entry or can otherwise reduce the quantity of the product or service provided.**

almost universal phenomenon in industries producing consumer goods and capital goods, the monopolistically competitive market structure is found only infrequently in practice. Although many industries produce a vast array of differentiated products, these are often produced by only a few firms. For example, a mere three firms produce most of the many breakfast cereals. Similar circumstances exist in soap powder, chemicals, cigarettes, and numerous other industries. These industries are clearly not perfectly competitive, and neither are they monopolies. Are they monopolistically competitive? The answer is no, because they contain few enough firms for each to take account of the others' reactions when determining its own behaviour (thus violating the second assumption above). Furthermore, these firms often earn large profits without attracting new entry (thus violating the prediction of zero profits in the long run).

One possible example is the restaurant market in a city such as London. Each competes in the 'eating out' market, but no individual restaurant is critically affected by any one other. Each has a slightly different product, and entry into the market is easy. The more entry there is, the smaller the market share of the others is likely to be, but each clearly has some discretion about the prices it charges. Some other retail service providers, such as hairdressers (see Box 9.2), provide similar examples, but good examples in other industries are hard to find.

While there are not many industries that even approximately fit the assumptions of monopolistic competition, there are two ways in which the model is a useful part of the toolbox of economics. First, it gives a simple illustration of the dynamics of competition by which entry of new firms tends to eliminate pure profit in the long-run. Second, the model shows how any market with differentiated products will tend to involve excess capacity and price unequal to marginal cost, though this apparent inefficiency needs to be set against the benefits of the more diverse choices available with product differentiation.

# Oligopoly

**Oligopoly** is imperfect competition among the few; it applies to an industry that contains only a few competing firms. Each firm has enough market power to prevent it from being a price-taker, but at the same time each firm is subject to enough inter-firm rivalry to prevent it from considering the market demand curve as its own. In most modern economies this is the dominant market structure for the production of consumer and capital goods as well as many basic industrial materials such as steel and aluminium. Services, however, are often produced in industries containing a larger number of firms—although product differentiation prevents them from being perfectly competitive. Also, the absence of symmetry prevents them from being monopolistically competitive. Since some firms' products are closer substitutes for each other than other firms' products, firms do tend to take account of the behaviour of their closest competititors.

In contrast to a monopoly, which has *no* competitors, and to a monopolistically competitive firm, which has *many* competitors, an oligopolistic firm faces *a few* competitors. Because there are only a few firms in an oligopolistic industry, each firm realizes that its competitors may respond to any move it makes. The prudent firm will take such possible responses into account. In other words, oligopolists are aware that all the decisions made by the various firms in the industry affect the other firms.

This is the key difference between oligopolists on the one hand and perfect competitors, monopolistic competitors, and monopolies on the other. The behaviour of oligopolists is **strategic**, which means that they must take explicit account of the impact of their decisions on competing firms and of the reactions they expect from competing firms. In contrast, firms in perfect and monopolistic competition engage in **non-strategic behaviour**, which means they make decisions based on their own costs and their own demand curves without considering any possible reactions from their large number of competitors. The behaviour of a monopolist is also non-strategic: it has no competitors with whom to interact.

Oligopolistic industries are of many types. In some industries there are only a few firms, but oligopoly is also consistent with a large number of small sellers, called a 'competitive fringe', as long as a 'big few' dominate the industry's production. For example, about 500 banks operate in the United Kingdom, but the big Five—Barclays, LloydsTSB, Royal Bank of Scotland (which owns NatWest), HSBC, and HBOS (formed by merger of the Halifax and the Bank of Scotland)—dominate the UK's retail commercial banking industry. Similarly, there are many small shops selling groceries, but a few large nationwide firms, such as Tesco, Sainsbury, Asda and Morrisons, dominate grocery retailing.

In oligopolistic industries prices are typically administered. Products are usually differentiated. Firms engage in rivalrous behaviour, although the intensity of the rivalry varies greatly across industries and over time. Some aspects of this rivalrous behaviour can be analysed using the tools of economics, but it is also the subject of strategy courses in business schools and the central topic running through thousands of business management books (a sample of which can be seen in any airport bookstore). Successful captains of industry, whose memoirs often sell millions of copies, are not those who are just good at deciding where marginal cost is equal to marginal revenue: rather, they are those who lead a large team of managers and workers in a complex competition to develop winning products and gain market share against teams of others trying to do the same.

*firms jostle for advantage by price and non-price competition, undercutting and outbidding rivals in the market-place by advertising outlays and promotional expenses, launching new differentiated products, new technical processes, new methods of marketing and new organisational forms, and even new reward structures for their employees, all for the sake of head-start profits that they know will soon be eroded. (Blaug 1997: 255)*

## Why bigness?

Several factors explain why a few large firms dominate so many industries. Some of these factors are 'natural', and some are created by the firms themselves.

### Natural causes of bigness

#### Economies of scale

Much manufacturing production applies the principle of the division of labour that we first studied in Chapter 1. The production of a complex product is broken up into hundreds of simple, repetitive tasks. This type of division of labour is the basis of the assembly line, which revolutionized the production of many goods in the early twentieth century, and still underlies economies of large-scale production in many industries.[4] The division of labour is, as Adam Smith observed long ago, dependent on the size of the market. If only a few units of a product can be sold each day, there is no point in dividing its production into a number of specialized tasks. So big firms have an advantage over small firms whenever there is great potential for economies based on division of labour. The larger the scale of production, the lower their average variable costs of production.

### Fixed costs

It is costly to design, test, and market a new product. In technologically dynamic industries it may be a matter of only a few years before each new version is replaced by some superior version of the same basic product. Yet the fixed costs of product development must be recovered in the revenues from sales of the product. The larger the firm's sales, the lower the cost that has to be recovered from each unit sold. Consider a product that costs £1 million to develop and market. If 1 million units can be sold before the product is replaced by a superior version, £1 of the selling price of each unit must go towards recovering the development costs. If, however, the firm expects to sell 10 million units, each unit need contribute only 10 pence to these costs, and the market price can be lowered accordingly. With the enormous development costs of some of today's high-tech products, firms that can sell a large volume have a distinct pricing advantage over firms that sell a smaller volume. Firms with large product development costs face downward-sloping average total cost curves even if their average variable costs are constant.

### Economies of scope

Economies of scope apply to a multi-product firm owing to the fact that some resources of the firms can be shared between different product areas. **Economies of scope** exist if production of several different products within one firm leads to the unit costs of production of each product being lower than if they had been produced in independent firms. Such economies may arise because some functions are shared, such as marketing and distribution, or they may arise because of some common skills in the firm that can be applied to more than one product.

Where size confers a cost advantage, through economies of either scale or scope, there may be room for only a few firms, even when the total market is quite large. This cost advantage of size will dictate that the industry be an oligopoly, unless government regulation prevents the firms from growing to their efficient size.

### Firm-created causes of bigness

The number of firms in an industry may be decreased while the average size of the survivors rises owing to the *strategic* behaviour of the firms themselves. Firms may grow by buying out rivals (acquisitions), by merging with them (mergers), or by driving rivals into bankruptcy, sometimes through predatory practices. This process increases the size and market shares of the survivors and may, by reducing competitive behaviour, allow them to earn larger profit margins. But these high profits will attract new entrants unless the surviving firms can create and sustain barriers to entry. Although most firms would like to behave in this manner, it is no easy task to create effective entry barriers when natural ones do not exist. We return to entry barriers later in the chapter.

### Is bigness natural or firm-created?

The answer to this question is probably: 'some of both'. Some industries have production in the hands of few firms because the efficient size of the firm is large relative to the overall size of the industry's market. Other industries may have more concentrated production than efficiency considerations would dictate, because the firms are seeking enhanced market power through large size combined with entry barriers. What is debatable is the relative importance of these two forces, the one coming from the efficiencies of large scale and scope, and the other from the desire of firms to create market power by growing large.

Harvard economist Alfred D. Chandler, Jr is a champion of the view that the major reason for the persistence of oligopolies in the manufacturing sector is the efficiency of large-scale production. His monumental work *Scale and Scope* (Chandler 1990) argues this case in great detail for the United States, the United Kingdom, and Germany.

## The basic dilemma of oligopoly

Oligopolistic behaviour is typically *strategic* behaviour. In deciding on strategies, oligopolists face a basic dilemma between competing and co-operating.

The firms in an oligopolistic industry will make more profits as a group if they co-operate; any one firm, however, may make more profits for itself if it goes it alone while the others co-operate.

This behaviour is similar to that established in Chapter 8 for the cartelization of a perfectly competitive

---

[4] This is sometimes referred to as *Fordism*, after Henry Ford who introduced the modern assembly line method of production.

industry.[5] In a perfectly competitive industry, however, there are so many firms that they cannot reach the co-operative solution unless some central governing body is able to force the necessary behaviour on all firms. In contrast, the few firms in an oligopolistic industry will themselves recognize the possibility of co-operating to avoid the loss of profits that will result from competitive behaviour.

### The co-operative solution

If the firms in an oligopolistic industry co-operate, either overtly or tacitly, to produce among themselves the monopoly output, they can maximize their joint profits. If they do this, they will reach what is called a **co-operative solution**, which is the position that a single monopoly firm would reach if it owned all the firms in the industry. Of course, explicit co-operation by firms may be forbidden by competition laws. However, even within the range of what is legal, firms can choose whether to compete aggressively or to be more passive. The more passive approach can be equivalent to tacit co-operation.

### The non-cooperative equilibrium

The analysis of a cartel in Chapter 8 shows that if all the firms in an oligopolistic industry adopt the co-operative pricing and output level, it would be profitable for any one of them to cut its price or to raise its output, as long as the others do not do so. However, if all do the same thing, they will be worse off as a group and may all be worse off individually. An equilibrium that is reached by firms when they proceed by calculating only their own gains, without co-operating with others, is called a **non-cooperative equilibrium** or a **Nash equilibrium**. This type of equilibrium is named after the US mathematician John Nash, who developed the concept in the 1950s and received the 1994 Nobel prize in economics for this work.[6] It is an equilibrium in which each firm's best strategy is to maintain its present behaviour, *given the present behaviour of the other firms*.

Nash equilibrium is a concept widely used in *game theory*, which is an approach to formal modelling of strategic interaction. We outline the game theory approach next.

## Oligopoly as a game

*Game theory* may sound trivial or humorous—after all we play 'games' for fun. However, game theory is a major branch of economic analysis that provides many insights into the real world behaviour of economic agents in situations where there is an actual or potential conflict of interest. **Game theory** is an approach to analysing rational decision-making behaviour in interactive or conflict situations. The 'game' element arises because the outcome depends not only on the choices made by one player but also on what other players choose to do at the same time (or subsequently).

In a game agents aim to maximize their own payoff by choosing specific actions, but the actual outcome also depends on what all other players do. The game consists of a specified interactive playing field (which in the case of firms would be the market for their product), a specification of all possible courses of action, and a schedule of the payoffs to each of the players under all possible outcomes. Players plan their own courses of action in order to maximize their expected payoff, under the knowledge that the other players are trying to do the same. A player's *strategy* is a complete specification of the actions to be taken in response to outcomes that are discovered as the game proceeds (though a strategy may include some random elements). One player's payoff from choosing a strategy depends on what the other players do, but players cannot make binding agreements with each other.

Given all the players' strategies, there will be a set of possible outcomes to the game. These determine the potential payoffs for each of the players. A specific outcome is called an *equilibrium* if no player can take actions to improve her own payoff while all other players continue to follow their optimal strategies.

There is a circularity to the problem that has to be solved, as, in order to select her best strategy, a player must know what other players will do, but they in turn are in the same position. In **normal (or strategic) form games**

---

[5] The basic reason is that when only one firm increases its output by 1 per cent the price falls by less than when all firms do the same. Thus, when the point is reached at which profits will be *reduced* if all firms expand output together, it will still pay one firm to expand output *if* the others do not do the same.

[6] Nash was immortalized by Hollywood in the 2002 film of his life, *A Beautiful Mind*, starring Russell Crowe.

players choose their moves simultaneously. Whenever the choices available are discrete and finite, the game can be represented in the structure of a table setting out the possible outcomes for each of the players depending on what the other players do. In an **extensive form game** players make moves in some order over time, so the analysis of the game needs a specification of the payoffs and information at each point in time. Real business interactions are obviously more closely analogous to an extensive form game, as firms interact dynamically over time; however, whenever the precise timing of moves is not essential to the outcome, a 'game' can often be represented more simply as a normal form game.

A game that is played only once is a 'one-shot' game. Repeated games open possibilities of learning and of acting in order to punish or reward the other players. A **supergame** is a game that is repeated an infinite number of times.

## Example 1

Let us think of a simple example in order to gain an intuitive feel for the issues involved. Suppose that you are in your first year at university and you are planning for your summer vacation. In all the previous years of your life you have gone on a summer vacation with your parents. This year you would like to go away with your own friends instead. However, you think that your parents will be offended if you say that you do not want to go on holiday with them—after all, they are helping to finance your education. So what do you say when your parents phone up and say that they are booking the summer vacation and are assuming that you will come?

What happens and the payoffs (i.e. level of happiness of all involved) depend upon what your parents' true preferences are. In one possible case, they would prefer to go on holiday without you, as they have had to have holidays that suit their children for the last twenty years or so. However, they think they should give you the option of going with them, even though they hope you will say no, because they do not want to offend you.

Clearly, the best solution for everybody, which would be called the **co-operative solution**, is for everyone to reveal their true preferences, in which case you can agree to have separate holidays and will all end up happy. However, a likely outcome in a one shot-game is that each of you tries to avoid the really bad outcome (as you perceive it) of offending the other; so your parents ask you to join them and you agree to go. This is not as bad as everybody feeling offended, but it is inferior to the best outcome of everyone having the holiday they want. Thus, each of you choosing a strategy of avoiding the worst

possible outcome leads to a solution, but one that is not the best that could be achieved for all concerned.

Of course, if this game were repeated for several years in a row then the preferences of each side might be revealed more clearly and the optimal solution of separate holidays could be arrived at.

The other possibility is that your parents really would prefer you to come on holiday with them while you really would prefer not to. In this situation there is no way in which you can both achieve your preferred solution. If you say no to them they will be upset, but if you say yes you will not have as good a holiday as you could with your friends. Your decision will depend on how you weigh up the psychic cost of offending your parents against the loss of having a good time without them.

This is obviously a rather special case, and in a family situation happily there are other ways of communicating and solving problems where objectives conflict. But hopefully it can give a feel for what is going on in a game structure. Individuals have a range of possible choices, but the outcomes are affected by what other players do at the same time. In business games we normally consider the potential payoffs in terms of profit, but strategy can just as easily be based on other types of preference—such as avoiding offending your parents.

## Solutions to games

The first thing to look for in a game is whether each player has a **dominant strategy**. This is a strategy that is the best response independent of what the other players do. If each player has a dominant strategy, this is what they will do, and the outcome of the game will be the payoff associated with all players following this strategy. *Dominated strategies*, which are all those other than the dominant strategy, will not be played, so these can be eliminated from consideration. If there are only two strategies to choose from and one is dominant the other must be dominated, but it is possible to have dominated strategies with no dominant strategy.

If there is no obvious dominant strategy for each player, it is necessary to look for possible equilibria of the game. A **Nash equilibrium** occurs when each player chooses his strategy to maximize the payoff, assuming that all other players are playing their Nash equilibrium strategies. In this situation, no player would want to change his strategy as it is believed that all other players would not change theirs.

According to the **Nash theorem**, every game with a finite number of players and a finite number of strategies will have at least one Nash equilibrium. For this to hold,

**Box 9.3 Games and their applications**

### The 'prisoner's dilemma' game

This is the story that lies behind the name:

Two men, John and Bill, are arrested for jointly committing a crime and are interrogated separately. They know that if they both plead innocent they will get only a light sentence. Each is told, however, that if either protests innocence while the other admits guilt, the one who claims innocence will get a severe sentence while the other will be let off. If they both plead guilty, they will both get a medium sentence.

The table shows the payoff matrix for that game.

|  |  | John's plea | |
|---|---|---|---|
|  |  | Innocent | Guilty |
| Bill's plea | Innocent | J light sentence<br>W light sentence | J no sentence<br>W severe sentence |
|  | Guilty | J severe sentence<br>W no sentence | J medium sentence<br>W medium sentence |

John reasons as follows: 'If Bill pleads innocent, I get a light sentence if I also plead innocent, but no sentence at all if I plead guilty, so guilty is my better plea. Second, if Bill pleads guilty, I get a severe sentence if I plead innocent and a medium sentence if I plead guilty. So once again guilty is my preferred plea.' Bill reasons in the same way, and as a result they both plead guilty and get a medium sentence; whereas if they had been able to communicate, they could both have agreed to plead innocent and both would have got off with a light sentence.

The prisoner's dilemma has many business applications, as it is the classic case in which co-operation would maximize joint income, but the strategic interaction of firms is more likely to lead to the non-cooperative outcome, as in a Nash equilibrium.

### Battle of the sexes

|  |  | Jane | |
|---|---|---|---|
|  |  | Soccer | Theatre |
| John | Soccer | 100, 200 | 0, 0 |
|  | Theatre | 0, 0 | 200, 100 |

Imagine a situation where a husband and wife have a choice between going to the theatre and going to a soccer game. John really wants to go to soccer and Jane really wants to go to the theatre. Jane's payoff is the first number in each box and John's is the second. Each would get some satisfaction from going along with the other's preferred choice, but neither would be at all happy to go alone to either of the potential activities. There are two Nash equilibria in the game as set out here, as both have an incentive to move from the off-diagonal outcomes. However, in a one-shot game it is not clear which of the two possible equilibria will emerge. In a repeated game the outcome may depend on who moves first and on whether they can agree to alternate the outcome—theatre this time, soccer next time.

The structure of this game illustrates some business situations in which it pays to co-operate rather than compete. The choice between VHS and betamax as a video standard shows that it does not pay to go it alone. Betamax was technically the better standard, but once VHS got to be on top in usage it paid all producers to adopt it. The same applies to mobile phones, computer operating systems and many integrated trading systems.

### Zero sum game

As the name suggests, a zero sum game is one in which whatever is won by one player is lost by the other. This is not the normal outcome of economic games, as in most economic interactions both parties can become better off and so there is some positive net gain to be shared out. However, the zero sum game is a frequently used reference point in economics for any interactive situation in which there is a distributional impact but no net increase in income or wealth for the participants.

A sweepstake is a zero sum game, as each player gets one horse in the race or one team in the competition and the winner takes all the stakes put in by others. An auction is also a form of zero sum game, as the article for sale changes hands from seller to winning bidder under all outcomes and all that has to be decided is how much the buyer pays the seller (and of course which buyer gets the goods). Many takeover bids are close to a zero sum game, where most of what gets determined is the distribution of gains and losses between shareholders of the bidding and bid-for firms.

however, there has to be the possibility of some random element to strategies. A strategy with some random elements is referred to as a *mixed strategy*. Another problem is that there may be multiple Nash equilibria and it is not always obvious which one will arise. Finally, it is generally true that the Nash equilibrium is not the global optimum in the sense that, if players could co-operate, they could all become better off.

A game theory framework can often help us understand the strategic choices available, but it does not always help predict which of many possible outcomes may occur.

We now discuss a hypothetical example to illustrate the above concepts. Box 9.3 outlines some classic interactive decision dilemmas that can be analysed in the game theory framework.

## Example 2

Firms that are competing head-to-head with a small number of other firms have to decide how aggressive to be. Suppose for example that there are just two firms producing a similar product and that each firm has two possible strategies. One is to act aggressively by increasing output and trying to increase market share. The other is to act passively and keep producing at the current level of output, which involves each firm having roughly half the market and jointly sharing the monopoly profit. The possible outcomes illustrate the relevance of game theory to oligopoly.

When game theory is applied to oligopoly, the players are firms, their game is played in the market, their strategies are their price/output decisions, and the payoffs are their profits.

The basic dilemma of oligopolists is shown in Figure 9.2 for the case of a two-firm oligopoly. The simplified game, adopted for the purposes of illustration, allows only two strategies for *each firm*. Each firm can produce an output equal to either one-half of the monopoly output (the passive strategy) or two-thirds of the monopoly output (the aggressive strategy). Note that the passive strategy amounts to tacit co-operation while the aggressive strategy is clearly non-cooperative. This simple game is sufficient to illustrate several key propositions in the modern theory of oligopoly.

Figure 9.2 presents the *payoff matrix*. The data in the matrix show the profits that result from the four possible combinations of strategies.

### 1. The passive (co-operative) solution

If both sides tacitly co-operate, *each producing* one-half of the monopoly output, they share the monopoly profits by *jointly producing* the output that a monopolist would produce. As a group, they cannot do better.

### 2. The aggressive (non-cooperative) solution

There is one Nash equilibrium in Figure 9.2. In the bottom-right cell, the best decision for each firm, given that the other firm is producing two-thirds of the monopoly output, is to produce two-thirds of the monopoly output itself. Between them they produce a joint output of one-and-a-third times the monopoly output. Neither firm has an incentive to depart from this position, except by co-operating with the other. In any other cell, each firm has an incentive to alter its output, *given the output of the other firm*.

This shows that the basis of a Nash equilibrium is rational decision-making in the absence of co-operation. Its particular importance in oligopoly theory is that it is the only type of equilibrium that is *self-policing*. It is self-policing in the sense that there is no need for group behaviour

**Figure 9.2  The oligopolist's dilemma: co-operate or compete**

**Co-operation to determine the overall level of output can maximize joint profits, but it leaves each firm with an incentive to alter its production.** The figure gives what is called a 'payoff matrix' for a two-firm duopoly game. Only two levels of production are considered in order to illustrate the basic problem. A's production is indicated across the top, and its profits (measured in millions of pounds) are shown in the blue circles within each square. B's production is indicated down the left side, and its profits (in millions of pounds) are shown in the green circles within each square. For example, the top right square tells us that, if B produces one-half, while A produces two-thirds, of the output that a monopolist would produce, A's profits will be £22 million, while B's will be £15 million.

If A and B co-operate, each produces one-half the monopoly output and earns profits of £20 million, as shown in the upper left box. In this 'co-operative solution' either firm can raise its profits by producing two-thirds of the monopoly output, provided that the other firm does not do the same.

Now let A and B behave non-cooperatively. A reasons that, whether B produces either one-half or two-thirds of the monopoly output, A's best output is two-thirds. B reasons similarly. They then reach the non-cooperative equilibrium, where each produces two-thirds of the monopoly output, and each makes less than it would if the two firms co-operated.

to enforce it. Each firm has a self-interest to maintain it because no move that it can make on its own will improve its profits, given what other firms are currently doing.

If a Nash equilibrium is established—by any means whatsoever—no firm has an incentive to depart from it by altering its own behaviour. It is self-policing.

### 3. Strategic behaviour

The Nash equilibrium will be attained if each firm behaves strategically, by choosing its optimal strategy taking into account what the other firm may do. Let us see how this works.

## Box 9.4 Real-world strategic games

There are many situations in which firms have to make strategic decisions about reactions to their main rival suppliers. Here are some examples.

### Supermarket price wars

Major supermarket chains are in competition with each for growth and market share in a relatively static business area— demand for food grows only slowly. They can grow by opening stores in new areas, by trying to attract customers from other stores by advertising, or by lowering prices.

Managers of supermarkets would like to run their businesses with comfortable profit margins, and in normal times there is a standard mark-up on most products that gives an adequate return on the company's capital employed. From time to time one of the major players decides that it will make a push for more customers and significantly cuts its prices on a wide range of standard products. Frequently, in order to stem the loss of customers, the rival players will then cut their prices too.

This may look like pure price competition. However, supermarkets are multi-product firms, and the aim of price wars is not to lose money, but rather to get more customers into the store so that they will buy a range of other products on which the prices have not been cut. Of course, if other stores also cut their prices then the price war could reduce the combined profits of all supermarkets. But it is also possible that the big players will end up better off as a result of attracting more customers from smaller grocery shops.

### Airline pricing

The European airline business has long had barriers to entry, often designed to protect inefficient state-owned carriers. Deregulation of pricing occurred slowly over time, but some barriers to entry still existed in the form of restriction in the available landing slots at major airports, such as London's Heathrow.

As discussed in Box 8.2 on page 169, established carriers have developed a pricing structure that enables them to segment the market between business and leisure passengers. This means that, unless booking ahead (on some routes) or staying over a Saturday night, fairs can be high—for example over £500 for an economy flight to Rome if returning within the week, while staying over a weekend might reduce this below £200.

This situation creates incentives for new entry into the market. Companies like easyJet and Ryanair introduced 'no frills' services between various European cities at dramatically lower fares and with no restrictions such as the weekend stay. They circumvented the entry barriers created by lack of access to landing slots by flying between smaller airports—easyJet built a hub at Luton and Ryanair at Stansted. EasyJet even targeted the business traveller market.

The result was a boom in the business of the low-cost carriers and a decline in the use of traditional carriers, such as BA. In April 2002, BA announced that it was slashing its fares on some short-haul domestic routes. A day return from London to Manchester, for example, would be cut from £233 to £69 (on some flights).

The strategic issue for BA was whether to ignore the new players and maintain their old fare structures, which clearly involved some monopoly profit, or to compete on price with the new entrants. For a while BA could ignore the other players, as they were small. However, once they started to hit their profitable segment of the market, BA felt it had to fight back. In previous bouts of new entry, in this case into the trans-Atlantic market, the new entrants (such as Laker Airways) were driven out by intense price competition from existing carriers. After driving out the upstarts a new equilibrium was established. In 2006 it seemed clear that BA intended to compete with low-cost airlines only on some routes, and largely by offering cheap fares at inconvenient times or for restricted periods of travel. Its main strategy was to attract premium-price travellers with better beds, executive lounges and other luxury features. In this way it could make profit on its first class and business class business, while pricing aggressively some of its economy class seats.

### Digital TV

UK satellite TV provider BskyB built up its business by bidding for exclusive coverage of live sporting events such as Premier League football, rugby internationals, and cricket test matches. This strategy proved to be successful in attracting subscribers who had to pay a premium for these extra channels.

A new company was set up in 2000 called On Digital (later renamed ITV Digital). It tried to follow a similar strategy of buying exclusive rights to some live sporting events, paying over £300 million for the rights to televise Football League games, i.e. lower divisions than the Premier League. However, in this case the strategy failed; there was little demand to watch the games they were showing and the company went into administration while attempting to renegotiate the terms of its contract with the League.

In effect, the aggressive strategy failed not because of reactions from rivals, but because the revenue to be generated by the aggressive strategy was misjudged. Rival suppliers could just sit back and wait for ITV Digital to fail. The only puzzle is why the managers of this company ever thought that large numbers of consumers would pay a premium to watch lower-division football in the first place. A successful strategy clearly needs a good assessment of the payoffs on which such a decision is to be based.

Suppose that firm A reasons as follows: 'B can do one of two things; what is the best thing for me to do in each case? First, what if B produces one-half of the monopoly output? If I do the same, I receive a profit of 20, but if I produce two-thirds of the monopoly output, I receive 22. Second, what if B produces two-thirds of the monopoly output? If I produce one-half of the monopoly output, I receive a profit of 15, whereas if I produce two-thirds, I receive 17. Clearly, my best strategy is to produce two-thirds of the monopoly output in either case.' Aggressive behaviour is the dominant strategy.

B will reason in the same way. As a result, they end up by jointly producing one-and-a-third times the monopoly output, where each earns a profit of 17.

This type of game, where the non-cooperative equilibrium makes both players worse off than if they were able to co-operate, is like the **prisoner's dilemma** shown in Box 9.3. The important insight following from prisoner's dilemma games is that individual maximization does not always lead to an optimum allocation of resources. In the Nash equilibrium of the prisoner's dilemma game, both players can be made better off if they co-operate and so move to the top left-hand box. But if both make individual maximizing decisions, they end up in the bottom right-hand box.

### 4. Breakdown of co-operation

The Nash equilibrium is attained by the strategic reasoning just outlined. It can, however, be used to give an intuitive argument for why tacit co-operation tends to break down.

Assume that the co-operative position has been attained. Each firm is producing one-half of the monopoly output and each is earning a profit of 20. The data in Figure 9.2 show that if, A cheats by increasing its output, its profits will increase. However, B's profits will be reduced. A's behaviour drives the industry's prices down, so B earns less from its unchanged output. Because A's cheating takes the firms away from the joint profit-maximizing monopoly output, their joint profits must fall. This means that B's profits fall by more than A's rise.

Figure 9.2 shows that similar considerations also apply to B. It is worthwhile for B to depart from the joint maximizing output, as long as A does not do so. So both A and B have an incentive to depart from the joint profit-maximizing level of output.

Finally, Figure 9.2 shows that, when either firm does depart from the joint-maximizing output, the other has an incentive to do so as well. When each follows this 'selfish' strategy, they reach a non-cooperative equilibrium at which they are jointly producing one-and-a-third times as much as the monopolist would. Each then has profits that are lower than at the co-operative solution.[7]

Game theory is an extremely flexible tool that has been applied to many branches of economics. Box 9.4 outlines some real-world situations that illustrate the strategic choices that firms have to make in practice.

## Dynamics of oligopolistic industries

Suppose that firms in an oligopolistic industry succeed in raising prices above long-run average total costs and earn substantial profits that are not completely eliminated by non-price competition. In the absence of significant barriers to entry, new firms will enter the industry and erode the profits of existing firms, as they do in monopolistic competition. Natural barriers to entry are an important part of the explanation of the persistence of profits in many oligopolistic industries. Where such natural barriers do not exist, oligopolistic firms can earn profits in the long run only if they can create entry barriers.

### Entry barriers

We have already discussed the importance of entry barriers on pages 170–1, and here we extend this discussion with some cases that are most relevant to oligopoly.

### Brand proliferation

By altering the characteristics of a differentiated product, it is possible to produce a vast array of variations on the general theme of that product. Think, for example, of cars with a little more or a little less acceleration, braking power, top speed, cornering ability, petrol mileage, and so on, compared with existing models.

Although the multiplicity of existing brands is no doubt partly a response to consumers' tastes, it also discourages the entry of new firms. Say, for example, that an industry contains three large firms, each selling one brand of cigarettes, and that 30 per cent of all smokers change

---

[7] This is why we do not speak of the co-operative *equilibrium*. It is a solution to the problem of finding the best co-operative behaviour, but it is not an equilibrium, since, once achieved, each firm has an incentive to depart from it.

**Box 9.5  Brand proliferation in alcoholic drinks**

Allied Domecq plc is one of Britain's largest companies. It is a major producer of wines and spirits and an owner of restaurants and food outlets including Baskin-Robbins, Dunkin' Donuts, and Togo's.

At one time Allied was a major producer of beers and retailer of alcohol through pubs, but it sold its beer and pub interests in the late 1990s in order to concentrate on its extensive portfolio of wine and spirits businesses. If you are into scotch whisky you might try Ballantine's, Teachers, and Laphroaig, or perhaps go for Canadian Club or Maker's Mark bourbon—they are all Allied brands, as are Beefeater gin, Lamb's Navy Rum, Courvoisier brandy, Stolichnaya vodka, and Sauza, Kahlúa, and Tia Maria liqueurs. You may prefer fortified wines like Harvey's and La Ina sherries, or Cockburn's ports—you're still drinking Allied products. If you prefer drinking wine, start the evening with Mumm or Perrier-Jouet champagne then move onto some Montana sauvignon blanc from New Zealand, perhaps followed by Marques de Arienzo rioja from Spain or an Atlas Peak cabernet from California. You guessed it, these are all Allied products, as are many other wine labels from around the world, including Clos du Bois, Callaway Coastal, William Hill winery, Buena Vista in California, and Bodegas Balbi in Argentina.

Of course, Allied is not the only multi-brand producer; most of Allied's main competitors also have an extensive portfolio of brands. For example, Diageo also sells many alcoholic products. In the spirits line they have Archers, Baileys, Bell's scotch whisky, Cacique rum, Captain Morgan rum, Crown Royal Canadian whisky, Cuervo tequila, Gilbey's and Gordon's gin, Hennessy cognac, Johnnie Walker and J&B scotch, Pimms, Smirnoff vodka, and Tanqueray gin. For drinkers of single malts they have Cragganmore, Dalwhinnie, Glenkinchie, Lagavulin, Oban, and Talisker. But if you prefer beer they have Guinness, Harp lager, Kilkenny Irish beer, and Red Stripe lager. Wine drinkers are not forgotten, as Diageo owns Beaulieu Vineyard, Blossom Hill and Sterling Vineyards in California and has distribution rights for Moet and Chandon champagne.

The production of such a wide range of differentiated products helps to satisfy consumers' clear demand for diversity. It also has the effect of making it more difficult for a new firm to enter the industry. If the new firm wishes to compete over the whole range of differentiated products, it must enter on a massive scale. If it wishes to enter on only a small scale, it faces a formidable task of establishing brand images and customer recognition with only a few products over which to spread the expenses of entry. There may also be significant economies of scope for the big liqueur companies, as they can share distribution channels for most of their products.

---

brands in a random fashion each year. If a new firm enters the industry, it can expect to pick up one-third of the smokers who change brands.[8] This would give the new firm 10 per cent (one third of 30 per cent) of the total market the first year merely as a result of picking up its share of the random switchers, and it would keep increasing its share for some time thereafter. If, however, the existing three firms have five brands each, there would be 15 brands already available. A new firm selling one new brand could then expect to pick up only one-fifteenth of the brand switchers, giving it 2 per cent of the total market the first year, with smaller gains also in subsequent years. This is an extreme case, but it illustrates a general result:

**The larger the number of differentiated products sold by existing oligopolists, the smaller is the market share available to a new firm entering with a single new product.**

An example of brand proliferation drawn from the alcoholic drinks industry is given in Box 9.5.

### Advertising

Existing firms can create entry barriers by imposing significant fixed costs on new firms that enter their market. This is particularly important if the industry has only weak natural barriers to entry, because the minimum efficient scale occurs at an output that is low relative to the total output of the industry.

Advertising serves the useful function of informing buyers about their alternatives, thereby making markets work more smoothly. Indeed, advertising is essential to make consumers aware of new products, whether produced by existing firms or new entrants.

None the less, advertising can also operate as a potent entry barrier by increasing the setup costs of new entrants. Where heavy advertising has established strong brand images for existing products, a new firm may have to spend heavily on advertising to create its own brand images in consumers' minds. If the firm's initial sales are small, advertising costs *per unit sold* will be large, and price will have to be correspondingly high to cover those costs.

---

[8] Since there are now four brands to choose from, you might think that the new brand would pick up one-quarter of the switchers. But this is not correct because, by definition, the switcher rejects his old brand and chooses one of the others. Each switcher's choice-set therefore consists of three brands: two of the pre-existing brands and the one new brand.

The combined use of brand proliferation and advertising as an entry barrier helps to explain one apparent paradox of business life: one firm often sells multiple brands of the same product, which compete actively against each other as well as against the products of other firms.

The soap and cigarette industries provide classic examples of this behaviour. Because quite small plants can realize all available scale economies, both industries have few natural barriers to entry. Both contain a few large firms, each of which produces an array of heavily advertised products. The numerous existing products make it harder for a new entrant to obtain a large market niche with a single new product. The heavy advertising, although it is directed against existing products, creates an entry barrier by increasing the setup costs of a new product that seeks to gain the attention of consumers and to establish its own brand image.

### Product innovation and new technologies

New products, which may be protected from imitation by patents for up to 20 years, give the inventing firms (or the firm that holds the licence to produce) a period in which they can profit from their discoveries. The pharmaceuticals and electronics industries provide copious examples. With them the competitive process is a race to invent the next blockbuster drug or the next communication device or the next standard software package. An example from the drugs industry is provided by Tamiflu, discussed on pages 176–7 above. Drugs giants like Roche, Pfizer, and GlaxoWelcome have a portfolio of products that are most profitable while under patent protection, and they are always working on finding new ones, as they know that there is only a limited period during which their existing products will yield high revenues. Competition in this world is not about co-operative or aggressive strategies relating to pricing and production of the same product: rather, it is about seeking out new products (either by R&D or by licensing products invented by others) that replace the drugs of other companies or provide cures for diseases that other companies do not have cures for.

The electronics industry is similar to the drugs industry. IBM lost out in the computer mainframe industry (which declined) as Apple invented the PC, but then IBM fought back with a new PC of its own. In turn, IBM lost out again as it was unable to stop cheaper clones of the PC sweeping the market and the key operating system was owned by Microsoft (who had the protection of a patent). Apple survived as a computer supplier as result of niche devotees to its Mackintosh computer and operating system, but it hit the big time again in 2004/5 with the takeoff of its iPod player of downloadable music. Many competitors emerged in the MP3 music player market, but Apple had a patent on one of the key features of its iPod, so exact imitation was not possible, at least for some time.

This process is one of competition to find new technologies or new products that are sufficiently different from existing ones that they can achieve patent protection, or a window of advantage until rivals catch up. This then gives the patent-holding firm a period of time during which profit can be made on the new product and effort (and money) can be invested in looking for the next new product. This process is found in industries as diverse as those producing mobile phones, cameras, aircraft and teaching devices.

### Contestable markets and potential entry

The theory of contestable markets shows that pure profits may be eliminated even though the industry contains only a few firms and experiences no actual entry. *Potential* entry can do the job just as well as actual entry, as long as two conditions are fulfilled. First, entry must be easy to accomplish, and, second, existing firms must take potential entry into account when making price and output decisions.

Entry is usually costly to the entering firm. It may have to build a plant, it may have to develop new versions of the industry's differentiated product, or it may have to advertise heavily in order to call attention to its product. These and many other initial expenses are often called **sunk costs of entry**, which are defined as costs that a firm must incur to enter the market and that cannot be recovered if the firm subsequently exits.

A market that new firms can enter and leave without incurring any sunk costs of entry is called a perfectly **contestable market.** A market can be perfectly contestable even if the firm has to pay some costs of entry, as long as these can be recovered when the firm exits. Because all markets require at least some sunk costs of entry, contestability must be understood as a variable. The lower the sunk costs of entry, the more contestable the market.

**In a contestable market the existence of profits, even if they are due to transitory causes, will attract entry. Firms will enter to gain a share of these profits and will exit when the transitory situation has changed.**

Consider, for example, the market for air travel on the lucrative London–Paris route. This market would become quite contestable *if* counter and loading space were easily available to new entrants at the two cities' airports. An airline that was not currently serving the cities in question could shift some of its existing planes to the market with small sunk costs of entry. Some training of personnel would be needed for them to become familiar with the route and the airport. This is a sunk cost of entry that cannot be recovered if the cities in question are no longer to be served. However, most of the airline's costs of entering the London–Paris market are not sunk costs. If it subsequently decides to leave a city, the rental of terminal space will stop, and the aeroplanes and the ground equipment can be shifted to another location. The former head of the American Civil Aeronautics Board, and architect of airline deregulation, captured this point by referring to commercial aircraft as 'marginal cost with wings'.

Sunk costs of entry constitute an entry barrier. The larger they are, the larger the profits of existing firms can be without attracting new entrants. The flip side of this coin is that firms operating in markets without large sunk costs of entry will not earn such large profits. Strategic considerations will lead them to keep prices near the level that would just cover their total costs. They know that, if they charge higher prices, firms will enter to capture the profits while they last and then exit.

Contestability, where it is possible, is a force that can limit the profits of existing oligopolists. Even if entry does not occur, the ease with which it could be accomplished may keep existing oligopolists from charging prices that would maximize their joint profits.

Contestability is just another example, in somewhat more refined form, of the key point that the possibility of entry is the major force preventing the exploitation of market power. Notice that the entrants do not have to be new firms. They can be domestic firms entering new domestic markets or foreign firms entering the domestic market.

# Oligopoly and the functioning of the economy

Oligopoly is found in many industries and in all advanced economies. It typically occurs in industries where both perfect and monopolistic competition are made impossible by the existence of major economies of scale or of scope (or both). In such industries, there is simply not enough room for a large number of firms, all operating at or near their minimum efficient scales.

Three questions are important for the evaluation of the performance of the oligopolistic market structure. First, do oligopolistic markets allocate resources very differently from perfectly competitive markets? Second, in their short-run and long-run price–output behaviour, where do oligopolistic firms typically settle between the extreme outcomes of earning zero profits and earning the profits

that would be available to a single monopolist? Third, how much do oligopolists contribute to economic growth by encouraging innovative activity? We consider each of these questions in turn.

## The market mechanism under oligopoly

We have seen that under perfect competition prices are set by the impersonal forces of demand and supply, and changes in the market conditions for both inputs and outputs are signalled by changes in the prices of a firm's inputs and outputs. The market signalling system works slightly differently when prices are administered by oligopolists. Changes in prices still signal changes in market conditions for inputs. However, changes in the market conditions for outputs are typically signalled by changes in the volume of their sales at the administered prices.

Increases in costs of inputs will shift cost curves upward, and oligopolistic firms will be led to raise prices and lower outputs. Increases in demand will cause the sales of oligopolistic firms to rise. Firms will then respond by increasing output, thereby increasing the quantities of society's resources that are allocated to producing that output. They will then decide whether or not to alter their administered prices.

The market system reallocates resources in response to changes in demands and costs in roughly the same way under oligopoly as it does under perfect competition.

## Profits under oligopoly

Some firms in some oligopolistic industries succeed in coming close to joint profit maximization in the short run. In other oligopolistic industries firms compete so intensely among themselves that they come close to achieving competitive prices and outputs.

In the long run those profits that do survive competitive behaviour among existing firms will tend to attract entry. These profits will persist only in so far as entry is restricted either by natural barriers, such as large minimum efficient scales for potential entrants, or by barriers created, and successfully defended, by the existing firms.

## Very-long-run competition

Once we allow for the effects of technological change, we need to ask which market structure is most conducive to the sorts of very-long-run changes that we discussed in Chapter 6. These changes are the driving force of the economic growth that has so greatly raised living standards over the last two centuries. They are intimately related to Schumpeter's concept of creative destruction, which we first encountered in our discussion of entry barriers in Chapter 8 (page 171). Notice that 'very long run' does not necessarily mean a very long time—just enough time to change technology, which in some industries is a matter of a few months.

Examples of creative destruction abound. In the nineteenth century, railways began to compete with horse-drawn wagons and barges for the carriage of freight. In the twentieth century, lorries operating on newly constructed highways began competing with rail. During the 1950s and 1960s, aeroplanes began to compete seriously with lorries and rail.

In recent years the development of fax transmission and email has eliminated the monopoly of the Royal Mail in delivering hard-copy (as opposed to oral) communications. In their myriad uses, computers for the home and the office have swept away the markets of many once-thriving products and services. For instance, in-store computers answer customer questions, decreasing the need for salespeople. Aided by computers, 'just in time' inventory systems greatly reduce the investment in inventories required of existing firms and new entrants alike. Computer-based flexible-manufacturing systems allow firms to switch production easily and inexpensively from one product line to another, thereby reducing the minimum scale at which each can be produced profitably. Computers are involved in book production, having replaced the author's hand- and type-written copy and the publisher's laborious page makeup procedures—one day soon the multimedia CD-ROM or website may replace the textbook altogether. The internet and the computer have allowed distance leaning to flourish so that now people can take degrees in a vast number of subjects from a large number of universities worldwide, without ever setting foot in any of them—something that was totally impossible a mere couple of decades ago.

An important defence of oligopoly relates to this process of creative destruction. Many economists argue that intermediate market structures, such as oligopoly, lead to more innovation than would occur under either perfect competition or monopoly. Oligopolists face strong competition from existing rivals and cannot afford the more relaxed life of the monopolist. At the same time, however, oligopolistic firms expect to keep a good share of the profits that they earn from their innovative activity.

Everyday observation provides some confirmation of this view. Leading North American firms that operate in highly concentrated industries, such as Kodak, IBM, Microsoft, Du Pont, Intel, General Electric, and 3M, have been highly innovative over many years. Indeed, Kodak, which used to dominate the world market for photographic supplies, has had to reinvent itself recently to take account of the fact that digital technology has slashed demand for film. UK examples of innovative firms include Rolls Royce, Glaxo Wellcome, Vodafone, AstraZeneca, and BAE Systems. All of these firms operate in markets in which success depends critically on keeping products up to speed with the latest technology.

The technologies that have revolutionized agricultural production over the last century, allowing us to feed 6 billion people where a century ago it would have been impossible to feed 2 billion, have come from oligopolistic industries such as agricultural machine manufacturers and biological firms such as Monsanto and public-sector laboratories, while none of them came from the perfectly competitive industry of agricultural production.

## Conclusion

Oligopoly is an important market structure in modern economies because there are many industries in which the minimum efficient scale is simply too large to support many competing firms. The challenge to public policy is to keep oligopolists competing rather than colluding, and using their competitive energies to improve products and lower costs, rather than merely to erect entry barriers.

 CASE STUDIES

### 1. Oligopoly in action: newspaper price wars again

In Chapter 4 on pages 82–4 we discussed the impact of a price war between *The Times* and other UK broadsheet newspapers. What was unusual in that case was that one producer cut its price and none of the others followed for quite some time. This makes it a good example of what happens in a market when one price changes and no others do. Eventually there were some other price reactions as the other producers attempted to protect their market share. After the burst of price competition in the mid-1990s, the broadsheets settled into a long period of tacit co-operation during which they maintained a constant price differential between their various newspapers.

However, another price war broke out in May 2002, this time among the tabloid papers. The following reports (written for one of the broadsheets when this price war was still in its early stages) give a good picture of the actions involved.

*The* Express *is the early winner in the latest round of newspaper price wars after unofficial figures showed it has boosted circulation by as much as 14 per cent since it dropped its price to 20p. Owner Richard Desmond slashed the cover price of his daily and Sunday titles two weeks ago and is already seeing significant gains with a 23 per cent rise on weekend sales. The price war intensified yesterday when both the Daily Mirror and the Sun joined him with 20p newspapers.*

*The* Mirror *appears to have gained most ground so far in the early stages of the tabloid war. According to unaudited figures the newspaper's sales have risen by 8 per cent, adding 160,000 readers nationwide, since cutting its cover price from 32p to 20p. The* Sun, *which cut its cover price from 30p to 20p, has seen its sales go up by 5 per cent, adding 200,000 to its circulation. The* Daily Star, *already the fastest growing newspaper, has also benefited from price-cutting with a 12 per cent rise in sales in the London region. (Jessica Hodgson, media.guardian.co.uk, 14 May 2002; copyright Guardian Newspapers Limited, 2002)*

Notice that this initial report focuses on the apparent increase in sales for all of those involved in price-cutting. This is the impact of the general increase in quantity demanded of a fall in price. However, a month later some winners and losers were emerging, at least from the first round. Also, while the *Express* initiated the price cutting, the head-to-head competition had shifted to the closer rivalry between the *Sun* and the *Mirror*. The *Express*'s closest rival, the *Daily Mail*, had not reacted.

*The* Sun *has declared itself the undisputed victor in the circulation war, claiming its 'unbeatable mixture of the best news, sport and features' has sent the price-cutting* Mirror *into crisis. It says the first official circulation figures, including bulk sales, since both papers slashed their cover prices to 20p show the* Sun's *sales are up by 107,378 year on year, while the* Mirror's *are down by 64,473.*

*'The sales disaster is a serious blow for the* Mirror,'*the* Sun *gloated in Saturday's edition. The* Mirror *has 'spent £20 million on price cutting, posh telly ads, posters and marketing research and gained NOTHING but a bloody nose and LESS sales', continued the* Sun. *The latest figures show that the Sun's circulation for May 2002 was 3,458,803, a 0.42 per cent rise since the same time last year. Sales of the* Mirror *have dropped by 0.53 per cent over the same period to 2,128,755....*

*By June 6, however, the Mirror was in partial retreat and put its cover price back up to 32p in its northern heartland. In London, Meridian, central, the west and south-west regions, the* Mirror *is still on sale at 20p, while in Scotland it is selling for 10p.*

*The tabloid price war between the* Sun *and the* Mirror *has taken a particularly bitter twist because of a personality clash between the two editors.* (Ciar Byrne, media.guardian.co.uk, 17 June 2002; copyright Guardian Newspapers Limited, 2002)

Three further points that emerge from this second extract are worth emphasizing. First, although price competition is important in this case, it is only one element of the competitive interface: quality and marketing issues are also involved. Second, the interaction between the closest rivals can be very explicit and direct. We have not published some of the rude things that the editors of the *Sun* and *Mirror* said about each other, but it is clear who they were each competing with as they traded insults publicly. Third, notice that the *Mirror* was using some elements of price discrimination (see pages 166–9) between various segments of its markets. In its heartland it was able to charge a higher price as (presumably) demand there was more inelastic, while in areas where competition was stiffer it was setting a lower price.

## 2. Patents as entry barriers

A patent confers a monopoly right to the exclusive use of an invention. Patent laws differ from one country to another. In the UK, to be patentable an invention must be new, involve an inventive step, be capable of industrial application, and not be 'excluded'. Among exclusions are all discoveries, such as scientific theories or mathematical methods, that have no specific products as an outcome. Also excluded are works of art and literature (though these may be covered by copyright laws) and new designs that have no function other than appearance. Patents are granted for an initial four-year period, renewable annually for up to twenty years.

The benefit of patent protection is that it gives an inventor several years of monopoly trading and thereby creates an incentive to invest in R&D that can generate some patentable product. Drugs companies, as discussed above, invest large sums in searching for the new drugs.

Patents also have drawbacks. First, they create a tension, because there are social pressures to provide a potentially life-saving drug as cheaply as possible to as many people as possible, once it has been invented. For example, there has recently been considerable pressure on Western drugs companies to provide anti-Aids drugs to poor countries in Africa at their marginal cost of production, rather than at the monopoly price charged to the richer countries.

Second, the patent may hold up the spread of technology. One of the most famous examples in history is the patent protection granted to James Watt for his invention of the steam engine. This patent applied to any process using steam to drive a piston, and no one could infringe the patent until it ran out in 1800. This greatly inhibited the spread of existing engines by holding up their prices. It also held up the development of more effective engines because Watt had no faith in the potential of high-pressure engines. After his patent ran out, others showed how wrong he was by developing high-pressure engines without which steam could only be a stationary source of power. Steam engines powerful and light enough to be used for railways and ships had to be of the high-pressure variety.

Furthermore, patents provide strong protection only in a fairly narrow range of products where each version is distinctly different from its competitors—pharmaceuticals being one of the modern industries where patents work best. In many other industries firms do not even bother to prosecute believed patent violations, owing to the cost of legal proceedings. Rather, they rely on secrecy and a short product cycle to stay ahead of the field, so that by the time imitations come along some newer product has been developed.

Thus, patent protection has only a limited role in creating monopolies and this is at best temporary. Perhaps a more important product-protection device derives from laws relating to *trademarks* and to *passing off*. For example, there is no patent protection to stop a soft drinks manufacturer making a drink identical to Coca Cola. However, this firm would not be allowed to sell this product under the Coca Cola label or to sell it in red cans that might fool customers into believing that they were buying genuine Coca Cola. Here it is the brand that has commercial value rather then the specific product itself.

## 3. Creative destruction—an endless process

The steel-nibbed pen eliminated the quill pen with its sharpened bird's feather nib. The fountain pen eliminated the steel pen and its accompanying inkwell. The ball-point pen or 'biro' virtually eliminated the fountain pen. Rolling-ball and fibre-tipped pens have partly replaced the biro. Who knows what will come next in writing implements.

The hand-cranked adding machine replaced the Dickensian clerk adding up long columns of figures in his head. (This *was* an all-male occupation.) The electrically driven mechanical desk calculator eliminated the hand-cranked version. The electronic desk calculator eliminated the mechanical calculator, while the pocket calculator eliminated the slide rule (a device for doing calculations based on logarithms). The mainframe computer largely replaced the electronic calculator during the 1960s and 1970s (except for pocket use). In the late 1980s and early 1990s the increasingly powerful personal computer largely replaced the mainframe. A modern PC will do in a fraction of a second what the Dickensian clerk did in a week, and what a desk calculator could do in half a day.

The silent film eliminated vaudeville. The 'talkies' eliminated the silent film, and colour largely eliminated black-and-white films. The TV seriously reduced the demand for films (and radio) while not eliminating either of them. Satellites reduced the demand for terrestrial TV reception by offering better pictures and a more varied selection. For a while it looked like fibre optic cable might do the same to satellite transmission, but at the time of writing it seems that cable will be made redundant by both simpler satellite systems and technical changes in the ability to deliver fast signals (suitable for broadband internet) down telephone lines.

In the 1920s and 1930s the American supermarket threatened the small grocery store as the main shopping place for the typical family. The small store fought back with assistance from the courts and the regulators, and was able to slow the advance of the supermarkets. But in the end, the big stores were seen to offer a superior product and they pushed the small operations into the niche of the convenience store or corner shop. In the 1960s supermarkets spread throughout Britain. In the 1980s and 1990s out-of-town shopping malls and hypermarkets threatened town-centre supermarkets. But by the late 1990s and early 2000s major supermarket groups had slowed their out-of-town expansion and focused on town-centre 'metro' stores close to where people live or work.

For long-distance passenger travel by sea, the steamship eliminated the sailing vessel around the late nineteenth century. The aeroplane eliminated the ocean liner in the 1950s and 1960s. For passenger travel on land the train eliminated the stagecoach, while the long-distance bus competed with the train without eliminating it. The aeroplane wiped out the passenger train in most of North America while leaving the bus still in a low-cost niche, used mainly for short and medium distances. In Europe distances are such that bus, train, and plane all compete over many routes while air transport dominates the longer trips.

The above are all product innovations. Production processes also undergo the same type of creative destruction. The laborious hand-setting of metal type for printing was replaced by linotype, which allowed lines of type to be set by a keyboard operator but still involved a costly procedure for making corrections. The linotype was swept away by computer typesetting, and many of the established printing shop operations have recently been replaced by digital publishing technology.

Masses of assembly-line workers, operating highly specialized and inflexible machines, replaced the craftsman when Henry Ford perfected the techniques of mass production at the beginning of the twentieth century. A smaller number of less specialized flexible-manufacturing workers, operating sophisticated and less specialized machinery, have now replaced the assembly-line workers who operated the traditional factory in many industries.

The list of such cases can be extended almost indefinitely, and they all illustrate the same general lesson. The process of creative destruction transforms the products we consume, how we make those products, and how we work. It continually sweeps away positions of high income and economic power established by firms that were in the previous wave of technological change and by those who work for them. It is an agent of dynamism in our economy, an agent of change and economic growth. But it is not without its negative side. Some firms go bust, owners lose wealth, and workers become redundant.

# SUMMARY

### Imperfectly competitive market structures

■ Firms in market structures other than perfect competition face negatively sloped demand curves and must administer their prices.

### Monopolistic competition

■ In the theory of large-group monopolistic competition, many firms compete to sell differentiated products. Each may make pure profits in the short run. In the long run, freedom of entry shifts its demand curve until it is tangent to the *ATC* curve, leading to excess capacity and production at average costs above the minimum possible level.

■ Not all industries comprising a large group of firms are monopolistically competitive within the terms of the theory. One of the main reasons is that all differentiated products are seldom if ever equally good substitutes for each other (as required by the symmetry assumption). Firms will therefore pay attention to the actions of those firms that produce the products that are closest substitutes for their own.

### Oligopoly

■ Oligopoly involves competition between a few rivals and the outcome for each is dependent on the behaviour of the others. In planning its production and pricing decisions, each firm must attempt to anticipate the reactions of the others.

■ Competitive behaviour among oligopolists may lead to a non-cooperative equilibrium. It is self-policing in the sense that no one has an incentive to depart from it unilaterally.

■ Oligopolistic profits can persist only if there are entry barriers. Natural barriers include economies of large-scale production and large fixed costs of entering the market. Artificial barriers include brand proliferation and high levels of advertising.

### Oligopoly as a game

■ Small-group interaction can be analysed using a game theory framework, which sets out the available actions and the payoffs under various actions.

■ In a Nash equilibrium each firm is doing the best it can, given the choices that other firms have made.

■ A co-operative solution is likely to be the one that maximizes joint profits, but each firm will typically have an incentive to cheat, and explicit co-operation between firms may be proscribed by competition laws.

### Dynamics of oligopoly industries

■ In qualitative terms, the workings of the allocative system under oligopoly are similar (but not identical) to perfect competition.

■ Oligopolistic industries appear to have contributed much more to the technological changes that underlie the long-run growth of productivity than have perfectly competitive industries.

# TOPICS FOR REVIEW

■ The assumptions of monopolistic competition
■ Excess capacity under monopolistic competition
■ Dominant and dominated strategies in games
■ Nash equilibrium
■ The prisoners' dilemma

■ The co-operative solution and the non-cooperative equilibrium
■ Entry barriers
■ Resource allocation under oligopoly

# QUESTIONS

1 Consider the following payoff matrixes for the interaction of two firms, A and X. For each, there is an aggressive or a passive strategy that it could adopt. The first payoff in each pair is for A and the second for X. In each case attempt to identify:
   (a) The dominant strategy for each player
   (b) The Nash equilibrium
   (c) The co-operative equilibrium

(i)

| | | Firm X choice | |
|---|---|---|---|
| | | Aggressive | Passive |
| Firm A choice | Aggressive | 100, 100 | 150, 50 |
| | Passive | 50, 150 | 175, 175 |

(ii)

| | | Firm X choice | |
|---|---|---|---|
| | | Aggressive | Passive |
| Firm A choice | Aggressive | 100, 75 | 160, 60 |
| | Passive | 50, 60 | 110, 80 |

(iii)

| | | Firm X choice | |
|---|---|---|---|
| | | Aggressive | Passive |
| Firm A choice | Aggressive | 250, 110 | 320, 120 |
| | Passive | 130, 160 | 300, 240 |

2 In each of the games set out above, would the outcome be likely to change if the game were repeated?

3 Explain the short-run equilibrium condition for a firm under monopolistic competition. If this is characterized by the existence of pure profit, what will happen to bring about the long-run equilibrium of the industry?

4 Give examples of barriers to entry and explain why it is beneficial for existing firms to attempt to create such barriers.

5 What is a Nash equilibrium and why is it self-policing?

6 Why do you think that non-price competition is an important factor where there is a small group of interacting competitors?

# PART THREE

# MARKETS FOR INPUTS

# Chapter 10

# DEMAND AND SUPPLY OF INPUTS

Up to now we have been studying markets for consumer goods where firms are the suppliers and individuals are the demanders. For the next few chapters we focus on the markets for the inputs that the firms use to make their outputs—mainly labour and capital. In these markets it is firms that are typically the demanders, and the suppliers may be either other firms or individuals; for example, in labour markets firms are the demanders and individuals are the suppliers. Fortunately, we can analyse these markets with demand and supply tools just as we did for consumer goods.

How do firms decide how many workers to hire? Under what circumstances will employers dismiss workers and substitute machines to do the work instead? Do input prices determine the prices of final goods or is it the other way round?

In this chapter you will learn that:

- Firms' demand for inputs is derived from the demand for their output.
- Firms will hire inputs up to the point where the extra cost is just equal to the extra contribution to revenue.
- Cheaper inputs will be substituted for dearer ones in the long run.
- The supply of inputs is more elastic for one specific use than for the economy as a whole.
- Economic rent is the return achieved in one use in excess of the highest available alternative return in another use.

We first study the forces that determine the demand for inputs, then the forces that determine supply, and finally how these interact in competitive markets to determine the prices of inputs.

## Overview of input markets

### A theory of distribution?

Markets for inputs are of interest in their own right. Workers are interested in the market for their labour; firms want to understand the markets for all the inputs that they buy; and the prices of certain key inputs, such as oil, have important effects on the economy as a whole. However, there is another reason for analysing input markets, which is to understand the determinants of the distribution of income between different groups in society—hence the term *distribution theory*. The approach that used to be common was to think of inputs as being divided into groups of resources such as land, labour, and capital, each of which was owned by a different class of society: rentier, workers, and capitalists. The prices assigned to these different resources would then determine how income was divided between these different classes of society. Hence the analysis of input pricing was also a theory of income distribution among these different groups. The distributional implications of input

**Box 10.1  Theories of the distribution of income**

The term **distribution theory** refers to any theory that explains how the total national income is divided up among the nation's citizens. Any theory that explains distribution on the basis of market forces is a **factor-price theory** of distribution, and a **market theory** of **resource allocation**. Theories of this type use the marginal products of inputs to explain their demands. They are thus often called **marginal productivity theories**. Marginal productivity theories were first developed by a group of neoclassical economists writing about a century ago, hence the often-used term **neoclassical theory of distribution**.

Early economists were interested in explaining the distribution of income between the owners of the main resources, or *factors of production*: labour, land, and capital. This is called the **functional distribution of income** because it divides income by functional classes, namely the three groups that provide the services of labour, land, and capital.* There was a long and heated debate about how the distribution of income would be affected by rising population, the accumulation of capital, and advancing technological knowledge. Would all three social groups benefit from the progress of society? Or would capitalists and/or landowners receive a larger and larger share of the national income while the workers received an ever-shrinking share?

Modern economists are more concerned with another way of looking at the distribution of incomes, called the **size distribution of income**. This is the distribution of income between different households without reference to the source of their incomes or each individual's social class.

The functional distribution of income refers to the share of total national income going to owners of different resources

and so focuses on the source of income, in particular distinguishing income from employment and income from property. The size distribution of income refers to the proportion of total income received by various groups and so focuses on inequality of income between various income-earners, irrespective of the source from which that income is derived.

Today economists devote most of their attention to the size distribution of income rather than the functional distribution. If someone is poor, it matters little whether that person is a landowner or a worker. Moreover, some capitalists, such as the owners of small retail stores, are in the lower part of the income scale, and some wage-earners, such as professional footballers, are at the upper end. Furthermore, the vast majority of company shares are owned by wage-earners through pension funds and life insurance policies. This fact alone makes irrelevant to the modern world the old class division between the workers who supply labour, the capitalists who own the means of production and the rentiers (or the landed gentry) who owned the land. In most cases, workers are owners and owners are workers. Class distinctions may still exist, but they do not divide those who are and are not the owners of firms or property.

---

\* The founders of classical economics, Adam Smith and David Ricardo, were concerned with the distribution of income among what were then the three great social classes of workers, capitalists, and landowners. To match these classes, they defined three *factors of production*: labour, capital, and land. The return to each factor determined the share of total national income going to each social class. This is why the theory of factor pricing is also called the *theory of distribution*.

---

pricing are still of interest today but they are no longer associated with simplistic class divisions. Much of the nation's capital, for example, is now owned by the pension funds of workers rather than by some separate class of capitalists. Box 10.1 explains some of the concepts associated with distribution theory.

Before proceeding, a word of warning. Beware of confusing the terms 'unequal' and 'inequality' with 'unjust' and 'inequitable'. For example, a completely equal distribution of the nation's income among all individuals—those who worked hard and those who loafed about on the job, those who did dangerous jobs and those in safe ones, those on whose skills we relied on and those who relied on others' skills—would not satisfy many people's idea of a just distribution of income. In any case, the analysis we develop below is designed to explain how incomes are determined, not to evaluate whether the outcome is equitable or inequitable, just or unjust. The policy implications of income inequalities and attempts

by government to redistribute income are discussed in Chapter 14.

## The link between output and input decisions

In Chapter 6 we saw how firms' costs vary with their output and how they can achieve cost minimization by finding the least costly combination of inputs to produce any given output. In Chapter 7 we saw that firms in perfect competition decide how much to produce by equating their marginal cost to the market price. We also saw how the market supply curve interacts with the market demand curve in each goods market. This interaction determines the market price as well as the quantity that is produced and consumed.

These events in goods markets have implications for input markets. The decisions of firms on how much to produce and how to produce it imply specific demands for various quantities of inputs. These demands, together with the supplies of inputs (which are determined by the owners of resources), come together in markets for inputs. Together they determine the quantities of the various inputs that are employed, their prices, and the incomes earned by their owners.

The above discussion shows that there is a close relationship between the production and pricing of firms' outputs on the one hand and the pricing, employment, and incomes earned by the owners of the inputs that firms hire on the other. These are two related aspects of how the market economy determines the production of goods and services and the allocation of the nation's resources among their various possible uses. This discussion provides a brief introduction to one of the great insights of economics:

**When demand and supply interact to determine the allocation of resources between various lines of production, they also determine the incomes of the owners of inputs that are used in making the outputs.**

The way this works can be summarized as follows.

1. The income of owners of different types of input depends on the price that is paid for these inputs and the amount that is used.

2. Demands and supplies in input markets determine input prices and quantities in exactly the same way that the prices and quantities of goods and services are determined in product markets.

3. All that is needed to explain input pricing is to identify the main determinants of the demand for, and supply of, various inputs (and to adjust for any distortion in free markets caused by governments, unions, or monopoly firms).

Figure 10.1 illustrates the theory of input pricing by showing how competitive market forces determine the income accruing to owners of a specific input. The rest of this chapter is an elaboration of this important theme. We first study the demand for inputs, then their supply, and finally how they come together to determine input prices and quantities.

## Two assumptions

Before we begin, we need to make explicit two assumptions that will underlie our analysis.[1]

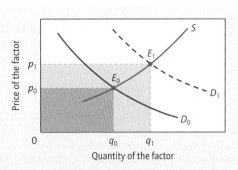

**Figure 10.1 Income of owners of primary resources determined in competitive markets**

The interaction of demand and supply in competitive input markets determines resource owners' equilibrium price and quantity, and hence their income. The original demand and supply curves are $D_0$ and $S$. Equilibrium is at $E_0$, with price $p_0$ and quantity employed $q_0$. The resource owners' incomes are shown by the dark blue area in the figure. When the demand curve shifts to $D_1$, equilibrium shifts to $E_1$, with price $p_1$ and quantity $q_1$. The resource owners' incomes rise by the amount of the light blue area.

### Other prices constant

In order to ensure that we are speaking of relative rather than absolute prices and quantities, we make the following assumption. When the changes studied in Figure 10.1 occur, *the prices of all other inputs, the prices of all goods, and the level of national income are held constant.* Under these circumstances, fluctuations in an input's equilibrium price and quantity cause fluctuations (*a*) in the money earnings of the owners of that input, (*b*) in their earnings relative to owners of other inputs, and (*c*) in the share of national income going to those owners.

### Competitive markets

We confine ourselves to perfectly competitive markets in this chapter. This means that individual firms are price-takers in both output and input markets. On the one hand they face a given price for the product they produce, and that price is both their average and marginal revenue. On the other hand they face a given price of each input that they buy, and that price is both the average and marginal cost of the input. These input and output prices may change, but they cannot be influenced by the actions of any single firm (or any single seller of inputs).

Dealing first with firms that are price-takers in product and input markets allows us to study the principles of input price determination in the simplest context. Once these are understood, it is relatively easy to allow for monopolistic elements in both input and output markets. This is done in Chapter 11.

---

[1] These assumptions are only a simplifying device: they do not affect the generality of the conclusions.

**Box 10.2  Economics of produced inputs**

It may seem strange that throughout this and the next few chapters we concentrate on analysing demand and supply of primary resource inputs, especially labour and capital. Most firms buy many of their inputs from other firms. A car manufacturer, for example, will buy in many of the components that go into its cars as well as hiring assembly workers, designers, marketing experts and accountants, etc., and will use its own capital and land for its factory. So why not analyse the markets for these other produced inputs?

The answer is that we do, but only indirectly. The principles that are set out in this chapter apply just as easily to manufactured inputs as they do to labour, capital, and other inputs. Demand for produced inputs is a derived demand depending on demand for the final product. Profit-maximizing firms (as we shall see below) will buy these inputs up to the point where the extra cost of the last unit is just equal to the value of the extra output that input generates. The demand curve for produced inputs will be negatively sloped as it is for all inputs (as we can rule out the Giffen-good case that arises with consumer demand), so markets for produced inputs can be analysed with demand and supply tools just like any other market.

By focusing on demand for primary resource inputs, we are aggregating across the entire supply chain of produced goods and services, and focusing on the inputs for industry as a whole rather than on each link in that supply chain. We do this because we are interested in resource allocation for the economy as a whole. But analysis of each intermediate market between firms and their suppliers of produced inputs is straightforward.

Individual firms do have some issues to resolve relating to their produced inputs. First, should they buy in the input or make it for themselves? So long as quality and reliability of supply are guaranteed, the answer will be: buy from another firm if that firm can make the product more cheaply than we can make it ourselves. Second, if the product is bought in, should the firm simply set up a long-term supply contract with the input producer or should it try to buy on the market from the cheapest supplier in each period? The answer here will depend on whether this is a standardized product that is widely available at short notice, or a highly specific input that needs special skills or equipment to produce. In the latter case, a longer-term supply contract is more likely.

# The demand for inputs

Firms use the services of land, labour, capital, and natural resources[2] as inputs. They also use products; such as steel, plastics, and electricity, that are produced by other firms. These products are in turn made by using land, labour, capital, natural resources, and other produced inputs. If we continue following through the chain of outputs of some firms that are used as inputs by other firms, we can account for all of the economy's output in terms of inputs of the basic resources—land, labour, capital, and natural resources. The theory of input pricing applies to *all* inputs used by a firm, as explained in Box 10.2.

Firms require inputs not for their own sake, but as a means to produce goods and services. For example, the demand for computer programmers and technicians is growing as more and more computers are used. The demand for carpenters and building materials rises and

falls as the amount of housing construction rises and falls. Thus, demand for any input is derived from the demand for the goods and services that it helps to produce; for this reason, the demand for all inputs is called a **derived demand**.

**Derived demand provides a link between the markets for output and the markets for inputs.**

An important point to note is that the quantity demanded of any input *always* varies negatively with its price. As its price falls more is demanded, and as its price rises less is demanded. In other words:

**The demand curve for any input is negatively sloped, with price and quantity demanded always varying in the opposite direction.**

This is an important result, which we explain below. It means that we can rule out Giffen goods so far as demand for inputs is concerned. The reasons for the negative slope to input demand curves differ in the long and the short run.

---

[2] Although natural resources are often included with land as a single type of resource, they have so many important special characteristics that it is sometimes worthwhile treating them as a separate type of primary input.

## Input demand in the long run

In the long run all inputs are variable. In this case, both the substitution and the income effects contribute to the negative slope of the demand curve. We consider the case of a price reduction and leave a price rise as a simple variation, which is easy to work through for yourself.

### The substitution effect

A fall in an input's price makes it less expensive relative to other inputs, and more of it will be used relative to those whose price has not fallen. This is true at all levels of aggregation. It is true if the price of all labour falls relative to capital, or if the price of one type of labour falls relative to other types of labour. We showed in Chapter 6 that a fall in the price of all types of labour will lead profit-maximizing firms to substitute labour for capital. According to the principle of substitution (see page 127), they will use more of the now cheaper input and less of the relatively more expensive ones. A fall in the wage of one type of labour will lead to more of that type being used as a replacement for other types of labour whose wage has not fallen. For example, some time ago the wages of building labour rose dramatically. This led builders to substitute prefabricated parts made in factories for parts made to order on the building site. Window frames, door jambs, walls, and a host of other parts of buildings that used to be custom made on the site were prefabricated to standard designs in factories where wages were much lower than on construction sites. In effect, factory labour whose price had not risen was substituted for building labour whose price had risen.

### The income effect

A fall in the price of one input reduces the cost of making all products that use that input. The cost curves of these products thus shift downwards, shifting the sum of the marginal cost curves—which is the industry supply curve. As a result, more will be produced and sold. To make more output, an increase in all the inputs is required. This leads to a rise in the amount demanded of the input whose price has fallen, as well as a rise in the demand for all other inputs that co-operate with it in production.

## Input demand in the short run

In the short run some inputs are fixed and some can be varied. If we think of an extreme situation in which only one input can be varied, we can derive a famous proposition that is true for each and every input as long as the firms that hire them are maximizing their profits.

## The maximizing firm

In Chapter 7 we set out the rules for maximizing a firm's profits in the short run. When one input is fixed and another is variable, the profit-maximizing firm increases its output until the last unit produced adds just as much to cost as to revenue, that is until marginal cost equals marginal revenue. An equivalent way of stating that the firm maximizes profits is to say that *the firm will increase production up to the point at which the last unit of the variable input employed adds just as much to revenue as it does to cost.*

The addition to total cost resulting from employing one more unit of an input is its price. (The firm is buying its inputs in a competitive market, so the extra purchase does not affect the market price.) So if one more worker is hired at a wage of £15 per hour, the addition to the firm's costs is £15 (and other workers' wages remain unchanged).

The amount that a unit of a variable input adds to revenue is the amount that the unit adds to total output multiplied by the change in revenue resulting from selling an extra unit of output.

In Chapter 6 we called the variable input's addition to total output its *marginal product*. When dealing with demand for inputs, we use the term **marginal *physical* product** (*MPP*) to avoid confusion with the revenue concepts that we also need to use.

The change in revenue resulting from selling one extra unit of output is just the price of the output, $p$ (since the firm is a price-taker in the market for its output). The resulting amount, which is $MPP \times p$, is called the input's **marginal revenue product** and given the symbol *MRP*.

For example, if the variable input's marginal physical product is two widgets per hour and the price of a widget is £7.50, then the input's marginal revenue product is £15 (£7.50 × 2).

We can now state the firm's profit maximization condition in two ways. First,

| Addition to total costs caused by hiring another unit of the variable input | = | the input's marginal revenue product (*MRP*). | (1) |

First note that if the firm is a price-taker in input markets the left-hand side is just the price of a unit of the variable input, which we now call $w$ (as the variable input is often labour and its price is the wage rate). Also note that, as long as the firm is a price-taker in the market for its output, the right-hand side is the input's marginal physical product, *MPP*, multiplied by the price at which the output is sold, which we call $p$. We can now restate (1) as follows:

Price of a unit of = the input's marginal (2)
the variable input    physical product multiplied
                      by the product's
                      market price

and in symbols,

$$w = MPP \times p. \qquad (2')$$

Here is an example to clarify the meaning of equation (2). Suppose that the extra labour is available to the firm at a cost of £10 an hour ($w = £10$). Suppose also that employing another hour's work adds three units to output ($MPP = 3$). Suppose further that output units sell for £5 each ($p = £5$). Then, the additional hour of input adds £15 to the firm's revenue and £10 to its costs. Hiring one worker for an extra hour brings in £5 more than it costs. *The firm will take on more of the variable input whenever its marginal revenue product exceeds its price, as this adds more to revenue than to cost.*

Now suppose that the last hour of work by the variable input has a marginal physical product of one unit of output—it adds only one extra unit to output—and so adds only £5 to revenue. Clearly, the firm can increase profits by reducing its use of the input, since hiring for one hour less reduces revenues by £5 while reducing costs by £10. *The firm will hire less of the variable input whenever its marginal revenue product is less than its price.*

Finally, suppose that the last hour of a worker hired has an $MPP$ of two units, so that it increases revenue by £10. Now the firm cannot increase its profits by altering its employment of the variable input in either direction. *The firm cannot increase its profits by altering employment of the variable input whenever the input's marginal revenue product equals its price.*

We are doing nothing new here. We are merely looking at the firm's profit-maximizing behaviour from the point of view of its inputs rather than its output. In Chapter 7 we analysed the firm varying its output until the marginal cost of producing the last unit of output was equal to the marginal revenue derived from selling that unit. The same profit-maximizing behaviour involves the firm varying its inputs until the marginal cost of the last input hired is just equal to the revenue derived from selling the marginal product of that extra input. These are exactly the same, because the variable input is the only component of marginal cost (and its MRP is the same as MR for the firm).

### The firm's demand curve for the input

It is now easy to see why in the short run, with only one variable input, the firm's demand curve for that input is negatively sloped. Suppose the firm starts in equilibrium.

The relationship shown in (2) above must hold, which means that that input's marginal revenue product is equated to its price. Now the price of the input falls. The unchanged marginal revenue product is now higher than the lowered price. So it pays the firm to hire more of the input. As it hires more inputs the marginal physical product falls, and since the firm is a price-taker so does the marginal revenue product. The firm goes on hiring more of the variable input until the marginal revenue product falls to the level of the new lower price.

What this tells us is that

**In the short run, with only one variable input, the firm's demand for its variable input is negatively sloped.**

We now show more precisely where this demand curve comes from. Here we explain the case where there is one variable input, and in Box 10.3 we extend the analysis to cover more than one input.

Equation (2′) above tells us what determines the quantity of a variable input a firm will demand when faced with some specific price of the input and some specific price of its output. The firm's demand curve shows how much the firm will buy at *each* price of the variable input. To derive this curve, we start by considering the right-hand side of equation (2′), which tells us that the input's marginal revenue product is composed of a physical component and a value component.

### The physical component of *MRP*

As the quantity of the variable input used changes, output will vary. The hypothesis of diminishing returns, first discussed in Chapter 6, predicts what will happen. As the firm adds further units of the variable input to a given quantity of the fixed input, the additions to output will eventually get smaller and smaller. In other words, the input's marginal physical product will decline. This is illustrated in part (i) of Figure 10.2, which uses hypothetical data that have the same general characteristics as the data in Table 6.3 on page 120. The negative slope of the *MPP* curve reflects the operation of the law of diminishing returns: each unit of labour adds less to total output than the previous unit.

### The value component of *MRP*

To convert the marginal physical product curve of Figure 10.2(i) into a curve showing the marginal revenue product of the variable input, we need to know the value of the extra physical product. As long as the firm is selling its output on a competitive market, this value is simply the marginal physical product multiplied by the market price at which the firm sells its product.

(i) The *MPP* curve                              (ii) The *MRP* and the demand curve

**Figure 10.2** **From marginal physical product to demand curve**

Each additional unit of the input employed adds a certain amount to total product (part (i)) and hence a certain amount to total revenue (part (ii)), and this determines the amount of the input that firms will demand at each price. Part (i) assumes data that are consistent with marginal productivity theory; it shows the addition to the firm's *output* produced by additional units of labour hired. The curve is negatively sloped because of the law of diminishing returns.

Part (ii) shows the addition to the firm's *revenue* caused by the employment of each additional unit of labour. It is the marginal physical product from part (i) multiplied by the price at which that product is sold. In this case the price is assumed to be £5. (The multiplication is by market price because the firm is assumed to be a price-taker in the market for its output.)

Since the firm equates the price of the variable input, which in this case is labour, to the input's marginal revenue product, it follows that the *MRP* curve in part (ii) is also the demand curve for labour, showing how much will be employed at each price.

This operation is illustrated in part (ii) of Figure 10.2, which shows a marginal revenue product curve for labour on the assumption that the firm is selling its product in a competitive market at a price of £5 a unit. This curve shows how much would be added to revenue by employing one more unit of the input *at each level of total employment of the input*. Notice that part (ii) of the figure measures money values on the vertical axis, whereas part (i) was measuring physical units of output.

Profit-maximizing firms should equate the addition to cost of buying another unit of a variable input with the addition to revenue caused by selling the output of that unit, which we call the input's *marginal revenue product*, *MRP*. The *MRP* is always composed of a physical component, which is the input's *MPP*, and a value component, which is the marginal revenue of selling those extra physical units of output. Because our firms are price-takers in their output markets, the marginal revenue is just the price that they face in that market. If the firms faced a negatively sloped demand curve for their output, we know from Chapter 8 that the addition to revenue from selling further units would not be the market price, because marginal revenue is less than price.

### From *MRP* to the demand curve

Equation (2′) states that the profit-maximizing firm will employ additional units of the input up to the point at which the *MRP* equals the price of the input. If, for example, the price of the variable input were £2,000 per month, then it would be most profitable to employ 60 workers. There is no point in employing a sixty-first, since that would add just less than £2,000 to revenue but a full £2,000 to costs. So the profit-maximizing firm hires the quantity of the variable input that equates the marginal revenue product with the price of the variable input. Thus, the curve that relates the quantity of the variable input employed to its *MRP* is also the curve that relates the quantity of the variable input the firm wishes to employ to its price.

The *MRP* curve of the variable input is the same as the demand curve for that input. The reason why both are negatively sloped is as a result of the operation of the law of diminishing returns.

The case of multiple inputs is discussed in Box 10.3.

## The industry's demand curve for an input

So far we have seen how a single firm that takes its market price as given will vary its quantity demanded for an input as that input's price changes. But when an input's price changes, and *all firms* in a competitive industry vary the amount of the input that they demand in order to vary

**Box 10.3 Demand for inputs where there is more than one variable input**

When a firm can vary the amounts of several inputs that it uses, profit maximization requires that the last £1 it spends on each input brings in the same amount of revenue.

To see how this works out for two inputs, call their prices $p_A$ and $p_B$ and their marginal revenue products $MRP_A$ and $MRP_B$. The amount of extra revenue per £1 spent on hiring more of input A is $MRP_A/p_A$, while the amount of extra revenue per pound spent on hiring more of input B is $MRP_B/p_B$. For example, if one more unit of A costs £3 and adds £6 to revenue, it yields £2 of revenue per £1 spent on it. If one more unit of B costs £5 and adds £10 to revenue, it too yields £2 of revenue per £1 spent on it. If the firm wants to equate these $MRP$s per pound spent on the inputs, it must set

$$\frac{MRP_A}{p_A} = \frac{MRP_B}{p_B}. \qquad (1)$$

The marginal revenue product is the marginal physical product multiplied by the product's selling price. We now have three prices, two for the variable inputs and one for output. To prevent confusion, we call the output price $p_S$, which stands for selling price. So $MRP = MPP \times p_S$. So we can rewrite equation (1) as

$$\frac{(MPP_A)(p_S)}{p_A} = \frac{(MPP_B)(p_S)}{p_B}. \qquad (2)$$

If we eliminate the common $p_S$ term, we have

$$\frac{MPP_A}{p_A} = \frac{MPP_B}{p_B}. \qquad (3)$$

Equation (3) can be rewritten as follows:

$$\frac{MPP_A}{MPP_B} = \frac{p_A}{p_B}. \qquad (4)$$

In equation (4) the firm is given prices of the two inputs, and it adjusts to these by altering the quantities of the two inputs until it has the profit-maximizing amount of each. This behaviour is similar to that of the consumer described on page 88. The consumer is given the prices of two commodities and she adjusts her consumption until her utility is maximized (which she does by making the ratios of the marginal utilities equal the ratio of their prices).

**Profit-maximizing firms hire inputs up to the point where the ratio of the marginal products of inputs is equal to the ratio of the inputs' prices.**

their output, the price of the industry's product changes. That change will have repercussions on desired output and the quantity of the input demanded.

For example, a fall in carpenters' wages will reduce the cost of producing houses, thus shifting the supply curve of houses to the right. Price-taking construction firms therefore plan to increase construction, and hence increase the quantity of carpenters demanded, by some specific amount if the price of houses does not change. Because the demand curve for houses is negatively sloped, however, the increase in output leads to a fall in the market price of houses. As a result, each individual firm will increase its desired output by *less* than it had planned to do before the market price changed.

An increase in carpenters' wages has the opposite effect. The cost of producing houses rises, the supply curve shifts to the left, and the price of houses rises. As a result, the individual firm will cut its planned output and employment of inputs by less than it would have done if market price had not changed.

**The industry's demand curve for an input is steeper than it would be if firms faced an unchanged product price, because the reaction of market price must be allowed for.**

It may be useful to summarize the argument so far.

1. In the short run, the derived demand curve for an input on the part of a *price-taking* firm will have a negative slope because of the law of diminishing returns. As more of the input is employed in response to a fall in its price, its marginal product falls. No further units will be added once its marginal revenue product falls to the input's new price.

2. An industry's short-run demand curve for an input is less elastic than suggested by point 1. As the industry expands output in response to a fall in an input's price, the price of the firm's output will fall, causing the final increase in each firm's output, and hence its demand for employment of inputs, to be less than it would be if output price remained unchanged.

## Elasticity of demand for inputs

The elasticity of demand for an input measures the *degree* of the response of the quantity demanded to a change in its price. The influences that were discussed in the preceding sections explain the *direction* of the response; that is, the quantity demanded is negatively related to price.

You should not be surprised, therefore, to hear that the amount of the response depends on the strength with which these influences operate. This section gives the four principles of derived demand that were first set out by the British economist Alfred Marshall (1842–1924).

## Diminishing returns

The first influence on the slope of the demand curve is the diminishing marginal productivity of an input. If marginal productivity declines rapidly as more of a variable input is employed, a fall in the input's price will not induce many more units to be employed. Conversely, if marginal productivity falls only slowly as more of a variable input is employed, there will be a large increase in quantity demanded as price falls.

**The faster the marginal productivity of an input declines as its use rises, the lower is the elasticity of each firm's demand curve for the input.**

For example, both labour and fertilizers are used by market gardeners who produce vegetables for sale in nearby cities. For many crops additional doses of fertilizers add significant amounts to yields over quite a wide range of fertilizer use. Although the marginal product of fertilizer does decline, it does so rather slowly as more and more fertilizer is used. In contrast, although certain amounts of labour are needed for planting, weeding, and harvesting, there is only a small range over which additional labour can be used productively. The marginal product of labour, although high for the first units, declines rapidly as more and more labour is used. Under these circumstances, market gardeners will have an elastic demand for fertilizer and an inelastic demand for labour.

## Substitution

In the long run all inputs are variable. If one input's price rises, firms will try to substitute relatively cheaper inputs instead. For this reason, the slope of the demand curve for an input is influenced by the ease with which other inputs can be substituted for the input whose price has changed.

**The greater the ease of substitution, the greater is the elasticity of demand for the input.**

The ease of substitution depends on the substitutes that are available and on the production technology. It is often possible to vary input proportions in surprising ways. For example, in car manufacturing and in building construction glass and steel can be substituted for each other simply by varying the dimensions of the windows. As another example, more durable parts can be substituted for repair work in the case of most manufactured goods. This is done by making the product more or less durable and more or less subject to breakdowns and by using more or less expensive materials in its construction.

Such substitutions are not the end of the story. Manufacturing equipment is being replaced continually, and this allows more or less capital-intensive methods to be built into new factories in response to changes in input prices. Similarly, car engines that use less fuel per mile tend to be developed when the price of fuel rises significantly.

## Importance of the input

**Other things being equal, the larger the fraction of the total costs of producing some product that are made up of payments to a particular input, the greater is the elasticity of demand for that input.**

To see this, suppose that wages account for 50 per cent of the costs of producing a good, and raw materials for 15 per cent. A 10 per cent rise in the price of labour raises the cost of production by 5 per cent (10 per cent of 50 per cent), but a 10 per cent rise in the price of raw materials raises the cost of the product by only 1.5 per cent (10 per cent of 15 per cent). The larger the increase in the cost of production, the larger is the shift in the product's supply curve, and hence the larger the decreases in quantities demanded of both the product and the inputs used to produce it.

## Elasticity of demand for the output

The fourth and final principle of derived demand is:

**Other things being equal, the more elastic is the demand for the product that the input helps to make, the more elastic is the demand for the input.**

If an increase in the price of the product causes a large decrease in the quantity demanded—that is, if the demand for the product is elastic—there will be a large decrease in the quantity of an input needed to produce it in response to a rise in the input's price. However, if an increase in the price of a product causes only a small decrease in the quantity demanded—that is, if the demand for the product is inelastic—there will be only a small decrease in the quantity of the input required in response to a rise in its price.

In Box 10.4 the forces affecting the elasticity of the derived demand curves that have just been discussed are related more specifically to the market for the industry's output.

**Box 10.4  The principles of derived demand**

This box demonstrates two of the four principles of derived demand using demand and supply curves.

**1. The larger the proportion of total costs accounted for by an input, the more elastic is the demand for it.**

Consider part (i) of the figure. The demand curve for the *industry's product* is D and, given the input's original price, the *industry supply curve* is $S_0$. Equilibrium is at $E_0$ with output at $q_0$.

Suppose that the input's price then falls. If the input accounts for a small part of the industry's total cost, each firm's marginal cost curve shifts downward by only a small amount. So also does the industry supply curve, as illustrated by the supply curve $S_1$. Output expands only a small amount to $q_1$, which implies only a small increase in the quantity of the variable input demanded.

If the input accounts for a large part of the industry's total costs, each firm's marginal cost curve shifts downward a great deal. So also does the industry supply curve, as illustrated by the curve $S_2$. Output expands greatly to $q_2$, which implies a large increase in the quantity of variable input demanded.

**2. The more elastic the demand curve for the product, the more elastic is the demand for the input.**

Consider part (ii) of the figure. The original demand and supply curves for the industry's product intersect at $E_0$ to produce an industry output of $q_0$. A fall in the price of an input causes the industry's supply curve to shift downward to $S_1$.

When the demand curve is relatively inelastic, as shown by the curve $D_i$, the industry's output increases by only a small amount to $q_1$. The quantity of the variable input demanded will increase by a correspondingly small amount.

(i)    Quantity of output

(ii)    Quantity of output

When the demand curve is relatively elastic, as shown by the curve $D_e$, the industry's output increases by a large amount to $q_2$. The quantity of the variable input demanded will then increase by a correspondingly large amount.

# The supply of inputs

When we consider the supply of any input, we must consider the amount supplied to the economy as a whole, to each industry and occupation, and to each firm. The elasticity of supply of an input will normally be different at each of these levels of aggregation. We start with the highest level of aggregation, the total supply of each resource input to the economy as a whole.

## Total supply of resources

At any one time, the total quantity of inputs of each resource is given. For example, in each country the labour

force is of a certain size, there is so much arable land available, there is so much machinery installed in factories, and there is a given supply of discovered raw materials. However, these supplies can and do change in response to both economic and non-economic forces. Sometimes the change is very gradual, as when climatic changes slowly turn arable land into desert or when a medical discovery lowers the rate of infant mortality and hence increases the rate of population growth. Sometimes the changes can be quite rapid, as when the UK discovered oil in the North Sea, or when a boom in business activity brings retired people back into the labour force, or when a rise in the price of agricultural produce encourages the draining of marshes to add to the supply of arable land.

## Total supply of capital

The supply of capital in a country consists of the stock of existing machines, factories, equipment, and so on. Capital is a manufactured input, and its total quantity is in no sense fixed, although it changes only slowly. Each year the stock of capital goods is diminished by the amount that becomes physically or economically obsolete and is increased by the amount that is newly produced. The difference between these is the net addition to, or net subtraction from, the capital stock. On balance, the trend has been for the capital stock to grow from decade to decade over the past few centuries. In Chapter 12 we will discuss the determinants of investment in capital.

## Total supply of land

The total area of dry land in a country is almost completely fixed, but the supply of *fertile* land is not fixed. Considerable care and effort are required to sustain the productive capacity of land. If farmers earn low incomes, they may not be able to provide the necessary care and the land's fertility may be destroyed within a short time. In contrast, high earnings from farming may provide the incentive to increase the supply of arable land by irrigation and other forms of reclamation.

## Total supply of labour

The number of people willing to work is called the *labour force*; the total number of hours they are willing to work is called the **supply of effort** or, more simply, the **supply of labour**. The supply of effort depends on three influences: the size of the population, the proportion of the population willing to work, and the number of hours worked by each individual. Each of these is partly influenced by economic forces.

### Population

Populations vary in size, and these variations are influenced to some extent by economic forces. There is some evidence, for example, that the birth rate and the net immigration rate (immigration minus emigration) are higher in good times than in bad. Much of the variation in population is, however, explained by factors outside economics.

### The labour force

The proportion of the total population, or of some subgroup such as men, women, or teenagers, that is willing to work is called that group's **labour force participation rate**. This rate varies in response to many influences. One non-economic influence is change in attitudes and tastes. The substantial rise in female participation rates in the second half of the twentieth century is a case in point. One economic influence is change in the demand for labour. A rise in demand is usually accompanied by a rise in earnings. This then leads to an increase in the proportion of the population willing to work. More married women and elderly people enter the labour force when the demand for labour is high. For the same reasons, the labour force tends to decline when earnings and employment opportunities decline.

### Hours worked

Not only does the wage rate influence the number of people in the labour force (as we observed above), it is also a major determinant of hours worked. By giving up leisure in order to work, workers obtain the incomes they need to buy goods. They can, therefore, be thought of as trading leisure for goods.

A rise in the wage rate implies a change in the relative prices of goods and leisure. Goods become cheaper relative to leisure, since each hour worked buys more goods than before. The other side of the same coin is that leisure becomes more expensive, since each hour of leisure consumed is at the cost of more goods forgone.

This change in relative prices has both the income and the substitution effects that we studied on pages 102–4. The substitution effect leads the individual to consume more of the relatively cheaper goods and *less* of the relatively more expensive leisure—that is, to trade more leisure for goods. The income effect, however, leads the individual to consume more goods *and* more leisure, since the rise in the wage rate makes it possible for the individual to have more of both. For example, if the wage rate rises by 10 per cent and the individual works 5 per cent fewer hours, more leisure and more goods will be consumed.

Because the income and the substitution effects work in the same direction for the consumption of goods, we can be sure that a rise in the wage rate will lead to a rise in income earned and goods consumed. Because, however, the two effects work in opposite directions for leisure,

a rise in the wage rate leads to less leisure being consumed (more hours worked) when the substitution effect is the dominant force and to more leisure being consumed (fewer hours worked) when the income effect is the dominant force.

Box 10.5 provides an optional analysis of these two cases using indifference curves.

Much of the long-run evidence tends to show that, as real hourly wage rates rise for the economy as a whole, people wish to reduce the number of hours they work.

**Box 10.5** **The supply of labour**

The discussion in the text can be formalized using indifference curves. The key proposition is the following:

**Because a change in the wage rate has an income effect and a substitution effect that pull in opposite directions, the supply curve of labour may have a positive or a negative slope.**

Part (i) of the figure plots leisure (in hours) on the horizontal axis and the consumption of goods (measured in pounds) on the vertical axis. The budget line always starts at 24, indicating that everyone is endowed with 24 hours a day that may be either consumed as leisure or traded for goods by working.

At the original wage rate the individual could obtain $q_a$ of goods by working 24 hours (i.e. the hourly wage rate is $q_a/24$). Equilibrium is at $E_0$, where the individual consumes $l_0$ of leisure and works $24 - l_0$ hours in return for $q_0$ of goods.

The wage rate now rises, so that $q_b$ becomes available if 24 hours are worked (i.e. the hourly wage rate is $q_b/24$). Equilibrium shifts to $E_1$. Consumption of leisure falls to $l_1$, and the

individual works $24 - l_1$ hours in return for a consumption of $q_1$ goods. The rise in wages increases hours worked.

The hourly wage rate now rises further to $q_c/24$, and equilibrium shifts to $E_2$. Consumption of leisure rises to $l_2$, whereas $24 - l_2$ hours are worked in return for an increased consumption of $q_2$ goods. This time, therefore, the rise in the wage rate lowers the number of hours worked.

Part (ii) of the figure shows the same behaviour as in part (i), using a supply curve. It plots the number of hours worked against the wage rate. At wage rates of up to $w_1$ the individual is not in the labour force, since no work is offered. As the wage rate rises from $w_1$ to $w_2$, more and more hours are worked so the supply curve of effort has the normal, positive slope. The wage rates that result in $E_0$ and $E_1$ in part (i) of the figure lie in this range. Above $w_2$ the quantity of effort falls as wages rise, so that the supply curve has a negative slope. This latter case is often referred to as a *backward-bending supply curve of labour*. The wage that gives rise to equilibrium $E_2$ in part (i) lies in this range.

**(i) Indifference curves**

**(ii) A supply curve of effort**

## The supply of inputs for a particular use

Most primary resources have many uses. A piece of land can be used to grow any one of several crops, or it can be subdivided for a housing development. A computer programmer in Oxford can work for one of several firms, for the government, or for the University. A lathe can be used to make many different products, and it requires no adaptation when it is turned for one use or another. Plainly, it is easier for any one user to acquire more of a scarce resource than it is for all users to do so simultaneously.

One user of an input can bid resources away from another user, even though the total supply of that input may be fixed.

When we are considering the supply of an input for a particular use, the most important concept is *resource mobility*. An input that shifts easily between uses in response to small changes in incentives is said to be *mobile*. Its supply to any one of its uses will be elastic, because a small increase in the price offered will attract many units of the input from other uses. Inputs that do not shift easily from one use to another, even in response to large changes in remuneration, are said to be *immobile*. It will be in inelastic supply in any one of its uses, because even a large increase in the price offered will attract only a small inflow from other uses. Often a specific input may be immobile in the short run but mobile in the long run.

An important key to input mobility is time. The longer the time interval, the easier it is to convert an input from one use to another.

Consider the mobility between uses of each of the three key types of input.

### Capital

Some kinds of capital equipment—lathes, lorries, and computers for example—can be shifted easily between uses; many others are difficult to shift. A great deal of machinery is quite specific: once built, it must be used for the purpose for which it was designed, or it cannot be used at all. (It is the immobility of much fixed capital equipment that makes the exit of firms from declining industries a slow and difficult process.)

In the long run, however, capital is highly mobile. When capital goods wear out, a firm may simply replace them with identical goods, or it may exercise other options. It may buy a newly designed machine to produce the same goods, or it may buy machines to produce totally different goods. Such decisions lead to changes in the long-run allocation of a country's stock of capital between various uses.

### Land

Land, which is physically the least mobile of inputs, is one of the most mobile in an economic sense. On agricultural land one crop can be harvested and a totally different crop can be planted. A farm on the outskirts of a growing city can be sold for a housing development at short notice—as long as planning permission is forthcoming. Once land is built on, its mobility is much reduced. A site on which a hotel has been built can be converted into a warehouse site, but it takes a large differential in the value of land use to make that transfer worthwhile, because the hotel must be demolished.

Although land is highly mobile between alternative uses, it is completely immobile as far as location is concerned. There is only so much land within a given distance of the centre of any city, and no increase in the price paid can induce further land to be located within that distance. This locational immobility has important consequences, including high prices for desirable locations and the tendency to build tall buildings to economize on the use of scarce land, as in the centres of large cities.

### Labour

Labour is a unique input, as supply of the services of labour usually requires the physical presence of the person who owns it. Most people in employment have to attend their place of work each day. In other cases, however, labour services, such as consulting, designing a product, or writing advertising copy, can be supplied at a distance and their product communicated to the purchaser by such means as phone, fax, email, or post.

Absentee landlords, while continuing to live in the place of their choice, can obtain income from land or buildings located in another part of the world. While physical capital needs to be present at the production site, its owner need not be. However, when a worker who is employed by a firm that produces men's ties in York decides to supply labour service to a firm that produces women's shoes in Northampton, the worker must physically travel to Northampton. This has an important consequence.

Because of the need for labour's physical presence when its services are provided for the production of many commodities, non-monetary considerations are much more important for the supply of labour than for other inputs.

People may be satisfied with, or frustrated by, the kind of work that they do, where they do it, the people with whom they do it, and the social status of their occupation. Since these considerations influence their decisions about what they will do with their labour services, they will not always move just because they could earn a higher wage.

Nevertheless, labour does move between industries, occupations, and areas in response to changes in the signals provided by wages and opportunities for employment. The ease with which movement occurs depends on many forces. For example, it is not difficult for a secretary to shift from one company to another in order to take a job in Cheltenham instead of in Hull, but it can be difficult for a coal miner to become an editor, a model, a machinist, or a doctor within a short period of time. Workers who lack skills, training, or inclination find certain kinds of job moves difficult or impossible.

Some barriers to movement may be virtually insurmountable once a person's training has been completed. It may be impossible for a farmer to become a surgeon or for a lorry-driver to become a professional athlete, even if the relative wage rates change greatly. However, the *children* of farmers, doctors, lorry-drivers, and athletes, when they are deciding how much education or training to obtain, are not nearly as limited in their choices as their parents, who have already completed their education and are settled in their occupations.

In any year some people enter the labour force directly from school or further education, and others leave it through retirement or death. The turnover in the labour force owing to these causes is 3 or 4 per cent per year. Over a period of ten years the allocation of labour can change dramatically merely by directing new entrants to jobs other than the ones that were left vacant by workers who left the labour force.

The role of education in helping new entrants adapt to available jobs is important. In a society in which education is provided to all, it is possible to achieve large increases in the supply of any needed labour skill within a decade or so. These issues are discussed at greater length in the first part of Chapter 11.

The labour force as a whole is mobile, even though many individual members of it are not.

## The supply of inputs to individual firms

Most firms usually employ a small proportion of the total supply of each input that they use. As a result they can usually obtain their inputs at the going market price. For example, a firm of accountants can usually augment its clerical staff by placing an advert in the local paper and paying the going rate for accounts clerks. In hiring just one more person, the firm will not affect the rate of pay earned by accounts clerks in its area. Similarly, most individual firms are price-takers in markets for their inputs.

# The operation of input markets

The determination of the price, quantity, and income of an input in a single market poses no new problem. Figure 10.1 on page 209 has already shown a competitive market for an input in which the intersection of the demand and supply curves determines the input's price and the quantity of it that is employed. As we saw at that time, the input's price times its quantity employed is its total income; and that amount, divided by the total income earned by all resource owners in the economy, represents that specific resource owner's share of the nation's total income. (We will study total national income and total national output in some detail in later chapters.)

## Reward differentials

If every worker were the same, if all benefits were monetary, and if workers moved freely between markets, then wage rates would tend to be the same in all jobs. Workers would move from low-priced jobs to high-priced ones. The quantity of labour supplied would diminish in occupations in which wages were low, and the resulting labour shortage would tend to force those wages up; the quantity of labour supplied would increase in occupations in which wages were high, and the resulting surplus would force wages down. The movement would continue until there were no further incentives to change occupations—that is, until wages were equalized in all uses.

As it is with labour, so it is with other type of input. If all units of capital or land were identical and moved freely between markets, all units would have the same market price in equilibrium.

In reality, of course, different units of any specific input type receive very different rewards. These differentials may be divided into two distinct types: those that exist only in disequilibrium situations and those that persist in equilibrium.

Disequilibrium differentials lead to, and are eroded by, movements of inputs between alternative uses; equilibrium differentials are not eliminated by mobility.

### Disequilibrium differentials

Some price or wage differentials reflect a temporary state of disequilibrium. They are brought about by circumstances such as the growth of one industry and the decline of another. The differentials themselves lead to a reallocation of inputs, and such reallocations in turn act to eliminate the differentials.

Over the past century there has been a steady rise in the demand for products of information and communications technology (ICT for short) firms and a decline in the demand for output of some traditional industries such as coal mining. In input markets the ICT industry's demand has increased while the coal mining industry's demand has decreased. Relative wages and return on capital have gone up in ICT and down in mining. The differential in rewards has caused a net movement of resources from mining (and other traditional industries) to the new ICT industries, and this movement itself has caused the differentials to lessen. How long such a process takes depends on how easily factors can be reallocated from one industry to the other, that is, on resource mobility. Of course, not many coal miners have become computer engineers or internet designers. What did happen, however, was that the UK coal mining industry went from employing over 1 million in the 1930s to under 10,000 in 2006, while ICT in the UK went from employing around zero in the 1930s to over 2 million in 2006.[3]

The behaviour that causes the erosion of disequilibrium differentials is summarized in the assumption of the *maximization of net benefit*[4]: the owners of inputs will allocate them to uses that maximize the net benefit to themselves, taking both monetary and non-monetary rewards into consideration. If net benefits are higher in occupation A than in occupation B, inputs will move from B to A. The increased supply in A, and the lower supply in B, will drive earnings down in A and up in B until net benefits are equalized, after which no further movement will occur. This analysis gives rise to the prediction of equal net benefit:

In equilibrium, inputs will be allocated among alternative possible uses in such a way that the net benefits in all uses are equalized.

Although non-monetary benefits are important in explaining differences in levels of pay for labour in different occupations, they tend to be quite stable over time. As a result monetary rewards, which vary with market conditions, lead to changes in *net benefits*.

A change in the relative price paid for the same inputs in any two industries will change the net benefits to the owner and create an incentive to shift some inputs into the activity in which relative rewards have increased.

This implies a positively sloped supply curve for an input in any particular use. When the price of an input rises in that use, more will be supplied to that use. This input supply curve (like all supply curves) can also *shift* in response to changes in other variables. For example, an improvement in the safety record in a particular occupation will shift the labour supply curve to that occupation.

### Equilibrium differentials

Some price differentials persist in equilibrium without generating any forces that will eliminate them. These **equilibrium differentials** can be explained by intrinsic differences in the type and quality of inputs and, for labour, by differences in the cost of acquiring skills and by different non-monetary advantages of different occupations. These were first called *compensating differentials* by Adam Smith over two hundred years ago.

### Intrinsic differences

If some inputs of the same general type have different specific characteristics, their market prices will differ. For example, if intelligence and dexterity are required to accomplish a task, intelligent and manually dextrous workers will earn more than less intelligent and less dextrous workers. If land is to be used for agricultural purposes, highly fertile land will command a higher rental value than poor land. These differences will persist even in long-run equilibrium.

### Acquired differences

It takes time and money to acquire qualifications. If this did not lead to higher expected future earnings, there would be no incentive to invest the time and money. So those employers that wish to hire highly qualified people will have to pay sufficiently higher salaries to compensate for that investment. Obtaining an MBA, for example, can cost well over £50,000 in terms of fees and lost earnings. Few people would study for this qualification unless they thought it would sufficiently enhance their earnings prospects.

### Non-monetary benefits

Whenever working conditions differ, workers will earn different equilibrium amounts in different occupations. The difference between a test pilot's wage and a chauffeur's wage is only partly a matter of skill; the rest is compensation to the worker for facing the higher risk of testing new planes as compared with driving a car. If both were paid the same, there would be an excess supply of chauffeurs and a shortage of test pilots.

Academics commonly earn less than they could earn in the world of commerce and industry because of the substantial non-monetary advantages of academic employment, such as flexible working hours and long breaks from teaching, which can be devoted partly to research and partly to leisure. If chemists, for example, were paid the same in universities and industry, many chemists would prefer academic to industrial jobs. Excess demand for industrial chemists and excess supply of academic chemists would then force chemists' wages up in industry until the two types of job seemed equally attractive on balance.

---

[3] Precise numbers depend on definitions adopted, but that there has been a general decline in jobs in production industries and a strong rise of jobs in ICT-related industries is not in doubt.

[4] This is just another form of 'utility' maximization and 'profit' maximization. Here the payoff is a mixture of financial reward and (especially in the case of labour) non-financial reward, such as status and job satisfaction.

The same forces account for equilibrium differences in regional earnings of otherwise identical workers.[5] People who work in remote logging or mining areas are paid more than people who perform jobs requiring similar skills in large cities. Without higher pay, too few people would be willing to work at sometimes-dangerous jobs in unattractive or remote locations.

## Pay equity

The distinction between equilibrium and disequilibrium wage differentials raises an important consideration for policy. Trade unions, governments, and other bodies often have explicit policies about earnings differentials, sometimes seeking to eliminate them in the name of equity. The success of such policies depends to a great extent on the kind of differential that is being attacked. Policies that attempt to eliminate equilibrium differentials will encounter severe difficulties.

Some government legislation seeks to establish *equal pay for work of equal value*, or *pay equity*. These laws can work as intended whenever they remove pay differentials that are due to prejudice. They run into trouble, however, whenever they require equal pay for jobs that have different non-monetary advantages.

To illustrate the problem, say that two jobs demand equal skills, training, and everything else that is taken into account when deciding what is work of equal value but that, in a city with an extreme climate, one is an outside job and the other is an inside job. If some pay commission requires equal pay for both jobs, there will be a shortage of people who are willing to work outside and an excess of people who want to work inside. Employers will seek ways to attract outside workers. Higher pensions, shorter hours, longer holidays, overtime paid for but not worked, and better working conditions may be offered. If these are allowed they will achieve the desired result, but they will defeat the original purpose of equalizing the monetary benefits of the inside and outside jobs. They will also cut down on the number of outside workers that employers will hire, since the total cost of an outside worker to an employer will have risen. If the authorities prevent such 'cheating', the shortage of workers for outside jobs will remain.

In Chapter 11 we discuss the effects of discrimination on wage differentials. Although discrimination is often important, it remains true that many wage differentials are a natural market consequence of supply and demand conditions that have nothing to do with inequitable treatment of different groups in society.

**Policies that seek to eliminate wage differentials without considering what caused them or how they affect the supply of specific types of worker are likely to have perverse results.**

# Economic rent

*Economic rent* is one of the most important concepts in economics. The owner of an input must earn a certain amount from the input's present use to prevent him from moving the input to another use. This is called its **reservation price** (Alfred Marshall called it the input's *transfer earnings*). If there were no non-monetary advantages in alternative uses, the input's reservation price would equal what it could earn elsewhere (its opportunity cost). This usually holds for capital and land. Labour, however, gets non-monetary advantages that differ between jobs: it must earn enough in one use to equate the two jobs' total benefits—monetary and non-monetary.

*Any excess that the owner of an input earns over its reservation price* is called its **economic rent**. Economic rent is analogous to economic profit as a surplus over the opportunity cost of capital. The concept of economic rent is crucial in predicting the effects that changes in earnings have on the movement of inputs between alternative uses. However, the terminology of rent is confusing because economic rent is often called simply *rent*, which can of course also mean the full price paid to hire something, such as a house or a piece of land. How the same term came to be used for these two different concepts is explained in Box 10.6.

## How much of earnings is rent?

In most cases economic rent makes up part of the actual earnings. The distinction is most easily seen, however, by examining two extreme cases. In one case all of earnings is rent; in the other, none is rent.

---

[5] Many regional wage differences are disequilibrium phenomena, where a wage in a declining industry is not yet sufficiently low to compensate for costs of moving.

**Box 10.6** Origin of the term 'economic rent'

In the early nineteenth century there was a public debate about the high price of wheat in England. The price was causing great hardship because bread was a major source of food for the working class. Some people argued that wheat had a high price because landlords were charging high rents to tenant farmers. In short, it was argued that the price of wheat was high because the rents of agricultural land were high. Some of those who held this view advocated restricting the rents that landlords could charge.

David Ricardo, a great British economist who was one of the originators of classical economics, argued that the situation was exactly the reverse. The price of wheat was high, he said, because there was a shortage, which was caused by the Napoleonic Wars. Because wheat was profitable to produce, there was keen competition among farmers to obtain land on which to grow wheat. This competition in turn forced up the rent of wheat land. Ricardo advocated removing the tariff so that imported wheat could come into the country, thereby increasing its supply and lowering both the price of wheat and the rent that could be charged for the land on which it was grown.

The essentials of Ricardo's argument were these. The supply of land was fixed. Land was regarded as having only one use, the growing of wheat. Nothing had to be paid to prevent land from transferring to a use other than growing wheat because it had no

other use. No landowner would leave land idle as long as some return could be obtained by renting it out. Therefore, all the payment to land—that is, 'rent' in the ordinary sense of the word—was a surplus over and above what was necessary to keep it in its present use.

Given a fixed supply of land, the price of land depended on the demand for land, which depended on the demand for wheat. *Rent*, the term for the payment for the use of land, thus became the term for a surplus payment to a resource owner over and above what was necessary to keep the resource in its present use.

Later two facts were realized. First, land often had alternative uses, and, from the point of view of any one use, part of the payment made to land would necessarily have to be paid to keep it in that use. Second, owners of resources other than land also often earned a surplus over and above what was necessary to keep those resources in their present use. Television stars and great athletes, for example, are in short and fairly fixed supply, and their potential earnings in other occupations are often quite moderate. However, because there is a huge demand for their services as television stars or athletes, they may receive payments greatly in excess of what is needed to keep them from transferring to other occupations. This surplus is now called *economic rent*, whether the input is land, labour, or a piece of capital equipment.

---

The possibilities are illustrated in Figure 10.3. When the supply curve is perfectly inelastic (vertical), the same quantity is supplied whatever the price. Evidently, there is no minimum that the owners of this input need to be paid to keep it in its present use, since the quantity supplied does not decrease no matter how low the price goes. In this case the whole of the payment is economic rent. The price actually paid allocates the fixed supply to those who are most willing to pay for it.

When the supply curve is perfectly elastic (horizontal), none of the price paid is economic rent. If any lower price is offered, nothing whatsoever will be supplied. All units of the input will be transferred to some other use.

The more usual situation is that of a gradually rising supply curve. A rise in the price paid for an input attracts more resources into the market in question, but the same rise provides additional economic rent to all units of the input that are already employed. We know that the extra pay that is going to the units already employed is economic rent because the owners of these units were willing to supply them at the lower price. The general result for a positively sloped supply curve is as follows:

**If there is an upward shift in the demand for a specific input in some sector, its price will rise. This will attract additional inputs into that sector. It will also increase the economic rent going to all the owners of the inputs already employed in that sector.[6]**

### Determinants of the split

The proportion of earnings that is economic rent varies from situation to situation. We cannot point to owners of any specific resource and assert that some fixed fraction of their income is always economic rent. The proportion of its earnings that is rent depends on the alternatives that are available.

Consider first a narrowly defined use of a specific input, say the use of a specific worker by a particular firm. From that firm's point of view the worker will be highly mobile, since he or she could readily move to another firm in the same industry. The firm must pay the going

---

[6] In this context the term 'sector' can stand for occupation, industry, or geographical area.

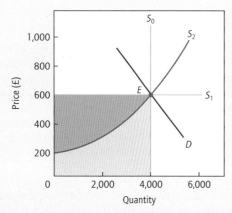

**Figure 10.3 The determination of rent in resource owners' incomes**

**The amount of rent in earnings depends on the shape of the supply curve.** A single demand curve is shown with three different supply curves. In each case the competitive equilibrium price is £600, and 4,000 units of the input are hired. The total payment (£2.4 million) is represented by the entire dark and light blue areas.

When the supply curve is vertical ($S_0$), the whole payment is economic rent, because a decrease in price would not lead any units of the input to move elsewhere. When the supply curve is horizontal ($S_1$), none of the payment is rent, because even a small decrease in price offered would lead all units of the input to move elsewhere. When the supply curve is positively sloped ($S_2$), part of the payment is rent. Although the 4,000th unit is receiving just enough to persuade it to offer its services in this market, the 2,000th unit is earning well above what it requires to stay in this market. The aggregate of economic rents is shown by the dark blue area, and the aggregate of what must be paid to keep 4,000 units in this market is shown by the light blue area.

wage or risk losing that worker. Thus, from the perspective of the *single firm*, a large proportion of the payment made to a worker is needed to prevent it from transferring to another use.

Now consider a more broadly defined use, for example the worker's use in an entire industry. From the industry's point of view the worker is less mobile, because it will be more difficult for her to gain employment quickly outside the industry. From the perspective of the particular *industry* (rather than the specific *firm* within the industry), a larger proportion of the payment to an input is economic rent.

From the even more general perspective of a particular *occupation*, mobility is likely to be less, and the proportion of earnings that is economic rent is likely to be more. The often controversial large salaries that are received by some highly specialized types of labour, such as superstar singers and professional athletes, illustrate these distinctions. These performers have a style or a talent that cannot be duplicated, whatever the training. The earnings that they receive are mostly economic rent from the viewpoint of the occupation: these performers enjoy their occupations and would pursue them for much less than the high remuneration that they actually receive. For example, David Beckham would choose football over other alternatives even at a much lower salary than he was earning in 2006. However, because of Beckham's skills as a football player, most teams would pay handsomely to have him, and he is able to command a high salary from the team he does play for. From the perspective of his employers, Real Madrid, most of Beckham's salary is required to keep him from switching to another team and hence is not economic rent. From the point of view of the 'football industry', however, much of his salary is economic rent. Similar arguments apply to top pop stars, who may earn several million pounds from record sales and concerts but would earn little in alternative occupations.

The notion of *rent seeking* is also commonly in use in the business world. Modern businesses are all trying to find products that give them some advantage over their rivals that generates economic profits and cannot be quickly competed away. Patent protection of a new invention can give such an advantage for some time, but reputation and brand loyalty may also create economic rents for some companies.

# CASE STUDIES

## 1. Electricity generation: substitution in practice

The principle of substitution has been important in the choice of fuels used to generate electricity, but it has not always worked in the same direction.

During the 1950s and 1960s increasing economies of scale in shipping crude oil from the Middle East to Western Europe made oil-based fuels more and more competitive. The relative price of fuels for industrial use fell by even more than the production cost of petrol, as it was the demand for petrol that was mainly responsible for the derived demand for crude oil. Other outputs of the oil-refining process were by-products. The Central Electricity Generating Board (CEGB), as it was then called (it has since been privatized as National Power and Powergen, and other electricity suppliers have entered the market), responded to the falling relative price of 'bunker' oil by building more and more oil-fired power stations and gradually closing down (or converting) the older coal-fired stations. From 85 per cent of electricity generated from coal and 11 per cent from oil in 1962, the CEGB steadily changed the 'mix', so that by 1971 it was generating about 65 per cent from coal and 25 per cent from oil.

Then came the 'oil shocks' of 1973 and 1979–80, when the OPEC countries dramatically raised the price of crude oil, leading to correspondingly dramatic increases in the prices of all oil products. Even though people in coal mining saw an opportunity to raise coal prices substantially, the *relative* price of oil was significantly higher in the 1980s than it had been in the 1960s and early 1970s. The CEGB accordingly switched back to an increasing reliance on coal-firing, which generated around 80 per cent of its electricity with only 5 per cent from oil in 1983.

Nevertheless, the electricity industry clearly retained the ability to switch back to oil rapidly if required. In 1984–5 a coal miners' strike which lasted nearly a full year led to an amazing 41 per cent of electricity being generated from oil (with total output slightly higher than the previous year) and only 42 per cent from coal. After the strike the figures quickly returned to their 1983 levels. However, the proportion of coal used declined in the late 1980s and 1990s owing to the growing use of natural gas and nuclear power (and environmental problems caused by high sulphur content of British coal). By 2005 the percentages of fuels used in UK electricity generation were coal 29, nuclear 24, gas 38, oil 1, and others (including hydroelectric, wind, and imports[7]) 8.

There is also a big controversy about future energy supply. Some want to build a new generation of nuclear power stations, which would generate electricity without adding to carbon emissions, while others are opposed to nuclear plants because of the long-term problems of waste disposal. It remains to be seen how energy production will actually evolve.

## 2. Employment in manufacturing.

The UK used to be known as the 'workshop of the world'. The industrial revolution started in Britain, and the British manufacturing sector used to be the largest source of both employment and output in the UK economy. In global terms, Britain was overtaken long ago as a centre for manufacturing, first by Germany, then by the United States, and more recently by Japan and China (among others).

Within the UK, employment in manufacturing has declined more or less continuously since the 1950s. Even in the past three decades or so, manufacturing employment has continued its

---

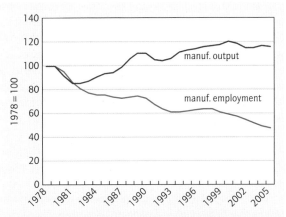

**Figure 10.4** UK manufacturing employment and output, 1978–2005

decline from over 7 million jobs in the late 1970s to under 3.5 million in 2005. Many commentators have concluded that this is evidence of the terminal decline of manufacturing as an activity in the UK. However, the reality is not so simple.

It is certainly true that the share of world manufacturing made in Britain has been in decline, but this decline started in the mid-1800s as other countries industrialized. It is also true that the share of manufacturing in UK GDP has been declining steadily since the Second World War, and that the share of employment in manufacturing continues to decline, as it has in most other developed industrialized countries. However, the fact is that the volume of manufacturing output in the UK in the year 2000 was at an all time high (see Figure 10.4, which shows an index of output and employment with 1978 set to equal 100). That is to say, despite its relative decline as a world player, and despite the absolute fall in employment in manufacturing, and despite the relative growth of the service sector in the economy, UK manufacturing industry produced a greater volume of output in 2000 than in any previous year in its history.

Thus, a key element of the UK manufacturing story is that the industry has achieved growing output with fewer and fewer employees. In effect, output per worker, or labour productivity, has been rising. A central reason for this is that real wages in the UK have risen relative to the cost of other inputs, such as capital and raw materials. Costs of computers, in particular, have fallen dramatically in the past two decades. Hence capital has been substituted for labour, so that many routine tasks are now done by computerized machinery that would previously have been performed by a line of assembly workers.

A major part of the story lies in the nature of modern technological change. For example, a mass production car factory in 1960 had a large number of workers operating dedicated and inflexible machinery on an assembly line. The modern car factory uses automated machines to do most of the things that these highly paid workers used to do. The paint is sprayed on at just the right moment by a computer-operated spraying machine. As with cars, so it is with many other manufacturing processes. The advent of computer-driven automated machines and robots, as well as the new method of lean production in which small groups of workers do multiple jobs, has drastically reduced the labour requirement per unit of output. So output has risen while employment has fallen. (Since the freed-up labourers are available to do other jobs, the net effect is a rise in living standards as more is produced throughout the economy per unit of labour employed.)

Another part of the story is globalization. A UK-based manufacturer has to pay high real wages to UK workers, but can buy in ready-made parts or materials from other parts of the world where wages are lower. Thus, a product that is finished in the UK may have inputs made by employees in many parts of the world.

A final part of the story relates to the restructuring of companies that has taken place since the 1980s. In the 1950s and 1960s a large manufacturing company would have groups of workers hired directly to provide virtually all of the services that it needed: catering, building maintenance, transport, etc. However, in the past two decades or so firms have moved to focus mainly on their core activities and now buy in other services needed from external firms. Thus, a large firm that has a canteen for its workers would previously have hired its own kitchen staff, but now it is most likely to have its catering provided by an external catering company. Before the change the same kitchen staff would have been classified as workers in manufacturing; now they are service-sector workers in the catering industry.

Accordingly, some of the decline in manufacturing employment is due to restructuring which has changed the boundaries of the manufacturing sector, even though these services are still purchased by manufacturing firms; some is due to the substitution of expensive domestic labour by cheaper foreign labour; and some is due to the direct substitution of capital for labour in domestic production. All of these are processes that are being driven by the relative prices of inputs.

## Conclusion

The key driving force of resource allocation in a market economy is that inputs are attracted into uses where they receive the highest rewards. In the case of capital and other non-human inputs, the reward sought is typically financial. However, in the case of labour financial rewards are only part of the story, as working conditions, job satisfaction, and other psychic benefits may also matter. Firms will demand inputs in relation to the value that those inputs add to output. Hence inputs will tend to be drawn towards those industries in which they are most productive and for which output demand is highest—the demand for inputs is derived from the demand for the outputs that they help produce. Thus there is a direct link from consumer demand for final products to demand for inputs and the rewards that the owners of those inputs receive.

## SUMMARY

- The determination of prices in input markets depends on demand and supply just as in markets for final goods and services.

- The distribution of income is determined in input markets.

- The income of owners of inputs depends on the price paid per unit of the input and the quantity of the input used.

### The demand for inputs

- The firm's decisions on how much to produce and how to produce it imply demands for inputs, which are derived from the demand for goods that they help to produce.

- A profit-maximizing firm equates an input's marginal cost to its marginal revenue product, which is its marginal physical product multiplied by the marginal revenue associated with the sale of another unit of output. When the firm is a price-taker in input markets, the marginal cost of the input is its price per unit. When the firm sells its output in a competitive market, the marginal revenue product is the input's marginal physical product multiplied by the market price of the output.

- A firm's demand for an input is negatively sloped in the long run because cheaper inputs will be substituted for dearer ones and a fall in an input's price leads to an increase in the output of the commodities used to make it. It is negatively sloped in the short run because of the law of diminishing returns.

- The industry's demand for an input will be more elastic: (a) the slower the marginal physical product of the input declines as more of it is used, (b) the easier it is to substitute one input for another, (c) the larger is the proportion of total variable costs accounted for by the cost of the input in question, and (d) the more elastic is the demand for the good that the input helps to make.

## The supply of inputs

- The total supply of land and capital is fixed at any moment but can vary over time. The total supply of labour varies with the size of the population, the participation rate, and the number of hours worked. The latter two vary with the wage rate. A rise in the wage rate has a substitution effect, which tends to induce more work, and an income effect, which tends to induce less.

- The supply of an input to a particular use is more elastic than its supply to the whole economy because one user can bid units away from other users. The elasticity of supply to a particular use depends on resource mobility, which tends to be greater the longer the time allowed for a reaction to take place.

## The operation of input markets

- Disequilibrium price differentials induce resource movements that eventually remove the differentials. Equilibrium differentials persist indefinitely.

## Economic rent

- Whenever the supply curve is positively sloped, part of the total return going to owners of a resource is needed to prevent them from transferring it to another use, and the rest is economic rent. The proportion of each depends on the potential mobility of the resource.

# TOPICS FOR REVIEW

- Distribution theory
- Derived demand
- Marginal physical product
- Marginal revenue product

- Input mobility between alternative uses
- Disequilibrium and equilibrium differentials
- Equal net benefit
- Economic rent

# QUESTIONS

1  A firm making lawnmowers has an existing factory and machinery but can vary the number of workers it hires. The following are data for total numbers of lawnmowers produced per week when hiring between 7 and 16 workers.

| Workers per week | Lawnmowers produced per week |
| --- | --- |
| 7 | 99 |
| 8 | 110 |
| 9 | 120 |
| 10 | 129 |
| 11 | 137 |
| 12 | 144 |
| 13 | 150 |
| 14 | 155 |
| 15 | 159 |
| 16 | 162 |

(a) Calculate the marginal physical product of workers number 8 to 16.
(b) Calculate the marginal revenue product of each worker if the lawnmowers can all be sold at £100.
(c) How many workers will this firm wish to hire if it is profit-maximizing and the going wage is £500 per week?

2  Suppose that the firm has the same production relationships as in question 1 but faces a downward-sloping demand curve for lawnmowers. The demand curve is $P = 400 - 1Q$ (so the marginal revenue curve is $MR = 400 - 2Q$), where $Q$ is the output of lawnmowers per week. If workers can again be hired at £500 per week, how many workers will be hired?

3  If the firm is faced with an upward-sloping supply curve of labour: $W = 300 + 20M$ (where $W$ is the wage per week and $M$ is the number of men hired per week), and the demand conditions in question 2 obtain, how many men will be hired?

4  Explain how demand for inputs is linked to the demand for the final outputs that those inputs help produce.

5 What determines the elasticity of demand for an input in one specific use and in general use?

6 Is the high price of hotel rooms in central London determined by high demand or by the scarcity of land on which hotels can be built (or something else)?

7 Rank the following occupations in terms of the likely proportion of rent (compared with transfer earnings) in typical earnings: pop stars, professional footballers, taxi drivers, computer consultants, university teachers, shop assistants, doctors.

8 What are the implications for input markets of rising demand for the following products: mobile phones, cheap flights, organic vegetables?

# Chapter 11

# THE LABOUR MARKET

The labour market is the most important market for most people, as that is where they find employment and earn their living. Can a labour market be analysed just like any other market? How do we explain wide differences in pay between different occupations? How do potential employers select employees when their quality is uncertain? What incentives are there for workers to perform once they land a job? These are some of the questions we address in this chapter.

In particular, you will learn that:

- Some long-lasting wage differentials arise from differences in skills and educational attainments; others arise from differences in age and sex.

- Some wage differentials arise from the type of market in which labour is sold; different wages are likely to be produced by competitive markets, where there are many buyers and sellers, monopoly markets, in which unions control the supply, and markets in which there are so few employers that each has power to influence the outcome.

- The full characteristics of many of today's workers are hard to ascertain in advance, so labour market practices evolve to cope with imperfect and asymmetric information.

- Efficiency wages are above the minimum that would be required to hire a worker, thereby providing an incentive for the employee to perform well.

- Selection and management procedures evolve to provide effective monitoring and incentive mechanisms.

- Internal labour markets within firms are like tournaments in which employees compete for promotion to more senior and better paid jobs.

The first part of the chapter is devoted to explaining wage differentials between different types of labour.[1] These are due partly to different skills and educational attainments, partly to age and sex, and partly to the type of market in which labour services are supplied. Workers can improve upon free market outcomes if they are organized as a single seller dealing with a large number of buyers, but they may do worse if they are unorganized and selling to a single buyer.

The first part of the chapter uses theories that assume that wages are set in competitive markets. These markets clear, in the sense that neither excess demand nor excess supply persists unless strong buyers or sellers are able to

exercise power over the market to prevent it from clearing. These theories can explain quite a bit about the forces that create wage differentials in the real world, because competitive markets where neither buyers nor sellers can significantly influence the price are more common in input markets than in goods markets. But they are not the whole story, since they treat labour as a homogeneous commodity, which is far from the truth.

Today, more and more employees are hired for their brain rather than their brawn. This introduces many complications to the labour market. Because people are heterogeneous, their contributions to the firm's success are difficult to assess and their motives may not always conform to the firm's objective of maximizing its profits. In the final part of the chapter, we study the many institutions and practices that have evolved to deal with these modern labour market problems.

---

[1] By 'labour' we mean all human resources of both workers and management, and by 'labour income', or 'wages', we mean all income earned from work, whether in the form of wages or salaries.

# Wage differentials

We noted in the previous chapter that if labour were homogeneous, jobs all had the same non-financial characteristics, and labour markets were perfectly competitive, every person would earn the same income in equilibrium. Disequilibrium differentials in wages would arise whenever demand or supply curves shifted. However, workers would then move from lower-wage to higher-wage jobs until the differentials had disappeared. In reality, some workers receive low rates of pay, others receive modest but higher wages, while yet others are paid very high wages (or salaries). These are equilibrium differentials which persist even after all markets have reached equilibrium. For full-time employees who work a standard week and have no income from assets, rates of pay translate into incomes.

- *Incomes vary with the type of job.* Cleaners and casual staff in fast-food restaurants earn less than electricians and IT support staff.
- *Incomes vary with education.* The average earnings of people with university degrees exceed the average earnings of those with only A levels, which in turn exceed the average earnings of those with only GCSEs, which exceed the average earnings of those with no qualifications at all.
- *Incomes vary with age.* Average earnings tend to rise until a person's mid-40s and fall thereafter (though this pattern varies with occupation).
- *Incomes vary with years on the job.* Generally, the longer one stays with one firm or organization, the higher the income one earns.
- *Incomes vary with sex and race.* On average, men earn more than women, and members of some minority ethnic groups earn less than members of majority groups —even when differences in education and experience are allowed for.
- *Incomes vary with the type of market in which labour is selling its services.* Workers who sell their labour in markets dominated by unions often earn more than similar people who sell their labour in more competitive markets.

We now consider some of the major causes of these equilibrium differentials in the earnings of various types of labour.

## Differentials arising from basic differences: non-competing groups

More highly skilled jobs pay better wages than less highly skilled jobs. Why does a movement from the latter to the former not erode these differentials?

One obvious answer lies in human differences that are either innate or acquired so early in life as to be beyond each individual's personal control. Some people are brighter than others; some are more athletic; some are blessed with a good singing voice; others are better endowed with manual skills. People may be separated by their natural endowments of intelligence, skills, and abilities into separate groups between which no movement is possible. We then have many *non-competing groups*. They will be selling their services in a number of *segmented labour markets*.

Figure 11.1 shows that wage differentials between non-competing groups arise from the positions of both the demand and the supply curves. One group will earn higher incomes than another only if its supply is low *relative to the demand for it*. It is not good enough to have a rare skill—that skill must be rare in relation to the demand for it.

Over time, wage differentials change. On the demand side, economic growth constantly alters the derived demand for many specific groups of labour, creating new differentials and eroding old ones. On the supply side there may be exogenous shifts. For example, a new group of immigrants may alter the mix of skills available in the local market. Furthermore, human differences notwithstanding, substantial mobility between groups does occur—particularly in the long run, when older people with specific skills leave the labour force and young people with different skills enter.

None the less, one lesson of the simple theory of non-competing groups is important:

Some income differentials arise because basic human characteristics cause the supplies of some types of labour to remain low relative to the demand for them, even in the long run.

## Differentials arising from human capital

The key to mobility among occupations is education. Many skills are learned rather than inherited. These may be thought of as a stock of human capital acquired by each worker.

A machine is physical capital. It requires an investment of time and money to create it, and, once built, yields valuable services over a long time. In the same way, the acquisition of labour skills requires an investment of time

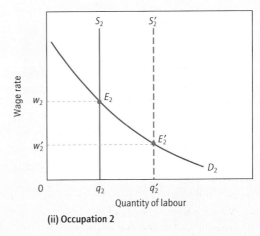

**Figure 11.1 Wage differentials in segmented labour markets**

**When labour cannot move from one market to another, wage differentials of any size can persist.** Because of basic differences in abilities, the supply of labour is fixed at $q_1$ in occupation 1 and at $q_2$ in occupation 2. Demand and supply curves intersect at $E_1$ and $E_2$ to produce the high wage of $w_1$ in occupation 1 and the low wage of $w_2$ in occupation 2. A fall in demand from $D_1$ to $D_1'$ in occupation 1 takes equilibrium to $E_1'$, lowering its wage to $w_1'$. A rise in supply in occupation 2 to $q_2'$ takes equilibrium to $E_2'$, lowering its wage to $w_2'$.

and money, and, once acquired, these skills yield an increased income to their owner over a long time. Since investment in labour skills is similar to investment in physical capital, acquired skills are called **human capital**.

Because acquiring human capital is costly, the more highly skilled the job, the more it must pay if enough people are to be attracted to train for it.

The stock of skills acquired by individual workers is called human capital; investment in this capital is usually costly, and the return is higher labour productivity and hence higher earning power.

The two main ways in which human capital is acquired are through formal education and on-the-job training.

### Formal education

Compulsory education provides some minimum human capital for all citizens. Some people, either through luck in the schools they attended or through their own efforts, profit more from their early education than do others. Those who decide to stay in school beyond the years of compulsory education are deciding to invest voluntarily in the acquisition of further human capital.

### Costs and benefits

The cost of higher education is the income that could have been earned if the person had entered the labour force immediately after compulsory education, plus any out-of-pocket costs for such things as fees and equipment, minus any student grant or scholarship. The return

is the difference between the income that would have been earned if she had left school and the income that she eventually earns as a result of going on to higher education. (There is also a *consumption return* whenever higher education is something that students enjoy more than work.) These costs and benefits are analysed in Figure 11.2.

### Changes in costs and benefits

If the demand for labour with low amounts of human capital falls, as it has in recent times, the earnings of low-skilled people will fall. This will raise the expected return from higher education for those currently deciding whether or not to make the investment themselves. A rise in unemployment will also lower such costs, because the probability of earning a steady income will be reduced, and this will reduce the expected loss from not entering the labour force early. If the demand for labour with high human capital rises, the earnings of such labour will rise. This will raise the expected return to those currently deciding whether or not to make such an investment.

### Individual decisions

For any *given* state of these incentives, why do some people decide to acquire human capital while others do not?

First, there are differences between individuals. For reasons related to inherited abilities or early educational experience, some people at the age of 16 (or 18) correctly decide that they have a low chance of profiting from further formal education. For them the return from such

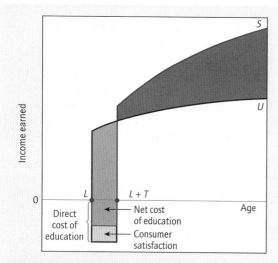

**Figure 11.2 The costs and benefits of higher education**

Acquiring human capital through formal education beyond minimum school-leaving age implies costs now and benefits later. Age is plotted on the horizontal axis and income earned on the vertical axis. Income is zero until age $L$, which is the minimum school-leaving age. After that the pink line $U$ shows the income of a typical person who leaves school at age $L$ and takes the relatively unskilled job for which her human capital is suitable.

The blue line $S$ shows the more complicated stream of payments and income receipts of someone who stays on for $T$ years of formal training after $L$. At first receipts are negative, reflecting the net out-of-pocket expenses related to attending school and university. Deducting the consumption value placed on being at school rather than at work (light pink area) yields the net cost associated with being in school. Adding this to the income that could have been earned by going directly into the labour force at age $L$ yields the total cost of the education, which is the medium pink area.

The benefit is shown by the dark pink area, representing the difference between the income earned in the skilled job that is acquired at year $L+T$ (line $S$) and the income that would have been earned if the labour force had been entered at age $L$ (line $U$). The investment in human capital could not possibly be worthwhile unless the dark pink benefit area exceeded the medium pink cost area. The net benefit to a particular individual depends on how she discounts the more distant gain in order to compare it with the more immediate costs.

education is lower than for others who have the necessary aptitudes and inclination.

Second, some people have special talents for types of work that do not require further human capital. For them the cost of acquiring more human capital is higher than it is for others; the earnings they would forgo by not entering the labour force are higher than the earnings that would be forgone by the average school-leaver. Obvious examples are pop singers and professional football players —Sir Mick Jagger did not suffer any loss of income by quitting his economics degree at the LSE and joining the Rolling Stones!

Third, different people have different time-preferences. The cost of acquiring human capital is income forgone *now*, and the return is a *probability* of higher income *later*. Tastes differ. Some people put a high value on income now and are not willing to pay the cost of postponing it. Others place a higher value on income to be earned later in life and are willing to have less now in return for the chance of much more later on.

Fourth, different people put different values on the consumption aspects of education. Those who enjoy the experience find the costs of acquiring human capital lower than those who do not. Those who would prefer to be at work rather than at school or university find the cost increased by the negative value they place on the educational experience.

**Market forces adjust the overall costs and benefits of acquiring human capital, while individuals respond according to their varying personal evaluation of these costs and the benefits.**

In the long run, decisions to acquire human capital help to erode disequilibrium differentials in incomes. Market signals change the costs and benefits of acquiring human capital in specific forms, for example skill in electronics, accountancy, law, or medicine. By reacting to these signals, young people increase the supply of high-income workers and reduce the supplies of low-income workers, thereby eroding existing disequilibrium differentials.

## On-the-job training

Wage differentials according to age are readily observable in most firms and occupations. To a significant extent, these differentials are a response to human capital acquired on the job. This type of human capital falls into two types.

### Firm-specific human capital

Three examples of firm-specific information are the way in which the firm makes its decisions, the way in which the firm's various departments interact, and the way in which customer complaints are dealt with. As employees acquire familiarity with such internal workings of their firm, they become more valuable to that firm. But this knowledge is not of value to other firms; workers who move to similar jobs with other firms will have to learn from scratch the new firm-specific characteristics of their working environment.

Firms do not want to lose long-term employees who have large amounts of firm-specific human capital since other employees will then have to be trained. But as it is firm-specific, this type of human capital is of no value to other firms. So if the firm pays its employees a wage that reflects the productivity conferred by this capital, they will have an incentive to stay in the job rather than to move to another firm where their value would initially be much less.

### General human capital

If a firm trains a clerical assistant through various ranks up to becoming the PA of the managing director, able to run his office efficiently, the PA skills he has acquired will be potentially useful to other firms. Some of the PA's human capital can be acquired only through on-the-job training; hence it must be acquired within the firm. However, unlike the firm-specific capital, a PA who is paid the value of his marginal product has no monetary incentive to stay with the firm that taught these transferable skills, as he could earn a similar income elsewhere. The same is true of any non-firm-specific human capital acquired through on-the-job experience by any of the firm's employees.

So why would firms invest in training employees if the resulting human capital is free to walk out of the door and move to another employer? Firms have no incentive to provide training when they cannot capture the benefit themselves but have to see it accruing to individual employees. One solution is to pay each worker less than her marginal product in the early years and more later on. The low pay can be seen as the employees' payment to the firm for helping them to acquire marketable human capital. The high pay later in life is partly a return on that capital, and partly a reward for loyalty to the firm.

**Human capital acquired through on-the-job experience provides a reason why earnings rise with the length of time spent with a firm. Firms tend to pay employees the value of their current marginal products for firm-specific capital, but for general human capital they pay less than the marginal products early in life and more later in life.**

Box 11.1 discusses some other ways in which a firm can have a longer-term grip on the capital embodied in its employees, and some in which it cannot.

Another reason why rewards tend to rise with length of service is that competition tends to be strongest at the initial point of entry into the firm and to weaken thereafter, when promotions to more senior posts typically go to internal candidates. This will tend to hold wages down to competitive levels at entry points but allow them to rise

 **Box 11.1  The rental and purchase price of labour**

If you wish to farm a piece of land, you can buy it yourself, or you can rent it for a specific period of time. If you want to set up a small business, you can buy your office and equipment, or you can rent them. The same is true for all capital and all land; a firm often has the option of either buying or renting.

Exactly the same would be true for labour if we lived in a slave society. You could buy a slave to be your assistant, or you could rent the services either of someone else's slave or those of a free person. Fortunately, slavery is illegal throughout most of today's world. As a result, the labour markets that we know deal only in the services of labour; we do not go to a labour market to buy a worker, only to hire her services.

You can, however, buy the services of a worker for a long period of time. In professional sports multi-year contracts are common, and ten-year contracts are not unknown. Football clubs for example pay a transfer fee to buy a player if he is still contracted to another club, so long as all parties agree. Publishers sometimes tie up their authors in multi-book contracts, and film and television production firms often sign up their actors on long-term contracts. In all cases of such *personal service contracts*, the person is not a slave, because his or her personal rights and liberties are protected by law. None the less, the purchaser of the long-term contract is buying ownership of the person's services for an extended period of time. The price of the contract will reflect the person's expected earnings over the contract's lifetime. If the contract is transferable, the owner can sell these services for a lump sum or rent them out for some period. As with land and capital goods, the price paid for this *stock* of labour services depends on the expected rental prices over the contract period.

above those levels for employees in more senior posts and with years of experience. This pattern does not always hold, of course—in universities, for example, new faculty members are often paid more than those who have been in place for some time. This is because the university is trying to recruit the brightest and best on the market and has to pay high rates to attract them, while the existing staff have some job security (so cannot easily be dismissed) but might not be the strongest candidates if applying in the current market situation.

### Market solutions

The above discussion illustrates the subtlety of market solutions to the issues posed by the human capital acquired through on-the-job experience. What may look arbitrary, or unfair, to the casual observer is often a rational response that has evolved to handle some aspect of the employment relationship—such as the fact that on-the-job training creates capital that is sometimes firm-specific and sometimes transferable, but in all cases is embodied in the employee rather than the firm itself.

To illustrate the importance of these insights, consider two jobs that employ people with equal initial requirements. One provides on-the-job training that is mainly firm-specific, and the wage follows the time-path of the employee's evolving marginal product fairly closely. The second job provides training that builds up transferable skills, and the wage paid is less than marginal product for younger employees and greater for older ones. Now assume that government policy-makers get worried about the discrimination between workers in different jobs and introduce legislation requiring equal pay for 'work of equal value'. Both types of employee must now be paid the value of their marginal products. Firms then become reluctant to invest in training their employees to acquire transferable human capital, because it is now illegal to use a time-pattern of wages that allows the firm to recover the cost of providing this capital. However fair it may appear to some, this government policy, designed to enhance equity, may not be in the interests of the workers affected by it.

# Differentials arising from sex and race

Aggregate statistics show that incomes vary by race and sex. More detailed studies suggest that much of these differences can be explained by such influences as amount of human capital acquired through both formal education and on-the-job experience. When these influences are taken into account, however, a core of difference remains that is consistent with discrimination based on race and sex. This is further discussed with respect to male–female earnings differentials in Box 11.2.

Some forms of discrimination make it difficult, or impossible, for particular groups to take certain jobs, even if skill and education equip them for these jobs. Until fairly recently, non-whites and women found many occupations closed to them. Even today, when overt discrimination is illegal, many feel that more subtle forms of discrimination are applied.

To the extent that such discrimination occurs, it reduces the supply of labour in the exclusive jobs—by keeping out the groups that are discriminated against. It also increases the supply in non-exclusive jobs, which are the only ones open to the groups subject to discrimination. This raises the wages in the exclusive jobs and lowers them in the non-exclusive jobs. Since discrimination prevents movement from the lower to the higher-wage jobs, the resulting wage differences are equilibrium, not disequilibrium, differentials.

## A model of labour market discrimination

To isolate the effects of discrimination, we begin by considering a non-discriminating labour market. We then introduce discrimination between two groups of equally qualified workers, group X and group Y. The analysis applies to workers who are distinguished on any ground other than their ability, such as female and male, black and white, alien and citizen, Catholic and Protestant.

Suppose that, except for the fact that half of the people are marked with X and the other half are marked with Y, the groups are the same. Each group has the same number of members, the same proportion who are educated to various levels, identical distributions of talent, and so on. Suppose also that there are two occupations. Occupation E (for elite) requires people of above-average education and skills, and occupation O (ordinary) can use anyone. If wages in the two occupations are the same, employers in occupation O will prefer to hire the above-average worker. Finally, suppose that the non-monetary advantages of the two occupations are equal.

In the absence of discrimination, the wages in E occupations will be bid up above those in O occupations in order that the E jobs attract the workers of above-average skills. Both Xs and Ys of above-average skill will take the E jobs, while the other Xs and Ys will have no choice but to seek O jobs. Because skills are equally distributed, each occupation will employ one-half Xs and one-half Ys.

Now discrimination enters in an extreme form. Suppose that all E occupations are hereafter open only to Xs, and all O occupations are hereafter open to either Xs or Ys. The immediate effect is to reduce by 50 per cent the supply of job candidates for E occupations: candidates must now be *both* Xs *and* above average. The discrimination also increases the supply of applicants for O jobs by 50 per cent; this group now includes all Ys *and* the below-average Xs.

### Wage-level effects

As shown in Figure 11.3, wages now rise in E occupations and fall in O occupations.

**Discrimination, by changing supply, can decrease the wages and incomes of a group that is discriminated against.**

**Box 11.2** Why are women paid less than men?

Wage discrimination can affect women (or any other group that is discriminated against) in at least two ways. They may earn less than men when doing the same job, or they may be forced into jobs that typically pay lower wages than the jobs from which they are excluded. Non-discriminatory wage differentials arise when men and women differ on average in relevant labour market characteristics. For example, men and women differ significantly in their average educational qualification and in their labour market experience, with women typically spending somewhere between five and ten years out of the labour market raising children.

Across the whole economy, the average pay of women is less than that of men. This has been known since at least the 1880s, when reliable records started. Indeed, at the Trades Union Congress of 1888 a motion was passed stating that where men and women do the same jobs they should get the same pay. However, it was 1970 before the Equal Pay Act finally legislated that pay must be the same 'for the same or broadly similar work'.

Since 1975, when the Equal Pay Act came into effect, the full-time mean pay gap has closed considerably, from 29.5 to 17.2 per cent in 2006. Using the median, the full-time gender pay gap was 12.6 per cent in 2006.

Research published by the Government in December 2001—*The Gender Pay Gap*—authoritatively identifies the key drivers behind the gender pay gap. It finds that the reasons for the pay gap are complex and interconnected:

*Key factors include:*

- *Human capital differences: i.e. differences in educational levels and work experience. Historical differences in the levels of qualifications held by men and women have contributed to the pay gap. However, women are still more likely than men to have breaks from paid work to care for children and other dependants. These breaks impact on women's level of work experience, which in turn impacts on their pay rates.*
- *Part-time working: the pay gap between men and women's part time hourly earnings and men's full time hourly earnings is particularly large and, because so many women work part-time, this is a major contributor to the gender pay gap. Some of this gap is due to part-time workers having lower levels of qualifications and*

less work experience. However, it is also due to part-time work being concentrated in less well-paid occupations.

- *Travel patterns: on average, women spend less time commuting than men. This may be because of time constraints due to balancing work and caring responsibilities. This can impact on women's pay in two ways: smaller pool of jobs to choose from and/or lots of women wanting work in the same location (i.e. near to where they live) leading to lower wages for those jobs.*
- *Occupational segregation: women's employment is highly concentrated in certain occupations (60 per cent of working women work in just 10 occupations). And those occupations which are female-dominated are often the lowest paid. In addition, women are still under-represented in the higher paid jobs within occupations—the 'glass ceiling' effect.*
- *Workplace segregation: at the level of individual workplaces, high concentrations of female employees are associated with relatively low rates of pay. And higher levels of part-time working are associated with lower rates of pay, even after other factors have been taken into account.* (http://www.womenandequality unit.gov.uk/pay/pay_facts.htm)

On a narrow interpretation, the pay differentials according to different labour market experiences are a reflection of the resulting lower marginal products. On a wider view of discrimination, however, these different experiences are merely convenient excuses for paying women less. This wider view is given some plausibility by the fact that in Sweden, the most egalitarian country in Europe, female earnings average over 90 per cent of male earnings.

It is harder to estimate the effects of discrimination that excludes women from certain jobs and crowds them into others. Studies suggest, however, that if the discrimination in type of employment were eliminated, wages in occupations that are currently dominated by females would rise by as much as 50 per cent! In contrast, wages in male-dominated jobs would fall by only a few percentage points.

Broadly, the evidence suggests two things. First, there almost certainly remains some discrimination against women in labour markets today. Second, we have to be very careful in interpreting the raw data. The measured average differentials have to be adjusted for labour force characteristics in order to identify any residual that is due to discrimination.

In the longer run, further changes may occur. Notice that total employment in the E industries falls. Employers may find ways to utilize slightly below-average labour and thus lure the next-best-qualified Xs out of O occupations. Although this will raise O wages slightly, it will also make these occupations increasingly 'Y occupations'. If dis-

crimination has been in effect for a sufficient length of time, Ys will learn that it does not pay to acquire above-average skills. Regardless of ability, Ys are forced by discrimination to work in unskilled jobs.

Now suppose that a long-standing discriminatory policy is reversed. Because they will have responded to

(i) Elite market (E)     (ii) Ordinary market (O)

**Figure 11.3  Economic discrimination**

**If market E discriminates against one group and market O does not, the supply curve will shift to the left in E and to the right in O.** Market E requires above-average skills, while market O requires only ordinary skills. When there is no discrimination, demands and supplies are $D_E$ and $S_E$ in market E, and $D_O$ and $S_O$ in market O. Initially the wage rate is $w_0$ and employment is $q_0$ in each market. (The actual wage in market E will be slightly higher than the wage in market O.) When all Ys are barred from E occupations, the supply curve shifts to $S_E'$ and the wage earned by the remaining workers, all of whom are Xs, rises to $w_1$. Ys put out of work in the E occupations now seek work in the O occupations. The resulting shift in the supply curve to $S_O'$ brings the wage down to $w_2$ in the O occupations. Because all Ys are in O occupations, they have a lower wage than many Xs. The average X wage is higher than the average Y wage.

discrimination by acquiring fewer skills than Xs, many Ys will be locked into the O occupations, at least for a time. Moreover, if both Xs and Ys come to expect that Ys will have less education than Xs, employers will tend to look for Xs to fill the E jobs. This will reinforce the belief of Ys that education does not pay. This and other kinds of subtle discrimination can persist for a very long time, making the supply of Ys to O jobs higher than it would be in the absence of the initial discrimination, thereby depressing the wages of Ys and poor Xs.

The kind of discrimination that we have considered in our model is extreme. It is similar to South Africa's former apartheid system (which was eliminated by 1994), in which blacks were excluded by law from prestigious and high-paying occupations. In most Western countries labour market discrimination against a specific group usually occurs in somewhat less obvious ways. First, it may be difficult (but not impossible, as in our model) for members of the group to get employment in certain jobs. Second, members of groups subject to discrimination may receive lower pay for a specific kind of work than members of groups not subject to discrimination.

It is interesting to note that falling transport and communication costs over the past century have expanded firms' choice of location for the production of goods: from local markets, to national markets, to wider regional markets, and now often to global markets. This has greatly reduced the power of local prejudices to impose discriminatory employment policies on firms. If firms are unhappy about local pressures to employ one group rather than another, production can be transferred to other sites and the customers will quickly lose any concern about, or even awareness of, the nature of the far-distant workforce that makes the products they consume.

## Differentials arising from labour market structures

In this section we see how differences in the degree of competition can contribute to income differentials between market segments. We then go on to study unions in a little more detail.

### The determination of wages without unions

When labour is supplied competitively, each individual worker must take the existing wage rate as given and decide how many hours to work at that wage.[2] Each worker has a supply curve showing how many hours of work

---

[2] In practice, the individual decision may be whether or not to work the standard working week at the going wage.

she will supply at each wage. The sum of these curves yields a market supply curve showing the total supply of work hours to this market as positively related to the real wage rate. The determination of wages under competitive supply can now be divided into three possible cases. The distinguishing characteristic of these cases is whether labour is bought by competitive purchasers, by a single-wage monopsonist, or by a discriminating monopsonist.

### Case 1: A competitive market

We first assume that there are so many purchasers of labour services that no one of them can influence the market wage rate. Instead, each merely decides how much labour to hire at the current rate. Since both demanders and suppliers are price-takers and quantity-adjusters, this labour market is perfectly competitive. Demand and supply as shown in Figure 10.1 on page 209 then determine the wage rate and volume of employment.

### Case 2: A single-wage monopsonist—a single purchaser

Now consider a labour market containing only a few firms. For simplicity we deal with a case in which the few purchasers form an employers' association and act as a single decision-taking unit in the labour market. In this section the single buyer is constrained to paying a single wage to all workers of one type that it employs.

When there is a single purchaser in any market, that purchaser is called a **monopsonist.** A monopsonist can offer any wage rate it chooses, and workers must either work for that wage or move to other markets (i.e. change occupation or location).

Suppose that the monopsonist decides to hire some specific quantity of labour. The labour supply curve shows the wage that it must offer. To the monopsonist this wage is the *average cost curve* of labour. In deciding how much labour to hire, however, the monopsonist is interested in the marginal cost of hiring additional workers. It wants to know how much its costs will rise if it takes on more labour.

Whenever the supply curve of labour has a positive slope, the marginal cost of employing extra units will exceed the average cost (the wage) because the increased wage rate necessary to attract an extra worker must also be paid to *everyone already employed*.

Consider an example. If 100 workers are employed at £2 per hour, then total cost is £200 and average cost per worker is £2. If an extra worker is employed and this drives the wage rate up to £2.05, then total cost becomes £207.05 (101 × £2.05); the average cost per labourer is £2.05, but the total cost has increased by £7.05 as a result of hiring one more labourer.

Monopsony results in a lower level of employment and a lower wage rate than when labour is purchased competitively.

The reason is that the monopsonistic purchaser is aware that, by purchasing more, it is driving up the price against itself. It will, therefore, stop short of the point that is reached when the input is purchased by many different firms, none of which can exert an influence on its price.

### Case 3: A discriminating monopsonist

What happens if the monopsonist can discriminate between different units of a single type of labour that it hires? By discrimination here we mean that the employer negotiates a different contract with each individual employee. We do not imply that this is related to any ethnic and gender characteristics whose impact we discussed above. As with the discriminatory monopolists that we studied in Chapter 8, the ability to discriminate has two effects:

A discriminating monopsonist will hire more labour and earn more profits than will a monopsonist who must pay the same wage to everyone.

In Figure 11.4 the monopsonist who must pay the same wage to all did not hire more labour, because doing so would have driven up the wage of its existing workers. For this reason the monopsonist's marginal cost of hiring labour exceeds the average costs. If the monopsonist can split its labour into groups, it can hire a second group without driving up the price of the first group. Consider the extreme case in which the monopsonist can make a separate bargain with each worker, paying just what is needed to persuade that person to accept a job. The supply curve is then the marginal cost curve of labour and the monopsonist employs the same amount of labour as would a perfectly competitive industry; but only the last worker hired gets the equivalent of the competitive wage—all others get less.

A perfectly discriminating monopsony is the extreme case. However, whenever the monopsonist can discriminate between two or more groups, employment and profits will be higher than when a single wage must be paid to all.

### The determination of wages with unions

Unions affect wages and employment in two ways, depending on whether labour is hired competitively or monopsonistically.[3]

---

[3] For simplicity, we deal here with only the single-wage monopsonist. Combining a union with a discriminating monopsonist complicates the analysis substantially without adding any new insights.

**Figure 11.4  A monopsonist facing many sellers**

**Under monopsony employment and wages are less than under competition.** The competitive wage and employment are $w_c$ and $q_c$, where the demand and supply curves intersect. The monopsonist firm that must pay the same wage to all equates the marginal cost of hiring labour with labour's marginal revenue product, which occurs at point $E_m$. The firm hires $q_m$ workers at a wage of $w_m$. (According to the supply curve, $w_m$ is the wage at which $q_m$ workers will be supplied.) Labour's income is shown by the dark pink and dark blue areas enclosed by $q_m$ and $w_m$.

A perfectly discriminating monopsonist can pay each worker her supply price, so the $S$ curve is also its marginal cost curve. It will hire $q_c$ labour and pay labour a total income equal to the dark and light blue areas *under* the $S$ curve. The light pink area between $w_m$ and $w_c$ is now part of the monopsonist's profits, as is the dark pink area between $w_m$ and the $S$ curve (whereas under perfect competition both pink areas are part of labour's income).

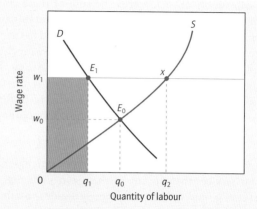

**Figure 11.5  A single union facing many employers**

**A union that faces many employers can raise wages above the competitive level.** Competitive equilibrium is at $E_0$. When the union sets the wage at $w_1$, it creates a perfectly elastic supply curve of labour up to the quantity $q_2$, which is the amount of labour willing to work at the wage $w_1$. Equilibrium is at $E_1$, with $q_1$ workers employed and $q_2 - q_1$ willing to work at the going wage rate but unable to find employment. Labour income is shown by the blue area.

A union can raise wages above the competitive-market level, but only at the cost of lowering employment and creating an excess supply of labour, with the consequent pressure for wage-cutting.

## Case 5: A monopsony versus a monopoly

We now consider the effects of introducing a union into the monopsonistic labour market first illustrated in Figure 11.4.

The (single-wage) monopsonistic employers' organization now faces a monopoly union, and the two sides will settle the wage through collective bargaining. The outcome of this bargaining process will depend on the objective that each side sets and on the skill that each has in bargaining for its objective. We have seen that, left to itself, the employers' organization will set the monopsonistic wage shown in Figure 11.4.

To understand the range over which the wage may be set after the union enters the market, let us ask what the union would do if it had the power to set a wage below which its members would not work. There is now no point in the employers holding off hiring for fear of driving the wage up, or of reducing the quantity demanded in the hope of driving the wage rate down. Here, just as in the case of a wage-setting union in a competitive market, the union presents the employer with a horizontal supply

## Case 4: Monopoly—a single seller

Suppose a union enters a competitive labour market and raises the wage above its equilibrium level. By so doing, it is establishing a minimum wage below which no one will work. The industry can hire as many units of labour as are prepared to work at the union wage, but none at a lower wage. Thus, the industry (and each firm) faces a supply curve that is horizontal at the level of the union wage up to the quantity of labour willing to work at that wage.

This is shown in Figure 11.5. The intersection of this horizontal supply curve and the demand curve establishes a higher wage rate, and a lower level of employment, than would occur at the competitive equilibrium.

There will be a group of workers who would like to obtain work in the industry or occupation but cannot. Pressure from the unemployed to cut the wage rate may develop, but the union must resist this pressure if the higher wage is to be maintained.

**Figure 11.6 A single union facing a single employer**

A union can raise both the wage and employment above their monopsonistic levels. The monopsonist facing competitively supplied labour is in the equilibrium analysed in Figure 11.4, with $q_m$ workers employed at a wage of $w_m$. If a newly entering union sets its wage at $w_0$, the supply curve runs from $w_0$ to $E_0$ and then rises along the line $S$. Equilibrium is at $E_0$ with employment at $q_0$.

If the union seeks a wage higher than $w_0$, it must accept a lower level of employment than $q_0$. The union can, for example, set a wage of $w_u$, creating a supply curve that runs from $w_u$ to $x$ then up the $S$ curve. This yields the same level of employment, $q_m$, as when the monopsonist dominated the market, but at the much higher wage of $w_u$. At that wage rate there are $q_2 - q_m$ people who would like to work but who are unable to find employment.

curve (up to the maximum number of workers who will accept work at the union wage). As demonstrated in Figure 11.6, the union can raise wages *and employment* above the monopsonistic level.

Because the union turns the firm into a price-taker in the labour market, it can stop a firm from exercising its monopsony power and thereby raise both wages and employment to the competitive level.

The union may not be content merely to neutralize the monopsonist's power. It may choose to raise wages further. If it does, the outcome will be similar to that shown in Figure 11.5. If the wage is raised above the competitive level, the employer will no longer wish to hire all the labour that is offered at that wage. The amount of employment will fall, and unemployment will develop. This is also shown in Figure 11.6. Notice, however, that the union can raise wages substantially above the competitive level before employment falls to a level as low as it was in the pre-union monopsonistic situation.

We know that the employer would like to set the monopsonistic wage and that the union would not want a wage below the competitive wage. The union may target a still higher wage depending on what trade-off it is willing to make between employment for its members and the wage that they earn. If the union is willing to accept the resulting low amount of employment, it could target a wage rate substantially higher than the competitive wage.

Simple demand and supply analysis can take us no further. As we have already observed, the actual outcome will depend on such other things as the target wage that the two sides seek to achieve, their relative bargaining skills, how each side assesses the cost of concessions, and how serious a strike would be for each.

## Differentials arising from product market structures

The ability of a union to raise wages above the competitive level depends partly on the profitability of the industry in which it is operating. Some industries are highly competitive because they contain a large number of small firms and entry and exit are easy. Typically, firms in such industries will be earning enough to cover the opportunity cost of their capital, but no pure profits. A strong union might still raise wages in such an industry. This would increase costs and lead to exit until prices rose sufficiently for the remaining firms fully to cover their now higher costs. Thus, the rise in wages would be accompanied by a fall in output and employment. However, even this limited gain may not be possible. If the union does not have a closed shop new firms may enter, with lower costs achieved by hiring non-union labour. Also, if there is competition from foreign firms that do not face strong unions, the domestic industry may suffer a drastic contraction.

In other industries scale economies allow only a few firms, each one of which may earn significant profits. Government regulation that restricts competitive behaviour can also create profits over and above the opportunity cost of capital. Evidence suggests that unions can appropriate a share of these profits for their members through aggressive collective bargaining. Wages fell significantly in the UK newspaper industry after new technology gave the opportunity to break the union monopoly on print workers.

## Minimum wage laws

When unions set wages for their members, they are in effect setting a minimum wage. Governments can cause similar effects by legislating specific *minimum wages*, which define the lowest wage rates that may legally be paid. Such minimum wages are common in the United States and Canada and some EU countries. The UK introduced a minimum wage on 1 April 1999 with a minimum wage of £3.60 an hour for adult workers and £3.00 for 18–21 year olds (16 and 17 year olds were exempt at that time). By February 2006 the adult rate stood at £5.05, while that for 18–21 year olds was £4.25 per hour. There was also a rate of £3.00 for 16 and 17 year olds.

To the extent that minimum wages are effective, they raise the wages of employed workers. However, an effective floor price (which is what a minimum wage is) may well lead to a market surplus—in this case, unemployment. Thus, minimum wages benefit some groups of workers while hurting others.

Analysis of the impact of a minimum wage is complicated because not all labour markets are competitive, because only a small proportion of the labour force is affected by minimum wage laws, and because many firms do not sell in perfectly competitive markets and so earn pure profits, some of which may be transferred to employees by such laws. Moreover, some groups in the labour force, especially youth and minorities, are affected more than the average worker. Also, it is worth bearing in mind that labour is not a homogeneous commodity (even though much of our demand and supply analysis assumes that it is). A change in employment conditions that encourages workers to work harder or to invest in improving their skills may have effects that differ from those that would occur in a market where the 'product' is unchanging.

### A comprehensive minimum wage

Consider a minimum wage law that, as in the UK, applies uniformly to all occupations. The occupations and the industries in which minimum wages are effective will be those paying the lowest wages. They will usually involve unskilled or, at best, semi-skilled labour. In most of them the workers will not be members of unions. Thus, the market structures in which minimum wages are likely to be most effective include both those in which competitive conditions obtain and those in which employers exercise monopsony power. The effects on employment are different in the two cases.

### Competitive labour markets

The consequences for employment of an effective minimum wage are unambiguous when the labour market is competitive and labour is homogeneous. By raising the wage that employers must pay, minimum wage legislation leads to a reduction in the quantity of labour that is demanded and an increase in the quantity of labour that is supplied. As a result, the actual level of employment falls, and a pool is created of people who would like to work in those jobs but cannot find employment. This does not necessarily lead to an increase in recorded unemployment, because those who are unsuccessful in seeking a highly paid job can be expected to settle for a lower-paid one after some time. This situation is exactly analogous to the one that arises when a union succeeds in setting a wage above the competitive equilibrium wage, as was illustrated in Figure 11.5. The excess supply of labour at the minimum wage also creates incentives for people to evade the law by working below the legal minimum wage.

In competitive labour markets, effective minimum wage laws raise the wages of those who remain employed but also cause some reduction in employment.

### Monopsonistic labour markets

By effectively flattening out the labour supply curve, a minimum wage law can simultaneously increase both wages and employment in monopsonistic labour markets. The circumstances in which this can happen are the same as those in which a union that is facing a monopsonistic employer succeeds in setting a wage above the wage that the employer would otherwise pay, as was shown in Figure 11.6. Of course, if the minimum wage is raised above the competitive wage, employment will start to fall, as in the union case. When it is set at the competitive level, however, the minimum wage can protect workers against monopsony power *and* lead to increases in employment.

A summary of the evidence of the impact of minimum wages in the UK and elsewhere is provided as a case study at the end of this chapter.

# Heterogeneity, incentives, and monitoring costs

In the first part of this chapter we studied the broad forces that create wage differentials between different groups of workers. For some purposes, it is a useful simplification to assume that workers of each type are identical individuals. But to understand other labour market issues, we need to recognize that no two workers are identical, while each can choose how to behave on the job. Labour market institutions evolve in subtle ways to cope with problems that arise from heterogeneity of employees and incomplete information about worker characteristics.

Individuals differ from each other. They all respond to the same incentives, but they respond differently. Given the same wage, some will work harder than others; some have more ability than others; with the same amount of effort, some produce more and get better results than others. This applies to all employees, whether working in production, design, planning, or supervision.

## Asymmetric information

Firms might like to reward good workers more than indifferent workers, but it is difficult to know one from the other in many work situations. Generally, workers know more about their effectiveness than does their employer.

### Adverse selection

**Adverse selection** is a problem that arises most commonly in insurance markets where, faced with the same rates, high-risk individuals are more inclined to apply for insurance than low-risk ones. The relevance of this to labour markets is that firms do not know all the characteristics of workers before they are hired and they want to act in such a way as to attract 'good' workers and not 'bad' ones. A firm seeking to hire people usually advertises a particular job with an associated pay or pay range. From the pool of those who meet the paper specifications, more of the applicants are likely to be lower-quality workers, who find that wage a good bargain, than higher-quality workers, who know they can get a good wage elsewhere. This would not be a problem if the employer knew as much about his prospective employees as did the employees themselves. But this is an obvious case of asymmetric information—you know more about yourself, your work habits, and your strengths and weaknesses than any outsider.

### Moral hazard

**Moral hazard** is defined as an adverse change of behaviour that results from an agreement or contract. A common example is an insurance-induced alteration of behaviour that makes the event insured against more likely to occur. For example, accident insurance may make a car driver act with less caution, and fire insurance may make a home owner be less careful about turning off electrical appliances before going out. Thus, moral hazard arises when insurance leads people to take risks that they would avoid if they did not have an insurance policy. In the context of labour markets, the relevance of moral hazard is that some forms of labour contract may lead the employee to change her behaviour in ways that are harmful to the firm. For example, if the employee is on a fixed salary for life, she may decide to take it easy and just put in the minimum amount of effort consistent with fulfilling the contract. Incentives for good performance and the monitoring of the outcome thus become important.

## Costly monitoring

It is difficult and costly for management to monitor its employees to find out how well each is contributing to the production process.

### Contracts and performance monitoring

When you purchase a haircut, you have a clear idea of what you expect to get and you can accurately judge the quality of the service you receive. When a firm hires a divisional manager, it knows that it wants good work but cannot say specifically what the manager should be doing at each moment in her work day. Furthermore, it is not easy to judge how much of the division's subsequent performance is due to the manager's efforts and how much to forces beyond the manager's control.

Many modern employment situations are better thought of as an ongoing relationship rather than as the equivalent of a purchase of a specific, exactly definable labour service. Hence employment contracts are often referred to as *relational contracts*. These contracts do not attempt to cover all of the many contingencies that could arise in a job. Instead, they set out general duties to be fulfilled in the post and leave the details to be decided by an evolving interaction between employer and employee. In many modern jobs it is not even desirable in principle to establish an exact job description because the nature of the work is continually evolving. For example, as recently as the 1980s a secretary's job involved taking handwritten notes from dictation and creating hard copy using a typewriter. Today the same job typically involves taking draft documents already in electronic form and developing them using a word-processor package. Instead of typing letters and addressing envelopes, the secretary (who is now more likely to be called a PA) will be sending email messages and taking on a much wider range of organizational functions. A precise 1980 job description would have been a hindrance to needed changes.

**Under relational contracts, neither employer nor employee has an exact or agreed expectation of each other's detailed behaviour.**

The firm does not know the marginal product of each employee. The employees do not know precisely what they need to do to get promoted and avoid being sacked. Neither workers nor firms can make accurate decisions based upon full information.

### The principal–agent problem

The management wishes to motivate employees to work in the firm's best interest, while employees often have different and conflicting motivations. Management would like to design incentive systems that motivate workers to provide the type of effort that it requires. This is known as the **principal–agent problem**. One context in which this problem arises is in the potential conflict of interest between owners of firms (shareholders), who are the principals in this context, and the managers of the firm, who are the agents. Shareholders want to maximize the value of their shares, but managers may have an incentive to overpay themselves and to empire-build. Solutions to this version of the problem are generally sought by trying to align the interests of both groups, for example by giving senior managers share options or profit-related bonuses. A similar analysis can help us to understand the relationship between senior management and all other employees. The bosses want workers to work hard and achieve production targets, but not all forms of employee behaviour can be observed or measured. So what incentives will persuade employees to buy into the goals set by senior management and behave productively?

An obvious principal–agent problem that arises with relational contracts, from the perspective of the firm, is that employees have some range of discretion about how hard they work, and they may have objectives of their own that are different from those of the employer.

The firm (the principal) cannot monitor accurately the performance of many of its employees (the agents).

It is often too costly even to try, and in many jobs it would be impossible even if money were no object. In such circumstances, the firm needs to design mechanisms that will induce its employees to act in the firm's interests. In general, unless there is costly monitoring of the agents' behaviour, the problem cannot be completely solved.

**Principal–agent analysis shows that, when employees have some range of discretion, their self-interested behaviour will make profits lower than in a 'perfect', frictionless world in which principals act as their own agents, or agents always do exactly what the principals want.**

Much labour market behaviour that seems odd at first sight has evolved to deal—more or less effectively—with the principal–agent problem. For example, people put in positions of trust are often paid much more than is needed to induce them to take these jobs. Why should principals pay their agents more than they need to pay to fill the jobs? The explanation is that agents who are paid much more than they could earn in other jobs have an incentive not to violate the trust placed in them. If they do violate the trust and are caught, they lose the premium attached to the job and are unlikely to find another such job elsewhere.

## Efficiency wages

The theory of competitive markets predicts that excess supply causes price to fall until the excess supply is eliminated—that is, until demand equals supply. Often this does not happen in labour markets. In the face of excess supply, firms do not typically cut wages, even though such a move would seem to enhance profits. Why?

Employers are worried about the quality and performance of the heterogeneous workers that they hire as well as their price. The wage that yields the best combination of price and quality of worker is known as the **efficiency wage**.

The theory of the *efficiency wage* helps to explain why it may be optimal for firms to set wages that are permanently above the level that would clear the labour market. Efficiency wage theory applies to hiring, to productivity on the job, and to worker turnover.

### Efficiency in hiring

Firms do not know the characteristics of specific workers until after they have sunk costs into hiring and training them. Good workers know who they are and are likely to have a higher reservation wage than bad workers. The *reservation wage* is the lowest wage at which a person is prepared to work for a particular firm. By lowering the wage it is offering, a firm will significantly lower the average ability of the workers applying for its jobs. This tendency for a firm that pays lower wages to attract poor-quality workers is a case of *adverse selection*. As a result, paying lower wages can make the firm worse off.

In labour markets with informational asymmetries, where unobserved characteristics of workers are correlated with the reservation wage, it will generally be optimal for firms to pay wages that exceed their employees' reservation wages.

### Productivity on the job

If wages are so low that workers are just indifferent between staying and losing their job, they are unlikely to do more than the minimum required. Workers are likely to give greater effort if they feel they are being well rewarded. A worker will then expect to be much worse off if she loses the job, and will be aware of a queue of good-quality workers prepared to work for the high wage. The high wage improves on-the-job efficiency.

### Minimizing turnover

Many firms find that high quit rates are costly because they must invest in training new workers. Firms are therefore reluctant to lower wages for existing workers, even in the face of an excess supply of labour. Workers who are already inside the company and know its work practices are worth retaining, even at premium wages. New workers, though possibly cheaper, may not be as good, and will be costly to train.

Efficiency wage theory says that firms will find it advantageous to pay high enough wages that working is a clearly superior alternative to being laid off. This will minimize labour turnover and improve the quality of workers' effort.

When considering the supply curve of labour, we saw that high wages may induce less work from workers who can choose how many hours they work—because of an income effect that is stronger than the substitution effect (see page 218). High efficiency wages give the workers a different choice, which is to work hard for a high reward or not to work at all (or, perhaps, to work in another job at the much lower average wage). By posing an all-or-nothing choice, employers alleviate the disincentive effects of high wages. Workers who do not work hard enough risk losing their high-paying job. This *potential-loss-of-income effect* reinforces the substitution effect, and for many workers encourages them to adopt the hard-work/high-pay solution—at least for those who are fortunate enough to have this choice.

## Signalling

Participants in markets with asymmetric information will develop informal criteria for signalling information about some of these unseen characteristics. Employers who pay a high efficiency wage signal that they are interested in high-quality staff and are prepared to pay them well. Educational qualifications provide a signal from potential employees. Hopefully your university degree, or higher education certificate, will indicate that you have acquired some useful knowledge and skills. However, another important function of the degree you will acquire is to convince potential employers that you are ambitious, hard working, intelligent, and committed to self-improvement—just the kind of person that every employer is looking for! The degree creates a signal about your personal characteristics independent of the subject of the degree. In selection situations the signal about who you are may play as important a role as what you have learned.

## Internal labour markets

Most manual and other unskilled workers have little or no expectation of advancement or even of long-term employment. They are often paid an hourly rate and have little job security. In contrast, many skilled manual workers, most white-collar workers, and virtually all technical, managerial, and professional staff have a long-term employment relationship, which provides a career path within the firm. Typically, there are limited entry points into the firm and most senior posts are filled by promotions from within the firm. These workers operate in what is known as an **internal labour market**, composed of a firm and its long-term employees—that is, the market is internal to the firm. Such a market has only limited connections with external labour markets and its structure reflects the needs and traditions of each specific firm. The market offers a *job ladder* for the firm's long-term employees, with most employees starting somewhere near the bottom of the ladder and working their way up throughout their career.

### Pay and promotion

Firms with internal labour markets do not generally try to assess their employees' marginal productivity and then pay them accordingly. Instead, firms have a number of defined job grades, with pay rates attached to the job rather than to any individual's productivity. Employees generally improve their pay by moving up the ladder of promotion. Good work in the current job has a potential payoff more in terms of promotion prospects than in terms of dramatically increased current pay.

There are at least three reasons why internal labour markets may be more efficient than tying individuals' pay to their individual performance. First, most of the relevant jobs involve a great deal of learning. A long-term employment relationship, with a potential for promotion, creates an incentive for employees to invest in acquiring skills that will benefit the firm. These firm-specific skills will take time to acquire and will take even longer to generate a payoff to the firm. Hence to achieve the benefits of this learning effect, firms have to offer the prospect of both long-term employment and future promotion.

The second reason why internal labour markets may be efficient derives from efficiency wage theory. The incentives for good performance built into the efficiency wage require a long-term employment relationship. The 'good' workers are attracted to the firm by high rewards and also by a commitment on the part of firms to a high degree of employment stability and 'good prospects'. Hence both employees and employers are likely to generate a more productive relationship via mutual longer-term commitment than via temporary employment contracts and minimal mutual commitment.

The third factor supporting internal labour markets is that successful firms require long-term strategic thinking from their senior staff. The ability to take and implement long-term strategies is not something that shows up or can be tested over a short horizon. Hence successful firms have significant numbers of senior managers who have been selected as a result of observing their performance within the company, and who have sufficient expectation of continuing employment that they are prepared to take a long-term view. A manager who does not expect to stay with a firm very long may postpone important investments, while one who sees his own future as tied to the success of the firm will want to ensure its continued survival.

**The internal labour market increases the convergence of interests between the employee and the firm, thereby reducing principal–agent problems.**

## Tournaments

One way to think of an internal labour market is as a *tournament*. Workers enter the tournament when they join a firm on the lower rungs of the ladder. Workers at each level compete with each other to show the senior management that they are most worthy of promotion. Periodically, when a more senior job becomes vacant, someone from the grade immediately below the vacant post is chosen to progress up the ladder. As there are fewer senior jobs than junior jobs, not everybody can progress up the ladder at the same pace. The winner of the tournament is the one who reaches the post of chief executive.

In an internal-labour-market tournament, the pay of senior executives is as much about motivating everybody in the organization as it is about paying a 'fair' compensation for the incumbent of any specific post. The £1 million salary paid to a chief executive officer (CEO) may be more important in terms of motivating junior staff to strive to rise to that exalted post than in terms of rewarding the current CEO for his efforts. Even though those who enter a golf or tennis tournament know that they cannot all win, tournaments with the greatest prize for winning still attract the best players and tend to bring out the best in them. The issue of CEO pay is discussed further in Case Study 2 at the end of this chapter.

The tournament structure of rewards has three advantages for firms. First, when a candidate is selected for promotion, only enough information is needed to make relative judgements among potential candidates. No absolute or detailed performance measures are needed. This economizes on the need to acquire costly information, which may in any case be unreliable.

The second advantage is that pay ranges are set in advance for each job, so time is not wasted on individual pay negotiations with each and every employee. An employee who wants more pay must work for a promotion, so bargaining time is saved. Equally, there is no incentive for employers to argue about performance in order to avoid having to pay bonuses.

The third advantage is that tournaments reduce the problems of asymmetric information. Employees who are chosen for promotion from within the firm will have become well known to their superiors, and so there is little uncertainty about their characteristics. Equally, employees who are promoted already know a great deal about the functioning of the company, so they can become effective in their new position more quickly than would be likely with an outsider.

**The promotion path in an internal labour market can be thought of as a tournament in which higher pay rates in more senior jobs create an incentive for employees to progress up the career ladder.**

## Seniority and MRP

The incentive issues discussed above suggest that, where there is a long-term relationship between firm and workers, firms will find it efficient to reward loyalty and long service. Hence it will generally be true that longer-serving workers will get higher rewards than younger workers. The rewards for long service will come via higher wages and company pension schemes, which will naturally reward long service with a higher pension. A pension can be thought of as deferred wages.

The need to reward long service means that on average there is a cross-subsidy passing from young workers, who get less than their current marginal revenue products, to older workers, who get more. However, the young workers have the encouragement of knowing that they themselves will eventually benefit from this cross-subsidy when they themselves become older workers, provided they stay with the firm. Thus, *ceteris paribus*, expectations of lifetime earnings will be the same for both groups.

# CASE STUDIES

## 1. The earnings of superstars

Small groups of people in many professions are often paid extraordinarily large salaries. In July 2006 Chelsea signed Andre Shevchenko from AC Milan for a transfer fee reported to be in excess of £30 million. He was given a four-year contract which was said to include a wage in excess of £110,000 per week. In 2004 David Beckham was transferred to Real Madrid from Manchester United for £25 million and Beckham himself was reported to have earned a total income of around £17 million in 2004 alone, when all his sponsorship deals were added to what his club paid him. In 2007 Beckham signed a five-year contract to play for LA Galaxy reported to be worth $250 million over five years. In 2005 Michael Schumacher earned $60 million from driving Formula 1 racing cars. In 2004 pop singer Robbie Williams was reported to have signed a £40 million five-record deal with EMI. The earnings of Coldplay in 2005 were reported at £37 million and those for U2 at £35 million. These rewards for pop stars and top sports stars are not new. Michael Jordan, the basketball player, made US$100 million in 1998, Mike Tyson the boxer made US$75 million in 1996, and singer/songwriter Sir Paul McCartney amassed a nearly £1 billion fortune out of his career in popular music and still had an income of £25 million in 2005—even though his earliest hit records with the Beatles were in the 1960s.

Why are superstars so highly paid? Shouldn't market incentives encourage others to compete for these large rewards, with the end result that the massive rewards for a few would fall and be replaced by more modest rewards for many? On the contrary, forces in the modern economy appear to be increasing the gap between superstars and the rest. There are three components to the explanation.

First, the general increase in real wealth over time has created an increase in demand for output in the sectors in which superstars perform.

Second, in some of these activities there is a premium to being the very best over what the merely competent can command. For example, if you are wealthy and need a lawyer or a heart surgeon, you are going to pay for the best; someone who is good but not the best will not do. Equally, if you want your team to win the Premier League, you need the best striker in the country—coming second is commendable but not good enough. Hence those who are 'the best' may be only, say, 10 per cent better than the bunch behind them, but they may command a substantial wage premium just because there is no one better. (The *MRP* of being the best greatly exceeds the *MRP* of being second.)

Tiger Woods, for example, the world's number one ranked golfer for five years in a row between 2000 and 2004, earned about US$6 million in prize money in 2003 alone and over US$60 million in endorsements. In 2005 he earned around $87 million. However, he is only on average about two shots per 18-hole round better than a player ranked around number 100. Yet the 100th ranked player earned around $1 million in prize money and endorsements combined. So Tiger, who was less than 2 per cent better at golf than the 100th ranked player, earned 85 times as much.

Third, modern communications have increased the size of the market over which stars compete. What used to be a series of local markets where the person who was the best in each market earned a moderately high income have become a single global market in which people compete to be the best in the world. The winners earn huge sums because they serve huge markets—TV, films, and pop stars are obvious examples. Why listen to a local opera company when you can listen to Pavarotti and Domingo on a CD? Why listen to a local band when you can access the latest global music hits, played by those who wrote them? The marginal revenue products of top stars have been vastly increased by modern communications media that allow them to reach audiences thousands of times larger than could be reached a century ago.

## 2. CEO pay—fat cats or optimal incentives?

Can chief executives of large companies possibly be 'worth' their very large salaries? Multi-million dollar salaries are not uncommon in the United States; neither are salaries of £1 million or more for UK chief executives and chairmen. Some people believe that these high salaries for British and American CEOs are an inefficiency caused by the principal–agent problem. In this view, CEOs have escaped shareholders' control. Their high pay is evidence that shareholders are being ripped off. If this were true, the solution would be to give genuinely independent non-CEOs more power in setting compensation, or to give shareholders a vote on CEO pay. There are good economic reasons, however, why high payments to CEOs are often needed for the incentives they create within the company. There are three elements to the incentive issue.

The first is the tournament model of internal incentives. High pay for CEOs provides an incentive for all the workers in the firm to aspire to the top job. Therefore, the pay is not justified solely by the performance of the specific incumbent CEO: rather, it is desirable for the extra effort it motivates from those who have any serious prospects of eventually becoming CEO. For them, high CEO pay may increase loyalty and the ambition to achieve promotion.

The second element is that the CEO does have to be motivated by his rewards, because there is no further promotion available. Hence, while middle-managers may be motivated partly by the prospect of moving up the promotion ladder, the CEO needs other motivation.

The third element relates to the incentives to take risks. If employees are risk-averse, they will take the safe option rather than risk being dismissed for making a difficult decision that goes wrong. However, in a modern dynamic economy firms need to be at least risk-neutral, if not risk-taking. This means that CEOs need an incentive to take risks in the interest of the long-term health of the company. One way to encourage this is to offer a reward if risk-taking pays off, while imposing no penalty when failures occur. Just such a reward profile is offered by **share options**. These options become valuable if the company's shares rise in value, but carry no cost to the CEO if the options expire worthless. Share options may encourage senior executives to take risks. A significant proportion of CEO compensation involves just such incentives.

One further important use of employment-contingent options to buy shares in the future is to bind managers to the firm. A young firm in a dynamic industry may not be able to pay its executives a large current salary. It thus risks having them leave, taking their firm-specific experience with them. As well as providing an incentive to take risks, options to buy the firm's shares in the future reduce the incentive to leave for a higher-paying job. After all, the stock options become worthless when the manager leaves.

Of course, the actual rewards of top management cannot always be justified on incentive grounds. There are undoubtedly many cases where senior executives have overpaid themselves, and others where they have expropriated funds of both shareholders and pension fund members.

## 3. The impact of minimum wages

The UK introduced a statutory national minimum wage in 1999 and there has now been a considerable amount of research on its impact. The following extract from *Government Evidence to the Low Pay Commission on the National Minimum Wage* summarizes the evidence.[4]

### Employment effects

*In the main the UK academic literature has not found significant evidence of negative employment consequences from the introduction and subsequent upratings of the adult national minimum wage (NMW). Stewart . . . used individual-level longitudinal data to compare the employment experience of individual workers whose pay would have had to be increased to comply with the new minimum, with that of a similar group who were not directly affected. He found little evidence that the introduction of the NMW had an adverse impact on the probability of subsequent employment of those affected. There was also little evidence that the 2000 and 2001 upratings had adverse employment consequences. Dickens and Draca . . . considered the 2003 uprating, finding insignificant disemployment effects.*

*Some exceptions to the evidence include Galindo-Reuda and Pereira . . . who, using a matched employer–employee data set, found some evidence that employment growth had been significantly lower in some exposed service sectors around the introduction of the minimum wage. They suggested that the minimum wage might have a slight disemployment effect that could have gone unnoticed (in absolute terms) when the level of the minimum wage was low and economic conditions benign. Machin and Wilson . . . , looking at employment in the UK care homes sector before and after the introduction of the NMW, found some evidence of employment reductions, but were unable to detect any effect on home closures.*

*International evidence on the employment effects on adults also tends to point to these being limited. An OECD study [by] Gregg . . . confirms only small employment effects from increases in minimum wage. Wolfson and Belman . . . found that the increase in the US federal minimum wage between 1947 and 1997 raised average wages in many low-paid industries, but the effects on employment were typically mixed and insignificant. Neumark, Schweitzer and Wascher . . . do however present evidence that the employment and hours of low-paid workers fall following increases in the minimum wage.*

### Effects of working hours

*There is some evidence that the introduction of the NMW in the UK may have led to a reduction in working hours. Stewart and*

---

[4] The full document and the literature references (not reproduced here) are available on http://www.dti.gov.uk/er/nmw/government_evidence_LPC_2005.pdf

*Swaffield . . . found that the introduction of the NMW led to a fall in the paid hours of both male and female low-wage workers. Their New Earnings Survey estimates indicate a reduction of between one and two basic hours per week. Labour Force Survey estimated total effects on basic hours were greater for men and lower for women than the corresponding NES estimates. But no evidence was found of an impact of either the October 2000 or the October 2001 uprating on adult men.*

## Effects on the distribution of earnings

*The academic evidence of the effects of the NMW on the distribution of earnings tends, on balance, to suggest that there is little evidence of spillovers further up the earnings distribution. This is somewhat at odds with the empirical observation in the UK that the bottom quarter of the earnings distribution has experienced faster growth than the median since the introduction of the NMW. But clearly other factors could also have impacted on the distribution over this period, and it is a legitimate area for further research.*

*Dickens and Manning . . . investigated the impact of the NMW on the distribution of wages in care homes. They concluded that there was virtually no evidence for spillovers from the NMW. Metcalf . . . also finds no evidence for spillovers, with workers in the bottom decile of pay experiencing above-average pay rises between 1998 and 2002 and there being no effects further up the wage distribution. Similarly, in the UK Neumark, Wchweitzer and Wascher present evidence that increases in the minimum wage are felt by low wage individuals, while individuals higher up the wage distribution are little affected.*

## Young workers

*The academic evidence for the impacts of minimum wages on the young is a little more mixed, with somewhat more evidence for disemployment effects than is the case with adults.*

*In the UK it is probably too early to draw any firm conclusions on the introduction of the minimum wage for 16–17 year olds, although there are a number of recent studies. Frayne and*

*Goodman . . . estimated the impact of introducing an NMW for 16 and 17 year olds on employment and education outcomes. They found that every 1 per cent increase in the 16–17 year old wage resulted in a 3.6 per cent decrease in employment in hours amongst this group, implying that a minimum wage of £3 would reduce employment in hours by around 6 per cent. Dickerson and Jones . . . found that the largest single influence on the decision to remain in full-time education at 16 is GCSE attainment. Using GCSE attainment as an indicator of ability suggests that a minimum wage set between £2.50 and £4.00 will have negligible effects on education participation. Neathey. Ritchie and Silverman . . . found little evidence in the retail and hospitality sectors of a link between the minimum wage and decisions to employ young workers of various ages.*

*Several international studies have found evidence that minimum wages can have disemployment effects on the young. Campolieti, Fang and Gunderson compared transitions from employment to non-employment by youths in Canada over the period 1991–99. They found that minimum wage increases during the period of interest increased the transitions from employment to non-employment by around 6 percentage points. These effects implied minimum wage elasticities of around −0.4. Wessels . . . found that increases in the NMW in the USA had a negative effect on the labour force participation of 16–19 year olds.*

## Effects on firms

*UK research has not found strong evidence of negative effects of the NMW on firms. Machin, Draca and Van Reenen . . . showed that although profitability fell in firms that were most affected by the introduction of the NMW, low wage firms were not forced out of business by the higher wage costs resulting from its introduction. They were also unable to detect evidence of higher wage costs being passed on in terms of higher prices. Forth and O'Mahony . . . also found no evidence of the NMW leading to a general increase in unit labout costs. (Department of Trade and Industry, November 2005: www.dti.gov.uk)*

# Conclusion

Labour is the most important input into any modern firm. A hundred years ago it was mainly the manual effort of workers that was being hired. Today, however, the vast majority of workers are hired not for their physical strength, but rather for their mental skills. Today brainpower rather than muscle power drives business success.

Brainpower is a much more complicated input to manage than was muscle power. The mental ability of

potential new employees is difficult to assess and the effort of brain workers is hard to monitor accurately. Yet the success of a firm in the long term depends crucially upon selecting, keeping, and motivating a stock of brainpower. The institutions and practices discussed in this chapter have evolved to provide the structure within which a company's most talented employees are nurtured, motivated, and developed.

# SUMMARY

### Wage differentials

- Equilibrium wage differentials can arise between jobs because (*a*) each requires different degrees of physical or mental abilities, (*b*) each requires different amounts of human capital acquired through costly formal education or on-the-job training, (*c*) some jobs are closed to people who could fill them as a result of discrimination, and (*d*) the markets for the types of worker needed in different jobs have different competitive structures.

- In perfectly competitive input markets, wages are set by demand and supply and there is no unemployment in equilibrium. In monopsonistic markets, wages and employment are less than their competitive levels, but there is no unemployment in equilibrium.

- If a union enters a perfectly competitive market, it can raise wages above the competitive level at the cost of lowering employment and creating a pool of people who would like to work at the union wage but cannot. If a union enters a monopsonistic labour market, it can raise wages *and* employment to the competitive level. If it raises wages beyond that point, employment will fall.

- Unions and professional associations can sometimes restrict the supply of labour and thereby achieve wages above the competitive equilibrium without creating a pool of unemployed.

- Minimum wage laws have a similar effect to the setting of wages by unions. If the market was monopsonistic before the minimum wage is imposed, wages *and* employment can be raised. If it was competitive, wages can be raised only at the expense of some (possibly small) reduction in employment in the affected occupation.

### Heterogeneity, incentives, and monitoring costs

- Today's labour markets are complicated by the fact that brainpower is extremely heterogeneous but it is hard for employers to discern the full characteristics of individual workers.

- Many employment contracts are relational contracts, which do not specify in detail what workers have to do. This creates the potential for principal–agent problems, where the hired employees act, in part, in their own interest rather than that of the employer.

- Solutions to the principal–agent problem involve some combination of incentives and monitoring.

- Most skilled, managerial, and professional workers now find themselves in internal labour markets that have some of the characteristics of a tournament. Here the main incentive for lower- and middle-ranking staff is to achieve promotion. Higher pay generally attaches to more senior jobs, and the competition to gain promotion can be thought of as a tournament.

# TOPICS FOR REVIEW

- Causes of equilibrium wage differentials
- Human capital
- Formal education and on-the-job training
- Wage differentials arising from the departure from perfect competition on the demand and the supply sides of labour markets

- Relational contracts
- Principal–agent problems in labour markets
- Efficiency wages
- Signalling in the labour market
- Internal and tournament labour markets

# QUESTIONS

1 Using the MRP data and the supply curve of labour from questions 1–3 of Chapter 10 on page 227, calculate how many workers would be hired and what wage would be paid if the hiring firm were a profit-maximizing monopsonist.

2 How would the outcome in question 1 differ if the monopsonist could price-discriminate and pay each worker the minimum wage for which she would work?

3 How would the outcome in question 1 change if a trade union were able to impose a going wage for all workers of £500 per week?

4 Why are wage rates not equal in different jobs, even in equilibrium?

5 What are the main difference between labour markets and markets for homogeneous commodities?

6 How does the efficiency wage help to solve the problems of recruitment, monitoring, and retention?

7 In what ways is the principal–agent problem manifested in employment relationships, and what measures are available to ameliorate the problem?

8 How does asymmetric information affect labour hiring decisions, and what role might signalling play in this process?

9 What is different about an internal labour market (as compared with the goods markets that we have studied earlier in this book)?

# Chapter 12

# CAPITAL, INVESTMENT, AND NEW TECHNOLOGY

After studying human inputs into production, we now turn to physical inputs. What differences are there between the firm's decisions on how much capital equipment to put in place and how much labour to hire? What factors have to be taken into account in the decision to invest? How does technical change influence the way in which firms operate, and how does it affect the competitive process? These are some of the questions we address in this chapter.

In particular, you will learn that:

- Physical capital differs from other variable inputs in that it is sometimes 'lumpy' and is generally durable.

- In order to evaluate a potential investment in capital equipment, firms need to calculate whether it adds net value to the firm.

- The present value of any future income stream is what it would be worth paying today to obtain that future income stream.

- An investment adds net value to a firm if the present value of the income stream generated exceeds the present value of the extra costs incurred.

- Firms will invest up to the point where the net present value of the project ceases to be positive. This is conceptually equivalent to the principle that a profit-maximizing firm will set marginal cost equal to marginal revenue.

- All investments are risky to some degree, as their value relies on future income streams and the future is uncertain.

- The recent revolution in information and communication technology (ICT) has important implications for the way firms work and for the economy in general.

Inputs that can be replaced, either by being manufactured, as is the case with machines, or by reproducing themselves, as do people, animals, or plants, are called **renewable resources**. Inputs that cannot be replaced, such as fossil fuels, are called **non-renewable** or **exhaustible resources**. Physical capital and non-renewable resources are similar inputs in that each is a stock of valuable things that gets used up in the process of producing goods and services. They are different in that physical capital can be replaced while non-renewable resources cannot. A new machine can always be created to replace one that wears out, but when a barrel of oil is used there is a permanent reduction in the world's total stock of oil. In this chapter we focus on renewable inputs, but we provide an extended discussion of the issues surrounding non-renewable resources on our website.[1]

---

[1] Reference here to our web link: http://www.oxfordtextbooks.co.uk/orc/lipsey11e/

# Capital as an input

The capital stock consists of all those produced goods that are used in the production of other goods and services. Factories, machines, tools, computers, roads, bridges, houses, and railways are a few examples. Because capital is a produced input, it is a renewable resource, though technical changes over time mean that the characteristics of capital change over time. Here we are always talking about physical capital, such as machines, and not about financial capital. Clearly, the two are connected, as firms often need to raise finance in order to purchase capital equipment. But our focus is on the equipment itself and not on the way in which it is financed.

## The pure return on capital

For a firm, the decision to invest in capital will be guided by whether the extra revenue that the capital generates justifies the cost.[2] To calculate the *return on capital*, we take the receipts from the sale of the output that the capital helps to make and subtract all variable costs of production. This gives us the **gross return on capital**.[3] It is convenient to divide this gross return into four components using concepts defined in Chapter 6 (see pages 115–18).

1. *Depreciation* is an allowance for the decrease in the value of a capital good over time resulting from its use in production and its obsolescence. Depreciation is often assumed to occur at a constant rate.

2. The *pure return on capital* is the amount that capital could earn in a riskless investment in equilibrium. When expressed as a return per £1 worth of capital invested, the result is called the **pure rate of interest**.

3. The *risk premium* compensates the owners for the actual risks of the enterprise.

4. *Pure* or *economic profit* is the residual after all other deductions have been made from the gross return. It may be positive, negative, or zero.

The *gross return* on capital is the sum of these four items. The *net return* is the sum of the last three—that is, the gross return minus depreciation.

In a competitive economy, positive and negative pure profits are a signal that resources should be reallocated, because earnings exceed opportunity costs in some lines of production and fall short of costs elsewhere. Economic profits are thus a disequilibrium phenomenon.

To study the return on capital in its simplest form, consider an economy that is in a competitive equilibrium. Thus, economic profits are zero in every productive activity. This does not mean that the owners of capital get nothing; it means only that the gross return to capital does not include an element of pure profit. The *equilibrium* net return on capital is therefore composed of components 2 and 3 minus 1.

To simplify things further at the outset, imagine a world of perfect certainty: everyone knows what the return on an existing new unit of capital will be in any of its possible uses. Since there is no risk, the gross return on capital would not include a risk premium.

We have now simplified to the point where the net return on capital is all pure return (item 2 on the above list), while the gross return is pure return plus depreciation (items 1 and 2). What determines this pure return on capital? This is the return that varies from time to time and from place to place under the influence of economic forces. Broadly speaking, it will be determined by the overall balance between saving and investment in the economy as a whole. Risk and disequilibrium differentials are merely additions to that pure return.[4]

## Implications of durability

Next we consider an important issue that arises because capital is durable—a machine, a factory building, or a computer programme lasts for years. To see some of the implications of durability, it is helpful to think of a capital good's lifetime as being divided into short periods which we refer to as production periods, or rental periods. The present time is the current period. Future time is one, two, three (and so on) periods hence.

The durability of capital goods makes it necessary to distinguish between the capital good itself and the flow of services that it provides in a given production period. For example, a firm could rent the use of a building for some

---

[2] Households and governments may have slightly different reasons to invest, but firms can be assumed to wish to maximize profits.

[3] This simplified example assumes that capital is the only fixed input.

[4] We are implicitly assuming a constant price level. Under inflationary conditions we would need to distinguish the nominal return on capital, where everything is measured in nominal monetary units, from the real return, where nominal values are deflated by a price index. This distinction is discussed in Chapter 3.

period of time, or it could buy the building outright. This distinction is just a particular instance of the general distinction between flows and stocks that we first encountered in Box 3.1 on page 38.

If a firm hires a piece of capital equipment for some period of time—for example, one lorry for one month—it pays a price for the privilege. If the firm buys the lorry outright, it pays a different (and higher) price for the purchase. Consider each of these prices in turn.

### Rental price

The *rental price of capital* is the amount that a firm pays to obtain the services of a capital good for a specific period of time. The rental price of one week's use of a piece of capital is analogous to the weekly wage rate that is the price of hiring the services of labour.

Just as a profit-maximizing firm operating in competitive markets continues to hire labour until its marginal revenue product (*MRP*) equals its wage, so will the firm go on hiring capital until its *MRP* equals its rental price. Since in a competitive market all firms will face the same rental price, all firms that are in equilibrium will have the same *MRP* of each type of capital.

A capital good may also be used by the firm that owns it. In this case the firm does not pay out any rental fee. However, the rental price is the amount that the firm could charge if it leased its capital to another firm. It is thus the *opportunity cost* to the firm of using the capital good itself. This rental price is the *implicit* price, reflecting the value to the firm of the services of its own capital that it is using during the current production period.

Whether the firm pays the rental price explicitly or calculates it as an implicit cost of using its own capital, the profit-maximizing firm will employ capital up to the point where the rental price of a capital good is just equal to its marginal revenue product.

### Purchase price

The price that a firm pays to buy a capital good, say a machine, is the *purchase price of capital*. When a firm buys such a machine outright, it obtains the marginal revenue product that the machine is expected to yield over its lifetime. The firm's willingness to buy the machine is, naturally enough, related to the value that it places now on this stream of *expected* receipts over future time-periods and how this compares with the cost of the machine.

The term 'expected' emphasizes that the firm is usually uncertain about the prices at which it will be able to sell its outputs in the future. For the sake of simplicity, we assume that the firm knows the future *MRP*s.

## Implications of lumpiness of some capital goods

While virtually all physical capital is durable, some capital is also *lumpy*. This means that it cannot be divided into small units and still serve the same purpose. The Channel Tunnel, for example, would not be much use if it stopped half way between England and France; and the Severn Bridge has to be long enough to span the river—a shorter structure would not do. Some manufacturing plants may also have a minimum functional scale and/or involve pieces of equipment that are large and thus also costly.

The economic implication of lumpiness is that the option of having a bit more or a bit less may not always be available in investment decisions. Rather, the choice will be of an 'all or nothing' nature. For example, you either build a fifth terminal at Heathrow Airport or you make do with four. And if you do build, then it has to be of a sufficient scale to handle a substantial number of large aircraft and the thousands of passengers that they will carry. This in turn implies the need for space for maintenance facilities, luggage handling, customs halls, restaurants, executive lounges, airline offices, etc. So the facility is either of substantial size or it is not built at all, although on the drawing board you can make a marginal decision to build it a bit bigger or a bit smaller.

Big investment projects, like the Channel Tunnel or the new Wembley Stadium, once started, take a long time to complete, in some cases many years. This makes it particularly difficult to estimate the cost of the project in advance, as prices and wages may change over time and unexpected technical problems may emerge along the way. We return to this issue below when we discuss how the riskiness of a project affects the decision to invest.

For now, a key issue to notice about decisions relating to capital projects is that a central problem is how to evaluate costs and revenues from a project when they accrue at different periods of time. Most capital projects will involve up-front costs, but the revenue will be generated over some future time-periods, which could be many years.

## Present value of future returns

When we looked at decisions of firms on how much of a variable input to hire, we came to the conclusion that, to maximize profits, inputs should be hired up to the point where the marginal cost of the last unit of input was just equal to the value of the extra revenue generated by hiring that last unit. These values were easy to compare because they were happening at the same point in time.

**Box 12.1** **The value of a brand**

Why is a Rolex watch more expensive than a similar watch that looks as good and tells the time just as well? Why are Gucci shoes more expensive than similar leather shoes from a less well-known shoemaker? Why are specific designer labels associated with higher priced fashion items in clothing shops? This is to do with the economics of branding. Designers and manufacturers of cars, clothes, watches, and many other consumer items attempt to create a distinctive image of quality associated with their own product which creates consumer loyalty and adds value to the product that is additional to the cost of the materials that go to make the product. Establishing a valuable brand is not straightforward,

but it is clearly something that many producers would wish to do. In part this may be achieved by advertising, which establishes a good image of the product and perhaps gives the impression that this product is used by top media stars or sports personalities.

How to establish a good brand is a topic for business studies courses. From the perspective of economics, what matters is that a good brand adds a dimension to a product for which consumers are prepared to pay. In effect, they have a taste for specific brands and are prepared to pay extra to buy these brands. A brand is thus a capital asset that is of value to the firm that owns it and it can be valued just like any other capital asset.

In investment decisions the costs and revenues are accruing at different points in time. So how can a firm compare revenue in the future with costs today? We first ask how we compare income today with income at a future period of time. This question is relevant to the issue of how to value assets, as well as to the issue of how much capital firms should install. Box 12.1 discusses the valuation of brands as capital assets.

How much is an asset that generates a particular income stream in the future worth *now*? How much would someone be willing to pay now to buy the right to receive that flow of future payments? The answer is called that asset's *present value*. In general, **present value** (*PV*) refers to the value *now* of one or more payments to be received *in the future*.

### Present value of a single future payment

#### One period hence

Let us start with the simplest possible case. How much would a firm be prepared to pay *now* to purchase an asset that will produce a single payment of £100 in one year's time? One way to approach this question is to ask how much the firm would have to lend out in order to have £100 a year from now. Suppose for the moment that the interest rate on a riskless loan (say, a government bond) is 5 per cent, which means that £1.00 invested today will be worth £1.05 in one year's time.[5]

If we use *PV* to stand for this unknown amount, we can write *PV*(1.05) = £100. (The left-hand side of this equation means *PV* multiplied by 1.05.) Thus, *PV* = £100/1.05 =

£95.24. This tells us that the present value of £100 receivable in one year's time is £95.24 when the interest rate is 5 per cent. Anyone who lends out £95.24 for one year at 5 per cent interest will get back £95.24 plus £4.76 in interest, which makes £100 in total. When we calculate this present value, the interest rate is used to *discount* (i.e. reduce to its present value) the £100 to be received one year hence. The maximum price that a firm would be willing to pay for this asset is £95.24 (assuming that the interest rate relevant to the firm is 5 per cent).

To see why, let us start by assuming that the firm is offered the asset at some other price, say £98. If, instead of paying this amount for the asset, a firm lends its £98 out at 5 per cent interest, it would have at the end of one year more than the £100 that the asset will yield. (At 5 per cent interest, £98 yields £4.90 in interest, which, together with the principal, comes to £102.90.) Clearly, no profit-maximizing firm would pay £98—or, by the same reasoning, any sum in excess of £95.24—for the asset. It could do better by using its funds in other ways.

Now suppose that the good is offered for sale at £90. A firm could borrow £90 to buy the asset and would pay £4.50 in interest at 5 per cent on its loan. At the end of the year, the asset will yield £100. When this is used to repay the £90 loan and the £4.50 in interest, £5.50 is left as profit to the firm. Clearly, it would be worthwhile for a profit-maximizing firm to buy the asset at a price of £90—or, by the same argument, at any price less than £95.24.

The actual present value that we have calculated depended on assuming that the interest rate was 5 per cent. What if the interest rate is 7 per cent? At that interest rate, the present value of the £100 receivable in one year's time would be £100/1.07 = £93.46.

These examples are easy to generalize. In both cases we have found the present value by dividing the sum that is

---

[5] The analysis in the rest of this chapter assumes *annual* compounding of interest.

receivable in the future by 1 plus the rate of interest.[6] In general, the present value of £R one year hence at an interest rate of $i$ per year is

$$PV = \frac{R}{(1 + i)}. \qquad (1)$$

### Several periods hence

The next step is to ask what would happen if the sum were receivable at a later date. What, for example, is the present value of £100 to be received *two* years hence when the interest rate is 5 per cent? This is £100/(1.05 × 1.05) = £90.70. We can check this by seeing what would happen if £90.70 were lent out for two years. In the first year the loan would earn an interest of (0.05)(£90.70) = £4.54, and hence after one year the firm would receive £95.24. In the second year the interest would be earned on this entire amount; it would equal (0.05)(£95.24) = £4.76. Hence in two years the firm would have £100. (The payment of interest in the second year on the interest income earned in the first year is known as *compound interest*.)

In general, the present value of £R after $t$ years at $i$ per cent is

$$PV = \frac{R}{(1 + i)^t}. \qquad (2)$$

All this formula does is discount the sum, $R$, by the interest rate, $i$, repeatedly, once for each of the $t$ periods that must pass until the sum becomes available. If we look at the formula, we see that the higher $i$ or $t$ is, the bigger is the whole term $(1 + i)^t$. This term, however, appears in the denominator, so $PV$ is *negatively* related to both $i$ and $t$.

The formula $PV = R/(1 + i)^t$ shows that the present value of a given sum payable in the future will be smaller the more distant the payment date and the higher the rate of interest.

### Present value of a stream of future payments

Now consider the present value of a stream of receipts that continues indefinitely.[7] At first glance that $PV$ might seem very high, because the total amount received grows without reaching any limit as time passes. The previous section suggests, however, that people will not value the far-distant money payments very highly.

To find the $PV$ of £100 a year, payable for ever, we ask how much would have to be invested now, at an interest rate of $i$ per cent per year, to obtain £100 each year. This

is simply $iPV = £100$, where $i$ is the interest rate and $PV$ the investment required. Dividing through by $i$ shows the present value of the stream of £100 a year for ever to be

$$PV = \frac{£100}{i}. \qquad (3)$$

For example, if the interest rate were 10 per cent, the present value would be £1,000. This merely says that £1,000 invested at 10 per cent yields £100 per year, for ever. Notice that, as in the previous sections, $PV$ is negatively related to the rate of interest: the higher the interest rate, the less is the present value of the stream of future payments.

In the text we have concentrated on finding the present value of amounts available in the future. Box 12.2 reverses the process and discusses the future value of sums available in the present.

### Implications for firms' desire to invest in capital

Profit-maximizing firms will want to invest in capital so long as it offers a return that is at least as good as could be achieved by investing a similar sum of money at the going market interest rate. Equivalently, if firms are borrowing the funds to finance the investment, they will want to purchase capital that offers a return in terms of revenue that exceeds the cost of the loan. Clearly, the costs of the capital and revenues that arise from using the capital will accrue at different points in time. In order to compare payments and receipts at different times, the firm needs simply to calculate the present value of the extra revenues and deduct the present value of the costs. This gives the **net present value** of the investment project.

Profit-maximizing firms should undertake any investment project for which the net present value is positive, as this means that it is increasing the present value of profits and thus adding value to the firm. On the plausible assumption that firms are faced with diminishing returns to capital, they will invest up to the point where the net present value of investment is zero. Beyond this point, further investment is adding more to the present value of costs than to the present value of revenues, and thus will lower the value of the firm.

Notice that when firms must compare income streams at different points in time we must generalize our interpretation of the assumption that firms maximize profits. This is because it may be rational for a firm to make losses (by investing) in one period in order to make even more profit in future. Hence when intertemporal revenue transfers are possible, the objective of the firm would not be to maximize profit in one specific period, but rather to maximize the present value of all current and expected future profit streams. This is the same thing as maximizing the present value of the firm.

---

[6] Notice that in this type of formula the interest rate, $i$, is expressed as a decimal fraction; for example, 7 per cent is expressed as 0.07, so $(1 + i)$ is 1.07.

[7] Some government securities, known as *perpetuities*, have the characteristic that they pay out a specific sum at regular intervals with no terminal (or maturity) date.

**Box 12.2** **The future value of a present sum**

In the text we have concentrated on the present value of amounts to be received in the future. We can, however, turn the question around and ask, 'What is the future value of an amount of money that is available in the present?'

Assume that you have £100 available to you today. What will that sum be worth next year? If you lend it out at 5 per cent, you will have £105 in a year's time. Letting *PV* stand for the sum you have now and *FV* for the value of the sum in the future, we have $FV = PV(1.05)$ in this case. Writing the interest rate as we have in the text, we get

$$FV = PV(1 + i).$$

If we divide through by $(1 + i)$, we get equation (1) in the text. (In the text we denote the future value by *R*.)

Next, if we let the sum build up by reinvesting the interest each year, we get

$$FV = PV(1 + i)^t.$$

If we divide both sides by $(1 + i)^t$, we get equation (2) in the text.

This tells us that what we did in the text is reversible. If we have an amount of money today, we can figure out what it will be worth if it is invested at compounded interest for some number of future periods. Similarly, if we are going to have some amount of money at some future date, we can figure out how much we would need to invest today to get that amount at the specified date in the future.

Our argument tells us that the two sums, *PV* and *FV*, are linked by the compound interest expression $(1 + i)^t$. To go from the present to the future, we *multiply PV* by the interest expression; and to go from the future to the present, we *divide FV* by the interest expression.

The so-called rule of 72 is a convenient way of going from *PV* to *FV* by finding out how long it takes for *FV* to become twice the size of *PV* at any given interest rate. According to the rule, the time it takes for any amount to double in size is given approximately by $72/100i$. So, for example, if *i* is 0.1 (an interest rate of 10 per cent), any present sum doubles in value in $72/10 = 7.2$ years.

When considering the decision to invest, firms can be assumed to wish to maximize the present value of the firm itself. The value of the firm will increase if it undertakes projects that have a positive net present value.

Investment decisions are very important for firms, so we now look in more detail at the investment decisions for profit-maximizing firms and what this implies for demand for capital.

## Equilibrium of the firm

When putting a present value on future income flows, each firm will discount them at a rate that reflects its own opportunity cost of capital, often called its *internal rate of discount*. With perfect capital markets in which the firm can borrow all that it needs, the internal rate of discount will equal the market rate of interest (suitably adjusted for risk in each case). The evidence suggests, however, that most firms do not face perfect capital markets and have internal rates of return that exceed market rates. Thus, when firms evaluate an internally financed investment project, they will use an internal rate of discount that exceeds the relevant market rate of interest. The general points made in the text are not affected by this complication, as long as *i* is interpreted in each case to mean the 'appropriate rate of discount'. For the time being we make the simplifying assumption that firms face perfect capital markets so that the internal rate of discount is equal to the market rate of interest, but we discuss the appropriate discount rate further in the next section.

In adjusting to market forces, an individual firm faces a given interest rate and given purchase prices of capital goods. The firm can vary the quantity of capital that it employs, and as a result the marginal revenue product of its capital varies. The law of diminishing returns tells us that the more capital the firm uses, the lower will be the *MRP* of its capital.

### The decision to purchase capital

Consider a firm that is evaluating a potential increase in its capital stock. It can borrow (and lend) money at an interest rate of, say, 10 per cent per year. The first thing the firm needs to do is to estimate the expected marginal revenue product of the new piece of capital over its lifetime. That is, for example, the net addition to revenue generated by the extra output in each period of time made possible by installing the extra machine. Then it discounts this at the appropriate rate, 10 per cent in this example, to find the present value of that stream of receipts the machine will create.[8] Let us say it is £5,000.

The present value, by construction, tells us how much the flow of future net receipts is worth today. If the firm

---

[8] Suppose that the machine has an *MRP* of £1,000 each period. First, suppose the machine lasts only this period. The present value is then £1,000. Next, suppose it lasts two periods. The *PV* is then £1,000 + £1,000/1.10 = £1,909.09. If it lasts three periods, the *PV* is £1,000 + £1,000/1.10 + £1,000/(1.10)² = £2,735.53; and so on. Each additional period that it lasts produces an *MRP* of £1,000, but at a more and more distant date, so that the *present value* of that period's revenue gets smaller owing to heavier discounting.

can buy the machine for less than the *PV of the extra revenue stream it generates*, this is a good buy. If it must pay more, the machine is not worth buying.

**It is always worthwhile for a firm to buy another unit of capital whenever the present value of the stream of future *MRP*s that the capital provides exceeds its purchase price.**

### The size of the firm's capital stock

The *MRP* of each addition to the firm's capital stock is assumed to decline as the amount of capital is increased. The firm will go on adding to its capital stock until the *present value* of the flow of *MRP*s conferred by the last unit added is equal to the purchase price of that unit. The firm then has its equilibrium amount of capital.

**The equilibrium capital stock of the firm is such that the present value of the stream of net income that is provided by the marginal unit of capital is equal to its purchase price.**

This is yet another example of the condition that, for equilibrium, marginal cost will equal marginal revenue.

Now let the firm be in equilibrium with respect to its capital stock and ask what would cause it to buy more capital. Given the price of the machines, anything that increases the present value of the flow of income that the machines produce will have that effect. Two things will accomplish this. First, the *MRP*s of the capital may rise. That will happen, for example, if technological changes make capital more productive so that each unit produces more than before. (This possibility is dealt with later in the chapter.) Second, the interest rate may fall, causing an increase in the present value of any given stream of future *MRP*s. For example, suppose that next year's *MRP* is £1,000. This has a *PV* of £909.09 when the interest rate is 10 per cent and £952.38 when the interest rate falls to 5 per cent.

So when the interest rate falls, the firm will wish to add to its capital stock. It will go on doing so until the decline in the *MRP*s of successive additions to its capital stock, according to the law of diminishing returns, reduces the present value of the *MRP*, at the new lower rate of interest, to the purchase price of the capital.

**The size of a firm's desired capital stock increases when the rate of interest falls, and it decreases when the rate of interest rises.**

This relationship is shown in Figure 12.1. It can be considered as the firm's demand curve for capital plotted against the interest rate. It shows how the desired stock of capital varies with the interest rate. (It is sometimes called the *marginal efficiency of capital curve*.)

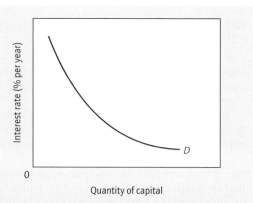

**Figure 12.1  The firm's demand curve for capital**
The firm's desired capital stock is negatively related to the rate of interest. The lower is the interest rate, the higher is the present value of any given stream of marginal revenue products, and hence the more capital the firm will wish to use.

## Equilibrium for the whole economy

The term **capital stock** refers to some aggregate amount of capital. The *firm's capital stock* has an *MRP*, showing the net increase in the firm's revenue when another unit of capital is added to its existing capital stock. The *economy's capital stock* can also be thought of as having a marginal revenue product; this is the addition to total national output (GDP) that is caused by adding another unit of capital to the economy's total stock. This capital stock also has an average product, which is total output divided by the total capital stock (i.e. the amount of output per unit of capital).

The same analysis that we used for one firm in the previous section applies to the whole economy. The lower the rate of interest, the higher is the desired stock of capital that all firms will wish to hold. Such a curve is shown as the economy's demand curve in Figure 12.2.

### Short-run equilibrium

In the short run the economy's capital stock is given, but for the economy as a whole the interest rate is variable.[9] Whereas the firm reaches equilibrium by altering its capital stock, the whole economy reaches equilibrium through variations in the interest rate.

---

[9] We know that the central bank sets the short-term nominal interest rate; however, we are talking here about long-term real interest rates. These are set by market forces, and are the rates relevant for long-term investment decisions.

**Figure 12.2 The equilibrium interest rate**

**In the short run the interest rate equates the demand for capital with its fixed supply.** The economy's desired capital stock is negatively related to the interest rate, as shown by the curve $D$. In the short run, when the stock is $K_0$, the equilibrium interest rate is $i_0$. When the capital stock grows to $K_1$ in the long run, the equilibrium interest rate falls to $i_1$.

**Figure 12.3 Changes in technology and the capital stock**

**Increases in technological knowledge and in the capital stock have opposite effects on the interest rate.** The original demand curve $D_0$ and capital stock $K_0$ produce an interest rate of $i_0$. Technological improvements shift the desired capital stock curve to $D_1$ and, with a constant stock of capital, would raise the interest rate to $i_1$. However, the capital stock increases to $K_1$, which *ceteris paribus* would lower the interest rate to $i_2$. In the figure the two effects exactly offset each other, and the interest rate remains unchanged at $i_0$, where $K_1$ and $D_1$ intersect.

For the economy as a whole, the condition that the present value of the *MRP*s should equal the price of capital goods determines the equilibrium interest rate.

Let us see how this comes about. If the price of capital were less than the present value of its stream of future *MRP*s, it would be worthwhile for all firms to borrow money to invest in capital. For the economy as a whole, however, the stock of capital cannot be changed quickly. As a result, the main effect of this demand to borrow would be to push up the interest rate until the present value of the *MRP* equals the price of a unit of capital goods. Conversely, if the price of capital were above its present value, no one would wish to borrow money to invest in capital, and the rate of interest would fall. This too is illustrated in Figure 12.2.

### Accumulation of capital in the long run

In an economy with positive saving, capital is accumulated over time and the stock of capital grows slowly. As this happens, other things being equal, the *MRP* falls. This will cause the equilibrium interest rate to fall over time, as is also shown in Figure 12.2.

### Changing technology in the very long run

In the very long run, technology changes. As a result, the capital stock becomes more productive as the old,

obsolete capital is replaced by newer, more efficient capital. This shifts the *MRP* curve rightward because any given amount of capital will have a higher *MRP*. This in turn tends to increase the equilibrium interest rate associated with any particular size of the capital stock—which is also, of course, the equilibrium return on capital. However, the accumulation of capital moves the economy downward to the right along any given *MRP* curve, and that tends to lower the return on capital associated with any one *MRP* curve. The net effect on the return on capital of both of these changes may be to raise it, to lower it, or to leave it unchanged, as shown in Figure 12.3. The very-long-run effects of changing technology, combined with a growing capital stock, are studied further in Chapter 26, and we discuss some aspects of recent changes in technology in the last section of this chapter.

So we see that the income going to owners of capital is the *pure risk-free rate of return* (multiplied by the amount of capital in use), plus a risk premium, plus any pure profits or minus any pure losses. The pure return serves to allocate capital to its most productive uses. All uses that yield more than the pure rate of return (plus any necessary risk premium) will be exploited; all uses that earn less than the pure rate will not be taken up.

# The investment decision

In the previous section we explained how a firm can evaluate whether or not an increase in its capital stock will increase its value. The message is that firms should undertake investment projects that have a positive net present value. This is easy to understand conceptually, but it is much harder to implement in practice. We now discuss some of the issues that inevitably arise in the practical evaluation of a potential investment project.

## Choice of discount rate

Assuming that the firm faces a perfect capital market, the discount rate appropriate for appraising an investment project is the true opportunity cost of the financial capital involved as valued by this market. There are two elements to this. First, there is the pure time value of money. This is usually measured by the market rate of interest on a risk-free investment, such as a government bond; to find this figure you have only to look in the daily financial press. However, even here there is slight complication, in that the yield on government bonds varies with the bond's term to maturity (the number of years before the principle is repaid). This means that calculation of the appropriate discount rate should take into account not just short-term interest rates, but also long-term rates, though for simplicity it is common to assume a single risk-free rate.

The second element of the opportunity cost of capital is the return in excess of the risk-free rate that is necessary to compensate for risk. The greater the risk associated with a project, the greater should be the risk premium attached to the discount rate used in evaluating the project. It should be stressed that the opportunity cost of capital relevant to these decisions is that set by the capital markets. It is not appropriate for a firm to argue, for example, that since the money used to finance the project is generated internally, the opportunity cost of the capital is lower than it would be if borrowed externally, so a lower discount rate can be used in investment appraisal. (Indeed, as discussed above, given the likelihood of market imperfections, the appropriate discount rate for internally generated funds may be *above* market rates.) The reason this would be an error is that the firm has the option of investing its capital in other projects via the capital markets, or of returning the money to shareholders. If it does not use the market valuation of the opportunity cost of capital in valuing its potential project, it will find that it has invested in an internal project that adds less value to the firm than could have been achieved by investing the resources elsewhere via the capital markets. Equivalently, it may accept a project as having a positive NPV when in fact it has a negative NPV when evaluated at the true opportunity cost of capital.

In practice, many firms use the weighted average cost of capital (WACC) as a discount rate for investment appraisal purposes. This is calculated on the basis of the average interest cost on all the sources of funds raised by the firm itself, such as equity, bonds, and bank loans. This is not a correct procedure from the perspective of economic theory, as the WACC reflects the average cost of capital to the firm, rather than marginal cost of funds and the riskiness of the project being assessed. However, for an investment project that is about as risky as the existing business and that still has access to its various sources of funds, this may not be a bad approximation to the true opportunity cost of capital.

## Treatment of inflation

Another factor that complicates investment appraisal is inflation. The problem here is that the value of money itself changes over time, so that care has to be taken to make sure that a project is generating added value *in real terms*.

The net present value method is ideally suited to judging real added value, because the assessment criterion is measured unambiguously in money values at the beginning period of the investment project. In other words, if we are making the decision in 2008, then the calculation is converted into 2008 pounds sterling. However, there are two different ways in which this can be done and it is important that one or other approach be applied consistently.

The first approach involves using expected current money values for all cash flows, that is, the actual money values that are expected to be recorded at the time the flows accrue. These money values are then discounted back to the initial-year present values using a nominal discount rate. The nominal discount rate is the actual money value of the interest rate in the markets for the appropriate level of risk.

The second approach measures all future cash flows in terms of, say, 2008 (base-year) money and discounts these back to the present using a *real* discount rate. The real discount rate is approximately equal to the nominal rate

**Box 12.3** Real and nominal interest rates

If you put £100 into a savings deposit today and the bank is offering 5 per cent interest, in one year's time you will receive interest of £5. If 'today' is 1 March 2009, the interest will be received on 28 February 2010. This 5 per cent is referred to as the *nominal rate of interest*. However, between these two dates it is likely that the purchasing power of each £1 of money will have changed. This is because of *inflation*, which by definition is a fall in the purchasing power of money. Inflation is typically measured by the annual percentage change in the retail price index (RPI) or the consumer price index (CPI).

If there is inflation in 2009–10, the £5 interest you receive in February 2010 will buy fewer goods and services than it would have done a year earlier. The real rate of interest is the figure that tells you how much extra goods your money interest will buy you. In order to calculate the real rate of interest *ex post*, you need to know what the inflation rate has been over the period in question. It is approximately true to say that the real rate of interest is the nominal rate of interest minus the rate of inflation.

We say 'approximately' for two reasons. First, the exact relationship between real rates, nominal rates, and inflation is

$$(1 + r) = (1 + i)(1 + p)$$

where $r$ is the nominal interest rate, $i$ is the real interest rate, and $p$ is the rate of inflation. If you multiply out the right-hand side of this equation, you get $1 + i + p + ip$. Hence the nominal rate is not exactly equal to the sum of the real interest rate and the inflation rate, because there is also the term $ip$. This term will be very small when both $i$ and $p$ are small, but not if they are large, such as when inflation is high. Second, the relationship is often used to apply to 'expected' interest rates. In this context expectations may be incorrect, so that the relationship holds subject to a random error. Expected real interest rates are what matter for most investment decisions by firms, because firms are converting a purchase of physical capital today into a stream of extra output of goods in future.

minus the rate of inflation. The reason why this is an approximation is discussed in Box 12.3.

If applied correctly, both of these methods will come up with exactly the same result. This is because they are just different ways of converting future cash flows into present real values: both methods use the same numeraire of base-period money values. However, mistakes will be made if a mixture of real and nominal data slips into the same calculation, for example if *nominal* cash flows are discounted by the *real* rate of interest.

## Sunk costs

There are two aspects to the problem of sunk costs, depending upon whether these costs have already been incurred or whether the expenditure is yet to be made and therefore is still an object of choice.

### In the past

A common error in investment decisions is to give weight to the past and try to rescue past mistakes. This is reflected in a statement such as: 'We need to spend more money on this factory because otherwise the investment we made last year will be wasted.'

A key element of rational decision-making in this context is that sunk costs from the past do not enter into the decision about new investments. Bygones are bygones. What matters is whether incremental spending adds to

present value or not. The success or failure of past investments is irrelevant to this decision.

What this implies is that decisions about whether to spend more on anything should be forward-looking. The question should always be asked: does the present value of the extra revenue generated exceed the present value of the extra spending incurred? If the answer is yes, then the spending will increase the value of the firm. If the answer is no, then the extra spending will decrease the value of the firm, and should not be undertaken.

This does not mean that present-value techniques cannot be used to take decisions about whether or not to scrap old plant and machinery: they can. Suppose that we have a factory that is declining in efficiency, and suppose also that it has zero scrap value. The question is whether to keep it going or close it down entirely. The answer will depend solely on the present value of the extra spending required to keep it going relative to the extra revenue that will be generated by keeping the plant operating. The original cost of the factory is irrelevant to the decision, though the scrap or resale value of the factory would be relevant if this were positive, as it would represent potential future cash flow.

Sunk costs should not influence future investment decisions.

### In the future

Until recently economists implicitly assumed that irreversible costs that had not yet been incurred should not

**Box 12.4  The option to invest**

Financial options come in two types. A *call option* is the right to buy an underlying asset at a specified price (the exercise price) within some period of time. A *put option* is the right to sell an underlying asset at a specified price within some period of time. These options can be exercised if the buyer so wishes, but there is no obligation so to do. If the buyer is better off not exercising the option then non-exercise is OK—hence the term 'option'. The option will expire worthless. Options have some value so long as they have some time left to run, and so long as there is even a faint possibility that the underlying value of the asset will exceed the exercise price of the call option, or be less than the exercise price of the put option.

Investment by firms that has not yet been implemented is just like the option to buy some underlying asset at some specified price. This is a call option. The value of this call option is conceptually separate from the value of the underlying asset itself. This is because the call option still allows you to back out without any further costs, whereas the investment itself incurs substantial sunk costs.

An example may help to illustrate these ideas. Suppose that a firm has a potential investment project. This project would involve an instant irreversible cost of £800 (these numbers can be thought of as millions). The revenue from the project will depend on which of two states of the world emerges in a year's time, affecting whether the output from the project sells for £150 or £50. These alternative states of the world are equally likely to arise, but only next year will it be clear what is going to

happen. For simplicity we can assume that the revenue streams established next year will then continue at that level for ever and that the appropriate discount rate is 10 per cent.

Suppose we do the NPV calculation relating to an immediate investment. The expected revenue on average will be £100, so the net present value is −£800 plus the present value of £100 for ever. The latter sum is £1,100. (We have £100 produced instantly plus the present value of a perpetual payment £100 for ever, which is £1,000.) Hence the NPV is £300 (calculated as −£800 + £1,100).

However, suppose we wait and then go ahead with the project only if the revenue received is £150, cancelling the project if it turns out to be £50. The present value of that alternative is £380 (calculated as half the present value of −£800 ('half' because there is a 0.5 probability of going ahead) plus half the present value of £150 in perpetuity, starting next year). Hence the present value of waiting one year is greater than the present value of investing now. The value of the wait-and-see option today is £80. The strategy that maximizes the present value of the firm is to do nothing until next year.

This approach gives important insights into how uncertainty about the environment can inhibit investment. Who will win the next election? Will the price of oil go higher? Will there be a war in the Middle East? Any event that increases uncertainty about future investment returns will increase the value of the option to invest and make it more likely that firms will wait and see.

---

be treated in any special way in investment appraisal. However, important insights have been derived from option pricing theory. Box 12.4 explains what 'options' are in this context and illustrates the idea with a numerical example.

There are two key features of many real-world investment projects. The first is that there is some significant chunk of costs that is irreversible, so that it cannot be recovered if it is later decided to abandon the project. The second is that implementation does not have to be done immediately: it is usually possible to delay. The advantage of being able to delay is that more information may come along later that would help the firm to avoid making a wrong decision.

The important idea is that some financial value should be assigned to the option to wait and see. Once the investment is undertaken, this option is killed and this value is lost. Hence an irreversible investment should be undertaken only if the net present value is sufficiently large to compensate for the loss in value of the option.

An investment that involves significant sunk costs should be undertaken only if the net present value of proceeding exceeds the value of the wait-and-see option.

One way to think about why this option must be valuable to a firm is to notice that, if the investment goes ahead, the sunk costs of the project will be incurred with certainty, and there is always some probability that the project itself will lose money, that is, have a negative NPV. By postponing the project, and perhaps cancelling it later when new information comes along, the firm is not losing money with certainty. Hence, by exercising the option to wait and see, the firm could end up creating extra value (by not throwing money down the drain on an unprofitable project).

This analysis helps us understand why it may be that may firms require a substantial estimated NPV of a project before they invest, whereas the theory set out above suggests that *any* positive NPV would be adequate to justify an investment.

Another application of the same idea relates to the close-down decision of firms. In Chapter 7 we argued that profit-maximizing firms would close down if they were not covering their average variable costs. In practice, many firms will stay in business for some time. Why is this? The prediction of immediate close-down ignored the value of the options that the firm may have to invest in value-enhancing projects once market conditions improve. If the firm closes down, these options will be lost. Hence the statement about close-down decisions should be modified to say that firms should close down if the present value of the losses exceeds the present value of the firm's investment options. We have, in effect, been ignoring the irreversibility that is built into a close-down decision. This also explains why other firms are often prepared to pay substantial sums to take over a loss-making business. Essentially, they are buying the investment options that the target firm owns.

# New technology[10]

So far we have talked about capital as if investment was just a matter of adding more of the same. In reality, technical change means that new capital almost always embodies new ways of doing things. In this section we illustrate the importance of technical change by examining the significance of the recent and ongoing revolution in information and communications technology.

## General purpose technologies

The technological changes that drive long-term economic growth range from small incremental improvements in existing technologies through to the introduction of what are called *general purpose technologies* (GPTs). GPTs share some important common characteristics. They begin as fairly crude technologies with a limited number of uses. As they diffuse throughout the economy, they evolve into much more complex technologies with dramatic increases in their efficiency, in the range of their use, in the range of economic outputs that they help to produce, and in the range of new product and process technologies that incorporate, or that otherwise depend on them.

Throughout history, the most important new GPTs have had major impacts on the economic, social, and political structures, creating what may be called a series of 'new economies'. Here are some of the main ones.

- **Information and communication technologies (ICTs):** writing, printing with movable type, the computer, which along with several related technologies is driving the current ICT revolution (see below)
- **Materials:** bronze, iron, and steel, and the current ability to create made-to-order materials invented specifically for use in newly developed products and processes

- **Power delivery systems:** domesticated animals, the water wheel, the steam engine, electricity, and the internal combustion engine
- **Transportation:** the three-masted sailing ship, railways, the iron steam ship, the motor vehicle, and commercial aircraft (the latter two of which were enabled by the internal combustion engine)
- **Organizational technologies:** the factory system, mass production, and flexible manufacturing (or lean production, or Toyotaism, as it is variously called)

As each new GPT diffuses through the economy, it creates a research programme for entrepreneurs to apply its principles to create new processes and new products and to improve old ones. These, in turn, create other new opportunities, and so on in a chain reaction that stretches over decades, even centuries. Think, for example, of all of the myriad ways that innovators have found to use electronic chips; how these ways have multiplied as the power and reliability of chips have increased; and how some of these ways have in turn enabled other developments; and so on in a complex linking of related innovations.

GPTs typically greatly reduce the cost of providing some good or service. Power GPTs reduced the cost of power, while information GPTs reduced the cost of creating, storing, transmitting, and analysing information. It is also important to note that some of the most important consequences to any new GPT depend on purely technological relations and not on how a given technology responds to a change in price. The use of water power, the main source of non-human power for manufacturing until well into the nineteenth century, required that factories be located near fast-running water. The introduction of steam power freed manufacturing from that constraint and allowed it to locate in the industrial cities

---

10  This section draws heavily on the material in: Lipsey *et al.* (2005).

of that grew up in the nineteenth century. No fall in the price of water power, even to zero, could have given rise to this transforming relocation of industry.

## The information and communication technology (ICT) revolution

To understand what is meant by the ICT revolution, we need to consider a few basic facts about technological change and economic growth. Long-term economic growth is driven by technological change, that is, by changes in the products that are produced, the process by which they are produced, and the ways in which productive activities are organized—what are called product, process, and organizational technologies. Although each person living in Western Europe and North America has about ten times as much 'real purchasing power' as did their forebears who lived a hundred years ago, they consume it largely in the form of *new commodities* made with *new techniques* and *new organizations*. Those who lived at the beginning of the twentieth century could not have imagined modern dental and medical equipment, penicillin, painkillers, bypass operations, safe births, control of genetically transmitted diseases, personal computers, compact discs, DVDs, television sets, digital cameras, the internet, efficient automobiles, opportunities for cheap fast world-wide travel, affordable education, safe food of great variety free from ptomaine and botulism, or the elimination of endless kitchen drudgery through the use of detergents, washing machines, electric stoves, microwaves, refrigerators, dishwashers, and a host of other labour-saving household products that we take for granted today. Nor could they have imagined the clean, robot-operated, computer-controlled modern factories that have largely replaced their noisy, dangerous, factories that spewed coal smoke and other pollutants over the surrounding countryside.

The point is important. Technological advance not only raises our incomes; it transforms our lives through the invention of new, hitherto undreamed of, things that are made in new, hitherto undreamed of, ways.

### Recent innovations

For the last few decades, the world has been living through a set of major structural adjustments associated with the so-called ICT revolution. Like all transforming GPTs, the ICT revolution has roots that go a long way back in technological history. This one began with the development of commercially useful electricity in the nineteenth century. True 'tele'communications started in the 1840s with the introduction of the telegraph and its associated communications language, the Morse Code. Submarine telegraphy started in 1851 with the first line from England to France. In 1866 the first commercial submarine cable came into regular use between Britain and the USA. The telephone was invented in 1876, and the wireless telegraph followed twenty years later. Wireless speech communication was first established in 1906, and in 1920 the first commercial radio station went on the air. Television first appeared in the late 1930s but became widely available, at prices most households could afford, only after 1945.

The modern ICT revolution is based on a new GPT that is driven by a cluster of technologies centred around the electronic computer, but also including efficient long-distance STD telephonic communication, faxes, satellite transmissions, lasers, fibre optics, and the internet (most of which either use computers directly or were developed with their assistance). These technologies are changing product design, production, marketing, finance, and the organization of firms. By managing information flows more effectively than the old, hierarchically organized mass of middle managers, computers have caused a major reorganization in the management of firms. They have also created a wide range of new products incorporating hard coded chips, computers and/or software. Computers are used to design products, fly aeroplanes, drive trains, operate machines, run buildings systems, facilitate scientific research, warn of unsafe driving practices, monitor health, and facilitate communication through the internet, email, and desktop publishing.

When computers were initially introduced, they entered structures designed for the paper world, merely substituting for human hands and minds. Before they could really pay off, administration and production facilities had to be redesigned, both physically and in their command structures. Slowly, as it was with electricity, the whole process of producing, designing, delivering, and marketing goods and services was, and still is being, reorganized along lines dominated by computing technologies:

*ICT not only affects every industry and service but also every function within each industry, that is R&D, design, production, marketing, transport, and general administration. It is systemization rather than automation, integrating the various previously separate departments and functions. In design and development every industry now depends on computers. This is not just a question of Computer-Aided-Design (CAD), although this is of great importance, especially in complex products, such as large buildings, chemical plants, aircraft, and ships as well as the products of the electronics industry itself. It is also a question of the accuracy, speed and volume of all kinds of calculations and access to data banks at all stages of the R&D process.* (Christopher Freeman, Chapter 2 in Mansell, 1994, pages 14–15)

### New economies

Each of the GPTs mentioned earlier issued in a set of economic, social, and political transformations that could be called the creation of a 'new economy'. Two examples from earlier ICT revolutions illustrate that this is not a new phenomenon.

#### Writing

The invention of writing around 3500 BC caused a radical transformation of the societies of the Tigris–Euphrates valley. Written records permitted the development of sophisticated systems of taxation and public spending that were quite impossible when all records were held in human memory. The new public savings financed the world's first major irrigation works, the technology of which evolved rapidly. The area under cultivation increased and agricultural surpluses rose. The populations of the largest settlements, which typically had been measured in the hundreds for millennia, increased over the span of a mere two centuries into the tens of thousands.

#### Printing

In the fifteenth century the invention of printing with movable type greatly lowered the total cost of reproducing a manuscript. It also altered the ratio of variable to fixed costs—the major cost of manuscript reproduction was the variable cost of the scribe's time; the major cost of printing was the high fixed cost of typesetting, while the marginal cost of printing an extra copy was low. This new cost structure made mass communication feasible. Costs of large-scale publications fell and learning exploded. Monopolies of knowledge were upset. The results of new scientific experiments were quickly disseminated and results duplicated and expanded upon at a speed that would have seemed miraculous a century earlier. Mass communication helped the Protestant Revolution, since its direct appeal to the people would have been impossible without the many low-cost printed pamphlets written in the vernacular.

In the sixteenth century, the tiny Netherlands rose to become a world power. A key contributor to its success was its liberal attitude towards the technology of printing and the learning that it embodied—unlike the Islamic nations and China, which suppressed it and stayed with hand-copied manuscripts or word block reproductions for centuries. The creation of the Dutch information network, which was based on low-cost reproduction of the printed word, greatly increased the economy's productive efficiency and the government's tax revenues. Between 1590 and 1620, the multinational corporations, the stock exchange, efficient year-round financial intermediation, the federal state, and a systematically drilled army all made their first appearances.

## The current 'new economy'

The current ICT revolution is similarly transforming many economic, social, and political relations. The term 'new economy' has, however, been used in more than one sense in recent years, which can be a cause of confusion. Some use the term to refer to an economy in which the laws of supply and demand no longer hold and there are neither business cycles nor inflations. Not many academic economists were gullible enough to believe that the ICT revolution would so alter normal economic behaviour. Others define the 'new economy' as the sector producing computing power and related things. By this supply-side definition, the 'new economy' covers only a small fraction of the whole economy. Yet others define a 'new economy' as occurring only when there is a sustained acceleration in the rate of growth of productivity. In contrast to all these, we follow a well established procedure of using the term in a wider sense to refer to the social, economic, and political changes brought about by the current ICT revolution. It is an economy-wide *process*, not located in just one hi-tech *sector* any more than the new economy initiated by electricity was confined to the electricity-generating sector.

Below we list just a few of the many changes that have been driven by the ICT revolution since 1970. They are grouped loosely under the headings of process, product, and organizational technologies and social and political implications, although the categories clearly overlap.

### Process technologies

• Computerized robots and related technologies have transformed the modern factory and eliminated most of the high-paying, low-skilled jobs that existed in the old Fordist assembly-line factories.

• Computer-assisted design (CAD) is revolutionizing the design process and eliminating much of the need for 'learning by using', whereby complex products such as new aircraft had to be built before their behavioural characteristics could be fully established.

• Surgery on hips, knees, and other delicate parts of the body is more and more often conducted by computers. These will soon facilitate distant surgery, permitting specialists working in major urban hospitals to operate on patients in remote parts of the world.

• Research in everything from economics to astronomy has been changed dramatically by the ability to perform complex calculations that were either impossible or prohibitively time-consuming without electronic computers.

• Computer-age crime detection is much more sophisticated than it was in the past. Here the biological and the ICT revolutions complement each other, as is so often the case with co-existing GPTs.

• Traffic control in the air and on the ground has been revolutionized in many ways, while navigation at sea is now so easy that lighthouses, the sailor's friend for several millennia, are slowly being phased out as unnecessary, since ships can determine their distance to within a few yards using satellites and computers.

### Product technologies

• Many goods now contain chips that allow them to do new things, or to do old things more efficiently. New applications continue to be developed. For example, cars will soon be equipped with systems that warn drivers of oncoming dangers and take over the controls if the driver fails to take evasive action.

• ATMs have enormously facilitated accessing one's bank account and obtaining funds in any currency in almost any part of the world.

• Email has largely replaced conventional mail, with a large increase in volume and speed of transmission, from days or weeks in the past, depending on the two locations, to minutes today.

• Computerized translation is a now a reality and will be transformed from its present crude form to a high degree of sophistication within the lifetimes of most of us. We are witnessing the arrival of Douglas Adam's vision in *The Hitch Hiker's Guide to the Galaxy*: the ability to hear in one's own language words spoken in any other, and to be understood in any other language while speaking one's own. The only difference is that, instead of inserting a fish into one's ear, a small computer will be attached to one's body.

• Distance learning is growing by leaps and bounds, and many are enrolled in education courses where they never (or only rarely) set foot inside the institution offering the course.

• Cars will soon receive real-time information on traffic conditions at all points in their projected journey, just as Tokyo taxis now do.

• Smart buildings and factories already exist and will grow rapidly in number. Among many other things, power consumption can be adjusted continually in response to real-time price signals sent out by the electricity supply company and calculated in response to current loads.

• The electronic book looks like it might defeat consumer resistance to reading books on screen. The book's blank pages fill up on demand with any one of a hundred or more books stored in a chip that is housed in its cover. A touch of a button, and one is reading a physics text in what looks like a conventional book; with another touch, a chemistry text replaces it.

### Organizational technologies

• The management of firms has been reorganized as direct lines of communication opened up by computers have eliminated the need for the old pyramidal structure in which middle managers processed and communicated information. Today's horizontally organized loose structure bears little resemblance to the management structure of the 1960s.

• Firms are increasingly disintegrating their operations. Virtually no firm in Silicon Valley, California's pioneering hi-tech sector, now produces physical products. In other industries, the main firm is increasingly becoming a co-ordinator of subcontractors who do everything from designing products to manufacturing them, and finally to distributing them.

• The e-lance economy—groups of independent contractors who come together for a single job and then disperse—is growing and, incidentally, becoming difficult for authorities to track.

• Just as the first industrial revolution took work out of the home, the ICT revolution is putting much of it back, as more and more people find it increasingly convenient to do all sorts of jobs from home rather than in 'the office'.

• ICTs have been central to the globalization of trade in manufactured goods, and of the market for unskilled workers. This has shifted the location of much manufacturing and has allowed poorer countries to industrialize, creating new opportunities and challenges for both developed and developing nations.

• Digitalized special effects have changed the movie industry in many ways, for example by reducing the need for shooting on location and for myriad extras whose presence can often be produced digitally.

### Political and social technologies

• The computer-enabled internet is revolutionizing everything from interpersonal relations to political activity.

Chat rooms form the basis for new forms of community, making interpersonal relations possible on a scale never before seen. Non-governmental organizations (NGOs) are able to organize activities to protest such things as clear-cut logging, WTO efforts to reduce trade barriers, and the push for a Free Trade Area of the Americas (FTAA). Never again will trade negotiations take place in the relative obscurity that they enjoyed from 1945 to 1990.

• Dictators find it much harder to cut their subjects off from knowledge of what is going on in the outside world, and hence to maintain their power.

• Driven by the internet, English is becoming a *lingua franca* for the world and, unlike Latin in the Middle Ages, its use is not limited to the intelligentsia.

• In former times, a physical presence was required from virtually everyone providing a service. With computers, email links, and a host of other ICTs, this link between physical presence and provision has been broken in many services, with profound social and political effects on such things as place of residence and the ability to regulate and tax many activities.

## Falling cost curves

Most of the firms that we have looked at in earlier chapters are assumed to have U-shaped cost curves—after an initial decline, the curves slope upwards. However, many ICT firms are working with cost curves that decline over their whole range. Typically, there are very large fixed costs associated with the R&D and setup costs of creating and establishing a new technology in the ICT sector. In contrast, marginal costs of producing another unit of output are very small or virtually zero. As a result, the average total cost curve (*ATC*) declines throughout its whole relevant range. Microsoft, for example, spent a lot of money and effort developing its Windows software (and MS DOS before that), but once it existed an extra copy of the software could be made at virtually no cost. Similarly, modern telephone cables have a very high capacity, so once the lines are in place the extra cost of delivering a marginal call is virtually zero.

Increasing returns tend to generate natural monopolies (discussed in Chapter 8). Such industries tend to be characterized by *winner takes all* outcomes, as new entrants find it virtually impossible to break into an industry where an established player is selling its product at very low marginal cost. (A contrasting case in which the 'winner' can be the loser is discussed in Box 12.5.) This is reinforced by the *network externalities* that arise from the adoption of common standards. For example,

computer compatibility is helpful, enabling computers to exchange messages and software. When Microsoft Windows emerged as the standard platform, most software was developed to be compatible with it and new operating systems found it hard to break in. Similarly, because a telephone network is more useful to any one user the more other users there are on the same system, new phone companies found it hard to break into the UK telephone market while BT owned all the lines. Regulators tried to offset this advantage by insisting that BT give other companies access to the network. Later, in an example of Schumpeter's creative destruction, the new technology of mobile phones made traditional phone lines less important.

Increasing returns are not unique to ICT industries. Pharmaceuticals also have some products, such as major drugs, that incur huge costs to develop, but then can often be produced at low marginal cost. These products tend to gain a dominant position while patent protection lasts (see pages 200–1) and the companies making them will hope to recoup their development cost during the patent period. Once the patent expires, such drugs are typically copied and sold by other drug companies at close to marginal cost.

It is not always the best product that obtains the winner-take-all advantage. The VHS format became the dominant standard for videotapes, because it established a critical mass ahead of Betamax, even though the latter was a better system. But videotape formats of both types were later superseded by digital recording technologies.

The nature of competition is different in constant or falling marginal cost industries. Where costs are rising, firms are competing at the margin—a small price change or quality initiative will take a bit of business at the margin from several main rivals. Market share may rise or fall, but only a small amount at a time (see the example of newspapers on pages 82–4). However, constant or falling-marginal-cost industries tend to see big jumps from one dominant player to another. Companies like Intel, Microsoft, Amazon, AOL, Nokia, and Vodafone grew to be huge within less than two decades. They may disappear just as quickly if some new and better technology removes their edge. In contrast, traditional retailers, banks, and manufacturers tend to grow slowly and fade slowly. They may merge or be taken over and so lose their name, but they are rarely made redundant by the sudden appearance of a new technology.

In these and many other ways, new ICTs have already revolutionized society and will continue to do so throughout the twenty-first century. Some of these are minor while others are transforming—e.g. globalization and its

**Box 12.5 The winner's curse**

In any auction market, the sale price is determined by what the highest bidder is prepared to pay. In a standard auction, the price keeps rising until all but one bidder drops out. The highest bidder, who ends up acquiring the object, is often described as 'the winner'. However, in the context of the 'winner' of a takeover bid, the winner of an auction may not be a winner at all.

The winner of a takeover fight has to pay a price so high that not only are the existing owners prepared to sell, but all other bidders have dropped out. This means that the so-called winner has paid a price for the target firm that is higher than the valuation placed on it by any other party in the auction.

The winner may know something about the value of the target firm that nobody else knows. More often, however, all bidders have roughly the same information. But there is always some uncertainty about how to assess the importance of this information. The uncertainty gives rise to differences in the potential purchasers' assessments of the true value of the target firm. The auction guarantees that the winner will be the bidder with the most optimistic estimate. If the average of all the bidders' estimates is close to the true value, the firm that wins will always pay more than the true value. Fortunately for the winner, uncertainty is such that sometimes even the most optimistic estimate is less than the true value. Also the target firm is sometimes worth more to the winner than to any other bidder. In such cases the winner really does win.

In other cases, however, the firm that wins a takeover battle does not increase the value of its own company. Indeed, in a hotly contested bidding war in which there are rival bidders and the winning bid is well above the initial bid, the successful bidder may end up paying more than the target firm is really worth. This is why this phenomenon is known as **the winner's curse**.

The true winners in a takeover war may be not only the shareholders of the target company, but also the rival bidders who failed to 'win'. The shareholders win because they sell their shares for more than they are really worth, at least in the opinion of most potential buyers. The losing bidders win because their rival who 'won' the auction may be saddled with a capital loss that could weaken its ability to compete in other ways.

A good example of this phenomenon is the takeover of the Crocker Bank of California by the UK's Midland Bank. This so weakened Midland that it ended up being taken over itself by HSBC. Another example is the takeover of RJR Nabisco by Kolberg Kravis and Roberts (KKR) in one of the most famous (and biggest—$25 billion) takeover auctions of all time. KKR survived, but the firm's ability to raise capital for other activities was severely dented for most of the following decade.

The winner's curse applies not just to takeover bids but also to any transaction in which there is competitive bidding, such as for supply contracts which go to the lowest bidder. That bidder may have underestimated the true costs and hence may lose on the deal.

Telecom companies such as BT and Vodafone were stock market stars when they entered an auction for 3G telecoms licences in April 2000. They 'won' licences in the auction but at a very high price, and the companies' share prices declined dramatically in the two subsequent years. The beneficiary in this case was the UK government, which received a total revenue for the five licences on offer of £23 billion. Its earlier estimate of the likely revenue was £3 billion.

---

many ramifications; the dramatic changes in the organization of firms; the end of mass production and its associated labour and management requirements; the alternations in the political power structure; the emergence of the civil society and its effects on the conduct of international negotiations.

# CASE STUDIES

## 1. The value of an entry restriction: taxis in Toronto and London

The system of regulating taxicabs in London is very different from the one in use in Toronto. An entry restriction in Toronto makes it worth investing a significant sum of money to be able to operate a taxi. This entry cost can be thought of as an investment in an asset that will yield a positive stream of income in the future. The market-clearing entry price is thus the present value of the extra income that be earned in this occupation as compared with the best alternative.

The supply of Toronto taxicabs, and the fares they charge, are rigidly controlled by a licensing system. The number of cabs is kept well below what it would be in a free-market situation. The 'medallion', which confers the right to operate a cab, acquires a scarcity value. In October 2004 a standard medallion sold for about CAN$110,000, but a medallion permitting operation out of Toronto airport sold for about CAN$450,000. As the population increases and people earn higher incomes, the demand for the services of taxicabs rises. In a free market fares would rise, increasing the earnings of taxi owners. The higher earnings would attract new entrants until earnings were reduced to what could be earned in other comparable lines of activity. But regulations imply that neither of these things can happen, so existing cabs spend less time empty and therefore earn more for their owners. Since investment in a taxi now earns more than comparable other investments, investors will want to enter the industry. The only way to do so, however, is to buy one of the fixed supply of medallions. So the market price of medallions is bid up. The price rises to equal the present value of the extra earnings that can be obtained by investing in a taxicab rather than in a comparable line of activity. As a result, new entrants earn only normal returns on their investment, which includes the price of the medallion. Eventually the regulating authority will raise fares in response to the excess demand. If the demand proves inelastic, the gross income from operating a cab will rise. But the price of the medallion is bid up correspondingly. The fare increase thus amounts to a free gift to the current holders of medallions; it does nothing to raise the net incomes of cab operators newly entering the industry, or to make it more attractive to enter.

In London, on the other hand, the fares of black cabs are rigidly regulated, but entry is free to anyone who can pass a set of tests.[11] The fares of minicabs are unregulated and entry is free (but they are prohibited from cruising the streets in search of fares). Periodically black cab fares are raised in an effort to raise incomes. If demand is inelastic, incomes will rise in the short run. But this will attract new entrants, who will continue to enter until each existing cab is carrying just enough fares to cover its full opportunity cost, at which price economic profits will have been reduced to zero. This case is analytically identical to the case of hairdressers discussed in Box 9.2 on page 187.

## 2. The economics of land prices and the height of skyscrapers

The larger is a city's population, the larger is the demand for all the inputs that are required to run its industries and to service its residents. One of these inputs is land. So, according to the principles of derived demand, the larger the city, the higher the demand for land on which to site all of its activities. A high demand for labour in the city will attract more people to the city. But land cannot move from one place to another. So, the higher the demand for land, the higher its rental and purchase price.

Since land in the centre of cities is a more desirable location for almost all commercial activities than land on the periphery, the demand for city-centre land is higher than that for land on the periphery. As a result, virtually all cities show a 'rent gradient' with rents and property prices looking like a tent, highest in the centre and declining towards the edges. Figure 12.4 shows typical gradients for two cities, one larger than the other. If land were physically mobile, it would be reallocated until these gradients disappeared. Since it is immobile, the gradients persist indefinitely.

It follows from what has just been said that the margin between the price of land in the centre of the city and that on the edges will increase as the city grows. So the margin is higher in London than in Bristol, and higher in Bristol than in Shrewsbury.

What determines the height of buildings? Construction costs per square metre of usable space rise as the height of buildings rises. There are many reasons for this, including the requirements that higher buildings must be stronger, with more and faster lifts than smaller buildings. Profit-maximizing developers will go on adding to a building's designed height until the extra cost per square metre can just be covered by rentals. So for any piece of land, the larger the city and the closer to the centre its location, the higher the demand for the space it provides—thus the higher the building that can be profitably erected on it. For this reason most large cities display a profile of average building height that is similar to their rent profile, highest in the centre and lowest at the peripheries.

Why is this predicted profile much clearer in New York than in London? The reason is that until the last half of the twentieth century, construction technology did not permit the erection of very high buildings on the clay that underlies London. In contrast, New York is built largely on rock, and for more than a hundred years technology has been adequate for the construction of very high buildings on rock. When the technology of construction improved in the last half of the twentieth century, the average height of new London buildings began to increase, just as the theory predicts.

Why, when the technology changed, did London's profile not immediately change to mimic New York's? One reason is related to sunk costs. It can take a long time for durable physical capital to exit a declining industry. Similarly, it takes a long time for old buildings to wear out and be replaced. The buildings are already there, and all the associated construction costs are sunk. They cannot be recovered by exiting. A new building must earn, over and above what the old building can earn, enough to repay the full costs of construction. So, as the theory predicts, we see large variations in the sizes of buildings, even on the most expensive land in the centre of the city. But old buildings are eventually demolished, either because they reach the limit of their age, or because their productivity falls sufficiently below what a new building would earn on the same site. So old and new coexist, but gradually the old go and new higher buildings take their place.

A second reason is related to government regulations. Many of the older London boroughs and hamlets had long-standing

---

[11] The main test is known as 'the Knowledge' as it involves learning street names and locations.

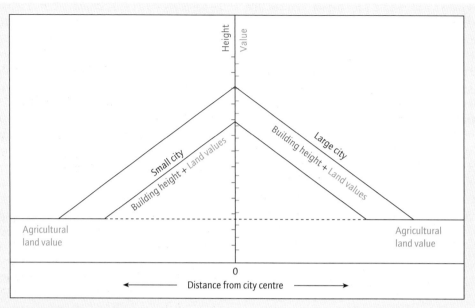

**Figure 12.4  Rent and height profiles**

**Both land rents and building heights tend to be highest at the city centre.** The figure shows two typical rent gradients for cities of two different sizes. Rents are highest at the city centre and fall towards the periphery. At the boundary between the city and the countryside, the rent that urban users can pay just equals the rent that can be paid for the same land in agricultural uses. Building heights will show a similar profile, being highest at the centre and tending to fall towards the periphery.

restrictions on building heights. These tended to push the new higher buildings away from the centre of the city to the nearest convenient location where these restrictions do not apply. Canary Wharf and Docklands are, literally and figuratively, monuments to the new construction technologies and the response of the market to economic and political forces.

What this case study tells us is that a city is an evolving entity whose past history determines much of its present character. None the less, its evolution over time is determined to a great extent by the size and type of buildings that the market shows to be currently most profitable, and this involves a decision about the installation of new capital.

## Conclusion

Capital is an important input into production. Increases in the capital stock are central to the process of generation of productivity gains that underpin the growth of real living standards over time. All businesses that invest in new capital have to make a careful assessment of the contribution of additional capital to the value of the firm.

New capital often embodies new technology, and technical change often has substantial implications for the range of employment opportunity and for the organization of firms and the economy as a whole. Recent and ongoing changes in information and communication technology are transforming the world in which we all live and work.

# SUMMARY

### Capital as an input

- Because capital goods are durable, it is necessary to distinguish between the stock of capital goods and the flow of services provided by them, and therefore between their purchase price and their rental price. The linkage between them relies on the ability to assign a present value to future returns. The present value of a future payment will be lower when the payment is more distant and the interest rate is higher.

- Firms will hire capital goods up to the point where the rental price of capital in each period equals its marginal revenue product in that period. The rental price is the amount that is paid to obtain the flow of services that a capital good provides for a given period. The purchase price is the amount that is paid to acquire ownership of the capital, and firms will buy capital goods up to the point where their price is just equal to the present value of the future net income stream generated by the capital. This is the present value of capital's future stream of marginal revenue products.

- An individual firm will invest in capital goods as long as the present value of the stream of future net incomes that are provided by another unit of capital exceeds its purchase price. For a single firm and for the economy as a whole, the size of the total capital stock demanded varies negatively with the rate of interest.

### The investment decision

- A central element of an investment appraisal is the choice of discount rate. Firms should discount future cash flows at a rate that reflects the cost of funds to them and the riskiness of the project involved.

- Present value calculations should allow for inflation appropriately.

- Sunk costs should not influence future investment decisions.

- The option value of an investment that has not yet been made may justify delaying the investment.

### New technology

- The revolution in information and communication technologies (ICTs) has roots that go back to the nineteenth century, but it accelerated in the latter part of the twentieth century when a new general purpose technology, the electronic computer and a few related technologies, began to transform much of the economic, social, and political structure of society.

- The revolution has been associated with many new products, new production processes, and new forms of organization.

- None the less, resources still move in response to price signals and profit motives and recessions and inflations have not been banished for ever.

- Two of the special features of ICT industries are increasing returns and network externalities. These generate a winner-take-all competition between firms.

# TOPICS FOR REVIEW

- The rental price and purchase price of capital
- The present value of a future sum
- The net present value (NPV) investment criterion
- The interest rate and the capital stock
- The risk-free rate and the risk premium
- Nominal and real interest rates
- Sunk costs
- The value of option to wait-and-see

- The ICT revolution
- General purpose technologies
- Declining cost curves resulting from high costs of R&D and setup for entry.
- Network externalities
- Winner takes all
- Winner's curse

## QUESTIONS

1 An extra tractor will lead to an increase in revenue for a farmer in successive years of £500, £4,000, £3,000, £3,000 and £1,000, after which the tractor is sold for £1,000. Assuming that the first revenue is treated as current and the interest rate is 8 per cent, what is the present value of the extra income stream?

2 If a new tractor costs £10,000 in the current period, would the purchase of the tractor increase the present value of profit?

3 If the tractor could be paid for in five equal instalments of £2,000 in each of the five years, would this make the purchase of the tractor more attractive?

4 Suppose you are offered, free of charge, one from each of the following pairs of assets: (a) a perpetuity that pays £20,000 per year for ever, or an annuity that pays £100,000 per year for five years; (b) an oil-drilling company that earned £100,000 after corporate taxes last year, or British government bonds that paid £100,000 in interest last year; (c) a 1 per cent share in a new company that has invested £10 million in a new cosmetic that is thought to appeal to middle-income women or a £100,000 bond that has been issued by the same company. What considerations would determine your choice in each case?

5 How would you go about evaluating the present value of each of the following? (a) a long-term bond, issued by a very unstable Third World government, that promises to pay the bearer £1,000 per year for ever; (b) a lottery ticket that your neighbour bought for £10 which was one of 1 million tickets sold for a draw to be held in one year's time that will pay £2 million to a single winner; (c) the value of a plot of land on the edge of a city which may get planning permission for a housing development.

6 List some of the ways in which increasing-returns industries differ from traditional diminishing-returns industries.

7 In what ways has the internet changed the education sector?

8 What threats and opportunities has digital music recording (including downloads) created for the market in recorded music?

# PART FOUR

# GOVERNMENT AND THE MARKET

# Chapter 13

# MARKET FAILURE

So far our main aims have been to understand how individual markets work, and how the market economy as a whole allocates resources between competing uses. We now ask whether market forces alone can be relied upon to deliver what are regarded as ideal outcomes. Do markets always generate efficient allocations of scarce resources? If they do not, in what circumstances do they fail to do so? Where markets fail, what alternative methods are available to deliver desired outcomes?

In particular, you will learn that:

- A perfectly competitive economy is allocatively efficient since it operates where price equals marginal cost.[1]

- Free markets can fail to achieve an efficient outcome for one of several possible causes of 'market failure'.

- Private markets will tend to overexploit common-property resources.

- Goods that can be jointly consumed by many people simultaneously are called public goods and cannot be provided efficiently by the market.

- The costs and benefits of production that are external to the producer cause the level of production that is achieved by the free market to deviate from the socially optimal level.

- Government policy towards competition is designed to encourage competitive practices and discourage monopoly.

In this chapter we first look at the basic functions that all governments have undertaken since the dawn of history: to provide institutions that protect the security of life, limb, and property. We see that if these functions are reasonably well performed, the free-market economy will allocate resources with relative efficiency. Indeed, an idealization of the free market, in which there is perfect competition in all markets, allocates resources optimally. We go on to see that in the real world markets fail to achieve complete efficiency under a number of well defined circumstances, including common property resources, public goods, harmful externalities, and excessive market power. These market failures provide the potential for government intervention to improve market efficiency. We see what government policies could achieve this objective under ideal circumstances. In Chapter 14 we study the role of government more broadly.

Because we are here concerned to assess how well the economy is doing at delivering the needs of society, the issues covered in this chapter and the next are sometimes called 'welfare economics'.

---

[1] We demonstrated this result in Chapter 7.

# Basic functions of government

Organized governments arose shortly after the neolithic agricultural revolution turned people from hunter–gatherers into settled farmers. An institution that has survived that long must be doing something right! Over the intervening 100 centuries, the functions undertaken by government have varied enormously. But through all that time, the function that has not changed is to provide what is called a *legal monopoly of violence*. Violent acts can be legally conducted only by the military and the civilian police arms of government. Also, through its judicial system the government can deprive people of their liberty by incarcerating them or, in extreme cases, by executing them. This is a dangerous monopoly that is easily abused, as is any monopoly, but with more serious consequences than when monopolies of production are abused. For these reasons, satisfactory governments have systems of checks and balances designed to keep the use of their monopoly power directed to the general good rather than to the good of individuals in a narrow government circle.

The importance of having a monopoly of violence can be seen in those countries whose governments do not have it. Somalia and Afghanistan in recent decades, and China in the 1920s, provide examples of countries in which individual warlords commanded armies that could not vanquish each other. Colombia, and to some extent Russia, provide examples of organized criminals with substantial power to commit violence that the government cannot control. In extreme cases where many groups have almost equal ability to exert military violence, power struggles can create havoc with normal economic and social life. Life then becomes 'nasty, brutish, and short'—to use the words of the seventeenth-century English political philosopher Thomas Hobbes.

The importance of having checks on the arbitrary use of such monopoly by a selfish government is seen in the disasters that ensue in the many dictatorships that misuse their power. The USSR under Stalin, Uganda under Idi Amin, Nigeria under Sanni Abacha, Cambodia under Pol Pot, Liberia under Charles Taylor, and Zimbabwe under Robert Mugabe are a few of the many modern-day examples.

When the government's monopoly of violence is secure and functions with reasonable restraints against its arbitrary use, citizens can safely carry on their ordinary economic and social activities.

So governments are, as they always have been, institutions to which people give over the legal monopoly of violence in return for the enforcement of 'law and order'.

A related government activity is to provide security of property. Governments define and enforce property rights that give people a secure claim to the fruits of their own labour. These property rights include clear definitions and enforcement of the rights and obligations of institutions such as joint-stock companies, banks, insurance companies, and stock exchanges as well as provisions for bankruptcy and protections against the rise and/or abuse of monopoly power over markets.

As the founder of British classical economics, Adam Smith, put it a long time ago:

*The first duty of the sovereign [is] that of protecting the society from the violence and invasion of other independent societies. . . . The second duty of the sovereign [is] that of protecting, as far as possible, every member of the society from the injustice or oppression of every other member of it.* (Smith 1776, pp. 653 and 669 of 1939 edition)

In a modern complex economy, providing these 'minimal' government services is no simple task. Countries whose governments are not good at doing these things have seldom prospered economically.

Before proceeding to discuss specific market outcomes in detail, it is important to recall that the market economy also determines the distribution of income by establishing the prices of resources (such as land, labour, and capital) that provide incomes for their owners. The income distribution that results may have characteristics that are regarded as undesirable, in that some people may have incomes on which it is impossible to live, either at all or at the minimum socially acceptable standard. Governments step in to ensure a safety net of some kind by redistributing the income that a pure market outcome would deliver. We do not list 'unacceptable, market-determined distributions of income' as a 'market failures' below because what is socially acceptable is a value judgement that is not a dimension of efficiency. We discuss the role of government in redistributing income in the following chapter.

# Market efficiency

Within a secure framework of law and order, with well defined and enforced property rights and other essential institutions, a modern economy can function at least moderately well without further government assistance. In this section we see how and why this is so. In subsequent sections we study government functions that arise when free markets fail to produce results that are regarded as acceptable.

Free markets are impressive institutions. Consumers' tastes and producers' costs help to generate price signals. These signals co-ordinate the separate decisions taken by millions of independent agents, all pursuing their own self-interest and oblivious to national priorities. In doing so, they allocate the nation's resources without conscious central direction. Furthermore, in modern market economies firms compete to get ahead of each other by producing better goods more cheaply, and in the process generate the technological changes that have raised average living standards fairly steadily at least over the past two centuries.

## How markets work

The most general case in support of market economies is that they fulfil their functions better than any known alternative. We observed that this *was* so in Chapter 1, but now we develop a deeper insight into *why* this is so.

### Better information

Market-generated prices convey an enormous amount of information about constantly changing market conditions. The central planners of the former Soviet Union found that generating this information by conscious planning was a massive job. For example, the Soviet authorities had to set prices for over 5 million items. Yet their economy was much simpler than any Western economy because the planners suppressed most of the vast range of differentiated products available to consumers in modern industrial economies.

### Greater flexibility

Compared with any known alternative, the decentralized market system is more flexible and leaves more scope for personal adaptation at any moment in time. If, for example, a scarcity of oil raises its price, one individual can elect to leave her heating on full and economize on her car's petrol consumption, while another may wish to do the opposite. In order to obtain the same overall reduction in consumption by non-price rationing, the government typically forces the same reduction in heating and driving on both individuals, independent of their tastes, doctor's advice, and other perceived needs.

### Better adaptability

In market economies prices change as conditions change. Decentralized decision-takers can react continuously to these changing signals, whereas government quotas, allocations, and rationing schemes are slower to adjust. Millions of adaptations to millions of changes in tens of thousands of markets are required every year. The Eastern European planners discovered that it is a Herculean task to anticipate these and plan the necessary adjustments.

### Decentralization of power

The market economy decentralizes power and thus requires less coercion of individuals than do other types of economy. Governments must coerce if markets are not allowed to allocate people to jobs, and products to consumers. The power to allocate creates major opportunities for bribery, corruption, and allocation according to the tastes of the central administrators. If, at the going prices and wages, there are not enough flats or coveted jobs to go around, the bureaucrats must allocate them. Some will go to those who pay the largest bribe, some to those with religious beliefs, hairstyles, or political views that they like, and only the rest to those whose names come up on the waiting-list.

Of course, large firms and large unions exercise substantial economic power in market economies. However, that power tends to be constrained both by the competition of other large entities and by the emergence of new products and firms.

## The efficiency of perfect competition

While they accept the general case for the superiority of the market economy just outlined, many professional economists want to be more precise about just what it is that the market economy does so well. They attempt to do this by proving that an idealization of the market economy (perfect competition) leads, in equilibrium, to an optimum, or efficient, allocation of resources. This result is often referred to as **Pareto optimality** after the great Italian economist Vilfredo Pareto (1848–1923), who studied it in great detail.

In Chapter 7 we showed that perfect competition was efficient because it maximized the sum of producers' and consumers' surplus. In Chapter 8 we showed that monopoly was not efficient because it restricts output below what is required to maximize these surpluses. In this section we develop an alternative proof of the proposition that perfect competition leads to efficient allocation of resources. As a first step, we enquire in a little more depth into the meaning of the term *efficiency*.

## Productive efficiency

Production is efficient when it is impossible to reallocate resources so as to produce more of some product without producing less of some other product. Watch the double negative! An allocation of resources is productively *in*efficient when it is possible to produce more of some product without producing less of any other product. It is efficient when this cannot be done—in other words, when the only way to produce more of one product is to produce less of some other product.

Productive efficiency has two aspects: one concerns the allocation of resources within each firm, and the other, the allocation of resources among the firms in an industry. The first condition for productive efficiency is that each firm should produce any given output at the lowest possible cost. Any firm that is not being productively efficient is producing at a higher cost than is necessary. This must reduce its profits. Thus, any perfectly competitive profit-maximizing firm will be productively efficient.[2]

The second condition for productive efficiency is that all firms producing the same product have the same marginal cost. This ensures that the total output of each industry is allocated among its individual firms in such a way that the total cost of producing the industry's output is minimized. If all firms' marginal costs were not the same, resources could be transferred from the firm with the highest marginal cost to the firm with lowest. The same output would be produced, but at a lower cost.

Perfect competition produces productive efficiency. First, all firms are motivated to produce at the lowest possible cost. Second, since firms in any one industry face the same price to which they equate their marginal cost, all firms have the same marginal cost.

Look again at the production possibility frontier in Figure 1.1 on page 6. An economy that is productively inefficient will be at some point inside the curve, such as point *c*. It will be possible to produce more of some goods without producing less of others.

Productive efficiency implies being on, rather than inside, the economy's production possibility frontier.

## Allocative efficiency

Allocative efficiency relates to the allocation of resources among the industries that supply all the goods and services that are produced within an economy. In other words,

Allocative efficiency relates to the choice among alternative points on the production possibility frontier.

It concerns, for example, the choice between points such as *a* and *b* in Figure 1.1 on page 6. Changing the allocation of resources implies producing more of some goods and less of others, which in turn means moving from one point on the production possibility curve to another.

**Allocative inefficiency** means that resources can be reallocated from their present uses so as to make at least one person better off while making no other person worse off. Conversely, **allocative efficiency** means that it is impossible, by producing a different bundle of goods, to make any one person better off without making at least one other person worse off.

How do we find the allocatively efficient point on the production possibility curve? For example, how many shoes, dresses, and hats should be produced to achieve allocative efficiency? The answer is as follows:

The economy's allocation of resources is efficient when the marginal cost of producing each good is equal to its market price.

To understand the reasoning behind this answer, we need to look at the significance of price and marginal cost.

First, look at price. The price of any product indicates the value that each consumer places on the last unit purchased of that product. Faced with the market price of some product, the consumer goes on buying units until the last one is valued exactly at its price. Consumers' surplus arises because each consumer would be willing to pay more than the market price for all but the last unit bought (see the discussion on page 91). On the last unit bought (i.e. the marginal unit), however, the consumer only 'breaks even', because the valuation placed on it is just equal to its price.

---

[2] This result is restricted to price-taking firms, because inefficient production, using more fixed capital than is necessary, can be an entry-barring strategy for oligopolistic firms. It may pay firms in such markets to produce above the minimum attainable cost in order to maximize profits in the long run by restricting entry.

Now consider marginal cost. This is the value of the resources used to produce the last unit of output. Thus, when marginal cost is equated to price, the value that consumers place on the last unit they consume is exactly equal to the value of the resources required to produce that unit of output.

For the next step in the argument, suppose that the entire economy is perfectly competitive. Marginal cost will then equal price in all lines of production. The value that consumers place on the last unit of each and every commodity that they consume will be equal to the cost of producing that unit.

In a perfectly competitive economy, £1 worth of resources reallocated from the production of any one product would produce £1 worth of value for consumers, whatever product it was then used to produce.

To illustrate, assume that marginal cost equals price in all lines of production except blue jeans. Jeans sell for £25 but initially cost £30 to produce at the margin. If one fewer pair of jeans is produced, consumers lose the £25 of value that they place on it. But resources worth £30 are freed. If those resources move to any industry in which marginal cost equals price, they will produce £30 worth of value. Society will have gained £5 in total value, and it will be possible to make someone better off by £5 worth of consumption without making anyone else worse off.

Now let the output of jeans be such that they cost only £20 to produce at the margin but still sell for £25. If one more pair of jeans is now produced, resources worth £20 will have to be withdrawn from some other line of production. But since marginal cost equals price in all other lines, only £20 worth of consumer satisfaction will be lost when these resources move. When they produce one more pair of jeans, consumers get a product they value at £25. So there is a net gain of £5 on the transfer.

Finally, let the output of jeans increase until the marginal cost of the last pair produced is equal to its £25 price. If *one pair of jeans fewer* is produced, £25 worth of value is sacrificed and the £25 worth of resources that are freed could produce £25 worth of value anywhere else in the economy. If *one pair of jeans more* is produced, the producers of jeans create £25 of value but £25 of value is lost when the resources are taken from some other industry. So there is no gain in reallocating resources either into or out of the production of blue jeans. The current allocation is efficient.

When marginal cost equals price in all industries, it is impossible to reallocate resources between alternative lines of production and increase consumer satisfaction. The economy is allocatively efficient.

A perfectly competitive economy is allocatively efficient because it equates marginal cost to price in all lines of production and (as we saw in earlier chapters—see page 154) because it maximizes the sum of producers' and consumers' surplus. Unfortunately, such perfectly competitive economies do not, and could not, exist in the world in which we live.

## How markets fail

The term **market failure** describes the failure of the market economy to achieve an efficient allocation of resources. We observed in Chapter 9 that firms in most lines of production have some market power over their prices because they face negatively sloped rather than perfectly elastic demand curves for their products. When firms face negatively sloped demand curves, price will exceed marginal cost in equilibrium. For this reason, no real market economy has ever achieved anything even close to perfect allocative efficiency. The conditions for efficiency are meant only as a benchmark to help in identifying sources of allocative inefficiency, called market failures. These sources provide scope for possible government intervention designed to improve market efficiency—even if not to achieve complete efficiency. (But there are also costs of such intervention, which we consider later in this chapter.)

There are several important circumstances under which markets fail to allocate resources with reasonable efficiency, let alone to achieve the optimal allocation of resources:[3]

1. Producers with excess capacity set positive prices, referred to as inefficient exclusion.

2. There are resources that can be used by everyone but belong to no one—called common property resources.

3. Public goods exist. A public good is a good that is non-rivalrous, so your consuming it does not preclude my consuming it at the same time, and non-excludable, so that I cannot prevent you from consuming it once it is produced.

4. People not party to some market bargain are none the less significantly affected by it, i.e. externalities.

5. One party to a market transaction has fuller knowledge of its consequences than is available to the other party—a situation referred to as asymmetric information.

6. Needed markets do not exist—known as missing markets.

7. Substantial monopoly power causes prices to diverge from marginal costs.

---

[3] New terms introduced in this list are explained below in this chapter.

Coping with these market failures provides govern-ments with major functions in addition to the law and order functions discussed earlier. In the rest of this chapter we study these sources of market failure and how government policies could conceivably alleviate them. In Chapter 14 we study the costs of government intervention, which must be set against the possible bene-fits before an intervention is justified on economic grounds. This raises the question of how well government policies actually work in coping with market failures as well as in achieving all the other goals that governments set for themselves.

# Rivalrous and excludable goods

Economies must allocate resources between the produc-tion and consumption of the four major classes of goods and services that are shown in Table 13.1. A good is **rival-rous** if no two people can *consume* the same unit. For example, if you buy and eat an apple, no one else can buy and eat that same apple. A good is **excludable** if people can be prevented from *obtaining* it. Excludability requires that an owner be able to exercise effective property rights over the good or service in order to determine who uses it—typically, only those who pay for the privilege.

Most of the goods and services that you and I buy are rivalrous and excludable. If I buy a chocolate bar and eat it, no one else can buy and eat that same bar, and the owner can prevent me from having it if I am unwilling to pay for it (unless I steal it). If an airline sells you a seat on a particular flight, it cannot let another person occupy that seat as well as you.

Obvious though these characteristics may seem, there are important classes of goods and services that lack one or both of them. Goods and services are **non-rivalrous** when the amount that one person consumes does not affect the amount that other people can consume. They are **non-excludable** when, once produced, there is no way to stop anyone from consuming them.

Rivalrousness is usually fixed once and for all by the nature of the good or service. An apple is rivalrous; a work of art is not. In contrast, excludability depends on the specific circumstances and the state of technology.

## What determines which is which?

### Circumstances

The Fastnet lighthouse guides all shipping making a land-fall on southwest Ireland, and there is no way to force passing ships to pay for its services. The New Brighton lighthouse illuminates the entrance to the River Mersey and the Port of Liverpool, and if its operators had turned it off (prior to the invention of radar) many ships would have passed on to another, better-lit harbour entrance. In this case private owners could sell the lighthouse's services not to passing ships, but to the port authorities, who knew they needed it in order to compete with rival ports.

### Technology

Early TV programmes were all broadcast openly to anyone who had a set. But the development of satellites, encoded signals, and cable transmission has allowed some forms of TV signals to be provided only to those who pay for the service. The programmes are still non-rivalrous, in the sense that there is no limit to the number of people who can watch a given programme. But the new technologies made them excludable so that private companies would

**Table 13.1  Four types of goods**

|  | Excludable | Non-excludable |
|---|---|---|
| Rivalrous | *Normal goods* | *Common property* |
|  | Apples | Fisheries |
|  | Dresses | Common land |
|  | TV sets | Wildlife |
|  | Computers | Air |
|  | A seat on an aeroplane | Streams |
| Non-rivalrous (up to capacity) |  | *Public goods* |
|  | Art galleries | Defence |
|  | Museums | Police |
|  | Fenced parks | Public information |
|  | Roads | Broadcast signals |
|  | Bridges | Some navigation aids |

**Markets cope best with rivalrous excludable goods.** The table gives examples of items in each of the four categories. The market can produce goods that are excludable but non-rivalrous, but their efficient use requires a zero price. Goods that are non-excludable but rivalrous are common property resources, which get overused by free markets. Goods that are non-rivalrous and non-excludable are public goods, which will usually not be produced at all by the free market.

be willing to provide them. As another example, until recently it has been impracticable to charge tolls for the use of urban roads and to exclude non-payers because of the excessive costs involved in the many tollbooths needed to service a road in a densely populated urban area. Today it is possible to implant in each car a device that tracks its location at very small cost. Fees for the use of urban roads can now be assessed and non-payers denied use of the roads, or charged a fine.

### Cost

In some cases it is technically possible to make a good excludable but too costly to do so. One could put a fence around the Lake District National Park and charge hikers a fee for walking in the area, but the cost of erecting and policing the fence would make it uneconomic to exclude non-payers.

In what follows, we look at the characteristics of goods and services that fall into the four possible combinations of excludable and non-excludable and rivalrous and non-rivalrous as shown in Table 13.1.

## Excludable goods

Private agents who produce goods and services for sale on the free market must be able to prohibit consumption of their output by those who will not pay for the privilege; otherwise the producers cannot gain the revenue they need to cover their production costs.

So excludability is necessary for a good to be produced by a firm for sale on the market.

### Ordinary goods: excludable and rivalrous

The market works best when goods and services are rivalrous and excludable.

Private firms can produce and sell such goods and services. Furthermore, these firms will fulfil the condition for allocative efficiency by operating where marginal cost equals price as long as they are price-takers.

### Art galleries, museums, and parks: excludable but non-rivalrous

Some excludable goods and services are non-rivalrous, at least up to a large capacity constraint. This is the first reason on our list of market failures. A park with a fence around it provides an excludable service, but one person's use does not interfere with another person's use—at least, not until there are so many users that overcrowding becomes a serious problem. Such goods can be provided by private firms, but since the marginal cost of adding

another user is zero (until capacity is reached), any admission fee that the owner charges will result in a non-optimal use of the facility. It costs nothing to add another user, but to cover their costs the providers must charge each user a fee. Thus, under private provision, price will exceed marginal cost and some people who are willing to pay more than this marginal cost but less than the current price do not use it. This market failure is called **inefficient exclusion**.

To avoid inefficient exclusions, the government often provides non-rivalrous but excludable goods and services.

The costs are then met out of taxation, and the service is provided free. Parks, art galleries, roads, and bridges often come under this category. Box 13.1 reviews the debate that arose in the early 1990s when the Conservative government in the UK reduced the grants to galleries and museums and the trustees of some felt they had little option but to levy charges for admission. The subsequent Labour government later abolished admission charges. (See also the evidence on what happened when these charges were abolished, in Chapter 4 on page 82.)

## Non-excludable goods

This class provides the next two sources on our list of major market failures: those associated with common property resources and public goods.

### Common property: non-excludable but rivalrous

If you catch a fish in the open ocean, I cannot catch it, so it is rivalrous. But in a free market there is no way for you to exclude me from catching it, so it is non-excludable. This is the second reason on our list of causes of market failures. A **common property resource** is one that is rivalrous but non-excludable. No one has an exclusive property right to it, and it can be used by anyone. No one owns the ocean's fish until they are caught. No one owns common grazing land. The world's international fishing grounds are common property for all fishermen, as is common grazing land for all livestock owners. If, by taking more fish, one fisherman reduces the catch of other fishermen, he does not count this as a cost, although it is a cost to society. If, by grazing her own sheep, a peasant reduces the grass available for other people's goats, she does not count this as a cost. The result has been called *the tragedy of the commons*—the tendency for commonly held property to be overexploited, often to the extent of destruction.

It is socially optimal to add to a fleet that is fishing any given fishing area until the last boat increases the *value of*

## Box 13.1  Pricing of galleries and museums

Art galleries, museums, fenced parks, bridges, and similar public institutions are examples of goods that are excludable—admission is easily controlled at entrances—but non-rivalrous, at least up to substantial capacity. Except on crowded days, one person's use does not reduce another person's ability to use the facility. The efficient solution is to allow everyone to use the facility free of charge on non-crowded days but to charge a price on days when the crowds do make the facility's use a rivalrous activity.

The argument *against* the policy of free admission runs along the following lines. Many taxpayers who never use the facility, and do not even care that it exists, are forced to help to pay for it. Many of these people may have lower-than-average incomes and be less well educated. So the free-admission policy is to a great extent a subsidy for middle-class persons with particular tastes. In times of financial stringency, those who want the facility should pay for it.

Whatever the reasons, in the early 1990s the UK Conservative government decided to curtail its support for the arts drastically. In response, many museum and gallery trustees decided that the only course open to them was to introduce admission charges, although others did not. Controversy was sustained and often bitter.

Those who opposed the imposition of charges argued several points. The admission fees would lead to inefficient exclusion. Institutions that were underused and could add more visitors would be excluding potential users by their not-insignificant charges. Those excluded would be from lower-income classes that had contributed little to the costs of operation in the past because they paid little in income tax.

There is no easy resolution of such debates. They tend to pit those who worry about equity against those who worry about efficiency. But even that is not always a clear division. It is an equity argument that those who benefit from the facilities should pay for them. But it is also an equity argument that positive admission fees should not be used to preclude the poor from taking part in an activity that has a zero marginal cost.

In 2001 the Labour government abolished admission charges. (See the evidence on the increase in admissions that followed the price reductions on page 82.) What is not clear is whether the government was swayed more by concerns about equity or about efficiency in reaching this decision.

of fishing fleet and flock of sheep that a social planner or a private monopolist would choose.

**The socially optimal exploitation of a common property resource occurs when the marginal cost of the last user equals the value of the marginal addition to total output.**

The free market will not, however, produce that result. Consider the fishery. Potential new entrants will judge entry to be profitable if the *value of their own catch* is equal to the costs of operating their boats. But a new entrant's catch is *partly* an addition to total catch and *partly* a reduction of the catch of other fishermen—because of congestion, each new boat reduces the catch of all other boats. Thus, under competitive free entry there will be too many boats in the fleet and too many sheep on the common.

How does a potential new fisherman judge the value of entering the industry? He will expect to do about as well as the average boat. So it pays him to enter, adding a new boat to the fleet, until the *average* value of the catch of a typical boat in the fleet is equal to the cost of running the newly entering boat.[4]

**The free market will add users to a common property resource until the marginal cost of the last entrant equals the *average* output of all existing producers.**

At this point, however, the *net* addition to the *total* catch brought about by the last boat will be substantially less than the cost of operating the boat, and it may even be negative.

**With common property resources the level of output will be too high, because each new entrant will not take account of the cost that he or she imposes on existing producers.**

This tendency towards overexploitation of a common property resource is illustrated by the example in Figure 13.1. Free-market entry proceeds until the cost of the last boat, which is the average total cost per boat, equals the revenue it expects, which is the average revenue per boat. This is the same as saying that total cost equals total revenue—so there are no economic profits to attract further entrants. The surplus over cost that could be earned with a smaller fleet is dissipated by entry. In this example, the fishing fleet is 100 vessels. Each boat costs £10,000 to run and catches £10,000 worth of fish. If the fleet were

---

the fleet's *total catch* by as much as it costs to operate the boat. Similarly, it is optimal to add another sheep to the flock that grazes on the commons as long as the total supply of meat (and milk) is increased by as much as the cost of maintaining the extra animal. These are the sizes

[4] This subtle point is the same as the difference between the perfectly competitive producer and the monopolist. The monopolist knows that if it sells more, it will reduce the market value of what it is already selling. The perfect competitor must take the market price as given and so will value a marginal unit of production at the market price, i.e. at the *average value* of all units already being sold.

**Figure 13.1** Overfishing of a common property fishery

A common property resource is exploited beyond the socially optimal level. Adding boats to the fleet adds to the total catch but at a diminishing rate up to 140 boats, after which additional boats lower the total catch. With the old technology, the cost (capital and current) of running each boat is £10,000, giving the steeper of the two total cost curves. The socially optimal level is 35 boats, where the addition to total catch, as shown by the slope of the tangent to the total catch curve, just equals the addition to the total cost of running one more boat, as shown by the slope of the total cost curve. At that point there is a surplus of revenue over total cost of £150,000. At that fleet size, a new boat expects to catch about £14,300 (i.e. £500,000/35) worth of fish, so entry is profitable from the private point of view. When the fleet reaches 100 boats, a new boat expects to catch £10,000 worth of fish, which just matches its cost. With new technology, each boat costs only £4,000 to run. The fleet expands to 200 boats catching £800,000 worth of fish. This yields revenue of £4,000 per boat, which just matches cost. Production has been pushed beyond the point of negative marginal returns.

restricted to 35 boats, each £10,000 boat would catch fish worth just over £14,000. The new technology reduces the cost of running each. Entry then proceeds well beyond the 140-boat level where each additional boat actually begins to reduce the total catch.

Fishing grounds, common pastures, and other common property resources often show a pattern of overexploitation.

This is true of almost all of today's fishing grounds, except where the catch is effectively regulated by government intervention. Case study 2 at the end of this chapter discusses the issue of fishing further.

One solution to the common property problem is to agree on the optimal level of use and then police the resource to reduce its use to that level. This is done with such items as fishing quotas and hunting licences. The problem here is to enforce the restrictions. It is possible to

control the number of fish caught in the high seas, but doing so is difficult and costly, as attested by the frequent international disputes over alleged quota violations.

Another method is for the state to create property rights that make the resource excludable. Its private owners then have an incentive to exploit it efficiently. The English enclosure movement that peaked between 1793 and 1815 did just that. Although those who had previously used the common grazing land were hurt by the measure, the land was used much more efficiently under private ownership. Issuing licences for the use of each particular wavelength can control the airwaves. State-owned forests that are being destroyed by excessive wood gathering can be sold to private owners. Property rights to wildlife can be given to local villages. And so on. This last case is controversial and is further discussed in Box 13.2. The problem of the tropical rainforests is discussed in case study 1 on page 296.

All of these cases involve a trade-off between efficiency and equity. When a common property resource is 'privatized', the efficiency of its use typically rises but the former users typically suffer some losses. The difficult issue of trading off efficiency of the resource's use against justice for the present users has no easy resolution. What is sure, however, is that, if the resource is being exploited to the point of destruction, little is achieved for either equity or efficiency by preserving its common property status.

### Public goods: non-excludable and non-rivalrous

Goods that are neither excludable nor rivalrous are called **public goods**, or sometimes **collective consumption goods**. They provide the third reason on our list of the causes of market failure. The classic case is national defence. An army of a given size protects all the nation's citizens equally, no matter how many citizens there are and whether or not a particular individual pays taxes to support it. Similarly, a police force that keeps the public streets safe protects all of the street's users, no matter how many there are. If some do not pay their share of the costs, they cannot be denied protection as long as they continue to use the safe street. Information is often a public good. It is clearly non-rivalrous and often non-excludable. Suppose a certain food additive causes cancer. The cost of discovering this has to be paid only once. The information is then of value to everyone who might have used the additive. Once it is in the public domain, no one can be stopped from learning about it. Other public goods include lighthouses (in most but not all circumstances) and publicly available weather forecasts.

Because public goods are non-excludable, private firms will not provide them.

**Box 13.2 Buffalo, cows, and elephants**

For centuries North American bison—commonly called buffalo —were a common property resource for the Plains Indians, whose populations were small enough that they could kill all they needed without endangering the ability of the herds to reproduce themselves. In a little over a decade following the end of the American Civil War in 1865, white hunters decimated the herds. Buffalo Bill Cody may have been a folk hero, but he, and those like him, were the buffalo's executioners.

The buffalo was replaced by cattle, which did not follow the buffalo into extinction. The difference was that cattle were the private property of the ranchers. Rustlers and other predators attacked the herds, but the self-interest of ranchers made it worthwhile for them to protect their cattle.

Many people, watching the decimation of wildlife in Africa and Asia, have argued that property rights should be used to turn these animals from the modern equivalent of the buffalo into the modern equivalent of cattle. Wildlife is a common property resource. When it becomes endangered, laws are passed to prevent predatory hunting. But no one has any profit motive in enforcing these laws. Government officials are employed to do this job, but they are often few in number and poorly paid. Some

become corrupted by the large sums that poachers are willing to pay to avoid enforcement. Others find the policing job impossible, given the inadequate resources that their governments devote to enforcement.

Some African governments have dealt with the problem by giving ownership of the wild animals to local villages and allowing them to use the animals as a commercial asset. The animals are the subjects of camera safaris, whose organizers pay the locals for the privilege. They are also prey for hunters, who pay large sums for licences to kill a selected number of animals. Local tribesmen control the poachers and keep the licensed kill rate below the reproduction rate because they have a profit motive in protecting what has become their very valuable property.

These schemes have many opponents as well as many supporters. Some opponents object to any permissible 'sports hunting' and other commercial use of wild animals. They argue for more effective public enforcement of anti-poaching laws. Supporters counter that leaving the animals as common property is bound to result in their extinction. Farming them is, they argue, better than presiding over their extinction.

---

The obvious remedy in such cases is for the government to provide the good and pay for its provision out of general tax revenue.

### When should a public good be provided?

To illustrate the basic principle, consider a community composed of just two consumers. The government is considering whether or not to provide a park. Arthur is prepared to pay up to £200 for use of the park, while Julia is willing to pay up to £100. The total value to the two individuals of having the park is £300. If it can be produced for £225, there is a £75 gain on its production since it provides services that the community values at £300 at a cost of only £225.

### The optimal quantity of a public good

The above example reveals a key point about public goods. If one person consumes a unit of an ordinary good, another person cannot also consume that unit; thus, to satisfy all the demand at any given price, the sum of all the quantities demanded must be produced. With a public good, however, everyone can consume any specific unit. A new defence system, for example, protects everyone in the country, and the fact that one person is protected does not reduce the protection received by all others.

The demand for a unit of the good is represented by the sum of the prices that each individual consumer would be

willing to pay for that unit. Therefore, the community's demand curve for a public good is the vertical sum of the demand curves of the individual consumers.

If the amount of a public good can be varied continuously, the optimal quantity to produce is that quantity for which the marginal cost of the last unit is just equal to the sum of the prices that all consumers would be willing to pay for that unit.

This equilibrium, which is analysed in Figure 13.2, guarantees that the last unit of the public good costs as much to produce as the value that it gives to all of its consumers.

### Who pays?

One way to pay for a public good is to charge each person the same proportion of the maximum amount he or she would be prepared to pay rather than go without the good, while fixing that proportion so as to cover the total costs of production. In the two-person community discussed above, Arthur is prepared to pay £200 and Julia £100 for the park rather than go without. If it costs £150 to produce, then each can be charged one-half of their own maximum, making £100 for Arthur and £50 for Julia. Each of them then gets the use of the park for half of what he or she is prepared to pay. Their payments just cover total costs of production, leaving £150 of total consumers' surplus.

**Figure 13.2  A public good**

The society's demand curve for a public good is the vertical sum of all the individuals' demand curves. The demand curves $D_a$ and $D_b$ refer to two individuals. Their collective demand is shown by $D_m$, which is the vertical summation of $D_a$ and $D_b$. For example, individual a would pay $p_0$ for quantity $q_0$, while individual b would pay $p_1$ for the same quantity. Together they are willing to pay the sum of $p_0$ and $p_1$, which is $p_2$.

The optimal quantity of the good to produce is $q_0$, where the marginal cost curve $MC$ cuts the collective demand curve. At this point the marginal cost of another unit is just equal to the sum of the values that each person places on that unit.

The practical problem in using any formula based on what people are willing to pay for the public good lies in getting people to reveal their preferences. Suppose, for example, that the government is considering building a public park to serve a community of 1,000 people. It asks each of them how much they are prepared to pay. If I am one of those 1,000, it is in my interests to understate my true valuation, as long as everyone else does not do the same. Indeed, I might say I valued the park at zero, while others reported enough value to cover the costs between them. The public good would then be produced, and I would get the use of it at no cost whatsoever to me.

The **free rider problem** refers to each person's motivation to understate the value of a non-rivalrous good in the hope that others will end up paying for it. This motivation makes it difficult to cover the costs of such goods by any formula based on people's individual valuations.

**The free rider problem can be avoided by covering the costs of public goods out of tax revenue.**

Goods such as national defence, weather forecasts, navigation aids, police, and fire protection are typically paid for from tax revenue and provided free to all users. This allows the goods to be produced above the levels at which the free market would produce them. (Often the free market would produce nothing.) It also avoids the problem of *inefficient exclusion* that we encountered in the context of discussion of the first source of market failure above. Those who value a particular good more highly than the average valuation gain more than those who value it at below the average valuation. The hope is that over a large number of public goods these individual differences will cancel out. Everyone will then gain on balance as a result of the government's provision of public goods out of tax revenue.

# Externalities

A perfectly competitive economy allocates resources optimally because price equals marginal cost in all lines of production. For this outcome to happen, it is necessary that all costs are incurred by the producers and all benefits are reaped by their customers. This localization of costs does not occur when there are **externalities**, which are costs or benefits of a transaction that are incurred or received by other members of the society but are not taken into account by the parties to the transaction. They are also called *third-party effects* and sometimes *neighbourhood effects*, because parties other than the primary participants in the transaction (the consumers and the producers) are affected. Externalities are the fourth item on our list of causes of market failure.

Externalities arise in many different ways, and they may be beneficial or harmful. A harmful externality occurs, for example, when a factory generates pollution. Individuals who live and work in the neighbourhood bear costs arising from the factory's production, including adverse health effects and clean-up costs. Profit-maximizing factory owners do not take these effects into account when they decide how much to produce. The element of social cost that they ignore is external to their decision-making process.

A beneficial externality occurs, for example, when I paint my house and enhance my neighbours' views and the values of their properties. Other cases arise when some genius—an Einstein, a Mozart, a van Gogh—gives the world discoveries and works of art whose worth is far in excess of what he or she is paid to create them.

Externalities create a divergence between the private benefits and costs of economic activity and the social benefits and costs. **Private costs** are those costs that are incurred by the parties directly involved in some economic activity. When a good is produced, the private costs are those borne by the producing firm. **Social costs** are the costs incurred by the whole society. These are the private costs *plus* any costs borne by third parties. **Private benefits** are the benefits received by those involved in the activity. In the case of a marketed good, these are the utilities obtained by buyers. **Social benefits** are the benefits to the whole society. They are the private benefits *plus* any benefit to third parties.

Society's resources are optimally allocated when social marginal cost equals social marginal benefit.

When this is the case, there can be no social benefit in reallocating resources among different lines of production. Free markets will not produce social optimality when there are discrepancies between private and social costs and private and social benefits. The reason is that under perfect competition *private* marginal cost is equated to *private* marginal benefit (the price of the product).

Two important results follow immediately.

1. The outputs of firms that create harmful externalities will exceed the socially optimal levels.

When marginal private cost is equated to price and hence to marginal private benefit, marginal social cost, which is higher because of harmful externalities, will exceed marginal social benefit. Thus, there is social gain from reducing the level of output. The reason for this discrepancy is that the private firm takes no account of the costs imposed on others.

2. The outputs of firms that create beneficial externalities will be less than the socially optimal levels.

When marginal private cost is equated to price and hence to marginal private benefit, the marginal social benefit, which is higher because of beneficial externalities, will exceed marginal social cost. Thus, there is social gain from increasing the level of output. The reason is that the private firm takes no account of the benefits received by others.

Consider a simple example in which an electric power station produces 1 million units of electricity per day at a marginal cost of 5p per unit and sells power for 5p per unit to consumers. If there are no externalities, this is the socially optimal output, because the 5p valuation that

**Figure 13.3 Private and social cost**

Negative externalities cause marginal social cost to exceed price in competitive equilibrium. Marginal social cost, $MC_s$, exceeds marginal private cost, $MC_p$, by the amount of the external cost imposed on others. At the competitive output, $q_0$, marginal private cost equals price, but marginal social cost exceeds it. The socially optimal output is $q^*$, where $MC_s$ = price. For every unit between $q^*$ and $q_0$ marginal social cost exceeds price and hence its production involves a social loss.

each consumer puts on the last unit consumed is equal to the 5p opportunity cost of producing that unit. Now let there be 2p of negative externalities created when each unit is produced (perhaps from pollution of the atmosphere from a coal or gas-fired station). The marginal social cost of 7p exceeds the marginal social benefit of 5p on the last unit produced. To move towards the social optimum, output should be reduced. Alternatively, suppose the externality is beneficial instead of harmful, conferring external benefits valued at 3p a unit on third parties. Now marginal social benefit of 8p exceeds marginal social cost of 5p. To approach a social optimum, output should be increased.

To achieve the optimal allocation of resources in the face of externalities, the production of goods with positive externalities needs to be encouraged and the production of those with negative externalities to be discouraged, compared with what would be produced under free market conditions.

Figure 13.3 illustrates the market failures caused by externalities as well as their optimal correction.

## Externalities and the Coase theorem

Externalities arise because of a lack of property rights. A factory throws its liquid waste into the river and its smoke into the atmosphere because no one owns the river or the atmosphere. Both are common property resources. If they were in private hands, the owners would have a self-interest in preserving them. Let us see how this might come about.

### An example

Say, for example, that a manufacturing plant needs pure water for one of its processes. It gets this from a short mountain stream that then tumbles into the ocean. A chemical plant is established upstream and dumps its waste into the river. The river is a common property resource so the plant cannot be stopped from imposing negative externalities on the downstream user, who must now set up an expensive water purification system.

#### A downstream owner

Assume that the downstream plant owns the stream. Its owner might say to the chemical plant's managers, 'Do not dump *your* waste into *my* stream.' The managers might counter that they were willing to pay for the privilege. The downstream owner asks, 'How much?' After considering the cost of alternative waste-disposal mechanisms, the chemical plant's managers answer, '£6 per tonne of waste'. The owner of the downstream plant determines that the cost of purifying the water in the stream is £8 per tonne of waste. 'No deal,' she says. The upstream chemical plant opens an alternative waste-disposal system at a cost of £6, and the least costly method of dealing with the waste is thus used.

Later, technological improvements in water purification allow the downstream plant to purify its water for only £3 per tonne. The owner calls the upstream managers and says, 'I hear your disposal plant is coming up for renewal next year. I am prepared to let you dump the waste in my stream for a fee of £4 per tonne.' 'Done,' say the upstream managers, and next year the waste is disposed of in the river. The water is then cleaned up by the downstream user at a cost of £3 per tonne, instead of at a cost of £6 when the chemical plant treated the waste. Once again, the cheapest method of disposal and use is adopted.

#### An upstream owner

What would have happened if the river had been owned by the chemical plant instead of the downstream user? The managers of the chemical plant decide to use their stream for disposing of their waste. But the downstream users of water complain and offer to pay for the use of the fresh water. Their costs of making the water usable are £8 per tonne of waste. So they can offer up to that much

to dissuade the chemical plant from dumping its waste. The plant can use an alternative waste-disposal method at a cost of £6 per tonne. So the managers say, 'Yes, how about giving us £7 for every tonne of our waste that we do not dump into our river?' A deal is struck and the cheapest method is undertaken.

Later, when the new water purification technology is developed, the downstream users can purify the water at a cost of only £3 per tonne. So they will offer no more than that to prevent the chemical plant from dumping its waste. When the upstream plant's alternative waste-disposal system wears out, it will not be replaced. The waste will be dumped, and the downstream plant will purify its water at a cost of £3 per tonne. Once again, the cheapest method of dealing with the waste will have been adopted.

### The theorem

This example illustrates a remarkable result developed some years ago by the British-born economist Ronald Coase, who received the 1991 Nobel Prize in economics. The result is now called the **Coase theorem**:

If the two sides to an externality—the one causing it and the one suffering from it—can bargain together with zero transaction costs, they will produce the efficient use of resources.

What is needed is that one of the two has a property right that forces the other side to bargain. Surprisingly, however, it does not matter which side has the property right. We saw this in the above example, where the same result was arrived at independently of who owned the river. Property rights will determine who gets most of the consumers' surplus on the bargain, because they determine who has to pay whom. But, given that both sides will bargain for their own self-interest, the allocation of resources to deal with the externality will be independent of where the property right resides.

### High transaction costs

What makes the Coase theorem work is (*a*) that someone has a property right over what is affected by the externality, (*b*) that both sides can bargain effectively together, *and* (*c*) that nothing can go ahead until they have reached an agreement. The second condition is a matter of transaction costs. It was easy enough for the owners of the two plants to talk on the phone and reach an efficient bargain; it is another matter for all the citizens of the cities of London or São Paulo to bargain with the hundreds of factory owners, car drivers, and other producers of pollution in order to reach an efficient solution to dealing with air and water pollution in and around their cities.

In cases in which property rights cannot be assigned and/or where transaction costs are excessive, there are only two possibilities. We may accept the externality and learn to live with it, or governments may intervene on our behalf to deal with it.

We will see however that, although governments often do improve matters somewhat, arriving at the most efficient solution is no easy task.

# The control of pollution

In this section we illustrate government policies with respect to negative externalities in the context of one of their most important applications: environmental damage caused by pollution. Steel plants produce heat and smoke in addition to steel. Farms produce chemical runoff as well as food. Household consumption produces human waste and refuse. Indeed, there are few human activities that do not produce some negative pollution externalities.

For this reason, it is impossible to reduce pollution to zero. Instead, the optimal amount of pollution abatement occurs when the marginal benefit of a unit of abatement is just equal to the marginal cost of abatement.

Unregulated markets tend to produce excessive amounts of environmental damage. Zero environmental damage, however, is neither technologically possible nor economically efficient.

Some types of pollution are a global problem and international agreements are required in order to achieve results. Of major current concern is the problem of climate change, which is (at least in part) caused by emissions of greenhouse gases such as carbon dioxide, which result from the burning of fossil fuels such as coal and oil. One attempt to conclude an international agreement to limit global greenhouse gas emissions is the Kyoto Protocol of 1997, which was a modification of the United Nations Framework Convention on Climate Change. Signatories to the Kyoto Protocol agreed on average cuts of greenhouse gas emissions of around 5 per cent of the 1990 level by 2010 (which would amount to more like 30 per cent of the predicted 2010 level). As of July 2006, 164 countries had signed the Kyoto Protocol, but this does not include the United States (the world's biggest emitter of greenhouse gases) and Australia. China and India are signatories but they have no effective limits under the Protocol, even though they are among the fastest growing economies in the world.

Where it has been agreed that greenhouse gas emissions are to be limited, the issue arises as to how this can be achieved.

## Pollution control through direct regulation

Direct controls are a common method of environmental regulation. For example, UK car emissions standards must be met by all new cars, and by cars over three years of age when they take their annual MOT test. Many cities and towns prohibit the private burning of leaves and other rubbish because of the air pollution that the burning would cause. The 1956 UK Clean Air Act gave local authorities powers to require people to switch from coal to smokeless fuels. Similarly, the government gradually reduced the amount of lead allowed in petrol and provided tax incentives for drivers to switch to unleaded petrol. Since the mid-1970s, petrol consumption has increased by about 50 per cent while lead emissions have fallen by about 75 per cent.

### Problems with direct controls

Direct controls are often economically inefficient. This is because controls typically mandate the same response from different polluters independently of their costs of pollution abatement. Although these requirements may seem reasonable, they will be inefficient unless the polluters face the same pollution abatement costs. Alternative, more flexible, methods can often provide the same amount of abatement at a lower cost.

Direct pollution controls are usually inefficient because, by mandating the same response from all agents, they do not minimize the cost of any given amount of pollution abatement.

Efficient allocation of pollution abatement between firms with different prevention costs is analysed in Figure 13.4. As long as one firm has a lower abatement cost than another, it pays to reallocate a given amount of abatement. The lower-cost firm should abate more and the higher-cost firm less. The general conclusion is that

Efficient abatement requires that each firm have the same marginal cost of the last unit of abatement undertaken.

None the less, direct controls are effective when it is important not to exceed certain dangerous thresholds. They are also useful in situations where production is undertaken by a very small number of publicly owned natural monopolies. In other cases, policies that create economic incentives not to pollute are more effective than those that operate on the command principle.

## Control through emissions taxes

The great British economist A. C. Pigou (1877–1959), who did path-breaking work on externalities of all sorts, was a pioneer in developing public policy tools for their control. Pigou's name is associated particularly with pollution

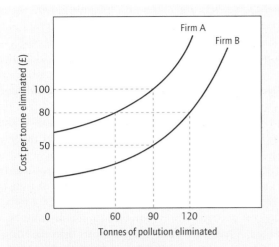

**Figure 13.4 Pollution abatement**

Efficient methods of abating pollution take account of differences in costs of abatement among firms. The figure shows the different marginal costs of pollution abatement for two firms. For any given amount of abatement, firm A has a higher cost of a further unit of abatement than has B. When they are both mandated to reduce pollution by 90 units, A's marginal cost of £100 exceeds B's marginal cost of £50. This is inefficient. A could cut its abatement by one unit, saving £100, while B increased its abatement by one unit, adding £50 to its costs. Total abatement would then be unchanged but costs would fall by £50.

An emissions tax of £80 per tonne of pollution is now imposed. Low-cost firm B now abates pollution by 120 tonnes, while high-cost firm A abates by 60 tonnes. This is the efficient way of producing 180 tonnes of abatement since the two firms have the same abatement costs at the margin, thus minimizing the total cost of reducing pollution by 180 tonnes.

taxes, which provide an alternative method to direct controls. The advantage of such taxes is that they *internalize the externality*, which means increasing the firm's private cost by the amount of the external cost. This makes private and social costs the same, with the result that efficient outcomes can result from decentralized decisions made by individual producers.

Look again at the example in Figure 13.4. If all firms are required to pay a tax of £80 on each unit of pollution, profit maximization will lead them to reduce emissions to the point at which the marginal cost of further reduction is equal to the tax. This means that firm B will reduce emissions much more than firm A, and that in equilibrium both will have the same marginal cost of further abatement that is required for efficiency.

A second great advantage of using emissions taxes is that they do not require the regulators to specify *how* polluters should abate pollution. Firms can be left to find the most efficient abatement techniques. The profit motive

will lead them to do so, because they will want to minimize their tax bill.

In principle, emissions taxes can perfectly internalize pollution externalities, so that profit-maximizing behaviour on the part of firms will lead them to produce the efficient amount of pollution abatement at minimum cost.

### Emissions taxes in practice

Emissions taxes can work only if it is possible to measure emissions accurately. In some cases this does not pose much of a problem, but in many other cases there are no effective measuring devices that can be installed at reasonable cost. One important example is automotive pollution. Today (but possibly not at some future date) it would be very expensive to attach a reliable monitor to every car and lorry and then to assess taxes based on readings from the monitor. In this case, as in many others, direct controls are the only cost-effective method.

Another problem involves setting the tax rate. The regulatory agency needs to estimate the marginal social damage caused per unit of each pollutant and set the tax equal to this amount. This would perfectly internalize the pollution externality. However, the required information is often difficult to obtain. If the regulatory agency sets the tax rate too high, too many resources will be devoted to pollution control. If the tax is set too low, there will be too much pollution. Also, if technological change causes the social damage to change, the optimal tax rate is also changed.

For a period in the late 1990s and early 2000s, the UK government was increasing taxes on petrol with the deliberate intention of discouraging the use of road transport and thereby reducing emissions from this source. However, in 2004 there were protests about the high price of petrol. The government postponed its planned tax increases and was continuing this policy in 2006. Hence political expediency conflicted with a rational policy of taxing carbon emissions.

### Control through tradable emissions permits

Tradable emissions permits can solve many of the problems associated with direct controls and emissions taxes. To use them, the regulator must decide how much pollution to permit. In Figure 13.4 you can see that the original regulations required each firm to reduce its total pollution by 90 tonnes. This is exactly the same as permitting the firms to pollute by their original amount of pollution *minus* 90 tonnes. Put another way, the regulators issue to each firm a right to pollute by that amount. To illustrate, if each firm had been generating 150 tonnes of pollution, exactly the same reduction occurs whether the firms are ordered to reduce pollution by 90 tonnes or are permitted to pollute to a maximum of 60 tonnes.

## Tradable permits in theory

Now, however, comes the new twist. A large efficiency gain can be achieved by making these rights to pollute tradable. This allows a firm with a low cost of pollution abatement to sell its right to pollute to the high-abatement-cost firm. Total pollution and total pollution abatement will be unchanged, but more abatement will be done by the firm with the low abatement cost (which sold its rights to pollute to the other firm), thus reducing the total cost of meeting the target for any given amount of pollution reduction.

Figure 13.5 illustrates this case. Where Figure 13.4 showed the amount of abatement, Figure 13.5 shows the amount of emissions. The cost curves now rise to the left instead of to the right as they did in Figure 13.4. Starting from the 150 tonnes of pollutants that each firm is emitting with zero abatement, the abatement cost rises as less and less pollution is allowed. Production with zero pollution is impossible, so the costs rise rapidly as very low

pollution levels are achieved. The government wishes to cut pollution from its existing level of 300 tonnes to 120 tonnes. So it gives each firm 60 tonnes' worth of pollution permits. When they each cut their pollution to 60 tonnes, firm A has a much higher marginal cost than firm B. So B sells A some permits: B then abates more and A pollutes more. Total pollution is unchanged but total abatement costs fall. Trade will be profitable as long as A's marginal abatement costs exceed B's. In the final equilibrium, both firms have the same marginal cost of abatement, which equals the price of a permit to abate by 1 tonne. Now each firm is indifferent between abating by 1 tonne and buying a permit to avoid abating by 1 tonne. The cost of abatement is minimized and both firms have gained. A has saved more clean-up costs than the cost of the permits it has bought. The prices of the permits that B sells exceed the cost of the extra abatement it must incur because of having fewer permits.

Everyone is better off. Society gets its abatement at the least cost in terms of valuable resources. Both firms have more money in their pockets than if each had been ordered to cut pollution by an identical amount.

Notice that the £90 price of a permit to produce 1 tonne of pollution is the same as the pollution tax required to induce 150 tonnes of abatement at the least cost. The difference is that permits require less information than taxes. The authorities just issue the number of permits they decide upon and let the market fix the price. If taxes are to be used, the government must determine the best tax rate and then impose it.

**Tradable emissions permits can be used to achieve the same allocation of resources as would occur with emissions taxes, while reducing the amount of information required by the regulatory authorities.**

## Tradable emissions permits in practice

A policy that sets a limit on emissions and allows permits to be traded is referred to as 'cap and trade'. The United States implemented an Acid Rain Program that started in 1995. This is targeted on reducing sulphur dioxide emissions from around 18 million tons a year as it was in the 1980s to a level of just under 9 million tons by 2010. This programme has been successful: 'The US Acid Rain Program has achieved greater emission reductions in such a short time than any other single program to control air pollution' (http://www.epa.gov/airmarkets/trading/basics/).

European governments until recently have shown a preference for 'ecotaxes' over tradable pollution permits. However, a UK Emissions Trading Scheme began in March 2002.

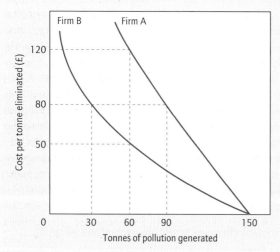

**Figure 13.5  Tradable pollution permits**

Tradable permits achieve the same results as the most efficient tax. Each firm produces 150 tonnes of pollution when no abatement procedures are followed. Abatement reduces the amount of pollution but at a rising marginal cost. Each firm is originally given an endowment of permits to emit 60 tonnes of pollution. If no trading is allowed, the marginal costs of abatement are then £120 for A and £50 for B. With trading, B sells 30 tonnes' worth of permits to A. Firm A then pollutes by 90 tonnes and firm B by 30 tonnes. The price of a permit is £80, which is the same as both firms' marginal cost of abatement at their new levels of pollution.

*Thirty-three organizations ('direct participants' in the scheme) have voluntarily taken on emission reduction targets to reduce their emissions against 1998–2000 levels. They have committed to reducing their emissions by 3.96 million tonnes of carbon dioxide equivalent ($CO_2e$) by the end of the Scheme. Over the lifetime of the scheme (2002–2006), this equates to 11.88 million tonnes of $CO_2e$ emissions releases avoided. In the first year (2002), the Participants achieved emission reductions of 4.64 million tonnes $CO_2e$ against their baselines. Over the first two years (2002 and 2003) the Scheme delivered emissions reductions of almost 5.2 million $tCO_2e$, and over the first three years (2002, 2003 and 2004), the Scheme delivered emissions reductions totalling 5.9 million $tCO_2e$. (http://www. defra.gov.uk/environment/climatechange/trading/uk/index.htm)*

In March 2006, a government report showed that:

*UK greenhouse gas emissions were 14.6 percent below base year levels in 2004 and, with current policy measures, are projected to be around 19.6 percent below base year levels in 2010. Under the Kyoto Protocol, the UK agreed to ensure that emissions of greenhouse gases were at least 12.5 percent lower than base year levels. (http:/www.defra.gov.uk/news/latest/2006/climate-0309.htm)*

An EU Emissions Trading Scheme commenced on 1 January 2005. The first phase runs from 2005 to 2007 and the second phase will run from 2008 to 2012 to coincide with the first Kyoto commitment period. Further five-year phases are expected after this.[5] Other countries introducing cap and trade systems include Canada and Australia.

### Conclusion

Much environmental pollution is caused by the failure of markets to account for externalities. At the same time, market-like mechanisms can be used to internalize the externalities. Pollution is an example of a problem in which markets themselves can be used to correct market failure.

The problem of externalities arises because of the absence of property rights. For example, the polluting firm is using the free air to dump its waste. If it owned the air, it would worry about the loss of the value of its property caused by the pollution. If those affected by the pollution owned the air, they would not allow it to be used unless they were paid sufficient compensation.

**Since many externalities arise from an absence of property rights, externalities can often be internalized if appropriate property rights can be created.**

---

[5] See: http://www.defra.gov.uk/environment/climatechange/trading/eu/index.htm

Box 13.3 outlines some of the main policies that governments have used to give effect to desired environmental control.

## Asymmetric information

Markets work best when everyone is well informed. People cannot make maximizing decisions if they are poorly informed about the things they are buying or selling. Lack of relevant information is the fifth item on our list of reasons for market failure.

Rules requiring that products and prices be described correctly are meant to improve the efficiency of choices by providing people with correct and relevant information. In many cases where the consequences of errors are not dramatic, consumers can be left to discover, through trial and error, what is in their own best interests. In other cases, however, the results of error can be too drastic to allow consumers to learn from their own experiences which products are reliable and which unreliable; for example, botulism, caused by poorly preserved foods, can cause death. In such cases the state intervenes to impose standards and testing requirements in the consumers' own best interests.

Standards are also set in the workplace. Some people argue that firms should be left to set their own safety standards. High-risk firms would then have to pay wage premiums to induce workers to accept these risks voluntarily. Those who favour government regulation of work standards argue it on two grounds. First, firms are often better informed than workers on changing safety conditions in work, particularly in small factories. Government regulation then compensates for the inefficiencies caused by this unequal access to information. Second, people who are desperate for work will take risks that are socially unacceptable, or that their own desperation causes them to assess imperfectly. In this case the purpose of government intervention is either to impose social values not held by specific individuals, or to act paternalistically in the belief that the state can assess the self-interests of the workers better than the workers themselves.

In some situations governments cannot easily remove the differences in information available to buyers and sellers. The party with the superior knowledge can then use it to change the nature of the transaction itself. For example, doctors, lawyers, and other specialists typically know much more than their clients about what they are doing. They can, therefore, influence the demand for their services by what they do and do not tell their clients. In countries where doctors are paid for on a fee-for-service basis—whether by the government, private insurers, or

**Box 13.3  Policies for environmental regulation**

Governments throughout the world are experimenting with many of the methods of environmental control discussed in the text. Here is a sampling of some of these policies.

• In the United Kingdom the Environmental Protection Act of 1989 lays down minimum standards for all emissions from thousands of chemical, waste incineration, and oil-refining factories. Performance is monitored by HM Inspectorate of Pollution, the costs of which are paid for by the factory owners themselves. The release of genetically engineered bacteria and viruses is also regulated. Strict regulations are imposed on waste disposal operations and on most forms of straw and stubble burning. Litterers are subject to on-the-spot fines of up to £1,000.

• The Sixth Environment Action Programme (6th EAP), which was adopted by the European Parliament and Council in 2002 and runs until 2012, requires the European Commission to prepare Thematic Strategies covering seven areas: Air Pollution, Prevention and Recycling of Waste, Protection and Conservation of the Marine Environment, Soil, Sustainable Use of Pesticides, Sustainable Use of Resources, and the Urban Environment.

*The Thematic Strategies represent the next generation of environment policy. As their name suggests, they work with themes rather than with specific pollutants or economic activities as has been the case in the past. They take a longer-term perspective in setting clear environmental objectives to around 2020 and will thus provide a stable policy framework. Finally, they focus on identifying the most appropriate instruments to deliver European policy goals in the least burdensome and most cost effective way possible. (http://europa.eu.int/comm/environment/newprg/strategies_en.htm)*

• The Kyoto Protocol, which was initiated in 1997 and came into force in February 2005, called for major reductions in greenhouse gas emissions over the following 15 years. This is discussed in the text.

• Under the United States Clean Air Act, utilities had to cut emissions of sulphur dioxide from a national total of 19 million tonnes to 9 million tonnes by the year 2000. This was accomplished by issuing 9 million tonnes worth of tradable permits to pollute. Such 'cap and trade policies' as applied in other countries are discussed in the text.

• According to the 'polluter-pays' principle used by the OECD, the polluter has to bear the cost of government-imposed measures designed to reduce pollution. This principle has been adopted in all member states so as to avoid the distortions in trade flows that could arise if countries tackled environmental problems in widely different ways with widely different effects on prices. In other cases, it is the sufferer who is paying. For example, Sweden assists Poland to reduce the acid rain that is damaging Swedish lakes and forests. Similarly, the Montreal Protocol includes provisions by which developing countries are to be compensated by richer countries for agreeing to limit their use of CFCs.

• The UK strategy for water pricing gives water companies the freedom to pass on any extra costs of environmental improvements and ensures that those companies have an economic incentive to undertake such improvements. The policy violates the 'polluter-pays' principle by putting the costs on the consumer. Non-market incentives are also widely applied to water. Under the UK Control of Pollution Act, a licence is required for the discharge of pollutants into rivers and coastal waters. These licences, called Discharge Consents, are issued by the National Rivers Authority. They specify the type and quantity of substances that may be discharged.

---

individual patients—elective surgery is often observed to vary with doctors' other workloads, being low in regions where doctors are busy and high in regions where they are underemployed. The explanation lies not in the different needs of patients in these various areas, but in the varying demands for these services created by the different advice that doctors give to their patients.

Two potential sources of market failure are moral hazard and adverse selection which we first discussed in the context of labour markets in Chapter 11 (page 241). An example of moral hazard is an insurance-induced alteration of behaviour that makes the event insured against more likely to occur. Thus, *moral hazard* arises when insurance leads people to take risks that they would avoid if they did not have an insurance policy. Where moral hazard affects behaviour, social costs are unnecessarily high. For example, more houses may be destroyed by fire because insured people take risks that they would avoid if they had to bear the full cost of any fire losses themselves. *Adverse selection* can arise when there is unequal knowledge of participants in a market about product characteristics. This arises, for example, when some types of insurance are bought heavily by those who know better than the insurers that they are bad risks, and is avoided by those who know better than the insurers that they are good risks. In general, adverse selection may cause the market outcome to be less efficient than if all participants were equally well informed.

## Missing markets

In the 1950s two American economists, Kenneth Arrow and Gerard Debreu, who were subsequently awarded Nobel Prizes in economics, studied the necessary conditions for optimality in resource allocation. One of the conditions is that there must exist a separate market in which each good and service can be traded to the point where the marginal benefit equals the marginal cost. Missing markets are the sixth item on our list of causes of market failure.

Not only do markets not exist for such prominent things as public goods and common property resources: they are also absent in a number of less obvious but equally important cases.

One important set of missing markets involves risk. You can insure your house against its burning down. This is because your knowledge of the probability of this occurrence is not much better than your insurance company's, and because the probability of your house burning down is normally independent of the probability of other houses burning down.

If you are a farmer, you cannot usually insure your crop against bad weather. This is because the probabilities of yours and your neighbour's crop suffering from bad weather are interrelated. If the insurance company has to pay you, the probabilities are it will also have to pay your neighbour and everyone else in the county—perhaps even throughout the country. An insurance company survives by pooling independent risks. It cannot survive if the same event affects all its clients in the same way. (This is why, although you can insure your house against a fire from ordinary causes, you cannot insure it against fires caused by war.)

If you are in business, you cannot insure against bankruptcy. Here the problem is adverse selection. You know much better than your would-be insurance company the chances that your business will fail. If insurance were offered against such failure, it would be taken out mainly by people whose businesses had developed a high chance of failure.

Another set of missing markets concerns future events. You can buy certain well established and unchanging products, such as corn or oil, on futures markets. But you cannot do so for most manufactured products, such as cars and TV sets, because no one knows the precise specifications of future models. Futures markets for these products are missing, so there is no way that the costs and benefits of planned future expenditure on these products can be equated by economic transactions conducted today.

# Public policy towards monopoly and competition

The seventh and last item on our list of reasons for market failure concerns market power. Cartels and price-fixing agreements among oligopolists, whether explicit or tacit, have long met with public suspicion and official hostility. These, and other non-competitive practices, are collectively referred to as monopoly practices. Note that these are not just what monopolists do: they include non-competitive behaviour of firms that are operating in other market structures such as oligopoly. The laws and other instruments that are used to encourage competition and discourage monopoly practices make up competition policy and are used to influence both the market structure and the behaviour of individual firms.

The goal of controlling market power provides rationales both for competition policy and for economic regulation. Competition can be encouraged and monopoly practices discouraged by influencing either the *market structure* or the *market behaviour* of individual firms. By and large, UK competition policy has sought to create more competitive market structures where possible. Where such structures could not be established, policy has sought to discourage monopolistic practices and to encourage competitive behaviour. In addition, the government employs economic regulations, which prescribe the rules under which firms can do business, and in some cases determine the prices that businesses can charge for their output.

We study three aspects of these policies: the direct control of natural monopolies, the direct control of oligopolies, and the creation of competitive conditions. The first is a necessary part of any competition policy, the second has been important in the past but is less so now, and the third constitutes the main current thrust of UK competition policy.

## Direct control of natural monopolies

The clearest case for public intervention arises with a **natural monopoly**, which is an industry in which economies of scale are so dominant that there is room for only one firm to operate at the minimum efficient scale. UK policy-makers have not wanted to insist on the establishment of several smaller, less efficient producers whenever a single firm would be much more efficient; neither have they wanted to give a natural monopolist the opportunity to restrict output, raise prices, and reap monopoly profits.

One response to natural monopoly is for government to assume ownership of the single firm, setting it up as

**(i) Losses in a falling-cost industry**     **(ii) Profits in a rising-cost industry**

**Figure 13.6 Pricing policies for natural monopolies**

**Marginal cost pricing leads to profits or losses; average cost pricing is inefficient.** In each part the output at which marginal cost equals price is $q_1$ and price is $p_1$.

In part (i) average costs are falling at output $q_1$, so marginal costs are less than the average cost of $c_1$. There is a loss of $c_1 - p_1$ on each unit, making a total loss equal to the blue area.

In part (ii) average cost of $c_1$ is less than price at output $q_1$. There is a profit of $p_1 - c_1$ on each unit sold, making a total profit equal to the blue area.

In each part of the diagram the output at which average cost equals price is $q_2$ and the associated price is $p_2$. In part (i) marginal cost is less than price at $q_2$, so output is below its optimal level. In part (ii) marginal cost exceeds price at $q_2$, so output is greater than its optimal level.

a nationalized industry. Another response has been to allow private ownership but to regulate the monopoly firm's behaviour. Until the 1980s UK policy favoured public ownership. Recently such industries have been privatized—that is, sold to members of the public—and then regulated to some extent. Examples are telecommunications, gas, water, and electricity. Whichever choice the government makes, it will be able to exert an influence on the behaviour of these industries.

### Short-run price and output

What is the correct price–output policy that the government should encourage these industries to adopt?

### Marginal cost pricing

Sometimes the government dictates that price should be set equal to short-run marginal cost so as to maximize consumers' plus producers' surpluses. According to economic theory, this policy, which is called marginal cost pricing, provides the efficient solution.

Marginal cost pricing does, however, create some problems. The natural monopoly may still have unexploited economies of scale and hence may be operating on the falling portion of its average total cost curve. In this case

marginal cost will be less than average total cost and pricing at marginal cost will lead to losses, as shown in Figure 13.6.

*A falling-cost natural monopoly that sets price equal to marginal cost will suffer losses.*

### Average cost pricing

Sometimes natural monopolies are directed to produce the output that will just cover total costs, thereby earning neither profits nor losses. This means that the firm produces to the point where average revenue equals average total cost, which is where the demand curve cuts the average total cost curve. Figure 13.6 shows that for a falling-cost firm this pricing policy requires producing at less than the optimal output in order to avoid the losses that would occur under marginal cost pricing.

*Average cost pricing is usually allocatively inefficient.*

### The very long run

Natural monopoly is a long-run concept, meaning that, given existing technology, there is room for only one firm to operate profitably. In the very long run, however, technology changes. Not only does today's competitive industry sometimes become tomorrow's natural monopoly, but also today's natural monopoly sometimes becomes tomorrow's competitive industry.

A striking example is the telecommunications industry. Not long ago the transmissions of voice and hard-copy messages were natural monopolies. Now technological developments such as satellite transmission, electronic mail, the internet, and fax machines have made these activities highly competitive. Also, new firms can be given access to existing infrastructure such as cables, thereby greatly lowering setup costs and encouraging competition from new entrants. As a consequence, in many countries an odd circumstance has arisen: nationalized industries, such as the UK Post Office and the nationalized telephone system, have sought to maintain their profitability by prohibiting entry into what would otherwise have become a fluid and competitive industry. Since it has the full force of the legal system behind it, the public firm may be more successful than the privately owned firm in preserving its monopoly long after technological changes have destroyed its 'naturalness'.

Government policies need to be adjusted frequently to keep them abreast of more or less continuous technological change.

## Regulation of natural monopolies

Now that most UK nationalized industries have been privatized, those that are natural monopolies are regulated by public regulatory authorities such as OFCOM (telecoms and media), OFGEM (gas and electricity), and OFWAT (water). In the United States, such regulatory bodies were often captured by the firms they were supposed to regulate and ended up working against the interests of consumers. An opposing pitfall that some worry about in the United Kingdom is that prices may be pushed so far down in the short-term interests of consumers that the regulated industries will have little incentive to invest in technological innovations. In response to this worry, firms have been given the right to appeal if they feel prices are being pushed too low. In today's world of rapid technological change, this could work to the long-term disadvantage of consumers.

## Direct control of oligopolies

Governments have from time to time intervened in industries that were oligopolies rather than natural monopolies, seeking to enforce the type of price and entry behaviour that was thought to be in the public interest. Such intervention has typically taken two distinct forms. In the United Kingdom from 1945 to 1980, interven-

tion primarily took the form of nationalization of whole oligopolistic industries such as airlines, railways, steel, and coal mining, which were then run by government-appointed boards. In the United States, firms in such oligopolistic industries as airlines, railways, and electric power were left in private hands, but their decisions were regulated by government-appointed bodies that set prices and regulated entry.

## Deregulation and privatization

The last two decades of the twentieth century witnessed a movement in virtually all advanced industrial nations, and the vast majority of less developed nations as well, to reduce the level of government control over industry.

### Causes

A number of forces had been pushing in this direction:

- Expectations that nationalized industries would be superior to private firms in the areas of efficiency, productivity growth, and industrial relations proved to be unrealistic.

- Falling transportation costs, and the information and communications revolutions, have exposed domestic industries to much more international competition than they had previously experienced. This has lowered concern over high national concentration ratios.

- Regulatory bodies sometimes had the effect of reducing, rather than increasing, competition.

- In spite of being allocatively inefficient, because price exceeds marginal cost (by virtue of each firm's negatively sloped demand curve) oligopolistic market structures provided much of the economic growth of the twentieth century. New products, and new ways of producing old products, have followed each other in rapid succession, all leading to higher living standards and higher productivity. Many of these innovations have been provided by firms in oligopolistic industries such as motor cars, agricultural implements, steel, petroleum refining, chemicals, and telecommunications. As long as governments can keep oligopolists competing with each other rather than co-operating to produce monopoly profits, most economists see no need to regulate such things as the prices at which they sell their products and the conditions of entry into their industries.

The world-wide movement towards privatization and deregulation was part of a growing belief among policy-makers that private firms operating in free markets are more efficient producers and innovators than governments.

The call was for a diminished role of government in resource allocation compared with what it was throughout most of the second half of the twentieth century—but not for a zero role. Although the belief that government intervention had been excessive is almost world-wide, there are many reasons why the public interest may still require significant intervention. Externalities and other market failures are some of the reasons why it is not necessarily efficient to allow the free market to decide all issues of resource allocation.

The natural outcome of these revised views has been the privatization of nationalized industries and the deregulation of privately owned ones. This latter policy was intended, among other things, to return price-setting and entry decisions to market determination.

Privatization has gone a long way in the United Kingdom. The majority of the nationalized industries have been returned to private ownership. Some details are given in Box 13.4.

---

 **Box 13.4  Privatization in the United Kingdom**

Privatization has been a complex development in the United Kingdom. Some nationalized industries were sold outright; in others the government maintained substantial holdings while selling off the rest of its shares. In yet other cases profitable parts of unprofitable enterprises were separated off and sold. In still other cases the government sold shares that it held in private companies that had never been nationalized.

The first step towards UK privatization was the sale of council houses, which began in 1979. Over the succeeding decade there was a major reduction in the stock of publicly owned housing, with almost 700,000 dwellings being sold to their occupiers.

The next phase covered a number of relatively small operations in markets where competition was strong. These included the British Sugar Corporation, British Rail Hotels, Sealink Ferries, British Ports, Jaguar, and British Aerospace. These companies have operated successfully, under relatively competitive conditions, since their privatization.

The third phase covered the great industrial giants. It began with British Telecom in 1984 and continued with British Gas in 1986, British Airways in 1987, and British Steel in 1988. Sale of shares in the publicly owned electricity industry began in 1990, with water following soon thereafter. Sale of the remaining coal pits was completed in 1994. The privatization of British Rail was completed by 1997, with the track going to Railtrack and the train services going to several private operators (though owing to financial problems Railtrack was temporarily taken back under government control in 2001/2).

---

### Outcomes

The evidence on the effects of privatization is largely encouraging. Prices have fallen markedly in the gas, electricity, and telecommunications industries. Some former state-owned companies have become world leaders in a manner that did not occur under state control—the most obvious examples are BT, and British Airways. Many have been attractive targets for takeover bids by foreign utilities. All of this is strong evidence that their performance has been improved by having been transferred to private ownership.

Privatization has also spread to other EU countries. For example, Deutsche Telekom was privatized in 1996. Part of the pressure to privatize has come from stiff competition from efficient foreign firms and part from the Maastricht Treaty, which limits public spending and government borrowing. There has also been a trend towards deregulation of many markets. Major pressure in this direction has been exerted by the Single Market Act, which is discussed in Chapter 27. A notable example is air travel, where state-imposed restrictions, often designed to protect state-owned national airlines, are being phased out. Many new private carriers are entering the industry, such as Easyjet and Ryanair based in the UK. The ensuing competition has pushed many fares down.

## Intervention to keep firms competing

The least stringent form of government intervention is designed to create conditions of competition by preventing firms from merging unnecessarily or from engaging in certain anti-competitive practices such as colluding to set monopoly prices. Such policies seek to create the most competitive market structure possible and then to prevent firms from reducing competition by engaging in certain forms of co-operative behaviour. (See Box 13.5 for more details on UK competition policies.)

### Why worry?

Up until the early 1990s, industrial concentration increased in Britain, with the percentage of industrial production accounted for by the five largest firms growing steadily. Two major causes were the growth of large firms at the expense of smaller ones, and mergers of existing firms. Although very recent data are difficult to come by, those that exist suggest that recent developments have been mixed. Concentration has increased, for example, in pharmaceuticals, where Glaxo merged with Wellcome, and then again with Smithkline-Beacham to form GlaxoSmithKline; and Zeneca merged with Astra to form AstraZeneca. In other industries, however, large firms have been broken up by their owners, reducing concentration ratios.

**Box 13.5** UK competition policies

Ultimate responsibility for competition policy in the United Kingdom lies with the Secretary of State for Trade and Industry, but application of the policy is in the hands of two main institutions (plus the utility regulators mentioned in the text): the Office of Fair Trading (OFT) and the Competition Commission (CC).* The goal of the OFT is to make markets work well for consumers. It has powers of enforcement of competition and consumer protection rules; it can initiate investigations into how any specific market is working; and it is involved in communication to explain and improve awareness of competition rules and policy. The OFT may refer mergers that it deems to be anti-competitive to the CC, and it may also refer markets where competition is perceived to be not working well.

*The Competition Commission is an independent public body established by the Competition Act 1998. It replaced the Monopolies and Mergers Commission on 1 April 1999. The Commission conducts in-depth inquiries into mergers, markets and the regulation of the major regulated industries. Every inquiry is undertaken in response to a reference made to it by another authority: usually by the Office of Fair Trading (OFT) but in certain circumstances the Secretary of State, or by the regulators under sector-specific legislative provisions relating to regulated industries. The Commission has no power to conduct inquiries on its own initiative.*

*The Enterprise Act 2002 introduces a new regime for the assessment of mergers and markets in the UK. In most merger and market references the Commission is responsible for making decisions on the competition questions and for making and implementing decisions on appropriate remedies. Under the legislation which the Act replaces, the Commission had to determine whether matters were against the public interest. The public interest test is replaced by tests focused specifically on competition issues. The new regime also differs from the previous regime where the Commission's power in relation to remedies was only to make recommendations to the Secretary of State. . . . [also] The newly established Appeal Tribunals hear appeals against decisions of the Director General of Fair Trading and the Regulators of Utilities in respect of infringements of the prohibitions contained in the [1998] Act concerning anti-competitive behaviour and abuse of a dominant position.* (http://www.competition-commission.org.uk/)

For an overview of EU competition policy, see http://europa.eu.int/comm/competition/index_en.html

* For more information see their respective websites: www.oft.gov.uk and www.competition-commission.org.uk

---

Globalization—the growing internationalization of competition—is one reason why this increasing domestic concentration in production has not necessarily implied less market competition. (Globalization is further discussed in Chapter 27.) The size of most markets now extends well beyond the boundaries of a single nation. A firm with an apparent monopoly in the United Kingdom may well be operating in a highly competitive international market that includes German, French, and Japanese firms. None the less, some intervention to keep firms competing rather then colluding is still thought necessary in most countries.

## Unsettled questions: market structure in the very long run

The case against monopoly and monopolistic practices is based on the allocation of resources with a given technology. In the very long run, however, technology is constantly changing as a result of both the discoveries of lower-cost methods of producing old products and the introduction of new and improved products. Does market structure affect the rate of innovation in the very long run?

### The incentive to innovate

#### Who gets the profits?

Both the monopolist and the perfect competitor have a profit incentive to introduce cost-reducing innovations. A monopoly can always increase its profits if it can reduce costs. Furthermore, since it is able to prevent the entry of new firms into the industry, these additional profits will persist into the long run. Thus, a firm that is either a monopoly or an oligopolist with entry barriers has both a short-run and a long-run incentive to reduce its costs.

Firms in perfect competition have the same incentive in the short run, but not in the long run. In the short run a reduction in costs will allow a firm that was just covering costs to earn profits. In the long run other firms will be attracted into the industry by these profits. Existing firms will copy the cost-saving innovation, and new firms will enter the industry using the new techniques. This will go on until the profits of the innovator have been eliminated.

**Monopolies and oligopolists with entry barriers have both a short- and a long-run incentive to innovate; perfectly competitive firms have only a short-run incentive.**

### Funds for research and development

The large profits available to oligopolistic firms provide a ready fund out of which research and development can be financed. The typical perfectly competitive firm, however, is earning only enough to cover all its production costs, and it will have few funds to spare for research and development. As an empirical illustration, farmers producing under perfect competition did not develop the innovations that have vastly raised agricultural productivity over the last century. These were developed by a few oligopolistic manufacturers of farm equipment and by researchers in universities and in government-financed research institutions.

### Schumpeter's defence of oligopoly and monopoly

In Joseph Schumpeter's theory (mentioned previously on page 171), monopolistic and oligopolistic market structures are more conducive to growth than is perfect competition.[6] He claimed that, since it is the incentive of profits that leads individuals and firms to take the great risks of innovation, market power is much more important than perfect competition in providing the climate under which innovation occurs. The large short-run profits earned by firms with market power provide the incentive for others to try to usurp some of these for themselves. Oligopolistic firms compete for each other's profits, as well as for the new profits that will be generated by major innovations. If they do not compete, or if they have a genuine monopoly, outsiders will seek to enter in order to share in the profits of the sitting firm or firms. If a frontal attack on the major barriers to entry is not possible, then the barriers will be circumvented by such dodges as the development of similar products against which the established firms will not have entry protection. Schumpeter called the replacing of one entrenched position of market power by another through the invention of new products or new production techniques the *process of creative destruction.*

*In this respect, perfect competition is not only impossible but inferior, and has no title to being setup as a model of ideal efficiency. It is hence a mistake to base the theory of government regulation of industry on the principle that big business should be made to work as the respective industry would work in perfect competition.* (Schumpeter 1950, page 106)

Schumpeter's theory is not easy to test. None the less, business school studies of firm behaviour show that much, probably most, inter-firm competition is in product and process innovation. Firms rarely fail because they set the wrong prices—for one reason, it is easy to alter prices that turn out to be uncompetitive. Firms do fail, however, when they fall behind their competitors in the constant battle to produce new and better products by ever more cost-efficient methods.

## The future of competition policy

Even though governments on the whole are no longer in the business of owning industries or tightly controlling their pricing and output decisions, government has an important role as both rule-maker and referee of the market economy. Even the strongest advocates of Schumpeter's theory of creative destruction accept that the public interest is better served when oligopolists are induced to compete with each other rather than colluding to avoid such rivalrous activity.

 # CASE STUDIES

## 1. Property rights and the destruction of tropical rain forests

A key factor leading to the destruction of tropical rain forests has been the lack of property rights assigned to these forests.

With lack of ownership, nobody has an incentive to plan for the long-term preservation of the trees and sustainability of forest industries. Rather, the incentive is to cut down the trees, sell the timber, and then move on—that is, take what money can be made immediately and move on.

The following two extracts from the 2003 World Development Report give examples of how Brazilian state authorities are creating incentives for preservation of the Amazon forest. In the first, tax rebates on value added tax (ICMS) are related to the areas of protected forest. The second has introduced tradable conservation permits.

---

[6] At the time that Schumpeter first wrote, economists recognized only two market structures: perfect competition and monopoly. He thus applied his arguments about creative destruction to monopolies. Now that oligopoly is seen to be the dominant market form in manufacturing, it is clear that his arguments apply with more force in oligopoly, where the threat of competition is more immediate, than in monopoly.

**Figure 13.7** Newfoundland cod catches

*Source*: Dr R. Meyers, Canadian Department of Fisheries and Oceans, St John's, Newfoundland.

*The ICMS Ecologico is a unique Brazilian mechanism that uses state-to-municipality transfers to reward the creation and maintenance of protected areas for biodiversity conservation and watershed protection. The intent is to counteract the local perceptions that maintenance of protected areas reduces municipal revenue.... Since the programs were adopted, about 1 million hectares have been placed under environmental zoning restrictions in Parana, and about 800,000 in Minas Gerais.*

*The Brazilian state of Parana has created a market for conservation by allowing trade in landholder obligations to maintain forests. A long-standing Brazilian law has required that property owners maintain 20 percent of each property under native vegetation (50 percent to 80 percent in the Amazon region). But noncompliance was common.... A preliminary analysis of a hypothetical similar program for the nearby state of Minas Gerais illustrates how efficiency-enhancing programs such as this might increase biodiversity conservation and economic output.... When landholders are free to trade within the biome, compliance costs drop by almost three-quarters, while the proportion of higher-ecological-quality forest reserve increases to 72 percent.* (*World Development Report 2003*, page 173; © 2003 by the International Bank for Reconstruction and Development / World Bank; all rights reserved)

This illustrates the point that socially suboptimal exploitation of resources can arise when property rights are not appropriately assigned. However, incentives can be introduced to encourage a socially efficient outcome.

Another case of property rights misallocation has arisen in Canada. It has been seriously argued that some of the incentives for non-sustainable logging in the vast forests of western Canada are created by the system of property rights in place there.[7] The government owns the forests and leases them out to the lumber companies for specific periods of time. As a result, the company logging a particular area has little incentive to act

in a way that is compatible with efficient reforestation. So laws are needed to force the companies to behave in the way that they would behave if they owned the land themselves. Once the laws are in place they must be enforced, which is not always easy, particularly in remote areas. If the logging companies owned the land, they would have a self-interest in preserving the forests for their own future logging. More efficient logging practices and more effective reforestation would be the result.

## 2. Endangered fish

The fish in the ocean are a common property resource, and theory predicts that such a resource will be overexploited if there is a high enough demand for the product and suppliers are able to meet that demand. In past centuries there were neither enough people eating fish nor efficient enough fishing technologies to endanger stocks. Over the last fifty years, however, the population explosion has added to the demand for fish and advances in technology have vastly increased the ability to catch fish. Large boats, radar detection, and more murderous nets have tipped the balance in favour of the predator and against the prey. As a result, the overfishing prediction of common property theory has been amply borne out. Today fish are a common property resource; tomorrow they could become no one's resource.

### Overfishing

Since 1950 the world's catch has increased fivefold. The increase was sustained only by substituting smaller, less desirable, fish for the diminishing stocks of the more desirable fish, and by

---

[7] Much of the concern of environmentalists is with another issue: whether or not the remaining first-growth lands should be logged at all. Our concern here is with the efficient management of those areas that it is agreed will be logged.

penetrating ever further into remote oceans. Today all available stocks are being exploited, and now even the total tonnage is beginning to fall. The UN estimates that the total value of the world's catch could be increased by nearly $30 billion if fish stocks were properly managed by governments interested in the total catch, rather than exploited by individuals interested in their own catch.

The developed countries have so overfished their own stocks that Iceland and the European Union could cut their fleets by 40 per cent and catch as much fish as they do today. This is because more fish would survive to spawn, allowing each boat in a smaller fleet to catch about 40 per cent more than does each boat in today's large fishing fleet.

The problem became so acute that Canada shut down its entire Atlantic cod fishing industry in 1985 and its Pacific salmon industry in 1988. Tens of thousands of Newfoundland residents lost their livelihoods in the demise of what had been the province's largest industry—the catching, freezing, and canning of fish—an industry that had flourished for five centuries (see Figure 13.7). Canada and the European Union have since been in conflict over what Canada claims is predatory overfishing by EU boats just outside Canadian territorial waters. As of 2006, the Canadian cod stocks still show no signs of recovery.

The Mediterranean has been so overfished that seafood that was once the staple for the poor is now an expensive luxury eaten mainly by rich tourists.

### Policy response

The European Union has a Common Fisheries Policy covering the territorial waters of its member countries. Since 1983, total allowable catches for all main species have been set annually and divided up into catch quotas for each member country. Minimum mesh size on nets and other ways of protecting young fish have also been imposed. Inspection and monitoring measures are applied to give force to the regulations. However, measures in place up to 2002 failed to solve the problem. In May 2002, the EU announced a new radical plan:

*Dwindling fish stocks, diminishing catches, too many vessels chasing too few fish, steady job losses and a lack of effective control and sanctions . . . the Common Fisheries Policy (CFP) needs fundamental change. . . . The Commission proposes to do away with the annual ritual of setting fishing quotas at too high levels. In future, total admissible catches would be fixed within a multi-annual management plan, on the basis of the most recent scientific advice to ensure that enough fish stay in the sea to replenish stocks. . . . the necessary cut in fishing effort (between 30 and 60 per cent according to the state of stocks and the regions) under multi-annual plans would result in an estimated withdrawal of some 8,600 vessels which represents 8.5 per cent of the number of EU fishing vessels and about 18 per cent in tonnage. . . . To achieve sustainable fisheries beyond EU waters on the basis of stronger international co-operation, the reform package includes an action plan against illegal fishing and a strategy for EU fisheries development partnerships with third countries. (Press release, 28 May 2002: see: http://europa.eu.int/comm/fisheries)*

The UN World Summit on Sustainable Development, held in Johannesburg in September 2002, agreed that there should be a strategy for restoring fish stocks at the global level. It was agreed to implement an action plan to address illegal fishing, and to set up a network of marine protected areas by 2012. The longer-term target was to restore fisheries to their maximum sustainable yields by 2015.

It remains to be seen how many types of fish will be caught to extinction and how many will recover as nations slowly learn the lesson of economic theory. Common property resources need central management if they are not to be overexploited to an extent that risks extinction.

# Conclusion

Some see everything that the government does as useless and would do away altogether with its activities in respect to the free market. The all-important function of providing the background against which the free market can effectively function—by maintaining a monopoly of violence and defining and protecting property rights—discredits this case.

Others see a very limited role for government but would take government activity no further than absolutely necessary. Just provide an effective basis for law and order, they say, and the miracle of Adam Smith's hidden hand will do the rest. Most people, although not quite all, reject this view. The case against the minimalist state lies in what we observed at the outset of this chapter: although markets work—and work very effectively much of the time—markets also fail—and sometimes fail quite seriously.

We have devoted much space to explaining the *why*, *how*, and *where* of these market failures. We have also explained what might be done to alleviate the most serious of these failures.

In the next chapter we discuss further the role of government in the economy. The balance between government intervention and the free market is often controversial, and opinions about what is the appropriate balance change over time and from place to place. However, there is no doubt about three points. First, markets do fail in many important ways. Second, governments provide the only institutions available to deal with many of these failures. Third, economists have designed many instruments, some of them highly subtle, by which governments can deal with these failures.

As Adam Smith long ago observed (see Chapter 1), altruism, no matter how valuable a motive in many situations, cannot be the basis for the day-to-day functioning of a market economy, which must be based on the pursuit of self-interest. Similarly, altruism, although often a highly effective motive behind locating and publicizing market failures, cannot be the basis for a systematic and sustained handling of these failures. Instead they are best coped with by creating incentives that direct self-interested behaviour towards alleviating them.

## SUMMARY

### Basic functions of government

- Effective governments have a legal monopoly of violence. They also define and protect the rights and obligations of property owned by individuals and institutions.

- Key characteristics of market economies are (a) their ability to co-ordinate decentralized decisions without conscious control, (b) their determination of the distribution of income, and (c), compared with the alternatives, their minimization of arbitrary economic power.

### Market efficiency

- A perfectly competitive economy is allocatively efficient because it produces where price, which measures the value consumers place on the last unit produced, equals marginal cost, which measures the value to consumers that the resources used to produce the marginal unit could produce in other uses. Equating price to marginal cost maximizes the sum of producers' and consumers' surpluses.

- Free markets fail to achieve efficiency because of inefficient exclusion of users from facilities with excess capacity, common property resources, public goods, externalities, asymmetric information, missing markets, and market power.

### Non-rivalrous and non-excludable goods

- The optimal price for the service of a facility with excess capacity is zero. Since private owners will charge a positive price, their facility will be inefficiently underused.

- The private market will exploit a common property resource to the point where the average revenue per producer equals the production cost of a new entrant instead of to the socially optimal level, where the marginal addition to total product caused by a new entrant equals its production cost.

- The optimal quantity of a public good is provided when the marginal cost of production is equal to the sum of the prices that all its consumers would be willing to pay for the marginal unit produced. This is difficult to attain because of the free rider problem—the incentive for individuals to understate the true value that they place on a public good.

### Externalities

- The Coase theorem shows that, if those parties that create an externality and those that are affected by it can bargain together with minimal transaction costs, all inefficiencies can be removed.

- Where private bargaining is impossible, the government can alleviate externalities by imposing rules and regulations or, more efficiently, by internalizing externalities through such measures as taxes and tradable permits to pollute.

### Public policy towards monopoly and competition

- Government policy with respect to market power is designed to encourage competitive practices and discourage monopolistic ones.

- Direct control of pricing and entry conditions of some key oligopolistic industries has been common in the past, but deregulation is reducing such control.

- An important issue concerns the effect of market structure on economic growth. The productively inefficient resource allocation that results whenever firms have market power may be more conducive to the technological change than is the productively efficient allocation that results from perfect competition.

## TOPICS FOR REVIEW

- Government as a monopolist of violence and a protector of property rights
- The efficiency of a perfectly competitive economy
- Rivalrous and non-rivalrous goods
- Excludable and non-excludable goods
- Inefficient exclusion
- Common property resources and the tragedy of the commons
- Rules for providing and pricing public goods

- Harmful and beneficial externalities
- Emissions taxes
- Tradable emissions permits
- Government control of market power
- Marginal and average cost pricing
- Competition policy
- Privatization
- Deregulation

## QUESTIONS

1 Your local authority undoubtedly provides a police station, a fire brigade, and a public library.
   (a) What are the market imperfections, if any, that each of these seeks to correct?
   (b) Which of these are closest to being public goods?
   (c) Which are furthest from being public goods?
   (d) What would happen if governments were prevented from offering these services?

2 Not counting the ones mentioned in the text, how many goods and services can you think of that are
   (a) non-rivalrous but excludable?
   (b) non-excludable but rivalrous?
   (c) non-rivalrous and non-excludable?

3 An industry consists of two firms producing the same product but using different technologies. Each emits 50 tonnes of pollution each year. One firm can clean up the first tonne at a cost of £1,000, while the cost of each additional tonne cleaned up rises by £1,000 per tonne until the last tonne costs £50,000. The second firm's cost for the first tonne cleaned up is £20,000, and the cost rises by £1,000 per tonne until the fiftieth tonne is cleaned up at a cost of £70,000. The government wishes to cut the industry's total emissions from 100 to 50 tonnes a year. It gives each firm 25 tradable permits, each one allowing 1 tonne of pollution.
   (a) What will be the equilibrium price of a permit to pollute by 1 tonne?
   (b) How many permits will be traded?
   (c) By how much will each firm clean up its own pollution?
   (d) What would you infer if, in a subsequent year, the price of a pollution permit fell by 50 per cent?

4 Why do we worry about the behaviour of natural monopolies and about collusion among oligopolists? What can be done to prevent the undesirable effects of their behaviour without stifling technological advance?

5 'There would be no externalities, harmful or beneficial, if everyone were well informed and could bargain with each other with no transactions cost.' Explain why you agree or disagree.

6 What are public goods, and why cannot markets easily provide such goods?

7 Why do common property resources tend to be over exploited, and what solutions are available?

8 Why would it be inefficient to exclude people from using a facility that had excess capacity?

# Chapter 14

# THE ROLE OF GOVERNMENT

In Chapter 13 we established three important results. First, free markets are effective ways of co-ordinating decentralized decision-taking. Second, although markets work quite well most of the time, they seldom work optimally because of the almost universal presence of one type of market failure or another (such as the absence of perfect competition.) Third, government policy can alleviate some of the most serious market failures, either by imposing more efficient behaviour by rules, regulations, and public production or by internalizing externalities. But while government interventions may have potential to improve the workings of markets, this does not mean that governments always get it right. What objectives do governments actually have for their economic actions? Do they usually succeed in improving economic outcomes by their interventions, or do they often make outcomes worse? What costs do government interventions impose on the private sector? Do governments sometimes pursue objectives of their own, objectives that do not reflect the interests of the community as a whole?

In particular, you will learn that:

- Governments have objectives for stability, growth, and equity as well as for efficiency.
- Equity, efficiency, and growth objectives may often conflict.
- Tools of government policy include taxation and spending, the law, and regulation, as well as public production of goods and services.
- Government interventions usually involve both direct costs of administration and indirect costs associated with interference with the price mechanism.
- The incentives facing specific governments may deviate from those needed to deliver economic efficiency.

We start by outlining the objectives that governments may have in addition to correcting market failures. We then outline the many tools that are available to the government to achieve its policies, showing how these tools can be applied to areas other than market failure. After that, we allow for the *costs* of government activity. These must be offset against the benefits in order to assess the net value of any proposed government intervention.

Finally, we note that governments do not always act in the best interest of society as a whole. Elected politicians often have agendas of their own, or of the section of society that elected them. We discuss potential outcomes when governments in these circumstances act in ways that generate either inefficiency in resource allocation or undesirable inequities in income distribution.

# Government objectives

Governments have multiple objectives, only some of which we studied in the previous chapter. The main ones are as follows:

1. To protect life and property by exercising a monopoly of force and establishing property rights

2. To improve economic efficiency by addressing the various causes of market failure

3. To protect the environment

4. To achieve some accepted standard of equity

5. To protect individuals from others and from themselves

6. To influence the rate of economic growth

7. To stabilize the economy against income and price-level fluctuations

The first three of these objectives were considered in the previous chapter. The next three are considered in this one. (Chapter 26 is also devoted to the sixth objective.) The final objective is a major subject of the second half of this book, which deals with macroeconomic theory and policy. The explicit policy goals for the UK government are set out in a case study towards the end of this chapter.

## Policies for equity

Markets generate reasonably efficient allocations of the nation's resources because, most of the time, the information that they need to allow them to perform well, even if not optimally, is derived from agents' desires to improve their private circumstances. No one should be surprised, therefore, that markets do not efficiently allocate resources towards achieving such broad social goals as establishing an 'equitable' distribution of income and promoting shared community values. Markets do not directly foster these goals, precisely because individuals do not seek to achieve them when they are purchasing goods and services in markets. Instead, they look to the political system to achieve desired outcomes in this respect.

### The distribution of income

An important characteristic of any market economy is the *distribution* of income that it determines. People whose skills are scarce relative to supply earn large incomes, whereas people whose skills are plentiful relative to supply earn much less.

As we have seen in earlier chapters, differentials in earnings serve the important function of motivating people to adapt. The advantage of such a system is that individuals can make their own decisions about how to alter their behaviour when market conditions change. The disadvantage is that temporary rewards and penalties are dealt out as a result of changes in market conditions that are beyond the control of the affected individuals. The resulting differences in incomes will seem inequitable to many—even though they are the incentives that make markets work.

Concerns about equity have two dimensions: horizontal and vertical. **Horizontal equity** means that people in similar circumstance should be treated similarly. Although this type of equity appeals to many people as desirable, it is not always a goal of government policies. For example, people who are exposed to similar natural risks are given more government assistance when they are planting crops than when they are mining ore, cutting trees, or extracting oil. This may be because farmers have more political power than others, or it may stem from a gut feeling on the part of the electorate that food production is more basic than any other economic activity. **Vertical equity** means treating people in different economic situations differently in order to reduce inequalities between them.

Figure 14.1 shows what is called a **Lorenz curve**. It shows how much of total income is received by various proportions of the nation's income earners. It indicates how total income is *distributed* among individuals or groups. The further the curve bends away from the diagonal, the more unequal are the incomes of the people in society. The curve shows, for example, that in 2003/4 the bottom 20 per cent of all UK individuals received only 2.6 per cent of all taxable income earned, while the bottom 80 per cent received only 51 per cent of total taxable income. The remaining 49 per cent went to the top 20 per cent of income-earners. The income shown in the figure is taxable income, measured before taxes and benefits.[1] After the impact of taxes and benefits is included, the share of the bottom 20 per cent rises to 9 per cent and the share of the top 20 per cent falls to 39 per cent. Thus, the UK tax-benefit system has the effect of substantially

---

[1] The data refer only to income with some tax liability and therefore exclude all income that escapes the notice of the tax authorities or is otherwise exempt from income tax.

**Figure 14.1** A Lorenz curve of individual pre-tax income in the UK, 2003/4

**The size of the shaded area between the Lorenz curve and the diagonal is a measure of the inequality of income distribution.** If there were complete income equality, the Lorenz curve would coincide with the diagonal line. The extent of income inequality (e.g. the lower 40 per cent receive only 15 per cent of the income) determines how far the Lorenz curve lies below the diagonal.

*Source*: ONS, *Annual Abstract of Statistics*, 2006.

narrowing the large disparities in the distribution of income between the various income classes.

Figure 14.2 shows how UK income inequalities have changed over time (before allowing for taxes and benefits). Average income has been rising over time, so the figure does not tell us anything about the level of income. But it

does tell us that the inequalities produced by the market have increased over time. For example, while about 13 per cent of the population had incomes that were less than 60 per cent of median income in 1961, the figure rose to over 20 per cent in the early 1990s, but had fallen back to around 17 per cent in 2003/4.

Redistributive policies are of two general types. Some, such as the progressive income tax, are concerned with vertical equity. They seek to alter the size distribution of income in quite general ways. High marginal rates of income tax, combined with a neutral spending system that benefits all income groups more or less equally, will narrow income inequalities.

Other policies seek to mitigate the effects of markets on particular individuals. They seek not to narrow income gaps in general, but rather to deal with specific unfortunate events. Should farmers bear all the losses associated with the destruction of livestock after an outbreak of foot and mouth or mad cow disease? Should heads of households be forced to bear the full burden of their misfortune if they lose their jobs through no fault of their own? Even if they lose their jobs through their own fault, should they and their families have to bear the whole burden, which may include starvation? Should the ill and the aged be thrown on the mercy of their families? What if they have no families? Policies designed to deal with such situations usually seek horizontal equity in treating similarly all those who fall into some group.

**Both private charities and a great many government policies are concerned with modifying the distribution of income that results from such things as one's parents' abilities, luck, and how one fares in the labour market.**

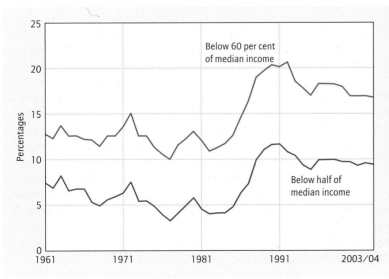

**Figure 14.2** Income inequalities in the UK, 1961–2004

**The figure shows the percentage of people whose income is below various fractions of median income.** The proportions of people below 60 per cent of median income (and below 50 per cent) were falling slightly in the 1960s and 1970s, but from the early 1980s these proportions rose sharply. In the 1990s they levelled off or even fell slightly.

*Source*: ONS, *Social Trends*, 2005.

## The distribution of wealth

It is sometimes argued that egalitarian economic policy should devote more attention than it does to the distribution of *wealth* and less to the distribution of *income*. Wealth confers economic power, and wealth is more unequally distributed than is income. Heavy estate duties in the United Kingdom, however, caused a gradual reduction in the inequality of wealth distribution during most of the twentieth century. The trend was slowed, if not reversed, over the last two decades of that century, largely because of the buildup of pension wealth in the hands of 50–70-year-olds. None the less, in 2005 just less than 20 per cent of all marketable wealth was held by the top 1 per cent of people in the UK wealth distribution, and a little over 90 per cent of all marketable wealth was owned by those in the top half of the distribution.

There are two main ways in which inequalities in the distribution of wealth can be reduced. The first is to levy taxes on wealth at the time that wealth is transferred from one owner to another, either by gifts during the lifetime of the owner or by bequest after death. In Britain such transfers used to be subject to a capital transfer tax. The rate of tax was progressive and rose to 60 per cent on taxable transfers in excess of £2 million. Currently, however, gifts among individuals during their lifetime are potentially exempt from tax. They become taxable only if made within seven years of the donor's death. In 2005/6 UK inheritance tax was set at the rate of 40 per cent on all estates over £275,000, and in the March 2006 Budget it was announced that this threshold would rise to £325,000 by 2009/10.

The second method is an annual tax on the value of each person's wealth. A wealth tax of this sort has been considered in the past, but it has never been instituted in the UK and it has not been actively debated in the past two decades.

## Equity versus efficiency

Problems arise when government measures designed to improve equity seriously inhibit the efficient operation of the price system.

**Often the goal of a more equitable distribution conflicts with the goal of a more efficient economy.**

Suppose we were so extreme as to believe that equity demanded that everyone receive the same income. All incentives to work hard and to move from job to job would be eliminated. Some command economies came close to this extreme position, and the results were predictably disastrous. Suppose that, to be less extreme, we believed that earnings received by some owners of resources should not reflect short-term fluctuations in demand and supply. The UK controls on rented accommodation did just that during much of the twentieth century, as do controls in several other countries today. When such intervention is effective, the incentive system for resource allocation is eliminated. A rise in demand creates extra earnings, which attract resources to meet the demand. Remove the price reaction and there is no reason for the resources to be reallocated.

## Policies to protect individuals

### Protection from others

People can use and even abuse other people for economic gain in ways that the members of society find offensive. Child labour laws and minimum standards of working conditions are responses to such actions. In an unhindered free market, the adults in a household usually decide how much education to buy for their children. Selfish parents might buy no education, while egalitarian parents might buy the same education for all of their children, regardless of their abilities. Members of society may want to interfere in these choices, both to protect the child of the selfish parent and to ensure that some of the scarce educational resources are distributed according to ability rather than a family's wealth. All households are forced to provide a minimum of education for their children, and a number of inducements are offered—through public universities, scholarships, loans, and other means—for talented children to consume more education than they or their parents might choose if they had to pay the entire cost themselves.

### Protection from oneself

Members of society, acting through the government, often seek to protect adult (and presumably responsible) individuals not from others, but from themselves. Laws prohibiting the use of heroin, crack cocaine, and other drugs, and laws prescribing the installation and use of car seat belts, are intended primarily to protect individuals from their own ignorance or short-sightedness. This kind of interference in the free choices of individuals is called **paternalism**. Whether such actions reflect the wishes of the majority in society or the interference of overbearing governments, there is no doubt that the market will not provide this kind of protection. Buyers do not buy what they do not want, and sellers have no motive to provide it.

Paternalism is often closely related to **merit goods.** Merit goods are goods that society, operating through the government, deems to be especially important, or that those in power feel individuals should be encouraged to consume. Housing, education, health care, and cultural amenities such as museums and art galleries are often cited as merit goods. Critics argue that the concept is merely a way of imposing the tastes of an elite group on others.

## Policies to promote social obligations

In a free-market system, if you can persuade someone else to clean your house in return for £40, both parties to the transaction are presumed to be better off. You prefer to part with £40 rather than to clean the house yourself, and the person you hire prefers to have £40 than to avoid cleaning your house. Normally society does not interfere with people's ability to negotiate mutually advantageous contracts.

Most people do not feel this way, however, about activities that are regarded as social obligations. For example, during major wars when military service is compulsory, contracts similar to the one between you and your housekeeper could also be negotiated. Some people, faced with the obligation to do military service, could no doubt pay enough to persuade others to do their tour of service for them. By exactly the same argument as we just used, we can presume that both parties will be better off if they are allowed to negotiate such a trade. Yet such contracts are usually prohibited as a result of widely held values that cannot be expressed in the marketplace. In times of major wars, of the sort that were experienced twice in the twentieth century, military service by all healthy males in the right age group is held to be a duty that is independent of an individual's tastes, income, wealth, or social position.

Military service is not the only example of a social obligation. Citizens are not allowed to buy their way out of jury duty or to sell their votes, even though in many cases they could find willing trading partners. Even if the price system allocates goods and services with complete efficiency, members of a society do not wish to rely solely on the market for all purposes, since they have other goals that they wish to achieve.

## Policies for economic growth

Over the long haul, economic growth is the most powerful determinant of living standards (see Chapter 26). Whatever their policies concerning efficiency and equity, people who live in economies with rapid rates of growth find their living standards rising on average faster than those of people who live in countries with low rates of growth. Over a few decades, these growth-induced changes tend to have much greater effects on living standards than any policy-induced changes in the efficiency of resource allocation or the distribution of income.

For the last half of the twentieth century, most economists viewed growth mainly as a macroeconomic phenomenon related to total savings and total investment. Reflecting this view, most textbooks do not even mention growth in their chapters on microeconomic policy.

More recently there has been a shift back to the perspective of earlier economists, who saw technological change as the engine of growth, with individual entrepreneurs and firms as the agents of innovation. This is a microeconomic perspective that is meant to add to, not replace, the macroeconomic stress on capital accumulation.

Governments are aware of this microeconomic perspective on growth. Today few microeconomic policies escape being exposed to the question, 'Even if this policy achieves its main goal, will it have unfavourable effects on growth?' Answering yes is not a sufficient reason to abandon a specific policy. But it is a sufficient reason to think again. Is it possible to redesign the policy so that it can still achieve its main objective, while removing its undesirable side-effects on growth?

# Tools and performance

The main sets of tools available to governments to achieve their goals are taxes, spending, rules, and public ownership. In this section we discuss these tools and show how they are used to achieve the specific objectives outlined earlier.

## Taxation

Taxes and spending are by far the most important items on this list. Governments spend money to achieve many objectives, and that money must be either borrowed or

**Table 14.1** Spending and revenue of UK central and local government, 2005/6

| Spending | £billion | Revenue | £billion |
|---|---|---|---|
| Health | 90 | VAT | 74 |
| Education | 70 | Income tax | 136 |
| Defence | 28 | National insurance | 84 |
| Social protection | 147 | Corporation tax | 42 |
| Personal social services | 25 | Excise duties | 40 |
| Debt interest | 26 | Council tax | 21 |
| Public order and safety | 31 | Business rates | 20 |
| Industry, agriculture, employment, and training | 21 | Other | 66 |
| Housing and environment | 17 | | |
| Other | 65 | | |
| Total managed spending | 520 | Total revenue | 483 |

*Source*: HM Treasury, *Pre-Budget Report*, December 2005.

raised through taxes. We leave borrowing aside here, as it is only a temporary measure. Interest must be paid on borrowed money, and if that too is borrowed the total government debt will eventually explode to unmanageable proportions.

**Sooner or later, all government spending must be paid for out of taxes. Borrowing only postpones the need to tax.**

Table 14.1 shows the major sources of tax revenues, along with the major classes of government spending, for the UK in 2005/6.

As well as providing the revenues needed to finance all of the government's activities, taxes are also used as tools in their own right for a wide range of purposes. They can be used to alter the incentives to which private maximizing agents react, and to alter the distribution of income.

### Indirect taxes

Taxes are divided into two broad groups, depending on whether it is people or transactions that are taxed. An **indirect tax** is levied on a transaction and is paid by an individual by virtue of being involved in that transaction. Taxes and stamp duties on the transfer of assets from one owner to another are indirect taxes, since they depend on the assets being transferred. Inheritance taxes, which depend on the size of the estate being inherited and not on the circumstances of the beneficiaries, are another indirect tax.

The most important indirect taxes in today's world are those on the sale of currently produced products. These taxes are called *excise taxes* when they are levied on manufacturers, and *sales taxes* when they are levied on the sale of goods from retailer to consumer. The EU countries levy a comprehensive tax of this sort on all transactions, whether at the retail, wholesale, or manufacturer's level, called the **value added tax** (VAT). Value added is the difference between the value of inputs that a firm purchases from other firms and the value of its output. It therefore represents the value that a firm adds by virtue of its own activities. VAT is an indirect tax, because it depends on the value of what is made and sold and not on the wealth or income of the maker or seller. Thus, two self-employed fabric designers, each with a value added of £50,000 in terms of designs produced and sold, would pay the same VAT even if one had no other source of income while the other was independently wealthy.

Indirect taxes may be levied in two basic ways. An **ad valorem tax** is a percentage of the value of the transaction on which it is levied. The UK's 17.5 per cent VAT on most transactions is an ad valorem tax. A **specific** or **per-unit tax** is a tax expressed as so many pence per unit, independent of the commodity's price. Taxes on cinema and theatre tickets, and on each litre of petrol or alcohol, and on each packet of cigarettes are all specific, indirect taxes. Box 14.1 outlines the main impact of a per-unit tax on the price and output of firms.

### Direct taxes

Taxes in the second broad group are called **direct taxes**. These are levied on people and vary with the status of the taxpayer. The most important direct tax is the income tax. The personal income tax falls sometimes on the income of households and sometimes separately on each member of the household. It varies with the size and source of the taxpayer's income and various other characteristics, such as marital status and number of dependants.

Firms also pay taxes on their incomes. UK companies are subject to corporation tax, which is levied on their profits. This is a direct tax, both in the legal sense that the company is an individual in the eyes of the law, and in the economic sense that the company is owned by its shareholders so that a tax on the company is a tax on them. The impact of taxes on profits is discussed in Box 14.2. An *expenditure tax*—as advocated some years ago for the United Kingdom by the Royal Commission headed by Nobel Prize-winning economist James Meade (1909–96)— is also a direct tax. It is based on what a person spends, rather than on what she earns, and has exemptions that are specific to the individual taxpayer. A poll tax, which is

## Box 14.1 The impact of a per-unit tax in a competitive industry

Many kinds of taxes affect the costs of firms. We illustrate here a tax that is levied on each unit produced.

From the firm's point of view, the tax on each unit produced is just another cost of production. It shifts each firm's marginal cost curve vertically upwards by the amount of the tax, where marginal cost now refers to the firm's total outlay—costs and taxes—associated with each additional unit of production.

The figure shows a competitive market in equilibrium with the demand and supply curves $D$ and $S$ intersecting at $E_0$ to produce equilibrium price and output of $p_0$ and $q_0$. A tax of $T$ per unit is then placed on the product. We show the effect of the tax by adding it to the supply curve. The 'costs' of producers now comprise production costs plus the tax that must be paid to the government. Every point on the supply curve shifts vertically upwards by the amount of the tax. The intersection of the new supply curve $S_T$ and the demand curve $D$ yields the new quantity and market price of $q_1$ and $p_1$. Producers' after-tax receipts are read from the original supply curve $S$ and are $p_2 (= p_1 - T)$ per unit.

The upward shift in marginal cost curves makes the industry's supply curve shift upward by the amount of the tax. The impact is similar to that of an increase in costs for a firm in perfect competition (see Chapter 7, especially Box 7.3 on page 148).

A per-unit tax on the output of a competitive industry will:

1. raise price in the short run, but by less than the amount of the tax, so that the burden will be shared by consumers, who pay a higher price, and by producers, who do not cover their average total costs;

2. cause the industry to contract in the long run until the losses disappear, and the whole burden will fall on consumers;

3. if the cost curves of firms remaining in the industry are unaffected by the contraction in the size of the industry, cause the price to rise in the long run by the full amount of the tax.

The second of the above consequences is an example of a most important general proposition. This is that in an industry with freedom of entry or exit, and where there is room for a large number of firms, profits will always be pushed to zero in the long run. Thus, any temporary advantage or disadvantage given to the industry by any public policy or private action must be dissipated in the long run—free entry and exit always ensures that surviving firms earn zero pure profits.

Government intervention in a competitive industry can influence the size of the industry, the total volume of its sales, and the price at which its goods are sold; but intervention cannot influence the long-run profitability of the firms that remain in the industry.

Many government policies have started out raising the profitability of a particular industry but ended up increasing the number of firms, each operating at an unchanged level of profits. It illustrates the point that any intervention policy will fail to secure economic profits in the long run, unless it creates entry barriers and thereby creates monopoly power.

---

simply a lump-sum tax levied on each person, is another direct tax.

It is important for many purposes to distinguish average from marginal rates of any tax. The *average rate* of income tax paid by a person is that person's total tax divided by her income. The *marginal rate* of tax is the rate she would pay on her next pound's worth of income.

### Progressivity

The general term for the relation between the level of income and the percentage of income paid as a tax is **progressivity**. A **regressive tax** takes a *smaller percentage* of people's incomes the larger is their income. A **progressive tax** takes a *larger percentage* of people's incomes the larger is their income. A **proportional tax** is the boundary case between the two, since it takes the *same percentage* of income from everyone. Taxes on food, for example, tend to be regressive, because the proportion of income spent on food tends to fall as income rises. Taxes on alcoholic spirits tend to be progressive, since the proportion of income spent on spirits tends to rise with income. (Taxes on beer, on the other hand, are regressive.) Different types of progressivity are shown in Figure 14.3.

Progressivity can be defined for any one tax or for the tax system as a whole. Different taxes have different characteristics. Inevitably, some will be progressive and some regressive. The impact of a tax system as a whole on high-, middle-, and low-income groups is best judged by

**Box 14.2 The effect of taxes on profits**

A famous prediction is that a tax levied as a percentage of profits will have no effect on price and output under any market structure. Let us first see how the prediction is derived, and then consider its application to real-world situations.

Given free entry, there will be no profits in long-run equilibrium. Thus, the firms in a perfectly competitive industry will pay no profit tax in the long run. (*X* per cent of zero is zero.) It follows that the tax does not affect any firm's long-run behaviour and hence has no effect on industry price and output.

A tax on profit as defined in economics affects neither price nor output of a competitive industry in equilibrium. Hence it does not affect the allocation of resources.

Does this prediction apply to those taxes on firms' profits that are actually levied in many countries? The answer is no, because profits are defined in tax law according to accountants' rather than economists' usage. In particular, the tax-law definition includes the opportunity cost of capital and the reward for risk-taking. To economists this is a cost; for tax purposes it is profit. (To review economists' definition of profit see pages 117–19.)

A tax on the return to capital will have some effects. First, perfectly competitive firms will pay such taxes even in long-run equilibrium, since they use capital and must earn enough money to pay a return on it. Second, the tax will affect costs differently in different industries. To see this, compare two industries. One is very labour-intensive, so that 90 per cent of its costs of production go to wages and only 10 per cent go to capital and other factors. The other is very capital-intensive, so that fully 50 per cent of its costs (in economists' sense) are a return to capital. The tax on the return to capital will take a small part of the total earnings of the first industry and a large part of those of the second industry. If the industries were equally profitable (in an economic sense) before the tax, they would not be afterwards, and producers would be attracted into the first industry and out of the second one. This would cause prices to change until both industries became equally profitable (post-tax), after which no further movement would occur.

A tax on profits as they are defined in tax law does affect price and output and hence alters the allocation of resources. It also implies a higher effective tax rate in capital-intensive industries (though the impact of real tax systems would have to look at the entire range of taxes, including those on labour).

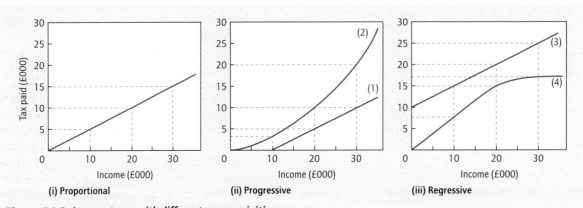

**Figure 14.3 Income taxes with different progressivities**

**Income taxes may be proportional, progressive, or regressive.** In part (i) the proportional tax's average and marginal rates remain unchanged at 50 per cent as income changes. In part (ii) tax (1) has a constant marginal rate of 50 per cent; but the average rate rises with income, being zero at income £10,000, 25 per cent at income £20,000, and 33.3 per cent at income £30,000. With tax (2) both the marginal and the average tax rates rise as income rises. In part (iii) tax (3) has a constant marginal rate of 50 per cent; but the average rate falls as income rises, being 150 per cent at £10,000, 100 per cent at income £20,000, and 83.3 per cent at £30,000. With tax (4) both the marginal and the average rates fall as income rises.

looking at the progressivity of the whole set of taxes taken together. For example, income taxes are progressive in the United Kingdom, rising to a maximum marginal rate of 40 per cent. The overall tax system is also progressive, but much less so than one would guess from studying only the income tax rates. This is because much revenue is raised by indirect taxes, which are much less progressive than income taxes.

## Expenditure

Some government expenditures involve the hiring of people and/or the purchase of land or capital to produce public services, such as health and education. Clearly, when the government hires these inputs, and uses them to produce goods and services in the public sector of the economy, these resources are unavailable to produce private sector output. A civil servant who works full time for the government cannot also work for a private company. This type of spending is sometimes called **exhaustive expenditure**. Among their many uses, exhaustive expenditures are a tool for filling in gaps in what the free market provides. For example, public goods, such as national defence, the legal system, and coastal navigation aids, must be produced by the government or not at all. In such cases the failure of the free market, and the potential for a remedy by government action, are obvious.

The remainder of government spending consists of **transfer payments**, which are payments *not* made in return for any contribution to current output. Old-age pensions, unemployment insurance and supplementary benefits, welfare payments, disability payments, and a host of other expenditures made by the modern welfare state are all transfer payments. They do not add to current marketable output; they merely transfer the power to purchase output from those who provide the money (usually taxpayers) to those who receive it. Their main purpose, therefore, is to alter the *distribution* of income. Tax-induced redistributions are not just from rich to poor. The government also makes transfers from those working to those retired and unemployed, from the healthy to the sick, and from city-dwellers to farmers (through CAP subsidies in the EU). None of these transfer payments represents a claim by the government on real productive resources. Revenue must none the less be raised to finance them. Table 14.2 shows UK government spending expressed as a proportion of national output.

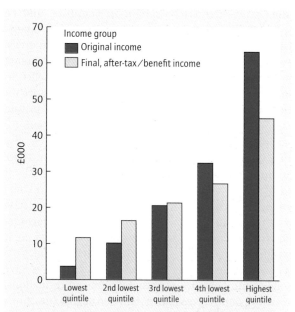

**Figure 14.4** UK households' original and final annual income, 2003/4

**The distribution of original income is much more unequal than the distribution of final income.** Original income obtained from private sector activities is altered by the subtraction of direct and indirect taxes and the addition of cash benefits and benefits in kind to obtain final, or after-tax/benefit, income.

*Source*: ONS, *Social Trends*, 2005.

Figure 14.4 shows the overall redistributive effect of the UK tax–spending system. While there were some increases in inequality in the 1980s (see Figure 14.2), the UK fiscal system still redistributes incomes from rich to poor. The main benefits to lower-income groups come from cash payments, such as welfare and unemployment benefits, and in-kind benefits, mainly education and the NHS. High-income groups contribute to the income redistribution because, although they receive many benefits, they pay even higher amounts of both direct and indirect taxes.

## Rules and regulations

Rules and regulations are potent tools for redressing market failures. Governments use rules both to set the framework within which market forces operate and to alter the workings of unhindered markets. Rules pervade economic activities. Shop hours and working conditions are regulated. Rules govern the circumstances under which various types of union can be formed and operated. Discrimination between labour services provided by males and females is illegal in the UK and in many other countries. Children cannot be served alcoholic drinks.

**Table 14.2** UK government spending as a percentage of GDP

| Spending on | 1956 | 1976 | 1997 | 2005 |
|---|---|---|---|---|
| Goods and services | 20.7 | 25.9 | 20.8 | 21.3 |
| Transfer payments | 13.2 | 21.0 | 18.6 | 16.5 |
| Total spending | 33.9 | 46.9 | 39.2 | 37.8 |

*Source*: ONS, UK National Accounts.

They must attend school in most countries, and be inoculated against communicable diseases in many. Laws prohibit people from selling or using certain drugs. Prostitution is prohibited in many societies even though it usually involves a willing buyer and a willing seller. In many countries you are forced to purchase insurance for the damage you might do to others with your private motor car. In some countries people who offer goods for sale cannot refuse to sell them to someone just because they do not like the customer's colour or religion. There are rules against fraudulent advertising and the sale of substandard, adulterated, or poisonous food. In some countries, such as the United States, anyone can purchase a variety of firearms ranging from pistols to machine-guns; in other countries, such as the United Kingdom, it is difficult for a private citizen to obtain a handgun.

As we saw in Chapter 13, most business practices have some control exerted on them by rules and regulations. In many countries agreements between oligopolistic firms to fix prices, or divide up markets, are illegal. The mere existence of monopoly is outlawed in some countries. When large economies of scale create a natural monopoly, the prices that a firm can charge, and the return it can earn on its capital investment, are often regulated.

## Public ownership

In the past many governments have used public ownership of nationalized industries as a tool for achieving policy goals. In the UK today most of these industries have been privatized. The remaining publicly owned industries in the UK (as of 2006) are the Royal Mail Group plc (which owns the Post Office), state education, and the National Health Service (NHS). The Royal Mail Group is in the market sector in the sense that it finances its activities by selling its services on the open market. We say nothing more about it here. We deal briefly with education and then in more detail with the NHS. The provision of both education and health services has been largely removed from the UK private sector and is provided free to consumers.

### The inefficiency of free goods

Of course, there is no such thing as a costless good or service. The production of anything requires resources, which have opportunity costs. So a 'free good' is not a costless good, only one whose costs are not borne by its users. Instead, the costs of state-provided free goods are borne by taxpayers.

Providing any good or service free to its users poses efficiency problems. We illustrate with a product that has neither positive nor negative externalities, so that private

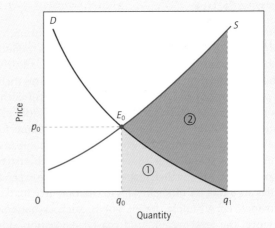

**Figure 14.5 The inefficiency of free goods**

Consumption of a free good exceeds what it would be at the efficient competitive equilibrium. Competitive equilibrium is at $E_0$ with price $p_0$ and quantity $q_0$. At a zero price $q_1$ is consumed. Since each extra unit that is produced adds its marginal cost to the total cost of production, total costs rise by the area under the industry's marginal cost curve (its supply curve). The two shaded areas 1 and 2 show this extra cost. The additional consumers' surplus is given by the light blue shaded area 1. So the efficiency loss is the dark blue shaded area 2.

and social costs and benefits coincide. If such a product is provided free and all demand is met, then people will go on consuming it until the last unit has a zero value to them. But that unit will have a positive marginal cost of production which represents the value to consumers that the resources used in its production could create in other lines of activity.

**Providing without charge goods and services that are costly to produce is allocatively inefficient because their price (of zero) is less than their marginal cost.**

Figure 14.5 shows the resource waste. It is obvious that the size of the waste will depend on the elasticity of the demand curve for the subsidized product. With a highly inelastic demand curve, the policy induces only a small increase in output, so only a small quantity of resources is inefficiently allocated. With a highly elastic demand, the quantity of misallocated resources is large.

From the point of view of improving equity in income distribution, free goods also have major shortcomings. Much of the money spent goes to subsidize their consumption by higher-income groups. Since there are few goods that are not bought by all income groups, the policy is much like shooting at a target with a shotgun—the bull's-eye will be hit, but so will almost everything else.

Transfer payments can be targeted at specific income groups; free goods cannot.

This lack of targeting makes the free-good policy an unnecessarily expensive way of helping low-income groups.

A further problem with free goods is that the government often does not provide a sufficient quantity to meet the demand at a zero price. Some alternative rationing scheme must therefore arise. Sometimes queues do the rationing. At other times sellers' preferences do the job. This happens, for example, when those considered most worthy by administrators or doctors are given expensive health care while others get cheaper alternatives.

## Education

Education could be left completely to the private sector. Those who were willing to pay would choose from the many schools at all levels that the private sector would no doubt provide. Most countries leave a substantial amount of education to be provided in this way. In the UK in 2006, about 6 per cent of 5–16 year olds were being educated in the private sector; thus, state schools still account for the vast majority of pupils. This raises three questions that are distinct although often confused. First, why is education made compulsory? Second, who should pay for education? Third, who should provide it?

### Why compulsion?

There are three main reasons for making education compulsory up to some allowable school-leaving age, which is 16 in the UK. The first is the protection of children. If selfish parents decided to spend money on themselves and nothing on their children, they would hamper their children's ability to function in the economy when they grew up. The second is income redistribution. It is held that no one should be prevented from gaining some minimum level of education because of lack of parental income. The third reason is externalities. Everyone gains from living in a society where everyone else has some minimum level of education. A well trained person is seldom of value on her own. One machinist in a society with no others would not be able to take most jobs that machinists do because they are done with other similarly trained workers. Because of externalities, we insist that everyone attend school up to some legal leaving age.

### Why free?

If an expensive service is made compulsory because it is of benefit to everyone, the obvious way to pay for it is through taxes. This is more acceptable, because the proposition that free goods are consumed in inefficient amounts does not apply to any good or service whose consumption is compulsory. Because everyone of school age must attend school, the elasticity of demand for such education is zero. Thus, the amount of resources allocated to compulsory education is independent of who pays for it. The method of payment will affect the distribution of income but will not cause any allocative inefficiency.

### Who should provide it?

There is no universal agreement on the question of provision. In the UK many parents opt out of the system and provide private education for their children. For this they must pay (in addition to the taxes that they already pay to support the state system). Those who go through the state system have little choice. They must go to the local school (possibly choosing between two nearby ones if space is available). They must accept the current curriculum and whatever educational practices are currently being mandated. They cannot purchase an alternative educational experience that does not currently have ministry approval (without opting out of the state sector entirely). In short, as with any other nationalized industries, there is little market choice available and innovation is centralized.

There are several arguments commonly advanced for state provision of education: it creates a desirable uniformity of standards; pay and working conditions will be the same throughout the system; the state with all its educational experts knows better than the child and its parents what educational experience is in the child's best interest; ministries can research new methods and techniques, and institute them efficiently when they seem to be improvements on current practices.

Opponents of the state monopoly in the provision of state-funded education argue for more market determination. The state could give every child education vouchers to the value of what the state is providing. These vouchers could be used to purchase education in any establishment that accepts them.

Proponents of this type of system argue several alleged advantages. First, it would give parents more choice among various schools—parents and their children usually have a better idea of what kind of education is needed and of whether or not they are getting it at the school currently being attended. Second, it would penalize schools with poor academic and discipline records. Salaries would not be uniform across all schools; instead, the earnings of schools and the salaries of teachers would vary with the success of individual schools in attracting students. Poorer schools would get few vouchers and hence little revenue out of which to pay their staff. Third, the system would encourage experimentation—anyone with a new idea could try it out, provided only that she could fill one classroom with students. The small amount of current centralized experimentation would be replaced with a large amount of decentralized experimentation. If some new educational ideal or fad gained majority acceptance it would not be forced on all students, as anyone who disagreed with it would need only find a school that was not following the herd.

These are some of the arguments advanced by some for exposing education to market forces while ensuring that it remains available to everyone. Many others worry about such exposure and prefer the system of state monopoly.

Although state financing of education is not in dispute in modern countries, the value of a state monopoly in providing free education is debated. Some think it the best system; others wish to inject market competition into the provision of free education.

### Health and medical care

The case for providing hospital and medical services at a price below cost (zero in the limit) rests on three considerations. First, private provision is prone to market failure. Second, it is alleged that the inefficiencies of free medical care are not large. Third, serious equity issues arise when health care is left to private markets.

#### Market failure

In the previous chapter we studied the types of market failure that emerge when all sides to a transaction are not equally informed. So we merely need note how these failures apply to the market for medical and health care. First, doctors are better informed about their patients' needs than are the patients themselves. So doctors are in a position to influence the demand for their services rather than responding to the demands of their patients. As a result, elective surgery and other treatments of non-life-threatening medical conditions are observed to vary with the supply of doctors. Second, patients are better informed than their medical insurers on the state of their own health. This creates the problem of adverse selection first mentioned in Chapter 11 (page 241). Third, people who are fully insured are likely to be more careless with their health than those who must pay for it themselves. This is the problem of moral hazard, also discussed in Chapter 11. It is worth noting that the first problem exists with any fee-for-service system, no matter who pays the bill. The second exists only when insurance companies

pay the bill, while the third exists in all systems where anyone but the patient pays.

With medical care, social and private costs and benefits are thought to diverge substantially. If I do not cure my infectious disease, the effects are not felt by me alone. More generally, everyone gains by living in a healthy rather than a disease-ridden society. Thus there are arguments for reducing the private costs of these services below the market rate by means of a subsidy.

Insurers can do little to avoid some adverse selection, but they will not insure those whom they know to be already ill or serious risks for other reasons. This means that a considerable number of people simply cannot get medical insurance under free-market provision. This group includes those who were born with serious health problems or acquired them while still living at home. It also includes those with serious health problems whose medical coverage runs out when they leave their present employer to change firms or retire; when they try to reinsure themselves in a private plan they often find themselves uninsurable.

#### Small inefficiencies?

Recall that the magnitude of the resource cost of a free-good policy depends on the slope of the demand curve between the free-market price and the subsidized price. Studies suggest a low incidence of unnecessary hospitalization in free-hospital systems. If the demand for services is not much larger than it would be in the free market (where most people would be privately insured) then the magnitude of the waste caused by divergence between the zero price and the positive marginal cost will be small.

Other potential inefficiencies also exist. Governments typically do not provide facilities to meet all the demand for free services, so scarce funds must be allocated within the system. However, bureaucratic decisions are seldom efficient in allocating scarce funds so that their marginal benefits are the same in all uses. In the mid-1990s a controversial internal-market mechanism was introduced into the NHS. Patients got treatment free, but doctors had a notional budget that they used to buy services from hospitals. Hospitals priced operations, and these prices varied substantially over the country. This internal-market system was abolished by the Labour government in 1999. A ten-year plan was embarked upon in 2000 to improve health service resources and the efficiency of the internal allocation mechanisms. The impact of this plan is still hard to judge, but it seems unlikely to solve the problem created by virtually permanent excess demand at a zero price. Indeed, in 2006 many local health authorities and hospital trusts found themselves with severe financial deficits, despite significant increases in government funding.

### Equity considerations

There are also more subtle arguments about social values. It has been argued that in richer societies decisions about basic medical care should be taken out of the economic arena. It is degrading for a person to have to balance medical care for a child against the other family needs. Therefore, it was argued, the inefficiency cost of freely provided basic medical care is worth accepting in order to produce a society where choices about basic medical services are eliminated.

Notice the use of the word 'basic' in the previous paragraph. The above position is arguable if it is confined to basic services for all. Modern medical technology is so expensive that the state could not afford to make all conceivable services freely available to all. The more expensive services must be rationed. This can be done either by prices or by decisions about need taken by medical and hospital authorities.

For all its problems, the NHS remains one of the most popular of the government's many activities. It seems likely, therefore, to stay in place for a long time to come. As a result, understanding its shortcomings and using economic analysis to alleviate the worst of its inefficiencies is an important social activity.

## Economic growth

Economic growth has been the cause of the sustained long-term increase in living standards that began sometime early in the nineteenth century, i.e. about 200 years ago. However, the contemporary focus on the interface between microeconomic policies and economic growth is relatively new. A few decades ago, growth policies would have been considered solely a macroeconomic issue relating to aggregate demand and aggregate investment. However, in recent times the focus on growth policies or 'supply-side policies' has concentrated on microeconomic issues, such as flexibility of labour markets, incentives for invention and innovation, and disincentive effects of taxation and red tape. One issue for policy-makers is the unintentional side-effects on growth of policies with other primary objectives. Another issue is the effectiveness of micro policies that are directly focused on encouraging growth. Both are relevant when policy tools are chosen.

### Taxation policies for growth

Almost all taxes can affect growth by altering incentives either to save, to work, or to take risks.

#### Taxation of consumption or income

Income taxes apply to income when it is earned; spending taxes (such as VAT) apply only to that part of income that is spent on consumption.

As an example, consider a woman in the 40 per cent marginal tax bracket who earns an extra £1,000 and pays £400 income tax. If she spends her after-tax income, she will be able to buy £600 worth of goods. If she saves the money, she will be able to buy a £600 bond. If the bond pays, say, a 4 per cent real return, she will earn £24 interest per year. But a 40 per cent tax must then be paid on the interest earnings, leaving only a £14.40 annual income. This is a 2.4 per cent after-tax return on the bond and a 1.44 per cent after-tax return on the original £1,000 income! 

This 'double taxation' of savings is a disincentive to save. Some economists who wish to encourage saving, which helps to finance growth-creating investment, argue for taxes on consumption rather than income. Under an expenditure tax, any income that is saved is untaxed. Our saver in the previous paragraph would be taxed only when the interest earned on the savings was actually spent on consumption.

#### Steeply progressive rates of tax

Steeply progressive tax rates are an incentive to emigrate or at least move one's business abroad. They also penalize people with fluctuating incomes, such as authors, self-employed builders, and small-scale innovators. Consider an innovator who tries to introduce one new product each year. She only covers costs on her first four attempts and then has a success that yields £250,000 over costs in the fifth year. Her income over the five years is the same as a salaried employee who has earned £50,000 for each of these five years. Yet under a steeply progressive tax regime she will pay much more tax. This was a really serious problem when the maximum rate of tax in the United Kingdom was 70 per cent. (Immediately after the Second World War, in 1945, it was well over 90 per cent!) In the 1980s the maximum rate was cut to 40 per cent, which greatly reduces the tax penalty paid by someone with a highly fluctuating income. But it is still there. In 2005/6, our innovator would have paid £92,542 in taxes, while over the same five-year period a salaried employee would have paid £62,708 (assuming each had no dependants).

Here we see one of the many possible conflicts between growth and equity. Policy-makers may favour steeply progressive tax rates on grounds of equity but be persuaded to moderate the degree of progressivity in the interest of encouraging the risk-taking that is necessary for promoting growth.

## Adjustment policies for growth

The innovations in products and production processes that underlie growth require continual changes and adaptations throughout the economy. If government policies discourage change, growth will be slowed. The realization that many policies designed to improve equity can discourage change has led to some policy re-evaluations.

### Labour market policies

When people lose jobs because of economic change, the various measures that constitute the welfare safety net provide them with income support. Although such passive support provides immediate relief, it provides no incentive for recipients to change their situation and can sometimes even discourage such efforts.

An alternative is to make some, or all, of the support conditional on adjusting to change, for example by retraining or relocating. The UK government, for example, has funded the Learning and Skills Council, to encouraged young people to undergo a period of training or work experience.

### Support of firms and industries

Governments are always tempted to support declining industries. Over the past century both Labour and Conservative governments have done a lot of this. Such policies reduce unemployment in the short run, but if economic forces are leading to a continual decline, the policies are only costly ways of postponing the inevitable. Furthermore, when it finally does come, the adjustment often comes suddenly. This is because the government support is withdrawn all at once when the growing cost of the support finally becomes unacceptable.

### Patents

If an innovation can be easily copied, new firms may enter an industry so quickly that the innovating firm is not compensated for the costs and risks of innovation. The innovation is, in effect, a public good, and private firms are not motivated to produce it. Patent laws are designed to provide the needed incentives by creating a temporary property right, i.e. a patent, over the invention, allowing the invention's owner to earn profits as a reward for inventing. Once the patent expires, others can legally copy the innovation and production will expand until

profits fall to normal. (See also our discussion on pages 200–1.)

### Reduction of entry barriers

Those who accept Schumpeter's theory of *creative destruction* (first introduced on page 171 and then further discussed on page 198) hold that anti-monopoly policy and public utility regulations are unnecessary as policies to influence behaviour in the very long run. They worry that state intervention will inadvertently create entry barriers that will protect existing firms from the growth-creating process of creative destruction. They believe that government policies directed at minimizing entry barriers are the only industrial and competition policies that are needed.

### Nationalization

Those who reject Schumpeter's theory often support anti-monopoly and public utility regulation policies. They feel that such policies are required to prevent monopolies from earning large profits at the expense of consumers.

Supporters of Schumpeter's theory argue that nationalization and public regulation will defeat their own purposes in the long term by inhibiting the process of creative destruction. A government monopoly provides the most enforceable entry barrier. It may inhibit the introduction of new products, and of new ways to produce old products, that would have occurred when new firms attacked the entrenched positions of existing firms. Supporters of this view point to the former Soviet Union's need to buy technology from Western countries, and argue that the rapid development of new products and processes in the oligopolistic and monopolistic industries operating in market-oriented economies gives support to Schumpeter's view. Box 14.3 deals with an important court case in which many of the issues relating to monopoly power and creative destruction arose.

### A short-term/long-term trade-off?

Economists who accept both the force of the argument that monopolistic firms can earn large exploitative profits in the short term *and* Schumpeter's argument about the very long run face a policy dilemma. In the short term, firms that gain monopoly power may earn very large profits at the expense of consumers. In the very long term, however, attempts to control these monopolies may inhibit the creative destruction that helps to raise living standards through productivity growth.

**The policy world is not a simple place, and policies that help to achieve desired goals over one time-span must be constantly scrutinized for undesired effects over other time-spans.**

**Box 14.3  The great Microsoft anti-trust case**

Some of the greatest innovations in information and communications technology have been due to Bill Gates and his firm Microsoft. Gates is one of the world's wealthiest people. He is a classic entrepreneur who entered the PC software industry when it was new, fiercely competitive, and rapidly developing. His Windows operating system achieved instant customer approval and now dominates the industry.

In 1998 the United States Department of Justice brought an anti-trust suit against Microsoft for alleged monopoly practices. The firm was accused of tactics designed to make entry difficult for smaller firms selling specialized products that competed with some parts of Microsoft's array. In particular, when customers buy any new version of the Windows operating system, they are automatically provided with Microsoft's Internet browser. This bundling of Microsoft products undoubtedly makes competition more difficult for smaller firms producing one type of product.

The suit reveals all the conflicting views that can be taken about competition and technical change.

• Technological innovations have transformed the lives of ordinary people several times since the first industrial revolution in the mid-eighteenth century.

• A new industry producing a wholly new range of products typically starts off as highly competitive as did cars, aircraft, and computers. Soon, however, the winners in the race to expand and improve the range of products eliminate most of the weaker competitors. They emerge as oligopolists in a mature industry.

• The dominant firm in the technological race often establishes something close to a monopoly position. This dominance is partly a result of continued successful innovation—established oligopolies have been the source of much growth-inducing technological change over the past 150 years. It is also partly a result of the firm's ability to suppress competition from smaller upstart firms.

• Over the long haul, even if the oligopolist becomes something close to a monopolist, it cannot perpetuate its position indefinitely—new firms with new products eventually arise to challenge and unseat the established firms.

So how should the US government react? Should it constrain Microsoft in order to create more growth-enhancing competition? Or should it accept Microsoft's dominant position in the industry as the reward for its amazing record as an innovator? Should it accept Schumpeter's argument that in the very long run neither Microsoft nor any other dominant firm will be able to maintain its position unless it outperforms actual and potential competitors in the race to provide consumers with more, better, and cheaper products?

Faced with that decision, the US Department of Justice took the line that Microsoft's behaviour was designed to stifle competition. Later a US appeals court took the opposite line. These early differences in legal opinions illustrate the difficulty in distinguishing successful competitive behaviour from behaviour designed to suppress competition. Later court hearings found Microsoft guilty in some aspects of anti-competitive behaviour but not in others. The US Justice Department proposed a final judgement that

*will stop recurrence of Microsoft's unlawful conduct, prevent recurrence of similar conduct in the future, and restore competitive conditions in the personal computer operating system market by, among other things, prohibiting actions by Microsoft to prevent computer manufacturers and others from developing, distributing or featuring middleware products that are threats to Microsoft's operating system monopoly; creating the opportunity for independent software vendors to develop products that will be competitive with Microsoft's middleware products; requiring Microsoft to disclose interfaces and license protocols in order to ensure that competing middleware and server operating system products can interoperate with Microsoft's desktop operating systems; and ensuring full compliance with the [final judgement]. (For details of the final judgement and subsequent monitoring of implementation see: www.usdoj.gov/atr/cases/ms_index.htm.)*

In 2006, EU antitrust action against Microsoft continued. In March, for example, the EU Commission was pursuing a complaint in the courts that Microsoft was not doing enough to comply with a 2004 ruling that ordered it to share information that would help rivals develop software to work with Windows servers. Hence this case may run and run.

# The costs of government intervention

We have seen that governments have many reasons to take action and many tools that help them to achieve their goals. However, to evaluate government intervention, we need to consider costs as well as benefits.

Large potential benefits do not necessarily justify government intervention, nor do large potential costs necessarily make it unwise. What matters are net benefits—the balance between benefits and costs.

Three types of cost of government intervention are important: costs that are internal to the government, costs that are external to the government but directly paid by others in the sector where the intervention occurs, and costs that are external to the government and felt more generally throughout the entire economy.

## Internal costs

Everything the government does uses resources. It costs money when government inspectors visit plants to check on compliance with government-imposed health standards, industrial safety, or environmental protection. The inspectors and their support staff must be paid and their offices maintained. The salaries of the judges, the clerks, and the court reporters that are needed when an anti-monopoly case is heard are costs imposed by the regulation.

Armies of office workers, backed up by computerized information technology, keep track of income tax and VAT receipts. Inspectors take to the field to enforce compliance, and the courts deal with serious offenders. Unemployment and other benefits must be administered.

## Direct external costs

External costs are costs that the government's action imposes on others; they may be either direct or indirect. Direct external costs fall on agents with whom the government is directly interacting. Regulation and control often add directly to the costs of producing goods. For example, firms must inspect machinery to ensure that it meets government safety standards.

Much business activity is devoted to understanding, reporting, and contesting regulatory provisions. Occupational safety and environmental control have increased the number of employees not working on the shop floor. The costs of complying with tax laws can run to large sums each year. Firms, and wealthy individuals, spend substantial sums on lawyers and accountants to help them comply with tax laws and choose tax-minimizing courses of action.

Quite apart from the actual cost to business, government intervention may reduce the incentive for experimentation, innovation, and the introduction of new products. Requiring advance government clearance before introducing a new method or product (on grounds of potential safety hazards or environmental impact) can reduce the incentive to develop it. New lines of investment may be chosen more for their tax implications than for their potential for reducing production costs and thereby contributing to productivity growth.

## Indirect external costs

Indirect external costs are costs of the government's action that spread beyond those immediately affected by it—sometimes to the entire economy. Here is an example of the many costs of this type.

### Externalities

Ironically, government intervention to offset adverse externalities can create new adverse externalities. For example, government regulations designed to ensure the safety of new drugs delay the introduction of all drugs, including those that are safe. The benefits of these regulations are related to the unsafe drugs kept off the market. The cost includes the delayed availability of new safe drugs.

The shifting of taxes often causes major externalities. **Shifting** refers to the passing of the incidence of a tax from the person who initially pays it to someone else. **Incidence** refers to who actually bears the tax. One major problem with the use of taxes to achieve a social goal such as redistributing income is that market forces may shift the burden of the tax from the person who initially pays it to others. In Box 14.1, we studied the effects of a tax levied in a single market and concluded:

If the supply curve is positively sloped and the demand curve negatively sloped, the burden of a tax is shared between producers and consumers.

This outcome does not depend on who actually makes the tax payment to the government. If producers initially pay the tax, the upward shift in the market supply curve will raise the price and pass some of the tax burden on to consumers. If consumers initially pay the tax, the downward shift in their after-tax demand curve will lower the price received by producers. This passes some of the burden on to producers.

There will also be repercussions in other markets. As the price of one product rises, the demand curves for substitutes will shift to the right, while the demand curves for complements will shift to the left. The resulting changes in their market prices will induce changes in other related markets. The effects of a tax on one market will therefore spread throughout the economy, making the final distribution of the burden difficult to ascertain.

### Inefficiencies

Many government interventions have some adverse efficiency effects. These have played an important part in the so-called supply-side criticisms of government policy, and we need to look at them in some detail.

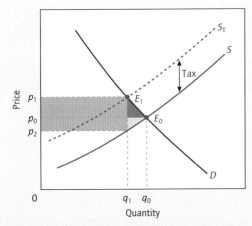

**Figure 14.6** **The efficiency loss from an indirect tax**

The tax causes a loss of consumers' surplus, which is a deadweight loss. The tax shifts the supply curve from $S$ to $S_T$. This moves equilibrium from $E_0$ with price $p_0$ and quantity $q_0$ to $E_1$ with price $p_1$ and quantity $q_1$. Consumers pay $p_1$, while the after-tax receipts of producers are $p_2$. The government gains tax revenue equal to the medium pink area, which is $p_1$ minus $p_2$ (the tax) multiplied by $q_1$. Part of this comes from producers and part from consumers. Consumers also lose surplus of the dark pink area. Producers also lose surplus of the light pink area. Since no one gets the surpluses that consumers and producers lose: they are the deadweight loss of the tax.

**Figure 14.7** **An income tax and the work–leisure choice**

An income tax results in an inefficient choice between work and leisure. This person earns £40 an hour. His budget line runs from 24 hours (no work) to £960 (no sleep!). He maximizes utility at $E_0$ with 16 hours of leisure (8 hours of work) and income of £320 per day. An income tax of 50 per cent shifts his after-tax budget line to run from 24 hours to £480 (no sleep). He maximizes utility by moving to $E_1$ with 18 hours of leisure (6 hours of work) and a gross pay of £240. This yields him an after-tax income of £120.

The government could raise its £120 through a tax that did not alter the income–leisure trade-off (say a poll tax). The after-tax budget line in this case shifts in to 21 hours (the tax is the equivalent of 3 hours' work) and £840. The individual now moves from $E_0$ to $E_2$, consuming 15 hours of leisure (working 9 hours) and consuming £240 worth of goods. $E_2$ is superior to $E_1$ because it lies on a higher indifference curve.

First, consider a sales tax on one specific good. The tax raises the relative price that consumers face for that good, so they will buy less of it and more of other products. Production falls below the competitive equilibrium level, which is the one that maximizes the sum of consumers' and producers' surplus. The result, as shown in Figure 14.6, is a loss of consumers' surplus exactly analogous to the deadweight loss of monopoly.

This result applies to any taxes that affect the prices of products in different proportions and hence change relative prices. It therefore applies to VAT whenever different products are taxed at different rates. The key is that

Consumers equate their marginal utilities to prices including tax, while producers equate their marginal costs to the price net of the tax. Hence the tax causes inefficiency, since the value that consumers place on the last unit consumed exceeds the marginal cost of making it.

Next, consider an income tax. It creates inefficiency by distorting the work–leisure choice. Employers pay one wage (pre-tax) and employees receive another wage (post-tax). Employees, reacting to after-tax wage rates, see a rate of substitution between work and leisure that differs from

the rate implied by the pre-tax wage the employer is prepared to pay.

To understand the source of the inefficiency, compare the income tax with a **poll tax**, which takes the same lump sum from everyone. Because it is not related to income, a poll tax leaves the marginal rate of substitution between goods and leisure unaffected. The tax exerts no disincentive to work at the margin, and thus is more efficient than the income tax.

Figure 14.7 demonstrates the inefficiency of an income tax. It shows that each individual achieves a higher indifference curve when she is forced to pay a given amount of tax revenue through a poll tax rather than through an income tax. The poll tax is more efficient because it leaves each person facing a choice at the margin that reflects the wage rate actually paid by employers in the labour market.

The importance of the figure lies in its demonstration that any practical tax does have negative efficiency effects, because it distorts relative price signals. The only tax that does not do so, under normal conditions, is the poll tax. It has no negative efficiency effects because the amount paid does not vary with the taxpayer's economic income or wealth or any of her economic decisions. It is precisely for this reason that most people find it *unacceptable* on equity grounds as anything other than a minor source of revenue.[2]

### Disincentive effects

If we consider a 'closed economy' where there is no possibility of emigration, then marginal rates of up to 40 per cent or so do not seem to have strong disincentive effects. Economic theory makes no general prediction about how altering income tax rates in this range would affect the supply of effort. On page 218 and in Box 10.5 we showed that a rise in the wage rate might increase, or decrease, the supply of effort, and, similarly, a fall in the wage rate might have either effect. Now observe that the after-tax wage rate is lowered by a rise in the rate of income tax, and raised by a fall in the rate. It follows immediately that any given change in the rate of income tax may either raise or lower the supply of effort. At some point, however, high marginal tax rates begin to have more serious disincentive effects. As marginal rates approach 100 per cent, the disincentive effect becomes absolute.

In an open society where emigration is possible, very high marginal rates of tax have major effects. Authors, artists, pop groups, and others who 'strike it rich' are strongly tempted to emigrate to countries that will allow them to keep a higher proportion of their incomes. Emigration of successful people of this type from the United Kingdom to the United States was significant between 1945 and 1980, when UK marginal rates of income tax were often double those in the United States.

From the point of view of maximizing tax revenues and reducing tax burdens on middle- and lower-income groups, it would be better to have high-income people still in the country paying tax rates of 40–50 per cent than out of the country avoiding much higher tax rates.

Governments throughout the world have come to accept that very high marginal rates of tax do exert vari-

---

[2] The argument in the text assumes a closed economy in which everyone actually pays the tax. In practice, however, even the poll tax will have some efficiency effects. A large enough poll tax will cause people to emigrate. It will also cause some people to choose jobs, and life-styles, that facilitate evasion. People with no fixed addresses, and no regular jobs, find evasion easier than people who are stuck with one job and own their own houses or flats. Thus, at the margin the poll tax will influence some people's job and residence decisions, which means that it does have some adverse efficiency effects.

**Table 14.3** UK marginal rates of income tax (tax rate on an extra £1 of income)

| Taxable income* | Marginal tax rate (%) | |
| --- | --- | --- |
| | 1978–79 | 2006–07 |
| 1,500 | 34 | 10 |
| 6,000 | 34 | 22 |
| 18,000 | 45 | 22 |
| 24,000 | 50 | 22 |
| 30,000 | 65 | 22 |
| 36,000 | 70 | 40 |
| 54,000 | 83 | 40 |

UK income taxes are much less progressive than they used to be. The figures have been converted to 1990 pounds to make them comparable. In 2006/7, the maximum marginal rate of 40 per cent sets in at about £33,000 taxable income. Twenty years earlier the marginal rate at that level of income was a full 65 per cent.

* Income after deducting allowances.

*Source*: ONS Financial Statement and Budget Report.

ous important disincentive effects. Table 14.3 shows marginal rates of income tax in the UK for 1978–79 and 2006–07. It is worth noting that the highest rate in 1978 was much lower than the highest marginal rate of 97.5 per cent levied in the UK in the period shortly after the Second World War. (This enormous rate included a surtax on investment income.)

Taxes are not the only government interventions that have disincentive effects. Payments designed to help certain low-income groups are often means-tested. Sometimes the welfare payments are reduced by £1 for every £1 of income received by welfare recipients. The person in effect faces a marginal tax rate of 100 per cent on every unit of income earned up to the level of the benefit payments. The effect, called the *poverty trap*, is a severe disincentive to work, and we should not be surprised when people respond rationally to these market signals.

Say, for example, that benefit payments are £25 a day and are cut by £1 for every £1 of income earned. If the person makes £5 a day, benefits fall to £20; if £10 is earned, benefits fall to £15, and so on. Only when more than £25 per day is earned will the person's disposable income begin to rise. Even if the benefits are reduced at a less sharp rate, say 50p per £1 earned, the disincentive of the high implicit tax rate is strong. Figure 14.8 illustrates this disincentive effect by showing how such schemes induce many people to reject employment that they would have accepted had the schemes not existed.

Benefit payments are required to help those in real need. If they are income-related, however, they tend to discourage recipients from working.

This does not argue against welfare payments. It does however suggest that welfare schemes should be designed to minimize their effects on efficiency.

## Costs versus benefits

It is difficult to estimate the overall direct and indirect costs of general government activity. About the most that can be said is that they are not insignificant. The level of uncertainty is great enough that those who wish to reduce the scope of government activity can argue that these costs are high, while those who wish to maintain or enlarge the present scope of government can argue that the benefits greatly outweigh the costs.

The costs are often clearer when specific government activities are considered, rather than all activities together. For example, when it became generally accepted that high marginal rates of income tax had serious consequences, governments (eventually) moved to lower these rates. When it became accepted that government-run business enterprises were no more efficient than privately run ones, and often much less efficient, many governments moved to privatize the industries that they owned. A great debate has raged over the costs of environmental regulation. Although full indirect costs are hard to measure, most estimates do not show these costs to be prohibitive. But the costs and inefficiencies of direct mandates to specific firms have seemed large enough that governments have searched for more efficient, less costly methods. In many cases the best solution seems to be tradable pollution permits.

So the lesson is that there is no general lesson about too much or too little government, but that government activity *is* costly, and in some circumstances can be very costly. So every activity, existing or projected, needs to be assessed on its individual merits. Only if the benefits appear to outweigh the measurable costs and the best guess about the unmeasurable costs should the activity be initiated or continued.

**Figure 14.8 Disincentives of welfare schemes**

**Income-tested benefits provide disincentives to work.** The individual is not employed but receives benefits of £25 per day from some income-related scheme. This puts him at point $E_0$, consuming 24 hours of leisure and receiving £25 pounds of income. He is now offered work at £5 per hour, presenting him with a budget line that ends at £120 (for 24 hours' work). In the absence of the benefit he would locate at $E_1$, consuming 16 hours of leisure (working 8 hours) and earning £40 of income. But for every £1 he earns he loses £1 of benefit, so the budget line starts at $E_0$ and is vertical to point $a$, where he is working 5 hours and still getting £25 but now all from work. Further work nets him £5 an hour, so the budget line has its normal slope below $a$. Since the indifference curve through $E_1$ is lower than the curve through $E_0$, his rational choice is not to work.

# Government failure

So far we have dealt with a government that is trying its best to achieve the goals that we laid out at the beginning of this chapter. It may impose costs, some expected and some unexpected, but it is seeking, as best it can, to achieve socially acceptable goals.

Is this too naïve a view of government and the political process? Today, many observers of the political scene, including not a few economists, would answer with an emphatic yes.

Without doubt, governments are far from perfect. This is not because bureaucrats and politicians are worse than other people—more stupid, more rigid, or more venal. Instead it is because they are like others, with flaws as well as virtues and with motives of their own. So, having found potential net benefits from perfect but costly government intervention, the final issue is whether the imperfect governments that we encounter in the real world will achieve some of these benefits. Where they do not succeed in achieving potential benefits that exceed the full direct and indirect costs, we speak of **government failure**—to distinguish it from market failure.

Governments may sometimes make isolated mistakes just as private decision-makers do. What is interesting, however, is why governments tend, under certain circumstances, to be more systematically in error than unhindered markets. There are many possible causes of systematic government failure.

## Rigidities

Rules and regulations, tax rates, and spending policies are hard to change. Market conditions, however, change continually and often rapidly. A rule requiring the use of a certain method to reduce pollution may have made sense when the cost of that method was low. It may, however, become a wasteful rule when some alternative method becomes less costly.

Today's natural monopolies often become tomorrow's competitive industries by technological innovations. For example, the near monopoly of the early railways was eliminated by the development of cheap road transport, and the falling cost of air transport is currently providing potent competition for surface transport in the movement of many products.

A centralized decision-taking body has difficulty in reacting to changing conditions as fast as decentralized decision-takers react to market signals.

Governments are often slow to admit mistakes even when they become aware of them. It is often politically easier to go on spending money on a project that has turned sour than to admit fault. A classic example was the development of Concorde, the supersonic airliner. Successive governments realized it was an enormous money-loser, but they went on supporting it long after any chance of commercial success was gone.

Markets are much harsher in judging success. When people are investing their own money, the principle that bygones are bygones is usually followed. No firm could raise fresh financial capital for what was currently a poor prospect just because the prospects had seemed good in the past. Neither could it do so because much money had already been spent on it, or because those who supported it in the past would lose face if it were now dropped.

## Decision-makers' objectives

An important cause of government failure arises from the nature of the government's own objectives. Why is economists' advice followed closely in some cases while it is systematically ignored in others? Governments are not faceless robots doing whatever economic analysis shows to be in the social interest. Instead they have their own objectives, which they seek to maximize.

Governments undoubtedly do care about the social good to some extent, but public officials have their careers, their families, and their prejudices as well. Elected MPs and local councillors no doubt care about the public good, but they must also worry about being re-elected. The resulting problems are similar to the principal–agent issues mentioned earlier as a source of market failure. In the present case the *principals* are the public; they want governments to do certain things. However, their *agents*—elected and appointed—are motivated by considerations that sometimes pull against what the public wishes.

An important advance in understanding economic policy came from modelling governments as maximizers of their own welfare, and then incorporating them into theoretical models of the working of the economy. One of the pioneers of this development was the American economist James Buchanan, who was awarded the 1986 Nobel Prize in economics for his work in this field. The theory that he helped to develop is called *public choice theory*.

The key idea is to view the government as just another economic agent engaging in its own maximizing behaviour. When this view is adopted, there is still room for many competing theories, depending on what variables are in the government's preference or utility function (i.e. what things the government cares about and is trying to achieve). Consider the other two main decision-taking bodies in orthodox economics. *Firms* have only profits in their utility functions, and they seek to maximize these. *Consumers* have only goods and services in their utility functions, and they seek to maximize their satisfaction from consuming them. An analogous theory of the government allows only one variable in its utility function, the variable being votes! Such a government would take all its decisions with a view to maximizing its votes at the next election.

## Public choice theory

Full-blown public choice theory deals with three maximizing groups. *Elected officials* seek to maximize their votes. *Civil servants* seek to maximize their salaries (and hence their positions in the hierarchy). *Voters* seek to maximize their personal level of satisfaction. To this end, voters look to the government to provide them with goods and services and income transfers that raise their personal utility. No one in this hypothetical world cares about the general public interest!

On the one hand, this surely is not a completely accurate characterization of motives. Elected statesmen have acted in what they perceive to be the public interest, hoping to be vindicated by history even if they know they risk losing the next election. Some civil servants have exposed inside corruption even though it cost them their jobs. And some high-income individuals vote for the political party that advocates the most, not the least, income redistribution.

On the other hand, the characterization is close to the mark in many cases. Most of us have read of politicians whose only principle is 'What will get me most votes?' And many voters ask only 'What is in it for me?' This is why the theory can take us a long way in understanding what we see, even though real behaviour is more complex.

Here is one example. Why, in spite of strong advice from economists, have governments persisted in subsidizing agriculture for decades, until the situation is reached where many governments face problems from the high cost of farm subsidies and international pressure over the associated protectionist trade policies? Public choice theory looks at the gainers and the losers among the voters.

The gainers from agricultural supports are domestic farmers. They are a politically powerful group, and are aware of what they will lose if farm supports are reduced. They would show their disapproval of such action by voting against any government that even suggests it. The main domestic losers are the entire group of consumers. Although the losers are more numerous than the gainers, and although their total loss is large, each individual loser suffers only a small loss. For example, a policy that gives £50 million a year to British farmers need cost each citizen only £1 per year.[3] Citizens have more important things to worry about, and so do not vote against the government just because it supports farmers. As long as the average voters are unconcerned about, and often

unaware of, the losses they suffer, the vote-maximizing government will ignore the interests of the many and support the interests of the few. The vote-maximizing government will consider changing the agricultural policy only when the cost of agricultural support becomes so large that ordinary taxpayers become aware of it and begin to protest. What is required for a policy change, according to this theory, is that those who lose become sufficiently aware of their losses for this awareness to affect their voting behaviour.

Another group of losers from agricultural protection (which usually accompanies farm subsidies) is foreign farmers in countries that do not provide similar support. They are often excluded from domestic markets by import levies or quantitative import restrictions, or are hurt by subsidies on foreign exports to their home markets. They are worse off as they are denied market access and therefore receive a lower price for their products than they otherwise might. Clearly, foreign farmers do not receive a vote, and this can explain why domestic politicians do not give them much weight in making their decisions. However, this can change when key foreign countries get together and use their collective negotiating strength to negotiate better access to rich country markets, perhaps in exchange for other concessions on market access. Such international organizations as the World Trade Organization (the WTO) are designed to provide a means whereby those in countries that suffer from policies adopted by other countries can exert pressure for these to be changed.

The ability of elected officials and civil servants to ignore the domestic public interest is strengthened by a phenomenon called **rational ignorance**. Many policy issues are extremely complex. For example, even the experts are divided when assessing the pros and cons of the UK's decision to stay out of the first wave of membership in the euro, the common European currency. Much time and effort is required for a layperson even to attempt to understand the issue. Similar comments apply to the evidence for and against capital punishment or lowering the age of criminal liability. Yet one person's vote has little influence on which party gets elected or on what the government really will do about the issue in question once elected. So the costs are large, the benefits small. Thus, a majority of rational, self-interested voters will remain innocent of the complexities involved in most policy issues.

Who will be the informed minority? The answer is: those who stand to gain or lose a lot from the policy, those with a strong sense of moral obligation, and those policy junkies who just like this sort of thing.

---

[3] 'Why worry?' you may ask. 'Isn't the small loss to each consumer a reasonable price to pay?' It may be in this one case. The problem, however, lies not in one such policy, but in the cumulative effects of many. If each of many special-interest groups secures a policy that costs each member of the public a small amount, the total bill over all such policies can be, and in many countries is, very large indeed.

## Inefficient public choices

A major principle of most people's idea of democracy is that each citizen's vote should have the same weight. One of the insights of public choice theory is that resource allocation based on the principle of one-person–one-vote will often be inefficient because it fails to take into account the *intensity of preferences*.

To illustrate this problem, consider three farmers, Al, Bob, and Charles. Farmers Al and Bob want the government to build an access road to each of their farms, and each road will cost £6,000. Suppose that the road to Al's farm is worth £7,000 to Al and that the road to Bob's farm is worth £7,000 to Bob. (Charles's farm is on the main road and so requires no new access road.) Suppose that, under the current taxing rules, the cost of building each road will be shared equally among the three farmers—£2,000 each. It is efficient to build both roads, since each generates net benefits of £1,000 (£7,000 gross benefits to the farmer helped, less £6,000 total cost). But each would be defeated 2 to 1 in a simple majority vote. (Bob and Charles would vote against Al's road; Al and Charles would vote against Bob's road.)

Now suppose that we allow Al and Bob to make a deal: 'I will vote for your road if you will vote for mine.' Although political commentators often decry such deals, they do enhance efficiency. Both roads now get 2 to 1 majorities, and both roads get built. However, such deals can just as well reduce efficiency. If we make the gross value of each road £5,000 instead of £7,000 and let Al and Bob make their deal, each road will still command a 2 to 1 majority because the total cost is £4,000 to each farmer while Al and Bob each gain £5,000 worth of road. It is, however, socially inefficient to build the roads, since the gross value of each road is now only £5,000, while the cost is still £6,000. Al and Bob will be using democracy to appropriate resources from Charles while reducing economic efficiency.

This case can be interpreted in a different way. Instead of being the third farmer, Charles might be all of the other voters in the county. Instead of bearing one-third of the costs, Al and Bob might each bear only a small portion of the costs. To the extent that Al and Bob are able to go to the local government and forcefully articulate the benefits that they would derive from the roads, they may be able to use democracy to appropriate resources from taxpayers in general. Much of the concern with the power of 'special interests' stems from the fact that the institutions of representative democracy tend to be responsive to benefits that focus on particular, identifiable, and articu-

late groups. Often the costs are diffused among all taxpayers, who hardly notice them and in any case are rationally ignorant about them.

## The effects of government failure

Suppose that, for any of the reasons discussed above, the government makes a mistake in regulation. Say it mistakenly specifies a method of pollution control that is less effective than the best method. If it insists on the level of control appropriate to the best method, but chooses the poorer method, it can convert a social gain from control into a social loss. This possibility is illustrated in Figure 14.9.

If governments pursue their own objectives such as vote-maximizing, they may sometimes fail to act in the voters' interest by design rather than by mistake. If government economists foresee that a politically popular

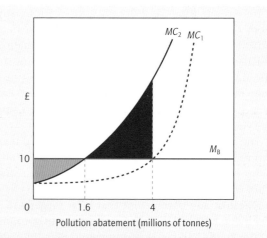

**Figure 14.9 Government failure**

Choice of an unnecessarily costly method of control reduces the optimal amount of abatement. Each tonne of pollution imposes a social cost of £10, so the marginal social benefit of abatement is £10 per tonne as shown by the $M_B$ line. The most efficient method of control has a marginal cost curve of $MC_1$, making it socially optimal to prevent 4 million tonnes of pollution. The government misguidedly chooses an abatement procedure that has a marginal cost curve of $MC_2$. Optimal abatement is now only 1.6 million tonnes. If the government insists on having 4 million tonnes abated, there is a loss of the pink shaded area above marginal benefit curve and below the $MC_2$ curve. That loss may exceed the benefit, which is given by the blue shaded area between the $M_B$ curve and the $MC_2$ curve. If so, the programme causes a net social loss. Having no programme would then be better than having the inefficient one imposed at too high a level of abatement.

policy will increase the degree of market failure in the long term, while seeming beneficial in the short term, the government may adopt the harmful policy, in spite of the unfavourable long-run consequences. The government could plead in such cases that it was only being democratic in following the public will. But if governments were to follow exactly where public opinion leads, they would not require experts who are able to foresee consequences that are not obvious to casual observers who are rationally ignorant about complex issues.

 # CASE STUDIES

## 1. UK government policy goals

In this chapter we have discussed the goals of governments in rather general terms. In this case study we report the goals of the UK Government as set out explicitly in the December 2005 *Pre-Budget Report*. The statement illustrates the complexity of what the Government was trying to achieve. The goals are influential in determining both taxation and spending policies, but there are obvious areas in which seemingly desirable goals can create conflicts. For example, redistributive taxes, which support the goal of fairness, may discourage productivity growth by discouraging enterprise. Similarly, carbon taxes or regulations, which discourage pollution, will raise business costs and hence discourage investment.

*The Pre-Budget Report describes the next steps the Government is taking to enhance its long term goals of:*

- *maintaining macroeconomic stability*, ensuring the fiscal rules are met and inflation remains low;

- *raising the sustainable rate of productivity growth*, through reforms that promote enterprise and competition, enhance flexibility and promote science, innovation and skills;

- *providing employment opportunity for all*, by promoting a flexible labour market which sustains a higher proportion of people in employment than ever before;

- *ensuring fairness*, by providing security for people when they need it, tackling child and pensioner poverty, providing opportunity for all children and young people and delivering security for all in retirement;

- *delivering world-class public services*, with extra investment alongside efficiency, reform and results; and

- *addressing environmental challenges*, such as climate change and the need for energy efficiency in response to rising oil prices. (HM Treasury, Pre-Budget Report, December 2005, page 3)

The first of these goals is covered extensively in the remaining chapters of the book, and we discuss the fiscal rules explicitly on page 437. For the other five goals, we report here some more detail on each of these goals, as set out in the same source.

### Productivity

*The Government's strategy focuses on five key drivers of productivity performance:*

- *improving competition*, which promotes consumer choice and encourages flexible markets and increased business efficiency;

- *promoting enterprise*, including through reducing the regulatory burden on business, to ensure that UK firms are well placed to respond to opportunities in a rapidly changing global market;

- *supporting science and innovation*, which is central to success in the international economy, as global restructuring focuses developed economies towards knowledge-based and high value-added sectors;

- *raising UK skills*, to create a more flexible and productive workforce, and to meet the long-term challenge of rising skill levels in the emerging markets; and

- *encouraging investment* to increase the stock of physical capital supported by stronger, more efficient capital markets. In the global economy, macroeconomic stability is important to attract international capital and investment, alongside a robust and efficient investment environment. (page 5)

### Employment

*The Government's strategy for extending employment opportunities to all builds on the strong performance of the UK labour market over recent years . . . through:*

- *delivering employment opportunity for all*, to provide everyone who is able to work with the support they need to move into work as quickly as possible and extending opportunities to those groups and regions which have faced the greatest barriers to work;

- *enhancing skills and mobility*, to ensure that everyone can fulfil their potential in the labour market and that business has access to the skilled workforce they need to compete in a global economy; and

- *making work pay*, through the National Minimum Wage and tax credits which deliver a system of support that provides greater rewards from work, improving incentives for individuals to participate in the labour market. (page 6)

## Fairness

*The range of reforms the Government has undertaken to achieve its goals in these areas [includes]:*

• **support for families and children**, *to lift children out of poverty and so ensure they have the opportunity to fulfil their potential;*

• **support for pensioners to tackle poverty and ensure security in retirement for all pensioners**, *with extra help for those who need it most and rewards for those who have saved modest amounts;*

• **steps to encourage saving**, *including through the introduction of the Child Trust Fund, Stakeholder pensions and Individual Savings Accounts (ISAs); and*

• **measures to reform and improve the tax system**, *and to ensure that everyone pays their fair share toward extra investment in public services.* (page 7)

## Public services

*The Government has taken steps to deliver lasting improvements in the delivery of public services, including:*

• **a new framework for managing public spending** *that strengthens incentives for departments to plan for the long term;*

• **significant extra resources for public services**, *consistent with the fiscal rules. The 2004 Spending Review set departmental spending plans for the three years to 2007–08, locking in previous increases in investment, while providing for further investment in priority areas of the public services; and*

• **challenging efficiency targets** *for all departments, delivering over £21 billion of efficiency gains a year by 2007–08 to be recycled to front-line public services.* (pages 8–9)

## Environment

*The steps the government has taken to deliver its environmental objectives [include]:*

• **tackling climate change** *and reducing emissions of greenhouse gases in line with domestic as well as international targets—in particular through the climate change levy and reduced VAT rates for energy saving materials;*

• **improving air quality** *to ensure that air pollutants are maintained below levels that could pose a risk to human health—including through support for cleaner fuels and vehicles;*

• **improving waste management**, *so that resources are used more efficiently and waste is re-used or recycled to deliver economic value —for example through increases in the landfill tax; and*

• **protecting the UK's countryside and natural resources** *to ensure that they are sustainable economically, socially and physically—in particular by introducing the aggregates levy.* (page 9)

Whether or not all of these goals will have been achieved fully, their statement illustrates the complexity of the issues that a government must face in practice.

## 2. Kicking up a stink over uncompetitive practices

The following newspaper report outlines a case in which a national competition authority has investigated a case of price fixing and then intervened by fining the companies involved.

**Leading cosmetics companies and distributors adopted heavy-handed tactics to keep prices high**, *reports Adam Sage*

*They are among the most famous names in cosmetics, linked with elegance, refinement and romance, enveloped in the enticing smell of luxury.*

*Yesterday an altogether more unpleasant odour clung to the world's biggest manufacturers of perfume and makeup after a damning report of their commercial practices in France. They were denounced by the French antitrust authorities for colluding in maintaining high prices to the detriment of consumers.*

*At the end of an extensive inquiry, the French Competition Council fined 13 of the leading brands in the global cosmetics industry and 3 of their French distribution chains a total of €46.2 million (£32 million) for price fixing.*

*In its ruling, the council said the manufacturers had adopted heavy-handed methods to force up prices and stamp out discounts for well-known perfumes and make-up.*

*It said that they had resorted to what it described as a 'price police' to control vendors and threaten recalcitrant shop-owners with reprisals. The council said that the brands had denied French shoppers any hope of cheaper products.*

*Among the famous names denounced in the ruling were L'Oreal, which was fined €4.1 million; Chanel, €3 million; Christian Dior, €2.2 million; Yves Saint Laurent, €1.8 million; Guerlain €1.7 million; and Elco, which markets Clinique and Estee Lauder, €1.6 million.*

*Three French distribution chains were also condemned for colluding in the price-fixing arrangements. They were Marionnaud, bought last year by the AS Watson group, which was fined €12.8 million; LVMF's chain, Sephora, fined €9.4 million; and the privately owned retailer Nocibe, fined €6.2 million. LVMH, which also owns four of the perfume brands fined by the council—Christian Dior, Guerlain, Givenchy and Kenzo—said that it would appeal. In a statement, the antitrust authority said: 'Each of these brands agreed with its distributors that each product should be sold in the shops at the same price, effectively eliminating any possibility of competition between sale points. Each agreement was accompanied by the creation of a price police, consisting of controls on the prices practised, pressures and threats of commercial reprisals against distributors who refused to apply the prices imposed on the brands.'*

*The council said that cosmetic manufacturers had argued that they needed to maintain prices to defend their 'image of luxury'. But it continued: 'This absence of competition . . . enabled all of them to increase and then share out the surplus obtained to the detriment of the consumer.'*

*It said that cosmetics manufacturers had sent letters to distributors complaining of 'abnormally low prices' and threatening vendors that refused to increase prices with 'delivery delays' and 'repeated errors'. Other vendors were told that deliveries would be stopped altogether. One shop complained of 'insidious' pressure, with frequent spot checks on prices. A shop in Lyons is quoted as saying of Christian Dior: 'Threats were clear. If we sold for more than 10 per cent under the recommended price, Dior would cut the brand out.'*

*An internal memo at Chanel about a discount sale in Paris said that the company's legal department was furious and advised 'frightening' shop owners. Another internal note at Thierry Mugler perfumes said that the price of a 100 ml bottle had been fixed at Fr590—about £59. 'This price, being unofficial, must never be stated on any document or letter from our company. It must only be communicated orally.' Yves Saint Laurent contacted a perfume distributor to complain about its low prices. 'After a telephone conversation, the customer has agreed to eliminate all discounts', a company memo said. (The Times, 15 March 2006, page 3)*

# Conclusion

Do governments intervene too little, or too much, in response to market failure? This question reflects one aspect of the continuing debate over the role of government in the economy.

Over the last three decades or so, in most of the advanced industrial countries the mix of free-market determination and government ownership and regulation has been shifting towards more market determination. No one believes that government intervention can, or should, be reduced to zero. Do we still have a long way to go in reversing the tide of big intrusive government that flowed through most of the twentieth century? Or have we gone too far and given some things to the market that governments could do better? These will be some of the great social debates of the early decades of the twenty-first century.

# SUMMARY

## Government objectives

- Governments seek to protect life and property, improve economic efficiency, protect individuals from others and (sometimes) from themselves, influence the rate of economic growth, and stabilize the economy against fluctuations in national income and the price level.
- Policies for equity include making the distribution of income and wealth somewhat less unequal.
- Equity, efficiency, and growth often come into conflict. Policies to increase equity may reduce efficiency and/or growth, while policies to increase efficiency or growth may make some situations less equitable.

## Tools and performance

- Governments may seek to achieve their policies using the tools of taxes, spending, rules and regulations, and public ownership.

## The costs of government intervention

- Government activity incurs many types of cost. Internal costs refer to the government's own costs of administering its

policies. Direct external costs refer to the costs imposed on those directly affected by these policies in such terms as extra production costs, costs of compliance, and losses in productivity. Indirect external costs refer to the efficiency losses that spread throughout the whole economy as a result of the alteration in price signals caused by government tax and spending policies.

## Government failure

- As well as showing the potential for benefits to exceed costs in a world where the government functioned perfectly, it is necessary to consider the likely outcome in the imperfect world of reality. Government failure— not achieving some possible gains—can arise because of rigidities causing a lack of adequate response of rules and regulations to changing conditions, poorer foresight on the part of government regulators compared with private participants in the market, and government objectives—such as winning the next election—that conflict with such objectives as improving economic efficiency.

## TOPICS FOR REVIEW

- Goals of government policy
- Measures of inequality at a point in time and over time
- Pre-tax and post-tax distribution of income
- Direct and indirect taxes
- Exhaustive expenditures and transfer payments

- Progressive, regressive, and proportional taxes
- Benefits and costs of government intervention
- Sources of government failure
- Public choice theory
- Rational ignorance

## QUESTIONS

1 What inefficiencies will be caused by (*a*) VAT, (*b*) the personal income tax, (*c*) farm subsidies, (*d*) free health care, (*e*) free elementary school education, (*f*) welfare payments to non-working persons? Explain why such inefficiencies do not provide *sufficient* reasons to end the activity.

2 How many rules, regulations, prohibitions, and other 'command-type' tools of government policy can you think of that could be replaced by market-based incentive schemes?

3 Can you think of government programmes that would have effects on all three goals of *equity*, *efficiency*, and *growth*? Select those programmes that have desirable effects on some and undesirable effects on others of these three goals. (Assume that your equity criterion is to have a less unequal distribution of income.) Discuss the trade-offs involved in these policy conflicts.

4 Discuss the relative efficiency and equity effects of two programmes designed to assist certain needy groups. One programme provides coupons that reduce the purchase price of groceries by 50 per cent. (The shop returns the coupons to the government and gets back the discount that it gave to the coupon-holder.) The other programme gives a money income supplement that has the same value as the food coupons.

5 List some things that *only* governments can do and some things that the government can do better than the private sector. Can you think of anything that the British government did thirty years ago, or that it does now, that the private sector could probably do better? Can you think of anything that the private sector did thirty years ago, or is doing now, that the government could probably do better?

6 Discuss the distinction between the initial incidence of a tax and the ultimate bearer of the tax.

7 Why is a role for government inevitable even in a market economy?

8 What difficulties arise in determining and implementing an optimal government intervention in the economy?

9 What are the arguments for and against government provision of health and education?

10 What government policies might best encourage economic growth?

# MACRO
# ECONOMICS

# PART FIVE

# MACROECONOMICS: ISSUES AND FRAMEWORK

# Chapter 15

# MACROECONOMIC ISSUES AND MEASUREMENT

So far in this book we have analysed individual markets or firms. Now we look at the economy as a whole. Why do some economies grow with sustained increases in their total outputs and living standards while others do not? Why are there cycles in economic activity with jobs being scarce and unemployment high at some times and jobs plentiful and unemployment low at other times? What can governments do to reduce such fluctuations? Why do we have inflations, and what harm do they do? What is the Bank of England trying to achieve when it sets interest rates? These are all issues addressed by macroeconomics and will be covered in the chapters ahead.

Here we start to analyse the economy as a whole and set out some key issues and concepts. In particular, you will learn that:

- Macroeconomics looks at the economy as a whole, dealing with such aggregate phenomena as growth in total output and living standards, commonly called 'economic growth', business cycles, inflation, unemployment, productivity, and the balance of payments.

- The macroeconomics we develop in the next few chapters of this book focuses on the cycle in activity, whereas growth theory (covered in Chapter 26) focuses on determinants of the long-run trend in output.

- The GDP gap is the difference between actual real GDP and its potential or trend value.

- The total output of the economy as a whole is the sum of the value added by each firm or enterprise.

- GDP can be measured as the sum of value added by all producers, as the sum of income claims generated in producing goods and services, or as the spending on all final goods and services produced.

- GDP measures the value of what is produced in this country, while GNI (or GNP) measures the income accruing to UK residents, including net income from overseas.

- GDP is a specific measure of output in the market economy, and is not a measure of welfare or happiness.

In this chapter we explain how macroeconomics differs in approach from the microeconomics of the first half of this book and outline the main issues addressed. We then look in detail at how the activity of the economy as a whole is measured before discussing the interpretation of these measures. In subsequent chapters we are concerned with explaining how the national product or national income is determined, and what government policy can do to influence it. Growth theory, which we discuss in Chapter 26, is about what determines the long-term trend in national output. The traditional focus of macroeconomic analysis, which we explain in subsequent chapters, is mainly on the short run and the issue of what explains deviations of output from its long-run trend level.

# What is macroeconomics?

**Macroeconomics** is the study of how the economy behaves in broad outline without dwelling on much of its interesting, but sometimes confusing, detail. Macroeconomics is concerned largely with the behaviour of economic *aggregates*, such as total national product, total investment, and exports for the entire economy. It is also concerned with the average price of all goods and services, rather than the prices of specific products. These aggregates result from activities in many different markets and from the behaviour of different decision-makers such as consumers, governments, and firms. In contrast, **microeconomics** (as outlined in Chapters 3–14) deals with the behaviour of individual markets, such as those for wheat, computer chips, or strawberries, and with the detailed behaviour of individual agents, e.g. firms and consumers.

In macroeconomics we add together the value of cornflakes, beer, cars, strawberries, haircuts, and restaurant meals along with the value of all other goods and services produced, and we study the aggregate *national product*. We also average the prices of all goods and services consumed and discuss the *general price level* for the entire economy—usually just called the price level. In practice, the averages of several different sets of prices are used. For example, one important index measures the average price of the goods and services bought by the typical consumer. In Britain it is known as the **retail price index** (RPI), while the equivalent in some other countries (and the measure used for the official inflation target in the UK) is called the *consumer price index* (CPI).

We know full well that an economy that produces much wheat and few cars differs from one that produces many cars but little wheat. We also know that an economy with cheap wheat and expensive cars differs from one with cheap cars and expensive wheat. Studying aggregates and averages often means missing such important differences, but in return for losing valuable detail we are able to view the big picture.

In macroeconomics we look at the broad range of opportunities and difficulties facing the economy as a whole. When national product rises, the output of most firms, and the incomes of most people, usually rise with it. When interest rates rise, most borrowers, including firms and homeowners, have to make bigger payments on their debts, though many savers will get a higher return on their savings. When the price level rises, virtually everyone in the economy is forced to make adjustments, because of the lower value of money. When the unemployment rate rises, workers are put at an increased risk of losing their jobs and suffering losses in their incomes. These movements in economic aggregates are strongly associated with the economic well-being of most individuals: the health of the sectors in which they work and the prices of the goods that they purchase. These associations between the health of the macroeconomy and the economic fortunes of many people are why macroeconomic aggregates (particularly inflation, unemployment, productivity, interest rates, and the balance of payments) are often in the news.

We also study how governments can use monetary and fiscal policy to stimulate economic activity when they are worried about recessions, and to dampen it down when they are worried about inflationary pressures caused by booms.

# Why do we need macroeconomics?

We need a separate subject called macroeconomics because there are forces affecting the economy as a whole that cannot be fully or simply understood by analysing individual markets and individual products. A problem that is affecting all firms, or many workers, in different industries may need to be tackled at the level of the whole economy. Certainly, if circumstances are common across many sectors of the economy, then analysis at the level of the whole economy may help us to understand what is happening. Let us look at some of the issues that are best thought about in a macroeconomic context.

## Major macroeconomic issues

### Economic growth

Both total and per capita output have risen for many decades in most industrial countries. These long-term trends have produced rising average living standards. In the United Kingdom the real value of the average wage doubled in the twenty years between 1953 and 1973. It stagnated for a while in the 1970s but then grew steadily again in the 1980s, 1990s, and into the early years of the twenty-first century.

Long-term growth is the predominant determinant of living standards and the material constraints facing a society from decade to decade and generation to generation. We discuss some of the influences on long-term growth in Chapter 26. Macroeconomics has traditionally taken the trend in output as given and looked at how to minimize deviations from that trend. However, in recent years there has been discussion of whether the policies used to stabilize activity may also influence the long-term trend. An important objective in macroeconomics is to ensure that world-wide growth will continue without the type of slowdown that happened in the 1970s or the serious recessions of the early 1980s and early 1990s. Growth is therefore a clear objective of macroeconomic policy.

## Business cycles

The economy tends to move in a series of ups and downs, called business cycles, rather than in a steady pattern. The 1930s saw the greatest world-wide economic depression in the twentieth century, with nearly one-fifth of the UK labour force unemployed for an extended period. In contrast, the twenty-five years following the Second World War were a period of sustained economic growth, with only minor interruptions caused by modest recessions. Then the business cycle returned in more serious form. There have been three major recessions in the United Kingdom during the past four decades (1973–5, 1979–81, and 1990–2), and most other major countries have experienced a similar pattern. From 1992 to 2006 there was no recession in the UK, but there were still cycles in the rate of growth of national income.

During recessions many businesses go bust, while profits fall for the survivors. In contrast, during a boom demand for most products rise, profits rise, and most businesses find it easy to expand. Understanding the business cycle is therefore important for successful businesses. Expanding capacity during the onset of a recession could be a recipe for disaster, while having too little capacity during a boom may result in a lost opportunity. Most importantly, although business cycles are beyond the control of individual firms, firms do need to understand that the economy moves in cycles. Governments sometimes claim that their policies will bring stable growth and the end to cycles, but business cycles have been around for a long time, and they are likely to be with us for much longer yet.

Macroeconomics as a subject was invented to help produce policies that could ameliorate economic fluctuations. Much of what follows is devoted to explanations of why the economy goes through these ups and downs, and what, if anything, the government can do about them.

## Productivity

Economic growth can be achieved either by using more inputs, such as increased capital or numbers of workers, or by getting more output for any given amount of inputs. The latter is known as productivity growth. Increasing productivity is a central target of most governments, as this is the most obvious way to make real incomes grow. Labour productivity (calculated as either output per worker or output per hour worked) is especially important in this regard, as growth in this is a necessary condition for sustained growth of real wages. Those who do not work do not produce, so the real living standards of the entire population are ultimately determined by the output per head of each of those who are in work. Labour productivity can increase if workers have more capital to work with, but over the long term what matters is technical progress.

We reported in the previous chapter (see page 323) that one of the central goals of the UK government is 'raising the sustainable rate of productivity growth, through reforms that promote enterprise and competition, enhance flexibility, and promote science, innovation, and skills'. None of the policies listed in this quotation would traditionally have been considered part of the macro policy tool box, which focuses on using monetary and fiscal policy to affect aggregate demand: rather, these would be considered supply-side policies. But a key point to note is that modern governments do put much greater emphasis than they used to on supply-side policies to foster economic growth and living standards.

## Inflation

In 1975 the annual UK inflation rate was over 25 per cent. Inflation at that rate means that retired people living on an income fixed in money terms, or savers who have made savings deposits fixed in money value, have their living standards, or their wealth, halved every three years! The government of Margaret Thatcher was elected in 1979 on the promise of eliminating inflation from the British economy. Inflation did fall below 5 per cent by 1984, but it rose again to around 10 per cent before the end of the decade. By the late 1990s the annual rate of inflation had fallen to around 2–3 per cent, which was the lowest level since the early 1960s. In May 1997 the incoming Labour government set a target level of inflation of 2.5 per cent and gave the Bank of England the power to set interest rates in order to achieve this target. From 1997 to 2002 inflation stayed within 1 percentage point of the target as intended. From 2003 onwards the inflation target was set at 2 per cent, using a slightly different measure of inflation. (We discuss the details in Chapter 20 below.) At least up to 2006, inflation remained within 1 percentage point of the official target.

Swings in economic activity have usually accompanied swings in inflation. Generally, attempts by governments to control high inflation have tended to bring about recessions. However, the relationship between inflation and recession has changed over time. The 1979–81 UK recession was accompanied by inflation of around 15 per cent, while the 1990–2 recession was accompanied by only single-figure inflation. The slowdown in major economies in 2000–2 was accompanied by very low levels of inflation, so was not explained by anti-inflation policies. Most major economies exhibited a pick-up in growth, but by 2006 there were few if any signs of inflation returning.

An important policy problem for governments in the past has been to stimulate economic activity without causing inflation. The rise in inflation during boom times has often led policy-makers to raise interest rates or taxes in order to bring inflation under control. When inflation falls after a recession, policy-makers have often felt that they have the leeway to stimulate the economy again. But they have to tread carefully to achieve a suitable balance between stimulus and contraction, and we will learn below that timing policy interventions in order to achieve a desired outcome is not a simple matter. More recently policy-makers have become much more cautious in their attempts to influence the cycle in the economy. In the UK at least, government taxation and spending policies have become focused on long-run stability, and interest rate policy on keeping inflation as close as possible to target.

### Unemployment

A recession in economic activity causes an increase in unemployment. Indeed, it was the high unemployment of the 1930s that led to the establishment of the subject now known as macroeconomics, and unemployment is still a central concern of economics. During the Great Depression of the 1930s UK unemployment rose to nearly 20 per cent of the labour force, and even higher levels were reached in some other countries. Although in the 1950s and 1960s unemployment was consistently very low in most industrial countries, higher unemployment returned in the 1980s and 1990s. UK unemployment[1] reached peaks of 12.2 per cent in 1986 and 10.8 per cent in 1993, while unemployment in France and Germany reached postwar highs of 12.5 and 11.7 per cent, respectively, in 1997. Japanese unemployment in June 2002 reached a level of 5.4 per cent not seen there since the Second World War. By 2006 unemployment had fallen to a thirty-year low in Britain, but it was still relatively high in several European countries, including Spain, Germany,

and France. Accordingly, analysis of the causes of, and potential cures for, unemployment is still very high on the agenda of macroeconomics today, especially in the EU and Japan. A new bout of high unemployment can never be ruled out, even for those countries where it has been low for some time; and even in countries where aggregate unemployment is not a major problem there are still big problems of youth unemployment or unemployment among certain ethnic groups, which are of great social and political concern.

The main method of reducing aggregate unemployment that economists developed early in the twentieth century was for governments to increase their spending and reduce taxes. Such deliberate use of government spending and taxes to influence the economy is known as **fiscal policy**. In Chapter 19 we will discuss why this long accepted policy no longer seems as promising as it once seemed.

### Government budget deficits

With the exception of two brief periods (1970 and 1988–9) the UK government has had a *budget deficit* since the Second World War—spending more than it was raising in taxation. In the mid-1970s the budget deficit rose to around 8 per cent of the value of the nation's total annual output (GDP). There was a deficit of about 3 per cent of GDP in 2005/6, although the government projected a return to surplus by 2008/9.[2] Deficits have to be financed by government borrowing. If this is from the public it raises the national debt; if it is from the Central Bank it increases the money supply and is inflationary.

At one time it was thought that budget deficits might be good for the economy because government spending created jobs. Nowadays there is more concern about the potential burden of the debt, in the form of interest, which has to be paid by taxpayers and which, therefore, keeps taxes high. In later chapters we will discuss how the budget deficit affects the economy and the conflict over the role of the government budget, which is central to macroeconomics. We will also discuss the implications of the limitations on budget deficits imposed on EU member states by the Maastricht Treaty and by the Stability and Growth Pact.

---

[1] There are two main measures of unemployment. The claimant count measures those registered for unemployment benefits, while the Labour Force Survey (LFS) asks a sample of people if they are actively seeking employment. The LFS number is usually higher than the claimant count. Numbers in the text refer to the LFS measure but charts of UK unemployment usually use the claimant count, as this measure has been available for longer.

[2] See: *Pre-Budget Report*, HM Treasury, December 2005.

## Interest rates

In addition to fiscal policy, government (or the monetary authority where this is independent of government) has available the tools of monetary policy. **Monetary policy** involves changing interest rates in order to influence the economy. High interest rates are a symptom of a tight monetary policy. When interest rates are high, firms find it more costly to borrow, and this makes them more reluctant to invest. Individuals with mortgages or bank loans are also hit by high interest rates, since it costs them more to make their loan repayments. Hence high interest rates tend to reduce demand in the economy—firms invest less, and those with mortgages have less to spend. Low interest rates tend to stimulate demand.

Another important channel of monetary policy is via the exchange rate, at least for countries whose exchange rates are flexible. Exchange rate changes can affect the relative prices, and thereby the competitiveness, of domestic and foreign producers. A significant rise in the cost of buying domestic currency on the foreign exchange market makes domestic goods expensive relative to foreign goods. This may lead to a shift of demand away from domestic goods towards foreign goods. Such shifts have an important influence on domestic economic activity.

## Targets and instruments

The issues that we have just discussed are of two types. First, there are issues that really matter for their own sake, things that affect living conditions and the state of the economic environment. Living standards, unemployment, business cycles, and inflation are outcomes that matter. Almost everyone wants growing living standards, high employment, and low unemployment, as well as an avoidance of recessions and inflation. These are known as the **targets** of policy. 'Good' values of these variables are what governments would like to achieve.

Fiscal and monetary policies (government spending, taxes, interest rates, and the money supply) are not valued so much for their own sake: rather, they are the **instruments** of policy and are valued for the effect they have on the targets. *Instruments* are the variables that the government can change directly in order to change the *targets*, which are the things that it would like to change.

The macroeconomic policy problem is to choose appropriate values of the policy instruments in order to achieve the best possible combination of the outcomes of the targets. This is a continually changing problem, because the targets are perpetually being affected by shocks from various parts of the world economy.

# The GDP gap

National output and national income are central topics in macroeconomics. For the most part we measure both of these by **gross domestic product**, which is usually shortened to GDP. We now introduce concepts known as *potential GDP* and the *GDP gap*, which are helpful in separating trends from cycles and will be important in the analysis of subsequent chapters. After this we go on to discuss how we measure GDP and other national income and output concepts.

## Potential GDP and the GDP gap

Economic growth is about the long-term trend in GDP, and we return to a study of this in Chapter 26. The cycle about this long-term trend is the topic on which much of the rest of macroeconomics focuses, and we study this from the next chapter onwards. In order to facilitate this separation, we use the concepts *actual* and *potential* GDP, and we refer to the difference between them as the *GDP gap*.

**Actual GDP** represents what the economy actually produces. An important related concept is **potential GDP**, which measures what the economy would produce if all resources—land, labour, and productive capacity—were fully employed at their normal levels of utilization. This concept is also referred to as *potential income* and is sometimes called *full-employment income* (or *high-employment income*).[3] We give it the symbol $Y^*$ to distinguish it from actual GDP (or national income), which is indicated by just $Y$.

What is variously called the **output gap** or the **GDP gap** measures the difference between what would have been produced if potential, or full-employment, GDP had been

---

[3] In everyday usage the words *real* and *actual* have similar meanings. In the National Accounts, however, their meanings are distinct. *Real* GDP is distinguished from *nominal* GDP, the latter being measured in current prices and the former in constant prices. *Actual* GDP—what is produced—is distinguished from *potential* GDP—which could have been produced. The latter two refer to real measures, so that the full descriptions are actual real GDP and potential real GDP.

produced and what is actually produced, as measured by the current GDP. The gap is calculated by subtracting potential GDP from actual GDP ($Y - Y^*$).

When potential GDP exceeds actual GDP, the gap measures the market value of goods and services that *could have been produced* if the economy's resources had been

fully employed but that actually went unproduced. The goods and services that are not produced when the economy is operating below $Y^*$ are permanently lost to the economy. Because these losses occur when employable resources are unused, they are often called the *deadweight loss* of unemployment. When the economy is

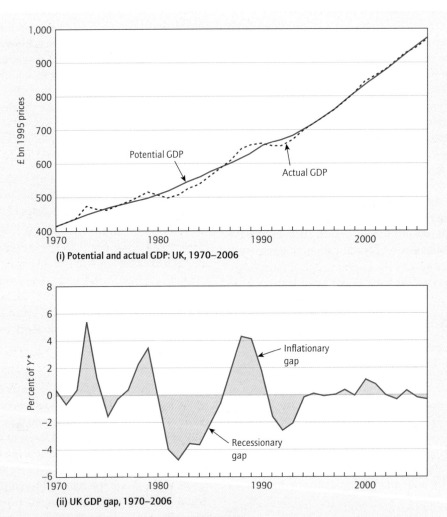

(i) Potential and actual GDP: UK, 1970–2006

(ii) UK GDP gap, 1970–2006

**Figure 15.1** UK potential GDP and the output gap, 1970–2006

**Potential and actual GDP have both displayed an upward trend in recent years, but actual GDP fluctuates around its potential level.**

(i)  Growth in the economy has been such that both potential and actual GDP have doubled since 1970. Both series are in real terms and are measured in 1995 pounds sterling. Measurement of potential GDP is controversial and there is no official UK series at present. These figures were calculated by the IMF. The data from 1970 to 1990 are from the *World Economic Outlook* (*WEO*), 2002, while the data for 1990 to 2005 are from the September 2005 *WEO*. The 2005 and 2006 figures are IMF projections.

(ii)  The cycles in the economy are apparent from the behaviour of the output gap. Slumps in economic activity produce large recessionary gaps, and booms produce inflationary gaps. The zero line indicates where actual and potential GDP are the same. The shaded areas below the zero line indicate the deadweight loss that arises from unemployment during periods when there is a recessionary output gap. Notice the large recessionary gaps in the early 1980s and the early 1990s.

*Source*: International Monetary Fund, *World Economic Outlook*, various issues.

operating below its potential level of output—that is, when $Y$ is less than $Y^*$—the negative output gap is called a **recessionary gap**.[4]

In booms actual GDP may *exceed* potential GDP, causing the output gap to become positive. Actual output can exceed potential output because potential GDP is defined for a *normal rate of utilization* of inputs, and these normal rates can be exceeded temporarily. Labour may work longer hours than normal; factories may operate an extra shift or not close for routine repairs and maintenance. Although many of these expedients are only temporary, they are effective in the short term. When actual GDP exceeds potential GDP, there is generally upward pressure on prices. For this reason, when $Y$ exceeds $Y^*$, the positive output gap is often called an **inflationary gap**.

Figure 15.1(i) shows one estimate of UK potential GDP for the years 1970–2006.[5] The rising trend reflects the growth in productive capacity of the UK economy over this period. The figure also shows actual real GDP, which has kept approximately in step with potential GDP. The distance between the two, which is the GDP gap, is plotted in part (ii) of the figure. Fluctuations in economic activity are apparent from fluctuations in the size of the gap.

Growth theory aims to explain the long-term trend in potential GDP, while the short-run macroeconomic model usually focuses on explaining the GDP gap.

## Measurement of national output

Macroeconomics has as its central goal the explanation of the determinants of national income and output. In the next chapter we start to build an analytical framework that helps us to understand the forces that influence these variables in the short term. In Chapter 26 we discuss the determinants of growth of national output in the longer term. First, however, we have to understand what it is we are talking about. What exactly do we mean by national income and the national output? What do we mean when we refer to GDP, and how does it differ from other related concepts such as GNI and GNP?

We start by discussing the measurement of national output, and find that, by summing the *value added* for each industry or sector, we arrive at a standard measure of national product. We then consider how it is that we can arrive at the same measure of national product both from the spending side of the economy and from adding up factor incomes. This discussion will demonstrate the equivalence of the concepts of national income and national product.

The national output or the national product is related to the sum of all the outputs produced in the economy by individuals, firms, and governmental organizations. To obtain it, however, we cannot just add up all of the outputs of individual production units.

### Value added as output

The reason that getting a total for the nation's output is not quite as straightforward as it may seem at first sight is that one firm's output is often another firm's input. A maker of clothing buys cloth from a textile manufacturer and buttons, zips, thread, pins, hangers, etc., from a range of other producers. Most modern manufactured products have many ready-made inputs. A car or aircraft manufacturer, for example, has hundreds of component suppliers.

Production occurs in stages: some firms produce outputs that are used as inputs by other firms, and these other firms in turn produce outputs that are used as inputs by yet other firms.

If we merely added up the market values of all outputs of all firms, we would obtain a total that was greatly in excess of the value of the economy's actual output. The error that would arise in estimating the nation's output by adding all sales of all firms is called **double counting**. 'Multiple counting' would be a better term, since, if we added up the values of all sales, the same output would be counted every time that it was sold from one firm to another.

The problem of double counting is resolved by distinguishing between two types of output. **Intermediate**

---

[4] Note that this is not the way the US President's Council of Economic Advisors defined it when they invented the concept in the early 1960s. For them, a positive GDP gap measured the economic waste of unemployment.

[5] Note that in both parts of Figure 15.1 the data for 2005 and 2006 are IMF projections as of mid-2005 rather than actual outturns. The estimates of UK potential GDP for 1970–90 are from the IMF *World Economic Outlook* (*WEO*), September 2002, and the estimates from 1990 onwards are from the September 2005 *WEO*.

goods and services are the outputs of some firms that are in turn used as inputs for other firms. **Final goods and services** are goods that are not used as inputs by other firms in the period of time under consideration. The term **final demand** refers to the purchase of final goods and services for consumption, for investment (including inventory accumulation), for use by governments, and for export. It does not include goods and services that are purchased by firms and used as inputs for producing other goods and services.

If the sales of firms could be readily separated into sales for final use and sales for further processing by other firms, measuring total output would still be straightforward. Total output would equal the value of all *final goods and services* produced by firms, excluding all intermediate goods and services. However, when a textile manufacturer sells a piece of cloth, it does not necessarily know whether it is being purchased by a fashion house, which will sell it on in the form of a dress, or is being purchased by a consumer for use as, say, a sofa cover. Thus, at the point of sale it is not always obvious if this is a final or intermediate sale. The problem of double counting must therefore be resolved in some other manner.

To avoid double counting, statisticians use the important concept of **value added**. Each firm's value added is the value of its output minus the value of the inputs that it purchases from other firms (which were in turn the

outputs of those other firms). Thus, a steel mill's value added is the value of its output minus the value of the ore that it buys from the mining company, the value of the electricity and other fuel that it uses, and the values of all other inputs that it buys from other firms. A bakery's value added is the value of the bread and cakes it produces minus the value of the flour and other inputs that it buys from other firms.

The total value of a firm's output is the *gross* value of its output. The firm's value added is the *net* value of its output. It is this latter figure that is the firm's contribution to the nation's total output. It is what its own efforts add to the value of what it takes in as inputs.

Value added measures each firm's own contribution to total output, the amount of market value that is produced by that firm. Its use avoids the statistical problem of double counting.

The concept of value added is further illustrated in Box 15.1. In this simple example, as in all more complex cases, the value of total output of final goods is obtained by summing all the individual values added.

The sum of all values added in an economy is a measure of the economy's total output. This measure of total output is called gross value added. It is a measure of all final output that is produced by all productive activity in the economy.

---

 **Box 15.1** **Value added through stages of production**

Because the output of one firm often becomes the input of other firms, the total value of goods sold by all firms greatly exceeds the value of the output of final goods. This general principle is illustrated by a simple example in which firm R starts from scratch and produces goods (raw materials) valued at £100; the firm's value added is £100. Firm I purchases these raw materials valued at £100 and produces semi-manufactured goods which it sells for £130. Its value added is £30 because the value of the goods

is increased by £30 as a result of the firm's activities. Firm F purchases the semi-manufactured goods for £130 and works them into a finished state, selling them for £180. Firm F's value added is £50. The value of final goods, £180, is found either by counting the sales of firm F or by taking the sum of the values added by each firm. This value is less than the £410 that we obtain by adding up the market value of the commodities sold by each firm. The table summarizes the example.

Transactions between firms at three different stages of production

| | Firm R | Firm I | Firm F | All firms |
|---|---|---|---|---|
| A: Purchases from other firms | £0 | £100 | £130 | £230 = Total interfirm sales |
| B: Purchase of factors of production (wages, rent, interest, profits) | 100 | 30 | 50 | 180 = Value added |
| Total A + B = value of product | 100 | 130 | 180 = Value of final goods and services | 410 = Total value of all sales |

**Table 15.1** Gross value added at current basic prices, by sector, UK, 2005

| Sector | £ million | % of GDP |
|---|---|---|
| Agriculture, hunting, forestry, and fisheries | 10,241 | 0.8 |
| Mining and quarrying | 25,458 | 2.1 |
| Manufacturing | 148,097 | 12.2 |
| Electricity, gas, and water supply | 24,953 | 2.0 |
| Construction | 65,923 | 5.4 |
| Wholesale and retail trade | 132,113 | 10.8 |
| Hotels and restaurants | 33,730 | 2.8 |
| Transport and communications | 81,059 | 6.6 |
| Financial intermediation and real estate | 266,485 | 21.8 |
| Public administration and defence | 54,935 | 4.5 |
| Education | 62,316 | 5.1 |
| Health and social work | 81,518 | 6.7 |
| Other services | 58,807 | 4.8 |
| **Gross value added at current basic prices** | **1,086,859** | |
| *plus* Adjustment to current basic prices (taxes minus subsidies on products) | 137,856 | 11.3 |
| **= GDP at market prices** | **1,224,715** | |

The table shows gross value added by industrial sector in the United Kingdom for 2005 at current basic prices. The sector values added combine to make gross value added. Gross value added is equal to the total output of goods and services minus the purchase of intermediate goods. It is also the sum of the factor rewards attributable to each sector. Percentages do not add up to 100 owing to rounding.

*Source*: ONS, *UK National Accounts* (the Blue Book), 2006.

Table 15.1 gives the gross value added by major industrial sectors for the UK economy in 2005. You will see from this table that gross value added becomes GDP by the addition of a further term (taxes on products minus subsidies). We will explain this step in moving from value added to GDP below.[6]

Notice that we have used 'gross' in two different senses: first in comparing the gross and net values of a firm's output, and then in the term 'gross value added'. The first usage relies on the common meanings of 'gross' and 'net'. The gross value of the firm's output is the total output before making any deductions, while the net value deducts inputs made by other firms. In 'gross value added' the usage is different. Value added is already defined as firms' net output; the word 'gross' is added because of its specific meaning in National Accounts statistics. 'Gross' in National Accounts aggregates refers to the fact that we are measuring currently produced outputs or incomes without taking into account the wearing out, or *depreciation*, of capital goods during their production. Thus, gross value added is the value added of the economy as a whole *before* any allowance for depreciation, and gross domestic product is the nation's output before allowing for depreciation. This latter meaning will be used in many measures considered below such as *gross* domestic product and *gross* national income.

# The circular flow of income, output, and spending

Figure 15.2 gives a stylized version of how income and expenditure interact with each other in what is called a circular flow diagram. To begin with, consider an economy that is made up solely of domestic individuals and domestic firms. For a moment we assume that the economy has no imports or exports and no government. The individuals provide labour for the firms and they buy the firms' output. The income that flows to individuals is represented by the black line in the figure running up

the left-hand side of the diagram, and their spending on the final output of firms is represented by the black line running down the right-hand side. National output (or national income) can be measured either from the

---

[6] Gross value added at basic prices is similar to what used to be called GDP at factor cost, but the latter term fell out of the National Accounts in 1998.

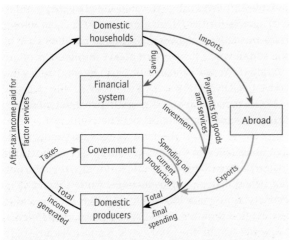

**Figure 15.2** An economy is made up of income and spending flows between firms and households.

In practice, final spending is not made up simply of individuals' consumption spending, so when we approach the explanation of GDP from the spending side we need to add in investment spending, government consumption, and exports (the green lines).

We will refer back to this diagram several times in future chapters. When we do so we will point out that, for the level of income and output to be constant (rather than rising or falling), the injections of spending from outside the circular flow must just equal the withdrawals (or leakages) from the circular flow. In the model to be developed in subsequent chapters, we call the injections *exogenous* or *autonomous* spending. These are investment, government consumption, and exports, and are shown in the diagram in green. The leakages or withdrawals are taxes, saving, and imports, shown in blue.

The circular flow diagram shows how incomes give rise to spending which gives rise to output which gives rise to incomes.

Withdrawals, or leakages, arise from income that is not passed on in the circular flow through spending; while injections are spending that does not arise out of incomes but is exogenous.

spending side in terms of spending on final goods produced, or on the income side. These incomes of resource owners can be measured either as the sum of values added in the economy or as the sum of individual incomes.

# GDP, GNI, and GNP

The measures of national income and national product that are used in Britain derive from an accounting system that has recently been standardized by international agreement and is thus common to most major countries. It is known as the System of National Accounts. A more detailed specification of this accounting system applies to all EU member states under the European System of Accounts 1995 (which was applied in all EU countries by April 1999 and was introduced into UK accounts in 1998). These accounts have a logical structure, based on the simple yet important idea that all output must be owned by someone. So whenever national output is produced, it must generate an equivalent amount of claims to that output in the form of national income.

Corresponding to the two sides of the circular flow in Figure 15.2 are two ways of measuring national income: by determining the value of what is produced and the value of the income claims generated by production. Both measures yield the same total, which is called gross domestic product (GDP). When it is calculated by adding up the total spending for each of the main components of final output, the result is called *GDP spending-based*. When

it is calculated by adding up all the incomes generated by the act of production, it is called *GDP income-based*.

All value produced in the form of output must also generate a claim to the income generated in the process of creating that value. For example, any spending you make when you buy a TV set must also be received by the supplier of that set. The value of what you spend is the spending; the value of the product sold to you is the output. Thus, the two values calculated on income and spending bases are identical conceptually, and they differ in practice only because of errors of measurement. Any discrepancy arising from such errors is then reconciled so that one common total is given as *the* measure of GDP. Both calculations are of interest, however, because each gives a different and useful breakdown. Also, having two independent ways of measuring the same quantity provides a useful check on statistical procedures and on unavoidable errors in measurement.

## GDP spending-based

GDP spending-based for a given year is calculated by adding up the spending going to purchase the final output produced in that year. Total spending on final output is expressed in the National Accounts as the sum of three broad categories of spending: consumption, investment, and net exports. Consumption is further divided into the consumption spending of government and that of private individuals (and non-profit organizations serving households). So there are four important categories of spending that we will discuss: private consumption, government consumption, investment, and net exports. In Chapter 16 we explain why these particular categories have received more attention in macroeconomics than have the net sector outputs listed in Table 15.1 and the income categories discussed below (Table 15.3). Here we define what these spending categories are and how they are measured. Remember that they are exhaustive: they are defined in such a way that *all* spending on final output falls into one of the four categories.

### Private consumption spending

Private consumption spending includes spending by individuals on goods and services produced and sold to their final users during the year—services such as haircuts, medical care, and legal advice; nondurable goods such as fresh meat, clothing, cut flowers, and fresh vegetables; and durable goods such as cars, television sets, and microwave ovens. However, it excludes purchases of newly built houses as these are counted as investment.[7] Also measured in the National Accounts as part of private consumption is the final consumption spending of non-profit-making institutions serving households (NPISH). These are institutions, such as charities, that are neither firms nor governmental organizations but nevertheless contribute some spending and so have to be included somewhere in the National Accounts. We denote actual, measured, private consumption spending by the symbol $C^a$.

### Government consumption spending

When governments provide goods and services that their citizens want, such as health care and street lighting, it is obvious that they are adding to the sum total of valuable output in the same way as do private firms that produce cars and CDs. With other government activities the case may not seem so clear. Should spending by the UK government to negotiate over the political situation in some foreign country, or to pay a civil servant to help draft legislation, be regarded as contributions to the national product? Some people believe that many (or even most)

activities in Whitehall and in town halls are wasteful, if not downright harmful. Others believe that governments produce many of the important things of life, such as education, law and order, and pollution control.

National Accounts statisticians do not speculate about which government spending is worthwhile. Instead, they include all government purchases of goods and services as part of national output. (Government spending on investment goods appears as public sector capital formation, which is a part of total investment spending.) Just as the national product includes, without distinction, the outputs of both gin and bibles, it also includes refuse collection and the upkeep of parks, along with the services of judges, members of Parliament, and even Inland Revenue inspectors.

The UK National Accounts distinguish two different categories of government consumption. When government pays for the goods and services that are consumed by private individuals, it is referred to as *individual government final consumption*. This applies among other things to health spending and education. If, for example, National Health Service doctors perform an operation, it is paid for by the government but the service is received by an identifiable individual. In contrast, the government also pays for street lighting, national defence, and law and order, but here the benefit is consumed by the population at large rather than some specific individual. This is spending on *public goods*, which we discussed in Chapter 14. Spending by the government where the consumption cannot be assigned to specific individuals is called in the National Accounts *collective government final consumption*. As a simplification (which we explain further in Chapter 16), in macroeconomics we lump together individual government final consumption and collective government final consumption into one term: *government consumption*, sometimes just called government spending. Actual government consumption spending is denoted by the symbol $G^a$.

Government output is typically valued at cost rather than at the market value. In most cases there is really no choice. The output of public services is not (generally) sold in the marketplace, so government output is not observed independently of the spending that produces it. What, for example, is the market value of the services of a court of law? No one knows. We do know, however, what it costs the government to provide these services, so we value them at their cost of production.

Although valuing at cost is the easiest way to measure many government activities, it does have one curious consequence. If, owing to an increase in productivity, one civil servant now does what two used to do, and the

---

[7] Private consumption does not include purchases of existing houses, as these are not part of current production. Instead, this involves a transfer of an existing asset.

displaced worker shifts to the private sector, the government's measured contribution to the national product will register a decline. On the other hand, if two workers now do what one worker used to do, the government's measured contribution will rise. Both changes could occur even though the services the government actually provides have not changed. This is an inevitable consequence of measuring the value of the government's output by the cost of the inputs, mainly labour, that are used to produce it, rather than by the value of outputs.[8]

It is important to recognize that only government spending on *currently produced goods and services* is included as part of GDP. A great deal of government spending is not a part of GDP. For example, when the Department of Health and Social Security (DHSS) makes a payment to an old-age pensioner, the government is not purchasing any currently produced goods or services from the retired. The payment itself adds neither to employment nor to total output. The same is true of payments on account of unemployment benefit, income support, student grants, and interest on the National Debt (which transfers income from taxpayers to holders of government bonds). All such payments are examples of **transfer payments**, which is government spending not made in return for currently produced goods and services. As it is not a part of spending on the nation's total output, it is not included in GDP.[9]

Thus, when we refer to government spending as part of GDP or use the symbol $G^a$, we include all government spending on currently produced goods and services, and we *exclude* all government transfer payments. (The term *total government spending* is often used to describe all government spending, including transfer payments.)

### Investment spending

Investment spending is defined as spending on the production of goods not for present consumption, but rather for future use. The goods that are created by this spending are called **investment (or capital) goods**. Investment spending can be divided into three categories: changes in inventories, fixed capital formation, and the net acquisition of valuables.

### Changes in inventories

Almost all firms hold stocks of their inputs and their own outputs. These stocks are known as inventories. Inventories of inputs and unfinished materials allow firms to maintain a steady stream of production in spite of short-term fluctuations in the deliveries of inputs bought from other firms. Inventories of outputs allow firms to meet orders in spite of temporary fluctuations in the rate of output or sales. Modern 'just-in-time' methods of production pioneered by the Japanese aim to reduce inventories held by manufacturing plants to nearly zero by delivering inputs just as they are needed. Most of the economy, however, does not achieve this level of efficiency and never will. Retailing, for example, would certainly not be improved if shops held no stocks.

An accumulation of stocks and unfinished goods in the production process counts as current investment because it represents goods produced (even if only half-finished) but not used for current consumption. A drawing down of inventories, also called *de-stocking*, counts as negative investment because it represents a reduction in the stocks of finished goods (produced in the current period) that are available for future use. Inventories are valued at what they will be worth on the market, rather than at what they have cost the firm so far. This is because the spending-based measure of GDP includes the value of what final spending on these goods would be if they were sold, even though they have not yet been sold.

### Fixed capital formation

All production uses capital goods. These are manufactured aids to production, such as machines, computers, and factory buildings. Creating new capital goods is an act of investment and is called *fixed investment* or **fixed capital formation**. The economy's total quantity of capital goods is called the **capital stock**. Much of the capital stock is in the form of equipment or buildings used by firms or government agencies in the production of goods and services. This includes not just factories and machines, but also hospitals, schools, and offices. A house or a flat is also a durable asset that yields its utility (housing services) over a long period of time. This meets the definition of fixed capital formation, so (as we pointed out above) housing *construction* is counted as investment spending rather than consumption spending. When a family purchases a house from a builder or another owner, the ownership of an already produced asset is transferred, and that transaction is not a part of current GDP.

### Net acquisition of valuables

Some productive activity creates goods that are neither consumed nor used in the production process. Rather,

---

[8] UK national income statisticians are developing some new measures of the output of government that will help improve measurement of productivity, but this exercise is in its infancy.

[9] When the recipients of transfer payments spend these on buying goods and services, their spending is measured as consumption spending, and thus as part of GDP, in the same way as any other consumption spending. We do not want to measure it twice, which we would be doing if we included in GDP both the government transfer and the spending by the recipient.

they are held for their intrinsic beauty or for their expected appreciation in value. Examples are jewellery and works of art. Such works are known as *valuables*. Acquisitions less disposals of valuables are treated as investments in the National Accounts.

### Gross and net investment

Total investment spending is called **gross investment** or **gross capital formation**. Gross investment is divided into two parts: replacement investment and net investment. **Replacement investment** is the amount of investment that just maintains the level of existing capital stock; in other words, it replaces the bits that have worn out. Replacement investment is classified as the **capital consumption allowance**, or simply **depreciation**. Gross investment minus replacement investment is **net investment**. Positive net investment increases the economy's total stock of capital, while replacement investment keeps the existing stock intact by replacing what has been used up or worn out.

All of gross investment is included in the calculation of GDP. This is because all investment goods are part of the nation's total output, and their production creates income (and employment) whether the goods produced are a part of net investment or are merely replacement investment. Actual total investment spending is denoted by the symbol $I^a$.

### Net exports

The fourth category of aggregate spending, and one that is very important to the UK economy, arises from foreign trade. How do imports and exports affect the calculation of GDP?

#### Imports

A country's GDP is the total value of final goods and services produced *in that country*. If you spend £15,000 on a car that was made in Germany, only a small part of that value will represent spending on UK production. Some of it represents payment for the services of the UK dealer and for transportation within this country; much of the rest is the output of German firms and spending on German products, though there may be component suppliers from several countries. If you take your next vacation in Italy, much of your spending will be on goods and services produced in Italy and so will contribute to Italian GDP.

Similarly, when a UK firm makes an investment spending on a UK-produced machine tool that was made partly with imported materials, only part of the spending is on British production; the rest is spending on production by the countries supplying the materials. The same is true for government spending on such things as roads and dams: some of the spending is for imported materials, and only part of it is for domestically produced goods and services.

Private consumption, government consumption, and investment all have an import content. To arrive at total spending on UK output, we need to subtract from total UK residents' spending actual spending on the imports of goods and services, which is represented below by the symbol $IM^a$.

### Exports

If UK firms sell goods or services to German consumers, the goods and services are a part of German consumption spending but also constitute spending on UK output. Indeed, all goods and services that are produced in the United Kingdom and sold to foreigners must be counted as part of UK GDP; they are produced in the United Kingdom, and they create incomes for the UK residents who produce them. They are not purchased by UK residents, however, so they are not included as part of $C^a$, $I^a$, or $G^a$. Therefore, to arrive at the total value of spending on the domestic product, it is necessary to add in the value of UK exports. Actual exports of goods and services are denoted by the symbol $X^a$.

It is convenient to group actual imports and actual exports together as **net exports**. Net exports are defined as total exports of goods and services minus total imports of goods and services ($X^a - IM^a$), which will also be denoted by $NX^a$. When the value of exports exceeds the value of imports, the net export term is positive. When the value of imports exceeds the value of exports, the net export term is negative.

### Market prices and basic prices

There is one important difference that arises when calculating the level of GDP from the spending side of the economy rather than calculating it by summing the values added in production. This difference arises because the price paid by consumers for many goods and services is not the same as the sales revenue received by the producer. There are taxes that have to be paid which place a wedge between what consumers pay and producers receive. Taxes attached to transactions are known as *indirect taxes*. Examples of UK indirect taxes include VAT and excise duties.[10] Thus, if you pay £100 for a meal in a restaurant, the restaurateur will receive only £85.10, and £14.90 will go to the government in the form of VAT.

---

10 The rate of VAT was 17.5 per cent in the UK in 2005/6 and applied to a wide range of goods and services. Excise duties applied mainly to tobacco, alcohol, and petrol.

In cases where products are subsidized by the government, the producer receives more than the consumer pays. In 2005 subsidies on UK products were minimal, amounting to only 0.8 per cent of GDP.

The term **basic prices** is used in the National Accounts to refer to the prices of products as received by producers. **Market prices** are the prices as paid by consumers. Thus, basic prices are equal to market prices *minus* taxes on products *plus* subsidies on products. In the example of the meal bill above, the market price was £100 but the basic price was £85.10.

If you look again at Table 15.1, you will see that the sum of sectoral values added that we presented there is referred to as gross value added *at basic prices*. You should also notice that, by adding to gross value added at basic prices a term labelled 'adjustment to current basic prices' we arrived at the total for GDP at market prices. This adjustment to current basic prices is made up of taxes minus subsidies on products.

Since our final spending categories are all measured at market prices—as these measure what is spent by purchasers rather than what is received by producers—we can proceed by adding up this final spending to arrive at GDP *at market prices* directly.

## Total spending

The spending-based measure of gross domestic product at market prices is the sum of the four spending categories that we have discussed above; in symbols,

$$GDP = C^a + I^a + G^a + (X^a - IM^a).$$

The actual spending components of GDP for the United Kingdom in 2005 are shown in Table 15.2.

GDP spending-based is the sum of private consumption, government consumption, investment, and net export spending on currently produced goods and services. It is GDP at market prices.

## GDP income-based

The production of a nation's output generates income. Labour must be employed, land must be rented, and capital must be used. The calculation of GDP from the income side involves adding up the income claims of owners of resource inputs (land, labour, capital, etc.) so that all of that value is accounted for. In essence, we are taking the value added displayed for the economy as a whole in Table 15.1 and dividing it up by types of income rather than by industrial sector. We have already noted that, because all value produced must be owned by some-

**Table 15.2** Expenditure-based GDP and its components, UK, 2005

| Expenditure categories | £ million | % of GDP |
|---|---|---|
| Individual consumption | | |
|   Household final consumption | 760,777 | 62 |
|   Final consumption of non-profit institutions serving households | 30,525 | 2.5 |
|   Individual government final consumption | 165,655 | 13.5 |
| Total actual individual consumption | 956,957 | 78.1 |
| Collective government final consumption | 101,875 | 8.3 |
| **Total final consumption** | **1,058,832** | **86.5** |
| Gross capital formation | | |
|   Gross fixed capital formation | 205,843 | 16.8 |
|   Change in inventories | 3,721 | 0.3 |
|   Acquisition less disposals of valuables | −337 | 0 |
| **Total gross capital formation** | **209,187** | **17.1** |
| Exports of goods and services | 322,298 | 26.3 |
|   *less* Imports of goods and services | −366,540 | −29.9 |
| **External balance of goods and services (net exports)** | **−44,242** | **−3.6** |
| Statistical discrepancy | 938 | |
| **Gross domestic product at market prices (money GDP)** | **1,224,715** | **100** |

**Expenditure based GDP is made up of consumption, investment, and net exports.** Consumption is by far the largest expenditure category, equal to about 86 per cent of GDP. Private consumption makes up most of this, around 65 per cent of GDP, and government consumption makes up the rest. Investment accounts for just over 17 per cent of GDP. Whereas exports and imports are both quite large (each over 25 per cent of GDP), net exports are small; in 2005 they represented (negative) 3.6 per cent of GDP. Government consumption is reported in two parts: that which is paid for by government but is consumed by individuals, such as health services and education, and that which is consumed collectively, such as defence and the legal system.

*Source*: ONS, *UK National Accounts* (the Blue Book), 2006.

one, the value of production must equal the value of income claims generated by that production.

National income accountants distinguish three main categories of income: operating surplus, mixed incomes, and compensation of employees.

### Operating surplus

Operating surpluses are net business incomes after payment has been made to hired labour and for material inputs but before direct taxes (such as corporation tax) have been paid. Direct taxes are those taxes levied on individuals or firms, usually in relation to their income. Operating surpluses are in large part the profits of firms, but also include the financial surplus of organizations other than companies, such as universities. Some profits are paid out as **dividends** to owners of firms; the rest are retained for use by firms. The former are called *distributed profits*, and the latter are called *undistributed profits* or *retained earnings*. Both distributed and undistributed profits are included in the calculation of GDP.

### Mixed incomes

This category covers the many people who are earning a living by selling their services or output but are not employed by any organization. It includes some consultants and those who work on short contracts but are not formally employees of an incorporated business; they are self-employed individuals running sole-trader businesses. Also included are some partnerships where the partners own the business. The reason why the incomes of this group are referred to as *mixed incomes* is that it is not clear what proportion of their earnings is equivalent to a wage or salary and what proportion is the profit or surplus of the business. They are a mixture of the two.

### Compensation of employees

This is wages and salaries (usually just referred to as *wages*). It is the payment for the services of labour. Wages include take-home pay, taxes withheld, national insurance contributions, pension fund contributions, and any other fringe benefits. In other words, wages are measured gross. In total, wages represent that part of the value of production that is attributable to hired labour.

The various components of UK income-based GDP in 2005 are shown in Table 15.3. Notice that the three income categories in Table 15.3 add up to gross value added at basic prices, as shown in Table 15.1. These income-based and output- or value-added-based measures are showing the same thing—the sum of factor incomes for the whole economy. In both cases we add taxes on production less subsidies to arrive at GDP at market prices.

## Income produced and income received

GDP at market prices provides a measure of total output produced in the United Kingdom and of the total income generated as a result of that production. However, the total income received by UK residents differs from GDP for two reasons. First, some domestic production creates factor earnings for non-residents who either do some paid work for UK residents or have previously invested in the United Kingdom; on this account, income received by UK residents will be less than UK GDP. Second, many UK resid-

**Table 15.3** Income-based GDP and its components, UK, 2005

| Income type | £ million | % of GDP |
|---|---|---|
| Operating surplus, gross (profits) | 312,026 | 25.5 |
| Mixed incomes | 76,112 | 6.2 |
| Compensation of employees | 684,618 | 55.9 |
| Taxes on production and imports | 162,267 | 13.2 |
| *less* Subsidies | −9,391 | −0.8 |
| Statistical discrepancy | −917 | 0.0 |
| **GDP at market prices** | **1,224,715** | **100** |
| Employees' compensation | | |
| Receipts from rest of world | 1,211 | |
| *less* Payment to rest of world | −1,137 | |
| Total | **74** | |
| *less* Taxes on production paid to rest of world *plus* Subsidies received from rest of world | −4,243 | |
| Other subsidies on production | 3,216 | |
| Property and entrepreneurial income | | |
| Receipts from rest of world | 185,826 | |
| *less* Payments to rest of world | −156,029 | |
| Total | **29,797** | |
| **Gross national income (GNI) at market prices** | 1,253,561 | |

**The income-based measure of GDP is made up of gross operating surplus (profit), mixed incomes, compensation of employees, and net taxes on goods.** Mixed incomes are largely incomes of the self-employed or non-incorporated businesses, where it is hard to distinguish profits from employee compensation. By far the largest income category is compensation of employees, which makes up 55 per cent of GDP. GNI is GDP at market prices plus various net income receipts from the rest of the world.

*Source*: ONS, *UK National Accounts* (the Blue Book), 2006.

ents earn income from work for overseas residents or on overseas investments; on this account, income received by UK residents will be greater than GDP.

While GDP measures the output, and hence the income, that is *produced in* this country, the **gross national income (GNI)** measures the income that is *received by* this country. To convert GDP into GNI, it is necessary to add three terms that combine to account for the difference between the income received by this country and the income produced in this country. The first term is *employees' compensation receipts from the rest of the world minus payments to the rest of the world*. Thus, if a London-based consultant sells her services to a French firm, the income received will contribute to UK GNI but will be part of French GDP.

The second term is *(minus) net taxes on production paid to the rest of the world plus subsidies received from the rest of the world*. The logic of this is that we are measuring GNI (like GDP) at market prices. If some element of the market prices paid is an indirect tax that generates revenue for a foreign government, then that tax represents a loss of income for the domestic economy as a whole and reduces domestic gross national income. Equally, if the product

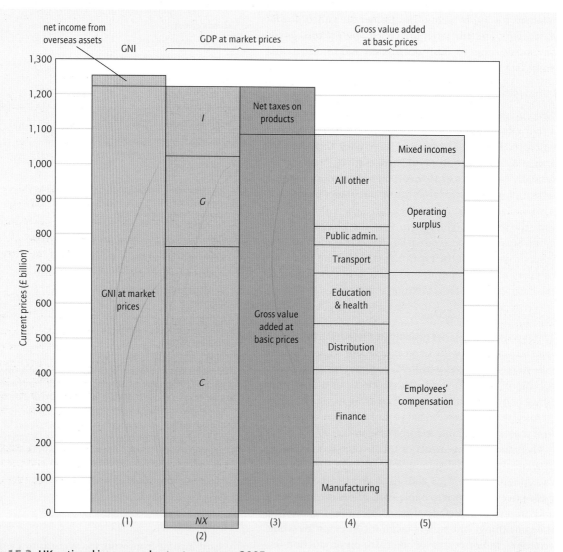

**Figure 15.3** UK national income and output measures, 2005

**Measurement of national income and output can be approached in three different ways, but they are all related.** The figure shows the actual UK aggregates GNI at market prices, GDP at market prices, and gross value added at basic prices for 2005. Column (1) is GNI at market prices. Columns (2) and (3) add up to GDP at market prices. Columns (4) and (5) add up to gross value added at basic prices (or what used to be called GDP at factor cost).

Column (1) exceeds column (2) by about 2.0 per cent. This difference is net income from abroad. In 2005 this was positive but small. Column (2) shows that GDP is made up of the spending components: consumption (*C*), investment (*I*), government spending (*G*), and net exports (*NX*). Notice that in 2005 net exports were negative, so *NX* has to be subtracted from the sum of *C* + *I* + *G* to arrive at GDP. Columns (3) and (4) show that gross value added at basic prices is equal to GDP at market prices minus net taxes on production.

Column (4) shows that gross value added is made up of the sum of the values added of each of the production sectors of the economy—manufacturing, for example, produces about 13.6 per cent of gross value added. Column (5) shows that gross value added can also be broken down by income type. Employees' compensation amounts to about 56 per cent of GDP at market prices.

*Source*: ONS, *UK National Accounts* (the Blue Book), 2006.

is subsidized by a foreign government, then this raises domestic incomes by enabling us to consume a given amount of goods at lower prices.

The third component of the difference between GDP and GNI is *property and entrepreneurial income receipts from the rest of the world minus payments to the rest of the world*. If, for example, you live in Manchester and own a holiday home in Spain that you rent out for part of the year, the revenue earned will count as part of GDP in Spain (as it is produced there), but the income accrues to a UK resident so it adds to UK GNI. Similarly, many UK firms have subsidiaries located in other countries. The value added of those subsidiaries counts as part of GDP in the host country, but profits remitted to the parent count as part of the UK's GNI. Conversely, a Japanese firm located in the UK contributes all its value added to UK GDP, but profits remitted back to Japan are deducted from GDP in order to arrive at GNI (as they are not part of UK income).

Total output produced in the economy, measured by GDP, differs from total income received, measured by GNI, because of net income from abroad.

It is important to note that the term *gross national income* was introduced as recently as 1998 to replace the term *gross national product* or GNP. GNI and GNP are conceptually identical. The latter has, however, been in use for several decades all over the world, so readers will continue to come across it for many years to come even if it is replaced by GNI in many new publications. This minor difference in terminology is not important for understanding macroeconomics, which is concerned primarily with GDP, but it is important not to be confused when these terms are encountered.

GDP and GNI (or GNP) at market prices are the most commonly used concepts of national output and national income. Once we move on to theory in the next chapter, we shall ignore the small difference between GDP and GNI and refer to GDP at all times unless stated otherwise. This is true even though we sometimes talk about 'national income' and sometimes about the 'national product', depending on the context. For analytical purposes, they are the same thing.

### Reconciling GDP with GNI

Table 15.3 shows the reconciliation of GDP with GNI. UK GNI was greater than GDP in 2005, but only by 2 per cent. This reflects slightly greater income from abroad for UK residents than UK-generated income paid out to foreigners. Clearly, GNI could be smaller than GDP if outward payments were greater than income earned from abroad.

Figure 15.3 provides a visual representation of the information in Tables 15.1–15.3. It shows both the relations between gross value added at basic prices and GDP at market prices, and the difference between GDP and GNI (at market prices). Components of the three possible decompositions of GDP are also displayed.

### Other income concepts

**Personal income** is income that is earned by or paid to individuals, before allowing for personal income taxes on that income. Some personal income goes on taxes, some goes on savings, and the rest goes on consumption. **Personal disposable income** is the amount of current income that individuals have available for spending and saving; it is personal income minus personal income taxes and national insurance contributions.

Personal disposable income is GNI *minus* any part of it that is not actually paid to persons (such as retained profits of companies) *minus* personal income taxes *plus* transfer payments received by individuals.

## Interpreting national income and output measures

The information provided by National Accounts data is useful, but unless it is carefully interpreted it can be misleading. Furthermore, each of the specific measures gives different information. Each may be the best statistic for studying a particular range of problems, but it is important to understand these differences if you are going to use the data for analytical purposes. Here we discuss some of the caveats to bear in mind.

### Real and nominal measures

It is important to distinguish between *real* and *nominal* measures of national income and output. When we add up money values of outputs, spending, or incomes, we end up with what are called *nominal values*. Suppose that we found that a measure of nominal GDP had risen by 70 per cent between 2000 and 2010. If we wanted to compare *real*

**Box 15.2  Calculation of nominal and real GDP**

To see what is involved in calculating nominal GDP, real GDP, and the implicit deflator, an example may be helpful. Consider a simple hypothetical economy that produces only two commodities, wheat and steel. Table I gives the basic data for output and prices in the economy for two years.

**Table I**

|  | Quantity produced | | Prices | |
|  | Wheat (bushels) | Steel (tons) | Wheat (£ per bu.) | Steel (£ per ton) |
|---|---|---|---|---|
| Year 1 | 100 | 20 | 10 | 50 |
| Year 2 | 110 | 16 | 12 | 55 |

Table II shows nominal GDP, calculated by adding the money values of wheat output and of steel output for each year. In year 1 the value of both wheat and steel production was £1,000, so nominal income was £2,000. In year 2 wheat output rose and steel output fell; the value of wheat output rose to £1,320, and that of steel fell to £880. Since the rise in value of wheat was greater than the fall in value of steel, nominal GDP rose by £200.

**Table II**

| Year 1 | $(100 \times 10) + (20 \times 50) = £2,000$ |
|---|---|
| Year 2 | $(110 \times 12) + (16 \times 55) = £2,200$ |

Table III shows real GDP, calculated by valuing output in each year by year 2 prices; that is, year 2 becomes the base year for weighting purposes. Using year 2 prices, the value of the fall in steel output between years 1 and 2 exceeded the value of the rise in wheat output, and real GDP fell.

**Table III**

| Year 1 | $(100 \times 12) + (20 \times 55) = £2,300$ |
|---|---|
| Year 2 | $(110 \times 12) + (16 \times 55) = £2,200$ |

In Table IV the ratio of nominal to real GDP is calculated for each year and multiplied by 100. This ratio implicitly measures the change in prices over the period in question and is called the *implicit deflator* or *implicit price index*. The implicit deflator shows that the price level increased by 15 per cent between year 1 and year 2 (calculated as $(13.04/86.96) \times 100$, where 13.04 is $(100 - 86.96)$).

**Table IV**

| Year 1 | $(2,000/2,300) \times 100 = 86.96$ |
|---|---|
| Year 2 | $(2,200/2,200) \times 100 = 100.00$ |

In Table IV we used year 2 as the base year for comparison purposes, but we could have used year 1. The implicit deflator would then have been 100 in year 1 and 115 in year 2, and the increase in price level would still have been 15 per cent. Or the base year could be some earlier year. No matter what year is picked as the year in which the index had a value of 100, the change in the implicit deflator between year 1 and year 2 is 15 per cent.

UK national income statisticians used to calculate UK real GDP using prices from the same base year for several years in a row. Thus, in the past, real GDP growth between 2000 and 1999 might have been calculated using 1995 as the base year for prices. They would then have big revisions some time later when they shifted to using a new base year. However, now they use a *chain-weighted* volume index of real output, which means that the price weights are adjusted each year on the basis of an average of prices in the most recent few years. This is similar to the way in which quantity weights are adjusted each year in construction of the UK retail price index (RPI) (see the case study on page 351 below).

---

GDP in 2010 with that in 2000, we would need to determine how much of that 70 per cent nominal increase was due to increases in the general level of prices and how much was due to increases in quantities of goods and services produced. Although there are many possible ways of doing this, the basic principle is always the same. It is to compute the value of output, spending, and income in each period by using a common set of *base-period prices*. When this is done, we speak of real output, spending, or income as being measured in *constant prices* or, say, 2000 *prices*.

GDP valued at current prices (i.e. money GDP) is a nominal measure. GDP valued at base-period prices is a real measure of the volume of national output and national income.

Any *change* in nominal GDP reflects the combined effects of changes in quantities and changes in prices. However, when real income is measured over different periods by using a common set of base-period prices, changes in real income reflect only changes in real output.

### The implicit deflator

If nominal and real GDP change by different amounts over some time-period, this must be because prices have changed over that period. Comparing what has happened to nominal and real GDP over the same period implies the existence of a price index measuring the change in prices over that period. We say 'implies' because no price index was used in calculating real and nominal GDP. However, an index can be inferred by comparing these two values. Such an index is called an *implicit price index* or an *implicit deflator*. It is defined as follows:

$$\text{Implicit deflator} = \frac{\text{GDP at current prices}}{\text{GDP at base-period prices}} \times 100 \ \%.$$

The implicit GDP deflator is the most comprehensive index of the price level because it covers all the goods and services that are produced by the entire economy. Although some other indexes use fixed weights, or weights that change only periodically, implicit deflators are variable-weight indexes. They use the current year's 'bundle' of production to compare the current year's prices with those prevailing in the base period. Thus, the 2000 deflator uses 2000 output weights, and the 2005 deflator uses 2005 output weights. Box 15.2 illustrates the calculation of real and nominal GDP and an implicit deflator for a simple hypothetical economy that produces only wheat and steel. See the case studies at the end of this chapter for a discussion of the construction of the retail price index.

A change in any nominal measure of GDP can be split into a change resulting from prices and a change resulting from quantities. For example, in 2005 UK nominal GDP ('money' GDP) was 3.8 per cent higher than in 2004. This increase was due to a 2.0 per cent increase in prices and a 1.8 per cent increase in real GDP. Table 15.4 gives nominal and real GDP and the implicit deflator for selected years since 1900.

## International comparisons of GDP

One purpose to which GDP measures are often put is international comparison of living standards or real income. It is natural to want to know if people have higher living standards in Britain or in, say, Germany or France. However, comparisons using measures such as GDP must be conducted with great care. There are many dimensions to living standards that are not measured by GDP or GNI.

For some purposes we may want to compare the absolute size of one economy relative to another, but normally

**Table 15.4** Nominal and real GDP at market prices, 1900–2005

| | Money GDP (£ billion) | Real GDP (1990 prices) (£ billion) | Implicit GDP deflator (1990 = 100) |
|---|---|---|---|
| 1900 | 1.9 | 109.5 | 1.7 |
| 1930 | 4.7 | 138.6 | 3.4 |
| 1950 | 13.1 | 200.4 | 6.5 |
| 1970 | 51.6 | 350.9 | 14.7 |
| 1980 | 231.2 | 426.8 | 54.2 |
| 2001 | 988 | 708 | 137.9 |
| 2005 | 1,225 | 777 | 152.3 |

**The data in the table are money GDP, real GDP, and the implicit GDP price deflator for selected years.** The first column shows that money (nominal) GDP increased 636-fold between 1900 and 2005. However, the second column shows that there was only a seven-fold increase in real GDP over the same period. The difference between the two is accounted for by the final column, which shows that the implicit price deflator for GDP rose nearly 90-fold in this period. Since 1950, real GDP has seen a nearly four-fold increase, while the GDP price deflator has increased over 23-fold.

*Sources: Economic Trends* and *100 Years of Economic Statistics* (Economist Pubications).

we are interested in how well off the average individual is in each country. For this purpose we want to look at GDP per head or per capita (or perhaps GNI per capita). To arrive at this figure, we divide GDP by the total population of the country. This tells us the share of total GDP that is available for the average citizen.

GDP in each country is measured in the local currency. So to make comparisons we have to convert different countries' nominal GDP into the same currency. To do this, we have to use an *exchange rate*. This is problematic because exchange rates fluctuate, sometimes dramatically. Even in normal conditions it is not unusual for exchange rates to move by 10 per cent in a few weeks, but the move could easily be reversed a little later.

To solve the problem of making comparisons using unreliable or atypical exchange rates, economists make comparisons of GDP using the exchange rate that equates the prices of a representative bundle of goods in two countries. This is known as the *purchasing power parity* (*PPP*) rate. We will discuss this concept more fully in Chapter 27.

Some comparisons of GNI per capita in 13 different countries (using PPP exchange rates) are given in Table 15.5. Figures are all expressed in US dollars. Several other indicators of material well-being are included in the table.

**Table 15.5** International comparisons of living standards

| | GNI per capita 2004 (US$) Atlas Method | Average annual real GDP growth 1990–2003 (%) | Fixed line and mobile telephones per 1,000 pop. 2004 | Infant mortality per 1,000 live births, 2004 | Personal computers per 1,000 pop. 2002 | Life-expectancy at birth 2004 | Internet users per 1,000 pop. 2004 | Doctors per 1,000 pop. 2003 |
|---|---|---|---|---|---|---|---|---|
| USA | 41,400 | 3.3 | 1,223 | 7 | 659 | 77 | 630 | 2.3 |
| Japan | 37,180 | 1.2 | 1,176 | 3 | 382 | 82 | 587 | 2.0 |
| UK | 33,630 | 2.7 | 1,584 | 5 | 406 | 79 | 628 | 2.2 |
| Germany | 30,690 | 1.5 | 1,525 | 4 | 485 | 78 | 500 | 3.4 |
| France | 30,090 | 1.9 | 1,299 | 4 | 347 | 80 | 414 | 3.4 |
| Canada | 28,390 | 3.3 | 1,053 | 5 | 487 | 80 | 626 | 2.1 |
| Australia | 27,070 | 3.8 | 1,359 | 5 | 565 | 80 | 646 | 2.5 |
| Spain | 21,530 | 2.8 | 1,321 | 3 | 196 | 80 | 336 | 3.2 |
| Mexico | 6,770 | 3.0 | 545 | 23 | 82 | 75 | 135 | 1.5 |
| Russia | 3,410 | −1.8 | 508 | 17 | 89 | 65 | 111 | 4.2 |
| Brazil | 3,000 | 2.6 | 587 | 32 | 75 | 71 | 120 | 2.1 |
| China | 1,500 | 9.6 | 499 | 26 | 28 | 71 | 73 | 1.6 |
| India | 620 | 5.9 | 85 | 62 | 7 | 63 | 32 | 0.6 |

**The table shows eight different indicators of living standards for 13 countries.** Most of the indicators tell the same story: wealthy countries have more goods and better life expectations. However, there are some interesting anomalies. Russia has more doctors per 1,000 people than any other country in the table, yet life expectancy is lower than in China, which has less than half as many doctors per person.

*Sources*: *World Bank Atlas*, 2004, and *World Development Indicators*, 2006. © 2004 and 2006 by the International Bank for Reconstruction and Development/World Bank. All rights reserved.

Broadly speaking, they tell the same story as the GNI figures—the inhabitants of the richer countries can purchase more goods and services and tend to have longer life expectancy. However, the rankings would be different for each possible indicator of well-being. The significance of this is that, while GNI per capita contains some useful information, other important indicators sometimes tell a slightly different story.

## What GDP does not measure

GDP measures the flow of economic activity in organized markets in a given year. But much economic activity takes place outside of the market economy. Although these activities are not typically included in GDP or GNI, they nevertheless use real resources and satisfy real wants and needs.

### Unreported activities

A significant omission from measured GDP is the so-called *underground* or *black economy*. The transactions that occur in the underground economy are perfectly legal in themselves; the only illegality is that such transactions

are not reported for tax purposes. One example of this is the carpenter who repairs a leak in your roof and takes payment in cash or in kind in order to avoid taxation. Because such transactions go unreported, they are omitted from GDP.

The growth of the underground economy could be encouraged by high rates of taxation and is facilitated by the rising importance of services in the nation's total output. The higher the tax rates, the more there is to be gained by 'going underground'. Of course, it is much easier for a carpenter or plumber to pass unnoticed by government authorities than it is for a manufacturing establishment.

Studies of the scale of the underground economy show its importance growing in recent years. Estimates have put the underground economy in Britain at about 7 per cent of GDP. A Canadian study concluded that 15 per cent of Canadian GDP went unreported because it was in the underground economy. In other countries the figures are even higher. The Italian underground economy, for example, has been estimated at about 20 per cent of GDP; for Spain estimates are close to 25 per cent, and for Greece 30 per cent!

## Non-marketed activities

If homeowners hire a firm to do some landscaping, the value of the landscaping enters into GDP; if they do the landscaping themselves, the value of the landscaping is omitted from GDP. Other non-marketed activities include the services of those who do their own housework, any do-it-yourself activity, and voluntary work such as canvassing for a political party, helping to run a volunteer day-care centre, or coaching an amateur football team.

One important non-marketed activity is leisure itself. If a lawyer voluntarily chooses to work 2,200 hours a year instead of 2,400 hours, measured GDP will fall by the lawyer's hourly wage rate times 200 hours. Yet the value to the lawyer of the 200 hours of new leisure, which is enjoyed outside of the marketplace, must exceed the lost wages (because the leisure has been voluntarily chosen in preference to the extra work), so total economic welfare has risen rather than fallen. Until recently, one of the most important ways in which economic growth benefited people was by permitting increased amounts of time off work. Because the time off is not marketed, its value does not show up in measures of GDP.

## Economic bads

When a coal-fired electricity generator sends sulphur dioxide into the atmosphere, leading to acid rain and environmental damage, the value of the electricity sold is included as part of GDP, but the value of the damage done by the acid rain is not deducted. Similarly, the petrol that we use in our cars is part of GDP, but the damage done by burning that petrol is not deducted. To the extent that economic growth brings with it increases in pollution, congestion, and other disamenities of modern living, GDP measures will overstate the value of the growth. They measure the increased economic output and income, but they fail to deduct the increased 'bads', or negative outputs, that generally accompany economic growth.

## Do the omissions matter?

GDP does a reasonable job of measuring the flow of goods and services through the market sector of the economy. Usually an increase in GDP implies greater opportunities for employment for those households that sell their labour services in the market. Unless the importance of unmeasured economic activity changes rapidly, *changes* in GDP will do an excellent job of measuring *changes* in economic activity and well-being. However, when the task at hand is the measurement of the overall flow of goods and services available to satisfy people's wants, regardless of the source of the goods and services, then the omissions that we have discussed above become undesirable and potentially serious. Still, in the relatively short term, changes in GDP will usually be good measures of the direction, if not the exact magnitude, of changes in economic welfare.

The omissions cause serious problems when GDP measures are used to compare living standards in structurally different economies, as was discussed above. Generally the non-market sector of the economy is larger in rural than in urban settings and in less developed than in more developed economies. Be cautious, then, when interpreting data from a country with a very different climate and culture. When you hear that the per capita GNI of India is about US$620 per year, you should not imagine living in Manchester on that income. The average Indian is undoubtedly poorer than the average Briton, but perhaps not one-fifty-fifth as well off, as the GNI figures suggest.

# CASE STUDIES

## 1. How the RPI is constructed

Two important questions must be answered when any price index is constructed. First, what group of prices should be used? This depends on what the index is intended to measure. The retail price index (RPI), which is calculated by the Office for National Statistics (ONS), covers prices of goods and services that are commonly bought by households. Changes in the RPI are meant to measure changes in the typical household's *cost of living*. (Other indexes, such as the wholesale price index or the producer price index, cover the prices of different baskets of commodities. The implicit deflator for GDP covers all of the nation's output, not just consumer prices.)

Second, how should the movements in consumer prices be added up and summarized in one price index? If all prices changed in the same proportion, this would not matter: a 10 per cent rise in every price would mean a 10 per cent rise in the average of all prices, no matter how the average was constructed. However, different prices usually change in different proportions. It then matters how much importance we give to each

**Table 15.6** Calculation of weights for a price index

| Commodity | Price (£) | Quantity | Spending (£) (price × quantity) | Proportional weight |
|---|---|---|---|---|
| A | 5 | 60 | 300 | 0.50 |
| B | 1 | 200 | 200 | 0.33 |
| C | 4 | 25 | 100 | 0.17 |
| Total | | | 600 | 1.00 |

**The weights are the proportions of total spending that are devoted to each commodity.** This simple example lists the prices of three commodities and the quantities bought by a typical household. Multiplying price by quantity gives spending on each, and summing these gives the total spending on all commodities. Dividing spending on each good by total spending gives the proportion of total spending that is devoted to each commodity, as shown in the last column. These proportions become the weights for the price indexes that are calculated in Table 15.7.

**Table 15.7** Calculation of a price index

| Commodity | Weight | Price (£) | | | Price × weight (£) | | |
|---|---|---|---|---|---|---|---|
| | | 2000 | 2005 | 2010 | 2000 | 2005 | 2010 |
| A | 0.50 | 5.00 | 6.00 | 14.00 | 2.50 | 3.00 | 7.00 |
| B | 0.33 | 1.00 | 1.50 | 2.00 | 0.33 | 0.495 | 0.66 |
| C | 0.17 | 4.00 | 8.00 | 9.00 | 0.68 | 1.36 | 1.53 |
| Total | 1.00 | | | | 3.51 | 4.855 | 9.19 |

| Index | 1980 | $\frac{3.51}{3.51} \times 100 = 100$ |
|---|---|---|
| | 1985 | $\frac{4.855}{3.51} \times 100 = 138.3$ |
| | 1990 | $\frac{9.19}{3.51} \times 100 = 261.8$ |

A price index expresses the weighted average of prices in the given year as a percentage of the weighted average of prices in the base year. The prices of the three commodities in each year are multiplied by the weights from Table 15.6. Summing the weighted prices for each year gives the average price in that year. Dividing the average price in the given year by the average price in the base year and multiplying by 100 gives the price index for the given year. The index is, of course, 100 when the base year is also taken as the given year, as is the case for 2000 in this example.

price change. Changes in the price of bread, for example, are much more important to the average consumer than changes in the price of caviar. In calculating a price index, each price is given a *weight* that reflects its importance.

Let us see how this is done for the RPI. Government statisticians periodically survey a representative group of households in what is called the Family Expenditure Survey. This shows how consumers spend their incomes. The average bundle of goods that is bought is determined, along with the proportion of spending that is devoted to each good. These proportions become the weights attached to the individual prices in calculating the RPI. As a result, the RPI weights rather heavily the prices of commodities on which consumers spend much of their income, and weights rather lightly the prices of commodities on which consumers spend only a little of their income. Table 15.6 provides a simple example of how these weights are calculated.

Once the weights are chosen, the average price can be calculated for each period. This is done, as shown in Table 15.7, by multiplying each price by its weight and summing the resulting figures. However, a single average price is not informative. Suppose, for example, you were told that the average price of all goods bought by consumers last year was £89.35. 'So what?' you might well ask, and the answer would be: 'So, not very much. By itself, this tells you nothing useful.' Now suppose you are told that this year's average price for the same set of consumers' purchases is £107.22. Now you know that, on average, prices paid by consumers have risen sharply over the year—in fact, the increase is 20 per cent.[11]

The average for each period is divided by the value of the average for the base period and multiplied by 100. The resulting series is called an *index number series*. By construction, the base-period value in this series equals 100; if prices in the next period average 20 per cent more, the index number for that period will be 120. A simple example of how these calculations are carried out is given in Table 15.7.

**Price indexes are constructed by assigning weights to reflect the importance of the individual items being combined. The value is set equal to 100 in the base period.**

Table 15.7 shows the calculation of what is called a *fixed-weight index*. The weights are the proportion of income that is spent on each of the three goods in the base year. These weights are then applied to the prices in each subsequent year. The value of the index in each year measures exactly how much the base-year bundle of goods would cost at that year's prices.[12] Fixed-weight indexes are easy to interpret, but problems arise because consumption patterns change over the years; the fixed weights represent with decreasing accuracy the importance that consumers *currently* place on each of the commodities.

---

[11] The change is £17.87, which is 20 per cent of the initial average price of £89.35.

[12] To verify this, calculate the total spending required to buy 60 units of commodity A, 200 units of commodity B, and 25 units of commodity C in each of the three years for which price data are given in Table 15.7. Divide the resulting amounts by £600, multiply by 100, and you will get exactly the index values shown in the table.

The RPI used to be calculated using fixed weights that were changed only every decade or so. Now they are revised annually. This avoids the problem of the fixed-weight index becoming steadily less representative of current spending patterns.[13]

### Measuring the rate of inflation

In February 2006 the RPI was 194.2. (The value for January 1987 equals 100.) This means that in February 2006 it cost just over 94 per cent more to buy a representative bundle of goods than it did in the base period, i.e. January 1987.[14] In other words, there was a 94 per cent *increase* in the price level over that period as measured by the RPI. The *percentage change* in the cost of purchasing the bundle of goods that is covered by any index is therefore the level of the index minus 100.

The *inflation rate* between any two periods of time is measured by the percentage increase in the relevant price index from the first period to the second period. In the rare event of a drop in the price level, we speak of a *deflation*. When the amount of the rise in the price level is being measured from the base period, all that needs to be done is to subtract the base-period index (100) from the later index, as we have just done. When two other periods are being compared, we must be careful to express the change as a percentage of the index in the first period.

If we let $P_1$ indicate the value of the price index in the first period and $P_2$ its value in the second period, the inflation rate is merely the difference between the two, expressed as a percentage of the value of the index in the first period:

$$\text{Inflation rate} = \frac{(P_2 - P_1)}{P_1} \times 100.$$

When $P_1$ is the base period, its value is 100, and the expression shown above reduces to $P_2 - 100$. In other cases the full calculation must be made. For example, suppose the index went to 144.7 in June 2008 from 141.0 in June 2007 (using a hypothetical base year later than 1987). The rise of 3.7 points in the index is a 2.6 per cent rise over its initial value of 141.0, indicating a rate of inflation of 2.6 per cent over the year.

If the two values being compared are not one year apart, it is common to convert the result to an *annual rate*. For example, suppose the RPI is 135.2 in January 2008 and 135.6 in February 2008 (on a base of, say, 1998 = 100). This is an increase of 0.296 per cent over the month ($(0.4/135.2) \times 100$). It is also an *annual rate* of approximately 3.55 per cent (0.296 per cent × 12) over the year.[15] This means that, if the rate of increase that occurred between January and February 2008 did continue for a year, the price level would rise by approximately 3.55 per cent over the year. In practice, inflation rates are usually expressed as the rate of change between the latest month and the same month a year earlier. So when we say that inflation was 2.4 per cent in February 2006, this means that the RPI was 2.4 per cent higher in February 2006 than it had been in February 2005. It does not mean that annualized inflation *between* January 2006 and February 2006 was 2.4 per cent.

### Variations on RPI

There are three additional, often-quoted variations on RPI in use in the United Kingdom:

1.  CPI is a consumer price index used to form the basis of the inflation target set by the government for the Bank of England's Monetary Policy Committee. (Chapter 20 discusses the Committee in some detail.) This index used to be called HICP (harmonized index of consumer prices). It is calculated on a different basis from the RPI in order to conform with EU statistical practices. This includes some differences in components and is calculated as a geometric rather than arithmetic average. The details of these differences are somewhat arcane and not important to understand at this stage.

2.  RPIX is an index calculated using the same components as RPI except that it excludes mortgage interest payments. This is the index that was used as the basis for the inflation target until 2003.

3.  RPIY is RPIX but with the further modification that it excludes the effects of indirect tax changes on prices. RPIY is sometimes referred to as 'underlying inflation' or 'core inflation' because it excludes the effects on inflation induced by changes in both monetary *and* fiscal policies.

In February 2006 the annual inflation rate according to each of these measures was:

- RPI = 2.4 per cent
- RPIX = 2.3 per cent
- RPIY = 2.3 per cent
- CPI = 2.0 per cent

The European Central Bank uses the CPI for the euro zone as a whole to judge whether it is meeting its objective of price stability. In February 2006, the euro zone CPI inflation stood at 2.2 per cent.

---

[13] In effect, the RPI is a 'chained' index of prices, comparable to the chained volume measures discussed above in Box 15.2.

[14] Notice that the base period relative to which the RPI is calculated could be changed at some time in the future, but the base period in current use in 2006 remained January 1987.

[15] We say *approximately* because a 0.296 per cent rise each month that is *compounded* for 12 months will give rise to an increase over the year that is greater than 3.55 per cent. The appropriate procedure is to increase the index in January by 0.296 per cent 12 times (calculate $[(1.00296)^{12} - 1] \times 100$) rather than just to multiply it by 12. The two results are the difference between simple and compound interest rates.

## 2. Revisions to National Accounts data

Tables 15.1–15.3 report the data for UK GDP in 2005 and its major components. Policy-makers use this type of information to assess what is going on in the economy, and to inform decisions about whether, for example, taxes or interest rates need to change. However, National Accounts statistics are frequently revised and sometimes by a large amount, so great caution has to be used in putting too much weight on what any particular statistical release reports.

One example of significant revisions to National Accounts arose in the early 2000s when the volume measures of GDP were converted from a fixed-base-period method of estimation to a chained-index basis. On the old basis, real growth in 1999 and 2000 had been estimated at 2.9 and 3.7 per cent respectively, but in 2003 these estimates were revised to 2.4 and 3.0 per cent. These changes may not seem large, but changes of this magnitude could have made policy-makers change their perception as to whether the economy was growing at well above its sustainable long-run trend or, as later appeared true, at very close to its long-run trend.

The most dramatic examples of revisions to data arise in the balance of payments figures, which broadly measure the difference between imports and exports of goods and services. (For further explanation see Chapter 22.) Table 15.8 shows first the official data for the UK current account balance of payments deficit for the years 1988–96, as reported in the 1997 Balance of Payments Pink Book, and then the figures for the same years as reported in that same source in 2005. There were substantial revisions to all of these figures, but the most dramatic revisions to the figures reported in 1997 were those for what were then the most recent three years, 1994–6. Of course, the current account balance is arrived at as the difference between two large numbers, so it requires only small percentage revisions to the measured totals for trade flows to lead to quite large percentage revisions to the deficit or surplus.

**Table 15.8** Revisions to UK current account balance of payments deficit between 1997 and 2005

|  | Data as of 1997 Pink Book (£ m) | Data as of 2005 Pink Book (£ m) |
|---|---|---|
| 1988 | −16,475 | −19,321 |
| 1989 | −22,398 | −26,321 |
| 1990 | −18,746 | −22,281 |
| 1991 | −7,954 | −10,659 |
| 1992 | −10,133 | −12,974 |
| 1993 | −10,295 | −11,919 |
| 1994 | −1,655 | −6,768 |
| 1995 | −3,672 | −9,015 |
| 1996 | −435 | −7,324 |

Some data, however, are not subject to revisions and which these are is also worth knowing. Most financial market data, such as exchange rates, interest rates, and share prices, do not get revised. These prices are recorded accurately at a point in time and so there is no reason for revision. The prices will of course change over time, sometimes quite significantly, but data for prices at a past point in time will not be later revised.

More surprising, perhaps, is the fact that inflation data do not get revised once they have been published. This does not mean that the statisticians could not have made an error. It is just that any such errors will not lead to data revisions. The main reason for this is that RPI data and other inflation measures get used in legal contracts, affecting some wage agreements, pension contracts, and the yield on some inflation linked securities (such as, indexed gilts), and it would cause chaos if the basis on which such payments are made were to be changed repeatedly in retrospect. Hence an inflation figure, once announced, can be taken as the truth, even if it isn't.

# SUMMARY

### What is macroeconomics?

■ Macroeconomics is about the economy as a whole. It studies aggregate phenomena, such as growth, business cycles, living standards, inflation, unemployment, and the balance of payments. It also asks how governments can use their monetary and fiscal policy instruments to help stabilize the economy.

### Why do we need macroeconomics?

■ Macroeconomics is useful because it enables us to study events that affect the economy as a whole without getting into too much detail about specific products and sectors.

### The GDP gap

■ Potential GDP is the level of national output that would be produced if the economy were operating at its normal capacity, or full-employment, level.

■ The GDP gap is the difference between actual GDP and its potential level.

- When actual GDP is above potential there is an inflationary gap, and when actual GDP is below potential there is a recessionary gap.

## Measurement of national output

- Each firm's contribution to total output is equal to its value added, which is the gross value of the firm's output minus the value of all intermediate goods and services—that is, the outputs of other firms—that it uses. Goods that count as part of the economy's output are called final goods; all others are called intermediate goods. The sum of all the values added produced in an economy is called gross value added at basic prices. Basic prices are the prices received by producers net of taxes on products (plus subsidies).

## The circular flow of income, output, and spending

- The determination of GDP and national income can be represented as a circular flow of income and spending.
- Withdrawals of spending arise when income received is not spent on the domestic economy.
- Injections of spending are those that are not the result of domestic income receipts, but rather come from sources other than domestic income recipients.

## GDP, GNI, and GNP

- Gross domestic product (GDP) can be calculated in three different ways: (i) as the sum of all values added by all producers of both intermediate and final goods; (ii) as the income claims generated by the total production of goods and services; and (iii) as the spending needed to purchase all final goods and services produced during the period. By standard accounting conventions these three aggregations define the same total, so long as we add taxes on products (minus subsidies) to the first two in order to measure GDP at market prices. Market prices are the prices paid by consumers.
- From the spending side of the National Accounts, GDP $= C^a + I^a + G^a + (X^a - IM^a)$. $C^a$ comprises private consumption spending. $I^a$ is investment in fixed capital (including residential construction), inventories, and valuables. Gross investment can be split into replacement investment (necessary to keep the stock of capital intact) and net investment (net additions to the stock of capital). $G^a$ is government consumption. $(X^a - IM^a)$ represents net exports, or exports minus imports; this is negative if imports exceed exports.

- GDP income-based adds up all factor rewards in production. The main income categories making up GDP are operating surpluses, mixed incomes, and compensation of employees.

- UK GDP measures production that is located in the United Kingdom, and UK gross national income (GNI) measures income accruing to UK residents. The difference between them is due to net income from overseas. GNI is the same thing as what used to be called gross national product (GNP).

- Real GDP is calculated to reflect changes in real volumes of output and real income. Nominal GDP reflects changes in both prices and quantities. Any change in nominal GDP (or GNI) can be split into a change in real GDP and a change due to prices. Appropriate comparisons of nominal and real measures yield implicit deflators.

- Personal income is income received by individuals before any allowance for personal taxes. Personal disposable income is the amount actually available for individuals to spend or to save, i.e. income minus taxes.

## Interpreting national income and output measures

- GDP and related measures of national income and output must be interpreted with their limitations in mind. GDP excludes production that takes place in the underground economy or that does not pass through markets. Moreover, GDP does not measure everything that contributes to human welfare.

- GDP is one of the best measures available of the total economic activity within a country. It is particularly valuable when changes in GDP are used to indicate how economic activity has changed over time.

## TOPICS FOR REVIEW

- Targets and instruments of macroeconomic policy
- Injections and withdrawals
- Potential GDP
- The GDP gap
- Value added
- Intermediate and final goods
- Spending-based and income-based GDP
- GNI and GNP
- Personal disposable income
- Implicit deflator
- What GDP does and does not measure

## QUESTIONS

1 Assuming an economy with no government and no foreign trade, calculate GDP for the following output scenario. There are three firms: firm A is a mining company, firm B is a steel producer, and firm C is a car manufacturer. In a specific year, firm A sells £100 million worth of iron ore to firm B, firm B sells £200 million worth of steel to firm C, and firm C sells £500 million worth of cars to the general public. If there are no changes in inventories, no taxes, and no other producers in the economy, what is GDP?

2 How would the answer to question 1 change if firm B had increased its inventories of iron ore by £20 million worth during this year?

3 How would the answer to question 2 change if firm C had sold £50 million worth of lorries to firm A in addition to its car sales?

4 Suppose again there are only three companies in an economy. Company A grows crops and extracts minerals from its land with no inputs from other companies. Its sales are £100 million per year, half of which goes to consumers and half to companies B and C in equal amounts. Company B buys inputs from A and sells its entire output of £200 million to company C. Company C buys inputs from A and B and sells its £450 million output directly to consumers (though 20 per cent of this is overseas). What is gross value added at basic prices? If there is only one indirect tax, value added tax, levied at 10 per cent, what is the value of GDP at market prices?

5 If the price index in February 2008 is 165 and by February 2009 it has risen to 171, what is the annual rate of inflation? If over the same time period nominal GDP has risen from £1,000 billion to £1,080 billion, what is the growth rate of real GDP?

6 Explain why we cannot calculate the national product simply by adding up the production of all firms.

7 What is the difference between real GDP and nominal GDP, and why does this distinction matter? Which measure would be appropriate for judging changes in standard of living?

8 What are the limitations of GDP per head as a measure of the quality of life?

9 What would it mean to be told that a country's GNI was greater than its GDP?

10 Using the expenditure-based definition ($C + I + G + NX$), explain where each of the following expenditures appears in the National Income Accounts measure of GDP, if at all: state pensions; company pensions; student loans; theatre receipts; judges' salaries; unsold cars in showrooms; receipts from beer sales in a students' union bar; receipts from purchases of new copies of this book; receipts from purchases of second-hand copies of this book.

# Chapter 16

# A BASIC MODEL OF THE DETERMINATION OF GDP IN THE SHORT TERM

For the next several chapters, we are going to build a model that explains the causes and consequences of deviations of GDP from its potential level. This is the behaviour of what we defined in Chapter 15 as the *GDP gap*. At some times GDP rises above its potential level, creating a positive GDP gap, and at other times it falls below it, creating a negative GDP gap. These variations can be thought of as the behaviour of GDP in the short term, or short run. Because the first macroeconomic models of the economy were developed to explain this short-term behaviour of GDP, the theory that underlies them is called *macroeconomics* without qualification, or *the theory of national income determination* also without qualification. But 'short term' should always be understood to apply to these models and theories. This is in contrast to growth theory, which deals with the determination of potential GDP over the long term (and is discussed in Chapter 26). So when we speak of macroeconomics and the theory of the determination of national income, we refer to *short-run macroeconomics* and *the theory of the determination of GDP gaps in the short run*.

Although the long-term living standard of a nation is determined by the growth of its potential GDP (which we discuss in Chapter 26), short-term deviations from the long-run trend also have important consequences. For example, the period in which the great UK economist, John Maynard Keynes, first developed macroeconomics was a period (the 1930s) when the actual GDPs of the industrialized countries stayed below their potential levels for almost a decade, with the consequence of massive levels of unemployment. More recently, actual GDP has several times stayed above its potential level for several years during which periods major inflations ensued. As a result, much of macroeconomic theory is devoted to examining the causes and consequences of such deviations. Also as a result, much economic policy is aimed at preventing the onset of the major bouts of unemployment and inflation that are associated with deviations of actual GDP from its potential and in mitigating these consequences when they do occur.

So we are now going to build a model of how GDP is determined in relation to its potential level, which level we can now take as given. This model will help us to study the forces that determine how actual GDP and the price level are determined from year to year. We seek to answer questions such as 'Why are there sometimes booms in activity and slowdowns at other times?' 'What happens to GDP when government spending is increased?' and 'Under what conditions do we get inflation?'

In this chapter you will learn that:

- The macroeconomic theory that we now study explains the deviation of actual from potential GDP, that is, the GDP gap.

- The determination of GDP in the short run depends on the behaviour of key categories of aggregate spending: consumption, investment, government spending, and net exports.

- Consumption spending depends on disposable income and wealth.

- Investment spending depends on real interest rates and business confidence.

- A necessary condition for GDP to be in equilibrium is that desired domestic spending is equal to actual output.

We start by setting out some of the conceptual foundations of the short-term analysis of macroeconomic activity. We then build the simplest possible model of GDP determination, under some very special assumptions. Later chapters make our model increasingly realistic. Whenever in the next chapters we say that something will happen or is true, we are referring to the assumptions and the behaviour of the model (often called its *predictions*). Whether or not these things are true of the world in which we live cannot, of course, be decided without appealing to factual observa-

tions. We would not, however, ask you to learn all of this if we did not think that much of the model's behaviour did agree with the facts—and we illustrate how it does in many cases along the way. Some things, however, are still open to debate, either because one or more of the model's assumptions are questioned (e.g. the effect of changes in the price level on wealth) or because it is not certain that the model's behaviour fits the facts fully (e.g. how well the long-run properties of the model describe real behaviour over various actual time periods).

## The macro problem: inflation and unemployment

Actual economies do not expand slowly and steadily as the level of potential GDP grows. Instead, virtually all economies have some periods when actual GDP is growing faster than potential and other periods when it is growing more slowly than potential, or even falling. In other words, actual economies exhibit cycles about the trend growth path.

The growth rate of UK GDP since 1886 is shown in Figure 16.1 (and the GDP gap since 1970 is shown in Figure 15.1 on page 336). This make clear that, while growth is generally positive, year-to-year changes in

actual GDP are quite volatile. There are some periods of very strong positive growth and others where growth is negative. The terminology associated with such cycles in economic activity is set out in Box 16.1.

Periods of decline in actual GDP (or even periods where growth in actual GDP is below potential) are costly because they are associated with a loss of output that is gone for ever. This is what we have referred to above as a *deadweight loss*. Economic downturns do not typically lead to all citizens losing some equal amount of income: rather, they lead to some people losing their jobs (or their

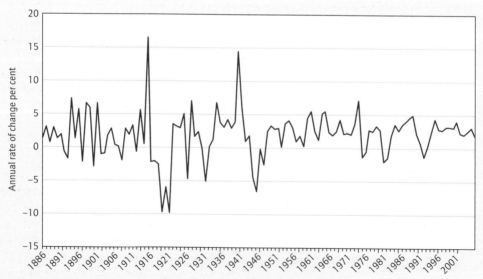

**Figure 16.1** UK real GDP growth, 1886–2005

**Actual growth in real GDP has displayed considerable volatility over time.**

*Source: 100 Years of Economic Statistics, The Economist, and UK National Accounts, ONS.*

**Box 16.1 The terminology of business cycles**

The pink line in the figure shows the hypothetical path of national output relative to trend, or potential, over time. Although the phases of business fluctuations are described by a series of commonly used terms, no two cycles are the same.

**Trough** A trough is characterized by high unemployment and a level of demand that is low in relation to the economy's capacity to produce. There is thus a substantial amount of unused productive capacity. Business profits are low; for some individual companies they are negative. Confidence about economic prospects in the immediate future is lacking, and as a result many firms are unwilling to risk making new investments.

**Recovery** The characteristics of a recovery, or expansion, are many—run-down equipment is replaced; employment, income, and consumer spending all begin to rise; and expectations become more favourable as a result of increases in production, sales, and profits. Investments that once seemed risky may be undertaken as the climate of business opinion starts to change from one of pessimism to one of optimism. As demand rises, production can be increased with relative ease merely by re-employing the existing unused capacity and unemployed labour.

**Peak** A peak is the top of a cycle. At the peak existing capacity is utilized to a high degree; labour shortages may develop, particularly in categories of key skills; and shortages of essential raw materials are likely. As shortages develop in more and more markets, a situation of general excess demand develops. Costs rise but, since prices also rise, business remains profitable.

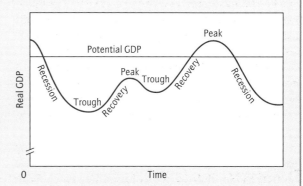

**Recession** A recession, or contraction, is a downturn in economic activity. Common usage defines a recession as a fall in real GDP for two quarters in succession. Demand falls off, and as a result production and employment also fall. As employment falls, so do personal incomes. Firms' profits drop, and some firms encounter financial difficulties. Investments that looked profitable with the expectation of continually rising demand now appear unprofitable. It may not even be worth replacing capital goods as they wear out, because unused capacity is increasing steadily. In historical discussions, a recession that is deep and long-lasting is often called a **depression**.

**Booms and slumps** Finally, two non-technical but descriptive terms are often used. The bottom of an abnormally deep recession is called a *slump*, and the top of an abnormally strong recovery is called a *boom*.

businesses) and thereby suffering a loss of income and well-being. Unemployment is therefore undesirable, and it is commonly agreed that policy-makers should aim to sustain unemployment at a low level. Indeed, macroeconomics as a subject was invented in order to explain why there was mass unemployment in the 1930s and to discover what could be done to eliminate it.

Another problem arises, however, when policy-makers try to make their economies grow too fast. This is especially so when governments try to encourage a growth of spending in the economy that is faster than the growth in productive capacity. The outcome of an excessive growth in demand relative to supply is inflation, and inflation itself is disruptive to the economy (for reasons that we discuss in Chapter 24).

Thus, the central problem for macroeconomic policy-makers is to decide how to manage the economy in such a way that inflation is kept under control while unemployment is also kept to a minimum.

This is not a trivial task, and many mistakes have been made in the past. Our job in the next several chapters is to understand how the macroeconomic system works in the short term and what policy-makers can do to keep the economy stable and close to potential output.

## Macroeconomics as theory

Our task is to understand what *causes* macroeconomic variables to behave as they do in the short term, and how they are interrelated. It is important to realize that we are about to discuss *theory*. In this process we will build up a conceptual model of the economy. This model will be simple. It needs to be simple so that we can understand how it works. This branch of macroeconomics has been around for well over half a century. It has developed and changed a great deal in this time. It is going to take several chapters before we get close to understanding contemporary macroeconomics. Hence readers should be patient and not rush to draw policy conclusions too soon.[1]

In what follows we start from a very simple structure and then add more features to it as we go along. Some clearly stated *assumptions* will define our macroeconomic model. Some of these assumptions will be relaxed as we go along, while others will remain throughout. The permanent or temporary nature of individual assumptions will be indicated as they are introduced.

# Key assumptions

In Chapter 15 we learned that 'national income' and 'national output' are the same thing, and can be measured by 'GDP'. From now on we will use these three terms equivalently. However, we refer to national income most frequently when discussing the determinants of domestic spending, as incomes are one of the most important determinants of consumers' spending. We refer to national output, or GDP, more commonly when discussing the responses of producers to changes in spending. Remember, though, that the actual values of these three concepts are identical.[2]

We also saw in Chapter 15 that we could arrive at a measure of GDP by three different routes. We could add up incomes of owners of resource inputs, we could add up the values added of each industrial sector, or we could add up total final spending. Now that we want to *explain* GDP determination rather than just describe it, we have to decide which of these three classifications we are going to rely on to structure our theories. We will learn very shortly that macroeconomics, as a subject, has developed by attempting to explain the major categories of final spending in the economy. We need to understand why this approach was adopted.

Suppose that we were to start our theory of GDP by trying to explain the net output (value added) of each major industrial sector—manufacturing, agriculture, etc. —as listed in Table 15.1. We could establish the capital stock and employment in each sector, and we could analyse demand forces for the output of each sector. In essence, we would be building a theory around demand and supply forces in each industry in the economy and then adding up the results to get total output.

One reason we do not do this in macroeconomics is that such an approach would not really be dealing with the aggregate economy at all. Models do exist in economics that explain output industry by industry, but such microeconomic models require so much detail that they make it difficult to handle many important issues that affect the whole economy simultaneously.

A second reason why we do not apply the tools of demand and supply on an industry-by-industry basis in macroeconomics is that those tools are not appropriate for handling the most important macro problems. In particular, macroeconomics seeks to explain why an economy might have unemployment and excess capacity for some time. In contrast, the microeconomic analysis of markets suggests that prices will move to clear markets. Macroeconomists also want to be able to study simultaneous (or near simultaneous) movements in output that are common to all sectors—the business cycle. An important question in macroeconomics is 'What causes the cycle in GDP, and can government policy stabilize it, i.e. smooth out the cycles?'

## Aggregation across industries

In macroeconomics we take the industrial structure of the economy as fixed. When national output expands or contracts, all sectors are assumed to expand and contract together. No consideration is given to relative prices of different goods or services. In this respect the economy of our model is best thought of as being made up of many competitive firms, all producing the same type of product.

---

[1] It also important to note that the approach we develop below sets out how macroeconomic analysis has traditionally been approached, but students who go on to study economics at a more advanced level will come across a different approach. The traditional approach assumes that there can be disequilibria in the economy, such as unemployment and output gaps, and tries to explain these in terms of aggregate spending flows compared with some hypothetical potential level of production. The newer, but not necessarily better, approach builds models of the economy in which all agents, e.g. consumers and firms, are continuously optimizing their behaviour and all markets are clearing continuously, so there are no disequilibria even in the short term. These models are useful for some purposes, but they are technically more demanding in that they require advanced mathematics, so they will not be discussed here. But students who go further in economics should be alert to a change in approach at some stage, even though courses that adopt this approach may still be called macroeconomics.

[2] As we have seen, there is a small difference between GDP and GNI; however, we are now assuming that this difference can be ignored. Recall also that GNI used to be called GNP, but GNI became standard in the UK National Accounts in 1998. You will no doubt see references to GNP in the economics literature for many years to come.

These firms are all aggregated into a single productive sector. It is the behaviour of this sector that will determine national output and national income.

In elementary macroeconomics, we assume the existence of a single productive sector producing a homogeneous output.

This assumption will remain throughout our study of macroeconomics. We will also analyse the behaviour of this single sector as if it were a manufacturing industry, though this is only a matter of convenience.

The fact that we assume a single production sector explains why we approach the determination of GDP by focusing on spending categories: there are no subdivisions of output by type of product. However, an important implication for final spending is that *in our model* it is all spent on the same final good—the product of 'United Kingdom plc'. This means that, while different categories of spending may be differently motivated, once implemented, they all have the same effect.

From time to time we use concrete examples, such as 'suppose the government increases spending on road building' or 'suppose firms decide to buy more machines (invest)'. The point to bear in mind is that all spending in the model has the same effect once it is made, because it is assumed to be demand for the output of the single-product, industrial sector.

### The government sector

Confusion can arise out of the assumption of a single sector when we come to discuss the role of government. In reality, part of government activity involves producing goods and services, such as health and education. However, in order to maintain the simplicity of the assumption that there is only one sector, in macroeconomics we ignore the fact that government is a producer and treat government as a purchaser of the output of the private industrial sector. In other words, we make no exceptions to our assumption about the homogeneity of productive activity. Such exceptions can be accommodated, but we do not do so in this book.

### Justification

The extreme assumption that there is only one output is of course not meant as a description of reality. It is a theoretical abstraction, meant to simplify our study without losing the essence of the problem in which we are interested. In this case the one-product model captures the assumption that, for what we are interested in, the similarities between the effects of £1 spent in each sector of the real-world economy are more important than the differences. Note that it is only similarities with respect

to the effects of spending that are in question. Causes of spending are not assumed to be the same. Indeed, much of our effort is directed to developing consumption, investment, and net export functions that explain the *different* motives that determine the various spending flows.

## Time-scale

The part of macroeconomics that we are about to study has traditionally been concerned with the short-run behaviour of an economy, while growth theory has been concerned with long-run trends. It is important to note, however, that the concepts of 'short run' and 'long run' have a different meaning in macroeconomics from the usage in microeconomics. Indeed, 'long run' itself is used in two different senses even within macroeconomics.

### Short run

In microeconomics 'short run' is used to analyse the behaviour of firms during the period in which their capital stock is taken as given and they can change only their variable inputs (labour and materials). In other words, the short run is a period during which the capital stock is fixed; none the less, firms are in short-run equilibrium because they are producing their optimal output given their capital stock. In macroeconomics, the short run is the period during which the economy maintains a deviation of actual from potential output, or a GDP gap. This deviation is associated either with the existence of excess capacity and unemployment, in the case of recession, or with unsustainable output and inflation, in the case of a boom. In practice, the short run may be measured in terms of several years, so it is not really short in the common-sense meaning of the term.

In its early days as a discipline, macroeconomics concentrated entirely on the short run as we have just defined it. Recent developments, however, have increasingly emphasized longer-run considerations.

Analysis of the short run in macroeconomics is concerned with explaining why national output can deviate from its potential level. It is about the GDP gap and how to keep both positive and negative gaps as small as possible—that is, how to keep actual GDP as close as possible to potential GDP.

### Long run

The long run is a period sufficient to allow time for the automatic adjustment mechanisms (discussed below) to return economic activity to equilibrium after it has been disturbed by an exogenous shock. This equilibrium is reached when the economy returns to producing the level of potential (or full-employment) output. For analytical purposes we will assume that the long-run level of output is constant and is associated with a fixed capital stock and a fixed level of technical knowledge. This contrasts markedly with the usage of 'long run' in microeconomics, where it relates to a period within which the capital stock can vary. Even in macroeconomics there is really a 'long run' and a 'longer run', the latter of which permits growth in productive capacity and, therefore, growth in potential output. For the most part we use the static concept of long run, unless we are explicitly discussing growth, as in Chapter 26.

The long run in macroeconomics is the period it takes the economy to return to the level of potential GDP once it has been disturbed.

## Temporary assumptions

In order to get us started in building a theory of macroeconomics, we need to make a few additional assumptions, but these will be relaxed in succeeding chapters.

### The price level

At the outset we will assume that the price level, that is, the money price of the economy's single output good, is fixed. All input prices are also fixed. Permitting the price level to vary simultaneously with output will be the main task addressed in Chapters 18 and 19. While the price level is held constant, all variables must necessarily be measured in real terms. But it is important to notice for the future that all spending (consumption, investment, government spending, and net exports) will continue to be defined in real terms even when the price level is permitted to vary.

### Excess capacity

Initially we will assume that the economy has excess capacity so that it is not constrained from producing more output by shortages of capital stock or labour. We start with the twin assumptions of a fixed price level and excess capacity, because it is easiest to begin in an environment where all changes in GDP are changes in real GDP. Explaining how changes in money GDP are divided between changes in the price level and changes in real GDP requires a more complicated model, which we come to in Chapter 18.

### Closed economy

In this chapter alone we will ignore the possibility that the output of our economy can be sold overseas and that domestic consumers can buy foreign-produced goods. We assume an economy with no foreign trade, so domestic spending and domestic output are equal. This is not an assumption we will need for very long. It will be dropped in the next chapter.

### No government

Government enters into macroeconomics in two ways: first, through decisions relating to taxation and spending, and second, through the setting of interest rates. A final simplifying assumption in this chapter is that there is no government sector either demanding goods (spending) or raising money through taxes. Again, we will drop this assumption in the next chapter.

Interest rates are one of the most important tools by which modern governments seek to control the macroeconomy. Interest rates have their main impact via influencing various categories of private spending and asset prices. In this and subsequent chapters we point out the impact that interest rate changes have on private spending. In Chapter 21 we provide a comprehensive analysis of the transmission mechanism of monetary policy, that is, of how changes in interest rates affect the GDP gap and inflation.

It is worth summarizing all these assumptions. We have a closed economy with a single industrial sector, producing a homogeneous output, at a fixed price, with no government. There is also excess capacity, so there are no resource constraints preventing the expansion of national output. By now readers may be wondering what is left after we have assumed away so many potentially important things. The answer is: final demand or spending on the output of the economy. Explaining final spending will enable us to understand what determines the national product and national income, that is, GDP.

In terms of the circular flow model introduced in Chapter 15, this, our simplest, model contains a flow of income from households to firms as spending and from firms to household as incomes (factor payments), when there is only one withdrawal or leakage—household savings—and one injection—investment spending. Later we will add the flows associated with the government and foreign trade.

There is a good reason for starting with an explanation of spending. We believe that variations in spending are the most important causes of variations in the gap between potential and actual income that we are seeking to explain.

# What determines aggregate spending?

Before we can answer this question, we must deal with a few more important preliminaries.

## Some important preliminaries

### From actual to desired spending

In Chapter 15 we discussed how statisticians divide actual GDP, calculated from the spending side, into its components: private consumption, investment, government consumption, and net exports.

In this chapter and the next we are concerned with a different concept. It is variously called *desired*, *planned*, or *intended* spending. Of course, all people would like to spend virtually unlimited amounts, if they had the resources. Desired spending does not refer, however, to what people would like to do under imaginary circumstances: it refers to what people want to spend out of the resources that are at their command. The *actual* values of the various categories of spending are indicated by $C^a$, $I^a$, $G^a$, and $(X^a - IM^a)$. We use the same letters without the superscript 'a' to indicate the *desired* spending in the same categories: $C$, $I$, $G$, and $(X - IM)$.

Everyone with income to spend makes spending decisions. Fortunately it is unnecessary for our purposes to look at each of the millions of such individual decisions. Instead, it is sufficient to consider four main groups of decision-makers: individual consumers (or households), firms, governments, and foreign purchasers of domestic output. The actual purchases made by these four groups account for the four main categories of spending that we studied in the previous chapter: private consumption, investment, government consumption, and net exports. These groups' desired spending—desired private consumption, desired investment, desired government consumption, and desired exports—account for total desired spending. (To allow for the fact that many of the commodities desired by each group have an import content, we subtract spending on imports to arrive at the value of spending on domestic output.) The result is total desired spending on domestically produced goods and services; this is called **aggregate spending**, or $AE$:[3]

$$AE = C + I + G + (X - IM).$$

Desired spending need not equal actual spending, either in total or in any individual category. For example, firms may not plan to invest in the accumulation of unsold stock this year but may do so unintentionally. If they produce goods to meet estimated sales but demand is unexpectedly low, the unsold goods that pile up on their shelves are undesired, and unintended, inventory accumulation. In this case actual investment spending, $I^a$, exceeds desired investment spending, $I$.

The National Accounts measure actual spending in each of the four categories: private consumption, investment, government consumption, and net exports. The theory of GDP determination deals with desired spending in each of these four categories.

Recall, however, that these spending categories differ because different agents are doing the spending and have different motivations for that spending. They are not different in the effects of their spending, because they all generate spending on the final output of the single productive sector.

### Autonomous and induced spending

In what follows it will be useful to distinguish between *autonomous* and *induced* spending. Components of aggregate spending that *do not* depend on current domestic incomes are called **autonomous**, or sometimes *exogenous*.[4] Autonomous spending can and does change, but such changes do not occur systematically in response to changes in income. Components of aggregate spending that *do* change in response to changes in income are called **induced**, or *endogenous*. As we will see, the induced response of aggregate spending to a change in income plays a key role in the determination of equilibrium GDP.

### A simple model

To develop a theory of GDP determination, we need to examine the determinants of each component of desired aggregate spending. In this chapter we focus on desired consumption and desired investment. Private consumption is the largest single component of aggregate spending (about 65 per cent of UK GDP in 2005), and as we will see it provides the single most important link between desired aggregate spending and actual GDP. Investment

---

[3] We use *AE*, which is short for 'aggregate *expenditure*', as we reserve *AS* to refer to 'aggregate supply'.

[4] 'Autonomous' means self-motivated, or independent. 'Exogenous' means determined outside the model.

is national output that is not used either for current consumption or by governments, and it is motivated by firms' desire to increase the capital stock.[5]

## Desired private consumption spending

We are now ready to study the determinants of desired spending flows. We start with private consumption.

People can do one of two things with their disposable income: spend it on consumption or save it. **Saving** is all disposable income that is not consumed.

By definition, there are only two possible uses of disposable income: consumption and saving. So when each individual decides how much to put to one use, she has automatically decided how much to put to the other use.

What determines the division between the amount that people decide to spend on goods and services for consumption and the amount that they decide to save? The factors that influence this decision are summarized in the consumption function and the saving function.

### The consumption function

The **consumption function** relates the total desired consumer spending of the personal sector to the variables that affect it. It is one of the central relationships in macroeconomics.

Although ultimately we are interested in the relationship between consumption and *national* income (GDP), the underlying behaviour of consumers depends on the income that they actually have to spend—their disposable income. Under the simplifying assumptions that we have made in this chapter, there are no taxes. Individuals receive all income that is generated.[6] Therefore, disposable income, which we denote by $Y_d$, is equal to national income, $Y$. (Later in our discussion $Y$ and $Y_d$ will diverge, because taxes are a part of national income that is not at the disposal of individuals.)

### Consumption and disposable income

It should not surprise us to hear that a consumer's spending is related to the amount of income available. There is, however, more than one way in which this relationship could work. To see what is involved, consider two quite different types of individual.

The first type behaves like the proverbial prodigal son. He spends everything he receives and puts nothing aside for a rainy day. When overtime results in a large pay cheque, he goes on a binge. When it is hard to find work during periods of slack demand, his pay cheque is small and spending has to be cut correspondingly. This person's spending each week is thus directly linked to each week's take-home pay, that is, to his current disposable income.

The second individual is a prudent planner. She thinks about the future as much as the present, and makes plans that stretch over her lifetime. She puts money aside for retirement and for the occasional rainy day when disposable income may fall temporarily—she knows that she must expect some hard times as well as good times. She also knows that she will need to spend extra money when her children are being raised and educated and that her disposable income will probably be highest later in life when the children have left home and she has finally reached the peak of her career. This person may borrow to meet higher expenses earlier in life, paying back out of the higher income that she expects to attain later in life. A temporary, unexpected windfall of income may be saved. Spending the savings that were put aside for just such a rainy day may cushion a temporary, unexpected shortfall. In short, this person's current spending will be closely related to her expected average *lifetime income*. Fluctuations in her *current income* will have little effect on her current spending, unless such fluctuations also cause her to change her expectations of lifetime income—as would be the case, for example, if an unexpected promotion came along.

John Maynard Keynes (1883–1946), the famous English economist who developed the basic theory of macroeconomics—and gave his name to 'Keynesian economics' —populated his theory with prodigal sons. For them current consumption spending depended only on current income. To this day, a consumption function based on this assumption is called a *Keynesian consumption function*.

Later two US economists, Franco Modigliani and Milton Friedman, both of whom were subsequently awarded the Nobel Prize in economics, analysed the behaviour of prudent consumers who take a longer-term view in determining their consumption. Their theories, which Modigliani called the *life-cycle theory* and which Friedman called *the permanent-income theory*, explain some observed consumer behaviour that cannot be explained by the Keynesian consumption function. Most modern approaches to private consumption behaviour are based on the life-cycle or permanent-income approaches, in which rational consumers plan their consumption over a broad time-horizon, and may even build in plans to leave money

---

[5] In practice government and consumers do some of the nation's investment, but we focus mainly on the investment behaviour of firms for simplicity. The principles involved can be generalized.

[6] We are assuming here that all firms pass on all their profits to the people who own them, so there is no retained profit.

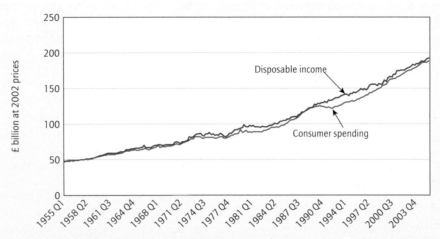

**Figure 16.2** Consumers' spending and personal disposable income, UK, 1955–2005 (£ billion at constant 2002 prices, quarterly data seasonally adjusted)

Consumer spending and income are closely related over time.

*Source:* ONS.

to their children (thereby planning consumption *beyond* their own lifetimes).

However, the differences between the modern theories and the Keynesian consumption function are not as great as they might seem at first sight. To see why this is so, let us return to our two imaginary individuals and see why their actual behaviour may not be quite so divergent as we have described it.

Even the prodigal son may be able to do some smoothing of spending in the face of income fluctuations. Most people have some money in the bank and some ability to borrow, even if it is just from friends and relatives. As a result, not every income fluctuation will be matched by an equivalent spending fluctuation.

In contrast, although the prudent person wants to smooth her pattern of consumption completely, she may not have the borrowing capacity to do so. Her bank may not be willing to lend money for consumption when the security consists of nothing more than the expectation that income will be much higher in later years. This may mean that in practice her consumption spending fluctuates more with her current income than she would wish.

This suggests that the consumption spending of both types of individual will fluctuate to some extent with their current disposable incomes and to some extent with their expectations of future disposable income. Moreover, in any economy there will be some people of both extremes, spendthrifts and planners, and a mix of the two types will determine aggregate consumption. As we develop

our basic theory, we will often find it useful to make the simplifying assumption that consumption spending is determined primarily by current disposable income. That is, we will often use a Keynesian consumption function and then indicate how things change if we consider more sophisticated theories of consumer spending. Figure 16.2 shows quarterly real personal disposable income and real consumers' spending in the UK from 1955 to 2005. It is clear that the two series are closely related.

The term 'consumption function' describes the relationship between private consumption and the variables that influence it. In the simplest theory, consumption spending is determined primarily by current personal disposable income.

When income is zero, a typical individual will still (via borrowing, or drawing down savings) consume some minimal amount.[7] This level of consumption spending is *autonomous* because it persists even when there is no income. The higher a person's income, the more he or she will want to consume. This part of consumption is *induced*; that is, it varies with disposable income and hence, in our simple model, with national income (GDP).

---

[7] Many individuals have no income but continue to consume, for example dependent children or non-working partners. In this case there is normally at least one earner in a household and it is the household income that is relevant. The household is the decision unit in that context. Such distinctions are important if we want to study the behaviour of individual spending units, but they are not critical in macroeconomics, which studies the aggregate behaviour of all consumers and relates their total spending to their total income.

**Table 16.1** The calculation of average and marginal propensity to consume (*APC* and *MPC*) (£ million)

| Disposable income ($Y_d$) (1) | Desired consumption ($C$) (2) | $APC = C/Y_d$ (3) | Change in $Y_d$ ($\Delta Y_d$) (4) | Change in $C$ ($\Delta C$) (5) | $MPC = \Delta C/\Delta Y_d$ (6) |
|---|---|---|---|---|---|
| 0 | 100 | — | | | |
| 100 | 180 | 1.800 | 100 | 80 | 0.80 |
| 400 | 420 | 1.050 | 300 | 240 | 0.80 |
| 500 | 500 | 1.000 | 100 | 80 | 0.80 |
| 1,000 | 900 | 0.900 | 500 | 400 | 0.80 |
| 1,500 | 1,300 | 0.867 | 500 | 400 | 0.80 |
| 1,750 | 1,500 | 0.857 | 250 | 200 | 0.80 |
| 2,000 | 1,700 | 0.850 | 250 | 200 | 0.80 |
| 3,000 | 2,500 | 0.833 | 1,000 | 800 | 0.80 |

*APC* measures the proportion of disposable income that households desire to spend on consumption; *MPC* measures the proportion of any increment to disposable income that households desire to spend on consumption. The data are hypothetical. We call the level of income at which desired consumption equals disposable income the break-even level; in this example it is £500 million. *APC*, calculated in the third column, exceeds unity—that is, consumption exceeds income—below the break-even level; above the break-even level *APC* is less than unity. It is negatively related to income at all levels of income. The last three columns are set between the lines of the first three columns to indicate that they refer to *changes* in the levels of income and consumption. *MPC*, calculated in the last column, is constant at 0.80 at all levels of $Y_d$. This indicates that, in this example, £0.80 of every additional £1.00 of disposable income is spent on consumption, and £0.20 is saved.

Consider the schedule relating personal disposable income to desired private consumption spending for a hypothetical economy that appears in columns (1) and (2) of Table 16.1. In this example autonomous consumption spending is £100 million, whereas induced consumption spending is 80 per cent of disposable income. In what follows we use this hypothetical example to illustrate the various properties of the consumption function.

## Average and marginal propensities to consume

To discuss the consumption function concisely, economists use two technical expressions.

The **average propensity to consume** (*APC*) is total consumption spending divided by total disposable income: $APC = C/Y_d$. Column (3) of Table 16.1 shows the *APC* calculated from the data in the table. Note that *APC* falls as disposable income rises.

The **marginal propensity to consume** (*MPC*) relates the *change* in consumption to the *change* in disposable income that brought it about. *MPC* is the change in disposable income divided into the resulting consumption change: $MPC = \Delta C/\Delta Y_d$ (where the capital Greek letter delta, $\Delta$, means 'a change in'). Column (6) of Table 16.1 shows the *MPC* that corresponds to the data in the table. Note that, by construction, *MPC* is constant.

## The slope of the consumption function

Part (i) of Figure 16.3 shows a graph of the consumption function, derived by plotting consumption against income using data from columns (1) and (2) of Table 16.1. The consumption function has a slope of $\Delta C/\Delta Y_d$, which is by definition the marginal propensity to consume. The positive slope of the consumption function shows that the *MPC* is positive; increases in income lead to increases in spending.

Using the concepts of the average and marginal propensities to consume, we can summarize the assumed properties of the short-term consumption function as follows.

1. There is a break-even level of income at which *APC* equals unity. Below this level *APC* is greater than unity; above it *APC* is less than unity. Below the break-even level consumption exceeds income, so consumers run down savings or borrow. Above the break-even level income exceeds consumption, so there is positive saving.

2. *MPC* is greater than zero, but less than unity, for all levels of income. This means that for each additional £1 of income, less than £1 is spent on consumption and the rest is saved. For a straight-line consumption function, the *MPC* is constant at all levels of income.

## The 45° line

Figure 16.3(i) contains a line that is constructed by connecting all points at which desired consumption (measured on the vertical axis) equals disposable income (measured on the horizontal axis). Because both axes are

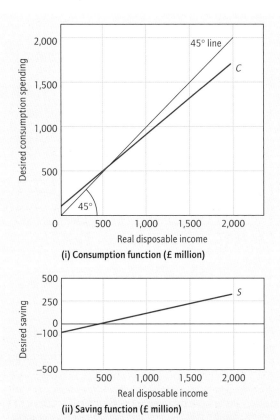

**(i) Consumption function (£ million)**

**(ii) Saving function (£ million)**

**Figure 16.3 The consumption and saving functions**

**Both consumption and saving rise as disposable income rises.** Line *C* in part (i) relates desired consumption spending to disposable income by using the hypothetical data from Table 16.1. Its slope, $\Delta C/\Delta Y_d$, is the marginal propensity to consume (*MPC*). The consumption line cuts the 45° line at the break-even level of disposable income, £500 million in this case. Note that the level of autonomous consumption is £100 million.

Saving is all disposable income that is not spent on consumption ($S = Y_d - C$). The relationship between desired saving and disposable income is derived in Table 16.2, and it is shown in part (ii) by line *S*. Its slope, $\Delta S/\Delta Y_d$, is the marginal propensity to save (*MPS*). The saving line cuts the horizontal axis at the break-even level of income. The vertical distance between *C* and the 45° line in part (i) is by definition the height of *S* in part (ii); that is, any given level of disposable income must be accounted for by the amount consumed plus the amount saved. Note that the level of autonomous saving is −£100 million. This means that at zero income consumers will draw down existing assets by £100 million a year or borrow this amount.

given in the same units, this line has a positive slope of unity; that is, it forms an angle of 45° with the axes. The line is therefore called the **45° line**.

The 45° line is a handy reference line. In part (i) of Figure 16.3 it helps to locate the break-even level of income at which consumption spending equals disposable income. The consumption function cuts the 45° line at the break-even level of income, in this instance £500 million. (The consumption function is flatter than the 45° line because *MPC* is less than unity.)

## The saving function

Individuals decide how much to consume and how much to save. As we have said, this is a single decision: how to divide disposable income between consumption and saving. It follows that, once we know the dependence of consumption on disposable income, we also automatically know the dependence of saving on disposable income. (This is illustrated in Table 16.2.)

There are two saving concepts that are exactly parallel to the consumption concepts of *APC* and *MPC*. The **average propensity to save** (*APS*) is the proportion of disposable income that households want to save, derived by dividing total desired saving by total disposable income: $APS = S/Y_d$. The **marginal propensity to save** (*MPS*) relates the *change* in total desired saving to the *change* in disposable income that brought it about: $MPS = \Delta S/\Delta Y_d$.

**Table 16.2 Consumption and saving schedules (£ million)**

| Disposable income | Desired consumption | Desired saving |
|---|---|---|
| 0 | 100 | −100 |
| 100 | 180 | −80 |
| 400 | 420 | −20 |
| 500 | 500 | 0 |
| 1,000 | 900 | +100 |
| 1,500 | 1,300 | +200 |
| 1,750 | 1,500 | +250 |
| 2,000 | 1,700 | +300 |
| 3,000 | 2,500 | +500 |
| 4,000 | 3,300 | +700 |

**Saving and consumption account for all household disposable income.** The first two columns repeat the data from Table 16.1. The third column, desired saving, is disposable income minus desired consumption. Consumption and saving both increase steadily as disposable income rises. In this example the break-even level of income is £500 million. At this level all income is consumed.

There is a simple relationship between the saving and consumption propensities. *APC* and *APS* must sum to unity, and so must *MPC* and *MPS*. Because income is either spent or saved, it follows that the fractions of incomes consumed and saved must account for all income (*APC* + *APS* = 1). It also follows that the fractions of any increment to income consumed and saved must account for all of that increment (*MPC* + *MPS* = 1). Calculations from Table 16.2 will allow you to confirm these relationships in the case of the example given. *MPC* is 0.80 and *MPS* is 0.20 at all levels of income, while, for example, at an income of £2,000 million *APC* is 0.85 and *APS* is 0.15.

Figure 16.3(ii) shows the saving schedule given in Table 16.2. At the break-even level of income, where desired consumption equals disposable income, desired saving is zero. The slope of the saving line $\Delta S/\Delta Y_d$ is equal to the *MPS*.

## Wealth and the consumption function

The Keynesian consumption function that we have been analysing can easily be combined with the permanent-income or life-cycle theories of consumption. According to these theories, households save in order to accumulate wealth to use during their retirement (or to pass on to their heirs[8]). Suppose that there is an unexpected rise in wealth. This will mean that less of current disposable income needs to be saved for the future, and will tend to cause a larger fraction of disposable income to be spent on consumption and a smaller fraction to be saved. Thus, the consumption function will be shifted upward and the saving function downward, as shown in Figure 16.4. A fall in wealth increases the incentive to save in order to restore wealth. This shifts the consumption function downward and the saving function upward.

## The interest rate and consumer spending

Higher interest rates will generally lead to lower consumer spending. Higher interest rates encourage saving, as the rewards for saving are increased. Higher interest rates also discourage borrowing, as the cost of credit rises. Many households have purchased houses with money borrowed in the form of a mortgage. Most mortgages in the UK have a variable interest rate so that monthly mortgage payments will increase as interest rates increase. Higher mortgage payments leave less out of any given income for spending on current consumption. Higher interest rates also tend to lead to lower asset values (for reasons we discuss in

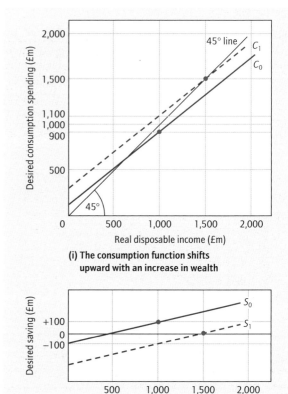

**(i) The consumption function shifts upward with an increase in wealth**

**(ii) The saving function shifts downward**

**Figure 16.4 Wealth and the consumption function**

**Changes in wealth shift the consumption function.** In part (i) line $C_0$ reproduces the consumption function from Figure 16.3(i). An increase in the level of wealth raises desired consumption at each level of disposable income, thereby shifting the consumption line up to $C_1$. In the figure the consumption function shifts up by £200 million; so with disposable income of £1,000 million, for example, desired consumption rises from £900 million to £1,100 million. As a result of the rise in wealth, the break-even level of income rises to £1,500 million.

The saving function in part (ii) shifts down by £200 million from $S_0$ to $S_1$. Thus, for example, at a disposable income of £1,000 million, saving *falls* from +£100 million to −£100 million.

Chapter 21), and this then generates a fall in wealth which lowers consumption as discussed above.

When we fully incorporate interest rates into our model in Chapter 21, we will have the main impact running from interest rates to investment. But it is also consistent with our analysis to think of higher interest rates lowering autonomous consumption.[9]

---

[8] Empirical evidence suggests that there is a significant 'bequest motive' for saving. This means that some individuals plan even further ahead than their own lifetime, because they want to leave money to their children.

[9] UK monetary policy-makers' own perception of how monetary policy works also includes an effect of interest rates working on consumer spending (see http://www.bankofengland.co.uk/publications/other/monetary/montrans.pdf).

# Desired investment spending

Investment spending is the most volatile component of GDP, and changes in investment spending are strongly associated with economic fluctuations. For example, the Great Depression witnessed a major fall in investment. Total investment fell by nearly a quarter between 1929 and 1932. A little less dramatically, at the trough of the UK recession of the early 1990s (in 1992), investment spending was 13 per cent less than the level two years earlier.

## Investment and the real interest rate

Other things being equal, the higher the real interest rate,[10] the higher is the cost of borrowing money for investment purposes and the less is the amount of desired investment spending. This relationship is most easily understood if we disaggregate investment into three parts: inventory accumulation, residential house building, and business fixed capital formation.[11]

### Inventory accumulation

Changes in inventories of finished goods, work in progress, or raw materials represent only a small percentage of private investment in a typical year, but their average size is not an adequate measure of their importance. They are one of the more volatile elements of total investment and therefore have a major influence on shifts in investment spending.

When a firm ties up funds by holding bigger inventories of inputs or outputs, those same funds cannot be used elsewhere to earn income. As an alternative to investing in inventories, the firm could lend the money out at the going rate of interest. Thus, the higher the rate of interest, the higher will be the opportunity cost of holding inventories of a given size; and the higher that opportunity cost, the smaller will be the inventories that will be desired.

The higher the real rate of interest, the lower is the desired inventory of goods and materials. Changes in the rate of interest cause temporary bouts of investment (or disinvestment) as inventories are either increased or decreased.

### Residential housing construction

Spending on new houses is both large and volatile and so exerts a major impact on the economy. Notice that what matters for investment is the demand for new housing. House purchases that involve the exchange of ownership of an existing house do not affect the demand for currently produced output and are, therefore, not relevant to determining current GDP.

Most houses are purchased with money that is borrowed by means of a mortgage. Interest on the borrowed money typically accounts for over half of the purchaser's mortgage payments over the life time of the loan; the rest is repayment of the original loan, called the *principal*. Because interest payments are so large a part of mortgage payments, variations in interest rates exert a substantial effect on the demand for housing. During the mid-1980s, UK interest rates fell sharply and there was a boom in the demand for housing; that boom persisted until late 1988, when interest rates started to rise again; the demand to purchase houses then dropped sharply and house prices fell. The lower interest rates that arrived in 1992 and 1993 caused the beginning of a recovery in the housing market; however, this recovery was very slow and house prices did not pick up until the second half of the 1990s. In the 2000–4 period, however, interest rates again fell to low levels and a further house price boom ensued. Higher interest rates in 2005 were associated with a slowing of house price inflation.

Spending for residential construction tends to vary negatively with interest rates.

### Business fixed capital formation

Investment by firms in fixed capital (factories, offices, and machines) is the largest component of domestic investment. Over one-half is financed by firms' retained profits (profits that are not paid out to their shareholders). This means that current profits are an important determinant of investment.

The rate of interest is thus a major determinant of investment in fixed capital. In the United Kingdom, both during the early 1980s and in 1989–92, high interest rates greatly reduced the volume of investment, as more and more firms found that their expected profits from investment did not cover the interest on borrowed investment funds. Other firms that had cash on hand found that purchasing interest-earning assets provided a better return than investment in factories and machinery. For them the increase in real interest rates meant that the opportunity cost of investing in fixed capital had risen.

---

[10] The *real* rate of interest is approximately equal to the nominal (money) rate of interest *minus* the expected rate of inflation. This important distinction was discussed in Chapter 12.

[11] These represent different motives for investment, and in practice would create demand for different kinds of goods. However, recall that they will all end up creating demand for the output of the single production sector. Thus, in our model, the impact of £1 worth of inventory accumulation is the same as £1 worth of fixed capital formation and, indeed, of £1 worth of consumption. The reason we distinguish investment from consumption is that it is affected by different factors, the most important of which is the interest rate. Note also that house building is part of gross fixed capital formation in the National Accounts. We ignore here the net acquisition of valuables, as this is very small.

## Expectations and business confidence

Investment takes time. When a firm invests, it increases its future capacity to produce output. If the new output can be sold profitably, the investment will prove to be a good one. If the new output does not generate profits, the investment will be a bad one. When the investment is undertaken, the firm does not know if it will turn out well or badly—it is betting on a favourable future which cannot be known with certainty.

When firms expect good times ahead they will want to invest so as to reap future profits. When they expect bad times they will not invest, because, given their expectations, there will be no payoff from doing so. For future reference, it is worth noting that one of the influences on firms' expectations and confidence will be the actions and credibility of the government and monetary policy-makers.

Business investment depends in part on firms' forecasts of the future state of the economy.

## Investment as autonomous spending

We have seen that many things influence investment. For the moment we treat investment as exogenous, meaning that it is not influenced by changes in GDP. But obviously, the policy-determined rate of interest is one of the things that could make investment change. The treatment of investment as exogenous allows us to study, first, how GDP is determined when there is an unchanged amount of desired investment spending and, second, how alterations in the amount of desired investment cause changes in equilibrium GDP.

# The aggregate spending function

The aggregate spending function relates the level of desired real spending to the level of real national income, that is, real GDP. Generally, total desired spending on the nation's output is the sum of desired private consumption, investment, government consumption, and net export spending. In the simplified economy of this chapter, aggregate spending is equal to $C + I$:

$$AE = C + I.$$

Table 16.3 shows how the $AE$ function is calculated, given the consumption function of Tables 16.1 and 16.2 and a constant level of desired investment of £250 million. In this specific case all of investment spending is autonomous, as is the £100 million of consumption that would be desired when national income is zero (see Table 16.1). Total autonomous spending is thus £350 million—induced

**Table 16.3** The aggregate spending function in a closed economy with no government (£ million)

| GDP (national income) (Y) | Desired consumption spending (C = 100 + 0.8Y) | Desired investment spending (I = 250) | Desired aggregate spending (AE = C + I) |
|---|---|---|---|
| 100 | 180 | 250 | 430 |
| 400 | 420 | 250 | 670 |
| 500 | 500 | 250 | 750 |
| 1,000 | 900 | 250 | 1,150 |
| 1,500 | 1,300 | 250 | 1,550 |
| 1,750 | 1,500 | 250 | 1,750 |
| 2,000 | 1,700 | 250 | 1,950 |
| 3,000 | 2,500 | 250 | 2,750 |
| 4,000 | 3,300 | 250 | 3,550 |

The aggregate spending function is the sum of desired consumption, investment, government, and net export spending. In this table government and net exports are assumed to be zero, investment is assumed to be constant at £250 million, and desired consumption is based on the hypothetical data given in Table 16.2. The autonomous components of desired aggregate spending are desired investment and the constant term in desired consumption spending (£100 million). The induced component is the second term in desired consumption spending 0.8Y.

The marginal response of consumption to a change in national income is 0.8, the marginal propensity to consume. The marginal response of desired aggregate spending to a change in national income, $\Delta AE / \Delta Y$, is also 0.8, because all induced spending in the economy is consumption spending.

spending is just equal to induced consumption, which is equal to 0.8Y. Thus, desired aggregate spending, whether thought of as $C + I$ or as autonomous plus induced spending, can be written as $AE = £350$ million $+ 0.8Y$. This aggregate spending function is illustrated in Figure 16.5.

## The propensity to spend out of national income

The fraction of any increment to national income (GDP) that will be spent on purchasing domestic output is called the economy's **marginal propensity to spend**. It is measured by the change in aggregate spending divided by the change in income, or $\Delta AE / \Delta Y$, the slope of the aggregate spending function. In this book we will denote the marginal propensity to spend by the symbol $c$, which will typically be a number greater than zero and less than one.

Similarly, the **marginal propensity not to spend** is the fraction of any increment to national income that does

**Figure 16.5** An aggregate spending function

The aggregate spending function relates total desired spending to national income. The *AE* line in the figure plots the data from the first and the last columns of Table 16.3, which are repeated in Table 16.4. Its intercept (which in this case is £350 million) shows autonomous spending, which in this case is the sum of autonomous consumption of £100 million and investment of £250 million. Its slope (which in this case is 0.8) shows the marginal propensity to spend.

not add to desired aggregate spending. This is denoted $(1 - c)$; if $c$ is the part of any £1 of incremental income that is spent, $(1 - c)$ is the part that is not spent.[12] In the example given in Table 16.3, $c$, the marginal propensity to spend, is 0.8. If national income increases by £1, then 80p will go into increased spending; 20 pence (£1 times 0.2, the value of $(1 - c)$) will go into increased saving and will not be spent.

The marginal propensity to spend, which we have just defined, should not be confused with the marginal propensity to consume, which we defined earlier in the chapter. The marginal propensity to spend is the amount of extra total spending induced when *national* income rises by £1, while the marginal propensity to consume is the amount of extra consumption spending induced when *personal disposable income* rises by £1. In the simple model of this chapter, the marginal propensity to spend is equal to the marginal propensity to consume, and the marginal propensity not to spend is equal to the marginal propensity to save. In later chapters, when we add government and the international sector, the marginal propensity to spend differs from the marginal propensity to consume. Both here and in later chapters, it is the more general measures $c$ and $(1 - c)$ that are important for determining equilibrium GDP.

# Equilibrium GDP

We are now ready to see what determines the *equilibrium* level of national income and output, that is, GDP. When something is in equilibrium, there is no tendency for it to change; forces are acting on it, but they balance out, and the net result is *no change*. Any conditions that are required for something to be in equilibrium are called *equilibrium conditions*. Here we determine the level of GDP that is consistent with spending decisions, and we will discover the full story about GDP determination only when we have added the supply behaviour of firms in Chapters 18 and 19. Thus, the conditions we analyse here are necessary for an equilibrium of GDP, but others will contribute to determine the total picture later.

Table 16.4 illustrates the determination of equilibrium GDP for our simple hypothetical economy. Suppose that firms are producing a final output of £1,000 million, and therefore GDP is £1,000 million. According to the table, at this level of national income aggregate desired spending is £1,150 million. If firms persist in producing a current output of only £1,000 million in the face of an

aggregate desired spending of £1,150 million, one of two things must happen.[13]

The first possibility is that consumers and investors will be unable to spend the extra £150 million that they would like to spend, so queues and unfulfilled order books will appear. These will send a signal to firms that they can increase their sales if they increase their production. When the firms increase production, GDP rises. Of course, the individual firms are interested only in their own sales and profits, but the inevitable consequence of their individual actions is an increase in GDP.

---

[12] More fully, these terms would be called the marginal propensity to spend *on the national product* and the marginal propensity not to spend *on the national product*. The marginal propensity not to spend, $(1 - c)$, is sometimes referred to as the *marginal propensity to withdraw*. Not spending some part of income amounts to a *withdrawal* or a *leakage* from the circular flow of income, as illustrated in Figure 15.2 on page 340.

[13] A third possibility—that prices could rise—is ruled out by assumption in this chapter.

**Table 16.4** The determination of equilibrium GDP (£ million)

| GDP (national income) (Y) | Desired aggregate spending (AE = C + I) | |
|---|---|---|
| 100 | 430 | |
| 400 | 670 | |
| 500 | 750 | Pressure on Y |
| 1,000 | 1,150 | to rise |
| 1,500 | 1,550 | ↓ |
| **1,750** | **1,750** | Equilibrium Y |
| 2,000 | 1,950 | ↑ |
| 3,000 | 2,750 | Pressure on Y |
| 4,000 | 3,550 | to fall |

**GDP is in equilibrium where aggregate desired spending equals national output.** The data are copied from Table 16.3. When GDP is below its equilibrium level, aggregate desired spending exceeds the value of current output. This creates an incentive for firms to increase output and hence for GDP to rise. When GDP is above its equilibrium level, aggregate desired spending is less than the value of current output. This creates an incentive for firms to reduce output and hence for GDP to fall. Only at the equilibrium level of GDP is aggregate desired spending equal to the value of current output.

The second possibility is that consumers and investors will spend everything that they want to spend. Then, however, spending will exceed current output, which can happen only when some spending plans are fulfilled by purchasing stocks of goods that were produced in the past. In our example, the fulfilment of plans to purchase £1,150 million worth of commodities in the face of a current output of only £1,000 million will reduce inventories by £150 million. As long as stocks last, more goods can be sold than are currently being produced.[14]

Eventually stocks will run out. But before this happens, firms will increase their output as they see their sales increase. Extra sales can then be made without a further depletion of inventories. Once again, the consequence of each individual firm's behaviour, in search of its own individual profits, is an increase in the national product and national income. Thus, the final response to an excess of aggregate desired spending over current output is a rise in GDP.

At any level of GDP at which aggregate desired spending exceeds total output, there will be pressure for GDP to rise.

---

[14] Notice that in this example actual national income (GDP) is equal to £1,000 million. Desired consumption is £900 million and desired investment is £250 million, but the reduction of inventories by £150 million is unplanned negative investment; thus, actual investment is only £100 million.

Next, consider the £4,000 million level of GDP in Table 16.4. At this level desired spending on domestically produced goods is only £3,550 million. If firms persist in producing £4,000 million worth of goods, £450 million worth must remain unsold. Therefore, stocks of unsold goods must rise. However, firms will not allow unsold goods to accumulate indefinitely; sooner or later they will reduce the level of output to the level of sales. When they do, GDP will fall.

At any level of GDP for which aggregate desired spending is less than total output, there will be pressure for GDP to fall.

Finally, look at the GDP level of £1,750 million in Table 16.4. At this level, and only at this level, aggregate desired spending is equal to national output (GDP). Purchasers can fulfil their spending plans without causing inventories to change. There is no incentive for firms to alter output. Because everyone wishes to purchase an amount equal to what is being produced, output and income will remain steady; GDP is in equilibrium.

The equilibrium level of GDP occurs where aggregate desired spending equals total output.

This conclusion is quite general and does not depend on the numbers that are used in the specific example.

Figure 16.6 shows the determination of the equilibrium level of GDP. In the figure the line labelled '*AE*' graphs the aggregate spending function given by the first and last columns of Table 16.3, also shown in Table 16.4. The line labelled '45° line (*AE = Y*)' graphs the equilibrium condition that aggregate desired spending equals national output. Since in equilibrium the variables measured on the two axes must be equal, the line showing this equality is a 45° line. Anywhere along that line the value of desired spending, which is measured on the vertical axis, is equal to the value of national output, which is measured on the horizontal axis.[15]

Graphically, equilibrium occurs at the level of GDP at which the aggregate desired spending line intersects the

---

[15] Because it turns up in many different guises, the 45° line can cause a bit of confusion until one gets used to it. The main thing about it is that it can be used whenever the variables plotted on the two axes are measured in the same units, such as pounds, and are plotted on the same scale. In that case equal distances on the two axes measure the same amounts. One centimetre may, for example, correspond to £1,000 on each axis. In such circumstances the 45° line joins all points where the values of the two variables are the same. In Figures 16.3 and 16.4 the 45° line shows all points where *desired consumption spending in real terms* equals *real disposable income*, because these are the two variables that are plotted on the two axes. In Figure 16.6 and all those that follow it, the 45° line shows all points at which *desired total spending in real terms* equals *real national output (GDP)*, because those are the variables that are measured on the two axes of these figures.

45° line. This is the level of GDP at which desired spending is just equal to total national output and therefore is just sufficient to purchase that output.

Exactly the same equilibrium is illustrated in panel (ii), but in terms of the saving–investment balance. The line labelled '$S$' is aggregate saving. In an economy without government and without international trade—the case we are studying here—aggregate saving is just equal to $Y - C$, the difference between national income and consumption. The line labelled '$I$' is investment, in this case assumed to be constant at all levels of income.

Notice that the vertical distance between $S$ and $I$ is just equal to the distance between the 45° line and $AE$. When desired investment exceeds desired saving, desired aggregate spending exceeds national output by the same amount. When desired investment is less than desired saving, desired aggregate spending is less than national output by the same amount.

Now we have explained the determinants of the equilibrium level of GDP at a *given price level*. A simple analogue, which will help us to understand why it is that equilibrium GDP is associated with equality of desired investment and saving, is set out in Box 16.2. In the next section we will study the forces that cause equilibrium income to change. We will see that shifts in autonomous consumption and investment spending cause changes in equilibrium GDP.

**Figure 16.6 Equilibrium GDP**

Equilibrium GDP occurs at $E_0$, where the desired aggregate spending line intersects the 45° line. If real GDP is below $Y_0$, desired aggregate spending will exceed national output, and production will rise. This is shown in part (i) by the arrow to the left of $Y_0$. If GDP is above $Y_0$, desired aggregate spending will be less than national output, and production will fall. This is shown by the arrow to the right of $Y_0$. Only when real GDP is $Y_0$ will desired aggregate spending equal real national output.

When saving is the only withdrawal and investment is the only injection, the equilibrium $Y_0$ is also the level of GDP at which saving equals investment, shown in part (ii). At levels of GDP greater than $Y_0$ saving exceeds investment (withdrawals exceed injections), so aggregate spending is less than output and the economy contracts. At levels of GDP below $Y_0$, investment exceeds saving (injections exceed withdrawals) so spending exceeds output and the level of GDP increases. Parts (i) and (ii) are just two different ways of looking at the same phenomenon.

---

**Box 16.2 A hydraulic analogue of GDP determination**

The key concept to understand in this chapter is how it is that GDP achieves its equilibrium level (for given values of exogenous spending). This is one of the most important ideas in macroeconomics, because it explains how GDP can be in equilibrium even when there is excess capacity in the economy.

Think of the economy as a water container, say a basin, which has inflows and outflows on a continuous basis—the tap is turned on and there is no plug in the plughole. Although the water is always changing, there is some condition under which the level of water in the basin will remain unchanged. This is when the volume of the inflow and the volume of the outflow are exactly equal.

Call the inflow 'investment', the outflow 'saving', and the level of water in the basin 'GDP'. GDP will stay at one level so long as the volume of investment just equals the volume of saving. (The same principle can be viewed in terms of the circular flow diagram in Figure 15.2 on page 340 when there is no foreign trade and no government. Only when $I = S$ will the level of the circular flow be stable.)

What happens if the basin fills up to overflowing? That is the problem of capacity constraints and full employment that we discuss in later chapters. Hopefully, the basin will never run empty, because that would mean that national income and output fall to zero—though the problem of the water getting undesirably low is what macroeconomics was invented to study.

Note also that in later chapters we will see that investment is not the only inflow, or injection (government spending and exports will be added), and saving is not the only leakage, or withdrawal (taxes and imports are also leakages).

# Changes in GDP

Because the *AE* function plays a central role in our explanation of the determination of the equilibrium value of GDP, you should not be surprised to hear that shifts in the *AE* function play a central role in explaining why GDP changes. (Remember that we continue to assume for the moment that the price level is constant.) To understand this influence, we must recall an important distinction first encountered in Chapter 3—the distinction between *shifts* in a curve and *movements along* a curve.

Suppose desired aggregate spending rises. This may be as a response to a change in GDP (and therefore in incomes), or it may be the result of an increased desire to spend at each level of GDP. A change in GDP causes a *movement along* the aggregate spending function. An increased desire to spend at each level of GDP causes a *shift* in the aggregate spending function. Figure 16.7 illustrates this important distinction.

## Shifts in the aggregate spending function

For any specific aggregate spending function, there is a unique level of equilibrium GDP. If the aggregate spending function shifts, the equilibrium will be disturbed and GDP will change. Thus, if we wish to find the causes of changes in GDP, we must understand the causes of shifts in the *AE* function.

The aggregate spending function shifts when one of its components shifts, that is, when there is a shift in the consumption function, in desired investment spending, in desired government spending on goods and services, or in desired net exports. In this chapter we consider only shifts in the consumption function and in desired investment spending. Both of these are changes in desired aggregate spending at every level of income. Such changes could, for example, be induced by a change in the level of the interest rate set by the monetary authorities.

### Upward shifts

What will happen if individuals permanently increase their levels of desired consumption spending at each level of disposable income, or if a major company desires to invest in more fixed capital because of improved confidence about the future health of the economy? (Recall that an increase in any component of spending has the same

(i) Movement along the *AE* line

(ii) A shift of the *AE* line

**Figure 16.7** Movements along and shifts of the *AE* function

A movement along the aggregate spending function occurs in response to a change in income; a shift of the *AE* function indicates a different level of desired spending at each level of income. In part (i) a change in income of $\Delta Y$ from $Y_0$ to $Y_1$ changes desired spending by $\Delta e$, from $e_0$ to $e_1$. In part (ii) a shift in the spending function from $AE_0$ to $AE_1$ raises the amount of spending associated with *each level* of income. At $Y_0$, for example, desired aggregate spending is increased by $\Delta e_1$; at $Y_1$ it is increased by $\Delta e_2$. (If the aggregate spending line shifts parallel to itself, $\Delta e_1 = \Delta e_2$.) (Note that from here on we drop 'aggregate' from the vertical axis label and write 'Desired spending'. The term 'aggregate' is always understood, even when we omit it to save space.)

effect, because it is an increase in demand for the output of the single production sector.) In considering these questions, remember that we are dealing with continuous flows measured as so much per period of time. An upward shift in any spending function means that the desired spending associated with each level of national income rises to and stays at a higher amount.

Because any such increase in desired spending shifts the entire aggregate spending function upward, the same analysis applies to each of the changes mentioned. Two important types of shift in AE need to be distinguished. First, if the same addition to spending occurs at all levels of income, the AE line shifts parallel to itself, as shown in part (i) of Figure 16.8. Second, if there is a change in the propensity to spend out of national income, the slope of the AE line changes, as shown in part (ii) of Figure 16.8. (Recall that the slope of the AE line is z, the marginal propensity to spend.) A change such as the one illustrated would occur if consumers decided to spend more of every £1 of disposable income, that is, if MPC rose.

Figure 16.8 shows that upward shifts in the aggregate spending function increase equilibrium GDP. After the shift in the AE line, output is no longer in equilibrium at

its original level, because at that level desired spending exceeds national output. Equilibrium GDP now occurs at the higher level indicated by the intersection of the new AE line with the 45° line, along which aggregate spending equals national output.

### Downward shifts

What happens to GDP if there is a decrease in the amount of consumption or investment spending desired at each level of income? These changes shift the aggregate spending function downward. A constant reduction in desired spending at all levels of income shifts AE parallel to itself. A fall in the marginal propensity to spend out of national income reduces the slope of the AE function. When we use the saving–investment relation, we must note that a downward shift in the consumption function causes an upward shift in the saving function, reducing the equilibrium level of income and output, at which saving equals investment.

### Summary

We have derived two important general propositions of the theory of GDP determination.

**(i) A parallel shift in AE**

**(ii) A change in the slope of AE**

**Figure 16.8 Shifts in the AE line**

**Upward shifts in the AE line increase equilibrium income and output; downward shifts decrease equilibrium income and output.** In parts (i) and (ii) the aggregate spending curve is initially $AE_0$ with national income $Y_0$. In part (i) a parallel upward *shift* in the AE line from $AE_0$ to $AE_1$ means that desired spending has increased by the same amount at each level of national income. For example, at $Y_0$ desired spending rises from $e_0$ to $e'_1$ and therefore exceeds national output. Equilibrium is reached at $E_1$, where output is $Y_1$ and spending is $e_1$. The increase in desired spending from $e'_1$ to $e_1$, represented by a *movement along* $AE_1$, is an induced response to the increase in GDP from $Y_0$ to $Y_1$.

In part (ii) a non-parallel upward shift in the AE line, say from $AE_0$ to $AE_2$, means that the marginal propensity to spend at each level of national income has increased. This leads to an increase in equilibrium GDP. Equilibrium is reached at $E_2$, where the new level of spending $e_2$ is equal to output $Y_2$. Again, the initial *shift* in the AE line induces a *movement along* the new AE line. Downward shifts in the AE line, from $AE_1$ to $AE_0$ or from $AE_2$ to $AE_0$, lead to a fall in equilibrium GDP to $Y_0$.

1. A rise in the amount of desired aggregate spending that is associated with each level of national income will increase equilibrium national output (GDP).

2. A fall in the amount of desired aggregate spending that is associated with each level of national income will lower equilibrium national output (GDP).

## The multiplier

We have learned how to predict the direction of the changes in GDP that will occur in response to various shifts in the aggregate spending function. We would like also to predict the *magnitude* of these changes.

During a recession the monetary authorities often lower interest rates in order to stimulate the economy. If this action has a larger effect than estimated, demand may rise too much and potential GDP may be reached with demand still rising. (We will see in Chapter 19 that this outcome will have an inflationary impact on the economy.) If the monetary authorities overestimate the effect of interest rate change, the recession will persist longer than is necessary. In this case there is a danger that the policy will be discredited as ineffective, even though the correct diagnosis is that too little of the right thing was done.

### Definition

The multiplier provides a measure of the magnitude of changes in GDP induced by a given change in autonomous expenditure. We have just seen that a shift in the aggregate spending curve will cause a change in equilibrium GDP. Such a shift could be caused by a change in any autonomous component of aggregate spending, for example an increase or decrease in desired investment. We will soon see that an increase in desired aggregate spending increases equilibrium GDP by a multiple of the initial increase in autonomous spending. The **multiplier** is the ratio of the change in GDP to the change in autonomous spending, that is, the change in GDP *divided by* the change in autonomous spending that brought it about.

### Why the multiplier is greater than unity

What will happen to GDP if GlaxoSmithKline plc spends £100 million more per year on new factories? Initially the construction of the factories will create £100 million worth of new demand for the output of the production sector (recall that there is only one type of output) and £100 million of new national income, and a corresponding amount of extra wages for workers and profits for firms (the income components of GDP). But this is not the end of the story. The increase in national income of £100 million will lead to an increase in disposable

income, which in turn will cause an induced rise in consumption spending.

Workers who gain new income directly from the building of the factory will spend some of it on consumer goods. (In reality they will spend it on many different goods, such as beer and cinema visits. In the simplified world of our model, all spending is on the final output of the single industrial sector.) When output and employment expand to meet this demand, further new incomes will then be created for workers and firms. When they then spend their newly earned incomes, output and employment will rise further. More income will be created, and more spending will be induced. Indeed, at this stage we might wonder whether the increases in income would ever come to an end. To deal with this concern, we need to consider the multiplier in somewhat more precise terms.

### The simple multiplier defined

Consider an increase in autonomous spending of $\Delta A$, which might be, say, £100 million per year. Remember

**Figure 16.9 The simple multiplier**

An increase in the autonomous component of desired aggregate spending increases equilibrium GDP by a multiple of the initial increase. The initial equilibrium is at $E_0$, where $AE_0$ intersects the 45° line. At this point desired spending, $e_0$, is equal to national output, $Y_0$. An increase in autonomous spending of $\Delta A$ then shifts the desired spending function upward to $AE_1$. If GDP stays at $Y_0$, desired spending rises to $e_1'$. (The coordinates of point $a$ are $Y_0$ and $e_1'$.) Because this level of desired spending is greater than national output, GDP will rise.

Equilibrium occurs when GDP rises to $Y_1$. Here desired spending, $e_1$, is equal to output, $Y_1$. The extra spending of $e_1$ represents the induced increases in spending. It is the amount by which the final increase in income and output, $\Delta Y$, exceeds the initial increase in autonomous spending, $\Delta A$. Because $\Delta Y$ is greater than $\Delta A$, the multiplier is greater than unity.

**Box 16.3** **The multiplier: a numerical example**

Consider an economy that has a marginal propensity to spend out of national income of 0.80. Suppose that autonomous spending increases by £100 million per year because a large company spends an extra £100 million per year on new factories. National income (and output) initially rises by £100 million, but that is not the end of it. The workers involved in factory building that received the first £100 million spend £80 million. This second round of spending generates £80 million of new income. This new income, in turn, induces £64 million of third-round spending. And so it continues, with each successive round of new income generating 80 per cent as much in new spending. Each additional round of spending creates new income (and output) and yet another round of spending.

The table carries the process through ten rounds. Readers with sufficient patience (and no faith in mathematics) may compute as many rounds in the process as you wish; you will find that the sum of the rounds of spending approaches a limit of £500 million, which is five times the initial increase in spending.

The graph of the cumulative spending increases shows how quickly this limit is approached. The multiplier is thus 5, given that the marginal propensity to spend is 0.8. Had the marginal propensity to spend been lower, say 0.667, the process would have been similar, but it would have approached a limit of three rather than five times the initial increase in spending. Notice that since our model has only a single productive sector, it makes no difference what the initial spending goes on: that, and all subsequent spending, is on the output of this single industry. In reality, the impact of spending increases may vary slightly depending on the product first demanded.

| Round of spending | Increase in spending (£m) | Cumulative total (£m) |
|---|---|---|
| Initial increase | 100.0 | 100.0 |
| 2 | 80.0 | 180.0 |
| 3 | 64.0 | 244.0 |
| 4 | 51.2 | 295.2 |
| 5 | 41.0 | 336.2 |
| 6 | 32.8 | 369.0 |
| 7 | 26.2 | 395.2 |
| 8 | 21.0 | 416.2 |
| 9 | 16.8 | 433.0 |
| 10 | 13.4 | 446.4 |
| 11–20 combined | 47.9 | 494.3 |
| All others | 5.7 | 500.0 |

that $\Delta A$ stands for any increase in autonomous spending; this could be an increase in investment or in the autonomous component of consumption. The new autonomous spending shifts the aggregate spending function upward by that amount. GDP is no longer in equilibrium at its original level, because desired aggregate spending now exceeds output. A movement along the new *AE* line restores equilibrium.

The **simple multiplier** measures the change in equilibrium GDP that occurs in response to a change in autonomous spending *at a constant price level*.[16] We refer to it as 'simple' because we have simplified the situation by assuming that the price level is fixed. Figure 16.9 illustrates the simple multiplier. Box 16.3 provides a numerical example.

## The size of the simple multiplier

The size of the simple multiplier depends on the slope of the *AE* line, that is, on the marginal propensity to spend, *c*. This is illustrated in Figure 16.10.

A high marginal propensity to spend means a steep *AE* line. The spending induced by any initial increase in income is large, with the result that the final rise in GDP is correspondingly large. By contrast, a low marginal propensity to spend means a relatively flat *AE* line. The spending induced by the initial increase in income is

---

[16] Recall that we have assumed that there is excess capacity in the economy, so an increase in spending *can* lead to extra real activity. The situation is very different when we begin with resources already fully employed. We consider this situation in later chapters.

**Figure 16.10** The size of the simple multiplier

The larger the marginal propensity to spend out of national income (z), the steeper is the AE line and the larger is the multiplier. In each part of the figure the initial aggregate spending function is $AE_0$ and equilibrium is at $E_0$, with income $Y_0$. The AE line then *shifts* upward to $AE_1$ as a result of an increase in autonomous spending of $\Delta A$. $\Delta A$ is the same in each part. The new equilibrium is at $E_1$. In part (i) the AE function is horizontal, indicating a marginal propensity to spend of zero ($z = 0$). The change in GDP, $\Delta Y$, is only the increase in autonomous spending, because there is no induced spending by those who receive the initial increase in income. The simple multiplier is then unity, its minimum possible value.

In part (ii) the AE line slopes upward but is still relatively flat ($z$ is low). The increase in GDP to $Y_2$ is only slightly greater than the increase in autonomous spending that brought it about.

In part (iii) the AE function is quite steep ($z$ is high). Now the increase in GDP to $Y_3$ is much larger than the increase in autonomous spending that brought it about. The simple multiplier is quite large.

small, and the final rise in GDP is not much larger than the initial rise in autonomous spending that brought it about.

**The larger the marginal propensity to spend, the steeper is the aggregate spending function and the larger is the multiplier.**

The precise value of the simple multiplier can be derived by using elementary algebra. (The derivation is given in Box 16.4.) The result is that the simple multiplier, which we call K, is

$$K = \frac{\Delta Y}{\Delta A} = \frac{1}{1-c}$$

where $c$ is the marginal propensity to spend out of national income. (Recall that $c$ is the slope of the aggregate spending function.)

As we saw earlier, the term $(1 - c)$ stands for the marginal propensity not to spend out of national income. For example, if £0.80 of every £1.00 of new national income is spent ($z = 0.80$), then £0.20 is the amount not spent. The value of the multiplier is then calculated as $K = 1/(0.20) = 5$.

**The simple multiplier equals the reciprocal of the marginal propensity not to spend.**

From this we see that if $(1 - c)$ is small (that is, if $c$ is large), the multiplier will be large (because extra income induces much extra spending). What if $(1 - c)$ is large? The largest possible value of $(1 - c)$ is unity, which arises when $z$ equals zero, indicating that none of any additional national income is spent. In this case the multiplier itself has a value of unity; the increase in equilibrium GDP is confined to the initial increase in autonomous spending. There are no induced additional effects on spending, so GDP increases only by the original increase in autonomous spending. The relation between $(1 - c)$ and the size of the multiplier is illustrated in Figure 16.10.

To estimate the size of the multiplier in an actual economy, we need to estimate the value of the marginal propensity not to spend out of national income in that economy, that is, $(1 - c)$. Evidence suggests that in the United Kingdom the value of the marginal propensity not to spend is much larger than the 0.2 used in the above example. This is because there are 'leakages' from the circular flow of income other than saving—income taxes and import spending (which will be added to our model

**Box 16.4 The derivation of the multiplier**

In models of short-run GDP determination, aggregate spending is divided into autonomous spending, $A$, and induced spending, $N$. In the simple model of this chapter, $A$ is just investment plus autonomous consumption, and $N$ is just induced consumption. When we add imports and government in the next chapter, $N$ will include induced imports, and $A$ will include government spending and exports. The derivation here is quite general, however. All that matters is that desired aggregate spending can be divided into one class of spending, $N$, that varies with income and another class, $A$, that does not.

Thus, we can write

$$E = N + A \qquad (A1)$$

where $E$ is total spending. Because $N$ is spending on domestically produced output that varies with income, we can write

$$N = cY, \quad 0 < c < 1 \qquad (A2)$$

where $c$ is the marginal propensity to spend out of national income. (In the simple model of this chapter, with no government and no foreign sector, it is equal to the marginal propensity to consume.) Substituting equation (2) into equation (1) yields the equation of the aggregate spending curve:

$$E = cY + A \qquad (A3)$$

Now we write the equation of the 45° line,

$$E = Y \qquad (A4)$$

which states the equilibrium condition that desired aggregate spending equals GDP. Equations (3) and (4) are two equations with two unknowns, $E$ and $Y$. To solve them, we substitute equation (3) into equation (4) to obtain

$$Y = cY + A. \qquad (A5)$$

Subtracting $cY$ from both sides, factoring out $Y$, and dividing through by $1 - c$ yields

$$Y = \frac{A}{1-c}. \qquad (A6)$$

To discover how GDP changes when autonomous spending changes, i.e. the multiplier $K$, we note that a change in $A$ will lead to a change in $Y$ that is equal to the change in $A$ multiplied by $1/1-c$. This is the value of the multiplier $K$ discussed in the text.*

---

\* For those who are familiar with calculus, we merely differentiate (6) to obtain

$$\frac{dy}{dA} = \frac{1}{(1-c)} = K$$

---

in the next chapter). Allowing for these extra withdrawals leads to a realistic estimate of something around 0.65 for $(1 - c)$.[17] Thus, the simple multiplier for the United Kingdom is just over 1.4, rather than 5 as in the above example.

The simple multiplier is a useful starting-point for understanding the effects of autonomous spending shifts on GDP. However, as we will see in subsequent chapters, many qualifications are needed before we can derive any policy significance from its value.

 # CASE STUDIES

## 1. The UK savings gap: why is the saving ratio so low?

One of the most important economic policy issues in the UK and many other major countries in the mid-2000s was the low level of private savings. This has been labelled by the UK media as the 'savings gap'. There are several reasons why this is important for policy-makers. The first is that, with life expectancy increasing

fast, the potential cost to the taxpayer of supporting increasing numbers of old people has become a cause of concern. Indeed, the UK Government set up a Pensions Commission to investigate the options. Its report in 2006 recommended a combination of later retirement and a compulsory savings scheme, to which employers as well as employees would contribute. This is a public recognition that savings rates have not been high enough to avoid a large number of people having to live on the basic state pension in old age, and that the basic state pension would accordingly be very basic indeed unless tax rates were much higher. That is to say, workers in the future would have to pay a lot more tax than they do now to support those on pensions in the future.

---

[17] This 0.65 is calculated using a marginal propensity to save of 0.2, a marginal propensity to import of 0.25, and an income tax rate of 0.25 (25p in the pound).

**Figure 16.11** UK personal savings ratio, 1963–2005

*Source*: ONS: www.statistics.gov.uk

The second reason why the savings issue is important is that the flip side of low saving is high consumption. High spending can be good for the economy, as it leads to high levels of demand, which in some circumstances can be helpful in keeping the economy operating at a high level, i.e. close to potential output. But a negative side of high consumer spending arises when it is associated with growing levels of personal debt—if some of that spending is financed by borrowing rather than out of current income. High levels of debt can be especially problematic if interest rates rise and existing debt levels need to be serviced with higher interest payments. This can lead ultimately to a collapse of consumer confidence and a sharp decline in consumer spending, leading to a slowdown in activity.

A third reason for concern about saving levels is that 'encouraging investment'[18] is one of the government's tools to help encourage productivity growth. Domestic personal savings are not necessarily a constraint on investment, as firms can finance investment out of their own savings or by borrowing in international capital markets. However, other things being equal, high domestic saving would generate a larger flow of finance for investment and is certainly helpful in building up national wealth.

Saving is the difference between personal disposable income and consumer spending. However, it includes only what is not spent out of current income, and not those increases in wealth that people enjoy from rises in the value of their houses or their investments (such as shares). Also, it is important to note that personal saving is not the same thing as national saving, as the latter would also include savings within the corporate sector and the public (government) sector.

Figure 16.11 shows the UK personal savings ratio since 1963. It has fluctuated over the past four decades or so from around 4 per cent of income to as much as 14 per cent of income. In the 1970s, the savings ratio was on a rise, but it fell sharply in the late 1980s during a credit-led consumer spending boom. It recovered strongly in the early 1990s, but in the early years of the twenty-first century the ratio fell into the 4–6 per cent range, and seemed to be firmly stuck there. This is the evidence underpinning the problem set out above.

So why have savings been stuck at such low levels? We cannot be sure about all the contributory factors, but here are some of them. Strong equity prices in the late 1990s and strong house prices in the 2002–5 period have made many households feel wealthy and so (possibly) not worried about saving for their future. In addition, interest rates have generally been low and cuts in tax relief on pension funds have reduced the incentives to save. Added to this, low inflation has probably reduced concern about an erosion of the value of savings, so that precautionary saving could have fallen, in contrast to the late 1970s when high inflation was associated with a high savings ratio. Falling unemployment and strong demand for labour have made people more confident that they can always find work even if they lose their current jobs; hence there is less reason to keep some funds aside for a rainy day.

## 2. Why is UK investment so low?

Another objective of the UK Government is 'encouraging investment to increase the stock of physical capital supported by stronger, more efficient capital markets.'[19] There was a boom in

---

[18] See *Pre-Budget Report* (HM Treasury, 2005), page 5.
[19] See *Pre-Budget Report* (HM Treasury, 2005), page 5.

**Figure 16.12**  UK business investment growth, quarter on corresponding quarter of previous year (1980 Q1–2005 Q4)

*Source*: ONS: www.statistics.gov.uk

investment in the late 1990s, especially associated with computer and communications technology, and related in part to investment intended to replace equipment that might be affected by the 'millennium computer bug'. But in the first five years of the twenty-first century UK business was either falling or rising very slowly.

Figure 16.12 shows the rate of growth of business investment since 1980. Generally, business investment is pro-cyclical. When the economy is booming investment is also growing strongly, and when the economy is depressed investment tends to fall. This should be not surprising, as firms will want to expand their productive capacity when demand for their output is strong. This explains why investment fell during the recessions of the early 1980s and early 1990s and why it was growing strongly during the booms of the late 1980s and late 1990s. However, it does not explain why investment was so weak in the 2002–5 period when the economy appeared to be performing well in terms of other indicators. There was, for example, falling unemployment during this period and steady positive growth of real GDP.

Again, we cannot be sure of the explanation for this slow investment growth in the first half of the 2000s, but there are some possible reasons. The first is the globalization of production. Many British businesses were highly profitable and expanding their activities in this is period, but they were investing in productive capacity outside the UK and this does not show up as part of the UK investment figures, even though these investments are owned by UK firms and the earnings on them will contribute to UK incomes.

A second possible reason is that the nature of much investment has changed in recent years. A few decades ago, if a car manufacturer built a new factory or installed a new set of machine tools, it was clear that this was an investment and would have been measured as such. However, if a bank installs a new software system for its employees or even replaces out-of-date desktop computers, it is not so clear that this is investment spending rather than just a current expense of the business. Investments in information technology and communication equipment are thus harder to identify as investments, and so the true level of investment may be underestimated.

A third possible reason is that the size of the UK service sector has grown relative to production industries. Service industries are increasingly based on the productive skills of their employees, and investment in skills and training is not counted as investment in the UK data. That is, investment in human capital is excluded from the data, as 'investment' relates only to 'gross fixed capital formation'.

# Conclusion

We can get a long way towards understanding the determinants of GDP in the short term by studying consumption and investment, two of the components of final expenditure. Consumer spending/saving and aggregate investment continue to be topics of major interest to policy-makers.

The key idea that emerges from the approach we have started to develop in this chapter is that aggregate spending on the output of the economy affects the outcome. The resulting level of GDP may or not be at a desirable level, and in particular could be one where there are underutilized resources and unemployment. We make the analysis increasingly more realistic in the following three chapters. Next we introduce a role for government and open the economy to external trade. After that we add a supply side to the economy and study the interaction of real activity and the level of prices.

## SUMMARY

### The macroeconomic problem: inflation and unemployment

- Models of the short-term determination of GDP explain why actual GDP deviates from potential GDP.

- Actual GDP above potential can be associated with inflation, while actual GDP below potential is associated with unemployment and lost output.

### Key assumptions

- For simplicity we aggregate all industrial sectors into one, so the economy produces only one type of output good. We explain GDP determination through the major spending categories: private consumption, investment, government consumption, and net exports.

### What determines aggregate spending?

- Desired aggregate spending includes desired consumption, desired investment, and desired government spending, plus desired net exports. It is the amount that economic agents want to spend on purchasing the national product. In this chapter we only consider consumption and investment.

- A change in personal disposable income leads to a change in desired private consumption and saving. The responsiveness of these changes is measured by the marginal propensity to consume (MPC) and the marginal propensity to save (MPS). These are both positive and sum to one, indicating that, by definition, all disposable income is either spent on consumption or saved.

- A change in wealth tends to cause a change in the allocation of disposable income between consumption and saving. The change in consumption is positively related to the change in wealth, while the change in saving is negatively related to this change.

- Investment depends, among other things, on real interest rates and business confidence. In our simple theory investment is treated as *autonomous*, or exogenous,

as is the constant term in the consumption function, called *autonomous* consumption.

- The part of consumption that responds to changes in income is called *induced* spending.

### Equilibrium GDP

- At the equilibrium level of GDP, purchasers wish to buy exactly the amount of national output that is being produced. At GDP above equilibrium, desired spending falls short of national output, and output will sooner or later be curtailed. At GDP below equilibrium, desired spending exceeds national output, and output will sooner or later be increased.

- In a closed economy with no government, desired saving equals desired investment at equilibrium GDP.

- Equilibrium GDP is represented graphically by the point at which the aggregate spending curve cuts the 45° line, that is, where total desired spending equals total output. This is the same level of GDP at which the saving function intersects the investment function.

### Changes in GDP

- With a constant price level, equilibrium GDP is increased by a rise in the desired consumption or investment spending that is associated with each level of national income. Equilibrium GDP is decreased by a fall in desired spending.

- The magnitude of the effect on GDP of shifts in autonomous spending is given by the multiplier. It is defined as $K = \Delta Y / \Delta A$, where $\Delta A$ is the change in autonomous spending and $\Delta Y$ the resulting increase in GDP.

- The simple multiplier is the multiplier when the price level is constant. It is equal to $1/(1 - c)$, where $c$ is the marginal propensity to spend out of national income. Thus, the larger $c$ is, the larger is the multiplier. It is a basic prediction of macroeconomics that the simple multiplier, relating £1 worth of increased spending on domestic output to the resulting increase in GDP, is greater than unity.

## TOPICS FOR REVIEW

- Aggregation across sectors
- Actual and potential GDP
- GDP gap
- Desired spending
- Consumption function
- Average and marginal propensities to consume and to save
- Aggregate spending function

- Marginal propensities to spend and not to spend
- Equilibrium GDP at a given price level
- Saving–investment balance
- Shifts of, and movements along, spending curves
- Effect on GDP of changes in desired spending
- The simple multiplier
- Size of the multiplier and slope of the $AE$ line

## QUESTIONS

1 Calculate GDP using the following information (where there is no government and no foreign trade and $C$ = consumption, $I$ = investment, and $Y$ = GDP): $C = 100 + 0.8Y$; $I = 1,000$.

2 How will the answer to question 1 change if $I$ increases to (a) 2,000, (b) 4,000, and (c) 10,000?

3 How would the answers to questions 1 and 2 change if the consumption function were (a) $C = 1,000 + 0.6Y$, (b) $C = -200 + 0.9Y$, and (c) $C = -200 + 1Y$?

4 Why is there a close relationship between personal disposable income and consumers' expenditure?

5 Explain why an increase in autonomous spending leads to a greater increase in GDP.

6 What factors do you think would put limits on how far increases in spending can lead to increases in real GDP?

7 What do you think are likely to be the main determinants of investment by firms?

8 Is it likely that individual consumers' marginal propensities to spend out of disposable income will vary with the age of the consumer? If so, how would you expect it to vary?

# Chapter 17

# GDP IN AN OPEN ECONOMY WITH GOVERNMENT

In this chapter we continue building a model of the short-run determination of GDP. Our model in Chapter 16 contained four simplifying, but temporary, assumptions: no government, no foreign trade, a fixed price level, and excess productive capacity. The current chapter relaxes the first two of these; the following chapter relaxes the last two.

In particular, you will learn that:

- Government consumption contributes to aggregate spending in the same way as any other component of autonomous spending.
- Taxes affect private consumption via their effect on disposable income.
- Net exports are negatively related to domestic income.
- A necessary condition for GDP to be in equilibrium is that desired aggregate domestic spending is equal to national output.
- The size of the multiplier is negatively related to the income tax rate and the marginal propensity to import.

In what follows we add first government and then a foreign sector to our simple model. Adding the government sector allows us to study fiscal policy, which is defined as the ability of the government to use its taxing and spending powers to affect the level of GDP. In an open economy, net foreign demand for domestic output is an important source of final spending, so it has to be included in any complete treatment of the spending components of GDP. After adding the government and the foreign trade sector, we examine how these additions alter both the structure of the model and its behaviour in response to changes in autonomous spending.

As we proceed, it is important to remember that the key elements of our theory of GDP determination in the short run are unchanged. The most important of these that will remain true, even after incorporating government and the foreign sector, are restated here.

1. Aggregate desired spending can be divided into autonomous (or exogenous) spending and induced spending. *Autonomous spending* is determined outside the model and is treated as a constant. We will ask what happens when some component of autonomous spending changes

but the changes are imposed from outside the system and can be thought of as external 'shocks'. *Induced spending* is spending that depends on the level of national income, and therefore on GDP, and so is determined within our model.

2. The equilibrium level of GDP (national income and output) is the level at which the sum of autonomous and induced desired spending in the domestic economy is equal to the level of output. Graphically, this is where the aggregate spending line intersects the 45° line.

3. The simple multiplier measures the change in equilibrium GDP that takes place in response to a unit change in autonomous domestic spending, with the price level held constant.

Recall that the spending-based measure of GDP is made up of private consumption, investment, government consumption spending, and net exports. We have already built a model of GDP determination that includes private consumption and investment. We are about to extend this model to include government consumption and net exports. Recall also that 'national income', 'national output', and 'GDP' are all equivalent terms for our purposes.

# Government spending and taxes

Government spending and taxation policies affect equilibrium GDP in two important ways. First, government spending is part of autonomous spending in our model; that is, it is an exogenous element of spending in the economy. Second, in deriving disposable income, taxes must be subtracted from national income, and government transfer payments must be added. Because disposable income determines private consumption spending, the relationship between desired private consumption and national income becomes more complicated when a government is added. A government's plans for taxes and spending determine its *fiscal policy*, which has important effects on the level of GDP in both the short and the long run.

## Government spending

In Chapter 15 we distinguished between *government consumption spending on goods and services* and *government transfer payments*. The distinction bears repeating here. Government consumption is part of GDP. When the government hires a civil servant, buys a paper clip, or purchases fuel for the navy, it is directly adding to the demand for the economy's current output of goods and services. Thus, desired government purchases, $G$, are part of aggregate spending. As explained in Chapter 16, in our model we assume that government consumption spending buys the output from the single industrial sector. This makes government spending have the same effect on GDP as any other component of autonomous spending.

The other part of government spending, transfer payments, also affects desired aggregate spending, but only indirectly. Consider, for example, state pensions or unemployment benefit. These are payments (transfers) made by government to individuals, who will spend at least some of the money. Since that spending is recorded as personal consumption, we do not want to count it twice by recording it under $G$ as well. Government transfer payments affect aggregate spending only through the effect that these payments have on personal *disposable* income. Transfer payments increase disposable income, and increases in disposable income, via the consumption function, increase desired consumption spending.

This distinction (between transfers and government consumption) is important when it comes to issues such as determining the amount of GDP that is accounted for by government. Measuring the size of government to include transfers makes it look as though government's share of GDP is much bigger than it really is. However, looking only at $G$ makes the government's revenue needs look smaller than they are, since transfers must be financed by taxes or borrowing, just as spending on goods and services must be. In what follows, government spending always excludes transfers, unless the contrary is stated.

## Tax revenues

Tax revenues may be thought of as negative transfer payments in their effect on desired aggregate spending. Tax payments reduce disposable income relative to national income; transfers raise disposable income relative to national income. For the purpose of calculating the effect of government policy on desired consumption spending, it is the net effect of the two that matters.

We define **net taxes** to be total tax revenues received by the government minus total transfer payments made by the government, and we denote net taxes as $T$. (For convenience, when we use the term 'taxes', we will mean *net* taxes unless we explicitly state otherwise.) Since transfer payments are smaller than total taxes, net taxes are positive, and personal disposable income is less than national income. Household disposable income was a fraction over 70 per cent of GDP at market prices in 2005.

## The budget balance

The **budget balance** is the difference between total government revenue and total government spending, or equivalently net taxes minus government spending, $T - G$. When revenues exceed spending, the government is running a **budget surplus**. The government will then reduce the national debt, since the surplus funds will be used to pay off old debt. When spending exceeds revenues, as it has for much of the period since the Second World War (1969–70, 1988–9, and 1998–2001 were the only exceptions between 1945 and 2005), the government is running a **budget deficit**. The government must then add to the national debt, since it must borrow to cover its deficit.[1] When the budget surplus (and deficit)

---

[1] It does this by selling government bonds (known as 'gilts' in the UK). When the government runs a surplus, it uses the excess revenue to purchase outstanding government bonds. The stock of outstanding bonds is termed the *national* or *public debt*. (Public debt is the debt of the entire public sector, which includes local authorities and nationalized industries; national debt is the debt of the central government only.)

is zero, the government has a **balanced budget**. Since the budget deficit is simply a negative budget surplus, we generally use the term 'budget surplus' to cover both cases, so bear in mind that the budget *surplus* can be negative.

## Tax and spending functions

We treat government spending as exogenous; that is, it does not vary with GDP. The government is assumed to decide how much it wishes to spend in real terms and to hold to these plans whatever the level of GDP. We also treat *tax rates* as exogenous. The government sets its tax rates and does not vary them as GDP varies. This makes *tax revenues* endogenous. As GDP rises with given tax rates, the tax revenue will rise. For example, when incomes rise, people pay more total tax, even if tax rates are unchanged.

Table 17.1 and Figure 17.1 illustrate these assumptions with a specific example. They show the size of the government's surplus when its desired purchases (G) are constant at £170 million and its net tax revenues are equal to 10 per cent of GDP (national income). Notice that the government budget surplus (or public saving) increases with GDP. This relationship occurs because net tax revenues rise with GDP but, by assumption, government spending does not. The slope of the budget surplus function is just equal to the income tax rate. The *position* of the function is determined by fiscal policy, as we discuss later in this chapter.[2]

For given tax rates, the government budget surplus (public saving) increases as GDP rises and falls as GDP falls.

**Table 17.1** The budget surplus function (£ million)

| GDP (Y) | Government spending (G) | Net taxes (T = 0.1Y) | Government surplus (T − G) |
|---------|-------------------------|----------------------|----------------------------|
| 500 | 170 | 50 | −120 |
| 1,000 | 170 | 100 | −70 |
| 1,750 | 170 | 175 | 5 |
| 2,000 | 170 | 200 | 30 |
| 3,000 | 170 | 300 | 130 |
| 4,000 | 170 | 400 | 230 |

**The budget surplus is negative at low levels of GDP and becomes positive at high levels of GDP.** The table shows that the size of the budget surplus increases with GDP, given constant spending and constant tax rates. For example, when GDP rises by £1,000 million, the deficit falls or the surplus rises by £100 million.

**Figure 17.1** Budget surplus function
**The budget surplus function increases as GDP increases.** This figure plots the T − G column from Table 17.1. Notice that the slope of the surplus function is equal to the income tax rate of 0.1.

# Net exports

The UK's foreign trade sector is significant in relation to its GDP. Exports of goods and services in 2005 were just over 26 per cent of GDP at market prices. Although the total volume of trade is important for many purposes, such as determining the amount by which a country gains from trade (see Chapter 27), the balance between exports and imports (the current account balance) is particularly important in determining GDP.

## The net export function

In macroeconomics we are interested in how the balance of trade responds to changes in GDP, the price level, and the exchange rate. Our theory covers trade in goods *and*

---

[2] The numerical example used here is designed only to illustrate the principles of GDP determination developed in this chapter. To avoid the appearance of direct applicability of overly simplified models, we have deliberately chosen not to use 'realistic' numbers. The example produces GDP of £2,000 million, whereas UK money GDP in 2005 was around £1,200,000 million.

*services*. The effect on GDP of selling a service to a foreigner is identical to that of selling a physical commodity. (Recall that we have only one type of product in our economy, and that all desired spending is treated as a demand for this product.)

Exports depend on spending decisions made by foreign consumers or overseas firms that purchase domestic goods and services. We assume, therefore, that exports are determined by influences outside of the home economy. This is autonomous, or exogenous, spending from the point of view of the determination of domestic GDP.

Imports, however, depend on the spending decisions of domestic residents. Most categories of spending have an import content; British-made cars, for example, use large quantities of imported components and raw materials in their manufacture. Thus, imports rise when the other categories of spending rise. Because consumption rises when the income of domestic consumers rises, imports of foreign-produced consumption goods, and of materials that go into the production of domestically produced consumption goods, also rise with domestic income. Total domestic (national) income, of course, rises identically with GDP.

**Desired net exports are negatively related to GDP because of the positive relationship between desired imports and GDP.**

This negative relationship between net exports and GDP is called the *net export function*. Data for a hypothetical economy with constant exports and with imports that are assumed to be 25 per cent of GDP are given in Table 17.2 and illustrated in Figure 17.2. In this example exports form the autonomous component and imports form the induced component of the desired net export function. The formulation in the table implicitly assumes that all imports are

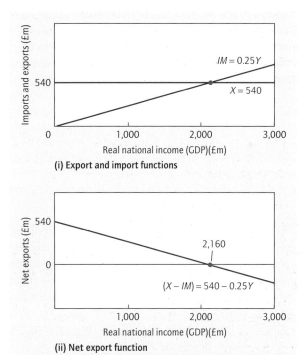

**(i) Export and import functions**

**(ii) Net export function**

**Figure 17.2** The net export function

Net exports, defined as the difference between exports and imports, are inversely related to the level of GDP. In part (i) exports are constant at £540 million, while imports rise with GDP. Therefore net exports, shown in part (ii), decline with GDP. The figure is based on hypothetical data in Table 17.2. With GDP equal to £2,160 million, imports are equal to exports at £540 million and net exports are zero. For levels of GDP below £2,160 million, imports are less than exports, and hence net exports are positive. For levels of GDP above £2,160 million, imports are greater than exports, and hence net exports are negative.

for final consumption. Imports rise when income rises, but imports do not change when *other* categories of autonomous spending change, so there is no direct import content of $G$, $I$, and $X$. This simplification will prove useful in our development of the determination of equilibrium income, and does not affect the essentials of the theory.

### Shifts in the net export function

We have seen that the net export function relates net exports $(X - IM)$, which we also denote by $NX$, to GDP. It is drawn on the assumption that everything that affects net exports, except domestic GDP, remains constant. The major factors that must be held constant are foreign GDP, relative international price levels, and the exchange rate. A change in any of these factors will affect the amount of net exports that will occur at each level of GDP and hence will shift the net export function.

**Table 17.2** The net export function (£ million)

| GDP (Y) | Exports (X) | Imports (IM = 0.25Y) | Net exports |
|---|---|---|---|
| 0 | 540 | 0 | 540 |
| 1,000 | 540 | 250 | 190 |
| 2,160 | 540 | 540 | 0 |
| 3,000 | 540 | 750 | −210 |
| 4,000 | 540 | 1,000 | −460 |
| 5,000 | 540 | 1,250 | −710 |

**Net exports fall as GDP rises.** We assume that exports are constant and that imports are 25 per cent of GDP. In this case net exports are positive at low levels of GDP and negative at high levels of GDP.

Notice that anything that affects domestic exports will change the values in the 'Exports' column in Table 17.2 and so will shift the net export function parallel to itself —upward if exports increase and downward if exports decrease. Also notice that anything that affects the proportion of income that home consumers wish to spend on imports will change the values in the 'Imports' column in the table, and therefore will change the slope of the net export function by making imports more or less responsive to changes in domestic income. What factors will cause such shifts?

### Foreign GDP

Other things being equal, an increase in foreign GDP will lead to an increase in the quantity of domestic-produced goods demanded by foreign countries, that is, to an increase in our exports. This is because as foreign GDP rises, foreign residents will receive higher incomes and will buy more of all goods, including imports. But foreign imports are domestic exports. Because the same additional amount is sold at each level of domestic GDP, the increase is in the constant of the domestic net export function, $X$. This causes $NX$ to shift upward, parallel to its original position. A fall in foreign GDP leads to a parallel downward shift in the net export function.

### Relative international prices

Any change in the prices of home-produced goods relative to those of foreign goods will cause both imports and exports to change. This will shift the net export function.

Consider first a rise in domestic prices relative to prices in foreign countries. On the one hand, foreigners will now see domestic-produced goods as more expensive relative both to goods produced in their own country and to goods imported from other countries. As a result domestic exports will fall. On the other hand, domestic residents will see imports from foreign countries becoming cheaper relative to the prices of home-produced goods. As a result they will buy more foreign goods, and imports will rise. Both of these responses will cause the net export function to shift downwards and change its slope, as shown in Figure 17.3.

Second, consider the opposite case of a fall in UK prices relative to prices of foreign-made goods. On the one hand, potential UK exports will now look cheaper in foreign markets relative both to their home-produced goods and to goods imported from third countries. As a result UK exports will rise. On the other hand, the same change in relative prices—British-made goods becoming cheaper relative to foreign-made goods—will cause UK imports to fall. Thus, the net export function will shift upwards, in exactly the opposite way to the movement in Figure 17.3.

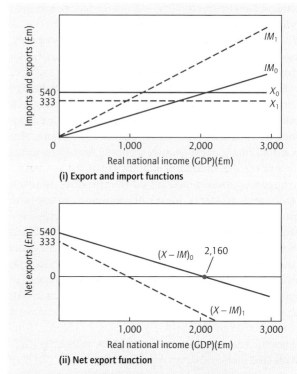

(i) Export and import functions

(ii) Net export function

**Figure 17.3  Shifts in the net export function**

**An upward shift in imports and/or a downward shift in exports shifts the net export function downward.** A rise in the domestic price level relative to foreign price levels, or a rise in the exchange rate, lowers exports from $X_0$ to $X_1$ and raises the import function from $IM_0$ to $IM_1$. This shifts the net export function downward from $(X - IM)_0$ to $(X - IM)_1$. (In the figure imports are 25 per cent of $Y$ along $IM_0$ and are assumed to rise to a third of $Y$ when domestic goods become more expensive relative to foreign goods, while exports fall from £540 million to £333 million.)

What circumstances will cause relative international prices to change? Two important causes of changes in competitiveness, for a country as a whole, are international differences in inflation rates and changes in exchange rates.

Consider inflation rates first, and assume that the UK is the home country. If the sterling exchange rate remains constant, UK prices will rise relative to foreign prices if the UK inflation rate is higher than the inflation rates in other major trading countries. In contrast, UK prices will fall relative to foreign prices if the UK inflation rate is lower than the rates in other major trading countries.

Now consider the exchange rate. Holding domestic and foreign price levels constant, a depreciation of sterling will make imports more expensive for domestic residents and UK exports cheaper for foreigners. This is because UK residents will get less foreign currency for each pound sterling and foreigners will get more pounds for each unit of their own currency. Both foreigners and domestic consumers will shift spending towards the UK-produced goods, which will have become cheaper relative to foreign goods. The net export function will thus shift upward.

An appreciation of sterling (holding price levels constant) has the opposite effect. It makes UK goods relatively expensive, thereby shifting the net export function downward.[3]

Exchange rate changes may be brought about by changes in interest rates implemented by the monetary authorities. Other things being equal, the domestic currency will generally appreciate when the domestic interest rate is raised, and *vice versa*. This is because more people will wish to buy assets denominated in the home currency to take advantage of the high domestic interest rates, and a high demand for anything including currency tends to push its price upwards. As we shall see, changes in the exchange rate are an important way in which monetary policy can exert leverage over domestic aggregate spending in an open economy. We discuss these influences in more detail in Chapters 22 and 23.

The results of this important chain of reasoning can now be summarized (continuing with the UK home country example).

1. UK prices rise relative to foreign prices either if the UK inflation rate exceeds the rate in other major trading countries (with exchange rates fixed) or if the pound sterling appreciates (with price levels constant). This discourages exports and encourages imports, causing the net export function to shift downwards.

2. UK prices fall relative to foreign prices either if the UK inflation rate is less than the rates in competitor countries (with exchange rates fixed) or if the pound sterling depreciates (with price levels constant). This encourages exports and discourages imports, causing the net export function to shift upwards.

## Equilibrium GDP

We are now ready to see how equilibrium GDP is determined in our new model which includes a government and a foreign sector. As in Chapter 16, we can determine the equilibrium in two ways that come to the same thing in the end: by relating output and spending, and by relating saving and investment.

### The aggregate spending approach

In Chapter 16 we determined equilibrium GDP by finding the level of GDP at which desired aggregate spending is equal to national output. The addition of government and the foreign sector changes the calculations that we must make but does not alter the basic principles that are involved. Our first step is to derive a new aggregate spending function that incorporates the effects of government consumption and foreign trade.

### Relating desired consumption to national income

Our theory of GDP determination requires that we relate each of the components of aggregate spending to national income, $Y$. Personal income taxes cause personal disposable income to differ from national income (by the proportion of income taxation net of transfers). We simply assume that disposable income is always 90 per cent of national income.[4] Thus, whatever the relationship between $C$ and $Y_d$, we can always substitute $0.9Y$ for $Y_d$. For example, if changes in consumption were always 80 per cent of changes in $Y_d$, changes in consumption would always be 72 per cent (80 per cent of 90 per cent) of changes in $Y$.

Table 17.3 illustrates how we can write desired consumption as a function of $Y$ as well as of $Y_d$. We can then derive the marginal response of consumption to changes in $Y$ by determining the proportion of any change in *national income (GDP)* that goes to a change in desired consumption.

The marginal response of consumption to changes in national income ($\Delta C/\Delta Y$) is equal to the marginal propensity to consume out of disposable income ($\Delta C/\Delta Y_d$) multiplied by the

---

[3] A depreciation of sterling that is exactly proportional to the excess of UK inflation over foreign inflation will leave the relative price of UK exports and imports unchanged. This would be referred to as a constant *real exchange rate*, or as preserving purchasing power parity (PPP). The real exchange rate is the relative price of home- and foreign-produced goods. It is also referred to as 'competitiveness' or the 'terms of trade'. A rise in the real exchange rate (a fall in competitiveness) shifts the net export function down because it lowers exports and increases imports at each level of GDP. These concepts are discussed more fully in Chapter 22.

[4] In this case $T$, desired net taxes, would be given by the function $T = 0.1Y$. Recall that for simplicity we ignore indirect taxes.

**Table 17.3** Consumption as a function of disposable income and national income (GDP) (£ million)

| National income (GDP) ($Y$) | Disposable income ($Y_d = 0.9Y$) | Desired private consumption ($C = 100 + 0.8Y_d$) |
|---|---|---|
| 100 | 90 | 172 |
| 1,000 | 900 | 820 |
| 2,000 | 1,800 | 1,540 |
| 3,000 | 2,700 | 2,260 |
| 4,000 | 3,600 | 2,980 |

If desired private consumption spending depends on disposable income, which in turn depends on national income, desired consumption can be written as a function of either income concept. The second column shows deductions of 10 per cent of any level of national income to arrive at disposable income. Deductions of 10 per cent of $Y$ imply that the remaining 90 per cent of $Y$ becomes disposable income. The third column shows consumption as £100 million plus 80 per cent of disposable income.

By relating the second and third columns, one sees consumption as a function of disposable income. By relating the first and third columns, one sees the derived relationship between consumption and national income. In this example the change in consumption in response to a change in disposable income (i.e. MPC) is 0.8, and the change in consumption in response to a unit change in national income is 0.72.

fraction of national income (GDP) that becomes personal disposable income ($\Delta Y_d / \Delta Y$).

This table shows how desired consumption spending varies as national income varies, including the effects of taxes and transfer payments ($C = 100 + 0.72Y$; arrived at from $C = 100 + 0.8Y_d$ by substituting $0.9Y$ for $Y_d$). This equation is part of the aggregate spending function.

## The aggregate spending function

In order to determine the equilibrium level of GDP, we start by defining the aggregate spending function,

$$AE = C + I + G + NX.$$

Table 17.4 illustrates the calculation of this function. It shows a schedule of desired spending for each of the components of aggregate spending, and it shows total desired *aggregate* spending at each level of national income (GDP). Figure 17.4 shows this aggregate spending function in graphical form.

## The marginal propensity to spend

The slope of the aggregate spending function is the *marginal propensity to spend* on national output ($c$). With the addition of taxes and net exports, however, the marginal propensity to spend is no longer equal to the marginal propensity to consume.

**Table 17.4** The aggregate spending function (£ million)

| National income (GDP) ($Y$) | Desired private consumption spending ($C = 100 + 0.72Y$) | Desired investment spending ($I = 250$) | Desired government spending ($G = 170$) | Desired net export spending ($IM = 540 - 0.25Y$) | Desired aggregate spending ($AE = C + I + G + (X - IM)$) |
|---|---|---|---|---|---|
| 0 | 100 | 250 | 170 | 540 | 1,060 |
| 100 | 172 | 250 | 170 | 515 | 1,107 |
| 500 | 460 | 250 | 170 | 315 | 1,195 |
| 1,000 | 820 | 250 | 170 | 290 | 1,530 |
| **2,000** | 1,540 | 250 | 170 | 40 | **2,000** |
| 3,000 | 2,260 | 250 | 170 | −210 | 2,470 |
| 4,000 | 2,980 | 250 | 170 | −460 | 2,940 |
| 5,000 | 3,700 | 250 | 170 | −710 | 3,410 |

The aggregate spending function is the sum of desired private consumption, investment, government, and net export spending. The autonomous components of desired aggregate spending are desired investment, desired government spending, desired export spending, and the constant term in desired consumption (first row). These sum to £1,060 million in the above example. The induced components are the second terms in desired consumption spending (0.72$Y$) and desired imports (0.25$Y$).

The marginal response of consumption to a change in national income is 0.72, calculated as the product of the marginal propensity to consume (0.8) and the fraction of national income that becomes disposable income (0.9). The marginal response of desired aggregate spending to a change in national income, $\Delta AE / \Delta Y$, is 0.47.

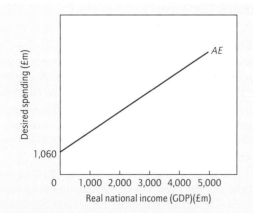

**Figure 17.4** **An aggregate spending curve**
**The aggregate spending curve relates total desired spending to national income.** The *AE* line in the figure plots the data from the first and last columns of Table 17.4. Its intercept shows £1,060 million of autonomous spending (£100 million autonomous consumption plus £250 million investment plus £170 million government spending plus £540 million autonomous net exports). Its slope is the marginal propensity to spend (which, following the calculations in Table 17.4, is 0.47 in this case).

Suppose that the economy produces £1 of extra income (and output) and that the response to this is governed by the relationships in Tables 17.1 and 17.2, as summarized in Table 17.4. Since £0.10 is collected by the government as net taxes, £0.90 is converted into disposable income, and 80 per cent of this amount (£0.72) becomes consumption spending. However, import spending also rises by £0.25, so spending on domestic goods—that is, aggregate spending—rises by only £0.47. Thus *c*, the marginal propensity to spend out of national income (GDP) is 0.47. What is not spent on domestic output includes the £0.10 in taxes, the £0.18 of disposable income that is saved, and the £0.25 of import spending, for a total of £0.53. Hence the marginal propensity not to spend, $(1 - c)$, is $1 - 0.47 = 0.53$.

### Determining equilibrium GDP

The logic of GDP determination in our (now more complicated) hypothetical economy is exactly the same as in the closed economy without government discussed in Chapter 16. We have added two new components of aggregate spending, *G* and *(X − IM)*. We have also made the calculation of desired private consumption spending more complicated: taxes must be subtracted from national income in order to determine personal disposable income. However, *equilibrium GDP is still the level of GDP at which desired aggregate spending equals national output (and income).*

The aggregate spending function can be used directly to determine equilibrium GDP. In Table 17.4 the equilibrium is £2,000 billion; when GDP is equal to £2,000 billion, it is also equal to desired aggregate spending.

Suppose that GDP is less than its equilibrium amount. The forces leading back to equilibrium are exactly the same as those described on pages 371–3 of Chapter 16. When domestic consumers, firms, foreign consumers, and governments try to spend at their desired amounts, they will try to purchase more goods and services than the economy is currently producing. Thus, some of the desired spending must either be frustrated or take the form of purchases of inventories of goods that were produced in the past. As firms see that they are (or could be) selling more than they are producing, they will increase production, thereby increasing the level of national output (and income).

The opposite sequence of events occurs when national output is greater than the level of aggregate desired spending at that level of GDP. Now the total of personal consumption, investment, government spending, and net foreign demand for the economy's output is less than the national product. Firms will be unable to sell all of their output. Their unsold stocks will be rising, and they will not let this happen indefinitely. They will seek to reduce the level of output until it equals the level of sales, and GDP (national output and income) will fall.

Finally, when national output is just equal to desired aggregate spending (£2,000 billion in Table 17.4), there is no pressure for output to change. Private consumption, investment, government consumption, and net exports just add up to the national product. Firms are producing exactly the quantity of goods and services that purchasers want to buy, given the level of national income.

**Equilibrium GDP is determined where desired aggregate spending equals national output. In our extended model aggregate spending includes private consumption, investment, government consumption, and net exports.**

### Graphical exposition

Figure 17.5 illustrates the determination of equilibrium GDP and the behaviour of the economy when it is not in equilibrium. The line labelled '*AE*' is simply the aggregate spending function shown in Figure 17.4. The slope of *AE* is the marginal propensity to spend out of national income (0.47 in our example). Recall that *AE* plots the behaviour of desired purchases. It shows demand for the domestic product at each level of national income (GDP). (The *AE* line is sometimes referred to as the 'aggregate demand curve' in this context. However, we reserve this term for another, related construct that we use in the

**Figure 17.5 Equilibrium GDP**

Equilibrium GDP occurs at $E_0$, where the desired aggregate spending line intersects the 45° line. Here the aggregate spending line is taken from Table 17.4; autonomous spending is £1,060 million, and the slope of AE is 0.47. If real GDP is below £2,000 million, desired aggregate spending will exceed national output, and production will rise. This is shown by the arrow to the left of Y = £2,000 million. If GDP is above £2,000 million, desired aggregate spending will be less than national output, and production will fall. This is shown by the arrow to the right of Y = £2,000 million. Only when real GDP is £2,000 million will desired aggregate spending equal real national output.

next chapter, once we have permitted the price level to be variable.)

The line labelled 'AE = Y' (the 45° line) depicts the equilibrium condition that desired aggregate spending be equal to actual national output (and income). Any point on this line *could* be an equilibrium, but only one is. Equilibrium occurs where behaviour (as depicted by the AE function) is consistent with equilibrium (as depicted by AE = Y). At the equilibrium level of GDP desired spending is just equal to national output (GDP) and is, therefore, just sufficient to purchase the total domestic product.

## The augmented saving–investment approach

An equivalent way of determining equilibrium GDP is analogous to finding the point where desired saving equals desired investment. Finding the level of income where $S = I$ was appropriate in Chapter 16, where we were dealing with a closed economy with no government. Now we have to take account of government as well as private saving, and net exports that provide an injection of spending that plays a similar role to investment.

### Additional injections and leakages

Saving and investment must be equal for GDP to be in equilibrium, as this provides a balance of inflows and outflows (injections and leakages). It may be helpful to review both the hydraulic analogue in Box 16.2 on page 373 and the circular flow of income and spending, illustrated in Figure 15.2 on page 340, at this stage. The principles involved are unchanged. Now, however, we have two additional sources of leakages and two additional sources of injections.

In Chapter 16 saving was the only leakage of spending from the circular flow. The marginal propensity to save told us how much was not spent out of each additional £1 of income received. Now we add personal income taxes. These are levied on individuals' gross incomes, so they too represent a proportion of income earned that cannot be spent. The second additional leakage is imports. Imports are a leakage because they create demand for foreign output, which does not generate domestic income.

Investment was the only injection in our model in Chapter 16. In this chapter we have added government spending. This is received as income by the private sector, and this extra income leads to further spending as before. Similarly, export demand comes from other countries, but it generates domestic incomes. Hence export demand is our second new injection.

The condition for GDP to be in equilibrium is now that the sum of desired injections should equal the sum of desired leakages. We can write this condition as an equation, with the sum of all leakages (saving, S, plus taxes, T, plus imports, IM) equal to the sum of all injections (investment, I, plus government spending, G, plus exports, X):

$$S + T + IM = I + G + X.$$

An equivalent equilibrium condition to AE = Y for the determination of equilibrium GDP is that injections (investment plus government spending plus exports) must equal leakages (saving plus taxes plus imports).

### Graphical exposition

In order to illustrate the determination of GDP via the equality of injections and leakages, it is convenient to rearrange the above equation. The graphical expression is made simpler, and the economic explanation more intuitive.

Subtracting G and IM from both sides of the above equation gives

$$S + (T - G) = I + (X - IM).$$

The brackets do not change the meaning of anything, but they do identify two terms we are already familiar with.

$(T - G)$ is the government budget surplus. In this context it can be thought of as public sector (government) saving. Since $S$ is private saving, $S + (T - G)$ is total domestic saving, or national saving. $(X - IM)$ is our old friend net exports. When there is no net income from abroad—that is, when GNI (or GNP) and GDP are equal (as was approximately true in the United Kingdom in 2005; GNI was about 2 per cent larger than GDP)—net exports equal the net accumulation of claims on foreigners. This is because if we sell to foreigners more than we buy from them, we must either acquire a new foreign asset or reduce some foreign liability. Hence net exports cause the net acquisition of foreign assets, or overseas investment. $I$ is domestic investment, so $I + (X - IM)$ is domestic plus overseas investment, or national asset formation. Thus, the equation $S + (T - G) = I + (X - IM)$ can be interpreted as a generalization of the condition that saving equals investment, since it says that national saving equals national asset formation.

Figure 17.6 illustrates how GDP is determined by the intersection of the national saving and national asset formation schedules. Notice that this is exactly the same level of GDP at which $AE = Y$.

**Figure 17.6** **National saving and national asset formation**

The economy is in equilibrium at $Y_0$, where desired national saving, $S + (T - G)$, equals desired national asset formation, $I + (X - IM)$. To the left of $Y_0$ desired national asset formation exceeds desired national saving. This implies that desired aggregate spending exceeds national output. Firms will respond to the imbalance by producing more, moving the economy towards equilibrium. To the right of $Y_0$ desired national asset formation is less than desired national saving, and aggregate spending is less than national output. Firms will cut back on output in order to avoid accumulating excess inventories, and the economy will move towards equilibrium.

# Changes in aggregate spending

Changes in any of the autonomous components of planned aggregate spending will cause changes in equilibrium GDP. In Chapter 16 we investigated the consequences of shifts in the consumption function and the investment function. Here we discuss fiscal policy—the effects of government spending and taxes. We also consider shifts in the net export function. First, we show that the simple multiplier is reduced by the presence of taxes and the marginal propensity to import.

### The simple multiplier revisited

In Chapter 16 we saw that the *simple multiplier*, the amount by which equilibrium GDP changes when autonomous spending changes by £1, was equal to $1/(1 - c)$. In the example considered throughout Chapter 16, $c$, the marginal propensity to spend, was equal to 0.8, and the multiplier was equal to 5, or $1/(0.2)$. In the example that we have developed in this chapter, with a marginal propensity to import of 0.25 and a marginal (net) income tax rate of 0.1, the marginal propensity to spend is 0.47. (One-tenth, or 10 per cent, of a £1 increase in autonomous spending goes to taxes, leaving 90p of disposable income.

With a marginal propensity to consume of 0.8, 72p is spent. Of this, 25p is spent on imports, leaving a total of 47p to be spent on domestically produced consumption goods.) Thus $(1 - c)$ is $(0.53)$, and the simple multiplier is $1/(0.53) = 1.89$.

## Fiscal policy

*Fiscal policy* involves the use of government spending and tax policies to influence total desired spending in order to achieve any specific goal set by the government.

Since government spending increases aggregate desired spending and taxation decreases it, the *directions* of the required changes in spending and taxation are generally easy to determine once we know the direction of the desired change in GDP. But the *timing*, *magnitude*, and *mixture* of the changes pose more difficult issues.

Any policy that attempts to stabilize GDP at or near any desired level (usually potential GDP) is called **stabilization policy**. The basic idea of stabilization policy follows from what we have already learned. A reduction in tax rates or an increase in government spending shifts the

**Box 17.1** The Keynesian revolution

In the 1930s there was a major slump affecting most of the industrial world. Unemployment in the United Kingdom reached levels around 20 per cent, and in the United States it was even higher. World trade collapsed and factories lay idle. The economic orthodoxy at the time suggested that the best course for policy-makers was to let market forces solve the problem. Prices would adjust to clear markets, and eventually excess supplies would be eliminated. Even if it was understood that this would take time, there was perceived to be nothing much that governments could do to help the process of recovery.

John Maynard Keynes challenged this conventional view in his path-breaking book, *The General Theory of Employment, Interest and Money* (Keynes, 1936). This work, and its subsequent interpretations and extensions, marks the beginning of macroeconomics as we are setting it out in Chapters 16–19.

One insight that Keynes expressed which would be considered valid today is that labour markets are not like conventional commodity markets, in that prices do not rapidly adjust to clear the market. This argument was discussed above in the context of the 'efficiency wage' in Chapter 11, and we shall return to it in Chapter 25 when we discuss unemployment. This means that unemployment can persist for a long time without the market mechanism doing much to eliminate it.

In the context where there is a general excess supply of productive resources, the question then arises: so why is demand not high enough to utilize these resources? Keynes's answer was 'effective demand failure'. What this means in terms of the analysis of this chapter is that the *AE* line is too low: it is leading to an equilibrium level of GDP (such as illustrated in Figure 17.5) that is well below its full-employment or potential level. Thus, the

cause of the 'great depression' was that one or all of $C + I + G + NX$ were too low, perhaps as a result of a collapse of consumer confidence (and the reinforcing effect of unemployment on incomes), a collapse of investor confidence (in the context of low demand for output), and/or a decline of world demand (as other countries were suffering too).

The analysis suggested not just the cause of the problem but also a potential solution. By increasing *G*, governments would create a positive multiplier effect, shift aggregate spending upwards, and lead to GDP being restored to its full-employment or potential level. Thus, the Keynesian revolution suggested an active role for fiscal policy in helping to stabilize the economy and a promise that mass unemployment could be a thing of the past. We discuss below (on pages 433–6) why these lofty ambitions for fiscal policy have more recently been tempered, but the idea did have a huge policy impact. It underpinned the New Deal policies of US President Roosevelt in the 1930s and was influential in many other countries, especially the UK, which in the post-Second World War period used fiscal policy actively to manage aggregate demand in an attempt to stabilize activity.

In December 1965, *Time Magazine* famously ran a cover story with the headline: 'We are all Keynesians now'. When President Nixon even more famously quoted the same statement in 1971, it was almost certainly no longer true. The problem most pressingly facing the world was moving on from unemployment to inflation and high energy prices. Concerning inflation, governments came closer to being villains rather than saviours and so limitations were imposed on fiscal discretion. As Keynes himself was quoted as saying, 'When the facts change, I change my mind—what do you do, sir?'

---

*AE* line upward, causing an increase in equilibrium GDP. An increase in tax rates or a decrease in government spending shifts the *AE* line downward, causing a decrease in equilibrium GDP.

If the government has some target level of GDP, it can use its taxation and spending as instruments to push the economy towards that target. First, suppose the economy is in a serious recession. The government would like to increase GDP. The appropriate fiscal tools are to raise spending and/or to lower tax rates. Second, suppose the economy is 'overheated'. In the next two chapters we will study what this means in detail. In the meantime we observe that an 'overheated' economy has such a high level of GDP (relative to potential) that shortages are pushing up prices and causing inflation. Without worrying too much about the details, just assume that the current level of GDP is higher than the target level that the government

judges to be appropriate. What should the government do? The fiscal tools at its command are to lower government spending and to raise tax rates, both of which will have a depressing effect on GDP.

The proposition that governments can alleviate recessions by deliberately stimulating aggregate demand created a major revolution in economic thought. This is still known as the Keynesian revolution. Box 17.1 gives further background on the origins of this revolution and its impact on policy. We have already done enough macroeconomics to understand what this was all about. According to the theory we have developed so far, an economy can reach an equilibrium level of GDP well below its full-employment or potential level. According to Keynesian theory, governments can use fiscal policy to increase aggregate spending by increasing government spending or reducing taxes (or both).

The aggregate spending model of national income and output determination predicts that GDP can get stuck at a level below its full potential. It also suggests how fiscal policy might be used to return an economy to its potential level of GDP.

Now let us look in a little more detail at how this might work out. Bear in mind, however, that we are still dealing with a special case in which prices are fixed and there is excess capacity, so we are just looking at how our present model works, not yet at how the real world works.

### Changes in government spending

Suppose the government decides to increase its road-building programme by £10 million a year.[5] Desired government spending ($G$) rises by £10 million at every level of income, shifting $AE$ upwards by the same amount. By how much would equilibrium GDP change? This can be calculated, in our simple model, using the multiplier. Government purchases are part of autonomous spending, so a *change* in government consumption of $\Delta G$ will lead to a *change* in equilibrium GDP of the multiplier times $\Delta G$. In this numerical example equilibrium GDP would rise by £10 million times the simple multiplier, or £18.9 million. Figure 17.7 shows the effect on GDP of an increase in government spending. It shows an upward parallel shift of the aggregate spending function, and a resulting increase in GDP. The same analysis could be applied equally to an increase in any other autonomous spending, such as investment or exports.

Reducing government spending has the opposite effect of shifting the $AE$ function downwards, parallel to itself, and reducing equilibrium GDP. For example, if the government were to spend £2 million less on new roads, equilibrium GDP would fall by £2 million times the simple multiplier, or £3.78 million.

A change in government spending, in this model, changes the equilibrium level of GDP by the size of the spending change times the simple multiplier.

### Changes in tax rates

If tax rates change, the difference between disposable income and national income changes. As a result the relationship between desired consumption spending and national income also changes. For any given level

**Figure 17.7** The effect of a change in government spending

A change in government spending changes GDP by shifting the $AE$ line parallel to its initial position. The figure shows the effect of an increase in government spending. The initial level of aggregate spending is $AE_0$, and the equilibrium level of GDP is $Y_0$, with desired spending $e_0$. An increase in government spending shifts aggregate spending upwards to $AE_1$. As a result GDP rises to $Y_1$, at which level desired spending is $e_1$. The increase in GDP from $Y_0$ to $Y_1$ is equal to the increase in government spending times the multiplier.

A reduction in government spending can be analysed in the same figure if we start with aggregate spending function $AE_1$ and GDP $Y_1$. A reduction in government spending shifts the $AE$ function downwards from $AE_1$ to $AE_0$, and as a result equilibrium GDP falls from $Y_1$ to $Y_0$. The fall is equal to the change in government spending times the multiplier.

of national income, there will be a different level of disposable income and thus a different level of consumption. Consequently, a change in tax rates will also cause a change in $c$, the marginal propensity to spend out of national income.

Consider a decrease in the tax rate. If the government decreases its rate of income tax so that it collects 5p less out of every £1 of national income, then disposable income rises in relation to national income. Thus consumption, which depends on disposable income, will also rise at every level of national income. This results in a non-parallel upward shift of the $AE$ line, that is, an increase in the slope of the line, as shown in Figure 17.8. The result of this shift will be a rise in equilibrium GDP.

A rise in the tax rate has the opposite effect. It causes a given percentage decrease in disposable income, and hence in consumption spending, at each level of national income. This results in a (non-parallel) downward shift of the $AE$ line and therefore decreases the level of equilibrium GDP.

---

[5] It does not matter what we assume the extra spending goes on. In our model it is always spent on the output of the single homogeneous industrial sector. Notice also that the value of the multiplier used in this section is hypothetical and is based on the numerical example in Table 17.4.

**Figure 17.8 The effect of changing the tax rate**

Changing the tax rate changes equilibrium GDP by changing the slope of the *AE* line. A reduction in the tax rate pivots the *AE* line from $AE_0$ to $AE_2$. The new curve has a steeper slope, because the lower tax rate withdraws a smaller amount of national income from the desired consumption flow. Equilibrium GDP rises from $Y_0$ to $Y_2$, because at every level of national income desired consumption, and hence aggregate spending, is higher. If we take $AE_2$ and $Y_2$ to be the initial equilibrium, an increase in tax rates will reduce the slope of the *AE* line, thereby reducing equilibrium GDP, as shown by $AE_0$ and $Y_0$.

## Tax rates and the multiplier

We have seen that the *simple multiplier* is equal to the reciprocal of one minus the marginal propensity to spend out of national income. That is, the multiplier equals $1/(1 - c)$. The simple multiplier tells us how much equilibrium GDP changes when autonomous spending changes by £1 and there is no change in prices.

When tax rates change, the multiplier also changes. Suppose that *MPC* is 0.8 and the tax rate *falls* by 5p per pound of national income. This would increase the marginal propensity to spend by 4p per pound of national income. (Disposable income would rise by 5p per pound at each level of national income, and consumption would rise by the marginal propensity to consume, i.e. 0.8, times 5p, which is 4p.) The increase in the value of *c*, the marginal propensity to spend, would cause the multiplier to rise, making equilibrium GDP more responsive to changes in autonomous spending from any source. In our example the multiplier has gone up from 1.89 to 1.96 (that is, $(1 - c)$ has fallen from 0.53 to 0.51).

The lower the income tax rate, the larger is the simple multiplier.

GDP may change as a result of a shift in any of the other exogenous components of spending—net exports, investment, and autonomous consumption. An increase in any of these would increase GDP by the shift times the multiplier, as illustrated (for the case of a government spending increase) in Figure 17.7. An increase in any exogenous spending shifts the *AE* line vertically upwards by the amount of the spending increase. The new intersection with the 45° line determines the new level of GDP, and its increase is measured relative to the original position on the horizontal axis. A reduction in any of these exogenous spending components would shift the *AE* line downwards by the amount of the fall in spending.

Changes that would alter the slope of the *AE* line are a shift in the marginal propensity to consume, a shift in the rate of income tax, and a shift in the propensity to import. A fall in the marginal propensity to save (hence a rise in *MPC*, the marginal propensity to consume), a fall in the income tax rate, and a fall in the propensity to import will all make the *AE* line steeper and increase the multiplier, as illustrated in Figure 17.8. A rise in any of these three has the opposite effect.

### Balanced budget changes

Another policy available to the government is to make a balanced budget change by altering spending and taxes equally. Say the government increases tax rates enough to raise an extra £100 million which it then uses to purchase goods and services. Aggregate spending would remain unchanged if, and only if, the £100 million that the government takes from the private sector would otherwise have been spent by that sector. If so, the government's policy would reduce private spending by £100 million and raise its own spending by £100 million. Aggregate demand, and hence national income and employment, would remain unchanged.

But this is not the case in our model. When an extra £100 million in taxes is taken away from households, they reduce their spending on domestically produced goods by less than £100 million. If the marginal propensity to consume out of disposable income is, say, 0.75, consumption spending will fall by only £75 million. If the government spends the entire £100 million on domestically produced goods, aggregate spending will increase by £25 million. In this case the balanced budget increase in government spending will have an expansionary effect because it will shift the aggregate spending function upwards and thereby increase GDP.

A balanced budget increase in government spending will have a mild expansionary effect on GDP, and a balanced budget decrease will have a mild contractionary effect.

The **balanced budget multiplier** measures these effects. It is the change in GDP divided by the balanced budget change in government spending that brought it about. Thus, if the extra £100 million of spending (combined with the tax increases to finance it) causes GDP to rise by £50 million, the balanced budget multiplier is 0.5; if GDP rises by £100 million, it is 1.0.

When government spending is increased with no corresponding increase in tax rates, we say it is deficit-financed. Because there is no increase in tax rates, there is no consequent decrease in consumption to offset the increase in government spending. With a balanced budget increase in spending, however, an offsetting increase in the tax rate and decrease in consumption do occur. Thus, the balanced budget multiplier is much lower than the multiplier that relates the change in GDP to a deficit-financed increase in government spending (with the tax rate constant).

## Monetary policy

Monetary policy influences aggregate spending through several channels which we will study in detail in Chapter 21. We have already mentioned the most important of these in this and the previous chapter. **Monetary policy** works via the effects of interest rates on aggregate spending, and the monetary authorities can set any short-term interest rate that they desire.

As we saw in Chapter 16, interest rate changes affect consumer spending. Higher interest rates encourage people to cut their spending in order to save more and discourage borrowing in order to spend more. In addition, they generate wealth effects on consumption via changes in the value of financial assets and property. We also saw that interest rates affect investment, with higher interest rates discouraging firms from borrowing in order to invest in such things as new equipment. Another channel from interest rates to aggregate spending is via the effect on the exchange rate to net exports (discussed further below).

Interest rate changes lead to a shift in spending (whether it be consumption, investment, or net exports) and can be analysed in the same way as a change of government spending shown in Figure 17.7. A rise in interest rates reduces some components of spending and thereby shifts the *AE* line downwards. A cut in interest rates raises spending and shifts the *AE* line upwards. There is thus a negative relationship between the interest rate and aggregate spending, and between interest rates and GDP from the spending side of the economy. We make use of this relationship again in Chapter 21.

The monetary authorities will aim to lower aggregate spending if actual GDP is above potential, that is, if demand in the economy is running ahead of the capacity to produce. They will wish to stimulate spending if actual GDP is below potential, that is, if demand is low compared to supply capacity. For the moment, however, the key point to notice is that monetary policy works by influencing one or more of the categories of aggregate spending that we have studied in this and the previous chapter.

## Net exports and equilibrium GDP

As with the other elements of desired aggregate spending, if the net export function shifts upward, equilibrium GDP will rise; if the net export function shifts downward, equilibrium GDP will fall. Again, we take the UK as the home country.

### Autonomous net exports

Net exports have both an autonomous component and an induced component. We have assumed that exports themselves are autonomous (exogenous) with respect to domestic GDP. Foreign demand for UK goods and services depends on foreign income, on foreign and UK prices, and on the exchange rate, but it does not depend on UK domestic income. Export demand could also change because of a change in tastes. Suppose that foreign consumers develop a taste for British-made goods (perhaps in reality Jaguars or Land Rovers, but in the model it is for the output of the single sector) and desire to purchase £500 million per year more of such goods than in the past. The net export function (and the aggregate spending function) will shift up by £500 million, and equilibrium GDP will increase by £500 million times the multiplier.

### Induced net exports

The domestic demand for imports depends in part on domestic income. The greater is domestic income, the greater will be UK residents' demand for goods and services in general, including those produced abroad. Because imports are subtracted to obtain net exports (net exports equal $X - IM$), the greater is the marginal propensity to import, the lower will be the marginal propensity to spend on the domestic product, and the lower will be the multiplier, $1/(1 - c)$.

#### The exchange rate regime

We have noted above that foreign demand for domestic exports will depend upon the exchange rate (and that this can be affected by the interest rate set by the monetary authorities). The way in which the exchange rate interacts with net exports will vary according to the exchange rate regime in operation at the time. For example, the adjustment of net exports will be different if the exchange rate is floating (determined by market forces) rather than pegged. It may be different again for countries that share a common currency, such as in the euro zone. We discuss the implication of various exchange rate regimes for external adjustment in some detail in Chapter 23, once we have added money to the model. For now we assume that there are no endogenous exchange rate changes affecting net exports, so our economy can best be thought of as one with a fixed exchange rate regime. The importance of this assumption will become apparent later.

## Lessons and limitations of the income–spending approach

In this and the preceding chapter we have discussed the determination of the four categories of aggregate spending and seen how they simultaneously determine equilibrium national income and output (GDP). The basic approach, which is the same no matter how many categories are considered, was first presented in Chapter 16 and has been restated and extended in this chapter.

Any factor that shifts one or more of the components of desired aggregate spending will change equilibrium GDP, *at a given price level*. Holding the price constant has been necessary because we do not yet have a supply side to our analysis. So the level of GDP that we have been determining is the one that would be determined by demand conditions alone. The true outcome will depend on supply behaviour as well as demand behaviour, so what we have done so far is only part of the story.

In the following chapters we augment the income-spending model by allowing the price level to change in both the short run and the long run. That is, we explicitly add a relationship that determines aggregate supply. When prices change, real GDP will change by amounts different from those predicted by the simple multiplier. We will see that changes in desired aggregate spending generally change both prices *and* real GDP. This is why the simple multiplier, derived under the assumption that prices do not change, is too simple.

However, there are three ways in which the simple income–aggregate spending model developed here remains useful, even when prices are incorporated. First, the simple multiplier will continue to be a valuable starting-place in calculating actual changes in GDP in response to changes in autonomous spending. Second, no matter what the price level is, the components of aggregate spending add up to GDP in equilibrium. Third, no matter what the price level is, equilibrium requires that desired aggregate spending must equal output (GDP) in equilibrium —or, equivalently, that injections equal leakages.

# CASE STUDIES

## 1. Fiscal stance: the cyclically adjusted budget deficit

As we saw in Figure 17.1, the government budget deficit (surplus) generally falls (rises) in a boom and rises (falls) in a recession. The reason for this is that tax revenues rise when the economy is booming and some spending components, such as unemployment-related benefits fall as activity rises. One implication of this is that you cannot judge from raw data on government budget deficits whether the budget is stimulating demand or is net contractionary. A deficit could have been caused by a recession, rather than by an attempt to alter the fiscal stance in order to stimulate the economy.

A clearer picture emerges if the actual budget is adjusted to what it would have been if the economy had been at potential GDP. In this way we can see whether there would have been a budget deficit even when the economy was running at its sustainable capacity level. This measure is referred to as the 'cyclically adjusted budget deficit'.

Figure 17.9 shows the net borrowing of the UK government as a percentage of GDP between 1972 and 2005 in actual and cyclically adjusted form. Net borrowing is the inverse of the overall budget deficit, so that larger borrowing arises from a bigger deficit and vice versa.

In the years between 1998 and 2005 there is little difference between the actual and the cyclically adjusted borrowing. This is because throughout this period GDP was close to potential (see Figure 15.1 on page 336). However, in the 1980s the pattern looks quite different when cycle adjustment is allowed for. In cycle-adjusted terms, fiscal policy was very tight in the mid-1980s, even though there was an actual budget deficit at the time. This resulted from an episode when taxes were raised sharply even though the economy was in recession (and 365 economists signed a protest letter as a result). Periods of fiscal looseness are evident in the mid-1970s and mid-1990s, and there were also signs of increasing fiscal looseness in 2003–5 after a period of tightness around the beginning of the new millenium.

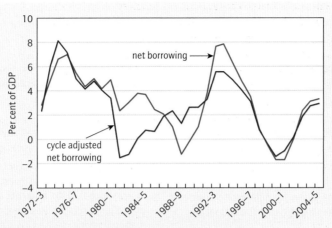

**Figure 17.9** UK government borrowing as percentage of GDP, 1972–2005
*Source*: *Pre-Budget Report*, 2005.

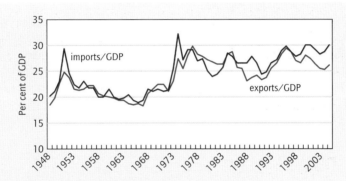

**Figure 17.10** Exports and imports as a percentage of GDP, UK, 1948–2005
*Source*: ONS National Accounts: www.statistics.gov.uk (annual data)

## 2. The openness of the economy

The UK is an open economy, and in many ways it has become more open in recent years, owing to falling transport costs, cheaper communication technology, and lower barriers to international trade. 'Globalization' has become the buzz word for the process that is alleged to be affecting us all. However, media hype and political agitation can create a mistaken impression of what has actually been happening.

Figure 17.10 shows the proportion of exports and imports of goods and services in GDP for the UK economy from 1948 to 2005. There has clearly been an upward trend. Imports and exports in 1948 were around 20 per cent of GDP, and in the mid-2000s they seemed to be fluctuating in the 25–30 per cent range. However, most of this upward movement happened in the late 1960s, and early 1970s. If we had drawn the chart

just since 1974, no upward trend would be evident. Indeed, the highest import-to-GDP ratio since the Second World War was achieved in 1974, presumably as a result of the rising price of imported oil, and the highest export to GDP ratio in this period was achieved in 1977.

This suggests that there is not a strong trend towards ever-increasing openness of the economy. Globalization of trade in some products, such as manufactured goods and food products (e.g. fresh fruit), is perhaps being offset by a growing proportion of services in GDP, and many services are provided locally rather than being traded in a global marketplace. What is also apparent from the chart is that imports and exports tend to move together in the long run. There are periods when the gap (the balance of trade in goods and services) tends to widen, but these deviations do not get ever wider even though they may persist for many years.

# SUMMARY

### Government spending and taxes

■ Government consumption is part of autonomous aggregate spending. Taxes minus transfer payments are called net taxes and affect aggregate spending indirectly. Taxes reduce disposable income, whereas transfers increase disposable income. Disposable income, in turn, determines desired private consumption, according to the consumption function.

■ The budget balance is defined as government revenues minus government spending. When this difference is positive the budget is in surplus; when it is negative the budget is in deficit.

■ When the budget is in surplus, there is positive public saving, because the government is spending less on the national product than the amount of income that it is withdrawing from the circular flow of income and spending. When the government budget is in deficit, public saving is negative.

### Net exports

■ Since desired imports increase as national income increases, desired net exports decrease as national income (GDP) increases, other things being equal. Hence the net export function is negatively sloped (net exports fall as GDP rises).

### Equilibrium GDP

■ GDP is in equilibrium when desired aggregate spending, $C + I + G + (X - IM)$, equals national output.

■ The sum of investment and net exports is called national asset formation, because investment is the increase in the domestic capital stock and net exports result in investment in foreign assets. At the equilibrium level of GDP, desired national saving, $S + T - G$, is just equal to national asset formation, $I + X - IM$.

### Changes in aggregate spending

■ The size of the multiplier is negatively related to the income tax rate.

■ A shift in exogenous spending changes GDP by the value of the shift times the simple multiplier.

■ A shift in aggregate spending can be brought about by fiscal policy changes or by a change in the official interest rate.

# TOPICS FOR REVIEW

■ Taxes and net taxes

■ Budget balance

■ Public saving

■ Net export function

■ Marginal propensity to spend

■ National asset formation

■ National saving

■ Calculation of the simple multiplier

■ Fiscal policy and equilibrium GDP

■ Monetary policy

# QUESTIONS

1 Using the same notation as in the text, solve for the value of GDP, given the following relationships and values of exogenous variables: $C = 100 + 0.8(Y - T)$; $IM = 0.25Y$; $I = 1,000$; $G = 100$; $T = 100$; $X = 500$ (where $T$ is a lump-sum income tax).

2 Repeat question 1 where income tax is a proportion of income so that the consumption function can be written $C = 100 + 0.8(1 - t)Y$ where $t$ is the income tax rate that can be taken as 0.2 (i.e. 20 per cent).

3 How does the answer to question 1 change if (a) $G$ rises to 200, (b) $X$ rises to 600, (c) $I$ rises to 1,100? (Take all other exogenous variables to be at their initial value in each case.)

4 Using the relationships in question 1, calculate (a) the impact on GDP of an equal increase in $G$ and $T$, (b) the impact of an equal increase in $X$ and $IM$. (Hint: increase each by the same number, say 100. In the case of $IM$, add the chosen number as an intercept to its equation.)

5 Explain how governments might try to use their fiscal policy instruments to end a recession. What practical difficulties might be encountered in implementing such a policy?

6 Why does the trade balance deteriorate as domestic income increases?

7 How is the size of the multiplier related to (a) the income tax rate, (b) the marginal propensity to import, (c) the marginal propensity to consume?

8 Explain how a change in foreign demand for UK goods will affect the level of UK GDP.

9 For the model of GDP determination set out above to be adequate, what must be assumed about the supply side of the economy? Are the necessary assumptions plausible?

# Chapter 18

# GDP AND THE PRICE LEVEL IN THE SHORT RUN

In this chapter we add supply forces to our analysis and as a result we are able to determine the price level in our model. So far the only changes affecting the economy have been shifts in categories of autonomous spending—variables such as investment, exports, and government spending. Changes in these variables, which we refer to as *shocks*, have an effect on the equilibrium value of real GDP. The shocks we have dealt with so far are all on the demand side of the economy, and so are referred to as *demand shocks*. However, other changes affect the supply side of the economy. A change in world oil prices, for example, or a change in the production technology will certainly have an impact, but this impact will be on the supply side, so we call these *supply shocks*. Virtually all shocks to the economy on both the demand and the supply sides affect *both* real GDP *and* the price level; that is, they affect both the volume of goods and services produced and the money values of those goods and services, at least initially. In other words, such shocks have both *real* and *nominal* effects. To understand these effects, we need to develop some further tools, called the *aggregate demand curve* and the *aggregate supply curve*.

In particular, in this chapter you will learn that:

- Aggregate demand is the level of desired real domestic spending at each price level.

- The aggregate demand curve plots the negative relationship between GDP and the price level.

- An exogenous change in autonomous spending (a *demand shock*) shifts the aggregate demand curve horizontally by the multiplier times the initial change in spending.

- The aggregate supply curve reflects a positive relationship between output and the price level, for given input prices.

- An exogenous change in input prices or technology (a *supply shock*) shifts the short-run aggregate supply curve.

- The equilibrium levels of GDP and the price level are determined where aggregate demand and supply are equal.

In order to determine the price level as well as real GDP, we need an explicit description of the supply side of our economy. No longer will we maintain the assumption that national output is purely demand-determined because there is excess productive capacity.

We make the transition to a variable price level in two steps. First, we study the consequences for GDP of *exogenous* changes in the price level—changes that happen for reasons that are not explained by our present model of the economy. This allows us to develop what we call the aggregate demand curve. Then we develop a theory of aggregate supply which, when combined with aggregate demand, explains simultaneous movements in both GDP *and* the price level. As a result, we can analyse more realistic situations where an economy operates close to potential GDP.[1]

---

[1] Recall that potential GDP may sometimes be referred to as *full-employment* or *capacity output*. Each of these concepts may have slightly different meanings in different contexts. The key feature for present purposes, however, is that we are talking about the maximum level of GDP that is currently sustainable without generating inflation.

# Aggregate demand

What happens to real GDP when all money prices change for some exogenous reason? We look at this question first from the spending side of the economy, then from the production side, and finally we put the two together. To find out what happens on the demand side, we need to understand how the change affects desired aggregate spending.

## Shifts in the *AE* line

There is one key result that we need to establish: a rise in the price level shifts the aggregate spending curve downward, while a fall in the price level shifts it upward. In other words, the price level and desired aggregate spending are negatively related to each other. A major part of the explanation lies in the way the change in the price level affects desired private consumption spending and desired net exports.

### Changes in private consumption

The link between a change in the price level and changes in desired consumption is provided by wealth. This link is in two parts.

The first part is provided by the effect of changes in the price level on the wealth of the private sector. Much of this wealth is held in the form of assets with a fixed nominal money value. One obvious example is money itself—cash and bank deposits. Other examples include many kinds of financial instruments, such as government bonds (gilts) and bills. When a bill or a bond matures, the owner is repaid a stated sum of money. What that money can buy—its real value—depends on the price level. The higher the price level, the less that sum of money can purchase. For this reason, a rise in the domestic price level lowers the real value of all assets that are denominated in money units.

How does this affect individuals? An individual who holds a bond has loaned money to the agent that issued it. When the real value of the asset falls the holder has his or her wealth reduced. However, the real wealth of the issuer of the bond has increased. This is because the money value of the bond buys fewer real goods and services as a result of the rise in the price level. So the agent that has to repay the bond will part with less purchasing power to do so, and so has more wealth. For example, if you are owed £100 in one year's time, that sum will be worth less to you if prices rise by 20 per cent over the year

than if they remain unchanged. However, the person who owes you the £100 will be better off by an amount equal to your loss if prices rise rather than remain unchanged, in that she will have to give up fewer goods to repay you.

A change in the price level affects the wealth of holders of assets denominated in money terms in exactly the opposite way to how it affects the wealth of those who issued the asset.

### Inside assets

An *inside asset* is one that is issued by some agent (an individual or a firm) in the private sector and held by some other agent in the private sector. It follows that, for inside assets, a rise in the price level lowers the real wealth of a bond-holder but raises the real wealth of the bond-issuer, who will have to part with less purchasing power when the bond is redeemed. With inside assets, therefore, the wealth changes are exactly offsetting. A rise in the price level lowers the real wealth of the person who owns any asset that is denominated in money, but it raises the real wealth of the person who must redeem the asset. So with inside assets a change in the price level has no net effect on private sector wealth.

### Outside assets

*Outside assets* are those held by an agent in the domestic private sector but issued by some agent outside that sector—in practice, this usually means the government or any foreign issuer. In this case the only private sector wealth-holders to experience wealth changes when the price level changes are the holders of the outside assets. There are no offsetting private sector wealth changes for the issuers of the assets, since they are not in the private sector. It follows that a change in the price level does cause a change in net private wealth held in outside assets denominated in nominal money units. A rise in the price level lowers the real wealth of holders of these assets.[2]

A change in the price level causes no net change in the wealth of the private sector with respect to inside assets, but it does cause a change with respect to outside assets, since the issuers are not in the private sector; private sector wealth and

---

[2] We are assuming that taxpayers do not include in their wealth calculations the real value of future tax liabilities. Taxpayers must pay taxes to service the national debt, and when a rise in the price level lowers its real value, it also lowers the real value of future tax liabilities by exactly the same amount. We ignore this possible offsetting change.

the price level vary in opposite directions, with wealth falling when prices rise and rising when prices fall.

The second link in the chain running from changes in the price level to changes in desired consumption is provided by the relationship between wealth and consumption that we stressed in Chapter 16 (see Figure 16.4 on page 368). Whenever individuals suffer a decrease in their wealth, they increase their saving so as to restore their wealth to the level that they desire for such purposes as retirement. At any level of income, of course, an increase in desired saving implies a reduction in desired consumption. Conversely, whenever individuals experience an increase in their wealth, they reduce their saving and consume more, causing an upward shift in the line that relates desired consumption spending and national income.

A rise in the domestic price level lowers the real value of total private sector wealth by lowering the real value of outside assets denominated in money units; this leads to a fall in desired private consumption; this in turn implies a downward shift in the aggregate spending curve. A fall in the domestic price level leads to a rise in wealth and desired private consumption, and thus to an upward shift in the aggregate spending line, AE.

We have concentrated here on the direct effect of a change in wealth on desired private consumption spending. There is also an indirect effect which operates through the interest rate. Although this effect is potentially very powerful, we cannot study it until we have studied the macroeconomic role of money and interest rates. Further discussion of this point must therefore be postponed until Chapter 21.

### Changes in net exports

When the domestic price level rises, domestically produced goods become more expensive relative to foreign goods. This change in relative prices causes domestic consumers to reduce their purchases of domestically produced goods (which have now become relatively more expensive) and to increase their purchases of foreign goods (which have now become relatively less expensive). At the same time, consumers in other countries reduce their purchases of the now relatively expensive domestic goods. We saw in Chapter 17 that these changes can be summarized as a downward shift in the net export function.

A rise in the domestic price level shifts the net export function downward, which shifts the aggregate spending curve downward. A fall in the domestic price level shifts the net export function and the aggregate spending curve upward.

To summarize, if home-produced goods and services become more expensive, fewer of them will be bought, so total desired spending on UK output will fall; if home-produced goods and services become cheaper, more will be bought, and total desired spending on them will rise.[3]

## Demand-induced changes in GDP

Because it shifts both the net export function and the consumption function downwards, a rise in the price level also shifts the aggregate desired spending curve downwards, as shown in Figure 18.1. This figure also allows us to reconfirm what we already know from Chapter 17: when the AE line shifts downward, the level of GDP falls.

A rise in the domestic price level reduces GDP because it causes the aggregate spending curve to shift downward—all other exogenous variables being held constant.

Since a fall in the domestic price level is the opposite of the case that we have just studied, we can quickly summarize the two key effects. First, domestic goods become relatively cheaper internationally, so net exports rise. Second, the real value of some money assets increases, so consumers spend more. The resulting increase in desired spending is represented by an upward shift of the AE line that raises GDP, as shown in Figure 18.1.

A fall in the domestic price level increases real GDP because it shifts the aggregate spending curve upward—all other exogenous variables being held constant.

Notice that level of GDP determined by aggregate spending (and the condition that injections equal leakages) would have been described in Chapter 17 as the 'equilibrium' level of GDP. This certainly would be the equilibrium for GDP if only demand side forces mattered, but we are soon going to combine demand-side and supply-side forces. Demand and supply combined will then determine the equilibrium level of GDP (and the price level). So only when we put aggregate demand and aggregate supply together will we have the full 'equilibrium' outcome.

## The aggregate demand (AD) curve

We now know from the behaviour underlying the aggregate spending curve (AE) that the price level and real GDP (as determined on the spending side of the economy) are

---

[3] This assumes that the price elasticity of demand for traded goods exceeds unity, so that a fall in price leads to both a greater volume and a greater value being bought.

**Figure 18.1 Aggregate spending and the price level**

Changes in the price level cause the *AE* line to shift and GDP to change. At the initial price level the *AE* line is given by the solid line $AE_0$, hence the level of GDP consistent with injections equal to leakages is $Y_0$. An increase in the price level reduces desired aggregate spending and thereby causes the *AE* line to shift downward to the dashed line $AE_1$. As a result GDP falls to $Y_1$. Starting with the dashed line $AE_1$, a fall in the price level increases desired aggregate spending, shifting the *AE* line up to $AE_0$ and raising GDP to $Y_0$.

**(i) Aggregate spending**

**(ii) Aggregate demand**

**Figure 18.2 The *AD* curve and the *AE* line**

GDP consistent with spending decisions is determined by the *AE* line for each given price level; the level of GDP and its associated price level are then plotted to yield a point on the *AD* curve. When the price level is $P_0$ the *AE* line is $AE_0$, hence demand-determined GDP is $Y_0$, as shown in part (i). (This reproduces the initial position from Figure 18.1.) Plotting $Y_0$ against $P_0$ yields the point $E_0$ on the *AD* curve in part (ii).

An increase in the price level to $P_1$ causes $AE_0$ in part (i) to shift downward to $AE_1$ and so causes GDP to fall to $Y_1$. Plotting this new, lower level of GDP $Y_1$ against the higher price level, $P_1$, yields a second point, $E_1$, on the *AD* curve in part (ii). A further increase in the price level to $P_2$ causes the *AE* line in part (i) to shift downward further, to $AE_2$, thereby causing GDP to fall further, to $Y_2$. Plotting $Y_2$ against $P_2$ yields a third point, $E_2$, on the *AD* curve in part (ii).

Thus, a change in the price level causes a shift in the *AE* line in part (i) and a movement along the *AD* curve in part (ii).

negatively related to each other. That is, a change in the price level changes GDP in the opposite direction, holding all other exogenous variables (such as government consumption, tax rates, exports, and investment) constant. This negative relationship can be shown in an important new construct called the *aggregate demand curve*.

Recall that the *AE* line relates national income (GDP) to desired spending for a given price level, plotting income on the horizontal axis. The **aggregate demand (*AD*) curve** relates GDP to the price level, again plotting GDP on the horizontal axis.[4] Because the horizontal axes of both the *AE* and the *AD* curves measure real GDP (national income), the two curves can be placed one above the other so that the level of GDP on each can be compared directly. This is shown in Figure 18.2.

Now let us see how the *AD* curve is derived. Given a value of the price level, equilibrium GDP is determined in part (i) of Figure 18.2 at the point where the *AE* line crosses the 45° line. In part (ii) of Figure 18.2 the combination of the level of GDP (for which injections equal leakages)

and the corresponding value of the price level is plotted, giving one point on the *AD* curve.

When the price level changes, the *AE* line shifts, for the reasons just seen. The new position of the *AE* line gives rise to a new level of GDP that is associated with the new price

---

[4] Don't forget that 'GDP' and 'national income' are the same thing. It is income that determines aggregate spending, and that spending in turn determines output. But any level of output generates an equivalent level of income. So income, output, and spending must all be consistent.

level. This determines a second point on the *AD* curve, as shown in Figure 18.2(ii).

Any change in the price level leads to a new *AE* line and hence to a new level of GDP consistent with injections and leakages being in balance. Each combination of GDP and its associated price level defines a particular point on the *AD* curve.

Note that, because the *AD* curve relates real GDP to the price level, changes in the price level that cause *shifts in* the *AE* line cause *movements along* the *AD* curve. A movement along the *AD* curve thus traces out the response of the level of GDP to a change in the price level that would be determined by aggregate spending alone. Notice also that the only exogenous change we are permitting at present is a change in the price level.

The aggregate demand curve shows, for each price level, the associated level of GDP for which aggregate desired spending equals total output, and is consistent with the level of income generated at that output.

In Chapter 17 we showed that points for which aggregate desired spending is equal to output are equivalent to points for which injections equal leakages (or, in the model of Chapter 16, for which investment equals saving). This equivalence carries through to the *AD* curve. Hence points on the *AD* curve are combinations of real GDP and the price level (for given values of all exogenous spending) for which injections equal leakages, that is, for which $I + G + X = S + T + IM$. Recall that this equation can be rearranged to make clear the further equivalence to the condition that national saving is equal to national asset formation: $S + (T - G) = I + (X - IM)$.

### The slope of the *AD* curve

Figure 18.2 shows that the *AD* curve is negatively sloped. Starting from some specific point on the *AD* curve,

1.  a rise in the price level causes the aggregate spending line, *AE*, to shift downward and hence leads to a movement upward and to the left along the *AD* curve, reflecting a fall in the associated level of GDP;

2.  a fall in the price level causes the aggregate spending line, *AE*, to shift upward and hence leads to a movement downward and to the right along the *AD* curve, reflecting a rise in the associated level of GDP.

In Chapter 3 we saw that demand curves for individual goods such as carrots and cars are negatively sloped. However, the reasons for the negative slope of the *AD* curve are different from the reasons for the negative slope of the individual demand curves that are used in microeconomics. This important point is discussed further in Box 18.1.

 **Box 18.1  The shape of the aggregate demand curve**

In Chapter 3 we studied the demand curves for individual products. It is tempting to think that the properties of the aggregate demand curve arise from the same behaviour that gives rise to those individual demand curves. However, this would involve committing the fallacy of composition; that is, assuming that what is correct for the parts must be correct for the whole.

Consider a simple example of this fallacy. An art collector can go into the market and add to her private collection of nineteenth-century French paintings provided only that she has enough money. However, the fact that any one person can do this does not mean that everyone could do so simultaneously. The world's stock of nineteenth-century French paintings is fixed. It is not possible for *all* of us to do what any *one* of us with enough money can do.

How does the fallacy of composition relate to demand curves? An individual demand curve describes a situation in which the price of one commodity changes while the prices of all other commodities and consumers' money incomes are constant. Such an individual demand curve is negatively sloped for two reasons. First, as the price of the commodity rises, each consumer's given money income will buy a smaller *total* amount of goods, so a smaller quantity of each commodity will be bought, other things being equal. Second, as the price of the commodity rises, consumers buy less of it and more of the now relatively cheaper substitutes.

The first reason has no application to the aggregate demand curve, which relates the total demand for all output to the price level. All prices and total output are changing as we move along the *AD* curve. Because the value of output determines income, consumers' money incomes will also be changing along this curve.

The second reason does apply to the aggregate demand curve, but in a limited way. A rise in the price level entails a rise in *all* domestic commodity prices. Thus, there is no incentive to substitute among domestic commodities whose prices do not change relative to each other. However, it does give rise, as we saw earlier in this chapter, to some substitution between domestic and foreign goods and services. Domestic goods and services rise in price relative to imported goods and services, and the switch in spending will lower desired aggregate spending on domestic output and hence will lower equilibrium GDP.

### Points off the *AD* curve

The *AD* curve depicts combinations of GDP and the price level at which aggregate desired spending is equal to actual output (and income). These points are said to be *consistent* with spending decisions.

The level of GDP given by any point on the aggregate demand curve is such that, *if* that level of output is produced, aggregate desired spending at the *given price level* will exactly equal total output.

We do not yet know if producers will really want to produce that output, as we have not modelled the supply decision, but we can say that the incomes generated by that level of GDP will be such as to generate the exact level of spending (via consumption and net exports, etc.) that can purchase all the output.

Points to the left of the *AD* curve show combinations of GDP and the price level that cause aggregate desired spending to exceed output. There is thus pressure for output to rise because firms could sell more than their current output. Points to the right of the *AD* curve show combinations of GDP and the price level for which aggregate desired spending is less than current output. There is thus pressure for output to fall because firms will not be able to sell all of their current output. These relationships are illustrated in Figure 18.3.

### Shifts in the *AD* curve

Because the *AD* curve plots demand-determined GDP as a function of the price level, anything that alters this outcome for GDP *at any specific price level* must shift the *AD* curve. In other words, any change in exogenous spending that we have been holding constant causes the aggregate spending curve to shift, and will also cause the *AD* curve to shift. (Recall that a change in the price level causes a *movement along* the *AD* curve.) Such a shift is called an *aggregate demand shock*.

Demand shocks could originate from changes in spending by the private sector, but they may also be induced by changes in monetary or fiscal policy. Higher interest rates will lower aggregate spending and thus shift the *AD* curve to the left. Lower rates will increase aggregate spending and shift the *AD* curve to the right. Higher government spending shifts the *AD* curve to the right, while higher taxes shift *AD* to the left, and vice versa for cuts in government spending and cuts in taxes.

A recent positive demand shock occurred in July 2002 when the UK Government announced substantial increases in spending on education and health (see Figure 17.9 on page 399, which shows the rise in net borrowing in the period 2003–5 which helped finance this increase in spending). This is represented by a rightward shift of the *AD* curve.

An example of a *negative* aggregate demand shock can be found in Germany in the early 1990s. The high costs for the German government associated with reunification

(i) Aggregate spending

(ii) Aggregate demand

**Figure 18.3** The relationship between the *AE* and *AD* curves

The *AD* curve plots the price level against the level of GDP consistent with spending decisions at that price level. With the price level $P_0$, GDP is $Y_0$, shown by the intersection of *AE* and the 45° line at $E_0$ in part (i) and by the point $E_0$ on the *AD* curve in part (ii).

With the price level constant at $P_0$, consider a level of GDP of $Y_1$, which is less than $Y_0$. As can be seen in part (i), if GDP were equal to $Y_1$, desired aggregate spending would be $e_1$, which is greater than $Y_1$. Hence $Y_1$ is not a level of GDP consistent with spending decisions when the price level is $P_0$, and the combination $(P_0, Y_1)$ is not a point on the *AD* curve in part (ii), as shown by point *X*. Now consider a level of GDP of $Y_2$, which is greater than $Y_0$. As can be seen in part (i), if GDP were equal to $Y_2$, desired aggregate spending would be $e_2$, which is less than $Y_2$. Hence $Y_2$ is not a level of GDP consistent with spending decisions when the price level is $P_0$, and the combination $(P_0, Y_2)$ is not a point on the *AD* curve in part (ii), as shown by point *Z*.

Repeating the same analysis for each given price level tells us that for all points to the left of the *AD* curve (the blue shaded area), output is tending to rise, because desired spending exceeds output, whereas for all points to the right of the *AD* curve output is tending to fall, because desired aggregate spending is less than output.

of East and West Germany required a sharp rise in German income tax rates. Although this was associated with higher spending in East Germany, there was a downward shift of the *AD* curve for West Germany which led to a downturn in output and a substantial rise in unemployment. The situation was made worse by a simultaneous fiscal tightening (cuts in government spending and/or tax increases) in several other European countries, including France, Belgium, and Italy, as they attempted to reduce their budget deficits to below 3 per cent of GDP to satisfy the Maastricht criteria for entry into the single European currency system in 1999. A simultaneous negative *AD* shock in, say, France would reinforce the fiscally generated *AD* shock in Germany, because it would lead to a downward shift in the German net export function, causing a further downward shift in Germany's *AD* curve.

Demand shocks also resulted from big wealth effects associated with swings in stock markets. In the years up to March 2000, there was a boom in technology stocks that led to a huge increase in the private sector's financial wealth, especially in the United States. This was associated with a consumer boom, as people whose wealth was rising increased their expenditures and reduced their savings. By the summer of 2002, however, stock markets had collapsed and consumer demand fell, with a resulting decline in economic activity.

We now summarize the factors that shift the *AD* curves as follows:

A rise in the amount of (autonomous) desired private consumption, investment, government consumption, or net export spending that is associated with each level of GDP shifts the *AD* curve to the right. A fall in any of these spending categories shifts the *AD* curve to the left.

## The simple multiplier and the *AD* curve

We saw in Chapter 17 that the simple multiplier measures the magnitude of the *change* in (what we then called) equilibrium GDP in response to a change in autonomous spending when the price level is constant. It follows that this multiplier gives the magnitude of the *horizontal* shift in the *AD* curve in response to a change in autonomous spending. This is shown in Figure 18.4.

The simple multiplier measures the horizontal shift in the *AD* curve in response to a change in autonomous spending.

(i) Aggregate spending

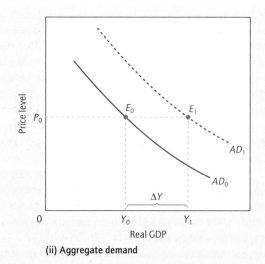
(ii) Aggregate demand

**Figure 18.4  The simple multiplier and shifts in the *AD* curve**

A change in autonomous spending changes GDP for any given price level, and the simple multiplier measures the resulting horizontal shift in the aggregate demand curve. The original desired spending line is $AE_0$ in part (i). The initial position is at $E_0$, with GDP $Y_0$ at price level $P_0$. This yields point $E_0$ on the curve $AD_0$ in part (ii).

The *AE* line in part (i) then shifts upwards from $AE_0$ to $AE_1$ because of an increase in autonomous spending of $\Delta A$. Output now rises to $Y_1$, with the price level still constant at $P_0$. Thus, the *AD* curve in part (ii) shifts to the right to point $E_1$, indicating the higher output $Y_1$ associated with the same price level $P_0$. The magnitude of the shift, $\Delta Y$, is given by the simple multiplier.

A fall in autonomous spending can be analysed by shifting the *AE* line from $AE_1$ to $AE_0$, which shifts the *AD* curve from $AD_1$ to $AD_0$ at the price level of $P_0$. The value of GDP determined by spending decisions falls from $Y_1$ to $Y_0$.

If the price level were to remain constant and firms were willing to supply everything that was demanded at that price level, the simple multiplier would show the change in equilibrium GDP that would occur in response to a change in autonomous spending. However, this will not normally be the case. To see how producers will actually respond to a shift in aggregate demand, we need to model supply responses.

# Aggregate supply and macroeconomic equilibrium

We have explained how the level of GDP is determined *when the price level is given*, and how that outcome changes as the price level is changed exogenously. We are now ready to take account of the supply decisions of producers. Once we have done this, we will be able to combine aggregate demand and aggregate supply to provide an explanation for the simultaneous determination of the price level and real GDP.

## The aggregate supply curve

*Aggregate supply* is the total output of goods and services that firms wish to produce, assuming that they can sell all that they wish to sell at the going price level. Recall, however, that in our simple model there is only one type of output, so *in our model* aggregate supply is the final output of the single good produced by all the firms in the economy. In the real world the national output is made up of thousands of different types of goods and services. In both our model and the real world, however, aggregate supply is the outcome of the decisions of all producers in the economy to hire workers and buy other inputs in order to produce goods (and services) to sell to consumers, governments, and other producers, as well as for export.

The *aggregate supply curve* relates the quantity of output supplied to the price level. It is useful to define two types of such curve, in order to allow for different stages of adjustment of the production sector to external shocks. The **short-run aggregate supply (*SRAS*) curve** shows the quantity of output that firms would like to produce and to sell at each price level *on the assumption that the prices of all inputs remain constant*. The **long-run aggregate supply (*LRAS*) curve** plots the desired quantity of output that firms would like to produce after the price level and input prices have fully adjusted to any demand shock. For the remainder of this chapter we confine our attention to the *SRAS* curve.

## The slope of the short-run aggregate supply curve

The slope of the *SRAS* curve depends on how production costs are related to output and on how goods prices and output are related.

### Costs and output

Suppose that firms wish to increase their outputs above current levels. What will this do to their costs per unit of output—often called their **unit costs**? The short-run aggregate supply curve is drawn on the assumption that the prices of all inputs that firms use, such as labour, remain constant. This does not, however, mean that unit costs will be constant. As output increases, less efficient standby machinery may have to be used, and less efficient workers may have to be hired, while existing workers may have to be paid overtime rates for additional work. For these reasons unit costs will tend to rise as output rises, even when input prices are constant.[5]

Unit costs and output tend to be positively related in the short run.

### Prices and output

To understand the relationship between price and output, we need to think about firms that sell in two distinct types of market: those in which firms are price-*takers*, and those in which firms are price-*setters*. Some industries contain many individual firms selling a homogeneous product. In these cases each one is too small to influence the market price, which is set by the overall forces of demand and supply. So each firm must accept whatever price is set on the open market and adjust its output to that price. The firms are said to be *price-takers* and *quantity-adjusters*. When the market price changes, these firms will react by altering their production.

Price-taking firms produce more only if price rises and produce less if price falls. This is because their unit costs tend to rise with output.

Firms in many other industries, including most of those that produce manufactured goods, are not price-takers. Whether there are few large firms or many small ones, each can influence the market price of its output. Most

---
[5] The law of diminishing returns (see Chapter 6) is one reason why costs rise in the short run, as firms try to produce more output with a fixed stock of capital equipment.

such firms on any one industry sell differentiated products, although all are similar enough to be thought of as the product of one industry. For example, no two makes of car are identical, but all cars are sufficiently alike that we can talk about 'the car industry' and the commodity 'cars'. In such cases each firm typically sets the price at which it is prepared to sell its products; that is, the firm is a *price-setter*.

Over some (small) range of output, price-setting firms will keep their prices constant and satisfy changes in demand by running down or building up inventories, such as numbers of cars in the showroom. However, if the demand for the output of price-setting firms increases sufficiently to take their production level into the range at which their unit costs start to rise (for example because overtime is worked and standby equipment is brought into production), profit-maximizing firms will not want to increase production further unless they can pass on at least some of these extra costs through higher prices. When demand falls they will reduce output, and competition among them will tend to cause a reduction in prices whenever unit costs fall.

Price-setting firms will increase their prices when they expand production into the range where unit costs are rising.

This is the basic behaviour of firms in response to changes in demand and prices when input prices are constant, and it explains the slope of the *SRAS* curve, such as the one shown in Figure 18.5.[6]

The actions of both price-taking and price-setting firms cause the price level and the desired supply of output to be positively related—the short-run aggregate supply curve is positively sloped.

### Real and nominal wages

Another way of explaining why the *SRAS* curve is positively sloped involves real wages. Consider price-taking firms, selling in competitive markets. With given money prices of their inputs—we will concentrate on the labour input—and a given price at which they can sell their output, each firm will produce output at the level where its marginal cost equals its marginal revenue (and average revenue, which is also equal to the market price of its output, as shown in Chapter 7).

Now what happens if an increase in total demand for final output leads to a rise in the output price? Firms

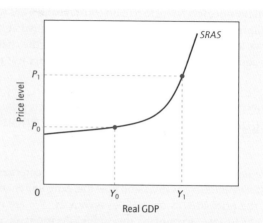

**Figure 18.5  A short-run aggregate supply curve**
The *SRAS* curve is positively sloped. The positive slope of the *SRAS* curve shows that, with the prices of labour and other inputs given, total desired output and the price level will be positively associated. Thus, a rise in the price level from $P_0$ to $P_1$ will be associated with a rise in the quantity of total output supplied from $Y_0$ to $Y_1$. The slope of the *SRAS* curve is fairly flat at low levels of output and very steep at higher levels.

will find that their marginal revenue curves (and average revenue) have shifted upwards. They will increase profits by expanding output up to the point where their new marginal revenue curve cuts their marginal cost curve. In the process they will also increase employment. Thus, as the price level rises, output increases. This is the positively sloped *SRAS* curve.

Notice, however, what is happening to the real wage rate. Money wages are fixed (by assumption, in the short run) in money terms. As the price of final output goes up, workers' money wages will buy fewer goods. The *real wage* has fallen. This is why firms choose to hire more labour and expand output. The relative price of their inputs has fallen in comparison with the price of their output.

Of course, this will not be the end of the story. Workers will resist a permanent fall in their real wage, and their representatives will bargain for higher wage rates. Money wages will eventually start to rise, and as they do the relative input and output prices faced by firms will tend to return to their initial level. So firms' output and employment will return to their original level. But this is the long-run story, to which we return in Chapter 19.

As we move upwards along a given *SRAS* curve, the rise in the price level and output is associated with a fall in the real wage—that is, with a rise in output prices relative to input prices.

### Shifts in the *SRAS* curve

Shifts in the *SRAS* curve, which are shown in Figure 18.6, are called *aggregate supply shocks*. Two sources of aggregate

---

[6] Notice that our argument here relating to two different types of firm is not really consistent with our assumption that there is only one type of output. However, since both price-takers and price-setters generate a positively sloped supply curve, for the purpose of building our macro model this does not cause any difficulties. It is worth bearing in mind, however, that in reality price-setting behaviour varies with product type and market structure.

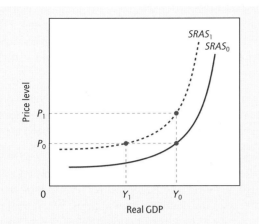

**Figure 18.6  Shifts in the *SRAS* curve**

**A shift to the left of the *SRAS* curve reflects a decrease in supply; a shift to the right reflects an increase in supply.** Starting from $(P_0, Y_0)$ on $SRAS_0$, suppose there is an increase in input prices. At price level $P_0$ only $Y_1$ would be produced. Alternatively, to get output $Y_0$ would require a rise to price level $P_1$. The new supply curve is $SRAS_1$, which may be viewed as being above and to the left of $SRAS_0$. An increase in supply—caused, say, by a decrease in input prices—would shift the *SRAS* curve downward and to the right, from $SRAS_1$ to $SRAS_0$.

supply shocks are of particular importance: changes in the price of inputs, and increases in productivity.

## Changes in input prices

Input prices are held constant along the *SRAS* curve; when they change, the curve shifts. If input prices rise, firms will find the profitability of their current production reduced. If output prices do not rise, firms will react by decreasing production. For the economy as a whole, this means that there will be less output at each price level than before the increase in input prices. Thus, if input prices rise, the *SRAS* curve shifts upward. (Notice that when a positively sloped curve shifts upward, indicating that any given quantity is associated with a higher price level, it also shifts to the left, indicating that any given price level is associated with a lower quantity.)

Similarly, a fall in input prices causes the *SRAS* curve to shift downward (and to the right). More will be produced and offered for sale at each price level.[7]

[7] Note that for either the *AD* or the *SRAS* curve a shift to the right means an increase, and a shift to the left means a decrease. Upward and downward shifts, however, have different meanings for the two curves. An upward shift of the *AD* curve reflects an increase in aggregate demand, but an upward shift in the *SRAS* curve reflects a decrease in aggregate supply.

## Increases in productivity

If labour productivity rises, meaning that each worker can produce more per hour, the unit costs of production will fall, as long as wage rates do not rise sufficiently to offset fully the productivity rise. If costs fall, firms will be willing to sell more at the same price, which causes a rightward shift in the aggregate supply curve. This is an increase in supply, as illustrated in Figure 18.6. Note that the same change can be thought of as a downward shift in the SRAS curve. Indeed, lower costs generally lead to lower prices. Competing firms cut prices in an attempt to raise their market shares, and the net result of such competition is that the fall in production costs is accompanied by a fall in the price at which any given output will be supplied.

A rightward (and downward) shift in the *SRAS* curve—brought about, for example, by an increase in productivity with no increase in input prices—implies that firms will be willing to produce more output with no increase in the price level.

A change in either input prices or productivity will shift the *SRAS* curve, because any given output will be supplied at a different price level than previously and a different amount will be supplied at any given price. An increase in input prices or a decrease in productivity shifts the *SRAS* curve upwards and to the left; an increase in productivity or a decrease in input prices shifts it downwards and to the right.

## Macroeconomic equilibrium

We have now added the *SRAS* curve to our model, and we are ready to see how real GDP and the price level are simultaneously determined by the interaction of aggregate demand and aggregate supply.

The equilibrium values of real GDP and the price level occur at the intersection of the *AD* and *SRAS* curves, as shown by the pair $Y_0$ and $P_0$ at point $E_0$ in Figure 18.7. We call the combination of real GDP and price level at the intersection of the *AD* and *SRAS* curves a *macroeconomic equilibrium.*

To see why the pair of points $(Y_0, P_0)$ is the only macroeconomic equilibrium, first consider what Figure 18.7 shows would happen if the price level were below $P_0$. At this lower price level the desired output of firms, as given by the *SRAS* curve, is less than desired aggregate spending at that level of GDP. The excess desired aggregate spending will cause prices to be bid up, and output will increase along the *SRAS* curve. Hence there can be no macroeconomic *equilibrium* when the price level is below $P_0$.

Similarly, Figure 18.7 shows that when the price level is above $P_0$, the behaviour underlying the *SRAS* and *AD*

**Figure 18.7  Macroeconomic equilibrium**

Macroeconomic equilibrium occurs at the intersection of the *AD* and *SRAS* curves and determines the equilibrium values for GDP and the price level. Given the *AD* and *SRAS* curves in the figure, macroeconomic equilibrium occurs at $E_0$, with GDP equal to $Y_0$ and the price level equal to $P_0$. At $P_0$ the desired output of firms, as given by the *SRAS* curve, is equal to the level of GDP that is consistent with spending decisions, as given by the *AD* curve.

If the price level is equal to $P_1$, less than $P_0$, the desired output of firms, given by the *SRAS* curve, will be $Y_1$. However, at $P_1$ the level of output that is consistent with spending decisions, given by the *AD* curve, will be $Y_2$, greater than $Y_1$. Hence when the price level is $P_1$, or any other level less than $P_0$, the desired output of firms will be less than the level of output that is consistent with spending decisions.

Similarly, for any price level above $P_0$, the desired output of firms, given by the *SRAS* curve, will exceed the level of output that is consistent with spending decisions, given by the *AD* curve.

curves is not consistent. In this case producers will wish to supply more than the output that is demanded at that price level. Desired spending will not be large enough to purchase everything that firms wish to produce at that price level.

Only at the combination of GDP and price level given by the intersection of the *SRAS* and *AD* curves are desired spending (demand) and desired production (supply) activities consistent.

When the price level is less than its equilibrium value, desired spending is consistent with a level of GDP that is greater than the desired output of firms. When the price level is greater than its equilibrium value, desired spending is consistent with a level of GDP that is less than the desired output of firms.

Macroeconomic equilibrium thus requires that two conditions be satisfied. The first is familiar to us because it comes from Chapters 16 and 17: at the prevailing price level, desired aggregate spending must be equal to national output (and consistent with the income generated by that output), which means that agents are just willing to buy all that is produced. The *AD* curve is constructed in such a way that this condition holds everywhere on it. The second requirement for equilibrium is introduced by consideration of aggregate supply: at the prevailing price level, firms must wish to produce the prevailing level of national output—no more and no less. This condition is fulfilled everywhere on the *SRAS* curve. Only where the two curves intersect are both conditions fulfilled simultaneously.

## Changes in GDP and the price level

The aggregate demand and aggregate supply curves can now be used to understand how various shocks to the economy change both real GDP and the price level.

A shift in the *AD* curve is called an **aggregate demand shock**. A *rightward* shift in the *AD* curve results from an *increase* in aggregate demand; it means that at all price levels spending decisions will now be consistent with a *higher* level of real GDP. Similarly, a *leftward* shift in the *AD* curve indicates a *decrease* in aggregate demand; it means that at all price levels spending decisions will now be consistent with a *lower* level of real GDP.[8]

A shift in the *SRAS* curve is called an **aggregate supply shock**. A *rightward* shift in the *SRAS* curve represents an *increase* in aggregate supply: at any given price level *more*

real national output will be supplied. A *leftward* shift in the *SRAS* curve is a *decrease* in aggregate supply: at any given price level *less* real national output will be supplied.[9]

---

[8] The factors that could shift *AD* are the same as those that could shift *AE* (*apart from the price level*). An autonomous increase in private consumption, government consumption, investment, or net exports, or a reduction in tax rates, will all shift *AD* upwards to the right. The opposite shift in any of these will move *AD* downwards to the left.

[9] The distinction between movements along and shifts of curves that we encountered in studying demand and supply in Chapter 3 is also relevant here. A *movement along* an aggregate demand curve indicates a change in the quantity demanded, whereas a *shift* in an aggregate demand curve indicates a 'change in demand'. A similar distinction applies to the supply curve.

**Box 18.2** The Keynesian *SRAS* curve

One extreme version of the *SRAS* curve, which is horizontal over some range of GDP, is called the Keynesian short-run aggregate supply curve. The reference is to John Maynard Keynes, who in his famous book *The General Theory of Employment, Interest and Money* (1936) pioneered the study of the behaviour of economies under conditions of high unemployment.

The following conjectured behaviour gives rise to the Keynesian *SRAS* curve. When real GDP is below potential GDP, individual firms are operating at less than normal-capacity output, and they hold their prices constant at the level that would maximize profits if production were at normal capacity. They then respond to demand variations below that capacity by altering output. In other words, firms will supply whatever they can sell at their existing prices as long as they are producing below their normal capacity. This implies that the firms have horizontal supply curves and that their output is *demand-determined*.*

Under these circumstances, the economy has a horizontal aggregate supply curve, indicating that any output up to potential will be supplied at the going price level. The amount that is actually produced is then determined by the position of the aggregate demand curve, as shown in the figure. Thus, we say that real GDP is demand-determined. If demand rises enough so that firms are trying to squeeze more than normal output out of their plants, their costs will rise, and so will their prices. Thus, the horizontal Keynesian *SRAS* curve applies only to situations below potential GDP.

---

* There is strong evidence that firms, particularly in the manufacturing sector, do behave like this in the short run. One possible explanation for this is that changing prices frequently is too costly, so firms set the best possible (profit-maximizing) prices when output is at normal capacity and then do not change prices in the face of short-term fluctuations in demand.

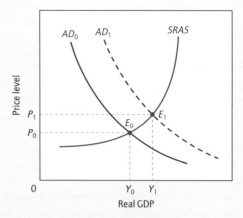

**Figure 18.8** Aggregate demand shocks

**Shifts in aggregate demand cause the price level and real GDP to move in the same direction.** An increase in aggregate demand shifts the *AD* curve to the right—say, from $AD_0$ to $AD_1$. Macroeconomic equilibrium moves from $E_0$ to $E_1$. The price level rises from $P_0$ to $P_1$, and real GDP rises from $Y_0$ to $Y_1$, reflecting a movement along the *SRAS* curve.

A decrease in aggregate demand shifts the *AD* curve to the left—say, from $AD_1$ to $AD_0$. Equilibrium moves from $E_1$ to $E_0$. Prices fall from $P_1$ to $P_0$, and real GDP falls from $Y_1$ to $Y_0$.

## Aggregate demand shocks

Figure 18.8 shows the effects of an increase in aggregate demand. This increase could have occurred because of, say, increased investment or government spending; it means that more national output will be demanded at any given price level. For now we are not concerned with the source of the shock; what we are interested in is its implications for the price level and real GDP.

An aggregate demand shock means that there is a shift in the *AD* curve (for example, from $AD_0$ to $AD_1$ in Figure 18.8). Adjustment to the new equilibrium following an aggregate demand shock involves a movement along the *SRAS* curve (for example, from point $E_0$ to point $E_1$).

As is shown in the figure, following an increase in aggregate demand, both the price level and real GDP rise.

Figure 18.8 also shows that both the price level and real GDP fall as the result of a decrease in aggregate demand.

Aggregate demand shocks cause the price level and real GDP to change in the same direction; both rise with an increase in aggregate demand, and both fall with a decrease in aggregate demand.

### The multiplier when the price level varies

We saw earlier in this chapter that the simple multiplier gives the extent of the horizontal shift in the *AD* curve in

---

What happens to real GDP and to the price level when either the aggregate demand or aggregate supply curve shifts?

A shift in either the *AD* or the *SRAS* curve leads to changes in the equilibrium values of the price level and real GDP.

Box 18.2 deals with the special case of a perfectly elastic *SRAS* curve. In that case, the aggregate supply curve determines the price level, while the aggregate demand curve determines real GDP. This is the special case where the model of Chapter 17 (with a fixed price level) is adequate to explain the determination of real GDP.

response to a change in autonomous spending. If the price level remains constant, and *if* firms are willing to supply all that is demanded at the existing price level (that is, if the aggregate supply curve is horizontal), then the simple multiplier gives the increase in equilibrium GDP.

Now that we can use aggregate demand and aggregate supply curves, we can answer a more interesting question: what happens in the more usual case where the aggregate supply curve slopes upward?

Figure 18.8 shows that, when the *SRAS* curve is positively sloped, the change in GDP that is caused by a change in autonomous spending is no longer equal to the size of the horizontal shift in the *AD* curve. A rightward shift of the *AD* curve causes the price level to rise, which in turn causes the rise in real GDP to be less than the horizontal shift of the *AD* curve. Part of the expansionary impact of an increase in demand is dissipated by a rise in the price level, and only part is transmitted to a rise in real output. Of course, there is still an increase in output, so there is still a positive multiplier effect, but its value is not the same as that of the simple multiplier.

When the *SRAS* curve is positively sloped, the multiplier is smaller than the simple multiplier.

Why is the multiplier smaller when the *SRAS* curve is positively sloped? The answer lies in the behaviour that is summarized by the *AE* line. To understand this, it is useful to think of the final change in GDP as occurring in two stages, as shown in Figure 18.9.

First, with prices remaining constant, an increase in autonomous spending shifts the *AE* line upward (part (i) of the figure) and therefore shifts the *AD* curve to the right (part (ii)). The horizontal shift in the *AD* curve is measured by the simple multiplier, but this cannot be the final equilibrium position because firms are unwilling to produce enough to satisfy the extra demand at the existing price level.

Second, we take account of the rise in the price level that occurs owing to the positive slope of the *SRAS* curve. A rise in the price level, via its negative effect on net exports and on wealth, leads to a downward shift in the *AE* line. This second shift of the *AE* line partially counteracts the initial rise in GDP and so reduces the size of the multiplier. The second stage shows up as a downward shift of the *AE* line in part (i) of Figure 18.9 and a movement upward and to the left along the *AD* curve in part (ii).

### The importance of the shape of the *SRAS* curve

The shape of the *SRAS* curve has important implications for how the effects of an aggregate demand shock are divided between changes in real GDP and changes in the

(i) Aggregate spending

(ii) Aggregate demand

**Figure 18.9** The *AE* line and the multiplier when the price level varies

An increase in autonomous spending causes the *AE* line to shift upward, but the rise in the price level causes it to shift part of the way down again. Hence the multiplier effect on GDP is smaller than when the price level is constant. Originally equilibrium is at point $E_0$ in both parts (i) and (ii), with real GDP at $Y_0$ and price level at $P_0$. Desired aggregate spending then shifts by $\Delta A$ to $AE_1'$, taking the aggregate demand curve to $AD_1$. These shifts are shown by arrow 1 in both parts. If the price level had remained constant at $P_0$, the new equilibrium would have been $E_1'$ and real GDP would have risen to $Y_1'$. The amount $Y_0Y_1'$ is the change called for by the simple multiplier.

Instead, however, the shift in the *AD* curve raises the price level to $P_1$ and shifts the aggregate spending curve down to $AE_1$, as shown by arrow 2 in part (i). This is shown as a movement along the *AD* curve, as indicated by arrow 2 in part (ii). The new equilibrium is thus at $E_1$. The amount $Y_0Y_1$ is $\Delta Y$, the actual increase in real GDP, whereas the amount $Y_1Y_1'$ is the shortfall relative to the simple multiplier owing to the rise in the price level.

The multiplier is the ratio $\Delta Y / \Delta A$ in part (i).

price level. Figure 18.10 highlights this point by considering *AD* shocks in the presence of an *SRAS* curve that exhibits three distinct ranges. Box 18.3 explores some possible reasons for such an increasing slope of the *SRAS* curve.

**Figure 18.10** **The effects of increases in aggregate demand**

The effects of increases in aggregate demand are divided between increases in real output and increases in prices, depending on the shape of the *SRAS* curve. Increases in aggregate demand up to $AD_0$ have virtually no impact on the price level. When aggregate demand increases from $AD_0$ to $AD_1$, there is a relatively small increase in the price level, from $P_0$ to $P_1$, and a relatively large increase in output, from $Y_0$ to $Y_1$. Successive further increases bring larger price increases and relatively smaller output increases. By the time aggregate demand is at $AD_5$, virtually all of the effect is on the price level.

---

### ◉ ◉ ◉ Box 18.3 More on the shape of the *SRAS* curve

The *SRAS* curve relates the price level to the quantity of output that producers are willing to sell. Notice two things about the shape of the *SRAS* curve that is reproduced in Figure 18.8: (i) it has a positive slope, and (ii) the slope increases as output rises.

**Positive slope**

The most obvious feature of the *SRAS* curve is its positive slope, indicating that a higher price level is associated with a higher volume of real output, other things being equal. Because the prices of all of the inputs to production are being held constant along the *SRAS* curve, why is the curve not horizontal, indicating that firms would be willing to supply as much output as might be demanded with no increase in the price level?

The answer is that, even though *input prices* are constant, *unit costs of production* eventually rise as output increases. Thus, beyond some low level of output (below which the SRAS curve may actually be flat, as argued in the previous box) a higher price level for increasing output—rising short-run aggregate supply—is necessary to compensate firms for rising costs.

The preceding paragraph addresses the question of what has to happen to the price level if national output increases, with the price of inputs remaining constant. Alternatively, one could ask what will happen to firms' willingness to supply output if product prices rise with no increase in input prices. Production becomes more profitable, and since firms are interested in making profits they will usually produce more. Thus, when the price level of final output rises while input prices are held constant, firms are motivated to increase their outputs. This is true for the individual firm and also for firms in the aggregate. This increase in the amount produced leads to an upward slope of the *SRAS* curve.

Thus, whether we look at how the price level responds in the short run to increases in output or at how the level of output responds to an increase in the price level with input prices being held constant, we find that the *SRAS* curve has a positive slope (although it may be flat or nearly flat at outputs well below the economy's potential output).

**Increasing slope**

A less obvious but in many ways more important property of a typical *SRAS* curve is that its slope *increases* as output rises. It is rather flat to the left of potential output and rather steep to the right. Why? Below potential output, firms typically have unused capacity—some plant and equipment are idle. When firms are faced with unused capacity, only a small increase in the price of their output (if any) may be needed to induce them to expand production—at least up to normal capacity.

Once output is pushed much beyond normal capacity, however, unit costs tend to rise increasingly rapidly. Many higher-cost expedients may have to be adopted. Standby capacity, overtime, and extra shifts may have to be used. Such expedients raise the cost of producing a unit of output. These higher-cost methods will not be used unless the selling price of the output has risen enough to cover them. The further output is expanded beyond normal capacity, the more rapidly unit costs will rise and hence the larger the rise in price that will be needed to induce firms to increase output even further.

This increasing slope is sometimes called the *first important asymmetry* in the behaviour of aggregate supply. (The second, 'sticky wages', will be discussed in the next chapter.)

The analysis of Chapter 7 is relevant here. This shows how a firm in a perfectly competitive market, when faced with a higher output price, expands output *along* its marginal cost curve until marginal cost is once again equal to price.

Over the *flat* range in Figure 18.10, from 0 to $Y_0$, any change in aggregate demand leads to no change in prices and a response of output equal to that predicted by the simple multiplier.

Over the *intermediate* range along which the *SRAS* curve is positively sloped, from $Y_1$ to $Y_4$, a shift in the *AD* curve gives rise to appreciable changes in both real GDP and the price level. As we saw earlier in this chapter, the change in the price level reduces the response of GDP to a change in autonomous spending.

Over the *steep* range, for GDP above $Y_4$, the economy is near its capacity constraint. Any change in aggregate demand leads to a sharp change in the price level and to little change in real GDP. The multiplier in this case is nearly zero.

How do we reconcile what we have just discovered with the analysis of Chapters 16 and 17, where a given shift in *AE* *always* changes real GDP by the same amount? The answer is that each *AE* line is drawn on the assumption that there is a constant price level and plenty of excess capacity. A rise in *AE* shifts the *AD* curve to the right. However, an upward-sloping *SRAS* curve means that the price level rises significantly (because there is little excess capacity), and this shifts the *AE* line downward, offsetting some of its initial rise.

This interaction is seen most easily if we study the extreme case, shown in Figure 18.11, in which the *SRAS* curve is vertical. An increase in autonomous spending shifts the *AE* line upward, thereby raising the amount demanded. However, a vertical *SRAS* curve means that output cannot be expanded to satisfy the increased demand. Instead, the extra demand merely forces prices up, and as prices rise the *AE* line shifts downward once again. The rise in prices continues until the *AE* line is back to where it started. Thus, the rise in prices offsets the expansionary effect of the original shift and, as a result, leaves both real aggregate spending and equilibrium real GDP unchanged.

The discussion of Figures 18.10 and 18.11 illustrates a general proposition:

The effect of any given shift in aggregate demand will be divided between a change in real output and a change in the price level, depending on the conditions of aggregate supply. The steeper the *SRAS* curve, the greater is the price effect, and the smaller is the output effect.

For reasons discussed in Boxes 18.2 and 18.3, the *SRAS* curve probably has the shape shown in Figure 18.10, that is, relatively flat for low levels of output and becoming steeper as the level of GDP increases (relative to potential GDP). This shape of the *SRAS* curve implies that at low levels of GDP (well below potential) shifts in aggregate demand primarily affect output, and at high levels of GDP

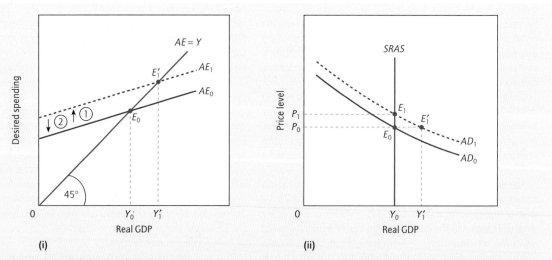

**Figure 18.11 Demand shocks when the *SRAS* curve is vertical**

If the *SRAS* curve were vertical, the effect of an increase in autonomous spending would be solely a rise in the price level. An increase in autonomous spending would shift the *AE* line upwards from $AE_0$ to $AE_1$, as shown by arrow 1 in part (i). Given the initial price level $P_0$, equilibrium would shift from $E_0$ to $E_1'$ and real GDP would rise from $Y_0$ to $Y_1'$. However, the price level does not remain constant. This is shown by the *SRAS* curve in part (ii). Instead, the price level rises to $P_1$. This causes the *AE* line to shift back down all the way to $AE_0$, as shown by arrow 2 in part (i), and equilibrium output stays at $Y_0$. In part (ii) the new equilibrium is at $E_1$, with GDP at $Y_0$ and price level $P_1$.

(above potential) shifts in aggregate demand primarily affect prices.

Of course, as we have noted already, treating wages and other input prices as constant is appropriate only when the time-period under consideration is short. Hence the *SRAS* curve is used only to analyse short-run, or *impact*, effects. In the next chapter we will see what happens in the *long run* when input prices (especially wages) respond to changes in GDP and the price level. First, however, our analysis of the short run needs to be completed with a discussion of aggregate supply shocks.

## Aggregate supply shocks

An aggregate supply shock means that there is a shift in the *SRAS* curve (for example, from $SRAS_0$ to $SRAS_1$ in Figure 18.12). Adjustment to the new equilibrium following the shock involves a movement along the *AD* curve (for example, from $E_0$ to $E_1$).

A decrease in aggregate supply is shown by a shift to the left of the *SRAS* curve and means that less national output will be supplied at any given price level. An increase in aggregate supply is shown by a shift to the right of the *SRAS* curve and means that more national output will be produced at any given price level.

Figure 18.12 illustrates the effects on the price level and real GDP of aggregate supply shocks. Following a decrease in aggregate supply, the price level rises and real GDP falls. This combination of events is called *stagflation*, a rather inelegant word that has been derived by combining *stagnation* (a term that is sometimes used to mean slow growth or even falling output) and *inflation*.

Figure 18.12 also shows that an increase in aggregate supply leads to an increase in real GDP and a decrease in the price level.

Aggregate supply shocks cause the price level and real GDP to change in opposite directions: with an increase in supply the price level falls and output rises; with a decrease in supply the price level rises and output falls.

Oil prices have provided three major examples of aggregate supply shocks in recent decades. The major industrial economies have been especially responsive to changes in the market for oil, because, in addition to its use in producing energy, oil is an input into many materials that are widely used in production and consumption, from plastics to cosmetics to fertilizer. Massive increases in oil prices during 1973–4 and 1979–80 caused leftward shifts in the *SRAS* curve for virtually all major economies. GDP fell while the price level rose, causing stagflation. During the mid-1980s oil prices fell substantially and stayed low for most of the 1990s (except for a blip after Iraq invaded Kuwait in 1990). This shifted the *SRAS* curve to the right, increasing GDP and putting downward

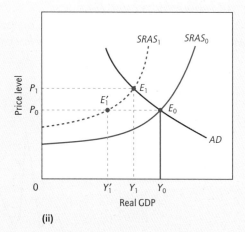

**Figure 18.12 Aggregate supply shocks**

**Shifts in aggregate supply cause the price level and real GDP to move in opposite directions.** The original equilibrium is at $E_0$ with GDP of $Y_0$ in both parts of the figure. The price level is $P_0$ in part (ii), and at that price level the desired aggregate spending curve is $AE_0$ in part (i).

An aggregate supply shock now shifts the *SRAS* curve in part (ii) to $SRAS_1$. At the original price level of $P_0$, firms are now willing to supply only $Y_1'$. The fall in supply, with no corresponding fall in demand, causes a shortage that leads to a rise in the price level along $SRAS_1$. The new equilibrium is reached at $E_1$, where the *AD* curve intersects $SRAS_1$. At the new, and higher, equilibrium price level of $P_1$, the *AE* line has fallen to $AE_1$, as shown in part (i), which is consistent with equilibrium GDP of $Y_1$.

pressure on the price level. However oil prices rose sharply again after 1999, reversing some of the earlier positive supply shock (see discussion on pages 173–6) and oil prices remained on an upward trend up to 2006. We can see now how a rightward shift in the *SRAS* curve, which is brought about by an increase in productivity or a fall in input prices, raises real GDP and lowers the price level.

# CASE STUDIES

## 1. Productivity and unit wage costs

The short-run aggregate supply curve that we have derived above is drawn for given technology and for given input prices. Technology is relevant because it influences the productivity of workers in the economy and the output per worker ultimately determines real living standards in the country. The technology that we are holding constant here implies both a given capital stock and a given state of technological knowledge embodied in that capital stock (and the skills of the workers). If output per worker is to increase, this could be achieved by giving each worker more capital equipment to work with, or by providing an improved type of capital (including human capital) that results from technical progress. An increase in output per worker is called an increase in labour productivity.

Increasing productivity in the UK economy is a major goal of the government, as the following extract from the December 2005 *Pre-Budget Report* makes clear:

### MEETING THE PRODUCTIVITY CHALLENGE
*Productivity growth, alongside high and stable levels of employment, is central to long-term economic performance. In the increas-ingly knowledge-driven global economy, science, innovation and creativity are important drivers of productivity growth, backed up by a high skilled workforce and a competitive and enterprising economy. The UK has historically experienced comparatively low rates of productivity growth. However, in recent years, UK performance has improved in relation to other major economies. The Government's long-term goal is for the UK to continue to close the productivity gap by achieving a faster rate of growth than its main competitors.* (UK *Pre-Budget Report*, 2005, page 5)

Figure 18.13 shows the annual growth of labour productivity and of unit labour costs for the whole economy. One measure of labour productivity is the growth of real GDP per person employed. What is clear from this chart is that there is no sign in the past few years of the pick-up of productivity that the government is hoping for. Indeed, productivity growth in the period 1995–2005 was consistently below the rates of increase achieved in the 1960s—as it was in most if not all industrial countries—suggesting that the 1950s and 1960s may have been the exceptional period, and not the present one. Average annual productivity growth for the UK by this measure was 2.8 per cent in the 1960s, 2.1 per cent in the 1970s, 1.8 per cent

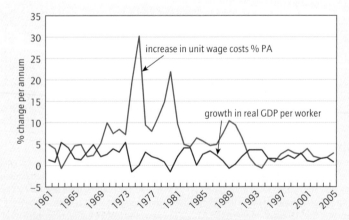

**Figure 18.13** UK annual changes in unit wage costs and productivity, 1961–2005

in the 1980s, 2.2 per cent in the 1990s, but only 1.5 per cent in the first six years of the 2000s.

Unit labour costs provide related information, but they are measured in money values and so reflect inflation in wage costs in addition to output per worker (which is a real concept unaffected by inflation). If there were no inflation in the money values of wages, there would be a simple inverse relationship between labour productivity and unit wage costs: as output per worker rises, the labour cost per unit of output falls. That inverse relationship is evident in Figure 18.13, but the big gaps in the 1970s and 1980s reflect the rapid wage inflation of those years, as well as the more modest variations in labour productivity. The years of rapid rises in unit wage costs are a good illustration of significant shifts to the left of the short-run aggregate supply curve. However, we cannot tell from the data alone to what extent these shifts in wage costs were the result of an exogenous supply shock or are an induced response to a demand shock that might have created an inflationary gap. We study induced changes in wages in detail in the next chapter.

Non-wage input prices that are largely the result of world market forces (at least in foreign currency terms), and therefore more likely to be exogenous to the home economy, are those of raw materials and fuels, and we look at these in the next case study.

## 2. Variations in input prices of materials and fuels

Labour is not the only input into the productive process whose price can change. Figure 18.14 shows monthly observations on the annual rate of change of prices of materials and fuels used as inputs into the UK manufacturing sector. Changes in these prices would generate a shift in the short-run aggregate supply curve, and some of these swings in input prices have been quite large. In September 1976, for example, these input prices were 30 per cent higher than a year earlier, and in March 1986 the prices of the same basket of inputs were 20 per cent lower than a year earlier.

One major influence on the price of fuels is obviously the world oil price (see our earlier discussion on pages 173–6). This has fluctuated considerably in this sample period. There was a major hike in oil prices in 1979 but the oil price was low from the mid-1980s to the mid-1990s. From 1999 to 2006 the oil price rose steadily from around $10 per barrel to around $70 per barrel. Other commodity prices were also strong in the mid-2000s, as were produced inputs such as steel (see our discussion of the price of steel on pages 57–8). These commodity price movements are all explicable using demand and supply analysis, but the key point to note for current purposes is that these prices are determined in the world market and hence are exogenous to the UK economy. The only exception to this arises from the fact that these prices are generally set by world markets in US dollar terms, so changes in the exchange rate of sterling against the US dollar will affect the sterling price of these inputs, and the exchange rate will be influenced by forces internal to the UK economy (see Chapter 22). Significant movements in these prices in sterling, as shown in Figure 18.14, cause shifts in the short-run aggregate supply curve.

Input prices, therefore, can be seen to show considerable variability. When these variations are due to forces external to the economy, they create a supply shock to which the economy must then adjust. However, there will also be some input price movements, especially in wages, which are themselves induced reactions to shocks on the demand side of the economy.

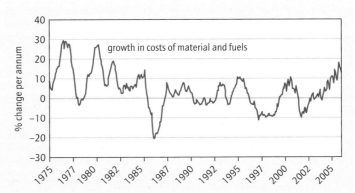

**Figure 18.14** Changes in non-wage input prices (materials and fuels), UK manufacturing, 1975–2006

*Source*: ONS website: www.statistics.gov.uk

## Conclusion

GDP and the price level are determined by the interaction of aggregate demand and aggregate supply. The aggregate demand curve is drawn for given values of exogenous expenditures. The aggregate supply curve is drawn for a given technology and given input prices. Demand and supply shocks disturb an existing equilibrium and lead to new values of GDP and the price level. In this chapter we have analysed the short-run response. In the next chapter we discuss the long run.

## SUMMARY

### Aggregate demand

■ A change in the price level shifts the *AE* line upward when the price level falls and downward when the price level rises. The new level of GDP that results would be the equilibrium level if it were solely demand-determined.

■ The *AD* curve plots the level of GDP (for which injections equal leakages) that corresponds to each possible price level. A change in GDP following a change in the price level is shown by a *movement along* the *AD* curve.

■ A rise in the price level lowers exports and lowers private consumption spending (because it decreases consumers' wealth). Both of these changes lower GDP and cause the aggregate demand curve to have a negative slope.

■ The *AD* curve shifts when any element of autonomous spending changes, and the simple multiplier measures the magnitude of the shift. This multiplier also measures the size of the change in equilibrium GDP when the price level remains constant *and* firms produce everything that is demanded at that price level.

### Aggregate supply and macroeconomic equilibrium

■ The short-run aggregate supply (*SRAS*) curve, drawn for given input prices, is positively sloped because unit costs rise with increasing output and because rising product prices make it profitable to increase output. An increase in productivity or a decrease in input prices shifts the curve to the right. A decrease in productivity or an increase in input prices has the opposite effect.

■ Macroeconomic equilibrium refers to values of real GDP and the price level determined by the intersection of the *AD* and *SRAS* curves. Shifts in the *AD* and *SRAS* curves, called aggregate demand shocks and aggregate supply shocks, change the equilibrium values of real GDP and the price level.

### Changes in GDP and the price level

■ When the *SRAS* curve is positively sloped, an aggregate demand shock causes the price level and real GDP to move in the same direction, the division between these effects depending on the shape of the *SRAS* curve. The main effect is on real GDP when the *SRAS* curve is flat, and on the price level when it is steep.

■ An aggregate supply shock moves equilibrium real GDP along the *AD* curve, causing the price level and output to move in opposite directions. A leftward shift in the *SRAS* curve causes a stagflation—rising prices and falling output. A rightward shift causes an increase in real GDP and a fall in the price level. The division of the effects of a shift in *SRAS* between a change in real GDP and a change in the price level depends on the shape of the *AD* curve.

## TOPICS FOR REVIEW

■ Effects of a change in the price level
■ Relationship between the *AE* and *AD* curves
■ Negative slope of the *AD* curve
■ Positive slope of the *SRAS* curve
■ Macroeconomic equilibrium

■ Aggregate demand shocks
■ The multiplier when the price level varies
■ Aggregate supply shocks
■ Stagflation

## QUESTIONS

1 Explain what happens to the UK *AD* curve in response to each of the following exogenous changes:
   (*a*) A rise in optimism leads to higher investment.
   (*b*) The government decides to build some new schools.
   (*c*) There is a recession in the United States.
   (*d*) Consumers become cautious about the future and decide to save more.
   (*e*) GDP in France and Germany rises.
   (*f*) New computer technology increases productivity in manufacturing industry.

2 Show what would happen to the *SRAS* curve if (*a*) investment in transport infrastructure lowers costs of shipping goods and raw materials; (*b*) oil prices rise; (*c*) workers agree to work for lower wages; (*d*) there is an increase in export demand; (*e*) there is technical innovation in manufacturing industry.

3 Outline how the interaction of the *AD* and *SRAS* curves determines the course of GDP and the price level in response to (*a*) a rise in wage rates; (*b*) an increase in investment; (*c*) a reduction in government consumption; (*d*) a boom in demand in neighbouring economies.

4 Explain why it is that changes in the price level lead to changes in desired aggregate spending for each level of GDP.

5 Explain why the change in GDP in response to an increase in export demand is smaller than that suggested by the simple multiplier. What happens to the size of this effect as GDP gets above its potential level?

6 Explain how it is that the outcomes of the shifts in *AD* set out in question 1 are consistent with the condition that injections equal leakages both before and after the shifts.

7 What determines the slope of the SRAS curve?

8 How do you think interest rates would affect aggregate demand?

# Chapter 19

# GDP AND THE PRICE LEVEL IN THE LONG RUN

Employees know that the best time to ask for a pay rise is during a boom, when the demand for labour is high. They also know that it is difficult to get significant wage increases during a recession, when high unemployment signals a low demand for labour. Managers in industry know that the cost of many materials tends to rise rapidly during business expansions and to fall—often dramatically— during recessions. In the case studies at the end of the previous chapter we saw examples of input price changes, some of which are exogenous to the economy while others are part of the internal adjustment mechanism of the economy. In this chapter we analyse those changes in input prices that are an endogenous response to demand and supply shocks. In short, input prices that are determined within the domestic economy change with domestic economic conditions, and we need to allow for these effects.

In particular, you will learn that:

- Output gaps will stimulate changes in both output and input prices.
- If actual output is greater than potential output, there is an inflationary gap associated with a high level of activity and a tendency for the price level to rise.
- If actual output is less that potential output, there is a recessionary gap associated with low levels of activity and a tendency for the price level to fall.
- The long-run aggregate supply curve is vertical at the level of potential output.
- Economic growth determines the position of the long-run aggregate supply curve.
- Shocks to aggregate demand and aggregate supply are associated with business cycles.
- In principle, fiscal and monetary policies can stabilize cycles and keep GDP close to its potential level.

In Chapter 18 we introduced the short-run aggregate supply, which is drawn holding input prices constant. In this chapter we analyse what happens when changes in GDP *induce* changes in input prices. Once we have completed this task, we can use our model of the short-run behaviour of the macro economy to investigate the causes and consequences of business cycles and to further our study of fiscal policy. In the following two chapters we study monetary policy.

# Induced changes in input prices

We begin by revising two key concepts that we first encountered in Chapter 15: potential output and the GDP gap.

## Another look at potential output and the GDP gap

Recall that potential output is the total output that can be produced when all productive resources are being used at their *normal rates of utilization*. When a nation's actual output diverges from its potential output, the difference is called the GDP gap or output gap (see Figure 15.1 on page 336).

Although growth in potential output has powerful effects from one decade to the next, its change from one *year* to the next is small enough to be ignored when studying the year-to-year behaviour of GDP and the price level. (See Chapter 26 for a discussion of the determinants of the growth of potential output.) Therefore, in this discussion we will continue with the convention, first adopted in Chapter 16, of ignoring the small changes in potential GDP caused by year-to-year changes in productivity. Variations in the output gap are then determined solely by variations in actual GDP around a given potential GDP.

Figure 19.1 shows actual GDP being determined by the intersection of the *AD* and *SRAS* curves. Potential GDP is constant, and it is shown by identical vertical lines in the two parts of the figure. In part (i) the *AD* and *SRAS* curves intersect to produce an equilibrium GDP that falls short of potential GDP. The result is called a *recessionary gap* because recessions often begin when actual output falls below potential output. In part (ii) the *AD* and *SRAS* curves intersect to produce an equilibrium GDP that exceeds potential output, resulting in an *inflationary gap*. The way in which an inflationary output gap puts upward pressure on prices will become clear in the following discussion.

## Input prices and the output gap

The output gap provides a convenient measure of the pressure of demand on input prices. When actual GDP is high relative to potential GDP, demand for inputs will

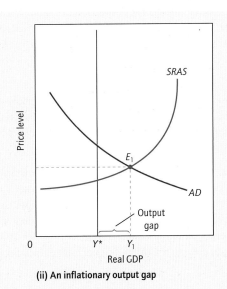

(i) A recessionary output gap

(ii) An inflationary output gap

**Figure 19.1  Actual GDP, potential GDP, and the output gap**

The output gap is the difference between actual GDP, *Y*, and potential GDP, *Y\**. Potential GDP is shown by a vertical line because it refers to a given, constant level of real GDP. Actual GDP is determined by the intersection of the aggregate demand (*AD*) and short-run aggregate supply (*SRAS*) curves.

In part (i) the positions of the *AD* and *SRAS* curves result in a recessionary gap: equilibrium is at $E_0$, so actual GDP is given by $Y_0$, which is less than potential output. The output gap is $Y_0 - Y^*$. In part (ii) the positions of the *AD* and *SRAS* curves result in an inflationary gap. Although potential output is unchanged at $Y^*$, equilibrium is now at $E_1$, so actual GDP is given by $Y_1$, which is greater than potential output. The output gap is $Y_1 - Y^*$.

also be high. When actual GDP is low relative to potential GDP, demand for inputs will be relatively low. This relationship is true of all inputs. The discussion that follows is simplified, however, by focusing on one key input, labour, and on its price, the wage rate.

When there is an inflationary gap, actual output exceeds potential, and the demand for labour services will be relatively high. When there is a recessionary gap, actual output is below potential, and the demand for labour services will be relatively low.

Each of these situations has implications for wages. Before turning to a detailed study of these, we first consider a benchmark for the behaviour of wages. Earlier we referred to average costs per unit of output as *unit costs*; to focus on labour costs, we now use average wage costs per unit of output, which we refer to as *unit labour costs*.

### Upward and downward wage pressures

Consider the *upward* and *downward* pressures on wages that are associated with various output gaps. Most wage bargaining starts from the assumption that, other things being equal, workers will get the benefit of increases in their own productivity by receiving higher wages. Thus, when GDP is at its potential level, wages will tend to be rising at the same rate as productivity is rising.[1] When wages and productivity change proportionately, *unit labour costs* remain unchanged. For example, if each worker produces 4 per cent more and earns 4 per cent more, unit labour costs will remain constant. This, then, is the benchmark:

When there is neither excess demand nor excess supply in the labour market, wages will tend to be rising at the same rate as labour productivity; as a result, unit labour costs will remain constant.

Note that, with unit labour costs remaining constant, there is no pressure coming from the labour market for the *SRAS* curve to shift. Hence there is no pressure for the price level to change. Indeed, a key characteristic of the definition of potential GDP is that there is no pressure for unit labour costs to rise or fall. So the state of the labour market and the level of potential GDP are inextricably connected.

In comparison with this benchmark of constant unit labour costs, *upward pressure on wages* means that there is pressure for wages to rise faster than productivity is rising. Thus, unit labour costs will also be rising. For example, if money wages rise by 8 per cent while productivity rises by only 4 per cent, labour costs per unit of output will be rising by about 4 per cent. In this case the *SRAS* curve will be shifting to the left, reflecting upward pressure on wage costs coming from the labour market (see Figure 18.13 on page 418).

*Downward pressure on wages* means that there is pressure for wages to rise more slowly than productivity is rising. When this occurs unit labour costs will be falling. For example, if productivity rises by 4 per cent while money wages rise by only 2 per cent, labour costs per unit of output will be falling by about 2 per cent. In this case the *SRAS* curve will be shifting to the right, reflecting downward pressure on wage costs coming from the labour market.

### Actual GDP exceeds potential GDP

Sometimes the *AD* and *SRAS* curves intersect where actual output exceeds potential, as illustrated in part (ii) of Figure 19.1. Firms are producing beyond their normal-capacity output, so there is an unusually large demand for all inputs, including labour. Labour shortages will emerge in some industries and among many groups of workers, particularly skilled workers. Firms will try to bid workers away from other firms in order to maintain the high levels of output and sales made possible by the boom conditions.

As a result of these tight labour market conditions, workers will find that they have considerable bargaining power with their employers, and they will put upward pressure on wages relative to productivity. Firms, recognizing that demand for their goods is strong, will be anxious to maintain a high level of output. To prevent their workers from either striking or quitting and moving to other employers, therefore, firms will be willing to accede to some of these upward pressures.

The boom that is associated with an inflationary gap generates a set of conditions—high profits for firms and unusually large demand for labour—that exerts upward pressure on wages.

### Actual GDP is less than potential GDP

Sometimes the *AD* and *SRAS* curves intersect where actual output is less than potential, as illustrated in part (i) of Figure 19.1. In this situation firms are producing below

---

[1] Ongoing inflation would also influence the normal pattern of wage changes. Wage contracts often allow for changes in prices that are expected to occur during the life of the contract. For now we make the simplifying assumption that the price level is expected to be constant; hence changes in money wages also are expected to be changes in real wages. The distinction between changes in money wages and real wages, and the important role played by expectations of price level changes, will be discussed later.

their normal-capacity output, so the demand for all inputs, including labour, is unusually low. The general conditions in the market for labour will be the opposite of those that occur when actual output exceeds potential. There will be labour surpluses in some industries and among some groups of workers. Firms will have below-normal sales, and will not only resist upward pressures on wages, but tend to offer wage increases below productivity increases. They may even seek reductions in money wages.

The slump that is associated with a recessionary gap generates a set of conditions—low profits for firms, unusually low demand for labour, and a desire on the part of firms to resist wage demands and even to push for wage concessions—that exerts a downward pressure on wages and unit labour costs.

### Adjustment asymmetry

Boom conditions, along with severe labour shortages, cause wages, unit labour costs, and the price level to rise rapidly. When there is a large excess demand for labour, wage (and price) increases may well run ahead of productivity increases. Money wages might be rising by, say, 4 per cent, while productivity is rising at only 1 per cent, so that unit labour costs would be rising by around 3 per cent.

The experience of most European economies (and other industrial economies, such as the United States and Canada) suggests, however, that the downward pressures on wages during slumps often do not operate as quickly as do the upward pressures during booms. Even in quite severe recessions, when the price level is fairly stable, money wages may continue to rise, although their rate of increase tends to fall below that of productivity. For example, productivity might be rising at 1.5 per cent per year while money wages are rising at 0.5 per cent. In this case unit labour costs are falling, but only by about 1 per cent per year. The rightward shift in the *SRAS* curve and the

downward pressure on the price level are correspondingly slight. Money wages may actually fall, reducing unit wage costs even more, but the reduction in unit labour costs in the times of deepest recession has not been as fast as the increases that have occurred during several of the strongest booms. This suggests that there is an asymmetry in the way in which the economy responds to each of the output gaps.

Both upward and downward adjustments to unit labour costs do occur, but there is a difference in the speed at which they typically operate. Excess demand can cause unit labour costs to rise very rapidly; excess supply normally causes unit labour costs to fall only slowly.[2]

### Inflationary and recessionary gaps

Now it should be clear why the output gaps are named as they are. When actual GDP exceeds potential GDP, there will normally be rising unit costs, and the *SRAS* curve will be shifting upward. This in turn will push the price level up. Indeed, the most obvious event accompanying these conditions is likely to be a significant inflation. The larger is the excess of actual output over potential output, the greater will be the inflationary pressure. The term *inflationary gap* emphasizes this salient feature.

When actual output is less than potential output, as we have seen, there will be unemployment of labour and other productive resources. Unit labour costs will fall only slowly, leading to a slow downward shift in the *SRAS* curve. Hence the price level will be falling only slowly, so that *unemployment* will be the output gap's most obvious result. The term *recessionary gap* emphasizes this salient feature that high rates of unemployment occur when actual output falls short of potential output.

The induced effects of output gaps on unit labour costs and the consequent shifts in the *SRAS* curve play an important role in our analysis of the long-run consequences of aggregate demand shocks, to which we now turn.

## The long-run consequences of aggregate demand shocks

We can now extend our study to cover the longer-run consequences of aggregate demand shocks, by incorporating changes in input prices. We need to examine separately the effects of aggregate demand shocks on input prices for expansionary and for contractionary shocks, because, as we have just seen, the behaviour of unit costs is not symmetrical for the two cases.

### Expansionary shocks

Suppose that the economy starts with a stable price level at full employment, so actual GDP equals potential

---

[2] This is the second asymmetry in aggregate supply that we have encountered. The first refers to the variable slope of the *SRAS* curve, as discussed in Box 18.3.

(i) Autonomous increase in aggregate demand

(ii) Induced shift in aggregate supply

**Figure 19.2 Demand-shock inflation**

A rightward shift of the *AD* curve first raises prices and output along the *SRAS* curve. It then induces a shift of the *SRAS* curve that further raises prices but lowers output along the *AD* curve. In part (i) the economy is in equilibrium at $E_0$, at its level of potential output $Y^*$ and price level $P_0$. The *AD* curve then shifts to $AD_1$. This moves equilibrium to $E_1$, with GDP $Y_1$ and price level $P_1$, and opens up an inflationary gap of $Y_1 - Y^*$.

In part (ii) the inflationary gap results in an increase in wages and other input costs, shifting the *SRAS* curve leftward. As this happens, output falls and the price level rises along $AD_1$. Eventually, when the *SRAS* curve has shifted to $SRAS_1$, output is back to $Y^*$ and the inflationary gap has been eliminated. However, the price level has risen to $P_2$.

GDP, as shown by the initial equilibrium in part (i) of Figure 19.2.

Now suppose that this stable situation is disturbed by an increase in autonomous spending, perhaps caused by a sudden boom in investment spending. Figure 19.2(i) shows the effects of this aggregate demand shock in raising both the price level and GDP. Now actual GDP exceeds potential GDP; i.e., there is an inflationary gap.

We have seen that an inflationary gap causes wages to rise faster than productivity, which raises unit costs. The *SRAS* curve shifts to the left as firms seek to pass on their increases in costs by increasing their output prices. For this reason the initial increases in the price level and in real GDP shown in part (i) of Figure 19.2 are *not* the final effects of the demand shock. As seen in part (ii) of the figure, the upward shift of the *SRAS* curve causes a further rise in the price level, but this time the price rise is associated with a fall in output.

The cost increases (and the consequent upward shifts of the *SRAS* curve) continue until the inflationary gap has been removed, that is, until output returns to $Y^*$, its potential level. Only then is there no excess demand for labour, and only then do wages and unit costs, and hence the *SRAS* curve, stabilize.

This important expansionary demand shock sequence can be summarized as follows.

1. Starting from full employment, a rise in aggregate demand raises the price level and raises output above its potential level as the economy expands along a given *SRAS* curve.

2. The expansion of output beyond its normal-capacity level puts pressure on input (especially labour) markets; input prices begin to increase faster than productivity, shifting the *SRAS* curve upward, such that prices are higher at every level of output.

3. The shift of the *SRAS* curve causes GDP to fall along the *AD* curve. This process continues *as long as* actual output exceeds potential output. Therefore, actual output eventually falls back to its potential level. The price level, however, is now higher than it was after the initial impact of the increased aggregate demand, but inflation will have come to a halt.

(i) Autonomous falls in aggregate demand

(ii) Induced shifts in aggregate supply

**Figure 19.3** Demand-shock deflation with flexible wages

A leftward shift of the *AD* curve first lowers prices and output along the *SRAS* curve and then induces a (slow) shift of the *SRAS* curve that further lowers prices but raises output along the *AD* curve. In part (i) the economy is in equilibrium at $E_0$, at its level of potential output $Y^*$ and price level $P_0$. The *AD* curve then shifts to $AD_1$, moving equilibrium to $E_1$, with output $Y_1$ and price level $P_1$, and opens up a recessionary gap of $Y_1 - Y^*$.

Part (ii) shows the adjustment back to full employment which occurs from the supply side of the economy. The fall in wages shifts the *SRAS* curve to the right. Real GDP rises, and the price level falls further along the *AD* curve. Eventually the *SRAS* curve reaches $SRAS_1$, with equilibrium at $E_2$. The price level stabilizes at $P_2$ when GDP returns to $Y^*$, eliminating the recessionary gap.

The ability to wring more output (and income) from the economy than its underlying potential output (as in point 2 above) is only a short-term possibility. GDP greater than $Y^*$ sets into motion inflationary pressures that tend to push GDP back to $Y^*$.

A once-and-for-all demand shock sets off an adjustment process that eventually returns GDP to its potential level, but (normally) at a different price level.

## Contractionary shocks

Let us return to that stable economy with full employment and steady prices. It appears again in part (i) of Figure 19.3, which is similar to part (i) of Figure 19.2. Now assume that there is a *decline* in aggregate demand, perhaps owing to a major reduction in investment spending, or to a fall in exports as a result of a fall in overseas demand.

The first effects of the decline are a fall in output and some downward adjustment of the price level, as shown in part (i) of the figure. As output falls, unemployment rises. The difference between potential GDP and actual GDP is the recessionary gap that is shown in the figure.

### Flexible wages

What would happen if severe unemployment caused a rapid fall in wage rates relative to productivity? For example, with productivity rising by 1 per cent per year, suppose that money wages fell by 4 per cent. Unit costs would then *fall* by 5 per cent. Falling wage rates would lower unit costs, causing a rightward shift of the *SRAS* curve. As shown in part (ii) of Figure 19.3, the economy would move along $AD_1$, with falling prices and rising output, until full employment was restored at potential GDP, $Y^*$. We conclude that, if wages were to fall whenever there was unemployment, the resulting fall in the *SRAS* curve would restore full employment.

Flexible wages that fell during periods of unemployment would provide an automatic adjustment mechanism that would push the economy back towards full employment whenever output fell below potential.

### Sticky wages

Boom conditions, along with severe labour shortages, do cause wages to rise rapidly, shifting the *SRAS* curve upward. However, as we noted earlier, the experience of many economies suggests that wages typically do not fall rapidly in response to recessionary gaps and their accompanying unemployment. It is sometimes said that wages are 'sticky' in a downward direction. This does not mean that wages never fall. In recession money wages often rise more slowly than productivity and some money wages actually fall. But during recessions there is typically only a small difference between the rate at which money wages are changing and the rate at which productivity is changing. Thus, unit labour costs fall only slowly. This in turn implies that the downward shifts in the *SRAS* curve occur slowly, and the adjustment mechanism that depends on these shifts will act sluggishly.

One reason why wage rates do not adjust quickly to clear labour markets will be discussed in Chapter 25. This explanation is associated with the idea of *efficiency wages*, which we first encountered in Chapter 11 (pages 242–3). Because labour is not a standardized commodity, employers face both a problem of attracting the best workers and a problem of motivating those workers who have been hired. Employers are reluctant to lower wages for their workforce, even when there is an excess supply of potential new workers, because lower wages are more likely to attract lower-quality workers at the margin, and existing staff would be discouraged by such actions.

**The *SRAS* curve shifts to the left fairly rapidly when GDP exceeds Y\*, but it shifts to the right only slowly when GDP is less than Y\*.**

The weakness of the adjustment mechanism does not imply that slumps must always be prolonged. It only requires that speedy recovery back to full employment be generated mainly from the demand side. If the economy is to avoid a lengthy period of recession or stagnation, the force leading to recovery must usually be a rightward shift of the *AD* curve rather than a downward drift of the *SRAS* curve.

Could government *stabilization policy* accomplish the needed shift in *AD*? This is one of the more important and contentious issues in macroeconomics, and one that we will return to later.

### The asymmetry

This difference in speed of adjustment is a consequence of the important asymmetry in the behaviour of aggregate supply that was noted earlier in this chapter. This asymmetry helps to explain two key facts about our economy. First, unemployment can persist for quite long periods without causing decreases in unit costs and prices of sufficient magnitude to remove the unemployment. Second, booms, along with labour shortages and production beyond normal capacity, do not persist for long periods without causing increases in unit costs and the price level.

## The long-run aggregate supply (*LRAS*) curve

The **long-run aggregate supply (*LRAS*) curve** shows the relationship between the price level and real GDP after wage rates and all other input costs have been fully adjusted to eliminate any unemployment or overall labour shortages.

### Shape of the *LRAS* curve

Once all the adjustments that are required have occurred, the economy will have eliminated any excess demand or excess supply of labour. In other words, full employment will prevail, and output will necessarily be at its potential level, Y\*. It follows that the aggregate supply curve becomes a vertical line at Y\*, as shown in Figure 19.4. The *LRAS* curve is sometimes called the classical aggregate supply

**Figure 19.4 The long-run aggregate supply (*LRAS*) curve**

The long-run aggregate supply curve is a vertical line drawn at the level of GDP that is equal to potential GDP, Y\*. It is a vertical line because the total amount of goods that the economy produces when all factors are efficiently used at their normal rate of utilization does not vary with the price level. If the price level were to rise from $P_1$ to $P_2$ and wages and all other input prices were to rise by the same proportion, the total desired output of firms would remain at Y\*.

If output were $Y_1$, which is less than Y\*, wages would be falling and the *SRAS* curve would be shifting rightward; hence the economy would not be on its *LRAS* curve. If output were $Y_2$, which is greater than Y\*, wages would be rising and the *SRAS* curve would be shifting leftward; hence, again, the economy would not be on its *LRAS* curve.

curve because many of the classical economists were concerned mainly with the behaviour of the economy in long-run equilibrium.

Notice that the vertical *LRAS* curve does not represent the same thing as the vertical portion of the *SRAS* curve (see Figure 18.10 on page 415). Over the vertical range of the *SRAS* curve, the economy is at the utmost limit of its existing productive capacity, as might occur in an all-out war effort. No more can be squeezed out. The vertical shape of the *LRAS* curve is due to the workings of an adjustment mechanism that brings the economy back to its potential output, even though actual output may differ from its potential level for considerable periods of time. It is called the long-run aggregate supply curve because it arises as a result of adjustments that take a significant amount of time.

Along the *LRAS* curve the prices of all outputs and all inputs have been fully adjusted to eliminate any excess demands or supplies. Proportionate changes in money wages and the price level (which, by definition, will leave real wages unaltered) will also leave equilibrium employment and total output unchanged. In the next section we will ask what does change when we move from one point on the *LRAS* curve to another.

## Long-run equilibrium

Figure 19.5 shows equilibrium GDP and the price level as they are determined by the intersection of the *AD* curve and the vertical *LRAS* curve. Because the *LRAS* curve is vertical, shifts in aggregate demand change the price level but not the level of equilibrium GDP, as shown in part (i). By contrast, a shift in aggregate supply changes both GDP and the price level, as shown in part (ii). For example, a rightward shift of the *LRAS* curve increases real GDP and leads to a fall in the price level.

With a vertical *LRAS* curve, in the long run total output is determined solely by conditions of supply, and the role of aggregate demand is simply to determine the price level.

What changes when the economy moves from one point on the *LRAS* curve, such as $E_0$ in part (i) of Figure 19.5, to another point, such as $E_1$? Although total output and total desired spending do not change, their *compositions* do change. The higher the price level, the lower is personal wealth (for a given nominal stock of assets) and hence the lower is private consumption. (Recall from Chapter 16 that private consumption is positively related to wealth.) Also, the higher the price level, the lower are exports and the higher are imports, and hence the lower are net exports.

**(i) A rise in aggregate demand**

**(ii) A rise in long-run aggregate supply**

**Figure 19.5  Long-run equilibrium and aggregate supply**

**When the *LRAS* curve is vertical, aggregate supply determines the long-run equilibrium value of GDP at Y\*.** Given Y\*, aggregate demand determines the long-run equilibrium value of the price level. In both parts of the figure the initial long-run equilibrium is at $E_0$, so the price level is $P_0$ and GDP is $Y_0^*$.

In part (i) a shift in the *AD* curve from $AD_0$ to $AD_1$, with the *LRAS* curve remaining unchanged, moves the long-run equilibrium from $E_0$ to $E_1$. This raises the price level from $P_0$ to $P_1$ but leaves GDP unchanged at $Y_0^*$ in the long run.

In part (ii) a shift in the *LRAS* curve from $LRAS_0$ to $LRAS_1$, with the aggregate demand curve remaining constant at $AD_0$, moves the long-run equilibrium from $E_0$ to $E_2$. This raises GDP from $Y_0^*$ to $Y_1^*$ but lowers the price level from $P_0$ to $P_2$.

Suppose the economy starts at a point on the *SRAS* curve and an increase in government spending then creates an inflationary gap. Money wages and the price level rise until the gap is removed. At the new long-run equilibrium, the higher level of government spending is exactly offset by lower private consumption and net exports, leaving total output unchanged. A similar analysis holds for an increase in investment. In the new long-run equilibrium, the higher level of investment spending will be exactly offset by lower consumption spending and net exports.

The vertical *LRAS* curve shows that, given full adjustment of input prices, potential GDP, *Y\**, is compatible with any price level although its composition among private consumption, investment, government consumption, and net exports may vary with different price levels.

In Chapter 21 we will discover circumstances under which a rise in the price level has *no real effect*, so that not only are real GDP and total spending the same at all points on the *LRAS* curve, but also the composition of spending among *C*, *I*, *G*, and $(X - IM)$ is the same. We will also learn, once we have added a monetary sector, that interest rate changes have important effects on the composition of spending.

# Real GDP in the short and long run

We have now identified two distinct equilibrium conditions for the economy:

1. In the short run the economy is in equilibrium at the level of GDP and the price level where the *SRAS* curve intersects the *AD* curve.

2. In the long run the economy is in equilibrium at potential GDP, the position of the vertical *LRAS* curve. The price level is that at which the *AD* curve intersects the *LRAS* curve.

The *position* of the *LRAS* curve is at *Y\**, which is determined by past economic growth. Deviations of actual output from potential output—GDP gaps—are generally associated with business cycles. Changes in total real output (and hence in employment, unemployment, and living standards) may take place as a result of either growth or the business cycle.

Demand and supply shocks may be positive or negative. Such shocks may results from policy changes by the government or monetary authorities, or they may result from autonomous changes in private sector behaviour, such as an autonomous change in consumer spending. They may also result from changes in other countries that affect the domestic economy via a shift in net exports.

This discussion suggests a need to distinguish three ways in which GDP can be increased. These are illustrated in Figure 19.6.

## Increases in aggregate demand

As shown in part (i) of Figure 19.6, an increase in aggregate demand will yield a one-time increase in real GDP. If that increase occurs when there is a recessionary gap, it pushes GDP towards its potential level. It therefore short-circuits the working of the automatic adjustment mechanism that would eventually have achieved the same outcome by depressing unit costs, as discussed earlier in this chapter.

If the demand increase pushes GDP beyond its potential level, the rise in GDP will be only temporary; the inflationary gap will cause wages and other costs to rise, shifting the *SRAS* curve to the left. This drives GDP back towards its potential level, so that the only lasting effect is on the price level. Box 19.1 presents a number of reasons why we might expect the effect of demand shocks on GDP to be cyclical, that is, to cause GDP to move first one way, then the other.

## Increases in aggregate supply

Increases in aggregate supply will also lead to increases in GDP. Here it is useful to distinguish between two possible kinds of increase that might occur—those that leave the *LRAS* curve unchanged, and those that shift it.

Part (ii) of Figure 19.6 shows the effects of a positive shock to short-run aggregate supply that leaves potential GDP unchanged, such as would be caused by a fall in the prices of imported raw materials. This will shift the *SRAS* curve to the right but will have no effect on the *LRAS* curve. The shock will thus cause GDP to rise towards potential if it starts out below, but an increase that takes GDP beyond potential will eventually be reversed.

Part (iii) of Figure 19.6 shows the effects of permanent increases in aggregate supply that shift the *LRAS* curve. A once-and-for-all increase due to, say, a labour market policy that reduces the level of structural unemployment will lead to a one-time increase in potential GDP. A recurring increase that is due, say, to population growth, capital accumulation, or ongoing improvements in productivity causes a continual rightward shift in the *LRAS* curve, giving rise to a continual increase in the level of potential GDP.

# Economic growth

A gradual but continual rise in potential GDP, or what we have called *economic growth*, is the main source of improvements in the standard of living over the long term.

**Figure 19.6 Three ways of increasing GDP**

**GDP will increase in response to an increase in aggregate demand or an increase in aggregate supply.** The increase will be permanent if the *LRAS* curve shifts, but if the *LRAS* curve does not shift any divergences of GDP from potential will be only temporary; the output gap that is created will set in motion the wage adjustments that we studied earlier in this chapter. In part (i) the *AD* curve shifts to the right. If the initial level of output is $Y_1$, then the shift from $AD_0$ to $AD_1$ eliminates the recessionary gap and raises GDP to $Y^*$. If the initial level of GDP is $Y^*$, then the shift from $AD_1$ to $AD_2$ raises GDP to $Y_2$ and thereby opens up an inflationary gap.

In part (ii) the *SRAS* curve shifts to the right. If the initial level of output is $Y_1$, then the shift from $SRAS_0$ to $SRAS_1$ eliminates the recessionary gap and raises GDP to $Y^*$. If the initial level of output is $Y^*$, then the shift from $SRAS_1$ to $SRAS_2$ raises GDP to $Y_2$ and thereby opens up an inflationary gap.

In the cases shown in parts (i) and (ii) any increase in output beyond potential is temporary, since in the absence of any additional shocks the inflationary gap will cause wages and other input prices to rise; this will cause the *SRAS* curve to shift upward, and therefore GDP to converge to $Y^*$.

In part (iii) the *LRAS* curve shifts to the right, causing potential GDP to increase. Whether or not actual output increases immediately depends on what happens to the *AD* and *SRAS* curves. Since in the absence of other shocks actual GDP eventually converges to potential GDP, a rightward shift in the *LRAS* curve eventually leads to an increase in actual GDP. If the shift in the *LRAS* curve is recurring, then GDP will grow continually.

---

 **Box 19.1  Demand shocks and business cycles**

Aggregate demand shocks are a major source of fluctuations in GDP around $Y^*$. As we have seen, an expansionary demand shock, starting from a position of full employment, will lead to an increase in output, followed by a fall in output accompanied by an increase in prices as the adjustment mechanism restores the economy to equilibrium. Depending on the nature and magnitude of the shock, the adjustment will take many months, often stretching to one or two years.

Suppose that the government increases spending on roads or that economic growth in Germany leads to an increase in demand for UK exports. No matter what the source of growth in demand, the economy will not respond instantaneously. In many industries it takes weeks or months, or even longer, to bring new or mothballed capacity into production and to hire and train new workers. The multiplier process itself takes time, as people and firms respond to the change in income that results from an initial increase in autonomous spending.

Because of these lags in the economy's response, changes in demand give rise to changes in output that are spread out over a substantial period of time. An increase in demand may lead to a gradual increase in output that builds up over several months. Then, as output does change, the adjustment mechanism comes into play. As an inflationary gap opens up, wages and costs start to rise, shifting the *SRAS* curve to the left.

Thus, a once-and-for-all positive demand shock can give rise to a *cyclical* output response, with GDP first rising because of the rightward shift in the *AD* curve, and then falling because of the upward shift in the *SRAS* curve. A negative demand shock is likely to play out even more slowly because of the asymmetry of response. Again, however, the behaviour of output will be cyclical: starting from potential output, GDP will fall over a period of time, because of a leftward shift in the *AD* curve, and then rise slowly as the adjustment mechanism shifts *SRAS* to the right.

Each major component of aggregate spending—private consumption, investment, net exports, and government consumption—is subject to continual random shifts, which are sometimes large enough to disturb the economy significantly. Adjustment lags can convert such shifts into cyclical oscillations in GDP.

Eliminating a severe recessionary gap could cause a once-and-for-all increase in GDP of, say, 4 per cent, while eliminating structural unemployment will raise it by somewhat less. However, a growth rate of 3 per cent per year raises GDP by 10 per cent in 3 years, *doubles* it in 24 years, and *quadruples* it in 48 years.

In any given year the position of the *LRAS* curve is at potential GDP, $Y^*$. The long run to which the *LRAS* curve refers is thus one in which the resources available to the economy do not change, but all markets reach equilibrium. Economic growth moves the *LRAS* curve to the right, year by year. Here the long run is not a period in which everything settles down, because growth is a continuing process: rather, the movement in *LRAS* causes a continuing movement in $Y^*$.

Determinants of long-run shifts in potential GDP, or economic growth, used to be regarded as beyond the scope of macroeconomics. However, it is clearly one of the most important factors in determining living standards. There is now a much stronger case for treating growth as an integral part of macroeconomics, which is that many of the forces of growth are endogenous; that is, apparently short-term policies may have implications for long-term growth. No longer is it safe to assume that the determinants of growth are independent of the determinants of the short-term cycle.

## Cyclical fluctuations

Figure 19.6 distinguishes the causes of trend growth in potential GDP, which is the gradual rightward shifting of the *LRAS* curve, from the causes of cyclical fluctuations, which are deviations from that trend.

Cyclical fluctuations in GDP are caused by shifts in the *AD* and *SRAS* curves that cause actual GDP to deviate temporarily from potential GDP.

These shifts in turn are caused by changes in a variety of factors, including interest rates, exchange rates, consumer and business confidence, and government policy. Although the resulting deviations of actual from potential GDP are described as 'temporary', recall from the discussion above that the automatic adjustment mechanism may work slowly enough that the deviations can persist for some time, perhaps several years.

It is worth looking at this stage at Figures 26.1 on page 590 and 16.1 on page 358. The first shows the level of UK real GDP since 1885. The dominant feature of this graph is the continued upward trend that has led to a more than five-fold increase in real GDP in just over 100 years. The average year-to-year increase is only about 2 per cent, but the cumulative effect of this slow but steady growth has been spectacular. The long-term trend reflects the steady rightward shift in the *LRAS* curve associated with sustained increases in potential GDP.

Figure 16.1 shows the year-to-year percentage changes in UK real GDP. Fluctuations in the annual rate of growth reflect the effects of aggregate demand and supply shocks. The two largest positive shocks derive from the increases in aggregate demand associated with the First and Second World Wars. The two largest negative demand shocks appear to be associated with the ends of those two wars, though there were sharp recessions in the early 1920s and early 1930s. The three post-1970 recessions look trivial in comparison with these earlier events, even though many who lived through them suffered severe loss of income and/or employment.

## Government policy and the business cycle

The short-run analysis of the macroeconomy that we set out in this and the previous three chapters was developed not just to explain the sources of GDP gaps, but also to suggest policies that could be used to alleviate major recessions—where there is persistent high unemployment and excess capacity—and to avoid inflation. Central to the so-called Keynesian revolution in economic policy-making was the idea that government policy could be used in a countercyclical manner to stabilize the economy. Accordingly, in the remainder of this chapter we discuss how changes in governments' taxing and spending policies and interest rates might be used as tools of stabilization

policy. The use of taxes and spending by the government in an attempt to control the economy is known as *fiscal stabilization policy*. We discuss monetary policy only briefly in this section, as the monetary system and monetary policy are the topic of the next two chapters.

Since increases in government spending raise aggregate demand and increases in taxation reduce it, the *directions* of the required changes in spending and taxation are generally easy to determine, once we know the direction of the desired change in GDP: cutting taxes and raising expenditure will tend to increase GDP while the opposite policy changes will tend to lower it. However, the *timing*, *magnitude*, and *mixture* of the changes pose more difficult issues.

There is no doubt that the government can exert a major influence on GDP. Prime examples are the massive increases in military spending during major wars. British government spending during the Second World War rose from 13.4 per cent of GDP in 1938 to 49.2 per cent of GDP in 1944. At the same time, the unemployment rate fell from 9.2 per cent to 0.3 per cent. Most observers agree that the increase in government spending helped to bring about the rise in GDP and the associated fall in unemployment. Similar experiences occurred during the rearmament of most European countries before, or just following, the outbreak of the Second World War in 1939 and in the United States during the Vietnam War in the late 1960s and early 1970s.

It might seem from what we have just said that fiscal policy can be an important tool for stabilizing the economy. In the heyday of fiscal policy activism, from about 1945 to about 1970, many economists were convinced that the economy could be stabilized adequately just by varying the size of the government's taxes and spending. That day is past. Today most economists are aware of the many limitations of fiscal policy.

# The basic theory of fiscal stabilization

A reduction in tax rates or an increase in government spending will shift the *AD* curve to the right, causing an increase in GDP. An increase in tax rates or a cut in government spending will shift the *AD* curve to the left, causing a decrease in GDP.

A more detailed look at how fiscal stabilization works will provide a useful review. It will also help to show some of the complications that arise in using fiscal policy.

## A recessionary gap

The two possible ways in which a recessionary gap can be removed are illustrated in Figure 19.7.

First, the gap may eventually cause wages and other input prices to rise sufficiently more slowly than productivity growth to shift the *SRAS* curve to the right and thereby reinstate full employment and potential GDP (at a lower price level). The evidence, however, is that this process takes a substantial period of time.

Second, the *AD* curve could shift to the right, restoring the economy to full employment and potential GDP (at a higher price level). The government can cause such a shift by using expansionary fiscal policy, lowering taxes, or raising spending (or the monetary authorities might cut

interest rates in order to stimulate spending). The advantage of using fiscal policy is that it may substantially shorten what would otherwise be a long recession. One disadvantage is that the use of fiscal policy may stimulate the economy just before private sector spending recovers on its own. As a result, the economy may overshoot its potential output, and an inflationary gap may open up. In this case fiscal policy that is intended to promote economic stability can actually cause instability.

## An inflationary gap

Figure 19.8 shows the ways in which an inflationary gap can be removed.

First, wages and other input prices may be pushed up by the excess demand. The *SRAS* curve will therefore shift to the left, eventually eliminating the gap, reducing GDP to its potential level, and raising the price level.

Second, the *AD* curve could shift to the left, restoring equilibrium GDP. The government, by raising taxes or cutting spending, can induce such a shift, reducing aggregate demand sufficiently to remove the inflationary gap. The advantage of this approach is that it avoids the inflationary increase in prices that accompanies the first method. One disadvantage is that if private sector spending falls GDP may be pushed below potential, thereby opening up a recessionary gap.

### A key proposition

This discussion suggests that, in circumstances in which the economy fails to adjust quickly enough on its own, or gives rise to undesirable side-effects such as rising prices, there is a potential stabilizing role for fiscal policy.

**Government taxes and spending shift the *AD* curve and hence can be used to remove persistent GDP gaps.**

### Automatic stabilizers

The government budget surplus increases as GDP increases. This is because tax revenues rise, some transfer payments —especially unemployment-related benefits—fall, while government consumption is generally unaffected by cyclical fluctuations. Thus, net taxes move in the same direction as GDP (unless there are changes in policy, that involve, for example, changes in tax rates). This means that there are increases in leakages as the economy expands and reductions in leakages as the economy contracts.

For example, in Chapter 17 we assumed that the net income tax rate was 10 per cent. This implies that a £1 rise in autonomous spending will increase disposable income by only 90p, dampening the multiplier effect of the initial increase. Generally, the wedge that income taxes place between national income and disposable income reduces

(i) A recessionary gap removed by a rightward shift in *SRAS*

(ii) A recessionary gap removed by a rightward shift in *AD*

**Figure 19.7  Removal of a recessionary gap**

**A recessionary gap may be removed by a (slow) rightward shift of the *SRAS* curve, a natural revival of private sector demand, or a fiscal-policy-induced increase in aggregate demand.** Initially equilibrium is at $E_0$, with GDP at $Y_0$ and the price level at $P_0$. The recessionary gap is $Y_0 - Y^*$.

In part (i) the gap might be removed by a shift in the *SRAS* curve to $SRAS_1$ as a result of reductions in wage rates and other input prices. The shift in the *SRAS* curve causes a movement down and to the right along $AD_0$ and establishes a new equilibrium at $E_1$, achieving potential GDP, $Y^*$, and lowering the price level to $P_1$.

In part (ii) the gap might also be removed by a shift of the *AD* curve to $AD_1$. That occurs either because of a natural revival of private sector spending or because of a fiscal-policy-induced increase in spending. The shift in the *AD* curve causes a movement up and to the right along $SRAS_0$ and shifts the equilibrium to $E_2$, raising GDP to $Y^*$ and the price level to $P_2$.

(i) An inflationary gap removed by a leftward shift in *SRAS*

(ii) An inflationary gap removed by a leftward shift in *AD*

**Figure 19.8  Removal of an inflationary gap**

**An inflationary gap may be removed by a leftward shift of the *SRAS* curve, a reduction in private sector demand, or a fiscal-policy-induced reduction in aggregate demand.** Initially equilibrium is at $E_0$, with GDP at $Y_0$ and the price level at $P_0$. The inflationary gap is $Y_0 - Y^*$.

In part (i) the gap might be removed by a shift in the *SRAS* curve to $SRAS_1$, which could occur as a result of increases in wage rates and other input prices. The shift in the *SRAS* curve would cause a movement up and to the left along $AD_0$ and establish a new equilibrium at $E_1$, reducing GDP to its potential level, $Y^*$, and raising the price level to $P_1$.

In part (ii) the gap might also be removed by a shift of the *AD* curve to $AD_1$, which could occur either because of a fall in private spending or because of contractionary fiscal policy. The shift in the *AD* curve would cause a movement down and to the left along $SRAS_0$. This movement would shift the equilibrium to $E_2$, lowering GDP to $Y^*$ and the price level to $P_2$.

the marginal propensity to spend out of national income, thereby reducing the size of the multiplier. The lower the multiplier, the less will equilibrium GDP tend to change for a given change in autonomous spending. The effect is to stabilize the economy, reducing the fluctuations in GDP that are caused by changes in autonomous spending. Because no policies need to be changed in order to achieve this result, the properties of the government budget that cause the multiplier to be reduced are called **automatic fiscal stabilizers**.

**Even when the government does not undertake to stabilize the economy via discretionary fiscal policy, the fact that net tax revenues rise with GDP means that there are fiscal effects that cause the budget to act as an *automatic stabilizer* for the economy.**

Of course, a government might try to follow a balanced budget policy, which means tying its spending in each period to the tax revenue it raises. This would change the impact of fiscal policy in a major way by making it *pro-cyclical*. With a pro-cyclical fiscal policy the government will restrict its spending during a recession because its tax revenue is low, and will increase its spending during a recovery when its tax revenue is rising. In other words, it moves with the economy, raising and lowering its spending in step with everyone else, exactly counter to the theory of fiscal stabilization that we just discussed. Some politicians have proposed changing the law so that governments must balance their budget in every year. However, most economists rarely call for anything more restrictive than a policy whereby governments aim to balance their budget on average over the course of the business cycle. A budget that was balanced on average would still permit the automatic stabilizer that is built into fiscal policy to work.

## Limitations of discretionary fiscal policy

The discussion of the previous few pages might suggest that returning the economy to potential GDP when the automatic stabilizers do not do the whole job, as they typically do not, is simply a matter of making discretionary changes in tax rates and government spending. However, many economists argue that such policies would be as likely to harm as to help. Part of their reasoning is that the execution of successful discretionary fiscal policy is anything but simple.[3]

---

[3] Another part has to do with the long-term consequences of budget deficits. Governments that run deficits for long periods build up substantial debts. These debts require significant tax revenues just to pay the interest, and this limits the ability of governments to spend on other programmes. Also, depending on the exchange rate regime, international considerations may reduce (but not eliminate) fiscal policy's effectiveness as a stabilization tool.

## Lags

Changing fiscal policy in response to GDP gaps requires changing tax rates and government spending and this can take much time for several reasons. First, it takes time to collect and process the statistics, so some time will have passed before the size of the current gap can be discerned. This reason for delay is known as an **information lag**.

There is then a much more serious delay caused by the policy-making process itself. In the UK the changes must be agreed upon by the Cabinet and passed by Parliament. Major changes in taxes are normally announced only once a year, in the spring Budget Statement, although 'mini-Budgets' are possible if 'crisis' measures need to be taken at other times of year. In December 2005 the Chancellor of the Exchequer announced spending plans for the succeeding three years. In the United States and most European countries, the budgetary process involves an annual round of policy proposals and legislation, though many spending programmes are for much longer horizons.

The political stakes in such changes are usually very large. Taxes and spending are called 'bread-and-butter' issues precisely because they affect the economic well-being of almost everyone. Thus, even if experts agreed that the economy would be helped by a tax cut, politicians may spend a good deal of time debating *which* taxes should be cut and *by how much*. The delay between the initial recognition of a recession or inflation and the enactment of legislation to change fiscal policy is called a **decision lag**.

Once policy changes are agreed upon, there is still an **execution lag**, adding time between the enactment and the implementation of the change. Furthermore, once policies are in place, it will usually take still more time for their economic consequences to be felt.

**Because of these lags, it is quite possible that by the time a given policy decision has any impact on the economy circumstances will have changed such that the policy is no longer appropriate.**

Figure 19.9 illustrates the problems that can arise in these circumstances.

To make matters even more frustrating, tax measures that are known to be temporary are generally less effective than measures that are expected to be permanent. If consumers know that a given tax cut will last for only a year or so, they may recognize that the effect on their long-run consumption possibilities is small and may adjust their short-run consumption relatively little. The more closely household consumption spending is related to lifetime (or 'permanent') income rather than current income, the smaller will be the effects on current consumption of tax changes that are known to be of short duration.

**Figure 19.9** Effects of fiscal policies that are not reversed

Fiscal policies that are initially appropriate may become inappropriate when private spending shifts. The initial position is on $AD_0$, at $Y^*$ and price level $P_0$. Suppose a slump in private investment shifts aggregate demand to $AD_1$, lowering GDP to $Y_1$ and causing a recessionary gap of $Y_1 - Y^*$.

The government now introduces fiscal expansion to restore aggregate demand to $AD_0$. But private investment then recovers, raising aggregate demand to $AD_2$. If fiscal policy can be quickly reversed, aggregate demand can be returned to $AD_0$ and GDP stabilized at $Y^*$. If the policy is not quickly reversed, the economy is at $E_2$ with an inflationary gap $Y_2 - Y^*$. This gap will cause wages to rise which will shift the $SRAS$ curve leftward and eventually restore $Y^*$ at price level $P_3$.

### The role of discretionary fiscal policy

**Fine-tuning** refers to the use of fiscal and monetary policy to offset virtually all fluctuations in private sector spending and so hold GDP at, or very near, its potential level at all times. However, the lags just discussed prevent policy-makers from undoing the consequences of every aggregate demand shock.

None the less, many economists would still argue that when a recessionary gap is large enough and persists for long enough, gross-tuning may be appropriate. **Gross-tuning** refers to the occasional use of fiscal and monetary policy to remove large and persistent GDP gaps. Advocates of gross-tuning hold that fiscal policy can and should be used to push the economy towards full employment when a GDP gap is large and has persisted for a long time. Other economists believe that fiscal policy should not be used for economic stabilization under any circumstances. They argue that tax and spending behaviour should be the

outcome of public choices regarding the long-term size and financing of the public sector and should not be altered for short-term considerations.

## Monetary policy

The difficulties in using fiscal policy to fine-tune the economy have caused current fiscal policy to be targeted on funding long-term government spending plans rather than as a tool for stabilizing the economy over the cycle (other than what is done by the automatic stabilizers). For this reason **monetary policy**, that is, the setting of interest rates in order to influence output or inflation, has become the main tool for short-run demand management.

Many monetary authorities, typically the central bank, have been allowed to set the official interest rate, but they have not been given the task of stabilizing macroeconomic activity. Rather, they have been set the objective of stabilizing inflation. The UK Monetary Policy Committee (MPC), for example, is charged with targeting an inflation rate of 2.0 per cent, while the European Central Bank (ECB) is charged with achieving 'price stability'. Fortunately, stabilizing inflation and offsetting aggregate demand shocks requires similar policy actions. Thus, where demand shocks are the main source of disturbances, stabilizing inflation and stabilizing output will amount to more or less the same thing. For example, a positive demand shock that takes actual GDP above potential GDP will cause inflation. To control inflation, interest rates will generally need to rise. This will lower domestic spending and hence actual GDP relative to potential, and thereby reduce inflationary pressures.[4]

Monetary policy has some advantages over fiscal policy. Although the information lag is the same, the other two lags are much shorter. Policy can be changed frequently. The UK MPC, for example, meets every month, the ECB meets every two weeks, and the US Federal Open Market Committee meets every six weeks (but can react more quickly if necessary via a video conference). The execution lag is even shorter. Once a policy decision has been made, interest rates can be changed within minutes of the policy decision being taken.

However, monetary policy is subject to a further time lag before its full effect is felt on the economy. The

---

[4] Deciding how to respond to supply shocks is more difficult, as a shock that raises prices will lower output and vice versa. Tightening monetary policy (raising interest rates) to control inflation would make the output loss even worse. We postpone a discussion of this case to Chapter 21.

traditional rule of thumb is that a change in monetary policy today takes about one year to have its maximum impact on output and a further year to have its maximum

impact on the inflation rate. Lags of this magnitude are considered by monetary policy-makers to be plausible even today.

# CASE STUDIES

## 1. UK fiscal rules

After winning the general election in 1997, the incoming Labour Chancellor, Gordon Brown, imposed a fiscal framework that involved two key rules designed to support the goal of 'maintaining macroeconomic stability':[5] the golden rule, and the sustainable investment rule:

*We have also put in place a new fiscal policy framework set out in the Code for Fiscal Stability requiring the Government to conduct fiscal policy in a transparent and responsible way. And we have set two strict fiscal rules: the golden rule requires that over the cycle we balance the current budget, and the sustainable investment rule requires that, as we borrow for investment, debt is set at a prudent and stable level.* (Gordon Brown speech, May 1999)

An assessment of these rules conducted within HM Treasury in 2005 reported as follows:

### The golden rule

*The projections show that the government is meeting the golden rule, on the basis of cautious assumptions, with an average annual surplus on the current budget over this economic cycle of 0.1 per cent of GDP. On this basis, and based on cautious assumptions, the Government is meeting the golden rule and there is a margin against the golden rule of £16 billion in this cycle. . . . The cyclically adjusted surplus, which allows underlying or structural trends in the public finances to be seen more clearly by removing the estimated effects of the economic cycle, shows a small deficit in 2005–6, but a surplus of 0.7 per cent of GDP or higher from 2006–7 onwards.*

### The sustainable investment rule

*The sustainable investment rule is also met over the economic cycle. In 1996–7, public sector net debt stood at 44 per cent of GDP. The tough decisions on taxation and expenditure taken by the Government, including the decision to use the proceeds from the auction of spectrum licences to repay debt, reduced debt to around 30 per cent of GDP by the end of 2001–2. It is now projected to rise slowly, as the Government borrows modestly to fund*

*increased investment in public services, reaching just over 38 per cent by the end of the economic cycle—£27 billion below the 40 per cent level—and stabilising at that level for the remainder of the forecasting period. The projections for core debt, which exclude the estimated impact of the economic cycle, rise to just under 36 per cent of GDP by the end of the projection period. This is consistent with the fiscal rules, and with the key objective of intergenerational fairness that underpins the fiscal framework.* (HM Treasury, *Pre-Budget Report*, December 2005, page 209)

What is notable from these statements is that there is no mention of using fiscal policy in a countercyclical manner to keep activity close to potential, even though the policy is explicitly intended to support macroeconomic stability. Automatic fiscal stabilizers are permitted to operate, but the golden rule makes clear the intention to maintain the current budget in balance when averaged over the whole of an economic cycle.

There was criticism in 2005 that the Treasury had redefined the dates of the cycle in order to make the golden rule achievable, but the golden rule itself clearly puts real constraints on the scale of budget deficits that could be incurred. Notice, however, that the 'current budget' excludes government investment expenditure. This is covered by the sustainable investment rule, which says that the Government will increase debt (on average over the cycle) only to finance investment but that the debt to GDP ratio will be kept below 40 per cent. This is claimed to be a prudent level, in that it does not put an unreasonable burden on future taxpayers who would have to pay the interest on the accumulated debt.

## 2. Earnings growth and inflation

In this chapter we have seen how an inflationary or a recessionary gap will lead to an adjustment of money wages and a shift in the short-run aggregate supply curve. We argued that in the case of recessions wages could be slow to adjust but that adjustment would be more rapid when there was inflationary pressure. In the major inflationary episodes that have occurred in the past few decades in the UK economy, the link between wage and price movements, the so-called wage–price spiral, was very strong.

Figure 19.10 shows monthly data for UK annual earnings growth and RPI inflation from 1964 to 2006. Earnings growth is generally slightly above inflation, reflecting growing real earnings,

---

[5] We first saw this in studying the objectives of the government in Chapter 14, page 323.

**Figure 19.10** UK earnings growth and RPI inflation, 1964–2006

*Source*: ONS on www.statistics.gov.uk

but the two series are clearly very closely correlated. When inflation is high, earnings growth is high and vice versa.

Although there were recorded recessions in the early 1970s, 1980s, and 1990s, there were no episodes of negative earnings growth or of negative inflation during this forty-year period. There were, however, a few brief periods when inflation exceeded earnings growth so that real earnings at these times fell.

There is unlikely to be any consistent pattern in which either wages are leading prices or prices are leading wages. Inflationary episodes could be triggered by supply shocks or demand shocks, but both earnings and prices are endogenous variables that respond to the excess demand or supplies represented by the GDP gap. We will study the dynamics of the inflation process in more detail in Chapter 24.

## Conclusion

We have now added a supply side to our macro model and have seen how aggregate supply and aggregate demand interact in that model to determine real GDP and the price level. The long-run aggregate supply curve is vertical at the level of potential GDP, but actual GDP may be above or below potential GDP in the short run. If it is above potential there will be an inflationary gap and this will lead to rising prices and wages; if it is below potential there will be unemployed workers and other resources, and eventually there will be downward pressure on wages and prices. In reality, on the basis of recent history, this is most

likely to be observed as a slow rise in wages and prices rather than an absolute fall.

It would be hard to go much further in a discussion of inflation and cycles in real activity without a more detailed discussion of money and monetary policy, as inflation *is* a fall in the purchasing power of money, and monetary policy-makers are charged with controlling inflation. So in the next two chapters we turn to the monetary system, monetary policy, and how they impact upon inflation and real activity.

## SUMMARY

- Potential GDP is represented by a vertical line at $Y^*$, which means that it does not vary with the price level.
- The output gap is equal to the horizontal distance between the actual level of GDP and $Y^*$, as determined by the intersection of the *AD* and *SRAS* curves.

### Induced changes in input prices

- An inflationary gap means that actual GDP, $Y$, is greater than $Y^*$, and hence there is excess demand in the labour market. As a result wages rise faster than productivity, causing unit labour costs to rise. The *SRAS* curve shifts leftward, and the price level rises.

- A recessionary gap means that *Y* is less than *Y\**, and hence demand in the labour market is relatively low. Although there is some resulting tendency for wages to fall relative to productivity, this force is much weaker than in the case of an inflationary gap. Unit labour costs fall only slowly, so the output gap persists for a considerable length of time.

- An expansionary demand shock creates an inflationary gap.

- A contractionary demand shock creates a recessionary gap.

### The long-run consequences of aggregate demand shocks

- The long-run aggregate supply (*LRAS*) curve relates the price level and real GDP after all wages and other costs have been adjusted fully to long-run equilibrium. The *LRAS* curve is vertical at the level of potential GDP, *Y\**.

- Because the *LRAS* curve is vertical, output in the long run is determined by the position of the *LRAS* curve, and the only long-run role of the *AD* curve is to determine the price level. Economic growth determines the position of the *LRAS* curve.

- Because of asymmetries in the shape of the SRAS curve, and in the adjustment mechanism that shifts that curve, the automatic adjustments that tend to return the economy to its LRAS curve tend to be much slower in the face of deflationary than inflationary gaps.

### Real GDP in the short and long runs

- GDP can increase (or decrease) for any of three reasons: a change in aggregate demand, a change in short-run aggregate supply, or a change in long-run aggregate supply (which is called economic growth). The first two changes are typically associated with business cycles.

### Government policy and the business cycle

- In principle, fiscal policy can be used to stabilize the position of the *AD* curve at or near potential GDP. To remove a recessionary gap, governments can shift *AD* to the right by cutting taxes and increasing spending. To remove an inflationary gap, governments can pursue the opposite policies.

- Because government tax and transfer programmes tend to reduce the size of the multiplier, they act as automatic stabilizers. When national income changes, in either direction, disposable income changes by less because of taxes and transfers.

- Discretionary fiscal policy is subject to information, decision, and execution lags that limit its ability to stabilize the economy at or near potential GDP.

- Monetary policy-makers can react quickly, but the impact of interest rate changes is subject to a lag.

## TOPICS FOR REVIEW

- The GDP gap and the labour market
- Inflationary gaps
- Recessionary gaps
- Asymmetry of wage adjustment
- Changes in aggregate demand and induced wage changes
- Wages, productivity, and unit costs
- Adjustment mechanism

- Long-run aggregate supply (*LRAS*) curve
- Economic stabilization
- Information, decision, and execution lags
- Automatic stabilizers
- Fiscal policy
- Monetary policy

## QUESTIONS

1 Starting with the economy at *Y\**, explain what happens to the price level and real GDP in the short run and the long run in response to (*a*) an increase in export demand, (*b*) an increase in oil prices (assuming that oil is an input into production), (*c*) a permanent increase in productivity, and (*d*) an increase in income tax rates.

2 Starting with the economy below *Y\**, (*a*) explain how the economy will eventually adjust back to *Y\**, (*b*) explain how fiscal and monetary policy could help return the economy to *Y\**.

3 Repeat question 2 but starting from a position where current GDP is above *Y\**.

4 Set out the reasons why fiscal policy was once thought to be able to offset shocks to the economy. Why is the effectiveness of fiscal policy now thought to be much more limited?

5 Outline the reasons for asymmetry in the adjustment mechanism to external shocks. How would the response to a positive demand shock differ from the response to a negative demand shock?

6 Explain what is meant by 'automatic stabilizers'. How do these help to reduce the amplitude of the business cycle?

7 Explain carefully the differences between the adjustment of the economy in a recessionary gap and in an inflationary gap.

8 Why is the *LRAS* curve vertical? What does this imply about the impact of aggregate demand shifts on equilibrium real GDP?

# MACROECONOMIC POLICY IN A MONETARY ECONOMY

# Chapter 20

# MONEY AND MONETARY INSTITUTIONS

What role does money play in the economy and how did it evolve? How does money get into the economy and how is the total amount of money determined? What role do banks play in the creation of money? These are some of the questions that we address in this chapter. In the following chapter we add a monetary sector to our macro model and analyse how monetary policy works.

In this chapter you will learn that:

- Money acts as a medium of exchange, a unit of account, and a store of value.
- The existence of money facilitates a wider range of transactions than would otherwise be feasible.
- Money was originally composed of commodities such as gold and silver.
- Paper currency was originally convertible into gold or silver, but now has nothing backing it except its acceptability in payment.
- The money multiplier is the ratio of broad money to high-powered money.
- Bank deposits are now the biggest part of the total amount of money in the economy, so the behaviour of the banking system is central to determining that total.

Many people believe that money is one of the more important things in life, and that there is never enough of it. However, increasing the amount of money in any one country or in the world as a whole would not make the average person better off. Although money allows those who have it to buy someone else's output, the total amount of goods and services available for everyone to buy depends on the total output produced, not on the total amount of money that people possess. In the terminology of Chapter 19, an increase in the total quantity of money will not increase $Y^*$, the level of potential GDP. However, the link between money and real activity has been a source of considerable debate.

## Money and the economy

### The classical view

Money's role in the economy has been a controversial topic for some time. Early theories argued for the independence of $Y^*$ from monetary factors in terms of an economic analysis that distinguished sharply between the 'real sector of the economy' and the 'monetary sector'. This approach led to a view of the economy that is now referred to as the *classical dichotomy*, which meant that the real sector of the economy (the production and consumption of real goods and services) could be analysed separately from the monetary sector. In other words, economic forces originating in the monetary sector did not affect real activity, at least not in the long term.

According to this view, the allocation of resources, and hence the determination of real GDP, is fully determined in the real sector. It is *relative prices*, including the level of wages relative to the price of commodities, rather than money (nominal) prices, that matter for this process.

According to the classical dichotomy, the price *level* is determined in the monetary sector of the economy. If the quantity of money were doubled, other things being equal, the prices of all commodities and money incomes would eventually double. Relative prices would remain unchanged, and the real sector would be unaffected.

According to the classical dichotomy, an increase in the total amount of money leads in the long run to a proportionate increase in all money prices, with no change in the allocation of resources or the level of real GDP.

The doctrine that the quantity of money influences the level of money prices but has no effect on the real part of the economy is called the **neutrality of money**. Because many early economists believed that the most important questions—How much does the economy produce? What share of it does each group in society get?—were answered in the real sector, they spoke of money as a 'veil' behind which occurred the real events that affected material well-being. Of course, if the classical dichotomy were correct even in the short term, we would not need to study monetary factors in trying to explain the determination of real GDP.

## The modern view

Most contemporary economists still accept the insights of the early economists that relative prices are a major determinant of the allocation of resources and that the quantity of money has an association with the absolute level of prices. They accept the neutrality of money in long-run equilibrium when all the forces causing change have fully worked themselves out. However, they do not accept the neutrality of money when the economy is adjusting to shocks, that is, when the economy is not in a state of long-run equilibrium. Thus, they reject the classical dichotomy as a statement of how the economy acts from day to day.

### Money and the price level

It is widely accepted today that there is a clear link between money and the price level, especially over long periods of time, when the conditions of long-run equilibrium are apt to be most relevant. However, many would argue that the causation runs from prices to money rather than from money to prices. What is generally agreed is that it is desirable to keep inflation under control and that it is the job of the monetary authorities to achieve this.

We now focus on how the monetary system works before returning to the issue of monetary policy in the next chapter.

# The nature of money

There is probably more widespread misunderstanding of money and the monetary system than of any other aspect of the economy. In this section we describe the functions of money and briefly outline its history.

Before we proceed, it is important to note that the amount of money in an economy is a *stock* (in the UK it is so many billions of pounds), not a *flow* of so many pounds per unit of time. Previously we have been talking about flows of output or spending *per period*. It is also important to notice that the money supply is a nominal variable measured in money units, whereas the other variables in our macro model are real variables measured in purchasing power units, or holding prices constant.

## What is money?

Money is defined as any generally accepted medium of exchange. A *medium of exchange* is anything that will be widely accepted in a society in exchange for goods and services. Although being a medium of exchange is usually regarded as money's defining function, money can also serve other roles:

Money acts as a medium of exchange and can also serve as a store of value and a unit of account.

### A medium of exchange

As we saw in Chapter 1, if there were no money, goods would have to be exchanged by barter (one good being swapped directly for another). The major difficulty with barter is that each transaction requires a double coincidence of wants: I can only buy from someone who wants what I can offer in exchange. Anyone who specialized in producing one commodity would have to spend a great deal of time searching for suitable trading partners. Thus, a thirsty economics lecturer would have to find a brewer who wanted to learn economics before he could swap a lesson in economics for a pint of beer.

The use of money as a medium of exchange alleviates this problem. People can sell their output for money and subsequently use the money to buy what they want from others. So a monetary economy typically involves exchanges of goods and services for money and exchanges of money for goods and services—but not exchanges of goods and services for other goods and services.

**The double coincidence of wants, which is required for barter, is unnecessary when a medium of exchange is used.**

By facilitating transactions, money makes possible the benefits of specialization and the division of labour, which in turn contribute to the efficiency of the economic system. It is not without justification that money has been called one of the great inventions contributing to human freedom and well-being.

To serve as an efficient medium of exchange, money must have a number of characteristics. It must be readily acceptable and therefore of known value. It must have a high value relative to its weight. (Otherwise it would be a nuisance to carry around.) It must be divisible, because money that comes only in large denominations is useless for transactions having only a small value. Finally, it must be difficult, if not impossible, to counterfeit.

### A store of value

Money is a convenient way to store purchasing power; goods may be sold today, and the money taken in exchange for them may be stored until it is needed. To be a satisfactory store of value, however, money must have a relatively stable value. A rise in the price level leads to a decrease in the purchasing power of money, because more money is required to buy a typical basket of goods. When the price level is stable, the purchasing power of a given sum of money is also stable; but when the price level is highly variable this is not so, and the usefulness of money as a store of value is undermined.

Although in a non-inflationary environment money can serve as a satisfactory store of accumulated purchasing power for a single individual, even in those circumstances it cannot do so for society as a whole. A single individual can accumulate money and, when the time comes to spend it, can command the current output of some other individual. However, if all individuals in a society were to save their money and then retire simultaneously to live on their savings, there would be no current production to purchase and consume. Society's ability to satisfy wants depends on goods and services being available. If some of this want-satisfying capacity is to be stored up for society as a whole, some goods that are produced today must be saved for future periods. In other words, money may be accumulated as savings to help individuals buy future goods, but it is the future real capital stock and labour resources that will determine future real output. Money and real wealth should not be confused.

**Money is a store of value for individuals but not for society as a whole.**

### A unit of account

Money also may be used purely for accounting purposes, without having a physical existence of its own. For instance, a government store in an imaginary centrally planned society might say that everyone had so many 'pounds' to spend or save each month. Goods could then be assigned prices and each consumer's purchases recorded, the consumer being allowed to buy until his or her allocated supply of pounds was exhausted. These pounds need have no existence other than as entries in the store's books, yet they would serve as a perfectly satisfactory unit of account.

Whether they could also serve as a medium of exchange between individuals would depend on whether the shop would agree to transfer credits from one customer to another at the first customer's request. Banks will transfer pounds credited to current account deposits in this way, and so a bank deposit can serve as both a unit of account and a medium of exchange. Notice that the use of 'pounds' in this context suggests a further sense in which money is a unit of account. People think about values in terms of the monetary unit with which they are familiar.

A related function of money is that it can be used as a standard of deferred payments. Payments that are to be made in the future, on account of debts and so on, are reckoned in money. Money's ability to serve as a unit of account over time in this manner can be diminished if there is significant inflation.

# The origins of money

The origins of money go far back into antiquity. Many primitive tribes seem to have made some use of it.

## Metallic money

All sorts of commodities have been used as money at one time or another, but gold and silver proved to have great advantages. They were precious because their supplies were relatively limited, and they were in constant demand by the wealthy for ornament and decoration. Thus, these metals tended to have a high and stable price. Further, they were easily recognized, they were divisible into extremely small units, and they did not easily wear out.

Before the invention of coins, it was necessary to carry the metals in bulk. When a purchase was made, the requisite quantity of the metal was carefully weighed on a scale. The invention of coinage eliminated the need to weigh the metal at each transaction, but it created an important role for an authority, usually a monarch, who made the coins by mixing gold or silver with base metals to create convenient size and durability, and affixed his or her seal, guaranteeing the amount of precious metal that the coin contained. This was clearly a great convenience, as long as traders knew that they could accept the coin at its 'face value'. The face value was nothing more than a statement that a certain weight of gold or silver was contained therein.

However, often coins could not be taken at their face value. A form of counterfeiting—clipping a thin slice off the edge of the coin and keeping the valuable metal—became common. This, of course, served to undermine the acceptability of coins, even if they were stamped. To get around this problem, the idea arose of minting the coins with a rough edge; then the absence of the rough edge would immediately indicate that the coin had been clipped. This practice, called milling, survives on some coins (such as the current UK 5p, 10p, £1, and £2 coins) as an interesting anachronism to remind us that there were days when the market value of the metal in the coin was equal to the face value of the coin.

Not to be outdone by the cunning of their subjects, some rulers were quick to seize the chance of getting something for nothing. The power to mint coins placed rulers in a position to work a really profitable fraud. They often used some suitable occasion—a marriage, an anniversary, an alliance—to re-mint the coinage. Subjects would be ordered to bring their coins into the mint to be melted down and coined afresh with a new stamp. Between the melting down and the recoining, however, the rulers had only to toss some further inexpensive base metal in with the molten coins. This debasing of the coinage allowed the ruler to earn a handsome profit by minting more new coins than the number of old ones collected, and putting the extras in the royal vault.

The result of debasement was inflation. The subjects had the same number of coins as before, and hence could demand the same quantity of goods. When rulers paid their bills, however, the recipients of the extra coins could be expected to spend them. This caused a net increase in demand, which in turn bid up prices.

**Debasing the coinage was a common cause of increases in prices.**

It was the experience of such inflations that led early economists to stress the link between the quantity of money and the price level. The relationship, known as the 'quantity theory of money', will be discussed in Chapter 21. A famous law in economics that owes its origins to the era of metallic money is set out in Box 20.1.

To this day, the revenue generated from the power to create currency is known as *seigniorage*. Today the possibility of debasement does not enter. The term applies to the revenue that accrues from the powers to print banknotes (which have very low production costs relative to their face value) and to require private banks to place non-interest-bearing deposits at the central bank.

The benefits of seigniorage could arise simply because the monetary authorities print money and spend it, so its value would be equal to the increase in note issue each period. In practice, the relevant monetary authority is the **central bank**, which is a government-owned institution that is the sole money-issuing authority and acts as banker to the commercial banking system.[1] The UK central bank is the Bank of England; for the United States it is the Federal Reserve Board, and for the euro area it is the European Central Bank (ECB). When the central bank provides bank notes to the private sector, it typically buys interest-bearing bonds with each new issue of notes. The seigniorage from the notes in circulation is thus equal to the interest per period on those bonds. So, for example,

---

[1] 'Commercial banks' are the private sector banks that provide deposit and loans services to personal and corporate customers, such as Barclays, NatWest, and HSBC.

**Box 20.1 Gresham's law**

The early experience of currency debasement led to the observation known as Gresham's law, after Sir Thomas Gresham, an adviser to the Elizabethan court, who stated that 'bad money drives out good'.

When Elizabeth I came to the throne of England in the middle of the sixteenth century, the coinage was severely debased. Seeking to help trade, Elizabeth minted new coins that contained their full face value in gold. However, as fast as she fed these new coins into circulation, they disappeared. Why?

Suppose that you possessed one new and one old coin, each with the same face value, and had a bill to pay. What would you do? Clearly, you would use the debased coin to pay the bill and keep the undebased one. (You part with less gold that way.) Again, suppose that you wanted to obtain a certain amount of gold bullion by melting down the gold coins (as was frequently done). Which coins would you use? Clearly, you would use new, undebased coins because you would part with less 'face value' that way. For these reasons, the debased coins would remain in circulation, and the undebased coins would disappear.

Gresham's insights have proven helpful in explaining the experience of a number of modern high-inflation economies.

For example, in the 1970s inflation in Chile raised the value of the metallic content in coins above their face value. Coins quickly disappeared from circulation as private citizens sold them to entrepreneurs who melted them down for their metal. Only paper currency remained in circulation, and this was used even for tiny transactions such as purchasing a box of matches. Gresham's law is one reason why modern coins, unlike their historical counterparts, are merely tokens, containing a metallic value that is only a minute fraction of their face value.

Gresham's law has had another modern interpretation in regimes of pegged exchange rates, where the values of two currencies are pegged together artificially. If one currency is overvalued and widely expected to have to be devalued, this causes people to spend it fast, while building up their holdings of the undervalued currency. The combination of hoarding one currency and running down balances of the other often brings about the devaluation that was feared—as when the pound sterling was forced to leave the European Exchange Rate Mechanism (ERM) in September 1992, and when Argentina was forced to break the link of its currency to the US dollar in 2001.

---

if the note issue was £100 and the central bank had bought £100 worth of bonds in issuing those notes, and the yield on the bonds was 5 per cent, then seigniorage would be £5 per year. Some seigniorage also arises from the policy of many central banks of forcing commercial banks to place non-interest-bearing deposits with them, which the central bank can also use to purchase interest-bearing securities. In the United Kingdom the Bank of England returns all of the revenue from seigniorage to HM Treasury.[2]

## Paper money

The next important step in the history of money was the evolution of paper currency, one source of which was goldsmiths. Since goldsmiths had secure safes, the public began to deposit their gold with them for safekeeping. Goldsmiths would give their depositors receipts promising to hand over the gold on demand. When any depositor wished to make a large purchase, she could go to her goldsmith, reclaim some of her gold, and hand it over to the seller of the goods. If the seller had no immediate need

for the gold, he would carry it back to the goldsmith for safekeeping on his behalf.

If people knew the goldsmith to be reliable, there was no need to go through the cumbersome and risky business of physically transferring the gold. The buyer needed only to transfer the goldsmith's receipt to the seller, who would accept it as long as he was confident that the goldsmith would pay over the gold whenever it was needed. If the seller wished to buy a good from a third party who also knew the goldsmith to be reliable, passing the goldsmith's receipt from the buyer to the seller here too could effect the transaction. The deposit receipt was 'as good as gold'. The convenience of using pieces of paper instead of gold is obvious.

When it came into being in this way, paper money represented a promise to pay so much gold on demand. In this case the promise was made first by goldsmiths and later by banks.[3] Such paper money, which became

---

[2] The Bank of England's 2005 *Annual Report* shows that it paid about £1.6 billion to HM Treasury from this source in 2003/4.

[3] Banks grew out of at least two other trades in addition to that of the goldsmiths. There were scriveners, who had writing skills and sold their services managing other people's financial affairs; there were also merchant bankers, who started trading in commodities but ended up specializing in trade finance—Barings and Rothschilds started this way, and their surviving successors are still sometimes referred to as 'merchant banks'. (In US terminology they are called 'investment banks'.)

banknotes, was backed by precious metal and was convertible on demand into this metal.[4]

## Fractionally backed paper money

Early on, many goldsmiths and banks discovered that it was not necessary to keep a full ounce of gold in the vaults for every claim to an ounce circulating as paper money. At any one time, some of the bank's customers would be withdrawing gold but others would be depositing it, and most would be trading in the bank's paper notes without indicating any need or desire to convert them into gold.

As a result, the bank was able to issue more money (initially notes, but later deposits) redeemable in gold than the amount of gold that it held in its vaults. This was good business, because the money could be invested profitably in interest-earning loans (often called advances) to individuals and firms. The demand for loans arose, as it does today, because some customers wanted credit to help them over hard times or to buy equipment for their businesses. To this day, banks have many more claims outstanding against them than they actually have in reserves available to pay those claims. We say that the currency issued in such a situation is *fractionally backed* by the reserves.

The major problem with a fractionally backed, convertible currency was maintaining its convertibility into the precious metal by which it was backed. The imprudent bank that issued too much paper money would find itself unable to redeem its currency in gold when the demand for gold was even slightly higher than usual. It would then have to suspend payments, and all holders of its notes would suddenly find that their notes were worthless. However, the prudent bank that kept a reasonable relationship between its note issue and its gold reserve would find that it could meet a normal range of demand for gold without any trouble.

If the public lost confidence and demanded redemption of its currency *en masse*, however, the banks would be unable to honour their pledges. The history of nineteenth- and early-twentieth-century banking around the world is full of examples of banks that were ruined by 'panics', or sudden runs on their gold reserves. When this happened, the banks' depositors and the holders of their notes would find themselves with worthless pieces of paper.[5]

## Fiat money

As time went on, note issue by private banks became less common, and central banks, which are (usually) state-owned institutions, took control of the currency. Over time central banks have assumed a monopoly in the provision of money to the economy.[6] As a result, they have the job of controlling monetary conditions and are ultimately responsible for determining the value of a nation's (or group of nations') currency.

Originally central banks issued paper currency that was fully convertible into gold. In those days gold would be brought to the central bank, which would issue currency in the form of 'gold certificates' which asserted that the gold was available on demand. The gold supply thus set some upper limit on the amount of currency. However, central banks, like private banks before them, could issue more currency than they had in gold, because in normal times only a small fraction of the currency would be presented for payment at any one time. Thus, even though the need to maintain convertibility under a **gold standard** put an upper limit on note issue, central banks had substantial discretionary control over the quantity of currency outstanding.

During the first half of the twentieth century almost all of the countries of the world abandoned the gold standard; their currencies were hence no longer convertible into gold. Money that is not convertible by law into anything else derives its value from its acceptability in exchange. *Fiat money* is widely acceptable because government order, or fiat,[7] declares it to be legal tender. Legal tender is anything that by law must be accepted when offered either for the purchase of goods or services or to discharge a debt. Bank of England notes have been legal tender in England and Wales since 1833.

Today almost all currency is fiat money.

Bank of England notes still say on them 'I promise to pay the bearer on demand the sum of $x$ pounds', and they are signed by the chief cashier. Until 1931 (apart from occasional temporary suspensions of convertibility) you could take these notes into the Bank of England and

---

[4] One of the earliest issuers of formal banknotes was the Riksbank of Sweden, established in 1668. It is 26 years older than the Bank of England, which was established in 1694. The Riksbank, which is now the central bank of Sweden, instituted the Nobel Prize for economics in 1968 to commemorate its tercentenary.

[5] In the early 1930s about 10,000 banks, or a third of the total, went bust in the United States. The personal and corporate losses involved were a major contributor to the Great Depression.

[6] In England and Wales no new banks have been permitted to issue notes since the 1844 Bank Charter Act, though in Scotland banks such as the Bank of Scotland, the Royal Bank of Scotland, and the Clydesdale Bank still issue the main notes in circulation. (Since 1845, however, the Scottish note issue has had 100 per cent backing with Bank of England liabilities, and hence has been fully under Bank of England direction.) In 2002 euro notes were issued by the European Central Bank to replace the previous currencies of the member states of the euro zone (see pages 484–5 below).

[7] Fiat means 'let there be' in Latin, and hence 'by decree'.

demand gold of equivalent value in return for your notes. Today, however, the promise is a quaint tradition rather than a real contract. The pound sterling, like all major currencies, is a fiat currency that is not backed by gold or any other commodity (though some people still argue for the return to a gold standard).

**Fiat money is valuable because it is accepted by convention and in law in payment for the purchase of goods or services and for the discharge of debts.**

Many people are disturbed to learn that present-day paper money is neither backed by, nor convertible into, anything more valuable—that it consists of nothing but pieces of paper whose value derives from general acceptance. Many people believe that their money should be more substantial than this.

If fiat money is acceptable it is a medium of exchange, and if its purchasing power remains stable it is a satisfactory store of value. If both of these things are true, it will also serve as a satisfactory unit of account.

# How does money get into the economy?

When gold was the basis of money, it was not too difficult to see how more gold got into circulation. It was either produced from gold mines, or converted from non-monetary uses (such as jewellery), or imported from other countries. In effect, it was received in payment for some transaction from the owners of gold mines, or from the previous owner of the gold, wherever in the world they happened to be. However, it is not so obvious how fiat money gets into the economic system. In fact, as suggested above, it comes from the central bank—in the UK the Bank of England, in the USA the Federal Reserve, in the euro area the European Central Bank (ECB).

The central bank does not just drop money from the sky, or even just give it to the government to spend. What the central bank has direct control over is referred to as high-powered money, *the cash base*, or the monetary base. (In the United Kingdom it is also defined as M0; see Box 20.2.) This consists of currency (banknotes and coin) held by the public and the banks, and of deposits held by the banks with the central bank.[8] The monetary base is referred to as 'high-powered money' because it is the basis upon which a much bigger stock of monetary assets is built (including the biggest component of the money stock, bank deposits). High-powered money is an asset to anyone in the private sector who holds it, but to the central bank it is a liability.

The central bank gets high-powered money into the economy simply by buying securities (usually government debt instruments). It pays for these purchases with newly issued high-powered money.

Hence in creating new high-powered money, the central bank is expanding both sides of its own balance sheet. At the same time as it increases its liabilities, it purchases assets of equal value. Of the two components of high-powered money, in the UK case bankers' deposits are the liability of the Banking Department of the Bank of England and currency is the liability of the Issue Department. The balance sheets of these two departments are shown in Table 20.1.

It is simplest to think of the process of high-powered money creation in two steps. First, using the UK example, we will discuss how the purchase of securities by the Bank of England creates bankers' deposits. Then we will see how currency gets into circulation.

## Bankers' deposits

Consider a situation in which there are initially no net transactions between the Bank of England and the rest of the economy. The Bank now buys £1 million worth of securities from an agent in the private sector. The seller receives a cheque for £1 million from the Bank of England which is paid into the recipient's bank account at, say, Barclays Bank. Barclays' deposits rise by £1 million, but at the same time Barclays receives an increase of £1 million in its deposits at the Bank of England. The balance in Barclays' account at the Bank of England is an example of what are called *bankers' deposits*. This increase in its bankers' deposits at the Bank of England arises when Barclays clears the cheque drawn on the Bank of England. (A cheque deposited in Barclays drawn on HSBC Bank would simply transfer bankers' deposits from HSBC to Barclays, but a cheque drawn on the Bank of England creates new bankers' deposits at the central bank.)

---

[8] M0 includes bankers' working balances at the Bank of England but it excludes compulsory cash ratio deposits. The latter are a form of tax on the banks that finance the Bank of England, making it not reliant on government funding.

**Table 20.1** Bank of England balance sheet, 22 February 2006

| Assets | (£m) | Liabilities | (£m) |
|---|---|---|---|
| (i) Balance sheet of Issue Department | | | |
| Government securities | 13,370 | Notes in circulation | 36,834 |
| Other securities | 23,470 | Notes in Banking Department | 6 |
| Total assets | 36,840 | Total liabilities | 36,840 |
| (ii) Balance sheet of Banking Department | | | |
| Government securities | 2,173 | Public deposits | 788 |
| Advances | 15,406 | Bankers' deposits | 2,884 |
| Premises, equipment, and other securities | 7,485 | Reserves and other accounts | 21,383 |
| Notes and coin | 6 | Balancing item | 15 |
| Total assets | 25,070 | | 25,070 |

**The Bank of England is divided into the Issue Department and the Banking Department.** The table shows the balance sheets of these two departments at 22 February 2006. The only function of the Issue Department is to issue currency (bank notes). It does this in exchange for purchases of securities, normally through a transaction with the Banking Department. The Banking Department acts as banker to the government and also holds deposits from the banks.

*Source*: Bank of England, *Monetary and Financial Statistics*.

This is not be the end of the story so far as Barclays is concerned, because as we shall see bankers' deposits constitute reserves against which the commercial banks can create new deposits. We will soon explain how this is done. In the meantime, this is most of what we need to know about how the Bank of England expands the monetary base, though we will look more closely below at how the Bank of England uses its money market operations to set interest rates. Contraction of the monetary base simply reverses the process—the Bank sells securities. A member of the public then writes a cheque drawn on, say, NatWest Bank, payable to the Bank of England, and NatWest transfers bankers' deposits to the Bank of an equivalent amount. The monetary base falls.

## Currency

The above discussion explains how central banks such as the Bank of England create or destroy high-powered money. The division of high-powered money between bankers' deposits and currency is determined by the demand for currency on the part of the general public. If private individuals (or firms) choose to increase their currency holdings, relative to bank deposits, they simply go to their bank and withdraw deposits in cash. The bank (if it did not have enough cash in its tills) would go to the Bank of England and withdraw some bankers' deposits in cash from the Banking Department. The Banking Department, in turn, would replenish its own stock of cash by

selling securities to the Issue Department. The Issue Department would print the new currency. Currency is made available on demand to the economy in this way and is not restricted in supply by the Bank of England.

**The stock of currency in circulation is determined entirely by the demands of the economy and is not set by any policy-makers.**

In the current UK financial system the total stock of high-powered money is also demand-determined. This is because the authorities choose to set short-term interest rates and supply whatever high-powered money is demanded at those rates. A discussion of the implementation of monetary policy follows in the next chapter.

## Modern money

The total amount of money in the economy is called the **money supply** or the **money stock**.[9] The creation of high-powered money is only part of the story of how the money supply is created, because most measures of the money supply include a wider range of assets than just the monetary base. In particular, money is usually defined to include bank deposits.

---

[9] Those who have studied microeconomics should note that the concept of a money supply is different from the concept of the supply of some commodity. In microeconomics supply refers to a desired quantity: how much the producer would like to make and sell. In macroeconomics the money supply is the actual amount of money that is in existence.

## Deposit money

Today's bank customers frequently deposit coins and paper money with the banks for safekeeping, just as in former times they deposited gold. Such a deposit is recorded as a credit to the customer's account. A customer who wishes to pay a debt may come to the bank, claim the money in currency, and then pay the money to someone else, who may himself redeposit the money in a bank.

As with gold transfers, this is a tedious procedure. It is more convenient to have the bank transfer claims to money on deposit. As soon as cheques, which are written instructions to the bank to make a transfer, became widely accepted in payment for commodities and debts, bank deposits became a form of money called 'deposit money'. Deposit money is defined as money held by the public in the form of deposits in commercial banks that can be withdrawn on demand. Cheques, unlike banknotes, do not circulate freely from hand to hand; thus cheques themselves are not currency. However, a balance in a current account deposit is money; the cheque simply transfers that money from one person to another. Because cheques are easily drawn and deposited, and because they are relatively safe from theft, they have been widely used. New technology has recently replaced many cheque transactions by computer transfer. Plastic cards such as Visa, Mastercard, and Switch enable holders of bank accounts to transfer money to another person's account in new ways.[10] The principle is the same, however: the balance in the bank account is the money that is to be transferred between customers, not the cheque or the plastic card.

When commercial banks lost the right to issue notes of their own, the form of bank money changed, but the substance did not. Today banks have money in their vaults (or on deposit with the central bank) just as they always did. Once it was gold; today it is the legal tender of the times—fiat money. It is true today, just as in the past, that most of the banks' customers are content to pay their bills by passing among themselves the banks' promises to pay money on demand. Only a small proportion of the value of the transactions made by the banks' customers involves the use of cash.

**Bank deposits are money.** Today, just as in the past, banks can create money by issuing more promises to pay (deposits) than they have cash reserves available to pay out.

The main reason that we are interested in the money stock is that if it grows too fast it will cause inflation. For this purpose, it is the broad measure of the money stock that includes bank deposits that is most relevant, as bank deposits can be used in payment for goods and it is often said that 'too much money chasing too few goods' is the source of inflation. Which specific measure of broad money we choose to use is of second-order importance.

Box 20.2 shows the various measures of the money stock that were in use in the United Kingdom in 2006. The main aggregates are M0, a narrow measure that excludes all private sector bank and building society deposits, and M4, a broad measure that includes all such bank and building society deposits. Notice also that there is now an EU harmonized measure of broad money known in the UK as M3H. This is slightly larger than M4 because it adds residents' foreign currency deposits (and some public sector deposits) to M4. The only other monetary aggregate current in the UK is M2, which is also known as 'retail M4' as it excludes the wholesale deposits in M4.

We now turn to a discussion of the role of banks in determining the broad money supply and in transmitting policy-determined interest rate changes to the economy.

# Two models of banking

We now present two models of the creation of deposit money. The first shows how banks can create a large volume of deposit money on the basis of a given amount of reserves. It is called the 'ratios approach' to the creation of money. The second shows how banks work in a competitive environment to attract the reserves they need in order to create deposit money. This model is better suited to understanding both the forces of competition between banks themselves and the competition between banks and other channels of financial intermediation (such as securities markets).

---

[10] With credit cards such as Visa or Mastercard, if you buy, say, petrol today, the petrol company will receive a credit in its bank account after a few days and you will have to settle with the credit card company once a month. With so-called EFTPOS (electronic funds transfer at the point of sale) cards like Switch, however, the funds are transferred directly from your account to the account of the petrol company very quickly. The technology is likely to keep changing, but it does not fundamentally alter the nature of the bank account transfer that is involved.

**Box 20.2  Definitions of UK monetary aggregates**

The way in which 'money' is defined has changed a great deal over time and is likely to change again in future. In 1750 money would almost certainly have been defined as the stock of gold in circulation (specie). By 1850 it would probably have been defined as gold in the hands of the non-bank public plus ban-knotes in circulation. In 1950 the most likely definition would have been currency held by the public plus current account bank deposits. In 1998 money was usually defined to include currency held by the public plus all deposits (current and savings) in banks and building societies. By 2050, who knows? Perhaps money on the internet will be included.

There have been many changes in the definition of money even in the last few years. Many of these are the result of the financial innovations of the 1980s. We should not expect this to be the end of the story. UK money measures such as M1 and £M3 (sterling M3), which were at the centre of monetary policy debates into the first half of the 1980s, have disappeared. These had to be dropped after 1989, when the Abbey National Building Society converted into a bank (and other conversions followed later). Thereafter, any monetary aggregate that contained bank deposits but not building society deposits became distorted. M0 contains neither; M2 and M4 contain both.

The money measures current in 2002 were as follows:

- **M0 (the monetary base)** This measure refers to all the currency in circulation outside the Bank of England plus bankers' deposits (in excess of their cash ratio deposits) with the Bank of England.

- **M2** This encompasses UK non-bank and non-building society holdings of notes and coins, plus sterling retail deposits with UK banks and building societies. The definition of M2 was changed in 1992 to make it a subset of M4, and it is now referred to in official statistics as 'retail M4'.

- **M4** M4 is M2 plus all other private sector sterling interest-bearing deposits at banks and building societies, plus sterling certificates of deposit (and other paper issued by banks and building societies of not more than five years' original maturity). (£M3 was effectively M4 minus building society deposits.)

**UK money supply, February 2006 (£ million, NSA)**

| | | |
|---|---:|---:|
| Notes and coins ouside bank | 43,559 | |
| Bankers' deposits | 808 | |
| **M0** | 44,367 | |
| Notes and cash with public (part of M0) | | 36,297 |
| NIB bank deposits | | 51,485 |
| Other bank retail deposits | | 660,396 |
| Building society retail deposits | | 176,282 |
| **M2 (retail M4)** | | 924,459 |
| Wholesale bank deposits + CDs, etc. | | 392,242 |
| Wholesale building society deposits + CDs | | 16,577 |
| **M4** | | 1,333,278 |
| **M3H** | | 1,430,582 |

*Note*: M0 is not a subset of M2 and M4 because it includes notes and coin held by banks, which are excluded from M2 and M4. If notes and coin held by banks were included in the latter, there would be double counting, because notes and coin held by banks are assets, and the deposits (liabilities) that are counterparts to those assets are included in M2 and M4 already. CDs are certificates of deposit.

*Source*: Bank of England, *Monetary and Financial Statistics*.

- **M3H** This is a new harmonized measure created to have standard money definitions throughout the EU. It is equal to M4 plus residents' foreign currency deposits in UK banks and building societies plus public corporations' sterling and foreign currency deposits in UK banks and building societies.

The accompanying table presents data for these monetary aggregates for February 2006.

## The ratios approach to the creation of deposit money

If you deposit cash with a bank, that deposit is an asset to you and a liability to the bank—because the bank owes that amount to you. Because the bank has the cash as an asset, its assets equal its liabilities. If a bank gives you a loan, it writes an extra balance into your account. This creates a deposit for you, but it is also a loan that you have to repay. So the process of overdraft or loan creation creates both deposits and loans simultaneously. In general,

banks' deposits are their liabilities, and whatever loans they make or securities they purchase constitute their assets. We will see below how banks can create deposits (and loans) that are some multiple of their cash reserves. This *fractional reserve* banking is analogous to the fractional backing of the note issue discussed above. Notice two slightly different meanings of the term *cash*. 'Cash' held by the banks can be currency in their tills *or* deposits at the central bank; 'cash' for the public means currency.

Suppose that, in a system with many banks, each bank obtains new deposits in cash. Say, for example, that there

## Table 20.2 A new cash deposit

| Liabilities | (£) | Assets | (£) |
|---|---|---|---|
| Deposit | 100 | Cash | 100 |

**A new cash deposit has 100 per cent backing.** The balance sheet shows the changes in assets and liabilities resulting from a new cash deposit. Both cash assets and deposit liabilities rise by the same amount.

are ten banks of equal size and that each receives a new deposit of £100 in cash. Each bank now has on its books the new entries shown in Table 20.2. The banks are on a fractional reserve system, and we assume for purposes of this illustration that they wish to hold 10 per cent cash reserves against all deposits. The new deposits put the banks into disequilibrium, since they each have 100 per cent reserves against these new deposits.

First, suppose that only one of the ten banks begins to expand deposits by making new loans (advances). When a bank makes a loan to a customer, it simply writes a larger balance into the customer's account, thereby increasing the size of its deposits. Now when cheques are written on these deposits, the majority will be deposited in other banks. If, for example, this one bank has only 10 per cent of the total deposits held by the community, then, on average, 90 per cent of any new deposits it creates for its customers—and thus much of its £100 in cash—will drain away to other banks. On this basis, the bank will make loans of £90, expecting that it will suffer a cash drain of £81 on account of these loans, leaving it with a £19 cash reserve (£100 new deposit minus the £81 cash drain). This is the position shown in Table 20.3.

One bank in a multi-bank system cannot produce a large multiple expansion of deposits based on an original accretion of cash when other banks do not also expand their deposits.

Now assume, however, that all ten banks begin to expand their deposits based on the £100 of new reserves that each received. On the one hand, since each bank does one-tenth of the total banking business, 90 per cent of the value of any newly created deposits will find its way into other banks as customers make payments by cheque to various members of the community. This represents a cash drain to these other banks. On the other hand, 10 per cent of the new deposits created by each other bank should find its way into this bank. Thus, if all banks receive new cash, and all start creating deposits simultaneously, no bank should suffer a significant cash drain to any other bank. Instead of finding itself with its surplus cash drained away, a bank with the balance sheet shown in Table 20.3 would have cash reserves of close to 53 per cent (£100 reserves against £190 deposits) rather than only 10 per cent as desired.

When all banks can go on expanding deposits without losing cash to each other, they need only worry about keeping enough cash to satisfy those depositors who occasionally require cash. So the expansion can go on, with each bank watching its own ratio of cash reserves to deposits, expanding its deposits as long as the ratio exceeds 1:10 and ceasing to do so when it reaches that figure. Assuming no cash drain to the public, the process will not come to a halt until each bank has created £900 in additional deposits, so that, for each initial £100 cash deposit, there is now £1,000 in deposits backed by £100 in cash. Now each of the banks will have new entries in its books similar to those shown in Table 20.4.

## Table 20.3 Deposit expansion in expection of a cash drain

| Liabilities | (£) | Assets | (£) |
|---|---|---|---|
| Deposit | 190 | Cash | 100 |
| | | Loans | 90 |
| | 190 | | 190 |

**If a bank expands deposits in the expectation of a cash drain, it will end up with excess reserves.** The table shows the position if a bank expands deposits on the basis of receiving £100 in new cash deposits and in the expectation that 90 per cent of any new deposits will drain out of the bank in a cash flow. The bank obtains new assets of loans and bonds of £90 by creating new deposits of that amount. It expects £81 of these to be withdrawn in cash, leaving it with £19 to provide a 10 per cent reserve against £190 of deposits.

## Table 20.4 Restoration of a 10 per cent reserve ratio

| Liabilities | (£) | Assets | (£) |
|---|---|---|---|
| Deposit | 1,000 | Cash | 100 |
| | | Loans | 900 |
| | 1,000 | | 1,000 |

**With no cash drain, a new cash deposit will support a multiple expansion of deposit liabilities.** The table shows the changes in assets and liabilities when all banks engage in deposit expansion after each has received a new cash deposit of £100. New assets are £900 and new deposits are £900. The accretion of £100 in cash now supports £1,000 in deposits, thus restoring the 10 per cent reserve ratio.

A multi-bank system creates a multiple increase in deposit money when all banks with excess reserves expand their deposits in step with each other.

## A complication: cash drain to the public

So far we have ignored the fact that the public actually divides its money holdings in a fairly stable proportion between cash and deposits. This means that when the banking system as a whole creates significant amounts of new deposit money, the system will suffer a cash drain as the public withdraws enough cash from the banks to maintain its desired ratio of cash to deposits.

### An example

Assume that the public wishes to hold a proportion of cash equal to 10 per cent of the size of its bank deposits. This means that for a given stock of cash in the system, the amount that will be held in bank reserves is reduced, so the maximum amount of deposit creation is also reduced. In this special case in which banks have a reserve ratio of 10 per cent and the public holds cash to the value of 10 per cent of the size of its bank deposits, the outcome will be as in Table 20.5. Half of the cash in existence (assumed to be £100 in total) will be held in banks' reserves, and the public will hold the other half. On the basis of their £50 reserves, banks will extend £450 of loans, so total deposits will be £500. This is only half of the value of deposits that were created when the entire £100 of cash was held in bank reserves (as shown in Table 20.3).

**Table 20.5 Deposit creation with a cash drain to the public**

| Liabilities | (£) | Assets | (£) |
| --- | --- | --- | --- |
| Deposit | 500 | Cash | 50 |
| | | Loans | 450 |
| | 500 | | 500 |

**A cash drain to the public greatly reduces the amount of new deposits that can be created on the basis of a given amount of cash.** The table shows the balance sheet of the banking system on the assumption that there is £100 of cash in the system but the public desires cash holdings equal to 10 per cent of their bank deposits. The outcome which satisfies both banks' desired reserve ratio and the public's cash to deposit ratio is such that the banks hold £50 in reserves and issue £450 worth of loans. Total deposits are £500, and £50 is held in cash by the public. The total money stock is £550 (deposits plus cash held by the public). An example in which the banks' reserve ratio differs from the public's cash to deposits ratio is given in Table 20.6.

A cash drain to the public reduces the expansion of deposit money that can be supported by the banking system.

## The general case of deposit creation

The two ratios that we have discussed (the banks' reserve ratio and public's ratio of cash to deposits) can now be used to determine the total level of deposit creation in a formal way. Let $R$ be the cash held in bank reserves, $C$ be the cash held by the non-bank public, $H$ (for high-powered money) be the total cash in the economy, and $D$ be the size of bank deposits. Thus,

$$C + R = H. \tag{1}$$

This says that the total cash in the economy is held either by the banks or by the public. Let the desired reserve ratio of banks be $x$. This allows us to write

$$R = xD. \tag{2}$$

Finally, let the public hold a fraction, $b$, of its bank deposits in cash:

$$C = bD. \tag{3}$$

Substituting the second and third equations into the first gives

$$bD + xD = H,$$

and solving for $D$ yields

$$D = \frac{H}{(b + x)}. \tag{4}$$

Equation (4) shows that, if the public's desired cash ratio is zero, deposits rise by the reciprocal of the cash reserve ratio. (If the banks' reserve ratio were 0.1 (10 per cent), then deposits would be ten times the cash in the economy.) A positive value of $b$, however, means that the resulting cash drain lowers the increase in deposits since it raises the value of the denominator in (4).

## The money multiplier

The total money supply in an economy with a banking system is defined as $D + C$. (It does not include $R$ because the deposit that created the original bank reserves is already counted in with deposits, $D$, and should not be counted twice.) Hence the money supply, $M$, is

$$M = C + D. \tag{5}$$

We can arrive at an expression that links $M$ and $H$ by substituting (2) into (5) for $C$ and then (4) into (5) for $D$. This gives

$$M = \frac{b + 1}{b + x} H. \tag{6}$$

Expression (6) is known as the *money multiplier*, because it tells us how much bigger is the money supply than the cash base of the system. In the modern UK banking system, where reserve ratios and cash ratios are very small, the money multiplier could be of the order of 30, since M4 was 30 times greater than M0 in 2006 (Q1).

The money multiplier should not be confused with the multiplier that links changes in exogenous spending with changes in GDP. The same term is used for two different concepts.

The size of the money multiplier is greater, the smaller is the banks' desired reserve ratio x and the smaller is the public's desired cash ratio b.

A diagrammatic exposition of the above algebra is given in Figure 20.1. It shows that the two ratios, combined with a given cash base, can be used to determine the level of deposits that result and also the money supply. A numerical example of the same ideas is given in Table 20.6.

## A competitive banking system

The ratios approach to bank behaviour gives us important insights into how deposit money is created as some multiple of high-powered money, but it does not provide an accurate picture of how modern banks work. They do not just sit around waiting for cash deposits to be made and then lend some multiple of the deposit (though it is certainly true that their deposits are some multiple of their reserves, and since equation (6) above is an identity it cannot be 'wrong'). Instead, modern banks usually start from the other end. They wait until they have found a profitable lending opportunity, and they then take steps to make sure that funds are available to make the loan. This they can do by either offering higher interest on deposits or borrowing from other banks.

In the ratios world, banks passively receive deposits and then use them to make loans. In the modern world, however, banks are trading in highly competitive markets for both deposits and loans. In a competitive market there will be a market-clearing interest rate for both deposit money and loans. Banks cannot expand their activity in either of these markets without taking into account the supply curve of deposits and the demand curve for loans that they face.

The market for bank loans is illustrated in Figure 20.2. This shows a positively sloped supply curve for the loans that banks are willing to make to the public and a negatively sloped demand curve for the loans that the public is willing to take. The supply curve of loans is determined by two factors: the supply curve of deposits, and the

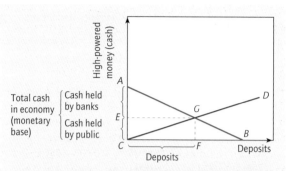

**Figure 20.1** The ratios approach to the determination of the money supply

The money supply is determined by the stock of high-powered money (monetary base), the reserve ratio of the banks, and the cash–deposit ratio of the non-bank public. The diagram illustrates the size of deposit creation, given the banks' reserve ratio x (= AC/CB), the public's cash–deposit ratio b (= EC/CF), and the total cash in the economy AC. Deposits plus cash held by the public make up the total money supply. The total stock of high-powered money, or cash, in the economy has to be held by either the banks or the public. At point A the public holds all the cash available so there are no bank deposits, and the total money supply is just AC, which is all cash. At point C the banks hold all the cash and on that reserve base they create deposits of CB. The line AB thus plots the level of deposit creation resulting from each level of cash reserves (where point A represents the point where banks have no cash or deposits and point C represents the point where all the cash in the economy is held in bank reserves and CB is the value of bank deposits created on that reserve base). The banks' reserve ratio AC/CB is thus equal to (minus) the slope of AB.

The line CD represents the cash–deposit ratio for the non-bank public. Its slope, measured by EC/CF, is equal to that cash–deposit ratio. For a given base of high-powered money (cash), deposit creation will be determined at the point where these two ratios are both satisfied. This will be where CD and AB intersect. So the actual outcome is at point G, where banks have AE cash in reserves and create CF of deposits. The public holds EC of cash and CF of deposits. The total money supply at G is given by CF plus EC.

spread. The **spread** is the difference between what the banks have to pay to borrow money and what they get by lending it (which has to provide a margin to cover staff costs, return on capital employed, and default risk). Remember that banks have to take in deposits in order to make loans. They borrow from one set of people or firms and lend to another.

The supply curve of deposits is positively sloped because, for given interest rates elsewhere in the economy, banks can attract more deposits by offering higher interest rates. (Not all deposits in banks pay interest, but the deposits that banks can increase by offering high interest rates—their marginal deposits—do.) To make the explanation easier, we assume that the spread is a constant absolute

**Table 20.6** High-powered money, deposits, and the money supply

| Banks | | Non-bank public | | High-powered money $(H = C + R)$ | Money supply $(M = C + D)$ |
| --- | --- | --- | --- | --- | --- |
| Reserves $(R)$ | Deposits $(D)$ $(R \times 20)$ | Cash $(C)$ $(1,000 - R)$ | Deposits $(D)$ $(C \times 10)$ | | |
| (1) | (2) | (3) | (4) | (5) | (6) |
| 1,000 | 20,000 | 0 | 0 | 1,000 | |
| 600 | 12,000 | 400 | 4,000 | 1,000 | |
| 400 | 8,000 | 600 | 6,000 | 1,000 | |
| **333.3** | **6,666.6** | **666.6** | **6,666.6** | **1,000** | **7,333.3** |
| 200 | 4,000 | 800 | 8,000 | 1,000 | |
| 100 | 2,000 | 900 | 9,000 | 1,000 | |
| 0 | 0 | 1,000 | 10,000 | 1,000 | |

**For a given stock of high-powered money, the amount of bank deposits created will be the amount that is consistent with the banks' reserve ratio and the non-bank public's cash–deposit ratio.** The table sets out a range of desired positions for banks and the non-bank public independently. Only one of these positions satisfies the desired positions for both the banks and the public, such that the deposits the banks wish to create are the same as the deposits the public wishes to hold.

The example assumes that high-powered money (the cash base or monetary base) is fixed at £1,000. This can be held in some proportion between the banks and the public, but it cannot be changed other than by the monetary authorities. Banks are assumed to have a reserve ratio of 5 per cent, and the non-bank public is assumed to wish to hold cash at a level 10 per cent of their holding of bank deposits. Column (1) shows a range of possible levels of reserve holding for the banks, ranging from all of the £1,000 to none of it. Column (2) shows the level of deposits they would like to create (by making loans) in order to satisfy their desired reserve ratio for each level of reserve holding in column (1). Column (3) shows the cash holding by the public that is implied for each level of banks' reserves in column (1), so it is equal to £1,000 minus the number in column (1). Column (4) shows the level of deposits that the public would like to hold given their cash holdings in column (3). Column (5) reminds us that the stock of high-powered money is fixed at £1,000 throughout. Column (6) shows the value of the money supply for the unique position that satisfies the desires of both the banks and the public.

The actual outcome is the single position where the deposits that the banks wish to create are exactly equal to the deposits the public wishes to hold. This is where the level of deposits is £6,666.6. At this point the banks hold £333.3 in reserves and the public holds £666.6 in cash. The money supply is £7,333.3 (deposits plus cash held by the public) and the money multiplier is 7.333 ($MIH$). We could also calculate this from equation (6) on p. 454: $(b + 1)/(b + x)$ is 1.1/0.15 (where $b = 0.1$ and $x = 0.05$); this is 7.333.

size, so that the supply curve of loans is drawn parallel to the supply curve of deposits, but above it by the constant amount of the spread.[11]

The public's demand curve for loans is negatively sloped because the higher the interest rate being charged, the less customers will wish to borrow. Equilibrium in the market for bank loans occurs where the demand and supply curves intersect, i.e. where the amount customers wish to borrow is equal to the amount banks wish to lend.

## Money supply and competitive banking

The ratios approach to money supply creation and the competitive model of banking present two rather differ-

ent ways of looking at the banking system, but they are compatible. Indeed, each helps us understand the other better, and both are necessary for a complete understanding of modern monetary control techniques.

The ratios approach tells us that the total money supply is related to the stock of high-powered money, this relationship being determined by the reserve ratio of banks and the cash–deposits ratio of the public. For given reserve ratios, the total money supply would be determined if the authorities fixed the supply of high-powered money. However, the UK monetary authorities (and most other central banks, including the ECB) do not operate this way. Rather, they aim to control total deposits via the demand for bank loans. If they wish to lower deposits (and loans), they force up short-term interest rates, as shown in Figure 20.2. In other words, the authorities use the knowledge of the market demand curve for loans in order to influence the total stock of deposits, and therefore also the money supply. Box 20.3 discusses whether the evolution of electronic money, sometimes called 'e-money', will have an impact of the way the monetary system works.

---

[11] Although, the spread may vary from loan to loan depending, among other things, on the size of the loan and the creditworthiness of the customer, on average the spread over all loans is driven down by competition among banks to an amount that will just cover costs with no pure profits. Hence its average value can be reasonably assumed to be a constant.

**Figure 20.2 Competitive banking: supply of and demand for loans**

**The volume of bank loans is determined by the intersection of the supply curve of loans and the demand curve for loans.** The diagram shows the positively sloped supply curve of loans and the negatively sloped demand curve for loans. The supply curve of loans is determined by the supply curve of deposits and the spread, or the interest margin that banks require to cover costs and risk. For given interest rates elsewhere in the economy, the supply curve of deposits is positively sloped because higher interest will attract more savings. The demand curve for loans is negatively sloped—high interest rates discourage borrowing and low rates encourage borrowing. Competition in banking drives the margin between deposit and loan rates to a level like $i_1-i_d$, where the spread is just enough to allow banks to cover costs and make a normal return on capital. With the demand and supply curves shown there will be $0A$ deposits and loans, and depositors will receive an interest rate of $i_d$ while borrowers pay the loan rate $i_1$.

---

### ◐ ◓ ◑ Box 20.3 The implications of electronic money for the monetary system

Some people have argued that electronic money will fundamentally change the nature of the monetary system and perhaps even eliminate the power of central banks either to control the stock of high-powered money or to set the short-term interest rate in money markets. Is this likely?

Our answer is that this is possible but very unlikely. There are two main forms of electronic money.

First, there is what is sometimes called an 'electronic purse', which involves loading some prepaid credits on to a plastic card (which has either a magnetic strip or a computer chip recording information). The carrier of the card can then use this to make retail payments in various shops where some of the balance on the card can be transferred to the retailer. Such cards are just a more general form of pre-paid telephone cards that carry some credit paid for in advance. They are certainly feasible methods of facilitating some payments. But whether they catch on remains to be seen. The key thing to note is that they offer no difference in principle from earlier payment methods. In effect, they are just a new way of transferring ownership of bank deposits from one person to another. They may lead to the general public needing to hold less cash, but they do not change the reality that bank deposits are the main component of money. The amount of cash loaded onto one of these cards is in effect a bank deposit, and this is transferred to the retailer when a purchase is made. This is just a new way of ordering your bank to transfer money from your account to that of someone from whom you buy goods.

Second, there are some forms of money that are transferred via the internet. Here the answer depends on the nature of the transaction involved. If all you are doing is using an internet message to transfer funds from your bank account to someone else's, then again this is just a new way of writing a cheque and no new principles are involved. If, however, new types of institution become able to issue tokens that become widely accepted in payment, this would be a new departure, and these new forms of money could provide a substitute for existing moneys. However, if such new moneys did emerge, it is most likely that governments would regulate them. The money issuers would be regulated like banks, and as banks they would have to hold deposits with the central bank—in which case, again, no new principles would be involved. Indeed, most large payments, in both the domestic and the international economy, have been made electronically for many years. This trend started with the invention of the telegraph in the 1830s and continued with the opening of the trans-Atlantic telegraph cable in the 1880s. The internet is a new technology for authorizing payments, but the monetary principles involved are not new.

This all suggests that e-money is not going to break the monopoly of central banks to issue high-powered money, and so is not going to weaken their ability to set interest rates in wholesale money markets. Neither is e-money going to affect the ability of central banks to control inflation, as that depends on the impact of interest rates on spending decisions and this is not affected in any obvious way by the nature of the payments technology.

Having chosen what they think is the correct interest rate to generate the desired demand for loans, the UK monetary authorities supply whatever high-powered money is demanded at that going interest rate. So the authorities do not fix the supply of high-powered money: this is demand-determined at the interest rate that policy-makers have set. The competitive model of banking helps us to see how this can be done by moving up or down the market demand curve for bank loans. We will return to this issue in more detail below.

Before moving on, however, there are two other important insights provided by the competitive model of banking. First, in the absence of reserve requirements imposed on the banking system by the monetary authorities,[12] we can see that the reserve ratio that banks will choose will be the outcome of an internal optimization process. Banks will try to keep the level of reserves as low as possible, subject to the need to supply cash on demand when customers wish to withdraw deposits. This is because reserves earn no interest and banks would like to devote as much as possible of the funds that are available to them

to profitable uses. Thus, in the absence of high legal reserve requirements, banks' chosen reserve ratios tend to be very small, especially where they can access liquid funds very quickly by borrowing in the inter-bank market. The money multiplier has, as a result, become quite large (as mentioned above).

Second, the competitive model helps us to understand that the banking system as a whole is in competition with other financial channels in the economy for the available amount of borrowing and lending (intermediation) business at any point in time. The real size of the banking sector, relative to other channels of finance (and, indeed, other industries), is determined by how efficient it is in channelling funds from savers to borrowers in the economy. Issues relating to the nominal size of bank deposits and the money supply should be kept separate from the question of the real relative size of the banking system compared with other channels of borrowing and lending flows (such as through securities markets).

In the next chapter we look at how money fits into our short-term model of the macroeconomy.

# CASE STUDIES

## 1. The changing roles of paper and plastic in the payments system

A well established trend in the UK payments system over the past two or three decades has been the rise in the use of plastic cards as a means of making payments, the decline in the use of cheques, the increasing use of automated payments methods such as direct debits and standing orders, and the relative (but not absolute) decline in the role of cash. These developments are documented in the following key facts provided by the UK Payments Association (APACS).

### Plastic cards in the UK and how we used them in 2004

• *Total spending on plastic cards outstripped cash spending for the first time ever in 2004.*

• *There were 141 million multi-function payment cards in issue at the end of 2004 with a further 25 million cards whose sole function is to withdraw cash, 800,000 standalone cheque guarantee cards, and some 23 million store cards.*

• *There were 66.8 million debit cards and 74.3 million credit/charge cards in issue.*

• *There were 20 million personal debit cardholders and 30.6 million credit cardholders.*

• *The average adult in the UK had 3.6 cards (1.6 debit and 2.3 credit cards).*

• *The number of transactions on all types of card reached 8.3 billion in 2004; the vast majority of these transactions (8.1 billion) took place in the UK. This splits into:*
  *purchases—5.6 billion transactions*
  *cash advances—2.4 billion transactions.*

• *The total value of all transactions was £463.9 billion, with £443.8 billion worth of transactions taking place in the UK.*

• *The number of plastic card transactions made by British cardholders abroad was 264 million, accounting for more than £20 billion of overall spending. Almost a third of transactions abroad are for cash acquisition.*

• *Debit cards account for the large majority of all card transactions. However, in the online world credit cards dominated, accounting for 72 per cent of transactions.*

• *The average value of credit card purchases was £58, with the average total purchases put on each credit card reaching £1,455 in the year.*

• *73 per cent of credit card purchases were made by people who repaid their balance in full each month.*

---

[12] In the United Kingdom in April 2006, reserves (known as the cash-ratio deposit, or CRD) held with the Bank of England were required to be 0.15 per cent of deposits for institutions with deposits above £500 million and zero for smaller deposit-taking institutions.

- *Plastic card spending online grew by 27 per cent to more than £16 billion. 11p in every £1 spent on credit cards was over the Internet.*

### Key cheque facts and figures

- *There were just over 6 million cheques issued each day in 2004, compared to 11 million in the peak year for cheque volumes, 1990. By 2014 there will be only 3.5 million per day.*

- *On average, each adult made 1.9 cheque payments per month in 2004, compared with 4.3 per month in 1991.*

- *The typical adult receives less than seven cheques per year.*

- *Only 7 million adults still use guaranteed cheques on a regular basis, compared to 16 million in 1996.*

- *Women make almost 50 per cent more guaranteed cheque payments than men.*

- *Only one in seven regular bills is paid by cheque, compared with one in three as recently as 1995. By 2014 only one in 25 regular bills will be paid by cheque.*

- *By 2014 personal cheques will account for only 3.9 per cent of all non-cash payments made by individuals.*

- *The average value of a personal cheque payment is £126.*

- *Only 6 per cent of retail spending is still paid by cheque, compared with over half by debit or credit card.*

- *Business cheque use peaked in 1997. Since 2001 business-to-business cheques have seen rapid decline as businesses increasingly move to the use of automated payments for their trade suppliers.*

### History of cash machines

*The world's first cash machine was introduced in the UK and installed in London on 27 June 1967 by Barclays Bank. The early machines had limited functions, dispensing fixed amounts of cash in exchange for tokens. In the early 1970s magnetic stripe technology enabled plastic cards to be used to withdraw cash.*

### The numbers

- *At the end of 2004 there were 57,000 cash machines in the UK, 60 per cent of which are owned by banks and building societies (21,683 machines are supplied by IADs—the non-bank independent ATM deployers, the rest by banks and building societies).*

- *Cash machines dispensed £161.3 billion in 2004 in 2.53 billion cash withdrawals, with an average cash withdrawal of £60.*

### Bank and building society owned ATMs—facts and figures
*In 2004:*

- *The total number of transactions undertaken at BBS machines was 2.4 billion (over £155.7 billion in cash withdrawals).*

- *95.1 per cent of all cash machine withdrawals and 96.6 per cent of all cash withdrawn were from cash machines owned by banks and building societies.*

- *The average amount of cash typically drawn from each BBS machine in a day is £13,000.*

- *The average number of cash withdrawals per day at a BBS cash machine was 204.*

- *The average withdrawal made at a BBS cash machine is £64.*

- *Of the 54,412 cash machine in operation in the UK 32,729 are BBS owned.*

- *Of the 45 institutions that deploy cash machines in the UK 31 are BBS institutions.*

### The trends

- *Higher daily allowances for cash machine withdrawals, greater convenience of their siting and wider availability of cashback, are inducing customers to shift away from using cheques and passbooks as the means by which they withdraw cash from their accounts.*

- *Going forward, the total volume of cash machine withdrawals is forecast to rise to 3 billion by 2013. Underlying demographic trends, such as a greater preference amongst younger customers to use cash machines, are major factors behind these projections. The other substantial influence is the introduction of automated benefit payment, which will result in many benefit recipients drawing cash from cash machines rather than over post office counters.* (http://www.apacs. org.uk/resources_publications/)

Additional data from APACS show that numbers of transactions involving cash were roughly constant at around 25 billion per year in the decade from 1995–2005, but the average value of each cash transaction almost certainly rose over this period as notes and coin in circulation rose from about £20 billion in 1995 to around £36 billion in early 2006. Over the same period the numbers of automated bank payments doubled from around 2.4 billion in 1995 to around 5 billion in 2005. In short, it is clear that payment methods have been evolving rapidly as the technology develops and an ever higher proportion of payments is made via plastic or digitally.

## 2. The core purpose of the Bank of England

The following quotation from the website of the Bank of England (www.bankofengland.co.uk) sets out the core purposes of the Bank as determine by the Court of the Bank, which is equivalent to its board of directors.

*In pursuing its goal of maintaining a stable and efficient monetary and financial framework as its contribution to a healthy economy, the Bank has two core purposes; achieving them depends on the work of the Bank as whole. This part of the website describes and explains each core purpose and some of the work that is undertaken to achieve them. . . . Other parts of the website provide more information about each of the Bank's activities.*

   *The Bank's Core Purposes are determined by Court as part of its role in setting the Bank's Objectives and Strategy. The statement below was reaffirmed by Court in May 2005.*

*Core Purpose 1–Monetary stability*

*Monetary stability means stable prices and confidence in the currency. Stable prices are defined by the Government's inflation target, which the Bank seeks to meet through the decisions on interest rates taken by the Monetary Policy Committee, explaining those decisions transparently and implementing them effectively in the money markets.*

*Core Purpose 2–Financial stability*

*Financial stability entails detecting and reducing threats to the financial system as a whole. Such threats are detected through the Bank's surveillance and market intelligence functions. They are reduced by strengthening infrastructure, and by financial and other operations, at home and abroad, including, in exceptional circumstances, by acting as the lender of last resort.*

*In pursuit of both purposes the Bank is open in communicating its views and analysis and works closely with others, including:*

- *Other central banks and international organizations to improve the international monetary system.*

- *HM Treasury and the Financial Services Authority, under the terms of the Memorandum of Understanding, to pursue financial stability.*

*The Bank will also play its part in promoting an open and internationally competitive financial centre in the UK, using its expertise to help make the UK financial system more efficient, where such efforts would be in the public interest and provided that they do not conflict with its primary responsibilities or those of other agencies.* (www.bankofengland.co.uk)

We look at how monetary policy works in more detail in the next chapter.

## SUMMARY

### Money and the economy

- In the classical dichotomy, money affects the price level but does not affect real activity.

### The nature of money

- Money is a medium of exchange, a unit of account, and a store of value.
- Money avoids the need for a double coincidence of wants and thus facilitates a wider range of transactions.

### The origins of money

- Money has evolved from being based primarily on a precious metal to being mainly in the form of bank deposits.
- Early moneys were based on commodities, and especially precious metals like gold and silver.
- Paper currency started as a claim to a deposit of precious metal.
- Bank deposits account for most of modern money.

### How does money get into the economy?

- Central banks create the monetary base or high-powered money, which is made up of notes and coins and bankers' deposits at the central bank.
- Banks create deposit money by expanding loans and deposits.

### Two models of banking

- Banks create deposits to some multiple of their cash reserves.
- In a competitive market in which banks pay interest on deposits and charge interest on loans, banks' behaviour is best understood in terms of demand and supply curves of deposits and loans. Banks must pay competitive interest rates to attract deposits, and they must charge competitive rates on their loans.

## TOPICS FOR REVIEW

- Neutrality of money
- Medium of exchange
- Unit of account
- Store of value
- Gold standard
- Reserve ratio
- Fiat money
- Money multiplier
- Competitive banking systems
- Interest rate spread

# QUESTIONS

1 Suppose that the monetary base is £20 billion, that the general public wishes to hold 20 per cent of its money in cash and the remaining 80 per cent in bank deposits, and that banks wish to hold a 5 per cent cash reserve. What will be the size of the broad money stock?

2 How does the answer to question 1 change for bank reserve ratios of (a) 0 per cent, (b) 1 per cent, and (c) 10 per cent?

3 How does the answer to question 1 change for general public cash holdings of (a) 0 per cent, (b) 5 per cent, (c) 100 per cent?

4 How would the answers to questions 2 and 3 change if the monetary base were £40 billion?

5 How is the broad money stock determined in a system where the monetary base is demand-determined, the central bank sets an interest rate, and the banking system is competitive?

6 Why do people hold money when there is normally a higher yielding asset available?

7 What role does money play in a market economy?

8 What difference would it make to the economy if there were no money? What types of commodity might serve as money instead?

# Chapter 21

# THE ROLE OF MONEY IN MACROECONOMICS

Does the quantity of money in circulation matter for the real economy? How do interest rates influence aggregate demand and inflation? What do the monetary policy-makers aim to achieve? These are some of the important questions addressed in the chapter.

In particular, you will learn that:

- There is an important distinction between money values and real (or relative) values.
- The market price of bonds is inversely related to the current interest rate.
- Monetary equilibrium occurs where people are willing to hold the existing stock of money and bonds at the current interest rate.
- A rise in interest rates reduces aggregate demand, and vice versa.
- Monetary and fiscal polices may assist the stabilization of the economy and control of inflation, but inappropriate policies can make things worse.
- Central banks have the power to set interest rates because they are the monopoly supplier of high-powered money (notes and coin plus bankers deposits at the central bank).
- UK monetary policy is focused on an inflation target.
- The goal of European Central Bank monetary policy is price stability across the euro zone.

In this chapter we add money to our model of the short-term determination of GDP and the price level. We want to know how monetary forces affect economic activity and how inflation can be kept under control. We approach this issue in a number of steps. First, we offer some context for discussing the role of money in the economy by emphasizing the distinction between money prices and relative prices. Second, we discuss the factors that influence the demand for and supply of money balances in the economy. Third, we ask how influences originating in the monetary system spill over into real activity. We can then accomplish the final task of integrating money and monetary policy into the aggregate demand and aggregate supply framework of Chapters 16–19, to see how monetary and fiscal policy can be used to influence the GDP gap and the price level.

## Money values and relative values

Money is our measuring rod in most economic activities. We value our wealth, our incomes, what we buy, and what we sell—all in money terms. When we think of a commodity's market value we usually think of its money price. 'What', we might ask, 'is the value of this refrigerator?' 'It costs £X', might go the reply. 'Is this refrigerator worth more than this TV set?' is another type of value question we frequently ask. Assuming the TV set costs £200, the answer is 'yes' if the refrigerator is priced at more than £200 and 'no' if it is priced at less. 'Have I saved enough money this winter to afford a week's holiday in Spain next summer?' is another common type of question. The answer depends on how much money you have saved up and what you expect the Spanish trip will cost you.

Money prices are our measure of economic value. They allow us to compare different values at any point in time, as with the refrigerator and the TV set. They also allow us to compare values over time, as with the amount saved now and the package holiday to be taken later.

## Money as a veil

Suppose you tell a man, newly arrived from Patagonia, that the price of a refrigerator is £200. If he knows no other sterling values, this would convey no useful information to him.

But let us say that he entered Britain with £2,000. Then he knows that his funds are sufficient to buy 10 refrigerators. He has compared two money values: the market value of the refrigerator and the value of the funds he has brought in with him. But is the £2,000 he has with him a little or a lot? Now he needs to know the prices of all the things he might want to buy, either individually or expressed as an average. This requires that he relate the amount of his funds to the *general level* of prices.

Consider a further example. How much meat, beer, and travel can we buy for a day's wages? Such 'exchange rates'—between the labour that we sell and the goods that we buy—are what determine our living standards. If a worker sells his labour for £40 a day and buys a suit for £120, then what matters is that it costs him three days' work to buy the suit. If instead he only received £20 a day while a suit cost him just £60, the *real* exchange rate would be unchanged, at three days' work to obtain the suit.

Adam Smith, writing in 1776, saw what the above examples illustrate: that individual sums of money, and individual money prices, in isolation convey no useful information. It is the *comparison* of two or more monetary values that conveys significant information. Such comparisons allow us to look behind individual money prices to find real opportunity costs: how much of one thing must be given up to obtain something else.

The important insight is that value is *relative*; the monetary unit in which values are expressed is irrelevant. If, for example, wheat is worth twice as much as is barley per bushel, it does not matter, as far as their exchange rate is concerned, whether wheat is £2 and barley £1, or wheat £4 and barley £2 or wheat £100 and barley £50. Early economists thus talked of money as a *veil* behind which real economic relations occurred and were reacted to.

## The neutrality of money

Out of this insight grew the doctrine of the *neutrality of money*. Correctly stated, this doctrine states that the units chosen to measure values have no effect on 'real values'— real values are 'relative values', and it is relative values that affect behaviour. It follows from the doctrine of the neutrality of money that, if we change *all* monetary values by the same proportion, nothing real happens—no change in real incomes, output, or wealth occurs.

The neutrality of money is most easily seen with a currency reform, such as those instituted in many European countries after the Second World War and later after major inflations caused by monetary excesses. By taking the same number of zeros off the prices of all goods and services and all assets and liabilities, nothing real was changed. Everyone's money incomes were reduced by a factor of 100, but so were the money values of all debts, and all other contracts, as well as all money prices. As a result, everyone's real income and wealth was unchanged. No new value was created and no existing value was destroyed. The change was solely in the 'monetary' or 'nominal' aspects of the economy.

### Money illusion

A person who understands the real choices facing her will be unaffected by changes that merely add or subtract the number of zeros on *all* prices and all money values. If that person's money income, and money wealth, is multiplied by 10, and all the prices she faces are also multiplied by 10, she will see that no real change has occurred. Her economic behaviour will therefore be unaffected. Such a person has penetrated the veil of money and is responding to the real choices that lie behind it.

Economists use the term **money illusion** to refer to behaviour that responds to purely nominal changes in money prices and values in either direction. Say for example that, faced with a ten-fold increase in all prices, a second person felt poorer and increased his savings in response, even though his money income and money wealth had also been increased ten-fold. That person is experiencing money illusion, which leads him to alter his behaviour in response to changes in money values that leave all real choices unaffected.

Some people may suffer from money illusion in the short term, feeling harmed by inflation even though their incomes, and the values of all their wealth, rise in step with the rise in prices. Over longer periods of time, however, money illusion seems less common. People may not at first realize that an inflation that leaves unchanged the relation between the incomes they earn and the prices they pay leaves them unaffected, but they appear to make the adjustment sooner or later. This means that, over the long term, real expenditure decisions are affected relatively little by purely nominal changes in money prices.

### The real and the monetary parts of the economy

The doctrine of the neutrality of money leads to a conceptual division of the economy into two parts. In the 'real part', *relative* prices, quantities, and the allocation of resources are determined by such things as consumers' tastes, production technology, and the degrees of competition among buyers and sellers. In the monetary part, the *absolute level of prices* is determined by monetary forces.

Thus, for example, the relative price of wheat and barley might be determined in the real part of the economy at 1 bushel of wheat = 2 bushels of barley, their outputs at 1 and 5 million tonnes, and the resources of land and labour allocated to each at 1 and 2.5 million hectares and 10 and 20 thousand person-hours, respectively. These are determined by the real forces of tastes and production possibilities operating through the markets for commodities and for productive inputs. The monetary part of the economy would then set the price level at which transactions would take place. For example, wheat might be priced at £4 and barley at £2 a bushel, and agricultural wages at £3 an hour; or wheat at £8 and barley at £4 and wages at £6. Both of these levels of absolute prices yield the same *price relatives*.

### The process of price-level changes

Will changes in the price level always leave real (relative) values unaffected? The answer is 'yes' when all adjustments have been fully made, but 'no' until then—and 'until then' may be a very long time. To see why, compare the French monetary reform referred to earlier with a change in the price level that comes about through the normal workings of the market. The French currency reform was carried out overnight by the stroke of a pen, and hence had virtually no real effects—the new long-run equilibrium set of money prices was established instantaneously. All prices, and all wealth holdings, were adjusted by legal decree at the same instant.

In most real-world situations, however, a major change in the price level is spread over a great deal of time—sometimes years and even decades. Consider a case in which a rapid doubling of the quantity of money leads to an eventual doubling of the price level. It may take years for this new price level to be achieved through the operation of normal market forces. Some prices will adjust quickly, others will take time. At the outset, all existing contracts—wage contracts, mortgages, loans, orders to buy output not yet produced, etc—will reflect the old price level. New contracts reflecting the new price level will be written as the old ones expire. But many contracts last for years, so it will take years for the full adjustment to be completed. Thus, in the process of moving from one price level to another, real changes in relative prices occur, and hence the process of inflation has real effects.

**The doctrine of the neutrality of money holds as a long-run equilibrium concept: it does not hold in transitory situations when the price level is changing.**

We now want to start the process of building a monetary sector that fits into the model of the economy that we developed in Chapters 16–19. The aim is to investigate linkages between events in the 'monetary sector' and those in the sector that delivers real outputs and incomes. The monetary sector that we build will consist not just of the money stock; it will include other financial assets that have a rate of return and whose market value can change.

In previous chapters we have discussed the determinants of *flows* of output and spending. Once we incorporate money and financial markets, we are also talking about *stocks* of assets and financial instruments. The central issue then is how markets for financial assets and liabilities interact with goods markets. This occurs through two important prices—the interest rate, which is the price we pay to borrow money, and the exchange rate, which is the price we pay to obtain foreign currency—and through wealth effects that arise when the real value of assets changes. First, we need to understand some important characteristics of financial assets and interest rates.

# The valuation of financial assets

At any particular moment, people have a stock of wealth that they can hold in many forms. Some of it may be money in a bank or building society; some may be cash in hand or under the mattress; some may be in shares; and some of it may be in property, such as a house.

In order to concentrate on money, we group wealth into just two categories: *money*, and everything else which we call *bonds*. By 'money' we mean the assets that serve as a medium of exchange—paper money, coins, and deposits on which cheques may be drawn or which can be transferred by plastic payment cards. We outlined the various definitions of money in Chapter 20 (see Box 20.2 on page 452). For present purposes it is adequate to think of money as including cash held by the public plus deposits in banks and building societies. By 'bonds' we mean all other forms of financial wealth; these include interest-earning financial assets *plus* claims on real capital. For simplicity, however, our analysis of bonds will assume an asset that is exactly like the debt of the central government (known in the UK as a *gilt*), rather than having the characteristics of corporate bonds or equities.[1]

Money and bonds have different characteristics as assets. The market price of bonds can rise or fall, but the price of money is fixed in money terms. (Obviously, £1 is always worth £1.) The price of bonds is related to market interest rates, so our first task is to understand this relationship.

## The rate of interest and present value

A bond is a financial asset that promises to make one or more interest payments and to repay a capital sum at a specified date in the future. The **present value (PV)** of a bond, or of any asset, refers to the value now of the future payment or payments to which the asset represents a claim. The concept of present value was discussed in more detail in Chapter 12 on pages 253–5. For those of you who have read Chapter 12 what follows is a review; for the rest it is essential reading.

Present value depends on the rate of interest, because when we calculate present value, the interest rate is used to *discount* the future payments. Two extreme examples help illustrate this relationship between the rate of interest and present value.

### A single payment one year hence

We start with the simplest case. How much would someone be prepared to pay *now* to purchase a bond that will produce a single payment of £100 in one year's time?

Suppose that the interest rate is 5 per cent, which means that £1.00 invested today will be worth £1.05 in one year's time. Now ask how much someone would have to lend out in order to have £100 a year from now. If we use *PV* to stand for this unknown amount, we can write *PV*(1.05) [which means *PV multiplied by* 1.05] = £100. Thus, *PV* = £100/1.05 = £95.24.[2] This tells us that the present value of £100 receivable in one year's time is £95.24; anyone who

lends out £95.24 for one year at 5 per cent interest will get back the £95.24 plus £4.76 in interest, which makes £100.

What if the interest rate is 7 per cent? At that interest rate the present value of the £100 receivable in one year's time would be £100/1.07 = £93.46, which is less than the present value when the interest rate was 5 per cent.

### A perpetuity

Now consider another extreme case—a perpetuity that promises to pay £100 per year to its holder *for ever*. The *present value* of the perpetuity depends on how much £100 per year is worth, and this again depends on the rate of interest.

A bond that will produce a stream of income of £100 per year for ever is worth £1,000 at 10 per cent interest, because £1,000 invested at 10 per cent per year will yield £100 interest per year for ever. However, the same bond is worth £2,000 when the interest rate is 5 per cent per year, because it takes £2,000 invested at 5 per cent per year to yield £100 interest per year. The lower the rate of interest obtainable on the market, the more valuable is a bond paying a fixed amount of interest.

Similar relations apply to bonds that are more complicated than single payments but are not perpetuities. Although in such cases the calculation of present value is more complicated, the same negative relationship between the interest rate and present value still holds.

**The present value of any asset that yields a given stream of money over time is negatively related to the interest rate.**

## Present value and market price

Present value is important because it establishes the market price for an asset.

**The present value of an asset is the amount that someone would be willing to pay now to secure the right to the future stream of payments conferred by ownership of the asset.**

To see this, return to our example of a bond that promises to pay £100 one year hence. When the interest rate is 5 per cent, the present value is £95.24. To see why this is the maximum that anyone would pay for this bond, suppose that some sellers offer to sell the bond at some other price, say £98. If, instead of paying this amount for the bond, a potential buyer were to lend her £98 out at 5 per cent interest, at the end of one year she would have more than the £100 that the bond would produce: at 5 per cent interest, £98 yields £4.90 in interest, which when added to the principal makes £102.90. Clearly, no well informed individual would pay £98—or by the same reasoning any sum in excess of £95.24—for the bond.

Now suppose that the bond is offered for sale at a price less than £95.24, say £90. A potential buyer could borrow

---
[1] This simplification can take us quite a long way and is necessary in order to keep our model straightforward.

[2] Notice that in this type of formula the interest rate, *i*, is expressed as a decimal fraction. For example, 5 per cent is expressed as 0.05, so (1 + *i*) equals 1.05.

£90 to buy the bond and would pay £4.50 in interest on the loan. At the end of the year the bond yields £100. When this is used to repay the £90 loan and the £4.50 in interest, £5.50 is left as profit. Clearly, it would be worthwhile for someone to buy the bond at the price of £90 —or by the same argument at any price less than £95.24. But at £90 no holder would want to *sell* the bond. If she needed £90 she could borrow it for a year then cash in the bond at the end of the year, pay back the £90 plus £4.50 interest, and be £5.50 better off than if she had sold the bond at the beginning of the year.

Thus, *all* bond-holders would want to sell at £98 and *none* would want to sell at £90, so £95.24 is the only price at which there are both buyers and sellers—it is the market price.

This discussion should make clear that the present value of an asset determines its market price. If the market price of any asset is greater than the present value of the income stream that it produces, no one will want to buy it, and the market price will fall. If the market value is below its present value, there will be a rush to buy it, and the market price will rise. These facts lead to the following conclusion:

In a free market, the equilibrium price of any asset will be the present value of the income stream that it produces.

## The rate of interest and market price

The discussion above leads us to three important propositions. The first two stress the negative relationship between interest rates and asset prices:

1. If the rate of interest falls, the value of an asset producing a given income stream will rise.

2. A rise in the market price of an asset producing a given income stream is equivalent to a decrease in the rate of interest earned by the asset.

Thus, a promise to pay £100 one year from now is worth £92.59 when the interest rate is 8 per cent and only £89.29 when the interest rate is 12 per cent: £92.59 at 8 per cent interest (£92.59 × 1.08) and £89.29 at 12 per cent interest (£89.29 × 1.12) are both worth £100 in one year's time.

The third proposition focuses on the term to maturity of the bond:

3. The nearer the maturity date of a bond, the less the bond's value will change with a change in the rate of interest.

To see this, consider an extreme case. The present value of a bond that is redeemable for £1,000 in one week's time will be very close to £1,000 no matter what the interest rate is. So its value will not change much even if the rate of interest leaps from 5 per cent to 10 per cent during that week. Note that any interest-earning components of *money* are so short-term that their values remain unchanged when the interest rate changes.

As a second example consider two bonds, one that promises to pay £100 next year and one that promises to pay £100 in ten years. A rise in the interest rate from 8 to 12 per cent will lower the value of £100 payable in one year's time by 3.6 per cent, but it will lower the value of £100 payable in ten years' time by 37.9 per cent.[3]

# The supply of money and the demand for money

We now return to our central task of adding a monetary sector to the macro model built up in Chapters 16–19. We proceed in several small steps. In this chapter we make some simplifying assumptions about the international financial environment in which our economy operates. In effect, we assume that the exchange rate is fixed, and that there is some segmentation of domestic and international financial markets. This will enable us to analyse domestic monetary equilibrium without fully incorporating international influences. In Chapter 22 we introduce international transactions explicitly, and in Chapter 23 we incorporate the influences of international financial markets and the exchange rate regime.

## The supply of money

In a modern economy the supply of money is determined by the interaction of the banking system and the non-bank private sector. We have already discussed the variety of definitions of the money stock and the way in which

---

[3] The example assumes annual compounding. The first case is calculated from the numbers of the previous example: (92.58 − 89.29)/92.58. The ten-year case uses the formula

$$\text{Present value} = \text{principal}/(1 + i)^n,$$

which gives £46.30 at 8 per cent and £28.75 at 12 per cent. The percentage fall in value is thus (46.30 − 28.75)/46.30 = 0.379, or 37.9 per cent.

the money supply is determined in detail in Chapter 20. For present purposes we use the broad definition of money, M4 (see page 452).

In most major countries the authorities implement monetary policy by setting interest rates and letting the money stock be determined by how much is demanded at that interest rate. We say more about how the authorities set interest rates later in this chapter; for now we just assume that the authorities set the interest rate and focus on the implications of this fact for money demand. We can then see how policy-determined changes in interest rates affect the real economy. Our analysis, therefore, now focuses on the factors influencing money demand because at the set interest rate the money stock is demand-determined.

## The demand for money

The amount of wealth that everyone in the economy wishes to hold in the form of money balances is called the demand for money. Because people can choose how to divide their given stock of wealth between money and bonds, it follows that if we know the demand for money, we also know the demand for bonds. With a *given level of wealth*, a rise in the demand for money necessarily implies a fall in the demand for bonds; if people wish to hold £1 billion more money, they must wish to hold £1 billion less of bonds. It also follows that, if households are in equilibrium with respect to their money holdings, they are in equilibrium with respect to their bond holdings.

When we say that in first quarter of 2006 the quantity of money demanded was £1,300 billion (the approximate value of the broad money stock, M4, at that time), we mean that at that time the public wished to hold money balances that totalled £1,300 billion. But why do firms and individuals wish to hold money balances at all? There is a cost to holding any money balance. The money could have been used to purchase bonds, which earn higher interest than does money.[4] For the present we assume no ongoing inflation, so there is no difference between real and nominal interest rates.

The opportunity cost of holding any money balance is the extra interest that could have been earned if the money had been used instead to purchase bonds.

Clearly, money will be held only when it provides services that are valued at least as highly as the opportunity cost of holding it. Three important services that are provided by money balances give rise to three motives for holding money: the transactions, precautionary, and speculative motives.

### The transactions motive

Most transactions require money. Money passes from consumers to firms to pay for the goods and services produced by firms; money passes from firms to employees to pay for the labour services supplied by workers to firms. Money balances that are held to finance such flows are called transactions balances.

In an imaginary world in which the receipts and disbursements of consumers and firms were perfectly synchronized, it would be unnecessary to hold transactions balances. If every time a consumer spent £10 she received £10 as part payment of her wages, no transactions balances would be needed. In the real world, however, receipts and payments are not perfectly synchronized.

Consider the balances that are held because of wage payments. Suppose, for purposes of illustration, that firms pay wages every Friday and that employees spend all their wages on goods and services, with the spending spread out evenly over the week. Thus, on Friday morning firms must hold balances equal to the weekly wage bill; on Friday afternoon the employees will hold these balances.

Over the week, workers' balances will be drawn down as a result of their purchasing goods and services. Over the same period, the balances held by firms will build up as a result of selling goods and services until, on the following Friday morning, firms will again have amassed balances equal to the wage bill that must be met on that day.

The transactions motive arises because payments and receipts are not synchronized.

What determines the size of the transactions balances to be held? It is clear that in our example total transactions balances vary with the value of the wage bill. If the wage bill doubles for any reason, the transactions balances held by firms and households for this purpose will also double, on average. As it is with wages, so it is with all other transactions: the size of the balances held is positively related to the value of the transactions.

It is the average value of money balances that people choose to hold over a particular period that is relevant for

---

4 Many of the bank and building society deposits that are included in M4 now yield interest. This complicates, but does not fundamentally alter, the analysis of the demand for money. In particular, it means that the opportunity cost of holding those interest-bearing components of money is not the *level* of interest rates paid on bonds but the *difference* between that rate and the rate paid on money. Because the interest earned on deposits tends to fluctuate less than rates on marketable securities, the difference tends to move with the level of interest rates in the economy, rising when rates rise and falling when rates fall. For simplicity, we talk of the demand for money responding to the *level* of interest rates, although in reality it is the *difference* that is the opportunity cost of money.

macroeconomics, but we need to know how money demand relates to GDP rather than to total transactions. In fact, the value of all transactions exceeds the value of the economy's final output. When the miller buys wheat from the farmer and when the baker buys flour from the miller, both are transactions against which money balances must be held, although only the value added at each stage is part of GDP.

Generally there will be a stable, positive relationship between transactions and GDP. A rise in GDP also leads to a rise in the total value of all transactions and hence to an associated rise in the demand for transactions balances. This allows us to relate transactions balances to GDP.

The larger the value of GDP, the larger is the value of transactions balances that will be held.

### The precautionary motive

Many reasons for spending arise unexpectedly, such as when your car breaks down, or you have to make an unplanned journey to visit a sick relative. As a precaution against cash crises, when receipts are abnormally low or disbursements are abnormally high, firms and individuals carry money balances. **Precautionary balances** provide a cushion against uncertainty about the timing of cash flows. The larger such balances are, the greater is the protection against running out of money because of temporary fluctuations in cash flows.

The seriousness of the risk of a cash crisis depends on the penalties that are inflicted for being caught without sufficient money balances. A firm is unlikely to be pushed into insolvency, but it may incur considerable costs if it is forced to borrow money at high interest rates in order to meet a temporary cash crisis.

The precautionary motive arises because individuals and firms are uncertain about the degree to which payments and receipts will be synchronized.

The protection provided by a given quantity of precautionary balances depends on the volume of payments and receipts. A £100 precautionary balance provides a large cushion for a person whose volume of payments per month is £800 and a small cushion for a firm whose monthly volume is £250,000. To provide the same degree of protection as the value of transactions rises, more money is necessary.

The precautionary motive, like the transactions motive, causes the demand for money to vary positively with the money value of GDP.

For most purposes the transactions and precautionary motives can be merged, as they both show that desired money holdings are positively related to GDP. Indeed, they both show money being held in relation to transactions, either planned or potential.

### The speculative motive

Money can be held for its characteristics as an asset. Firms and individuals may hold some money in order to provide a hedge against the uncertainty inherent in fluctuating prices of other financial assets. Money balances held for this purpose are called **speculative balances**. This motive was first analysed by Keynes. Professor James Tobin, the 1981 Nobel Laureate in economics, developed the modern analysis.

Any holder of money balances forgoes the extra interest income that could be earned if bonds were held instead. However, market interest rates fluctuate, and so do the market prices of existing bonds (whose present values depend on the interest rate). Bonds are risky assets, because their prices fluctuate. Many individuals and firms do not like risk; they are said to be *risk-averse*.[5]

In choosing between holding money and holding bonds, wealth-holders must balance the extra interest income that they could earn by holding bonds against the risk that bonds carry. At one extreme, if individuals hold all their wealth in the form of bonds, they earn extra interest on their entire wealth, but they also expose their entire wealth to the risk of changes in the price of bonds. At the other extreme, if people hold all their wealth in the form of money, they earn less interest income, but they do not face the risk of unexpected changes in the price of bonds. Wealth-holders usually do not take either extreme position. They hold part of their wealth as money and part of it as bonds; that is, they *diversify* their holdings. The fact that some proportion of wealth is held in money and some in bonds suggests that, as wealth rises, desired money holdings will also rise.

The speculative motive implies that the demand for money varies positively with wealth.

Although one individual's wealth may rise or fall rapidly, the total wealth of a society changes only slowly. For the analysis of short-term fluctuations in GDP, the effects of changes in wealth are fairly small, and we will ignore them for the present. Specific individuals may undergo large wealth changes in response to bond price changes, but with inside wealth the total effect is

---

[5] A person is risk-averse when she prefers a certain sum of money to an uncertain outcome for which the expected value is the same. See our website www.oxfordtextbooks.co.uk/orc/lipsey11e/ for a discussion of risk aversion.

small.[6] When lenders gain, borrowers lose; and when lenders lose, borrowers gain. Over the long term, however, variations in aggregate wealth can have a major effect on the demand for money.

Wealth that is held in cash or deposits earns less interest than could be earned by holding bonds; hence the reduction in risk involved in holding money carries an opportunity cost in terms of interest earnings forgone. The speculative motive leads individuals and firms to add to their money holdings until the reduction in risk obtained by the last pound added is just balanced (in each wealth-holder's view) by the cost in terms of the interest forgone on that pound. A fall in the rate of return on bonds for the same level of risk will encourage people to hold more of their wealth as money and less in bonds. A rise in their rate of return for a given level of risk will cause people to hold more bonds and less money.

**The speculative motive implies that the demand for money will be negatively related to the rate of interest.**

The precautionary and transactions motives may also be negatively related to interest rates at the margin, because higher returns on bonds encourage people to economize on their money holding. However, in practice we only observe total money holdings, so we cannot distinguish the components held for different motives. Hence demand for money, as a whole, is likely to be positively related to GDP and wealth, and negatively related to the interest rate.

### Real and nominal money balances

The money supply is a nominal quantity, but it is important to distinguish demand for *real* money balances from *nominal* money demand. Real money demand is the number of units of purchasing power that the public wishes to hold in the form of money balances. For example, in an imaginary one-product (wheat) economy, the number of bushels of wheat that could be purchased with the money balances held would be the measure of their real value. In a more complex economy it could be measured in terms of the number of 'baskets of goods', represented by a price index such as the RPI, that could be purchased with the money balances held. When we speak of the demand for money in real terms, we speak of the amount demanded in constant pounds (that is, with a constant price level):

The real demand for money (or the demand for real money balances) is the nominal quantity demanded divided by the price level.

In the twenty-four years from March 1982 to February 2006, on the M4 definition, the nominal quantity of money balances held in the United Kingdom increased nearly ten-fold, from around £140 billion to around £1,333 billion. Over the same period, however, the price level, as measured by the RPI, approximately trebled. This tells us that the real quantity of money rose from £140 billion to about £500 billion, measured in constant 1982 prices, roughly a three-fold increase.

So far we have held the price level constant, and so we have identified the determinants of the demand for real money balances as real GDP, real wealth, and the interest rate. Now suppose that, with the interest rate, real wealth, and real GDP held constant, the price level doubles. Because the demand for real money balances will be unchanged, the demand for nominal balances must double. If the public previously demanded £300 billion in nominal money balances, it will now demand £600 billion. This keeps the real demand unchanged at £600/2 = £300 billion. The money balances of £600 billion at the new, higher price level represent exactly the same purchasing power as £300 billion at the old price level.

Other things being equal, the nominal demand for money balances varies in proportion to the price level; when the price level doubles, desired nominal money balances also double.

This is a central proposition of the quantity theory of money, which is discussed further in Box 21.1.

### Total demand for money

Figure 21.1 summarizes the influences of the nominal rate of interest, real GDP, and the price level, the three variables that account for most of the short-term variations in the nominal quantity of money demanded. The function relating money demanded to the rate of interest is often called the **demand for money function**, even though the demand for nominal money depends also on GDP, wealth, and prices.

We have seen that the public has a fixed stock of wealth at any point in time. When it decides how much money to hold, for the reasons just mentioned, it is also deciding how many bonds to hold. In other words, the public can be seen as adjusting the balance of its portfolio of wealth between the two assets, money and bonds. When it is in disequilibrium, it is trying to alter that balance either by selling bonds and getting money, or by buying bonds and giving up money. When it is in equilibrium, it has the desired balance between the two assets.

---

[6] 'Inside wealth' is not net wealth for the economy *as a whole*—one agent's assets are another agent's liabilities.

### Box 21.1 The quantity theory of money

The quantity theory of money can be set out in terms of four equations. Equation (i) states that the demand for money balances depends on the value of transactions as measured by nominal GDP, which is real GDP multiplied by the price level:

$$M^D = kPY. \tag{i}$$

Equation (ii) states that the supply of money, $M$, is exogenously determined:

$$M^S = M. \tag{ii}$$

Equation (iii) states the equilibrium condition that the demand for money must equal the supply:

$$M^D = M^S. \tag{iii}$$

Substitution from (ii) and (iii) into equation (i) yields

$$M = kPY. \tag{iv}$$

The original classical quantity theory assumes that $k$ is a constant given by the transactions demand for money and that $Y$ is constant because full employment (equilibrium GDP) is maintained. Thus, increases or decreases in the money supply lead to proportional increases or decreases in prices.

Often the quantity theory is presented by using the *equation of exchange*:

$$MV = PY, \tag{v}$$

where $V$ is the **velocity of circulation**, defined as nominal GDP divided by the quantity of money:

$$V = PY/M. \tag{vi}$$

*Velocity* may be interpreted as showing the average amount of 'work' done by a unit of money. If annual money GDP is £600

billion and the stock of money is £200 billion, on average each pound's worth of money is used three times to create the values added that compose GDP.

There is a simple relationship between $k$ and $V$. One is the reciprocal of the other, as may be seen by comparing (iv) and (vi). So it makes no difference whether we choose to work with $k$ or $V$. Further, if $k$ is assumed to be constant, this implies that $V$ must also be treated as a constant.

An example may help to illustrate the interpretation of each. Suppose the stock of money that people wish to hold equals one-fifth of the value of total transactions. Thus $k$ is 0.2 and $V$, the reciprocal of $k$, is 5. If the money supply is to be one-fifth of the value of annual transactions, each pound must be 'used' on average five times.

The modern version of the quantity theory does not assume that $k$ and $V$ are exogenously fixed. However, it does argue that they will not change in response to a change in the quantity of money.

In the long run GDP tends to equal its potential. If we take the extreme case in which $Y$ always equals $Y^*$, we can derive the famous predictions of the quantity theory.

Substituting $Y^*$ for $Y$ into equation (v) and dividing through by $Y^*$, we get

$$P = MV/Y^*.$$

If we assume that $V$ is constant, we can use $\alpha$ for the constant value of $V/Y^*$ and then write

$$P = \alpha M.$$

In words, the price level is determined by the quantity of money. By taking first differences ($\Delta P = \alpha \Delta M$), we derive the prediction that changes in the price level will be proportional to changes in the quantity of money.

**Figure 21.1** **The demand for money as a function of interest rates, GDP, and the price level**

The quantity of money demanded varies negatively with the nominal rate of interest and positively with both real GDP and the price level. In part (i) the quantity of money demanded varies negatively with the interest rate. When the interest rate rises from $i_0$ to $i_1$, the quantity of money demanded falls from $M_0$ to $M_1$. In part (ii) the quantity of money demanded is positively related to real GDP. When GDP rises from $Y_0$ to $Y_1$, the quantity demanded rises from $M_2$ to $M_3$. In part (iii) the quantity of money demanded is proportional to the price level. When the price level doubles from $P_0$ to $P_1$, the quantity demanded doubles from $M_4$ to $M_5$. In the text we refer to the $M^D$ curve in (i) as the money demand function. It is drawn for given values of real GDP, wealth, and the price level.

# Monetary forces and aggregate demand

We are now in a position to examine the relationship between monetary forces on the one hand, and the equilibrium values of GDP and the price level on the other. The first step in explaining this relationship is a new one: the link between monetary equilibrium and aggregate demand. The second is familiar from earlier chapters: the effects of shifts in aggregate demand on equilibrium values of GDP and the price level. The first step we set out in this section, and the second we analyse in the last section of this chapter, where we compare monetary and fiscal polices as tools for controlling the economy.

## Monetary equilibrium and the interest rate

**Monetary equilibrium** occurs when the demand for money equals the supply of money. In Chapter 3 we saw that in competitive markets the price will adjust so as to ensure equilibrium. The rate of interest is the relevant price in the money markets. However, as we saw in the previous chapter, in UK and European money markets (as well as those of most major countries) the monetary authorities set the level of interest rates and the money supply adjusts to become equal to the quantity of money demanded at the policy-determined rate of interest.[7]

The easiest way to understand how this works is to start by showing how interest rates would adjust to clear the money market (i.e. equate demand and supply) if there were a given money supply. We then show how the money stock adjusts to equate demand and supply when the authorities choose to change the interest rate for macro policy reasons.

### Equilibrium interest rate

Figure 21.2 shows supply and demand curves for money. The supply of money that is in existence at the initial point in time is shown as a vertical line, indicating that the money supply is a given nominal quantity. The money demand curve is based upon the speculative demand illustrated in Figure 21.1(i). It is negatively sloped because people wish to hold less money as interest rates rise. The money demand curve is drawn for given levels of

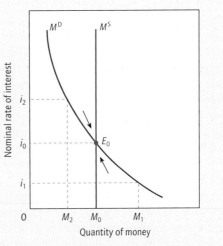

**Figure 21.2** **The equilibrium interest rate**

**The equilibrium interest rate arises where demand for money equals the supply of money.** A given quantity of money, $M_0$, is shown by the vertical supply curve $M^S$. The demand for money is $M^D$; its negative slope indicates that a fall in the rate of interest causes the quantity of money demanded to increase. Equilibrium is at $E_0$, with a rate of interest $i_0$.

If the interest rate is $i_1$, there will be an excess demand for money of $M_1 - M_0$. Bonds will be offered for sale in an attempt to increase money holdings. This will force the rate of interest up to $i_0$ (the price of bonds falls), at which point the quantity of money demanded is equal to the fixed supply, $M_0$. If the interest rate is $i_2$, there will be an excess supply of money $M_0 - M_2$. Bonds will be demanded in return for excess money balances. This will force the rate of interest down to $i_0$ (the price of bonds rises), at which point the quantity of money demanded has risen to equal the fixed money supply, $M_0$.

real GDP, the price level, and wealth, and will shift to the right if any of these variables increases.

Figure 21.2 also shows how the interest rate would move in order to equate the demand for money with its supply, given the initial money stock and the existing stock of bonds. When a few people find that they have less money than they wish to hold, they can sell some bonds and add the proceeds to their money holdings. This transaction simply redistributes given supplies of bonds and money among individuals; it does not change the total supply of either money or bonds.

Now suppose that all of the firms and households in the economy have excess demands for money balances. They all try to sell bonds to add to their money balances, but what one person can do, all cannot necessarily do. At any moment the economy's total supply of money and bonds

---

[7] The authorities actually set a specific rate at which they trade with the wholesale money markets. All other rates are determined relative to this policy rate by market forces. We will talk as if there is only one interest rate and this is the one the authorities set. More institutional detail on the process of interest rate setting is given in the last section of this chapter.

is fixed—there is just so much money and there are just so many bonds in existence. If everyone tries to sell bonds, there will be no one to buy them, and the price of bonds will fall.

We saw earlier in this chapter that a fall in the price of bonds means a rise in the rate of interest. As the interest rate rises, people economize on money balances, because the opportunity cost of holding such balances is rising. This is what we saw in Figure 21.1(i), where the quantity of money demanded falls along the demand curve, in response to a rise in the rate of interest. Eventually the interest rate will rise enough that people will no longer be trying to add to their money balances by selling bonds. At that point there is no longer an excess supply of bonds, and the interest rate stops rising. The demand for money again equals the supply.

Suppose now that all firms and households hold larger money balances than they would like. A single household or firm would purchase bonds with its excess balances, achieving monetary equilibrium by reducing its money holdings and increasing its bond holdings. However, just as in the previous example, what one individual can do, all cannot do. At any moment the total quantity of bonds is fixed, so not everyone can simultaneously add to personal bond-holdings. When all agents enter the bond market and try to purchase bonds with unwanted money balances, they bid up the price of existing bonds, and the interest rate falls. Individuals and firms then become willing to hold larger quantities of money; that is, the quantity of money demanded increases along the money demand curve, in response to a fall in the rate of interest. The rise in the price of bonds continues until firms and households stop trying to convert bonds into money. In other words, it continues until everyone is content to hold the existing supply of money and bonds.

Monetary equilibrium occurs when the rate of interest is such that the demand to hold money equals the supply available to be held, and hence the demand to hold bonds equals the supply available to be held.

The determination of the interest rate depicted in Figure 21.2 is often called the *liquidity preference theory* of interest and sometimes the *portfolio balance theory*.

As we will see, a monetary shock—an autonomous shift in the demand for money or a change in the policy-determined interest rate—will lead to an adjustment in the money supply. However, the critical factor is that aggregate spending, especially investment but also consumption and net exports (as we saw in Chapters 16 and 17), is sensitive to changes in the interest rate. Here, then, is a link between monetary factors and real spending flows.

## Interest rates as the monetary policy instrument

In the previous section we have seen how the interest rate adjusts to clear the money market for a given level of the money stock and a given money demand curve. Figure 21.3 illustrates how this works. If the authorities wished to relax monetary policy, they could do so by increasing the money supply. If they did this, there would initially be an excess supply of money. Holders of this money would demand more bonds, and via the process discussed above this would raise the price of bonds and lower the interest rate.

However, this is not what happens. Rather than setting a level of the money supply, the authorities set the level of the interest rate. When the Bank decides to loosen monetary policy it lowers the interest rate. At this lower interest rate, the public wishes to hold more money. So there is excess demand for money. In order to achieve portfolio balance (that is, the desired composition of asset holding), the public tries to sell bonds for money. If the Bank did nothing, the sales of bonds would raise the interest rate. However, the Bank is setting the interest rate, so in order to maintain that rate it accommodates the public's desire

**Figure 21.3** **Interest rates and money supply changes**

**A change in the policy-determined interest rate requires the money supply to change.** In the figure the initial money supply is shown by the vertical line $M_0^S$, and the demand for money is shown by the negatively sloped curve $M^D$. The initial equilibrium is at $E_0$, with corresponding interest rate $i_0$. The monetary authorities choose to lower the interest rate from $i_0$ to $i_1$. In order to achieve this they must generate an increase in the money supply, from $M_0^S$ to $M_1^S$. The new equilibrium is at $E_1$. Starting at $E_1$, with $M_1^S$ and $i_1$, it can be seen that a decrease in the money supply to $M_0^S$ would be required to achieve an increase in the interest rate from $i_1$ to $i_0$.

to switch from bonds to money by buying bonds and supplying money.[8] The money supply thus increases to whatever is demanded at the new interest rate.[9]

Notice that the outcome in Figure 21.3 is exactly the same when the authorities fix interest rates and let the money supply adjust as it is when they fix the money supply and let interest rates adjust—it makes no difference to the equilibrium of our macro model which way it is done. We will see, however, that when the authorities are responding to an exogenous shock to aggregate demand, fixing interest rates and fixing the stock of money can lead to widely different adjustment paths.

The monetary authorities in most industrial countries (or currency zones) set the interest rate and let the money stock adjust to demand.

### The transmission mechanism

The mechanism by which changes in monetary policy affect aggregate demand is called the **transmission mechanism**. The transmission mechanism operates in two stages: the first is as the link between the interest rate and investment spending, and the second is as the link between investment spending and aggregate demand. For this discussion we assume that the authorities are setting the interest rate. The case where the authorities set the exchange rate is discussed in Chapter 23. The views of the UK Monetary Policy Committee on the transmission mechanism of their interest rate decisions are available on: http://www.bankofengland.co.uk/publications/other/monetary/montrans.pdf.

### From changes in the interest rate to shifts in investment

The first step in the transmission mechanism relates interest rates to aggregate spending. For simplicity we focus here only on the link via changes in investment. We saw in Chapter 16 that investment, which includes spending on inventory accumulation, residential construction, and business fixed investment, responds to changes in the real rate of interest. Other things being equal, a decrease in the real rate of interest makes borrowing cheaper and generates new investment spending.[10] This negative relationship between investment and the rate of interest is called the **investment demand function**.

This link between the interest rate and investment is shown in Figure 21.4. In part (i) we see that if the authorities wish to lower the interest rate they can do so (as discussed above) by buying all the extra bonds offered for sale at the new interest rate and thereby increasing the money supply. In part (ii) we see that a change in the interest rate causes the level of investment spending to change in the opposite direction.[11] A fall in the interest rate causes investment to rise, and a rise in the interest rate causes investment to fall.

A fall in the interest rate leads to an increase in investment spending. A rise in the interest rate leads to a decrease in investment spending.

The change in investment spending shifts the aggregate spending curve, *AE*, as shown in Chapters 16 and 17. Box 21.2 discusses some forces additional to interest rates that help explain investment.

### From shifts in aggregate spending to shifts in aggregate demand

Now we are back on familiar ground. In Chapter 18 we saw that a shift in the aggregate spending curve leads to a shift in the *AD* curve. This is shown again in Figure 21.5.

A change in the interest rate, by causing a change in desired investment spending (which in previous chapters was assumed to be exogenous) and hence a shift in the *AE* curve, causes the *AD* curve to shift. A fall in the interest rate causes an increase in investment spending and hence an increase in aggregate demand. A rise in the interest rate causes a decrease in investment spending and therefore a decrease in aggregate demand.

The transmission mechanism connects monetary forces and real spending flows. A change in the interest rate causes a change in investment spending, which in turn leads to a shift in the aggregate demand curve.

Thus, a lowering of the interest rate increases investment and this shifts the *AD* curve to the right. A raising of interest rates lowers investment and this shifts *AD* to the left.

---

[8] The central bank's money market operators are instructed to buy or sell whatever short-term securities necessary to keep that rate at the target level. So in effect they are making up any discrepancy between the stock demand and the current stock supply by altering the stock in existence.

[9] In practice it is the monetary base, M0, that the authorities supply in order to maintain interest rates. Broader monetary aggregates are then determined by demand at whatever level the set interest rate determines (as a result of the public's demand for loans and deposits). This complication does not change the principles involved. The process was explained in Chapter 20.

[10] Consumption may also respond to changes in the real interest rate, and there may also be an impact on net exports via the exchange rate. In this chapter we concentrate on investment spending, which may be taken to stand for *all* interest-sensitive spending, and we maintain our simplifying assumption that expected inflation is zero so that the real and nominal interest rates are equal.

[11] Recall that we have assumed that real and nominal interest rates are the same. Generally, as long as inflation expectations are constant, the change in the nominal interest rate determined in part (i) of Figure 21.4 is equal to the change in the real interest rate in part (ii).

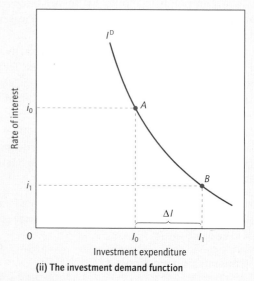

(i) Money demand and supply    (ii) The investment demand function

**Figure 21.4  The effect of changes in the interest rate on investment spending**

A reduction in the rate of interest increases desired investment spending. Initial equilibrium is at $E_0$, with a quantity of money $M_0$ (shown by the vertical money supply curve $M_0^S$), an interest rate of $i_0$, and an investment spending of $I_0$ (point $A$ in part (ii)). The monetary authorities then lower the rate of interest to $i_1$ (and increase the money supply to $M_1$), and this increases investment spending by $\Delta I$ to $I_1$ (point $B$). A policy-induced rise in the interest rate from $i_1$ to $i_0$ is accompanied by a fall in the money stock from $M_1$ to $M_0$ and leads investment to fall by $\Delta I$ from $I_1$ to $I_0$.

---

 **Box 21.2  The accelerator theory of investment**

In our macroeconomic model, investment changes in response to changes in interest rates. The **accelerator theory of investment** relies on another determinant of investment which can be formalized only in a dynamic model. This theory relates investment to GDP. The possibility of systematic fluctuations arises because the *level* of investment is assumed to be related to *changes* in GDP.

The demand for machinery and factories is obviously derived from the demand for the goods that the capital equipment is designed to produce. If there is a demand that is expected to persist, and that cannot be met by increasing production with existing industrial capacity, then new plant and equipment will be needed.

Investment expenditure occurs while the new capital equipment is being built and installed. If the desired stock of capital goods increases, there will be an investment boom while the new capital is being produced. But if nothing else changes, and even though business conditions continue to look rosy enough to justify the increased stock of capital, investment in new plant and equipment will cease once the larger capital stock is in place. This makes investment depend on changes in final demand, and hence on changes in GDP, as illustrated in the table.* The figure illustrates what happens to investment under the accelerator theory when GDP rises from one constant level to another.

The main insight that the accelerator theory provides is its emphasis on the role of net investment as a *disequilibrium* phenomenon—something that occurs when the stock of capital goods differs from what firms and households would like it to be. This makes the accelerator a possible explanation of *fluctuations* in GDP. As we will see, it can itself contribute to those fluctuations.

Taken literally, the simple accelerator assumes a mechanical and rigid response of investment to changes in sales (and thus, in the aggregate, to changes in GDP). It does this by assuming a proportional relationship between changes in output and changes in the desired capital stock. It also assumes that there is a fixed ratio between the level of output and the level of the capital stock. This ratio is called the *capital–output ratio*. Both assumptions are to some degree questionable.

The accelerator does not by itself give anything like a complete explanation of variations in investment in capital goods, and it should not be surprising that a simple accelerator theory provides a relatively poor overall explanation of changes in investment. Yet accelerator-like influences do exist, and they play a role in the cyclical variability of investment. Modern investment theories often include a flexible version of the accelerator, in which the capital–output ratio (coefficient $\alpha$ of the footnote)

**Box 21.2** *continued*

### An illustration of the accelerator theory of investment

| Year | Annual sales | Change in sales | Required stock of capital[a] | Net investment increase in required capital stock |
|------|------|------|------|------|
| (1) | (2) | (3) | (4) | (5) |
| 1 | £10 | £0 | £50 | £0 |
| 2 | 10 | 0 | 50 | 0 |
| 3 | 11 | 1 | 55 | 5 |
| 4 | 13 | 2 | 65 | 10 |
| 5 | 16 | 3 | 80 | 15 |
| 6 | 19 | 3 | 95 | 15 |
| 7 | 22 | 3 | 110 | 15 |
| 8 | 24 | 2 | 120 | 10 |
| 9 | 25 | 1 | 125 | 5 |
| 10 | 25 | 0 | 125 | 0 |

With a fixed capital–output ratio, net investment occurs only when it is necessary to increase the stock of capital in order to change output. Assume that it takes £5 of capital to produce £1 of output per year. In years 1 and 2 there is no need for investment. In year 3 a rise in sales of £1 requires investment of £5 to provide the needed capital stock. In year 4 a further rise of £2 in sales requires an additional investment of £10 to provide the needed capital stock. As columns (3) and (5) show, the amount of net investment is proportional to the *change* in sales. When the increase in sales tapers off in years 7–9, investment declines. When sales no longer increase in year 10, net investment falls to zero because the capital stock of year 9 is adequate to provide output for year 10's sales.

[a] Assuming a capital–output ratio of 5:1.

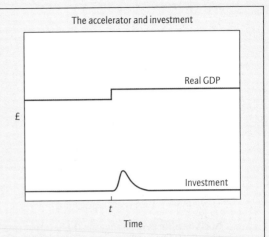

The accelerator and investment

When there is a change in the level of final output, there is a much bigger percentage change in the rate of investment. The figure illustrates the path over time of GDP and investment. We assume that GDP is constant but that at time *t* it jumps to a new, higher level and then continues at this level. Replacement investment carries on at some constant level, but the increase in output requires a higher capital stock. This in turn requires a burst of *new investment*. Once this burst of new investment is over (shown as being spread out over time), the level of new investment returns to zero.

\* A more formal derivation is as follows. Let the relationship between the GDP level and the amount of capital needed to produce it be

$$K = \alpha Y, \tag{i}$$

where $K$ is the required capital stock. The coefficient $\alpha$ is the capital–output ratio; $\alpha = K/Y$ and is also called the accelerator coefficient. Taking changes in (i), and noticing that investment is, by definition, the change in the capital stock, yields

$$I = \Delta K = \alpha \Delta Y$$

This says that investment is some constant times *the change* in GDP. This is called the 'simple', or sometimes the 'naïve', accelerator.

varies with other factors such as interest rates. Also, the actual coefficient will vary over the cycle since during a recession some existing capital will be unemployed, so a rise in income may not lead to a rise in new investment until all existing capital is once again utilized.

Later we will see that another important channel of the transmission mechanism is provided by the exchange rate.

A discussion of how the openness of the economy affects the transmission mechanism is presented in Chapter 23.

## Macroeconomic cycles and aggregate shocks

In Chapter 19 we discussed how fiscal policy could be used to return GDP to its potential level following an inflationary or deflationary shock. Now that we have added a monetary sector to our model we are able to tell a much more detailed story about how shocks work their way through the economy and about the policy options available to the authorities to respond to those shocks.

**Figure 21.5** The effects of changes in the interest rate on aggregate demand

Changes in the interest rate cause shifts in the aggregate spending and aggregate demand functions. In Figure 21.4 a fall in the interest rate increased desired investment spending by $\Delta I$. Here, in part (i) the aggregate spending function shifts up by $\Delta I$, from $AE_0$ to $AE_1$. At the fixed price level $P_0$, equilibrium GDP rises from $Y_0$ to $Y_1$, shifting the aggregate demand curve horizontally from $AD_0$ to $AD_1$ in part (ii).

When the interest rate rises (as from $i_1$ to $i_0$ in Figure 21.4), investment falls by $\Delta I$, thereby shifting aggregate spending from $AE_1$ to $AE_0$. At the fixed price level $P_0$, this reduces equilibrium income from $Y_1$ to $Y_0$ and shifts the $AD$ curve from $AD_1$ to $AD_0$.

## Aggregate demand and supply shocks

Let us now return to our complete model, where we can add the long-run and short-run aggregate supply curves developed in Chapters 18 and 19 to the aggregate demand curve. Now that we have incorporated monetary influences in to our model, we can give more complete answers to the questions we asked in these earlier chapters: first, how the economy responds to shocks to aggregate demand and supply and, second, what monetary and fiscal policy can do to influence the response.

### Aggregate demand shocks

How does the economy respond to an aggregate demand shock? Such shocks could come from a change in world demand for domestic exports, or from an autonomous shift in investment or consumption coming, perhaps, from a wave of optimism or a wave of pessimism. Some of the detail of the resulting changes will depend upon the precise nature of the shock, but the general principles will be the same. For simplicity, we assume that the shock is an autonomous shift in domestic investment. Box 21.3 discusses why the interaction of the multiplier and accelerator tends to be associated with cumulative responses to specific exogenous shocks.

### Positive demand shock

Figure 21.6 shows how the economy responds to an autonomous increase in investment. Starting at point $A$, the $AD$ curve shifts to the right. This rightward shift of $AD$ has two components. First, the rise in investment shifts the $AD$ to the right. With a given money supply, that would be the end of the story. However, the increase in GDP brought about by the increase in investment increases the transactions demand for money, and this puts upward pressure on interest rates. If the monetary authorities are to hold the initial level of the interest rate, they must buy bonds and so permit the money stock to rise. This increase in the money stock imparts a further rightward shift to $AD$ (such that the total horizontal shift is equal to the initial shift in investment times the simple multiplier).

With given initial input prices, the economy expands from point $A$ to point $B$ along the short-run aggregate supply curve $SRAS_0$. The economy is in a boom. In the first phase of this boom prices may be slow to respond, but as GDP moves further above its potential level, the price level will start to rise. Real wages fall because money wages are assumed to be fixed, at least initially. However, workers will not be happy for long to see their real wages fall while

**Box 21.3** Multiplier–accelerator interaction

The theory linking systematic fluctuations in GDP to systematic fluctuations in investment expenditure combines the accelerator theory discussed in Box 21.2 with the multiplier.

This **multiplier–accelerator theory** of the cycle is divided into three steps. First, a theory of cumulative upswings and downswings explains why, once started, movements tend to carry on in the same direction. Second, a theory of floors and ceilings explains why upward and downward movements are eventually brought to a halt. And third, a theory of instability explains how, once a process of upward or downward movement is brought to a halt, it tends to reverse itself.

Why does a period of expansion or contraction, once begun, tend to develop its own momentum? First, the multiplier process tends to cause cumulative movements. As soon as a revival begins, some unemployed people find work again. These people, with their newly acquired income, can afford to make much-needed consumption expenditures. This new demand causes an increase in production and creates new jobs for others. As incomes rise, demand rises; as demand rises, incomes rise. The reverse happens in a downswing. Unemployment in one sector causes a fall in demand for the products of other sectors, which leads to a further fall in employment and a further fall in demand.

A second major factor is the accelerator theory. New investment is needed to expand existing productive capacity and to introduce new methods of production. When consumer demand is low and there is excess capacity, investment is likely to fall to a very low level; once demand and output start to rise and entrepreneurs come to expect further rises, investment expenditure may rise very rapidly. Furthermore, when full employment of existing capacity is reached, new investment becomes one of the few ways available for firms to increase their output.

A third major explanation for cumulative movements is expectations. All production plans take time to fulfil. Current decisions to produce consumer goods and investment goods are very strongly influenced by business expectations. Such expectations can sometimes be volatile, and sometimes self-fulfilling. If enough people think, for example, that equity prices are going to rise, they will all buy equities in anticipation of the price rise, and these purchases will themselves cause prices to rise. If on the other hand enough people think that equity prices are going to fall, they will sell quickly at what they regard as a high price, and thereby actually cause prices to fall. This is the phenomenon of *self-realizing expectations*. It applies to many parts of the economy. If enough managers think the future looks rosy and begin to invest in increasing capacity, this will create new employment and income in the capital goods industries, and the resulting increase in demand will help to create the rosy conditions whose vision started the whole process. There is a bandwagon effect. Once things begin to improve, people expect further improvements, and their actions, based on this expectation, help to cause further improvements. On the other hand, once things begin

to worsen, people often expect further worsening; then their actions, based on this expectation, help to make things worse.

The multiplier–accelerator process, combined with changes in expectations that cause autonomous shifts of expenditure, can explain the cumulative tendencies of recessions and recoveries.

The next question that arises is why these upward and downward processes ever come to an end.

A very rapid expansion can continue for some time, but it cannot go on for ever because eventually the economy will run into bottlenecks (or ceilings) in terms of some resources. This will happen when firms cannot take on more workers without paying much higher wages to attract them from other firms. Inflation will begin to rise, and either the monetary authorities will put interest rates up or firms will cut investment in anticipation of a downturn. This expectation itself may become self-fulfilling.

A rapid contraction, too, is eventually brought to an end. Firms cannot postpone investment and run down stocks—and consumers cannot put off buying new clothes and new cars—indefinitely. Eventually some kinds of spending can be postponed no longer. Even a modest increase in sales can cause confidence to return. The small upturn in spending then leads to further spending and the start of an upswing of the cycle, through the interaction of the multiplier and accelerator together.

The accelerator also can explain how expansions and contractions reverse direction. We have seen that the accelerator causes the desired level of *new* (not replacement) investment to depend upon the rate of change of GDP. If GDP is rising at a constant rate, then investment will be at a constant *level*; if there is a slackening in the speed at which GDP is rising, the level of investment will decline. This means that a *levelling-off* in GDP at the top of a cycle may lead to a *decline* in the amount of investment. The decline in investment at the upper turning-point will cause a decline in the level of GDP. This will be intensified through the multiplier process.

The accelerator theory provides one possible explanation of why a slowdown in the growth of GDP may lead to negative growth in subsequent periods, via a fall in investment spending.

Recessions do not go on for ever. Investment theory predicts that sooner or later there will be an upturn. If nothing else causes an expansion of business activity, eventually there will be a revival of replacement investment. As existing capital wears out, the capital stock will fall below the level required to produce current output. At this stage new machines will have to be bought to replace those that are wearing out. The rise in the level of activity in the capital goods industries will then, by way of the multiplier, cause a further rise in incomes and output. The economy will have turned the corner. An expansion, once started, may trigger the sort of cumulative upward movement already discussed.

**Figure 21.6 Aggregate demand shocks**

A positive demand shock leads to a temporary boom in GDP and a permanent rise in the price level, while a negative demand shock leads to a temporary fall in output and (ultimately) lower prices. Consider an initial position at point $A$ with the economy at $Y*$ with an initial price level $P_0$. A positive demand shock shifts the $AD$ curve from $AD_0$ to $AD_1$. This shift will be greater with a pegged interest rate than with a fixed money stock, as the money supply will increase, reinforcing the rightward shift. The economy will move from point $A$ to a point such as $B$. The inflationary gap will now lead to upward pressure on money wages. As wages rise, the rise is partly passed on in higher prices, and the $SRAS$ curve shifts leftward from $SRAS_0$ to $SRAS_1$. At the equilibrium, point $C$, the economy has returned to the initial level of potential GDP, $Y*$, but at a higher price level.

A negative demand shock shifts the $AD$ curve from $AD_0$ to $AD_2$, and the economy moves from point $A$ to a point such as $D$. The recessionary gap eventually leads to wage cuts, and, as these are passed on into prices, output recovers and the economy moves to a point such as $E$ with price level $P_2$.

the economy is booming. Also, unemployment will be falling and excess demand for certain types of labour will develop. Soon workers will demand, and employers will concede, increases in money wage rates. Once money wages start to rise, the $SRAS$ curve starts to shift upwards to the left, the wage rises are partly passed on in the form of higher prices, and output starts to fall. The economy moves from $B$ to $C$ in the figure.

Once the economy has returned to point $C$ it is back in equilibrium, with GDP returned to its potential level but at a higher price level. This price level will be higher in the case where interest rates are pegged than it would be if the money stock were fixed, because the authorities have permitted an increase in the money stock to prevent interest rates from rising.

### Negative demand shock

Suppose instead that there was an autonomous fall in investment, starting from the same initial position as above. This is shown in Figure 21.6 as a leftward shift in the $AD$ curve from $AD_0$ to $AD_2$. The economy now moves into recession as GDP falls along the path from $A$ to $D$. As GDP falls, the transactions demand for money will also fall, and with a fixed money stock this would lead to a fall in interest rates. However, if the monetary authorities are pegging interest rates, they will reduce the money supply in order to stop interest rates falling. This imparts two steps to the leftward shift in $AD$ (as above but in reverse).

The major difference in this case, apart from the direction of change, is that, because the $SRAS$ curve is flatter to the left of $Y*$ than to the right, more of the initial adjustment falls on GDP and less on the price level. Indeed, if prices and money wages are slow to adjust downwards (as is often claimed), in the absence of a policy response, the economy may get stuck for some time in the neighbourhood of point $D$. Only as higher unemployment leads to *falling* money wages, and these falls then get passed on into lower prices (so that the $SRAS$ curve shifts down to $SRAS_2$ along the path $D$ to $E$), will the economy return to its potential level of output at a point like $E$.

The ultimate fall in the price level from point $A$ to point $E$ (assuming the economy returns smoothly to this point) will be greater in the case where interest rates are held constant than in the case where the money stock is fixed. This is because in the former case the money stock has been allowed to fall relative to its initial level. What then could policy-makers have done to moderate these responses to demand shocks?

### Policy responses

In order to understand the problem faced by policy-makers, we have to be clear that the economy is being hit more or less continuously by various shocks of differing strength. Also, the economy is continuing to respond in complex ways to past shocks. However, in order to get some insights into the nature of the policy problem, we study single discrete shocks, even though we know that in reality the authorities have to cope with a continually changing situation.

Let us consider first what could be done to offset the effects of a positive demand shock. Again we refer to Figure 21.6. If the authorities had known that investment was about to rise and could have implemented a policy change that had immediate effect (a very big IF), they could have acted to shift the $AD$ curve straight back down again so that it never shifted from $AD_0$ and the economy stayed put at point $A$. The monetary authorities could do this by raising interest rates, and the fiscal authorities could do this by increasing taxes or cutting government spending.

Even here there would still be a slight difference depending upon whether it was the monetary or fiscal authorities that acted. With higher interest rates, the reversal of the *AD* shift would be achieved by lowering investment (or other interest-sensitive spending) relative to the level it would otherwise have achieved. Higher taxes shift *AD* down to the left via a fall in personal consumption, while lower government spending obviously leads to a fall in *G*.

Thus, although monetary and fiscal policies have identical effects on the price level and aggregate GDP, they have different effects on the composition of GDP.

We will learn in Chapter 23 that changes in net exports are also part of this story, once exchange rate adjustments are incorporated.

Of course, it is not realistic to think that policy-makers can react at the same time as shocks occur, or that they can implement policy changes immediately. We discussed the problems created by information lags and policy lags for fiscal policy in Chapter 19. These problems also apply to monetary policy. Indeed, Milton Friedman said many years ago that the impact of monetary policy was subject to 'long and variable lags'. Box 21.4 explains the *Taylor rule*, which explains the policy changes made by monetary authorities as a reaction to deviation of inflation from target and of GDP from its potential.

If the monetary authorities respond in a timely way to the positive demand shock, they may be able to improve the outcome. This could be accomplished by helping the economy return from point *B* to point *A*, or at least some point between *A* and *C*, thereby reducing the inflation that results from the positive demand shock. However, the danger of mistimed policy interventions is a serious one. Suppose, for example, the impact of a monetary tightening starts to bite only when the economy is arriving at point *C*. This tightening will force the economy to the left of point *C* and will cause a recession that would not otherwise have occurred. The same error could obviously arise from badly timed fiscal policy, and this is the main case against attempts to use active monetary or fiscal fine-tuning of the economy.

The case for an active policy response may be much stronger in the event of a negative demand shock. This is because, as we saw in previous chapters, there is good reason to believe that the automatic adjustment processes are much slower working in a downward than an upward direction—because of the asymmetry in the aggregate supply curve and the (possible) fact that money wages are slower to adjust down than up. If this is true, with the economy stuck for some time around point *D* in Figure 21.6, a lowering of interest rates would help shift production back towards point *A*, as would a cut in taxes or an increase in government spending. Again, there would be differences in the composition of GDP but not in the level (in equilibrium).

---

 **Box 21.4  Monetary policy reactions and the Taylor rule**

Professor John B. Taylor of Stanford University noticed that the interest rates set by the US Federal Reserve could be explained in terms of a fairly simple rule. The authorities raise interest rates when inflation is above target and when actual GDP is above potential, and vice versa. This rule can be expressed in the following equation:

$$i_t = 2 + \pi_t + g_\pi(\pi_t - \pi^*) + g_x(Y_t - Y^*)$$

where $i_t$ is the official interest rate that monetary policy-makers set, $\pi_t$ is the latest annual inflation rate, $\pi^*$ is the target inflation rate, $Y_t$ is actual GDP, $Y^*$ is potential GDP, and $g_\pi$ and $g_x$ are weights attached to the inflation target and GDP gap, respectively.* The constant (2) in the equation is the long-run average real interest rate.

Policy-makers do not admit to operating any simple policy; as they say, 'we look at everything'. However, it is very plausible that

we should find some policy reaction of this sort. The UK Monetary Policy Committee, for example, is charged with targeting a specific inflation rate, so it should be expected that they will raise interest rates if actual inflation is above target. The reaction to the GDP gap can be interpreted in two ways. Either the authorities also care directly about keeping GDP close to potential, or the GDP gap is an important predictor of future inflationary pressure, so that by responding to the current GDP gap they are in effect reacting to control future inflation.

The behaviour summarized in the Taylor rule is consistent with our explanation of monetary policy in the text, but the actual process of making policy decisions is rather more complex than this simple rule suggests.

* Latest evidence on the Taylor rule and its application to many countries can be found on John Taylor's website: www.stanford.edu/~johntayl/

## Aggregate supply shocks

Let us now consider shocks to aggregate supply. For the purpose of this analysis, we will assume that the supply shock affects only the *SRAS* curve and does not affect $Y^*$, the level of potential output. In many cases supply shocks will also have long-run effects so that $Y^*$ changes—a productivity shock, for example, will increase aggregate supply in both the short and the long run. Where there are long-run effects, there is no potential for monetary and fiscal policies to influence the long-run outcome, as these policy tools only influence aggregate demand. It is for this reason that nothing is lost if we assume that the position of the *LRAS* curve is unchanged. This is equivalent to assuming that the position of *LRAS* is invariant to monetary and fiscal policy; but bear in mind that this assumption will not generally be true.[12]

### Positive supply shock

Figure 21.7 illustrates the effect of a positive supply shock. Starting at the initial point *A* at $Y^*$ and on $SRAS_0$, the supply shock, such as a fall in world raw material prices, shifts the *SRAS* curve down to the right. The economy will experience a rise in GDP and falling prices as it starts to move from *A* to *E*. These would be not unwelcome events, but a move to point *E* would not be the end of the story.

First, as the price level falls below $P_0$ the real money supply starts to rise (for a given nominal money stock), and this in turn leads to lower interest rates. It is this fall in interest rates causing an increase in investment that tends to increase real GDP. However, if the monetary authorities were pegging interest rates they would tend to reduce the money stock rather than let interest rates fall, and this would make the economy follow a path closer to $A \rightarrow D$ rather than $A \rightarrow E$.

Second, to the extent that the economy did move to the right of $Y^*$, this would set up inflationary pressure which would tend to make prices rise again until *SRAS* had shifted back up to its initial position at point *A*. Thus, with a fixed money stock, the economy would tend to move from *A* to *E* and back again to *A*, while with a fixed interest rate it would tend to move from *A* to *D* and then stop. (Here the assumption of unchanged $Y^*$ is important, as it is quite likely that the ultimate effect of a positive supply shock would be a new level of potential output to the right of $Y^*$.)

**Figure 21.7  Supply shocks**

**A positive supply shock increases output and lowers prices temporarily, while a negative supply shock lowers output and raises prices temporarily.** The economy starts at point *A* as in Figure 21.6. A positive supply shock shifts the *SRAS* curve from $SRAS_0$ to $SRAS_2$. This stimulates output and lowers the price level as the economy moves from *A* to *E*. However, if the monetary authorities peg the interest rate, they will resist the interest rate fall necessary to increase investment and instead will reduce the money supply, taking the economy from *A* to *D*. With a fixed money stock, the move from *A* to *E* will eventually be reversed as the inflationary gap leads to money wage rises and $SRAS_2$ shifts back to its original position.

A negative supply shock shifts the *SRAS* curve from $SRAS_0$ to $SRAS_1$. This raises prices and lowers output as the economy moves from *A* to *B*. With a fixed money stock the recessionary gap will eventually lead to lower wages and prices, *SRAS* will shift back to $SRAS_0$, and the economy will return to point *A*. However, with pegged interest rates the money stock will increase (as the authorities accommodate the supply shock) and the economy will move from *A* to *C*.

### Negative supply shock

Suppose that we start from the same initial equilibrium at point *A* and that there is now a rise in raw material prices, such as a rise in the price of oil. Here the short-run aggregate supply curve shifts upward to the left from $SRAS_0$ to $SRAS_1$. With the given initial aggregate demand curve $AD_0$, the economy will tend to move from point *A* to point *B*. This situation is characterized by both a rising price level and falling output—known (when it occurred in the 1970s) as *stagflation*. In practice, the move from *A* to *B* along a given *AD* curve will occur only if the money stock is held constant. Then the logic would be that the rising price level reduces the real money supply, forcing up interest rates, and hence leading to lower investment, which

---

[12] Indeed, some economists have proposed distinguishing supply shocks from demand shocks by the condition that demand shocks have no long-run effects on output while supply shocks do.

in turn would lower GDP. However, if the monetary authorities peg the interest rate, they will resist the rise in interest rates by increasing the money supply, and this will shift the $AD$ curve to the right, causing the economy to move along a path more like $A \rightarrow C$ than $A \rightarrow B$.

The contrast between the effects of supply shocks and demand shocks is worth emphasizing. The outcomes also differ depending on whether the monetary authorities are setting interest rates or fixing the money supply.

A monetary policy that holds the interest rate constant (until it is deliberately changed by policy-makers) stabilizes the effects of supply shocks on real GDP but amplifies the effects of demand shocks.

Notice that this applies to the automatic effects of the policy and *not* to discretionary policy changes, which could have quite different effects.

### Policy responses

The optimal policy response to supply shocks is far from clear, especially since mistiming is possible. With a fixed interest rate there will automatically be a stabilizing change in the money supply, although if policy-makers were fixing the money stock (which they are not in any major countries) there might be a role for temporary counter-cyclical monetary or fiscal changes to aid the return to equilibrium; however, these would have to be reversed rapidly as the economy returned to equilibrium. Otherwise policy action could lead to deviations from $Y^*$ that could have been avoided. That is, policy intended to return the economy to equilibrium could end up leading it to overshoot in the opposite direction. Indeed, the possibility that policy-makers might do more harm than good is much debated.

As we have discussed above, getting macro policy right is a difficult task in a complex world. Often, for example, the authorities do not know what shocks are hitting the economy until some time after the event, and even then they are uncertain about the quantitative significance of specific shocks. Stabilization policy is therefore an imperfect art, and the correct role of policy has been (and continues to be) a source of great controversy.

The appendix to this chapter outlines an alternative way of deriving the aggregate demand curve known as the *IS/LM* model. This can be skipped on first reading as the material in it will be needed only to follow the contents of Chapter 23—other chapters can be understood without it. We conclude this chapter with a discussion of how monetary policy is implemented in practice in the UK and the euro zone.

# Implementation of monetary policy

How is monetary policy implemented by the Bank of England in the United Kingdom, and by the European Central Bank (ECB) for the 12 members of the euro zone? In both cases the main objective of monetary policy is to maintain price stability, i.e. to control inflation, and in both cases this is done by setting a specific short-term interest rate which then influences other local-currency interest rates. The same is also true generally of other central banks in the major industrial countries. The institutional details vary from place to place. They are also likely to change over time. Indeed, the arrangements we describe were introduced in the UK only in 1997 and by the ECB in January 1999.

## The Bank of England

The Bank of England started life as a privately owned joint-stock company, but in 1946 it was nationalized. From 1946 to 1997 the Bank had a key role in implementing monetary policy, but the decisions about policy were all taken by the elected government of the day, in the person of the Chancellor of the Exchequer. However, in May 1997 the incoming Labour government decided to delegate the power to set interest rates to the Bank of England with effect from June 1997, and the new arrangements were embodied in the Bank of England Act of 1998. This formally established the Monetary Policy Committee and the framework within which it operates. First, we outline the make-up and procedures of this committee; then we explain what it tries to achieve; and finally, we describe how its interest rate decisions are transmitted to the financial markets.

### The Monetary Policy Committee

The Monetary Policy Committee (MPC) is made up of nine members. Five of these are senior Bank of England officials and four are outsiders appointed by the Chancellor of the Exchequer. The governor of the Bank of England chairs the committee. The outside members are each appointed for a three-year period, while the term of the Bank insiders depends upon the length of their Bank contract.

The MPC meets formally to set interest rates once every month, with announcements coming at noon on the first Thursday after the first Monday of each month. Decisions are made by a simple majority vote, with the governor having a casting vote in the event of a tie. Prior to making this decision, the MPC has three days of meetings to evaluate the latest data on the state of the economy and to debate among themselves the appropriate course of action. A record of the debate is published two weeks later in the form of the minutes of the meeting.

Four times a year the Bank also publishes its *Inflation Report*, which gives an in-depth assessment of the state of the economy. This contains the Bank's forecast of inflation and GDP growth over the succeeding two-year period. Members of the MPC are also summoned from time to time by the Treasury Select Committee of the House of Commons (the elected Parliament) to answer questions about how and why they reached the decisions they did on monetary policy in the past.

### Policy goals

The government sets the target for inflation that the MPC is meant to achieve. The target originally set in 1997 was to keep inflation at 2.5 per cent using RPIX as the measure of inflation targeted, and this remained the goal. RPIX is constructed by removing mortgage interest payments from the standard RPI (see Chapter 15, pages 351–3). The logic of using this measure is that, if inflation were expected to rise and the MPC tightened monetary policy in order to control it, this rise in interest rates would itself raise RPI but not RPIX. However, since November 2003 the target has been specified in terms of the CPI index (see page 353) and the target rate at least until 2007 has been set at 2 per cent.

Because it is impossible to hit an inflation target exactly, the MPC has been given a band of plus or minus 1 per cent. If CPI inflation turns out at more than 3.0 per cent or less than 1.0 per cent, the MPC has to write an open letter to the Chancellor of the Exchequer explaining why this deviation has happened and setting out what it intends to do about it. This covers the possibility that there will be unavoidable external shocks affecting inflation—for example an oil price rise—such that the return to low inflation will have to be managed over some time. Up to December 2006 no open letter had been written, as the outcome for inflation had remained within the specified band.

**The MPC has been given *instrument independence* in that it can set the official interest rate at whatever level it thinks**

appropriate; but it does not have *goal independence* as the government sets the inflation target.

Choosing an interest rate to achieve an inflation target is not a simple matter. It requires a detailed quantitative understanding of the transmission mechanism in the economy.[13] Because of time lags, the full effect of any policy change is spread over many months. This means that policy has to be forward-looking. In effect, policy-makers are targeting an inflation forecast rather than current inflation, because although there is nothing they can do about inflation already reported, they can take actions that will influence inflation in the future.

Figure 21.8 shows a 'fan chart' for inflation as published in the Bank of England *Inflation Report*. This shows the Bank's estimated probability distribution of future inflation over a three-year period looking forward. The Bank estimates this on the basis of previous forecasting errors. Each shaded band represents 10 per cent probability and the shaded area represents 90 per cent of the potential possibilities. Clearly, an important piece of information in the policy process is the mean of this probability distribution, which expresses the central forecast for the inflation rate. If the mean forecast inflation rate two years ahead is well above the target of 2.0 per cent, the MPC will be likely to raise interest rates in order to curb the expected inflation. If the mean forecast inflation rate is well below 2.0 per cent, it will be likely to bring interest rates down because inflation is expected to be well under control. If the mean forecast is very close to target, there is likely to be a fine balance between raising and lowering interest rates, with a strong likelihood of an unchanged policy.

**The monetary regime in the United Kingdom is one where interest rates are adjusted in order to hit an inflation target up to about two years forward. A key intermediate target is the inflation forecast, which indicates whether monetary policy needs to be tightened or loosened.**

### Implementation

Suppose that the MPC has decided to change interest rates. How does it act in order to make this change stick? In practice it announces the new rate to the media and it appears on Reuters and Bloomberg screens around the City at noon on the announcement day. Banks then change

---

[13] For the MPC's own explanation of this see: http://www.bankofengland.co.uk/publications/other/monetary/montrans.pdf

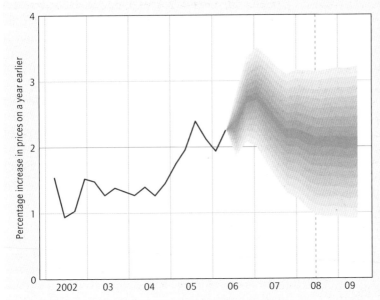

**Figure 21.8 Bank of England CPI inflation forecast\***

The Bank of England forecasts the probability distribution of inflation for three years ahead, but aims to target inflation at the two-year horizon. Each level of shading represents 10 per cent of the probability distribution. There are nine bands, so the bank is 90 per cent sure that inflation will lie somewhere in the shaded area. The mean of the forecast is in the dark area at the centre of the distribution. The target inflation rate is 2.0 per cent.

\* Projections based on market interest rate expectations.

*Source*: Bank of England, *The Inflation Report*, August 2006.

their base rates[14] more or less immediately. Why do money markets have to adjust their interest rates in this way?

The reason is that they know that the Bank of England has changed the interest rate at which it will lend high-powered money (M0) to the banks. And they also know that *the Bank of England can force them to borrow from it on a regular basis*. Banks will not wish to lend to their customers at a rate lower than they themselves might have to borrow. So the general level of money market rates is set by the rate at which the central bank will provide base money (cash plus bankers' deposits at the Bank of England in the UK case) to the participants in the money markets.

The Bank of England can force other banks to borrow from it because it is the monopoly supplier of high-powered money, and it can conduct security sales (open-market operations) to ensure that the banks are short of cash. Thus, suppose the Bank wishes to raise its official interest rate. It announces that this is the rate at which it will lend to the private banks, and the banks know that they may be forced to borrow from the Bank at this new rate. Very quickly, the banks raise the rates at which they will lend to their customers (and borrow and lend between each other, the inter-bank rate). Any subsequent borrowings by

the banks from the Bank of England are then at the new higher interest rate. So the Bank of England official interest rate has been passed on into other money market rates.

The standard instrument through which the Bank of England lends money to the banks is known as a **repo**. 'Repo' is short for 'sale and repurchase agreement'. It sounds complicated, but it is actually very simple. The basic problem is that the Bank of England needs to be able to lend high-powered money to private banks, but it does not want to take on any credit risk—it does not want the risk that some counterparty (some institution to which it has lent money) may go bust and not be able to repay. Accordingly, it makes only secured loans. 'Secured' means that the borrower gives up the claim to some asset as security for the loan. (A mortgage on a house is a secured loan—if you do not repay the loan, the lender can take your house.) A repo is a loan secured upon a government security.

A repo has two parts. Suppose the Bank of England does a repo transaction with NatWest for £100 million. NatWest needs cash but it starts with some government securities (gilts) on its balance sheet. It borrows money from the Bank, using the gilts as security. Step 1: it sells £100 million of gilts to the Bank of England in exchange for a credit in NatWest's account at the Bank. Step 2: it agrees to buy back the gilts on some future date. But it will not pay back £100 million: rather, it will pay back a bit more—the extra representing the interest rate for the loan over that period. This interest rate is known as the repo rate, *and this is the interest rate that the Bank of England sets*.

---

[14] The base rate is an interest rate set by each bank as a reference point for the loan rates charged to customers. For example, a large corporate client may be charged interest at the base rate plus 1 per cent, while a (more risky) smaller business may be charged base rate plus 4 per cent.

The two steps in the repo deal are both agreed at the outset, so the sale and repurchase are structured as part of a single contract. A *reverse repo* would involve a bank lending, rather than borrowing, in the same way. In practice, it is the two-week repo rate that is set by the Bank of England.

Interest rate decisions of the MPC are implemented by the Bank of England fixing the interest rate at which it will do two-week repo deals. In effect, this is just the rate at which the Bank will lend high-powered money to private sector banks.

There is a connection between the setting of the official repo rate and the money supply. When the repo rate is high, banks will be reluctant to increase their lending (and so increase the money supply) because they do not want to risk having to borrow reserves from the Bank of England, and there will be a lower demand for loans from the banks when loan rates are higher. When the repro rate is low, banks will be more inclined to increase lending (and hence the money supply) because the penalty for having to borrow reserves from the Bank is low, and because demand for borrowing from the banks is high.

# The European Central Bank

The ECB runs monetary policy for the 13 EU countries that adopted the euro in place of their former currencies.[15] The ECB is at the centre of the European System of Central Banks (ESCB), which includes also the central banks of other EU member countries. For monetary policy purposes, only central banks of euro zone members have a say in ECB monetary policy. The ECB has an Executive Board of six members responsible for implementation of monetary policy decisions. The Governing Council of the ECB is responsible for taking monetary policy decisions, and it is made up of the Executive Board plus the governors of the member central banks (of the euro zone).

The Maastricht Treaty defined the primary objective of the ESCB to be 'to maintain price stability'. But 'without prejudice to the primary objective of price stability' the ESCB has to support the general economic policies of the European Union. In October 1998 the Governing Council of the ECB decided that 'price stability shall be defined as a year-on-year increase in the Harmonized Index of Consumer Prices (HICP) for the euro area of below 2 per cent', and that the goal would be to maintain price stability according to this criterion over the medium term. This goal has remained unchanged through to 2006 (at least).

In order to achieve its goal of price stability, the ECB announced in December 1998 a reference value for the growth rate of broad money of 4.5 per cent per annum. It also defined the monetary aggregate that it would monitor as M3 for the euro area as a whole. (See Box 20.2 on page 452 for the European harmonized definition of M3. Note that definitions may vary slightly for each member of the euro zone.) However, in addition to this explicit reference rate for monetary growth, 'a broadly based assessment of the outlook for price developments and the risks to price stability in the euro area will play a major role in the ECB's strategy'.

The ECB has both target and instrument independence but with a general objective to maintain price stability.

## Implementation

The general principles of how the ECB operates are very similar to those for the Bank of England, though the ECB currently operates through its member central banks (just as the US Federal Reserve Board operates mainly through the Federal Reserve Bank of New York). There are three main elements to the operating procedures.

### Open-market operations

These involve repo-style secured lending and borrowing operations *vis-à-vis* the money markets. This is the main day-to-day operating procedure, and it is the rate at which the ECB lends to the money markets (on secured terms) that determines the general level of short-term interest rates within the euro area. As with the Bank of England, repo operations are the key activity, and this is similar to the way that many other central banks already operate.

### Standing facilities

The ECB also offers a standing facility for participating banks to make deposits with, and take loans from, the ECB for overnight duration. The deposit and loan rates so specified in effect put upper and lower bands around the short-term interest rate that can rule in the market for overnight money, and are in themselves an adequate instrument for setting very-short-term market rates even without participation in the repo market. The lending facility must be secured on eligible assets (such as government securities). These facilities are open on a daily basis and provide and absorb overnight liquidity as well as providing a tool for signalling monetary policy stance.[16]

---

[15] The 12 original member countries are France, Germany, Italy, Spain, Portugal, Belgium, the Netherlands, Luxembourg, Austria, Finland, Greece, and the Republic of Ireland. Slovenia joined on 1 January 2007.

[16] The Bank of England announced plans to introduce similar standing facilities in May 2006, and it also announced plans to pay interest on bankers' deposits.

### Minimum reserves

The ECB has the power to set minimum reserves required from private banks within the system. In October 1998 the ECB announced that the required reserve would initially be 2 per cent of bank deposits. However, the ECB pays interest on these reserves at a level determined by its repo rate. A change in reserve requirements may be used from time to time to influence the money supply, as we explained in our discussion of the money multiplier earlier in this chapter, but this had not been used up to 2007.

It seems that the target of maintaining euro zone inflation at less than 2 per cent over the medium term is likely to endure for the foreseeable future. The reference rate for monetary growth currently used in 2006 was 4.5 per cent per annum. This will no doubt be adjusted from time to time, and the ECB will use other information about the state of the economy, including economic forecasts, in order to inform its decisions.[17]

The success of the new monetary arrangements in the United Kingdom and the euro zone will be judged by how well the respective monetary authorities do in controlling inflation, as well as by the price that has to be paid, if any, in terms of lost output and employment. Up to 2006 the verdict was very positive. UK inflation from 1997 to 2006 was consistently within the target range, and euro zone inflation had exceeded its target for a while but was very close to the 2 per cent ceiling in the 2002–6 period.

 # CASE STUDIES

## 1. The EU Stability and Growth Pact

In the section above we discussed the making of monetary policy in the euro area. The fact that a single interest rate for the whole euro area has replaced separate rates in each country has clearly put a constraint on the use of monetary policy as a stabilization tool in each individual country. Monetary policy has to be aimed at the behaviour of euro-area aggregates and has to ignore individual country differences. This has caused some problems in the early years of euro-area operation, as some countries like France and Germany were experiencing high unemployment and slow growth while others, such as Ireland, were enjoying fast growth and low unemployment. It might be thought that fiscal policy could compensate for this inflexibility associated with a 'one-size-fits-all' monetary policy, but fiscal policy was also constrained.

The Maastricht Treaty of 1992 required potential members of the euro area to get their budget deficits below 3 per cent of GDP in order to qualify for membership. Subsequently an agreement was reached, known as the Stability and Growth Pact, that extended the commitment to keep deficits below 3 per cent indefinitely.

Countries are allowed to breach the 3 per cent limit 'in exceptional and temporary circumstances'. A government deficit greater than 3 per cent of GDP is considered 'exceptional and temporary' if it results from an unusual event outside the control of the member state in question or from a severe economic downturn, provided also that, once the temporary cause has passed, EU Commission projections for the following year forecast the deficit to fall back to 3 per cent or less. A decline in GDP of 2 per cent or more in one year will, as a rule, be regarded as a severe downturn.

Countries that are identified as having excessive deficits are potentially subject to financial penalties, though they have a further year in which to remove the excess deficit after being warned. Sanctions have not so far been imposed on any country, but there is a possibility that fines may be imposed.

IMF staff have calculated that an average EU country that had a fiscal balance when its GDP was at its potential level would tend to reach a 3 per cent deficit with a GDP gap of around 5 per cent of GDP. (Recall that tax revenues fall as GDP falls and some government expenditures, like unemployment benefit, rise.) This means that automatic stabilizers could accommodate a fluctuation of up to 5 per cent of GDP around trend while meeting the limits of the Stability and Growth Pact, and this is well within the normal range of business cycle fluctuations.

Thus, so long as member states have a fiscal balance when the economy is at potential GDP—a situation referred to as one of *structural balance*—then budget deficits will be able to rise during recessions and fall during booms without breaching the 3 per cent limit. However, problems will be caused if member states change their fiscal stance, and it remains to be seen whether any member will really end up being fined or whether some political fudge will be resorted to. It would be ironic if the outcome were to increase political tensions when the aim of the single currency is to enhance the integration of EU member states.

It is tempting to conclude that the Stability and Growth Pact will leave member states with very severe restrictions on their fiscal freedom. However, the restrictions under this regime may

---

[17] The latest information about policy statements from the Bank of England can be found via the internet at www.bankofengland.co.uk, and at www.ecb.int for the ECB.

actually be less severe than in the recent past, when governments have been trying to eliminate high budget deficits in order to meet the Maastricht criteria. As an IMF assessment put it,

*In any event, concerns about the potentially constraining effects on countries' abilities to pursue countercyclical fiscal policies need to be put into the perspective of the constraints imposed by large deficits in most EU countries over much of the past twenty-five years. From this viewpoint, the increased discipline involved in adhering to the pact may well permit a greater stabilizing role for fiscal policy than has been possible in most of these countries in many years. At the same time, the achievement of a high degree of price stability, together with the focus of the European System of Central banks on conditions throughout the euro area (in contrast to the dominant influence of German economic conditions on monetary policy in countries participating in the exchange rate mechanism (ERM)), should allow monetary policy to play a greater stabilizing role than in the past for the euro area as a whole.*

(IMF 1997, page 59; © International Monetary Fund)

One reason why policy may be better in future than it has been in the past is that policy-makers have often made mistakes. It would be an error to compare regimes on the assumption that policy changes in the past have always been stabilizing. In practice, mistimed policy interventions have often made the business cycle worse. Hence the merging of monetary policy under the aegis of one authority and the restraints on budget deficits may improve the policy outcome simply by making it harder for governments to get it wrong. As US Nobel laureate Robert Solow once said, 'If you don't know what you're doing, don't do much of it!'

The following extract provides an outline of issues facing the Pact and changes introduced in 2005.

*Despite the clear consensus that emerged in the early 1990s over the need to formulate statistical rules to co-ordinate the multinational undertaking of EMU, the pact has been highly disputed since its inception, with critics and academics arguing especially fervently on the 'arbitrary' selection of the three per cent threshold.*

*The Stability and Growth Pact is emerging from a major crisis after the Commission took the Council to the European Court of Justice on procedural grounds after the [Council] failed to take further action against France and Germany for persistent breaches of the pact's rules.*

*EU finance ministers reached a hard won deal on reforms to the Stability and Growth Pact at an extraordinary meeting in advance of the EU summit of heads of state and government on 22 and 23 March 2005.*

*In essence, big countries such as France and Germany have won concessions making the pact more 'flexible' in various parts, adding up to a considerable relaxation of the rules. In return, countries such as Austria and Netherlands have won references to 'enhanced surveillance, peer support and peer pressure'.*

*The two thresholds—60 per cent for the debt and 3 per cent for the deficit—remain unchanged.*

*However, the following has changed:*

### Trigger for an excessive deficit procedure

*No excessive deficit procedure will be launched against a member state experiencing negative growth or a prolonged period of low growth. Previously the exception was for countries in a recession defined as 2 per cent negative growth, something which has been virtually unheard of among EU member states.*

### 'Relevant factors' letting a country off an EDP

*Member states recording a 'temporary' deficit or one close to the 3 per cent reference value will be able to refer to a series of 'relevant factors' to avoid an excessive deficit procedure. Factors will include potential growth, the economic cycle, structural reforms (pensions, social security), policies supporting R&D plus medium-term budgetary efforts (consolidating during good economic times, debt levels, public investment).*

*Rather than referring to an exhaustive list of 'relevant factors' as had been mooted at one stage, the deal sets out chapter headings. These will take the form of general principles whose application will be thrashed out between member states and EU institutions.*

*Leeway will be given where countries spend on efforts to 'foster international solidarity and to achieving European policy goals', notably the reunification of Europe if it has a detrimental effect on the growth and fiscal burden of a member state'.*

*The first part of this phrase will go some way to pleasing France, which failed to ensure that development aid and some military expenditure would be explicitly taken into account in its budgetary assessment. Germany will also be pleased as it wanted special treatment for what it regards as its high contribution to the EU budget and will no doubt try to justify this as part of efforts 'to achieve European policy goals'. Germany also appears to have got its way as regards the last part of the above text in that it is expected to cite the cost of German reunification.*

*The Council and Commission have recognised the importance of pension reforms in an ageing society by agreeing to give 'due consideration' to the implementation of these reforms in their budgetary assessments relating to the excessive deficit procedure. They note that carrying out such reforms leads to a short-term worsening of public deficits but a long-term improvement in the sustainability (public debt) of public finances.*

### Extension of deadlines in connection with excessive deficit procedures

*Countries will have two years (previously one) to correct an excessive deficit. This may be extended in cases of 'unexpected and adverse economic events with major unfavourable budgetary effects occurring during the procedure'. To benefit from these, countries must show proof that they have adopted the correction measures that were recommended to them.*

*Member states have committed to using unexpected fiscal receipts during periods of strong growth to reduce their deficits and debt.*

### Country-specific medium-term objectives

*Medium-term objectives will be tailored to individual member states based on their current debt ratio and potential growth. This will vary*

*from −1 per cent of GDP for low debt/high potential growth countries to balance or surplus for high debt/low growth countries.* (http://www.euractiv.com/Article?tcmuri=tcm:29-133199-16&type=LinksDossier)

## 2. Limits of monetary policy: Japan in the early 2000s

Japan was one of the most successful economies of the post-Second World War period. It experienced spectacular growth rates of real GDP in the 1950s and 1960s, which averaged nearly 10 per cent. This rapid growth moderated somewhat in the 1970s, but in the ten-year period 1979–88 Japan still had the highest average growth rate of all the major industrial countries at 3.8 per cent, compared with an average for the seven major industrial countries (the G7) of 2.9 per cent. Over the next ten years, 1989–98, however, Japanese economic growth at 2.4 per cent had fallen very close to the G7 average of 2.2 per cent. Then in 1998–2004 Japan had the *lowest* rate of economic growth of all the major economies and it exhibited a recessionary gap throughout this period, with GDP appearing to return to potential only in 2006 (see Figure 21.9).

The problems of the Japanese economy in the second half of the 1990s and early 2000s were to an important extent a product of the extreme success of the Japanese economy in the previous four decades. Rapid real growth became the norm, and expectations of continued rapid growth got built into market prices. In 1991 the Japanese stock market index peaked at around 38,000, but in August 1998 it stood at around 15,000 and by October 2002 it was around 8,500—less than a quarter of its peak value. This collapse of share prices was mirrored in property prices, which also fell dramatically in the second half of the 1990s and early 2000s.

Asset prices are an important influence on spending decisions. We discussed the importance of wealth effects on consumer spending in Chapter 16. As wealth rose in the 1980s, Japanese consumers felt very well off, and they increased their spending on both consumer goods and property. However, a collapse of wealth had the reverse effect, causing them to cut their spending and feel increasingly cautious about the future.

Asset prices are also very important in the spending decisions of companies and lending decisions by banks. Companies with high stock market values find it easier to raise more capital, and banks are happy to lend on the basis of high property values or share holdings. Banks in Japan also hold shares in companies directly, so a fall in share values affects the capital of the banks, and hence their ability to make further loans.

Thus, falling asset prices, falling spending, and a loss of confidence create a process that can spiral downwards for some time. Some elements of this downward spiral are evident in any recession. However, the situation was worse than a normal cyclical recession in Japan in the late 1990s because of the abnormally large falls in asset prices. This situation was labelled by American economist Irving Fisher (1867–1947) **debt deflation**.

The process of debt deflation will not go on for ever, but it may take the economy into a very deep recession before it is reversed. At some stage, however, goods and asset prices will fall to so low a level that they appear cheap. Consumers then start spending again, and firms want to invest. Once confidence returns, the interaction of the multiplier and the accelerator (see Box 21.3 on page 477) help to run any initial increase in spending into an upturn as the spiral starts moving in an upward direction.

Given the overall scenario of an economy exhibiting a large negative GDP gap, what could the Japanese authorities do to help improve the situation? The main policy tools at their disposal are the monetary and fiscal policy instruments that we have discussed extensively in our analysis of macroeconomics.

### Monetary policy

A standard monetary policy intervention involves the authorities' changing the interest rate at which they will lend to the money markets. In Japan this is the official discount rate. For an economy in recession, a monetary policy reaction intended to stimulate the economy would involve lowering the interest rate.

Figure 21.10 shows that the Japanese monetary authorities did indeed lower their interest rate steadily from 1991. This was

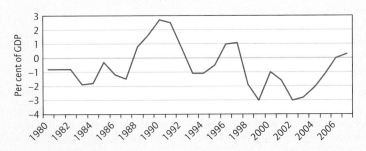

**Figure 21.9 GDP gap, Japan, 1980–2007**
*Source: IMF, World Economic Outlook.*

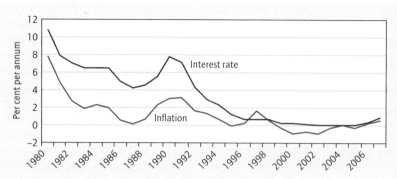

**Figure 21.10** Inflation and the interest rate, Japan, 1980–2007

*Source*: IMF *World Economic Outlook*, April 2006.

almost certainly an attempt to moderate the rise in the exchange rate, rather than to stimulate output directly, as at that time the Japanese economy was above potential GDP. However, in the late 1990s and early 2000s when the economy was running well below potential, but there was no room to lower interest rates further. At this stage the problem became a somewhat unusual one. *When interest rates have already been pushed down as low as they can go, what can the monetary authorities do then in order to stimulate aggregate demand?* The answer is: not much with monetary policy tools.

This problem was encountered during the recession of the early 1930s in the US and UK economies, and it was extensively discussed in debates associated with the Keynesian revolution. The problem was known as the **liquidity trap**. It arises when interest rates are so low that nothing else can be done to stimulate spending via even lower rates. If investors cannot be encouraged to invest when interest rates are close to zero, it is not clear what else the monetary authorities can do to increase aggregate demand.

Even if the government were simply to print more money and give it to people,[18] in a liquidity trap this does not necessarily increase spending, as people may simply save the money (owing to their lack of confidence in the future). Keynes described this powerlessness of monetary policy in a liquidity trap as trying to move an object by 'pushing on a string'.

In the postwar period most economists in the major economies had dismissed the liquidity trap as a phenomenon that was possible in theory but did not arise in practice. It *is* a rare occurrence, but it helps to explain the problems of Japan in the late 1990s and early 2000s.

Figure 21.10 also shows the inflation rate in Japan and provides a clear example of a situation where the recessionary gap of 1999–2005 is clearly associated with a period when the price level is falling.

### Fiscal policy

When monetary policy becomes powerless, fiscal policy is an alternative. Cuts in taxes and increases in spending by the government can create public demand where private demand is lacking.

In the 1980s Japanese fiscal policy was generally designed to reduce aggregate demand, but from 1992 to 1996 fiscal policy was stimulatory. In 1997 fiscal policy was tightened sharply, but by late 1997 it became clear that Japan was heading into a major slowdown. In April 1998 the Japanese government announced a package of fiscal stimuli in addition to some financial support for weak financial institutions. The net effect of the fiscal package was claimed to be a boost to demand by about 2–3 per cent of GDP, though some commentators thought that the effect would be less, and the net effect did little more than reverse the tightening of the previous year. In any event, the fiscal stimulus was insufficient to keep Japan from recession. The budget deficit rose to 8 per cent of GDP in 2002, but much of this was the product of lower tax revenues as output growth slowed. By 2002 government debt had reached 140 per cent of GDP, well above what is generally considered prudent. So there seemed to be limited scope for further fiscal stimulus.

The recovery of domestic and world demand that helped Japan recover in 2005 also helped bring down its budget deficit from over 8 per cent of GDP in 2003 to 5.8 per cent in 2005, but concerns remained that it would have to reduce its budget deficit much further if its government debt was to be stabilized at sustainable levels.

**The Japanese economy exhibited a severe recessionary gap in the late 1990s and early 2000s. Monetary policy actions were constrained by the fact that interest rates could go no lower, and the fiscal authorities were unable or unwilling to introduce a further major fiscal stimulus as they already had a large deficit and substantial debt.**

---

[18] In practice, the monetary authorities would not usually literally print money and spend it: rather, as we explained in Chapters 20 and 21, they would buy long-term government debt with high-powered money. This increases the liquidity of both the public and the banks with possible positive effects on spending.

# SUMMARY

## Money values and relative values

- Money prices do not matter if they all change at once along with all money incomes and assets. What matters for the real economy is relative prices.

- Money illusion arises when people are deceived by changes in all relevant money prices into thinking that something real has changed when it has not.

## The valuation of financial assets

- For simplicity we group all forms in which wealth is held into money, which is a medium of exchange, and bonds, which earn a higher interest return than money and can be turned into money by being sold at a price that is determined on the open market.

- The price of existing bonds varies negatively with the rate of interest. A rise in the interest rate lowers the prices of all outstanding bonds. The longer a bond's term to maturity, the greater the change in its price will be for a given change in the interest rate.

## The supply of money and the demand for money

- The value of money balances that the public wishes to hold is called the *demand for money*. It is a stock (not a flow), measured in the United Kingdom as so many billions of pounds.

- Money balances are held, despite the opportunity cost of bond interest forgone, because of transactions, precautionary, and speculative motives. They have the effect of making the demand for money vary positively with real GDP, the price level, and wealth, and negatively with the nominal rate of interest. The nominal demand for money varies proportionally with the price level.

- When there is an excess demand for money balances, people try to sell bonds. This pushes the price of bonds down and the interest rate up. When there is an excess supply of money balances, people try to buy bonds. This pushes the price of bonds up and the rate of interest down. Monetary equilibrium is established when people are willing to hold the existing stocks of money and bonds at the current rate of interest.

## Monetary forces and aggregate demand

- With given inflationary expectations, changes in the nominal interest rate translate into changes in the real interest rate. A change in the real interest rate causes desired investment to change along the investment demand function. This shifts the aggregate desired spending function and causes equilibrium GDP to change.

- A rise in interest rates (or a decrease in the supply of money) reduces aggregate demand; that is, it shifts *AD* to the left. A cut in interest rates (or an increase in the money supply) increases aggregate demand; that is, it shifts *AD* to the right.

- The negatively sloped aggregate demand curve indicates that the higher the price level, the lower the equilibrium GDP. The explanation lies in part with the effect of money on the adjustment mechanism: other things being equal (for a given money stock), the higher the price level, the higher the demand for money and the rate of interest, the lower the level of investment, and therefore the lower the aggregate spending function and the lower the level of GDP (for which injections equal leakages).

## Macroeconomic cycles and aggregate shocks

- A positive demand shock (starting at potential GDP) will trigger a temporary boom in output and lead to a permanent increase in the price level. The latter will be greater if interest rates are pegged than if the money stock is fixed.

- A negative demand shock will cause a recession, and the automatic adjustment mechanisms may be slow to return the economy to equilibrium.

- A positive supply shock will increase output and reduce the price level temporarily, but inflationary pressure will eventually return the economy close to its initial position (where there is no permanent impact on potential GDP).

- A negative supply shock is associated with rising prices and falling output—a situation known as stagflation.

- Monetary and fiscal policies can assist the return of the economy to equilibrium, but inappropriate policies can also make things worse.

- Monetary authorities' reactions are well described by the Taylor rule: interest rates are raised when inflation exceeds target and when GDP exceeds potential, and *vice versa*.

## Implementation of monetary policy

- Central banks are the ultimate suppliers of cash to the monetary system, and they have the power to set short-term interest rates in the money markets.

- The Bank of England uses the two-week repo rate as its policy instrument.

- The UK inflation target is set by the government, and the Monetary Policy Committee has been delegated the responsibility to keep inflation close to target.

## TOPICS FOR REVIEW

- Neutrality of money
- Money illusion
- Money as a veil
- Interest rates and bond prices
- Transactions, precautionary, and speculative motives for holding money
- Negative relationship between the quantity of money demanded and the interest rate

- Monetary equilibrium
- Transmission mechanism
- Investment demand function
- Demand and supply shocks
- Monetary and fiscal policy reactions
- The Taylor rule

## QUESTIONS

1 Suppose a bond is issued that is a perpetuity, which pays £5 per year and is issued for £100. What will this bond be worth if the current interest rate is (a) 2 per cent, (b) 10 per cent, and (c) 20 per cent?

2 At an interest rate of 5 per cent, what is the present value of £1000 in (a) one year's time, (b) 5 years' time, and (c) 10 years' time?

3 Starting from a given price level and with GDP at its potential, explain what happens to real GDP and the price level in the short term and long term in response to (a) a rise in the interest rate, (b) an increase in export demand, (c) a fall in government spending, and (d) a fall in income tax rates.

4 Explain how a change in monetary policy works its way through the economy to influence GDP and the price level in both the short and the long term.

5 Compare and contrast monetary and fiscal policies as tools for controlling output and inflation.

6 When the monetary authorities set interest rates, what role does the money stock play in monetary policy?

7 Why does the *AD* curve have a negative slope, and what factors determine this slope?

8 What factors cause the *AD* curve to shift?

## Appendix  An alternative derivation of the *AD* curve: *IS/LM*

We show here a slightly more detailed exposition of the monetary sector and its links with aggregate spending. This helps us derive the aggregate demand curve explicitly. There are no new economic relationships or even different assumptions involved.

This particular diagrammatic exposition was devised by the English Nobel Laureate Sir John Hicks (1904–89). It is so familiar to economists who have trained over the last half century that it is frequently quoted. If you have followed the macroeconomics chapters this far, you already know the economics behind the *IS/LM* model, but it is also helpful to know what specific bit of analysis '*IS/LM*' refers to. The diagrammatic apparatus has one important addi-

tional payoff. It shows the differences between the transmission mechanisms of monetary and fiscal policy. The only place where we use this apparatus again in this book is in Chapter 23.

For purposes of the present analysis, we assume that real wealth is constant and that there are no relative price changes between domestic and foreign goods—these were the factors that gave us a negatively sloped aggregate demand curve in Chapters 18 and 19. By eliminating them, we focus on the way in which money markets, acting through interest rates on spending, contribute to the negative slope of the *AD* curve.

## The *IS* curve

Figure 21.4(ii) on page 474 plots the negative relationship between interest rates and investment, called the investment demand function. We have also seen (in Figure 21.5 on page 476) that an increase in investment shifts the *AE* curve upwards and that this is associated with an increase in equilibrium GDP (a rightward shift of *AD*).

The *IS* curve shows the equilibrium[19] level of GDP that is associated with each possible interest rate. Recall that GDP is in equilibrium when desired expenditure equals actual output—or, what is the same thing, when injections equal withdrawals (and in the simplest possible closed-economy model, investment equals saving).

An *IS* curve is plotted in Figure 21A.1. It is negatively sloped because higher interest rates cause investment to fall, which shifts *AE* down and lowers equilibrium GDP. In contrast, lower interest rates cause investment to rise, which shifts *AE* up and raises equilibrium GDP.

In all cases, the *IS* curve shows the relationship between interest rates and the level of income at which desired expenditure flows are equal to actual output—or, what is the same thing, desired withdrawals are equal to desired injections. But because the flows of withdrawals and injections are different in a closed and an open economy, the relationship given by the *IS* curve can be stated somewhat differently for each. In a closed economy with no government, the *IS* curve shows the combinations of the interest rate and GDP for which saving and investment are equal. In an open economy with a government, the *IS* curve shows the combinations of the interest rate and GDP for which withdrawals in the form of saving, taxes, and imports $(S + T + IM)$ are equal to injections in the form of investment, government purchases, and exports $(I + G + X)$. In this case the *IS* curve is drawn for given values of government spending, exports, and autonomous consumption as well as the tax rate.

The *IS* curve is the locus of interest rates and levels of GDP that are consistent with equality between desired spending and output or, what is the same thing, injections equal leakages. It is drawn for given values of government spending, exports, and autonomous consumption as well as given tax rates and a given price level.

Now let us see what shifts the *IS* curve. In particular, we are interested in the effects of shifts in exogenous

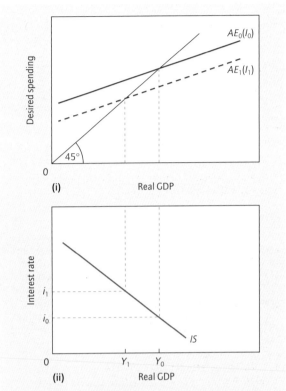

**Figure 21A.1 The *IS* curve**

The *IS* curve shows the equilibrium level of GDP associated with each given rate of interest. It shows combinations of the interest rate and GDP for which desired spending equal actual national output, and for which injections equal withdrawals. Part (i) shows a fall in *AE* resulting from a fall in investment from $I_0$ to $I_1$. This fall in *I* is caused by a rise in the interest rate from $i_0$ to $i_1$. The fall in investment produces a fall in GDP from $Y_0$ to $Y_1$.

Part (ii) shows the resulting combinations of the interest rate and real GDP. For given values of exogenous spending, $i_0$ leads to a level of GDP $Y_0$, and $i_1$ leads to level of GDP $Y_1$. Choosing any other level of the interest rate and following through its effect on GDP via investment produces another point on the *IS* curve.

---

[19] 'Equilibrium' in this section should be taken to mean the level of GDP that would be determined by aggregate spending if there were no supply constraints, that is, if there were no aggregate supply curve and GDP were entirely demand-determined at an exogenously given price level. This is the level of GDP at which injections and leakages are equal.

spending. An increase in exogenous spending shifts the *AE* curve up in Figure 21A.1(i), so it shifts the *IS* curve to the right. The size of the horizontal shift in the IS curve is the same when measured on the GDP axis as is the affect of the change in *AE* on GDP. This change (for a given interest rate and holding the price level constant) is simply equal to the increase in exogenous spending times the multiplier. This means that there is nothing new here, just a new way of representing what we knew already. A fall in exogenous spending shifts the *AE* curve down, so it shifts the *IS* curve to the left. These shifts in the *IS* curve are illustrated in Figure 21A.2.

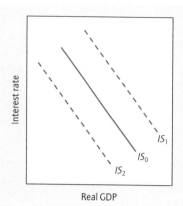

**Figure 21A.2 Shifts in the *IS* curve**

An increase in exogenous spending shifts the *IS* curve to the right, while a decrease shifts it to the left. The initial *IS* curve is $IS_0$. Suppose there is an autonomous increase in government consumption. The *IS* curve shifts right to $IS_1$. This means that for each level of the interest rate there is a higher level of GDP consistent with injections being equal to withdrawals. Increases in any other autonomous spending give the same shift. In contrast, if the change is a fall in autonomous spending the *IS* curve shifts left to $IS_2$.

## The *LM* curve

The *LM* curve shows the combination of GDP and interest rate that will produce equilibrium in the money market so that people are just willing to hold the stocks of money and bonds that are in existence. Initially we assume that there is a given money supply and that interest rates are free to vary. Later we show how this can be used to handle an interest rate that is set by the monetary authorities.

Figure 21.2 on page 471 illustrates equilibrium in the money market at the point where the money demand curve intersects the money supply curve. The money demand curve is plotted for given levels of real GDP, the price level, and wealth. We continue to assume that wealth and the price level are constant, but what happens in that figure when real GDP increases? The answer is shown in Figure 21A.3(i). As GDP increases, the transactions and precautionary demands for money both increase, and so the money demand curve shifts to the right. People will now try to sell bonds to get more money. But the stock of money is fixed so the price of bonds must fall, which means that the interest rate rises, until the quantity of money demanded returns to its original level. This requires that the quantity of money demanded for speculative purposes falls by just enough to offset the increase in the amount of money demanded for transactions purposes.

The *LM* curve is shown in Figure 21A.3(ii). This curve is drawn for given values of the price level, wealth, and the money supply. The curve is positively sloped because a rise in income must, for reasons outlined in the previous paragraph, lead to a rise in the interest rate if people are to be made willing to hold only the same amount of money in spite of needing more for transactions purposes.

The *LM* curve plots combinations of GDP and the interest rate, for a given money supply and given price level, that are consistent with the equality of money demand and money supply.

Now let us see how the curve shifts. As with any other curve, a change in any of the variables held constant along the curve causes the curve to shift. We focus here on the effect of a change in the money supply. An increase in the money supply shifts the *LM* curve to the right, while a decrease in the money supply shifts the *LM* curve to the left. To see this, shift the vertical money supply curve in part (i) of Figure 21A.3.

An increase in the money supply produces a lower equilibrium interest rate for each level of $Y$ (and therefore for each $M^D$ curve). This is shown as a shift of the *LM* curve from $LM_0$ to $LM_1$ in Figure 21A.3(ii). People try to buy bonds with their newly acquired money, but the stock is fixed so the price of bonds must rise, which means that the interest rate must fall until people are willing to hold the larger stock of money and the unchanged stock of bonds. A decrease in the money supply produces a higher equilibrium interest rate for each level of real GDP, as shown by a shift of the *LM* curve from $LM_0$ to $LM_2$.

## *IS/LM* and aggregate demand

The *IS* and *LM* curves each tell part of the story of the determination of aggregate demand. The *IS* curve determines GDP for given interest rates, while the *LM* curve determines the interest rate for given levels of GDP. In effect, they are two simultaneous equations in GDP and the interest rate. One (*IS*) represents the set of points for which desired spending equals national output (and injections equal leakages). The other (*LM*) represents the set of equilibrium points for which money demand equals money supply. Equilibrium for the whole economy (but still excluding the aggregate supply side) must be on both the *IS* and *LM* curves. This will be where they intersect, as is shown in Figure 21A.4.

In the past the *IS/LM* model was widely used to analyse the effects on GDP of either changes in monetary policy that altered the quantity of money (shifts in *LM*) or changes in fiscal policy (shifts in *IS*). However, this

**Figure 21A.3** The *LM* curve

The *LM* curve shows the combinations of real GDP and the interest rate that are consistent with the equality of money demand and supply for a given nominal money supply and given price level. Part (i) shows equilibrium in the money market with a given money supply and an $M^D$ function that is negatively sloped. At an initial level of GDP $Y_0$ the demand curve for money is given by $M_0^D$ and the equilibrium interest rate is $i_0$. At higher levels of GDP the $M^D$ curve shifts to the right (higher levels of GDP cause higher transactions demand for money). When GDP increases to $Y_1$, the money demand curve shifts to $M_1^D$ and the associated equilibrium interest rate rises to $i_1$.

In part (ii) the *LM* curve $LM_0$ plots out the equilibrium interest rate associated with each possible $Y$ and the given money stock $M^S$. This is a positively sloped curve. An increase in the nominal money supply shifts the *LM* curve parallel to the right, such as to $LM_1$, and a decrease in the nominal money supply shifts the *LM* curve to the left, such as to $LM_2$.

**Figure 21A.4** *IS/LM* and aggregate demand

The *AD* curve plots the *IS/LM* equilibrium level of GDP for each given price level (holding all exogenous spending and the nominal money supply constant). Part (i) has the initial position as the intersection of $LM_0$ (which is drawn with price level $P_0$) with the *IS* curve. This gives the overall equilibrium levels of real GDP and the interest rate as $Y_0$ and $i_0$. At higher price levels the *LM* curve shifts to the left (because the real money supply falls). At price level $P_1$ the *LM* curve is given by $LM_1$, and this leads to equilibrium GDP and interest rate of $Y_1$ and $i_1$. Part (ii) plots the resulting combinations of the price level and GDP. This is the aggregate demand curve, *AD*.

framework has the limitation that it can only be used either if the price level is fixed and output is variable, or if output is fixed and the price level is variable. When output and prices are simultaneously variable, we need to use the *AS/AD* model.

There is nothing wrong with the *IS/LM* model. It is just incomplete. Indeed, it can be used to derive the *AD* curve (thereby illustrating that the *IS/LM* model is consistent with our approach to *AD*). The *AD* curve implied by our *IS/LM* model is derived in Figure 21A.4(ii).

To derive *AD*, we take a given *IS* and *LM* curve and ask what happens to the level of GDP (determined by their intersection) as the price level rises. The answer is that a higher price level shifts the *LM* curve to the left (as it reduces the real money supply for a given nominal money supply, and given all exogenous spending) and leads to a lower level of equilibrium GDP.

The reason why an increase in the price level shifts the *LM* curve to the left is that the given money supply is *nominal* but money is demanded in relation to its *real* purchasing power. This means that as the price level rises there is an increase in the nominal quantity of money demanded to finance a given volume of real transactions. This in turn leads to an upward shift in the $M^D$ curves in Figure 21A.3(i) and so to a higher equilibrium interest rate for each level of real GDP. And this shifts the *LM* curve (upwards) to the left. An alternative way of making the same point (that a higher price level shifts the *LM* curve to the left) is to draw Figure 21A.3(i) with the *real* money stock on the horizontal axis. Then an increase in the price level simply reduces the real money supply and shifts the money supply curve to the left. These two different ways of expressing the point are equivalent and lead to the same impact of price level changes on the *LM* curve.

By taking different values of the price level, we plot out the aggregate demand curve. Notice that the *AD* curve is drawn for given levels of the money supply and exogenous spending, but *not* for given levels of endogenous variables like the interest rate, consumption, investment, net exports, and GDP.

This derivation also helps us to understand the determinants of the slope of the *AD* curve. Since it is determined by the intersection of the *IS* and *LM* curves, its slope depends upon the slopes of both. These in turn depend on four factors: the interest and income elasticities of demand for money, the interest elasticity of investment, and the size of the multiplier.

This reinforces our earlier argument that the reason for the slope of the *AD* curve is not logically the same as that for the slope of any micro demand curve. The logic here is more tortuous—a higher price level lowers real money supply; this raises equilibrium interest rates; this lowers investment; this lowers GDP via the multiplier. In addition, there is the wealth effect and the effect of relative prices (domestic and foreign) on net exports, which we explained in Chapter 17.

We now show that an increase in the money supply will shift the *AD* curve to the right while a decrease in the money supply will shift the *AD* curve to the left. This is shown in Figure 21A.5 simply by shifting the *LM* curve. With a given *IS* curve, each level of the money supply will be associated with a different equilibrium level of GDP for any given price level. A reduction in the money supply is represented by a leftward shift of the *LM* curve, and this leads to a leftward shift of the *AD* curve. Hence an exogenous fall in the nominal money supply shifts the *AD* curve to the left. An exogenous increase in the nominal money supply shifts the *AD* curve to the right.

(i) *IS/LM*

(ii) *AD*

**Figure 21A.5  Shifts in the *AD* curve**

A change in the money supply leads to a shift in the *AD* curve. The curves are drawn with an initial money stock $M_0$, leading to *LM* curve $LM_0$ and *AD* curve $AD_0$. An increase in the money stock to $M_1$ shifts the *LM* curve right to $LM_1$ and with a given *IS* curve produces the *AD* curve $AD_1$. Thus, a higher GDP is associated with each level of *P*. The reverse happens for a fall in the money stock—*LM* and *AD* shift left.

So far we have assumed when using the LM curve that the monetary authorities control the amount of money, leaving interest rate to be determined in the market. Now let us allow for the fact that they usually fix the interest rate and let the amount of money be determined by the demand for it. When the central bank lowers interest rates it needs to permit the money stock to increase, since more money will be demanded the lower is the interest rate. When it raises interest rates it needs to lower the money stock, which it does by selling bonds and accepting high-powered money in return. Thus, changes of monetary policy can be interpreted as shifts of the *LM* curve irrespective of whether the authorities are fixing the interest rate or the money supply. Hence once we are in the *IS/LM* framework, we have an analytical tool that is equally suitable for either policy environment. The reason this is true is that the *LM* curve represents equilibrium states in the money market. It does not matter whether that equilibrium is achieved by the interest rate adjusting to the money stock or the money stock adjusting to the interest rate—the outcome is the same. A relaxation of monetary policy involves the *LM* curve shifting to the right, while a tightening of monetary policy involves the *LM* curve shifting to the left.

We now look more closely at how we can use our macro model to understand the role of monetary and fiscal policies in stabilizing activity.

## Monetary policy and aggregate demand

We have already explained in Chapter 21 that the aggregate demand curve is drawn for a given money stock. However, since most monetary authorities set the interest rate rather than the money supply, we need to understand how monetary policy changes work in our model.

We saw in Figure 21A.4 on page 493 how the *AD* curve can be derived from the intersection of the *IS* and *LM* curves as we vary the price level. And we also saw in Figure 21A.5 that a change in the money stock shifts the *AD* curve. We now want to make the connection between shifts of the *AD* curve and changes in monetary policy, that is, changes in the interest rate. This is shown in Figure 21A.6.

The initial position is shown in part (i) by the intersection of *IS* and $LM_0$ and in part (ii) by the aggregate demand curve $AD_0$. Suppose now that the monetary authorities decide to relax monetary policy by lowering interest rates. To do this they buy bonds. This raises the price of bonds and, what is the same thing, lowers the rate of interest. Their purchases provide the extra money supply that will be demanded at the lower interest rate. In providing this money, they shift the *LM* curve to the right. At each price level this gives us a point on the new *AD* curve, which has shifted to the right. Notice that the size of the horizontal shift in *AD* depends not only on the size of the shift in *LM* (necessary to equate demand and supply of money at the new lower interest rate) but also on the slope of the *IS* curve. The slope of the *IS* curve is important, because it is determined by the amount of the increase in investment in response to a fall in the interest rate and by the multiplier. And it is the change in investment times the multiplier that determines how much real GDP increases. (This will not be the actual increase in GDP as we do not have the aggregate supply curves in this figure.)

A monetary policy loosening that involves a policy-induced lowering of interest rates shifts the *AD* curve to the right. A

**Figure 21A.6  Interest rate changes and aggregate demand**

**A policy-induced fall in the interest rate shifts the *AD* curve to the right.** In part (i), from an initial position with interest rate $i_0$ at the intersection of *IS* and $LM_0$, which is associated with aggregate demand curve $AD_0$ in part (ii), a fall in the interest rate to $i_1$ requires an increase in the money stock, which shifts the *LM* curve rightward to $LM_1$. In part (ii) this implies that the *AD* curve has shifted from $AD_0$ to $AD_1$ and at a price level such as $P_0$ there has been an increase in GDP from $Y_0$ to $Y_1$. A rise in interest rates would have the reverse effect, requiring a lowering of the money stock and a leftward shift of *AD*.

monetary policy tightening involves raising interest rates and shifts the *AD* curve to the left.

## Fiscal policy and aggregate demand

We have seen in Chapter 19 how fiscal policy can be used to shift the aggregate demand curve. However, now that we have added a monetary sector to our model, we can see more clearly how the size of that shift is determined. In particular, it turns out that the effects of a fiscal policy change depend in part on what the monetary authorities are doing.

**(i) IS/LM**

**(ii) AD**

**Figure 21A.7 Fiscal policy changes and aggregate demand**

**An expansionary fiscal policy shifts the AD curve to the right, but the shift is greater if the monetary authorities peg interest rates than if they fix the money stock.** The initial position is shown in part (i) by point $A$ and in part (ii) by point $D$, with a given price level of $P_0$ and initial values of the interest rate of $i_0$ and of GDP of $Y_0$. The introduction of an expansionary fiscal policy shifts the $IS$ curve to the right from $IS_0$ to $IS_1$. With a given money stock the $LM$ curve would stay put at $LM_0$ and the interest rate would rise to $i_1$, illustrated by point $B$. Accordingly, the new $AD$ curve would now pass through point $E$, reflecting an increase in GDP from $Y_0$ to $Y_1$.

However, if the monetary authorities act to prevent interest rates rising, they will permit an increase in the money supply, represented by a shift of the $LM$ curve to $LM_1$ where it intersects $IS_1$ at point $C$. The associated $AD$ curve passes through point $F$, so the new $AD$ curve is $AD_2$. At the given price level $P_0$ GDP has increased to $Y_2$. This shift in $AD$ is equal to the change in government spending that triggered it times the simple multiplier. A contractionary fiscal policy change would lead to a symmetrical leftward shift in $AD$.

The initial position is shown in Figure 21A.7(i) by the intersection of $IS_0$ and $LM_0$, and in part (ii) of the figure by the aggregate demand curve $AD_0$. An expansionary fiscal policy, for example an increase in government spending, shifts the $IS$ curve to the right in part (i). With a given $LM$ curve associated with a fixed money supply, interest rates will rise, and this rise in interest rates will *crowd out* some investment expenditure. The $AD$ curve will shift from $AD_0$ to $AD_1$ and GDP will increase from $Y_0$ to $Y_1$ for a price level such as $P_0$.

However, if the monetary authorities are pegging the interest rate at $i_0$, this will not be the outcome. Once the $IS$ curve starts to shift to the right, this will put upward pressure on interest rates (because the rise in spending increases GDP and this increases demand for money). To obtain the extra money, people sell bonds. The monetary authority purchases the bonds, thereby stabilizing the interest rate and supplying the extra money that people require. Accordingly, the $LM$ curve will also shift to the right and so the $AD$ curve will shift to $AD_2$, which involves a horizontal shift of $Y_0 - Y_2$. This is clearly a greater horizontal shift than would have been the case if the money stock had been unchanged.

Notice that, when the monetary authorities peg the interest rate, the effect of a given fiscal policy change on GDP is larger than when they fix the money supply. With a fixed money stock, a rise in the interest rate will offset some of the expansionary effect of the fiscal stimulus; but with a pegged interest rate this offsetting effect is eliminated. Of course, the monetary authorities could *choose* to raise interest rates in response to a fiscal policy relaxation, but this would be an independent policy choice rather than something that happens automatically within the economy. Notice also that the shift in $AD$ *when interest rates are held constant* is equal to the direct change in spending times the simple multiplier. In effect, the monetary sector is passive to the changes in fiscal policy, and the analysis we set out in Chapters 16–19 is adequate to understand the determinants of GDP. In reality, of course, although the monetary authorities are setting interest rates, they do not hold them constant for ever. Rather, they change them in an attempt to control inflation and (perhaps) to avoid large deviations of GDP from its potential level.

# Chapter 22

# THE BALANCE OF PAYMENTS AND EXCHANGE RATES

Is a balance of payments deficit a sign of economic failure? Why are floating exchange rates so volatile? These are two of the questions we address in this chapter.

In particular, you will learn that:

- Balance of payment accounts measure the net transactions between domestic residents and the rest of the world over a specific period.
- The current account balance is identically equal and opposite to the capital and financial account balance.
- There is nothing inherently 'good' or 'bad' about a current account deficit or surplus.
- In a floating exchange rate regime, the exchange rate is determined by the demand and supply of domestic currency.
- Exchange rates often overshoot the long-run equilibrium, and they can be volatile as they react to 'news'.

We now focus on the linkages between the economy and the rest of the world. We have mentioned some of these linkages before, but here they are the main concern. There are financial (or monetary) linkages, through the international money and capital markets, and there are 'real' linkages, through international trade and travel. The real and the monetary links are not independent of each other. Real transactions cannot take place without money and finance, and are influenced by monetary forces; equally, money markets are influenced by the fundamentals of the real economy.

Discussion of these issues will bring together much material from elsewhere in this book: the theory of supply and demand (Chapter 3), the nature of money (Chapter 20), international trade (yet to come in Chapter 27), and short-run macroeconomics (Chapters 16–21). Indeed, we have had the balance of payments (net exports of goods and services, $NX$) explicitly in our macroeconomic model since Chapter 16. We now need to look at these issues in much greater detail, to prepare the ground for our policy discussions in the next chapter.

In the first part of this chapter we discuss the balance of payments. This is an important concept, concerned with net transactions between one country and the rest of the world. We ask what the 'balance of payments' means, how it is measured, and why it matters. In the second part we discuss the exchange rate—what role it plays in connecting the domestic economy with foreign economies, and what economic forces determine its value.

## The balance of payments

The economy's balance of payments has had a high profile in political arguments over economic policy throughout the past century in countries such as the United Kingdom that had recurrent balance of payments problems. In the past decade or two, balance of payments issues have been most problematic for developing and transition economies, though in the mid-2000s there was considerable concern about the large current account deficit of the

United States and the large surplus of China. We will first explain how the balance of payments is recorded, using the United Kingdom as an example, and will then ask in what ways the balance of payments matters.

## Balance of payments accounts

In order to know what is happening to international payments, governments keep track of the transactions between countries. The record of such transactions is made in the *balance of payments accounts*. Each transaction, such as a shipment of exports or the arrival of imported goods, is classified according to the payments or receipts that would typically arise from it.

Transactions that lead to a receipt of payment from foreigners, such as a commodity export or the sale of an asset abroad, are recorded in the balance of payments accounts as a *credit*. In terms of our later objective of analysing the market for foreign exchange, these transactions represent the supply of foreign exchange and the demand for sterling on the foreign exchange market. This is because foreigners have to buy our currency in order to pay us in sterling for the goods or assets they have bought. Transactions that lead to a payment to foreigners, such as a commodity import or the purchase of a foreign asset, are recorded as a *debit*. These transactions represent the demand for foreign exchange and the supply of sterling on the foreign exchange market, because we have to buy foreign currency with sterling in order to pay for our overseas purchases.[1] In calculating the *balance*, credits are positive and debits are negative, so the overall balance is simply credits minus debits.

Balance of payments accounts are divided into two broad parts. One part deals with payments for goods and services, income, and transfers. This is known as the **current account**. The other part records transactions in assets and is, accordingly, known as the **capital and financial account**. A summary of the balance of payments accounts of the United Kingdom for 2005 is given in Table 22.1.[2]

### Current account

The current account records transactions arising from trade in goods and services, from income accruing to residents of one country from another, and from transfers by residents of one country to residents of another. The current account is divided into three main sections.

The first of these is the *goods and services* account. This has two parts. The component of this relating to 'goods' trade is often called the **visible account**, the **trade account**, or the **merchandise account**. It records payments and receipts arising from the import and export of tangible goods, such as computers, cars, wheat, and shoes. UK imports require payments to be made to foreign residents in foreign exchange, and hence are entered as debit items on the visible account. In 2005 UK residents spent just over £278 billion on goods imported from overseas. UK exports earn payments from foreign residents in foreign exchange (though the foreign exchange will be converted into sterling through the foreign exchange market), and hence are recorded as credit items. In 2005 UK exports amounted to about £211 billion. Exports represent goods leaving the country, and payment for those goods passes in the opposite direction. With imports, goods enter the country and payment has to be made to the foreign manufacturers. We can see that in 2005 there was a goods trade deficit of just over £67 billion, which is the difference between the value of exports and imports.

The second part of the goods and services account is services. Trade in services covers transactions that do not involve a physical commodity (or asset) changing hands, such as insurance, banking, shipping, and tourism.[3] Trade in services showed a surplus of just over £23 billion in 2005; however, this was smaller than the deficit in goods trade, so that trade in goods and services had a (negative) balance of just over –£44 billion.

The second element of the current account is the *income* account. This again has two components. The first is employee compensation. Credit items involve UK residents being paid for working for non-residents, while the debit items result from UK residents employing non-residents. The second component is investment income. Credit items involve interest and dividend income received by UK residents from assets overseas, while debits reflect similar payments to non-resident owners of assets in the UK. The income component of the current account showed a surplus of £29.9 billion in 2005.

The third element in the current account is *current transfers*. This is subdivided into central government and other transfers. An example of a central government transfer is payment of a UK old-age pension to a former

---

[1] In the euro zone, it is the payments for the euro zone as whole *vis à vis* the rest of the world that matters for the exchange market of the euro. In this chapter we assume that external payments or receipts generate demands or supplies of foreign exchange. However, for countries within a single-currency area or for regions of a single country, this would not be true.

[2] This format for balance of payments accounts was introduced in 1998, so earlier accounts may look different. This is now an international standard format, so balance of payments accounts for other countries have a similar structure.

[3] The symbols $X$ and $IM$ as used in this book refer to exports and imports of both tangible goods *and* services, but do not include payments of interest, dividends and profits, or transfers.

**Table 22.1** UK Balance of payments, 2005 (£ m)

|  | Credits | Debits | Balances |
|---|---|---|---|
| **1 Current account** | **525,648** | **552,198** | **−26,550** |
| A Goods and services |  |  |  |
| 1 Goods | 211,175 | 278,473 | −67,298 |
| 2 Services | 111,123 | 88,067 | 23,056 |
| B Income |  |  |  |
| 1 Compensation of employees | 1,211 | 1,137 | 74 |
| 2 Investment income | 185,826 | 156,029 | 29,797 |
| C Current transfers |  |  |  |
| 1 Central government | 4,071 | 13,499 | −9,428 |
| 2 Other sectors | 12,242 | 14,993 | −2,751 |
| **2 Capital and financial accounts** | **737,271** | **717,393** | **19,878** |
| A Capital account | **4,178** | **1,776** | **2,402** |
| 1 Capital transfers | 3,964 | 1,094 | 2,870 |
| 2 Acquisition/disposal of non-produced, non-financial assets | 214 | 682 | −468 |
| B Financial account | **733,093** | **715,617** | **17,476** |
| 1 Direct investment | 87,725 | 55,539 | 33,186 |
| 2 Portfolio investment | 127,021 | 160,710 | −33,689 |
| 3 Financial derivatives (net) |  | 2,451 | −2,451 |
| 4 Other investment | 518,347 | 495,261 | 23,086 |
| 5 Reserve assets |  | 656 | −656 |
| Total (1 + 2) |  |  | **−6,672** |
| Net errors and omissions |  |  | **+6,672** |

*Source*: ONS, *Balance of Payments Pink Book*, 2006.

UK resident now living in Spain. An Italian restaurant owner in London sending money to his mother in Milan is an example of an 'other' transfer. Current transfers contributed a deficit of around –£12 billion to the UK current account in 2005.

All components of the current account *other than trade in goods* are sometimes referred to as **invisibles** because you can see goods entering the country but you cannot see, for example, the services of a consultant crossing borders.

Overall the current account of the UK balance of payments showed a negative balance (or deficit) of around –£26 billion in 2005.

## Capital and financial accounts

The other major component in the balance of payments is the capital and financial accounts, which record transactions related to international movements of ownership of financial assets. It is important to notice right away that the 'capital' and financial accounts do not relate to imports and exports of physical capital: trade in such things as machine tools and construction equipment is part of the

*goods trade account*. Rather, the capital and financial accounts of the balance of payments relate only to cross-border movements in ownership of *assets*, a large part of which involves financial instruments such as ownership of company shares, bank loans, or government securities.

The capital and financial accounts used to be referred to just as the 'capital account', and we will continue this usage below. However, in the UK accounts shown in Table 22.1 the 'capital account' and 'financial account' are itemized separately. In the accounting conventions used today, the item labelled 'capital account' is a relatively insignificant one. It is made up of 'capital transfers' and 'acquisition/disposal of non-produced, non-financial assets'. Included in the former are items such as a government investment grant to build a hospital overseas, and debt forgiveness between the UK government and an overseas government. The latter includes overseas sales or purchases of patents, trademarks, or copyrights.

The second component of the capital and financial accounts is the financial account. This is made up of four elements: direct investment, portfolio investment, other investment, and reserve assets. **Direct investment** relates to changes in non-resident ownership of domestic firms and resident ownership of foreign firms. One form of direct investment, called 'greenfield investment', is the building of a factory in the United Kingdom by a foreign firm—for example the Toyota car factory near Derby. Another form of direct investment, called 'brownfield investment',[4] is a takeover in which a controlling interest in a firm previously controlled by residents is acquired by foreigners—such as when Ford acquired Jaguar from its domestic owners. **Portfolio investment**, on the other hand, is investment in bonds or a minority holding of shares that does not involve legal control. Direct and portfolio investment combined is sometimes referred to as the *long-term capital* element of the capital and financial accounts.

'Other investments' is made up mainly of what are called *short-term capital flows*. These include transfers into overseas banks, and sales or purchases of short-term financial instruments, such as Treasury bills or commercial bills. The large size of these other investment flows in the UK balance of payments accounts reflects in part the role of the City of London as an international financial centre. 'Reserve assets' reflects changes in the official foreign exchange reserves that are held by the Bank of England.

From now on we adopt the convention that the terms 'capital flows' and 'capital account' refer to all items in the 'capital and financial accounts' of the balance of payments. UK purchases of foreign investments (which then become assets to the UK) are called a *capital outflow*. They use foreign exchange in order to buy the foreign investment, and so they are entered as a debit item in the UK payments accounts.[5] Foreign investment in the United Kingdom (which thereby increases UK liabilities to foreigners) is called a *capital inflow*. It earns foreign exchange and so is entered as a credit (positive) item.

As shown in Table 22.1, in 2005 UK residents increased their investments abroad by just over £717 billion, while foreigners increased their investments in the United Kingdom by just over £737 billion. These may seem like very large amounts, and indeed they are. However, as already mentioned, a high proportion of this activity relates to the international borrowing and lending of the financial institutions in the City of London. The net capital inflow resulted in a surplus in the capital and financial accounts of about £20 billion. This means that there was a net decrease in foreign assets (or increase in borrowing from foreigners) of £20 billion.[6]

## The meaning of payments balances and imbalances

We have seen that the payments accounts show the total of receipts of foreign exchange (credit items) and payments of foreign exchange (debit items) on account of each category of payment. It is also common to calculate the *balance* on separate items or groups of items. Interest in 'the balance of payments' and its interpretation has a number of aspects, so we approach this issue in a series of steps.

### The balance of payments must balance overall

The notion that the balance of payments accounts must balance should present no great mystery. The accounts are constructed so that this has to be true. The idea behind this proposition is quite general. Take your own personal income and spending. Suppose you earn £100 by selling your services (labour) and you buy £90 worth of clothing. You have exports (of services/labour) worth £100, and imports (of clothing) worth £90. Your current account surplus is £10. However, that £10 surplus must be invested in holding a financial claim on someone else—if you hold cash, it is a claim on the Bank of England; if you deposit the money in a bank, it becomes a claim on the bank; and so on.

Whichever way you look at it, the £10 you have acquired is the acquisition of an asset. It represents a capital outflow from your personal economy that is the inevitable consequence of your current account surplus. So you have a current account surplus of £10 and a capital account deficit (outflow) of £10. The main difference between your accounts and those for the UK economy as a whole is that with the latter, payments across the foreign exchange markets are involved.[7] A country with a current

---

[4] The terms are used slightly differently in the context of, for example, house-building. Here 'greenfield' building means building on what used to be agricultural or park land, while 'brownfield' means building on land that had previously had an industrial or commercial use.

[5] Capital outflows are sometimes also referred to as *capital exports*. It may seem odd that, whereas a merchandise export is a credit item on current account, a capital export is a debit item on capital account. To understand this terminology, consider the export of UK funds for investment in a German bond. The capital transaction involves the purchase, and hence the *import*, of a German bond, and this has the same effect on the balance of payments as the purchase, and hence the import, of a German good. Both items involve payments to foreigners, and both use foreign exchange. Both are thus debit items in UK balance of payments accounts.

[6] Note that this figure relates only to transactions in assets. It does not account for capital gains or losses resulting from valuation changes of existing asset holdings. Thus, the capital and financial accounts balance is *not* a measure of the total change in indebtedness between the United Kingdom and the rest of the world.

[7] Areas that do not have their own currency still have a balance of payments. The member countries of the euro zone, for example, have balance of payments accounts even though they share a common currency. We could in principle also construct balance of payment accounts for Wales or Scotland.

**Box 22.1** Trade and modern mercantilism

Media commentators, political figures, and much of the general public often judge the national balance of payments as they would the accounts of a single firm. Just as a firm is supposed to show a profit, the nation is supposed to secure a balance of payments surplus on current account, with the benefits derived from international trade measured by the size of that surplus.

This view is related to the exploitation doctrine of international trade: one country's surplus is another country's deficit. Thus, one country's gain, judged by its surplus, must be another country's loss, judged by its deficit.

People who hold such views today are echoing an ancient economic doctrine called *mercantilism*. The mercantilists were a group of economists who preceded Adam Smith. They judged the success of trade by the size of the trade balance. In many cases this doctrine made sense in terms of their objective, which was to use international trade as a means of building up the political and military power of the state, rather than as a means of raising the living standards of its citizens. A balance of payments surplus allowed the nation (then and now) to acquire foreign exchange reserves. (In those days the reserves took the form of gold; today they are a mixture of gold and claims on the currencies of other countries.) These reserves could then be used to pay armies, to purchase weapons from abroad, and generally to finance colonial expansions.

People who advocate this view in modern times are called *neomercantilists*. In so far as their object is to increase the military power of the state, they are choosing means that could achieve their ends. In so far as they are drawing an analogy between what is a sensible objective for a business, interested in its own material welfare, and what is a sensible objective for a society, interested in the material welfare of its citizens, their views are erroneous, because their analogy is false.

If the object of economic activity is to promote the welfare and living standards of ordinary citizens, rather than the power of governments, then the mercantilist focus on the balance of trade makes no sense. The law of comparative advantage shows that average living standards are maximized by having individuals, regions, and countries specialize in the things that they can produce comparatively best and then trading to obtain the things that they can produce comparatively worst. The more specialization there is, the more trade occurs.

On this view, the gains from trade are to be judged by the volume of trade. A situation in which there is a *large volume* of trade but in which each country has a *zero balance* of trade can thus be regarded as quite satisfactory. Furthermore, a change in commercial policy that results in a balanced increase in trade between two countries will bring gain, because it allows for specialization according to comparative advantage, even though it causes no change in either country's trade balance.

To the business interested in private profit, and to the government interested in the power of the state, it is the *balance* of trade that matters. To the person interested in the welfare of ordinary citizens, it is the *volume* of trade that matters.

---

account surplus in its balance of payments must, at the same time, have acquired net claims on foreigners to the same value.

**The current and capital account balances are necessarily of equal and opposite size. When added together, they equal zero.**

There is one important caveat to the above statement with regard to actual official accounts. This is that, while conceptually the current and capital accounts are defined to be equal and opposite, in practice the national income statisticians are not able to keep totally accurate records of all transactions, and hence there are always errors in measurement. This means that a balancing item, called 'net errors and omissions', is included in the balance of payments table. The balancing item stands for all unrecorded transactions and is defined to be equal to the difference between the measured current account and the measured capital and financial account. So in practice, it is the sum of the current account, the capital and financial accounts, and net errors and omissions that is always zero by construction.

### Does the balance of payments matter?

The *balance of payments on current account* is the sum of the balances on the visible and invisible accounts. As a carry-over from a long-discredited eighteenth-century economic doctrine called *mercantilism*, a credit balance on current account (where receipts exceed payments) is often called a *favourable balance*, and a debit balance (where payments exceed receipts) is often called an *unfavourable balance*. Mercantilists, both ancient and modern, hold that the gains from trade arise only from having a favourable balance of trade. This misses the point of the doctrine of comparative advantage, first introduced in Box 1.4. This states that countries can gain from a *balanced increase* in trade because it allows each country to specialize according to its comparative advantage. The modern version of mercantilism is discussed in Box 22.1.

It would be tempting to refer to a deficit on capital account as an unfavourable balance as well. However, by now it should be clear that this would be nonsense, because a current account surplus is the same thing as a capital account deficit. Hence it is impossible for one to be

**Box 22.2  Balance of payments crises**

Many countries have experienced crises recently that have been linked to external payments problems. The Mexican crisis of 1994, the Asian crisis of 1997, the Russian crisis of 1998, and the Argentinean crisis of 2001/2 are but a few examples. We discuss the problems in the Argentinean and Asian crises in case studies in Chapter 23. Here we summarize some common features of these crises and discuss who bears the costs of the adjustments necessary to eliminate the problem.

We argued in the text that a current account deficit could be a healthy sign when it indicates that a country is borrowing from abroad to finance investment in real economic growth. But a current account deficit could be unhealthy if it involves borrowing to finance current consumption so that debts build up but there is no investment in real assets that can help repay the debt.

The most common reason for balance of payments crises is that potential investors in a specific economy revise their analysis of this economy's prospects and come to believe that its level of international borrowing is unsustainable. At this point capital inflows turn into outflows as foreigners try to get their money out and domestic residents too try to move their funds abroad. If the exchange rate is pegged by the domestic government (see the text page 507 for a discussion of how this is done), there will be a run on official foreign exchange reserves and this will put pressure on the domestic authorities to change their monetary and/or fiscal policies. If the currency is floating the exchange rate will fall sharply, and this will lead to a sharp increase in domestic inflation.

There could be many reasons for the change in assessment of an economy that triggers a crisis. It could be political instability or the introduction of profligate government spending plans. It could be a sharp fall in market price of the country's main export commodity. It could be a general rise in world interest rates that sharply increases the cost of servicing foreign debts.

Countries hit by such crises generally seek loans from the International Monetary Fund (IMF) that are intended to help provide finance while policies are put in place to correct the underlying problem. As a condition of the loan, the IMF usually requires a significant tightening of domestic monetary and fiscal policies—higher interest rates, cuts in spending, and higher taxes.

Two main groups suffer from the after-effects of the crisis. International banks and other investors who have lent to the country may find that the value of their investment has fallen sharply or in some cases that there is a debt default. The main sufferers however are typically domestic residents, who often suffer sharp falls in their income and wealth and may lose their jobs or their businesses. Critics of IMF policies have argued that the IMF loans and the conditions attached help to bail out international investors but do little to help the adjustment pains felt by domestic residents. This is controversial, but it seems unlikely that countries suffering such crises could be better off with no source of international financial support, even if it is conceded that the handling of such crises by the IMF could be improved.

---

'good' and the other 'bad'. However, this discussion does have one important implication.

The terms balance of payments *deficit* and balance of payments *surplus* must refer to the balance on some part of the payments accounts. In the United Kingdom these terms almost always apply to the current account.

A current account deficit is just as likely to be the product of a healthy growing economy as it is of an unhealthy economy. Suppose, for example, that an economy has rapidly growing domestic industries that offer a high rate of return on domestic investment. Such an economy would be attracting investment from the rest of the world, and as a result would have a capital account surplus (capital inflows) and a current account deficit. Far from being a sign of weakness, the current account deficit would indicate economic health. True, the economy is acquiring external debt; but if this debt is being used to finance rapid real growth, it can be repaid out of higher future output.[8]

In contrast, another economy may indeed have inefficient and unproductive domestic industry, and may be in a situation where domestic spending exceeds domestic output. (Recall from Chapter 15 that the balance of trade in goods and services is equal to the difference between total domestic spending and total domestic production.) Therefore, it will have a trade deficit and will be borrowing from abroad to finance the extra consumption.[9]

The existence of a current account balance of payments deficit tells us only that an economy's total spending exceeds its total income and that it has a capital inflow. The existence of such a deficit is consistent both with healthy, growing economies and with unhealthy, inefficient economies.

There are some times when balance of payments problems are associated with crises. The causes of these differ from place to place and time to time. Some of the issues that arise are discussed in Box 22.2.

---

[8] 'Debt' is used here in its general sense to refer to foreign liabilities rather than in the context of debt versus equity. These external debts could be in any specific form, including equity, bonds, or bank loans.

[9] It is assumed here that the balance of trade in goods and services and the current account balance are the same. The balance of trade is the difference between domestic spending and GDP, while the current account balance is the difference between domestic spending and GNI.

### Actual and desired transactions

The discussion in this section has focused on *actual* transactions as measured in the balance of payments accounts. It is the actual capital inflow that must equal the actual current account deficit. There is no reason at all, however, why *desired* (or planned) current account transactions should equal desired capital account transactions. In practice, it is movements in the exchange rate that play a key role in reconciling actual and desired transactions (at least for a country that has its own currency and a flexible exchange rate). We now turn to a discussion of the exchange rate and how it is determined.

## The market for foreign exchange

The foreign exchange markets are the markets in which one currency can be traded for another. We are used to thinking about markets in which goods are exchanged for money. In a foreign exchange market, it is one country's money that is exchanged for another country's money. As with all markets, the foreign exchange market can be analysed with the tools of demand and supply developed earlier in this book. Before proceeding with this exercise, it is helpful to remind ourselves why we need such markets.

Money is central to the efficient working of any modern economy that relies on specialization and exchange. Yet fiat money as we know it is a *national* matter, one that is closely controlled by national governments. Until recently each nation-state had its own currency, though in 1999 twelve EU nations adopted a common currency, the euro, and a thirteenth joined in 2007. For purposes of the following discussion, we treat the euro-zone countries as if they were a single country, as they have a single external exchange rate. Other nation-states each have their own currency. If you live in Sweden, you earn kronor and spend kronor; if you run a business in Australia, you borrow Australian dollars and meet your wage bill with Australian dollars. The currency of a country is acceptable within the bounds of that country, but usually it will not be accepted by people and firms in another country. The Stockholm buses will accept kronor for a fare, but not Australian dollars; the Australian worker will not take Swedish kronor for wages, but will insist on being paid in Australian dollars.

UK producers require payment in pounds sterling for their products. They need pounds to meet their wage bills, to pay for their raw materials, and to reinvest or distribute their profits. There is no problem when they sell to UK-based purchasers. However, if they sell their goods to, say, Indian importers, either the Indians must exchange their rupees for pounds to pay for the goods, or the UK producers must accept rupees;[10] and they will accept rupees only if they know that they can exchange the rupees for pounds. The same holds true for producers in all countries: they must eventually receive payment in the currency of their own country.

Trade between nations typically requires the exchange of one nation's currency for that of another. The major exception is the euro zone, where member states have a common currency.

International payments involve the exchange of currencies between people who have one currency and require another. Suppose that a UK firm wishes to acquire ¥3 million for some purpose. (¥ is the currency symbol for the Japanese yen.) The firm can go to its bank and buy a cheque, or money order, that will be accepted in Japan as ¥3 million. How many *pounds* the firm must pay to purchase this cheque will depend on the value of the yen in terms of pounds.

The exchange of one currency for another is a *foreign exchange transaction*. The term 'foreign exchange' refers to the actual foreign currency or various claims on it, such as bank deposits or promises to pay that are traded for each other. The UK *exchange rate* is the value of the domestic currency in terms of foreign currency; it is the amount of foreign currency that can be obtained with one unit of the domestic currency. For example, if £1 will buy ¥150, the yen–pound exchange rate is 150. Most other countries, however, express their exchange rate the other way round, that is, by the number of units of domestic currency that it takes to buy one unit of foreign currency (usually expressed in term of US dollars). In economic theory also, we usually express the exchange rate as a quantity of domestic currency per unit of foreign currency.

A rise in the external value of the pound (that is, a rise in the exchange rate) is called an **appreciation** of the pound; for example, if one can now obtain ¥175 for £1 instead of ¥150, the pound has *appreciated*. A fall in the external value of the pound (that is, a fall in the exchange rate) is called a **depreciation** of the pound; for example,

---

[10] Some trade, especially in primary commodities such as wheat and oil, is conducted in US dollars, even when US residents are not involved. In this respect the US dollar has a special role as an international medium of exchange or unit of account.

if one can now obtain only ¥125 for £1 instead of ¥150, the pound has *depreciated*.[11]

Because the exchange rate expresses the value of one currency in terms of another, when one currency appreciates the other must depreciate.

## The demand for and supply of pounds

The exchange rate is just a price, albeit a very important price. As with other prices, we will approach the explanation of exchange rates from the perspective of demand and supply. However, the exchange rate is potentially influenced by (and influences) all payments into and out of the national economy from abroad. Hence we must first be clear about what those payments are.

For the sake of simplicity, we use an example involving trade between the United Kingdom and the United States and the determination of the exchange rate between their two currencies, the pound sterling and the US dollar, for which we use the shorthand forms 'pound' and 'dollar'. The two-country example simplifies things, but the principles apply to all foreign transactions. Thus, 'dollar' stands for foreign exchange in general, and the value of the pound in terms of dollars stands for the foreign exchange rate in general.[12]

When £1 = $1.50, a US importer who offers to buy £1 million with dollars must be offering to sell $1.5 million. Similarly, a UK importer who offers to sell £1 million for dollars must be offering to buy $1.5 million.

Because one currency is traded for another in the foreign exchange market, it follows that a demand for foreign exchange (dollars) implies a supply of pounds, while a supply of foreign exchange (dollars) implies a demand for pounds.

For this reason, a theory of the exchange rate between the pound and the dollar can deal either with the demand for and supply of pounds or with the demand for and supply of dollars: both need not be considered. We will concentrate on the demand, supply, and price of the pound (quoted in dollars).

We develop our example in terms of the demand-and-supply analysis first encountered in Chapter 3. To do so, we need only recall that *in the market for foreign exchange* transactions that generate a receipt of foreign exchange (a credit in the balance of payments) represent a demand for pounds, and transactions that require a payment of foreign exchange represent a supply of pounds. We focus on the demand and supply of pounds arising from both the current and capital accounts. Later we turn to the important role of official intervention by the domestic government.

### The demand for pounds

The demand for pounds arises from all international transactions that generate a receipt of foreign exchange, that is, credits in the balance of payments.

#### UK exports

One important source of demand for pounds in foreign exchange markets is foreigners who do not currently hold pounds but wish to buy UK-made goods and services. A German importer of Scotch whisky is such a purchaser; an Austrian couple planning to take a holiday in Cornwall is another; the Chinese national airline seeking to buy Rolls Royce engines for its passenger aircraft is yet another. All are sources of demand for pounds arising out of international trade. Each potential buyer wants to sell its own currency and buy pounds for the purpose of purchasing UK exports.

#### Income payments and transfers

A UK resident who owns shares in, say, General Motors receives dividend payments on those shares. The dividend is paid by GM in dollars. But the UK resident wants to use the money for a meal out in London, so converts the dollars into pounds, thereby creating a demand for pounds. Thus, credit items in the balance of payments accounts for income or transfers create demand for pounds.

#### Capital inflows

A third source of a demand for pounds comes from foreigners who wish to purchase UK assets. In order to buy UK assets, holders of foreign currencies must first buy pounds in foreign exchange markets.[13]

#### Reserve currency

Governments often accumulate and hold foreign exchange reserves, just as individuals maintain savings accounts. The government of Nigeria, for example, may decide to increase its reserve holdings of pounds and reduce its reserve holdings of dollars; if it does so, it will

---

[11] When the external value of the currency changes as a result of an explicit policy of the central bank, it is often said to have been *devalued* when it falls and *revalued* when it rises.

[12] The foreign exchange market between the pound and the dollar is referred to in the market as 'cable', because it grew to its present structure by use of one of the first transatlantic telegraph cables.

[13] Capital inflows also arise when UK citizens sell foreign assets, because they enter the foreign exchange market and sell the foreign currency received for the assets and buy pounds.

be a demander of pounds (and a supplier of dollars) in foreign exchange markets. The pound sterling used to be a very important reserve currency, particularly for countries that were formerly British colonies. This role has been greatly reduced (relative to the US dollar and euro), but it still creates a significant overseas demand for pounds. Currency reserves are almost always held in an interest-bearing asset, so it is the expected return on these assets that is likely to influence the choice, just as with private sector capital flows.

### The total demand for pounds

The total demand for pounds by holders of foreign currencies is the sum of the demands for all of the purposes just discussed—for purchases of UK exports of goods and services, for income payments and transfers, for capital movements, or for adding to currency reserves.

Furthermore, because people, firms, and governments in all countries purchase goods from, and invest in, many other countries, the demand for any one currency will be the aggregate demand of individuals, firms, and governments in a number of different countries. Thus, the total demand for pounds, for example, may include Germans who are offering euros, Japanese who are offering yen, Australians who are offering Australian dollars, and so on. For simplicity, however, we continue with our two-country example and use only the United Kingdom and the United States.

### The demand curve for pounds

The demand for pounds in terms of dollars is represented by a negatively sloped curve, such as the one shown in Figure 22.1. This figure plots the price of the pound (measured in dollars) on the vertical axis and the quantity of pounds on the horizontal axis. Moving down the vertical scale, the pound is worth fewer dollars and hence is depreciating in the foreign exchange market. Moving up the scale, the pound is appreciating.

Why is the demand curve for pounds negatively sloped? Consider the demand for pounds for foreign purchases of UK exports. If the pound depreciates, the dollar price of UK exports will fall because holders of dollars require fewer of them to buy £1. US citizens will buy more of the cheaper UK goods and will require more pounds for this purpose. The quantity of pounds demanded will therefore rise. In the opposite case, when the pound appreciates, more dollars are required to buy £1, and so the price of UK exports rises in terms of dollars. US citizens will buy fewer UK goods and hence will demand fewer pounds.

Similar considerations affect other sources of demand for pounds. When the pound is cheaper UK assets become

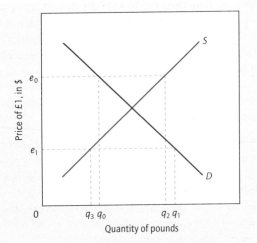

**Figure 22.1  The market for foreign exchange**

**The demand curve for pounds is negatively sloped, and the supply curve of pounds is positively sloped.** The demand for pounds is $D$. It represents the sum of transactions giving rise to receipts of foreign exchange. When the exchange rate is $e_0$, the quantity of pounds demanded is $q_0$. A depreciation of the pound is indicated by a fall in the exchange rate to $e_1$; foreign demand for UK goods and assets rises, and hence the quantity of pounds demanded also rises, from $q_0$ to $q_1$. An appreciation has the opposite effect: a rise in the exchange rate from $e_1$ to $e_0$ causes the quantity of pounds demanded to fall from $q_1$ to $q_0$.

The supply of pounds is given by line $S$. It represents the sum of transactions that require payments of foreign exchange. When the exchange rate is $e_0$, the quantity of pounds supplied is $q_2$. If the exchange rate falls to $e_1$, UK demand for foreign goods and assets falls, and hence the quantity of pounds supplied also falls, from $q_2$ to $q_3$. An appreciation has the opposite effect; a rise in the exchange rate from $e_1$ to $e_0$ causes the quantity of pounds supplied to rise from $q_3$ to $q_2$.

attractive purchases, and the quantity purchased will rise. As it does, the quantity of pounds demanded to pay for the purchases will increase.

The demand curve for pounds in the foreign exchange market is negatively sloped when it is plotted against the dollar price of £1.

### The supply of pounds

The sources of supply of pounds in the foreign exchange market are merely the opposite side of the demand for dollars. (Recall that the *supply* of pounds by people who are seeking dollars is the same as the *demand* for dollars by holders of pounds.)

Who wants to sell pounds? UK residents seeking to purchase foreign goods and services or assets will be supplying pounds and purchasing foreign exchange for this purpose. In addition, holders of UK assets may decide to sell their UK holdings and shift them into foreign assets, and if they do they will sell pounds; that is, they will be supplying pounds to the foreign exchange market. Similarly, a country with some sterling reserves of foreign exchange may decide that the sterling-denominated assets offer a poor return and that it should sell pounds in order to buy another currency.

### The supply curve of pounds

When the pound sterling depreciates, the sterling price of US exports to the UK rises. It takes more pounds to buy the same US goods, so UK residents will buy fewer of the now more expensive US goods. The quantity of pounds being offered in exchange for dollars in order to pay for US exports to the UK (UK imports) will therefore fall.[14]

In the opposite case, when the pound appreciates US exports to the United Kingdom become cheaper, more are sold, and a greater quantity of pounds is spent on them. Thus, more pounds will be offered in exchange for dollars to obtain the foreign exchange that is needed to pay for the extra imports. The argument also applies to purchases and sales of assets.

The supply curve of pounds in the foreign exchange market is positively sloped when it is plotted against the dollar price of £1.

This too is illustrated in Figure 22.1.

# The determination of exchange rates

The demand and supply curves in Figure 22.1 do not include official foreign exchange market intervention by the domestic government (or by the monetary authorities,[15] depending on the institutional arrangements in the country concerned), though they do include any transactions in pounds by foreign monetary authorities. In order to complete our analysis, we need to incorporate the role of domestic official intervention.[16] Three important cases need to be considered:

1. When there is no official intervention by the monetary authorities or the government, the exchange rate is determined by the equality between the supply and demand for pounds arising from the capital and current accounts. This is called a *flexible* or *floating exchange rate regime*.

2. When official intervention is used to maintain the exchange rate at (or close to) a particular value, there is said to be a *fixed* or *pegged exchange rate regime*.

3. Between these two 'pure' regimes are many possible intermediate cases, including the *adjustable peg* and the *managed float*. Under an adjustable peg, governments set and attempt to maintain par values for their exchange rates, but they explicitly recognize that circumstances may arise in which they will change the par value. In a managed float, the authorities seek to have some stabilizing influence on the exchange rate but do not try to fix it at some publicly announced par value.

## Flexible exchange rates

Consider an exchange rate that is set in a freely competitive market, with no intervention by the authorities. Like any competitive price, this rate fluctuates according to the conditions of demand and supply.

Suppose that the current price of the pound is so low (say, at $e_1$ in Figure 22.1) that the quantity of pounds demanded exceeds the quantity supplied. Pounds will be in scarce supply in the foreign exchange market; some people who require pounds to make payments to the United Kingdom will be unable to obtain them; and the price of the pound will be bid up. The value of the pound *vis-à-vis* the dollar will appreciate. As the price of the pound rises, the dollar price of UK exports to the United States rises and the quantity of pounds demanded to buy UK goods decreases. At the same time as the sterling price of imports from the United States falls, a larger quantity will be purchased and the quantity of pounds supplied

---

[14] As long as the demand for imports is elastic (price elasticity greater than 1 (in absolute terms)), the fall in the volume of imports will swamp the rise in price, and hence fewer pounds will be spent on imports. If the elasticity of demand for imports is less than 1 (in absolute terms), the volume of imports will fall but the amount of domestic money spent on them will still rise. In what follows, we adopt the case of elastic demand, which is usual in this area. In a more general form this is called the *Marshall–Lerner condition*, after two famous British economists who first studied the problem.

[15] In the UK the official reserves used to be entirely owned by the government but managed by the Bank of England. However, following the 1998 Bank of England Act, the Bank was given some of the UK reserves, so foreign exchange market intervention could be performed with either the Treasury's or the Bank's reserves. The European Central Bank can also intervene in foreign exchange markets as it has its own foreign exchange reserves.

[16] Official intervention is included in the balance of payments accounts in Table 22.1 under 'reserve assets'.

will rise. Thus, a rise in the price of the pound reduces the quantity demanded and increases the quantity supplied. Where the two curves intersect, quantity demanded equals quantity supplied and the exchange rate is in equilibrium.

What happens when the price of the pound is above its equilibrium value? The quantity of pounds demanded will be less than the quantity supplied. With pounds in excess supply, some people who wish to convert pounds into dollars will be unable to do so. (Equivalently, we could say that there is an excess demand for dollars.) The price of the pound will fall, fewer pounds will be supplied, more will be demanded, and an equilibrium will be re-established.

**A foreign exchange market is like other competitive markets in that the forces of demand and supply lead to an equilibrium price at which quantity demanded equals quantity supplied.**

In a floating exchange rate regime it is exchange rate adjustment that determines the actual current and capital account transactions, even though planned, or desired, trade and investment decisions may have been inconsistent. Suppose that at the beginning of some period importers and exporters had plans that would have created a current account deficit and domestic investors had plans to buy foreign securities (while foreigners had no such plans). The attempt to implement these plans would create a massive excess supply of pounds (demand for dollars). This would force a sterling depreciation, which would continue until it moved far enough to force changes in plans. Indeed, it would depreciate just far enough so that any supply of pounds generated by a current account deficit was just balanced by a capital inflow (or any current account surplus was just balanced by a capital outflow).

# Fixed exchange rates

When there is official intervention in the foreign exchange market to maintain a particular exchange rate, this stops some movements in the exchange rate that would otherwise have happened. In this way it may prevent the exchange rate from adjusting sufficiently to guarantee that the current account balance and the (private sector) capital account balance are equal and opposite. In this situation the authorities must satisfy any private sector excess demand or supply of pounds. In the process of intervention, the authorities will be building up or running down their foreign exchange reserves.

**The official foreign exchange reserves are the stock of foreign-currency-denominated assets that the monetary** authorities hold in order to be able to intervene in the foreign exchange markets.

When the authorities peg the exchange rate, they do so not at one specific rate, but rather within some range. In the postwar exchange regime that existed until 1972 (in the UK case) exchange rates were pegged within one percentage point on either side of a central (or 'par') rate. This regime was known as the Bretton Woods regime, after the town in the United States where the agreement was drawn up. In the European Exchange Rate Mechanism (ERM) of the 1980s and early 1990s, the range of permitted fluctuation was 2.25 per cent for some countries and 6 per cent for others (including the United Kingdom from October 1990 to September 1992), though the band was widened to 15 per cent after a crisis in 1993.

Let us consider a simplified analysis of how such pegged exchange rate regimes operate. Assume for simplicity that the domestic authorities peg the UK exchange rate between, say, $1.50 and $1.60. This case is illustrated in Figure 22.2. The authorities will then enter the market to prevent the rate from going outside this range. At the price

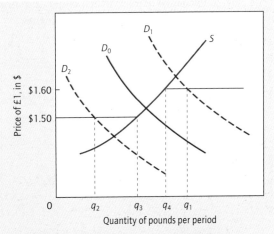

**Figure 22.2 Managing fixed exchange rates**

Under a fixed exchange rate regime, the authorities intervene in the foreign exchange market to ensure that the exchange rate stays within specified bands. The supply curve is $S$, and the exchange rate is pegged within the range $1.50–$1.60. If the demand curve is given by $D_0$, the equilibrium exchange rate is within the bands so no intervention by the authorities is required. With demand curve $D_1$ the equilibrium exchange rate would be above $1.60. To stop the exchange rate rising above $1.60, the authorities have to sell $q_4q_1$ pounds per period and buy dollars of equivalent value. (For every £100 sold, they will acquire $160.) If the demand curve were $D_2$, the exchange rate would fall below $1.50 in a free market, so the authorities have to buy $q_2q_3$ pounds per period with dollars.

of $1.50 the authorities will offer to buy pounds (in exchange for dollars) in unlimited amounts; at the price $1.60 they will offer to sell pounds (in exchange for dollars) in unlimited amounts. When the authorities buy dollars (sell pounds) their exchange reserves rise, but when they sell dollars (buy pounds) their foreign exchange reserves fall.

If on average the demand and supply curves intersect in the range $1.50–$1.60, exchange reserves will be relatively stable. However, if demand for pounds intersects the supply curve below $1.50, the authorities will find themselves losing reserves each period, and such a situation cannot be sustained indefinitely (because the authorities will run out of reserves). They must then either move the bands of fluctuation (devalue), or take action to shift the demand or supply curves. This could be done, for example, by trade restrictions, or by raising interest rates to attract short-term capital inflows.

In a fixed exchange rate regime with an overvalued currency, the balance of payments becomes a problem. In this case it is not necessarily a current account deficit that is the problem, but rather the overall excess supply of domestic currency (excess demand for foreign currency) in the foreign exchange market, which could arise from any of the components of the balance of payments.

With fixed exchange rates and an overvalued currency, the monetary authorities will be suffering a loss of reserves. It is this that causes balance of payments crises for governments operating under fixed exchange rate regimes.

The problems associated with fixing the exchange rate provide a good example of the difficulties that governments often have in trying to manage market prices. In the remainder of this chapter we focus on flexible exchange rates, which is the regime under which sterling, the euro, the US dollar, and most other major currencies operate today.

## Changes in exchange rates

What causes flexible exchange rates to move? The simplest answer to this question is changes in demand or supply in the foreign exchange market. Anything that shifts the demand curve for pounds to the right or the supply curve of pounds to the left leads to an appreciation of the pound. Anything that shifts the demand curve for pounds to the left or the supply curve of pounds to the right leads to a depreciation of the pound. This is nothing more than a restatement of the laws of supply and demand, applied now to the market for foreign currencies; it is illustrated in Figure 22.3.

**(i) Demand shifts**

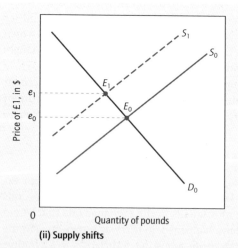
**(ii) Supply shifts**

**Figure 22.3  Changes in exchange rates**

An increase in the demand for pounds or a decrease in the supply will cause the pound to appreciate; a decrease in the demand or an increase in supply will cause it to depreciate. The initial demand and supply curves, $D_0$ and $S_0$, are shown as solid lines. Equilibrium is at $E_0$ with an exchange rate of $e_0$. An increase in the demand for pounds, as shown by a rightward shift in the demand curve from $D_0$ to $D_1$ in part (i), or a decrease in the supply of pounds, as shown by a leftward shift in the supply curve from $S_0$ to $S_1$ in part (ii), will cause the pound to appreciate. In both parts the new equilibrium is at $E_1$, and the appreciation is shown by the rise in the exchange rate from $e_0$ to $e_1$.

A decrease in the demand for pounds, as shown by a leftward shift in the demand curve from $D_1$ to $D_0$ in part (i), or an increase in the supply of pounds, as shown by a rightward shift in the supply curve from $S_1$ to $S_0$ in part (ii), will cause the pound to depreciate. The equilibrium will shift from $E_1$ to $E_0$, and the depreciation is shown by the fall in the exchange rate from $e_1$ to $e_0$ in both parts.

What causes the shifts in demand and supply that lead to changes in exchange rates? There are many causes, some of which are transitory and some of which are persistent. We will discuss some of the most important ones.

### A rise in the domestic price of exports

Suppose that the sterling price of UK-produced telephone equipment rises. The effect on the demand for pounds depends on the price elasticity of foreign demand for the UK products.

If the demand is inelastic (say, because the United Kingdom is uniquely able to supply the product for which there are no close substitutes), then more will be spent; the demand for pounds to pay the bigger bill will shift the demand curve to the right, and the pound will appreciate. This is illustrated in Figure 22.3(i).

If the demand is elastic, perhaps because other countries are supplying the same product to competitive world markets, the total amount spent will decrease and so fewer pounds will be demanded; that is, the demand curve for pounds will shift to the left, and the pound will depreciate. This too is illustrated in Figure 22.3(i), by a reverse of the previous shift.

### A rise in the foreign price of imports

Suppose that the dollar price of US-produced computers increases sharply. Suppose also that UK consumers have an elastic demand for US computers because they can easily switch to UK substitutes. In this case they will spend fewer dollars for US computers than they did before. Hence they will supply fewer pounds to the foreign exchange market. The supply curve of pounds shifts to the left, and the pound will appreciate. If the demand for US computers were inelastic, spending on them would rise and the supply of pounds would shift to the right, leading to a depreciation of the pound. This is illustrated in Figure 22.3(ii).

### Changes in price levels

Suppose that, instead of a change in the price of a specific exported product, there is a change in *all* prices because of inflation. What matters here is the change in the UK price level *relative to* the price levels of its trading partners. (Recall that in our two-country example the United States stands for the rest of the world.)

If UK inflation is higher than that in the United States, UK exports are becoming relatively expensive in US markets while imports from the United States are becoming relatively cheap in the United Kingdom. This will shift the demand curve for pounds to the left and the supply curve to the right. Each change causes the dollar price of £1 to fall; that is, it causes the pound to depreciate.

If the price level of one country is rising relative to that of another country, the equilibrium value of its currency will be falling relative to that of the other country.

Indeed, the price level and the exchange rate are both measures of a currency's value. The price level is the value of a currency measured against a typical basket of goods, while the exchange rate values a currency against other currencies.

### Capital movements

Major capital flows can exert a strong influence on exchange rates, especially as the size of capital flows (in the modern globalized financial system) can swamp trade payments on any particular day. An increased desire by UK residents to invest in US assets will shift the supply curve for pounds to the right, and the pound will depreciate. This is illustrated in Figure 22.3(ii).

A significant movement of investment funds has the effect of appreciating the currency of the capital-importing country and depreciating the currency of the capital-exporting country.

This statement is true for all capital movements—short-term and long-term. Because the motives that lead to large capital movements are likely to be different in the short and long terms, however, it is worth considering each separately.

#### Short-term capital movements

A major motive for short-term capital flows is a change in interest rates. International traders hold transactions balances just as domestic traders do. These balances are usually lent out on a short-term basis rather than being left in a non-interest-bearing deposit. Naturally, other things being equal, the holders of these balances will tend to lend them in those markets where interest rates are highest. Thus, if one major country's short-term rate of interest rises above the rates in most other countries, there will tend to be an inflow of short-term capital into that country (or at least of deposits in major financial centres denominated in that country's currency) in an effort to take advantage of the high rate, and this will tend to appreciate the currency. If these short-term interest rates should fall, there will most likely be a sudden shift away from that country as a location for short-term funds, and its currency will tend to depreciate.

A second motive for short-term capital movements is speculation about a country's exchange rate. If foreigners expect the pound to appreciate, they will rush to buy assets denominated in pounds; if they expect the pound to depreciate, they will be reluctant to buy or to hold UK financial assets.

### Long-term capital movements

Long-term capital movements are largely influenced by long-term expectations about another country's profit opportunities and the long-run value of its currency. A US firm would be more willing to purchase a UK firm if it expected that the profits in pounds would buy more dollars in future years than the profits from investment in a US factory. This could happen if the UK business earned greater profits than the US alternative, with exchange rates remaining unchanged. It could also happen if the profits were the same but the US firm expected the pound to appreciate relative to the dollar.

### Structural changes

An economy can undergo structural changes that alter the equilibrium exchange rate. 'Structural change' is an all-purpose term for a change in technology, the invention of new products, or anything else that affects the pattern of comparative advantage. For example, when a country's products do not improve in quality as rapidly as those of some other countries, that country's consumers' demand (at fixed prices) will shift slowly away from its own products and towards those of its foreign competitors. This will cause a slow depreciation in the first country's currency, because the demand for its currency is shifting slowly leftward as illustrated in Figure 22.3(i).

An important example of a structural change in recent UK history was the production of oil and gas from the North Sea. This reduced UK demand for imported oil, leading to a reduced supply of pounds in the foreign exchange market and an appreciation of the UK exchange rate.

## The behaviour of exchange rates

The degree of exchange rate variability experienced since the advent of floating in the early 1970s has been greater than was expected.

Why have exchange rates been volatile? This question remains at the centre of debate and controversy among researchers and policy commentators. In this section we provide only a cursory view of this and related questions about the behaviour of exchange rates.

First, we look at one measure of the value that the exchange rate would take on if it were subject to the influence of what might be called the underlying, or fundamental, market determinants. We can then compare this with the actual value of the exchange rate. Second, we provide one explanation for the divergence of the exchange rate from the path determined by these fundamentals.

### Purchasing power parity

**Purchasing power parity (PPP)** theory holds that over the long term the average value of the exchange rate between two currencies depends on their relative purchasing power. The theory holds that a currency will tend to have the same purchasing power when spent in its home country as it would have if it were converted to foreign exchange and spent in the foreign country.

If, at existing values of relative price levels and the existing exchange rate, a currency has a higher purchasing power in its own country, it is said to be undervalued. There is then an incentive to sell foreign exchange and buy the domestic currency in order to take advantage of this higher purchasing power (that is, the fact that goods seem cheaper) in the domestic economy. This will put upward pressure on the domestic currency.

Similarly, if a currency has a lower purchasing power in its own country, it is said to be overvalued; there is then an incentive to sell the domestic currency and buy foreign exchange in order to take advantage of the higher purchasing power (cheaper goods) abroad. This will put downward pressure on the domestic currency.

**The PPP exchange rate is determined by relative price levels in the two countries.**

For example, assume that the UK price level rises by 20 per cent, while the US price level rises by only 5 per cent over the same period. The PPP value of the dollar then appreciates by approximately 15 per cent against sterling. This means that in the United States the prices of all goods (both US-produced and imported UK goods) will rise by 5 per cent, measured in dollars, while in the United Kingdom the prices of all goods (both UK-produced and imported US goods) will rise by 20 per cent, measured in pounds.

**The PPP exchange rate adjusts so that the relative prices of the two nations' goods (measured in the same currency) are unchanged, because the change in the relative values of two currencies compensates exactly for differences in national inflation rates.**

If the actual exchange rate changes along with the PPP rate, the competitive positions of producers in the two countries will be unchanged. Firms that are located in countries with high inflation rates will still be able to sell their outputs on international markets, because the exchange rate will adjust to offset the effect of the rising domestic prices. An exchange rate that adjusts in line with the PPP exchange rate is also referred to as a constant

**Box 22.3 Exchange rates and the quantity theory of money**

A simple expression for the exchange rate can be derived from the quantity theory of money (as set out in Box 21.1) when there are two countries and an exchange rate that follows its PPP value.

Let the foreign country be denoted by an asterisk (*), so that it has an equation linking money, prices, income, and velocity:

$$M^*V^* = P^*Y^*. \tag{i}$$

Using values for home money supply, prices, velocity, and income, we already had

$$MV = PY. \tag{ii}$$

All we need to add is the relationship implied by PPP. This is that prices will be the same in both economies when converted at the current exchange rate:

$$PE = P^*, \tag{iii}$$

where $P$ is the home country price level, $P^*$ is the foreign country price level, and $E$ is the exchange rate (expressed as the number of units of foreign currency required to buy a unit of home currency). Now all we do is rearrange (i) and (ii) as expressions for $P$ and $P^*$, then substitute into (iii) and arrange as an expression for $E$. This gives†

$$E = \frac{M^*}{M} \cdot \frac{Y}{Y^*} \cdot \frac{V^*}{V}. \tag{iv}$$

This equation gives us some new insights into the exchange rate. The first term is the ratio of the home and foreign money supplies. $E$ falls in proportion to the home money supply and rises in proportion to the foreign money supply. This means that, when the home money supply rises, the exchange rate depreciates in the same proportion. The logic of this has two steps. First, a rise in home money supply leads to a proportional increase in the home price level (for given levels of $Y$ and $V$). Second, a rise in the home price level leads to a proportional depreciation of the home currency to preserve PPP.

The second term in (iv) has an important implication. Domestic real national income is positively related to $E$. This means that, other things being equal, a rise in domestic national income leads to an appreciation of the home currency. The reason for this is that an increase in $Y$ leads to an increased transactions demand for the home currency. As we have learned in this chapter, anything that increases demand for the home currency will tend to appreciate its exchange rate.

Although this simple model of exchange rates gives important insights, it is only a beginning. Many other factors affecting interest rates and expectations can easily be incorporated by a more detailed specification of the determinants of $V$. However, the main elements of (iv) are recognizable in many of the empirical exchange rate models of the past two decades.

† The steps are as follows:

1. $P^* = M^*V^*/Y^*$ and $P = MV/Y$.
2. Substituting into (iii), $E(MV/Y) = M^*V^*/Y^*$.
3. Rearranging gives (iv).

real exchange rate.[17] A simple model of the exchange rate implied by the quantity theory of money and PPP is set out in Box 22.3.

Figure 22.4 shows an index of the real exchange rate for the United Kingdom, the United States, Japan, and Germany for 1975–2005. PPP requires that the real exchange rate should be constant in the long term. This is broadly true. Notice also, however, the large fluctuations around the PPP rate. The United Kingdom had a high real exchange rate in the early 1980s, associated with its emergence as an oil producer. This led to a sharp loss of competitiveness of the non-oil sectors of the economy (especially manufacturing), causing a sharp decline in UK manufacturing output which in turn contributed to the 1979–81 recession. The UK real exchange rate fell significantly between 1981 and 1986. The UK real exchange was high again at the end of the 1990s and in the early years of the twenty-first century. The most dramatic swing in the 1980s, however, was in the US real exchange rate, which increased 50 per cent between 1980 and 1985, and then fell back to its 1980 level by 1987.

**PPP governs exchange rate behaviour in the long term, but there often are significant deviations from PPP in the short to medium term.**

Why have these wide fluctuations occurred? One of the most important reasons is associated with international differences in interest rates. Another, related reason—responses to new information—is discussed in Box 22.4.

### Exchange rate overshooting

Differences in interest rates between countries, arising from differences in monetary and fiscal policies, among

---

[17] The real exchange rate is the inverse of competitiveness. A country whose goods were becoming relatively cheap in world markets would be said to be improving its competitiveness but to be having a falling real exchange rate, and vice versa. The real exchange rate is not an actual price of currency: it is an index number of the relative prices of home and foreign goods.

**Figure 22.4** Real exchange rates for Germany, Japan, the UK and the USA, 1975–2005

**Deviations from PPP can be substantial in the short run, but over the long run exchange rates tend to revert to their PPP values.** At the PPP exchange rate the real exchange rate will be constant. The chart shows real exchange rates for four countries, calculated by adjusting actual exchange rates by indexes of relative unit labour costs, and set to a value of 100 in January 2000. The UK real exchange rate rose between 1978 and early 1981. It then fell in stages. It rose again at the end of the 1980s but fell sharply after September 1992, when Britain left the ERM. It rose again in 1996 and stayed high up to 2005.

The United States experienced a dramatic appreciation of its real exchange rate from 1980 to 1985, after which time it fell back sharply. The dollar was strong again in real terms during the internet boom of the late 1990s but it fell again after 2001.

The real exchange rate of Germany was low in the early 1980s but then rose up to the mid-1990s before easing again after Germany tied its currency with those of other euro zone members.

The Japanese real exchange rate was strong in the mid-1990s, but in the early 2000s Japan suffered a major depression and its currency weakened in real terms.

*Source*: IMF, *International Financial Statistics*, online database.

other factors, can trigger large capital flows as investors seek to place their funds where returns are highest. These capital flows will in turn result in swings in the exchange rate between the two countries. Some economists argue that this is the fundamental reason for the wide fluctuations in exchange rates that have been observed.

To illustrate, suppose that an exogenous change in monetary policy causes UK interest rates to rise 4 percentage points above those in New York. The interest rate differential will lead to a capital inflow into the United Kingdom. UK and foreign investors alike will sell assets denominated in US dollars and will buy UK assets that earn higher interest. These capital inflows will lead to an increased demand for pounds on the foreign exchange market as investors exchange dollars for pounds to buy UK assets. The increased demand will in turn lead to an appreciation of sterling.

**A relative rise in domestic interest rates will cause a capital inflow and an appreciation of the home currency.**

When will the process stop? It will stop only when expected returns on UK and foreign assets are again roughly equalized; as long as the return on UK assets is above that on foreign assets, the capital inflows will continue, and the upward pressure on the pound will continue. The key is that the expected return includes not only the interest earnings, but also the expected gains or losses that might arise because of changes in the exchange rate during the period of the investment. A foreign investor holding a UK asset will receive pounds when the asset is sold, and will at that time want to exchange pounds for foreign exchange. If the value of the pound has fallen, that will be a source of loss that has to be balanced against the interest income in assessing the net return on holding the asset.

**Equilibrium in the above example occurs when the rise in value of the pound sterling in foreign exchange markets is large enough that investors will expect a future depreciation which just offsets the interest premium from investing funds in sterling-denominated assets.**

**Box 22.4  'News' and the exchange rate**

Foreign exchange markets are different from markets for consumer goods in that the vast bulk of trading takes place between professional foreign exchange dealers of banks. These dealers do not meet each other face to face. Rather, they conduct their transactions over the telephone or via computers, and the other party to the deal can be anywhere in the world. The structure of this market has one interesting implication: exchange rates respond to news. Let us see why this is and what it means.

Deals done by the professional dealers are all on a large scale, typically involving sums no smaller than £1 million and often very much larger. Each dealer tends to specialize in deals between a small number of currencies, say the pound sterling and the euro. But the dealers in all currencies for each bank sit close together, in a dealing room, so that they can hear what is going on in other markets. When a big news event breaks, anywhere in the world, this will be shouted out to all dealers in the room simultaneously.

Each dealer is also faced with several computer screens and many buttons which will connect him or her very quickly by telephone to other dealers. Speed of transaction can be very important if you are dealing with large volumes of money in a market that is continuously changing the prices quoted. Latest price quotes from around the world appear on the screens. However, contracts are agreed over the telephone (and nowadays are recorded in case of disagreement) or via an online trading system and the paperwork follows within two days.

As exchange rates are closely related to expectations and to interest rates, the foreign exchange dealers have to keep an eye on all major news events affecting the economic environment. Since all the players in the foreign exchange markets are professionals, they are all well informed—not just about what has happened, but also about forecasts of what is likely to happen. Accordingly, the exchange rate, at any point in time, reflects not just history but also current expectations of what is going to happen in future.

As soon as some future event comes to be expected, it will be reflected in the current exchange rate. Events expected to happen soon will usually be given more weight than distant events. The only component in today's news that will cause the exchange rate to change is what was *not* expected to happen. Economists attribute the unforecastable component of news to a random error. It is random in the sense that it has no detectable pattern to it and it is unrelated to the information available before it happened.

Some events are clearly unforecastable, like an earthquake in Japan or a head of state having a heart attack. Others are the production of economic statistics for which forecasts have generally been published. In the latter case it is the deviation of announced figures from their forecast value that, if large, tends to move exchange rates.

Exchange rates are moved by news. Since news is random and unpredictable, changes in exchange rates will tend to be random.

Some people, observing the volatility of exchange rates, conclude that foreign exchange markets are inefficient. However, with well-informed professional players who have forward-looking expectations, new information is rapidly transmitted into prices. Volatility of exchange rates may, therefore, reflect the volatility of relevant, but unexpected, events around the world.

---

Suppose investors believe that the PPP rate is £1 = $1.50, but as they rush to buy pounds to take advantage of higher UK interest rates, they drive the rate to, say, £1 = $1.75. (Because £1 now buys more dollars, the pound has appreciated, and because it takes more dollars to buy £1, the dollar has depreciated.) They do not believe that this rate will be sustained and instead expect the pound to lose value in future periods. If foreign investors expect the pound to depreciate by 4 per cent per year, they will be indifferent between lending money in London and doing so in New York. The extra 4 per cent per year of interest that they earn in London is exactly offset by the 4 per cent that they expect to lose when they turn their money back into their own currency.

A policy that raises domestic interest rates above world levels will cause the external value of the domestic currency to appreciate enough to create an expected future depreciation that will be sufficient to offset the interest differential.

While interest differentials persist, the exchange rate must deviate from its equilibrium or PPP value; this is often referred to as exchange rate *overshooting*, because at the time interest rates are raised the exchange rate will jump beyond its long-run equilibrium level. This is illustrated in Figure 22.5.

The argument that a rise in domestic interest rates will cause an appreciation of the home currency requires an important proviso. The interest rate rise has to occur with all other factors—especially long-run inflation expectations—held constant. If, for example, it was a rise in expectations of future inflation that triggered off events, the story would be quite different. In this case the interest rate rise would be responding to these expectations and to the consequent expectation of a long-run *depreciation* in the home currency. Now the change in the exchange rate would depend upon the size of the interest rate rise relative to the size of the expected long-run depreciation. In short, we

**Figure 22.5 Exchange rate overshooting**

The adjustment of exchange rates to policy changes often involves overshooting the long-run equilibrium. The figure illustrates how the exchange rate may move over time after a monetary policy tightening. The initial exchange rate is $e_0$. At time $t_1$ the central bank raises domestic interest rates and the exchange rate appreciates to $e_1$. Over time it then depreciates back towards the new long-run equilibrium level of $e_2$.

need to be careful when applying economic analysis that works *holding other things constant* to a world where many things are changing simultaneously.

## Implications of overshooting

One policy implication of exchange rate theory is that a central bank that is seeking to use its monetary policy to attain its domestic policy targets may have to put up with large fluctuations in the exchange rate. Indeed, overshooting of the exchange rate in response to interest rate changes may be one of the most important elements of the monetary transmission mechanism.

In the case of a tightening of monetary policy which raises interest rates, the overshooting (appreciation) of the pound beyond its PPP rate would put export- and import-competing industries under temporary but severe pressure from foreign competition, because UK goods would become expensive relative to imported goods. The resulting fall in demand for UK goods would open up a recessionary gap, thereby providing a further mechanism by which the restrictive monetary policy could be transmitted to the rest of the economy. This is discussed further in Chapter 23.

The two recessions in the United Kingdom in the early 1980s and early 1990s both illustrate this mechanism at work. Both were associated with tight monetary policy and an overvalued exchange rate, although, as there were world-wide recessions at roughly the same time, domestic factors cannot be the whole story.

In the run-up to the 1979–81 recession the pound had appreciated strongly. In 1979 interest rates were raised sharply and the pound appreciated further, as the Thatcher government implemented its commitment to control inflation by tight monetary policy. The high exchange rate meant that domestic producers became very uncompetitive, and so imports of cheaper foreign goods rose. Between late 1979 and early 1981, domestic manufacturing output fell by nearly 20 per cent and unemployment subsequently rose to over 3 million.

The high exchange rate cannot be blamed on tight monetary policy alone, because this was also the time when the United Kingdom was emerging as an oil producer (and the price of oil had doubled in 1979). However, monetary policy—especially the sharp rise in interest rates in 1979—certainly contributed to the overshooting of sterling, and the extremely high exchange rate was undoubtedly a central element in the transmission mechanism between the monetary sector and the real economy.

The recession of 1990–2 was made worse by an attempt to maintain an overvalued exchange rate. From 1981 to 1988 the UK economy had seen a sustained recovery, and by 1988 inflationary pressures had built up. The government tightened monetary policy in the autumn of 1988 by raising interest rates. Higher interest rates created a higher foreign exchange value of the pound than would otherwise have happened. Then in October 1990 the pound was pegged in the European Exchange Rate Mechanism (ERM). The onset of recession and fall of inflation, which was evident from 1991, would normally have permitted a reduction in interest rates (and a subsequent decline in the foreign exchange value of sterling), but ERM membership prevented this, because of the need to keep interest rates consistent with those of other ERM members, notably Germany, in order to defend the exchange rate. In September 1992 sterling was forced to leave the ERM by speculative pressure which caused reserve losses (as illustrated in Figure 22.2). This permitted a sharp fall in UK interest rates, which was associated with a fall in the exchange rate. (Sterling fell from nearly $2.00 per pound in the summer of 1992 to around $1.50 after September, and stayed around that level for the next couple of years.) The fall in interest rates and in the exchange rate led fairly quickly to economic recovery by the spring of 1993.

The UK exchange rate experienced another period of high valuation from mid-1996 until 2006. Initially it is likely that the strength of sterling was due to the uncertainty affecting other EU currencies (especially the Deutschmark) over prospects for the creation of a single currency. Sterling was regarded as something of a 'safe haven' for investors of funds. This was reinforced by the extra credibility attached to the UK monetary policy regime once the Bank of England was given monetary policy independence in May 1997 (see Chapter 21). The strength of the pound in this period made UK exporters (and producers of import-competing goods) less competitive, and was associated with the large balance of trade deficit reported in Table 22.1.

A more detailed analysis of the role of the exchange rate in macroeconomic adjustment follows in the next chapter. What we have learned in this chapter is that the exchange rate is an essential element of the transmission mechanism that turns monetary policy shocks into real shocks in an open economy under flexible exchange rates.

# CASE STUDIES

## 1. The current account and the UK's international investment position

The UK has run a current account balance of payments deficit in every year from 1985 to 2005. The 2005 deficit of £32 billion was the largest deficit in nominal terms on record, though as a percentage of GDP the deficits in the late 1980s were larger. Current account deficits must be financed by external borrowing or the running down of overseas assets. Hence the sustained deficits of this period inevitably reduced the UK's ownership of overseas assets compared with what it would otherwise have been.

Figure 22.6 shows the UK current account deficit and its components over this period. A large positive contribution to the current account balance comes from investment income. This is a bit odd, since the cumulative effect of the current account deficit

itself is that the UK has officially become a net debtor to the rest of the world. The following extracts from the Bank of England's *Inflation Report* elaborate on this puzzle.

*Official estimates imply that the United Kingdom is a net external debtor. In other words, the combined value of overseas claims on UK resources (UK external liabilities) exceeds the value of UK residents' claims on resources in the rest of the world (UK external assets)—by almost 20 per cent of annual GDP. That primarily reflects the counterpart to cumulated deficits on the current account. . . . Given the state of its external balance sheet, it is perhaps surprising that the United Kingdom receives a net inflow of investment income. UK residents appear to earn a significantly higher rate of return on their foreign assets than overseas residents earn on UK liabilities. What could explain that puzzle?*

*Most assets offer uncertain returns. The difference between the rate of return earned by UK and overseas residents could therefore simply reflect good luck. . . . Investors may also demand an additional return —or risk premium—to hold assets which offer uncertain returns. So the difference in rates of return could also reflect greater uncertainty about returns on overseas assets, relative to those on UK assets.*

*The negative international investment position is largely driven by the large stock of deposits held in UK banks. Overseas residents may have a motive for holding these assets over and above earning a return to fund future consumption—for example, these deposits may facilitate transactions in the UK financial system. In that case, overseas residents may be willing to accept a low return on these assets. . . .*

*Finally, the puzzling size and direction of the net flow of investment income received by UK residents, given the state of the external balance sheet, may reflect mismeasurement. Some assets—and in particular direct investments in physical capital—are recorded at what is called 'book value', rather than the amount the owner would raise if they sold the asset. For example, when UK companies open a plant overseas, the data may only measure the value of the buildings and machinery the company has purchased. The data may not capture the valuable knowledge that the company uses to combine capital and labour overseas to produce output.*

**Figure 22.6  The current account**

*Source: Inflation Report*, Bank of England, May 2006, page 16.

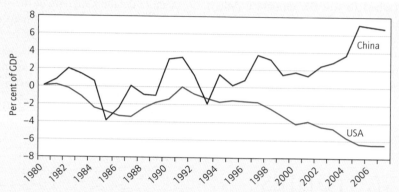

**Figure 22.7** China and US current account balance of payments as percentages of GDP, 1980–2007

*Source:* IMF, *World Economic Outlook.* (Figures for 2006–7 are IMF forecasts.)

*As a result of this mismeasurement, foreign direct investments are likely to generate surprisingly large returns given the measured book value of the investment. These assets appear on both sides of the United Kingdom's external balance sheet. But the value of FDI assets far exceeds that of the liabilities on the balance sheet. So if these assets were properly measured—at market value—then the UK's estimated international investment position would look healthier.* (*Inflation Report*, Bank of England, May 2006, pages 16–17)

Note that capital gains and losses on overseas assets and liabilities do not get measured, even in principle, in the balance of payments accounts. So the mismeasurement here refers to estimates of the current value of external assets and liabilities which are published annually. This reinforces the message from the text above that great care needs to be taken in interpreting what balance of payments figures tell us about the economic health of the country concerned.

## 2. International imbalances: China and the United States

In the mid-2000s one of the biggest issues affecting the global economy was the very large current account balance of payments deficit of the United States and the surplus of China. These were the most significant components of important global imbalances, but also important were surpluses of oil-exporting countries associated with high oil prices and surpluses in other emerging Asian countries.

Figure 22.7 shows the overall current account surplus of China and the US deficit as a percentage of their respective GDPs. In percentage terms these seem to be of comparable size, around 7 per cent of GDP. However, US output remains much larger than that of China, so that the dollar value of its deficit in 2005 was over $800 billion while the surplus of China was only around $160 billion.

US politicians attempted to blame Chinese policies for their own deficit. Certainly the fact that the Chinese currency was

pegged to the US dollar up to 2005 prevented the possibility of a Chinese currency appreciation helping the adjustment. However, the US deficit was also associated with low levels of US domestic saving, which is the same thing as high levels of domestic spending relative to domestic production.

The following assessment of the problem was offered by the IMF:

*As a matter of simple arithmetic, the global imbalances remain on an unsustainable trend over the long run, as they would lead to ever-accumulating stocks of emerging Asian and oil exporter's assets and US external liabilities. Therefore, the issue is not whether but how and when they adjust. . . . It is possible that there will be an orderly private-sector led adjustment in imbalances even without policy action, with US private savings rising gradually as interest rates increase and the housing market slows, accompanied by substantial real exchange rate adjustment, including through rising inflation in Asia. This benign scenario assumes that foreigners will continue to purchase US assets and that protectionist pressures can be avoided. If this does not happen, . . . the implication could be a much more abrupt and disorderly adjustment, characterised by a substantial overshooting of exchange rates; a large increase in interest rates; and a sharp contraction of global economic activity.*

*The question then becomes how public policy can best assist an orderly rebalancing. The World Economic Outlook has long argued that the key actions in this regard include measures to increase savings in the United States; exchange rate appreciation in the context of greater exchange rate flexibility, along with measures to boost domestic demand in emerging Asia; structural reforms to boost domestic demand and growth in the euro area and Japan; and measures to increase demand in oil exporters.* (IMF, *World Economic Outlook*, April 2006, pages 28–9)

Readers should visit the IMF website and read the latest edition of the *World Economic Outlook* to find out how much progress has been made.[18]

---

[18] See: http://www.imf.org/external/pubind.htm

# SUMMARY

- International trade normally requires the exchange of the currency of one country for that of another. The major exception is trade within the euro zone. The exchange rate between two currencies is the amount of one currency that must be paid in order to obtain one unit of another currency.

## The balance of payments

- Actual transactions among the firms, consumers, and governments of various countries are recorded in the balance of payments accounts. In these accounts any transaction that uses foreign exchange is recorded as a debit item, and any transaction that produces foreign exchange is recorded as a credit item. If all transactions are recorded, the sum of all credit items necessarily equals the sum of all debit items, because the foreign exchange that is bought must also have been sold.

- The two major categories in the balance of payments accounts are the current account and the capital and financial accounts. When we talk about a balance of payments surplus or deficit, we are normally referring to the current account balance alone. A balance on the current account must be matched by a balance on the capital and financial accounts of equal magnitude but opposite sign.

- There is nothing inherently good or bad about deficits or surpluses on the current account. Persistent deficits or surpluses involve a build-up or run-down of a country's net foreign assets.

## The market for foreign exchange

- The demand for pounds arises from UK exports of goods and services, income payments from overseas, capital inflows, and the desire of foreign governments to use sterling assets as part of their reserves.

- The supply of pounds to purchase foreign currencies arises from UK imports of goods and services, income payments to overseas, capital outflows, and the desire of holders of sterling assets to decrease the size of their holdings.

- The demand curve for pounds is negatively sloped and the supply curve of pounds is positively sloped when the quantities demanded and supplied are plotted against the price of pounds, measured in terms of a foreign currency.

## The determination of exchange rates

- When the authorities do not intervene in the foreign exchange market, there is a flexible exchange rate. Under fixed exchange rates the authorities intervene in the foreign exchange market to maintain the exchange rate within a specified range. To do this, they must hold sufficient stocks of foreign exchange reserves.

- Under a flexible (or floating) exchange rate regime the exchange rate is market-determined by supply and demand for the currency.

- Fluctuations in exchange rates can be understood as fluctuations around a trend value that is determined by the purchasing power parity (PPP) rate. The PPP rate adjusts in response to differences in national inflation rates. Deviations from the PPP rate are related, among other things, to international differences in interest rates.

- Exchange rates tend to overshoot their long-run equilibrium in response to shocks. A relaxation of monetary policy, which lowers domestic interest rates, will cause the exchange rate to depreciate. However, it will tend to depreciate to a point from which it can then appreciate at a rate sufficient to compensate for the interest rate fall. A rise in domestic interest rates will tend to make the exchange rate overshoot in the opposite direction (upwards).

# TOPICS FOR REVIEW

- Balance of trade in goods and services
- Balance of income payments and transfers
- Current and capital accounts
- Mercantilist views on the balance of trade and volume of trade
- Foreign exchange and exchange rates
- Appreciation and depreciation

- Sources of the demand for and supply of foreign exchange
- Effects on exchange rates of capital flows, inflation, interest rates, and expectations about exchange rates
- Fixed and flexible exchange rates
- Adjustable pegs and managed floats
- Purchasing power parity
- Exchange rate overshooting

# QUESTIONS

1 If PPP holds and the same basket of goods that is priced at $100 in the USA costs £80 in the UK, what should be the exchange rate between £ and $?

2 Starting from the position in question 1, if UK prices now rise by 10 per cent while US prices rise by 5 per cent, what will the new exchange rate be?

3 Where (if at all) do each of the following appear in the balance of payments accounts: (*a*) money earned by an Italian waiter in London that is sent to his family in Italy, (*b*) a purchase by a UK resident of a house in France financed entirely by a loan from a French bank, (*c*) a purchase of shares in an American company by a UK pension fund, (*d*) the cost of an airline flight from the UK to the USA on a US airline? (Would it change if it were a UK airline?)

4 Does the balance of payments matter? If so how?

5 Is it a good thing or a bad thing for a country to have a strong currency?

6 Why do floating exchange rates tend to overshoot?

7 'Capital outflows are a bad thing for the home economy as they mean that we are investing in jobs overseas.' Critically evaluate this statement.

8 Is it desirable to have a current account surplus in the balance of payments?

9 Would you expect PPP to hold in the short run?

# Chapter 23

# MACROECONOMIC POLICY IN AN OPEN ECONOMY

How is macroeconomic policy affected by international influences? Do domestic policy-makers have any power over their own economy, or is it the world economy that matters? How do macro policy choices change with the exchange rate regime adopted? Should stabilization policy be conducted at the world level? These are some of the questions we study in this chapter.

In particular you will learn that:

- Openness of the economy matters, as international factors directly affect real demand, world financial forces influence domestic financial markets, and the exchange rate regime affects the policy choices that are available.

- Monetary policy is powerless to affect domestic aggregate demand under a fixed exchange rate regime when capital is perfectly mobile.

- The exchange rate is an important element of the monetary transmission under a floating exchange rate regime.

- The effects of fiscal policy depend on the exchange rate regime and the monetary policy rule that is used.

- The long-run impact of fiscal policy is mainly on the trade balance.

- Financial and spending linkages between economies cause business cycles to have similar patterns in many major economies.

We now focus on how the exchange rate regime and the explicit incorporation of international financial capital flows affect the impact of fiscal and monetary policies. This will give us a much better grasp of how the transmission mechanism works in a world of globalized finance.[1]

In Chapters 21 we expanded our model of the economy to incorporate monetary forces in the determination of aggregate demand. In that analysis we did make some allowances for openness, as net exports were a component of aggregate demand. Chapter 22 discussed the determinants of the exchange rate, and capital flows were an important part of that analysis. In this chapter we incorporate financial capital flows explicitly into our model and then go on to reconsider the impact of monetary and fiscal policies, under the alternative regimes of fixed and floating exchange rates.

Before proceeding, it might help to revise Chapter 21. It is also necessary to understand the *IS/LM* model, so it is advisable to read the appendix to Chapter 21 before proceeding (if you have not already done so). In Chapter 21 we neglected the role of external influences, such as capital flows and the exchange rate, in the adjustment process. Now they must be incorporated in order to complete our formal development of the short-run model of the macroeconomy.

---

[1] For a detailed explanation of how the UK Monetary Policy Committee (MPC) perceives the transmission mechanism of monetary policy to work in an economy that has a floating exchange rate and in which the MPC sets a specific interest rate in order to hit the inflation target, see http://www.bankofengland.co.uk/publications/other/monetary/montrans.pdf

# Why does openness matter?

There are three main reasons why we have to take a much closer look at the interactions between our macro model and the rest of the world. First, while we have always had net exports in our model, we have not paid attention to all the possible implications of trade imbalances. Second, as we have mentioned several times in earlier chapters, financial markets have become more integrated around the world. This is often referred to as the globalization of financial markets, and Box 23.1 discusses some of its causes. The high international mobility of financial capital implies that money markets in one country are influenced by what happens in the rest of the world's financial markets. Third, the exchange rate regime matters for the conduct of monetary policy because it affects the possibilities for *arbitrage* between domestic and overseas financial markets (and therefore the link between domestic and overseas interest rates). **Arbitrage** involves buying where a price is low and selling where it is high, in order to make profit. The process of arbitrage tends to drive prices of the same commodity or asset towards equality in different locations.

---

  **Box 23.1** **The globalization of financial markets**

Technological innovations in communication and financial liberalization have led to a globalization of the financial services industry over the past few decades. Computers, satellite communication systems, reliable telephones with direct world-wide dialling, electronic mail, and fax machines have put people in instantaneous contact anywhere in the world.

As a result of these new technologies, borrowers and lenders can learn about market conditions anywhere in the world and then move their funds instantly in search of the best loan rates. Large firms need transaction balances only while banks in their area are open. Once banks close for the day in each area, the firms will not need these balances until the following day's reopening. So the funds can be moved to another market, where they can be used until *it* closes, and then moved to yet another market. Funds are thus free to move from, say, London to New York to Tokyo and back to London on a daily rotation. This is a degree of global sophistication that was inconceivable before the advent of the computer, when international communication was much slower and costlier than it now is. To facilitate the movement in and out of various national currencies, increasing amounts of bank deposits are denominated in foreign rather than domestic currencies.

One of the first developments in this movement towards globalization was the growth of the foreign currency markets in Europe in the 1960s. At first the main currency involved was the US dollar. (The market for dollar-denominated bank deposits and loans outside the United States was known as the Eurodollar market—not to be confused with the foreign exchange market in which the euro exchanges for the dollar today.) The progressive world-wide lifting of domestic interest rate ceilings and other capital market restrictions that occurred in the 1980s led to a further globalization of financial markets. Particularly important was the abolition of exchange controls in country after country.

The United Kingdom abolished its exchange controls in 1979, Japan did so in 1980, France and Italy in 1989, Spain in 1991, Portugal and Ireland in 1992, and Greece in 1994. Once such restrictions were abolished, the wholesale money markets integrated with the international money markets very quickly. This is because sophisticated borrowers and lenders dealing with large amounts of money have an incentive to shop around for the best terms.

The increasing sophistication of information transfer has also led to a breakdown of the high degree of specialization that had characterized financial markets in earlier decades. When information was difficult to obtain and analyse, an efficient division of labour called for a host of specialist institutions, each with expertise in a narrow range of transactions. New developments in communications technology created economies of scale that led to the integration of various financial operations within one firm. For example, in many countries banks have moved into the markets where securities are traded, while many security-trading firms have begun to offer a range of banking services. As the scale of such integrated firms increases, they find it easier to extend their operations geographically as well as functionally. The introduction of the euro in 1999 added further impetus to globalization as it increased the integration of EU financial markets and created a currency that has become an important international instrument.

The heavy government intervention in domestic capital markets and government control over international capital flows that characterized the 1950s and 1960s is no longer possible. International markets are just too sophisticated. Globalization is here to stay; and, by removing domestic restrictions and exchange controls, governments in advanced countries were only bowing to the inevitable.

We need to expand a little on each of these three reasons before we proceed to an explicit analysis of the macro model in which capital flows are included and explicit attention is paid to the trade balance.

## Net exports

Our macro model, from Chapter 17 onwards, included net exports, *NX*. The first thing we learned about the *NX* function was that it is negatively sloped. This means that net exports fall as GDP rises—because induced imports rise while autonomous exports are constant.

We also discovered that the net export function will shift if there is an exogenous (autonomous) change in export demand, and if there is a change in the domestic price level relative to foreign prices (caused either by an exchange rate change with given price level, or a price level change with a given exchange rate). An autonomous rise in exports increases net exports (shifts the *NX* function upwards for each level of GDP—see Figures 17.2 and 17.3 on pages 387–8). A rise in domestic relative prices reduces net exports (shifts the *NX* function down and changes its slope).

When we studied how fiscal and monetary policy can be used to speed up the adjustment of GDP back to equilibrium (see pages 476–9), we ignored any repercussions that might be induced by changes in the balance of trade. We can no longer do so. We now analyse the impacts of monetary and fiscal policies taking explicit account of the forces that are put in play by the change in the trade balance as GDP changes. The nature of these impacts is influenced by the degree of mobility of financial capital and by the exchange rate regime. We will focus on the case of highly mobile financial capital, because this conforms closely to the modern world.

## Mobile capital

Recall that, when we talk about capital flows in the context of the balance of payments, we are *not* talking about imports and exports of capital goods, such as machine tools and heavy equipment. Rather, we are talking about trade in assets and liabilities, such as shares and bonds, or about lending by banks in one country to customers in another.

Capital flows matter for two reasons. First, as we saw in Chapter 22, net capital flows must be equal in magnitude (but with the opposite sign) to the current account balance. Since this relationship is true by definition, it must always hold. It is important to realize, however, that changes affecting capital flows have implications for net exports

(possibly via exchange rate changes), just as shifts affecting net exports have implications for the capital account. We will be more specific about these linkages below.

The second reason why capital flows matter for the macro model is that they influence the domestic interest rate. If everyone is free to borrow and lend both domestically and internationally, they will borrow where the interest rate is lowest and lend where it is highest. Mobile capital tends to drive the domestic interest rate towards the level of interest rates in world markets. In effect, the domestic economy is close to being a price-taker in world financial markets.

We will examine how capital mobility affects our model below. The key point to notice now is that, in an open economy with mobile financial capital, we cannot analyse the determination of the domestic interest rate using domestic demand and supply forces alone. Changes in the domestic interest rate brought about by domestic shocks and policy responses will generate reactions through international capital flows and net exports that will inevitably complicate the picture.

It may seem that what we are saying here conflicts with the fact that domestic monetary authorities set interest rates. How can they also be set in world financial markets? These are not inconsistent. Monetary authorities set a specific nominal interest rate for short-term borrowing in money markets, but as we shall see below, their freedom of manoeuvre depends on the exchange regime in which they operate. With a pegged exchange rate they have no choice in the interest rate they set.

Under floating exchange rates they have more discretion, but world market forces also matter. In our model developed above we have only one interest rate. However, in the real world there are many interest rates for loans of different type and duration. Monetary authorities set short-term *nominal* rates, but world markets set longer-term *real* rates.

We continue to assume a simple financial structure in our model, but this need not stop us making statements about the more complicated financial forces that operate in the real world.

## The exchange rate regime

The exchange rate regime matters because it determines which variables are free to adjust. Fixing the exchange rate ties down other variables as well as the exchange rate. Fixed exchange rates tie together the value of domestic and foreign money, which implies that the domestic price level cannot deviate from the foreign price level in the long run.

Fixed exchange rates, with mobile capital, also tie domestic and foreign interest rates together because there is no exchange rate uncertainty. In such circumstances the domestic monetary authorities have no discretion in setting the domestic interest rates. The money supply is endogenously determined by demand, at whatever interest rate is dictated by world money markets. This explains why the UK authorities had no discretion to lower interest rates (as would have been dictated by internal considerations alone) during October 1990–September 1992, when the UK was a member of the ERM. It is also relevant to understanding the behaviour of the economies of the 12 members of the euro zone after January 1999. For these countries there is only one interest rate,—that set by the European Central Bank—so monetary policy is the same for all.

We shall see that, in general, the monetary authorities of nations with independent currencies can fix any one (but only one) of the interest rate, the exchange rate, and the money supply. Once they choose one of these, the other two become endogenous. Fixing the exchange rate is one possible monetary policy, but having done this the authorities cannot also control either the interest rate or the money supply. Most major countries (outside the euro zone) set short-term interest rates and let the money supply and the exchange rate adjust.

Under floating exchange rates, much of the adjustment to shocks comes through exchange rate changes and the resulting effect on the relative prices of domestic and foreign goods (and assets). In contrast, under fixed exchange rates, much more of the adjustment to shocks is worked out via aggregate demand, money stock, and output changes at given relative prices. These differences will become clearer as we work through specific examples below.

We now turn to a discussion of how the macro model is modified by the inclusion of capital flows, and how the presence of capital flows alters the impact of monetary and fiscal policies.

# Macro policy in a world with perfect capital mobility

As we have seen, financial flows in the balance of payments accounts include net cross-border sales of a wide variety of domestic and foreign assets—shares and bonds, etc. To keep things as simple as possible, we assume that there are just two types of asset: domestic bonds and foreign bonds. Domestic bonds are denominated in pounds sterling and foreign bonds are denominated in US dollars. (Which foreign currency we select is not critical; in our model it represents the rest of the world.)

When asset-holders switch from foreign bonds to domestic bonds, capital flows into the home economy. When asset-holders switch from domestic bonds to foreign bonds, capital flows out of the home economy. The process of switching involves sales of one currency for the other, so it creates a demand or supply of foreign exchange in the foreign exchange market.

An important assumption we make throughout is that net exports (the goods and services balance) and the current account of the balance of payments are identical. In effect, this means that we are ignoring the net income and transfers components of the current account.[2] This is a reasonable assumption for the United Kingdom in 2005; as Table 22.1 on page 499 shows, the balance of these was around 1.6 per cent of GDP in that year. Even if this item were not so small, it could be ignored for analytical purposes, because it does not vary much in response to short-run changes in exchange rates or GDP.

In order to incorporate capital flows into the macro model, we need to use the *IS* and *LM* curves discussed on pages 490–6. Recall that the *IS* and *LM* curves are just a convenient way of showing how the monetary sector interacts with the determinants of aggregate spending to determine the position of the aggregate demand curve.

## The macro model with capital flows

Two relationships must be kept in mind when incorporating capital flows into our model. First, since net capital flows must be of equal size and opposite sign to the current account balance of payments surplus or deficit, an actual capital inflow implies a current account deficit of equal size. Second, the foreign demand for domestic bonds depends in part upon the differential in interest rates between domestic and foreign bonds.

We need to make some assumption about how sensitive demand for domestic bonds will be to this interest differential. The analysis of Chapter 21 implicitly assumed immobile financial capital, so that there would be no switching between domestic and foreign bonds at any

---

[2] This assumption is equivalent to assuming that GNI is equal to GDP.

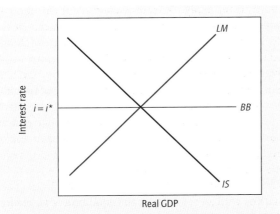

**Figure 23.1** The macroeconomic implications of perfect capital mobility

With perfect capital mobility, the domestic interest rate must be equal to the foreign interest rate in equilibrium. The $BB$ line shows the combinations of interest rates and GDP for which a current account surplus (deficit) equals the associated capital outflow (inflow). The $BB$ line is drawn horizontally at the point where the domestic interest rate is equal to the foreign rate $i^*$. The shape of $BB$ means that any size of current account deficit can be financed by borrowing at the going interest rate on world capital markets.

feasible interest rate. Now we make the opposite assumption that foreign demand for domestic bonds is perfectly elastic with respect to the interest differential. In effect, we are assuming that domestic and foreign bonds are perfect substitutes.[3] This is only one of several possible assumptions, but it is closer to the realities of the modern world of globalized finance and highly mobile international capital than the assumption of perfect immobility. Hence it is a reasonable simplifying assumption to make in the UK context, and for most other major countries, though it is inappropriate for economies that still have official exchange controls affecting capital flows.

Perfect substitutability between domestic bonds and foreign bonds is called perfect capital mobility. Its implications are illustrated in Figure 23.1, which shows the $IS/LM$ diagram explained in the appendix to Chapter 21, with the addition of a horizontal line labelled $BB$. Points on the $BB$ line represent combinations of the interest rate and GDP for which there is equality between the current account balance of payments and capital flows. It joins short-run balance of payments equilibrium points. Its horizontal slope reflects the assumption that capital is perfectly mobile. If the return on domestic bonds were

slightly higher than that on foreign bonds, there would be an immediate huge demand for them; this would drive up the price of domestic bonds and drive down their yield. Similarly, if domestic bonds had a yield below foreign bonds, holders would sell them to buy foreign bonds; this would drive their price down and their yield up. The result is that the domestic interest rate must equal the world interest rate $i^*$.[4] The intuition is that any two commodities that are perfect substitutes must have a common price (because they are, in effect, one commodity).

It is important to notice that the $BB$ curve does not represent points for which the current account balance is zero. Indeed, for a given net export function, the current account balance deteriorates as we move to the right (GDP increases). If this involves a deficit, however, borrowing from abroad at the going world rate of interest can finance this. Thus, any point on $BB$ for which there is a current account imbalance will also be associated with an equal and opposite capital account imbalance. The horizontal shape of $BB$ reflects the perfectly elastic supply curve of capital, as discussed above.

How can we be sure that the $BB$ line cuts the $IS$ and $LM$ curves at their intersection? The answer is that initially it may not do so; but if it does not, there will be endogenous adjustments of exchange rates and/or money supply. These will shift either the $IS$ or the $LM$ curve (or both) until all three have a common intersection. We will shortly be discussing cases where policy changes create such non-intersections, and we will then see in detail how such adjustment works. The exact process depends upon the exchange rate regime in operation as well as the monetary policy regime.

The implication that domestic and foreign interest rates are equal requires further comment. Recall that domestic and foreign bonds are denominated in different currencies. When exchange rates are fixed (and expected to remain fixed), this causes no complications. The comparative yield is given by the interest differential. Perfect capital mobility does indeed require exact equality of domestic and foreign interest rates—as it would also do for risk-free bonds within the euro zone.

However, under floating exchange rates, where exchange rates are expected to change, the position is more complicated. Here there can be a differential in nominal interest rates that will be equal to the expected rate of change of the exchange rate. This effect is associated with exchange rate overshooting, and was discussed in

---

[3] Since corporate bonds vary in riskiness, at best there will be perfect substitutability only between the bonds issued by governments of major industrial countries, as these have virtually no default risk.

[4] If capital flows were imperfect, the $BB$ line would be positively sloped because net exports decrease as GDP increases, and the higher capital flows required to finance an increasing current account deficit could be attracted only at increasing interest rates.

Chapter 22 and illustrated in Figure 22.5 on page 514. Suppose, for example, that holders of bonds expect sterling to depreciate against the US dollar by 5 per cent over the next year. If the yield on US bonds is 10 per cent per year, they will need a yield of about 15 per cent per year on sterling bonds to compensate for the expected currency depreciation. In this case the expected returns will be equal, but the nominal interest rates will not.[5]

This means that, when we discuss floating exchange rates, points on the horizontal *BB* line represent the full equilibrium, when there are no further expectations of exchange rate changes—but the economy can deviate from the line during the adjustment process. With fixed exchange rates, on the other hand, the economy must be on it all the time.

Perfect capital mobility means that with fixed exchange rates the domestic interest rate must always equal the foreign interest rate. With floating exchange rates any interest differential must equal the expected exchange rate change. This will be zero in full equilibrium.

The explicit addition of capital flows to our model introduces a new adjustment mechanism that reconciles differences in the desired trade surplus and desired net capital flows via either official reserve changes (under fixed exchange rates) or exchange rate changes (under floating rates). This we will explain using specific examples.

## Policy changes with fixed exchange rates

Now we can trace through the effects of monetary and fiscal policy changes in a model that allows for perfect capital mobility. Of particular interest will be the new predictions that follow from the addition of capital flows to the model.

To make it easier to understand how the adjustment mechanism works with capital flows included, initially we consider the effects of policy changes starting from a position of full equilibrium, where $Y = Y^*$. Of course, policy changes would normally be made to correct a disequilibrium that had been caused by some exogenous shock. If we start our analysis from disequilibrium, however, there can be many different reasons for disequilibrium (that is,

shocks from many different sources), and the effect of policy changes may depend upon what has caused the deviation of $Y$ from $Y^*$. When we start at $Y^*$, there should be no surprise to find that eventually we return to $Y^*$. What matters is to understand how the adjustment mechanism of the economy works when perfect capital mobility is assumed, and how the exchange rate regime affects this. We will discuss how the result might change if we start with disequilibrium later. We first consider a fixed exchange rate regime.

### Monetary policy

Starting with an economy in full equilibrium, we assume that the monetary authorities relax the monetary policy stance by reducing the domestic interest rate. The analysis, which is shown in Figure 23.2, is simple under a fixed exchange rate regime.

The policy change, if it could be made to stick, would shift the *LM* curve to the right (because a lower interest rate would lead to a higher money stock, as discussed in Chapter 21), which in turn would shift the *AD* curve to the right. However, we do not bother to translate this shift into an aggregate demand shift, because it will have to be reversed immediately. As soon as domestic interest rates

**Figure 23.2 Monetary policy with fixed exchange rates and perfect capital mobility**

Monetary policy is powerless to influence economic activity under fixed exchange rates and perfect capital mobility. An attempted cut in domestic interest rates increases the money supply and shifts the *LM* curve to the right from $LM_0$ to $LM_1$. However, the smallest fall in domestic interest rates causes a massive desired capital outflow. This puts downward pressure on the exchange rate. The monetary authorities are forced to buy sterling immediately in order to stop the exchange rate falling, and the *LM* curve shifts back to its original position, $LM_0$.

---

[5] The exact expression that must hold for expected yields on the two bonds denominated in different currencies to be equal is: $(1 + i) = (1 + i^*)(e_t/e_{t+1})$, where $i$ is the yield on UK bonds (expressed as a decimal, so 10 per cent is 0.1), $i^*$ is the yield on foreign bonds, $e_t$ is the exchange rate ($ per £) at the beginning of the holding period, and $e_{t+1}$ is the exchange rate expected to obtain at the end of the holding period.

dip slightly below world rates, there will be a massive sale of domestic bonds. This will create an excess supply of sterling in the foreign exchange market (because holders are selling sterling bonds and converting the proceeds into dollars to buy dollar bonds), and the authorities will have to buy sterling (and sell reserves) in order to stop the exchange rate from falling.

As they buy back sterling, just as when they sell bonds in Chapter 21 (here they are selling dollars), the domestic money supply is reduced, and the *LM* curve shifts back to its initial position. In effect, the domestic monetary authorities are forced to abandon their attempt to lower domestic interest rates by the massive capital outflows (and loss of foreign exchange reserves) that follow. The conclusion is that, with perfect capital mobility and fixed exchange rates, the monetary authorities have control over neither domestic interest rates nor the stock of money. If they do not set the domestic interest rates at the ruling world interest rate, they will be swamped with massive inflows or outflows of financial capital (bond sales or purchases). Thus, perfect capital mobility implies that it is

impossible to use monetary policy to influence real economic activity under fixed exchange rates. For exactly the same reasons, there cannot be independent monetary policies in the member states of the euro zone. The ECB can change the interest rate for all member countries, but no single country can change its own interest rate. (Indeed, there is only one interest rate for all member countries.)

**Monetary policy under fixed exchange rates and perfect capital mobility cannot exert any independent influence over real economic activity.**

### Fiscal policy

The analysis of what happens when fiscal policy changes is more complicated than in the case of a monetary policy change. It is also very different from events in the absence of capital flows. The course of events is illustrated in Figure 23.3.

Again, we start with the economy in full equilibrium. We need also to clarify what the monetary authorities are doing. As we explained above, the monetary authorities

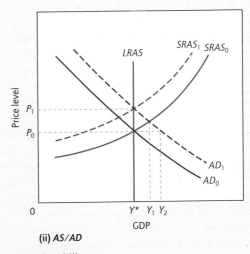

(i) *IS/LM*    (ii) *AS/AD*

**Figure 23.3 Fiscal policy with fixed exchange rates and perfect capital mobility**

**Starting from full equilibrium, an increase in government spending creates a significant stimulus to real activity in the short run, but in the long run it leads to a higher price level and a current account deficit.** The increase in government spending shifts the *IS* curve from $IS_0$ to $IS_1$ in part (i). With a given money supply, this puts upward pressure on domestic interest rates. The slightest rise in domestic interest rates causes a massive capital inflow, which puts upward pressure on the exchange rate. To stop the exchange rate rising, the monetary authorities sell sterling in the foreign exchange market. This increases the money supply and shifts the *LM* curve to the right, from $LM_0$ to $LM_1$. The combined effect of the *IS* and *LM* curves shifting is that *AD* shifts right, from $AD_0$ to $AD_1$, as shown in part (ii).

The increase in aggregate demand causes GDP to increase from $Y^*$ to $Y_1$ in the short run, and there is a small initial increase in the price level. (This price level rise shifts the *IS* and *LM* curves slightly leftward to $IS_2$ and $LM_2$ so that they intersect at $Y_1$ rather than $Y_2$.) Net exports become negative. In the long run, inflationary pressure causes the price level to rise to $P_1$ as the *SRAS* curve shifts up to $SRAS_1$ and GDP returns to $Y^*$. However, the sustained rise in the price level (for given foreign prices) causes a permanent trade deficit, which is equal to the budget deficit. At price level $P_1$ the real money supply has fallen, so the *LM* curve shifts back to $LM_0$. The higher price of domestic goods causes net exports to shift downwards, so *IS* also shifts back to its original position, $IS_0$.

cannot set both the domestic interest rate *and* the exchange rate. Since we are studying the fixed exchange rate case here, we must temporarily drop the assumption that the monetary authorities are fixing the domestic interest rate. Rather, the monetary policy is pegging the exchange rate, and the interest rate is determined by world interest rates.

The assumed fiscal policy change is an increase in government spending. The initial effect of this increase is to shift the *IS* curve to the right. With a given initial nominal money stock (given *LM* curve), this will put upward pressure on domestic interest rates. However, even the smallest rise in domestic interest rates generates a capital inflow (foreign demand for domestic bonds) and creates excess demand for sterling in the foreign exchange markets. To stop the exchange rate rising, the monetary authorities have to sell sterling and buy foreign currency. These sales of sterling increase the supply of money and shift the *LM* curve to the right.

Thus, the initial rightward shift of the *IS* curve has been reinforced by a rightward shift of the *LM* curve. The *AD* curve shifts to the right as a result of each of these shifts. The combined effect is shown in part (ii) of the figure. This is a bigger shift of *AD* than would have resulted from a shift in the *IS* curve alone. Indeed, the size of the horizontal shift of *AD* is equal to the full value of the simple (open-economy) multiplier, because there is no negative feedback (via higher interest rates) from the monetary sector. This comes about because interest rates cannot rise, so the authorities have to increase the money supply to avoid an exchange rate appreciation.

This is not the end of the story. The increase in aggregate demand shifts the aggregate demand curve to intersect the initial short-run aggregate supply curve at a level of GDP well above its potential level. The resulting inflationary gap causes a short-term boom in the economy, and real GDP rises temporarily above its potential level.

The inflationary gap, once created, puts upward pressure on the domestic price level. Initially this is felt only in output prices. The increase in output prices, combined with the increase in real GDP, creates a trade deficit. The current account balance deteriorates because (induced) imports increase with domestic income. The price level rise reinforces this increase because (with a fixed exchange rate and given foreign prices) domestic goods become more expensive relative to foreign goods. Thus, there is a change in the import propensity and a fall in net exports. Indeed, it is this price level rise that moves the economy back up the *AD* curve and reduces the impact on GDP, compared with the full impact of the simple multiplier (as measured by the horizontal shift in *AD*).

In the longer term, inflationary forces pass through to input prices, and the short-run aggregate supply curve shifts up to the left. This raises the price level further, as the economy moves back up the *AD* curve and GDP returns to its potential level. The higher price level reduces the real money supply, and so the *LM* curve shifts back leftwards to its initial position. It also further increases the trade deficit, and this downward shift in net exports also shifts the *IS* curve back leftwards to its original position.

Thus, instead of crowding out investment (as would happen in the absence of capital flows), the increase in government spending has led to a trade deficit of equal value. (Real GDP returns to its original level but real national spending has risen by the amount of extra government spending. The excess of national spending over national output is equal to the trade deficit.)

**An increase in government spending (starting at full equilibrium), with fixed exchange rates and perfect capital mobility, creates a short-run economic boom, but the long-run effect is an increase in the domestic price level and a trade deficit.**

This trade deficit will be equal to the government budget deficit if the initial position was one of budget balance and trade balance. Notice also that the mechanism that brought about the trade deficit was a rise in domestic prices (relative to foreign prices). This is equivalent to a rise in the real exchange rate, even though the nominal exchange rate is fixed. However, in this case there has been no crowding out of investment because fiscal policy is powerless to influence interest rates. In effect, domestic investment can be financed at the going world interest rate. The trade deficit is matched by a capital inflow (foreign purchases of domestic bonds) of equal size.

This is the end of the story in our model, but it cannot be the end of the story in reality. We have an equilibrium in which there is a current account deficit on the balance of payments and, therefore, continuing capital inflows. The domestic economy is borrowing from the rest of the world to finance the excess of spending over output.

If this borrowing is financing current consumption (government consumption in this case), the wealth of the economy will be falling (relative to the initial trend position), and that cannot go on for ever—although, as the current experience of the United Sates illustrates, it can go on for quite a long time. At some point, however, the wealth effects will lead to either a (downward) shift in domestic spending or a reversal of government policy. (The government cannot build up infinite debt, and any financing problems may cause reserve losses.) The modelling of such wealth effects is beyond the scope of this

**Figure 23.4** Reactions to monetary and fiscal policy changes under fixed exchange rates

**Monetary policy is powerless under fixed exchange rates, but fiscal policy is not.** Any change in monetary policy generates capital flow and a change in reserves which force the monetary authorities to reverse their actions. A fiscal policy change shifts the *IS* and *AD* curves to the right and takes GDP above potential. The extra spending in the economy makes domestic spending greater than domestic output so net exports become negative. The excess of output over potential starts to put upward pressure on domestic prices. As prices rise, *Y* falls back to *Y\**, and at the new equilibrium *Y* is equal to *Y\**, the price level is higher, and the increase in *G* is just equal to the (negative) increase in net exports.

book. Readers should merely note that some further adjustment must occur sooner or later.

However, if the borrowing is financing real investment (or if an equivalent amount of real investment is taking place anyway), the story could be quite different. If the return on real investment is greater than the interest rate on foreign borrowing, the economy will be increasing its wealth over time. So long as investment returns continue to exceed interest costs, such a position can be sustained and potential GDP will continue to grow over time. Therefore, one cannot assume that a current account balance of payments deficit is always undesirable. This reinforces the point first stated in Chapter 22.

A summary of the main reactions to monetary and fiscal policy under fixed rates is shown in Figure 23.4.

## Policy changes with floating exchange rates

We now turn to an analysis of policy changes under a regime of floating exchange rates. This is the current regime in the United Kingdom, as it is for most major countries (where the euro zone is counted as one country), so this analysis is the one that is appropriate for analysing the effects of macroeconomic policy in most major economies today. It represents the culmination of all our efforts to build a macroeconomic model. We return to a framework in which the monetary authorities set the interest rate (as the exchange rate is set by market forces in a floating exchange rate regime).

### Monetary policy

Again, we start with a relaxation of domestic monetary policy in the form of a reduction in the interest rate initi-

ated by the domestic monetary authorities from a position of full equilibrium, as illustrated in Figure 23.5. This shifts the *LM* curve downward to the right (because the authorities buy bonds and increase the money stock in order to lower the market interest rate).

The fall in domestic interest rates, with perfect capital mobility, will normally cause a massive capital outflow. However, since the exchange rate is floating, the emergence of an excess supply of sterling causes an immediate drop in the exchange rate. It drops to the point where it is expected to appreciate at a rate sufficient to compensate for the lower domestic interest rate; in other words, it overshoots its long-run equilibrium in a downward direction. We discussed this notion of overshooting in Chapter 22, pages 514–15.

The fall in the nominal exchange rate also represents a fall in the real exchange rate, because the domestic price level does not change quickly, while the exchange rate has fallen instantaneously. So the relative price of domestic goods has fallen. This leads to an upward shift in the net export function, which causes a shift of the *IS* curve to the right. The combined effect of the rightward shifts of the *LM* and *IS* curves causes a rightward shift in the *AD* curve.

The increase in aggregate demand takes GDP beyond its potential level and creates an inflationary gap. In the short run the economy experiences a boom in output and a small increase in the domestic price level. This increase in prices reduces the real money supply slightly and also offsets a little the upward shift in net exports; so both the *IS* and *LM* curves shift back a fraction relative to their initial new positions. However, the full adjustment takes place in the longer term, when inflationary pressure works through into input costs and the short-run aggregate supply curve shifts upwards.

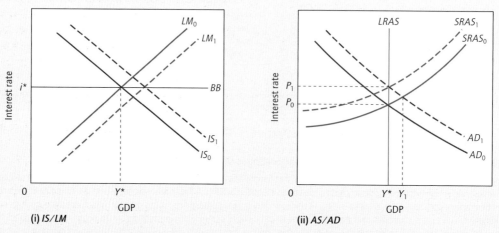

**Figure 23.5** Monetary policy with floating exchange rates and perfect capital mobility

Starting at full equilibrium, a monetary loosening causes an output boom in the short run but in the long run causes only higher prices and currency depreciation. The *LM* curve shifts to the right. Any fall in the domestic interest rate causes the exchange rate to depreciate to a point from which it is expected to appreciate. This involves overshooting and a fall in the real exchange rate. This fall in the real exchange rate shifts the net export function upwards, so, as part (i) shows, there is a shift in the *IS* curve from $IS_0$ to $IS_1$ accompanying the initial shift in the *LM* curve from $LM_0$ to $LM_1$. The combined effect of these two shifts on aggregate demand is shown in part (ii) as the shift from $AD_0$ to $AD_1$.

The increase in aggregate demand creates an inflationary gap. GDP increases from $Y^*$ to $Y_1$ in the short run, and the price level starts to rise to the level indicated by the intersection of $AD_1$ and $SRAS_0$. Eventually inflationary pressure works through to input prices, and the short-run aggregate supply curve shifts upwards to $SRAS_1$. The price level rises to $P_1$, and GDP falls back to $Y^*$. The *LM* curve shifts back to $LM_0$ as the rise in price level reduces the real money supply. The *IS* curve shifts back to $IS_0$ as higher domestic prices raise the relative price of domestic goods and the net export function shifts downwards. The long-run outcome is an increase in prices but the same real GDP.

As the price level rises to its long-run equilibrium, the real money supply returns to its original level, so the *LM* curve shifts back to its initial position, reversing the initial interest rate fall. Also, the real exchange rate returns to its initial position (the price level rises in proportion to the long-run currency depreciation), so net exports shift back to where they started. Notice, however, that during the adjustment period the current account has been in surplus because of the lower real exchange rate (and therefore there have been capital outflows), and so there has been an accumulation of net foreign assets (or a rundown of foreign liabilities). This accumulation has occurred because national spending has been less than national output during the adjustment process (i.e., there has been a trade surplus). The current account is back in balance at the long-run equilibrium.

An expansionary monetary policy under floating exchange rates with perfect capital mobility causes a boom in real economic activity in the short run, but the long-run effect is a higher price level and a depreciation of the nominal exchange rate, with no permanent gain in real output and an unchanged real exchange rate.

Although we assume in the context of our model that GDP returns to its potential level, in practice there may be some long-run real effects. During the transition period, which may be quite a long time, national wealth increases. Lower interest rates cause a temporary rise in investment, which creates domestic assets, and the temporary trade surplus causes an accumulation of foreign assets. These effects are ignored in our model, but in reality they may be significant.

Notice also the change in the monetary adjustment mechanism when there is perfect capital mobility. In the absence of capital flows the monetary expansion creates a desired current account deficit, whereas in the presence of capital flows it creates an exchange rate depreciation, which results in an actual current account surplus and a capital outflow. In the long run the outcome is the same (a higher price level and proportional depreciation of the currency with the same real GDP), but external payments adjustment during the transition to full equilibrium is quite different.

### Fiscal policy

The case of a fiscal policy expansion under floating exchange rates with perfect capital mobility is illustrated

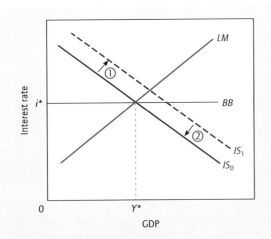

**Figure 23.6 Fiscal policy with floating exchange rates and perfect capital mobility**

Starting at full equilibrium, a fiscal expansion leads to a currency appreciation which crowds out an equivalent volume of net exports, causing a current account deficit but little or no stimulus to GDP. The initial increase in government spending shifts the IS curve to the right from $IS_0$ to $IS_1$. But the resulting appreciation of the exchange rate (real and nominal) shifts the net export function downwards, which shifts the IS curve back to the left.

in Figure 23.6. Again, we take as our policy change an increase in government spending at full equilibrium.

The increase in government spending shifts the IS curve to the right. What happens next depends on what the monetary authorities do. We examine two cases. In the first the authorities adjust the domestic interest rate upwards in order to maintain a constant money stock; and in the second case the authorities hold the domestic interest rate fixed by buying bonds and increasing the money stock.

### Fixed money stock

With a given money supply (fixed LM curve), a rightward shift of the IS curve, resulting from the expansionary fiscal policy, puts upward pressure on domestic interest rates. Any rise in domestic interest rates creates massive desired capital inflows and thereby puts upward pressure on the exchange rate. The exchange rate immediately appreciates to a point from which it can be expected to depreciate at a rate equal to the interest differential.

The exchange rate appreciation, for a given initial price level, also appreciates the real exchange rate, which means that domestic goods become more expensive than foreign goods. This rise in the relative price of domestic goods shifts the net export function downwards, and therefore

also shifts the IS curve back towards its original position. The result is a current account balance of payments deficit, which is matched by net capital inflows.

There is ambiguity about the precise course of aggregate demand in the short run. The increase in government spending shifts AD to the right, but the downward shift in net exports shifts it back to the left. On balance, the likely outcome is that it will remain roughly at its initial position. The factors affecting the adjustment of net exports to an exchange rate change are discussed in Box 23.2. In any event, the effect on real GDP, even in the short run, may well be negligible.

The long-run outcome is that there is a trade deficit that matches the government budget deficit. There is also a permanent increase in the real exchange rate, brought about by a sustained appreciation of the nominal exchange rate, though less than the appreciation achieved during the overshooting phase. There is a significant difference between short-run adjustment to a fiscal policy expansion under floating exchange rates with perfect capital mobility and the case with no capital flows. With no capital flows the increase in G creates an inflationary gap and a currency depreciation, the domestic price level rises, and interest rates rise, thereby crowding out investment. With capital flows the same increase in the relative price of domestic output is brought about by exchange rate appreciation, but there is no interest rate rise, and no sustained crowding-out of investment. There is, however, a trade deficit that matches the budget deficit.

Again, this cannot be the end of the story, because there is ongoing borrowing by the government and increasing indebtedness to foreigners. Thus, similar wealth effects arise to those we discussed in the context of fiscal policy under fixed exchange rates. The big difference, however, is that under floating exchange rates a fiscal expansion, holding M constant, creates a minimal stimulus to real GDP, whereas under fixed rates a fiscal expansion leads to a short-run boom.

An expansionary fiscal policy, under floating exchange rates, has little impact on real GDP in the short run when the money stock is fixed; instead, it causes an exchange rate appreciation and a trade deficit. In the long run there is a permanent appreciation of the real exchange rate, and the government budget deficit is equal to the trade deficit.

### Fixed interest rate

The response to a fiscal policy change is somewhat different if the monetary authorities maintain a fixed interest rate, rather than raising rates in order to keep the money supply constant. Indeed, the outcome is initially similar

**Box 23.2  The J-curve**

In this chapter we consider what happens when there is a change in monetary or fiscal policy under fixed or floating exchange rates. We have not yet asked what happens under a fixed exchange rate regime if there is a discrete devaluation. In such a devaluation there is a sudden fall in the exchange rate at which the currency is pegged.

Devaluations usually occur when a persistent current account deficit is causing a serious drain on official reserves. Their purpose is to reduce the deficit and thereby reduce outflows of official international reserves. However, the effect on the current account is often not immediately positive. A common pattern is for the current account first to deteriorate further and then later to improve. This pattern is known as the J-curve because of the shape of the curve that the current account traces over time. The figure plots the path of the current account over time, starting in deficit. Devaluation at time $t_0$ initially makes the deficit worse, but eventually it leads to a surplus after a lag of perhaps two years.

The reason for the initial deterioration in the current account is that volumes of imports and exports take time to adjust to the new relative prices. Devaluation makes domestic goods cheaper than foreign goods, and if volumes did not change at all, the domestic currency value of exports would stay the same but the domestic currency value of imports would rise (because their price has gone up in domestic currency terms).

It is only when the volumes of imports and exports adjust more than in proportion to the change in relative goods prices that the current account of the balance of payments improves. After the

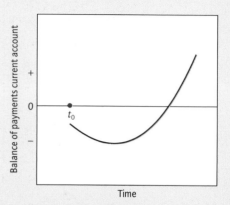

1967 devaluation of sterling, it took between eighteen months and two years for the current account to move into surplus.

The J-curve is also applicable to a world of floating exchange rates after a sudden sustained exchange rate change. It helps us to understand that it takes many months, if not years, for the trade account to adjust fully to such exchange rate changes. Thus, when the UK left the ERM in September 1992 its currency devalued by about 20 per cent against the US dollar, and the effects of this took several years to work through. When exchange rates change in small steps, the economic adjustments are still there, but they are harder to detect. Once the exchange rate is endogenous, of course, it becomes virtually impossible to determine the direction of causation—the exchange rate and the balance of payment are jointly determined by many other factors.

to that illustrated in Figure 23.5. The fiscal policy expansion shifts the *IS* curve to the right, and the money supply increase that results from the authorities' attempts to keep the interest rate from rising shifts the *LM* curve to the right. Thus, the *AD* curve shifts to the right and GDP goes from $Y^*$ to $Y_1$, as shown in Figure 23.5(ii). This creates an inflationary gap, and wage rises eventually shift the *SRAS* curve to the left, returning the economy to equilibrium at the original level of GDP but with a higher price level.

This is different from the case where the money stock is fixed because the fiscal expansion has given a temporary stimulus to real output. The increase in aggregate spending coming from higher government consumption does not crowd out net exports via a rapid rise in the real exchange rate. Instead, an expansion of the money stock acts to keep the real exchange rate down. Thus, the money stock expansion created by the monetary authorities reinforces the expansionary effect of fiscal policy in the short run. However, this expansion of the money stock must

eventually lead to a higher price level, and this rise in the price level will eventually crowd out net exports. Investment is not crowded out because interest rates do not change. But something has to be crowded out once the level of GDP returns to its potential level, $Y^*$: because $G$ is bigger, some other component of $C + I + G + NX$ must be smaller. Thus, the economy returns to equilibrium with a current account deficit. Borrowing from abroad will finance this deficit.

**A fiscal policy expansion does have a short-run expansionary effect on the economy if the monetary authorities increase the money supply to accommodate the increase in GDP at a constant interest rate. But net exports are crowded out in the long run by a higher domestic price level which raises the real exchange rate.**

Again, this cannot be the end of the story, as the current account deficit will lead to declining national wealth. The decline in wealth will eventually lead to a spending

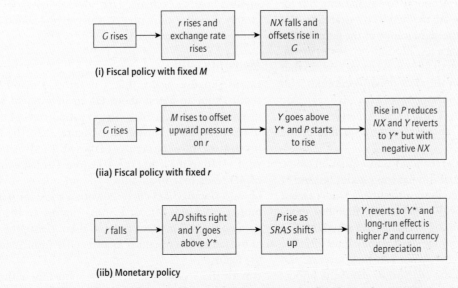

**Figure 23.7** Reactions to monetary and fiscal policy changes under floating exchange rates

With floating rates, monetary policy is more powerful than fiscal policy, though the effects of the latter depend on what monetary policy is followed. If the monetary authorities are fixing the money stock, case (i), a rise in G leads to a rise in the domestic interest rate and an appreciation of the currency. This leads to a fall in net exports which offsets the increase in G, so the government spending expansion just crowds out net exports with minimal impact on Y. If the monetary authorities are setting the interest rate, as in case (iia), and hold it constant in the face of an increase in G, then the money stock will rise (to offset upward pressure on r, and this stops the exchange rate rising) and the rightward shift in AD will take Y above Y*. Prices will then tend to rise and net exports will be crowded out. Ultimately Y will equal Y*, P will be higher, and the increase in G will be offset by a fall in NX.

A monetary expansion is implemented by lowering r, case (iib). This shifts the LM and AD curves to the right. The lower r permits an increase in M and stimulates an increase in I. This extra spending takes Y above Y* and upward pressure on prices results. As prices rise, the SRAS curve shifts leftwards and the currency depreciates. In equilibrium there is no gain in real output, a higher price level, and a depreciated currency.

fall that will correct the imbalance in external payments; however, this is where our analysis stops.

Let us now summarize what we have learned about the adjustment to monetary and fiscal policy changes in the presence of perfect capital mobility, assuming that we start in full equilibrium. We will then see whether starting in disequilibrium makes any difference.

1. *Under fixed exchange rates* monetary policy is powerless to influence real economic activity. The money supply is demand-determined, and the authorities have no discretion over interest rates. A fiscal policy expansion under fixed exchange rates causes a short-run boom in real activity, but this leads to inflation. The long-run effect is a permanent rise in the domestic price level and the real exchange rate, a budget deficit, and a trade deficit financed by capital inflows.

2. *Under floating exchange rates* an expansionary monetary policy creates an inflationary boom in real activity in the short run; in the long run the price level rises in proportion to the money stock increase, and the nominal

exchange rate depreciates in the same proportion. A fiscal policy expansion under floating exchange rates creates little or no increase in real GDP if the money stock is held fixed, even in the short run. In the long run there is a sustained real and nominal exchange rate appreciation, and the government budget deficit is matched by a trade deficit and capital account surplus. In contrast, if the monetary authorities maintain a fixed interest rate, and therefore increase the money stock to accompany the fiscal policy expansion, there will be a short-term stimulus to real GDP. In the long run the price level will rise and net exports will be crowded out, via a real exchange rate rise as before.

A summary of these main channels of causation for floating rates is shown in diagrammatic form in Figure 23.7.

## Policy changes to correct disequilibrium

We now need to see if our conclusions are specific to the case in which the economy is initially in equilibrium. In reality, policy-makers use monetary and fiscal policies as tools for returning the economy to equilibrium, not for moving it away. There are many possible examples, but we can get a feel for the significance of the equilibrium assumption by studying a few illustrative cases in depth. We will look closely only at flexible exchange rates, as that is the current situation for most major economies, and we will consider only the response to a negative aggregate demand shock. However, the fixed exchange rate case is easy to summarize, and we will now do that before proceeding.

Let us suppose that the economy is in a situation where $Y$ is less than $Y^*$, and that this has come about because of an autonomous fall in domestic investment. Under a fixed exchange rate regime with perfect capital mobility, monetary policy can do nothing to change this situation. The monetary authorities cannot lower interest rates (because of the horizontal $BB$ curve), nor can they increase the money supply. Hence the conclusion about the impotence of monetary policy under fixed exchange rates is robust, even when we start in disequilibrium. This result carries over to the individual economies of those EU countries that are members of the euro zone. Essentially, the national monetary authorities have no power to affect monetary conditions in their own country. Only the ECB can change the monetary stance (for all 13 member countries at once).

Fiscal policy, however, can have a beneficial effect. The fall in investment shifts the $IS$ and $AD$ curves to the left. An increase in government spending shifts these two curves back to their initial position without any of the longer-term harmful effects that arise when $G$ is increased starting from full equilibrium.[6] There is no real exchange rate appreciation or crowding-out of the balance of payments, though there is a budget deficit. Certainly, government spending has replaced investment spending in equilibrium GDP, but this is not crowding-out since the causation is reversed—$G$ is filling the gap left by an autonomous fall in $I$. Crowding-out involves higher $G$ causing lower $I$ through higher interest rates.

Now let the initial negative demand shock be an exogenous fall in export demand, rather than an autonomous fall in investment. The offsetting increase in $G$ and the accompanying budget deficit will be matched by a current account balance of payments deficit in equilibrium. But again, this is not crowding-out, because of the reversed causality. Also, the increase in $G$ will only improve the outcome if it is timed correctly. This point also arises

under a floating exchange rate, so let us now look more closely at policy responses to a negative demand shock under floating exchange rates.

## Monetary policy

Let us suppose, again, that a negative demand shock results from an autonomous fall in investment with a given initial money stock. The situation created by this investment fall is illustrated in Figure 23.8. The fall in investment shifts the $IS$ curve to the left. This is associated with a shift to the left of the $AD$ curve. The leftward shift of $AD$ leads to a small fall in the price level, given an upward-sloping $SRAS$ curve; so with a constant nominal money stock the $LM$ curve shifts slightly to the right, because the real money stock has risen. Hence the effect of the fall in investment is to lower GDP from $Y^*$ to $Y_1$ in the figure.[7]

With the economy at $Y_1$, if the monetary authorities permit interest rates to fall in order to keep the nominal money stock fixed, desired capital outflows will cause the exchange rate to depreciate. It will fall to the point where it is expected to appreciate at just the right rate to compensate for the lower domestic interest rate. The currency depreciation, combined with the lower price level, means that domestic goods have fallen in price relative to foreign goods. There has been a real exchange rate depreciation. This causes an upward shift in the net export function and an associated current account balance of payments surplus.

The upward shift in the net export function shifts the $IS$ curve back to the right, and this could be sufficient to return the economy to equilibrium at $Y^*$. However, it is possible that the initial recessionary gap may also cause the $SRAS$ curve to shift to the right, via a reduction in money wage rates. Both of these responses, however, take some time, so the monetary authorities could, in principle, speed up the return to $Y^*$ by increasing the nominal money supply, which would shift the $LM$ curve to the right.

The advisability of such a monetary response depends upon the authorities being able to achieve their effects quickly. Some economists believe that monetary policy works with 'long and variable lags'. If the effects of this monetary stimulus are not felt until GDP has already returned to a level close to potential, then, rather than

---

[6] Notice, however, that the Stability and Growth Pact imposes some restrictions on the size of budget deficits for EU member countries. These were discussed on pages 485–7.

[7] The initial fall in GDP would be much greater if the monetary authorities were pegging the interest rate rather than the nominal money stock. In that case GDP would initially fall to $Y_2$ in the figure. The authorities would have to abandon this pegged interest rate policy in order to use monetary policy to stimulate the economy, so we revert to the assumption of an initially fixed nominal money supply.

**Figure 23.8 Macro policies to correct a disequilibrium**

Monetary and fiscal policy can help the economy recover from a negative demand shock, so long as they are appropriately timed. The negative demand shock is assumed to be an autonomous fall in investment. The economy is initially in full equilibrium at $Y^*$. The fall in investment shifts the IS curve from $IS_0$ to $IS_1$ in part (i), and it shifts the AD curve from $AD_0$ to $AD_1$ in part (ii). The resulting fall in the price level from $P_0$ to $P_1$ increases the real money supply (assuming the authorities adjust interest rates to hold the money stock constant), which shifts the LM curve to $LM_1$. The economy thus goes to GDP level $Y_1$, where there is a recessionary gap.

In the absence of policy changes, the automatic adjustment mechanism will eventually bring GDP back to $Y^*$. Monetary policy can speed up this adjustment process by lowering domestic interest rates and causing currency depreciation shifting LM and AD to the right. Fiscal policy can shift the IS and AD curves back to their original positions.

help end the recession, it could cause the economy to overshoot into an inflationary boom. In any event, the monetary stimulus will have to be reversed at some stage if inflation is to be avoided in the longer term.

Thus, monetary policy can be used in the short term to offset the recessionary effects of a negative demand shock, but whether this can be done with enough accuracy to improve on the automatic adjustment mechanisms is controversial.

Monetary policy affects the real economy, via the effects of the exchange rate on net exports and via the effects of interest rate changes on investment, but timing this response correctly is difficult.

### Fiscal policy

Now let us consider the possibilities of a fiscal reaction to the same negative demand shock that is illustrated in Figure 23.8. As a result of the fall in investment, GDP has fallen from $Y^*$ to $Y_1$, assuming that the authorities have adjusted interest rates downward to maintain a constant money stock.

An appropriate increase in government spending would shift the IS and AD curves back to their initial positions and thereby restore GDP to $Y^*$. If this could be timed exactly to coincide with the fall in investment, there would be no need for a fall in interest rates and no exchange rate depreciation, and so there would be no shift in the net export function. The only change at full equilibrium would be lower investment and a budget deficit (assuming that the budget was in balance before the increase in government spending).[8]

However, as with monetary policy, there is the problem of getting the timing right. If the increase in government spending takes effect after the automatic adjustment process does its job, then the increased spending could create an inflationary gap (as happens when $G$ is increased with the economy starting at $Y^*$ as above).

There is, however, an important difference between fiscal and monetary stabilization in response to this same negative demand shock. Monetary stabilization policy speeds up the automatic response mechanism by lowering the interest rate and exchange rate further than they would otherwise go. If monetary policy is timed accurately, the long-run outcome is the same as if automatic stabilizing forces did the work. Monetary policy just helps to get the economy to full equilibrium more quickly.

By contrast, fiscal policy cuts out the automatic adjustment mechanism and leads to a different composition of final demand in equilibrium. The increased budget deficit crowds out an equivalent volume of net exports, relative to what would have happened if the automatic

---

[8] If the negative demand shock was caused by an exogenous fall in net exports rather than investment, the net effect would be a sustained budget deficit and a balance of payments deficit in full equilibrium.

adjustment had been left alone. This is because the fiscal stimulus stops the fall in the nominal and real exchange rate that would otherwise have shifted the net export function upwards.

In the case of an initial fall in investment, the automatic adjustment mechanism creates a current account balance of payments surplus at full equilibrium. A fiscal stimulus replaces this with a budget deficit (and a current account balance at full equilibrium). If the initial negative demand shock is caused by a fall in net exports, the automatic adjustment mechanism will restore the current account balance at full equilibrium. But an offsetting fiscal stimulus would mean that there was both a current account deficit and a budget deficit at full employment.

Fiscal policy can be used to help return GDP to potential when a recessionary gap has been created by a negative demand shock, but its precise impact will depend on the nature of the original shock.

In short, when the economy starts at less than potential GDP and has a flexible exchange rate, both monetary and fiscal policies can speed up the adjustment of GDP back to its potential level. However, whether actual fiscal and monetary policies improve on the automatic adjustment mechanism in practice depends crucially on timing. If the impact of policy is felt too late, it will push the recovery of GDP beyond potential GDP and into an inflationary boom, even though it was conceived as a response to an earlier recessionary gap.

## Some implications

Readers will probably have found the material in this chapter hard going, on first reading. However, the effort is worthwhile, because we have now reached a very advanced level of understanding of a coherent model of the macroeconomy. In the following chapters we will discuss a number of important policy issues. Before doing so, it is worth drawing together some of the implications of what we have already learned.

### The transmission of monetary policy

When we first introduced a monetary sector into our macro model in Chapter 21, we discussed the way in which changes in monetary policy are transmitted to the real economy via changes in domestic interest rates.

The transmission mechanism was set out as follows. The monetary authorities decide to stimulate the economy by lowering the interest rate. In order to lower the interest rate they buy bonds, and this leads to an increase in the money supply. The lower interest rate increases investment, which, via the multiplier, increases desired aggregate spending. This increase in desired aggregate spending means that there is an increase in aggregate demand. The increase in aggregate demand then leads to an increase in real GDP and a rise in the price level. As the price level rises further, in response to inflationary pressure, the real money stock falls and GDP returns to its potential level at a higher price level.

We have now learned that the transmission of monetary policy does not work quite like this in most forms of open economy. With fixed exchange rates monetary policy is powerless to influence the real economy, because excess supply of the home currency in the foreign exchange market will rapidly force a policy reversal. This happens especially quickly in the modern world of highly mobile financial capital.

Under floating exchange rates with perfect capital mobility, monetary policy is able to stimulate real activity in the short run. It does so largely because an expansionary monetary policy depreciates the real exchange rate, which stimulates net exports. Deliberate use of monetary policy can be helpful in speeding the adjustment to a negative demand shock. In our model, nominal interest rates fall temporarily and this stimulates investment. However, in practice the effect on investment may be small. Hence it is likely that the principal link in the transmission mechanism from the monetary sector to real activity in an open economy, with floating exchange rates, is through the exchange rate to net exports.

The views of the Bank of England's MPC of the transmission mechanism are available on www.bankofengland.co.uk/publications/other/monetary/montrans.pdf. They are entirely consistent with what we have said, though they include some other channels. There are, for example, some direct effects of interest rates on consumption, there are wealth effects via asset prices, and there are effects via expectations and confidence. Textbook models are intended to illustrate the main channels while making some simplifying assumptions for the sake of clarity. The real-world policy-makers need to take on board the full reality of what they are doing. If you have understood our exposition so far, you should have no difficulty in following what a real-world monetary authority thinks it is doing when it changes interest rates.

## The efficacy of fiscal policy

We have found that fiscal policy is a very powerful tool for stimulating real activity in the short run in an economy with fixed exchange rates and mobile international capital. In that case the monetary authorities are forced by capital inflows to reinforce the fiscal expansion with an increase in the money supply.

Under floating exchange rates with mobile capital and a fixed money supply, however, the expansionary fiscal policy creates a currency appreciation, which neutralizes the stimulation to real activity. A fiscal stimulus would give a temporary boost to the real economy where the monetary authorities peg the interest rate—and would thereby create an accommodating rise in the money stock. The long-run effect of a fiscal expansion, with no capital flows, is to crowd out investment. But with mobile capital, a fiscal expansion crowds out net exports via an appreciation of the real exchange rate.

There is a potential role for fiscal policy in offsetting the negative demand shocks that cause recessionary gaps. In such cases, at best, fiscal adjustment would replace the automatic adjustment mechanism of the economy and would lead to a deterioration of the budget balance in equilibrium. However, there may be situations in which this is preferable to waiting for recovery.

In general, the role of fiscal policy in influencing macroeconomic activity is much more limited in a world of floating exchange rates and mobile international capital than it is under a fixed exchange rate regime, or in the world of restricted capital flows.

## Global transmission of cycles

Small countries may be price-takers in globalized financial markets, so that they have only limited freedom to influence domestic nominal interest rates, and even less freedom to influence domestic real interest rates. But this does not mean that world interest rates will not move: rather, it means that interest rates will tend to move up and down together as the demand and supply of savings and loans moves up and down at the world level.

World interest rate movements will be transmitted to real activity through our original transmission mechanism. Correlation of interest rate movements around the world also causes correlation of the cycles in real activity. Chart (i) in Box 23.3 shows the growth rate of world GDP since 1970, and chart (ii) shows the growth rates of real GDP since 1980 for several of the major economies. Clearly, there is a very high level of correlation of the business cycles in the major industrial countries of the world. This suggests that any one country acting alone cannot succeed in stabilizing its economic cycle, as it will still be subject to fluctuations in world demand (and supply). The world cycle may be controllable, if at all, only by co-ordinated stabilization policy among groups of countries, or at the world level.

This argument should not be taken to mean that domestic macro policies do not matter; the point is that they are not the only things that matter. External influences are much more important today than they were, say, in the 1950s. But there are many things that domestic policymakers can do that affect the performance of their home economy for better or worse. Despite the clear existence of a global business cycle, there have been widely differing experiences with regard to inflation and unemployment among economies more or less equally exposed to external forces. It is to the causes and cures of inflation and unemployment that we turn in Chapters 24 and 25.

# CASE STUDIES

## 1. The Asian financial crises of 1997–8

In the summer of 1997 a major financial crisis broke out affecting several countries in Southeast Asia. This crisis was largely unforeseen, as many of the countries involved appeared to have rapidly growing economies and governments with sound fiscal positions. However, crisis there was, and its aftermath affected some of the countries involved for many years.

We first examine the nature of financial crises. We then look at the events before drawing some conclusions about the problems revealed.

### Financial crises

There are four general types of economic or financial crisis, and any actual crisis situation may have elements of one, some, or all of these. We consider each in turn.

**Box 23.3** International linkages and the world business cycle

The analyses of macroeconomic policy in this chapter have taken place in the context of a single economy. However, openness to foreign trade and the globalization of financial markets have caused all major countries in the world to be influenced by global economic forces as well as by local conditions. An important component of aggregate demand in each country is net exports, and this is affected by world demand.

Chart (i) shows the growth rate of real GDP for the world as a whole since 1970. It shows that there were three periods of significant slowdown during the past four decades, though growth at the world level has remained positive throughout. These general slowdowns were in the mid-1970s, the early 1980s, and the early 1990s.

Chart (ii) shows the real GDP growth of six major countries since 1980. Clearly, the cycles in all these countries are related. All had strong growth in the late 1980s, and slowdowns (or recessions) in the early 1990s, though the slowdown in France, Germany, and Japan was later that that in the other three countries. All except Japan (see pages 487–8) had strong growth in the late 1990s, and all experienced slowdowns in 2001–2.

Open economies are ultimately constrained by world aggregate demand and appear unable significantly to offset swings in world demand by local monetary or fiscal policy changes. No one country acting alone (except perhaps the United States, or the EU countries acting together) can influence world aggregate demand substantially. So it should not be surprising that there is a common element of business cycles across countries. This may imply that the only possibility of stabilizing world aggregate demand is for countries to co-ordinate their macroeconomic policies.

However, the realities of the politics of policy formation create formidable obstacles to co-ordinated action. There are already decision lags and implementation lags in the policy formation process in each country. These would be magnified if policy were to be determined at the supranational level. Realistically, explicit co-ordination of macroeconomic policies is not going to happen in the foreseeable future. This may mean that the global business cycle is a phenomenon that countries will have to continue to live with.

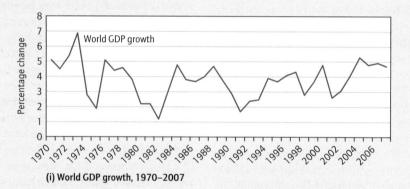

**(i) World GDP growth, 1970–2007**

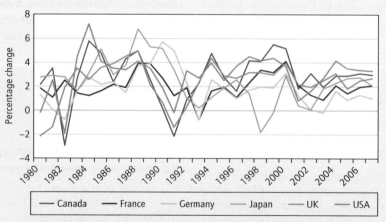

**(ii) Real GDP growth, Canada, France, Germany, Japan, UK and USA, 1980–2007**

*Source*: IMF, *World Economic Outlook*, April 2006. Data for 2006 and 2007 are IMF projections.

## Currency crisis

A currency crisis shows up when there is a speculative attack on the exchange rate, resulting in a devaluation of a pegged currency or sharp depreciation of a floating currency. (See Chapter 22 for an analysis of currency pegging.) When a currency crisis occurs the domestic monetary authorities usually lose large amounts of their international reserves and/or raise interest rates very sharply in order to try to discourage capital outflows.

## Banking crisis

A banking crisis may occur because depositors lose confidence in the solvency of banks and attempt to withdraw their deposits, thereby causing a run on the banks. Alternatively, it may occur because banks make so many bad loans and investments that they become insolvent without any depositors' panic. In either case, banks are forced to close or seek financial support from their governments. Failure of one small bank might not produce a crisis, but failure of a bank that has a large share of deposits would, as would failure of a number of banks at the same time.

## Systemic financial crisis

The third type of financial crisis involves severe disruption in domestic financial markets that hampers the working of the real economy. Such a crisis is harmful to real activity because it disrupts the payments system and leads to a breakdown of all those markets that channel funds from savers to borrowers. Banking and currency crises may be components of a systemic financial crisis, but this is something bigger than either of these two, involving equity and bond markets as well as money market institutions.

## Foreign debt crisis

The final type of crisis arises when one or more countries find that they are unable to keep up the interest payments on their foreign debt. This situation may trigger loss of confidence in the economy or the government, and so could bring about a currency and banking crisis. It also frequently involves application to the IMF for financial assistance (which could happen in response to any of the other types of crisis, especially a currency crisis). When granting a loan, the IMF typically imposes some *conditionality*, or special terms, which often involve monetary and fiscal policy tightening. There will also usually be some negotiation between debtors and creditors in order to reschedule the debt, that is, turn unpaid interest into a further loan. As the IMF reported,

*Crises of all types have often had common origins: the buildup of unsustainable economic imbalances and misalignments in asset prices or exchange rates, often in a context of financial sector distortions and structural rigidities. A crisis may be triggered by a sudden loss of confidence in the currency or banking system, prompted by such developments as a sudden correction in asset prices, or by disruption to credit or external financing flows that expose underlying economic and financial weaknesses. Crises may involve sharp declines in assets, and failures of financial institutions and nonfinancial corporations. Of course, not all corrections of imbalances involve a crisis. Whether they do or not depends, apart from the magnitude of the imbalances themselves, on the credibility of policies to correct the imbalances and achieve a 'soft landing' and on the robustness of the country's financial system. These factors together determine the economy's vulnerability to crises. Crises may then be considered to be the consequence of financial or economic disturbances when economies suffer from a high degree of vulnerability.*
(IMF, *World Economic Outlook*, May 1998, page 75)

There have been many financial crises in recent history. There was a currency crisis in Europe in September 1992 when the United Kingdom and Italy were forced to leave the ERM. There was another in the summer of 1993 when the remaining ERM members adopted wide fluctuation bands in order to accommodate exchange rate changes without destroying the principles of the exchange rate mechanism.

The most famous banking crisis of all time happened in the United States in the early 1930s, when over 10,000 banks became insolvent. More recent examples include the secondary banking crisis in Britain in 1974, the collapse of many savings and loans institutions (equivalent to UK building societies) in the United States in the 1980s, and a crisis in Sweden in 1993.

Systemic financial crises have, fortunately, been less frequent, but they have arisen when there has been political breakdown, often associated with war or revolution. A recent example occurred in Serbia in 1993, when the breakdown of the financial system was accompanied by hyperinflation (see Box 24.1 on page 552).

Foreign debt crises have been all too frequent in the last two decades. A major crisis affecting many countries in Latin America, including Mexico, Brazil, and Argentina, broke out in 1982. This crisis was so severe that it threatened the survival of many major US and UK banks that had lent large amounts of money to these countries. Mexico had a further severe debt crisis in 1994. The crisis in Argentina in 2001/2 is discussed below.

## Events in Southeast Asia, 1997–8

The Asian crisis that broke out in the summer of 1997 had elements of a currency crisis, a banking crisis, and a foreign debt crisis, though the currency and banking crises were the dominant elements. The worst effects of the crisis were felt by five countries: Korea, Thailand, Malaysia, the Philippines, and Indonesia. Indonesia was affected worst of all, as the economic effects led to political turbulence that brought down President Suharto in May 1998, and the new government had trouble restoring confidence. While the situation was slightly different in each country, we concentrate on the common factors.

## The currency crisis

The background to the crisis in this region, as with Japan, was a sustained period of high real growth. Collectively these economies, together with some others such as Singapore, Taiwan, and Hong Kong, were called the 'Asian Tigers', and through the early 1990s they were the success story of the world economy. In the 1980s their average real growth rate was 7.7 per cent, and in the 1990s it was still over 6 per cent.

Because the region was growing quickly at a time when many of the industrial countries were stagnating, or growing only slowly, financial capital was attracted to invest in these so-called emerging markets. Most of the countries involved pegged their exchange rates to the dollar, and the substantial inflows of capital during the first half of the 1990s allowed the monetary authorities to build up healthy reserves of foreign exchange. This increased both the confidence of foreign investors and the belief of domestic borrowers that they did not face any exchange rate risk on dollar debts.

Thailand was the first country to feel the onset of a currency crisis. There had already been concerns in 1996 about the sustainability of the dollar peg, and there was renewed pressure on the currency in early 1997. Also there had been falls in equity prices from 1996 and a collapse of property prices. The concerns were increased by a growing current account deficit on the balance of payments and worries that the short-term external debt was becoming excessive.

As a result, capital flowed out of Thailand in increasing volume, and on 2 July 1997 the Thai authorities abandoned the exchange rate peg to the dollar. The value of the *baht* (the Thai currency) fell initially by 10 per cent but then continued to fall

as concerns built up about the political situation and the delay by policy-makers in taking corrective action. The stability of major financial institutions came into question as elements of a banking crisis started to take over.

The currency crisis in Thailand and the resulting collapse in the exchange rate turned the focus on to neighbouring countries. Speculative pressure forced the Philippines, Malaysia, and Indonesia to follow Thailand in floating their currencies, and all floated downwards by substantial amounts, as shown in Figure 23.9(i) for Korea, Thailand, and Indonesia. Last of the five most affected countries to be hit by a currency crisis was Korea, but its exchange rate fall, when it came, was as severe as any but Indonesia's. At the worst point the value of these five currencies had fallen by amounts ranging from around 40 per cent (for Malaysia and the Philippines) to over 80 per cent (for Indonesia).

Currency devaluations of such large size have one good effect: they lower domestic output prices relative to foreign goods and so boost net exports. However, they have several bad effects that tend to dominate in the short run. First, prices of imported materials rise, which boosts domestic inflation—this effect alone led to riots in Indonesia as petrol and food prices rose very sharply. Second, the domestic value of foreign-currency debts rises sharply, putting the viability of companies and financial institutions at risk. Third, domestic authorities tend to raise interest rates and taxes, both to defend the currency and to avoid further capital flight. This puts severe financial pressure on all those who have borrowed money at floating interest rates, since their repayments rise sharply. Fourth, the resulting financial squeeze forces investors to sell assets and causes profits to fall. This in

(i) Dollar exchange rates of Korea, Thailand, Indonesia, and Japan, July 1997–July 1998

(ii) Equity prices in Korea, Thailand, Malaysia, and Indonesia, January 1997–June 1998

**Figure 23.9** **Dollar exchange rates and equity prices during the Asian crisis**

**The exchange rate of Thailand was the first to fall, in July 1997.** The Korean collapse started in October 1997. Equity prices also fell in late 1997, recovering temporarily in early 1998, but falling again in April–May 1998.

*Sources:* part (i): *Financial Times*, 1 July 1998, p. 23; part (ii): Thomson Datastream.

turn leads to a collapse of equity and property prices (see Figure 23.9(ii) for equity prices). Domestic economic activity slows sharply as both consumer spending and investment spending are severely curtailed.

### The banking crisis

The currency crisis soon also developed into a banking crisis, as a result of which many banks were forced to close or to be restructured.[9] There were three main components to the banking crisis in Asia in 1997–8.

First, the countries involved had experienced many years of high growth. It is easy to make good loans in such periods because profits are generally rising, as are equity prices and property prices. Loan defaults comprise a very small percentage of loans made, and so bankers tend to get overconfident about the ability of borrowers to repay their loans. This is especially true of young bankers who have never known anything but boom conditions. So as time goes by they start to make loans that are increasingly risky. Indeed, even safe loans in good times will turn out to be bad loans once a major downturn occurs. The profusion of unsound loans tends to be reinforced by asset price bubbles, where speculators borrow money to buy assets, which in turn drives asset prices up further and feeds even more speculative buying. Widespread bankruptcies result when the asset price bubble bursts.

The second element behind the banking crisis was the false assumption by many banks that the currency would remain pegged to the US dollar. This encouraged them to borrow in dollars in order to make domestic currency loans. As US dollar interest rates were low relative to domestic interest rates, this was a highly profitable strategy for a while. However, once the exchange rate peg was broken, the true level of foreign exchange rate risk was revealed when the domestic value of interest payments denominated in US dollars rose, making many banks insolvent in the process.

Finally, the rapid growth in these countries had disguised the fact that many banks were badly run and that the system of banking regulation was inadequate. The 1982 debt crisis had already led to the introduction of a new global bank regulatory regime from 1992. However, the crisis revealed inadequate application of these new prudential regulations in some of the countries of Southeast Asia. This served to make worse a crisis that would have brought down some banking institutions even under an adequate regulatory regime.

**The currency and banking crises in Asia caused major disruption to the economies involved, imposing bankruptcy and financial hardship on millions of people.**

As in the case of Japan, discussed above (pages 487–8), there were also other structural problems in the economies involved. Many of these resulted from government intervention that led to inefficiencies and lack of international competitiveness in various sectors. However, the detail is different in each country, and a detailed examination of these issues is beyond our scope.

## 2. The exchange rate crisis in Argentina, 2001–2

In 1989 Argentina had an annual inflation rate of 3,080 per cent and in 1990 its inflation was 2,314 per cent. This was caused by big fiscal deficits and rapidly expanding money supply (in part, printing money to finance the deficit). In 1991 the government decided that inflation had to be brought under control, and it pegged its currency rigidly to the US dollar by setting up a currency board. Currency boards maintain the convertibility of a currency by ensuring that domestic currency issuance is only such as can be converted into the international reserve currency that is held by the board; in effect, they limit the issuance of domestic currency. This policy was remarkably successful in bringing down inflation. In 1991 inflation was down to 170 per cent and by 1994 it was in single figures and stayed very close to zero throughout the rest of the decade (see Figure 23.10).

At the same time, real economic growth, which had been erratic throughout the 1970s and 1980s, improved noticeably in the 1990s. Apart from 1995 (when there was a spill-over from the 1994 Mexican debt crisis), Argentina experienced strong positive growth in every year during 1991–8 (see Figure 23.10). Low inflation and high growth after years of economic instability seemed like good news at last for Argentina.

Unfortunately, it did not last. Real GDP fell by about 10 per cent in 2002 (IMF 2006) and inflation rose to around 25 per cent in the same year. So what went wrong?

According to Anne Kreuger, Deputy Managing Director of the IMF, 'Two factors came together in a destructive cocktail: weak fiscal policy and mounting overvaluation.'

The weak fiscal policy led to a growing debt burden, which eventually became unsustainable:

*The protracted weakness of the public finances soon made its impact felt on Argentina's consolidated public debt burden, which rose from less than 33 per cent of GDP in early 1990s to more than 41 per cent in 1998 . . . and much of the debt had to be serviced in foreign currency, which was made more difficult by Argentina's low export-to-GDP ratio. . . . In addition, the fixed exchange rate regime under the convertibility plan further reduced the degrees of freedom for fiscal deficits and debt. External debt had already climbed to 50 per cent of GDP in 2000, but of course markets feared that in the absence of fiscal and other policies strong enough to support the convertibility plan, the currency board would collapse, the exchange rate would plummet, and the debt plan would balloon. These fears were duly realised and by the end of 2001 the debt-to-GDP ratio stood at 130 per cent.* (Kreuger 2002)

---

[9] Restructuring could involve a takeover by, or a merger with, another institution, a change of management, a recapitalization or nationalization by the government, or some combination of these.

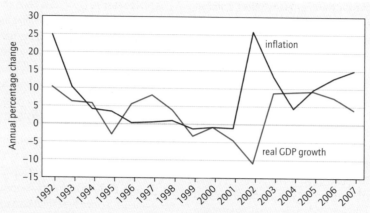

**Figure 23.10** Inflation and real GDP growth, Argentina, 1992–2007

*Source*: IMF, *World Economic Outlook*, April 2006; data for 2006 and 2007 are IMF projections.

The other problem for Argentina was being tied to the US dollar at a time when the dollar was strong; this made the Argentine real exchange rate very high relative to those of its competitors. The situation became even worse in 1999 when Brazil devalued its currency. GDP growth was negative in Argentina for four years in a row 1999–2002, with 2002 being worst of all. By early 2002 the currency board had collapsed and the peso was floated, falling substantially in value against the dollar. This in turn led to a substantial burst of inflation.

The ending of the rigid exchange rate peg to the US dollar was clearly very painful for Argentina, which experienced both a deep recession and high inflation in 2002. But for the next three years floating seemed to be working well, as output recovered strongly in the 2003–5 period and inflation fell to below 5 per cent in 2004. However, projections from the IMF (published in April 2006) were for a slowdown in growth and a pickup of inflation in 2006 and 2007.

Thus, while the pegging of its currency to the US dollar helped to bring hyperinflation under control in the early 1990s, the breakdown of this regime was very painful, and it seems unlikely that Argentina will operate with anything other than a floating exchange rate regime for the foreseeable future.

## SUMMARY

### Why does openness matter?

■ Openness of the economy matters because trade and capital flows influence real activity, international financial markets influence domestic money markets, and the exchange rate regime determines which monetary instruments are available to the authorities.

### Macro policy in a world with perfect capital mobility

■ Perfect capital mobility can be represented by a horizontal *BB* line in the *IS/LM* diagram.

■ Under fixed exchange rates and perfect capital mobility, an expansionary monetary policy is rapidly reversed through losses of foreign exchange reserves. It has no real impact.

■ Starting from equilibrium GDP, an increase in government spending, under fixed exchange rates and perfect capital mobility, creates an inflationary gap and a significant stimulus to real GDP in the short run. In the long run there is a rise in the relative price of domestic goods, a budget deficit, and a trade deficit.

■ Starting from equilibrium, a monetary policy expansion, under floating exchange rates and perfect capital mobility, leads to a currency depreciation and creates an inflationary gap. In the long run the price level rises in proportion to the money supply increase and the exchange rate depreciates in the same proportion.

■ Starting from equilibrium, an increase in government spending, with floating exchange rates and perfect capital mobility, creates little or no stimulus to real GDP if the money stock is held constant; but it does create a temporary stimulus if the interest rate is held constant. In the long run in both cases this leads to a real exchange rate appreciation and a trade deficit. The budget deficit and the trade deficit are of equal size.

- Starting with a recessionary gap, both monetary and fiscal policies can speed up the return to potential GDP if they are timed correctly. Fiscal policy can be used to increase final demand, while monetary policy can lower interest rates and/or the exchange rate.

**Some implications**

- The transmission mechanism of monetary policy and the efficacy of fiscal policy are both affected by openness and capital mobility.
- Financial and spending linkages between economies mean that business cycles are a global phenomenon, and cycles in one country are often closely related to cycles in other important economies.

## TOPICS FOR REVIEW

- Monetary policy
- Fiscal policy
- Fixed exchange rates
- Floating exchange rates

- Capital mobility
- Overshooting
- Crowding-out

## QUESTIONS

1 If UK annual interest rates are currently 4 per cent and those in the USA are 2 per cent, while the sterling–dollar exchange rate is $1.5 per £, what do the markets expect the sterling dollar rate to be in one year's time?

2 What would the answer to question 1 be if UK interest rates were 4 per cent and US rates were 10 per cent?

3 Using the initial position in question 1, an interest rate in the euro area of 6 per cent, and an initial exchange rate between dollar and euro of $1.0 per euro, what is the market's expectation of the exchange rate between the euro and sterling in one year's time?

4 Explain how monetary and fiscal policies influence GDP and the price level under fixed exchange rates with perfect capital mobility.

5 Explain how monetary and fiscal policies influence GDP and the price level under floating exchange rates with perfect capital mobility.

6 Does the globalization of financial markets mean that monetary authorities have lost the power to influence their own economy?

7 What macroeconomic policy options are available for a single member of the euro zone?

8 Should macro policy be co-ordinated between major countries?

# PART SEVEN

# GLOBAL ECONOMIC ISSUES

# Chapter 24

# INFLATION

Policies to avoid inflation and unemployment and to encourage growth are the big macroeconomic issues of our time. We discuss growth in Chapter 26. In this chapter we focus on inflation, while the following chapter concentrates on unemployment. Is inflation a thing of the past? How are today's policies influenced by the desire to prevent its return? Is there a trade-off between inflation and unemployment? Are the causes of sustained inflations different from those of one-off price level changes? These are some of the questions we address in this chapter.

In particular you will learn that:

- Because inflation and unemployment are closely related, at least in the short term, macroeconomic policy-makers must walk a tightrope with inflation on one side and unemployment on the other.

- Attempts to reduce unemployment have often been accompanied by a rise in inflation, and attempts to reduce inflation have usually led to episodes of increased unemployment, which although temporary are often severe.

- Inflation is related to the output gap and to expected inflation.

- Inflation is currently under control in most countries, but this could change if policy-makers change their priorities.

- Inflation is generally considered to be undesirable, especially when it is unexpected, because it distorts the signals that are provided by the price system; it creates arbitrary redistribution from debtors to creditors; it creates incentives for speculative as opposed to productive investment activity; and it is usually costly to eliminate.

The recent history of inflation and unemployment in the United Kingdom is set out in Figure 24.1(i). In the 1960s inflation was generally below 5 per cent and unemployment was always below 750,000 or under 2 per cent of the workforce. However, this picture changed dramatically in the 1970s. Inflation rose to over 25 per cent in 1975 (the highest peace-time inflation rate in the United Kingdom for at least 300 years) and unemployment fluctuated about a rising trend, reaching 1.5 million in 1977 and over 3 million by 1983, which represented over 10 per cent of the workforce. Inflation fell to under 5 per cent by the mid-1980s, but it rose again to around 10 per cent as a result of the late-1980s boom. This boom also brought unemployment down to around 1.5 million, but it rose again to around 3 million in the recession of the early

1990s. Over the same period, inflation fell to around 2 per cent. The negative relationship between inflation and unemployment, at least from the end of the 1970s to the late 1990s, is evident from the figure. However, in the late 1990s and the first six years of the twenty-first century, inflation and unemployment were both low.[1] Inflation was consistently within 1 percentage point of the target that the government had set for it (see pages 481–4) and unemployment fell to levels not seen since the early 1970s.

Figure 24.1(ii) shows a GDP-weighted average of world inflation since 1970. This shows a rising trend in the 1970s,

---

[1] There have been some changes in the way unemployment is measured, which are discussed in the next chapter.

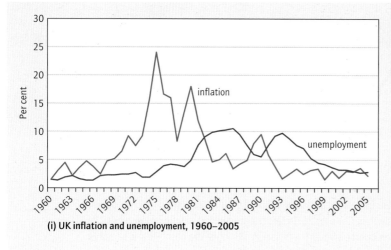

(i) UK inflation and unemployment, 1960–2005

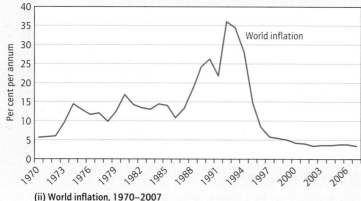

(ii) World inflation, 1970–2007

**Figure 24.1** UK and world inflation

**Many countries in the world have experienced inflation.** Part (i) shows that UK inflation was high in the 1970s and unemployment was high in the 1980s. But by the early 2000s both inflation and unemployment had fallen to historically low levels. Part (ii) shows that inflation was a rising world-wide problem in the 1970s, but that it did not peak until the early 1990s. This was affected by very high inflation in some countries even though inflation in the major industrial countries had fallen to low levels by this time. By the early years of the twenty-first century inflation was low world-wide. Data for 2006 and 2007 are IMF staff projections.

*Sources*: part (i): ONS, *Economic Trends*; part (ii): IMF, *World Economic Outlook*, May 2006.

a slight fall in the mid-1980s, followed by a strong surge in the late 1980s and early 1990s. Since the mid-1990s there has been a sharp fall to historically low levels.

We want to understand the forces that caused inflation in the 1970s–1990s so that we can understand the current policies that are designed to prevent the mistakes of the past from being repeated. Inflation may finally be under control around the world, but it could easily return if anti-inflation policies were relaxed.

We start by using our macroeconomic model to investigate the causes of inflation. We then set out a theoretical framework for analysing the trade-off between inflation and unemployment. Finally, we discuss the implications of our analysis for counter-inflationary policy-making.

## Inflation in the macro model

Although any increase in the price level is usually called an inflation, we need to distinguish between the forces that cause a once-and-for-all increase in the price level and those that cause a continuing, or sustained, increase. Any event that tends to drive the price level upwards is called an *inflationary shock*. To examine such shocks, we begin with an economy in long-run macroeconomic equilibrium operating under a flexible exchange rate regime. The price level is stable, and GDP is at its potential level. We then study the economy as different types of inflationary shock buffet it.

### Supply shocks

Suppose there is a negative supply shock that shifts the *SRAS* curve upwards. This might be caused by a rise in the cost of oil, imported raw materials, or domestic wage costs per unit of output, such as from a large increase in the minimum wage. With a given *AD* curve, the impact effect is for output to fall and the price level to rise; that is, GDP falls while inflation picks up. What happens next depends on how the monetary authorities react. The authorities now have two alternatives.

First, they can lower the interest rate sufficiently to shift the *AD* curve rightwards, so that it intersects the new *SRAS* curve at potential GDP. To achieve this, they must buy bonds and supply money in return. This injects new money into the system, thereby shifting *AD* rightwards. The supply shock is then said to be 'accommodated' by an increase in the money supply. This is a case of monetary **accommodation**.

Second, the authorities can adopt an interest rate policy that keeps the money supply constant and the *AD* curve in its initial position.[2] We then say that the supply shock is 'not accommodated' by an increase in the money supply. This is the case of *no monetary accommodation*.

What happens also depends on whether the supply shock is an isolated event or one of a series of continued shocks. We take these two cases in turn.

### Isolated supply shocks

Suppose that the leftward shift in the *SRAS* curve is an isolated event. It might, for example, be caused by a once-and-for-all increase in the cost of oil.

#### No monetary accommodation

The leftward shift in the *SRAS* curve causes the price level to rise and pushes GDP below its potential level, opening up a recessionary gap. As a result of this recessionary gap, market pressures tend to cause wages and other input prices to fall relative to productivity. When this happens, the *SRAS* curve shifts downward, causing a return of GDP to its potential level, and a fall in the price level. The period of inflation accompanying the original supply shock is followed by a period of deflation, which continues until long-run equilibrium is re-established. This sequence is illustrated in Figure 24.2. Since money wages tend to react only sluggishly to excess supply in the labour market, unit costs of production fall only slowly, so the recovery to full equilibrium at *Y\** may take a long time.

**Figure 24.2  A single supply shock**

The final effect of a single supply shock depends on whether or not it is accommodated by monetary expansion. A supply shock causes the *SRAS* curve to shift leftward from $SRAS_0$ to $SRAS_1$, as shown by arrow 1. Short-run equilibrium is established at $E_1$. If there is no monetary accommodation, the unemployment will exert a downward pressure on wage costs, causing the *SRAS* curve to shift slowly back to the right to $SRAS_0$. Prices will fall, and output will rise, until the original equilibrium is restored at $E_0$. If there is monetary accommodation, the *AD* curve will shift from $AD_0$ to $AD_1$, as shown by arrow 2. This re-establishes full-employment equilibrium at $E_2$, but with a higher price level, $P_2$.

#### Monetary accommodation

Now suppose that the monetary authorities react by loosening their monetary stance, lowering interest rates and increasing in the money supply. This shifts the *AD* curve to the right, causing both the price level and output to rise. (Part of this adjustment may come from currency depreciation, causing an upward shift of the net export function.) When the recessionary gap is eliminated, the price level, rather than falling back to its original value, will have risen further. These effects are also shown in Figure 24.2.

The monetary authorities might decide to accommodate the supply shock because relying on cost deflation to restore activity to its potential level forces the economy to suffer an extended slump.

Monetary accommodation can return the economy to potential GDP relatively quickly, but at the cost of a once-and-for-all increase in the price level.

### Repeated supply shocks

As an example of a repeated supply shock, assume that powerful unions are able to raise money wages faster than

---

[2] Whether this requires higher, constant (or even lower) interest rates depends on what happens to demand for money. Output has fallen, lowering money demand; but prices have risen, raising money demand. If there is a net increase in money demand following the supply shock, interest rates will have to rise to maintain a constant money supply. If money demand is unchanged, constant interest rates will be consistent with a constant money stock.

productivity is increasing, even in the face of a significant excess supply of labour. Firms then pass these higher wages on in the form of higher prices. This type of supply shock causes what is called a wage-cost push inflation—an increase in the price level arising from increases in money wages that are not associated with an excess demand for labour.

### No monetary accommodation

Suppose the monetary authorities do not accommodate these supply shocks. The initial effect of the leftward shift in the SRAS curve is to open up a recessionary gap, as shown in Figure 24.2. If unions continue to negotiate increases in wages, subjecting the economy to further supply shocks, prices will continue to rise while output and employment continue to fall. Eventually the trade-off between higher wages and unemployment will become obvious to everyone. Long before everyone is unemployed, unions will cease forcing up wages in order to maintain jobs for those who are still employed.

Once the wage-cost push ceases, there are two possibilities. First, the unions may succeed in holding on to their high real wages, but will not push for further increases of money wages in excess of productivity increases. The economy will then come to rest with a stable price level and a large recessionary gap. Second, the persistent unemployment may eventually erode the power of the unions, so that real wages and hence unit costs begin to fall, because money wages rise more slowly than productivity is rising. In this case the supply shock is reversed, and the SRAS curve will shift downward until full employment is eventually restored.

A non-accommodated wage-cost push tends to be self-limiting because the rising unemployment that it causes tends to restrain further wage increases.

### Monetary accommodation

Now suppose that the monetary authorities accommodate the shock by relaxing their monetary policy stance, lowering interest rates relative to where they would otherwise be by buying bonds and increasing the money supply. This shifts the AD curve to the right, as shown in Figure 24.3. In the new full-employment equilibrium, where GDP is at its potential level, both money wages and prices have risen. The rise in wages has been offset by a rise in prices. Workers are no better off than they were originally, although those who remained in jobs were temporarily better off in the transition period when wages had risen (taking equilibrium to $E_1$ in Figure 24.2) but before the price level had risen enough to restore full employment (taking equilibrium to $E_2$).

**Figure 24.3 Monetary accommodation of a repeated supply shock**

**Monetary accommodation of a repeated supply shock causes a continuous inflation in the absence of excess demand.** The initial equilibrium is at $E_0$. A supply shock then takes equilibrium to $E_1$, just as in Figure 24.2. This is the stagflation phase of rising prices and falling output; it is indicated by arrow 1. If the monetary authorities then accommodate the supply shock, the AD curve shifts to $AD_1$, taking equilibrium to $E_2$. This is the expansionary phase of rising prices and rising output (arrow 2). A second supply shock takes equilibrium to $E_3$ (arrow 3), and a second round of monetary accommodation takes it to $E_4$ (arrow 4). As long as the supply shocks and the monetary accommodation continue, the inflation will continue.

The stage is now set for the unions to try again. If they succeed in negotiating further increases in money wages, they will hit the economy with another supply shock. If the monetary authorities again accommodate the shock, full employment will be maintained, but at the cost of a further round of inflation. If this process goes on repeatedly, it can give rise to a continual wage-cost push inflation as shown in Figure 24.3. The wage-cost push tends to cause a *stagflation*, with rising prices and falling output. Monetary accommodation tends to reinforce the rise in prices and to offset the fall in output. It will also be associated with the home currency falling in value in foreign exchange markets.

There are two requirements for continuing wage-cost push inflation. First, powerful groups, such as industrial unions or government employees, must press for, and employers must grant, increases in money wages in excess of productivity growth, even in the absence of excess demand for labour and goods. Second, the monetary authorities must accommodate the resulting inflation by loosening their monetary stance, in order to prevent the rising unemployment that would otherwise occur.

The process set up by this sequence of wage-cost push and monetary accommodation is often called a wage–price spiral.

### Is monetary accommodation desirable?

Once started, a wage–price spiral can be halted only if the monetary authorities stop accommodating the supply shocks that are causing the inflation. The longer they wait to do so, the more entrenched will become the expectations of continuing inflation. These entrenched expectations may cause wages to continue to rise after accommodation has ceased. Because employers expect prices to rise, they go on granting wage increases. If expectations are firmly enough entrenched, the wage push can continue for quite some time, in spite of the downward pressure caused by the rising unemployment associated with the growing recessionary gap.

Evidence suggests that, when politicians run monetary policy, they typically accommodate supply shocks to avoid the short-term unpopularity that is generated by rising unemployment. For this reason many economists have recommended that central banks be given the clear objective of maintaining a stable price level and then insulated from further political direction. This is what has been done in the United Kingdom since May 1997.[3] Although the Bank of England's Monetary Policy Committee may elect to accommodate some isolated supply shocks, the Bank's independence makes it unlikely that persistent wage–price spirals will be permitted to develop through continued monetary accommodation. The same applies in the euro zone, where the ECB has been given the goal of achieving price stability and has been insulated from short-term political pressures.

**Accommodating a negative supply shock risks setting off a wage–price spiral, but accommodating the first-round effects of shocks may limit the output and employment losses that are otherwise inevitable.**

This may not seem like a big issue in the first decade of the twenty-first century, but it certainly was important in the 1970s and 1980s, and may be again in the future. Notice also that wage shocks are not the only type of possible supply shock. The energy price rises of 1973 and 1979 (oil shocks) were very important, and their effects can be analysed just as above. The high energy prices in 2005–6 have had less of an impact so far, as production is generally of lower energy intensity than it used to be, but if energy prices rise even higher some impact may be felt. Equally, a price rise in any imported materials will have a similar effect. Exchange rate depreciations contribute to input price shocks because the price of imported materials rises, but exchange rate changes have demand dimensions as well, as they shift the net export function.

## Demand shocks

Now suppose that an initial equilibrium is disturbed by a rightward shift in the aggregate demand curve, a shift that could have been caused by either an increase in some category of autonomous spending or a relaxation of monetary policy. This causes the price level and output to rise. If the monetary authorities react to the increase in the demand for money that accompanies an increase in autonomous spending by permitting the money supply to rise, they are said to be **validating** the shock. (Notice that this terminology distinguishes between the response to a supply shock, which is described as 'accommodating' the shock, and the response to a demand shock, which is described as 'validating' the shock.)

### No monetary validation

This is the standard case of a once-and-for-all increase in aggregate demand, such as shown in Figure 21.6 on page 478. Because the initial *AD* shock takes output above the full-employment level, an inflationary gap opens up. The pressure of excess demand soon causes wages to rise faster than productivity, shifting the *SRAS* curve upwards. As output and prices are higher, money demand increases. In order to hold the money supply constant in the face of a higher money demand, the monetary authorities will have to sell bonds and raise interest rates, thereby choking off the excess demand for money. As long as the authorities follow an interest rate policy that holds the money supply constant, the rise in the price level moves the economy upwards along its fixed *AD* curve. The rise in the price level thus eventually eliminates the inflationary gap. In this case the initial period of inflation is followed by further inflation, which continues until the new long-run equilibrium is reached. The potential level of GDP and a stable price level are then restored.

### Monetary validation

Next suppose that, once the initial demand shock has created an inflationary gap, the monetary authorities frustrate the forces that would return GDP to its potential level by relaxing monetary policy, thereby permitting the nominal money supply to rise when output starts to fall. This is the case illustrated in Figure 24.4. Two forces are now brought into play. Spurred by the inflationary gap,

**Figure 24.4** **A validated demand-shock inflation**

Monetary validation will cause the *AD* curve to shift, offsetting the leftward shift in the *SRAS* curve and maintaining an inflationary gap in spite of the ever-rising price level. An initial demand shock shifts equilibrium from $E_0$ to $E_1$ (along the path indicated by arrow 1), taking GDP to $Y_1$ and the price level to $P_1$. The resulting inflationary gap then causes the *SRAS* curve to shift to the left. This time, however, the money supply increases, shifting the *AD* curve to the right. By the time the aggregate supply curve has reached $SRAS_1$, the aggregate demand curve has reached $AD_2$, taking equilibrium to $E_2$. GDP remains constant at $Y_1$, while the price level rises to $P_2$.

The persistent inflationary gap continues to push the *SRAS* curve to the left, while the continued monetary validation continues to push the *AD* curve to the right. By the time aggregate supply reaches $SRAS_2$, aggregate demand has reached $AD_3$. The price level has risen still further to $P_3$, but the inflationary gap remains unchanged at $Y_1 - Y^*$. As long as this monetary validation continues, the economy will move along the vertical path of arrow 2.

the wage increases cause the *SRAS* curve to shift to the left. Fuelled by the expansionary monetary policy, the *AD* curve shifts to the right. As a result of both of these shifts, the price level rises. But if the shift in the *AD* curve offsets the shift in the *SRAS* curve, the inflationary gap does not diminish. The validation of an isolated demand shock thus creates a series of repeated demand shocks that permit the inflation to continue.

**Validation of a demand shock turns what would have been a transitory inflation into a sustained inflation fuelled by monetary expansion.**

We can now see why a rise in the price level may not remove an inflationary gap. Because the money supply may expand endogenously to meet any demand for it, when the monetary authorities are pegging nominal

interest rates, there is no automatic adjustment mechanism to eliminate the inflationary gap. As the price level rises, the nominal money supply rises sufficiently to keep the real money supply constant, and the inflationary gap is not reduced. This sequence requires either that the monetary authorities do not pick up the warnings of impending inflation coming from the rising money supply figures, or that they decide on an inflationary policy.

Although there is controversy over how much control the monetary authorities can have over the money supply, few economists doubt that a determined enough anti-inflationary policy can stop the nominal money supply from expanding as fast as prices are rising. Most monetary authorities have pursued such a policy at one time or another over the past few decades, thereby ending an inflation in their own country. Thus, in the world in which we live, inflations cannot go on indefinitely unless they are validated by policy decisions taken by the monetary authorities. Notice also that the Taylor rule (explained in Box 21.4 on page 479) has monetary authorities reacting to deviations of inflation from its target rate and to deviations of GDP from its potential level. Thus, in a world of inflation targeting, central banks are unlikely to validate any inflation that does occur as the result of a temporary shock. The authorities will raise interest rates both when inflation goes above target and when actual GDP exceeds potential GDP, and this will prevent the validation of demand-shock inflations.

Figure 24.5 summarizes all the cases of supply and demand shock with or without accommodation or validation.

## Inflation as a monetary phenomenon

Economists have debated the extent to which inflation is a monetary phenomenon. Does it have purely monetary causes—increases in the supply of money? Does it have purely monetary consequences—only the price level is affected? The US economist Milton Friedman made popular one slogan stating an extreme position on this issue: 'Inflation is everywhere and always a monetary phenomenon.' This could be a mere tautology, since inflation is by definition a fall in the purchasing power of money. However, avoiding semantics, let us summarize what we have already learned about the causes of inflation.

1. Many forces can cause the price level to rise. On the demand side, anything that shifts the *AD* curve to the right will have this result—*ceteris paribus*, increases in desired spending on exports, government spending, investment, and consumption, as well as a relaxation

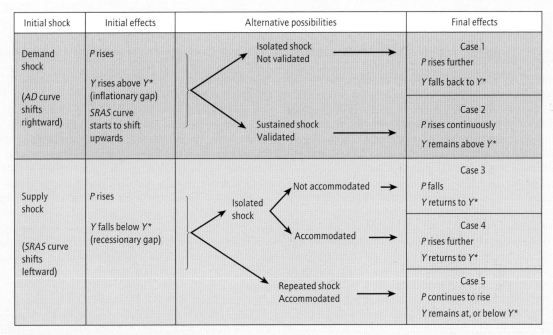

| Initial shock | Initial effects | Alternative possibilities | | Final effects |
|---|---|---|---|---|
| Demand shock<br><br>(*AD* curve shifts rightward) | *P* rises<br><br>*Y* rises above *Y\** (inflationary gap)<br>*SRAS* curve starts to shift upwards | Isolated shock<br>Not validated | | Case 1<br>*P* rises further<br>*Y* falls back to *Y\** |
| | | Sustained shock<br>Validated | | Case 2<br>*P* rises continuously<br>*Y* remains above *Y\** |
| Supply shock<br><br>(*SRAS* curve shifts leftward) | *P* rises<br><br>*Y* falls below *Y\** (recessionary gap) | Isolated shock | Not accommodated | Case 3<br>*P* falls<br>*Y* returns to *Y\** |
| | | | Accommodated | Case 4<br>*P* rises further<br>*Y* returns to *Y\** |
| | | Repeated shock<br>Accommodated | | Case 5<br>*P* continues to rise<br>*Y* remains at, or below *Y\** |

**Figure 24.5 The effects of inflationary shocks**

**Demand and supply shocks have different final effects, depending on whether they are isolated or sustained and are validated or accommodated.** This figure summarizes the analysis of each of the five cases given in the text. It should be referred to after reading the text discussion of each of the cases. All comparisons assume that GDP starts at its potential level and that initially the price level is stable.

The initial effects of a demand shock are to raise GDP and the price level. If the shock is isolated, the price level continues to rise until GDP falls back to its potential level (case 1). If the shock is sustained and validated (validation turns an isolated shock into a sustained shock), the price level continues to rise while GDP stays above its potential level (case 2).

The initial effects of a supply shock are to raise the price level but to reduce GDP. Once the shock is over, GDP will return to its potential level, with a lowered price level if there is no accommodation (case 3), and with a higher price level if there is accommodation (case 4). If the shock is sustained and accommodated, the price level can continue to rise, with or without a persistent recessionary gap (case 5).

of monetary policy or decreases in money demand. On the supply side, anything that increases unit costs of production will shift the *SRAS* curve to the left and cause the price level to rise.

2. Such inflation can continue for some time without any increases in the money supply.

3. The rise in prices must eventually come to a halt, unless monetary expansion occurs.

Points 1 and 2 indicate that a temporary burst of inflation may or may not be a monetary phenomenon; it need not have monetary causes, and it need not be accompanied by monetary expansion. Point 3 implies that a sustained inflation must be a monetary phenomenon. If a rise in prices is to continue, it must be accompanied by continuing increases in the money supply (or decreases in money demand). This is true regardless of what first set the rise in prices in motion. What happens when monetary validation gets out of hand is discussed in Box 24.1.

Now let us summarize what we have learned about the consequences of an inflation, assuming that the economy begins from a situation of full employment and a stable price level.

1. In the short run a demand-shock inflation tends to be accompanied by an increase in GDP.

2. In the short run a supply-shock inflation tends to be accompanied by a decrease in GDP.

3. When all adjustments have been fully made, so that the relevant supply-side curve is the *LRAS* curve, shifts in either the *AD* or *SRAS* curve leave GDP unchanged and affect only the price level.

Points 1 and 2 are saying that inflation is not, in the short run, a purely monetary phenomenon; it has real consequences for output and employment. Point 3 states that, from the point of view of long-run equilibrium, inflation *is* a purely monetary phenomenon.

**Box 24.1** Hyperinflation

Monetary validation of ongoing inflation sometimes gets out of hand. In extreme cases it leads to hyperinflation, in which inflation is so rapid that money ceases to be useful as a medium of exchange and a store of value. However, inflation rates of 50, 100, and even 200 per cent or more per year have occurred year after year in some countries and have proven to be manageable as people adjust their contracts in real terms. Although there are strains and side-effects, the evidence shows such situations to be possible without causing money to become useless.

Does this mean that there is no reason to fear that rapid inflation will turn into a hyperinflation that will destroy the value of money completely? The historical record is not entirely reassuring. There have been a number of cases in which prices began to rise at an ever-accelerating rate until a nation's money ceased to be a satisfactory store of value, even for the short period between receipt and spending, and hence ceased also to be useful as a medium of exchange.

The index of wholesale prices in Germany before and after the First World War is given in the table. The index shows that a product purchased with one 100 mark note in July 1923 would have required 10 million 100 mark notes for its purchase only four months later! Although Germany had experienced substantial inflation during the war, averaging more than 30 per cent per year, the immediate postwar years of 1920 and 1921 gave no sign of an explosive inflation; indeed, during 1920 price stability was experienced. In 1922 and 1923, however, the price level exploded. On 15 November 1923 the mark was officially repudiated, its value wholly destroyed. How could this happen?

### German wholesale price index (1913 = 1)

| | |
|---|---:|
| January 1913 | 1 |
| January 1920 | 13 |
| January 1921 | 14 |
| January 1922 | 37 |
| July 1922 | 101 |
| January 1923 | 2,785 |
| July 1923 | 74,800 |
| August 1923 | 944,000 |
| September 1923 | 23,900,000 |
| October 1923 | 7,096,000,000 |
| November 1923 | 750,000,000,000 |

When inflation becomes so rapid that people lose confidence in the purchasing power of their currency, they rush to spend it. People who have goods become increasingly reluctant to accept the rapidly depreciating money in exchange. The rush to spend money accelerates the increase in prices until people finally become unwilling to accept money on any terms. What was once money ceases to be money.

The price system can then be restored only by repudiation of the old monetary unit and its replacement by a new unit. This destroys the value of monetary savings and of all contracts specified in terms of the old monetary unit.

There are about a dozen documented hyperinflations in world history, among them the collapses of the 'continental'* during the American War of Independence, the rouble during the Russian Revolution, the drachma during and after the German occupation of Greece in the Second World War, the pengo in Hungary during 1945–6, and the Chinese national currency during 1946–8. Every one of these hyperinflations was accompanied by great increases in the money supply; new money was printed to give governments the purchasing power that they could not or would not obtain by taxation. Further, every one occurred in the midst of a major political upheaval in which grave doubts existed about the stability and the future of the government itself.

Is hyperinflation likely in the absence of civil war, revolution, or collapse of a government? Most economists think not. Further, it is clear that high inflation rates over a period of time do not mean the inevitable or even likely onset of hyperinflation.

However, do not assume that hyperinflation is a curiosity only to be found in the history books. The following is an extract from a newspaper report on events in Serbia in 1993 and 1994:

*Worried that Serbian cities might starve during the winter, the government announced [in July 1993] that it would buy a million tons of the wheat harvest from private farmers at guaranteed prices. . . . The entire country, now highly attuned to living with an unstable currency, realised what this would mean. The government could only pay by printing a lot more money, which the peasants would switch into marks the moment they were paid. It would, in short, kill the currency.*

*Sure enough, three times during July, the dinar/mark exchange rate lurched downwards. Then it spun out of control.*

*The exponential growth of inflation during these months still astonishes even the Yugoslav economists who had seen it coming. Between July and the end of the year it went from 500 per cent to 2,000 per cent a month, to 20,000 per cent, then 500,000 per cent and onwards. By January, prices were rising faster than 100 per cent an hour.*

*At the final assessment before the recovery plan was put into effect on January 24th [1994], the monthly inflation rate had reached a mind-blowing 302 million per cent. Compare that with the inflation rate in Germany, which at its height in 1923 reached only 332 per cent per month, while inflation in Latin American countries during the 1980s never went beyond 300 per cent per year.* ('Inflation hero is a man in a billion', *Independent on Sunday*, 9 October 1994, page 9)

---

* This is the name given to the notes issued by the American Continental Congress at that time.

We have now established three important conclusions:

1. Without monetary accommodation, supply shocks cause temporary bursts of inflation accompanied by recessionary gaps. The gaps are removed if, and when, unit costs of production fall, restoring equilibrium at potential GDP and at the initial price level.

2. Without monetary validation, demand shocks cause temporary bursts of inflation accompanied by inflationary gaps. The gaps are removed as wages rise, returning GDP to its potential level, but at a higher price level.

3. With an appropriate response from the monetary authorities, an inflation initiated by either supply or demand shocks can continue indefinitely; an ever-increasing money supply is necessary for an ever-continuing inflation.

Fortunately, the lessons from the inflation episodes of the 1970s, 1980s, and 1990s have been learned by policymakers, and in many countries central banks have been told that their job is to maintain low inflation. So sustained periods of rapid inflation are much less likely to occur in the near future. Politicians have learned these lessons the hard way, rather than by reading textbooks such as this.

# The Phillips curve

Up to now it has been enough to say that an inflationary gap implies excess demand for labour, low unemployment, pressure on wages to rise faster than productivity, and hence an upward-shifting *SRAS* curve. But now we need to look in more detail at the influence of wages on inflation. To do this, we make use of a famous relation called the **Phillips curve**, which helps us understand how fast the *SRAS* curve shifts. We first present the Phillips curve in its original form and then transform into a form more applicable to the *AD–AS* model. Since the original curve uses unemployment rather than GDP as its indicator of excess demand in labour markets, we must first show the relation between the two.

## The NAIRU

When current GDP is at its potential level, unemployment is not zero, even though we sometimes refer to this situation as 'full employment'. This is because there may be a substantial amount of *frictional unemployment*, caused by the movement of people among jobs, and *structural unemployment*, caused by a mismatch between the characteristics of the demand for labour and the characteristics of its supply. The amount of frictional and structural unemployment that exists when GDP is at its potential level is called the **NAIRU** or the **natural rate of unemployment** ($U^*$).[4] We use the term NAIRU rather than natural rate because the latter term may create the

erroneous impression that nothing can be done to reduce unemployment below a rate that is 'natural'.

It follows from the definition of the NAIRU that, when GDP exceeds potential GDP ($Y > Y^*$), unemployment will be less than the NAIRU ($U < U^*$); and when GDP is less than potential GDP ($Y < Y^*$), unemployment will exceed the NAIRU ($U > U^*$).[5]

We can now use the NAIRU terminology to restate our earlier assumptions about the pressure that is put on wage rates, and through them on the *SRAS* curve, by inflationary and recessionary gaps.

When the unemployment rate is below the NAIRU, demand forces put pressure on wages to rise faster than productivity. When the unemployment rate is above the NAIRU, demand forces put pressure on wages to rise more slowly than productivity, or even to fall. When unemployment is at the NAIRU, demand forces exert neither upward nor downward pressure on wages relative to productivity.

## The theory of the Phillips curve

In the 1950s Professor A. W. Phillips (1914–75) was doing research on stabilization policy at the London School of Economics. He was interested in the question of the speed with which input prices responded to excess demand and excess supply. To study this question, he looked at the rate of change of money wage rates in the United Kingdom over a period of 100 years. By relating these wage changes to the level of unemployment, he discovered a

---

[4] 'NAIRU' is an acronym for Non-Accelerating-Inflation Rate of Unemployment. The reason for this name will become apparent later in the chapter. We talk about the natural rate of unemployment and the NAIRU as if they were the same concept. In reality, they are different except when the economy is in full equilibrium.

[5] In more complex models it is possible that the correspondence between the NAIRU and $Y^*$ may not hold, but for simplicity here we assume that it does hold.

remarkable relationship, which came to be known as the Phillips curve. This was an empirical relationship which later theoretical work tried to explain. We will incorporate the key elements of Phillips curve theory into the context of our macro model.

The Phillips curve relates the percentage rate of change of money wage rates (measured at an annual rate) to the level of unemployment (measured as the percentage of the labour force unemployed). Unemployment is plotted on the horizontal axis, and wage changes on the vertical axis. Thus, any point on the curve relates a particular level of unemployment to a particular rate of increase of money wages. At first we assume that the price level is expected to remain relatively stable. Later we consider what happens to the curve when people expect a significant rate of inflation to persist.

So far in this book we have dealt with the levels of variables. The Phillips curve relates the amount of unemployment to the rate of change of money wages. Letting $\Delta W$ stand for the change in money wage rates from one year to the next, and $W$ for the level of wage rates in the first year, the equation of the Phillips curve is

$$(\Delta W/W) = f(U), \qquad (1)$$

where f stands for a functional relation.

A numerical example of a Phillips curve is shown in Figure 24.6. The numbers on the figure are hypothetical. (The original curve became negative at high rates of

unemployment.) We will see that, appropriately interpreted, the Phillips curve can handle all of the causes of inflation. For the moment we will concentrate on the influence of demand forces.

## The shape of the Phillips curve

### A negative slope

Note first that the Phillips curve has a negative slope, showing that the lower is the level of unemployment, the higher is the rate of change of money wages. This should not surprise us. Low rates of unemployment are associated with boom conditions, when excess demand for labour cause money wages to rise rapidly. High rates of unemployment, on the other hand, are associated with slump conditions, when the slack demand for labour leads to low increases, or possibly even decreases, in money wages.

### A flattening slope

Moving along the Phillips curve from left to right, the curve gets flatter. This shape is another way of showing the asymmetry of aggregate supply, namely that input prices change more rapidly upwards than downwards. Let us recall why.

First, assume that a recovery is increasing the excess demand for labour. As a boom develops, the unemployment rate will decrease towards, but will never reach, zero. (There will always be some frictional and structural unemployment.) At the same time, the growing excess demand for labour will be bidding up wage rates more and more rapidly. This behaviour causes the Phillips curve to get very steep and to lie far above the horizontal axis at its left-hand end. The further the curve is above the axis, the faster wages are rising.

**The steepness of the curve in the range of low unemployment shows that wage inflation is very responsive to changes in unemployment in that range.**

Second, consider the onset of a recession that raises unemployment. This recession restrains wage increases. As a result, the Phillips curve comes closer and closer to the horizontal axis, indicating less and less upward pressure on wages the higher the level of unemployment. If the curve fell below the axis, then money wages would actually be falling over some range of high unemployment. We do not show this case in the figure but instead assume that, as unemployment gets very high, the rate of increase in money wages approaches zero but never becomes negative.

**The flatness of the Phillips curve in the range of high unemployment shows that the rate of wage inflation is relatively unresponsive to changes in unemployment over that range.**

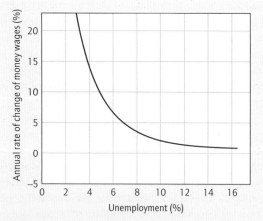

**Figure 24.6  A Phillips curve**

The Phillips curve relates the level of unemployment to the rate of change of money wage rates. The figure shows a numerical example of a Phillips curve. According to the example, an increase in unemployment by four percentage points, from 8 to 12 per cent, will lower wage inflation from 3 to 2 per cent, while a reduction in unemployment by four percentage points, from 8 to 4 per cent, will raise wage inflation from 3 to 14 per cent.

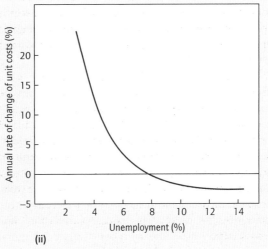

**Figure 24.7 The Phillips curve transformed**

**The Phillips curve is transformed in two steps into a curve relating GDP to the rate of change of unit costs.** Part (i) repeats the numerical example from Figure 24.6. It also adds a straight line labelled '*g*', indicating a 3 per cent rate of increase in labour productivity. Part (ii) shows unemployment related to the rate of change of unit costs, which is the rate of change of money wages minus the rate of change of productivity. Part (iii) substitutes *Y* for *U*, making use of the negative relation between the two variables. It shows the rate of change of unit costs positively related to GDP.

## The Phillips curve and the *SRAS* curve

To see what is happening to unit costs of production, we need to relate the increase in wage rates to the increase in labour productivity. For simplicity, in the rest of the discussion we will assume that labour is the only variable factor used by firms. This allows us to associate the labour costs of each unit of output with total variable costs per unit of output. (We could equally well have assumed that all input prices change at the same rate as the price of labour.)

What happens to unit costs of production now depends only on the differences between what labour costs the firm and what labour produces for the firm. To illustrate what is involved, we repeat in part (i) of Figure 24.7 the Phillips curve from Figure 24.6. We then add to it a horizontal line

labelled *g*, for growth in output per unit of labour input, which shows the rate at which labour productivity is growing year by year. In the hypothetical example of the figure, we have assumed that productivity is rising at 3 per cent per year. The intersection of the Phillips curve and the productivity line at the point *x* now divides the graph into an inflationary and a deflationary range described in the numbered points below. Given the assumptions about wage behaviour made earlier, point *x* must occur at the NAIRU (labelled *U\**)—which corresponds to a level of output equal to potential GDP, *Y\**.

1. At unemployment rates less than at the intersection point, wages are rising faster than productivity and thus unit costs of production (input costs per unit of output) are rising. If unit costs are rising, the *SRAS* curve must be shifting upwards.

2. At unemployment rates greater than at the intersection point, money wage rates are rising more slowly than productivity is rising. Therefore unit costs are falling. If unit costs are falling, the *SRAS* curve must be shifting downwards.

Notice that, although we have drawn the Phillips curve to show complete downward inflexibility of money wages, this does not imply complete downward inflexibility of unit costs. As long as money wages rise less than productivity rises, unit costs of production will be falling and the *SRAS* curve will be shifting downwards. Complete downward inflexibility of unit costs—and hence the total absence of the equilibrating mechanism that comes from downward shifts in the *SRAS* curve—requires more than the downward inflexibility of money wages: it requires that money wages never rise by less than the increase in productivity.

We will now derive from the Phillips curve a new curve that expresses the verbal argument just given.

Part (ii) of Figure 24.7 shows a new curve that relates the rate of unemployment to the change in unit costs, rather than to the change in money wage rates. The new curve still has unemployment on the horizontal axis, but now it is plotted against the rate of increase in unit costs on the vertical axis. Since this is merely the rate of increase in money wage rates minus the rate of increase of productivity, the new diagram is the same as part (i) of the figure, except that the origin on the vertical axis has been shifted by the rate of productivity growth.

The new curve tells us the rate at which unit costs of production are changing—and thus the rate at which the *SRAS* curve is shifting upwards or downwards—at each level of unemployment.

So far we have followed Phillips in plotting unemployment on the horizontal axis. The *SRAS* curve, however, plots GDP on its horizontal axis. To get a curve that relates the change in unit costs of production to the level of GDP, we note that unemployment is negatively related to the level of GDP. As GDP rises, unemployment tends to fall.

To make the relation precise, we assume that the labour force remains constant. Now any short-run increase in GDP, which means that more labour is employed, must mean that less labour is unemployed. In this case, any increase in GDP must mean a decrease in unemployment.

We can now transform the curve in part (ii) of Figure 24.7, which plots changes in unit costs of production against the unemployment rate, into a new relationship, shown in part (iii) of the figure. This curve shows the same rate of change in unit costs of production, but plots it

against the level of GDP. Since GDP and unemployment vary negatively with each other, the curve in part (iii) of the figure has the opposite slope to that in part (ii).[6] We call this new curve the transformed Phillips curve.

### Shifts in the *SRAS* curve

Figure 24.8(i) shows the familiar aggregate demand/aggregate supply diagram. Part (ii) shows the transformed Phillips curve (*PC*), relating the rate of change of unit costs to GDP. Both parts have GDP on their horizontal axes, and by lining these up we can compare one with the other. The *AD* and *SRAS* curves in part (i) determine the short-run levels of prices and GDP. Given the GDP so determined, the transformed Phillips curve tells us the rate at which the *SRAS* curve is shifting. Since from now on we will always be working with this transformed curve, we will just call it a Phillips curve. (Notice that, to emphasize that we are dealing with rates of change, we place a dot over the variable to indicate its annual percentage rate of change—in this case the symbol is $\dot{c}$.)

The long-run equilibrium of the economy is at potential GDP. All that the curve in part (ii) tells us is how fast the *SRAS* curve in part (i) is shifting, moving the economy towards its long-run equilibrium. The steepness of the curve for $Y$ greater than $Y^*$ (i.e. above equilibrium) shows the rapid adjustment towards equilibrium after a single expansionary shock. The flatness of the curve below equilibrium shows the slowness of adjustment towards equilibrium after a single contractionary shock.

The nonlinearity of the transformed Phillips curve expresses the asymmetry of aggregate supply: that costs, and hence prices, rise rapidly in the face of an inflationary gap, but fall only slowly in the face of a recessionary gap.

### The micro underpinnings of the asymmetry

The micro behaviour that lies behind the flat part of the Phillips curve to the left of $Y^*$ is explained in two parts. The first concerns the theory of short-run oligopoly pricing described in Chapter 9: firms tend to absorb cyclical demand fluctuations by varying their outputs rather than their prices. The second concerns the theory that money wage rates do not fall rapidly in the face of an

---

[6] We started with the relation $\Delta W/W = f(U)$, which is the original Phillips curve. We then subtracted productivity growth, $g$, to get a unit-cost-increase curve: $\Delta c/c = f(U) - g$. Then we substituted a relation between unemployment and national income, $U = u(Y)$, to get a curve relating the rate of increase in unit costs to the level of unemployment: $\Delta c/c = f(u(Y))$.

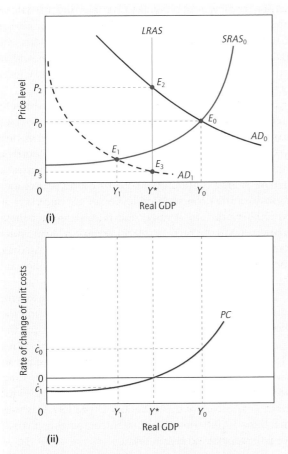

**(i)**

**(ii)**

**Figure 24.8 The Phillips curve and the *AS–AD* relationship**

The transformed Phillips curve shows the speed with which the *SRAS* curve is shifting upwards. When the curves are $AD_0$ and $SRAS_0$ in part (i), they intersect at $E_0$ to produce equilibrium GDP of $Y_0$. Part (ii) shows that when GDP is $Y_0$, the rate of change of unit costs, and hence the rate of increase in the *SRAS* curve, is $\dot{c}_0$ per cent per year. Thus, equilibrium GDP is moving rapidly towards $Y^*$ as the point of macroeconomic equilibrium moves up the fixed *AD* curve towards the long-run equilibrium at $E_2$.

When the curves are $AD_1$ and $SRAS_0$ in part (i), equilibrium is at $E_1$, with GDP $Y_1$. Part (ii) shows that when GDP is $Y_1$, unit costs, and hence the *SRAS* curve, will be shifting downwards at the rate of $\dot{c}_1$ per cent per year. Thus, equilibrium GDP is moving slowly along $AD_1$ towards a long-run equilibrium at $E_3$. Each long-run equilibrium has the same level of GDP but a different price level.

excess supply of labour, although they can rise rapidly in the face of excess demand for labour. This issue of wage inflexibility is central to the modern New Keynesian attempts to understand labour markets, and will be discussed in Chapter 25.

The overall microeconomics of wage behaviour is thought to be as follows. When demand falls, oligopolistic firms reduce their outputs and their demands for labour, holding their mark-ups approximately constant. The unemployment does not force money wage rates down significantly, so firms' unit costs, and hence their prices, fall no faster than productivity is rising. There will also be some downward pressure on money wages (particularly in non-unionized markets) and on prices in more competitive markets, and the result will be a slow downward drift of the price level. When demand rises above potential output, firms try to expand output by hiring more labour, and the labour shortages that develop cause wages to rise. As costs rise, firms pass these on in higher prices. This is a continuing process, which goes on as long as excess demand holds GDP above its potential level.

## Expectational forces

We must now drop our assumption that people expect that the price level will remain relatively stable in order to consider the effect of expectations of inflation. Suppose, for example, that both employers and employees expect a 4 per cent inflation rate next year. Unions will start negotiations from a base of a 4 per cent increase in money wages, which would hold their real wages constant. Firms also may be inclined to begin bargaining by conceding at least a 4 per cent increase in money wages, since they expect that the prices at which they sell their products will rise by 4 per cent. Starting from that base, unions will attempt to obtain some desired increase in their real wages. At this point such factors as profits, productivity, and bargaining power become important.

The general expectation of an *x* per cent inflation creates pressures for wages to rise by *x* per cent more than productivity, and hence for the *SRAS* curve to shift upwards by *x* per cent.

The key point is that the *SRAS* curve can be shifting upwards even if there is no inflationary gap. As long as people expect prices to rise, their behaviour will push money wages and unit costs up. This brings about the rise in prices that was expected. This is an example of the phenomenon of self-fulfilling expectations—if everyone thinks that event X is going to occur, their actions in anticipation of X may *make* X occur.

### Expectations formation

We have already discussed expectations in Chapter 22, in the context of exchange rate determination. Expectations are also important in investment behaviour, since firms invest in the expectation of increasing future profits. Here we consider the importance of inflation expectations in the context of the Phillips curve.

### Backward-looking theories

Keynesian theories of expectations assume that expectations are slow to change. The theory of *extrapolative expectations* says that expectations depend on extrapolations of past behaviour and respond only slowly to what is currently happening to costs. In one simple form of the theory the expected future inflation rate is merely a moving average of past actual rates. The rationale is that, unless a deviation from past trends persists, firms and workers will dismiss the deviation as transitory. They do not let it influence their wage- and price-setting behaviour.

The theory of *adaptive expectations* states that the expectation of future inflation rates adjusts to the error in predicting the current rate. Thus, if you thought the current rate was going to be 6 per cent and it turned out to be 10 per cent, you might revise your estimate of the next period's inflation rate upwards by, say, half of your error, making the new expectation 8 per cent.

These two theories make expectations about future inflation depend on past actual rates. In an obvious sense such expectations are backward-looking, since the expectation can be calculated using data on what has happened already.

### Forward-looking theories

**Rational expectations** are forward-looking. The rational expectations hypothesis assumes that people do not continue to make persistent, systematic errors in forming their expectations. Thus, if the economic system about which they are forming expectations remains stable, their expectations will be correct *on average*. Any individual's expectations at any time about next year's price level can thus be thought of as the actual price level that will occur next year plus a random error term which has a mean of zero.

Rational expectations have the effect of speeding up the adjustment of expectations. Instead of being based on past inflation rates, expected inflation is based on an informed forecast of the outcome of existing (and expected) policies.

Backward-looking expectations are overly naïve. People do look ahead to the future and assess future possibilities rather than just blindly reacting to what has gone before. Yet the assumption of unbiased forward-looking expectations requires that workers and firms have a degree of understanding of inflation forecasting that few economists would claim to have. It is possible that in reality wage-setting is a mixture of rational, forward-looking behaviour and expectations based on the experience of the recent past. Depending on the circumstances, expectations will tend sometimes to rely more on past experience, and at other times to rely more on present events whose effects are expected to influence the future.

Of course, people will not make the error of consistently underpredicting (or overpredicting) the inflation rate for decades, but it can go on for several years, whenever people do not fully understand the causes of current inflation. Every past period of inflation has led to intense debate among economists about its causes, cures, and probable future course. If professionals are uncertain, it would be surprising if wage- and price-setters got these matters right even on average. None the less, economists can use assumptions such as rational expectations in their models and then test the predictions to see if they are consistent with the data.

The belief that expectations are, at least to some extent, rational is one of the reasons why politicians around the world have sought to establish *credible* regimes for the control of inflation. Independent central banks with clearly defined low-inflation objectives have been put in place not just to control inflation directly, but also to *make people believe that inflation really will be kept under control*. Once people believe that inflation will be low, it is very much easier (in terms of output and employment costs) for policy-makers to keep it low.

## Random shocks

Forces other than excess demand and expectations of inflation also affect wage changes. These forces can be positive, pushing wages higher than they would otherwise go, or negative, pushing wages lower than they would otherwise go. One such shock occurs when an exceptionally strong union, or an exceptionally weak management, comes to the bargaining table and produces a wage increase that is a percentage point or two higher than would have occurred under more typical bargaining conditions.

One simple approach is to assume that there are many sources of shock, and that they are independent of one another. This means that, overall, they exert a random influence on wages—sometimes speeding wage changes up a bit, sometimes slowing them down a bit, but having a net effect that more or less cancels out when taken over several years. Over the long term they may be regarded as random events and are referred to as random shocks.

Random shocks may have a large positive or negative effect in any one year. Over the period of a sustained inflation, however, positive shocks in some years will tend to be offset by negative shocks in other years, so that overall they contribute little to the long-term trend of the price level.

## The overall effect on wages

The overall change in wage costs is a result of the three basic forces just studied. We may express this as follows:

$$
\begin{matrix}
\text{Percentage} \\
\text{increase} \\
\text{in unit} \\
\text{wage costs}
\end{matrix}
= \underset{\text{effect}}{\text{demand}} + \underset{\text{effect}}{\text{expectational}} + \underset{\text{effect}}{\text{shock.}} \quad (2)
$$

## The expectations-augmented Phillips curve

We can now add the forces of expectations and random shocks to the Phillips curve determining the behaviour of unit labour costs. The Phillips curve in Figure 24.7 shows only the effects of demand pressures. It will predict actual inflation only if the expected inflation rate is zero and there are no random shocks.

The relationship set out in (2) above defines a whole set of Phillips curves. Each curve is drawn for zero shocks and a given expected rate of inflation, which enters as an additive constant. At $Y^*$ there are no demand pressures on wages, so the height of the Phillips curve above the axis at that point is determined by the expected rate of inflation. The whole Phillips curve then shows how much the rate of change of unit costs varies from the expected inflation rate as a result of excess demand or excess supply in the labour market. Any particular Phillips curve drawn for a given expected rate of inflation is called a **short-run Phillips curve** (*SRPC*) or an **expectations-augmented Phillips curve**.

Figure 24.9 gives an example of one short-run curve and uses it to illustrate the relationships shown in equation (2). It shows unit costs rising as a result of increases in wage costs brought about by demand pressures (shown by the Phillips curve), expectations of inflation (which determine the height of the Phillips curve above the axis at $Y^*$), and random shocks (which are shown as deviations from the Phillips curve).

## The long-run Phillips curve

Is there any level of GDP in this model that is compatible with a constant rate of inflation? The answer is yes: potential GDP. When GDP is at $Y^*$, the demand component of inflation is zero, as shown in Figure 24.8. This means

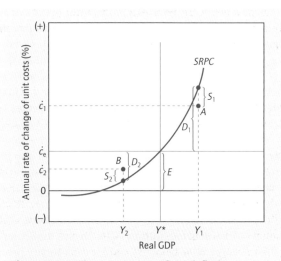

**Figure 24.9 The components of cost inflation illustrated**

**The rate of cost inflation can be separated into three components: expectational inflation, demand inflation, and shock inflation.** The Phillips curve is drawn for a given expected rate of inflation and hence is labelled a short-run Phillips curve (*SRPC*). The given expected inflation rate, $\dot{c}_e$, is shown by the height of the horizontal solid blue line. Point A indicates a GDP of $Y_1$ combined with a rate of cost inflation of $\dot{c}_1$. This rate is composed of a rate to match expected inflation, shown by the bracket *E*; a positive demand component, shown by the bracket $D_1$ (determined by the shape of *SRPC*); and a negative shock component, shown by the bracket $S_1$. Point B indicates a GDP of $Y_2$ combined with a rate of cost inflation of $\dot{c}_2$. This rate is composed of a rate to match expected inflation, once again shown by the bracket *E*; the demand component, shown by the bracket $D_2$, which is now negative (since income $Y_2$ is less than $Y^*$); and a positive shock component, shown by the bracket $S_2$.

that actual inflation equals expected inflation. There are no surprises. No one's plans are upset, so no one has any incentive to alter plans as a result of what actually happens to inflation.

**Provided the inflation rate is fully validated, any rate of inflation can persist indefinitely as long as GDP is held at its potential level.**[7]

---

[7] We now see why the level of unemployment associated with potential GDP is called the non-accelerating-inflation rate of unemployment (NAIRU). At any lower level of unemployment GDP exceeds potential GDP and the inflation rate will tend to rise; at any higher level of unemployment GDP is below potential GDP and inflation will tend to fall. (Money wage increases are lower than the rate of productivity growth.)

We now define the **long-run Phillips curve** (*LRPC*) as the relationship between GDP and stable rates of inflation that neither accelerate nor decelerate. This occurs when the expected and actual inflation rates are equal. On the theory just described, the long-run Phillips curve is vertical, because only at $Y^*$ can the expected and actual rates of inflation be equal. The long-run Phillips curve is shown in Figure 24.10.

Points on the *LRPC* are consistent with any stable rate of inflation. This could be zero, but it could also be some large positive number. Of course, to remain at a stable high rate, the inflation would have to be validated by the monetary authority permitting the money stock to rise. If the inflation rate were not validated the real money stock would fall, shifting *AD* to the left and eventually causing $Y$ to be below $Y^*$ and for deflationary pressure to rise.

The long-run Phillips curve is vertical at $Y^*$; only $Y^*$ is compatible with a stable rate of inflation; and any stable rate is, if fully accommodated, compatible with $Y^*$.

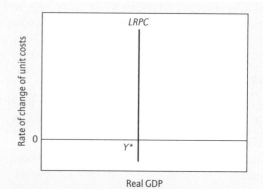

**Figure 24.10   The vertical long-run Phillips curve**

When actual inflation equals expected inflation, there is no trade-off between inflation and unemployment. In long-term equilibrium the actual rate of inflation must remain equal to the expected rate (otherwise expectations will be revised). This can occur only at potential GDP $Y^*$, that is, along the *LRPC*. At $Y^*$ there is no demand pressure on the price level; hence the only influence on actual inflation is expected inflation. Any stable rate of inflation (provided it is accommodated by the appropriate rate of monetary expansion) is compatible with $Y^*$ and its associated NAIRU.

# The Lucas aggregate supply function

A concept that is closely related to the expectation-augmented Phillips curve under rational expectations is the Lucas aggregate supply curve. This is associated with the New Classical approach to macroeconomics that was popular in the 1970s. The key element in the New Classical approach is a particular specification of the aggregate supply function that was formulated by US economist Robert Lucas (the 1995 Nobel Laureate in economics).

In Chapter 18, where we first set out the *SRAS* curve, we assumed that in the short run output prices are variable (they can respond to changes in demand in the current period) while input prices (we will concentrate here on wages) are fixed. In the long run, if output prices rise, wages are negotiated upwards to catch up with prices. This is what makes the *LRAS* curve vertical.

In the Lucas approach, wages are not just given on the basis of last period's equilibrium: rather, they are set at the beginning of the current period at the market-clearing level for *given expectations of what output prices in the current period will be*. In other words, they are set on the basis of forward-looking expectations of what the market outcome will be.

This may seem like a harmless modification of our original assumption, but it turns out to have fundamental implications. Figure 24.11 illustrates the implications for aggregate supply behaviour. The key point is that any shift in aggregate demand that is expected at the time wages are set, such as an announced (or anticipated) increase in the money supply, will cause the *SRAS* curve to shift up immediately. The economy will therefore experience an immediate increase in the price level and no increase in GDP. Only an *unexpected* increase in *AD* will lead to an increase in GDP in the short run. Lucas assumed that this shock to *AD* would be an unexpected increase in the money supply.

In the New Classical approach, cycles in real economic activity are triggered by unexpected increases in the money supply.

New Classical economists assume that the actors in the private sector of the economy have *rational expectations* and that all market prices, including those for labour, fluctuate to equate current demands with current supplies. This requires that agents form expectations based upon all available information about the future at the time they

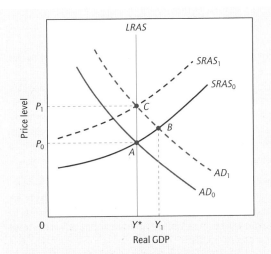

**Figure 24.11** **The Lucas aggregate supply curve**

In the New Classical approach, a given *SRAS* curve applies only to unexpected shifts in *AD*. Suppose there is a shift in aggregate demand from $AD_0$ to $AD_1$. If the shift is unexpected, the economy will move from the initial position at point A to point B, at the intersection of $SRAS_0$ and $AD_1$. However, if the shift in *AD* is expected, agents will negotiate higher wages immediately on the basis of this expectation, and the *SRAS* curve will shift up to $SRAS_1$. The price level will go straight from $P_0$ to $P_1$, and the economy will move from A to C, with no increase in GDP.

Policy ineffectiveness follows from the same analysis. Any predictable change in monetary or fiscal policy causing a change in aggregate demand, such as the shift in *AD* from $AD_0$ to $AD_1$, will lead to an immediate rise in prices from $P_0$ to $P_1$ and will have no effect on real GDP. An unexpected policy change of the same magnitude, however, would take the economy from point A to point B in the short run, and to C only in the long run.

take the decision. So agents make only random errors in forecasting the future course of economic variables. This implies that the expectational errors that trigger cycles cannot be systematic. (If they were systematic, agents could learn from the pattern of mistakes and improve their forecasts.) It would be tempting to conclude from this that deviations from potential output must, therefore, be random—which is clearly contradicted by evidence. However, to avoid this erroneous implication, Lucas added a lagged adjustment process to his model. This implied that any random shock can cause a slow adjustment process within the economy that has some persistence.

### Policy invariance

A perhaps surprising implication of the New Classical approach is that changes in monetary or fiscal policy, which may be intended to influence economic activity by shifting the *AD* curve, will have real effects only if they are unexpected. For example, a stimulus to demand involving an announced reduction in interest rates (and a consequent increase in the money supply) will create expectations of rising prices. These expectations will influence wage-setting, so the *SRAS* curve will shift up immediately and prices will rise straight away with no temporary increase in output. This outcome is illustrated in Figure 24.11, where an anticipated interest rate reduction shifts the *AD* curve to the right and the *SRAS* curve to the left, the net effect being that the economy moves straight up the *LRAS* curve, with the price level rising but real GDP remaining unchanged.

According to the New Classical approach, only unanticipated policy changes lead to changes in real GDP. Systematic policy changes will be predictable and will have no real effects.

Most economists do not accept the proposition that only unexpected policy changes will have real effects. One reason is that there is so much inertia in price- and wage-setting behaviour that very few contracts can be renegotiated as soon as a policy change is announced.

A second reason is that the massive complexity of the economy makes it impossible for individual agents to know how some shock will affect all the relevant prices and quantities that matter to them over any specified period of time. The idea of everyone knowing the exact nature of some policy disturbance and solving the equations of the economy to determine the exact outcome, and of their acting to anticipate these outcomes, is far-fetched. After all, the great virtue of the price system is that it co-ordinates activity without the need for anyone having knowledge of all the prices and quantities that exist.

However, the New Classical presumption that private agents have expectations of what policy-makers are going to do, and that this influences private behaviour, is important. Without assuming omniscience, just reasonably approximate expectations can cause private anticipation of government action to affect the outcome of policies. This realization has had a fundamental impact on macroeconomic policy analysis. In our model above the government is exogenous to the model. However, in the New Classical framework the government and the private sector interact by trying to guess what the other is going to do. The conduct of policy becomes more like a 'game', where strategy and perception of the other players matter.

It follows that policy-makers certainly have some leverage over real activity, even when making policy changes that are predictable, but that this leverage is less certain the more that private agents anticipate the effects of policy changes and react quickly to offset them.

**Box 24.2 The Lucas Critique**

The assumption that private agents are forming expectations of government behaviour has important implications for how economic models can be used to predict the effects of changes in policy.

A great deal of effort over the last thirty years has gone into building empirical econometric macroeconomic models of the economy for forecasting purposes (such as the National Institute model and the Bank of England model). Lucas pointed out that such models contain estimates of key behavioural parameters that were derived from past data. These data were collected under particular policy regimes.

Any attempt to use such a model to predict the consequences of significant policy changes may be erroneous. This is because the behaviour of private agents may change when the behaviour of policy-makers changes, as they are interdependent in some areas.

One example is the failure of the government to understand (and of the forecasters to forecast) the buildup of inflationary pressures in the UK economy in the late 1980s, following the financial innovations of the mid-1980s. Another is the difficulty of forecasting behaviour of agents in the EU following the introduction in January 1999 of the new single currency, the euro.

The Lucas Critique suggests that there will be shifts in many private sector behaviour functions when there are significant changes in the policy regime. Hence the effects of such regime changes will be impossible to forecast accurately using traditional macro models.

---

This change in perception of policy as interactive rather than exogenous has two important implications. The first follows below and the second, known as the Lucas Critique, is explained in Box 24.2.

### Policy credibility

If private agents are watching the government (and the monetary authorities, where these are different) and are trying to form expectations of its future behaviour, not only does it matter what the government does, but it also matters what agents think it will do in future. This means that a government needs more than just the correct current policies. It also needs to establish credibility that it will follow correct policies in future.

Suppose, for example, that a government enters office with a commitment to control inflation. It introduces tight monetary and fiscal policies, which in due course succeed in bringing down inflation but at the cost of a temporary recession. Now, however, there is an election approaching, and the government would like to increase real GDP to improve its chances of re-election. It may be tempted to break its original commitment to anti-inflationary policies.[8] However, private agents know that this incentive exists, so it matters to the outcome whether or not the private agents anticipate that the government will break its word. In other words, the government's credibility actually affects private behaviour. Once the government has broken its commitments, it will be more difficult for it to establish credibility in the future—at least, not without a change in personnel.

Recognition of the importance of credibility has been behind the ceding of power to set interest rates to independent central banks. They have an incentive to behave transparently and with high credibility, as this influences inflationary expectations and makes actual inflation much easier to control.

## Is inflation dead?

In Figure 24.1 on page 546 we saw that inflation is projected to stay low in the world economy at least for much of the first decade of the twenty-first century. One should not conclude from this that inflation no longer matters. On the contrary: the correct conclusion is that high inflation is so disruptive to a modern economy—and the costs of eliminating it once entrenched are so great—that it is important that the lessons of the recent past be learned and remembered by future generations, so that similar mistakes are not repeated.

It is not an accident that central banks around the world, from New Zealand to the United Kingdom and within the euro zone, have been given the power to determine monetary policy independently of elected politicians. This is to avoid the inflationary bias created when

---

[8] US economists F. Kydland and E. Prescott labelled the fact that it may now be rational for the government to renege on its commitments *time inconsistency*.

politicians are tempted to generate pre-election booms in order to aid their re-election. This problem is known as time-inconsistency, since it is in the self-interest of politicians to promise low inflation, but then also in their interests to break their promise at a later date, once inflation expectations are low. This implies that leaving the control of inflation to elected politicians can bring into question the credibility of counterinflationary credentials. A central bank with, at least, instrument independence can solve this problem. It is in the interest of the appointed central bankers to deliver on the imposed objective of price stability. Central bankers, who do not stand for re-election, have less problem in establishing a highly credible low-inflation regime.

This regime change is an important component in explaining why inflation is expected to stay low. However, the underlying cause has been both a public determination to support anti-inflation policies and a realization by the politicians themselves that inflation does not deliver prosperity in the long term. Economists have played an important role in the debate about the causes of and cures

for inflation, and it was economic analysis that underpinned the case for independent central banks.

While inflation has generally been conquered today, there is no guarantee that it will stay low for ever. After all, it was low throughout the 1950s and 1960s, yet erupted in the 1970s. Only sound monetary policies can deliver continued low inflation. Monetary policy is made by human beings, as are the institutions within which monetary policies are formulated. Therefore it is important that economists continue to study, and increase their understanding of, inflation so that future generations can learn by past mistakes rather than from their own.

The efforts of the 1980s and 1990s to bring down inflation have not been costless. Many millions of workers have spent time in unemployment, and many owners of businesses have seen their businesses go bust, in the recessions that followed episodes of sharp monetary tightening. The issue is not just how to control inflation, but rather how to control inflation *and* maintain a high level of employment and economic activity. It is to the issue of unemployment that we turn in the next chapter.

 # CASE STUDIES

## 1. Inflation and the price level in the long run

Figure 24.12 shows the UK price level and inflation rates since 1661. Looking at the price level in part (i), it is dramatically obvious that the price level was very stable from 1661 until the 1930s, since when it has risen considerably. It is literally true that the UK[9] price level in 1699 was the same as in 1906, a period of just over two hundred years. But, while the price level had no upward (or downward) trend (and was thus what we would now call 'mean-reverting'), it was certainly not constant, as part (ii) of the figure shows. Indeed, prices were quite volatile; they went up and down a lot. However, whenever they went up, sooner or later, they came back down again, and generally this was sooner rather later.

The main reason for the mean reversion of prices up to the early 1930s was that the value of sterling was tied to a physical commodity, gold. Thus, the quantity of money could not be increased by policy-makers in an attempt to hold interest rates below their market value and thereby stimulate the economy. This is the period of the so called 'gold standard'. Prices were volatile under

the gold standard because most of the products that are counted in the price index at that time were agricultural, and hence were subject to variations in supply due to weather. It is still true today that many agricultural prices are highly variable, for the same reasons, but they now have a much smaller weight in the consumer price index. Many of the products we now buy did not exist twenty years ago, let alone two hundred years ago.

After the abandonment of the gold standard in 1931 sterling floated for a while, but after the Second World War it was pegged to the US dollar until 1972. After that time there was no 'nominal anchor', and it is from then on that the UK price level rose rapidly. By the 1990s an inflation target had been adopted as the method for keeping inflation under control. While this has clearly helped to keep inflation low and stable, it is none the less positive. Hence the price level keeps rising, and has risen in every year since the 1930s (with the one exception of 1960 when inflation was zero). Thus, the price level is no longer mean-reverting. Even at an inflation rate of only 2 per cent, the price level doubles every 35 years or so. For these reasons, unless there is another regime change there is little chance that prices in 2199 will be on average the same as those in 1999.

Why then does the government not ask the Bank of England to target a constant price level, thereby duplicating the experience

---

[9] Of course the United Kingdom did not exist in 1661. Price indexes for this time are generally based on prices in England and were constructed much later.

of the earlier centuries? One reason is that the prices of most of the commodities that we buy today are not as volatile as the basic goods providing food and shelter that took up most of the public's spending in earlier centuries. The prices of manufactured goods and labour inputs tend to be rather inflexible downwards. Given a long and severe enough slump, wages and prices will come down, but they tend to do so only slowly. To hold the average level of prices constant, an upward shock to the price level, such as is often caused by a rise in the prices of energy or raw materials, would have to be accompanied by a fall in wage costs and other goods prices. Since this would not happen quickly, the transition effect would be a recession of the sort caused by an adverse input price shock as shown in Figure 24.2. Since the transition would sometimes be spread over years rather than months, holding the price level constant in the face of periodic upward price shocks would require periodic and, often

persistent, recessions. Most of us would probably agree that the preferred alternative to such a situation is a mild inflationary trend that accommodates occasional upward shocks in some prices by allowing all other prices to rise to restore equilibrium relative prices.

## 2. Asset price bubbles

Monetary policy-makers in the Bank of England and the ECB (and some other central banks) are charged with keeping prices under control. However, the targets that are used for this purpose are based upon consumer prices, i.e. prices of currently produced retail goods and services. In recent years consumer price inflation has generally been under control, and in this respect monetary policy has been very successful. However, there have been other prices, notably asset prices, that have

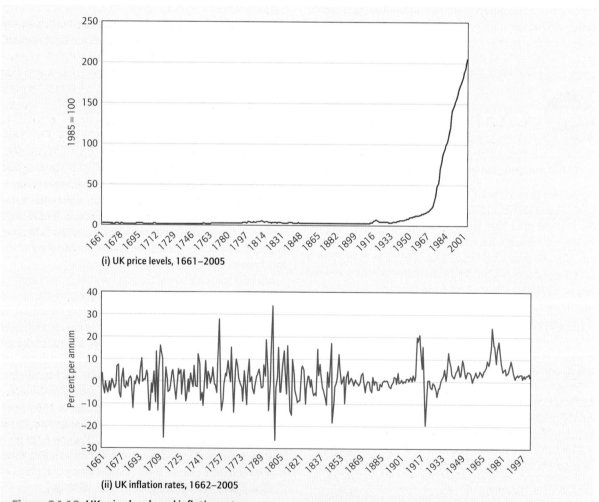

(i) UK price levels, 1661–2005

(ii) UK inflation rates, 1662–2005

**Figure 24.12** UK price levels and inflation rates

been very volatile, and the boom and bust in these prices have been associated with considerable disruption to the economy as a whole. The question then arises: should monetary policy-makers try to influence asset prices as well as consumer prices? Notice that asset prices are partly the prices of physical assets, such as houses and factories produced in the past, and partly the prices of securities, such as company shares, the values of which are determined by the profit streams that are expected in the future.

The conventional view until recently has been that monetary policy should stick to targeting consumer price inflation, that is the prices of currently produced goods and services. If it succeeds in controlling these, it cannot achieve much more. Some go further and argue that, because asset prices are so volatile, any attempt to target them would make monetary policy too un-stable and would induce policy cycles that caused unnecessary volatility in real activity. It is also hard to see how the monetary authorities could decide what is an appropriate level of asset prices and what weight they should give to different classes of assets, such as housing and shares.

The counter-argument to this is that if bubbles in asset prices are ignored they can cause significant disruption to real activity, which might have been avoided by timely policy interventions. Stock market bubbles in Japan and the United States in recent decades have been associated with major boom and bust cycles in their respective economies. Figure 24.13 shows share prices in Japan for 1981–92 and for US share prices over 1991–2002. The boom and bust patterns are remarkably similar. We have outlined above the severe problems experienced by Japan sub-sequent to this boom and bust cycle. The United States did not suffer as much as Japan did after its asset price collapse, but the US economy did experience a significant slowdown after the internet bubble burst in 2001. Cause and effect are hard to disentangle, but it is certainly possible that the downturn in

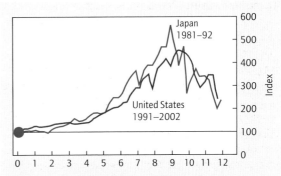

**Figure 24.13** **US (1991–2002) and Japanese (1981–1992) share prices**

Index: USA—1 January 1991 = 100; Japan—1 January 1981 = 100.

*Source: The Economist,* 28 September 2002, supplement, p. 29.

2001/2 would have been less severe if the stock market boom and bust had been more moderate.

Many countries, including the United Kingdom, have been affected by the same sort of stock market bubble as happened in the United States, though less so. However, the UK has seen an asset price bubble associated with house prices, and similar concerns about the influence that this should have on monetary policy have been raised.

It is unlikely that inflation targets will be changed to include asset prices. But it is likely that monetary policy-makers them-selves will be very careful in future in assessing the significance of asset price volatility and in deciding if there is anything that policy should be doing to avoid the bubble over-inflating, or possibly to help deflate it gently. This means that assets prices are unlikely to be included explicitly in inflation targets, but monetary policy-makers will take account of the information imparted by asset prices in making their policy decisions.

## SUMMARY

### Inflation in the macro model

■ A shift in the *SRAS* curve is called a supply shock, while a shift in the *AD* curve is called a demand shock.

■ A single leftward shift in the *SRAS* curve causes a rise in the price level and a fall in GDP. Full employment can be restored either by a fall in unit wage costs, which shifts the *SRAS* curve to the right, or by a monetary expansion, which shifts the *AD* curve to the right.

■ Repeated supply shocks in terms of leftward shifts of the *SRAS* curve carry their own restraining force in terms of

ever-rising unemployment if they are not accommodated by monetary expansion. If accommodated, they can give rise to a sustained supply-side inflation.

■ An isolated expansionary demand shock leads to a temporary rise in GDP and a rise in the price level. If it is not validated, output will fall while the price level rises as GDP returns to its potential level.

■ Sustained demand shocks that are validated by monetary expansion lead to sustained inflation with GDP remaining above potential.

## The Phillips curve

■ The original Phillips curve relates wage inflation to the level of unemployment; suitably transformed, it relates unit cost inflation to GDP. It thus determines the rate at which the *SRAS* curve is shifting.

■ Unit cost inflation depends on the state of demand— it is positive when $Y > Y^*$ and negative when $Y < Y^*$— and on expectations of inflation and random shocks. The expectations-augmented Phillips curve relates GDP to unit cost inflation and is displaced from the point of zero demand inflation at $Y = Y^*$ by the amount of expectational inflation.

■ A sustained inflation at a constant rate is possible only when $Y = Y^*$ and the monetary authorities accommodate the inflation. Expected inflation is then equal to actual inflation.

## The Lucas aggregate supply curve

■ With the Lucas aggregate supply curve only unexpected shifts in aggregate demand will have real effects, but this result is not generally accepted to apply to today's economies with their short-term rigidities and long adjustment lags.

■ Policy credibility is important once it is perceived that private agents' behaviour is influenced by their expectations of the government's future policy actions.

## Is inflation dead?

■ The establishment of a low-inflation environment at the end of the 1990s and into the 2000s was aided by the institutional changes that put monetary policy in the hands of central banks with independent control over the monetary policy instruments (as discussed in Chapter 21).

## TOPICS FOR REVIEW

■ Causes and consequences of demand and supply shocks

■ Once-and-for-all and sustained inflations

■ Wage inflation, productivity growth, and unit costs

■ NAIRU

■ Original, transformed, and expectations-augmented Phillips curves

■ Causes of sustained inflations

■ Lucas aggregate supply curve

■ Time inconsistency

■ The credibility of independent central banks

## QUESTIONS

1 If inflation cannot occur without money, does this mean that changes in the money stock always cause changes in inflation and that controlling the money stock is the only way to control inflation?

2 What is the relationship between the short-run Phillips curve and the *SRAS* curve?

3 What is the relationship between the long-run Phillips curve and the *LRAS* curve?

4 Starting from equilibrium, explain what happens to inflation when there is a one-off rise in the price of oil but the monetary authorities do not accommodate the shock.

5 Repeat question 4, but now assume that the monetary authorities relax monetary policy in an attempt to avoid any output loss from the supply shock.

6 Using the Phillips curve framework, outline how inflation and unemployment respond (starting from zero inflation and at the NAIRU) to a permanent positive exogenous shock to aggregate demand. Make clear what you are assuming about the monetary policy response.

7 Repeat question 6 but now assume that there has been an exogenous negative supply shock.

8 What factors lay behind the high inflation of the 1970s, and what changed by the 1990s to bring about the apparent elimination of inflation?

# Chapter 25

# UNEMPLOYMENT

Can the economy create jobs for all who want to work? Is mass unemployment a thing of the past? Will technology destroy jobs? These are some of the issues we address in this chapter.

In particular, you will learn that:

- Prospects for UK unemployment to remain low are better in the first decade of the twenty-first century than they appeared to be in the 1980s and early 1990s.

- Unemployment can be thought of as being made up of cyclical, frictional, and structural unemployment. The latter two make up equilibrium unemployment.

- Nominal wage rigidities help explain why cycles in demand cause cycles in unemployment.

- Equilibrium unemployment arises from frictions in the economy, structural changes in the nature of economic activity, and the benefit system.

- Aggregate demand management can reduce cyclical unemployment.

- Lower benefits, active manpower policies, and reformed wage bargaining institutions can reduce equilibrium unemployment.

- It is neither possible nor desirable to reduce unemployment to zero.

In the previous chapter we learned that inflation was a major problem in the 1970s and 1980s but that it had largely been brought under control by the late 1990s and remained low in the early part of the 2000s. Part of the price paid for bringing inflation down was higher unemployment, although the high unemployment levels often associated with lowering inflation are usually temporary. Indeed, unemployment too has fallen in several countries, such as the United States and the United Kingdom, where in the second half of the 1990s and into the mid-2000s it fell to levels not seen since the early 1970s. But unemployment remained a problem in many economies, including some countries within the European Union. As the International Labour Office reported,

*The world's unemployment rate stood at 6.3 per cent (in 2005), unchanged from the previous year and 0.3 percentage points higher that a decade earlier. In total, nearly 191.8 million people were unemployed around the world in 2005, an increase of 2.2 million since 2004 and 34.4 million since 1995. Almost half of the unemployed people in the world are young people, a*

*troublesome figure given that youth make up only 25 per cent of the working age population. Young people are more than three times as likely as adults to be unemployed.* (ILO, *Global Employment Trends Brief*, January 2006; © 2006 ILO)

The Keynesian revolution, which established the branch of economics we now call macroeconomics, was stimulated by the need to explain and then solve the high-unemployment problems of the 1930s. The proposed solution focused on the use of countercyclical aggregate demand policies to cure unemployment. But the simple message that stimulating demand can cure unemployment is no longer accepted in its original form. This is because these policies did not distinguish between unemployment that arises because the economy is below potential output and the unemployment that exists even when the economy is in equilibrium at the potential level of GDP. Unemployment that is associated with actual GDP being below potential is called *cyclical* unemployment. But *equilibrium* unemployment is also important, and this can exist even when GDP is at its potential level. Hence we need explanations of both cyclical and equilibrium unemployment.

In this chapter we first introduce some definitions and measurement issues relating to unemployment. Next we set out some of the main facts. We then study cyclical unemployment. Finally, we discuss equilibrium unemployment and the NAIRU[1] in much more detail. In particular, we ask why equilibrium unemployment exists and why it changes. We then consider whether government policy can do anything to reduce the NAIRU.

# Unemployment characteristics

## Measurement and definitions

For purposes of study, the unemployed can be classified in various ways. They can be grouped by personal characteristics such as age, sex, degree of skill or education, and ethnic group. They can also be classified by geographical location, by occupation, by the duration of unemployment, or by the reasons for their unemployment. In this chapter we are concerned with explanations of unemployment. Although it is not always possible to say why a particular person does not have a job, it is usually possible to test hypotheses about the causes of differences in aggregate unemployment, both over time for one country and between countries at the same point in time.

The ways in which unemployment is measured have changed many times over the years. UK figures used to include only those people actively looking for work and registering for benefits. This is referred to as the *claimant count*. The claimant count is still published, but it is more common to use a measure of unemployment based upon a survey of the labour force. These two measures of unemployment are explained in Box 25.1.

The recorded figures for unemployment may significantly understate or overstate the numbers who are actually willing to work at the existing set of wage rates. Overstatement arises because measured unemployment includes people who are not interested in work but who say they are in order to collect unemployment benefits. Understatement arises because of the voluntary withdrawal from the labour force of people who would like to work but have ceased to believe that there are any suitable jobs available; although these people may not be measured in the unemployment figures, they are unemployed in the sense that they would accept a job if one were available at the going wage rate. People in this category are referred to as *discouraged workers*. They have voluntarily withdrawn from the labour force, not because they do not want to work, but because they believe that they cannot find a job given current labour market conditions.

In this chapter we refer to three main types of unemployment. **Cyclical** or **demand-deficient unemployment** occurs when aggregate spending in the economy is insufficient to purchase the output that would be supplied when the economy is at potential GDP. An alternative definition of cyclical unemployment focuses on the labour market rather than the goods market. In this approach cyclical unemployment is that unemployment in excess of the NAIRU. **Frictional unemployment** is unemployment that arises as part of the normal turnover of labour. For example, in a market economy firms and products are continually changing and workers are moving from one job to another, or from work to training and from training to work. In the course of this dynamic movement there will always be some workers who are between jobs, or just entering the labour force and looking for the first job, and are classified as unemployed. **Structural unemployment** occurs when there is a mismatch between the characteristics and skills of the people looking for work and those desired by potential employers. Jobs may exist in London while the available workers are in Liverpool, or there may be plenty of opportunities for computer programmers but an oversupply of individuals looking for jobs in social work. Frictional and structural unemployment make up **equilibrium unemployment**, which is defined as the unemployment that exists when GDP is at its potential level (and when unemployment is at the NAIRU), and hence when there is neither a recessionary nor an inflationary gap. In what follows we assume that equilibrium unemployment and the NAIRU are the same.

### UK experience

Figure 25.1 shows UK unemployment since 1885.[2] There was highly cyclical unemployment before the First World War, very high unemployment in the interwar period,

---

[1] The non-accelerating-inflation rate of unemployment (NAIRU) was explained in Chapter 24.

[2] There have been many changes in the definition of unemployment over the years. Data since the 1950s that we use here are based on the claimant count. This has been affected by changes in the benefits rules, which influence who can register.

**Box 25.1  How is unemployment measured?**

Figure 25.1 shows data for the percentage of the workforce unemployed in the United Kingdom from 1885 to 2005. This figure uses a measure of unemployment known as the *claimant count*. The claimant count gives us the longest available data series on UK unemployment, but it has been replaced as the standard measure of unemployment by a different series. This alternative measure is an international standard defined by the United Nations International Labour Office; hence it is known as *ILO unemployment*. The European Union and the OECD have adopted the ILO unemployment definition. So what is the difference between the claimant count and ILO unemployment?

**The claimant count**

The UK claimant count is all those people claiming unemployment-related benefits at Employment Service offices. In 2006 the relevant benefits that could be claimed were the Jobseeker's Allowance and National Insurance credits. The percentage of unemployment is then expressed using the numbers of claimants as a percentage of 'workforce jobs' plus claimant unemployment. *Workforce jobs* is a measure of the number of full-time and part-time jobs in the economy.

One big advantage of the claimant count is that it is an accurate measure of *all* those claiming benefits. It gives a correct picture of who is registered for benefits both at national and local level, and it is timely in that it does not take long to produce an unemployment figure. But there are several disadvantages. First, as the benefits system changes, so the numbers able to claim benefits change. Second, it does not measure anyone who is unemployed but does not bother to claim benefit. Third, the measure of workforce jobs overestimates the numbers in work because it counts twice anyone with two jobs, so the *percentage* of persons unemployed is underestimated.

**ILO unemployment**

Under the ILO approach all people aged 16 and over are classified into one of three states: in employment, ILO unemployed, or economically inactive. ILO unemployed are those who either

- are out of work, want a job, have actively sought work in the last four weeks, and are available to start work in the next two weeks; or

- are out of work, have found a job, and are waiting to start it in the next two weeks.

Anyone who carries out at least one hour's paid work in a week, is on a government-supported training scheme, does unpaid work for a family business, or is away temporarily from a job (such as on vacation) is counted as being in employment. Those who are out of work but do not meet the criteria for ILO unemployment are defined as economically inactive. The unemployment percentage expresses numbers of ILO unemployed as a percentage of the total numbers of economically active.

ILO unemployment is measured by means of a monthly survey, which in the United Kingdom is called the Labour Force Survey (LFS), and hence ILO unemployment is sometimes also referred to as *LFS unemployment*. About 40,000 individuals are interviewed each month, and the unemployment figure announced is the average of data for the previous three months.

The advantage of the ILO measure of unemployment is that it is comprehensive—it measures those who say they are unemployed and not just those claiming benefits. The disadvantages are that it is based on a survey and so is subject to sampling error; it takes time to produce; it lumps together as 'employed' anyone who takes even one hour's paid work with those who work much longer hours; and, because of the small numbers involved, it is not accurate at the local level.

In April 2006 UK unemployment by the ILO definition was 1.59 million, while the claimant count was 0.945 million. The unemployment percentage was 5.1 by the ILO definition and 3.1 by the claimant count definition. These are by no means insignificant differences; missing half a million people who are looking for work from the unemployment measure is not a trivial matter. In the same period the ILO unemployment percentage was 4.1 per cent in Japan, 4.7 in the United States, 11.3 in Germany, and 9.5 in France.

and then very low and stable unemployment from the Second World War until the 1970s. There was a rising trend in UK unemployment, in successive cycles, through the 1970s and into the 1980s, followed by a steady fall in the 1990s and early 2000s. A perspective over the last century or so suggests that there is no long-term upward or downward trend. Rather, there is a high degree of persistence. Once unemployment is high it tends to stay high; once low it tends to stay low. In the interwar period unemployment was consistently high, but in the 1950s and 1960s it was consistently low. In the 1980s and early 1990s it was high, but not as high as in the 1930s.

Unemployment varies much more between business cycles than within them. For example, in the 1920s and 1930s unemployment cycled about a high average level, but in the 1950s it cycled about a low level. Also, compare the low average unemployment levels of the 1960s and early 1970s with the high levels of the 1980s. This evidence suggests that there are long-term changes in social institutions affecting employment and unemployment, and perhaps that big shocks to the economic system—a major war being the obvious example—have long-lasting effects.

The trend of total employment in the United Kingdom has been slowly rising over the postwar period. The

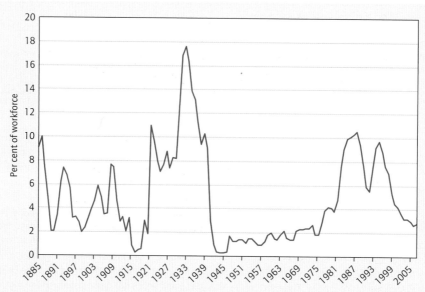

**Figure 25.1** UK claimant count unemployment 1885–2005

UK unemployment has varied considerably over the past century and a quarter. Unemployment was high in the interwar period and in the 1980s, but it was low in the 1950s and 1960s.

number of people who were economically active[3] rose from 25.5 million in 1971 to around 30 million in 2005. The numbers in employment over the same period rose from 24.5 million to 28.5 million.[4] This steady but fairly slow growth is explained partly by the low rate of population growth. Indeed, the proportion of the population over the age of 16 who were economically active was exactly the same in 2005 as it was in 1971: 63.1 per cent. However, there have also been some big structural changes in the pattern of employment. There were, for example, big shifts between sectors, such as a decline in manufacturing employment and a rise in services. Also there have been changes in the composition of the labour force. Declining male employment has offset increased female participation rates.[5] For example, the proportion of males over the age of 16 who were economically active declined from 84 per cent in 1971 to 70 per cent in 2005, while the

proportion of women in the same age group who were economically active rose from 45 per cent in 1971 to 56 per cent in 2005.

## International comparisons

Unemployment has not been a uniquely UK problem; hence international comparisons are instructive. Figure 25.2 shows unemployment in major EU countries, as well as in the United States and Japan, since 1980.[6]

Part (i) of the figure shows France, Germany, Japan, the United Kingdom, and the United States. Japan had very low measured unemployment in the 1980s, but it started to rise in the 1990s before declining again after 2002. France and the United Kingdom had high unemployment rates in the 1980s. This declined in the 1990s in the UK but stayed high in France. Germany joined France as a high-unemployment country in recent years, while the UK, USA, and Japan experienced much lower levels.

Part (ii) of the figure shows data for Denmark, Greece, Italy, the Netherlands, and Spain. The latter had extremely high unemployment in the 1980s, as did Ireland. However, rapid economic growth transformed the Irish economy such that by 2006 it was among the low-unemployment countries. The Spanish unemployment position improved

---

[3] The 'economically active' are those of working age who are either in work or are actively seeking work (the unemployed). It excludes people of working age who are not seeking work.

[4] Employment here includes self-employed as well as employees, and the difference between those economically active and those employed is the unemployed. The economically inactive are thus defined as those who are over 16 but who are neither employed nor seeking work.

[5] The 'participation rate' is the proportion of a particular group that is in employment. For example, the 'female participation rate' measures the proportion of women of working age who are in work.

[6] All the data in this section use the ILO definition of unemployment.

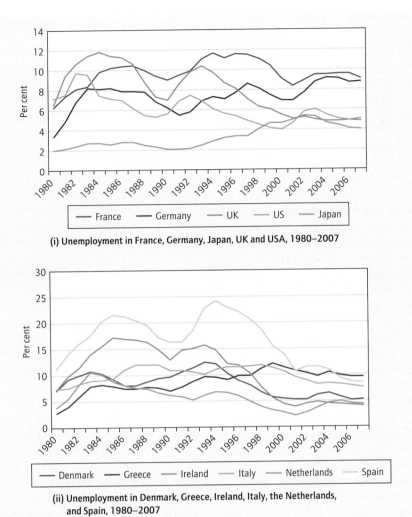

(i) Unemployment in France, Germany, Japan, UK and USA, 1980–2007

(ii) Unemployment in Denmark, Greece, Ireland, Italy, the Netherlands, and Spain, 1980–2007

**Figure 25.2 Unemployment in 11 countries, 1980–2007**

**The behaviour of unemployment has varied considerably within the industrialized world.** Part (i) shows that unemployment was high in France from the early 1980s onwards. In Japan it was very low in the 1980s, but starting to rise in the 1990s. UK unemployment was high in the 1980s but fell sharply in the 1990s. US unemployment was high in the early 1980s but cycled about a declining trend thereafter.

Part (ii) shows that Spain and Ireland had very high unemployment in the 1980s. It fell in Ireland in the 1990s, to reach low levels by 2006. Unemployment in Spain also fell in the late 1990s, but was still relatively high at 8.7 per cent in 2006. Italy and Greece also had relatively high unemployment in 2006, while Denmark and the Netherlands were among those countries with relatively low unemployment.

*Source*: IMF, *World Economic Outlook*, May 2006 (data for 2006 and 2007 are IMF projections).

considerably in the late 1990s, but it was a still a relatively-high unemployment country in the mid-2000s. Italy and Greece also experienced relatively high unemployment in the early 2000s, while the Netherlands and Denmark joined Ireland in the ranks of the low unemployed.

There is one broad generalization that will be helpful in understanding the causes of unemployment, and the differences in experience between countries. Unemployment is the result of the balance of two continuous flows: the flow of potential workers into unemployment (leaving employment but seeking work, or joining the labour force but not finding employment immediately), and the flow of workers out of unemployment (finding jobs, or withdrawing from the labour force).

In EU countries the flow into unemployment has been quite small and does not change much over time. However, the outflow is also small, so very high proportions of workers who are unemployed have been unemployed for a long time. For example, in Belgium, Ireland, and Italy around 60 per cent of the unemployed (at the peak of the unemployment upturn in the early 1990s) had been unemployed for more than 12 months, which is defined as long-term unemployment. The figures for Germany, France, and the United Kingdom were all around 35 per cent. This contrasts with Canada and the United States, where only just over 10 per cent of the unemployed had been without jobs for more than 12 months. In the United States, in particular, flows into unemployment are high, but flows out are just as high, so the level of long-term unemployment is low.

This may give an important clue as to the reasons for the higher persistence of unemployment in several EU countries. Skills and human capital deteriorate during periods out of employment, so the long-term unemployed are perceived (rightly or wrongly) as being less employable than those who have recently been in work.

A common pattern across countries is that low-skilled workers are four or five times more likely to be unemployed than skilled or professional workers. About 75 per cent of unemployed men are manual workers. This suggests that it is the unemployment of unskilled manual workers that should be the main focus of study.

Older workers are less likely to be unemployed than younger workers. Youth unemployment is universally higher than adult unemployment. Extreme cases at the height of the recession in the early 1990s included Spain with 43 per cent youth unemployment and Italy with 30 per cent. The UK figure was 17 per cent at this time, when the overall unemployment, rate was around 10 per cent.

In most EU countries female unemployment is greater than male unemployment. The United Kingdom is the exception, with 4.2 per cent female unemployment compared with around 5.7 per cent for males in 2005 (although a high proportion of female employment is part-time).

Another universal feature of unemployment is that movement into the ranks of the unemployed is predominantly the result of redundancy rather than voluntary job leaving. This may seem obvious, but it is important from an economic theory perspective because some economists have attempted to explain unemployment as a voluntary choice made by workers. There is certainly some element of choice involved in deciding whether or not to accept a job offer once one has been located, but that is very different from having chosen to be unemployed in the first place. Hence most economists believe that the majority of those who are recorded as unemployed are involuntarily unemployed. Someone is **involuntarily unemployed** if she would accept an offer of work in a job for which she is trained, at the going wage rate, if such an offer could be found.

# Consequences of unemployment

Involuntary unemployment is regarded by most people as a social 'bad' just as much as output is regarded a social 'good'. The harm caused by involuntary unemployment is measured in terms of the output lost to the whole economy and the harm done to the individuals who are affected.

## Lost output

Every involuntarily unemployed person is someone willing and able to work but unable to find a job. Unemployed workers are valuable resources whose potential output is wasted. The material counterpart of unemployment is the recessionary gap—i.e. the potential GDP that is not produced. The cumulative loss of UK output in 1991–7 was £55 billion (at 1990 prices);[7] this is nearly £1,000 for every member of the population, or about £2,000 for each member of the labour force. In a world of scarcity with many unsatisfied wants, such a loss is serious. It represents goods and services that could have been produced but are gone for ever. From 1997 until 2006 UK output was very close to potential, so there were no further losses over this period.

## Personal costs

The social welfare system, designed to alleviate the short-term economic consequences of unemployment, has been extended in the postwar period. Being unemployed in the United Kingdom, even for a substantial period of time, is no longer quite the personal disaster that it once was. But the longer-term effects of high unemployment rates for those who have become so disillusioned that they have given up trying to make it within the system, and who may be contributing to social unrest, should be a matter of serious concern to the haves as well as the have-nots. As UK economists Richard Layard, Stephen Nickell, and Richard Jackman put it,

*Unemployment matters. It generally reduces output and aggregate income. It increases inequality, since the unemployed lose more than the employed. It erodes human capital. And, finally, it involves psychic costs. People need to be needed. Though unemployment increases leisure, the value of this is largely offset by the pain of rejection.* (Layard *et al.* 1994; by permission of Oxford University Press)

Next we study the causes of cyclical and structural unemployment.

---

[7] This figure is calculated using the IMF estimates of actual and potential GDP shown in Figure 15.1 on page 336. The loss is just the sum of the gaps between actual and potential output in each of these seven years.

# Cyclical unemployment

*Cyclical unemployment*, or demand-deficient unemployment, occurs whenever total demand is insufficient to purchase all of the economy's potential output, causing a recessionary gap in which actual output is less than potential output. Cyclical unemployment can be measured as the number of people who would be employed if the economy were at potential GDP minus the number of persons currently employed. When cyclical unemployment is zero, all existing unemployment is either structural or frictional, and the rate of unemployment is the NAIRU. Notice that cyclical unemployment can be less than zero, because GDP can be above potential GDP, at least temporarily.

**Macroeconomic theory has traditionally sought to explain only cyclical unemployment.**

Equilibrium unemployment was once presumed to be outside the scope of macroeconomics. However, we will see below that it is unwise to try to establish a simple dichotomy between cyclical unemployment (as being due to macro causes) and equilibrium unemployment (as being due to micro causes). Both micro and macro factors contribute to both cyclical and equilibrium unemployment. (The microeconomics of labour markets is discussed in Chapter 11.) Indeed, we will find that a strong case can be made for the view that high cyclical unemployment raises the level of equilibrium unemployment for some time. Hence we must caution against the presumption that cyclical unemployment and equilibrium unemployment have different causes—or, indeed, that they are unrelated. However, it is useful to analyse cyclical unemployment separately, because this is the component of unemployment that can potentially be reduced by monetary and fiscal policies, via their effect in shifting aggregate demand.

Fluctuations in GDP are not sufficient to create fluctuations in involuntary unemployment. Something else is needed. Suppose, for example, that aggregate demand is fluctuating, causing GDP to fluctuate around its potential level. This fluctuation will cause the demand for labour to fluctuate as well, rising in booms and falling in slumps. If the labour market had fully flexible wage rates, then wages would fluctuate to keep quantity demanded equal to quantity supplied. We would observe cyclical fluctuations in employment (and therefore also in voluntary unemployment) and in the wage rate, but no changes in involuntary unemployment. Employment and wages

would vary procyclically (i.e. rising in booms and falling in slumps), but there would be no significant amounts of involuntary unemployment. Such behaviour is shown for a typical labour market in Figure 25.3.

The hypothetical situation we have just described is not what we actually observe. Instead we see cyclical fluctuations not only in employment, but also in involuntary unemployment. Furthermore, the changes in wage rates that do occur are insufficient to equate demand and supply, as is shown in Figure 25.4. Unemployment exceeds the NAIRU in slumps and falls below it in booms. Although wages do tend to vary procyclically over the cycle, the fluctuations are not sufficient to remove all cyclical variations in unemployment. Why is this so?

Two types of explanation have been advanced over the years. The one that we consider first is associated with the New Classical school. This explanation assumes that labour markets are always in equilibrium, in the sense that quantity demanded is continually equated with quantity supplied. While the New Classical approach is hard to accept as a description of the causes of unemployment, for reasons already mentioned (such as the assumptions that there are no involuntary lay-offs and that wages are flexible even in the short run), the New Classical school set down a challenge which was met by what is called the New Keynesian agenda. Also, it is worth noting that the predictions of New Classical models and New Keynesian models, while based on very different assumptions, are difficult to distinguish empirically, although their implications for appropriate anti-unemployment policies differ greatly.

## The New Classical approach

The major characteristic of the New Classical approach is that agents continuously optimize and markets continuously clear; hence there can be no involuntary unemployment. The New Classicists then seek to explain unemployment as the outcome of voluntary decisions made by rational people who are choosing to do what they do, including spending some time out of employment. Notice the contrast with traditional Keynesian (and early monetarist) macroeconomics. Theories in this class assume that unemployment is a sign of market failure, associated with non-market-clearing prices and/or wages, and that a high proportion of unemployment is involuntary.

(i)                                    (ii)

**Figure 25.3 Employment and wages in a single competitive labour market**

In a perfectly competitive labour market, wages and employment fluctuate in the same direction when demand fluctuates and in opposite directions when supply fluctuates; in both cases there is no involuntary unemployment. The figure shows a single perfectly competitive market for one type of labour. In part (i) the demand curves $D_1$, $D_2$, and $D_0$ are the demands for this market when there is a slump, a boom, and when aggregate GDP is at its potential level. As demand rises from $D_1$ to $D_0$ to $D_2$, wages rise from $w_1$ to $w_0$ to $w_2$, and employment rises from $q_1$ to $q_0$ to $q_2$. At no time, however, is there any involuntary unemployment.

In part (ii) the supply of labour fluctuates from $S_1$ to $S_0$ to $S_2$, and wages fluctuate from $w_1$ to $w_0$ to $w_2$. In this case wages fall when employment rises and vice versa, but again there is no involuntary unemployment.

**Figure 25.4 Unemployment in a single labour market with sticky wages**

When the wage rate does not change enough to equate quantity demanded and quantity supplied at all times, there will be unemployment in slumps and labour shortages in booms in each individual labour market. When demand is at its normal level, $D_0$, the market is cleared with wage rate $w_0$, employment is $q_0$, and there is no unemployment. In a recession demand falls to $D_1$, but the wage falls only to $w_1'$. As a result $q_1$ labour is demanded, but $q_1'$ is supplied. Employment is determined by the quantity demanded at $q_1$; the remainder of the supply for which there is no demand, $q_1q_1'$, is unemployed. In a boom demand rises to $D_2$, but the wage rate rises only to $w_2'$. As a result the quantity demanded is $q_2'$, whereas only $q_2$ is supplied. Employment rises to $q_2$, that is, the amount supplied; the rest of the demand cannot be satisfied, making an excess demand for labour of $q_2q_2'$.

One New Classical explanation of cyclical fluctuations in employment assumes that they are caused by fluctuations in the willingness of people to supply their labour, as shown in part (ii) of Figure 25.3. If the supply curve of labour fluctuates cyclically, this will lead to cyclical variations in employment. This explanation of cyclical behaviour in the labour market has two problems. First, it implies that wages will tend to rise in slumps and

fall in booms, which is not what we observe. Second, it predicts that there will still be no systematic cyclical *involuntary unemployment*, since labour markets always clear, leaving everyone who wishes to work actually working. Supply-induced fluctuations in employment form part of the basis of what is called real business cycle theory. However, the real supply shocks that trigger 'real' business cycles cause changes in the NAIRU, so at best this explains variations in equilibrium but not cyclical unemployment.[8]

A second line of the New Classical explanation lies in errors on the part of workers and employers in predicting the course of the price level over the business cycle. To understand this argument, start by assuming that each of the economy's markets is in equilibrium, that there is full employment, that prices are stable, and that the actual and expected rates of inflation are zero. Now suppose that the government relaxes monetary policy to permit the money supply to increase unexpectedly by 5 per cent in such a way that inflation expectations are unaffected. People find themselves with unwanted money balances, which they seek to spend. For simplicity, assume that the increased money supply leads to an increase in desired expenditure on *all* commodities. The demand for each commodity shifts to the right, and all prices rise, since they are assumed to be competitively determined. Individual decision-makers seeing their selling prices go up mistakenly interpret the increase as a rise in their own relative price. This is because they expect the overall inflation rate to be zero. Firms will produce more, and workers will work more, because both groups think they are getting an increased *relative* price for what they sell. Thus total output and employment rise. (This assumes that producers are not aware of changes in the prices of competing products and that consumers are not aware of changes in the prices of what they buy.)

When both groups eventually realize that their own relative prices are in fact unchanged, output and employment fall back to their initial levels. The extra output and employment occur only while people are being fooled. When they realize that *all* prices have risen by 5 per cent, they revert to their initial behaviour. The only difference is that now the price level has risen by 5 per cent, leaving relative prices unchanged.

A similar argument shows that an unanticipated monetary contraction would cause output to fall below its full-employment level.

All New Classical explanations assume that labour markets clear, and then look for reasons why employment fluctuates. They all imply, therefore, that people who are not working have voluntarily withdrawn from the labour market, either because this is their optimal decision or because they have misinterpreted market signals.

## The New Keynesian agenda

Many economists find the New Classical explanations implausible. They believe that people read market signals more or less correctly but react in ways that do not cause markets to be in equilibrium at all times. These economists believe that many who are recorded as unemployed are involuntarily unemployed, just as they tell those who survey them that they are.

The New Classical approach does have attractions to some economists because it assumes rational agents who are always optimizing. In other words, it has rigorous micro foundations which are attractive to economists trained to analyse the utility-maximizing behaviour of agents interacting in clearing markets. Economists so trained were uncomfortable with the early Keynesian assumptions of arbitrary price and wage stickiness (in the face of sustained excess supply) and of markets that do not clear. Those who are unhappy to assume no involuntary unemployment therefore seek to explain why there could be a labour market *equilibrium* in which there is an excess supply of labour at the going wage. We refer to this as the New Keynesian 'agenda' rather than 'theory', because there are many different theories encompassed by it and it is ongoing.[9]

Most attempts to explain involuntary unemployment examine the forces that determine wage-setting and hiring decisions in what are thought to be more realistic labour market institutions. They look for reasons (consistent with optimizing behaviour by participants) why wages do not respond quickly to shifts in supply and demand in the labour market.[10] So quantity supplied and quantity demanded may *not* be equated for extended periods of time even though people are behaving rationally. Labour markets will then display unemployment during recessions and excess demand during booms. This is shown for one typical labour market in Figure 25.4.

These theories start with the everyday observation that wage rates do not change every time demand or supply shifts. When unemployed workers are looking for jobs, they do not knock on employers' doors and offer to work at lower wages than are being paid to current workers.

---

[8] The distinction here is semantic if the NAIRU is cyclical. We do not pursue the argument further because, although supply shocks are undoubtedly important, the assumption of continuous market-clearing seems unnecessarily restrictive and implausible.

[9] Many economists working in this area might not accept the label 'Keynesian'. Indeed, some of the new approaches explain why real wages may be held 'too high' to generate employment for all those seeking work at the going wage. This used to be called 'Classical' unemployment. 'Keynesian' used to be reserved for demand-deficient unemployment. Thus, much of the new work makes these old taxonomies irrelevant.

[10] We discuss some reasons why employers may not change wage rates in response to demand and supply in Chapter 11. One argument is that efficiency wages are used to provide incentives for existing workers. This and other explanations are further discussed below.

Instead, they answer job advertisements and hope to get the jobs offered, and often are disappointed. Similarly, employers, seeing an excess of applicants for the few jobs that are available, do not reduce the wages of their current workers until potential applicants for a job have all lost interest.[11]

In discussing New Keynesian approaches, it is helpful to divide them into two groups. The first seeks to explain nominal wage and price rigidities that slow the adjustment towards full equilibrium. The second focuses on real wage rigidities that are not eliminated over time, but continue in full equilibrium. We will associate the former approaches with long-term relationships and menu costs, while we will discuss the latter in the context of efficiency wages and union bargaining models. Chapter 11 also discusses labour markets and covers some of the same issues in more detail.

### Long-term relationships

One set of theories explains the familiar observation that money wages do not adjust to clear labour markets as resulting from the advantages to both workers and employers of relatively long-term, stable employment relationships. Workers want job security in the face of fluctuating demand; employers want workers who understand the firm's organization, production, and marketing plans. Under these circumstances, both parties care about things in addition to the wage rate, and wages become somewhat less sensitive to fluctuations in current economic conditions. Wages are in effect regular payments to workers over an extended employment relationship, rather than a device for fine-tuning the current supplies and demands for labour. Given this situation, the tendency is for employers to 'smooth out' the income of employees by paying a steady money wage and letting profits and employment fluctuate to absorb the effects of temporary increases and decreases in demand for the firm's product.

A number of labour market institutions work to achieve these results. Employment contracts provide for a schedule of money wages over a period of several years. Fringe benefits, such as membership of the company pension scheme, a company car, and perhaps private health insurance, tend to bind workers to their employers. A worker's pay tends to rise with years of service, despite the known fact that the output attributable to workers rises rapidly as they gain experience, reaches a peak, *and then falls off*

as they age. Under gradually rising wages, workers who spend a long time in the same firm tend to get less than the value of their marginal products when they are young and more than the value of their marginal products as they near retirement. But over the long haul they are paid, on average, the value of their marginal products, just as microeconomic theory predicts. Such features help to bind the employee to the company, whereas redundancy pay, related to years of service, tends to bind the employer to the long-term worker, who would cost the firm more to dismiss than to keep employed.

In labour markets characterized by long-term relationships, the wage rate does not fluctuate to clear the market. Wages are written over what has been called the long-term 'economic climate' rather than the short-term 'economic weather'. Optimizing firms in such an environment will adjust employment rather than wages during the cycle. Although employees might prefer to accept a lower wage than be laid off, in many work environments seniority rules imply that it is those most recently hired who are at greatest risk of being laid off when demand is low, so the majority of long-term employees will not see any disadvantage to cyclically sticky wages.

### Menu costs and wage contracts

A typical large manufacturing firm sells differentiated products numbered in the thousands and employs hundreds of different types of labour. Changing prices and wages in response to every minor fluctuation in demand is a costly and time-consuming activity. Firms find it optimal to keep their price lists (*menus*) constant for significant periods of time. Since all manufacturing firms are operating in imperfectly competitive markets, they have some discretion over price. Hence it may be optimal for firms to react to small changes in demand by holding prices constant and responding with changes in output and employment. If many firms are behaving this way, output and employment will respond to changes in aggregate demand. However, in some product areas such as air travel, internet sales platforms have greatly reduced this problem, and prices have become more flexible.

The UK evidence is consistent with the existence of sluggish price adjustment by manufacturers. This, of course, is where Keynesian economics came in (with an assumption of price stickiness). One line of the New Keynesian literature attempts to model it as an optimal response to adjustment costs and adverse customer reactions.

Money wages tend to be inflexible in the short term because wage rates are generally set on an annual basis. In some other countries they are set for longer periods— three years is not uncommon with union contracts in

---

[11] This observation concerns cyclical variations in the demand for labour. It does not conflict with the different observation that, when firms get into long-term competitive trouble, workers sometimes renegotiate contracts and agree to wage cuts in order to save the firm, and their jobs.

North America. Such short-term inflexibility of wages, particularly in the face of negative supply shocks such as the oil price shocks of the 1970s, will lead to increases in unemployment.

We now turn to a discussion of the New Keynesian approaches that focus on real rigidities in labour markets.

### Efficiency wages

The idea of the *efficiency wage* forms the core of a strand of thinking about why it may be optimal for firms to set wages permanently above the level that would clear the labour market. Efficiency wage theory applies to hiring, to productivity on the job, and to worker turnover.

Workers are not homogeneous. There are good workers and bad workers, but there is *asymmetrical information*: firms do not know the characteristics of a specific worker until after they have sunk costs into hiring and training her. Good workers know who they are and are likely to have a higher reservation wage (the wage at which they are prepared to work) than bad workers. By lowering the wage they offer, firms will significantly lower the average ability of the workers who apply to them for jobs, and so they could find that paying lower wages makes them worse off. This is known as *adverse selection*. It is a concept we have already met in the context of our discussion of market failure, especially in the context of insurance markets (see page 241), but it is also an essential feature of labour markets.

In labour markets with informational asymmetries, where unobserved characteristics of job applicants are correlated with the reservation wage, it may not be optimal for firms to pay the market-clearing wage.

Once in employment, workers are likely to give greater effort if they feel they are being well rewarded and that the costs of losing their job are high. If wages are so low that workers are just indifferent between staying and losing their jobs, they are likely to please themselves about how hard they work as they will not be afraid of getting the sack. Employers have a problem of monitoring and enforcing efficient work practices—this is another case of the principal–agent problem discussed on page 242. Paying a high wage reduces the problem, both because workers will expect to be much worse off if they lose their current job, and because there will be a queue of good-quality workers prepared to work for the higher wage. The high wage improves efficiency—hence the term *efficiency wages*.

Another way in which higher wages may improve productivity is through the direct effects on worker nutrition and general health. In improving the physical well-being of the worker, the marginal productivity of workers may be increased. This is a very important effect in developing countries, but it may also apply in some sectors of developed economies. However, an effect that clearly does apply in developed countries is that workers who are paid well above their best alternative wage have an incentive to invest in self-education and skill acquisition in order to secure their continued employment prospects.

Finally, firms for which high quit rates are costly will be reluctant to lower the wages of existing workers, even in the face of an excess supply of labour. It would be possible for firms to pay lower wages to new workers, but tiered wage structures, in which several people doing the same job get different rates of pay, often cause morale problems. This does not prevent firms from paying experienced workers more than inexperienced ones; but it does restrain firms from responding to job queues by offering new workers a lower lifetime earnings profile than that enjoyed by existing workers.

Efficiency wage theory implies that firms may find it advantageous to pay high enough wages so that working is clearly a superior alternative to being laid off. This will improve the quality of workers' output without firms having to spend heavily to monitor workers' performance.

Efficiency wage theory helps us to understand much about labour markets. It also explains why firms may wish to pay wages above market-clearing levels. This helps to explain why involuntary unemployment can persist in equilibrium when GDP is at its potential level.

### Union bargaining

The final theoretical approach to be considered under the New Keynesian agenda assumes that those already in employment ('insiders') have more say in wage bargaining than those out of work ('outsiders'). Typically, a union negotiates the wage rate with firms. The union will generally represent the interests of its members, the bulk of whom will be in employment. It will not necessarily reflect the interests of those excluded from employment.

It is easy to see that insiders will wish to bid up wages even though to do so will harm the employment prospects of outsiders. Hence this framework can generate an outcome to the bargaining process between firms and unions in which the wage is set higher than the market-clearing level, just as with the efficiency wage.

Again, these models help explain the existence of involuntary unemployment even when GDP is at its potential level. However, they do add one important new insight into the causes of international differences in unemployment.

In some countries unions bargain at the level of the firm; in others they bargain at the level of the whole industry or the whole economy. Where bargaining is decentralized, the union can push for higher wages for the insiders without worrying about effects on the rest of the economy or on outsiders. However, where bargaining is centralized the effects on the rest of the economy become internalized into the bargaining process, because union negotiators are bargaining on behalf of all workers (and potential workers), rather than just those in one firm.

The prediction is that decentralized bargaining with strong unions will lead to higher than market-clearing wages, resulting in outsiders being excluded from jobs, whereas centralized bargaining will produce an outcome closer to the market-clearing outcome (because outsider concerns are voiced), so unemployment will be low.

The third alternative to centralized and decentralized union bargaining is no union bargaining at all. This is the case when unionization is low and unions are weak. It too will produce an outcome close to the free-market rate even in the absence of efficiency wage considerations. This analysis may explain why unemployment is relatively high in EU countries, where unions are strong but bargaining is decentralized, but lower in Scandinavia, where again unions are strong but bargaining is centralized, and the United States, where unions are weak.

**The basic message of New Keynesian theories of unemployment is that labour markets cannot be relied upon to eliminate involuntary unemployment by equating current demand for labour with current supply.**

The New Keynesian theories have concentrated on explaining why wages do not fluctuate to clear labour markets instantaneously. This helps to explain the existence of involuntary cyclical unemployment in the face of fluctuations in aggregate demand. These demand fluctuations are, however, still a necessary part of the explanation of cyclical fluctuations. They leave the emphasis of anticyclical policy on demand-side measures whenever the automatic adjustment mechanism does not work fast enough. To the extent that the theories explain why wages do not clear labour markets even in the long term, they help to explain high *equilibrium unemployment*. It is to this that we now turn.

# Equilibrium unemployment: the NAIRU

Equilibrium unemployment, or the NAIRU, is composed of *frictional* and *structural* unemployment.

## Frictional unemployment

Frictional unemployment results from the normal turnover of labour. An important source of frictional unemployment is young people who enter the labour force looking for jobs. Another source is people who are in the process of changing their jobs and are caught between one job and the next. Some may quit because they are dissatisfied with the type of work or their working conditions; others may be sacked. Whatever the reason, they must search for new jobs and this takes time. People who are unemployed while searching for jobs are said to be frictionally unemployed or, alternatively, in *search unemployment*.

**The normal turnover of labour would cause some frictional unemployment to persist even if the economy were at potential GDP and the structure of jobs in terms of skills, industries, occupations, and location were unchanging.**

## Structural unemployment

Structural adjustments can cause unemployment. When the pattern of demand for goods changes, the pattern of the demand for labour changes. Until labour adjusts fully, structural unemployment develops. Such unemployment may be defined as unemployment caused by a mismatch between the structure of the labour force—in terms of skills, occupations, industries, or geographical locations—and the structure of the demand for labour.

# Endogenous change

Changes that accompany economic growth shift the structure of the demand for labour. One of the more dramatic recent structural changes has been in the organization of the firm. Large firms used to be organized much like an army, with a pyramid command structure. Most key strategic decisions were made near the top, with lesser ones concerning implementation made at lower levels. This structure required an array of middle-level managers who passed information upward to the top level and downward to the production level and who made various secondary decisions themselves. Changes associated with the IT revolution in the 1980s and early 1990s led to a much looser organization with much more local autonomy among the subsections of the firm. As a result large numbers of middle managers were made redundant. They found themselves on the labour market at middle age and with many of their skills rendered obsolete.

Another key structural change in the UK (and in many other economies) has been the decline in manufacturing and the rise in service employment. Employment in manufacturing has been declining since the late 1950s, but the UK real exchange rate appreciation of the late 1970s and early 1980s (partly associated with another structural change, the emergence of North Sea oil production) accelerated this adjustment in the UK. Many factories closed in the early 1980s or were replaced by capital-intensive rather than labour-intensive plant. Although the total of available jobs did not change much, it was not always easy for a newly unemployed factory worker to find employment in the expanding service sector, particularly when many of the new jobs were requiring new skills.

Increases in international competition can have effects similar to those of economic growth and change. As the geographical distribution of world production changes, so does the composition of production and of labour demand in any one country. Labour adapts to such shifts by changing jobs, skills, and locations, but until the transition is complete, structural unemployment exists.

Structural unemployment increases if there is either an increase in the speed at which the structure of the demand for labour is changing or a decrease in the speed at which labour is adapting to these changes.

## Policy influences

Government policies can influence the speed with which labour markets adapt to change. Some countries have adopted policies that discourage movement among regions, industries, and occupations. These policies tend to raise structural unemployment, though state subsidies may disguise it for a while. The EU Common Agricultural Policy (CAP), for example, is intended in part to resist the decline of incomes and employment in agriculture, even though employment in agriculture has been declining in Europe since the late eighteenth century. Other countries, such as Sweden, have adopted the reverse approach and have encouraged workers to adapt to change. Partly for this reason, Sweden's unemployment rates were well below the European average during the 1980s.

Policies that discourage firms from replacing labour with machines may protect employment over the short term. However, if such policies lead to the decline of an industry because it cannot compete effectively with innovative foreign competitors, serious structural unemployment can result in the long run.

High minimum wage laws may cause structural unemployment by pricing low-skilled labour out of the market. As explained in Chapter 16, minimum wage laws have two effects when they are imposed on competitive markets: they reduce employment of the unskilled, and they raise the wages of the unskilled who retain their jobs.

## Why does the NAIRU change?

We have noted that structural unemployment can increase because the pace of change accelerates or the pace of adjustment to change slows down. An increase in the rate of growth, for example, usually speeds up the rate at which the structure of the demand for labour is changing. The adaptation of labour to the changing structure of demand may be slowed by such diverse factors as a decline in educational achievement and regulations that make it harder for workers in a given occupation to take new jobs in other areas or occupations. Any of these changes will cause the NAIRU to rise. Changes in the opposite direction will cause the NAIRU to fall.

### Demographic changes

Because people usually try several jobs before settling into one for a longer period of time, young or inexperienced workers have higher unemployment rates than experienced workers. The proportion of inexperienced workers in the labour force rose significantly as the postwar baby boom generation entered the labour force in the late 1960s and 1970s, along with an unprecedented number of women who newly elected to work outside the home. In the 1980s youth unemployment became an even bigger problem, because school-leavers found it hard to get a foothold on the career ladder when unemployment was rising and even experienced workers were being laid off.

Even if youth unemployment should fall in future, many observers worry about the long-term consequences for some individuals. Learning through on-the-job experience is a critical part of developing marketable labour skills, and those who suffered prolonged unemployment during their teens and twenties have been denied that experience early in their working careers. These workers may have little option later in life but to take temporary jobs at low pay and little future job security, or drop out of the labour force entirely.

The significant increase in female participation rates, and the related increase in the number of households with more than one income-earner, has also affected the NAIRU. When both husband and wife work, it is possible for one to support both while the other looks for 'a really good job' rather than accepting the first job offer that comes along, or decides to spend time in retraining. This can increase recorded unemployment while not inflicting excessive hardship on those involved.

## Hysteresis

Recent models of unemployment show that the size of the NAIRU can be influenced by the *size* of the actual current rate of unemployment. Such models get their name from the Greek word **hysteresis**, meaning 'coming late'.[12] In economics it means that the current equilibrium is not independent of what has gone before—it is path-dependent. This means that the NAIRU will be higher after periods of high unemployment than after periods of low unemployment. If this is correct, we have to distinguish between the short-run NAIRU and the long-run **natural rate**. The latter is the true long-run equilibrium towards which the short-run NAIRU will adjust slowly over time.

One mechanism that can lead to hysteresis in labour markets has already been noted. It arises from the importance of experience and on-the-job training. Suppose, for example, that a period of recession causes a significant group of new entrants to the labour force to have unusual difficulty in obtaining their first jobs. As a result the unlucky group will be slow to acquire the important skills that workers generally learn in their first jobs. When demand increases again, this unlucky group of workers will be at a disadvantage relative to workers with normal histories of job experience, and so may have unemployment rates that will be higher than average. Thus, the NAIRU will be higher than it would have been had there been no recession.

Another force that can cause such effects is insider–outsider segregation in a heavily unionized labour force with decentralized bargaining, discussed above. In times of high unemployment, people who are currently employed (insiders) may use their bargaining power to ensure that their own status is maintained and to prevent new entrants to the labour force (outsiders) from competing effectively. In an insider–outsider model of this type a period of prolonged high unemployment, whatever its initial cause, will tend to become 'locked in'. If outsiders are denied access to the labour market, their unemployment will fail to exert downward pressure on wages, and the NAIRU will tend to rise.

Hysteresis is part of the explanation of the high levels of persistence of unemployment in many EU countries, including the United Kingdom.

## Increasing structural change

The amount of industrial restructuring, both locally and internationally, increased in the 1980s and continued in the 1990s. In part this was the result of the increasing integration of the UK economy with the European Union and the rest of the world, and the globalization of world markets. External influences continued to be important in the 2000s. There was, for example, a significant inflow of workers into the UK from eastern Europe following the expansion of the EU in 2004.[13]

The following numerous structural changes have created a continuing need for rapid adjustments:

- the collapse of communism and the conversion of the countries of eastern Europe to market economies;

- increases in the supply of agricultural products, owing to the green revolution in less developed countries and heavy agricultural subsidization in the European Union;

- enormous OPEC-induced increases in the price of oil in the 1970s and early 1980s, followed by almost equally precipitous declines in the mid-1980s that carried through into the 1990s, before more rises again in 2004–6;

- the emergence of several Asian countries as industrial economies, of which China and India will, in the long run, be the most important;

- the communications revolution, leading to the decentralization of industry, with components produced in various countries and assembled in others;

- robotization, which increased industrial productivity and reduced the demand for assembly-line workers so that, although the long-run trend in manufacturing output is still positive, manufacturing employment is falling;

- the growth of knowledge-intensive industries, which require highly educated and geographically mobile workforces;

- the globalization of competition, with fewer and fewer domestic markets that are sheltered by artificial barriers;

- changes in the organization of firms;

- the privatization of large sections of formerly state-owned industries;

- the enormous growth in service employment.

Although evidence is difficult to obtain, some observers argue that the increasing pace and the changing nature of

---

[12] It was first used in electronics to relate to effects coming after their causes, i.e. lagged effects.

[13] UK official estimates released in August 2006 showed that 447,000 people from the accession countries had applied to work in the UK between May 2004 and June 2006. Half of these were from Poland. This figure excludes the self-employed, who were estimated to make up another 36,000.

technological change since the mid-1970s have contributed to an increase in the level of structural unemployment.

### Mismatch

Structural change that creates unemployed workers with the wrong characteristics (skills, experience, location) for the available jobs is known as *mismatch*. As we saw above, the biggest mismatch is likely to be the requirement of modern industry for skilled and flexible workers while the majority of the unemployed are unskilled. Intuitively this makes sense—a Yorkshire coal miner who lost his job in the 1980s is unlikely to have found work (quickly) as an advertising executive, even if vacancies for the latter existed.

Researchers studying UK unemployment have found mismatch to be important in increasing the NAIRU, but mismatch does not appear to have increased markedly since the early 1970s. Thus, it explains the rise in the NAIRU between the 1960s and 1970s but not subsequent rises—though further studies may produce different evidence.

### Unemployment benefits

Workers who lose their jobs receive unemployment benefit. The size of the benefits paid, relative to pay levels in work, is known as the **replacement ratio**. A high replacement ratio raises the NAIRU. It affects the willingness of the unemployed to accept job offers and it affects the intensity with which they search for work.

Changes in the replacement ratio do have significant statistical effects on the NAIRU, but in *The Unemployment Crisis* Layard, Nickell, and Jackman (1994) found that it explains only 0.8 percentage point of the 6.2 percentage point rise in equilibrium unemployment between the 1960s and 1980s.

However, differences in benefit systems between countries do seem to play a very important role in explaining international differences in unemployment. It is not just the replacement ratio faced by a newly unemployed worker that matters; also important is the duration for which that benefit is provided (if it is for only a short period, the worker has an incentive to find work very quickly) and the degree to which the benefit is conditional on job-seeking activity. Countries with only temporary benefits and both incentives and assistance with finding work tend to have lower equilibrium unemployment rates.

### Other effects

Two other factors are often reported to have at least a temporary effect on the NAIRU. The first is the *tax wedge*. This is the difference between what an employer has to pay to hire a worker and what the worker receives in take-home pay. Increasing the tax wedge for a given quantity of labour demanded reduces take-home pay. This is likely to increase wage-bargaining pressure as a result of workers' reluctance to accept lower real wages. In effect, this shifts up the short-run Phillips curve, thereby worsening the inflation–unemployment trade-off in the short run. However, this has no long-run effect on the NAIRU, as the tax wedge cannot keep increasing.

The second factor is associated with a *terms-of-trade loss*, or *real exchange rate depreciation*. This is argued to have a similar effect; because it raises import prices, it also reduces real wages. Real wage resistance shifts the short-run Phillips curve upwards and we get the same result as in the previous paragraph.

## Explaining unemployment

By combining the analysis of demand and supply shocks and the Phillips curve of Chapter 24 with what we have learned about labour markets above, we can now produce an explanation for the unemployment experience that we summarized at the beginning of this chapter. This explanation is broadly that set out by Layard, Nickell, and Jackman in *The Unemployment Crisis* (Layard *et al.* 1994).

### Supply shocks

Most countries were subjected to two major supply shocks associated with the oil price rises of 1973 and 1979. Countries with more centralized wage bargaining suffered less unemployment than others, because wage negotiators were more prepared to accept cuts in real wages. The shock was complicated in the United Kingdom by structural adjustment resulting from the emergence of an oil-producing sector. The pace of technological and organizational change has speeded up and affected unemployment most in those countries with inflexible labour market institutions and regulations.

### Demand shocks

Governments reacted to high inflation in the 1970s with tight monetary and fiscal policies. Slow downward adjustment of inflation expectations, combined with negative demand shocks, created recessionary gaps and rising unemployment. The short-run impact of these demand shocks on unemployment was less, the more flexible were wage contracts.

### Persistence

Unemployment became persistent in those countries with open-ended unemployment benefits and, once in place, was sustained by hysteresis effects. Countries that did least to get the long-term unemployed back to work suffered most in terms of rising equilibrium unemployment rates.

Government policies that encourage job security also encourage persistence. Labour laws (designed to protect workers) that make it difficult and costly to make workers redundant also make firms reluctant to hire workers in the first place. This is especially true of the young who miss out on the crucial early work experience. For example, in France in January 2006 the unemployment rate of people aged 18–25 was 20 per cent, while the national unemployment rate was 9.6 per cent. The French government tried to enact legislation that encouraged the hiring of the young by making it easier to fire them, in the hope that firms would be more willing to take them on. However, there were strikes and street protests, which made the government eventually give in and leave the employment-destroying laws largely in place.

# Reducing unemployment

Other things being equal, all governments would like to reduce unemployment. The questions are 'Can it be done?' and 'If so, at what cost?' Some commonly aired 'solutions' that will almost certainly not help are discussed in Box 25.2.

In this section we review the policies that governments could use to help lower unemployment once it is high. The simple solution, in view of what we have learned about persistence, is: don't start from here! That is to say, governments should not wait for high unemployment to get established before they start to worry about it. It may be easier to prevent it from getting high that to bring it down once it is entrenched. This is so whatever the size of the NAIRU. And it suggests that the authorities should act quickly to accommodate the effects of a negative shock to aggregate supply before it generates high unemployment.

With GDP close to its potential level, however, an increase in aggregate demand intended to reduce equilibrium unemployment would rapidly lead to a rise in inflation. By definition, inflation will start to accelerate once unemployment falls below the NAIRU.

This means that the most that demand management can do about equilibrium unemployment is to try to make sure that it does not rise as a result of hysteresis effects associated with major deflations. Unfortunately, it was attempts to eliminate inflation rapidly by restrictive aggregate demand policies that contributed to high unemployment in the first place.

Once inflation is low and the unemployment level is close to the NAIRU, aggregate demand policy should be neutral; that is, it should aim to maintain GDP at its potential level.

## Reducing persistence

The reduction of persistence and hysteresis effects is a major challenge. It probably requires both a reform of the benefits system and active policies to ensure that those in danger of long-term unemployment get work experience and training. The feature of the benefits system that seems to be most harmful (in the sense of creating long-term unemployment) is an indefinite period of benefits payments. This reduces the incentive of the recently unemployed to seek work urgently. Some commentators advocate compulsory public sector work for the unemployed after some period of time; others advocate state subsidies towards private sector employment as a way of getting people back into the labour market. The general point however is that, whatever the policies are, they have to be targeted directly on the unemployed, rather than in the form of general reflation. In the United States, where unemployment is much lower than in Europe, benefits are strictly limited and are related to the amount of time a worker was last in employment.

Another aspect of persistence is mismatch. Policies to reduce this must involve making it easier for workers to change occupations by offering assistance in retraining and relocation. It could be argued that it is the responsibility of individuals or firms to finance retraining. However, individuals may be financially constrained, and firms may feel that it is not worth training a worker who may go elsewhere. The state funds education for the young, so there is no reason, in principle, why those needing retraining should be treated differently.

## Labour market reform

A third class of policies that may help to reduce unemployment involves labour market reforms, especially the structure of wage bargaining. We have seen that insiders may hold wage rates high, to the detriment of outsiders. We have also seen that centralized wage bargaining may generate lower unemployment than decentralized bargaining. However, union structures have evolved over decades, and it is no easy matter in a free society to scrap the lot and start again.

**Box 25.2 False trails: what won't cure unemployment**

The existence of persistent high unemployment in many European countries prompts many well meaning but ill considered suggestions for solving the problem. The most common error made when thinking about unemployment is to assume that there is a fixed number of jobs available to be shared out. This leads to proposals for compulsory job sharing and enforced early retirement to divide existing jobs among available workers, proposals to halt new technology 'destroying' jobs, and protectionism to stop 'our jobs' being taken by low-wage foreigners. Also, as in France, a lowering of the work week tended to raise unit costs (because the weekly wage was not changed) and so led to a fall in employment.

The following arguments have been made against these false assumptions.

### Job sharing

Enforced job sharing and involuntary early retirement reduce potential GDP because they prevent those who are willing and able to work productively from doing so. It makes the individuals so restricted worse off, and it makes society as a whole worse off. Indeed, it is a form of forced unemployment. As an *OECD Jobs Study* puts it,

*Legislated, across-the-board, work-sharing addresses the unemployment problem not by increasing the number of jobs through more economic activity, but through rationing gainful work. Enforced work-sharing has never succeeded in cutting unemployment significantly, not least because of workers' resistance to reduced income. (OECD Jobs Study, 1994, page 27)*

This is not to say that flexible working practices, which enable part-time working for those who would otherwise be unable to work, are a bad thing: on the contrary, the key is that each individual should be able to maximize her productive activity in the manner most suited to her needs and commitments. Anything that limits the opportunities to work is harmful.

### Technology

In 1811 Nottinghamshire frameworkers (led by the probably mythical Ned Ludd) smashed new machinery. This was because they thought that the new technology of the industrial revolution was doing them out of a livelihood, as indeed it would for those not prepared and able to learn new skills. Before the industrial revolution real wages had been constant, possibly for centuries. Since that time real wages have multiplied at least ten-fold even for manual workers, and job opportunities have multiplied in many ways. To quote the OECD study again,

*History has shown that when technological progress accelerates, so do growth, living standards and employment. Technological progress would lead to high unemployment only in a world of saturated wants or perpetual restriction of demand, conditions that have not occurred in the past, and seem unlikely in the foreseeable future. Furthermore, worries about a new era of 'jobless growth' appear unfounded: the current upswing in the United States and a number of other countries has brought job growth in its train, and broadly in line with past relationships between growth and employment. (OECD Jobs Study, 1994, page 29)*

### Protectionism

It is an erroneous but widely held view in Europe that competition from low-wage countries, especially in Asia, is responsible for much of the current unemployment. This is an argument that the OECD economists are able to dismiss:

*The weight of low-wage countries' exports in the overall expenditure of OECD countries on goods and services is only about 1.5 per cent. The number of markets which they contest is greater, and their effect on the intensity of competition is increasing. But the judgement on present evidence is that both the overall impact of imports from these countries and their contestation of OECD markets is too small to account for a significant part of either current unemployment or falling relative wages of the low-skilled. On the other hand, these countries represent a large and growing potential market for OECD exports of goods and services, and hence represent an important source of current and future growth and employment. (OECD Jobs Study, 1994, page 28)*

On the case for using protectionism to 'keep jobs at home', the OECD has no doubts:

*Protectionism reduces overall economic welfare; increases costs to consumers, often hurting most those with lowest incomes; penalises successful enterprise; harms exports; encourages tariff factories; harms developing countries' trade; and increases the pressures for international migration. It encourages domestic monopolies, while cutting the economy off from mainstream developments in the world outside. Producers, dependent on protection for their survival, ultimately become prepared to spend large sums to preserve its continuance. Lobbying, and even bribery and corruption, become more widespread. (OECD Jobs Study, 1994, page 29)*

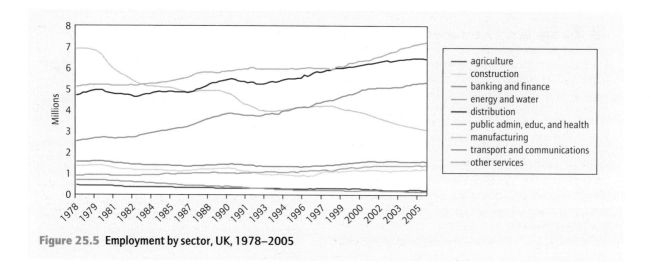

**Figure 25.5** Employment by sector, UK, 1978–2005

# CASE STUDIES

## 1. Changing patterns of employment

Changes in the pattern of employment have been rapid in the past few decades. Figure 25.5 shows the changing industrial structure of UK employment between 1978 and 2005. The dominant trends evident from this chart are very clear. There is high and rising employment in three main sectors: public administration, education and health; distribution; and banking and finance. These three sectors combined provided just over 70 per cent of UK employee jobs in 2005, up from 50 per cent on 1978. Over the same period, the manufacturing sector fell from providing around 7 million jobs to providing around 3 million. Significant numbers were also employed in three other sectors: construction (1.2 million in 2005); transport and communications (1.6 million); and other services (1.4 million). But the UK primary industries were small employers and continued to decline still further. Agriculture, hunting, and fishing employed only 230,000 in 2005 and energy and water only 162,000—less than 1.5 per cent of the working population combined.

The shift out of agriculture in the United Kingdom is a process that started at the time of the industrial revolution in the late 1700s. However, this shift is nothing like so far advanced in many other countries, as the following extract from a recent ILO *Global Employment Trends Brief* illustrates:

*In 2005, the agricultural sector accounted for 40 per cent of total employment in the world. This meant it still had the highest employment share of all three sectors (agriculture, industry, services) with a total of 1.1 billion people working in the sector.*

*Agriculture continues to dominate in East Asia, South-East Asia, South Asia and sub-Saharan Africa, where more that 60 per cent of the world's working age population lives. And given that the vast majority of the world's poor live in these regions, working out of poverty means ensuring that jobs in the agriculture sector provide a decent living. Much development theory is based on the assumption that, over time, people will move out of agriculture in rural areas into industry and then into services. The overall share of agriculture has decreased over the ten years between 1995 and 2005 from 44.4 to 40.1 [per cent]. But did all the workers really move into the industry sector?*

*The industry sector has grown over time in terms of total numbers of workers; there were 598 million people working in industry in 2005, a 16 per cent increase from ten years earlier. Still, the share in total employment decreased from 21.1 per cent to 21 per cent. . . . At the same time, employment in the service sector has changed the most in ten years. The share of total employment in services increased in all regions with one exception —the Middle East and North Africa. If the service sector continues to grow the way it has over the last ten years, it will soon overtake agriculture as the largest provider of employment. East Asia (where employment in China accounts for nearly 94 per cent of the region's total employment) saw the smallest changes in terms of sectoral distribution over time. Even though one would have expected big changes in the manufacturing sector in China, employment in new manufacturing export industries has grown, but this has been matched by a similarly rapid decline in jobs in the older state-owned manufacturing sector.*

Given these trends, there is a need to reformulate development strategies; reality no longer follows economic theory. Workers are moving directly from agriculture to services. It is important to bear in mind that this transition does not necessarily mean an upgrade in terms of working conditions or in personal welfare. The service sector covers the whole range of jobs, from decent jobs in the 'formal economy' to low paid precarious jobs under bad conditions in the 'informal economy'. The fact that the agriculture to services shift typically implies the rural to urban migration of workers can also be a factor in the welfare development of the worker, in that the person loses access to land where food might be gathered and must henceforth rely on the market, and thus on earning a wage for sustenance. This is no simple matter for the very poor who might find themselves with no means of earning income from one day to the next. Such issues need to be addressed by policy-makers if they are to make sure that the development process will lead to poverty reduction. (ILO, Global Employment Trends Brief, pages 8 and 9; © International Labour Organization)

**Figure 25.6** Male and female employment, UK, 1978–2005

## 2. Male and female employment

Male and female employment have evolved quite differently in the United Kingdom over the past few decades (see Figure 25.6). Female employment has grown consistently, while male employment fell sharply between the late 1970s and the mid-1990s before subsequently recovering. Britain was unique among industrial countries in the 1990s in having a majority of female workers, and it was still unusual in the 2000s in having approximately equal numbers of male and female workers.

The decline in male employment in the 1980s and 1990s was largely associated with the decline in manufacturing employment, and to a lesser extent mining. Female employment has been associated with expansion of the service sector, and especially of the public administration, education and health sector, which in 2005 employed 2 million men and 5 million women. The other two fast growing parts of the service sector—banking and finance, and distribution—employ roughly equal numbers of men and women.

These figures do not distinguish between full-time and part-time jobs. In 2005 nearly 40 per cent of female jobs were part-time, while only just over 10 per cent of male jobs were part-time. This clearly reflects the needs of women when they are bringing up families. However, the rising participation of women in the labour force has been a clear trend for several decades, and increased job flexibility and changing technology, which sometimes permits home working, are assisting this trend.

## 3. Unemployment in Europe

One of the stylized facts that emerges from Figure 25.2 above is that most European countries experienced high unemployment

in the 1980s, but by the 2000s they had divided into two groups: those that still had high unemployment and those that now had relatively low unemployment.

In 2006 Olivier Blanchard, a French economist working at MIT, published a comprehensive review of the recent history and causes of European unemployment (Blanchard 2006). The following is a summary of that paper by Charles Bean of the Bank of England, written as part of his discussion at a conference when the paper was first presented.

*Broadly speaking, Blanchard's tale runs thus. Unemployment first rose in the 1970s as a result of real wage resistance[14], which raised the natural rate of unemployment in the face of the oil price shocks and the slowdown in productivity growth. International differences could be traced at least in part to differences in wage bargaining structures. Initially policy-makers sought to maintain growth and employment, but in doing so ran demand above potential, leading to a pickup of inflation. Subsequently policies were tightened to squeeze inflation out of the system so that the hitherto suppressed component of unemployment emerged.*

*But as the 1980s wore on this unemployment persisted, leading researchers to focus on mechanisms that amplified the effects of the original shock and propagated them over time. Key mechanisms included those operating via the impact of capital decumulation on labour demand and insider-outsider effects on wage setting, whether operating through the disenfranchisement of the unemployed in the wage bargaining process or the progressive disconnection from the labour market of the long-term unemployed.*

---

[14] 'Real wage resistance' means that when prices rose workers bargained for higher money wages to ensure that their real wages did not fall.

*As we move into the 1990s, unemployment continued to remain high in some countries—particularly the big four continental economies—but fell back in others. Researchers and policy-makers focused increasingly on institutional differences in labour markets, and to a lesser degree, product market institutions and regulations. In some cases, poorly designed responses to the initial rise in unemployment that were focused on the symptoms rather than the causes had aggravated matters. Elsewhere, reforms had caused unemployment to fall. The research effort here was spurred by theoretical advances in modelling worker flows which permitted a rigorous analysis of the implications of alternative labour market arrangements, as well as the development of multi-dimensional measures of labour market institutions on a comparable basis, so facilitating cross-country empirical work.*

*As a result of all this effort we have a good, though still imperfect, idea of which labour market reforms work and which don't. The principles can be summarised thus: protect workers, not jobs; couple unemployment benefits with pressure on the unemployed to take jobs and measures to help them find them; ensure that employment protection merely internalises social costs and does not inhibit job creation and labour reallocation; and avoid artificial restrictions on individual employment contracts wherever possible.* (Bean 2006)

## Conclusion

Unemployment is a major problem of our time. We have been able to understand, with a combination of the tools provided by the macro model and our new understanding of labour markets, how unemployment came about and why it is characterized by persistence. We have also learned why the traditional macroeconomic approach to reducing unemployment is no longer adequate. The bad news is that reducing equilibrium unemployment is likely to be a slow process. The good news is that persistence does not mean permanence. Normal economic change and new economic policies can make progress against persistence, which need not be accepted as inevitable.

## SUMMARY

### Unemployment characteristics

- Unemployment appeared to have an upward trend in the 1970s and 1980s. However, unemployment is untrended in the long run, and the prospects for keeping unemployment low seemed very good in the first decade of the twenty-first century.

- It is useful to distinguish among several kinds of unemployment: (*a*) cyclical unemployment, which is caused by too low a level of aggregate demand; (*b*) frictional unemployment, which is caused by the length of time it takes to find a first job and to move from job to job as a result of normal labour turnover; and (*c*) structural unemployment, which is caused by the need to reallocate resources among occupations, regions, and industries as the structure of demands and supplies changes. Together, frictional and structural unemployment make up equilibrium unemployment, or the NAIRU, which is then expressed as a percentage of the total labour force.

### Cyclical unemployment

- New Classical theories look to explanations that allow the labour market to be cleared continuously. Such theories can explain cyclical variations in employment but do not explain involuntary unemployment, i.e. the unemployment of workers who would like to work at the going wage rates but for whom jobs are not available.

- Recent New Keynesian theories have focused on the long-term nature of employer–worker relationships which keep wage rates constant over cyclical fluctuations in employment, and on the possibility that it is efficient for employers to pay wages that are above the level that would clear the labour market. These explain why wages may be rigid enough for demand fluctuations to produce cyclical fluctuations in unemployment.

### Equilibrium unemployment

- The NAIRU will always be positive because it takes time for new workers to find their first jobs and for existing workers to move between jobs, both in normal turnover and in response to changes in the structure of the demand for labour. Government policies can also influence the NAIRU.

- Changes in the NAIRU can result from demographic changes, hysteresis effects, structural change in the economy, or changes in the unemployment benefit system.

### Reducing unemployment

- Cyclical unemployment can be reduced by aggregate demand policies.

- Equilibrium unemployment can be reduced by lowering benefits (level and duration), imposing active manpower policies, and reforming wage bargaining institutions and other labour market policies that inhibit hiring workers.

- In a growing, changing economy populated by people who wish to change jobs for many reasons, it is neither possible nor desirable to reduce unemployment to zero. Most important is the avoidance of the buildup of long-term unemployment.

## TOPICS FOR REVIEW

- Cyclical unemployment
- Frictional unemployment
- Structural unemployment
- Efficiency wages

- Hysteresis
- Persistence
- Determinants of the size of the NAIRU
- Policies to reduce unemployment

## QUESTIONS

1 Explain the differences between cyclical, frictional, and structural unemployment.

2 Why does it matter whether unemployment is voluntary or involuntary?

3 Why does the issue of whether or not wage rates are sticky enter into the question of what determines unemployment?

4 How do efficiency wage theories explain why firms are unwilling to adjust wages in response to an excess supply of labour?

5 Outline potential policy solutions to (a) cyclical and (b) structural unemployment.

6 What are the main determinants of the NAIRU?

7 What is the difference between claimant count and Labour Force Survey (LFS) unemployment?

# Chapter 26

# ECONOMIC GROWTH

Why are some countries getting richer while others seem to be getting poorer? Why are we so much better off than our grandparents? Will our children be better off than us? These are questions about economic growth and what determines it. Growth is one of the most important topics in economics, as it affects how well off people are, and how this changes over time.

In particular, you will learn that:

- Economic growth theory studies the determinants of the long-run trend in GDP, while macroeconomics was developed to explain the cycles around this trend.

- Even small differences in growth rate can lead to big differences in living standards between generations.

- While growth has many benefits, it brings with it significant costs and serious risks.

- Growth of output depends on growth in inputs (capital, labour, etc.) plus changing technology, which raises productivity (i.e. output per unit of input).

- Continued growth puts pressure on supplies of non-renewable resources and on the environment.

In this chapter we first discuss the distinction between the long-term growth in the productive capacity of the economy and the cycle about that long-term trend. We then emphasize the importance of growth, and discuss the costs and benefits of economic growth. After that we outline some of the theories that economists use to understand the growth process. We deal with these first at a highly aggregated (or macro) level, then at a more disaggregated (or micro) level. We end with a brief discussion of possible limits to growth.

## Trend and cycle

### Macroeconomics and growth theory

In Chapters 15–23 we built up a model of the macro economy. The emphasis in that model was on explaining the deviations of actual GDP from its potential level. For all of that analysis we took the current level of potential GDP as exogenously given. Macroeconomic policy was largely assumed to be aimed at keeping the economy as close to potential as possible. In this respect traditional stabilization policy has emphasized the need to reduce cycles in the economy, and especially to avoid both recessionary gaps, which are associated with high unemployment, and inflationary gaps, which generate inflation.

The focus on studying the GDP gap does not imply that it is unimportant to understand the determinants of potential GDP. On the contrary, as we shall see, the determination of potential GDP over the longer term is the most important influence on living standards and welfare and is thus one of the most important topics in economics. We separate the study of the cycle around potential GDP from the study of the trend in potential GDP because the determinants of the trend are generally very different from the determinants of the deviation from the trend. To oversimplify slightly, the trend in potential is driven largely by long-term supply-side factors, such as the growth of the capital stock, labour supply and technical change, while deviations from trend are driven by short-term shocks, especially demand components or some prices, or even temporary changes in sentiment. It is to the explanation of the determinants of the long-term trend in potential GDP that this chapter is devoted.

Economic growth theory is concerned to explain the determinant of the long-term trend in potential GDP.

## Growth in potential GDP

Economic growth is the economy's most powerful engine for generating long-term increases in living standards. Throughout most of the nineteenth and twentieth centuries, per capita GDP rose steadily while its distribution became somewhat less unequal. As a result, the citizens of the countries in the European Union, the United States, and Japan became materially better off decade by decade, and children typically were substantially better off on average than their parents were at the same age.

During the late 1970s, 1980s and 1990s growth rates fell in many countries compared with the very rapid growth experienced during the period of recovery after the Second World War. At the same time the distribution of income became somewhat more unequal. As a result, the real incomes of many European and Japanese families grew less rapidly than in the early postwar years. In contrast, there was a feeling in some other countries, such as the USA, that from the mid-1990s onwards we were entering a new age of rapid growth linked to new technologies (see also pages 261–6). By the mid-2000s attention had shifted to a concern that a few emerging economies, like China and India, were growing rapidly while most of the old industrial countries, particularly those in Europe, were locked into relatively slow growth rates[1]. The environmental impact of continued growth, especially global warming, has also come to the forefront as a global policy issue.

### Continued annual growth has a big impact over long periods

Since 1885, the annual average growth rate of real output (GDP) per head of population in the UK has been around 2 per cent. Two per cent per year may not sound like much

and may not seem much from one year to the next, but it has very large effects over the average person's lifetime. A 2 per cent growth rate doubles real incomes every 36 years and quadruples it every 72 years. This means that each generation has on average been more than twice as well off as its parents and there has been, on average, a four-fold increase in living standards during each person's lifetime!

What look like quite modest annual growth rates have a powerful effect in raising living standards over the decades *because growth can go on indefinitely and its effects accumulate.*

Table 26.1 illustrates the cumulative effect of what seem to be very small differences in growth rates. Notice that if one country grows faster than another, the gap in their respective living standards will widen progressively. If, for example, two countries start from the same level of income, and the first country grows at 2 per cent per year while the second grows at 1 per cent, the first country's per capita income will be twice that of the second country's in about 70 years. Having started from equality, the citizens of the second country will within one lifetime come to look poor and backward to the citizens of the first country.

Figure 26.1 shows the level of UK real GDP since 1885. The steady upward trend throughout this period is clearly evident. Total national output increased more than

**Table 26.1  How national incomes change when growth rates differ**

| Year | Country (rate of growth per year) | | | | |
|------|--------|--------|--------|--------|--------|
|      | A (1%) | B (2%) | C (3%) | D (5%) | E (7%) |
| 2000 | 100 | 100 | 100 | 100 | 100 |
| 2010 | 110 | 122 | 135 | 165 | 201 |
| 2030 | 135 | 182 | 246 | 448 | 817 |
| 2050 | 165 | 272 | 448 | 1,218 | 3,312 |
| 2070 | 201 | 406 | 817 | 3,312 | 13,429 |
| 2100 | 272 | 739 | 2,009 | 14,841 | 109,660 |

**Small differences in growth rates cause enormous differences in national incomes over even a few decades.** In the year 2000 all five countries in the table have the same level of national income equal to 100 but they have different growth rates. Within ten years there are large differences between the national incomes of the various countries, and by 2070, the span of one lifetime, there are massive differences. By 2070 even the country with a 2 per cent growth rate has twice the income of the country with the 1 per cent rate, while the others have vastly more.

---

[1] The concern in this chapter is mainly about growth in the established industrial countries. Growth in developing countries is discussed extensively on our website: www.oxfordtextbooks.co.uk/orc/lipsey11e/

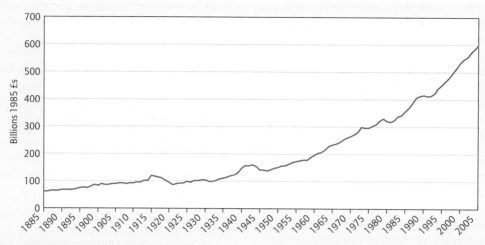

**Figure 26.1** UK Real GDP growth, 1885–2005

**Real GDP, which measures the total production of goods and services for the whole economy over a year, has grown steadily over the past century.** Long-term growth is reflected in the upward trend of real GDP. There were significant declines in real GDP after each of the world wars, there was a recession in the 1930s, and there have been three notable recessions since 1970. Otherwise the trend dominates the cycle in the long term.

eight-fold between 1885 and 2005 while the population increased by only about 60 per cent over the same time, which means that incomes per head rose by over five-fold.

In terms of levels of real GDP, the strong upward trend shows only a few small blips around an otherwise relentless upward drift. There were periods of faster growth during the two world wars as national resources were mobilized for the war effort, and these periods were both followed by postwar recessions (periods of negative growth). Since the Second World War, however, growth has always been positive except for three short periods of negative growth: 1974–5, 1980–2, and 1991–2.

While growth throughout the past 120 years has been generally positive, and this is what generates the upward drift in incomes, the annual growth rates have been quite variable. Figure 16.1 on page 358 shows the same data as those that lie behind Figure 26.1 but expressed as annual growth rates. UK economic growth was extremely volatile in the interwar period. Since 1950 growth has generally been positive and much less variable, with most annual growth rates falling in the range of 0–5 per cent.

# Benefits and costs of growth

We look first at the benefits of growth, and then consider the costs.

## Benefits of growth

### Growth and living standards

For those who share in it, growth is a powerful weapon against poverty. A family that is earning £25,000 today can expect an income of about £30,500 within ten years (in constant pounds and with no promotion) if it shares in a 2 per cent growth rate, and £37,000 if that rate is 4 per cent.

The transformation of the life-style of ordinary workers in advanced industrial nations over the last two centuries shows the massive improvements in living standards and quality of life that growth makes possible. Much of the recent concern over economic problems facing Europeans stems from the decline of growth that occurred in the mid-1970s and in the recessions of the early 1980s and early 1990s. Partly because growth slowed in those periods and partly because the distribution of income has changed unfavourably for them, the real incomes of many working families grew little in the 1970s and only modestly in the 1980s and 1990s. Several European countries continued to grow slowly in the early 2000s and exhibited high levels of unemployment (see previous chapter).

### Growth and life-style

A family often finds that a big increase in its income can lead to a major change in the pattern of its consumption—that extra money buys important amenities of life. In the same way, members of society as a whole may change their consumption patterns as their average income rises. Not only do markets in a country that is growing rapidly make it profitable to produce more cars, but also the government is led to construct more roads and to provide more recreational areas for its newly affluent and mobile citizens. At yet higher levels of income, a concern about litter, pollution, and congestion may become important, and their correction may then begin to account for a significant fraction of GDP. Such 'amenities' usually become matters of social concern only when growth has ensured the provision of the basic requirements for food, clothing, and housing to a substantial majority of the population.

More subtle, but in the long term more important, are the effects of technological change on the whole nation's life-style. Today's real incomes are five to ten times those of Victorians who lived in the second half of the nineteenth century. But we do not spend this higher purchasing power on more of what Victorians consumed; instead, we buy new and better products made in new and better ways. We return to this point later, and Box 26.3 on page 597 expands on this.

The new products and production processes created by technological change transform our entire way of living.

### Growth and income redistribution

Not everyone benefits equally from growth. Many of the poorest are not even in the labour force and thus are unlikely to share in the higher wages that, along with higher profits, are the primary means by which the gains from growth are distributed. Some lose their jobs as a result of technical change, and the older workers may find it difficult to retrain for anything like as good a job as they lost. For this reason, even in a growing economy, redistribution policies will be needed if poverty and extreme hardship are to be averted.

If a constant total of national income is redistributed, some people's standards of living will actually have to be lowered. However, when there is economic growth, and when only a part of the increment in income is redistributed (through government intervention), it is possible to reduce income inequalities while raising everyone's real income.

It is much easier for a rapidly growing economy to be generous towards its less fortunate citizens—or neighbours—than it is for a static economy.

## Costs of growth

Other things being equal, most people would probably regard a fast rate of growth as preferable to a slow one; but other things are seldom equal.

### The opportunity cost of growth

In a world of scarcity, almost nothing is free. Growth requires heavy investment of resources in capital goods, as well as in activities such as education. Often these investments yield no immediate return in terms of goods and services for consumption; this implies that sacrifices have been made by the current generation of consumers.

Growth, which promises more goods tomorrow, is achieved by consuming fewer goods today. For the economy as a whole, this sacrifice of current consumption is the primary cost of growth.

### Social and personal costs of growth

A growing economy is a changing economy. Innovation renders some machines obsolete and also leaves some people partly obsolete. No matter how well trained workers are at age 25, in another 25 years many will find that their skills are at least partly obsolete. A rapid growth rate requires rapid adjustments, which can cause much upset and misery to the people who are affected by them. It is often argued that costs of this kind are a small price to pay for the great benefits that growth can bring. Even if this is true in the aggregate, such personal costs are very unevenly borne. Many of those for whom growth is most costly (in terms of lost jobs) share least in the fruits that growth brings.

Ever more growth does not appear to make us any happier once we have reached a certain standard of living (see Layard 2005). In the United States, for example, surveys show that the percentage of the population feeling 'very happy' was no higher in the year 2000 than it had been in 1960, despite a doubling of real incomes over that period. Indeed, the pressures of competing in an ever more stressful world have led to increases in depression and other stress-related illnesses. Societies do not get happier just by getting richer. The single biggest factor that people say makes them happy is family relationships, and pressures to succeed (which can include working long hours) can make family relationships much more strained. The relative deprivation associated with not working can be even worse.

**Box 26.1   The end of work?**

From time immemorial, people have observed that technological change destroys particular jobs and have worried that it will destroy jobs in general. Two points are important in assessing this issue.

First, technological change does destroy particular jobs. When waterwheels were used to automate the fulling of cloth in twelfth-century Europe there were riots and protests among the fullers who lost their jobs. A century ago, half of the labour force in North America and Europe was required to produce the food needed to feed the population. (The figure was a little lower in the UK because British manufactured goods were exported in return for imported foodstuffs.) Today less than 3 per cent of the labour force is needed in high-income countries to feed all their citizens. In other words, out of every 100 jobs that existed in 1900, 50 were in agriculture, and 47 of those have been destroyed by techno-logical progress over the course of the last century.

The second point is that new technologies create new jobs just as they destroy old ones. The displaced agricultural workers did not join the ranks of the permanently unemployed—some of the older ones may have done, but their children did not. Instead they and their children took jobs in manufacturing and service industries and helped to produce the mass of new goods and services that have raised living standards over the century—including cars, refrigerators, computers, foreign travel, and a vast list of new things.

New technologies usually require new skills. Those who are unable to retrain may suffer, but their children can train appro-priately from the outset.

**Technological change raises living standards by destroying jobs in existing lines of production and freeing labour to produce new commodities as well as more of some existing commodities.**

Modern technologies have two new aspects that worry some observers. First, they tend to be knowledge-intensive. A fairly high degree of literacy and numeracy, as well as familiarity with computers, is needed to work with many although not all of these new technologies. Second, owing to the globalizing of world markets—through falling costs of transporting goods and the co-ordination of their production worldwide—unskilled workers in advanced countries have come into competition with unskilled workers everywhere in the world. Both of these forces are decreasing the relative demand for unskilled workers in developed countries. This may lead to falling relative wages for the unskilled and, if labour markets are sufficiently inflexible, to some structural unemployment.

For these reasons, some people blame the high unemploy-ment rates in Europe on the new technologies. This is hard to reconcile, however, with the fact that the lowest unemployment rates in the industrialized countries are currently being recorded in the United States, which is the most technologically dynamic of all countries and the one where policy-makers have worried least about the unemployment effects of new technologies. This suggests that the cause of high European unemployment rates may be not enough technological change and too much govern-ment interference, rather than too much technological change.

Worries that technological change will cause general unem-ployment have been recorded for at least two hundred years but, so far at least, there is no sign that those displaced by tech-nological change or their children are being forced into the ranks of the permanently unemployed.

**Over all of recorded history so far, technological change has created more jobs than it has destroyed.**

Growth creates new jobs and destroys some old ones. Those who were trained for the jobs that are lost can, and often do, suffer. Box 26.1 deals with a less well founded worry: that growth may destroy more jobs than it creates, leading to long-term heavy unemployment for a growing body of structurally unemployed workers.

### Time distribution of costs and benefits

The costs of technological change tend to be borne imme-diately. Jobs are lost, and people trained in the old tech-nologies lose their jobs and find their skills obsolete. The forgone consumption needed to finance the investment that embodies the new technologies happens right away. In contrast, the benefits are felt by many in the present generation and by almost everyone in the future. We are all better off for having most of the new products that are created by past technological changes, even though those

who made the older competing products probably suf-fered when the new ones were first introduced. As a result, everyone is a beneficiary of past growth-inducing techno-logical change—the costs have been paid and the benefits are still with us. But not everyone is a beneficiary of cur-rent change. Most benefit, but some suffer, and some of those would have been better off if the change that affected them adversely had never happened.

### Negative externalities of growth

One of the greatest recent concerns about growth has been about growing greenhouse gas emissions and the resulting effect on global warming. This is a concern not about growth itself, but rather about the burning of fossil fuels (such as coal and oil), releasing carbon into the atmosphere, that has characterized the industrial growth of the past cen-tury or so. Growth in some countries has also led to the cutting down of forests which then reduces their natural function of absorbing carbon dioxide and releasing oxygen. We return to this negative aspect of growth below (on page 603), but for the present it is worth noting that for growth to be beneficial it must be sustainable, and this may well require the incorporation of strategies to limit carbon emissions and preserve the environment.[2] It will also inevitably require the development of alternative tech-

nologies that generate energy without the burning of fossil fuels which release carbon dioxide. Such alternative energy sources are feasible, but they are unlikely to be developed rapidly without public assistance as long as fossil fuels remain available and are not excessively expensive.

Before returning to the problems that can be caused by growth, however, we turn to explanations of what drives growth in the first place.

## Theories of economic growth

In this section we study some of the theories that attempt to explain economic growth. This is an exciting area. Ideas are changing rapidly as both theoretical and empirical research expands our knowledge.

Before going further, it is helpful to clarify the distinction between what has been called *extensive growth* and *intensive growth*. Extensive growth relates to the growth of total GDP, whereas intensive growth is about GDP per head. The former is thus relevant to discussions of total market size and income of the economy as a whole, while the latter is relevant to understanding the real living standard of average individuals in the economy. The former tells us about the size of the cake, while the latter tells us how much cake is available for each citizen.

### Determinants of growth

The four of the most important determinants of growth of total output are as follows:

1. *growth in the labour force*, such as occurs when the population grows or participation rates rise;

2. *investment in human capital*, such as formal education and on-the-job experience;

3. *investment in physical capital*, such as factories, machines, transportation, and communications facilities;

4. *technological change*, brought about by innovation that introduces new products, new ways of producing existing products, and new forms of business organization.

One line of investigation studies how these four forces operate in what is called the **aggregate production function**. This is an expression for the relationship between the total amounts of labour (*L*), physical capital (*K*), and

human capital (*H*) that are employed[3] and the nation's total output, its GDP:

$$GDP = f(L, K, H).$$

This is an aggregate function because it relates the economy's total output, its GDP, to the total amount of the three main inputs that are used to produce that output. (A micro production function, such as is discussed in Chapter 6, relates the output of one firm to the inputs employed by that firm.) The function, indicated by the letter 'f', shows the relation between the inputs of *L*, *K*, and *H* and the output of GDP. The production function tells us how much GDP will be produced for given amounts of labour and capital employed. For example, the function may tell us that, when 200 million units of labour per period[4] of time, 400 million units of physical capital per period, and 100 million units of human capital per period are used, the GDP will be 4,000 million units of output per period.[5]

In growth theory we ignore short-term fluctuations of output around its trend. Thus, the GDP in the above

---

[3] Growth theory focuses on the production of manufactured goods and services, where, in contrast to agriculture, land is rarely a limiting factor. All the relatively small amounts of land that are needed can be obtained, and hence nothing significant is lost by ignoring land in the analysis of an industrialized economy—although this cannot be done for an agricultural economy. A service-based economy, of course, needs even less land than manufacturing.

[4] These would be flows of inputs and flows of outputs; so, for example, labour input would be measured as worker-hours or worker-weeks.

[5] A simple example of a production function is $GDP = z(LKH)^{1/3}$. This equation says that, to find the amount of GDP produced, multiply the amount of labour by the amount of physical capital and by the amount of human capital, take the cube root, and multiply the result by the constant $z$. This production function has positive but diminishing returns to each input. This can be shown using calculus by evaluating the first and second partial derivatives and showing that the first derivatives are positive while the second derivatives are negative. In the numerical example in the text $z$ is taken as 20, making $20[(200)(400)(100)]^{1/3} = 4,000$.

---

[2] Some of these issues were discussed in the context of market failure and the role of government in Chapter 14.

production function can be interpreted as the trend level of GDP, i.e. potential GDP.

We now use this aggregate production function to structure a discussion of some theories of economic growth.

## Neoclassical growth theory

One early branch of neoclassical theory deals with growth when the stock of technological knowledge remains unchanged. There are no innovations—no new ways of making things, and no new products. As a result, the relation between inputs and output, as shown by the production function, does not change. The key aspects of what is called the neoclassical model are that the aggregate production function displays *decreasing returns* when any input is increased on its own, and *constant returns* when all inputs are increased together and in the same proportion. We explain these concepts below.

### Decreasing returns to a single input

To start with, suppose that the population of the country grows while the stocks of physical and human capital remain constant. More and more people go to work using the same fixed quantity of physical capital and knowledge. The amount that each new unit of input adds to total output is called its *marginal product*. The operation of the famous **law of diminishing returns** tells us that the successive employment of equal additional amounts (or units) of labour will eventually add less to total output than the immediately previous unit of labour. In other words, sooner or later each additional unit of labour will produce a diminishing marginal product. This is referred to as *diminishing returns to a single input*. We first met it in Chapter 6, and it is illustrated in Figure 26.2.

The law of diminishing returns applies to any input that is varied while the other inputs are held constant. Thus, successive amounts of capital added to *a fixed supply of labour* will also eventually add less and less to GDP.

According to the law of diminishing returns, the increment to total production will eventually fall whenever equal increases of a variable input are combined with another input whose quantity is fixed.[6]

**Figure 26.2 Average and marginal products of a variable input**

The average and marginal products of any variable input decline as successive units of that input are added to a fixed amount of another input. This figure shows the marginal and average products of the variable input declining as more and more units of that input are used. The marginal products are plotted between the units of the variable input, since they apply to a change from one amount to the next.

### Constant returns to scale

The other main property of the neoclassical aggregate production function is **constant returns to scale**. This means that, if the amounts of labour and physical and human capital are all changed in equal proportion, the total output will change in the same proportion. For example, a 10 per cent increase in the amounts of labour and physical and human capital used will lead to a 10 per cent increase in GDP. We first met this relationship in Chapter 6.

### Sources of growth in the neoclassical model

Now consider each of the sources of growth listed above. To begin with, we let each source operate with the others held constant.

#### Labour force growth

In the long term we can associate labour force growth with population growth (although in the short term the labour force can grow if participation rates rise even though the population remains constant). As more labour is used, there will be more output and, consequently, a growth in total GDP. The law of diminishing returns tells us that sooner

---

[6] In some production functions marginal product may rise at first and begin to decline only after a certain critical amount of the variable input is used. In the neoclassical constant returns production function, however, marginal product declines from the outset, as shown in Figure 26.2.

or later each further unit of labour to be employed will cause a smaller and smaller addition to GDP. Eventually, not only will the marginal product of labour be falling, but the average product will fall as well. Beyond that point, although economic growth continues in the sense that total output is growing, living standards are falling in the sense that average GDP per head of population is falling. If we are interested in the growth in living standards, we are concerned with increasing GDP *per person*.

Whenever diminishing average returns apply, increases in population on their own are eventually accompanied by falling living standards.[7]

### Physical capital

Increases in the amount of physical capital on their own affect GDP in a manner similar to population growth alone. Eventually, each successive unit of physical capital will add less to total output than the previous unit of physical capital.

There is, however, a major contrast with the case of labour growth, because it is output per person that determines living standards, not output per unit of capital. Thus, as physical capital increases, living standards increase because output is rising while the population is constant. Indeed, per capita output can be increased by adding more physical capital as long as its marginal product exceeds zero. However, since the increases in output are subject to diminishing returns, successive additions to the economy's capital stock bring smaller and smaller increases in per capita output.

In the neoclassical model, the operation of diminishing returns implies that equal increases in physical capital on its own brings smaller and smaller increases in per capita GDP.

Box 26.2 shows a particular exposition of these elements of the neoclassical model known as the Solow–Swan model, named after the originators, US economist (and 1987 Nobel Laureate) Robert Solow and Australian economist Trevor Swan.

### Human capital

Human capital has several aspects. One involves improvements in the health and longevity of the population. Of course, these are desired as ends in themselves, but they also have consequences for both the size and the productivity of the labour force. There is no doubt that improvements in the health of workers have increased productivity per worker-hour by cutting down on illness, accidents, and absenteeism.

A second aspect of the quality of human capital concerns technical training—from learning how to operate a machine to learning how to be a scientist. This training depends on the current state of knowledge, and advances in knowledge allow us not only to build more productive physical capital, but also to create more effective human capital. Training is clearly required if a person is to operate, repair, manage, or invent complex machines. More subtly, there may be general social advantages to an educated population. Productivity improves with literacy. The longer a person has been educated, the more adaptable, and so the more productive in the long run that person will be in the face of new and changing challenges.

A third aspect of human capital is its contribution to growth and innovation.

Not only can current human capital embody in people the best current technological knowledge, but, by training potential innovators, it leads to advances in our knowledge and hence contributes to growth.

### Balanced growth

Now consider what happens if labour and physical and human capital all grow at the same rate. In this case the neoclassical assumption of constant returns to scale means that GDP grows at the same rate. As a result, per capita output (GDP/$L$) remains constant.[8] This is called a **balanced growth** path, along which all inputs and output are growing at the same constant rate. Per capita GDP, however, is unchanged.

This is not the kind of growth that concerns those interested in living standards. It is just more of the same: larger and larger economies, with more capital and more labour, doing exactly what the existing capital and the existing labour were already doing. There is nothing new. This is the kind of steady-state growth path illustrated in Box 26.2.

### Growth and living standards

In this constant-technology neoclassical model, the only way for growth to add to living standards is for the per capita stocks of physical and human capital to increase. The law of diminishing returns dictates, however, that the rise in living standards brought about by successive equal

---

[7] In the neoclassical model diminishing returns set in from the outset, so that there is no range over which population increases cause rising marginal or average product of labour. The issue of when diminishing returns set in need not concern us here, since all that matters for the text discussion is that, other things held constant, increases in any one input must eventually encounter diminishing returns.

[8] In all of these models a constant fraction of the population is assumed to be in the labour force, so that output per employed person and output per head of population always change in the same direction.

### Box 26.2  The Solow–Swan growth model

A well known model that helps us to understand some theories of growth is due to US economist Robert Solow and Australian economist Trevor Swan. It is also sometimes known as the neo-classical growth model.

The assumptions of the model are as outlined in the text, except that the aggregate production function expresses national output as a function of inputs of only two factors: labour and capital. As in the text, this function exhibits constant returns to scale. So if both capital and labour inputs are increased in the same proportion, output will also increase in that proportion: a 10 per cent increase in capital and labour will lead to a 10 per cent increase in output. But there are diminishing returns to each input. So if we hold the labour input constant, each successive unit of capital will produce a declining increase in units of output.

The figure illustrates the working of the model. The vertical axis measures output per worker and the horizontal axis measures capital per worker. With a given labour force, the accumulation of capital increases the amount of capital per head as well as income per head. But because of diminishing returns to any one input, output per head increases at a diminishing rate as capital, and hence capital per head, increases. Labour saves a constant fraction of its income which is always invested. So, as capital increases, so does output (and income) per head and, as

a result, so does saving and investment. This is shown by the line labelled 'Saving (and investment)'. As one moves out along this line income is rising, as is saving and investment, but at a diminishing rate.

The straight line labelled 'Capital replacement requirement' shows the investment in capital per worker needed to keep the capital–labour ratio at its original level in the face of a constant growth rate of the labour force and a constant depreciation rate of capital. This is a straight line because it represents points for which capital and labour are increasing in the same proportion and there are constant returns to scale (so an equal percentage increase in both inputs leads to the same percentage increase in output).

There are two possible cases, depending on what we assume about technical progress.

In the first case we assume that the technology is given, so there is no productivity growth. The 'steady state' in the model is at point A. The economy will be attracted towards point A because to the left of A investment is greater than is needed to keep the capital–labour ratio constant so capital per worker is rising; while to the right of A investment is too low to keep the capital–labour ratio constant so the capital–labour ratio is falling. At point A saving (and therefore investment) is just sufficient to generate a rate of growth of the capital stock which just keeps up with the growth of the labour force and compensates for any depreciation of capital. So at point A capital per worker is constant and output grows at the rate of growth of the workforce. But there is no growth in real living standards, for the expanding labour force delivers 'more of the same' in the sense that output per worker is constant and so real wages are also constant.

In the second case there is technical progress so that labour productivity grows over time at some exogenous rate. In this world total output grows at the rate of population growth plus the rate of productivity growth, but the rate of growth of output per head depends entirely on the rate of technical progress. In this second case, therefore, the rate of growth of real incomes depends entirely on the rate of technical change, but this is not explained within the model. More recent theories have focused on trying to explain technical change as an endogenous variable as discussed in the text.

increases in capital will inexorably diminish. Raising living standards becomes more and more difficult as capital accumulation continues.

### Technological change in the neoclassical growth model

So far we have held technology constant. In fact, over the centuries (and even decades) economic growth has been dominated by technological changes. As we have already

observed, we are not better off than our Victorian ancestors because we have more Victorian factories making more Victorian commodities—we are better off because technological change has provided us with new commodities often made in radically new ways. Box 26.3 discusses some of the many new products that have literally transformed life-styles over the past century. In the neoclassical model, technological change can be shown as shifting the production function so that the same amount

**Box 26.3** The transformative effects of technological change

*People living at the beginning of the twenty-first century experience measured real consumption that is over ten times as much as the consumption of those living at the beginning of the twentieth century. But they consume this enormous increment largely in terms of new commodities made with new techniques. People living in the first decade of the twentieth century did not know modern dental and medical equipment, penicillin, bypass operations, safe births, control of genetically transmitted diseases, personal computers, compact discs, television sets, automobiles, opportunities for fast and cheap world wide travel, affordable universities, central heating, air conditioning, and food of great variety free from ptomaine and botulism, much less the elimination of endless kitchen drudgery through the use of detergents, washing machines, electric stoves, vacuum cleaners, refrigerators, dish washers, and a host of other labour-saving household products, which their great-grandchildren take for granted.*

*Nor could our ancestors of one hundred years ago have imagined the robot-operated, computer-controlled, modern factories that* *have largely replaced their noisy, dangerous, factories that spewed coal smoke over the surrounding countryside.*

*Technological change has transformed the quality of our lives. It has removed terrible diseases that maimed, crippled, and killed—plague, tuberculosis, cholera, dysentery, smallpox, and leprosy, to mention only the most common. In 1700, average European life expectancy was about 30 years; in early eighteenth-century France one in five babies was dead by the end of its first year, and 50 per cent of registered children were dead by age ten. In 1900, death from botulism and ptomaine poisoning from contaminated food was common. Chemical additives virtually eliminated these killers and allow us to live long enough to worry about the long run cancer causing effects of some of these additives. Now they are being replaced by safer preservatives.*

*In summary, technological advance not only increases our incomes; it also transforms our lives through the invention of new, hitherto undreamed of products that are made in new, hitherto undreamed of ways.* (Lipsey, Carlaw, and Bekar 2005, pages 5–6; reprinted by permission of the publishers)

of labour, physical capital, and human capital produces more GDP. This result is depicted in Figure 26.3 by rightward shifts in the *MP* curves of each input: the same amount of input produces more output.[9]

The neoclassical growth model can accommodate technological change along balanced growth paths if physical and human capital are growing at a constant rate and technological change increases the efficiency of labour at the same rate, making labour grow at a constant exponential rate when measured in *efficiency units*. This is called labour-augmenting, or Harrod-neutral, technical change. The result is that there is no increase in output per efficiency unit of labour, but there is an increase in output per worker. Along such a balanced growth path labour is constant, measured in number of workers employed, while human and physical capital, the efficiency of labour, and total and per capita output are all growing at a constant rate. All that has been done here is that, instead of having labour grow at a constant rate in terms of physical numbers, leading to balanced growth

**Figure 26.3** Shifts in marginal product curves

**Technological change shifts the marginal product curve of each input so that any given amount will produce more.** In this example technological change shifts the marginal product curve of the input from $MP_0$ to $MP_1$. The amount $f_0$ of the input formerly produced a marginal product of $q_0$, but after the change it produces the larger amount $q_1$.

[9] In the neoclassical production function which allows for growth, we have GDP = $z(L^{\alpha}K^{\beta}H^{1-\alpha-\beta})$, $0 < \alpha$, $\beta$, $\alpha + \beta < 1$. The parameter $z$ is a constant that relates given inputs of $L$, $K$, and $H$ to a specific GDP. Increases in input productivity cause $z$ to rise, so the given amounts of $L$, $K$, and $H$ are associated with higher GDP. Exogenous technical progress at a constant rate can be shown as GDP$_t = z_t(L^{\alpha}K^{\beta}H^{1-\alpha-\beta})$, where $z$ grows at a constant rate as time passes.

with constant living standards, labour is growing at a constant rate measured in efficiency units (with the number of workers constant) so that per capita output is growing at the balanced growth rate.

## Kinds of technological change

Increases in productive capacity that are created by installing new and better capital goods are called **embodied technical change**. The historical importance of embodied technical change is clear: the assembly line and automation transformed most manufacturing industries, the aeroplane revolutionized transportation, and electronic devices now dominate the information and communications industries. These innovations, plus lesser known but no less profound ones—e.g. improvements in the strength of metals, the productivity of seeds, and the techniques for recovering basic raw materials from the ground—create new investment opportunities.

Less obvious but none the less important changes occur through **disembodied technical change**, that is, changes in the organization of production that are not embodied in particular capital goods. Examples are improved techniques of management, design, marketing, organization of business activity, and feedback from user experience to product improvement.

The modern understanding that technological innovation is at the heart of the growth process has led to two important developments in many economists' views on growth. First, technological change is largely endogenous to the economic system. Second, investment that increases the capital stock may encounter increasing rather than diminishing returns. These insights have led to new growth theories that go far beyond the neoclassical growth model.

## Endogenous growth

In the neoclassical model, innovation shifts the production function but is itself unexplained. In other words, technological change is treated as being *exogenous*. It has profound effects on economic variables such as GDP, but it is not influenced by economic causes. It just happens.

Yet microeconomic research by many scholars over the past several decades has established that technological change *is* responsive to such economic 'signals' as prices and profits. In other words, technological change is *endogenous* to the economic system. Much of the earliest work on this issue was conducted in the United Kingdom by scholars such as Christopher Freeman, who were associated with the Science Policy Research Unit (SPRU) at Sussex University. The most influential overall single study, however, was by the American professor Nathan Rosenberg, whose path-breaking book *Inside the Black Box* argued this case in great detail (Rosenberg 1982; see also Rosenberg 1994).

Technological change stems from research and development (R&D) and from innovating activities that put the results of R&D into practice. These are costly and highly risky activities, undertaken largely by firms and usually in pursuit of profit. It is not surprising, therefore, that these activities respond to economic incentives.

Rosenberg established two key relationships. First, R&D designed to apply known basic principles to new problems is responsive to economic signals. For example, if the price of some particular input such as petroleum or skilled labour goes up, R&D and innovating activities will be directed towards altering the production function to economize on these inputs. This process does not involve a substitution of less expensive inputs for more expensive ones within the confines of *known* technologies; rather, it focuses on the development of *new* technologies in response to changes in relative prices. Second, basic research itself is responsive to economic incentives. One reason for this is that the basic research agenda is strongly influenced by practical issues of the day. For example, university-based research in solid state physics became popular, and was heavily funded, only after the development of the transistor.

There are many important implications of this new understanding of the fact that, to a great extent, growth is achieved through costly, risky, innovative activity that occurs to a significant extent in response to economic signals. We will discuss a few of these below.

### The complexity of the innovation process

The pioneering theorist of innovation, Joseph Schumpeter, developed a model in which innovation flowed in one direction, from a pure discovery 'upstream', to more applied R&D, then to working machines, and finally to output 'downstream'.

In contrast, modern research shows that innovation involves a large amount of 'learning by doing' at all of its stages. (This phenomenon, whereby costs per unit of output fall steadily over time as firms learn how to manage new technologies, was discussed in more detail in Chapter 12.) What is learned 'downstream' then modifies what must be done 'upstream'. The best innovation-managing systems encourage feedback from the more applied steps to the purer researchers and from users to designers.

### The location of innovation

Innovation typically takes place in different parts of the producer–user chain in different industries—as shown, for example, by the research of Eric von Hippel of the Massachusetts Institute of Technology (MIT) in his book *The Sources of Innovation* (1988). Von Hippel shows that in some industries manufacturers make most of the product innovations, in others the users make most of them, and in yet others the innovating is done by those who supply components or materials to the manufacturer.

Unless these differences are appreciated, public policy designed to encourage innovation can go seriously astray. An example is provided by von Hippel:

*Consider the current concern of US policy-makers that the products of US semiconductor process equipment firms are falling behind the leading edge. The conventional assessment of this problem is that these firms should somehow be strengthened and helped to innovate so that US semiconductor equipment users (makers of semiconductors) will not also fall behind. But investigation shows that most process equipment innovations in this field are, in fact, developed by equipment users. Therefore, the causality is probably reversed: US equipment builders are falling behind because the US user community they deal with is falling behind. If this is so, the policy prescription should change. Perhaps US equipment builders can best be helped by helping US equipment users to innovate at the leading edge once more.* (von Hippel 1988, pages 9–10; by permission of Oxford University Press, Inc.)

More recent events suggest that the US semiconductor industry did subsequently improve its performance, but the message for economists and policy-makers is important: an understanding of the details of the innovating process in each industry is needed if successful innovation-encouraging policies are to be developed.

## Costly diffusion

The *diffusion* of technological knowledge from those who have it to those who want it is not costless (as it was assumed to be in Schumpeter's model). Firms need research capacity just to adopt the technologies developed by others. Some of the knowledge needed to use a new technology can be learned by plant managers, technicians, and operators only through experience. (Such knowledge is called *tacit knowledge.*) We often tend to think that once a production process is developed it can easily be copied by others. Indeed, some advanced economic theories use the 'hypothesis of replication', which holds that any known process can be replicated in any new location by using the same factor inputs and management as are used in the old location. In practice, however, the diffusion of new technological knowledge is not so simple.

For example, US economists Richard Nelson and Sidney Winter have argued that most industrial technologies require technology-specific organizational skills that can be 'embodied' neither in the machines themselves, nor in instruction books, nor in blueprints. Instead, they claim

that acquiring tacit knowledge requires a deliberate process of building up new skills, work practices, knowledge, and experience.

The fact that diffusion is a costly, risky, and time-consuming business explains why new technologies take considerable time to diffuse, first through the economy of the originating country and then through the rest of the world. If diffusion were simple and virtually costless, the puzzle would be why technological knowledge and best industrial practices do not diffuse very quickly. As it is, decades can pass before a new technological process is diffused everywhere that it could be employed.

## Market structure and innovation

Because it is highly risky, innovation is encouraged by a strongly competitive environment and is discouraged by monopoly practices. Competition among three or four large firms often produces much innovation, but a single firm, especially if it serves a secure home market protected by trade barriers, seems much less inclined to innovate.[10]

Although the ideas of Joseph Schumpeter lie behind much of modern growth theory, this emphasis on competition seems at first to conflict with his ideas. The apparent conflict arises because the theories available to Schumpeter in his time offered only two market structures: perfect competition and monopoly. He chose monopoly as the structure more conducive to growth, on the grounds that monopoly profits would provide the incentive to innovate, and innovation itself would provide the mechanism whereby new entrants could compete with established monopolies. (He called this latter process 'creative destruction'.) Modern economists, faced with a richer variety of theoretical market structures, find that competition among oligopolists is usually more conducive to growth-enhancing technological change than either monopoly or perfect competition.

Government assistance designed to encourage innovation often allows the firms in an industry to work together as one. Unless great care is exercised, and unless sufficient foreign competition exists, the result may be a national monopoly that will discourage risk-taking rather than encourage it as intended.

The United Kingdom provides many examples of this mistaken view of policy. For example:

*[UK policy in the 1960s] operated under the faulty theory that encouraging British companies to merge would create world-class competitors. Consolidation of steel, automobiles, machine*

---

[10] This is an important theme in much contemporary research, supported by evidence from such authors as Chandler (1990) and Mowrey and Rosenberg (1989).

*tools, and computers all led to notable failures. A program of research support for industry . . . proved disastrous. The British government tried to choose promising technologies and gave direct grants to firms to develop them. Most of the choices were failures. . . . [In contrast] unusually low levels of regulation in some service industries have avoided disadvantages faced by other nations and allowed innovation and change . . . in auctioneering . . . trading and insurance. British firms in these industries have been among the most innovative in the world.* (Porter 1998, page 507)

### Shocks and innovation

One interesting consequence of endogenous technical change is that shocks that would be unambiguously adverse to an economy operating with fixed technology can sometimes provide a spur to innovation that proves a blessing in disguise. A sharp rise in the price of one input can raise costs and lower the value of output per person for some time. But it may lead to a wave of innovations that reduce the need for this expensive input and, as a side-effect, greatly raise the productivity of labour.[11]

Sometimes individual firms will respond differently to the same economic signal. Those who respond by altering technology may do better than those who concentrate their efforts on substituting within the confines of known technology. For example, in *The Competitive Advantage of Nations*, Michael Porter (1998) tells of how US consumer electronics firms decided to move their operations abroad to avoid high, and rigid, labour costs. They continued to use their existing technology and went where labour costs were low enough to make that technology pay. Their Japanese competitors, however, stayed at home; they innovated away most of their labour costs—and then built factories in the United States to replace the factories of US firms that had gone abroad!

### Innovation as a competitive strategy

Managing innovation better than one's competitors is one of the most important objectives of any modern firm that wishes to survive. Firms often fail because they do not keep up with their competitors in the race to develop new and improved products and techniques of production and distribution. Success in real-world competition often depends more on success in managing innovation than on success in adopting the right pricing policies or making the right capacity decisions from already-known technological possibilities.

## Increasing returns theories

We saw earlier that neoclassical theories assume that investment is always subject to diminishing returns. Some new growth theories emphasize the possibility of *historical increasing returns to investment*. This means that, as investments in some new areas—products, power sources, or production technologies—proceed through time, each new increment of investment is more productive than previous increments. A number of sources of increasing returns have been noted. These fall under the general categories of once-and-for-all costs and ideas.

### Fixed costs

There are three ways in which once-and-for-all costs can cause increasing returns to investment.

1. Investment in the early stages of development of a country or region may create new skills and attitudes in the workforce that are then available to all subsequent investors, whose costs are therefore lower than those encountered by the initial investors. In the language of Chapter 13, the early firms are conferring an *externality* on those who follow them.

2. Each new investor may find the environment more and more favourable to its investment because of the infrastructure that has been created by those who came before.

3. The first investment in a new product will encounter countless problems, both technical problems of production and problems of product acceptance among customers. Once the technical problems are overcome, they do not exist for subsequent investors. When a new product is developed customers will often resist adopting it, partly because they may be conservative and partly because they know that new products often have teething troubles. Customers also need time to learn how best to use the new product—they need to do what is called 'learning by using'. The first firms in the field with a truly new idea, such as personal computers, usually meet strong customer resistance, but this resistance is eroded over time.

All of these cases, and many more that could be mentioned, are examples of a single phenomenon:

**Many investments require fixed costs, the advantages of which are then available to subsequent investors; hence the investment costs for 'followers' can be substantially less than the investment costs for 'pioneers'.**

---

[11] This is why in microeconomics we study three runs: the short run, the long run, and the very long run. Often the very-long-run response to a change in relative prices is much more important than either the short-run response, which is limited by fixed capital, or the long-run response, which is limited by existing technology.

More generally, many of the sources of increasing returns are variations on the following theme:

Doing something really new is difficult, both technically and in terms of customer acceptance, whereas making further variations on an accepted and developed new idea becomes progressively easier.

The implications of these ideas have been the subject of intense study ever since they were first embedded in modern growth models by Paul Romer of the University of California and Maurice Scott of Oxford University.[12]

### Ideas

An even more fundamental change in the new theories is the shift from the economics of goods to the economics of ideas.

Physical goods, such as factories and machines, exist in one place at one time. The nature of this existence has two consequences. First, when physical goods are used by someone, they cannot be used by someone else. Second, if a given labour force is provided with more and more physical objects to use in production, sooner or later diminishing returns will be encountered.

Ideas have different characteristics. In the first place, ideas can be used by one person without reducing their use by others. Thus, once someone has an idea and develops it, the idea can be used simultaneously by everyone. For example, if one firm is using a certain van, another firm cannot use that van at the same time; but one firm's use of a revolutionary design for a new suspension on a van or lorry does not prevent other firms from using that design as well. Ideas are not subject to the same use restrictions as goods. (In the language of Table 13.1 on page 278, physical goods are *rivalrous*; ideas are *non-rivalrous*.)

Second, ideas are not necessarily subject to decreasing returns. As our knowledge increases, each increment of new knowledge does *not* inevitably add less to our productive ability than each previous increment. A year spent improving the operation of semiconductors may be more productive than a year spent improving the operation of vacuum tubes (the technology used before semiconductors).

Modern growth theories stress the importance of ideas in producing what can be called knowledge-driven growth. New knowledge provides the input that allows investment to produce constant or increasing rather than diminishing returns. Furthermore, the evidence from modern research

is that new technologies are usually absolutely input-saving —they typically use less of all inputs per unit of output. Since there are no practical boundaries to human knowledge, there need be no immediate boundaries to finding new ways to produce more output using less of all inputs.[13]

Classical and neoclassical growth theories gave economics the name 'dismal science' by emphasizing that diminishing returns under conditions of given technology put a cap on growth based on capital accumulation. Modern growth theories are more optimistic, because they emphasize the unlimited potential of knowledge-driven technological change to economize on all resource inputs, and because they display increasing or constant returns to investment with constant population.

However, these theories refer to long-term trends. For reasons that are not fully understood, the dynamics of market systems cause growth rates to vary from decade to decade, fluctuating about their long-term trend which is the subject of growth theory. Over the long haul, however, there seems no reason to believe that equal increments of human inventive effort must inevitably be rewarded by ever-diminishing increments to material output.

## Further causes of growth

So far we have looked at increases in labour and capital and at technological change as causes of growth. Contemporary studies suggest other causes of growth that are also important. The effects of these other causes appear as shifts in the production function, so that any given number of hours of labour operating with a given amount of capital produces more and more output as time passes.

### Institutions

Almost all aspects of a country's institutions can foster or deter the efficient use of a society's natural and human resources. Social and religious habits, legal institutions, and traditional patterns of national and international trade are all important. So, too, is the political climate.

Historians of economic growth, such as Paul David and Nathan Rosenberg, attribute much of the growth of Western economies in the post-medieval world to the development of *new institutions*, such as the joint-stock company, limited liability, efficient forms of insurance, effective patent laws, and double entry bookkeeping (which allowed the firm's value to be assessed by those who wished

---

[12] As with so many innovations, these new views have many historical antecedents, including a classic article in the 1960s by Nobel Prize winner Kenneth Arrow of Stanford University (Arrow 1962).

[13] Possibly, at some distant date, we may know everything there is to know, but if that time ever comes, it is clearly going to be a long, long way in the future.

to invest in it—at least until modern managers began to manipulate these figures). Many students of modern growth suggest that institutions are as important today as they were in the past. They suggest that the societies that are most successful in developing the new institutions that are needed in today's knowledge-intensive world of globalized competition will be those that are at the forefront of economic growth.

### The role of the government

Governments play an important role in the growth process.

First, the government needs to provide the framework for the market economy that is given by such things as well defined property rights secure from arbitrary confiscation, security and enforcement of contracts, law and order, a sound money, and the basic rights of the individual to locate, sell, and invest where and how she decides.

Second, governments need to provide infrastructure. For example, transportation and communications networks are critical to growth in the modern globalized economy. Some of these facilities, such as roads, bridges, and harbours, are usually provided directly by governments; others, such as telecommunications, rail, and air services, can be provided by private firms, but government regulations and competition policy may be needed to prevent the emergence of growth-inhibiting monopolies in these areas.

Education and health (especially for the disadvantaged) are important forms of government expenditure. Creating the appropriate inputs to production is critical to creating comparative advantages in products that can be exported. This requires general education, trade schools, and other appropriate institutions for formal education, as well as policies to increase on-the-job training within firms. Such activities are even more important today than they were in the past, because so much of a nation's capacity to grow, and to compete in a world of rapidly developing ideas, lies in the quality of its human capital—in both those who produce goods and services and in those who do research and development (R&D) on new goods and services that can be produced in the future.

Other possible government policies include favourable tax treatment of saving, investment, and capital gains, R&D tax incentives and funding assistance, and policies to encourage some fraction of the large pools of financial capital held by pension funds and insurance companies to be used to finance innovation.

Finally, emphasis can be placed on poverty reduction for at least two reasons. First, poverty can exert powerful anti-growth effects. People living in poverty will not develop the skills to provide a productive labour force, and they may not even respond to incentives that are provided. Malnutrition in early childhood can affect a person's capacities for life. Second, although economic growth tends to reduce the incidence of poverty, it does not eliminate it.

What else governments can do to encourage the development of specific new technologies is much debated. Some argue that governments should never seek to interfere at the micro level in the development of new technologies. Certainly, there have been some spectacular and costly failures of this type, including the British government's failure to develop a gas-cooled nuclear reactor and to support successfully a UK challenger to IBM in the field of computers. Other economists, however, point out that many of the most important modern technologies have received substantial government support in the early stages of their development. For example, the vastly successful Japanese automobile industry was largely dependent in its early stages on tariff protection of the postwar Japanese market and the prohibition of US investment in that market. Within this protected environment, the Toyota Motor Company developed new techniques that allowed it to create new products faster and then produce them cheaper than their US competitors.

The massively successful Taiwanese electronics industry was largely the creation of the Taiwanese government. It built up the industry and brokered co-operative relations with US firms from which the Taiwanese firms learned. They then went on to become world leaders, no longer dependent on government support. The United States, which purports to rely on private initiative exclusively, has given government assistance to several of its most successful new technologies. In the 1950s the US Bureau of Standards encouraged the development of an American software industry primarily to assist in the cold war. Two major spin-offs were an infrastructure of academic experts, created largely with government funding, and high industry standards that were set by the rigorous demands of the Department of Defence. Military procurement also supported the growth of the US semiconductor industry, providing for the incubation of innovations that were not yet commercially viable. Firms supplying that market, often on a cost-plus basis, refined their innovations and often reduced their costs sufficiently to achieve commercial viability. The airframe of the Boeing 707, the first successful long haul passenger jet aircraft, was developed on a cost-plus basis in a military version before it was put into civilian production. So were the engines of the 747, the first successful jumbo aircraft. So there have been spectacular government successes and failures in attempts to assist new technologies in their early phases of development, and debate continues on the advisability of this type of assistance.

# Are there limits to growth?

Many opponents of growth argue that sustained world growth is undesirable; some argue that it is impossible. Of course, all things terrestrial have an ultimate limit. After all, astronomers predict that the solar system itself will die when the sun burns out in another five billion or so years. But to be of practical concern, a limit must be within our planning horizons.

## Resource exhaustion

The years since the Second World War have seen a rapid acceleration in the consumption of the world's resources, particularly fossil fuels and basic minerals. World population has increased from under 2.5 billion to over 6 billion in that period; this increase alone has intensified the demand for the world's resources. Furthermore, as economic development spreads to more and more countries, living standards are rising, in some cases at a rapid rate. As people attain higher incomes, they consume more resources. So not only are there more people in the world, but many of those people are consuming increasing quantities of resources.

Most economists believe that the technology and resources available at the beginning of the twenty-first century could not possibly support the world's population at a standard of living equal to that currently enjoyed by the average European family. To do so, for example, the annual consumption of oil would have to increase more than ten-fold. It seems evident that resources and our present capacity to cope with pollution and environmental degradation are insufficient to accomplish this rise in living standards with our present technology.

Most economists, however, agree that *absolute* limits to growth, based on the assumptions of constant technology and fixed resources, are not relevant. As modern growth theory stresses, technology changes continually, as do stocks of resources. For example, forty years ago few would have thought that the world could produce enough food to feed its present population of around 6 billion people, let alone the 10 billion at which the population is projected to stabilize sometime in the mid-twenty-first century. Yet this task now seems feasible, and major famines are associated not with our inability to produce enough, but often with political upheavals that reduce food production and distribution well below what could be achieved by existing technology.

In the first decade of the twenty-first century the developed world is struggling not with a food shortage, but with a food glut. Farm support policies in the European Union have turned the countries of Europe into food exporters rather than food importers, as they had been in the past. The mere 3 per cent of European, US, and Canadian labour applied to limited farmland with modern technology is producing more food than the world markets can consume. The problem in the early-2000s is how to reduce subsidized production, not how to produce more.

Although globally there is enough food for everyone, severe problems arise when primarily agricultural economies suffer drought and other natural disasters, or wars and other man-made disasters. The problem then is not to produce more food worldwide, but to be sure that it is available where it is needed.

It is possible that fifty years from now the global energy problem will be as much a thing of the past as the global food shortage problem is today. Technology could by then have produced a cheap, non-polluting energy source to replace our present reliance on fossil fuels. There are many candidates, most of which are used somewhere today and require only further R&D to reduced their costs to competitive levels. These include solar energy, geothermal heat, wind power, hydrogen-based fuel cells, and possibly nuclear fusion.

The typical innovation in production processes uses less of all inputs per unit of output. Thus, technological change is part of the *solution*, as well as being part of the problem. The problem is too many people aspiring to levels of consumption that cannot be sustained *with existing technologies*.

The future is always uncertain, and it is instructive to recall how many things that we accept as commonplace today would have seemed miraculous a mere twenty-five years ago.

Yet there is surely also cause for concern. Although many barriers can be overcome by technological advances, such achievements are not instantaneous and are certainly not automatic. There is a critical problem of timing: how soon can we discover and put into practice the knowledge required to solve the problems that are made ever more imminent by the growth in the population, the affluence of the rich nations, and the aspirations of the billions who now live in poverty? There is no guarantee that a whole generation will not be caught in transition between technologies, with enormous social and political consequences.

## Renewable resources

One possible limitation to growth relates to renewable resources. The demands placed on them threaten to destroy their natural recuperative cycle. Throughout history, for example, fishermen were a small part of the predatory process. Now the demands of 6 billion people have made fish a scarce resource, threatening to destroy the fish-generating capacity of many oceans, as we saw in the case study on page 297.

## Pollution

Another major problem is how to cope with pollution. Air, water, and earth are polluted by a variety of natural activities, and through billions of years the environment has coped with these. The earth's natural processes had little trouble dealing with the pollution generated by its 1 billion inhabitants in 1800. But the 6 billion people who now exist are putting demands on pollution abatement systems that are threatening to become unsustainable. Smoke, sewage, chemical waste, hydrocarbon emissions, spent nuclear fuel, and a host of other pollutants threaten to overwhelm the Earth's natural regenerative processes. Detailed analysis of some ways in which these problems may be dealt with was given in Chapters 13 and 14.

Conscious management of pollution and renewable resources was unnecessary when the world's population was 1 billion people, but such management has become a pressing matter of survival now that over 6 billion people are seeking to live in the same space and off the world's limited resources.

### Global warming

There is no doubt that global temperatures are rising. This is already having serious consequences such as the melting of Arctic ice, the migration of sea life to different regions, threats to coral reefs worldwide, increasing infestations of tree-killing beetles whose larvae used to be controlled by winter frosts that are no longer severe enough to do the job, and rising sea levels that so far are measured in inches but could reach meters within a few decades or less.

There is debate about how much of this climate change is due to human activity in the form of greenhouse gas emissions and how much to natural causes. But the majority of those who have studied it believe that humans are a major cause, possibly *the* major cause. There is also uncertainty about what the consequences will be if no steps are taken to curtail the emissions of greenhouse gases over the next decade or two. Many feel that the

consequences could be catastrophic and could include such things as the possible inversion of the Gulf Stream, which has happened several times in pre-history. Since the Gulf Stream is what makes much of the British Isles and northern Europe habitable, the consequences would be disastrous. Another possibility is a rise in sea levels sufficient to flood much of the world's coastal regions, including most of such low-lying countries as Bangladesh and the non-volcanic Pacific islands. The social consequences of millions of displaced people desperately searching for food and shelter are hard to imagine, and one must wonder if civil authority could be maintained in the face of such dislocations. These are now only possibilties, but enough researchers take them seriously (while others doubt them) that we need to be aware of them.

While almost everyone agrees that the problem is large, there is some disagreement as to how much harm will be done by any given change in temperatures and, therefore, how many resources it is worth investing now to alleviate the warming. These disagreements matter because they create political room for those who wish not to burden industry with more regulations.

However, if the world came to accept that the consequences of leaving the current warming trend unchecked would be serious, technology is available, or could be developed, to eliminate most of these causes within decades rather than centuries—although the short-run problems could still be formidable. The problem is not, therefore, with technology, but with human assessment of the costs and benefits of doing nothing versus adopting various costly prevention programmes now.

It is conceivable that we will so mismanage these problems as to destroy growth for a long time to come and even reduce living standards by large amounts. But if we do so, it will not be because the problems are unsolvable technologically. Humans are technological animals, and there are no practical limits to new technological knowledge. If we do create environmental disasters, it will more likely be because we have been unwilling to face up to our problems, or to create the institutions necessary to deal with them, or any number of other social, political, or psychological reasons—but not because solving them is technically impossible. (Note that a 'solution' might include abandoning the use of a particular technology because its harmful side-effects cannot be eliminated.)

One major caveat to this argument is that no one can rule out the possibility that our productive activities will produce some catastrophic effect, with a sufficient lag between cause and effect that, by the time the effect is understood, it is too late to remove the cause—or that a sudden 'phase state shift' will produce disastrous results faster than any reaction is possible, even with the most enlightened policy-makers. So the probability of such future events cannot be reduced to zero by foreseeable technological means. They are part of the uncertainties involved in technological change. But so far they have not been large enough to stop growth.

 # CASE STUDIES

## 1. A comparison of US and European growth performance

One of the big puzzles in growth experience is why European economic growth has been slower that US growth in recent years. One element of the story is the relatively slow rate of productivity growth in Europe. The following is an extract of a speech made by the President of the European Central Bank on this subject.

*The economic well being of the European people, as elsewhere, depends on a number of factors, but one fundamental factor is represented by the amount of goods and services that are available on average for each of us, that is, real output per capita. Let me discuss the development of this key macroeconomic measure for the euro area and the forces which can explain its evolution.*

*A comparative perspective with developments in the US can offer useful insights. Indeed, from a long term perspective, a comparison of real output per capita developments between the euro area and the US is not always unfavourable for Europe. For example, since the early 1960s real output per capita growth has been on average slightly higher in the euro area than in the US. From 1980 onwards developments have been on average similar, with real output per capita growth being on average just below 2 per cent in both economic areas. However, these average figures conceal very different patterns. While in the euro area real output per capita growth has been gradually declining over the past four decades from almost 5 per cent during the 1960s to just below 2 per cent in the 1990s, in the US it declined slightly between the 1960s and 1970s but then stabilised in the two subsequent decades from just below 3 per cent in the 1960s to just above 2 per cent in the 1970s, 1980s and 1990s. Hence, while up to the 1970s average real output per capita growth was higher in the euro area, in the 1980s it was similar and in the 1990s it became lower. More recently, since the mid-90s, while in the euro area trend real output per capita growth continued gradually to decline, in the US it even started to increase. As a result of these relative growth patterns, the level of euro area real output per capita which was gradually catching up with the US level up to the early 1980s [from about 55 per cent in 1960 to just above 70 per cent in the early 1980s] appeared to stop converging and then, since mid 1990s, the relative level has slightly started to fall again.*

## Productivity is the key to prosperity

*What then can explain these different output per capita growth patterns? There are various immediate sources of output per capita growth. These can be classified into three main categories: labour productivity, labour utilisation and demographic factors. Labour utilisation, which depends on factors such as average hours worked, the unemployment rate and the participation rate, can explain a significant part of the growth dynamics reviewed. For example, average hours worked have been declining during most of the past 40 years in the euro area, although in the recent decade to a lesser extent. By contrast, in the US after declining up to the 1980s, they have been broadly stable. As a result, while in 1970 euro area workers were working about the same number of hours per person as US workers, by 2004 we are working just 85 per cent of what North-American are doing. Moreover, despite some recent improvements in the most recent decade, the unemployment rate is significantly higher in the euro area and has declined less since the mid-1990s than in the US. By contrast, the participation rate has been increasing more strongly in the euro area than in the US since the 1990s, but this was possibly due to the significantly lower initial level of participation we had in the euro area. Also demographic factors, in particular the gradual process of ageing of the population, have been relevant and will undoubtedly become an important challenge, looking ahead.*

*However, I would like to focus today on labour productivity. There are good reasons to focus mainly on this factor of growth. We know, since at least the pioneering contributions of Professor Robert Solow to growth theory in the late 1950s, that productivity growth is the key factor to long term economic growth.*

*For the euro area this is confirmed by the fact that almost all of the average growth in real output per capita was determined by labour productivity growth in all of the past four decades, while the contribution from labour utilisation has been most often negative and demographic factors—or the changing age structure—have provided a very modest contribution in most decades since 1960, which turned even negative in the 1990s. Similarly, also for the US, labour productivity growth has been the main driving force of real output per capita growth in the past few decades, although on average to a lesser extent compared to the euro area.*

As regards labour productivity growth, from a longer term perspective the euro area and the US have one aspect in common: a decline in average productivity growth after the early 1970s. Unfortunately, while the stylised facts characterising this productivity growth slowdown are well documented, its causes are still debated. Various possible explanations have been proposed, ranging from sectoral shifts, to the impact of the oil shocks of the 1970s, to increasing measurement problems. However, none seems to provide a fully satisfactory interpretation.

More recently, labour productivity growth developments have diverged between the euro area and the US. While on average productivity growth was broadly unchanged between the 1980s and the first half of the 1990s, both in the euro area and the US, a substantial change can be observed in the second half of the 1990s.

In the euro area, average productivity growth (measured in terms of output per hour worked), after growing on average by about 2.5% from 1980 to 1995, declined to just above 1.5% in the period 1995–2000 and further to just above 1.0% on average in the period 2000–2004. By contrast in the US, growth in productivity per hour worked, after averaging just below 1.5% from 1980 to 1995, rose to an average of just below 2% in the period 1995–2000 and to just below 3% over the period 2000–2004. This rise in the US may partly reflect cyclical factors, but the apparent resilience of productivity growth during the past downturn and the significant further pick-up over the last two years tends to support the widespread view that the mid-1990s marked a structural improvement in US productivity growth.

I should note that the assessment that productivity growth in the euro area has fallen behind the US in the second half of the 1990s is independent of the way labour productivity growth is measured. Downward trends in productivity growth are observed for the euro area irrespective of whether productivity is measured per person employed or per hour worked. However, it is worth noting that due to the trend decline in average hours worked in the euro area (in contrast to stable hours in the US), the productivity growth gap with the US is more marked in terms of employed persons than in terms of hours worked.

Given then this striking recent divergence, it is worthwhile to focus on productivity developments since the mid-1990s.

## Proximate causes of labour productivity growth divergences

The decline in euro area labour productivity growth since the mid-1990s can be discussed in terms of its main immediate sources, i.e. total factor productivity growth, changes in labour quality and capital deepening.

Total factor productivity is a measure that corresponds to the theoretical concept of technological progress. However, in practice it captures the impact of several factors (such as improvements in organization and in the quality of capital), such that it is not immediate to associate its evolution to purely technological advances. Capital deepening is the increase in capital intensity, which is the amount of capital per unit of labour input.

Although the decomposition of labour productivity is subject to significant measurement uncertainty, there seems to be robust evidence that slower productivity growth in the euro area since the mid-1990s reflects both less capital deepening and lower growth in total factor productivity. During the period 1995–2000, capital deepening was only half of that observed over the period 1990–1995, hence accounting for a large part of the slowdown in aggregate labour productivity growth. While increases in Information and Communication Technology (ICT) investment are estimated to have had a positive, albeit limited, effect on the contribution of ICT capital deepening since the mid-1990s, this was more than compensated for by lower capital deepening in non-ICT. Available evidence also suggests that labour quality increased more moderately in recent years than in the first half of the 1990s.

Comparing the factors driving US labour productivity growth shows striking differences. The increasing contributions from ICT capital deepening and total factor productivity since the mid-1990s stand in stark contrast to developments in the euro area and results from accelerating investment in ICT and a higher growth in measured total factor productivity in the US. In fact, the shares of ICT investment in GDP and the pace of ICT capital deepening were both higher in the US, thus contributing to the labour productivity growth gap between the two economic areas. Diverging trends in total factor productivity growth are also remarkable, with the US showing significant improvements in recent years.

The decomposition of labour productivity growth per hour worked at the sectoral level sheds more light on the different developments in labour productivity growth in the euro area and the US. The main features of sectoral productivity contributions can be summarised as follows.

First, a significant deceleration in hourly labour productivity in non-ICT sectors from the first half of the 1990s explains most of the decline in euro area aggregate labour productivity growth over the late 1990s.

Second, productivity developments in the ICT producing sectors were in recent years relatively strong in the euro area, and even outperformed slightly the US in the segment of ICT producing services (software, computer and communication services). However, this sector represents a smaller share of the economy in the euro area than in the US, which implies that positive developments had a more limited impact on aggregate productivity in the euro area.

Third, the ICT using sectors in the euro area failed to experience the strong acceleration in labour productivity observed in the US in recent years. In particular, key ICT using services such as retail, wholesale and financial services saw broadly stable, or slightly lower, productivity growth in recent years in the euro area. At the same time productivity growth in these sectors surged in the US. This accounts for a large part of the difference in aggregate productivity growth between the euro area and the US [of around 1ppt] over the period 1996–2002. (Speech by Jean-Claude Trichet, President of the ECB, Annual Dinner Lloyd's, London, 10 November 2005; at http://www.ecb.int/press/key/date/2005/html/sp051110.en.html)

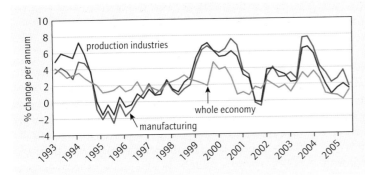

**Figure 26.4** UK productivity per hour, 1993–2005

Quarterly observations on annual rates of growth

*Source*: ONS, www.statistics.gov.uk

## 2. UK productivity growth

There are many different ways of measuring productivity growth, and different measures often tell different stories. In Figure 18.3 on page 418 we showed UK productivity growth measured as the rate of increase of real GDP per worker. This is one possible measure of labour productivity. However, it has at least two limitations. First, changes in output per worker could be due to each worker working longer hours rather than working more productively in the hours worked. Second, it does not allow for the fact that workers could be producing more output because they have more capital to work with, rather than being more productive in their own right.

The first problem can be handled by measuring instead output per hour worked. Figure 26.4 shows the growth rate of output per hour worked in UK manufacturing, in production industries (of which manufacturing is a significant subset) and in the whole economy. The latter, which is dominated by service industries, is generally slow but stable, while productivity growth in production industries is quite volatile and, apart from a period of decline in the mid-1990s, generally higher than that for the whole economy. This makes sense, because in production industries capital can enhance labour productivity more effectively than it can in service industries, many of which are necessarily more labour-intensive.

International comparisons of labour productivity can look very different depending upon whether output per worker or output per hour is used. For example, taking the UK as an index base of 100, in France in 2004 output per worker was 111, but output per hour was 129. This suggests that French workers work relatively few hours but are relatively more productive in each hour worked. In contrast, on the same basis, US output per worker was 127 but output per hour worked was only 116. This suggests that US workers work relatively more hours but are relatively less productive than the French for each hour worked.

The second problem mentioned above can be handled by measuring what is called 'total factor productivity' (TFP) rather than just labour productivity. This requires an index of the combination of labour and capital inputs relative to output (where the weights reflect the proportions of each input in the aggregate production function). The measurement of TFP is not straightforward,[14] and no official estimates are available for the UK (but some estimates are provided in the source mentioned in footnote 14).

Differences between the growth of output and the increase that can be explained by the growth of inputs are referred to as the 'Solow residual'. Some have tried to use the size of the Solow residual as a direct measure of technical progress, and this has given rise to what is sometimes called the *productivity paradox*. Solow (1987) himself has given apparent support for this paradox in his quote that 'You can see the computer age everywhere but in the productivity statistics.' While it is true, at least in the UK data, that there appears to be no big upturn in productivity growth by any of the available measures (either labour productivity or TFP), productivity growth by any measure remains positive and over time the cumulative effects of this on real incomes are substantial. It is also true that the relative productivity performance of the UK, on official measures (such as quoted above), is behind that of some competitors, such as France and the United States, but it is ahead of Japan and about equal with Germany, and it had improved in the international productivity league tables in 2004 in comparison with its position a decade earlier.

It is also important to note that, while TFP growth is a by-product of technical change, it is not a direct measure of such technical change. This means that the production implications of new technologies may take many years or even decades to produce results in output terms. So it is a mistake, for example, to downplay the significance of the ICT revolution on the basis that it has not shown up in the productivity data. Technical change in the ICT sector is undoubtedly rapid, but only time will tell what the implications of this might be for productivity.

---

[14] See 'Measuring total factor productivity for the United Kingdom', *Bank of England Quarterly Bulletin*, Spring 2004; available at: http://www.bankofengland.co.uk/publications/quarterlybulletin/qb040106.pdf

# Conclusion

Growth has raised the average citizens of advanced countries from poverty to plenty in the course of two centuries —a short time in terms of human history. Yet the world still faces many problems. Starvation and poverty are the common lot of citizens in many countries and are not unknown in the European Union and the United States, where average living standards are high. Further growth is needed if people in less developed countries are to escape material poverty, and further growth would help advanced countries to deal with many of their pressing economic problems. (The problems of producing growth in less developed countries are further considered in material available on our website www.oxfordtextbooks.co.uk/orc/lipsey11e/)

Rising population and rising per capita consumption, however, put pressure on the world's natural ecosystems, especially through pollution and congestion. Further growth must be sustainable growth, which in turn must be based on idea-driven technological change. Past experience suggests that new technologies will use less of all resources per unit of output. However, if they are to reduce dramatically the demands placed on the Earth's ecosystems, price and policy incentives will be needed to direct technological change in more 'environmentally friendly' ways. Just as present technologies are much less polluting than the technologies of 100 years ago, the technologies of the twenty-first century must be made much less polluting than today's.

There is no guarantee that the world will solve the problems of sustainable growth, but there is nothing in modern growth theory and existing evidence to suggest that such an achievement is impossible.

# SUMMARY

### Growth and cycles

- Growth theory studies the long-term trend in real output and living standards, while macroeconomics studies cycles about the trend.

- Growth is the most important determinant of changes in living standards over time.

### Benefits and costs of growth

- The most important benefit of growth lies in its contribution to the long-run struggle to raise living standards and to escape poverty. The cumulative effects of what may appear to be small growth rates become large over periods of a decade or more.

- Small differences in national growth rates can cumulate into large national differences in living standards over a few decades.

- It is easier to redistribute income in a growing society than in a static one.

- The opportunity cost of growth is the diversion of resources from current consumption to capital formation. For individuals who are left behind in a rapidly changing world, the costs can be high and more personal.

### Theories of economic growth

- The aggregate neoclassical model displays diminishing returns when one input is increased on its own, and constant returns when all inputs are increased together. In a balanced growth path, labour, capital, and national output all increase at a constant rate, leaving living standards unchanged. When labour-augmenting productivity growth occurs, a balanced growth path is consistent with rising per capita output and income.

- In the long term, technological change is the major cause of growth together with the new capital investment that is needed to embody new technologies. Modern growth theory treats technological change as an endogenous variable that responds to market signals. The diffusion of technology is also endogenous. It is costly and often proceeds at a relatively slow pace.

- Some modern growth theories display increasing returns as investment increases on its own. This is because investment creates externalities so that successive increments of investment may add constant or even successively *increasing* amounts to total output.

- The critical importance of increasing knowledge and new technology to the goal of sustaining growth is highlighted by the great drain on existing natural resources that has resulted from the explosive growth of population and output in recent decades. Without continuing technological change, the present needs and aspirations of the world's population cannot come anywhere close to being met.

### Are there limits to growth?

- Rising population and rising real incomes place pressure on resources. Although resources in general will not be exhausted, particular resources, such as petroleum, will be. Furthermore, resources that renewed themselves without help from humans when the world's population was 1 billion people will be exhausted unless they are consciously conserved, now that the world's population exceeds 6 billion.

■ The enormous increase in population also creates severe problems of pollution. The Earth's environment could cope naturally with most of the pollution caused by humans two hundred years ago, but the present population is so large that pollution has outstripped nature's coping mechanisms in many cases. Technological advance is needed to reduce the amount of pollution created by each unit of output.

## TOPICS FOR REVIEW

■ Short-run and long-run effects of investment and saving
■ Cumulative nature of growth
■ Benefits and costs of growth
■ Neoclassical aggregate production function
■ Balanced growth

■ Endogenous technical change
■ Increasing returns to investment
■ Embodied and disembodied technical change
■ Economics of goods and of ideas
■ Resource depletion and pollution

## QUESTIONS

1 GDP per head of population in the UK in 2005 was a fraction under £21,000. Supposing that there is no inflation and zero population growth, what will GDP per head be in 2015, 2025, and 2035 if the rate of economic growth continues at its long-term trend rate of 2 per cent per annum?

2 How would your answers to question 1 change if the average rate of growth over these periods rose to: (a) 3 per cent? (b) 4 per cent? (c) 5 per cent?

3 Using the actual data for GDP growth in Table 15.4 on page 349 and the GDP per head figure for 2005 given in question 1, and assuming the same population as today, calculate the real GDP per head in 1900 (at 2005 prices). In reality, the UK population was about 41 million in 1900,

and it grew to about 59 million in 2005. Recalculate your figure for real GDP per head in 1900 using this information.

4 Outline the costs and benefits of economic growth.

5 What actions could (a) governments, (b) firms, and (c) individuals take to increase the rate of economic growth?

6 What are the main determinants of economic growth?

7 List products that you use regularly that were not available when (a) your parents, and (b) your grandparents were born. What does the process of product innovation tell us about the nature of economic growth?

8 Must economic growth inevitably come to an end when various non-renewable energy (and commodity) sources are depleted?

# Chapter 27

# INTERNATIONAL TRADE

Do imports of goods made with cheap foreign labour destroy jobs at home? Is globalization making us worse off? Should our government subsidize domestic industries to help them compete internationally? Should we restrict imports of goods made in countries where working conditions are worse than our own? These are some of the questions we address in this chapter.

In particular, you will learn that:

- Gains from trade result from comparative advantage, which arises whenever there are differences in opportunity costs of production.
- Terms of trade determine how the gains from trade are distributed.
- Free trade tends to maximize world income.
- Protectionism may make one country better off, but it tends to make the world as a whole worse off.
- The World Trade Organisation polices world trade rules and the commercial policies of member governments.
- Regional free trade areas and common markets bring efficiency gains through trade creation and efficiency losses through trade diversion.

Sales and purchases of goods and services that take place across international boundaries are referred to as *international trade*. For example, the British buy BMWs made in Germany, Germans take holidays in Italy, Italians buy spices from Tanzania, Belgians import oil from Kuwait, Egyptians buy Japanese cameras, the Japanese depend heavily on American soybeans as a source of food, and the Taiwanese make many electronic goods whose parts are manufactured throughout Southeast Asia.

There is substantial evidence to show that international trade and economic growth are positively linked. In this chapter we explain why trade increases output and incomes. We then ask why, if trade is generally beneficial, governments have often attempted to restrict the freedom to trade. Finally, we discuss some of the institutional arrangements that affect world trade.[1]

## Sources of the gains from trade

An economy that engages in international trade is an **open economy**. One that does not is a **closed economy**. A situation in which a country does no foreign trade is called **autarky**. The advantages realized as a result of trade are called the **gains from trade**. Although politicians often regard foreign trade as different from domestic

trade, economists from Adam Smith on have argued that the causes and consequences of international trade are simply an extension of the principles governing domestic

---

[1] We focus in this chapter on the general issue of trade, but we provide a more detailed discussion of how trade affects developing countries on our website www.oxfordtextbooks.co.uk/orc/lipsey11e/

trade. What is the benefit from trade among individuals, among groups, among regions, or among countries?

## Interpersonal, interregional, and international trade

Let us start by thinking about trade between individuals. Without trade, each person would have to be self-sufficient; each would have to produce all the food, clothing, shelter, medical services, entertainment, and luxuries that she consumed. A world of individual self-sufficiency would be a world with extremely low living standards.

Trade between individuals allows people to specialize in those activities they can do relatively well and to buy from others the goods and services they themselves cannot easily produce. A good doctor who is a bad carpenter can provide medical services not only for her own family, but also for an excellent carpenter who lacks the training or the ability to practise medicine. Thus, trade and specialization are intimately connected. Without trade, everyone must be self-sufficient. With trade, everyone can specialize in what she does well and satisfy other needs by trading.

The same principles apply to regions. Without interregional trade, each region would be forced to be self-sufficient. With trade, each region can specialize in producing goods or services for which it has some natural or acquired advantage. Plains regions can specialize in growing grain, mountain regions can specialize in mining and forest products, and regions with abundant manpower can specialize in manufacturing. Cool regions can produce dairy products, wool, and crops that thrive in temperate climates, and hot regions can grow such tropical crops as rice, cotton, bananas, sugar, and coffee. Places with lots of sunshine and sandy beaches can specialize in the tourist trade. The living standards of the inhabitants of all regions will be higher when each region specializes in products in which it has some natural or acquired advantage and obtains other products by trade than when all regions seek to be self-sufficient.

The same principle applies to nations. Nations, like regions or persons, can gain from specialization. Almost all countries produce more of some goods than their residents wish to consume. At the same time, they consume more than they produce of some other goods.

International trade is necessary to achieve the gains that international specialization makes possible. Trade allows each individual, region, or nation to concentrate on producing those goods and services that it produces relatively efficiently, while trading to obtain goods and services that it would produce less efficiently than others.

Specialization and trade go hand in hand, because there is no motivation to achieve the gains from specialization without being able to trade the goods produced for the different goods desired. The term 'gains from trade' encompasses the results of both. This was first discussed in Chapter 1, and it would be worth rereading now pages 9–11 and Box 1.3.

There are three main sources of gains from trade. The first is those differences between regions of the world in climate and resource endowment that lead to advantages in producing certain goods and disadvantages in producing others. These gains would occur even if each country's costs of production were unchanged by the existence of trade. The second source is the reduction in each country's costs of production resulting from the greater production that specialization brings. The third is the international competition, which usually promotes more rapid technological change and economic growth than would occur if domestic firms produced solely for a protected home market.

## Gains from specialization with given costs

In order to focus on differences in countries' conditions of production, suppose that each country's average costs of production are constant. We will use an example below involving only two countries and two products, but the general principles apply as well to the real-world case of many countries and many products.

### Absolute advantage

Box 1.3 on page 10 described the simple case of absolute advantage. One region is said to have an **absolute advantage** over another in the production of good X when an equal quantity of resources can produce more X in the first region than in the second. If we rename the individuals in Box 1.3 as countries, we see what is obvious. Total production can be increased if each country specializes in producing the product for which it has an absolute advantage.

These gains from specialization make possible the gains from trade. If consumers in both countries are to get the goods they desire in the required proportions, each must export some of the commodity in which it specializes and import commodities in which other countries are specialized.

### Comparative advantage

When each country has an absolute advantage over others in a product, the gains from trade are obvious. But what if one country can produce all commodities more efficiently than other countries? In essence this was the question that English economist David Ricardo (1772–1823) posed 200 years ago. His answer underlies the *theory of comparative advantage*, which is still accepted by economists today as a valid statement of the potential gains from trade.

The gains from specialization and trade depend on the pattern of comparative rather than absolute advantage. Although this point was illustrated in Box 1.3, it is important enough to justify another example. Let us assume that there are two economies, the United States and the European Union. Both produce the same two goods, wheat and cloth, but the opportunity costs of producing these two products differ between countries. Recall from Chapter 1 that the *opportunity cost* in production is given by the slope of the production possibility frontier, and it tells us how much of one good we have to give up in order to produce one more unit of the other. For the moment we assume that this opportunity cost is constant in each country at all combinations of outputs.

For the purposes of our example, we assume that the opportunity cost of producing 1 kilogram of wheat is 0.60 metre of cloth in the United States and 2 metres of cloth in the European Union. These data are summarized in Table 27.1. The second column of this table gives the same information again but expressed as the opportunity cost of 1 metre of cloth (so the numbers there are the reciprocals of the numbers in the first column).

The sacrifice of cloth involved in producing wheat is much lower in the USA than it is in the EU. World wheat production could be increased if the USA rather than the EU produced it. Looking at cloth production, we can see that the loss of wheat involved in producing one unit of cloth is lower in the EU than in the USA. World cloth production could be increased if the EU rather than the

### Table 27.2 Gains from specialization with differing opportunity costs

| | Changes from each producing one more unit of the product in which it has the lower opportunity cost | |
| --- | --- | --- |
| | Wheat (kg) | Cloth (metres) |
| USA | +1.0 | −0.6 |
| EU | −0.5 | +1.0 |
| Total | +0.5 | +0.4 |

**Whenever opportunity costs differ between countries, specialization can increase the production of both products.** These calculations show that there are gains from specialization given the opportunity costs of Table 27.1. To produce one more kilogram of wheat, the USA must sacrifice 0.6 m of cloth. To produce one more metre of cloth, the EU must sacrifice 0.5 kg of wheat. Making both changes raises world production of both wheat and cloth.

USA produced it. The gains from a US shift towards wheat production and an EU shift towards cloth production are shown in Table 27.2.

**The gains from trade arise from differing opportunity costs in the two countries.**

The slope of the production possibility boundary indicates the opportunity costs, and the existence of different opportunity costs implies comparative advantages and disadvantages that can lead to gains from trade. Figure 27.1 illustrates how two countries can both gain from trade when they have different opportunity costs in production and the opportunity costs are independent of the level of production. An alternative diagrammatic illustration of the gains from trade appears in Box 27.1, where the production possibility frontier is concave (which means that opportunity cost varies with the composition of output).

Conclusions about the gains from trade arising from international differences in opportunity costs can now be summarized.

1. Country A has a *comparative advantage* over country B in producing a product when the opportunity cost (in terms of some other product) of production in country A is lower. This implies, however, that it has a comparative disadvantage in the other product.

2. Opportunity costs depend on the relative costs of producing two products, not on absolute costs.

3. When opportunity costs are the same in all countries, there is no comparative advantage and there is no possibility of gains from specialization and trade.

### Table 27.1 Opportunity cost of wheat and cloth in the USA and the EU

| | Wheat (kg) (1) | Cloth (metres) (2) |
| --- | --- | --- |
| USA | 0.60 m cloth | 1.67 kg wheat |
| EU | 2.00 m cloth | 0.50 kg wheat |

**Comparative advantages reflect opportunity costs that differ between countries.** Column (1) expresses opportunity cost per kilogram of wheat. Column (2) expresses the same information in terms of a metre of cloth. The USA has a comparative advantage in wheat production, the EU in cloth.

**Box 27.1** Gains from trade with varying opportunity costs

International trade leads to an expansion in the set of goods that can be consumed in the economy in two ways: by allowing the bundle of goods consumed to differ from the bundle produced, and by permitting a profitable change in the pattern of production. Without international trade, the bundle of goods produced is the bundle consumed. With international trade, the consumption and production bundles can be altered independently to reflect the relative values placed on goods by international markets.

The graphical demonstration of the gains from trade proceeds in two stages.

### Stage 1: fixed production

In each part of the figure the pink curve is the economy's production possibility boundary. If there is no international trade, the economy must consume the same bundle of goods that it produces. Thus, the production possibility boundary is also the consumption possibility boundary. (In contrast to Figure 27.1, opportunity cost here varies along the boundary.) Suppose the economy produces, and consumes, at point $a$, with $x_1$ of good X and $y_1$ of good Y, as in part (i) of the figure.

Next suppose that, with production point $a$, good Y can be exchanged for good X internationally. The consumption possibilities are now shown by the line $tt$ drawn through point $a$. The slope of $tt$ indicates the quantity of Y that exchanges for a unit of X on the international market.

Although production is fixed at $a$, consumption can now be anywhere on the line $tt$. For example, the consumption point could be at $b$. This could be achieved by exporting $y_1 - y_2$ units of Y and importing $x_2 - x_1$ units of X. Since point $b$ (and all others on

line $tt$ to the right of $a$) lies outside the production possibility boundary, there are potential gains from trade. Consumers are no longer limited by their country's production possibilities. Let us suppose they prefer point $b$ to point $a$. They have achieved a gain from trade by being allowed to exchange some of their production of good Y for some quantity of good X and thus to consume more of good X than is produced at home.

### Stage 2: variable production

There is a further opportunity for the expansion of the country's consumption possibilities: with trade the production bundle may be profitably altered in response to international prices. The country may produce the bundle of goods that is most valuable in world markets. This is represented by the bundle $d$ in part (ii). The consumption possibility set is shifted to the line $t't'$ by changing production from $a$ to $d$ and thereby increasing the country's degree of specialization in good Y. For every point on the original consumption possibility set, $tt$, there are points on the new set, $t't'$, which allow more consumption of both goods; compare points $b$ and $f$, for example. Notice also that, except at the zero-trade point, $d$, the new consumption possibility set lies everywhere above the production possibility curve.

The benefits of moving from a no-trade position such as $a$ to a trading position such as $b$ or $f$ are the gains from trade to the country. When the production of good Y is increased and the production of good X decreased, the country is able to move to a point such as $f$ by producing more of good Y, in which the country has a comparative advantage, and trading the additional production for good X.

(i) Stage 1: fixed production

(ii) Stage 2: variable production

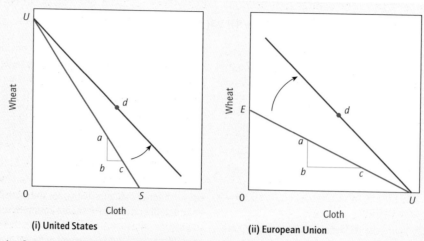

**Figure 27.1 Gains from trade with constant opportunity costs**

**International trade leads to specialization in production and increased consumption possibilities.** The blue lines in parts (i) and (ii) represent the production possibility boundary for the United States and the European Union, respectively. In the absence of any international trade, these also represent each country's consumption possibilities.

The difference in the slopes of the production possibility boundaries reflects differences in comparative advantage, as shown in Table 27.1. In each part the opportunity cost of increasing production of wheat by the same amount (measured by the distance *ba*) is the amount by which the production of cloth must be reduced (measured by the distance *bc*). The relatively steep production possibility boundary for the United States thus indicates that the opportunity cost of producing wheat in the United States is less than that in the European Union.

If trade is possible at some terms of trade between the two countries' opportunity costs of production, each country will specialize in the production of the good in which it has a comparative advantage. In each part of the figure, production occurs at *U*; the United States produces only wheat, and the EU produces only cloth.

Consumption possibilities are given by the pink line that passes through *U* and has a slope equal to the terms of trade. Consumption possibilities are increased in both countries; consumption may occur at some point such as *d* that involves a combination of wheat and cloth that was not obtainable in the absence of trade.

4. When opportunity costs differ in any two countries, and both countries are producing both products, it is always possible to increase production of both products by a suitable reallocation of resources within each country.

## Gains from specialization with variable costs

So far, apart from in Box 27.1, we have assumed that unit costs are the same whatever the scale of output, and we have seen that there are gains from specialization and trade as long as there are interregional differences in opportunity costs. If costs vary with the level of output, or as experience is acquired via specialization, *additional* sources of gain are possible.

### Scale and imperfect competition

Real production costs, measured in terms of resources used, often fall as the scale of output increases. The larger the scale of operations, the more efficiently large-scale machinery can be used and the more efficient the division of labour that is possible. Smaller countries such as Switzerland, Belgium, and Israel, whose domestic markets are not large enough to exploit economies of scale, would find it prohibitively expensive to become self-sufficient by producing a little bit of everything at very great cost.

Trade allows smaller countries to specialize and produce a few products at high enough levels of output to reap the available economies of scale.

One of the important lessons learned from patterns of world trade since the Second World War results from imperfect competition and product differentiation. Virtually all of today's manufactured consumer goods are produced in multiple differentiated product lines. In some industries many firms produce this range; in others only a few firms produce the entire product range. In both cases firms are not price-takers, and they do not exhaust all available economies of scale, as a perfectly competitive firm would do. This means that an increase in the size of the market, even in an economy as large as the USA or the EU, may allow the exploitation of some previously unexploited scale economies in individual product lines.

These possibilities were first dramatically illustrated when the European Common Market (now called the European Union, the EU) was set up in the late 1950s. Economists had expected that specialization would occur according to the classical theory of comparative advantage, with one country specializing in, say, cars, another in refrigerators, another in fashion clothes, another in shoes, and so on. This is not the way it worked out. Instead, much of the vast growth of trade was in intra-industry trade. Today one can buy French, English, Italian, and German fashion goods, cars, shoes, appliances, and a host of other goods in the shops of London, Paris, Berlin, and Rome. Ships loaded with Swedish furniture bound for London pass ships loaded with English furniture bound for Stockholm; and so on.

What free European trade did was to allow a proliferation of differentiated products, with different countries each specializing in differentiated sub-product lines. Consumers have shown by their expenditures that they value this enormous increase in the range of choice between differentiated products. As Asian countries have expanded into European and American markets with textiles, cars, and electronic goods, European and American manufacturers have increasingly specialized their production, and they now export textiles, cars, and electronic

equipment to Japan even while importing similar but differentiated products from Japan.

### Learning by doing

The discussion so far has assumed that costs vary only with the level of output. They may also vary with the experience accumulated in producing a good over time.

Some economists place great importance on what we now call *learning by doing*. They argue that, as countries gain experience in particular tasks, workers and managers become more efficient in performing them. As people acquire expertise, costs tend to fall. There is substantial evidence that such learning by doing does occur.

The distinction between this phenomenon and the gains from economies of scale is illustrated in Figure 27.2. This is one more example of the difference between a movement along a curve and a shift of the curve.

Recognition of the opportunities for learning by doing leads to an important implication: policy-makers need not accept *current* comparative advantages as given. Through such means as training and tax incentives, they can seek to develop new comparative advantages. Moreover, countries cannot complacently assume that their existing comparative advantages will persist. Misguided tax incentives and subsidies, or policies that discourage risk-taking, can lead to the rapid erosion of a country's comparative advantage in particular products. So, too, can developments in other countries.

  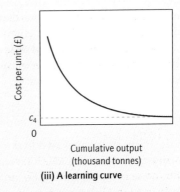

**Figure 27.2 Gains from specialization with variable costs**

Specialization may lead to gains from trade by permitting economies of larger-scale output, by leading to downward shifts of cost curves, or both. A country can produce output $q_0$ at an average cost per unit of $c_1$ and can export the quantity $q_1 - q_0$ if it produces $q_1$. This may lead to cost savings in two ways. (i) The increased level of production of $q_1$ compared with $q_0$ permits it to *move along* its cost curve, $C$, from $a$ to $b$, thereby reducing costs per unit to $c_2$. This is an economy of scale. (ii) As workers and managements learn, they may increase productivity and shift the cost curve from $C$ to $C'$. This is learning by doing. The downward *shift*, shown by the arrows, lowers the cost of producing every unit of output. At output $q_1$ costs per unit fall to $c_3$. The movement from $a$ to $b'$ incorporates both economies of scale and learning by doing.

Part (iii) shows a learning curve. This shows the relation between the costs of producing a given output per period and the total output over the whole time during which production has taken place. When all learning possibilities have been exploited, costs reach a minimum level, shown by $c_4$ in the figure.

# Trade as a source of technological change and economic growth

When countries protect their home markets with high tariffs, they reduce the amount of international competition faced by their domestic firms. This is particularly important when the countries are small so that there is room for only a few, or possibly even just one, domestic firm to serve the local market. In these circumstances, international trade can increase competitive pressures that face domestic firms. This in turn may lead to more product and process innovation than occurred under protection. Also, because firms throughout the world are innovating in both product and production processes, an open trading regime allows consumers to benefit from the many technological changes that occur in other countries as well as locally.

# Terms of trade

So far we have seen that world production can be increased when countries specialize in the production of the goods and services in which they have a comparative advantage, and then trade with one another. We now ask how these gains from specialization and trade will be shared between countries. The division of the gain depends on the **terms of trade**, which measure the quantity of imported goods that can be obtained per unit of goods exported.

A rise in the price of imported goods, with the price of exports unchanged, indicates a fall in the terms of trade; it will now take more exports to buy the same quantity of imports. Similarly, a rise in the price of exported goods, with the price of imports unchanged, indicates a rise in terms of trade; it will now take fewer exports to buy the same quantity of imports. Thus, the ratio of these prices measures the amount of imports that can be obtained per unit of goods exported.

Because actual international trade involves many countries and many products, a country's terms of trade are computed as an index number:

$$\text{Terms of trade} = \frac{\text{Index of export prices}}{\text{Index of import prices}} \times 100.$$

A rise in the index is referred to as a *favourable* change in a country's terms of trade. A favourable change means that more can be imported per unit of goods exported than previously. For example, if the export price index rises from 100 to 120 while the import price index rises from 100 to 110, the terms of trade index rises from 100 to 109. At the new terms of trade, a unit of exports will buy 9 per cent more imports than at the old terms.

A decrease in the index of the terms of trade, called an *unfavourable* change, means that the country can import less in return for any given amount of exports or, equivalently, that it must export more to pay for any given amount of imports. For example, the sharp rise in oil prices in the 1970s led to large unfavourable shifts in the terms of trade of oil-importing countries. When oil prices fell sharply in the mid-1980s, the terms of trade of oil-importing countries changed favourably. The converse was true for oil-exporting countries. Oil prices rose again in the mid-2000s. While they had been as low as $10 per barrel in 1998, they reached over $70 per barrel in 2006. An example showing falling terms of trade for coffee-exporting nations is shown on page 81.

There are two other concepts closely related to the terms of trade that we have come across before, especially in Chapter 22. These are the *real exchange rate* and *competitiveness*. They also are indexes of the relative prices of domestic and foreign goods. However, both competitiveness and the real exchange rate normally relate to the prices of domestic production relative to foreign production, while terms of trade apply just to the subset of outputs that are imported and exported.

Notice, however, an interesting ambiguity in terminology. We have said above that an improvement in the terms of trade is 'favourable'; but a rise in domestic prices relative to foreign prices could also be described as a *loss of competitiveness*. This would normally be considered 'unfavourable'. Clearly, the same event cannot switch from being good to being bad just because of what we call it. The reality is that whether a relative rise in domestic prices is good or bad depends upon why it came about. If the prices of the things we produce and sell in world markets rise because they are in high demand, then this is a good thing and we are better off for it (even though it could be described as a loss of competitiveness). However, if our prices rise because of domestic inefficiency or higher domestic wages bills, *for a given level of world demand for our output*, then we will lose sales to foreign competitors and we will be worse off.

We now turn to a discussion of the arguments for and against government intervention in international trade.

# The theory of commercial policy

Government policy towards international trade is known as **commercial policy**. Complete freedom from interference with trade is known as a **free trade** policy. Any departure from free trade designed to give some protection to domestic industries from foreign competition is called **protectionism**.

Today debates over commercial policy are as heated as they were two hundred years ago when the theory of gains from trade that we presented above was still being worked out. Should a country permit the free flow of international trade, or should it seek to protect its local producers from foreign competition? Such protection may be achieved either by **tariffs**, which are taxes designed to raise the price of foreign goods, or by **non-tariff barriers**, which are devices other than tariffs that are designed to reduce the flow of imports. Examples of the latter include quotas and customs procedures deliberately made more cumbersome than is necessary.

## The case for free trade

The case for free trade is based on the analysis presented above. We saw that *for any given set of costs*, whenever opportunity costs differ among countries, specialization and trade will raise world living standards. Free trade allows all countries to specialize in producing products in which they have a comparative advantage.

Free trade allows the maximization of world production, thus making it possible for each consumer in the world to consume more goods than she could without free trade.

This does not necessarily mean that everyone will be better off with free trade than without it. Protectionism could allow some people to obtain a larger share of a smaller world output so that they would benefit even though the average person would lose. If we ask whether it is possible for free trade to improve everyone's living standards, the answer is 'yes'. But if we ask whether free trade does in fact always do so, the answer is 'not necessarily'.

There is abundant evidence that significant differences in opportunity costs exist and that large gains are realized from international trade because of these differences. What needs explanation is the fact that trade is not wholly free. Why do tariffs and non-tariff barriers to trade continue to exist two centuries after Adam Smith and David Ricardo stated the case for free trade? Is there a valid case for protectionism?

## The case for protectionism

Two kinds of argument for protection are commonly offered. The first concerns national objectives other than total income; the second concerns the desire to increase one country's national income, possibly at the expense of world national income.

### Objectives other than maximizing national income

It is possible to accept the proposition that national income is higher with free trade, and yet rationally to oppose free trade, because of a concern with policy objectives other than that of maximizing income.

#### Non-economic advantages of diversification

Comparative advantage might dictate that a country should specialize in producing a narrow range of products. The government might decide, however, that there are distinct social advantages in encouraging a more diverse economy. Citizens would be given a wider range of occupations, and the social and psychological advantages of diversification would more than compensate for a reduction in living standards to, say, 5 per cent below what they could be with complete specialization of production according to comparative advantage.

#### Risks of specialization

For a very small country, specializing in the production of only a few products—though dictated by comparative advantage—may involve risks that the country does not wish to take. One such risk is that technological advances may render its major product obsolete. Everyone understands this risk, but there is debate over what governments can do about it. The pro-tariff argument is that the government can encourage a more diversified economy by protecting industries that otherwise could not compete. Opponents argue among other things that governments, being naturally influenced by political motives, are in the final analysis poor judges of which industries can be protected in order to produce diversification at a reasonable cost.

#### National defence

Another non-economic reason for protectionism concerns national defence. It used to be argued, for example, that the United Kingdom needed an experienced merchant navy in case of war, and that this industry should be fostered by protectionist policies even though it was less efficient than the foreign competition. The same argument is sometimes made for the aircraft industry. Agriculture has also been protected for strategic reasons in the past—we would need to feed ourselves if trade were disrupted by war. The United States does not allow foreign ships to transport cargo between its domestic ports on the grounds that a strong merchant navy, which would not exist without protection, is needed for times of war.

### Protection of specific groups

Although free trade will maximize per capita GDP over the whole economy, some specific groups may have higher incomes under protection than under free trade. An obvious example is a firm or industry that is given monopoly power when tariffs are used to restrict foreign competition. If a small group of firms, and possibly their employees, find their incomes increased by, say, 25 per cent when they get tariff protection, they may not be concerned that everyone else's incomes fall by, say, 2 per cent. They get a much larger share of a slightly smaller total income and end up better off. If they gain from the tariff, they will lose from free trade.

Tariffs tend to raise the relative income of a group of people who are in short supply domestically and to lower the relative income of a group of people who are in plentiful supply domestically. Free trade does the opposite.

### Conclusion

Other things being equal, most people prefer more income to less. Economists cannot say that it is irrational for a society to sacrifice some income in order to achieve other goals. Economists can, however, do three things when faced with such reasons for adopting protectionist measures. First, they can ask if the proposed measures really do achieve the ends suggested. Second, they can calculate the cost of the measures in terms of lowered living standards. Third, they can see if there are alternative means of achieving the stated goals at lower cost in terms of lost output.

## Maximizing national income

Here we consider five important arguments for the use of tariffs when the objective is to make national income as large as possible.

### Protection of infant industries

The oldest valid argument for protectionism as a means of raising living standards concerns economies of scale. It is usually called the **infant industry argument**.

This comes in a static and a dynamic form. The static form assumes that world technology is given and constant. If an industry has large economies of scale, costs will be high when the industry is small but will fall as the industry grows. In such industries the country first in the field has a tremendous advantage. A newly developing country may find that in the early stages of development its industries are unable to compete with established foreign rivals. A trade restriction may protect these industries from foreign competition while they grow. When they are large enough, they will be able to produce as cheaply as foreign rivals and then will be able to compete without protection.

The dynamic form emphasizes that technology is constantly changing endogenously and that those countries who are at the frontier of technological advance have an enormous advantage of experience and acquired ability in inventing and innovating over those who seek to industrialize later on. To develop these abilities, so goes the argument, a country needs to protect its domestic industries during the early stages of development. The object is not to move along a given falling long-run cost curve. Instead, it is to develop industries that will have cost curves that fall, over time, as fast as similar cost curves are falling in the advanced countries owing to invention and innovation. To prevent the new industries from becoming stagnant under the protection that shields them from foreign competition, protection must, it is argued, be contingent on achieving success in foreign markets within a stated period of time. Once they have developed the skills needed to hold their own in the intense international competition associated with new technologies, the protection can be removed. The advocates of this argument point out that virtually all the economically advanced countries developed their early industries under tariff protection. This was true of Germany and France (and to some extent also of the early English industries in the industrial revolution, which were helped by the prohibition of imports of Indian cotton goods), the United States, Canada, Australia, and New Zealand, as well as the most successful of the Asian economies, e.g. Taiwan, South Korea, and Singapore.

Those who support such polices argue that the assumption of fixed technology that is implicit in the major arguments for completely free trade is misleading in a world in which most competition is in terms of the technological change. They also point out that the argument does not deny the importance of trade: it just holds that, to take part in globalized trade as a fully developed country, early protection may be needed—for reasons found both in the theory of endogenous technological change and in the evidence of what most developed countries actually did in the early stages of their development. In so far as there is any validity in this argument, it provides a possible qualification to the proposition that free trade maximizes world income. If some limited protection actually raises the level of world innovation in new products and processes, world income may be higher with some protection than with pure free trade. What this possibility shows is that, just like all propositions that follow from economic theory, the proposition that free trade maximizes world income is open to empirical testing. It is not something that can be shown to be necessarily true in the real world by virtue of theoretical propositions alone.

### To encourage learning by doing

The dynamic version of the infant industry argument is supported by the argument based on learning by doing. Skills and other things that help to create comparative advantages are not fixed for ever: they can be learned by producing the new products if enough time is allowed for the learning to take place. Learning by doing therefore suggests that the pattern of comparative advantage can be changed. If a country learns enough through producing products in which it currently is at a comparative disadvantage, it may gain in the long run by specializing in those products, and could develop a comparative advantage as the learning process lowers their costs.

The successes of such newly industrializing countries (NICs) as Brazil, Hong Kong, South Korea, Singapore, and Taiwan are based largely on acquired skills. For example, nothing in Singapore or Taiwan in 1960—in terms of natural resources, capital, or skills—suggested that they would become major producers of state-of-the-art electronic products well before the end of the twentieth century. This type of experience provides evidence that comparative advantages can change, and that they can be developed by suitable government policies. Also, government policies created favourable business conditions and encouraged the development of specific industries that went on to develop comparative advantages—although the importance of such policies in contributing to these developments is subject to debate.

Protecting a domestic industry from foreign competition may give its management time to learn to be efficient, and its labour force time to acquire the needed skills.

If this is so, it may pay in the very long run to protect the industry against foreign competition while a dynamic comparative advantage is being developed.

Some countries have succeeded in developing strong comparative advantages in targeted industries, but others have failed. One reason such policies sometimes fail is that protecting local industries from foreign competition may make the industries unadaptive and complacent. Another reason is the difficulty of identifying the industries that will be able to succeed in the long run. All too often, the protected infant grows up to be a weakling requiring permanent tariff protection for its continued existence; or else the rate of learning is slower than for similar industries in countries that do not provide protection from the chill winds of international competition. In these instances the anticipated comparative advantage never materializes. Where such a 'picking of winners' has succeeded, it has almost always been the result of co-operation between government bodies and private sector firms, rather than civil servants picking and fostering potential winners on their own initiatives. Examples are Japan's auto industry, Taiwan's electronics industry, Singapore's software industry, and the software and semiconductor industries of the United States.

### Creation or exploitation of a strategic trade advantage

A recent argument for tariffs or other trade restrictions is that they enable the creation of a strategic advantage in producing or marketing some new product that is expected to generate profits. To the extent that all lines of production earn normal profits, there is no reason to produce goods other than ones for which a country has a comparative advantage. Some goods, however, are produced in industries containing a few large firms where large-scale economies provide a natural barrier to further entry. Firms in these industries can earn extra-high profits over long periods of time. Where such industries are already well established, there is little chance that a new firm will replace one of the existing giants.

The situation is, however, more fluid with new products. The first firm to develop and market a new product successfully may earn a substantial pure profit over all of its opportunity costs and become one of the few established firms in the industry. If protection of the domestic market can increase the chance that one of the protected domestic firms will become one of the established firms in the international market, the protection may pay off.

Many of today's high-tech industries experience declining average total cost curves because of their large fixed costs of product development. For a new generation of civilian aircraft, silicon chips, computers, software, and pharmaceuticals, a very high proportion of each producer's total costs goes on product development. These are the fixed costs of entering the market, and they must be incurred before a single unit of output can be sold. In such industries there may be room for only a few firms.

The production of full-sized commercial jet aeroplanes provides an example of an industry that possesses many of these characteristics. The development costs of a new generation of jet aircraft have risen with each new generation. If the aircraft manufacturers are to recover these costs, each of them must have large sales. Thus, the number of firms that the market can support has diminished steadily, until today there is room in the world aircraft industry for only two or three firms producing a full range of commercial jets.

The characteristics just described are sometimes used to provide arguments for subsidizing the development of such industries and/or protecting their home markets with a tariff. Suppose, for example, that there is room in the aircraft industry for only three major producers of the next round of passenger jets. If a government assists a domestic firm, this firm may become one of the three that succeed, and the profits that are subsequently earned may more than repay the cost of the subsidy. Furthermore, another country's firm, which was not subsidized, may have been just as good as the three that succeeded; without the subsidy, however, that firm may lose out in the battle to establish itself as one of the three surviving firms in the market.

This example is not unlike the story of the European Airbus. The European producers received many direct subsidies (and they charge that their main competitor, the Boeing 767, received many indirect ones). Whatever the merits of the argument, several things are clear: the civilian jet aircraft industry remains profitable; there is room for only two or three major producers; and one of these would not have been the European consortium had it not been for substantial government assistance.

Generalizing from this and similar cases, some economists advocate that their governments should adopt *strategic trade policies* more broadly than they now do. This means, for high-tech industries, government protection of the home market and government subsidization (either openly or by more subtle back-door methods) of the product development stage. These economists say that if their country does not follow their advice it will lose out in industry after industry to the more aggressive Japanese and North American competition—a competition that is adept at combining private innovative activity with government assistance.

Opponents argue that, once all countries try to be strategic, they will all waste vast sums trying to break into industries in which there is no room for most of them. Advocates of strategic trade policy reply that a country cannot afford to stand by while others play the strategic game.

Advocates also argue that there are key industries that have major 'spillovers' into the rest of the economy. If a country wants to have a high living standard, it must, they argue, compete with the best. If a country lets its key industries migrate to other countries, many of its other industries will follow. The country then risks being reduced to the status of a less developed nation.

Opponents argue that strategic trade policy is just the modern version of mercantilism, a policy of trying to enrich oneself at the expense of one's neighbours rather than looking for mutually beneficial gains from trade. They point to the rising world prosperity of the entire period following the Second World War, which has been built largely on a rising volume of relatively free international trade. There are real doubts that such prosperity could be maintained if the volume of trade were to shrink steadily because of growing trade barriers.

### Protection against 'unfair' actions by foreign firms and governments

Tariffs may be used to prevent foreign industries from gaining an advantage over domestic industries by use of predatory practices that will harm domestic industries and hence lower national income. Two common practices are subsidies paid by foreign governments to their exporters and price discrimination by foreign firms, which is called *dumping* when it is done across international borders. These practices are typically countered by levying tariffs known as countervailing and anti-dumping duties.

### Alteration of the terms of trade

Trade restrictions can be used to turn the terms of trade in favour of countries that produce, and export, a large fraction of the world's supply of some product. They can also be used to turn the terms of trade in favour of countries that constitute a large fraction of the world demand for some product that they import.

When the OPEC countries restricted their output of oil in the 1970s, they were able to drive up the price of oil relative to the prices of other traded goods. This turned the terms of trade in their favour; for every barrel of oil exported, they were able to obtain a larger quantity of imports. When the output of oil grew greatly in the mid-1980s, the relative price of oil fell dramatically, and the terms of trade turned unfavourably for the oil-exploring companies. These are illustrations of how changes in the quantities of exports can affect the terms of trade.

Now consider a country that provides a large fraction of the total demand for some product that it imports. By restricting its demand for that product through tariffs, it can force the price of that product down. This turns the terms of trade in its favour, because it can now get more units of imports per unit of exports.

Both of these techniques lower world output. They can, however, make it possible for a small group of countries to gain because they acquire a sufficiently larger share of the smaller world output. However, if foreign countries retaliate by raising their tariffs, the ensuing tariff war can easily leave every country with a lowered income.

## Conclusion

In today's world a country's products must stand up to international competition if they are to survive. Over time this requires that they hold their own in competition for successful innovations. Protection that is high enough to confer a national monopoly reduces the incentive for firms to fight to hold their own internationally. If any one country adopts high tariffs unilaterally, its domestic industries may become less competitive. Secure in its home market because of the tariff wall, the protected industries may become less and less competitive in the international market. As the gap between domestic and foreign industries widens, any tariff wall will provide less and less protection. Eventually the domestic industries will succumb to the foreign competition.

Although restrictive policies have sometimes been pursued following a rational assessment of the approximate cost, it is hard to avoid the conclusion that more often than not such policies are pursued for political objectives, or on fallacious economic grounds, with little appreciation of the actual costs involved.

One major exception to this tendency is the postwar Japanese car industry. The Japanese government protected the local market against imports and prevented foreign firms from establishing production facilities in Japan. But fierce competition among the local Japanese firms led to the development of the methods of 'lean production' which, after 20 years of internal development, allowed Japanese firms to challenge foreign automobile industries and become world leaders in the industry.

Some recent criticisms of the global trading system are discussed in Box 27.2.

## Methods of protection

We have now studied some of the many reasons why governments may wish to provide some protection for some of their domestic industries. The next task is to see how they do it. What are the tools that provide protection?

The two main types of protectionist policy are illustrated in Figure 27.3. Both cause the price of the imported good to rise and its quantity to fall. They differ, however,

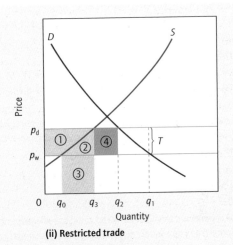

**(i) Free trade**          **(ii) Restricted trade**

**Figure 27.3 Methods of protecting domestic producers**
**The same reduction in imports can be achieved by using either a tariff or a quantity restriction.** In both parts of the figure $D$ and $S$ are the domestic demand and supply curves, respectively, and $p_w$ is the world price.

Part (i) of the figure shows the situation under free trade. Domestic consumption is $q_1$, domestic production is $q_0$, and imports are $q_0 - q_1$.

Part (ii) shows what happens when protectionist policies restrict imports to the amount $q_2 - q_3$. When this is done by levying a tariff of $T$ per unit, the price in the domestic market rises by the full amount of the tariff to $p_d$. Consumers reduce consumption from $q_1$ to $q_2$ and pay an extra amount, shown by the coloured areas 1, 2, and 4 for the $q_2$ that they now purchase. Domestic production rises from $q_0$ to $q_3$. Since domestic producers receive the domestic price, their receipts rise by the three pink areas, labelled 1, 2, and 3. Area 3 is revenue that was earned by foreign producers under free trade, while areas 1 and 2 are paid by domestic consumers because of the higher prices they now face. Foreign suppliers of the imported good continue to receive the world price, so the government receives as tariff revenue the extra amount paid by consumers for the $q_3 - q_2$ units that are still imported (shown by the blue area, 4).

When the same result is accomplished by a quantity restriction, the government—through either a quota or a *voluntary export agreement* (*VER*)—reduces imports to $q_2 - q_3$. This drives the domestic market price up to $p_d$ and has the same effect on domestic producers and consumers as the tariff. Since the government has merely restricted the quantity of imports, both foreign and domestic suppliers get the higher price in the domestic market. Thus, foreign suppliers now receive the extra amount paid by domestic consumers (represented by the blue area labelled 4) for the units that are still imported.

**Box 27.2** Anti-capitalism, anti-globalization, and fair trade

In recent years there have been many demonstrations against the World Trade Organisation (WTO), the International Monetary Fund (IMF), and the World Bank. These have been referred to as 'anti-capitalist' or 'anti-globalization' demonstrations. Some of the arguments made by the protesters are difficult to disagree with (like the desirability of reducing poverty in the poorest countries), but others are plain wrong. Virtually all economists, for example, would agree that globalization in the form of greater international trade in goods and services is both wealth- and welfare-increasing, and that closing down international trade would make the world a very much poorer place for all.

There have long been debates about free trade, and there have certainly been times when there have been doubts about whether capitalism is the best system. The collapse of communism helped to squash the latter doubts, but the case for a free and open trading system has come under renewed threat in recent years from a number of apparently rational sources.

Professor Jagdish Bhagwati of Columbia University identifies four different new critiques that question the benefits of an open trading system:

- *Demands for 'fair trade' that either mask protectionism or degenerate into it, in both cases charging that free trade lacks fairness and that fair trade restores it.*

- *Concerns that free trade harms the environment.*

- *Charges that free trade (and it chief institution, the WTO) is incompatible with the advancement of social and moral agendas.*

- *Fears that free trade hurts the real wages of workers and that rich countries trading with poor countries create poor in rich countries: and in poor countries, that free trade accentuates poverty.* (Bhagwati 2002, page 50)

Let us look at each of these issues in turn.

### Fair trade

'Fair' trade seems hard to object to—who could possibly support 'unfair' trade? One common form of this argument is similar to what used to be called 'the sweated labour fallacy'. This says that we should restrict imports from countries that have lower labour or environmental standards (in extreme cases using child labour) as this is not fair competition with domestic suppliers. However, to restrict such trade would hurt the poor country, whose best chance of reducing poverty and increasing labour standards is to export to rich countries. So this is just an excuse for protectionism and restricting the benefits that flow from comparative advantage. This is the version of fair trade that Bhagwati criticizes above.

There are two forms of the fair trade argument that are less problematic. The first is that industrial countries have pressured some developing countries to open their markets to the products of the richer countries while at the same time imposing restrictions on developing-country exports into rich-country markets. This is a case of uneven bargaining power, and the poorer countries clearly have a good case. The case for free trade has to apply to all and not in one direction only. The second argument for fair trade applies to some products like bananas and coffee, where some charitable groups argue that industrial countries' monopsony power has depressed the prices of commodities. They aim to counter these poverty-inducing low prices by offering a 'fair trade' product at a higher price, the revenues from which go to the poor-country producers. Rich-country consumers are free to buy these 'fair-trade' products as they are sold along side comparable but cheaper products in supermarkets. This form of fair trade allows people who so wish to direct charitable giving to specific producers, and there is nothing in economics to say that they should not do this. The only doubt is whether this will catch on in a big enough way to solve the underlying problem. Counteracting monopsony power in commodity markets is likely to require a stronger intervention from governments if this is the true nature of the problem. Notice, however, that our discussion of coffee prices on page 81 points out that the main problem in coffee markets is over-production.

### Trade and the environment

The environment is important for all of us and perhaps will be even more important for our children and grandchildren. Economic analysis clearly shows that free markets may not adequately protect the environment and government intervention is necessary to deliver the social optimum resource use (see pages 279–81 above). This applies to many common property resources such as fisheries and rain forests. It also applies to pollution issues like greenhouse gases and acid rain.

However, it makes no sense to address environmental problems by closing down world trade. Environmental issues should be handled directly with suitable policies to solve the problem in hand. World trade *per se* is not the cause of environmental problems. Indeed, the higher standards of living that world trade provides can be helpful in providing the extra output that takes living standards sufficiently above subsistence that quality of life is also in high demand.

### Social and moral agendas

Some politicians have sought to include a 'social clause' in the WTO rules. This would permit the use of trade sanctions against countries whose labour laws or social conventions we did not like. This is presented as a moral crusade to help poor people, but Bhagwati points out that these demands are widely seen as protectionism hiding behind a moral mask. And it is a mistake to bundle together two issues that should be dealt with by separate processes and institutions: 'By trying to kill these two birds (i.e.

---

**Box 27.2** *continued*

social agendas and free trade) with one stone (i.e. trade treaties and institutions), you are likely to miss both' (Bhagwati 2002, page 69). Rather, he argues, it is important to pursue these different goals in international agencies suited to the specific agendas for which they were set up: 'the WTO for trade liberalization, the International Labour Organization for labour standards, the UN Environment Program for environmental issues, UNICEF for children's rights, UNESCO for cultural preservation, and so on' (p. 69).

**Trade is bad for wages**

There are two elements to this argument depending on whether we are talking about workers in rich countries or poor ones. In rich countries, it is certainly true that some specific workers may be hurt if their employer loses business to cheaper imports from abroad. However, the overwhelming weight of evidence is that the growth of real GDP that is supported by growth in international trade during the past three decades or so has been associated with rising real wages for most classes of worker in the rich countries. Some have tried to argue that trade has hurt unskilled

workers in the rich countries, but the case remains unproven, as it is difficult to disentangle the effects of trade from changes in technology that have been occurring at the same time.

For the workers in poor countries, here is Bhagwati again:

*Speaking at least for India, I would say that autarky helped produce a slow average growth rate of 3.5 per cent annually for over a quarter of a century until early 1980s. During this period, it was virtually impossible to pull people up into gainful employment, and out of poverty, in a significant way. With the 1980s, the increasing pace of outward-oriented reforms has been associated with growth rates closer to 6–6.5 per cent annually; and after much controversy, there is a fair degree of consensus that poverty has been dented. Contradicting the anti-free-trade rhetoric that flows ceaselessly from the street theater and even from certain international agencies, the facts show that a shift out of autarky into closer integration into the world economy is producing better, not worse, results for poverty reduction.* (Bhagwati 2000, page 89)

---

in how they achieve these results. The caption to the figure analyses these two types of policy.

### Policies that directly raise prices

The first type of protectionist policy directly raises the *price* of the imported product. A tariff, also often called an *import duty*, is the most common policy of this type. Other such policies include any rules or regulations that fulfil three conditions: they are costly to comply with; they do not apply to competing, domestically produced products; and they are more than is required to meet any purpose other than restricting trade.

As shown in part (ii) of Figure 27.3, tariffs affect both foreign and domestic producers, as well as domestic consumers. The initial effect is to raise the domestic price of the imported product above its world price by the amount of the tariff. Imports fall, and as a result foreign producers sell less and so must transfer resources to other lines of production. The price received on domestically produced units rises, as does the quantity produced domestically. On both counts domestic producers earn more. However, the cost of producing the extra output at home exceeds the price at which it could be purchased on the world market. Thus, the benefit to domestic producers comes at the expense of domestic consumers. Indeed, domestic consumers lose on two counts: first, they consume less of the product because its price rises; and second, they pay a higher price for the amount that they do consume. This

extra spending ends up in two places: the extra that is paid on all units produced at home goes to domestic producers (partly in the resource costs of extra production and partly in profit), and the extra that is paid on units still imported goes to the government as tariff revenue.

### Policies that directly lower quantities

The second type of protectionist policy directly restricts the quantity of an imported product. Any implicit or explicit restriction on trade that does not involve a tariff is known as a **non-tariff barrier**. These can take various subtle forms, including quality standards that are complicated to interpret or customs forms that take weeks to get approved. But many non-tariff barriers are more obvious and easy to understand. A common example is the **import quota**, by which the importing country sets a maximum on the quantity of some product that may be imported each year. Increasingly popular in the recent past, however, has been the **voluntary export restriction** (VER), an agreement by an exporting country to limit the amount of a good that it sells to the importing country.

The European Union and the United States have used VERs extensively, and the EU also makes frequent use of import quotas. Japan has been pressured into negotiating several VERs with the European Union and the United States in order to limit sales of some of the Japanese goods that have had the most success in international competition. For example, in 1983 the United States and Canada negotiated VERs whereby the Japanese government agreed to restrict total sales of Japanese cars to these two countries for three years. When the agreements ran out in 1986, the Japanese continued to restrain their car sales by unilateral voluntary action. In 2005 the EU negotiated a voluntary export restraint for exports of textiles from China.

# Fallacious trade policy arguments

We saw above that there are potential gains from trade and specialization. We have also seen that there are some valid arguments for a moderate degree of protectionism for one specific country. There are also many claims that do not advance the debate. Fallacious arguments are heard on both sides, and they colour much of the popular discussion. These arguments have been around for a long time, but their survival does not make them true. We examine them now to see where their fallacies lie.

## Fallacious arguments for free trade

### Free trade always benefits all countries

This is not necessarily so. We saw above that a small group of countries may gain by restricting trade in order to get a sufficiently favourable shift in their terms of trade. Such countries would lose if they gave up these tariffs and adopted free trade unilaterally.

### Infant industries never abandon their tariff protection

It is argued that granting protection to infant industries is a mistake because these industries seldom admit to growing up, and will cling to their protection even when fully grown. But infant industry tariffs are a mistake only if these industries never grow up. In this case permanent tariff protection would be required to protect a weak industry that is never able to compete on an equal footing in the international market. But if the industries do grow up and achieve the expected scale and learning economies, the real costs of production will be reduced and resources freed for other uses. Whether or not the trade barriers remain, a cost saving has been effected by the scale economies. We have already given examples of industries that did 'grow up' to become world leaders. Examples of those that did not, in spite of substantial government protection and assistance, include the Irish steel industry, the UK computer industry, and the Japanese commercial aircraft industry.

## Fallacious arguments for protectionism

### It prevents exploitation

According to the exploitation theory, trade can never be mutually advantageous, as one trading partner must always reap a gain at the other's expense. Therefore, the weaker trading partner must protect itself by restricting its trade with the stronger partner. By showing that both parties can gain from trade, the principle of comparative advantage refutes the exploitation doctrine of trade. When opportunity-cost ratios differ in two countries, specialization and the accompanying trade make it possible to produce more of all products. This makes it possible for both parties to consume more as a result of trade than they could consume in its absence.

### It protects against low-wage foreign labour

Surely, this argument says, in industrialized nations the products of low-wage countries will drive domestic products from the market, and the high domestic standard of living will be dragged down to that of its poorer trading partners. Arguments of this sort have swayed many voters through the years.

As a prelude to considering them, stop and think what the argument would imply if taken out of the international context and put into a local one, where the same principles govern the gains from trade. Is it really impossible for a rich person to gain from trading with a poor person? Would the CEO of a high street retail chain be better off if she did all her own typing, gardening, and cooking? No one believes that a rich (and busy) person cannot gain from trading with those who are less rich (and less busy).

Why then must a rich *group* of people lose from trading with a poor group? 'Well,' some may say, 'the poor group will price their goods too cheaply.' Does anyone believe that consumers lose from buying in supermarkets just because the prices are lower there than at the old-fashioned corner shop? Consumers gain when they can buy the same goods at a lower price. If the Koreans pay low wages and sell their goods cheaply, Korean labour may suffer—but the EU will gain by obtaining imports at a low cost in terms of the goods that must be exported in return. The cheaper our imports are, the better off we are in terms of the goods and services available for domestic consumption.

Stated in more formal terms, the gains from trade depend on comparative, not absolute, advantages. World production is higher when any two areas, say the EU and Japan, specialize in the production of the goods for which they have a comparative advantage than when they both try to be self-sufficient.

Might it not be possible, however, that Japan will undersell the EU in all lines of production and thus appropriate all, or more than all, the gains for itself, leaving the EU no better off, or even worse off, than if it had no trade with Japan? The answer is no. The reason for this depends on the behaviour of exchange rates, which were discussed in

Chapter 22. As we saw in that chapter, equality of demand and supply in foreign exchange markets ensures that trade flows in both directions. The reason a country cannot import for long without exporting may also be stated intuitively as follows.

Imports can be obtained only by spending the currency of the country that produces the imports. Claims to this currency can be obtained only by exporting goods and services, or by borrowing. Thus, lending and borrowing aside, imports must equal exports. All trade must be in two directions; we can buy only if we can also sell.

In the long run, trade cannot hurt a country by causing it to import without exporting.

Trade, then, always provides scope for international specialization, with each country producing and exporting those goods for which it has a comparative advantage and importing those goods for which it does not.

### Exports raise living standards; imports lower them

Exports create domestic income and employment; imports create income and employment for foreigners. Therefore, other things being equal, exports tend to increase our total national income and imports reduce it. Surely, then, it is desirable to encourage exports by subsidizing them and to discourage imports by taxing them.

This is an appealing argument, but it is incorrect. Exports raise national income by adding to the value of domestic output, but they do not add to the value of domestic consumption. In fact, exports are goods produced at home and consumed abroad, while imports are goods produced abroad and consumed at home. The standard of living in a country depends on the goods and services available for consumption, not on what is produced.

The living standards of a country depend on the goods and services consumed in that country. The importance of exports is that they permit goods to be imported. This two-way international exchange is valuable because more goods can be imported than could be obtained if the same goods were produced at home.

### It creates domestic jobs and reduces unemployment

It is sometimes said that an economy with substantial unemployment, such as the EU in the 1990s and early 2000s, provides an exception to the case for free trade. Suppose that tariffs or import quotas cut the imports of Japanese cars, Korean textiles, US computers, and Polish vodka. Surely, the argument maintains, this will create more employment in local industries producing similar products. The answer is that it will—initially. But the Japanese, Koreans, Americans, and Poles can buy from the EU only if they earn euros by selling things to (or by borrowing euros from) the EU. The decline in their sales of cars, textiles, computers, and vodka will decrease their purchases of Spanish vegetables, French wine, and holidays in Greece. Jobs will be lost in EU export industries, and gained in those industries that formerly faced competition from imports. The likely long-term effect is that overall employment will not be increased but merely redistributed among industries. In the process, living standards will be reduced because employment expands in inefficient import-competing industries and contracts in efficient exporting industries.

Industries and unions that compete with imports often favour protectionism, while those with large exports usually favour more trade. Protection is an ineffective means to reduce unemployment.

## Global commercial policy

We now consider the supranational influences on commercial policy in the world today. We start with the many international agreements that govern current commercial policies and then look in a little more detail at the European Union.

Before 1947 most countries were free to impose any tariffs on its imports. However, when one country increased its tariffs, the action often triggered retaliatory actions by its trading partners. The Great Depression of the 1930s saw a high-water mark of world protectionism, as each country sought to raise its employment by raising its tariffs. The end result was lowered efficiency, less trade—but no increase in employment. Since that time, much effort has been devoted to reducing tariff barriers, on both a multilateral and a regional basis.

### The GATT and the WTO

One of the most notable achievements of the postwar era was the creation of the General Agreement on Tariffs and Trade (GATT). The principle of the GATT was that each member country agreed not to make unilateral tariff increases. This prevented the outbreak of tariff wars in which countries raise tariffs to protect particular domestic

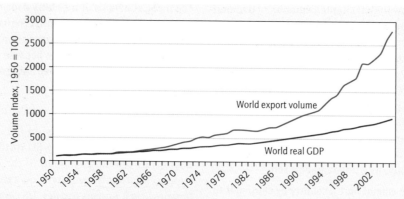

**Figure 27.4** World real GDP and export volume, 1950–2005

**Trade has grown more than GDP in the postwar period.** Since 1950 world real GDP had risen nearly ten-fold while export volume has risen twenty-eight-fold.

*Sources*: IMF, *International Financial Statistics* (online database and various issues of the publication itself).

industries and to retaliate against other countries' tariff increases. Such wars usually harm all countries as mutually beneficial trade shrinks under the impact of escalating tariff barriers.

There were eight 'rounds' of global trade talks under the GATT, beginning in 1948 and ending in 1993. The three most recently completed rounds of GATT agreements, the Kennedy round (completed 1967), the Tokyo round (completed 1979), and the Uruguay round (completed 1993), each reduced world tariffs substantially, the first two by about one-third each, and the last by about 40 per cent.

The Uruguay round created a new body, the World Trade Organisation (WTO), which superseded the GATT in 1995. It also created a new legal structure for multilateral trading. Under this new structure all members have equal mutual rights and obligations. Until the WTO was formed, developing countries who were in the GATT enjoyed all the GATT rights but were exempt from most of its obligations to liberalize trade—obligations that applied only to the developed countries. However, all such special treatments were phased out over seven years starting in 1995. There is also a new dispute settlement mechanism with much more power to enforce rulings over non-tariff barriers than existed in the past. In its first eight years the WTO dealt with around 300 disputes; while the GATT only heard 300 in 47 years!

In 1997 three strands of negotiation that had been left incomplete in the Uruguay round were completed, involving agreements to lower trade barriers in telecommunications, financial services, and information technology.

These agreements were important because they greatly increased the amount of trade covered by WTO rules and dispute settlement procedures, they may lead to larger trade volume gains than the entire Uruguay round, and they complete most of the unfinished business from Uruguay, clearing the way for a new global trade round. This was started in 2001 at the Qatar capital, Doha, and hence known as the Doha round. This round was still continuing in 2006.

By December 2005 the WTO had 149 member countries including China, with a further 30 or so, including Russia, at various stages of negotiation to join.[2] It is thus growing into a truly global forum for the regulation of government involvement in world trade. There is further discussion of some of the issues surrounding the WTO in the second case study below.

Figure 27.4 shows that world trade has grown faster than world GDP since 1950. Indeed, while real GDP has grown ten-fold, world export volumes have grown twenty-eight-fold. It is hard to believe that this could have occurred without the liberalization of international trade brought about through successive rounds of tariff negotiation.

## Types of regional agreement

Regional agreements seek to liberalize trade over a much smaller set of countries than WTO membership. Three

---

[2] The latest information about the WTO can be found on the internet at www.wto.org.

standard forms of regional trade-liberalizing agreement are free trade areas, customs unions, and common markets.

A **free trade area** (FTA) is the least comprehensive of the three. It allows for tariff-free trade among the member countries, but it leaves each member free to impose its own trade restrictions on imports from other countries. As a result, members must maintain customs points at their common borders to make sure that imports into the free trade area do not all enter through the member that is levying the lowest tariff on each item. They must also agree on rules of origin to establish when a good is made in a member country, and hence is able to pass duty-free across their borders, and when it is imported from outside the free trade area, and hence is liable to pay duties when it crosses borders within the free trade area.

A **customs union** is a free trade area plus an agreement to establish common barriers to trade with the rest of the world. Because they have a common tariff against the outside world, the members need neither customs controls on goods moving among themselves nor rules of origin.

A **common market** is a customs union that also has free movement of labour and capital among its members.

An **economic union** takes things still further and creates an area that shares many other aspects of economic policy and harmonized legal structures, such as in the European Union today.

## Trade creation and trade diversion

A major effect of regional trade liberalization is on resource reallocation. Economic theory divides these effects production into two categories.

### Trade creation

This occurs when producers in one member country find that they can undersell producers in another member country because the latter loses its tariff protection. For example, when the North American Free Trade Agreement (NAFTA) came into force, some Mexican firms found that they could undersell their US competitors in some product lines, while some US firms found that they could undersell their Mexican competitors in others, once tariffs were eliminated. As a result, specialization occurred and new international trade developed.

### Trade diversion

This occurs when exporters in one member country replace foreign exporters as suppliers to another member country as a result of preferential tariff treatment. For example, US trade diversion occurs when Mexican firms find that they can undersell competitors from the EU in the US market, not because they are the cheapest source

of supply, but because their tariff-free prices are lower than the tariff-burdened prices of imports from Europe. This effect is a gain to Mexican firms but a cost to the United States—which now has to pay more for any given amount of imports than before the trade diversion occurred.

From the global perspective, trade diversion represents an inefficient use of resources.

From the narrower national points of view of Mexico and the United States, however, trade diversion brings some gain as well as some loss. In so far as there is a shared desire to increase domestic manufacturing production, trade diversion brings mutual benefit to both countries. It gives producers within the two countries an advantage over producers in the rest of the world, which has the effect of increasing the total amount of production and trade that occurs among the member countries while reducing what comes in from third countries.

### EFTA, NAFTA, and other FTAs

The first important free trade area in the modern era was the European Free Trade Association (EFTA). This was formed in 1960 by a group of European countries that were unwilling to join the European Economic Community, as the EU was then called, because of its all-embracing character. Not wanting to be left out of the gains from trade, they formed an association whose sole purpose was tariff removal. First, they removed all tariffs on trade among themselves. Then each country signed a free trade area agreement with the EEC. This made the EEC–EFTA market the largest tariff-free market in the world (over 300 million people). Three of the EFTA countries—Austria, Finland, and Sweden—switched to full membership of the EU in 1995; by 2006 the only remaining members were Iceland, Liechtenstein, Norway, and Switzerland.

In 1988 a sweeping agreement was signed between Canada and the United States, instituting free trade on all goods and most non-government services and covering what is the world's largest flow of international trade between any two countries. In 1993 this agreement was extended into the North American Free Trade Agreement (NAFTA) by renegotiation of the Canada–USA agreement to include Mexico. Australia and New Zealand have also entered into an association that removes restrictions on trade in goods and services between their two countries, and a group of countries in Southeast Asia have formed the ASEAN trade group.

The countries of Latin America have been experimenting with free trade areas for many decades. Most earlier attempts failed, but in the last few years a more durable free trade area has been formed, known as Mercosur. In 1994 an initiative was started to put in place a free trade area for the whole of the Americas. Negotiations started in 1998 and were scheduled to be concluded by January 2005; however, this deadline was not met. The new free trade area was planned to create the Free Trade Area of the Americas (FTAA), but at the time of writing (June 2006) there is considerable doubt as to whether this will come about in the foreseeable future.

# Common markets: the European Union

By far the most successful common market, which is now referred to as a 'single market', is the European Union. Its origins go back to the period immediately following the Second World War in 1945. After the war there was a strong belief throughout Europe that the way to avoid future military conflict was to create a high level of economic integration between the existing nation-states. Later the motivation switched to creating a powerful economic bloc that could be competitive with Japan and the USA.

In 1952, as a first step towards economic union, France, Belgium, West Germany, Italy, Luxembourg, and Holland formed the European Coal and Steel Community. This removed trade restrictions on coal, steel, and iron ore among these six countries. In 1957 the same six countries signed the Treaty of Rome. This created the European Economic Community (EEC), which later became the European Community (EC), and after 1993 the European Union (EU). In 1973 the United Kingdom, Denmark, and Ireland joined, and they were followed in 1981 by Greece and in 1986 by Spain and Portugal. Austria, Sweden, and Finland entered in 1995. The European Union welcomed ten new countries in 2004: Cyprus, the Czech Republic, Estonia, Hungary, Latvia, Lithuania, Malta, Poland, Slovakia, and Slovenia. Bulgaria and Romania followed in 2007.

In the first two decades of its existence, the main economic achievements of the EEC were the elimination of internal tariff barriers and the establishment of common external tariffs (in other words, the establishment of a customs union), and the establishment of the Common Agricultural Policy (CAP), which guarantees farm prices by means of intervention and an import levy. There were other significant EEC policies, such as regional aid and protection of competition, but they did not have great economic impact to begin with.

By the mid-1980s it was clear that the intended 'Common Market' had not been achieved. There remained many non-tariff barriers to trade and to the mobility of labour. These included quality standards, licensing requirements, and a lack of recognition of qualifications. In financial services there were explicit exchange controls and other regulatory restrictions on cross-border trade. In response, a new push to turn the customs union into a genuine common market began in 1985.

## The Single Market Programme

The Single Market Act was signed in 1986. Its intention was to remove all remaining barriers to the creation of a fully integrated single market by the end of 1992. The Single Market Act did not in itself create the single market. Rather, it was a statement (or treaty) of intent which instituted a simplified administrative procedure whereby most of the single market legislation needed only 'weighted majority' support, rather than unanimity. The single market itself was to be created by a large number of Directives, which are drafted by the European Commission, the EU's civil service. These become Community law after they have been 'adopted' by the European Council (a committee of the heads of state or other ministers of member states). They then have to be ratified in the law of each member state. Once in force, they have precedence over the domestic laws of member states if there is a conflict.

The elimination of non-tariff barriers has been approached on a product-by-product basis. Only in this way could minimum quality standards be created that would permit cross-border trade without the threat of quality checks as a prerequisite to entry (a problem that plagues some branches of Canada–USA trade). This has required a complicated set of negotiations on quality standards, relating to everything from condoms to sausages and from toys to telecommunications. There is even a quality standard for the bacterial content of aqueous toys—transparent plastic souvenirs containing, perhaps, a model of Big Ben or the Eiffel Tower, which, when shaken, create a snow scene.

All countries have such safety or quality standards for their products, and what has been happening is the harmonization of these standards, which is something that Canada and the United States have been trying to do since their Agreement was put into force in 1989.

The Single Market Programme is an ongoing process, not a discrete jump. Some of the intended measures have been implemented, but many are still in the pipeline. The process will continue well into the twenty-first century.

## The single market in financial services

Perhaps the most significant achievements of the Single Market Programme to date have been in the area of trade in financial services. Although the Treaty of Rome called for free movement of capital as well as goods, this was ignored until the mid-1980s. Until recently, most member countries had exchange controls on capital movements until recently which prohibited residents of each country from investing in any other country. The Capital Liberalization Directive required all member states to abolish exchange controls by June 1990. Some member states, such as the UK and Germany, had already abolished controls. France and Italy, which had not, were forced to do so by the Directive. Spain, Portugal, Ireland, and Greece were given longer to comply. All except Greece fully abolished their controls by the end of 1992, and Greece abolished most of its controls by 1994.

Once exchange controls were abolished, it could be argued that nothing else had to be done to create a single market in financial services. Certainly wholesale financial markets rapidly integrated with the global financial system, once they were free to do so. Indeed, this is one of the key elements of globalization, which was discussed in Box 23.1 on page 520.

However, agreement was still needed on how to facilitate greater cross-border competition in retail financial markets. Each country in isolation had already created a domestic regulatory regime designed, in part, to protect the consumer. How was the EU to encourage competition but maintain a sensible regime of consumer protection? Financial services are particularly prone to fraud, because the profit margin for a crook is 100 per cent—even a used car salesman has to show you a car, but the seller of an investment product offers only future promises!

The European Union adopted a pragmatic approach based upon assuming the competence of existing regulators. Firms in each sector were to be authorized as 'fit and proper' by their home country regulator, and they would then be presumed to be fit and proper to trade in any member state. In effect, the home country gave a driving licence which then permitted an authorized company to 'drive' anywhere in the Union. This mutual recognition of regulators has been wrongly interpreted as permitting financial services firms to trade anywhere in the European Union on the basis of their home country's rules. A moment's thought will tell you why it has to be wrong. Imagine, for example, British drivers being permitted to drive on the left in France just because that is the law in Britain. It is just as disastrous to have banks in any one location trading under fifteen different legal structures.

The single market in financial services is built on a dual set of principles: home country authorization, and host country conduct of business rules. This means that a firm can be authorized to trade throughout the Union by the home regulator, but the trade itself must obey the local laws in the country concerned.

Allowing home countries to regulate entry and host countries to regulate performance is a simple application of the principle of *national treatment* that was developed in the context of the Uruguay round. It means that foreign firms get treated just the same as local firms.

The Cecchini Report of 1989 estimated that the completion of the Single Market Programme may increase the GDP of the European Union by up to 6 per cent. However, a well known American economist, Richard Baldwin, has challenged that figure, suggesting that the gains could be at least twice as large (owing to economies of scale external to firms). And this is only the gain in one year. Similar gains will continue to flow in future years. Thus, while politically tortuous, the process of reducing trade barriers, even within groups of countries, is capable of creating considerable gains in economic efficiency.

### The Lisbon Agenda

In 2000 a renewed agenda for economic progress in the European Union up to 2010 was adopted at a European Council meeting in Lisbon, Portugal (hence known as the Lisbon Agenda). It aims at making 'the EU the world's most dynamic and competitive economy' by 2010. Little progress towards this goal had been made by 2005 so it was relaunched:

> It is accepted that member states have not made the necessary progress on the Lisbon Agenda goals. There have been some advances on specific goals, for example the liberalisation of energy, telecoms and financial services sectors. But the headline objectives of boosting jobs by 20 million and ensuring annual growth of 3 per cent by 2010 a year will not be met. . . . European Commission President Jose Manuel Barroso said in February: 'Lisbon has been blown off course by a combination of economic conditions, international uncertainty, slow progress in the member states and a gradual loss of political focus.' Leaders are likely to address these problems by reducing the number of goals and focusing on boosting jobs and growth. Instead of the current confusing myriad of progress indicators there will be one national action programme and implementation report for each country. (BBC website, March 2005)

## The future of the multilateral trading system

At the end of the Second World War the United States took the lead in forming the GATT and in pressing for reductions in world tariffs through successive rounds of negotiations. Largely as a result of this US initiative, the world's tariff barriers have been greatly reduced, while the volume of world trade has risen steadily (see Figure 27.4 on page 626).

The next few years will be critical for the future of the multilateral trading system, which has served the world so well since the end of the Second World War. The dangers are, first, a growth of regional trading blocs that will trade more with their own member countries and less with others, and second, the growth of state-managed trade.

The 1920s and 1930s provide a cautionary tale. Arguments for major trade restrictions always have a superficial appeal and sometimes have real short-term payoffs. In the long term, however, a major worldwide escalation of tariffs would lower efficiency and incomes and restrict trade worldwide, while doing nothing to raise employment. Both economic theory and the evidence of history support this proposition. Although most agree that pressure should be put on countries that restrict trade, the above analysis suggests that these pressures are best applied using the multilateral institution, the WTO. Unilateral imposition of restrictions in response to the perceived restrictions in other countries can all too easily degenerate into a round of mutually escalating trade barriers.

In the first few years of the twenty-first century, the United States has been more protectionist than at any

other time during the last half of the previous century. New heavy anti-dumping duties on steel and softwood lumber and big new protectionist measures for the US agricultural industry are causing worrying ripples internationally. If the United States abandons the position it established over the last 60 years as the leader of the movement for trade liberalization, there is no obvious successor.

The European Union, although it has achieved something close to free trade within the Union, has been equivocal on free trade with the rest of the world. Anti-dumping duties, voluntary export agreements, and other non-tariff barriers have been used with effect against successful importers—particularly the Japanese. Although these measures may bring short-term gains, both economic theory and historical experience suggest that they will bring losses in the long term. Protectionism reduces incomes because low-priced goods are excluded to the detriment of current consumers, particularly those with lower incomes. It also reduces employment because restrictions on imports are sooner or later balanced by restrictions on exports as other countries retaliate. It also inhibits the technological dynamism that is the source of long-term growth, by shielding domestic producers from the need that free international competition forces on them: to keep up with all foreign competitors.

# CASE STUDIES

## 1. Changing shares of world trade

Figure 27.5 shows the percentage shares of world exports of goods and services of six major countries between 1957 and 2005. For most of this period, the United States has been the world's biggest exporter, though it was exceeded by Germany for a brief period in the late 1980s and then again in the three years 2003–5. The United Kingdom was the second biggest exporter in the late 1950s, but it was overtaken by Germany in about 1960 and by Japan and France in the early 1970s. Japan's exports grew to rival those of the United States and Germany by the mid-1980s, but then declined in relative importance. China's share of world exports grew slowly from low relative levels during the 1980s and 1990s to surge very rapidly in the first five years of the twenty-first century. If this trend continues it will become the world's largest exporter before 2010. Of course, extrapolating trends is a dangerous thing to do, as the trend of Japanese export growth did not continue in the same vein after 1986.

It would also be a mistake to think that those countries whose relative share of world exports has declined are in any sense a failure: far from it. All of these countries showed upwards trends of volumes of exports of goods and services and an upwards trend in real living standards for almost all of this period. Hence it is not a 'bad thing' for other countries that China has become so successful. Rather, a wealthier China provides an expanded market for goods and services produced by other countries, so its rapid growth does not provide any threat to living standards in other countries. Just remember that trade benefits both parties to the transaction, so growing trade is good for world incomes in general. As shown in Figure 27.4, world trade volumes do continue to grow rapidly.

## 2. The World Trade Organisation and its critics

The following article by one of the authors of this book summarizes some background information about the WTO and assesses some point made by its critics.

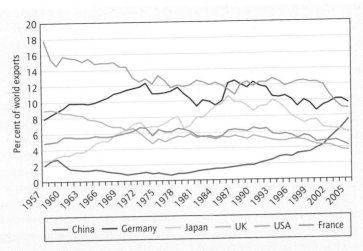

**Figure 27.5** Major countries' shares of world exports, 1957–2005

*Source:* IMF, International Financial Statistics database.

### Don't Give Up on WTO: Fix It

*The WTO may not be perfect, but its elimination is a recipe for trade chaos.*

*One major target of those protesting globalization on behalf of the poor is the World Trade Organisation. Yet, as the administrator of our rules-based international trading regime, it especially benefits the smaller, less powerful nations, and no feasible alternative has been suggested.*

*At one extreme, the WTO's opponents argue that all institutions supporting globalization should be abolished; the other extreme admits that globalization is inevitable, requiring some rules-based system, but the WTO is so defective that it does more harm than good. Before assessing these positions, we need to analyze globalization and the WTO.*

*New technologies and policies drove the globalization that began in the second half of the 20th century. Containerization and improvements in ship design greatly reduced transporting costs, while new information and communications technologies allowed worldwide coordinated production in ways that were impossible 50 years ago. As a result the 19th century pattern of globalized trade—with developed countries exporting manufactured goods to less developed countries in return for agricultural produce and raw materials—has given way to a new pattern in which parts of individual manufactured goods are made throughout the world in a supply-chain system. These far-reaching changes, and the globalization that they enable, cannot be rolled back by protesters any more than the 19th century Luddites could end the factory system.*

*In policy, governments have sought to reduce the high levels of tariff protection that were erected from 1918 to 1939. The vision*

*of post-World War II reformers was to remove high tariff walls thus reintegrating the world trading system and bringing prosperity to all participants. The General Agreement on Tariffs and Trade (GATT) was the enduring result. Through eight rounds of bargaining, members greatly reduced tariffs. World trade grew dramatically, and their economies prospered.*

*The GATT, an accidental creation resulting from US rejection of more ambitious initiatives, was replaced in 1995 by the WTO, which has what the GATT lacked, a substantial institutional structure.*

*Because the GATT had already reduced the trade barriers for which there was least resistance, the WTO has faced a tougher job. The powerful developed nations, who were the majority of the charter members, had—albeit often reluctantly—accepted the reductions of the trade barriers on manufactured goods for which they typically had competitive advantages. But they were reluctant to do the same in areas where they lacked competitive advantages, particularly agricultural commodities and textiles. So the tougher issues—trade in services, intellectual property protection and agricultural subsidies—had yet to be settled by an ever-growing membership that made the WTO rule of proceeding by consensus increasingly cumbersome.*

*At a series of bi-annual WTO ministerial conferences, the less developed countries applied pressure to deal with their priorities. The fourth conference began the Doha Round of negotiations, the first round since the WTO replaced the GATT. Progress has been slow, but considering the entrenched vested interests of the developed countries, this is not surprising. The fifth conference in Cancun broke down with little progress as a new grouping—22 developing nations called the G-22—refused to handle issues that concerned the developed countries while pressing for the end of EU and US agricultural subsidies.*

*The most recent conference in Hong Kong (December 2005) produced results that, although disappointing to many, were at least positive. Agreement was reached in principle to end all subsidies of agricultural exports by 2013, as well as giving more market access to the poorest nations' exports to the industrialized countries. The tough bargaining over details was postponed until 2006. Until then, skepticism is justified. Will the developed countries end export subsidization? This would be a good beginning, but not the end of the problem, since subsidization of production for the home market hurts producers in poor countries, denying them major export markets.*

*So, should the WTO be abolished as many of its harshest critics advocate? No, because the WTO is the best hope for those who would be most oppressed in a lawless world where the powerful, particularly the USA and the EU, could behave as they wished. In contrast, as part of its rule-based regime, the WTO has a dispute settlement function that has heard more than 300 cases and settled many. Furthermore, having the developed world listen to the G-22's complaints in Cancun, and then agreeing to international negotiations to address them, would have been inconceivable without the WTO.*

*But isn't the enforcement of dispute settlements hindered by the disparities in economic power? Nations with large economies can use trade sanctions against small nations, but the small nation that tries the same sanctions against a large nation often inflicts most harm on its own economy. This is a major defect. But the dispute settlement mechanism has accomplished much, and to discard it because of imperfect enforcement would be unfortunate. Reform is needed instead—with larger economies agreeing to graduated enforcement mechanisms, including stiffer penalties for themselves.*

*Is the WTO a failure because it does not permit trade sanctions on those who pollute their environments or exploit their laborers? To the contrary, the poorest countries fear that advanced countries would use environmental and labor standards written into the body of trade agreements, with trade sanctions for non-performers, as concealed non-tariff barriers. This is not to argue against WTO efforts to end slave labor and eliminate forms of pollution with worldwide effects. But it is policy imperialism to argue that the poor must accept the standards of environmental and labor protection that the rich countries can only now afford.*

*Don't the rich countries exert too much power over WTO negotiations? No doubt they do exert much influence on the behind-the-scenes negotiations needed to achieve unanimity, often ignoring the poorer countries. But at least the meetings provide a forum for poor nations to speak out and broker alliances, such as the G-22, and use them to exert influence on the developed nations. The alternative—no voice in a no-rules system—would be much worse.*

*Is the process undemocratic? Representatives of sovereign nations conduct the negotiations. So the protesters assume that they know better than their own governments what is good for their country. This, while possible, seems unlikely considering that 155 governments, of all political stripes, remain members.*

*Isn't the WTO a tool for those who advocate a doctrinaire form of laissez faire liberalism? Supporting the WTO are many who believe in the unaided market to meet all social requirements, as well as many, including this author, who believe that the free market needs public-sector assistance if it is to meet societal needs for justice and growth. Both sides agree that most, if not all, trade restrictions are harmful and, therefore, support attempts to lower them.*

*For sure, the WTO is a flawed institution—one that needs reform not abolition. Its bureaucracy is probably too small to handle the job. Decision-making by unanimous agreement is cumbersome, encouraging blocking coalitions. One reform would be a system of representation by countries selected according to such criteria as regions, levels of development, and trading interests, with a mechanism for rotation. In the meantime, until a better rules-based system for governing trade relations is developed we need to support the one we have. (Lipsey 2006)*

# SUMMARY

## Sources of the gains from trade

- Potential gains from trade exist whenever one country, region, firm, or individual has a comparative advantage in the production of some good or service.

- Comparative advantage occurs whenever countries have different opportunity costs of producing particular goods. World production of all products can be increased if each country transfers resources into the production of the products in which it has a comparative advantage, which means those in which it has the lower opportunity cost.

- The most important proposition in the theory of the gains from trade is that trade allows all countries to obtain the goods in which they do not have a comparative advantage at a lower opportunity cost than they would face if they were to produce all products for themselves. This allows all countries to have more of all products than they could have if they tried to be self-sufficient.

- As well as gaining the advantages of specialization arising from comparative advantage, a nation that engages in trade and specialization may realize the benefits of economies of large-scale production and of learning by doing.

- Classical theory regarded comparative advantage as being determined largely by natural resource endowments, and thus as difficult to change. Economists now believe that some comparative advantages are acquired and thus can be changed. In today's world acquired knowledge is often more important than natural resource endowments. A country may, in this view, influence its role in world production and trade to its advantage. Successful intervention leads to a country acquiring a comparative advantage; unsuccessful intervention fails to develop such an advantage.

## Terms of trade

- The terms of trade refer to the ratio of the prices of goods exported to those imported, which determines the quantity of imports that can be obtained per unit of exports. The terms of trade determine how the gains from trade are shared. A favourable change in the terms of trade—that is, a rise in export prices relative to import prices—means that a country can acquire more imports per unit of exports.

## The theory of commercial policy

- Protection can be a means to ends other than maximizing world living standards. It is also sometimes justified on the grounds that it may lead to higher living standards for the protectionist country than a policy of free trade would. Such a result might come about by developing a dynamic comparative advantage, allowing inexperienced or uneconomically small industries to become efficient enough to compete with foreign industries. A recent argument for protection is to operate a strategic trade policy whereby a country attracts firms in oligopolistic industries that, because of scale economies, can earn large profits even in equilibrium.

- Domestic industries may be protected from foreign competition by tariffs, which affect the prices of imports, or by non-tariff barriers, which affect the quantities of imports.

- Some fallacious free trade arguments are that (a) because free trade maximizes world income, it will maximize the income of every individual country; and (b) because infant industries seldom admit to growing up and thus try to retain their protection indefinitely, the whole country necessarily loses by protecting its infant industries.

- Some fallacious protectionist arguments are that (a) mutually advantageous trade is impossible because one trader's gain must always be the other's loss; (b) our high-paid workers must be protected against the competition from low-paid foreign workers; and (c) imports are to be discouraged because they lower national income and cause unemployment.

## Global commercial policy

- The World Trade Organisation (WTO) has taken over from the GATT the role of policing world trade rules relating to government commercial policies and providing a forum for further international co-operation in evolving the global trade regime.

- Regional trade-liberalizing agreements such as free trade areas and common markets bring efficiency gains through trade creation and efficiency losses through trade diversion. The North American Free Trade Agreement (NAFTA) is the world's largest and most successful free trade area, while the European Union is the world's largest and most successful common market (now called a single market).

# TOPICS FOR REVIEW

- Comparative advantage
- Gains from trade
- Terms of trade
- Free trade and protectionism
- Tariff and non-tariff barriers to trade
- General Agreement on Tariffs and Trade (GATT)

- World Trade Organisation (WTO)
- Common markets, customs unions, and free trade associations
- North American Free Trade Agreement (NAFTA)
- European Union (EU)

## QUESTIONS

1 It is quite common for governments from time to time to encourage their citizens to buy home-produced goods in preference to foreign-produced goods. (For example, in the United Kingdom a 'Buy British' policy has been encouraged.) In what ways if any could such encouragement be good for the domestic economy?

2 Outline the arguments for and against free trade.

3 Compare and contrast tariffs and quotas as methods of restricting trade.

4 Why does trading with countries where workers have lower real incomes *not* make us worse off?

5 Why is it that openness to foreign competition seems to be good for economic growth?

6 What is the basis of recent protests against globalization? Critically evaluate these claims.

# GLOSSARY

**absolute advantage** The advantage that one region is said to have over another in the production of some commodity when an equal quantity of resources can produce more of that commodity in the first region than in the second. Compare *comparative advantage*.

**absolute price** The price of a good or a service expressed in monetary units. Also called a *money price*.

**accelerator theory of investment** The theory that the level of investment depends on the rate of change of output.

**accommodation** Said to occur when the monetary authorities increase the money supply in response to a negative *aggregate supply shock*. Accommodation has the effect of offsetting the downward impact of the shock on real GDP at the cost of a permanently higher price level.

**actual GDP** The level of GDP actually produced over a given period.

**AD curve** See *aggregate demand curve*.

**ad valorem tax** A tax levied as a percentage of the value of some transaction.

**adaptive expectations** The expectation of the future value of a variable formed on the basis of an adjustment which is some proportion of the error in expectations made last period. The error is the difference between what was expected last period and what actually happened.

**administered price** A price that is set by the decisions of individual firms rather than by impersonal market forces.

**adverse selection** The tendency for people most at risk to insure, while people least at risk do not, so that the insurers get an unrepresentative sample of clients within any one fee category.

**agents** All decision-makers, including consumers, workers, firms, and government bodies.

**aggregate demand (AD)** The total desired purchases of all the nation's buyers of final output.

**aggregate demand curve** A curve that plots all combinations of the price level and national income that yield equilibrium in the goods and the asset markets—i.e. that yield *IS–LM* equilibrium.

**aggregate demand shock** A shift in the *aggregate demand curve* resulting from an autonomous change in exogenous expenditures or the money supply (or equivalently, a policy-induced change in interest rates).

**aggregate (desired) expenditure (AE)** The total volume of purchases of currently produced goods and services that all spending units in the economy wish to make.

**aggregate production function** The technical relation which expresses the maximum national output that can be produced with each possible combination of capital, labour, and other resource inputs. See also *production function*.

**aggregate spending** See *aggregate expenditure*.

**aggregate supply (AS)** The total desired output of all the nation's producers.

**aggregate supply curve** A curve relating the economy's producers' total desired output, $Y$, to the price level, $P$.

**aggregate supply shock** A shift in the *aggregate supply curve* resulting from an exogenous change in input prices or from technical change (exogenous or endogenous). One example is the oil price shocks of the 1970s.

**allocative efficiency** Situation in which production cannot be rearranged in order to make someone made better off without at the same time making someone else worse off.

**allocative inefficiency** Situation in which production *can* be rearranged to make someone better off while making no one else worse off.

**appreciation** When a change in the free market exchange rate raises the value of one currency relative to others.

**arbitrage** Trading activity based on buying where a product is cheap and selling where it has a higher price (from the French word *arbitrer*: to referee or arbitrate). Arbitrage activity helps to bring prices closer in different segments of the market.

**arc elasticity** A measure of the average responsiveness of quantity to price over an interval of the demand curve: $(\Delta q/q) \times (p/\Delta p)$. See also *point elasticity*.

**asymmetric information** A situation in which some economic agents have more information than others and this affects the outcome of a bargain between them.

**auction prices** Prices that are set by the continuous bidding of buyers, often against each other.

**autarky** Situation existing when a country does no foreign trade.

**automatic fiscal stabilizers** Stabilizers that arise because the value of some tax revenues and benefits changes with the level of economic activity. For example, income tax revenue rises as personal incomes rise, corporation tax revenue increases with company profits, and unemployment benefit falls as employment increases.

**autonomous expenditures** Expenditures that are determined outside the domestic economy or are independent of the current level of GDP.

**autonomous variable** See *exogenous variable*.

**average fixed costs (AFC)** *Total fixed costs* divided by the number of units produced.

**average product (AP)** Total output divided by the number of units of the *variable factor* used in its production.

**average propensity to consume (APC)** Total consumption expenditure divided by total national income, $C/Y$.

**average propensity to import** Total imports divided by total national income (or expenditure), $IM/Y$.

**average propensity to save (APS)** Total saving divided by total national income, $S/Y$. Also known as the savings ratio.

**average propensity to tax** Total tax revenue divided by total national income, $T/Y$.

**average revenue (AR)** *Total revenue* divided by the number of units sold.

**average total cost (ATC)** The total cost of producing any given output divided by the number of units produced, i.e. the cost per unit.

**average variable cost (AVC)** *Total variable cost* divided by the number of units produced. Also called unit cost.

**balance of payments accounts** A summary record of a country's transactions involving payment or receipts of foreign exchange.

**balance of trade** The difference between imports and exports.

**balanced budget** A situation in which current revenue is exactly equal to current expenditure.

**balanced budget multiplier** The change in GDP divided by the balanced budget change in government expenditure that brought it about.

**balanced growth** This occurs when most major sectors of the economy grow together at similar rates.

**barriers to entry** Anything that prevents new firms from entering an industry that is earning profits.

**barter** The trading of goods directly for other goods.

**base period** A time-period chosen for comparison purposes in order to express or compute index numbers. Values in all other periods are expressed as percentages of the base-period value.

**base rate** The interest rate quoted by UK banks as the reference rate for much of their loan business. For example, a company may be given a loan at 'base plus 2 per cent'. The base rate changes periodically when the monetary authorities signal that they want money market rates in general to change. The equivalent term used by US banks is 'prime rate'.

**base year** A *base period* that is a year.

**basic prices** Used in National Accounts to refer to prices received by producers that exclude taxes on products, as in 'gross value added at basic prices'.

**BB line** The locus of levels of the interest rate and real GDP for which the desired current account balance of payments surplus (deficit) just equals the desired capital account deficit (surplus).

**beta** The relationship between the price of a share and the share market in general. A beta of 1 implies a perfect correlation between the share in question and the market.

**bill** A tradable security, usually with an initial maturity of up to six months, which pays no explicit interest and so trades at a discount to its maturity value.

**black market** A market in which goods are sold at prices that violate some legally imposed pricing restriction.

**bond** In economic theory, any evidence of a debt carrying a legal obligation to pay interest and repay the principal at some stated future time. This concept covers many different debt instruments that are found in practice.

**boom** Period of high output and high employment. See also *slump*.

**break-even price** The price at which a firm is just able to cover all of its costs, including the opportunity cost of capital. See also *shutdown price*.

**budget balance** See *balanced budget*.

**budget deficit** The shortfall of current revenue below current expenditure, usually with reference to the government.

**budget line** Line showing all those combinations of commodities that are just obtainable, given a household's income and the prices of all commodities.

**budget surplus** The excess of current revenue over current expenditure, usually with reference to the government.

**built-in stabilizer** Anything that reduces the economy's cyclical fluctuations and is activated without a conscious government decision. See also *automatic fiscal stabilizers*.

**business cycles** Fluctuations in the general level of activity in an economy that affect many sectors at roughly the same time, though not necessarily to the same extent. In recent times, the period from the peak of one cycle to the peak of the next has varied in the range of five to ten years. Used to be known as trade cycles.

**buyout** What happens when a group of investors buys up a controlling interest in a firm.

**capacity** The output that corresponds to the minimum short-run *average total cost*.

**capital** All those man-made aids to further production, such as tools, machinery, and factories, which are used up in the process of making other goods and services rather than being consumed for their own sake.

**capital and financial account** Part of the balance of payments accounts that records international transactions in assets and liabilities.

**capital consumption allowance** An estimate of the amount by which the capital stock is depleted through wear and tear. Also called *depreciation*.

**capital goods** See *investment goods*.

**capital inflow** This arises when overseas residents buy assets in the domestic economy or domestic residents sell foreign assets.

**capital–labour ratio** The ratio of the amount of capital to the amount of labour used in production.

**capital outflow** This arises when overseas residents sell assets in the domestic economy or domestic residents buy foreign assets.

**capital stock** The total quantity of physical capital in existence.

**capital widening** Increasing the quantity of capital without changing the proportions in which the factors of production are used.

**cartel** A group of firms that agree to act as if they were a single seller.

**cash base** See *high-powered money* and M0.

**central authorities** See *government*.

**central bank** A bank that acts as banker to the commercial banking system and often to the government as well. In the modern world it is usually a government-owned institution that is the sole money-issuing authority and has a key role in the setting and implementation of *monetary policy*.

**centrally planned economy** See *command economy*.

**ceteris paribus** 'Other things being equal': commonly used to describe a situation in which all but one of the *independent variables* are held constant in order to study the effect that a change in the remaining independent variable has on the variables of interest.

**change in demand** A shift in the whole demand curve, i.e. a change in the amount that will be bought at each price.

**change in the quantity demanded** An increase or decrease in the specific quantity bought at a specified price, represented by a movement along a demand curve.

**circular flow of income** The flow of expenditures on output and factor services passing between domestic (as opposed to foreign) firms and domestic households.

**classical dichotomy** Concept in *classical economics* that monetary forces could influence the general price level but had no effect on real activity. Related to the concept of *neutrality of money*.

**classical economics** Usually refers to the body of thought on economics that evolved in the hundred years or so before the 1930s; often associated (probably incorrectly) with the notion that government policy cannot influence the level of economic activity. Contrasted with *Keynesian economics*, which attempted to break down the *classical dichotomy*.

**closed economy** An economy that does not engage in international trade (*autarky*).

**closed shop** A firm in which only union members can be employed. Closed shops may be either 'pre-entry', where the worker must be a member of the union before being employed, or 'post-entry', where the worker must join the union on becoming employed.

**Coase theorem** The proposition that, if those creating an externality and those affected by it can bargain together with zero transaction costs, the externality will be *internalized* independently of whether it is the creators of or the sufferers from the externality who have the property rights.

**collective consumption goods** See *public goods*.

**command economy** An economy in which the decisions of the central authorities (as distinct from households and firms) exert the major influence over the allocation of resources and the distribution of income. Also called a centrally planned economy.

**commercial policy** The government's policy towards international trade, investment, and related matters.

**commodities** A term that usually refers to basic goods, such as wheat and iron ore, that are produced by the primary sector of the economy. Sometimes also used by economists to refer to all goods and services.

**common market** An agreement among a group of countries to have free trade among themselves, a common set of barriers to trade with other countries, and free movement of labour and capital among themselves.

**common property resource** A resource that is owned by no one and may be used by anyone.

**comparative advantage** The ability of one nation (or region or individual) to produce a commodity at a lower opportunity cost in terms of other products forgone than another nation (or region or individual). Compare *absolute advantage*.

**comparative statics** Short for 'comparative-static equilibrium analysis': studying the effect of a change in some variable by comparing the positions of static equilibrium before and after the change.

**compensating variation** The amount of income that has to be taken away from a consumer following a price fall in one good in order to return the consumer to the original indifference curve and thereby leave her feeling equally well off.

**competition policy** Policy designed to prohibit the acquisition and exercise of monopoly power by business firms.

**complements** Two goods for which the quantity demanded of one is negatively related to the price of the other.

**concentration ratio** The fraction of total market sales (or some other measure of market occupancy) accounted for by a specific number of the industry's largest firms, four-firm and eight-firm concentration ratios being the most frequently used.

**constant returns to scale** Situation existing when a firm's output increases at the same rate as all its inputs increase.

**consumer** An agent who consumes goods or services.

**consumers' surplus** The difference between the total value that consumers place on all units consumed of a commodity and the payment they must make to purchase that amount of the commodity.

**consumption** The act of using goods and services to satisfy wants.

**consumption expenditure** The amount that individuals spend on purchasing goods and services for consumption.

**consumption function** The relationship between personal planned consumption expenditure and the variables that affect it, such as *disposable income* and wealth.

**contestable market** A market in which there are no *sunk costs* of entry or exit, so that potential entry may hold the profits of existing firms to low levels—zero in the case of perfect contestability.

**co-operative solution** A situation in which existing firms co-operate to maximize their joint profits.

**cost minimization** An implication of profit maximization that the firm will choose the method that produces any specific output at the lowest attainable cost.

**creative destruction** Schumpeter's theory that high profits and wages earned by monopolistic or oligopolistic firms and unions are the spur for others to invent cheaper or better substitute products and techniques which allow their suppliers to gain some of these profits.

**credibility** The extent to which actors in the private sector of the economy believe that the government will carry out the policy it promises in the future. Important in policy analysis in macro models which assume *rational expectations*, since expectations of future policy action influence current behaviour.

**cross-elasticity of demand** The responsiveness of demand for one commodity to changes in the price of another, defined as the percentage change in quantity demanded of one commodity divided by the percentage change in the price of another commodity.

**cross-sectional data** A number of observations on the same variable, such as individuals' savings or the price of eggs, all taken at the same time but in different places or for different agents.

**current account** Account recording all international transactions related to goods and services.

**customs union** A group of countries that agree to have free trade among themselves and a common set of barriers against imports from the rest of the world.

**cyclical unemployment** See *demand-deficient unemployment*.

**debt** Anything that is owed by one agent to another. In the context of corporate finance this applies to bonds or bank loans, but not equity.

**debt deflation** A fall in aggregate demand that is associated with falling asset values, causing a negative wealth effect on consumption. It could also involve a decline in investment as investors wait for asset values to stop falling.

**debt instruments** Any written documents that record the terms of a debt, often providing legal proof of the conditions under which interest will be paid and the principal repaid.

**decision lag** The time it takes to assess a situation and decide what corrective action should be taken.

**decreasing returns to scale** A situation in which output increases less than proportionately to inputs as the scale of production increases.

**deflation** A decrease in the general price level.

**degree of risk** A measurement of the amount of risk associated with some action such as lending money or innovating. When the nature of the risk is known, the degree can be measured by the variance of the probability distribution describing the possible outcomes.

**demand** The entire relationship between the quantity of a commodity that buyers wish to purchase per period of time and the price of that commodity, other things being equal.

**demand curve** A graphical relation showing the quantity of some commodity that households would like to buy at each possible price.

**demand-deficient unemployment** Unemployment that occurs because aggregate desired expenditure is insufficient to purchase all of the output of a fully employed labour force. Also called cyclical unemployment.

**demand for money** The amount of wealth that agents in the economy wish to hold in the form of money balances.

**demand for money function** The relation between the quantity of money demanded and its principle determinants such as income, wealth, and interest rates.

**demand function** A functional relation between quantity demanded and all of the variables that influence it.

**demand management** Policies that seek to shift the aggregate demand curve by shifting either the *IS* curve (fiscal policy) or the *LM* curve (monetary policy).

**demand schedule** A numerical tabulation showing the quantities that are demanded at selected prices.

**demand shock** In macroeconomics, a change of an exogenous variable that causes the AD curve to shift.

**dependent variable** The variable that is determined by the *independent variables*; e.g., in the consumption function consumption is the dependent variable.

**depreciation** (1) The loss in value of an asset over a period of time owing to physical wear and tear and obsolescence. (2) A fall in the free-market value of domestic currency in terms of foreign currencies. See also *capital consumption allowance*.

**depression** A prolonged period of very low economic activity with very high unemployment and high excess capacity.

**derived demand** The demand for a factor of production that results from the demand for the products it is used to make.

**developed countries** Usually refers to the rich industrial countries of North America, Western Europe, Japan, and Australasia.

**developing countries** See *less developed countries*.

**development gap** The gap between *less developed countries* and *developed countries*.

**differentiated product** A product that is produced in several distinct varieties, or brands, all of which are sufficiently similar to distinguish them, as a group, from other products (e.g. cars).

**diminishing marginal rate of substitution** The hypothesis that the less of one commodity is presently being consumed, the less willing the consumer will be to give up a unit of that commodity to obtain an additional unit of a second commodity; its geometrical expression is the decreasing absolute slope of an indifference curve as one moves along it to the right.

**direct investment** See *foreign direct investment*.

**direct taxes** Taxes levied on persons that can vary with the status of the taxpayer, e.g. income tax.

**discount rate** The difference between the current price of a bill and its maturity value expressed as an annualized interest rate.

**discouraged worker** Someone of working age who has withdrawn permanently from the labour force because of the poor prospects of employment.

**diseconomies of scale** See *decreasing returns to scale*.

**disembodied technical change** Technical change that is the result of changes in the organization of production that are not embodied in specific capital goods, e.g. improved management techniques.

**disequilibrium** A state of imbalance between opposing forces so that there is a tendency to change, as when quantity demanded does not equal quantity supplied at the prevailing price.

**disposable income** The after-tax income that individuals have at their disposal to spend or to save.

**distortions** Anything that creates a deviation from some optimality conditions, and thereby induces some inefficiency.

**distribution of income** The division of total national income among various groups. See also *functional* and *size distribution of income*.

**distribution theory** The theory of what determines the way in which the nation's total income is divided among various groups. See also *functional* and *size distribution of income*.

**dividends** Profits that are paid out to shareholders.

**division of labour** The breaking-up of a production process into a series of repetitive tasks, each done by a different worker.

**dominant strategy** A strategy that offers the best choices for one player independent of what the other players do.

**double counting** In national income accounting, adding up the total outputs of all the sectors in the economy so that the value of intermediate goods is counted both in the sector that produces them and in the sector that purchases them.

**dumping** The selling of a commodity in a foreign country at a price below its domestic sale price, for reasons not related to costs.

**duopoly** An industry containing exactly two firms.

**economic growth** The positive trend in the nation's total real output or GDP over the long term.

**economic models** A term used in several related ways: sometimes as a synonym for theory, sometimes for a specific quantification of a general theory, sometimes for the application of a general theory to a specific context, and sometimes for an abstraction designed to illustrate some point but not meant as a full theory on its own.

**economic profits** The difference between the revenues received from the sale of an output and the full opportunity cost of the inputs used to make the output. The cost includes the *opportunity cost* of the owners' capital. Also called pure profits or simply *profits*.

**economic rent** Any excess that a factor is paid above what is needed to keep it in its present use.

**economic union** A combination of a currency union and a customs union which may involve other harmonized economic policies and some common political institutions.

**economies of scale** See *increasing returns to scale*.

**economies of scope** Economies achieved by a multi-product firm owing to its overall size rather than its amount of production of any one product; typically associated with large-scale distribution, advertising, and purchasing and lower cost of borrowing money.

**economy** Any specified collection of interrelated marketed and non-marketed productive activities.

**effective exchange rate** An index number of the value of a nation's currency relative to a weighted basket of other currencies. Whereas an *exchange rate* measures the rate of exchange of one currency for another, specific, currency, changes in the effective exchange rate indicate movements in a single currency's value against other currencies in general.

**efficiency wage** A wage rate above the market-clearing level which enables employers to attract and keep the best workers as well as to provide their employees with an incentive to perform well so as to avoid being sacked.

**elastic** A percentage change in quantity that is greater than the percentage change in price (elasticity is greater than 1).

**elasticity of demand** See *price elasticity of demand*.

**elasticity of supply** See *price elasticity of supply*.

**embodied technical change** A technical change that is the result of changes in the form of particular capital goods.

**endogenous variable** A variable that is explained within a theory. Also called an induced variable.

**entrepreneur** One who innovates, i.e. takes risks by introducing new products and/or and new ways of making old products.

**entrepreneurship** The skill required to be an *entrepreneur*.

**entry barrier** Any natural barrier to the entry of new firms into an industry, such as a large *minimum efficient scale* for firms, or any firm-created barrier, such as a patent.

**envelope** Any curve that encloses, by being tangent to, a series of other curves. In particular, the envelope cost curve is the *LRAC* curve, which encloses the *SRAC* curves by being tangent to each without cutting any of them.

**equation of exchange** $MV = PT$, where $M$ is the money stock, $V$ is the velocity of circulation, $P$ is the average price of transactions, and $T$ is the number of transactions. As usually defined, it is an identity which says that the value of money spent is equal to the value of goods and services sold. However, with additional assumptions it provides a basis for the *quantity theory of money*.

**equilibrium** A state of balance between opposing forces so that there is no tendency to change.

**equilibrium differentials** Differentials in the prices of factors that persist in equilibrium without generating forces to eliminate them.

**equilibrium employment (unemployment)** The level of employment (unemployment) achieved when GDP is at its potential level. Traditionally referred to as full employment. Equilibrium unemployment (*frictional* plus *structural*) is total unemployment minus *demand-deficient unemployment*.

**equilibrium price** The price at which quantity demanded equals quantity supplied.

**equilibrium quantity** The amount that is bought and sold at the *equilibrium price*.

**equities** Certificates indicating part ownership of a joint-stock company.

**equivalent variation** The change in income that leaves a consumer just as well off as some specific change in the price of a good.

**excess capacity theorem** The prediction that each firm in a monopolistically competitive industry is producing below its minimum efficient scale and hence at an average cost that is higher than it could achieve by producing its capacity output.

**excess demand** The amount by which quantity demanded exceeds quantity supplied at some price; negative *excess supply*.

**excess supply** The amount by which quantity supplied exceeds quantity demanded at some price; negative *excess demand*.

**exchange rate** The rate at which two national currencies exchange for each other. Often expressed as the amount of domestic currency needed to buy one unit of foreign currency.

**excludable** The owner of an excludable good can prevent others from consuming it or its services.

**execution lag** The time it takes to initiate corrective policies and for their full influence to be felt.

**exhaustible resource** See *non-renewable resource*.

**exhaustive expenditures** Government purchases of currently produced goods and services. Also called government direct expenditures.

**exogenous variable** A variable that influences other variables within a theory but is itself determined by factors outside the theory. Also called an autonomous variable.

**expectations-augmented Phillips curve** See *short-run Phillips curve*.

**expected value** The most likely outcome of some procedure that is repeated over and over again; the mean of the probability distribution expressing the possible outcomes.

**explicit collusion** This occurs when firms explicitly agree to co-operate rather than compete. See also *tacit collusion*.

**extensive form game** Game in which players make moves in some order over time.

**external economies** Economies of scale that arise from sources outside the firm.

**externalities** Costs or benefits of a transaction that fall on people not involved in that transaction.

**extrapolative expectations** Expectation formation based on the assumption that a past trend will continue into the future. The simplest form of extrapolation would be to assume that next period's value of a variable will be the same as this period's.

**factor markets** Markets where factor services are bought and sold.

**factor price theory** The theory of the determination of the prices of factors of production.

**factors of production** Resources used to produce goods and services; frequently divided into the basic categories of land, labour, and capital. Sometimes entrepreneurship is distinguished as a fourth factor; sometimes it is included in the category of labour.

**fiat money** Inconvertible paper money that is issued by government order (or fiat).

**final demand** Demand for the *final goods and services* produced in the economy.

**final goods and services** The outputs of the economy after eliminating all *double counting*, i.e. excluding all intermediate goods.

**financial capital** The funds used to finance a firm, including both equity capital and debt. Also called money capital.

**financial innovation** Occurs when new products are introduced into the financial system, or when existing suppliers behave in new ways. Changes are often a complex interaction of regulatory changes, changing technology, and competitive pressures.

**financial intermediaries** Financial institutions that stand between those who deposit money and those who borrow it.

**fine-tuning** The attempt to maintain national income at, or near, its full-employment level by means of frequent changes in fiscal and/or monetary policy. Compare *gross-tuning*.

**firm** The unit that employs factors of production to produce commodities that it sells to other firms, to households, or to the government.

**fiscal consolidation** A situation in which governments that have been running substantial budget deficits decide to aim for a sustainable budgetary position, usually by getting their expenditure under control.

**fiscal policy** Attempts to influence the aggregate demand curve by altering government expenditures and/or taxes, thereby shifting the *IS* curve.

**fixed capital formation** See *fixed investment*.

**fixed cost** A cost that does not change with output. Also called overhead cost, unavoidable cost, or indirect cost.

**fixed exchange rate** An exchange rate that is held within a narrow band around some pre-announced par value by intervention of the country's central bank in the foreign exchange market.

**fixed factors** Inputs whose available amount is fixed in the short run.

**fixed investment** Investment in plant and equipment.

**fixed prices** See *administered prices*.

**flexible prices** See *auction prices*.

**floating exchange rate** An exchange rate that is left free to be determined on the foreign exchange market by the forces of demand and supply.

**flow variable** See *stock variable*.

**foreign direct investment (FDI)** Non-resident investment in the form of a takeover or capital investment in a domestic branch, plant, or subsidiary corporation in which the investor has voting control. See also *portfolio investment*.

**foreign exchange** Foreign currencies and claims to them in such forms as bank deposits, cheques, and promissory notes payable in the currency.

**foreign exchange market** The market where foreign exchange is traded—at a price that is expressed by the *exchange rate*.

**45° line** Used in macroeconomics to indicate points where expenditures and output are equal, so that what firms produce is just equal to what agents wish to buy.

**free-market economy** An economy in which the decisions of individuals and firms (as distinct from the central authorities) exert the major influence over the allocation of resources.

**free rider problem** The problem that arises because people have a self-interest in not revealing the strength of their own preferences for a *public good* in the hope that others will pay for it.

**free trade** An absence of any form of government interference with the free flow of international trade.

**free trade area** An agreement between two or more countries to abolish tariffs on all, or most, of the trade among themselves, while each remains free to set its own tariffs against other countries.

**frictional unemployment** Unemployment that is associated with the normal turnover of labour.

**function** Loosely, an expression of a relationship between two or more variables. Precisely, $Y$ is a function of the variables $X_1, \ldots, X_n$ if, for every set of values of the variables $X_1, \ldots, X_n$, there is associated a unique value of the variable $Y$. Also referred to as a *functional relation*.

**functional distribution of income** The distribution of income among major factors of production.

**functional relation** A mathematical relation between two or more variables such that, for every value of the independent variables, there is one and only one associated value of the dependent variable.

**gains from trade** Advantages realized as a result of specialization made possible by trade.

**game theory** The study of the strategic choices between firms, applicable when the outcome for one firm depends on the behaviour of the others.

**GDP** See *gross domestic product*.

**GDP gap** See *output gap*.

**general price level** Average level of the prices of all goods and services produced in the economy. Usually just called the price level.

**Giffen good** A good with a positively sloped demand curve.

**gilt-edged securities** UK government bonds; so called because they are considered to carry lower risk than private sector debt.

**given period** Any particular period that is being compared with a *base period* by an index number.

**globalization** The increased world-wide interdependence of most economies. Integrated financial markets, the sourcing of the production of components throughout the world, the growing importance of transnational firms, and the linking of many service activities through the new information and communications technologies are some of its many manifestations.

**GNI** See *gross national income.*

**GNP** See *gross national product.*

**gold standard** Currency standard whereby a country's money is convertible into gold.

**Goodhart's law** The view that many statistical relations (particularly those established by monetarists) cannot be used for policy purposes because they do not depend on causal relations and are, therefore, unstable.

**goods** Tangible production, such as cars or shoes. Sometimes all goods and services are loosely referred to as goods.

**goods markets** Markets where goods and services are bought and sold.

**government** In economics, all public agencies, government bodies, and other organizations belonging to, or owing their existence to, the government; sometimes (more accurately) called the central authorities.

**government direct expenditures** See *exhaustive expenditures.*

**government failure** Where government intervention imposes costs that would not have been accrued if it had acted efficiently.

**Gresham's law** Axiom that bad money (i.e. money whose intrinsic value is less than its face value) drives good money (i.e. money whose intrinsic value exceeds its face value) out of circulation.

**gross capital formation** See *gross investment.*

**gross domestic product (GDP)** The value of total output actually produced in the whole economy over some period, usually a year (although quarterly data are also available).

**gross investment** The total value of all investment goods produced in the economy during a stated period of time.

**gross national income (GNI)** A measure of what a nation earns from all its economic activity throughout the world. It differs from *gross domestic product*, which measures only what is produced in the domestic economy (some of which may generate income for non-residents). Used to be known as *gross national product.*

**gross national product (GNP)** A National Accounts concept equivalent to *gross national income* used prior to 1998. It measures income earned by domestic residents in return for contributions to current production, whether production is located at home or abroad, and is equal to GDP plus net property income from abroad.

**gross return on capital** The market value of output minus all non-capital costs: made up of depreciation, the pure return on capital, any risk premium, and the residual, which is *pure profit.*

**gross-tuning** Use of monetary and fiscal policies to attempt to correct only large deviations from potential national income. It is contrasted with *fine-tuning*, which aims to adjust aggregate demand frequently in order to keep national income close to its potential level at all times.

**high-powered money** The monetary magnitude that is under the direct control of the central bank. In the UK, it is composed of cash in the hands of the public, bank reserves of currency, and clearing balances held by the commercial banks with the Bank of England. Measured by M0.

**hog cycles** A term used to characterize cycles of over- and under-production because of time-lags in the production process. For example, high prices for pork today lead many farmers to start breeding pigs; when the pigs mature there will be an increased supply of pork, which will drive down its price; so fewer farmers will breed pigs and the price will later rise again, starting the cycle over again.

**homogeneous product** A product for which, as far as purchasers are concerned, every unit is identical to every other unit.

**horizontal equity** Treating similar groups equitably, which usually means treating them similarly. Compare *vertical equity.*

**household** All people living under one roof and taking, or subject to others taking for them, joint financial decisions.

**human capital** The capitalized value of productive investments in persons. Usually refers to value derived from expenditures on education, training, and health improvements.

**hyperinflation** Episodes of very rapid inflation.

**hysteresis** The lagging of effects behind their causes. In economics the term has come to relate to persistence or irreversibility of effects. An example is the difficulty of returning the long-term unemployed to work because their skills have deteriorated. It also implies path-dependency, which means that the ultimate equilibrium is not independent of how the economy gets there (i.e. it is not unique).

**identification problem** The problem of how to estimate both demand and supply curves from observed market data on prices and quantities actually traded.

**import quota** A maximum amount of some product that may be imported each year.

**imputed costs** The costs of using factors of production already owned by the firm, measured by the earnings they could have received in their best alternative employment.

**incentives** Motivational influences that drive the behaviour of economic agents. Consumers make choices to increase their satisfaction or utility, while firms respond to choices that increase their profit.

**incidence** In tax theory, where the burden of a tax finally falls.

**income–consumption line** On an indifference-curve diagram, a line showing how consumption bundles change as income changes, with prices held constant.

**income effect** The effect on quantity demanded of a change in real income, relative prices held constant.

**income-elastic** The percentage change in quantity demanded exceeds the percentage change in income.

**income elasticity of demand** The responsiveness of quantity demanded to a change in income as measured by the percentage change in quantity divided by the percentage change in income.

**income-inelastic** The percentage change in quantity demanded is smaller than the percentage change in income.

**increasing returns industry** One in which all firms operate under *increasing returns to scale*.

**increasing returns to scale** A situation in which long-run average total cost falls as output increases, enabling large firms able to produce at lower unit cost than small firms.

**incremental ratio** When *Y* is a function of *X*, the incremental ratio is the change in *Y* divided by the change in *X* that brought it about, $\Delta Y / \Delta X$. The limit of this ratio as $\Delta X$ approaches 0 is the derivative of *Y* with respect to *X*, $dY/dX$.

**independent variable** A variable that can take on any value in some specified range; it determines the value of the dependent variable.

**index number** An observation in a given time-period expressed as a ratio to the observation in a *base period* and then multiplied by 100.

**index of retail prices** See *retail price index*.

**indexation** When a contract for wages, pensions, or repayment of debt is specified in real terms. Any specified money payment would be increased to compensate for actual inflation. More generally, the term applies to any contingent contract tied to an index number.

**indicators** Variables that policy-makers monitor for the information they yield about the state of the economy.

**indifference curve** A curve showing all combinations of commodities that yield equal satisfaction to the consumer.

**indifference map** A set of indifference curves in which curves further away from the origin indicate higher levels of satisfaction than curves closer to the origin.

**indirect tax** A tax levied on a transaction that is paid by an individual by virtue of her association with that activity and does not vary with the circumstances of the individual who pays it, e.g. VAT on a restaurant meal.

**induced** Anything that is determined from within a theory. The opposite of autonomous or exogenous; also called endogenous.

**induced expenditure** Any expenditure flow that is related to national income (or to any other variable explained by the theory).

**induced variable** See *endogenous variable*.

**industrial union** A single union representing all workers in a given industry, whatever their trade.

**industry** A group of firms that sell a well defined product or closely related set of products.

**inefficient exclusion** Situation in which producers with excess capacity set positive prices.

**inelastic** The percentage change in quantity is less than the percentage change in price (elasticity is less than 1).

**infant industry argument** The argument that new domestic industries with potential economies of scale need to be protected from competition from established low-cost foreign producers so that they can grow large enough to achieve costs as low as those of foreign producers.

**inferior good** A commodity with a negative *income elasticity*; demand for it diminishes when income increases.

**inflation** A positive rate of growth of the general price level.

**inflationary gap** A positive output gap, i.e. where actual GDP exceeds *potential output* (GDP).

**inflationary shock** Any autonomous shift in aggregate demand or aggregate supply that causes the price level to rise.

**information lag** The time between an event happening and policy-makers learning about it. For example, National Accounts data for a quarter do not arrive until six weeks or so after the quarter ends and are then revised several times subsequently.

**infrastructure** The basic facilities (especially transportation and communications systems) on which the commerce of a community depends.

**injections** Exogenous expenditure flows into the home economy. The main injections in the macro model are government spending, exports, and investment.

**innovation** The introduction of something new, either a new product or a new way of making an old product. See also *entrepreneur*.

**innovators** Those who innovate. Also called *entrepreneurs*.

**inputs** The materials and factor services used in the process of production.

**insider–outsider model** An analysis of labour markets which gives more influence over market outcomes to those in employment (usually via trade union representation) than to the unemployed.

**instruments** The variables that policy-makers can control directly. (In econometrics, instruments are proxy variables used in regression equations because of their desirable statistical properties—usually independence from the equation error.)

**interest** The amount paid each year on a loan, usually expressed as a percentage (e.g. 5 per cent) or as a ratio (e.g. 0.05) of the principal of the loan.

**intermediate goods and services** All goods and services used as inputs into a further stage of production.

**internal economies** Economies of scale that arise from sources within the firm.

**internal labour market** The market inside the firm in which employees compete against each other, particularly for promotion.

**internalizing an externality** Doing something that makes an *externality* enter into the firm's own calculations of its private costs and benefits.

**inventories** Goods and materials that are held during the production or distribution process. See also *stocks*.

**investment** The act of producing or purchasing goods that are not for immediate consumption.

**investment demand function** A negative relationship between the quantity of investment per period and the interest rate, holding other things constant. Used to be more commonly called the marginal efficiency of investment.

**investment expenditure** Expenditure on capital goods.

**investment goods** Goods produced not for present consumption, i.e. capital goods, inventories, and residential housing.

**invisibles** Services, especially in the context of the balance of payments accounts, that we cannot see crossing the frontier, such as insurance, freight haulage, and tourist expenditures.

**involuntary unemployment** Unemployment that occurs when a person is willing to accept a job at the going wage rate but cannot find such a job.

**IS curve** The locus of combinations of the interest rate and the level of real GDP for which desired aggregate expenditure equals actual national output. So called because, in a closed economy with no government, it also reflects the combinations of the interest rate and national income for which investment equals saving, $I = S$. In general it reflects points for which *injections* equal *withdrawals*.

**IS/LM model** A diagrammatic representation of a model of aggregate demand determination based upon the locus of equilibrium points in the aggregate expenditure sector (*IS*) and the monetary sector (*LM*). It is incomplete as a model of GDP determination because it does not include an aggregate supply curve.

**isocost line** A line showing all combinations of inputs that have the same total cost to the firm.

**isoquant** A curve showing all technologically efficient factor combinations for producing a given level of output.

**isoquant map** A series of *isoquants* from the same production function, each isoquant relating to a specific level of output.

**J-curve** Pattern usually followed by the *balance of trade* after a devaluation of the domestic currency. Initially the trade balance deteriorates, and then after a lag it improves.

**joint-stock company** A firm regarded in law as having an identity of its own. Its owners, who are its shareholders, are not personally responsible for anything that is done in the name of the firm. Called a corporation in North America.

**Keynesian economics** Economic theories based on *AE*, *IS*, *LM*, *AD*, and *AS* curves and assuming enough short-run price inflexibility that *AD* and *AS* shocks cause substantial deviations of real GDP from its potential level.

**Keynesian revolution** Adoption of the idea that government could use monetary and fiscal policy to control aggregate demand and thereby influence the level of GDP. For a while it was believed that Keynesian economics had found ways in which policy-makers could smooth business cycles and eliminate unemployment.

**Kondratieff cycles** Long cycles in economic activity of around fifty years' duration. Sometimes referred to as long waves.

**labour** All productive human resources, mental and physical, both inherited and acquired.

**labour force** See *working population*.

**labour force participation rate** The percentage of the population of working age that is actually in the labour force (i.e. either working or seeking work).

**labour productivity** Total output divided by the labour used in producing it, i.e. output per unit of labour.

**Laffer curve** A curve relating total tax revenue to the tax rate.

**land** All free gifts of nature, such as land, forests, minerals, etc. Sometimes called natural resources.

**law of demand** Axiom stating that a lower price increases the quantity demanded and vice versa; that is, demand curves have a negative slope.

**law of diminishing returns** Law stating that, if increasing quantities of a variable input are applied to a given quantity of a fixed input, the *marginal product*, and the *average product*, of the variable input will eventually decrease.

**law of price adjustment** Law stating that, if there is an excess demand price will rise, and if there is an excess supply price will fall.

**leakages** See *withdrawals*.

**learning by doing** The increase in output per worker that often results as workers learn on the job through repeatedly performing the same tasks. It causes a downward shift in the average variable cost curve.

**legal tender** Currency that is recognized in law as the acceptable medium for payment of debts. Bank of England notes became legal tender in England and Wales in 1833. Euro notes became legal tender for members of the euro zone in 2002.

**less developed countries (LDCs)** The lower-income countries of the world, most of which are in Asia, Africa, and South and Central America. Also called underdeveloped countries and developing countries.

**life-cycle theory** A theory that relates a household's actual consumption to its expected lifetime income.

**limited partnership** A form of business organization in which the firm has two classes of owner: general partners, who take part in managing the firm and who are personally liable for all of the firm's actions and debts; and limited partners, who take no part in the management of the firm and who risk only the money that they have invested.

**liquidity** The ease with which an asset can be converted into money. Sometimes refers to money itself—*liquidity preference* used to be widely used in economics as an expression meaning demand for money.

**liquidity preference** The demand to hold wealth as money rather than as interest-earning assets. Also called the *demand for money*.

**liquidity trap** A situation that may arise when interest rates are so low that further reductions either are not possible or do not stimulate spending. In such situations the monetary authorities cannot stimulate aggregate demand by interest rate changes alone.

**LM curve** The locus of combinations of the interest rate and real GDP for which money demand equals money supply. So called because it represents the points where *liquidity preference* equals the money supply.

**logarithmic scale** A scale on which equal proportional changes are shown as equal distances (e.g. 1 cm may always represent doubling of a variable, whether from 3 to 6 or 50 to 100). Also called log scale or ratio scale.

**long run** A period of time in which all inputs may be varied but the basic technology of production is unchanged.

**long-run aggregate supply (LRAS) curve** A curve that relates the price level to equilibrium real GDP after all input costs, including wage rates, have been fully adjusted to eliminate any excess demand or supply.

**long-run average cost (LRAC) curve** Curve showing the least-cost method of producing each level of output when all inputs can be varied. Also sometimes called the long-run average total cost curve.

**long-run industry supply (LRS) curve** Curve showing the relation between equilibrium price and the output that the firms in an industry will be willing to supply after all desired entry or exit has occurred.

**long-run Phillips curve (LRPC)** Curve showing the relation between unemployment and stable rates of inflation that neither accelerate nor decelerate (and therefore for which actual and expected inflation are equal). Usually thought to be vertical at the *natural rate of unemployment* or *NAIRU*.

**long wave** See *Kondratieff cycles*.

**Lorenz curve** A curve showing the extent of departure from equality of income distribution. It graphs the proportion of total income earned by all people up to each stated point in the income distribution, such as the proportion earned by the bottom quarter, the bottom half, and the bottom three-quarters.

**Lucas aggregate supply curve** An aggregate supply curve which is positively sloped for unexpected increases in the price level but vertical for anticipated increases in the price level. Also known as the 'surprise' aggregate supply curve.

**Lucas critique** The proposition that empirical macro models will be inaccurate when used to predict the effects of changes in policy. This is because the behaviour of agents will be different under different policy regimes.

**M0** Currency held by the non-bank public plus bankers' deposits with the central bank. Also known as the monetary base, the cash base, or *high-powered money*.

**M1** A measure of the money stock which includes currency plus current account bank deposits. This measure is no longer reported by the Bank of England.

**M2** Currency held by the public plus retail current and savings accounts in banks and building societies. Also known as 'retail M4'.

**M3** Measure of broad money no longer used by the UK authorities. It was equal to M1 plus all savings deposits in banks. A harmonized measure of M3, **M3H**, is in use in the euro area as a monetary indicator; however, this has a different definition, as it is equal to M4 plus foreign currency and some other deposits.

**M4** Currency in circulation plus all sterling deposits in banks and building societies.

**macroeconomic policy** Any measure directed at influencing such macroeconomic variables as the overall levels of employment, unemployment, GDP, and prices.

**macroeconomics** The study of the determination of economic aggregates and averages, such as total output, total employment, the general price level, and the rate of economic growth.

**marginal cost (MC)** The increase in total cost resulting from raising the rate of production by one unit.

**marginal cost pricing** A policy of setting the price of a product equal to its marginal cost.

**marginal efficiency of capital** The rate at which the value of the stream of output of a marginal unit of capital must be discounted to make it equal to £1.

**marginal efficiency of capital schedule** A schedule that relates the marginal efficiency of each additional £1 worth of capital to the size of the capital stock.

**marginal efficiency of investment** The relation between desired investment and the rate of interest, assuming all other things are equal.

**marginal physical product (MPP)** See *marginal product*.

**marginal product (MP)** The change in total product resulting from using one more (or less) unit of the variable factor. Also

called marginal physical product. Mathematically, the partial derivative of total product with respect to the variable factor.

**marginal productivity theory** The demand half of the *neo-classical theory* of income distribution, in which the demand for any variable factor is determined by the value of that factor's *marginal revenue product*.

**marginal propensity not to spend** The proportion of any new increment of income that is not passed on in spending, and instead leaks out of (i.e. is withdrawn from) the circular flow of income. Also called the marginal propensity to withdraw and the marginal propensity to leak.

**marginal propensity to consume (MPC)** The proportion of any new increment of income that is spent on consumption, $\Delta C/\Delta Y$.

**marginal propensity to import** The proportion of any new increment of income that is spent on imports, $\Delta M/\Delta Y$.

**marginal propensity to leak** See *marginal propensity not to spend*.

**marginal propensity to save (MPS)** The proportion of any new increment of income that is saved, $\Delta S/\Delta Y$.

**marginal propensity to spend** The ratio of any increment of induced expenditure to the increment in income that brought it about.

**marginal propensity to tax** The proportion of any increment in income that is taxed away by the government, $\Delta T/\Delta Y$.

**marginal propensity to withdraw** See *marginal propensity not to spend*.

**marginal rate of substitution (MRS)** The rate at which one factor is substituted for another with output held constant. Graphically, the slope of the *isoquant*.

**marginal rate of transformation** The slope of the *production possibility boundary*, indicating the rate of substitution of production of one good for that of another.

**marginal revenue** The change in total revenue resulting from a unit change in the sales per period of time. Mathematically, the derivative of total revenue with respect to quantity sold.

**marginal revenue product (MRP)** The addition to a firm's revenue resulting from the sale of the output produced by an additional unit of the variable factor.

**marginal utility** The change in satisfaction resulting from consuming one unit more or one unit less of a commodity.

**market** An area over which buyers and sellers negotiate the exchange of a well defined commodity.

**market economy** A society in which people specialize in productive activities and meet most of their material wants through exchanges voluntarily agreed upon by the contracting parties.

**market failure** Any market performance that is less than the most efficient possible (the optimal) performance.

**market for corporate control** Where potential buyers and sellers (both willing and unwilling) bargain about transferring the ownership of firms.

**market prices** In National Accounts, refers to the fact that expenditures are measured in the prices actually paid by consumers and so include taxes on products. See also *basic prices*.

**market sector** That portion of an economy in which producers must cover their costs by selling their output to consumers.

**market structure** The characteristics of a market that influences the behaviour and performance of firms that sell in the market. The four main market structures are *perfect competition, monopolistic competition, oligopoly,* and *monopoly.*

**maturity** The length of time until the redemption date of a security such as a bond.

**medium of exchange** A commodity or token that is widely accepted in payment for goods and services.

**menu costs** Costs associated with changing prices, such as the costs of reprinting catalogues or menus. These costs make it rational for producers to keep output prices fixed until input prices have changed significantly, or to respond only periodically.

**mercantilism** The doctrine that the gains from trade are a function of the balance of trade, in contrast with the classical theory, in which the gains from trade are a function of the volume of trade.

**merchandise account** The part of the balance of payments accounts relating to trade in goods.

**merchandise trade** Trade in physical products. Same as *visible trade.*

**merger** The uniting of two or more formerly independent firms.

**merit goods** Goods which the government decides have sufficient merit that more should be produced and consumed than people would choose to do if left to themselves.

**microeconomics** The study of the allocation of resources and the distribution of income as they are affected by the working of the price system and by the policies of the central authorities.

**minimum efficient scale (MES)** The smallest level of output at which long-run average cost is at a minimum; the smallest output required to achieve all economies of scale in production.

**mismatch** See *structural unemployment.*

**mixed economy** An economy in which some decisions about the allocation of resources are made by firms and households and some are made by the government.

**monetarism** The doctrine that monetary magnitudes exert powerful influences in the economy and that control of these magnitudes is a potent means of affecting the economy's macroeconomic behaviour.

**monetary base** See *high-powered money* and *M0.*

**monetary equilibrium** A situation in which there is no excess demand for or supply of money.

**monetary policy** Policy of trying to control aggregate demand (and ultimately inflation) via the setting of short-term interest rates.

**monetary transmission mechanism** The mechanism that turns a monetary shock into a real expenditure shock and thus links the monetary and the real sides of the economy.

**money** Any generally accepted medium of exchange, i.e. anything that will be accepted in exchange for goods and services.

**money demand function** The function that determines the demand to hold money balances.

**money illusion** Refers to behaviour that responds to purely nominal changes in money prices and incomes in either direction, even though real incomes or relative prices have not changed.

**money income** Income measured in terms of some monetary unit. See also *real income.*

**money multiplier** The ratio of the money stock to the monetary base (*high-powered money*).

**money price** See *absolute price.*

**money rate of interest** The rate of interest as measured in monetary units.

**money stock** See *supply of money.*

**money supply** See *supply of money.*

**monopolist** The sole seller in a market.

**monopolistic competition** A market structure in which there are many sellers and freedom of entry but in which each firm sells a differentiated version of some generic product and, as a result, faces a negatively sloped demand curve for its own product.

**monopoly** A market structure in which the industry contains only one firm.

**monopsonist** The sole purchaser in a market.

**moral hazard** Any change in behaviour resulting from the fact that a contract has been agreed. One example is drivers who drive more recklessly because they have accident insurance; another is employees who do not work hard because employers cannot monitor their performance effectively.

**multinational enterprises (MNEs)** See *transnational corporations.*

**multiplier** The ratio of the change in GDP to the change in autonomous expenditure that brought it about.

**multiplier–accelerator theory** An element of business-cycle dynamics caused by the interaction of the multiplier and the accelerator, which can make the economy follow a cyclical path in response to a one-off exogenous shock.

**NAIRU** The amount of unemployment (all of it *frictional* or *structural*) that exists when GDP is at its potential level and that, if maintained, will result in a stable rate of inflation. The acronym stands for 'non-accelerating-inflation rate of unemployment'. In the long run the NAIRU is equivalent to the *natural rate of unemployment.*

**Nash equilibrium** In the case of firms, an equilibrium that results when each firm in an industry is currently doing the best that it can, given the current behaviour of all other firms.

**Nash theorem** Theory that every game with a finite number of players and a finite number of strategies will have at least one Nash equilibrium (so long as some random element to strategies is possible).

**national debt** The debt of the central government.

**national income** In general, the value of the nation's total output, and the value of the income generated by the production of that output. Measured in practice by *gross national income* and assumed in most of this book to be equivalent to GDP.

**national product** A generic term for the nation's total output, which might be measured more specifically by GDP. See *gross national product.*

**natural monopoly** An industry whose market demand is insufficient to allow more than one firm to cover costs at any positive level of output.

**natural rate of unemployment** The level of unemployment in a competitive economy that corresponds to potential GDP in long-run equilibrium and that is associated with stable inflation. For most purposes it is equivalent to the *NAIRU*, but the latter may differ when the economy is adjusting slowly back to full equilibrium following some large shock.

**natural scale** A scale on which equal absolute amounts are represented by equal distances. Compare *logarithmic scale*.

**negatively related** Refers to the relationship where an increase in one variable is associated with a decrease in another.

**neoclassical theory** In general, a theory based on the maximizing choices of well informed agents pursuing their own selfinterest. In *distribution* it is a theory that factor incomes are determined by demand and supply, where demand depends on the value of the factor's marginal product and supply depends on the maximizing decisions of those who own the factors.

**net exports** Total exports minus total imports ($X - IM$).

**net investment** Gross investment minus replacement investment, which is new capital that represents net additions to the capital stock.

**net present value** The difference between the present value of revenues and the present value of costs.

**net taxes** Total tax receipts net of *transfer payments*.

**neutrality of money** Hypothesis that the level of real national income is independent of the level of the money stock.

**New Classical theory** A theory that assumes that the economy behaves as if it were perfectly competitive, with all markets always clearing; where deviations from full employment can occur only if people make mistakes and where, given rational expectations, these mistakes will not be systematic.

**New Keynesian economics** Recent research agenda which has focused on explaining why prices do not adjust to clear markets, especially the labour market. It differs from the traditional Keynesian approach in its concern for *equilibrium unemployment* as well as *demand-deficient unemployment*.

**newly industrialized countries (NICs)** Formerly *less developed countries* that have become major industrial exporters in recent times. Sometimes called newly industrialized economies (NIEs).

**nominal interest rate** Actual interest rate in money terms. It is contrasted with the real interest rate, which is the nominal interest rate minus the inflation rate (or expected inflation rate).

**nominal money supply** The money supply measured in monetary units.

**nominal national product** Total output valued at current prices and usually measured by 'money GDP'.

**non-cooperative equilibrium** The equilibrium reached when firms calculate their own best policy without considering competitors' reactions and without explicit collusion.

**non-excludable** A good or service is non-excludable if its owners cannot dictate who will consume it.

**non-market sector** That portion of an economy in which producers must cover their costs from some source other than sales revenue.

**non-renewable (or exhaustible) resource** Any productive resource that exists as a fixed stock that cannot be replaced once it is used, such as natural petroleum.

**non-rivalrous** A good or a service is non-rivalrous if a given unit of it can be consumed by everyone. Thus, one person's consumption of it does not reduce the ability of another person to consume it—as with knowledge, national defence, police protection, and navigational aids.

**non-strategic behaviour** Behaviour that does not take account of the reactions of others, as when a firm acts in perfect or monopolistic competition.

**non-tariff barriers** Devices other than tariffs that are designed to reduce the flow of imports.

**non-tradables** Goods and services that are produced and sold domestically but do not enter into international trade.

**normal good** A commodity whose demand increases when income increases. Compare *inferior good*.

**normal form game** Players make choices based on expected payoffs simultaneously.

**normative** Things that concern what ought to be and thus depend on value judgements. Compare *positive*.

**oligopoly** An industry that contains only a few firms.

**open economy** An economy that engages in international trade.

**open-market operations** Sales or purchases of securities by the central bank aimed at influencing monetary conditions.

**open shop** A place of employment in which a union represents its members but does not have bargaining jurisdiction for all workers, and where membership of the union is not a condition of getting or keeping a job.

**opportunity cost** Measurement of cost by reference to the alternatives forgone.

**optimum output** See *profit-maximizing output*.

**option** Options come in two varieties. A *call option* is the right (but not the obligation) to buy some commodity or security at a specific price called the exercise price. A *put option* is the right (but not the obligation) to sell some commodity or security at a specific price.

**ordinary partnership** An enterprise composed of a group of individuals who are all jointly liable for the debts and other obligations of that enterprise.

**output** The goods and services that result from the process of production.

**output gap** The difference between potential output and actual output ($Y - Y^*$); negative output gaps are called *recessionary gaps*; positive output gaps are called *inflationary gaps*.

**overshooting** Occurs when the impact effect of a shock takes a variable beyond its ultimate equilibrium level. Most widely applied to the exchange rate. A characteristic of a wide class of exchange rate models under rational expectations is that when monetary policy is, say, tightened, the exchange rate initially appreciates to a point from which it will depreciate towards its long-run equilibrium level.

**Pareto optimality** A situation in which it is impossible to reallocate production activities to produce more of one good without producing less of some other good, and in which it is impossible to reallocate consumption activities to make at least one person better off without making anyone worse off. Also called Pareto efficiency.

**partnership** An enterprise with two or more joint owners, each of whom is personally responsible for all of the partnership's debts.

**paternalism** The belief that the individual is not the best judge of his or her own self-interest; i.e. the belief that someone else knows better.

**path-dependence** Non-uniqueness of equilibrium resulting from the possibility that what happens in one period affects the stock of physical and human capital for a long time thereafter. Sometimes referred to as *hysteresis*.

**per capita economic growth** The growth of per capita GDP or GNI (GDP or GNI divided by the population).

**per-unit tax** See *specific tax*.

**perfect competition** A market structure in which all firms in an industry are price-takers and in which there is freedom of entry into, and exit from, the industry.

**permanent income** The maximum amount that a person can consume per year into the indefinite future without reducing her wealth.

**permanent income theory** A theory that relates actual consumption to *permanent income*.

**perpetuity** A bond that pays a fixed sum of money each year for ever and has no redemption date. Sometimes called a consol.

**personal disposable income (*PDI*)** The gross income of the personal sector less all direct taxes and national insurance contributions.

**personal income** Income earned by or paid to individuals before personal income taxes are deducted.

**Phillips curve** Curve that relates the percentage rate of change of money wages (measured at an annual rate) to the level of unemployment (measured as the percentage of the *working population* unemployed).

**point elasticity** Uses the derivative at a point on the demand curve $(dq/dp) \times (p/q)$. See also *arc elasticity*.

**political business cycles** Cycles in the economy resulting from the political goals of incumbent (or potentially incumbent) politicians. The simplest form is the deliberate pre-election boom, though modern theories are more subtle.

**poll tax** A tax that takes the same lump sum from everyone.

**portfolio investment** Investment in bonds and other debt instruments that do not imply ownership, or in minority holdings of shares that do not establish legal control.

**positive** Refers to statements concerning what is, was, or will be; they assert alleged facts about the universe in which we live. Compare *normative*.

**positively related** Refers to the relationship whereby an increase in one variable is associated with an increase in another.

**potential output (GDP), *Y\*** The level of output at which there is a balance between inflationary and deflationary forces. It is also the level of output at which there is no *demand-deficient unemployment* (the economy is at the *NAIRU*) and the existing capital stock is being run at its normal rate of utilization.

**precautionary balances** The amount of money people wish to hold because of uncertainty about the exact timing of receipts and payments.

**present value** The value now of a sum to be received in the future. Also called discounted present value.

**price–consumption line** A line on an indifference curve diagram showing how consumption changes as the price of one commodity changes, *ceteris paribus*.

**price control** Anything that influences prices by law rather than by market forces.

**price discrimination** Situation arising when firms sell different units of their output at different prices for reasons not associated with differences in costs.

**price elasticity of demand** The percentage change in quantity demanded divided by the percentage change in price that brought it about. Often called elasticity of demand.

**price elasticity of supply** The percentage change in quantity supplied divided by the percentage change in price that brought it about. Often called elasticity of supply.

**price index** A statistical measure of the average percentage change in some group of prices relative to some base period.

**price level** See *general price level*.

**price-makers** Firms that administer their prices. See *administered price*.

**price system** An economic system in which market-determined prices play a key role in determining the allocation of resources and the distribution of the national product.

**price-taker** A firm that can alter its rate of production and sales within any feasible range without having any effect on the price of its products.

**principal** (1) The amount of a loan, or (2) the unit that employs agents to work on its behalf.

**principal–agent problem** The problem of resource allocation that arises because contracts that will induce agents to act in their principals' best interests are often impossible to write or too costly to monitor.

**principle of substitution** Methods of production reflecting the relative prices of inputs, with relatively more of the cheaper input and relatively less of the more expensive input being used.

**prisoner's dilemma** A term in game theory for a game in which the *Nash equilibrium* leaves both players less well off than if they co-operated with each other.

**private benefits** The benefits of some activity that accrue to the parties in that activity.

**private consumption spending** Spending for which the consumption of the goods bought is done by private individuals (even where payment may have been made by the government, such as on health services).

**private cost** The value of the best alternative use of the resources used in production as valued by the producer.

**private sector** That portion of an economy in which the organizations that produce goods and services are owned and operated by private units such as households and firms. Compare *public sector*.

**pro-cyclical** Positively correlated with the business cycle.

**producer** Any unit that makes goods or services.

**producers' surplus** Total revenue minus total variable cost; the market value that the firm creates by producing goods, net of the value of the resources currently used to create these goods.

**production** The act of making goods and services.

**production function** A mathematical relation showing the maximum output that can be produced by each and every combination of inputs.

**production possibility boundary** A curve that shows the alternative combinations of commodities that can just be attained if all available productive resources are used; the boundary between attainable and unattainable output combinations.

**productive efficiency** Production of any output at the lowest attainable cost for that level of output, so that it is impossible to reallocate resources and produce more of one output without simultaneously producing less of some other output.

**productivity** Output per unit of input employed.

**products** A general term referring to all goods and services. Sometimes also referred to as *commodities*.

**profit** (1) In ordinary usage, the difference between the value of outputs and the value of inputs. (2) In microeconomics, the difference between revenues received from the sale of goods and the value of inputs, which includes the opportunity cost of capital. Also called *pure profit* or *economic profit*. (3) In macroeconomics, a component of factor incomes (and thus income-based measures of national product) which is measured as trading surpluses plus a component of mixed incomes.

**profit-maximizing output** The level of output that maximizes a firm's profits. Sometimes also called the optimum output.

**progressive tax** A tax that takes a larger percentage of people's income the larger their income is. Compare *regressive tax*.

**progressivity** The general term for the relation between income and the percentage of income paid in taxes.

**proportional tax** A tax that takes the same percentage of people's income whatever the level of their income.

**protectionism** Any departure from free trade designed to give some protection to domestic industries from foreign competition.

**public corporation** A body set up to run a nationalized industry. It is owned by the state but is usually under the direction of a more or less independent, state-appointed board.

**public goods** Goods and services that, once produced, can be consumed by everyone in the society. Also called collective consumption goods.

**public sector** That portion of an economy in which production is owned and operated by the government or by bodies created by it, such as nationalized industries. Compare *private sector*.

**purchasing power parity (PPP) exchange rate** The exchange rate between two currencies that equates their purchasing powers and hence adjusts for relative inflation rates.

**purchasing power parity theory** Theory that the equilibrium exchange rate between two national currencies will be the one that equates their purchasing powers.

**pure market economy** An economy in which all decisions, without exception, are made by individuals and firms acting through unhindered markets.

**pure profit** Any excess of a firm's revenue over all opportunity costs including those of capital. Also called economic profit.

**pure rate of interest** See *pure return on capital*.

**pure return on capital** The amount that capital can earn in a riskless investment. Also called the pure rate of interest.

**quantity actually bought and sold** The amount of a commodity that consumers and firms actually succeed in purchasing and selling.

**quantity actually purchased** See *quantity actually bought and sold*.

**quantity demanded** The amount of a commodity that households wish to purchase in some time-period.

**quantity supplied** The amount of a commodity that firms offer for sale in some time-period.

**quantity theory of money** Theory predicting that the price level and the quantity of money vary in exact proportion to each other; e.g., changing $M$ by $X$ per cent changes $P$ by $X$ per cent.

**ratio scale** See *logarithmic scale*.

**rational expectations** The theory that people understand how the economy works and learn quickly from their mistakes, so that, while random errors may be made, systematic and persistent errors are not made.

**rational ignorance** This occurs when agents have no incentive to inform themselves about some government action because the costs of so doing greatly exceed the potential benefits of any action the agent could take as a result of having the correct information.

**reaction curve** The optimal choices that will be made by one firm in the light of each possible choice made by a rival firm. Could refer to the price reaction or the output reaction, but usually relates to output.

**real business cycles** An approach to the explanation of business cycles which uses dynamic equilibrium market-clearing models and relies on productivity shocks as a trigger. In such models all cycles are an optimal response to the real shock and there are no deviations from potential output: rather, it is the full equilibrium that fluctuates over time.

**real capital** Physical assets, including factories, machinery, and stocks of material and finished goods. Also called physical capital.

**real exchange rate** An index of the relative prices of domestic and foreign goods.

**real income** The purchasing power of *money income*, measured by deflating nominal income by an index of the price level.

**real money supply** The money supply measured in purchasing power units, measured as the nominal money supply divided by a price index.

**real national product** Total output valued at *base-year* prices, measured for example by GDP at 1999 prices.

**real product wage** The proportion of the sale value of each unit that is accounted for by labour costs (including the pre-tax nominal wage rate, benefits, and the firm's national insurance contributions).

**real rate of interest** The money rate of interest minus the inflation rate (or expected inflation rate), which expresses the real return on a loan.

**real wage** The money wage deflated by a price index to measure the wage's purchasing power.

**reallocation of resources** Some change in the uses to which the economy's resources are put.

**recession** A sustained drop in the level of economic activity.

**recessionary gap** A negative output gap, when actual GDP falls short of potential GDP.

**redemption date** The time at which the principal of a loan is to be repaid.

**regressive tax** A tax that takes a smaller percentage of people's incomes the larger their income is. Compare *progressive tax*.

**relative price** Any price expressed as a ratio of another price.

**renewable resources** Productive resources that can be replaced as they are used up, as with *real capital* or forests; distinguished from *non-renewable resources*, which are available in a fixed stock that when depleted cannot be replaced, such as natural oil and coal.

**replacement investment** Investment that replaces capital as it wears out but does not increase the capital stock.

**replacement ratio** Benefits received by those out of work as a proportion of the wage of those in employment.

**repo** Short for a 'sale and repurchase agreement', whereby a firm sells a security (such as a gilt) to a bank and agrees to buy it back at some future time. The difference in price between sale and repurchase reflects the ruling rate of interest. The deal is a loan (usually short-term) secured on the security involved. Central banks typically set the rate of interest in repo transactions for a specific term. In the UK the Bank of England sets the two-week repo rate.

**reservation price** The price below which some action will not be taken, such as selling a commodity or accepting a job.

**resource allocation** The allocation of the economy's scarce resources among alternative uses.

**retail price index (RPI)** An index of the general price level based on the consumption pattern of typical consumers.

**reverse repo** Similar to a *repo*, but here the bank sells the security to the firm and agrees to buy it back at some future date.

**risk-averse** Description of people who wish to avoid risks and so will play only those games that are sufficiently biased in their favour to overcome their aversion to risk; they will be unwilling to play mathematically fair games, let alone games that are biased against them.

**risk-loving** Description of people who are willing to play some games that are biased against them, the extent of the love of risk being measured by the degree of bias that they are willing to accept.

**risk-neutral** Description of people who are indifferent about playing a mathematically fair game and are also willing to play games that are biased in their favour but not games that are biased against them.

**risk premium** The return on capital necessary to compensate owners of capital for the risk of loss of their capital.

**rivalrous** A good or service is rivalrous if, when one person consumes a unit of it, no other person can also consume that unit, as with all ordinary goods and services such as apples or haircuts.

**saving** Income received by individuals that they do not spend through *consumption expenditure*.

**savings ratio** See *average propensity to save*.

**scatter diagram** Plots of a series of observations each made on two variables, e.g. the price and quantity of eggs sold in 20 different cities.

**seigniorage** The revenue that accrues to the issuer of money.

**self-employed** Those people who work for themselves.

**sellers' preferences** Allocation of a commodity that is in excess demand by the decisions of sellers.

**services** Intangible production that does not produce a physical product, such as haircuts and medical services.

**shares** See *equities*.

**share option** See *option*.

**shifting** The passing of tax incidence from the person who initially pays it to someone else.

**short run** The period of time over which the inputs of some factors cannot be varied.

**short-run aggregate supply (SRAS) curve** The total amount that will be produced and offered for sale at each price level on the assumption that all input prices are fixed.

**short-run equilibrium** Generally, equilibrium subject to fixed factors or other things that cannot change over the time-period being considered.

**short-run Phillips curve** Any particular Phillips curve drawn for a given expected rate of inflation.

**short-run supply curve** A curve showing the relation of quantity supplied to price when one or more factor is fixed; under perfect competition, the horizontal sum of marginal cost curves (above the level of average variable costs) of all firms in an industry.

**shutdown price** The price that is equal to a firm's average variable costs, below which it will produce no output. See also *break-even price*.

**simple multiplier** Usually applies to the value of the *multiplier* in the aggregate expenditure system before any account is taken of the feedback from the monetary sector and from aggregate supply.

**single proprietorship** An enterprise with one owner who is personally responsible for everything that is done. More commonly called a *sole trader*.

**size distribution of income** A classification of income according to the amount of income received by each individual irrespective of the sources of that income.

**slump** A period of low output and low employment. See also *boom*.

**small open economy (SOE)** An economy that is a price-taker for both its imports and its exports. It must buy and sell at the world price, irrespective of the quantities that it buys and sells.

**social benefits** The value of an activity to the whole society, which includes the internal effects on those who are involved in deciding on it and the external effects on those who are not involved in the activity.

**social cost** The value of the best alternative use of resources that are available to the whole society.

**sole trader** A non-incorporated business operated by a single owner. Modern UK terminology for a *single proprietorship*.

**specialization of labour** The organization of production so that individual workers specialize in the production of particular goods or services (and satisfy their wants by trading) rather than producing everything they consume (and satisfying their wants by being self-sufficient).

**specific tax** A tax expressed as so much per unit, independent of its price. Also called a per-unit tax.

**speculation** Taking a financial position that will yield profits if prices move in a particular direction in future but will yield losses if they move the other way.

**speculative balances** Monetary assets held for their expected rate of return rather than for transactions purposes.

**speculative motive** The motive that leads agents to hold money in response to the risks inherent in fluctuating bond prices. More generally, it refers to the asset motive, as opposed to the transactions motive, for holding money.

**spread** The difference between the prices or interest rates on specific assets or loans, such as the spread between deposit and loan rates offered by banks.

**SRAS curve** See *short-run aggregate supply curve*.

**stabilization policy** The attempt to reduce fluctuations in GDP, employment, and the price level by use of *monetary* and *fiscal policies*.

**stagflation** The simultaneous occurrence of a recession (with its accompanying high unemployment) and inflation.

**stock** See *equities*.

**stock variable** A variable that does not have a time dimension. It is contrasted with a flow variable, which does.

**stockbuilding** The process of building *stocks* or inventories.

**stocks** Accumulation of inputs and outputs held by firms to facilitate a smooth flow of production in spite of variations in delivery of inputs and sales of outputs. Now called inventories in National Accounts.

**strategic** Behaviour that takes into account the reactions of others to one's own actions, as when an oligopolistic firm makes decisions that take account of its competitors' reactions.

**strategic form game** See *normal form game*.

**structural unemployment** Unemployment that exists because of a mismatch between the characteristics of the unemployed and the characteristics of the available jobs in terms of region, occupation, or industry.

**substitutes** Two goods are substitutes if the quantity demanded of one is positively related to the price of the other.

**substitution effect** The change in quantity demanded of a good resulting from a change in the commodity's relative price, eliminating the effect of the price change on real income.

**sunk costs of entry** Those costs that must be incurred for a firm to enter a market and cannot be recouped when the firm leaves.

**supergame** A game that is repeated an infinite number of times.

**supply** The whole relation between the quantity supplied of some commodity and its own price.

**supply curve** The graphical representation of the relation between the quantity of some commodity that producers wish to make and sell per period of time and the price of that commodity, *ceteris paribus*.

**supply function** A mathematical relation between the quantity supplied and all the variables that influence it.

**supply of effort** The total number of hours people in the labour force are willing to work. Also called supply of labour.

**supply of labour** See *supply of effort*.

**supply of money** The total amount of money available in the entire economy. Also called the money supply or the money stock.

**supply schedule** A numerical tabulation showing the quantity supplied at a number of alternative prices.

**supply shocks** A shift in any aggregate supply curve caused by an exogenous change in input prices or technology.

**supply-side policies** Policies that seek to shift either the short-run or the long-run aggregate supply curve.

**surprise aggregate supply curve** See *Lucas aggregate supply curve*.

**tacit collusion** Occurs when firms arrive at the co-operative solution (which maximizes their joint profit) even though they may not have formed an explicit agreement to co-operate.

**takeover** When one firm buys another firm.

**targets** The variables in the economy that policy-makers wish to influence. Typical policy targets might be inflation, unemployment, or real growth.

**tariffs** Taxes on imported goods.

**term** The amount of time between a bond's issue date and its redemption date.

**terms of trade** The ratio of the average price of a country's exports to the average price of its imports.

**theory of games** The study of rational decision-making in situations in which each player must anticipate the reactions of competitors to the moves that she makes. It can be applied to analysis of the strategic interaction of firms in oligopolistic markets.

**third-party effects** See *externalities*.

**time-inconsistency** Problem that arises in rational expectations models when policy-makers have an incentive to abandon their commitments at a later time. The existence of this incentive is generally understood by private sector agents, and it may influence their current behaviour.

**time-series data** Data on some variable taken at different, usually regularly spaced, points in time, such as consumer spending in each quarter for the last 10 years.

**total cost (*TC*)** The total of all costs of producing a firm's output, usually divided into *fixed* and *variable costs*.

**total final expenditure** The total expenditure required to purchase all the goods and services that are produced domestically when these are valued at market prices.

**total fixed costs** The total of a firm's costs that do not vary in the short run.

**total product (*TP*)** Total amount produced by a firm during some time-period.

**total revenue (*TR*)** Total amount of money that a firm receives from the sale of its output over some period of time.

**total utility** The total satisfaction derived from consuming some amount of a commodity.

**total variable costs** The total of those of the firm's costs that vary in the short run.

**tradables** Goods and services that enter into international trade.

**trade account** The part of the balance of payments accounts relating to trade in goods.

**trade creation** Trade between the members of a customs union or free trade area where previously protected industries had served their own home markets.

**trade cycles** See *business cycles*.

**trade diversion** The diversion of the source of a member country's imports from other countries to union members as a result of the preferential removal of tariffs following the formation of a customs union or a free trade area.

**trade or craft union** A union covering workers with a common set of skills, no matter where, or for whom, they work.

**trade-weighted exchange rate** The average of the exchange rates between a particular country's currency and those of each of its major trading partners, with each rate being weighted by the amount of trade with the country in question. Also called the *effective exchange rate*.

**traditional economic system** Economic system in which behaviour is based primarily on tradition, custom, and habit.

**transaction costs** Costs involved in making a trade in addition to the price of the product itself, such as the time involved or the cost of transport.

**transactions balances** Holdings of money intended to be used for buying goods or services at some unknown future time.

**transactions demand for money** The amount of money that people wish to hold in order to finance their transactions.

**transfer earnings** The amount that a factor must earn in its present use to prevent it from moving (i.e. transferring) to another use.

**transfer payments** Payments not made in return for any contribution to current output, such as unemployment benefits.

**transition economies** Countries that have abandoned central planning and have been making the transition to market economies, such as the countries of eastern Europe and the former Soviet Union.

**transmission mechanism** See *monetary transmission mechanism*.

**transnational corporations (TNCs)** Firms that have operations in more than one country. Also called transnationals or multinational enterprises (MNEs).

**underdeveloped countries** See *less developed countries*.

**unit cost** See *average variable cost*.

**unit elasticity** An elasticity with a numerical measure of 1, indicating that the percentage change in quantity is equal to the percentage change in price (so that total expenditure remains constant).

**utility** See *marginal utility* and *total utility*.

**utils** An imaginary measure of utility used in the exposition of marginal utility theory, which assumes that utility is cardinally measurable.

**validation** When the authorities sustain an ongoing inflation by increasing the money supply.

**value added** The value of a firm's output minus the value of the inputs that it purchases from other firms.

**value added tax (VAT)** Tax charged as a proportion of a firm's *value added*.

**value of money** See *purchasing power of money*.

**variable** Any well defined item, such as the price of a commodity or its quantity, that can take on various specific values.

**variable cost** A cost that varies directly with changes in output. Also called direct cost or avoidable cost.

**variable factors** Inputs whose amount can be varied in the short run.

**velocity of circulation** The number of times an average unit of money is used in transactions within a specific period. Defined as the ratio of nominal GDP to the money stock.

**vertical equity** Equitable treatment of people in different income brackets. Compare *horizontal equity*.

**very long run** A period of time over which the technological possibilities open to a firm are subject to change.

**visible account** The part of the balance of payments accounts relating to trade in goods.

**visible trade** Trade in physical products. Same as *merchandise trade*.

**visibles** Goods such as cars, aluminium, coffee, and iron ore, which we can see when they cross international borders.

**voluntary export restriction (VER)** Restriction whereby an exporting country agrees to limit the amount it sells to a second country.

**voluntary unemployment** Unemployment that occurs when there is a job available but the unemployed person is not willing to accept it at the existing wage rate.

**winner's curse** The possibility that the agent who wins the bidding on a contested takeover may pay more than the target firm is really worth because the winner is the one with the highest valuation of all bidders.

**withdrawals** Spending that leaves the economy and does not create further incomes for domestic residents. Import spending, for example, creates incomes overseas. Also called *leakages*.

**working population** The total of the employed, the self-employed, and the unemployed, i.e. those who have a job plus those who are looking for work.

**X-inefficiency** Failure to use resources efficiently within the firm so that firms are producing above their relevant cost curves and the economy is inside its production possibility boundary.

**yield curve** A line on a graph plotting the yield on securities against the term to maturity.

# BIBLIOGRAPHY

Arrow, K. (1962). 'The Economic Implications for Learning by Doing'. *Review of Economic Studies*, vol. 29, pp. 155–73.

Barber, N. (2004). *Kindness in a Cruel World: The Evolution of Altruism*. New York: Prometheus.

Bean, C. (2005). 'European Employment: The Evolution of Facts and Ideas'. *Economic Policy*, vol. 21, pp. 47–51.

Bhagwati, J. (2002). *Free Trade Today*. Princeton, NJ: Princeton University Press.

Blanchard, O. (2006). 'European Unemployment: The Evolution of Facts and Ideas'. *Economic Policy*, vol. 21, pp. 5–47.

Blaug, M. (1997). *Economic Theory in Retrospect*. Cambridge: Cambridge University Press.

Chandler, A. D. Jr (1990). *Scale and Scope: The Dynamics of Industrial Capitalism*. Cambridge, Mass.: Harvard University Press.

Department of Trade and Industry (DTI) (2005). *Government Evidence to the Low Pay Commission on the National Minimum Wage*. London: DTI; at www.dti.gov.uk/files/file14450.pdf

Dickens, R. and Draca, M. (2005). *The Employment Effects of the October 2003 Increase in the National Minimum Wage*. London: Low Pay Commission.

HM Treasury (2005). *Pre-Budget Report*. London: HM Treasury.

International Monetary Fund (IMF) (various issues). *World Economic Outlook*. Washington: IMF.

Kaounides, L. C. (1995). 'New Materials and Simultaneous Engineering in the Car Industry: The Alcoa–Audi Alliance in Lightweight Aluminium Car Body Structures'. Based on L. C. Kaounides, *Advanced Material Management and Government Strategies in the 1990s*, Financial Times Management Report. London: Financial Times.

Keynes, J. M. (1936). *The General Theory of Employment, Interest and Money*. London: Macmillan.

Kreuger, A. (2002). Speech given to the NBER on 17 July; available at http://www.imf.org/external/np/speeches/2002/071702.htm

Layard, R. (2005). *Happiness: Lessons from a New Science*. New York and London: Penguin.

Layard, R., Nickell, S., and Jackman, R. (1994). *The Unemployment Crisis*. Oxford: Oxford University Press.

Lipsey, R. G. (2006). 'Don't Give Up on WTO: Fix It'. Yale Centre for the Study of Globalization, April; at http://yaleglobal.yale.edu/display.article?id=7213

——, Carlaw, K. I., and Bekar, C. T. (2005). *Economic Transformations: General Purpose Technologies and Long Term Economic Growth*. Oxford: Oxford University Press.

Mansell, R. (ed.) (1994). *Management of Information and Communication Technologies*. London: Association of Information Management.

Mowrey, D. and Rosenberg, N. (1989). *Technology and the Pursuit of Economic Growth*. Cambridge: Cambridge University Press.

Porter, M. (1998). *The Competitive Advantage of Nations*. London: Palgrave Macmillan.

Rosenberg, N. (1982). *Inside the Black Box: Technology and Economics*. Cambridge: Cambridge University Press.

—— (1994). *Exploring the Black Box: Technology, Economics, and History*. Cambridge: Cambridge University Press.

Schumpeter, J. (1950). *Capitalism, Socialism and Democracy*, 3rd edn. New York: Harper & Row.

Sigmund, K., Fehr, E., and Nowak, M. A. (2002). 'The Economics of Fair Play'. *Scientific American*, January, pp. 82–7.

Smith, A. (1776). *An Inquiry into the Nature and Causes of the Wealth of Nations*, ed. R. H. Campbell and A. S. Skinner. Oxford: Clarendon Press, 1976.

Solow, F. E. (1987). 'We'd Better Watch Out', book review, *New York Times*, 12 July, page 36.

UNCTAD (2001). *World Investment Report*. Geneva: UNCTAD.

von Hippel, E. (1988). *The Sources of Innovation*. New York: Oxford University Press.

Warsh, D. (2006). *Knowledge and the Wealth of Nations*. New York and London: W. W. Norton.

# INDEX

Note to index: definitions may be found in the glossary, pp 635–51